RSCCD

3 3065 00323 6878

Santiago Canyon College
Library

I0788444

Music in American Life

A list of books in the series appears at the end of this book.

THE INCREDIBLE BAND OF JOHN PHILIP SOUSA

ML
421
.S657
B54
2006

The Incredible Band of
JOHN PHILIP SOUSA

Paul Edmund Bierley

University of Illinois Press • Urbana and Chicago

ocm 673 5 796

Santiago Canyon College
Library

© 2006 by the Board of Trustees
of the University of Illinois
All rights reserved
Manufactured in the United States of America
c 5 4 3 2
∞ This book is printed on acid-free paper.

Library of Congress Cataloging-in-Publication Data
Bierley, Paul E.
The incredible band of John Philip Sousa / Paul E. Bierley.
p.   cm.
Includes discography (p.   ), bibliographical references (p.   ), and index.
ISBN-13: 978-0-252-03147-2 (cloth : alk. paper)
ISBN-10: 0-252-03147-4 (cloth : alk. paper)
1. Sousa Band. 2. Sousa, John Philip, 1854–1932. I. Title.
ML421.S657B54   2006
784.8'406073—dc22   2006011277

TO PAULINE, LOIS, AND JOHN

Contents

Illustrations

Acknowledgments

Four decades were required to complete this book, so credit must be given to many people who supplied vital information. My sincere appreciation goes to a few hundred of them.

PRIMARY SOURCES

Top priority was given to interviewing former members of Sousa's Band (plus a few individuals from the management staff). It was my privilege to personally interview sixty-four of the estimated three hundred who were still alive. Many others had passed on.

Personal interviews with the following former Sousa people led me to all four corners of the continental United States: Don Bassett, Frederick W. Bayers, John Weston Bell, William John Bell, Walter H. Bender, Joseph R. Browning, W. Fred Campbell, Robin W. Davis, Reuben Clinton Evans, Nora Fauchald, Lillian J. Finegan, Elver J. Fitchhorn, Earl Van Wyck Foote, George F. Ford, Arthur L. Frantz, Birley Gardner, Donald C. Gardner, Arthur R. Glenum, Lester M. Gray, Clyde L. Hall, Edward J. Heney, John J. Heney, Senta Hofman, Noble P. Howard, Paul E. Howland, Vane H. Kensinger, Richard E. Kent, Owen D. Kincaid, Otto J. Kraushaar, Mathias J. Kuhn, Joseph G. Lefter, Wayne Lewis, Estelle Liebling, Marcella Lindh, Joseph L. George Lucas, Robert Mayer, G. Rowe McRitchie, Albertus L. Meyers, Roy M. Miller, Marjorie Moody, Louis Morris, Oscar L. Nutter, Theodore Pashedag, Chester A. Perry, Fred E. Pfaff, Arthur H. Rosander Jr., Herman F. Schmidt, William Schneider, William P. Schueler, Elbert Severance, Frank Simon, Jay G. Sims, Eugene Slick, John Henry Spencer, Harold O. Stambaugh, Harold B. Stephens, John F. Van Fossen, Michael Vincinguerra, Edmund C. Wall, Albert L. Weber, Leon E. Weir, Robert G. Willaman, and Robert Meredith Willson. There was additional correspondence with these same individuals as well as with members of their families.

Among those just mentioned, Frank Simon, Louis Morris, Marjorie Moody, William Schneider, Robert Meredith Willson, and Nora Fauchald were the most influential in introducing me to the inner workings of Sousa's Band.

I corresponded, by either mail or telephone, with additional members of Sousa's Band: James C. Austin, Harry Baxter, Paul G. Blagg, Clarence Booth, James G. Borrelli, Jaroslav Cimera, Francis M. Crawford, William E. Duncan, Elvin L. Freeman, J. Ernest Harper, Benjamin Hudish, Herman R. Johnson, Frank J. Kapralek, Maurice Sackett, Henry A. Schueler, Arthur C. Schwaner, Paul C. Sexauer, Donald Snyder, Leopold Steinert, Frank W. Sullivan, Ernest L. Thompson, Sherley C. Thompson, Ralph N. Wige, Cedric Willson, Harold I. Woolridge, Arthur M. Wriggins, and Manuel Yingling.

Because the majority of band members had died before my research began I corresponded with family members of these additional Sousa Band members: Paul G. Blagg, Paul O. Christensen, Herman C. Conrad, Ralph H. Corey, William H. Decker, Louis P. Fritze, Pasquale C. Funaro, Guy G. Gaugler, Howard N. Goulden, William P. Heney, William Herb, William B. Holl, Frank Holt, Earl Keller, Albert A. Knecht, Alexander Laurendeau, John S. Leick, John S. Leigl, Abraham Levy, Theodore Levy, Robert J. Lorenz, Graydon C. Lower, Nathan C. Lower, Marcus C. Lyon, Louis Mehling, John J. Perfetto, Earle A. Poling, Albert A. Pons, Edgard I. Ricciardi, Eugene C. Rose, Carl T. Rundquist, Willard Rundquist, Clarence J. Russell, John P. Schueler, George B. Tompkins, Frederick L. Walen, Charles A. Wall, Edmund A. Wall, Orlando Edward Wardwell, Berthold K. Wavrek, Frederick J. Wavrek, and Leopold A. Zimmerman.

Next in order of priority was working with members of Sousa's own family. I am exceedingly grateful to his daughter, Helen Sousa Abert, who allowed me access to the family archives. Because she followed her father on some of the tours, her insight into the mechanics of the band's travel and her father's relationship with the musicians was especially helpful.

Other members of the family did not have detailed knowledge of travel arrangements. Some relatives did, however, provide encouragement: grandsons John Philip Sousa III and Thomas A. Sousa, granddaughter Jane Priscilla Abert, and great-grandsons John Philip Sousa IV and Thomas Abert.

HELP FROM PORTRAYERS

Two great friends of many years have inspired me in a multitude of ways because they are both John Philip Sousa personified: James G. (Jimmy) Saied and Keith Brion.

Jimmy Saied personified Sousa in both his philosophy of music and his personal appearance. As they say, he was the "spittin' image" of Sousa. In conducting his Sousa-style concerts with many bands around America, he left the unmistakable impression that Sousa was not only 100 percent an American but also 100 percent an artistic conductor and nice guy. In supporting the Integrity Research Foundation (which partially funded research), the Saied Family Foundation was another way in which Jimmy helped my work.

Brion, whose Sousa-style concerts and recordings are creating a stir throughout the world, portrays Sousa with symphony orchestras and bands—especially with his own New Sousa Band—and has reintroduced millions to the Sousa of old. Brion brought the New Sousa Band to Columbus, Ohio, on the day I received an honorary doctorate from Ohio State University. I am also grateful to him for finding new facets of Sousa's career while presenting concerts in the same cities where the Sousa Band played. Sousa left unforgettable memories wherever he went, and Brion is doing the same thing.

THE UNITED STATES MARINE BAND

The United States Marine Band played a major role in the writing of this book because its vast archive of Sousa music, memorabilia, and papers is something no serious Sousa researcher can do without. The Sousa Band press books, now carefully preserved in the band's fireproof vaults in Washington, D.C., were a major source of information. Making these and other documents available to me was of the utmost importance. I am particularly grateful to Michael Ressler, head librarian, for assistance in a variety of ways. Without his cheerful cooperation my research would have been much less complete.

The enthusiasm of Michael's staff members was uplifting. I am grateful to Dale Allen, Katherine Allen, Jane Cross, Preston Mitchell, and Meagan Benson. I am also grateful to former members of the staff: Susan Koutsky, Russ Girsberger, Dianna Eiland, Susan (Zafke) Bour, and Rick Zogaig. All came to my rescue many times.

The entire staff of the United States Marine Band, present and past, played an important part in the development of this book. Frank Byrne, for instance, shared his considerable knowledge of Sousa with me and led me on to greater heights. Joan Ambrose, publicist-historian, kept me up to date on the band's acquisitions. The esteemed leaders of recent years, Timothy W. Foley, John R. Bourgeois, and Dale Harpham, gave me a measure of inspiration that could have come only from those who followed in the footsteps of Sousa as leader of "The President's Own."

MILITARY BANDMASTERS

Speaking of inspiration coming from leaders of military bands, I must acknowledge the inspiration given by George S. Howard, Arnold D. Gabriel, Lowell E. Graham, Kenneth R. Force, Donald W. Stauffer, Brian Shelburne, Carl Chevallard, and Lewis J. Buckley.

DISCOGRAPHIC STUDIES

In compiling a list of recordings made by the group of musicians known as "Sousa's Band," plus the histories of the recording companies and the studio musicians involved, I am greatly indebted to discographer/historian Frederick P. Williams, who furnished an enormous amount of data on the Victor Talking Machine Company and other companies, as well as the dossiers of numerous recording artists. He also made available the catalog of his huge record and cylinder collection and referred me to countless sources that were of great help.

I am grateful as well to John L. Hubbard, who, along with Fred Williams, examined the discography of this book with extreme care and made many helpful suggestions. His unique collection of band and brass instrument recordings confirmed the listings of some very rare discs and cylinders.

In compiling the discography I am also indebted to Paul Charosh for sharing his knowledge of Berliner discs and to Loras J. Schissel for assistance in proper cataloging.

Had it not been for James R. Smart's *The Sousa Band, A Discography,* compiling the discography for this volume would have been much more difficult if not impossible. His follow-on advice was also of great help. Thanks go also to Oliver R. Graham and his brother E. J. (Mike) Graham, who made available the holdings of the Cameron-Graham Memorial Band Library. Special thanks also go to Jack E. Linker and Frank McGuire for sharing their knowledge of old recordings and band music.

SPECIAL THANKS

Many individuals helped in a variety of ways:

To Phyllis Danner, the former archivist of the Sousa Archives for Band Research at the University of Illinois at Urbana-Champaign, I express undying thanks for making the extensive holdings of that facility available for study. Her loving care of all things Sousa and her willingness to share her knowledge of Sousa's Band will continue to inspire me for many years to come.

Leonard B. Smith, composer, conductor, and cornet/trumpet virtuoso, helped immensely in my understanding of the great professional bands of the past. His association with many former Sousa Band musicians contributed to several databases I compiled. Playing under his direction in the Detroit Concert Band up until the very end helped me understand what life in Sousa's Band must have been like, and it gave meaning to excellence in music. Leonard learned from Sousa, and I learned from him. Thanks also go to Mary Lou Hornberger, his energetic business partner, for help in assembling a collection of photographs and other data for study.

Loras J. Schissel, music specialist at the Library of Congress and conductor of the Virginia Grand Military Band and the Blossom Festival Concert Band, helped in more ways than could be counted. His knowledge of Sousa's music, and the music that other professional bands were playing, was a great help in compiling several appendixes of this book. Loras also suffered through a complete reading of my manuscript, as did seven others to whom I express profound gratitude: Lois E. Walker, Keith Brion, Michael Ressler, William H. Rehrig, Barry Owen Furrer, James G. Saied, and John L. Hubbard.

Barry Owen Furrer, a serious collector of Sousa memorabilia, contributed a number of items from his extensive holdings. Many of his photographs appear in this book, and he also made sure that any items with critical information, such as programs, correspondence, and other papers, did not escape my attention. His wife Susan Furrer was especially helpful in gathering and reproducing important data.

William H. Rehrig, author of the most significant "band" document ever published—*The Heritage Encyclopedia of Band Music* and *Supplement*—added greatly to my knowledge of band history. He was constantly supplying information about former Sousa Band musicians that had not found its way to my doorstep. He also helped transcribe and interpret Albert A. Knecht's world tour diary (chapter 7).

Richard L. Harris, a dear friend of my family, helped in innumerable phases of my research, primarily in the study of the Sousa Band music library at the University of Illinois. He was a brilliant musician, and I often felt he had forgotten more about music than I could ever know.

Kenneth Berger, the real pioneer in Sousa Band research, graciously passed the torch to me.

Raymond Dvorak, a true devotee of Sousa, shared firsthand knowledge of the Sousa Band music library and inspired me through his enthusiasm. He was the man most responsible for having Sousa elected to the Hall of Fame for Great Americans, and it was my privilege to assist him in that effort.

William Lichtenwanger of the Music Division of the Library of Congress helped define the paths of my research and gave me the benefit of his wisdom in all things musical.

Glenn D. Bridges duplicated recordings of brass soloists of Sousa's Band and furnished much biographical information in addition to that included in his *Pioneers of Brass*.

Harold Bachman, founder and conductor of the famous Million Dollar Band, furnished knowledge of the Sousa Band music library. This resulted in saving a large portion of the original Sousa Band music library from extinction. In 1964 he led me to a cache of the band's music in storage and destined for disposal at Stetson University. I also thank Richard Feasel, band director there at the time, for having the music cataloged and making it available for study.

Seiichiro Takahashi, co-founder of the Japan Sousa Society, produced with loving care the now-famous set of Sousa march recordings with the Japan Ground Self Defense Force First Band.

Kozo Suzuki provided the privilege of collaborating with him on *All about Sousa Marches* (in Japanese) and studying the Sousa Band music library at the University of Illinois.

Gay Corrie of England, who knows more about Sousa than anyone on the other side of the Atlantic, shared his knowledge with me and arranged numerous pieces of Sousa's music so it could be recorded by the Detroit Concert Band.

Tom Spain made available the findings of his staff in the research that led to the epic television documentary *If You Knew Sousa.*

Raoul Camus spent countless hours unearthing information, which could be found only in the New York City area, on Sousa musicians.

Herbert N. Johnston contributed memories of the Sousa Band musicians he knew personally and also compared research notes with me.

George Foreman was the source of information on Sousa and Sousa Band musicians gathered during his career as one of the world's leading band historians.

Carole E. Nowicke helped me in many ways. Her in-depth study of Walter Smith, who played under Sousa in both the United States Marine Band and Sousa's Band, was of inestimable help. She also assisted in cataloging the music that Sousa's Band played at various St. Louis Expositions.

Kenneth B. Slater provided information on the working careers of numerous Sousa Band musicians.

Frederick Fennell gave helpful advice about collecting information on band history and provided inspiration by recording a great number of Sousa marches.

Betty McCloskey, daughter of Sousa Band saxophonist Albert A. Knecht, made available her father's world tour diary of 1911 (chapter 7) and provided several photographs.

Mark Foutch assisted in identifying music in the Sousa Band music library at the University of Illinois and was generous in his great hospitality as well.

Wilbur Crist, Paul Droste, and Donald E. McGinnis were sources of sage advice on how to clear academic hurdles.

David Byers and John L. Hubbard provided information on railroads, particularly those used by Sousa's Band.

George Class Jr. furnished detailed information on J. W. Pepper's manufacture of the first sousaphone.

John R. Taylor supplied biographical information on Sousa Band tubists.

Edmund Watkins, Betty Holling, and Steve Kelly made digital enhancements of photographs of Sousa Band musicians.

PASSING IT ON

The specialized research conducted by the students I assisted with dissertations and theses eventually yielded information and thus expanded my knowledge of Sousa and his musicians. Hats off to Alan L. Davis, Leon Bly, Lucinda Erickson, Daniel Frizane, Michael E. Hester, Michael R. Jorgensen, Jonathan Korzun, James T. Madeja, Vince Polce, William B. Stacy, James A. Strain, Victoria Ullery, Patrick Warfield, John A. Whisler, and Steven M. Wolfinbarger.

OTHER SCHOLARLY HELP

Researchers, authors, historians, or friends of Sousa Band musicians were of considerable help in documenting the activities of Sousa Band musicians. Among those I thank heartily are Lisa M. Akenhead, Jorgen Voigt Arnsted, Patricia Backhaus, Robert Bernat, John Beyrent, Michael Biel, Goeffrey Brand, George Brozak, John S. Burroughs,

Donald Callahan, Frank Cipola, Keith Clark, Ronald H. Demkee, Celeste Chapman Dent, John Dudd, James C. Dutton, Carl Ehrke, Mark Elrod, Lloyd Farrar, Robert Finzell, John Fowles, Sabina Freeman, Daniel Frizane, Harold Geerdes, Andrew Glover, Wilford Graham, Charles Greaven, Roberta Hagood, Ivan Hammond, Paul J. Harris Jr., Don Harry, Dennis Havens, Margaret H. and Robert M. Hazen, Ken Henderson, Margeret Heney, Malcolm Heslip, David Hoffman, Brian W. Holt, Ronald W. Holz, Frank Hosticka, Donald Hunsburger, John Hunsinger, John Jenkins, Martin Jenkins, Katherine Borst Jones, Walter Kaville, Craig Kirchhoff, Thomas J. Kirk, Earl Lauber, Paul Lavalle, Arthur W. Lehman, Leland A. Lillehaug, Laura J. Lineberger, Thomas Lloyd, Joe Losh, Earle Louder, June and Floyd Mackey, Doug MacLeod, Frank Mader, Keith Mann, Richard T. Mannisto, William McMahon, Larry McVey, William R. Miller, James Moore, Marcus Neiman, Susan Nelson, Roger Nixon, William O'Hara, Martin Oxley, Thomas C. Pardo, Allen Pergament, Helen Pettee, Harvey Phillips, William G. Pruyn, Ronald J. Putz, Jerry Rife, Deane Root, Toni Ryon, Lynn Sams, Stephen Secan, Karen A. Shaffer, Wayne Shirley, Beverly Sills, Andre Smith, Clayton F. Smith, Norman E. Smith, Ainsley Smithyman, Martin Snitzer, Hildreth Spencer, Stan Stanford, David H. Stanon, Loren Stephens, Anthony Thomas, Thomas J. Trimborn, Lavern Wagner, Christopher Weait, David Whitwell, Warren Wilson, Masahiro Yoshinaga, Robert C. Zimmer, and J. Herbert Zornes.

RESEARCH ASSOCIATES

Several research associates added substantially in gathering information for this book, performing investigations on a wide number of topics. Two in particular proved indispensable.

Kathryn Marie Morris worked for several years on a variety of projects, primarily reconstructing band tours (Appendix I) and compiling information on individual Sousa Band musicians (Appendix II) by systematic study of the Sousa Band press books and other documents.

Heather B. Doughty also worked on many facets of research, but her masterpiece was compiling the only known collection of Sousa Band concert programs that included all the surprise encores (Appendix IV). Her husband, Bryan, was also of great help, particularly in transcribing taped interviews and corresponding with libraries.

Family members assisted as well. My daughter, Lois E. Walker, an experienced U.S. Air Force historian and author, provided valuable editorial aid and keen insights on manuscript preparation. More important, following my unfortunate illness in August 2003, she prepared the entire manuscript for publication and shepherded it through the publishing process. I am particularly indebted to her for preparing the detailed index for this volume, pursuing photo permissions, and proofing the final published work. Had she not taken this project under her wing this book would have been many more years in the making. My son, John E. Bierley, worked wonders in compiling the database that appears as Appendix III, painstakingly scanned all photographs, helped with editing and proofreading, and assisted

Lois in details of final publication. Melissa J. Bierley, my granddaughter, worked in several capacities, mostly in compiling the discography and corresponding with libraries. Another granddaughter, Deborah Yousavich, helped document the band tours. Son-in-law William K. Walker and nephew Eric Allison solved many computer problems and patiently educated me in clever search techniques and other electronic tricks of the trade. Abby Pressler, my cousin, also helped document the band tours.

Other research associates helped in many capacities, most notably Ben Roush, Ruth C. Nichols, and Keith Denick. Jennifer Blair made a study of the Sousa Band's violin soloists, an inquiry funded by Rachel Barton, one of today's premier concert violinists.

LIBRARIANS

Thousands of letters were exchanged with libraries, historical societies, museums, and other institutions to confirm Sousa Band visits to various cities. This was necessary to reconstruct numerous band tours for which no itineraries were available. It is only fitting that I offer sincere appreciation to individuals and institutions, which are arranged by state or province.

Alabama: Thomas Hutchens, Huntsville–Madison County Public Library; Ken Tilley, State of Alabama Department of Archives and History (Montgomery); Les Wilsey, Public Library of Anniston and Calhoun County.

Arizona: Michael Wurtz, Sharlot Hall Museum (Prescott).

Arkansas: Donne Addison, Garland County Library; Bobbie Jones McLane, Garland County Historical Society; Gwendolyn L. Shelton, Pine Bluff/Jefferson County Library.

California: Terri M. Anderson, Needles Branch, San Bernardino County Library System; Roger Bonilla and Ralph Libby, Palo Alto City Library; Nannette Bricker-Barrett, San Bernardino County Library; Virginia Crook, Gwen Kraft, and John Light, San Luis Obispo City County Library; Steve Fjeldsted and Janet Harader, Kings County Library; Christie Hammond, Richard Hanks, and Don McCue, A. K. Smiley Public Library (Redlands); Anne Harder, Santa Ana Public Library; Rosemary Hardy, Berkeley Public Library; Sheila Holder, Tulare County Library; Bob Johnson, San Jose Public Library; Gregory J. Kelly, San Francisco Public Library; James E. Kern, Vallejo Naval and Historical Museum; Rosalie Longan, Tulare Public Library; Brandon C. McLintock, Woodland Public Library; Carrie Miller and Ken Warfield, Santa Barbara Public Library; La Verna Miller, Ontario City Library; Karen Rames, Stockton–San Joaquin County Public Library; Mary Robertson, Yuba County Library; Bonnie Roos, Monterey County Free Library; Mel Russell, Yolo County Archives and Records Center; Elke Faraci and Carol Schroeter, Orange County Public Library; Melissa Scroggins and Linda Sitterding, Fresno County Free Library; Mitch Ison, David Seagly, and Jill Stockinger, Sacramento Public Library; Millicent Sharma, City of Pasadena Department of Information Services Library; Jennifer Songster, Long Beach Public Library; Charles B. Teval, Stanislaus County Free Library; Charles Johnson,

Barbara Topping, and Dave Weber, Ventura County Library; John Walden, Kern County Library; staff, Napa City–County Library; staff, Riverside Public Library; staff, Santa Cruz City–County Library.

Connecticut: Tom Burnham, Manchester Public Library; Leon N. Flanagan, Silas Bronson Library (Waterbury); Betty D. Goldman, Bridgeport Public Library; Lee Jaworski, Ferguson Library (Stamford); Jean Luddy, Rockville Public Library (Vernon); John O'Donnell, Danbury Public Library; Denise Russo, Russel Library (Middleton).

Colorado: Emily Anderson and Jody Jones, Pikes Peak Library District (Colorado Springs); Linda Brown, Victor County Public Library; Linda Brown-Byrne, Fort Collins Public Library; Susan Cochran, Canon City Public Library; Debbie Cosper, Woodruff Memorial Library (La Junta); Barbara Dey, Colorado Historical Society (Denver); Pegga A. Ford, Greeley County Division of Museums; Kay Oxer, Mesa County Public Library; Philip Panum, Denver Public Library; Weldean Peto, Franklin Ferguson Memorial Library (Cripple Creek); Mary Jo Reitsema, Boulder Public Library; Noreen Riffe, McClelland Public Library (Pueblo); Heather Kimsey and Liz Roberts, La Junta Public Library; Doug Thompson, Rocky Ford Public Library.

Delaware: Jenifer Brown, Wilmington Public Library.

Florida: B. Young, Miami-Dade Public Library; Tom Hambright, Monroe County May Hill Russell Library; Paul Camp, Fowler Library, University of South Florida.

Georgia: Anne M. Isabell, Lake Blackshear Regional Library (Americus); Diane H. Jackson, Brunswick-Glynn Regional Library; Linda Litton, Dalton–Whitfield County Public Library; Amy S. Swann, *Savannah Morning News;* staff, Augusta Public Library.

Illinois: Carol Alanghuty, Reddick Library (Ottawa); Roberta Allen, Danville Public Library; Kim Bunner, Parlin-Ingersoll Library (Canton); Margaret Bush, Tazwell County Genealogical Society (Pekin); Emily Clark, Chicago Historical Society; Martha Clyde, Macomb Public Library; Bethany Corbett, Bloomington Public Library; Bernadette Duvernoy, Hayner Public Library (Alton); Susan Fagan, Newberry Library (Chicago); Esther May Ayers and Gladys Freeze, Stinson Memorial Library (Anna); Roger Gambral, Joliet Public Library; Sally Gardner, Pekin Public Library; Caryl M. Harris, Matson Public Library (Princeton); Marcia Heise, Galesburg Public Library; Glenn Humphreys and the G.I.S. Letter Reference Team, Chicago Public Library; Lou Ann James, Belleville Public Library; Roberts S. Jordan, Lasalle County Genealogical Guild (Ottawa); Betsy Kisler, John Mosser Public Library (Abingdon); Emily J. Knott, Kewanee Public Library; John L. Molyneux, Rockford Public Library; Mary Ann Pirone, Aurora Public Library; Betty Robertson and Elaine Pichaske Sokolowski, Peoria Public Library; Edward J. Russo, Lincoln Library (Springfield); David Siegenthaler, Gail Borden Public Library (Elgin); Dorothea Smith, Wilmington Area Historical Society; Richard Sumrall, Lincoln Public Library; Leslie Toldeh, Streator Public Library; Margaret G. Wollitz, Decatur Public Library; Jacksonville Public Library; staff, Quincy Public Library.

Indiana: Marion Boots, Hartford City Public Library; Pat Brooks, Carnegie Library (Muncie); Loretta Dodd, Elwood Public Library;

Shirley Doller, Jay County Public Library; Robert Eagen, La Porte County Public Library; Chris Hough, Porter County Public Library; Mary Johnson and Judy Spencer, Crawfordsville District Public Library; Nancy Gootee and Ed Szynaka, Indianapolis–Marion County Public Library; Vicki Green, Frankfort Public Library; Joan Keefer, Huntington City Township Public Library; Nancy Lee and Michael R. Pitts, Anderson Public Library; Barbara A. Love, Marion Public Library; T. Miller and Jeanina Rhodes, Elkhart Public Library; A. Pennington, Crawfordsville District Public Library; Rebecca S. Price and Joseph Sipocz, St. Joseph County Public Library; Dana L. Owen, Warsaw Community Public Library; Mary J. Snider, Logansport Cass County Library; Ann Unger, Wabash Carnegie Public Library; Sean Walton, St. Joseph County Public Library; Pamela Wasner, Monroe County Public Library; Donald L. Weaver, Putnam County Public Library; staff, Peru Public Library.

Iowa: Betty A. Baule, Carnegie-Stout Public Library (Dubuque); Virginia Borkowski, Red Oak Public Library; Linda Brown-Link and Rosie Springer, State Historical Society of Iowa; Margaret Carpenter, Council Bluffs Public Library; Treasure Elliot, Le Mars Public Library; Ellen V. Foland, Independence Public Library; Susie Guest, Burlington Public Library; Karen Manning, Maquoketa Free Public Library; Mary Ann Moore, Davenport Public Library; Nancy Neumann, Sioux City Public Library; Sue Pearson, Waterloo Public Library; staff, Cedar Rapids Public Library; staff, Iowa City Public Library; staff, Washington Public Library.

Kansas: K. Baker and Jim Riordan, Leavenworth Public Library; Claudia Basshammer, Atchison Library; Linda L. Clark, Kingman Carnegie Public Library; Katharine A. Commerford, Emporia Public Library; Kathy Hannah, Wichita Public Library; John Lance and Cecilia May, Lawrence Public Library; Susan Moyer, Dorothy Bramlage Public Library (Junction City); Mark Rustman, Topeka and Shawnee County Public Library; Linda Slack, Kingman Carnegie Public Library; staff, Burney Memorial Library (Cottonwood Falls); staff, Manhattan Public Library; staff, Newton Public Library; staff, Ottawa Library.

Kentucky: Elaine Allen, Fulton Public Library; Kathie L. Farmer, W. T. Young Library, University of Kentucky; Ron Steensland, Lexington Public Library; staff, Paris-Bourbon County Library.

Louisiana: Bandana Mukherjee, Shreve Memorial Library (Shreveport).

Maine: Laura Bean, Curtis Memorial Library (Brunswick); Anthony Douim, Maine State Archives; D. Povich, Bath Historical Society; Joyce Wanger, Rumford Public Library; staff, Portland Public Library.

Maryland: Marcia Dysart, Enoch Pratt Free Library (Baltimore); Anne Marie Reed, Washington County Free Library; Mae Talbott, Washington County Free Library.

Massachusetts: Margaret Banister, Concord Free Public Library; Freda Chabot, Fitchburg Public Library; Keith Chognette and Lucia M. Shannon, Brockton Public Library; Bethany Cove, Lynn Public Library; Pamela Donovan-Hall (who traveled to a neighboring town for information and was rewarded by a parking ticket); Ruth C. Gagliardi, Athol Public Library; Paul K. Graves, Holyoke Public Library; Betty Hamilton, Attleboro Public Library; Delores Henry, New Bedford Free Public Library; Marguerite M. Jacinto, Taunton Public Library; Dawn B. Jordan and Gregory H. Laing, Haverhill Public Library; Tom Madden, Gloucester Lyceum and Sawyer Free Library; Maureen Nimmo, Lawrence Public Library; Cecile Pimental, Newburyport Public Library; Esther Proctor, Manchester Historical Society; Barbara Oberlin, Marlboro Public Library; Patricia Redfearn, Fall River Public Library; Lee Regan and Throckmorton Hunt, Plymouth Public Library; Henry Scannell, Boston Public Library; Ann Tumavicus, Westfield Anthenaeum; Joyce Woodman, Concord Free Library; staff, Greenfield Public Library; staff, Salem Public Library; staff, Pollard Memorial Library (Lowell).

Michigan: Margaret Bentley, Shiawassee District Library (Owosso); Susan Brower, Catherine A. Larson, and Cathy Seria, Kalamazoo Public Library; Deborah Buzzard, Niles Community Library; Helen Constan, Capital Area District Library (Lansing); Maria Davis (Eastern Michigan University Archives); Paula C. Drummond, Ypsilanti District Library; Brigette Felix, Pontiac Public Library; Lawrence Frank, Blue Water District Library (Port Huron); Beverly Garrett, Willard Library (Battle Creek); Kay Hadley, Dowagiac Public Library; Richard LeSueur and Anthony Reed, Ann Arbor District Library; Agatha K. Kalkanis and Lillian Stefano, Detroit Public Library; Ann Kelly, Muskegon Public Library; Frederick J. Kirby and Jill Rauh, Benton Harbor Public Library; Michelle Klose, Niles Community Library; D. Larsen, Mt. Clemens Public Library; Doris Littlebrant, Jackson District Library; James Mac Lean, Clarence H. Rosa Public Library (Lansing); Robert C. Myers, Berrian County Historical Association (Berrien Springs); Alice Selfridge, Big Rapids Community Library; Carolyn Sutter, Vicksburg District Library; David G. Tacia, Pontiac Public Library; Suzanne Wayda-Slomski, Adrian Public Library; Angie Wesch, Flint Public Library; Mary W. Wessels, Oakland County Pioneer and Historical Society (Pontiac); staff, Bay Area County Library; staff, Detroit Public Library; staff, Grand Rapids Public Library; staff, Mt. Clemens Public Library; staff, Ypsilanti Historical Museum.

Minnesota: Linda Anderson, Austin Public Library; Bruce Burns and Kathryn Rynders, Red Wing Public Library; Carol Hannick, Minnesota Valley Regional Library (Mankoto); Bonnie Kreuger and Nancy Vaillancourt, Owatonna Public Library; Chris McArdle Rojo, Albert Lea Public Library; staff, Chatfield Brass Band Lending Library; staff, Stillwater Public Library.

Mississippi: Rosemary A. Fairchild, Warren County–Vicksburg Public Library; Perian P. Kerr, Starkville–Oktibbeha County Public Library.

Missouri: Randall Blomquist, Missouri Historical Society; Roberta Hagood, Hannibal Free Library; Noel C. Holobeck, St. Louis Public Library; John A. Horner, Kansas City Public Library; Robert Pigg, Livingston County Genealogical Society; Janice G. Cox Proffitt, Ray County Library; Mary Schumaker, Sedalia Public Library.

Montana: Milla L. Cummins and John Swenumosn, Livingston–

Park County Public Library; Jim Curry, Parmly Billings Library (Billings); Terry Dood, Bozeman Public Library; Esther Kornemann, Miles City Public Library; Karla Ritten, Lewis and Clark Library (Helena); Don Spitzer, Missoula Public Library; Ellen Thompson, Great Falls Public Library.

Nebraska: Becky W. Clark, Lincoln City Library; Jeff Gilderson-Due, Holdrege Public Library; Judy Hilkemann, Norfolk Public Library; Dan Kubick, Omaha Public Library; Darlene Mayer, Morton-James Public Library (Nebraska City); Myrtle Nygren, Memorial Library (Fremont); Linda Price, Kearney Public Library; Linda M. Rea, Hastings Public Library; Stan Schulz, Kilgore Memorial Library (York); staff, Beatrice Public Library.

Nevada: Susan Antipa, Carson City Library; Tim Bauer, Washoe County Library; Joyce M. Cox, Nevada State Library and Archives (Carson City).

New Brunswick, Canada: Elva Hatt, St. Croix Public Library of St. Stephen; Laura Master, York Regional Library (Fredericton); Margaret Rogers, St. John Regional Library; staff, Moncton Public Library.

New Hampshire: Margaret Banister, Concord Free Public Library; Dave Howlett, Keene Public Library; Cynthia N. O'Neil, Manchester City Library; Andrea Thorpe, Richards Free Library (Newport); Peggie Wood, Lebanon Public Library.

New Jersey: Valerie Austin and Paul D. Pattwell, Newark Public Library; Robert Barbanell, Free Library of Elizabeth; Bruce R. Bardarik, Patterson Free Public Library; Ted Bennicoff, Seely G. Mudd Manuscript Library, Princeton University; Bernadette A. Boucher, New Brunswick Free Public Library; Renee G. Cohen, Red Bank Public Library; Theresa M. Gorman, Camden Public Library; Ellen Kastel, Plainfield Public Library; James Lindemuth, Ocean Grove Camp Meeting Association; Arleen Maiden, Salem Free Public Library; Alice McMillan, Orange Public Library; Eileen Meyer-Sklar, Trenton Public Library; John J. Norton, Jersey City Public Library; Korin Rosenkrans, Morristown Public Library; Pat Rothenberg, Atlantic City Free Public Library; Mary Lou Skillin, Montclair Public Library; Robert W. Stewart, Asbury Park Public Library; Patricia Wardwell, Bergen County Department of Parks; staff, Princeton Public Library.

New Mexico: Judy Klinger, Santa Fe Public Library; John J. Vittal, Albuquerque–Bernalillo County Public Library.

New York: Donna Barnes, Niagara County History Department; Kathryn L. Barton, Guernsey Memorial Library (Norwich); Virginia B. Bowers, Albany City Historian; Robert Boyle and Barbara Zimmer, Colin Naylor Field Library (Peekskill); Barbara Brooks, Utica Public Library; Ronda Brown, Bartholomew County Public Library; Charles J. Browne and Michael F. Sackett, Broome County Public Library; Deborah Bucholtz, Gloversville Free Library; Katherine S. Cayea and Richard D. Ward, Plattsburgh Public Library; Lori Chien, Jervis Public Library (Rome); Sandy Chronhkite, Historian of Fort Plain; Maria Davis, Eastern Michigan University Archives; Ed Dunscombe, George F. Johnson Memorial Library (Endicott); Kathy Van Flue and Ronald Lagasse, Schenectady County Public Library; Rita Forrester, Newburgh Free Library; Ellen K. Gamache, Albany Public Library; Shirley Garrett, Mt. Vernon Public Library; Mary Gilmore, Seymour Public Library (Auburn); Tioga County Historical Society; Varney S. Greene and Patricia Monahan, Buffalo and Erie County Public Library; Joanie Hand, Pen Yan Public Library; Elizabeth Hardy and Joy Holland, Brooklyn Public Library; Antonia F. Houston, Blodgett Memorial Library (Fishkill); Gary Jones and Susan Spence, Onondago County Public Library; Deborah Jop, Rochester Public Library; Mary King, Madison County Historical Society; Lisa Kochik, Poughkeepsie Public Library; Rita A. McCormack, Richmond Memorial Library (Batavia); Gail Myker, Middletown Thrall Library; Grace M. Norcott, Newark Public Library; Susan R. Perkins, Herkimer County Historical Society; Sandra M. Putney, Ogdensburg Public Library; Laura M. Prievo, Carthage Village Historian; Deborah Scheffler, Geneva Free Library; Ann Schwartz, R. P. Flower Memorial Library (Watertown); staff, Frank J. Basloe Library (Herkimer); staff, Little Falls Public Library; staff, Lockport Public Library; staff, Economic and Public Affairs Division, New York Public Library.

North Carolina: Anne Berkley, Durham County Library; Jerry Carroll and Sharon Carter, Forsyth County Public Library; Patricia F. Ferguson and Wanda Hunter, Cumberland County Public Library; Peter R. Neal and Peter Vari, Durham Public Library; Robbie Owens and Helen Snow, Greensboro Public Library; Joseph Sheppard, New Hanover County Public Library; staff, Olivia Rarey Library (Raleigh); staff, Rowan Public Library (Salisbury); staff, Wayne County Public Library.

North Dakota: C. Boldish, Grand Forks City-County Library; Joyce Forland, Williston Community Library; Steve Hubbard, Fargo Public Library; staff, Bismarck Public Library; staff, North Dakota State Library (Bismarck).

Nova Scotia, Canada: Laura Bradley, Cathy d'Entremont, and Virginia Stoddard, Western Counties Regional Library (Yarmouth); Paula Coldwell, Kingstec Campus Library of Nova Scotia Community College; Martha K. MacDonald, New Glasgow Library; Garry D. Shutlak, Public Archives of Nova Scotia (Halifax); Beverly True, Cumberland Regional Library (Amherst); staff, Arcadia University Archives (Wolfville).

Ohio: Margaret J. Baker and Wendy Wise, Tiffin-Seneca Public Library; Amy E. Baldauf and Samuel A. Norris, Marion Public Library; Carol W. Bell, Warren–Trumbell County Public Library; Robert Bertrand and Ralph Waite, Lima Public Library; Gary Bransen, London Public Library; Sherie L. Brown, Massillon Public Library; R. Burton, Elyria Public Library; Inez Clark, Patsy Pace, and Sam Roshon and countless other associates, Columbus Metropolitan Library; Joan L. Clark, Cleveland Public Library; Wendy Contini, Dover Public Library; Ron Davidson and Susan Schwerer, Sandusky Library; Sandy Day, Schiappa Library (Steubenville); Betsy DeMent, Portsmouth Public Library; Carolyn Diersing, Cheryl Fulton, Barb Hauer, Erik Johansen, Laura Moorman, Belinda Mortensen, Patricia Ross, and Elaine Warren, Westerville Public Library; Doris Ebbert and Patty Rothermich, Otterbein College Library; Valerie E. Elliott, Smith Library of Re-

gional History (Oxford); Donna Ferguson, Wilmington Public Library; Karen Furlong, Mansfield/Richland County Public Library; Jim Gill, Tuscarawas County Public Library; Richard E. Goodwin, Guernsey County District Public Library; Ann Grimes, Salem Public Library; Anna J. Horton, Public Library of Cincinnati and Hamilton County; J. James, Akron–Summit County Public Library; Joe Jeffries, Loraine Public Library; Penelope H. Justice, Kaubisch Memorial Public Library (Fostoria); Deborah Keener, Wayne County Public Library; Marlo Keller and John Ransom, Rutherford B. Hayes Presidential Center (Fremont); Bianca E. V. Kelley, Logan County District Library; Pat Little, Defiance Public Library; Marianne Mahl, Susan Schillig, and Joseph A. Vondruska, Elyria Public Library; James C. Marshall, Toledo–Lucas County Public Library; Jennifer Morrow and Catherine Wilson, Greene County Public Library; Deborah Orth, Norwalk Public Library; Joanne D. Prisley, Athens County Historical Society; Deirdre Bray Root, Middletown Public Library; Tim Seman, Public Library of Youngstown and Mahoning County; Vicky Frey, Janine Shilling, and Jennifer Thompson, Chillicothe and Roth County Public Library; J. Thomas, Rodman Public Library (Alliance); Kim Van Blaricum, Stark County District Library; Dianna Wood and Local History Department, Findlay–Hancock County Public Library; staff, Ada Public Library; staff, Birchard Public Library (Fremont); staff, Bucyrus Public Library; staff, Champaign County Library; staff, Lane Public Library (Hamilton); staff, Mansfield–Richland County Public Library; staff, Newcomerstown Historical Society; staff, Stark County District Library.

Oklahoma: Delbert Amen, Oklahoma Historical Society (Oklahoma City); Dianne Costin, El Reno Carnegie Library; Ruth Ann Evans, Public Library of Enid and Garfield County; Larry Johnson, Metropolitan Library System (Oklahoma City); Pat Schubert, Chickasha Public Library; staff, Okmulgee Public Library.

Ontario, Canada: Brian Covill, Hamilton Public Library; B. Sears, Peterborough Public Library.

Oregon: George Domijon, Jackson County Library; Greg Wibe, Multnomah County Library.

Pennsylvania: Christa L. Bassett and David L. Smith, Cumberland County Historical Society; Wendy Bish-McGrew, Hanover Public Library; Fred Bomberger, Allentown Public Library; Jane Bradford, Thomas Beaver Free Library (Danville); Jerry Bruce, Lancaster Area Library; Carmen Rae Campbell, Northumberland County Historical Society; Jim Curry, Clearfield Historical Society; Lois Donovan, Historical Society of the Phoenixville Area; Dottie Fritton, Martin Library (York); Lila Fourhman-Shaull, Historical Society of York County; Linda Freedman, Bethlehem Area Public Library; Mike Geary, Coatesville Area Public Library; Gwen Gillespie, Dimmick Memorial Library (Jim Thorp); Andrea Glossner, Annie Halenbake Ross Library (Lock Haven); Audrey Iacone, Carnegie Library of Pittsburgh; William E. Irvin, Carnegie Free Library of Beaver Falls; Barbara Keiser, Eastern Monroe Public Library (Stroudsburg); Sabrina Kirby, Kauffman Public Library (Sunbury); Christine L. Mason, Lebanon County Historical Society;

Paul Savedow and Newspaper Center, Free Library of Philadelphia; Paula Schechter, Coyle Free Library (Chambersburg); Connie Weaver, Bosler Free Library (Carlisle); staff, Bradford County Historical Society; staff, Green Free Library (Canton); staff, Historical Society of Montgomery County; staff, Lebanon Community Library; staff, Norristown Public Library; staff, Osterhout Free Library (Wilkes-Barre); staff, Shaw Public Library (Clearfield); staff, Towanda Public Library.

Quebec, Canada: Stanley Brasgold, Bibliothèque Centrale (Montreal).

Rhode Island: Sandra Allen, Newport Public Library; Barbara Cussart, Woonsocket Harris Public Library; Susan Reed, Pawtucket Public Library.

South Carolina: Durk Spencer, Sheppard Memorial Library (Greenville); Winnie Walsh, Spartanburg County Public Library.

South Dakota: Jane A. Larson, Vermillion Public Library.

Tennessee: Laura J. Underwood, Knox County Public Library; staff, Morriston-Hamblen Library.

Texas: Brenda Edgar, Marshall Public Library; Amie Treuer, Dallas Public Library; staff, Waco–McLennan County Library.

Utah: Jeanne L. Brückner, Weber County Library; Linda A. Threlkeld, Weber County Library; Cherie Willis, Salt Lake City Public Library; Dina Wyatt, Provo City Library.

Vermont: Anita Danigelis, Fletcher Free Library (Burlington); Paul Donovan, Vermont Department of Libraries; Donna Fogarty, Windsor Public Library; Francis Inslie, Kimball Public Library (Randolph); Russell S. Moore, Springfield Town Library; Richard M. Shuldiner, Brooks Memorial Library (Brattleboro); Anne Wingate, Fletcher Memorial Library (Ludlow); staff, Kellogg Hubbard Library (Montpelier); staff, Rutland Free Library; staff, Vermont Historical Society Library.

Virginia: Lewis Hobgood Averett, Jones Memorial Library (Lynchburg); Jim Barns, Jefferson-Madison Regional Library (Charlottesville); Katrina M. Boston, Newport News Public Library; David Feinberg, The Library of Virginia (Richmond); Robert Kinney, Norfolk Public Library; Terry L. McFarland, Hampton Public Library; Jeanne D. Mead, Jones Memorial Library (Lynchburg); Bebe Wills, Staunton Public Library; staff, Lynchburg Public Library.

Washington: Chris Skaugset, Longview Public Library; staff, Timberland Regional Library (Olympia).

West Virginia: Louis Horacek, Ohio County Public Library (Wheeling); staff, Cabell County Public Library.

Wisconsin: Hans Baierl, Watertown Public Library; Shirley Chilson, Waukesha Public Library; Jay J. Chung and Judy Day, Racine Public Library; Erin Coppersmith, Kohler Public Library; A. Day, Kenosha Public Library; Nijole Etzwiler, Baraboo Public Library; Alan Jorgenson, Ripon Public Library; Roberta May, Mead Public Library (Sheboygan); Laura McMennamin, Albany County Public Library; Mara B. Munroe, Oshkosh Public Library; Larry A. Nickel, L. E. Phillips Memorial Library (Eau Claire); Karen M. Peterson, Berlin Public Library; Kathy Wodrich Schmidt, Manitowoc Public Library; Julie Zachau, Superior Public Library; staff, Beloit Public Library; staff, La Crosse Public Library.

Wyoming: Jean Brainard, Cindy L. Brown, and Ann Nelson, Wyoming State Archives; Robert Kalabus, Western Wyoming Community College Library (Rock Springs); Jennifer Mayer, Albany County Public Library; staff, Central Wyoming College Library (Rawlins).

SPONSORSHIP

After thirty-five years of footing the bills for my research, I organized the Integrity Research Foundation and was able to obtain a degree of financial support that enabled me to engage research associates who helped bring closure to the effort. To these organizations and individuals I extend heartfelt appreciation. Principal benefactors were the John Philip Sousa Foundation, led by Al G. Wright and John R. Bourgeois, and James G. Saied of the Saied Family Foundation.

I am exceedingly grateful to the following organizations and individuals: The Brass Band of Columbus, Judith Foulk and Mark Elrod, the American School Band Directors Educational Foundation, Rachel Barton, Harry Lucas Jr., the Sounds of Sousa Band (via the Corbin Corp.), the American Bandmasters Association Foundation, Keith Brion and the New Sousa Band, Donald E. and Ruth McGinnis, the Japan Sousa Society, Loras J. Schissel, Paul and Anne Droste, Pauline J. Bierley, Virginia Blankenship, Antoinette Cendali, Barry and Susan Furrer, the Ringgold Band (Reading), Windjammers Unlimited, Donald N. Ruff, Vernon Pack, John Philip Sousa IV, Al and Gladys Wright, *The Instrumentalist,* Mr. and Mrs. William F. Ludwig II, Kathy Samuelson, Volkwein Brothers, Wingert-Jones Publications, Thomas Edgar Ewing, Frank Fendorf, John Howard, and Hazel Sampson.

MY TOP ADVISOR

As usual in the acknowledgments sections of my books, the best has been saved until last. Pauline, my beloved wife of more than half a century, deserves much more credit than she will ever receive. Over the course of more than forty years of research and writing she has sacrificed much of her own time and interests to support my "addiction," as she affectionately refers to it. She has tolerated the impact to the family budget, managed household affairs while my mind was occupied elsewhere, foregone vacations, and kept the family on an even keel. She has fed and entertained hundreds of guests in our home and kept me healthy despite my proclivity for eating certain foods that I adore. She has sat through innumerable concerts, contests, conferences, and seminars and spent many long hours alone while I was busily engaged in my interests. She has tolerated the ego and multitudinous idiosyncrasies of a determined researcher with relatively little fuss and for that I am eternally grateful. On top of all that, she contributed directly to this volume in many ways. She graciously offered editorial comment and was another who spent long hours proofreading the entire manuscript. This one, Pauline, is dedicated to you.

Introduction

I WAS CURIOUS, YOU SEE

It was curiosity about the colorful titles of John Philip Sousa's marches that led me down a long trail to become his biographer. Take "The Fairest of the Fair," for instance. Who was the "fairest"? Of what fair? "King Cotton" was the ruler of what country? Who was "El Capitan"? "The Diplomat"? "The Belle of Chicago"? Which star is "The Golden Star"? Was "The Washington Post" a military base? Who were the "Nobles of the Mystic Shrine"? Who or what was "The Thunderer"?

I thought surely some day there would be a book explaining these mysterious titles and telling the story of this man called the "March King" and the band that was the standard of comparison for all others. No such volume ever appeared.

In a moment of weakness I brazenly thought I might be able to write such a book myself. I was an aeronautical engineer and only a part-time musician, however, so my credentials were in the wrong field. Nevertheless, because of my overgrown curiosity and an ability to work with intensity I thought I could easily produce such a book in my spare time in about two years.

That was forty years ago.

HITCHING MY WAGON TO A STAR

My research eventually led to five books and numerous other writings about Sousa and his music, but the comprehensive story of the band had yet to be told.

When I made the decision to write a book documenting the band's history, I was apprehensive. It meant telling the story of not one man but more than 1,200 men and women. Did Sousa's band deserve such a book? Yes, because of the part the band played in his "mission in music." In presenting more than fifteen thousand concerts he and the band had an enormous impact on the American music scene. Together, they carried the torch of a dynamic young America throughout the world.

Sousa's charisma, coupled with his skill as a conductor and creator of unique programs, attracted extraordinary musicians. The best in their field, they composed an unparalleled aggregation of wind and percussion musicians during that era. It was my privilege to interview five dozen of them.

INSPIRATION

From my earliest recollection I was inspired by Sousa's music—even before I knew the name *Sousa*. Several years passed before I became aware that he composed anything other than marches. For reasons I can't explain, those marches said something to me personally. I still have that fascination despite being exposed to the finest marches of the world's famous march writers.

Sousa stated repeatedly that he composed only when inspired. He could write at any hour of the day or night, but unless a piece of music was the result of a genuine inspiration he usually disposed of it.

He inspired his musicians, and they inspired me. Their stories about his kindness, gentlemanly deportment, and generosity left me awestruck.

A KING'S HONOR

Although called a "king," Sousa was actually a humble man, sincere in the belief that along with his God-given talents came an obligation to serve others with those talents.

Sousa's sense of morality, I learned, was beyond question. The editor of my first book took me to task for portraying him as somewhat of a saint, but I had been on the lookout for the least bit of gossip for ten years and had found none.

I will never forget the day William Schneider, Sousa's road manager, said with conviction, "In the years I knew Mr. Sousa, he impressed me as being the man who tried to be the most honorable person who ever walked the face of this earth."

LOYALTY

The loyalty of Sousa's musicians was legendary. In talking with them, I detected a hint of reverence and watched their faces light up as they eagerly told me about the most precious moments of their careers—the time they spent with Sousa and his band. What other conductor's musicians formed a fraternal society twelve years after his death—and met every year on the anniversary of his birth until none were still living?

MEMORIES

It is regrettable that most people now living did not hear Sousa's band in concert and that there are no recordings or films of his touring band in all its glory. In this book I have endeavored to preserve the memory of that incredible band.

CHAPTER ONE

The Legacy

A CENTURY AGO

Let us transport ourselves back through history to the end of the nineteenth century. It is Sunday evening, April 10, 1898, and we are attending a concert by John Philip Sousa and his legendary band.

We find ourselves in the revered Metropolitan Opera House in New York City, where Sousa is presenting a patriotic concert instead of the program he had originally planned. He and many others believe the United States is about to go to war with Spain.

The battleship *Maine* was blown up less than two months before, and "Remember the Maine" is a rallying cry around the country. Congress is petitioning Spain to free Cuba from what it considers harsh rule and oppressive conditions.

Five thousand people are present. They fill every seat, and hundreds more stand in the rear. The program will consist largely of Sousa's own works unless he elects to add other patriotic music, which he has been known to do on the spur of the moment.

The program is well received by the huge audience. A medley of patriotic songs, including "Yankee Doodle" and "Marching through Georgia," builds enthusiasm, and people begin to beat time with their feet.

Selections from "El Capitan" are played next, and then Sousa's new march "The Stars and Stripes Forever" brings thunderous applause. Cheering breaks out in earnest when the band strikes up "The Star-Spangled Banner," and many stand on their seats. All around the hall, people wave handkerchiefs, hats, canes, and other articles. The outburst is deafening.

The band launches into "Dixie," and there is bedlam. Rebel yells and Union cheers drown out the music, and the crowd goes wild. After the last note is played a man in a gray suit yells, "Three cheers for the stars and stripes! For the North and South! We're all ready!"

That is followed by another outburst. "Who says we're not ready for war?" a man in the balcony screams. The crowd lets loose again.

When order is restored the concert resumes. The band is assisted on the final number by a sizable chorus for Sousa's rousing "Unchain the Dogs of War." This draws more cheers, and band and chorus are obliged to repeat it several times before five thousand hoarse and tired individuals make their ways home.[1] The extraordinary display of patriotism was not typical of a Sousa concert, but the incident illustrates how he and his band could make any concert interesting and exciting. Such was the tradition for nearly forty years.

AN AMERICAN PHENOMENON

How a talented young American who had a promising future in theater music began his career as an orchestral violinist and ended that career as the most famous band conductor the world has known is a strange tale indeed.

Such is the story of John Philip Sousa, called the "March King" much as Johann Strauss is known as the "Waltz King." By the time Sousa reached fifty he was the most popular musical figure of the day and in all probability the highest paid.

His legendary band was made up of the finest musicians money could buy, several of whom were recognized as the very best on their respective instruments. The group was called a band but could more accurately be termed a wind symphony. It had substantial impact on America's cultural heritage and was, in a sense, a cultural export. This book is the story of that band.

---

1. This scene was described in six New York newspapers, the *Herald, Telegraph, News, Journal, Evening Sun,* and *Mail and Express.* War with Spain was declared eight days later.

THE SYMBOL OF AN ERA

The phenomenon of Sousa's Band could not have occurred at any time other than its own era. Sousa came along at the right moment in history, when America was emerging as a world power. The energy of his country is clear in his music, particularly the marches, which people welcomed with great enthusiasm. March music was very popular, and to a certain extent Sousa's mirrored the pulse of the nation.

"The Stars and Stripes Forever" was considered America's national march for more than ninety years before its official designation as such in 1987.[2] Many of Sousa's other marches, such as "The Liberty Bell," "The Invincible Eagle," and "Hail to the Spirit of Liberty," contributed to a wave of patriotism brought on by the Spanish-American War.

ENTERTAINMENT BEFORE MODERN CONVENIENCES

Sousa and his band came on the scene at a time when live entertainment was paramount. People generally did not travel far from home. Moreover, there was no television or radio, nor were there movies. The phonograph was still in its primitive stage and a novelty. Modern highways and automobiles were many years away, so live entertainment was the only practical way to partake of the musical arts.

Sousa's Band, in traveling throughout the land by railroad, was a welcome part of an average American's life. His band took entertainment directly to the people and at a remarkable pace. He was a great composer and also the greatest bandmaster of all time. To understand his impact on the American cultural scene, however, we must think of him as a traveling entertainer.

THE MAN BEHIND THE LEGEND

Sousa, the guiding light of this aggregation, was an American patriot through and through. He was born in Washington, D.C., on November 6, 1854, to a Portuguese Spanish father and a German mother and died in Reading, Pennsylvania, on March 6, 1932.[3]

He was educated in public grammar schools while simultaneously studying music at the Esputa Conservatory of Music, a small private school. For a short period he had his own dance band. At age thirteen he enlisted in the United States Marine Band as an apprentice musician.

The general education and music training Sousa received as a U.S. Marine were valuable, but far more important was the additional study taken with George Felix Benkert, a highly regarded orchestra conductor, violinist, and pianist. Benkert had studied in Vienna, and although he introduced Sousa to the European classical

John Philip Sousa is known as the "March King," but he also composed operettas and many other types of music while presenting more than fifteen thousand concerts with the Sousa Band and serving nineteen years in military service. It is possible that he made more personal appearances than any other major conductor. "I would rather be the composer of an inspired march than the composer of a manufactured symphony" was one of his favorite sayings. (Barry Owen Furrer Collection)

tradition, he strongly suggested that the talented student seek his own compositional style.

While studying with Benkert, Sousa also played in weekly string quartet recitals at the home of William Hunter, the assistant secretary of state. Hunter introduced him to philanthropist W. W. Corcoran, who likely would have sent Sousa to Europe for more formal music study had Sousa asked.

He left the Marine Band at age twenty and began to work as a violinist and conductor of theater orchestras in the Washington area and on tour. During the American Centennial Celebration in Philadelphia he was a member of the first violin section of the orchestra conducted by French composer Jacques Offenbach. Later, he conducted an *H.M.S. Pinafore* company on a tour of the eastern states.

Sousa's reputation as a journeyman musician and composer attracted the attention of Marine Corps officials, and he was recalled to Washington to serve as leader of the "President's Own," the United States Marine Band. Over a period of twelve years, from 1880 to 1892, he transformed that group into America's finest military band.

---

2. "The Stars and Stripes Forever" has probably been recorded more than any other single piece of music ever written, according to my research. That is not to say it has sold more records—only that it has been recorded more times.
3. Sousa, *Marching Along*; Bierley, *John Philip Sousa, American Phenomenon*.

Sousa resigned from the Marine Corps at age thirty-seven to form his own civilian band, which over the next forty years became a revered American institution, playing an astonishing 15,623 live concerts, not counting radio broadcasts.[4]

The only interruption came during World War I, when Sousa was commissioned by the U.S. Navy to train musicians for fleet duty at the Great Lakes Naval Training Station. The Sousa Band resumed operation after the war. On March 6, 1932, Sousa died between tours while in Reading, Pennsylvania, to guest-conduct the Ringgold Band. He was buried with full military honors in Washington's Congressional Cemetery.

UNEXPECTED POPULARITY

Surprisingly, it was not "The Stars and Stripes Forever" that launched Sousa to worldwide fame; it was a march composed for a newspaper three years before the formation of Sousa's Band. The proprietors of the *Washington Post* asked that he write a march for an award ceremony at a children's essay contest in 1889.

The rhythm of Sousa's new march was a perfect fit for a new dance craze, the two-step, and it gained astonishing popularity in America and abroad. In Germany and Austria, for example, all two-steps were called "Washington Posts." Unfortunately, however, Sousa sold the march outright for a mere $35, whereas the publisher made a fortune from the sheet music. For years it was demanded at nearly every Sousa Band concert.

NOT STARTING FROM SCRATCH

Sousa did not enter the concert field an unknown. People already recognized his name from seeing it on sheet music and hearing bands and orchestras play that music. He also had served under five presidents as leader of the United States Marine Band and made two national tours with the band.

The Sousa Band's founder and first manager, David Blakely, managed the two Marine Band tours and numerous other top attractions. Blakely had a strong advantage over other impresarios in that he had experience as both a conductor and publicity writer and also owned one of the nation's largest printing companies. The combination of Sousa and Blakely was destined for greatness.

MAKING MUSIC HISTORY

From the very beginning Sousa attracted widely experienced musicians to his band. It is an axiom in the music business that talent attracts talent, and within two years many leading instrumentalists had joined, several of whom had already attained wide reputations in Europe.

Sousa was a perfectionist, so the band began to set standards then unattainable by most other conductors. The first tour of Europe was made in 1900, and many critics were stating that Sousa's Band was the world's finest. It thus became an effective musical ambassador, emphatically serving notice that America could no longer be considered a cultural void.

Europe's stereotype of America as a country lacking in cultural refinement was a source of irritation to Sousa throughout his early life. He was sensitive to the fact that nearly all the world's major composers were European, whereas very few American composers were taken seriously abroad. Moreover, people in the fast-growing, unsophisticated New World showed little concern for that state of affairs.

Sousa helped rectify the situation in two ways. First, he educated audiences by presenting classics played to perfection, just as Theodore Thomas was doing with symphony orchestras. This played no small part in encouraging other American musical organizations to improve the quality of their products. Second, he took his band to Europe and demonstrated beyond a doubt that quality music was available in America, even without government support of the arts as was the custom in Europe. Critics overseas agreed almost unanimously on Sousa's originality and marveled at the band's polish and precision.

By the 1920s Sousa's role in the cultural growth of his country was aptly summed up by one midwestern writer: "John Philip Sousa has, without a doubt, done as much or more for music in America and for American music than any other person in the United States."[5]

"I AM MY OWN ANCESTOR"

The talented Sousa would no doubt have excelled in any field he chose. For both practical and idealistic considerations, he chose the band over the orchestra as a musical medium because of its versatility. A band has a wide variety of instrumental combinations and is mobile.

Sousa's Band was a compromise between a symphony orchestra and a nonmarching band. It had a wide range of dynamics, being able to play delicately as well as forcefully. Several musicians in the band had come from symphony or opera orchestras, and most of the others had orchestral experience. He disliked the bombastic sound of most bands and rehearsed sections of his until a balanced, cohesive sound resulted. As one critic put it, "In some of the selections with eyes closed one would have imagined a concert orchestra in his presence, the music being so much like that of a string orchestra."[6]

Audiences on both sides of the Atlantic were unaccustomed to hearing bands play so softly. German audiences were particularly surprised. A military band accompanying a violin soloist, for in-

---

4. The documentation is based on concert programs; tour itineraries; the Sousa band's eighty-five books of press clippings; schedules in music trade journals; and correspondence with hundreds of libraries, historical societies, museums, and newspapers.

5. *Daily Argus Leader* (Sioux Falls), Nov. 22, 1925.
6. *Wilkes-Barre Record,* Dec. 9, 1892.

stance, was unheard of. Most Europeans also appreciated the pleasing combinations of woodwinds that came to be one of Sousa's trademarks.

With a band instead of an orchestra Sousa was not obliged to follow any precedent in programming. In this regard he once quipped, "I am my own ancestor."[7] With a band, he was able to insert humor into programs. He did so in an obvious way, whereas with a symphony orchestra humor is often so subtle and reserved that only trained musicians can detect it. Another advantage of a band over an orchestra is that bands more widely use patriotic music. Humor and patriotism presented in a straightforward manner were staples of Sousa performances.

If those attending Sousa's concerts were to analyze what they heard, beneath the sparkle and excitement they would have found evidence of all his earlier influences: a European classical element, a light-opera element, a patriotic element, dance music, vaudeville music, and of course military music. This becomes obvious in a study of the concert programs (Appendix IV).

THE MIXMASTER

Some critics took Sousa to task for mixing transcriptions of orchestral or operatic masterpieces with other music on a program. He viewed this as unwarranted prejudice because he played them with a preci-

Sousa expressed patriotism in both his personal and professional life, as well as through his music, in a more profound manner than any other composer. (Library of Congress)

7. *Musical America*, Oct. 2, 1920.

sion and finesse that could be matched only by the world's finest orchestras.

Did composers of classical music object to Sousa's practice? Quite the opposite appears to be true; composers sent him numerous letters of appreciation. Any serious objection in print would have found its way into Sousa's massive press clipping books.

A few purists were critical of Sousa for playing any piece originally composed for orchestra. When one studies the Sousa Band press books, however, it becomes apparent that the most experienced critics were among Sousa's staunchest supporters. One gets the impression that critics of little renown sometimes imagine their stature is enhanced by being critical of acclaimed performers, that is, pointing out real or imagined shortcomings.

"ME SING WITH A *BAND!?"*

"What, *me* sing with a *band!?"* That was the response of Sousa's first soprano soloist, Marcella Lindh, to her manager when he suggested she make a tour with Sousa. He retorted that she should hear the band before deciding to pass on what he considered a golden opportunity for nationwide exposure. Together they slipped into the back of the auditorium where the band was rehearsing for its first tour. "I'll sing with *that* band!" Lindh said after hearing Grieg's *Peer Gynt Suite.*

ACCOUNTING FOR THE BAND'S POPULARITY

Why, modern scholars might ask, was Sousa's Band so popular? There are many reasons, the most significant being the aura of Sousa himself. When the band came to town, people came out en masse. Schools in many towns were dismissed and businesses closed for afternoon performances so people could see the March King. It was common for a town's mayor to declare a Sousa Day.

Another important reason for his popularity was that Sousa was taking his music directly to the people. The band was on the move, quite often presenting a matinee in one town and an evening concert in another. This was something a symphony orchestra could not do with great financial success, so Sousa saw to it that classical music was always represented on his programs. Bands such as Sousa's, not orchestras, were largely responsible for exposing the American public to the classics. Not all did it as artistically as Sousa, but bands did, in fact, introduce classical music to a large segment of the American public.

It has been estimated that in its first eight years of existence the Sousa Band played more concerts than all six of the country's major symphony orchestras put together.[8] Premium entertainment was not available to people in sparsely populated areas, so Sousa provided many classics to audiences that had never heard them. He often, for example, alluded to the fact that he played music from Wagner's

8. This can be illustrated by comparing a symphony orchestra's schedule with the schedule of Sousa's Band. A typical American major orchestra's schedule for a season in the 1890s consisted of fewer than a hundred concerts. By contrast, Sousa's Band played 661 concerts in 1894. Their busiest year was 1902, with 730.

At nearly every concert the band played "The Stars and Stripes Forever," named official march of the United States in 1987. Despite playing it thousands of times, the musicians played it with enthusiasm and claimed never to tire of it. "Stars" and some of Sousa's other popular marches were published for as many as eighteen different combinations of instruments, as seen at the bottom of the sheet music. (U.S. Marine Band)

Table 1. A Summary of Sousa Band Concerts

Year	Jan.	Feb.	Mar.	Apr.	May	Jun.	July	Aug.	Sept.	Oct.	Nov.	Dec.	Total
1892	—	—	—	—	—	—	—	—	8	46	30	20	104
1893	1	—	—	2	59	58	84	85	107	99	37	3	535
1894	5	7	56	56	45	46	81	79	107	97	55	27	661
1895	14	24	36	51	53	49	62	62	110	95	63	25	644
1896	44	47	51	15	55	49	62	62	20	—	—	7	412
1897	49	44	53	45	53	34	31	31	10	57	—	—	407
1898	43	49	45	28	41	—	—	—	88	119	48	6	467
1899	29	52	48	41	57	30	62	62	79	20	16	—	496
1900	1	53	59	13	38	38	45	42	27	51	—	1	368
1901	53	48	57	42	72	78	37	31	62	53	54	25	612
1902	36	49	57	5	45	72	124	124	75	57	58	28	730
1903	54	46	52	54	54	52	54	9	72	13	—	—	460
1904	—	—	—	52	86	16	—	16	70	52	55	9	356
1905	50	49	56	59	34	42	—	26	68	55	—	—	439
1906	45	54	62	44	11	—	—	82	51	46	—	—	395
1907	—	—	—	—	—	—	—	90	74	47	48	24	283
1908	46	52	6	—	—	—	—	66	88	31	1	—	290
1909	—	1	—	—	—	—	—	68	51	60	54	41	275
1910	2	—	—	—	—	—	—	74	68	—	47	37	228
1911	57	51	19	33	24	47	43	53	19	55	58	19	478
1912	—	—	—	—	—	—	—	44	98	59	59	16	276
1913	—	—	—	—	—	—	—	74	96	62	51	—	283
1914	—	—	—	—	—	—	—	54	106	62	35	—	257
1915	—	—	—	50	69	61	58	88	98	57	56	58	595
1916	58	54	59	54	55	6	—	52	40	53	58	60	549
1917	61	56	33	—	—	2	37	76	36	—	—	—	301
1918	—	—	—	—	—	10	63	89	32	—	—	—	194
1919	—	—	—	—	—	28	55	88	87	57	53	51	419
1920	18	—	—	—	—	—	2	94	80	55	38	—	287
1921	—	—	—	—	—	—	36	109	73	—	20	57	295
1922	55	44	53	2	—	—	25	60	79	56	30	—	404
1923	—	—	—	—	—	—	20	116	90	58	57	54	395
1924	53	58	13	—	—	22	124	124	88	61	30	—	573
1925	—	—	—	—	—	—	55	104	86	86	59	59	449
1926	62	50	12	—	—	—	98	124	84	62	38	—	531
1927	—	—	24	117	30	—	31	116	64	62	98	36	578
1928	—	—	—	—	—	—	39	89	60	60	60	45	353
1929	—	—	—	—	—	2	—	23	51	—	—	—	76
1930	—	—	—	—	—	—	—	26	22	47	37	—	132
1931	—	—	—	—	—	—	—	6	30	—	—	—	36
												Total	15,623

Parsifal ten years before that opera was performed in America.[9] As conductor of America's premier concert band, he believed it was his responsibility to lead the way to upgrading his country's musical tastes.

Because Sousa was an entertainer he knew the importance of playing what audiences wanted to hear. Even though his marches largely accounted for the band's popularity, he believed that well-played classics should be on every program to help elevate the public's musical taste. Hence, programs impressed both sophisticated and unsophisticated audiences.

Sousa's skill and poise as a conductor was yet another reason for the band's success. To say that he was a showman would be an understatement, although he was not flamboyant. He was also generous in promoting the music of local composers and sometimes had them conduct the band in their own compositions. The stature of many little-known composers grew quickly as a result of this generosity on Sousa's part.

Another factor that contributed to the band's renown was professional management. A management team painstakingly arranged all the band's tours and distributed a wealth of publicity materials. The band attracted the best managers as well as the best musicians. It was a mark of distinction to be associated with the world's best-known band and the world's most popular composer.

All these considerations led to the amazing prosperity the band enjoyed over the years, but had it not been for the magic of Sousa's innovative programming none of it would have happened. Without Sousa the band could not have existed for long. That was demonstrated by the smaller audiences when people learned that Sousa

9. Sousa played excerpts from *Parsifal* at the Manhattan Beach Resort in New York City in the summer of 1893. The opera was first performed in America at the Metropolitan Opera House on December 24, 1903.

The band's first tour abroad in 1900. Europeans were surprised to learn that America could produce a musical organization of such refinement. They marveled at the band's precision and Sousa's artistry as a conductor. First row: Marshall P. Lufsky, Eugene Rose, Giacomo Norrito, Darius Lyons, Paul Mohles, Eugene De Vaux, George Frederick Hinton (manager), John Philip Sousa, Arthur Pryor, August Grosskurth, Peter Nielsen, Holly Wilder, Henry Higgins, Walter B. Rogers, and Herbert L. Clarke. Second row: R. Engberg, Edward Locke, Henry Nelson, Ettore Pomo, Emil Preiss, Pasquale Marchese, Charles Otto, B. Kroeder, Thomas Hughes, John Hickey, Abraham Levy, William Langan, Franz Schuetz, Louis Christie, and Otto Fritsche. Third row: Thomas Mills, John Helleberg, Henry Thoede, Anton LeRoux, Helmar Dornheim, Giuseppe Boccavecchia, William Foerster, Carl Schroeder, A. Donati, Stanley Lawton, Maxwell Davidson, Louis Knittle, Homer Dickinson, and Franz Helle. Fourth row: Luca Del Negro, August Helleberg, Horace Seavey, Herman Conrad, Ross Chapman, Marcus Lyon, Edward Williams, Carl Wienelt, Philip Lotz, William Lange, Anton Horner, O. Edward Wardwell, Simone Mantia, and Edwin Clarke. Fifth row: Christopher Chapman and Herman Forster. (Author's Collection)

was temporarily indisposed. As a road manager astutely explained, "Mr. Sousa was the whole show."[10]

SELF-SUBSISTENCE AND INDEPENDENCE

Music historians would be hard-pressed to come up with the name of another musical organization the size of Sousa's Band that played as many concerts without subsidization or sponsorship of some kind. But Sousa and his band did so for four decades. Most income came from ticket sales.

Throughout history the most famous orchestras or bands have depended upon patrons or governments for their existence. The finest symphony orchestras, for example, could not survive without the assistance of generous patrons and occasional grants to guarantee against loss. Likewise, the finest bands in America are now the premier bands of the Armed Forces, financed by the government.

Sousa's Band, however, was the exception, being the most successful musical organization of an era. It took extraordinary efforts to maintain a profit. It was necessary to present two or more concerts each day for months on end. Such a schedule is unheard of today. Modern musicians would not tolerate such a schedule, yet the loy-

alty of Sousa's men was legendary. They were troupers of the first magnitude.

PROMOTING GOOD MUSIC

Sousa proclaimed, whether in numerous interviews or in several of his written pieces, that the purpose of putting his band through a rigorous schedule while offering only quality music was to raise the level of his country's appreciation of the art of music. In that respect he must be compared with Theodore Thomas, the celebrated orchestra conductor whose efforts were directed in a similar way.

Occasionally, someone in the media would realize what Sousa was doing and write about it. In 1900 one reporter went to the very heart of Sousa's mission: "It is the great band of the master American composer and conductor that has done more to promote the cause of good music throughout the length and breadth of the land than all the erudite symphony orchestras combined, for Sousa reaches the great body of people who love music for its inherent attractions rather than for its classical aspects."[11]

Sousa was selective in the orchestral transcriptions he used. He reviewed dozens issued by leading music publishers each year, al-

10. Author interview with William Schneider, 1968.

11. *Quincy* (Ill.) *Whig,* Feb. 27, 1900.

The band played 2,751 concerts at fashionable Willow Grove Park, just north of Philadelphia, known as the "summer music capital of America," between 1901 and 1926 (except for 1911, when on world tour). Four completely different concerts were played each day, including Sundays, with no rehearsals—attesting to the caliber of the band and Sousa's conducting. The musicians standing on each side of Sousa, facing the audience, are piccolo players performing the obbligato to "The Stars and Stripes Forever." Here, Sousa wears the white uniform he reserved for Sundays and special occasions. The special occasion on Wednesday, August 21, 1907, was Grand Army of the Republic Day. Postcards of this photograph are now collectors' items. (Author's Collection)

tered most to suit his requirements, and used only a few exactly as published. When he could not find a good edition of a masterwork he felt should be heard, he would often arrange one himself. His transcription of the *Peer Gynt Suite,* for example, influenced Marcella Lindh in her career path.

SMOOTH

The overall sound of the band, with its abundance of woodwind instruments, could accurately be described as smooth, perhaps owing to the fact that Sousa, a violinist, disliked the harsh sound of many bands. Critics around the world marveled at the distinctive sound, which can be explained by Sousa's insistence that each family of instruments has its own cohesive quality and that it does not clash with others. Cornetist Herbert L. Clarke, who joined the band in its second year, often described how Sousa would spend the entire morning of a first rehearsal working on just a few measures of an overture to get each member of the clarinet section to match the sound of the principal clarinetist, Joseph Norrito.

ALL THOSE MARCHES AND NO MARCHING?

Mixed with the wide variety of music found on every Sousa program

was a generous offering of his own marches, as anticipated by audiences. It is only natural to assume that Sousa's Band might have done a lot of marching, but nothing could be further from the truth. It was strictly a concert band. Nearly all concerts were presented at indoor concert halls except when the band was featured at fairs and expositions, and then concerts were usually given in pavilions or bandshells. The band did march, but only eight times in forty years. Sousa had his fill of marching while leader of the Marine Band.

The band's military-style uniforms also contributed to the impression that it was a marching unit. As part of the publicity strategy musicians were required to wear their uniforms at all times except off-days. That also applied to Sousa. Having uniformed men seen around a town before a concert added to the excitement and resulted in last-minute ticket sales.

SOUSA, CONDUCTOR AND GENTLEMAN

The press books compiled by the band office staff in New York over the years contain countless descriptions of Sousa's conducting. A study of those accounts leaves no doubt that he was among the most artistic, graceful conductors of his time. He was visibly moved by the music he conducted, his emotions reflecting a composer's intuition

To show the extent of Sousa Band activity, four and one half months of touring in 1899 are represented on the map. There were five tours that year, plus an additional engagement of eighty days at New York's Manhattan Beach, for a total of 496 concerts. By way of comparison, the band's busiest year was 1902, with an amazing 730 concerts.

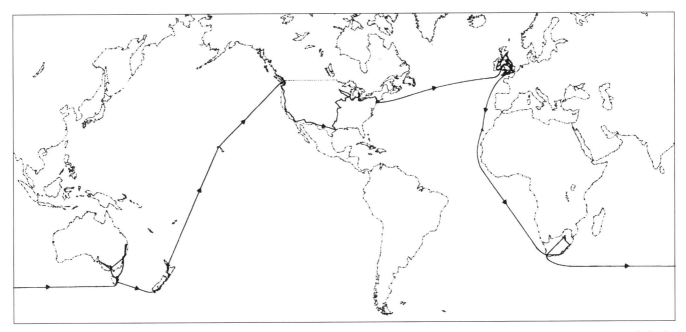

The tour around the world in 1911 started and ended in New York City. The 352–day tour covered 47,346 miles. Overseas arrangements were made by the Quinlan International Agency of London and included numerous countries of the British Empire. Saxophonist Albert Knecht kept a remarkable diary of the event (chapter 7).

The band made four tours of Europe between 1900 and 1905 and one tour around the world in 1911. The group was in Johannesburg, South Africa, on the world tour when this picture was taken. Nicoline Zedeler was the violin soloist, and Virginia Root was the soprano soloist. First row: George Ahlborn, Paul Senno, Julius Spindler, Nicoline Zedeler, Quinlan Agency tour representative Joseph Marthage, John Philip Sousa, Virginia Root, Herbert L. Clarke, Edwin Clark (manager), Quinlan Agency tour representative, Ross Millhouse, and Guy Gaugler. Second row: Carl Schroeder, Arthur Berry, Rene Magnant, Joseph Kapralek, Sol Eckstein, Walter Collins, Joseph Guerard, P. Lephilibert, Victor Welte, Harry Freeman, and Clarence J. Russell. Third row: Joseph Norrito, Ernest Gatley, Isadore Davis, William Robinson, James Lawnham, Harry Baldwin, George Kampe, Joseph Lomas, Walter Sheaffer, Edmund A. Wall, Clarence Livingston, William Culley, Edward Williams, Marcus Lyon, George Lucas, and Ralph Corey. Fourth row: Dr. William Lowe, Athol J. Garing, William Laendner, Arthur Kunze, Clarence Smith, Hermann Hand, Frank Snow, G. H. Cunnington, William Decker, Oskar Modess, John Perfetto, and Francis Haynes. Fifth row: Benjamin Vereecken, Albert Knecht, Stanley Lawton, August Helleberg Jr., Emil Mix, Arthur Griswold, and Arthur Storch. (U.S. Marine Band)

as well as a conductor's involvement. He sometimes spoke of being physically drained after conducting pieces he loved, such as works by Wagner, his favorite composer.

Sousa's movements on the podium were original and picturesque; the actor Otis Skinner once remarked that he was the best actor America had ever seen.[12] Music critics were quick to point out that he did not over-conduct. His motions were in harmony with the music at hand, expressing what it was intended to convey. One critic commented, "A deaf person might almost watch Sousa and understand the music."[13]

Sousa cut an immaculate figure on the podium. It was the responsibility of his personal valet, who traveled with the band, to see that his appearance, seen from any angle, was an appealing one. His uniforms did not contrast with the bands' other than that he wore a white uniform on Sundays and for special occasions. Expensive white kid gloves were one idiosyncrasy. The fact that they

were discarded when they showed the slightest soil mark gave rise to the story that he wore them only once. That was not true, but he did wear a pair only one time on many occasions. One press release for the 1925–26 tour stated that Sousa would be using his ten-thousandth pair on that tour.

Something that endeared Sousa to the public was the fact that he was approachable, always willing to give autographs after a concert, grant an interview, or honor requests from high-profile patrons and children alike.[14] The publicity issued by the management placed him on a high pedestal indeed, but he was actually a modest, retiring man who greeted everyone with the sincerity of a true gentleman.

It was not only musicians and friends who talked about Sousa's modest demeanor. Word of his many kindnesses got around. Even competitors loved him. As Mayhew Lester Lake, a composer-arranger, recalled, "During mornings at the [New York] Hippodrome where he was playing, there was an army of scrubwomen at work and, picking

12. Amy Leslie in *Chicago News* and undated clipping in the 1895–96 press book; also quoted in a booklet of testimonials published by Sousa's first manager, David Blakely.
13. *Duluth Herald*, May 23, 1893.

14. Sousa's daughter, Helen, often remarked that if her father had not been a musician he would have been a newspaper man. Indeed, he wrote seven books, more than a hundred articles, and the lyrics to several of his operettas and songs.

During the 1920s, Sousa often wore his U.S. Navy lieutenant commander's uniform at concerts. He was associated with the U.S. Marine Corps, Army, and Navy during his career. (Barry Owen Furrer Collection)

our way from the stage door to his dressing room, that old hat was raised to at least a dozen scrubwomen with the same gracious bow as he had made to the queen of England."[15]

What endeared him to his own musicians was his obvious respect for them, and that resulted in a degree of loyalty rarely seen in professional organizations. Sousa did not raise his voice or criticize a musician in the presence of others. He would ignore mistakes made at a concert, but when the same passage came up at the next concert he had subtle and sometimes humorous ways of letting the offending musician know he had heard the mistake.

A NEW KIND OF CONCERT

Sousa Band programs were as different as they were exciting. The most obvious difference was the use of quick encores, which were played during a program, immediately after the end of nearly every selection, rather than at the end of a concert. Actual programs were therefore approximately twice as long as printed programs indicated.

The innovation took most audiences by surprise, but they loved it and probably wondered why other concert organizations did not do likewise. It is especially amusing to consider the reaction to this style of programming in Britain. Critics there, steeped in the tradition

15. Lake, *Great Guys*, 116–17.

Table 2. A Concert Program, as Printed and as Played

As Printed	
1. *Mignon:* Overture	Thomas
2. "Showers of Gold"	Clarke
Herbert L. Clarke, cornet soloist	
3. *Dwellers of the Western World,* suite	Sousa
I. "The Red Man"	
II. "The White Man"	
III. "The Black Man"	
4. Mad Scene, from *Lucia di Lammermoor*	Donizetti
Leonora Simonsen, soprano	
Flute obbligato by Louis P. Fritze	
5. *Songs of Grace and Songs of Glory,* fantasy	Sousa
* INTERVAL *	
6. *Southern Rhapsody*	Hosmer
7. (a) "Annie Laurie," song	Traditional
Joseph Marthage, harp soloist	
(b) "Boy Scouts of America," march	Sousa
8. "Scotch Fantasie"	Boehm
Louis P. Fritze, flute soloist	
9. Rákóczy, March, from *The Damnation of Faust*	Berlioz

As Played	
1. *Mignon:* Overture	Thomas
Encore: "El Capitan," march	Sousa
Encore: "White Bird," novelette	Hager
2. "Showers of Gold"	Clarke
Herbert L. Clarke, cornet soloist	
Encore: "Brighten the Corner Where You Are"	Gabriel
Duet with Frank Simon	
Encore: "A Perfect Day," song	Bond
Herbert L. Clarke, cornet soloist	
3. *Dwellers of the Western World,* suite	Sousa
I. "The Red Man"	
II. "The White Man"	
III. "The Black Man"	
Encore: "King Cotton," march	Sousa
Encore: "The Gliding Girl," tango	Sousa
4. Mad Scene, from *Lucia di Lammermoor*	Donizetti
Encore: "Good Bye"	Tosti
Leonora Simonsen, soprano	
Flute obbligato by Louis P. Fritze	
5. "Songs of Grace and Songs of Glory," fantasy	Sousa
Encore: "The Pathfinder of Panama," march	Sousa
Encore [request]: "Mystic Potentate March"	F. A. Myers
* INTERVAL *	
6. *Southern Rhapsody*	Hosmer
Encore: "Good-bye, Girls, I'm Through"	Bellstedt
Encore: "Ragging the Scale"	Claypoole
Encore: Sextette, from *Lucia di Lammermoor*	Donizetti
Messrs. Clarke, Simon, Russell, Corey, Perfetto, and Williams	
7. (a) "Annie Laurie," song	Traditional
Encore: "Men of Harlech," patriotic air	Traditional
Joseph Marthage, harp soloist	
(b) "Boy Scouts of America," march	Sousa
Encore: "The Stars and Stripes Forever," march	Sousa
Encore: "Manhattan Beach," march	Sousa
8. "Scotch Fantasie"	Boehm
Encore: "The Waltzing Doll"	Poldini
Louis P. Fritze, flute soloist	
9. Rákóczy, March, from *The Damnation of Faust*	Berlioz

Note: A program given in Utica, New York, on December 20, 1916. The fact that encores began within ten seconds of a preceding piece meant that musicians had little rest except during vocal or violin solos, which had thin accompaniments.

of long waits before an encore and then only upon demand, were horrified by Sousa's generous use of encores. He began them within ten seconds after the finish of a main number, before the audience had stopped applauding. When critics got wise to the fact that audiences were accepting this with enthusiasm they admitted that the practice was not bad—just different.

Another practice that startled first-time concertgoers was Sousa's manner of starting a concert without delay. He did not walk onstage and take several bows, milking applause. Rather, he walked briskly to center stage, took one or two short bows, and stepped up on the podium. The first number would begin immediately. There was no rapping the baton or looking around to see if everyone was ready. The musicians were ready, and the concert began with no hesitation. Travel schedules were planned to the last minute, so starting times were precise—unless a late train made delay unavoidable. As Sousa often said, "Punctuality is the politeness of kings."

One of Sousa's personal standards, which some of his musicians thought unreasonable, was his insistence that soloists memorize every solo they played. He did not want a music stand between an audience and a soloist. Because there were often last-minute requests, soloists had to be ready to play everything in their repertoire—and sometimes pieces that were not. The nonrepertoire pieces created a hardship for even the most polished soloists. Years later they would reveal how they sometimes cheated by taping small pieces of music to the bells of their instruments or even writing notes on the exposed white cuffs of their uniforms.

The unique Sousa Band programs are seldom replicated other than in "tribute to Sousa" concerts, primarily because they require considerable stamina on the part of musicians. Modern musicians are unaccustomed to presenting two long concerts each day, each consisting of twenty pieces or more. Frank Simon, a cornetist, related that one evening he counted thirty-five pieces in a concert.[16] Sousa told of playing forty-two numbers at a concert in Berlin in 1903 as audiences shouted out names of extra pieces they wanted to hear (*"Voshington Pust!"*).[17]

SOUSA'S MANY INFLUENCES

Sousa and the Sousa Band had direct influence on many aspects of American social history. Musicologists are just now beginning to appreciate the magnitude of that impact. The most obvious was in the development of bands in the United States, particularly in the areas of repertoire and instrumentation. The chain reaction began with the effect Patrick S. Gilmore and his band had on Sousa. Gilmore inspired Sousa, and Sousa inspired others. Sousa had great respect for the legendary Irish American conductor and referred to himself

as the "King's lieutenant."[18] Gilmore died, however, just two days before the first concert of Sousa's Band, leaving Sousa with no close rival.[19]

Another influence was on the music publishing industry. More than thirty houses published Sousa's music during his lifetime, and double that number have since published it. The popularity of his marches, a staple of practically every band in America, did not diminish until many years after his death. As soon as a new one was published, better bands had to play it. Many were too difficult for beginning bands.

Sousa always featured his latest marches during concerts, with "(new)" noted on programs so conductors in the audience would take note. Those conductors also took note of Sousa's conducting and sometimes emulated his style.

Sousa's Band had a dramatic impact on the recording industry (chapter 5). The growth of the band's reputation coincided with the growth of that industry as exciting new technology was being introduced. The band's most often-played music was available to anyone with a phonograph, even though the sound was primitive.

The impact of Sousa's Band on the recording industry did not stop with Sousa. Many graduates of the band such as Arthur Pryor, Herbert L. Clarke, and Walter B. Rogers went on to establish enviable careers as studio conductors or recording artists. The list of alumni reads like a *Who's Who in American Music* (Appendix II). Several became famous as conductors or composers in their own right, while many others subsequently held important positions in symphony orchestras or bands. Some became prominent music educators. The accumulative influence of musicians who played with Sousa will reverberate in the music community for many years.

As the role model, the band's impact was considerable in the field of music education. Music students made up a large part of nearly any audience. Once the school band movement gained impetus in the 1920s, it was common for an outstanding high school band to be invited to play along with Sousa's Band for a short part of a program. On other occasions Sousa conducted school bands during an intermission, and thousands could say they "played with Sousa."

Typical of the impression Sousa made on student musicians was the recollection of a former member of the All-Ohio Boys Band, which Sousa guest-conducted at the Ohio State Fair in 1928: "Mr. Sousa, white gloves and all, came over to the grandstand platform each evening and directed our band in 'The Stars and Stripes Forever.' We kids played our hearts out with thrills and goosepimples, and Sousa's dignified warm smile and bow to us, as well as the audience, gave us a never to be forgotten impression of the great American and 'March King.'"[20]

16. Author interview with Frank Simon, 1963.
17. As told in "The World's Most Famous Conductor," *Cassell's Saturday Journal,* Feb. 22, 1905, 502.

18. One such reference was reported in the *New York Record* on July 13, 1893.
19. Sousa's Band eventually took over several engagements that had been awarded to Gilmore's.
20. Richard Lambert Harris to the Editor, *Columbus Dispatch,* Aug. 29, 1966.

Strange as it might seem, Sousa's Band also influenced aspects of music having little or nothing to do with bands. He was a pioneer in American operetta, composing fifteen during his career. The band played selections from those operettas, and in many instances individual songs were featured by vocal or instrumental soloists.

Sousa was always among the first to play new types of music, and ragtime was no exception. As it gained in popularity it became prominent in the band's programs. Significantly, it was his band that introduced ragtime to Europe in 1900, setting off a craze for the music in Paris. When jazz became popular during the 1920s he had small sections of the band, such as a saxophone sextet or octet, play it. Although Sousa himself was indifferent toward the new form of music, he respected the desires of his audiences.

The Sousa Band had only a minor influence on radio, broadcasting only thirty-seven programs between 1929 and 1932 (chapter 6).

THE MAGIC OF SOUSA'S PROGRAMMING

A book could be written about why audiences received the Sousa Band's programs so warmly. The primary factor was that he played music that people appreciated rather than music to impress colleagues. As he put it, "If musicians depended upon musicians for a living, there would be no musicians."[21]

Variety was the most important element of Sousa concerts. One could always expect a liberal dose of the classics despite programs being billed as "popular" (Appendix IV). There would also be a touch of patriotism, a touch of humor, and perhaps the latest tune in the style of the day—such as ragtime. Of course, there would be numerous Sousa marches.

Occasionally, a critic would comment that there was too much music by Sousa, particularly marches, but Sousa knew from experience what people expected to hear. During the final decade, when the band played four concerts a day at Willow Grove Park on the outskirts of Philadelphia, one day each week was devoted exclusively to Sousa's music.

The use of quick encores added excitement and probably played a greater part in the remarkable success of the band than is realized. The band broke box office records, both in America and abroad, and Sousa's encore policy was undoubtedly a major reason. When an encore began, a placard announcing the title was held up in the back of the band, usually by Sousa's valet or a percussionist. The refreshing use of multiple encores within a program surprised new audiences but was met with enthusiasm. As a critic in Australia noted:

> A new fashion in programme management has been set by Sousa, for which we should all be profoundly grateful. He puts American hustle into the time, both of the music and of the rate at which one

piece follows another. There are no dreary waitings while the performers slowly crawl up and down the steps of the artists' room to take calls or encores. Mr. Sousa stays "right there," and whoops up the encore before the clapping has half died out. Then a sensible man holds up an enormous card on which is legibly written the name of the encore piece.[22]

Sousa once defended his policy of immediate encores in a statement made to a Washington, D.C., reporter: "The inspiration that comes from physical activity on the part of the audience is the greatest compliment that a musician can have. It is his reward and deserves a return. . . . If I can please my audiences with more, I am willing to please them. It is the work that I was put in the world to do."[23]

Sousa was a master of the psychology of programming, notably in his construction of tour concerts. Selections were placed for maximum effect, and he learned early how to sense audience reaction. Pieces that did not produce the desired effect would be altered or replaced. That applied especially to orchestral transcriptions, which he sometimes abridged because he knew that his audiences were not made up of the same people who would sit through a long Wagnerian opera. If Sousa detected that an audience was bored he might stop at a logical spot, call out the name of one of his most popular marches, and play the remainder of the concert from encore books, which consisted of favorite selections. There was something for everyone on a Sousa program. If one number was not appealing, the next one probably would be. To avoid monotony he also took great care in alternating between fast and slow pieces, keys, and meters.[24]

Another factor contributing to the general interest of Sousa's programs was that many soloists composed their own pieces. The cornet solos of Herbert L. Clarke and the trombone solos of Arthur Pryor, for example, became standards of their day and are still being performed by accomplished players. The technical difficulty of the Clarke and Pryor solos taxes even the finest musicians. It is revealing to compare a modern performance with the somewhat primitive recordings made by Clarke and Pryor before the days of tape splicing and digital editing.

The matter of playing serious and popular pieces back to back was annoying to a few critics, but it was Sousa's way of maintaining contrast and keeping an audience wondering what would come next. An Ann Arbor, Michigan, reviewer once hinted strongly that a certain local conductor should learn from Sousa's example: "Professor Stanley was in attendance, it was noted, and it is hoped that he had his ear to the ground. A few popular airs would not spoil the Choral Union concerts, but would go far toward relieving people of that tired feeling when

---

21. When Sousa first said this is not known, but the words have been used frequently to explain his philosophy of programming.

22. *Sydney Sun,* May 19, 1911.
23. *Washington Star,* Jan. 20, 1900.
24. Keith Brion, who brilliantly portrays Sousa with symphony orchestras and his own New Sousa Band, has studied this technique in great detail and plans his programs accordingly.

they go home from an evening of pure classics. By interspersing these programs with something the popular taste craves, the correct thing that it does not crave is made more palatable."[25]

THE PHILOSOPHY BEHIND THE PROGRAMMING

Band members could easily tell when Sousa did not particularly like a given piece of music, but they also knew it was their duty to play every selection on the program with equal skill. He did avoid, however, lengthy music that was gloomy or dispiriting. Overall, he believed a concert should bristle with action, a reflection of his personal life and the vitality and industry of America.

Sousa's programs were not geared to one strata of a population or one section of a country. He believed that music was a universal language and that pieces played well would have appeal anywhere. He made sure, though, that every program would be appealing, no matter where it was played.

He was a progressive, always surprising audiences with new music. He wanted to be the first to introduce new pieces he felt might eventually be popular. Music publishers knew that and sent him new music as soon as the ink was dry. Advertising "as played by Sousa's Band" was good for business. Numerous pieces were scheduled once or twice and promptly deleted from the library. Many were played from manuscript before they were published (or they were never published). Sousa believed that he played more unpublished music than any other American bandmaster.[26]

Playing modern music could be risky, but Sousa had to see for himself whether an audience would be receptive. He tried Ernest Schelling's "Victory Ball" In 1923 with great success. As he reasoned, "The last season I played Schelling's 'At the Victory Ball,' a number which had been attempted for only a performance or two by orchestras in Philadelphia and New York. But it was enjoyed by my audiences, at least in the sense that they were glad for an opportunity to hear a much-discussed number of the modernistic school."[27]

SHOWMANSHIP

Sousa went to great lengths to determine which pieces of music might be appropriate to a city.[28] Upon arriving, he would seek a copy of the local newspaper or newspapers with the largest circulation, hoping to find an account of some event he could match with something in the library that might catch the public's fancy. He was eager to receive requests for the same reason. If he could obtain the music of a local composer he would add that to the program at the last minute.

Pieces known to be especially popular in an area were certain to be found on programs there. "Dixie," for example, was played quite often south of the Mason-Dixon Line. In a college town he would make every effort to slip in the school's fight song as a surprise encore. The same was done with a high school's song when there was only one high school in a city.

Given his quest for variety, the band would play pieces differently than other bands. On the finales of some of his marches, for instance, he would have the brass players come to the front of the stage. What is now a tradition was initiated by Sousa when playing "The Stars and Stripes Forever." Piccolo players came out and played their obbligato on the first repeat of the trio; on the final repeat they were joined by cornet, trumpet, and trombone players.

The band had several pieces memorized, particularly Sousa marches played often as encores. On one occasion the band displayed amazing showmanship by playing Rossini's *William Tell Overture* entirely from memory when the music was not in the folders and had not been played for several weeks. Sousa received a request for another piece at a concert in Richmond, Indiana, on September 30, 1912, and gambled on the musicians actually playing it. They did, "without a discordant note or mistake."[29]

THE SHOW MUST GO ON

Sousa's Band practiced an often-expressed phrase, "The show must go on." About the only thing that prevented a concert from beginning at the appointed hour was a late train, sometimes caused by a wreck of their own train or another train farther up the line. When that happened it was a rare audience that did not wait patiently until the band arrived. The band, being troupers, traditionally postponed lunches or dinners so as not to keep an audience waiting.

Sousa conducted at all times unless it was physically impossible for him to do so. Even so he would sometimes start a concert and be relieved by the assistant conductor. On at least two occasions he had to be carried offstage after beginning a concert. He was on crutches when he conducted rehearsals before the 1912 tour because of a tennis injury sustained just before the tour began. When he was on tour, however, the crutches disappeared and he endured the pain.

A mishap in 1921 put a permanent end to his graceful conducting style. While on his morning ride at Willow Grove Park he was thrown from his horse and cracked vertebrae in his neck. He was hospitalized, leaving John Dolan, a cornet soloist, to conduct in his absence until it was decided to cancel the remainder of the tour. When Sousa was able to resume touring two months later, he was still in such pain that he could not raise his left arm outward. He carried on, however. At first the musician closest to him had to turn the pages of Sousa's score, and Dolan would sometimes conduct while Sousa rested. Even after he was able to turn the pages himself, conducting was such an effort that he had to alter his style so as to use his left arm very little.

25. *Ann Arbor Courier-Weekly,* March 3, 1898. Sousa compared his programs to the works of Shakespeare, where comedy sometimes follows tragedy. According to the Sousa Band press books, critics disagreed on the matter of mixing serious and popular music; they both lambasted Sousa and gave him high praise. A study of Sousa Band press books, however, indicates that approvals outnumber objections by several dozen to one.

26. Sousa, *Marching Along,* 303.

27. *North American,* ca. Nov. 1924, Sousa Band Press Book 64, 4.

28. See "The Day Kelly Disappeared" in chapter 8.

29. Interview with Sousa, *Philadelphia Examiner,* Oct. 15, 1916.

It is unfortunate that the Sousa who conducted from 1921 to 1932 was only a shadow of the vigorous conductor of earlier years. He took an osteopath, John P. Brennan, along on the 1921–22 tour, but the treatments helped only slightly. For the remainder of the tour, his road manager William Schneider recalled, Sousa would slip exhausted into a chair during intermissions and after concerts, sometimes wet with sweat.[30] Audiences never knew the agony Sousa went through and that he tried to keep it from the press.

Later in life Sousa would reminisce about the mishap and joke that he was the "greatest one-armed conductor in captivity." It is surprising that he composed one of his most vigorous marches, "The Gallant Seventh," while recovering from the neck injury.

A FRATERNAL SOCIETY

Sousa was held in such esteem by his musicians that they formed the Sousa Band Fraternal Society twelve years after he died. They met each year in New York on the anniversary of his birthday until they were physically unable, and chapters were also formed in Philadelphia and Los Angeles (chapter 3).

"OUT OF THE CADENCES OF TIME"

John Philip Sousa might have been one of the greatest entertainers of all time, but until his dying day he remained as modest as when he was a struggling young man trying to make his way in the music world. In his autobiography, his parting words were, "If, out of the cadences of Time, I have evoked one note that, clear and true, vibrates gratefully on the heartstrings of my public—I am well content."[31]

30. Author interview with William Schneider, 1968.
31. Sousa, *Marching Along*, 365.

CHAPTER TWO

Sousa's Band, 1892–1932

THE DREAMS OF JOHN PHILIP SOUSA
AND DAVID BLAKELY

While John Philip Sousa was molding the United States Marine Band into America's finest military ensemble between 1880 and 1892 he often dreamed of having a group of his own—one unencumbered by limits on travel or salary. The sole purpose of such a band would be to present regularly scheduled concerts. It would not be required to march or be subjected to orders handed down by nonmusicians.

His dream band might never have come into existence had he not crossed paths with David Blakely, an impresario of the first order. It was Blakely, who had foresight and considerable business acumen, who provided the opportunity for Sousa to become an entertainment figure famous beyond his wildest imagination.

As leader of the Marine Band, Sousa longed to take the group on tour. He made no headway with his superiors, so he went over their heads. Cleverly, he worked through Secretary of the Navy Benjamin F. Tracy and First Lady Caroline Harrison and eventually convinced the president, Benjamin Harrison, that the band should make a tour to allow more of the country to appreciate the music then available only to Washington. With the president's approval a five-week tour was arranged for April and May 1891. Blakely was engaged as tour manager.[1] The tour was an artistic success, but by Blakely's standards it was only a moderate financial success. For Sousa, however, it was a different matter. His share of the five-week tour's profits was $2,635, an enormous sum compared to his annual government salary of approximately $1,500.

A second tour of seven weeks' duration, extending all the way to the West Coast, took place the following year, 1892. When Blakely met Sousa in Chicago as the band made its way back to Washington he offered financial backing if Sousa would leave government service and organize a civilian band. The second tour was producing even greater receipts than the first, so the idea was enticing. What clenched the deal was Blakely's offer to pay Sousa $6,000 per year plus a percentage of the profits. It did not take Sousa long to make a decision, taking into account the fact that Blakely had become known as America's leading manager of artists. At last he would have the freelance civilian band he had dreamed of.

Perhaps unbeknown to Sousa, Blakely had a dream of his own. He had managed several premier musical organizations, including America's finest civilian band at the time, the band of the popular Irish American Patrick S. Gilmore. Gilmore and Blakely parted company, however, and Blakely was looking for a well-known bandmaster around whom he could build a superb musical organization and challenge Gilmore for supremacy in the American market. He had even traveled across Europe, concentrating on Vienna, Paris, and London, to seek such a conductor. When he noted Sousa's rising popularity he realized he was working with the very man he had hoped to find. Because Sousa was also a promising composer, it was reasonable to assume he might develop into a superstar.

After the second tour ended and the receipts were counted, Sousa's share was $8,250.[2] Blakely was meanwhile busily organizing a syndicate in Chicago, hoping to raise a large amount of capital by selling stock. He was unable to find a sufficient number of investors, however, so he bought back all the shares and dissolved the syndicate. Blakely was facing possible financial disaster, but he weighed

---

1. This was the first tour of the Marine Band, "The President's Own." Annual tours still continue.

2. As determined by Margaret L. Brown in research of the ledgers and other documents in Blakely Ledger Books, David Blakely Collection, New York Public Library. Newsom, ed., *Perspectives on John Philip Sousa,* 123.

that risk against Sousa's unique combination of talents. He was also aware that Sousa was a confident and determined man and reasoned they would make a superb team.

BLAKELY'S UNIQUE BACKGROUND

David Blakely served as the Sousa Band's manager for four years, until his death in 1896. Had it not been for Blakely's spirit of adventure Sousa might never have had a career as a civilian bandmaster. It is also possible that Sousa might never have gained great wealth as a composer had Blakely not insisted on taking over negotiations with Sousa's publishers. Sousa was selling most of his compositions outright for $35 or less; after the association with Blakely, annual royalties averaged well over $10,000.

Blakely was the ideal manager for the new band, having a broad background in music and a proven track record in artist management. He was also an excellent writer and editor and, conveniently, president of one of the nation's largest printing companies (chapter 4). In addition to Gilmore's Band, he had already managed such premium attractions as the Theodore Thomas Orchestra, the Strauss Orchestra of Vienna, and the two tours of the United States Marine Band under Sousa's direction.

SOUSA AND AN ADMIRING WASHINGTON

Sousa's decision to leave military service and perhaps move to Chicago, the original location of the band's headquarters, was met by disbelief on the part of Marine Corps officials. Washingtonians, who had come to love the Marine Band's concerts and the atmosphere Sousa had created as a bandmaster and composer, were also disappointed. Reports of his resignation made him realize how popular he had become. The April 18 *Washington Post,* for example, stated, "Chicago will want the White House next."

There was no turning back. Sousa's final concert as a U.S. Marine was given on Saturday, July 30, 1892, on the White House lawn, with President Harrison attending. The band presented Sousa with a beautifully engraved baton as a token of esteem and affection.[3]

FORMATION OF THE BAND

The new band set up its office in New York City, where Blakely had another office. Sousa auditioned a large number of musicians, selected fifty-one of them, and began two weeks of rehearsals.

Blakely wanted the band to be known as "Sousa's New Marine Band," but Sousa objected. Although "marine band" was a generic term used at the time by several bands having no connection to the United States Marine Corps, Sousa predicted that U.S. Marine Corps officials back in Washington would object, which they did. Blakely finally yielded to the objections, but it took him several months to replace publicity already in use with new billing as "Sousa's Concert Band" or "Sousa's Band."[4]

Initially, none of Sousa's musicians from the Marine Band resigned to join the new organization, but Walter F. Smith, a cornetist, did so in April 1893, and a few others followed after that. More notably, several musicians of international repute soon became members. Among them were Pasquale Marchese, clarinet, from the Municipal Band of Milan; Robert Messinger, oboe, Hinrich's American Grand Opera; Ferdinand Jabon, bassoon, Brussels Grand Opera; Arthur H. Smith, cornet, the Coldstream Guards; John Saveniers, trumpet, the Belgian Guides Royal Symphonic Band; Edward A. Williams, trombone, Albaugh's Opera House, Washington; Matthias Cesky, tuba, Fahrbach's Band, Vienna; and Herman Forster, percussion, the Prussian Guards.

SUCCEEDING GILMORE

By a strange quirk of fate Gilmore died on September 24, 1892, just two days before the first scheduled concert of Sousa's new band. The group's chief rival was thus temporarily out of the picture until Gilmore's band could be reorganized under a new conductor.

Sousa was outspoken in his admiration for Gilmore and considered him the greatest bandmaster America had produced. Out of respect, he and Blakely had earlier agreed not to recruit musicians from Gilmore's band, but within months several had resigned and joined Sousa's Band, much to the chagrin of the remaining Gilmore musicians.[5] Eventually, at least nineteen went with Sousa, several of whom were prominent soloists or first-chair players, such as Herbert L. Clarke, E. A. Lefebre, and Frank W. Wadsworth.

HIGH EXPECTATIONS

Sousa agreed wholeheartedly with Blakely's goal of making the band one of the best in the world, if not the best. At that time the Garde Républicaine Band of France was considered the finest in the world, and Blakely was intent on making the new band its equal. One part of the five-year contract between Blakely and Sousa read, "It shall be the aim and duty of said Sousa by individual effort, and band rehearsal and practice, and by the preparation and furnishing of music, to make this band equal in executive ability of the Garde Républicaine in Paris."

Recruiting top players was vigorous once word was out about expectations for the group. Blakely arranged with Theodore Thomas, head of the music program for the 1892–93 World's Columbian Exposition in Chicago, for Sousa's Band to be the official band of the fair. That stimulated recruiting. In addition to the leading musicians already

---

3. The Sousa family returned the baton to the Marine Corps in 1953, and it now is passed from retiring leaders to their successors at impressive retirement ceremonies held on the parade ground of the Marine Barracks in Washington.

4. Between 1894 and 1899 the band was billed variously as "Sousa's Unrivalled Band," "Sousa's Grand Concert Band," or "Sousa's Peerless Band." From then on it was "Sousa and His Band" or "Sousa's Band," the latter now used predominately by historians. "Sousa's Band" was also the name used on phonograph records.

5. Angry letters between the two factions were printed in the *Musical Courier* issues of March, 1893.

mentioned, twenty members came from Philadelphia.[6] Harry Coleman, Sousa's publisher in that city, aided in recruiting and auditioning there.[7] The August 1892 issue of *Metronome* carried an announcement that a novel feature of the band would be a choir of boys. If that was indeed considered the plan was ruled out early on.

OTHER CONSIDERATIONS

The contract between Blakely and Sousa was unusual. Blakely assumed the responsibility of negotiating with the publishers of Sousa's music. In return he received 50 percent of the profits, including several works already composed for the band but not yet published. Moreover, Blakely was the sole owner of the band's music library, including Sousa's handwritten scores. That portion of the contract would come back to haunt Sousa after Blakely's death. Aside from the terms of the contract, other matters of interest concerning the band were provisions for first-class railroad travel and uniforms, which musicians could either purchase or rent.

THE FIRST CONCERT AND A TRIBUTE

The beginning of a new era in the history of American music began with the Sousa Band's first performance on Monday, September 26, 1892, at the Stillman Music Hall in Plainfield, New Jersey. Plainfield was chosen because the area was affluent and populated with people interested in culture, many with offices in New York. The city had a history of supporting artistic activities, and Blakely believed that audiences there were as critical as any in the United States.

The concert opened in a touching manner as the band stood and played Gilmore's "Voice of a Departing Soul" (also known as "Death's at the Door"), Sousa's sincere tribute to his late friend and colleague. He would sing Gilmore's praises for many years, not just because of his great esteem but because there inevitably would be comparisons between his band and Gilmore's, and he wanted no part of such a controversy. As he stated to the press in 1894, "It makes me hope that when I come to pass away, I may be remembered even half so kindly [as Gilmore]. . . . I do not believe that any one can or ever will have the place in the hearts of the people that Mr. Gilmore held." Referring to Gilmore's colossal National Peace Jubilee (1869) and World Peace Jubilee (1872), he declared that out of respect for his memory he would never use the word *jubilee* in any special festival at which the Sousa Band appeared.[8]

The concert was very well received according to accounts in three Plainfield newspapers. The program was lengthy and heavy on the classics.[9] Of course, those pieces were interspersed with popular numbers, including several Sousa compositions. One unusual feature was the introduction of a set of five-foot-long Egyptian trumpets performing Sousa's new "March of the Royal Trumpets."

TWO TOURS IN 1892

Plainfield was the first stop on two short tours that took place in 1892. In Chicago before the Columbian Exposition opened, the band played at the dedication of the New York Building.

Meanwhile, Blakely was hard at work sending publicity releases to newspapers in cities where the band was to perform. In this publicity he described Sousa as America's foremost bandmaster, unabashedly stating that the artist musicians of the band had been selected from the best orchestras of the world. Moreover, the band "produced results in finish, in refinement, in delicacy, feeling and expressions rivaling in beauty and charm the best efforts of the finest string orchestras."

Near the end of the first tour Sousa and Blakely had their first disagreement. Concert receipts had been lower than expected, and Blakely suggested that they cancel the last few scheduled concerts. Sousa objected strenuously, possibly thinking that Blakely intended to shut down the band altogether and move on to some other musical organization. Such was not the case. Blakely backed down, and the remainder of the tour was completed.[10]

The first group photograph of Sousa's Band, taken on October 10, 1892, appeared in the *Illustrated World's Fair* magazine of November, 1892. The occasion was the dedication of the New York Building. An original copy of the picture could not be located. (Author's Collection)

---

6. Author interviews with Philadelphia clarinetist Louis Morris, who was with the band from 1908 to 1921.

7. Coleman was not rewarded for his efforts; in fact, he suffered heavy losses in the end. He became wealthy as the publisher of Sousa's most popular marches while first paying Sousa only $35 per march and later very meager royalties in a somewhat inconsistent manner. Thus when Blakely negotiated with the John Church Company for a better deal for Sousa (and himself), Coleman lost a fortune.

8. *New York Advertiser,* July, 1894.

9. An actual program of this concert is not known to have survived, although I made a concerted effort to reconstruct it for Keith Brion, who portrays Sousa. The order, however, is probably inexact. Performed that night were the following works: "Death's at the Door" (Gilmore); "Overture to Semiramide" (Rossini); "My Mary Green" (Lamb); *Peer Gynt Suite* (Grieg); "Advance and Retreat of the Salvation Army" (Orth, repeated); "Bal des Enfants" (Jaxone); "Love's Dream after the Ball" (Czibulka); "March of the Royal Trumpets" (Sousa, repeated); the Mad Scene from *Lucia di Lammermoor* (Donizetti); "The Bob-o-link" (Bischoff); "Home Sweet Home" (Payne-Bishop); "Sheridan's Ride" (Sousa, repeated); "Arabasque" (Stasny); "Good-Bye" (Sousa); "The Star-Spangled Banner"; and several Sousa marches.

10. Sousa, *Marching Along,* 127.

Several changes in personnel and instrumentation were made at that time, some probably at the suggestion of Theodore Thomas, who had heard the band in Chicago. The second short tour of 1892 was more of a financial success than the first and also more satisfying artistically for Sousa and Blakely.

A CRITICAL YEAR AND BLAKELY'S CHALLENGE

The band was idle for the first few months of 1893 except for periodic concerts in New York City. The first big engagement was back in Chicago, where the group played for thirty-eight days at the World's Columbian Exposition (Chicago World's Fair). Theodore Thomas decided that the band should play for six months, but Blakely explained that the band had already been awarded a sixty-six-day contract during that time period by the management of Manhattan Beach, New York's fashionable summer resort. The group was beginning to inherit jobs that previously had been awarded to Gilmore's band, including that at the Chicago World's Fair and at the 1893 St. Louis Exposition (Appendix I).

Blakely was convinced that the band had already achieved the goal of becoming one of the finest in the world, but he wanted the public's confirmation. He boldly issued a challenge to the press and discriminating musicians of the New York area by inviting them to come to Manhattan Beach and judge for themselves.

Afternoon and evening concerts on July 15, 1893, were chosen for the test. Press releases were distributed, and invitations were sent to five hundred musicians and several noted composers and conductors. The guests made up a large portion of the immense crowd. Numerous accounts of the concerts in the Sousa Band press books attest to the success of Blakely's brazen challenge. Several of the musicians present went on record as saying they had never heard a better band. Blakely had the confirmation he sought.

TWO BUSY YEARS, 1894 AND 1895

Several lengthy engagements, with 661 concerts, kept the band extremely busy in 1894. There were thirty-six-day stays at the San Francisco Mid-Winter Exposition and at Madison Square Garden in New York and a sixty-six-day engagement at New York's Manhattan Beach. The Manhattan Beach booking had traditionally been awarded to Gilmore, and few thought his popularity could be eclipsed. It soon became obvious, however, that Sousa was equally successful.

During the fair at San Francisco the band encountered something that musicians have always experienced—prejudice. Sousa regarded

In its first widely reproduced group photograph, taken at the St. Louis Exposition in October 1893, the band wore its earliest style of uniform. First row: unidentified, William Langan, unidentified, Joseph Norrito, August Stengler, Albert Bode, Herbert L. Clarke, Frank Seltzer, William Griffin, and Joseph Raffayolo. Second row: Frank Wadsworth, Giacomo Norrito, Franz Schuetz, Joseph Lacalle, Fred Urbain?, Edouard A. Lefebre, Charles Kruger, Stanley Lawton, F. Heppner, Frank Martin, and August Haase. Third row: William Dougherty, Pasquale Marchese, Samuel Schaich, Thomas Shannon, Henry Geise, unidentified, Giuseppe Boccavecchia, unidentified, H. Narotsky, Harry Fricke, August Wagner, and Henry Koch. Fourth row: Emil Preiss, Paul Jahn, Chet Bronson?, Robert Messinger, unidentified, A. Pagliani, Henry Thoede, Edward Williams, Marcus Lyon, and Arthur Pryor. Fifth row: Eldon Baker, Charles Lowe, Herman Forster, William Jeschka, Dr. William Lowe, and Herman Conrad. (The Sousa Archives and Center for American Music, University of Illinois at Urbana-Champaign)

artistic snobbery as vicious, and members of his band came to appreciate his sentiments. In San Francisco they strongly resented the condescension they encountered from members of Fritz Scheel's Imperial Orchestra of Germany, with whom Sousa shared a program. The band's inspired reading of the overture to Rossini's opera *William Tell* was a revelation for Scheel and a source of great satisfaction for Sousa. "It was the most impeccable performance I have heard in my entire career!" Sousa would recall many years later.[11] Shortly thereafter Scheel's flugelhorn soloist, Franz Helle, became a star soloist with Sousa and remained with the band for ten years.

In 1895 the band experienced another exceedingly busy year, with 644 concerts. The Manhattan Beach booking was extended to eighty days, and the band played at the St. Louis Exposition for forty-six days. In St. Louis, a city known for its acceptance of quality music, Sousa experimented with the use of local talent. This, of course, added local interest. None of the local soloists went on to become regular touring soloists with the band, but it was Sousa's practice to be his own talent scout. He was always on the lookout for undiscovered artists who had not yet found their way to Chicago, New York, or Boston. The circumstances were different when the band played at Manhattan Beach. There was never a problem finding top talent, given the leading performers of the Metropolitan Opera House who were usually available.

The reception at a twenty-day engagement in Atlanta for the Cotton States and International Exposition provided a good example of Sousa's drawing power. Gate receipts had been far less than expected, and fair officials feared the expense of bringing Sousa and the band would bankrupt them. They tried to cancel the engagement, but it was the decision of both Blakely and Sousa to insist that the contract be honored. A compromise was reached whereby the band would charge admission for its concerts instead of playing at a bandstand where there was no admission charge. The result was a series of standing-room-only concerts, and many additional patrons were turned away. Concerts had to be moved indoors because of unruly crowds.[12] The officials asked for an extension of the contract, but the band had to move on to fulfill previously scheduled concerts.[13]

"THE STARS AND STRIPES FOREVER"

One could argue that 1896 was the most important year in John Philip Sousa's life. That was the year he composed his most famous and most financially rewarding work, "The Stars and Stripes Forever." It was also the year in which he lost David Blakely, the man responsible for founding the Sousa Band and guiding Sousa to national prominence as a bandmaster.

After tours lasting three months and six weeks, followed by a Manhattan Beach engagement of nearly three more months, he and

Blakely decided it was time for a well-deserved vacation. After all, the band had been in service almost constantly for four years. Blakely retreated to his home in Vermont. Sousa and his wife, Jane (Jennie), traveled to Europe with two purposes in mind. He could relax in a part of the world he had always longed to see and survey the cultural scene there to determine how the band might fare if Blakely could arrange a European tour. The Sousas' itinerary in Europe is not recorded, but it is known that they visited several cities in England, France, Switzerland, and Italy. Spain, Germany, and Austria are also possibilities.

In Naples he was shocked to read, in a four-day-old newspaper from Paris, that on November 7 Blakely had died suddenly in the New York office. Blakely's secretary sent a cablegram to Sousa, but it was not received. A new tour was to begin in less than two months, and untold responsibilities awaited him in New York. The Sousas sailed for home aboard the British liner *S.S. Teutonic*.

While walking the decks of the ship he experienced what he would describe as "one of the most vivid incidents of my career." His "brain-band" was playing a distinct melody again and again, and before the voyage was over he had mentally formulated "The Stars and Stripes Forever." He did not put the work to paper until Christmas Day of 1896. What was to become the official march of the United States was Sousa's Christmas present to the American people. Its two-page manuscript in the Library of Congress remains a national treasure.

AN UNEXPECTED LEGAL ENTANGLEMENT

Plans for a tour commencing December 27, 1896, had been laid before Blakely's death, so the tour began. Who was in charge, however, was the cause of much confusion, and there were frequent changes of management personnel. Sousa initially accepted the staff members appointed by Blakely's wife, Ada, but serious complications arose.

One person in the new Blakely management circle was a relative of Blakely who had little knowledge of concert management. When he reduced Sousa's salary to the amount specified in the original contract, $6,000 per year, Sousa was incensed. He had been paid, before Blakely's death, approximately $50,000 per year from the profits.[14] He demanded and eventually received greater sums several times, much to Ada Blakely's displeasure. A series of bitter lawsuits began. The crux of the matter was that Sousa assumed the contract terminated when Blakely died, whereas Ada Blakely assumed that she automatically inherited the contract. Ironically, had Blakely lived another seven months, the five-year contract would have been fulfilled and a new contract covering the very successful venture likely would have been negotiated.

It did not help matters when Sousa refused to turn over concert receipts to the Blakely faction. He did so because, he claimed, he had not been paid for all services rendered before Blakely died. To make

---

11. Ibid., 143.

12. *Atlanta Constitution*, Nov. 20, 1895.

13. The story of the conflict with the fair's management appears in Sousa's *Marching Along* (147–49). He composed one of his finest marches, "King Cotton," for the fair.

14. Blakely Ledger Books, David Blakely Collection, New York Public Library.

This 1895–96 grouping shows individual members of the band. The purpose of the montage is uncertain, because not all of them played in the band at the same time. Moreover, spellings of some of the names vary from spellings commonly used today. (Author's collection, courtesy of Leonard B. Smith)

matters worse, Blakely management people began to add new engagements to the schedule. For three days in April 1897, while negotiations were at a standstill, Sousa refused to let the band perform. He added to the confusion by making separate contracts with several theater owners. Also in contention was ownership of the band's music library.

The most hotly contested issue, however, was Sousa's percentage of the profits, which Blakely had increased a year earlier but by verbal agreement rather than by contract provisions. Still another issue was the use of the name *Sousa's Band*. Ada Blakely pointed out that Sousa had been an employee of Blakely. She could use the name and hire another bandmaster.

The controversy dragged on for nearly four years, until October 1900. The court ruled that Sousa had to forfeit $30,000, but he alone could use the name "Sousa's Band." The Blakely family retained the music library for many years and continued to receive royalties on

music composed by Sousa during the period covered by the contract. The final ruling reveals that the court deliberated extensively about the unique talents of both men. The original contract of June 27, 1892, which was central to the lawsuits, reads:

Whereas Mr. David Blakely, the manager of the late tours of the U.S. Marine Band, is desirous of perfecting a new organization for the purpose of securing high excellence in a military band, and with that view to secure the services of Mr. John Philip Sousa as its musical director, and said John Philip Sousa is willing, on the terms hereinafter expressed to accept said employment and position.

This agreement between said parties witnesseth as follows:

1. It is agreed that the said David Blakely shall be the business manager of the said band, in connection with his assistant managers or agents, and shall perform all acts and duties pertaining thereto, and shall be solely responsible for all expenses connected therewith, the said John Philip Sousa not to be liable in any event for any portion thereof.

2. It is agreed that John Philip Sousa shall be the musical director

of said band, and shall perform all acts and duties pertaining thereto, and that the organization shall be known as Sousa's Band, or shall have some title chosen by said Blakely with the name of Sousa as part thereof. Said name shall therefore be a part of the property of said band, and be owned and controlled by the business manager thereof, or his successors and assigns.

3. It is agreed that the contract shall take effect from the date of the acceptance of said Sousa's resignation as leader of the U.S. Marine Band, and severance of his connection therewith, and continue for the full term of five years thereafter.

4. It is agreed that the compensation of the said Sousa for the duties connected with his position as hereinafter mentioned during said period, shall be at the rate of $6,000 per year, from the time of his severance of connection with the U.S. Marine Service until the expiration of this contract, payable monthly by said Blakely, and, in addition thereto, ten per cent of the net profits of the business of the organization during the first year after the date of the organization of the band, and twenty percent during the remainder of this engagement, also payable by said Blakely. The said net profits to be the remainder of moneys on hand at the expiration of the first year, after deducting all expenses of conducting the band and its business, and including the aforesaid salary of the musical director, and a like annual salary of $6,000 to the said Blakely or his successor as business manager of the said new organization; and the said musical director shall receive twenty per cent of the said so described profits for the remaining years of the duration of this contract, after deducting all expenses, including salaries as aforesaid. And said Blakely will pay for first-class railroad transportation on all tours made by said Sousa in connection with said band.

5. The said John Philip Sousa, after the expiration of this contract, shall give the said David Blakely the refusal of his services in a similar capacity for another five years; provided the said Blakely shall agree to pay him as great a compensation as any other manager in good faith offers to do.

6. The work of securing the said new organization shall begin as soon as may be after the signing of this contract.

7. The number of musicians engaged for concert tours shall not be less than forty-six, unless agreed to by both Blakely and Sousa.

8. It shall be the aim and duty of the said Sousa by individual effort, and band rehearsal and practice, and by the preparation and furnishing of music, to make this band equal in executive ability to the band of the Garde Républicaine in Paris.

9. The musical direction of the aforesaid organization shall be in the hands of the said John Philip Sousa, and the business management in the hands of the said Blakely as aforesaid, but both shall mutually receive counsel in their respective positions, and especially regarding the preparation of programmes. It shall be the effort of the musical director to make programmes, which, while embodying a good class of music, shall be popular and pleasing, and have regard to business success.

10. The salaries to be paid to the musicians shall be paid by the business management, but the director may at all times advise and counsel the business management in this particular.

11. The musical director shall conduct as many concerts or other engagements, as are arranged for, or as the men are willing to play, but shall be entitled to one month's leave of absence in each calendar year, at a time or times when the band is not engaged on the road or otherwise, and the compensation of said Sousa shall not cease or be diminished by reason of such leave or any other cessation of work by said band.

12. The musical director shall, whenever able to do so in times of leisure, or when not occupied in conducting the band (except during such leave), rehearse and conduct any respectable organization composed of individuals of musical excellence, whenever requested by the said Blakely; and shall generally devote his time to the furtherance of the business interests of the said Blakely in this connection by his musical accomplishments and work; and in case of any musical compositions by said Sousa during or prior to said period, the profits of the sale or negotiations of any such musical compositions, and all other music now controlled by the said Sousa, or composed by him during or prior to this engagement, including his "Sheridan's Ride," "Ben Hur," etc. (already composed), shall be divided equally between the parties of this agreement; the publication of these, if published by him, to be at the expense of said Blakely, said expense to be deducted from the receipts of the sales of said music before any division of profits shall be made.

13. The said Sousa, party of the second part, agrees to transfer and deliver, and hereby does transfer to the said Blakely, party of the first part, as aforesaid, the original scores and orchestra music, or copies of the same of all his own musical library of band music; and such scores and music, or copies of all music of this class, composed, arranged, purchased, or in any way heretofore acquired, or to be acquired, for the use of said band, during the force of this agreement, shall be the property of the party of the first part, as a part of the permanent library of said band.

14. Should, for any reason, the said Sousa return to the government service, or resume his position as leader of the Marine Band, or any other organization, or engage in other business, then this contract shall cease and determine. But the said Sousa shall not so return or accept the direction of any other organization not herein specified, or engage in any musical or other work not connected with this engagement, without the written consent of the said David Blakely.

15. It is agreed that both parties to this agreement shall do all that within them lies to make the enterprise herein contemplated a success, both musically and financially; and, in general, they shall both spare no pains to forward the interests of the business connected directly and indirectly therewith.

16. In addition to conducting the concerts arranged for by the business management, the said John Philip Sousa shall conduct at all expositions, watering places, or other reputable engagements arranged for by the said David Blakely.

17. It is hereby further understood and agreed that in case of and as soon as the said David Blakely shall have perfected, and there shall have been organized, a stock company for the carrying out of the agreements herein set forth, this contract may be assigned to said company by said Blakely, and in case of its acceptance by said company, and its agreement to carry out its provision, it shall become the principal in the fulfillment of this contract in the place of the said David Blakely. But in case the said corporation shall not be formed, then it is understood and agreed that this contract shall be maintained intact by and be in full force as to both parties, as herein signed and executed.

In witness whereof, the parties hereto have signed their names and affixed their seals, in duplicate, this 27th day of June, A.D. 1892.

DAVID BLAKELY,　　　　[Seal]
JOHN PHILIP SOUSA.　　[Seal]
Witness:
　HOWARD PEW,
　FRANK CHRISTIANER.

CHILDREN CALLING

A review of the layout of the band's concert programs makes it obvious that many matinee concerts were intended primarily for children. It was not always that way; in the early years matinees were mostly for adults. If a date could be affixed on the time when Sousa decided on this change of repertoire it would be January 7, 1897. On that date the band was playing a matinee in Goldsboro, North Carolina. While the concert was in progress a large crowd of school children tried unsuccessfully to swarm through the doors of the auditorium. The fuss they raised disrupted patrons in the hall. Sousa sent a messenger outside with word that the band would play a special concert, just for them, if they would remain quiet until the regular concert ended. When the adults left the children rushed in, filling the main floor of the auditorium. Their applause and shouting were the most enthusiastic the band received. The band members and Sousa attempted to escape through the stage door after the concert, but the children descended upon them, showering them with flowers. Adults joined in, and all surrounded the band, shouting happily, as the band made its way to the train station. The train left half an hour late.[15] Sousa loved children, and from then on there was always something on matinee concerts for them to enjoy.

PATRIOTISM CALLING

What was billed as the "twelfth semi-annual tour" occupied the first three months of 1898, a period when the United States was having serious differences with Spain over its occupation of Cuba. The band played a patriotic concert at the Metropolitan Opera House in New York City on April 10 that ended in a patriotic frenzy. Two weeks later, on April 24, the Spanish-American War broke out.

Meanwhile, Sousa was busy preparing a pageant, *The Trooping of the Colors*. It was the main attraction on a two-month tour of twenty-three major American cities, and Sousa was hailed as America's musical patriot. He volunteered to leave the band and serve as a bandmaster in the Sixth Army Corps, but he was stricken with malaria complicated by typhoid and pneumonia and could not serve.

Much of the fighting in Cuba was over by the time he recovered, so he regrouped the band and fulfilled previously arranged engagements at the Pittsburgh Exposition and the St. Louis Exposition. These were followed by a short tour, mostly of the midwestern states, and the tour ended just as the war did.

A PROPOSED EUROPEAN TOUR

The band did not perform at Manhattan Beach in 1898 for two reasons. First, a tour of Europe was planned for that time although it was canceled because of the war. There was anti-American sentiment in Europe, and the presence of an American band in military-style uniforms would not have been prudent. Second, Sousa's illness meant that an assistant conductor, probably Arthur Pryor, would have had to lead the band. The result would have been decreased attendance at concerts, which was always the case when Sousa could not be on the podium.

ADMIRAL DEWEY'S HISTORIC PARADE

The year 1899 was another exceptionally busy one for the band, with five individual tours plus another lengthy engagement at Manhattan Beach. Perhaps the most important event was one of the band's rare appearances as a marching unit. It was chosen to lead a spectacular parade to celebrate America's victory in the Spanish-American War and honor Admiral George Dewey for his impressive naval victories.

The date was Saturday, September 30. The parade was four hours long, and the huge crowd cheered wildly as Sousa's Band led the way. The biggest reception was for Dewey, who rode in a carriage with New York's mayor, Robert Anderson Van Wyck, but all the returning service units and many other bands were received with great enthusiasm. Strutting at the head of the band was a man Sousa brought out of retirement for the occasion, Edward D. Hughes, who had been his drum major in the Marine Band. Among the marches the band played was Sousa's "El Capitan." Significantly, it was the same piece the band on Dewey's warship *Olympia* had played as they steamed out of Mirs Bay (Hong Kong) on the way to attack Manila.

A misunderstanding nearly prevented the band from appearing in the parade. At the time, the band was playing at the Philadelphia National Export Exposition. When Sousa's manager, Everett R. Reynolds, was asked what the band's fee would be he quoted a figure equal to that forfeited for canceling concerts in Philadelphia. Local musicians learned of the figure and spread the word that Sousa's price was exorbitant. To put an end to the bad publicity Sousa canceled the remainder of the Philadelphia engagement. Moreover, he enlarged the band to more than a hundred, paying the extra players out of his own pocket and charging nothing for the appearance.[16]

HAIL TO THE SPIRIT OF LIBERTY—THE FIRST EUROPEAN TOUR

Sousa and the band honed their skills on a tour extending deep into the Midwest during the first part of 1900. They were ready for their first tour of Europe, which had been canceled in 1898. Just before they left there was another unexpected change in management. Everett R. Reynolds resigned at the very last minute over a contract dispute, leaving his luggage behind on the ship. He had demanded that he and Sousa extend their contract (which was effective for another year) to well beyond the European tour. Sousa declined, perhaps influenced by the memory of the distasteful relationship with the family of David Blakely. He also wanted to wait until he could judge Reynolds's effectiveness in a foreign market.

Sousa, now fully responsible for a sixty-one-piece band, was en route to Europe as his own manager. They sailed on April 25 and stopped in England, where no concerts were played, on the way to France. In Southampton they met the band's publicity agent, George

---

15. Publicity release, David Blakely Collection, New York Public Library.

16. Newspapers say the band was 135 or 138 strong, but the only known photograph does not show that many players.

The parade for Admiral Dewey marked one of only eight times that Sousa's Band marched in the forty years of its existence. (Author's Collection)

Frederick Hinton, who had been arranging publicity overseas. Sousa appointed him the new manager.[17]

The next stop was Belgium. The positive impression made by the band there inspired the Academy of Arts, Science and Literature of Hainault (Henegouwen) to bestow a diploma of honor and also a medal, the Cross of Artistic Merit, on Sousa. He wore the medal, or its replica, on uniforms until the end of his career. Hinton received similar honors.

The band then headed to Paris for one day, May 19, to play at a party for a wealthy American, Harry Kimball Thaw. The next stop was Berlin via special railroad arrangements, and a European speed record was set in the process. The afternoon following the Thaw party, the band played a matinee in Berlin, a distance of some 620 miles (1,050 kilometers).

The band was back in Paris again on July 3 for the unveiling of the Washington Monument, and July 4 marked the unveiling of the La-fayette Monument. On that occasion the band premiered one of Sousa's finest marches, "Hail to the Spirit of Liberty." The activities of July 4 were especially significant in that the band made one of its rare appearances as a marching band. After performing at the dedica-tion of the American Pavilion they paraded through the principal streets of Paris accompanied by the mounted unit of the Garde Ré-publicaine and the American Guard. Later, they gave a concert of American music at the Esplanade des Invalides. Still later, they ser-enaded the American ambassador at a reception. After seventeen days in Paris the band returned to Germany for concerts and then went on to the Netherlands before heading home.

Sousa learned many lessons on this first tour of Europe, not the least of which was that Europe was ripe for future tours. He witnessed firsthand that his own "Washington Post" march was the most popu-lar piece of music in the world at that time and was used for dancing as well as for marching.

The band successfully introduced its style of fast-paced concerts to Europe and made a mark in two other ways as well. First, ragtime was introduced in a big way, causing one publisher, Leo Feist, to advertise that "Paris has gone ragtime wild."[18] Second, it is said that members of the band played one of the first baseball games to be played in Europe, defeating the team of the American Guard in Paris.

The band played a total of 175 concerts in thirty-four cities on the tour. Receipts were very high in Germany, where attendance was "far in excess of any ever known before."[19] Sousa and Hinton were over-whelmed by letters and telegrams from cities across Germany offering contracts. The situation was even more pronounced in Paris, where

17. Sousa's association with Hinton was long-standing. He was the prompter at perfor-mances of *The Queen of Hearts* in Washington in 1886 and later became an agent for numerous artists. The men had crossed paths many times.

18. Championing ragtime in the early days was the beginning of Sousa's role as a catalyst in the jazz movement. He played ragtime for several years until the novelty wore off. At first he believed jazz was a passing fad but years later conceded that it had become an integral part of American culture. He incorporated several jazz motives in his later works.

19. *Musical Courier,* n.d., Sousa Band Press Book 12.

Sousa's Band was the official American band at the Paris Exposition of 1900. Throughout its history, the band made appearances at this and many other great fairs and expositions, such as the Columbian Exposition (Chicago World's Fair, 1893); the Cotton States and International Exposition (Atlanta, 1895); the Pan-American Exposition (Buffalo, 1901); the Glasgow Exhibition (Scotland, 1901); the Louisiana Purchase Exposition (St. Louis, 1904); and the Panama-Pacific Exposition (San Francisco, 1915). It was to be the official band of the Century of Progress World's Fair in Chicago in 1933, but Sousa died in 1932. (U.S. Marine Band)

crowds were huge and the press hurled superlatives. "Wherever Mr. Sousa went after each performance," trombone soloist Arthur Pryor wrote, "he was followed by admiring, applauding crowds. From a distance we could tell his whereabouts within the grounds by the motion of a moving mass of humanity of which he was the central figure. . . . In a less conspicuous way, yet very noticeable, individual members of the band were similarly treated. . . . Proffers to pay for admission were useless. When in uniform our money was refused in nine cases out of ten."[20]

BRITAIN AND A COMMAND PERFORMANCE

Because of changes in the entertainment scene in New York City, 1901 was the last year Sousa and the band played at Manhattan Beach. There were, however, new engagements to keep them very busy. On their second European tour, also in 1901, they presented concerts in Britain for the first time and played their first command performance. Back home, they played the first of many engagements at Willow Grove Park in Philadelphia and made a grand appearance at the Pan-American Exposition in Buffalo. For the latter Sousa composed "The Invincible Eagle," a march he incorrectly predicted might surpass "The Stars and Stripes Forever" in popularity.

Britain had been bypassed on the band's first tour abroad in 1900

for reasons not subsequently explained.[21] Sousa might have sensed uncertain conditions in England when at the end of the 1900 tour he evaluated the situation there for a week while the band returned to America. His apprehension proved unfounded, because he and the band received high praise throughout the 1901 tour. Everywhere they played they were invited back.[22]

A command performance at Sandringham House on Sunday, December 1, was an unforgettable experience for both Sousa and the band members. The private affair was kept in such secrecy that even the musicians thought they were playing at another location until boarding the train. There were twenty guests, not counting the musicians, at a surprise party King Edward VII was hosting for Queen Alexandra. At the end of the concert the king handed a small casket containing the Royal Victorian Order to the prince of Wales for presentation to Sousa. Where, the prince asked, should he pin the medal? "Over my heart," Sousa replied. "How American!" exclaimed the prince. The queen summed up her appreciation in an aside to Sousa: "Your stirring marches, are like your people—fire, brilliance and sentiment."[23]

BAD PRESS IN BIRMINGHAM

The band's first concerts in England drew criticism for Sousa's energetic programming practices until reviewers realized that the pacing met with enthusiastic audience approval. On one occasion the criticism of an obviously prejudiced reporter was, according to Sousa, "the quintessence of vituperation and abuse."[24] A review of a concert on November 20, 1901, in the *Birmingham Gazette,* aroused the ire of the band's tour manager. The critic referred to Herbert L. Clarke's music as "rubbish," remarked that Sousa's conducting "smacks of the circus," and made numerous other insulting comments. The reviewer was also critical of the performance of Wagner's music, Sousa's favorite composer, and declared that the band would benefit from hearing half a dozen British bands he claimed were better. Sousa was content to ignore the matter, believing that audiences would know the attack was absurd. The tour manager, however, wanted revenge. When a letter to the newspaper brought no satisfaction he filed a lawsuit for £100,000 in damages.

That got their attention. The *Gazette* printed a retraction, alluding to the reviewer's personal prejudices. It noted Sousa's wide success in Britain, acknowledged that his "tuneful genius has been a source of infinite delight to thousands," and confirmed the band's worthiness in performing a command performance. With that the matter was dropped.

20. "Pryor Talks of European Trip," n.d., from a St. Joseph, Mo., publication and apparently reprinted from the *Music Trade Review,* Sousa Band Press Book 14.

21. There is nothing in Sousa's memoirs relating to that decision.
22. The *Musical Courier* reported that Sousa's share of the profits amounted to $6,000 per week (Sousa Band Press Book 14, 282).
23. *New York World,* Dec. 15, 1901. A listing of pieces played at the first command performance appears on page 276.
24. Sousa, *Marching Along,* 223–24; clippings, Sousa Band Press Book 15.

An important engagement during the band's second European tour was the Glasgow Exhibition of 1901. A fraternal relationship was established there with the band of His Majesty's Grenadier Guards of England, and both bands are shown in this portrait. Each band held a dinner in honor of the other. (U.S. Marine Band)

WILLOW GROVE

The band's fourteen-day stay at Willow Grove Park in 1901 was the first of twenty-seven important engagements at the "summer music capital of America." The band then played there every year through 1926 (two separate times in 1905 and for one day only in 1928) except in 1911, the year of the world tour. The park's owners were initially uncertain about Sousa's drawing power and uneasy over the price they had to pay. They eventually came to realize, however, that although numerous famous orchestras and bands performed at Willow Grove it was Sousa who assured a profit by the size of his crowds at the end of a season.[25]

ANOTHER MEDAL

Sousa's third medal from abroad came from France in 1901. In recognition of his bringing New World music of high quality to France during the Paris Exposition the French government awarded him the Palms and Rosette of the French Academy, another medal (or replica thereof) he wore throughout his career.

THE BUSIEST YEAR, 1902

The year 1902 was busier than any other for Sousa and the band. They performed 730 concerts, and an eighty-five-day engagement at the Steel Pier in Atlantic City was added to the normal schedule. The band would not play again at the Steel Pier for another twenty-four years; not until the late 1920s did that venue replace Willow Grove as the band's most important summer engagement.

At the time of the command performance in 1901 Sousa had asked Edward VII for permission to compose a march in his honor as well as a piece for the royal family, and the king granted his request. The march, "Imperial Edward," was completed and published in 1902, and George Frederick Hinton hand-carried a beautifully illuminated manuscript of the piece to the king. The trio of the march incorporated a subtle six-measure trombone countermelody of "God Save the King" for trombones, and when performed by the band it was customary for the trombones to stand for those six measures. The number had been composed rather hurriedly, and Sousa remarked later that he did not feel it to be among his better efforts.

The piece for the royal family was a majestic suite entitled "At the King's Court" (1904). In one movement Sousa added a modification of the earlier and unpublished "March of the Royal Trumpets," music unavailable for his reference because it was in the library kept by the Blakely heirs. Sousa reconstructed it from memory, however, and made major changes.[26]

A disappointment occurred for Sousa when the band appeared in Poughkeepsie, New York, for a matinee concert on December 2, 1902. His daughter, Jane Priscilla, was attending school there at Vassar College, but only she and a very few other students were permitted to attend the event because the school's lady principal had banned students from attending the theater, a ruling that made local theater owners unhappy.[27]

25. The standard Sousa Band fee, the highest for any performing arts group there, was $1,000 per day, or $7,000 per week, with four different concerts daily.

26. In 1964 I discovered the manuscript of "March of the Royal Trumpets" in an out-of-the-way section of the Sousa Band library, located in the basement of the library at Stetson University in DeLand, Florida. As of the time of writing, "March of the Royal Trumpets" had not been published. After Sousa completely revised the piece, the Blakely heirs could not claim ownership.

27. Clippings from the *Poughkeepsie Enterprise* and *New York Morning Telegraph*, Sousa Band Press Book 19. Vassar College's administration at that time included a male president as well as the lady principal.

SOUSA'S BAND - WILLOW GROVE PARK, PHILADELPHIA, PA.

Willow Grove Park concerts drew huge crowds, especially on weekends and holidays, and many of the nation's leading symphony orchestras and bands performed there. Sousa's Band played longer and was paid more than other groups because it attracted the largest audiences. The bandshell was inside the pavilion in this image, enlarged from a postcard around 1902, but two years earlier it stood alone as a separate building. The piece that was about to be played (or perhaps had just been played) was not a standard concert number because of the unusual seating arrangement. (Barry Owen Furrer Collection)

NOT QUITE A WORLD TOUR

A tour completely around the world was planned for 1903. In addition to European and African countries, the itinerary was to include India, Japan (Yokohama, Kobe, and Nagasaki), China, Hong Kong, the Philippines (Manila), and Hawaii (Honolulu). Satisfactory contracts could not be made in some countries, however, so the tour was scaled down drastically. The compromise tour was still ambitious, however. It included England, Wales, Ireland, Scotland, France, Belgium, Germany, Russia, Poland, Austria, Bohemia, Denmark, and the Netherlands.

Concerts in St. Petersburg were accompanied by unexpected difficulties. First, there was the matter of obtaining passports. Then the police demanded to see the words of all songs soprano Estelle Liebling was to sing, as well as the copy for all advertising. All went well, however. Liebling sang songs that included many "ahs" and even substituted the words of "Annie Rooney" for the possibly objectionable words of another song. Sousa was surprised and pleased at the exceptional responses of audiences and calls for pieces to be repeated. When the Russian national anthem was played, for example, applause was so intense that the band was obliged to play it four times.

In Vienna the band was a hit with Sousa's interpretation of "The Blue Danube Waltz." It was, one report remarked, the "first time it had really been heard since Johann Strauss' death."[28]

A SECOND COMMAND PERFORMANCE

A summary of the 1903 tour itinerary is impressive considering the state of transportation at the time. The tour covered all the leading cities of Northern and Central Europe, and the band played 362 concerts in 133 towns.

Among the tour's highlights was a second command performance in Great Britain, this time at Windsor Castle, on Saturday, January 31,

---

28. Sousa, *Marching Along,* 254; review not found in Sousa Band Press Books.

1903. Concerts in Manchester that day had to be canceled so the 10 P.M. program could be scheduled. In addition to members of the royal family, several foreign dignitaries and all members of His Majesty's Scots Guard Band were invited.[29] The event provided an unplanned demonstration of the outstanding caliber of the Sousa musicians when music did not arrive on time and the entire two-hour program had to be played from memory. En route to the concert the driver of the carriage transporting the music had lost control of the vehicle, causing the carriage to slide down an icy road and crash.

THE FINEST BAND?

Historians speculate about which year Sousa had his best band, and 1903 could certainly be brought up in such deliberations. That year he had the brilliant lyric soprano Estelle Liebling and two individuals still among the best soloists of all time on their instruments, Arthur Pryor on trombone and Simone Mantia on euphonium. Moreover, the legendary Maud Powell, considered the greatest American violinist until that time and for several years thereafter, was soloist. Other notables on the tour were Walter B. Rogers on cornet and Franz Helle on flugelhorn.

A FOURTH EUROPEAN TOUR

The band operated for only half of 1904, a less hectic year. Their most important engagement was at the World's Fair in St. Louis, known as the Louisiana Purchase Exposition. Arthur Pryor had resigned to form his own band, taking Simone Mantia with him, but they were replaced by two other young virtuos just beginning to make their mark in the music world: Leo Zimmerman on trombone and John Perfetto on euphonium.

An August-to-December tour took the band through Indian Territory and also to Mitchell, South Dakota, for its first engagement at the Corn Palace. The advance man questioned whether that sparsely populated part of South Dakota could support a week's worth of concerts but decided to risk the booking. Corn Palace officials paid cash in full, and the stop turned out to be a lucrative engagement. While in Mitchell, Sousa completed "The Diplomat" march, inspired, he said, by the best steak he had ever eaten.

The fourth European tour consumed the first four months of 1905 and was spent entirely in Great Britain. Because venues were close together the tour was less tiring for the musicians and travel expenses were reduced. Sousa had become much loved in England, and the tour was very profitable. The band continued in full stride, again featuring Maud Powell and Estelle Liebling.

Counting the trip to Great Britain, there were four individual tours in 1905. Concert bookings for the year were unusual because the schedule was open for much of the summer and the visits to Willow Grove and the Pittsburgh Exposition were each split into two separate engagements.

WINDING DOWN

After its four overseas tours the band had a period of less rigorous schedules. There were four relatively short tours in 1906, and the band was inactive for more than five months. In 1907, 1908, and 1909 there was even less activity, the band being idle for seven months of each year. There might be several explanations for the reduced activity, but they are not obvious from Sousa's writing. It was not a particularly slack period in the entertainment industry, so perhaps the inactivity was a deliberate choice on Sousa's part—he was now in his fifties. It could, however, have been caused by less aggressive planning on the part of the manager, Edwin G. Clarke. Clarke did have big things in mind, however. He wanted to complete the world tour that had been postponed in 1903 and made connections with the Quinlan International Music Agency in London (which also had a New York office) to manage most of the foreign segments of the tour, which finally took place in 1911.

THE WORLD TOUR OF 1911

A "warm-up" for the world tour took place in November and December of 1910 and nearly ended in a tragedy. The tour had scarcely begun when Sousa was struck with a recurrence of the malaria he had suffered during the Spanish-American War, and his illness was complicated by acute indigestion. His condition worsened, and during a concert at Woolsey Hall on the Yale University campus he was carried off the stage to the New Haven Hospital. Herbert L. Clarke stepped in as conductor until Sousa regained enough strength to return.

The world tour, ambitious and filled with adventure, covered 47,346 miles by land and sea.[30] The troupe consisted of sixty-nine persons: Sousa, sixty band members (including soprano Virginia Root and violinist Nicoline Zedeler), Jane Sousa, the Sousas' daughters Helen and Jane Priscilla, J. C. Simmons of the Quinlan Agency, Edwin G. Clarke, and the wives of three members of the band.

Members of the group narrowly escaped disaster on three occasions. The first occurred following a matinee on January 17 in Plymouth, England, when Zedeler was overcome by gas leaking from a stove in the theater's dressing room. Root, her roommate, entered the room later and was overcome in her effort to revive Zedeler. A cab driver, waiting impatiently to take them to their hotel, called Edwin Clarke, who smelled the gas as he approached the room. He rushed in and carried out the unconscious women, saving their lives. Neither was in any condition to perform that evening and were

---

29. A listing of pieces played at the second command performance appears on page 276. Detailed accounts of the event were printed in the *New York Evening Sun,* Feb. 11, 1903.

30. Sousa's Band was not the first band to travel around the world. The Kilties Band of Canada had launched a similar venture two years earlier, traveling from east to west (Sousa's Band traveled from west to east). The Kilties Band was roughly half the size of Sousa's and marched as part of its presentations. The tour lasted for four years.

In September 1907 the band paid the second of its four visits to the Corn Palace in Mitchell, South Dakota, decorated with corn of many different colors. (Barry Owen Furrer Collection)

barely able to perform the next day. One newspaper commented that Root sang "with amazing restraint"; Zedeler was amused when it was announced that she was suffering from gastritis.

Two days later in Merthyr Tydfil, Wales, a temporary stage extension collapsed when the brass players came to the front for the finale of "The Stars and Stripes Forever"; several of them crashed seven feet to the floor of the hall. Virginia Root ran screaming toward the stage, thinking Sousa might have been killed. No one was seriously injured, however. It was learned that the carpenter who built the stage extension was also the local undertaker.

The third mishap occurred when the ship transporting the group encountered a terrible storm while rounding the coast of southern Africa. Treacherous seas caused it to list to forty-five degrees and nearly capsize. Several passengers, including a few band members, were injured. Percussionist William Lowe, who was also a physician, helped the ship's physician care for the injured parties.

The tour included visits to Australia and New Zealand, where the band received what was probably the warmest reception it had re-

ceived from local musicians, sometimes with more than a thousand participating. Audiences were equally enthusiastic.

After a stop for two concerts in Honolulu, the band finally returned to the New World at Victoria, British Columbia, and continued on to an extensive tour of the United States. Its journey ended in New York City. Saxophonist Albert A. Knecht kept a detailed diary throughout the tour (chapter 7).

THREE LEAN YEARS

For three years after the world tour, in 1912, 1913, and 1914, band operations were curtailed to four months annually. Engagements at Willow Grove and the Pittsburgh Exposition had become annual events, and short tours were added to round out the touring seasons. Moreover, there were no off-tour concerts in New York during those years.

HIP! HIP! HOORAY!

The band became much busier in 1915. A six-month tour stretched to the West Coast and included a lengthy engagement in San Francisco at the Panama-Pacific Exposition, held to celebrate the opening of the Panama Canal. There were also the annual visits to Willow Grove and the Pittsburgh Exposition.

While in San Francisco Sousa received a telegram asking if the band could play in New York City for eight months to accompany acts for the upcoming *Hip! Hip! Hooray!* extravaganza. The promoter, Charles Dillingham, then sent a seasoned theater manager, Harry Askin, to San Francisco to make the arrangements. Askin had worked with Sousa on other occasions and was to become manager of the band three years later.

Hip! Hip! Hooray! was staged at New York's 5,200-seat Hippodrome Theatre, billed as the largest in the world. The show was called a "spectacular," but that description was inadequate. There was a wealth of variety—a series of mostly unrelated acts with no central theme—including numerous vocalists, dancing acts, comedy routines, instrumental groups, and even an ice ballet on a miniature rink. The stage was huge, and an army of employees was needed to keep the show progressing smoothly.[31]

An anamorphic diagram, artist unknown, was printed during the Australia-New Zealand part of the world tour. By holding the card aslant and reading from below, an announcement can be read: "Australasian Tour of the Great Sousa and His World Renowned Band of Sixty Performers. All Artists." (Author's Collection, courtesy of Antoinette Cendali)

The band did not play many "drive-in" concerts. In this huge Tacoma, Washington, High School stadium, where they played for seventeen thousand on July 27, 1915, one might wonder if the crowd could hear much of the music. Clarence J. Russell, the band's librarian, stated in an article he wrote for *Musical America* on September 11 that the acoustics were unusually fine. (Author's Collection, courtesy of Antoinette Cendali)

31. The Hippodrome was located at Sixth Avenue and Forty-third Street in Manhattan, south of the current Radio City Music Hall that replaced it.

As manager of New York's Hippodrome Theatre, impresario Charles Dillingham engaged the band to accompany *Hip! Hip! Hooray!* When the show went on the road, the band was again part of the show. Sousa dedicated the "New York Hippodrome" march to Dillingham and also wrote incidental music for *Cheer Up* and *Everything,* later Dillingham shows. (Loras J. Schissel Collection)

The band accompanied many acts, including an elaborate procession entitled "March of the States" in which costumed actors represented each state; Sousa composed the music. Two shows were staged every day except for Sundays, and each Sunday evening the band held its own concert, with many of the biggest names in show business appearing. Advance ticket sales for *Hip! Hip! Hooray!* were high, and it is remarkable that a theater of that size could be filled for eight months. A diary kept by band librarian Clarence J. Russell noted 425 performances of the band between October 30, 1915, and June 4, 1916.

HIP! HIP! ON THE ROAD

After twenty-two days at Willow Grove, Sousa and the band embarked on an unusual tour with the *Hip! Hip! Hooray!* show and played at the largest theaters in Philadelphia, Boston, Cincinnati, St. Louis, Kansas City, St. Paul, Chicago, and Cleveland. The tour lasted from October 14, 1916, to March 18, 1917. Dismantling the stage in one city, transporting the entire company to another city, and setting up required a minimum of two days. On off-days the band held regular concerts in cities between venues. Performers from the show provided many solo numbers at the concerts.

THE WORLD WAR I YEARS

On April 6, 1917, two weeks after the *Hip! Hip! Hooray!* tour ended, the United States entered World War I and several members of the band enlisted. Sousa, although sixty-two, wanted to join them in one way or another. The problem was, however, that the band was booked for two months in the summer of 1917 and a slightly longer period in the summer of 1918.

Capt. William A. Moffett, commandant at the Great Lakes Naval Training Center outside Chicago, asked Sousa to organize bands there. Moffett also offered a commission as a lieutenant. That appealed to Sousa, who had always been sensitive to the fact that he had never been made a commissioned officer while leader of the Marine Band. The Sousa Band's advance engagements, however, stood in the way.

A compromise was struck. Sousa agreed to serve, at a salary of only one dollar per month, with the provision that he be granted leave so he could bring the Sousa Band together for the prearranged 1917 and 1918 engagements. The war ended two months after the 1918 tour. Meanwhile, Sousa had developed a serious ear infection that caused him to take a vacation from the music business. The band was inactive for nine months.

During periods when the band was not in session the musicians had to find employment elsewhere; some played with symphony orchestras in the winter and with Sousa in the summer. When Sousa called them back together again, however, the band would respond readily. He never experienced difficulty reforming the group.

CHANGING TIMES

Following World War I, when the band had been out of operation for about nine months, the band's manager did have difficulty obtaining the services of the specific personnel he wanted. Thus there were a number of new faces in the band for the first postwar tour. Twenty-seven members of the 1919–20 tour had served in the Armed Forces overseas. There was no trouble finding musicians who sought work, but many of the mainstays had moved on to other jobs. Loyalty among the new musicians was not as pronounced as it had been in previous years—as Sousa was about to discover.

The 1919–20 tour began with a looping route around the Midwest and then into Canada for a series of engagements at fairs. Then came the annual Willow Grove visit, followed by an ambitious tour taking the band to the West Coast. Returning to New York by way of the southern states, the group began to grumble about travel conditions.

THE STRIKE

In the forty-year history of Sousa's Band there was only one occasion on which members refused to play. Two-thirds of the band did not appear for a matinee in Winston-Salem, North Carolina, on Monday,

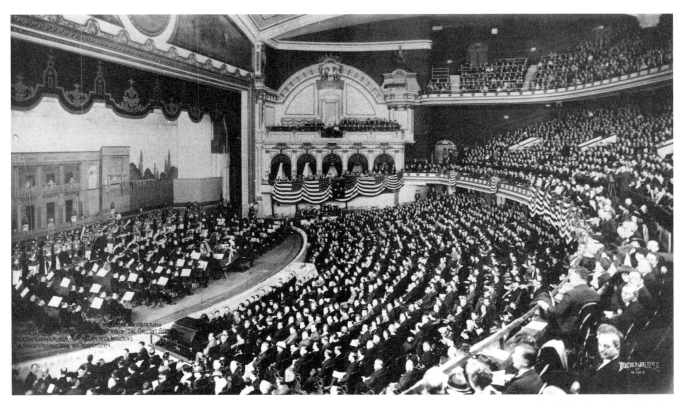

The Hippodrome Theatre was the scene of many Sousa Band concerts, In this March 5, 1922, concert the band was assisted by Keith's Boys Band. The Hippodrome, which had a huge stage, was torn down in 1939 and is now the site of a parking garage. (Barry Owen Furrer Collection)

January 5, 1920, during the last week of the 1919–20 tour. All played the evening performance, however, and finished the tour.[32]

They were irritated by inadequate hotel arrangements toward the end of the tour, unrest aggravated by an altered railroad connection. Poor lodging had been a concern several times earlier on the tour, but it is unclear who was responsible for making proper reservations.

Before the Winston-Salem incident, afternoon and evening concerts were played in Nashville, Tennessee, on Saturday, January 3. Sunday was an off day. The next concert was scheduled for Monday at Winston-Salem, 410 miles from Nashville, and a sleeper train left Nashville immediately after the Saturday night performance. The band arrived in Asheville, North Carolina, at 7 A.M. on Sunday with only a half-hour allowed for switching trains. The musicians hurried to the depot restaurant for breakfast, but many were not served.

Then something went terribly wrong. The passenger train expected to be available was scheduled to arrive in Winston-Salem at 3 P.M. That run was apparently canceled, however, and the cars that carried the band were attached to the back of a slow-moving freight with no dining service available. The three-car section consisted of a Pullman car for Sousa, the two female soloists, and a few band members; a regular passenger car for the remainder; and a baggage car. The freight train did not arrive in Winston-Salem until 3 A.M. on Monday.[33]

Then came another unpleasant surprise. No hotel rooms were available other than those for Sousa, the female soloists, and solo cornetist Frank Simon. Simon volunteered to share his bed with two band members, and the remainder of the group retired to hotel couches, chairs, and a few pool tables. The next morning those unable to find beds had an "indignation meeting." A majority voted to show their displeasure by not playing the matinee concert.

At concert time the stage held nineteen musicians and thirty-eight empty chairs. Sousa strode to the stage, took a bow, stared at Frank Simon, and asked, "Where is my band?" Simon replied that he had no idea. "If ever I saw fire in a pair of Spanish eyes," he recalled, "it was at that moment."

A concert with only nineteen instrumentalists rather than fifty-seven leaves much to be desired in sound. "Well," Simon would remark about the beginning of the overture, "I'll never forget that chord to my dying day!" There were no tubas, no French horns, no drums, and only skeletons of the other sections. Nineteen very busy musicians frantically played cues for as many of the missing instruments as they could, but the music remained painfully thin. Simon played a cornet solo as a substitute for H. Benne Henton's scheduled saxophone solo because Henton was one of those absent. The players

32. The following account is based on interviews with Frank Simon (solo cornetist), Simon's writings, interviews with other members of the band at the time, and research by historian Earl Lauber of Winston-Salem. The band stopped in seven cities after Winston-Salem.

33. It is also possible that an alternate route might have been taken. The trip from Asheville to Winston-Salem averaged about seven miles per hour.

limped through the remainder of the concert, which was attended mostly by school children who perhaps were unaware of how the band normally sounded.[34] At the end of the concert Sousa announced that something had happened to his band and the box office would issue refunds to anyone asking for them. No one did.

Sousa was furious. In his mind, it was inexcusable for musicians not to perform at a contracted engagement for a paying audience when physically able to do so, even under extenuating circumstances. He instructed his personnel manager, Jay Sims, never to hire any of the strikers for future tours. Percussionist Gus Helmecke, apparently considered indispensable, was the only exception. Sousa refused to speak publicly of the incident until nearly four years later:

> Once upon a time, I had twenty-eight [sic] vacancies all at once. There were a couple bolsheviks in the organization—men who growled and complained about everything. If the train was late they growled, and if it wasn't late they growled. It was undermining the whole group and one day when some of the men failed to turn up for [a] matinee because the train had been four hours late and they were going to "show the manager," I cleaned them out. I took out twenty-eight at one shot and some of them [were] my best musicians; one man had been with me fifteen years. I hated to do it, but to have a real organization you have to have harmony. Sometimes I'll get a man who has talent but doesn't keep up the standards of his work. I have to get rid of him. It's "4 o'clock for him" as they say back where I come from. A real musician must have more than talent; he must be sincere.[35]

Frank Simon was among those discharged. He had kept in touch with the musicians and reported on their complaints, and Sousa mistakenly assumed that he was the ringleader who called the strike. It was the striking musicians, however, who had called the "indignation meeting" without inviting Simon.[36]

Another long-standing member of the band, harpist Joseph Marthage, was also discharged. The morning after the strike he greeted Sousa on the platform of the railway station. "Don't you ever speak to me again [on] the longest day of your life," was Sousa's scowling response. Marthage, a ten-year veteran of the band, was crushed. He had been with Sousa on the world tour of 1911 but found himself forever banned. An amazing aspect of this incident was that the musicians themselves kept it a secret. Those who were fired seldom talked about it, and many of their replacements did not know a strike had taken place.[37]

A DIFFERENT BAND

It was more than six months after the strike that Sousa took the band on tour again. This time the majority of the musicians were new and had been screened very carefully. John Dolan, who replaced Frank Simon, proved a superb solo cornetist and reliable first chair. Although he was unsociable at times, both the band and the public marveled at his artistry.

SOUSA'S CRIPPLING ACCIDENT

Sousa was thrown while riding his favorite mount, Patrician Charley, at Willow Grove on the morning of September 6, 1921. Ironically, he had remarked earlier, "Some day that horse is going to break my neck," and the fall did indeed crack vertebrae in Sousa's neck. The horse was determined to have the "blinding staggers."[38] John Dolan conducted the band until September 25, when it was decided to terminate the tour and give the musicians severance pay.

Many believed the accident would end Sousa's career, but he resumed work two months later. A rearranged tour resumed on November 21 and continued until April 1, 1922, with nearly all of the same personnel. Because Sousa was in considerable pain it was necessary for Dolan to conduct part of the time.

It annoyed Sousa when newspapers would remark that they were not seeing the Sousa of old. When asked about retirement he had a number of blunt responses, among them, "Some day you'll pick up the paper and see 'Sousa Dead.' Then you'll know I've retired."

FORGING AHEAD

After laying off for three and a half months the band was back on tour again. The 1922 tour included a week in Cuba, its first and only visit there because the appearance was not a financial success. Not all was lost, however. Band members brought back a good supply of cheap liquor, and Sousa brought back a good supply of his favorite Fonseca cigars.

A BLUE LAW VIOLATION

From the time of the band's organization in 1892 Sousa had asked managers and booking agents to avoid scheduling concerts on Sundays where there might be objections by religious groups. If there was any hint of objection, concerts were advertised as a "sacred concert" and included at least a token amount of religious music. In Binghamton, New York, the band ran afoul of a blue law restriction prohibiting Sunday amusements where admission was charged.

As a gift to twelve thousand employees, the Endicott-Johnson

---

34. In 1993 I asked a local newspaper to run an article requesting information from anyone who had been present at the concert some seventy-two years earlier. One person was found, but she was in ill-health and unable to respond to my questions.

35. *Emporia Gazette,* Dec. 5, 1923.

36. Simon did not know he had been discharged until nearly two months later when rehearsals began for the next tour. When he received no "call sheet" (a letter informing members of rehearsal place and time) he assumed it had been lost in the mail and traveled from his home in Middletown, Ohio, to New York. He arrived at the rehearsal to find John Dolan sitting in his chair. Louis Morris, a clarinetist and Simon's closest friend in the band, was present when Sousa informed Simon that his services would not be needed for the tour. Morris and Simon related identical stories to me in interviews.

37. Nearly all the poststrike members of the band whom I interviewed could not recall the incident. Others who were in the band at the time and did play the concert preferred not to comment.

38. Equine meningo-encephalitis was known in those days variously as "staggers," "blind staggers," "sleep staggers," or "mad staggers." Scientists in the early twentieth century were trying to determine what caused the illness, although it appeared that some horses contracted it by feeding on immature corn infected with mold and worm dirt. In its early stages horses would stumble over low objects and exhibit colic and restlessness. As the condition advanced, the animals would fall or throw themselves down or become violent, running through fences and into stationary objects.

The 1921–22 season's band was photographed in San Francisco in December 1921. Sousa temporarily permitted the "bell-front" sousaphone in the back row while a "bell-up" model, like the other four, was being manufactured. First row: William Kunkel, Chester Barclay, George Ford, Meredith Willson, Robert Lorenz, William Brandenburg, Frank Zuber, Robert Ross, Lorenzo Engberg, Edward Johnson, Einar Frigga, William Schueler, James Borrelli, Joseph Norrito, local promoter A. M. Oberfelder, Sousa, Winifred Bambrick (harpist), Dr. John Paul Brennan (Sousa was still recovering from a riding accident), John Dolan, Arthur Danner, Henry Schueler, Edwin Newcomb, Clarence Russell, Arthur Brabrook, and Charles Koppitz. Second row: Fred Prohaska, Arthur Davis, Herman Johnson, Charles Schwartz, Otto Jacob, Fred Weaver, Michael Vincinguerra, John Leigl, Theodore Lubis, James Shepard, Earl Foote, John Albrecht, Henri Barron, Henry Seigfried, John Linde, Charles Loehmann, Sherley Thompson, Anton Maly, George Abeel, Paul Gerhardt, Herman Schmidt, Howard Grantham, John Silbach, Charles Lobber, Leon Weir, Richard Kent, Erling Sodohl, Howard Rowell, Mathias Kuhn, Gerald Byrne, and William Pierce. Third row: August Helmecke, George Carey, Howard Goulden, Willard Snyder (Sousa's valet), Nicola Ferrara, Daniel Markert, Earl Field, Donald Gardner, William Bell, William Parker, Oscar Nutter, Jay Sims, Arthur Gibbs, John Schueler, Carl Preble, and Joseph De Luca. (U.S. Marine Band)

Corporation in Binghamton sponsored matinee and evening concerts on Sunday, November 12, 1922. Ticket prices normally cost up to $2.50, but the company arranged employee tickets for only 25 cents and agreed to make up the difference in the band's expenses, approximately $800. Sousa promised to charge only what it would cost to bring the band there. George F. Johnson, the company's popular president, thought the blue law would be overlooked. In short speeches at the concerts he announced that he did not feel like a criminal because the good in the events outweighed the bad. He was loudly cheered.

The concerts caused an uproar among the Binghamton Ministerial Association, however, and made national headlines. The clergy demanded that the law be enforced. The police entered the auditorium during the matinee concert and arrested Harold F. Albert, director of the corporation's recreational department. Sousa made his feelings known to reporters, pointing out that he personally was not receiving a penny for the concerts and remarking that there seemed to be a strange double standard, because the objecting ministers themselves (as well as some choir members) were paid for working on Sundays. He added a final blast, "There is more inspiration in some of my marches than in all their sermons!"[39]

BUYING BACK THE LIBRARY

In July 1923 the band embarked on a coast-to-coast tour of seven months. The next tour, in 1924, lasted five months and covered the Midwest and South. The 1924 tour was unique in that the Willow Grove engagement was extended to eleven weeks. If there was ever a ques-

tion about the caliber of musicians in Sousa's Band, one should consider what they accomplished in those eleven weeks. They performed four completely different concerts each day, seven days a week, with no rehearsals.

A particularly significant event of the Willow Grove stay was the buy-back of the original band library from the heirs of former manager David Blakely. Very little of it was put to use, however, because Sousa had replaced most of the pieces he considered essential for effective concerts.[40]

CONCERT SPONSORSHIP AND ENHANCEMENTS

Sousa was a Freemason for most of his adult life but did not go further into Masonry by becoming a Shriner until 1922. The next year he honored Shriners by composing one of his finest marches, "Nobles of the Mystic Shrine" and dedicating it to Shriners everywhere. A lasting friendship began with Shrine organizations around the country. They sponsored quite a few of the band's concerts in cities where the fraternal organization was strong, and often members of a local Shrine band joined the Sousa Band for a march or two. Moreover, by the late 1920s more than half of the band were Shriners.

During this period the school band movement in America was gathering impetus, and Sousa was outspoken in his support of school music programs. Numerous high school bands (and sometimes college bands) were invited to play Sousa marches during intermissions at concerts, usually with Sousa conducting. This, of course, gave bragging rights to thousands of budding young musicians who could then say, "I played under John Philip Sousa." Bands were sometimes given trophies or loving cups.

---

39. Sousa learned early about resistance to Sunday concerts in certain locales. Against his wishes, the band was booked for a concert in Lima, Ohio, on Sunday, October 23, 1892. Ministers there condemned the concerts and, assuming that Sousa was Italian, said they "didn't want any dago and his band here" ("Sousa Tells of Visit to Lima Thirty-three Years Ago," clipping, Sousa Band Press Book, n.p., n.d.). In the case of Harold F. Albert of Endicott-Johnson, he insisted on a jury trial and was found not guilty two weeks later.

40. J. Fred Campbell, a flutist and Sousa's personal secretary, stated in a 1964 interview with me that the purchase price was about $500. That part of the library is significant in that it included quite a few of Sousa's handwritten manuscripts.

In some cities Sousa would be called upon to judge local band contests. For those competitions he usually asked members of the band to help adjudicate his decisions, and among those who did so were Clarence J. Russell, William Tong, Jay Sims, Raymond Williams, Leon Weir, and Arthur Davenport. On one occasion Sousa conducted one number with each of seven bands.

Another new feature of the band of the 1920s was the addition of a saxophone sextet, which became so popular it was expanded to an octet. The saxophonists worked up their own repertoire, usually including a comedy routine. At one point Sousa considered hiring the Brown Brothers Saxophone Sextet as a special feature, but negotiations could not be worked out.

THE INDOMITABLE SOUSA

Sousa turned seventy-one during the 1925–26 tour but did not slow down. The outing lasted eight months and was advertised as the "Third of a Century Tour." How a man of his age could conduct two concerts a day for weeks on end is beyond the comprehension of modern conductors. Sometimes he had no rest during intermissions because he was conducting guest bands.

EUROPE AGAIN?

The band toured the country for five months in 1926. Both Sousa and the management had been in favor of another European tour, but it was canceled, likely because of unsteady financial conditions in Europe following World War I.

Saxophone ensembles from within the band became popular with the beginning of the dance craze of the 1920s. The saxophone sextet of the 1919–20 tour included, back row, Albert Knecht (alto), M. B. Howard (tenor); H. Benne Henton (alto), and Andrew Jacobson (tenor); seated, Charles Weber (bass), and Arthur Rosander Sr. (baritone). (Author's Collection, courtesy of Betty McCloskey)

The saxophone sextet grew to an octet. These players at the Steel Pier in Atlantic City in July 1926 are, left to right, Edward Heney (alto), Owen Kincaid (alto), Benjamin Conklin (alto), John Bell (alto), Fred Monroe (bass), Leon Weir (tenor), Bert Madden (tenor), and James Schlanz (baritone). They jokingly referred to the octet as "our little German Band." (American Bandmasters Association Research Center)

A fifty-six-day Willow Grove engagement in 1926 was the last engagement for the band there other than one day in 1928. Before Willow Grove, the band played at Atlantic City's Steel Pier, which thereafter replaced Willow Grove as the major summer engagement. The reasons for terminating the Willow Grove series are unclear, but some band members surmised that Sousa and park owner Thomas A. Mitten might have had a serious disagreement. That seems unlikely, however, in light of the fact that Sousa dedicated a march to Mitten, "March of the Mitten Men."[41]

Former Sousa Band musicians liked to reminisce about a stop in Milwaukee on the 1926 tour. As the train pulled into the station on November 6, locomotives blew their whistles. When Sousa inquired about the reason for such noise, he was asked, "Mr. Sousa, don't you know it's your birthday?" "I wish the railroad would save their coal and pay more dividends on their stock" was the reply. At that day's matinee seventy-two children, all orphans, came forward with cakes, lighted with candles, and four boys carried a large cake onstage. One boy remained, keeping Sousa from continuing the concert. The honoree finally turned and said, "Well, young man, I'm not going to eat it *right now.*" After the concert the candle bearers had their fill of cake, and what was left was donated to charities.

AT THE MOVIES

The year 1927 was another unusual one for Sousa and the band, inasmuch as they were part of a double feature in movie houses on two separate tours. They played mini-concerts lasting from half an hour to an hour, four or five times a day, and those were followed by movies. On the first tour they played a week each in New York, Brooklyn, Boston, Buffalo, Detroit, and Chicago, an arrangement made in cooperation with the Publix Circuit. The second tour was planned as a standard concert tour of four months but extended by

---

41. "March of the Mitten Men" (1923) was later published as "Power and Glory." It incorporated Mitten's favorite hymn, "Onward Christian Soldiers."

The July 1926 engagement was the band's first at the Steel Pier after an absence of twenty-four years. Thereafter, the Steel Pier engagement was an annual event and the band's most important summer engagement. Front row: Carl Smith (Sousa's valet), Cal Porlatto, Charles Kardasen, John Van Fossen, Edward Williams, Edward Elliot, Frank Zuber, Fred Weaver, George Kampe, Einar Frigga, William Schueler, Lorenzo Engberg, Roy Schmidt, Marjorie Moody, Sousa, Winifred Bambrick, John Dolan, William Tong, Harold Stambaugh, Jacob Knuttunen, Clarence Russell, Maxwell Arnold, Walter Cameron, and Guy Gaugler. Second row: Paul Gerhardt, Russell Walt, John Bell, Maurice Sackett, George Ford, Paul Siebeneichen, John Petrie, Arthur Wriggins, Raymond Williams, William Kruse, John Silbach, J. Pheney, Edward Heney, Owen Kincaid, Benjamin Conklin, Leo Spalti, Leon Weir, Bert Madden, James Schlantz, Fred Monroe, Charles Strothcamp, and Clyde Hall. Third row: John Schueler, Cliff Braun, Lester Gray, Jay Sims, Arthur Wolf, Claude Hubley, William Vopni, Peter Biroschak, Stanley Byra, Charles Leiby, Otto Jacob, William Herb, Gabe Russ, John Richardson, O. J. Thompson, Earl Kilgour, Roy Miller, Fritz Frank, Howard Goulden, John Heney, Wayne Lewis, and Joseph De Luca. (Author's Collection)

making a similar concert/movie arrangement with the Loew theater chain for weekly engagements in Kansas City, St. Louis, Pittsburgh, and Baltimore.

The short movie concerts, made up mostly of tried-and-true favorites, consisted of a soprano solo by Marjorie Moody; a cornet solo by John Dolan; a generous mixture of Sousa marches, always including "The Stars and Stripes Forever"; and from one to three short concert numbers. Moody had become a popular favorite, but it was Dolan's solo—Sullivan's "The Lost Chord"—that won high praise. It was done in Sousa's own arrangement, with theater organ added for a grand finale. One reviewer described the event:

> A musician with a cornet steps forward and softly begins the sweet, familiar tones of "The Lost Chord." At intervals he is given soft assistance by Sousa and his men. He starts the second stanza, and then comes a volume of sound from the band, so tremendous and magnificent that it seems as if it will burst the very walls of the auditorium. The sound spreads out and rolls upward, seemingly gathering in one great tone in the dome. Then it dies almost as suddenly as it began, and the soft notes of the cornet are heard again. It is tremendous. Saturday afternoon there weren't many dry eyes in the auditorium afterward.[42]

THE GOLDEN JUBILEE

The five-month tour of 1928 was highly publicized, billed as the "Golden Jubilee Tour" to commemorate Sousa's fiftieth year as a conductor. In reality, he had been conducting for more than fifty years, but no one made an issue of the method of computation. For the tour, the band introduced a Sousa march entitled, appropriately, "Golden Jubilee."

That same year also marked the end of John Dolan's reign as

Sousa's top instrumentalist. In September the men had a heated exchange of words as the train made its way through the Midwest. The disagreement was over one of Dolan's favorite encore numbers, which Sousa thought was ineffective. At the next stop Dolan and his baggage were left standing on the depot platform. Band members watched in amazement as the train pulled away. Some musicians related that Dolan had been displeased with the poor audience reception to one of his encore numbers and made an obscene gesture that Sousa might have seen. He was never to play with the band again. For the remainder of the tour William Tong and Ralph Ostrom shared his solo spot.[43]

A MAKESHIFT TOUR IN 1929

No tour had been planned for 1929, but the band was offered four days of concerts in Minneapolis that would pay $20,000. The offer was from Wilbur B. Foshay, a public utilities magnate whose company was celebrating the opening of its new building. The "Foshay Tower" was unique. Foshay, who admired George Washington, had the structure built with sloped sides to resemble the Washington Monument. Sousa felt obligated to write a new march for the occasion, but there was not enough time. So he scratched the existing title from a march he had just completed and renamed it "Foshay Tower Washington Memorial."

Manager Harry Askin hurriedly put together a short tour extending as far west as Colorado. He had to use shifts of musicians, because many regulars were otherwise occupied and could play only

---

42. *St. Louis Daily Globe Democrat,* Nov. 21, 1927.

43. Marjorie Moody told me that she was seated next to Sousa and shocked to hear language she had not realized was part of his vocabulary. One band member told the exaggerated (and untrue) story that Sousa and Dolan had a fistfight. Traveling manager William Schneider and clarinetist John Van Fossen happened to be standing next to Dolan, and their stories corroborated Moody's account (author interview with Moody; author interview with Schneider).

The band played at the elegantly decorated Strand movie theater in Brooklyn during its 1927 "movie tour." (Author's Collection, courtesy of Leonard B. Smith)

The last group photo in which all band members have been identified. In front: Winifred Bambrick, Sousa, and Marjorie Moody. First row: Vane Kinsinger, Theodore Lubis, Charles Wall, Walter Bender, George Kampe, Edward Johnson, William Robinson, Fred Weaver, Robert Willaman, Jacob Knuttunen, Albert Hiltensmith, Earl Duncan, Clarence Russell, Walter Cameron, Victor Welte, and Jules Bolle. Second row: John Leigl, Walfred Holt, George Knuttunen, Cecil Tozier, Charles Strothcamp, Fred Wavrek, Eugene Slick, Charles Leiby, John Van Fossen, Florian Mueller, Edson Weiss, John Lammers, Edward Heney, Frank Sullivan, Paul Desmond, Felix Eau Claire, James Schlanz, and Fred Monroe. Third row: John Silbach, Andrew Reissner, G. Rowe McRitchie, Clarence Booth, Arthur Wriggins, Eric Evans, Henry Zlotnik, Earl Held, John Orosky, Hale Phares, Walter Ryba, Seelye Meagher, Bernard Mott, and William Muelbe. Last row: Frank Holt, Ralph Wige, Howard Goulden, Noble Howard, August Helmecke, Arbor Fuller, William Herb, Reuben Evans, John Richardson, Jay Sims, Cliff Braun, John Schueler, William Heney (Sousa's valet). The identifications were made by Sousa scholar Herbert N. Johnston. (Barry Owen Furrer Collection)

parts of the tour. As the band traveled westward after the Minne-apolis engagement the new march suddenly disappeared from the programs. When Sousa learned that Foshay had been accused of misrepresenting his stock he had the march removed so the Sousa name would not be associated with scandal.[44]

A TRAIN WRECK IN COLORADO

On Monday, September 9, 1929, the band was involved in a serious train wreck while traveling on seldom-used tracks between Pueblo and Trinidad, Colorado (chapter 3). With the track weakened by heavy rains, the train derailed and wrecked at a place called "Capps Spur" near Walsenburg. Seven members of the band sustained minor inju-ries although none filed claims. The incident put the group five hours behind schedule, but only one concert, a matinee in Trinidad, had to be canceled.

RADIO, FINALLY

Sousa steadfastly refused to let any of the band's concerts be broad-cast but finally agreed to a series of broadcasts before the 1929 tour and another series after (chapter 6).

After playing two concerts on the campus of Stanford University in Palo Alto, California, on November 6, 1928, the band serenaded Herbert Hoover outside his campus home. It had just been announced that Hoover, then the president of the university, had been elected thirty-first president of the United States. Were it not for the upright bells of the sousaphones, the band could not be found in the crowd. It was also Sousa's seventy-fourth birthday. (Palo Alto Historical Association, photo by C. Beringer, San Francisco)

---

44. Sousa took an unpublished march he had written for the College of Industrial Arts in Denton, Texas, and retitled it "Foshay Tower Washington Memorial." I discovered the retitled conductor's score in the Library of Congress, and the instrumental parts were later found in the archives of Sousa's Long Island home and subsequently published. Foshay's case resulted in a hung jury, but it came out later that his personal secretary had somehow been appointed to that jury. Disgraced, she committed suicide. Foshay was re-tried and imprisoned but was released three years later and eventually pardoned. Bierley, "Sousa's Mystery March"; Bierley, *The Works of John Philip Sousa,* 52–54.

THE FINAL YEARS

The Great Depression, beginning in October 1929, was the major factor in reducing the Sousa Band's operations. The shattered econ-omy took a terrible toll on people in all walks of life but was espe-cially difficult for the entertainment industry. Musicians at the top of their profession were among the hardest hit because average people could no longer afford premium entertainment.

The band traveled more than a million miles by rail and was involved in sev-eral mishaps, the worst of which occurred between Pueblo and Trinidad, Colorado, on September 9, 1929. No one was seriously injured. (Author's Collection)

Sousa and his band posed for their final portrait in September 1931 at the Steel Pier, the entire company (entertainers and employees) of which is shown in the top photograph. Among the other performers are the Horace Heidt Orchestra, Singer's Midgets, the Hawaiian Divers, and canine film star Rin Tin Tin. According to clarinetist John Van Fossen, "The Old Man was mad as hell!" because the day of the photograph was a hot one and it took a long time for everyone to get in place. The final four live concerts of Sousa's Band were played on Tuesday, September 8. (Author's Collection)

The activities of Sousa's Band were greatly diminished after the 1929 tour. The 1930 season consisted of three very short tours, only thirty-four days, and the 1931 tour lasted only eleven. By way of comparison the 1928 tour was 150 days, and the 1929 tour thirty-five. The band was heading in an obvious direction.

Other factors contributed to the reduction in the band's schedule, of course. Radio was bringing quality entertainment into people's homes with no admission charge. Movies had sound, which made them more attractive and also put hundreds of theater orchestra musicians out of work. Sousa was undeniably slowing down and was showing his age. The same was true of the band's manager Harry Askin and of personnel manager Jay Sims and librarian Clarence

Russell. Only Sims had definite plans for retirement. He asked former cornetist Albertus Myers to assume his position, but Myers was well established as conductor of the Allentown, Pennsylvania, band.[45]

The glorious touring years were now behind the March King, as was his amazing stamina. Early in the morning of March 6, 1932, after guest-conducting a rehearsal of the Ringgold Band in Reading, Pennsylvania, he died in his room at the Abraham Lincoln Hotel in Reading. John Philip Sousa, seventy-seven, had finally retired. His death marked the end of a saga unlike any other in musical history, so unique that it surely will never be duplicated.

---

45. Sims made his offer to Meyers the night before Sousa died; Meyers served as conductor of the Allentown Band for more than fifty years.

AN ILL-FATED REVIVAL

Throughout the history of the band its managers learned that the band could not exist for long without Sousa. Two years after he died that fact was demonstrated one last time. A revival was attempted on Easter Sunday, April 1, 1934, for an organization called the Ex-Sousa Men's Band.

Cornetist Eugene LaBarre dreamed of bringing the band back to its former glory, but he lacked the business acumen to make that happen. Those were the days of the Great Depression, and LaBarre himself was out of work. He enlisted Sousa musicians in the New York area for an outdoor concert at the Sunken Plaza in Rockefeller Center. The musicians were unaware that there was no financial backing for the event.

LaBarre planned to present a free concert to generate interest, trusting that a sponsor would come forward to finance the concert as well as a tour to follow. One of his writer friends created publicity, and finding volunteer musicians was easy because almost any kind of music employment during those troubled times would be welcome.

A fine band was assembled for one rehearsal in a hall that LaBarre rented at a minimum rate. It was quickly apparent that he was not a conductor of Sousa's caliber, but the rehearsal went well and the concert was well received. That was to be expected because a crowd would happily gather for free entertainment at almost any hour in that location. Perhaps those in the crowd wondered who was paying for the performance, but who cared?

The musicians began to ask that same question after the concert, and then stark reality set in. They had donated their time and talent for a concert to be followed by a possible tour, but there was no trace of a potential sponsor. LaBarre had no money and apparently had solicited few if any supporters. Some musicians came to regard the incident as a cruel hoax. LaBarre partially redeemed himself six years later, however, to at least some. He recruited thirty-eight former Sousa musicians, in addition to other fine musicians having no Sousa connection, and formed a magnificent concert band for a twenty-five-week engagement at the 1939–40 New York World's Fair. For being part of the World's Fair Band, the musicians were paid well.[46]

---

46. This story was based on information supplied by clarinetist Edmund C. Wall, a member of the revival band. Many of LaBarre's post-Sousa activities were reported in the *Sousa Band Fraternal Society News,* although the Ex-Sousa Men's Band was not mentioned.

CHAPTER THREE

A Closer Look at the Band

TRAVEL BY RAIL

The Sousa Band toured America and foreign countries exclusively by rail. During the "golden age of bands" travel by bus or automobile was not possible because superhighways had not been developed—indeed, many areas had no highways at all. Horse-drawn vehicles were out of the question, so the only way a "business" band or orchestra could stay in business was to travel by rail. Railroads made it possible for touring ensembles to exist, and Sousa proved that travel by rail could be done profitably. He did, of course, have an advantage over other bandmasters because of his popularity as a composer.

There was talk of traveling by truck in the 1920s, but that was abandoned. Scheduling, particularly on long jumps or in bad weather, would have made doing so impractical. Air travel was not available, even in the latter years of the band. During the early years, there were no airplanes or airports, and by the time of the band's demise air travel for large groups was still ten years away.

The Sousa Band never owned a private train or private cars. In its early years tickets were purchased for standard runs, and concert itineraries were planned around them; the musicians mixed with regular passengers. The band had gained renown and was operating with considerable profit by 1900 so the management decided to reserve three cars on various railroads exclusively for the group's use. Cars were kept as long as the band was using that railroad, sometimes only a day or two but usually longer. Other than the baggage car, it was rare that cars of one railroad were used on another's line, and when that happened they incurred the per-diem financial arrangements that were standard between lines.

By 1900 the band usually used three cars, two for passengers and one for baggage. In the late 1920s, when the band was larger, it was occasionally necessary to have three passenger cars, depending on the size of the rolling stock available. Whether they were coaches or sleepers (used sparingly because of cost) was dictated by the length of the run. On long overnight runs Sousa and the female soloists would generally have their own drawing rooms.

Much of the time the band played in two towns a day, particularly in the highly populated northeastern states. The average distance between venues on those days was forty-three miles; only in rare cases did it approach a hundred. Two-town days were, of course, not possible in most western states and in some parts of the South.

Once it was financially possible to do so management decided not to rely entirely on standard railroad timetables and arranged with numerous railroads for "specials," runs between regularly scheduled trains. It was a rare band that could afford to pay this extra expense, but Sousa's Band did. The management did not hesitate to do so if it meant adding an extra town or two to a tour, visiting a town that had not previously had the opportunity to hear the band, or making more efficient use of profitable tour areas.

According to the band's extant financial records, as much as a third of its rail travel was done on specials during the 1920s. Such arrangements were usually made because of time constraints, and former band members told hair-raising stories about how new speed records were set when train crews threw caution to the wind and made up lost time or hauled them over an unusually long distance to meet a commitment.

The luxury of traveling in air-conditioned cars in hot weather did not exist. Open windows meant that smoke from the locomotive was apt to drift through the cars, an unavoidable hazard. During the early years the group occasionally had to settle for cars not equipped with centralized heating but with stoves fired by porters.

Finding suitable meals on the road often posed difficulties. Diners on trains were not common until around 1905, although some lines provided buffet cars or snack bars. On short runs there was seldom time to visit diners, and musicians had to fend for themselves in restaurants in or near depots. The band's management attempted to provide in many ways, but meals were not their responsibility. When it was necessary to take meals on long train jumps, however, Sousa sometimes did pay because food in the diner cost more than at restaurants.

In traveling a total of approximately 1,272,000 miles by rail the band was involved in several train wrecks.[1] It is believed, however, that no band member ever suffered a career-ending injury. Sousa instructed tour planners to insist on steel rather than wooden cars. The most serious wreck occurred in 1929 when the band was traveling in Colorado over seldom-used tracks between Pueblo and Trinidad (chapter 2). It is a sad epilogue to railroad history that were Sousa's Band operating now it would be forced to travel by bus and truck. Many towns through which they traveled are no longer served by rail. With the coming of the American superhighway network, passenger car travel and trucking proved too much competition for railroads.

BUSINESS ASPECTS

A major musical organization, Sousa's Band needed an efficient management staff that knew the art of tour planning. The staff was relatively small—a general manager, a traveling manager/paymaster, a personnel manager, advance men, a treasurer, a publicist, a secretary, and other staff members as needed. Advance men and publicists were seasonal associates, hired as independent contractors. The personnel manager was a member of the band. He arranged for auditions, made contracts with musicians, and saw that personnel rela-

Band members did a lot of waiting for trains at depots. Seldom did anyone miss a train. Bass drummer Gus Helmecke once overslept in Albuquerque, New Mexico, and had to charter an old biplane to catch up with the train. The plane landed in an open field where the train had a lunch stop, and Helmecke was greeted with "three cheers for the Flying Dutchman!" (Lower right, Stanley Barney Smith Collection/Western Michigan University Archives and Regional History Collections; others from Author's Collection)

---

1. Wrecks or equipment failure were not the only things that caused delays. In rare instances trains were held up by heavy snowstorms or blizzards. In December 1919, during the worst snowstorm in Nebraska history, the band was scheduled to play in Holdrege for both matinee and evening concerts on the eighth, but the train was hopelessly mired in snow a hundred miles to the west. A telegram was sent so the concerts could be canceled, but people from surrounding towns had poured into Holdrege and were marooned there. Concerts scheduled for Omaha the next day were also canceled.

tions were always good. It was also his duty to make sure there were no irregularities in behavior that would reflect on the band.

The general managers of the band and their years of service were David Blakely (1892–96); Charles W. Strine (1897); Frank Christianer (1897); Everett R. Reynolds (1897–1900); George Frederick Hinton (1900–1902); James R. Barnes (1902–10); Edwin G. Clarke (1910–19); and Harry Askin (1919–32). Offices were located at the Broadway Theater Building, 1441 Broadway (1892–93); the Hotel Beresford, 1 West Eighty-first Street (1894); Carnegie Hall, Fifty-seventh Street and Seventh Avenue (1894–96); again at the Broadway Theatre Building (1897); and the Astor Court Building, 18–20 West Thirty-fourth Street (1898–1910). There were also offices at 1 West Thirty-fourth Street (1911–19) and 1451 Broadway (1919–32).[2]

The offices were not spacious or elaborate but had to be large enough to accommodate data such as railroad timetables for every passenger railroad in the country, statistics on theaters in any cities the band might visit, and other theatrical operational information. The old adage "ya gotta know the territory" applied to the business of managing a professional band. All information on any town to be visited was relevant because avenues of promotion had to be used to best advantage.

If planning a tour was difficult in the 1890s, so was securing the most desirable concert hall in each city. By the 1920s, however, railroad travel was more highly developed and the band had become so well known that the majority of concert applications could not be filled.

Touring with a large group of musicians was an expensive proposition. According to a breakdown of expenses for the 1925–26 eight-month tour, for example, $437,500 went toward musicians' salaries; $90,000 for standard railroad fares; $30,000 for Pullman fares; $40,000 for transfer companies (baggage); and $175,000 for billboard and newspaper advertising, yielding a grand total of $772,000.[3] Not included in that figure were such things as rehearsal expenses, music library expenses, insurance on the music library and large instruments belonging to the band, booking fees, office operation, and other incidentals.

Tours were laid out many months in advance, and the staff relied heavily on telegraph communication with presenters. Contracts covered all details of an appearance, including a guarantee of local newspaper publicity and the numbers of posters, circulars, and street banners. Contracts were drawn up by the Sousa organization, and the wording was similar for them all.[4]

The schedule was normally so full that additional engagements were rarely added once the band was on the road. A last-minute

When Sousa's Band came to town the event was advertised in many ways. An appearance was often announced by street banners such as this one across Detroit's Woodward Avenue in 1898. (Barry Owen Furrer Collection)

3. *Oklahoma City Oklahoman*, Nov. 29, 1925.

4. Although most financial records of the band were destroyed by the Sousa family, some dating from 1920–31 were preserved and are now stored in the archives of the U.S. Marine Band library in Washington. Among those records are several theater contracts. Several earlier theater contracts are found among the David Blakely Collection at the New York Public Library.

2. Before the band was organized, David Blakely had planned to make Chicago its headquarters, and addresses given in various types of directories are not always in agreement. Nor do they always agree with addresses found on Sousa Band stationery.

concert might be added in case of a cancellation, but that seldom happened. If there was extra time and a pressing need arose Sousa would sometimes schedule a short morning concert for institutions such as a hospital or children's home.

Advance men usually went out two weeks before a concert to smooth possible obstacles to an efficient presentation. They had to make certain the concert hall would be ready and properly staffed. It was also their job to see that the publicity strategy was in place and that arrangements had been made for baggage transfer between train depots, concert halls, and hotels. They also checked to see that adequate housing was available if the band was to stay overnight.

Four types of revenue apportionments were used. The first was a "percentage split" in gross receipts, for example, 75 percent for the band and 25 percent for the sponsor. The second was a "guarantee" of a set amount for the band. With "first money," not used often, the sponsor and/or band would receive a certain amount before the remainder of the receipts was divided. A fourth type, very rarely used, was "hall rental," whereby the band would rent a facility and be responsible for all arrangements.

The traveling manager, who accompanied the band, collected the band's share of proceeds shortly after concerts began. He was also paymaster, giving each musician a cash-filled envelope once a week, usually on Saturdays. In many cases "managing the manager" was necessary for reality checks with inexperienced local sponsors. The band's manager would point out that a mere announcement such as "Sousa Coming to Town" was only a first step. Many local presenters were not familiar with the complexity of bringing premium entertainment to their towns. They were perhaps unaware of local population data, trolley or interurban radius, excursion rates for concertgoers, aspects of newspaper publicity, the volume and nature of other advertising strategies, convenience of a hall's location, and differentials in ticket prices. Coming face to face with such realities was in the best interests of a sponsor, because a severe setback could be disastrous for musical enterprise in a community for several years.

PUBLICITY

Publicity was a major preoccupation for management throughout the history of the band. Advertising copy and publicity were sent out to newspapers with the largest circulations long before a concert date, but the same publicity was not sent to every newspaper. Press copy was generally of two types. The first announced the concert's time and place and added general information about the band and Sousa. The second type was a feature article detailing personal information on Sousa and his many interests, reminders of previous visits of the band, or stories about key musicians. The personal information was intended to satisfy the public's curiosity about the lives of prominent public figures.

Photographs were an important part of publicity packages, whether stock portraits of Sousa or ones of band members and their instruments. While Harry Askin was manager he created many situations in

Warming up, or "preluding," was done backstage or outside the concert hall so as to be out of earshot of the audience. Musicians were not permitted to warm up onstage unless there was no other alternative. Contracts for some years specified no "preluding" onstage once the house doors were opened. (Author's Collection)

Publicity photo featuring Paul Whiteman, the "King of Jazz"; Babe Ruth, the "Sultan of Swat"; and John Philip Sousa, the "March King," 1927. (The Sousa Archives and Center for American Music, University of Illinois at Urbana-Champaign)

order to obtain publicity, such as Sousa riding horses or bicycles, playing tennis, and posing with movie stars or other celebrities. Newspaper writers created additional publicity gags. One in Los Angeles thought it would make a nice story if Sousa would direct something besides the band—traffic. The photograph resulted in a colossal traffic jam.

On another occasion a photographer caught the seventy-year-old Sousa playing golf, apparently the first time he had tried the game.

Los Angeles, 1924. Sousa created a traffic snarl that took six officers half an hour to untangle. (Author's Collection, courtesy of George Foreman)

He evidently did not find that pursuit as exciting as baseball or trap-shooting and commented, "I'm too young for this sport!" The band's press books also yield the fact that earlier photographs of Sousa were often sent out as he aged, giving the impression that he was younger than his years.

Askin's creative publicity writers provided still other attention-getting stories or photographs. George Carey's xylophone was twelve feet long, supposedly large enough to accommodate eight players; the percussion section's gong, reportedly presented by a Chinese statesman, had been used by a Manchurian executioner to announce that a condemned's time had come; the chimes, made in 1924 specifically for effects in Sousa's "Liberty Bell" march, were alleged to have cost as much as $15,000; and Gus Helmecke had selected and cured his bass drum head from a zebra hide.

CONCERT SITES

The band performed in many of the world's finest auditoriums but occasionally played in less traditional places to avoid vacancies in the schedule, among them churches and in one instance a large garage. In Austin, they played in the Texas House of Representatives. It also toured four American territories before they gained statehood: Oklahoma, Arizona, New Mexico, and Hawaii. Former band members liked to muse about the names of some auditoriums, such as "Rink," "The Baths," "Feather Market," and "First Saloon."

When they played in sparsely populated areas of the West the group often wondered where a crowd would come from, but the hall was usually filled before concert time. Sousa's daughter, Helen, recalled the time that she, her sister, Priscilla, and their mother, Jane

Sousa, accompanied the band on part of a tour. She particularly remembered the engagement in Rock Springs, Wyoming:

[We] wandered about the town to see what we could see. Well, there wasn't much. The railroad station, the "opery" house where the band was playing, a few houses, and a large pile of coal, because it is a junction. So, as always, we drifted to the theater, while I envisaged a practically empty house, for there were not enough people in the town to fill two rows. But when we went back-stage, we peeked and the house was crowded, with the audience applauding and stamping their feet and just having one heck of a good time. They had come from all around, and this was before the days of the Model-T. By horseback or buckboards, but they got there, and except for the encores of which there were many, they were hearing the same program that audiences in Chicago, San Francisco, New York and all the other big cities heard and were eating it up. That's why when I read that So-and-So influenced the love of music in this country, I say to myself: Rubbish! My father did that.[5]

The musicians constantly had to adjust to extremes of lighting, ventilation, temperature, and stage size around the world. Varying acoustics were another problem, but they learned, as professionals do, to compensate for inadequacies while playing in as many as twelve different auditoriums in a week's time. As Sousa once joked about some of the theaters, "There wasn't a single acoustic to be found in them."[6]

EIGHT PARADES IN FORTY YEARS

Bands have been associated with marching for centuries, but not all bands march. Sousa's played 15,623 concerts but marched only eight times in the forty years of its existence. The eight appearances were documented from a detailed study of the eighty-five press clipping books compiled by the band office in New York, from mentions in Sousa's writings, and from other sources as well.

1. Thursday, October 20, 1892, Chicago: The Chicago World's Fair (the World's Columbian Exposition), originally scheduled for 1892 to commemorate Christopher Columbus's discovery of the New World five hundred years earlier, did not open until 1893. A few ceremonies and dedications were held late in 1892, however. On October 20 Sousa's Band led a civic parade that started at 12:30 P.M. and lasted for three and a half hours. Approximately seventy-five thousand people attended the parade.[7]

2. Thursday, May 5, 1898, Cleveland: The band was in Cleveland for afternoon and evening performances of the Trooping of the Colors Pageant. Troops A, B, and C of the Ohio Volunteer Cavalry had just been mobilized for the Spanish-American War, and on the morning of May 5 Sousa's Band escorted the units to the railway station.

5. The Rock Springs concert, one of four times the band played there, was held on Wednesday, November 6, 1907, Sousa's fifty-third birthday. Helen Sousa's story appeared in the *Sousa Band Fraternal Society News,* July 1962, 2.

6. *Minneapolis Evening Tribune,* November 22, 1907.

7. A remote possibility exists that the band also led a short procession to the New York Building for the official dedication on Saturday, October 22, but no record of that has been found.

On a London stage where they played in 1903 the band was placed between two sections of the audience and was on tiers, thus altering the usual seating arrangement. There was not room for the brass to come forward for the finale of marches. Sousa's tall music stand, which has been restored by collector Barry Owen Furrer, is evident here; the foot-high podium was gradually shortened as Sousa grew older. (U.S. Marine Band)

3. Sunday, September 11, 1898, Pittsburgh: The band was in Pittsburgh for a one-week engagement at the Pittsburgh Exposition when troops returned from Cuba after the war. The band led a long parade from the railway station to the Eighteenth Regiment Armory. Relatives marched alongside returning soldiers and were joined by members of the Grand Army of the Republic, other organizations, and an untold number of participants.

4. Saturday, September 20, 1899, New York: Sousa's Band led a spectacular victory parade for Admiral George Dewey to celebrate America's victory in the Spanish-American War. The band was playing in Philadelphia at the National Export Exposition at the time and canceled the remainder of the engagement so they could march in the parade that began at Grant's Tomb and ended at the Washington Arch. Sousa sacrificed the band's income from the exposition and augmented the band to more than a hundred musicians at his own expense.

5. Wednesday, July 4, 1900, Paris: The band, on its first tour of Europe, was the official American band at the Paris Exposition. After

the unveiling of the Lafayette Statue they marched through several principal streets and finally up the Champs-Elysée to the Arc de Triomphe.

6–7. Wednesday, April 12, 1916, and Thursday, April 12, 1917, New York: The New York Hippodrome Theatre organization held morning parades of its performers on these dates to promote the extravaganzas playing at the time. Sousa's Band was playing daily shows of *Hip! Hip! Hooray!* at the time of the 1916 parade but was not in session at the time of the 1917 parade, so it is probable that Sousa used members who lived in New York and hired extra musicians to increase the size of the unit.

8. Saturday, June 15, 1929, Princeton, New Jersey: The band played two off-tour concerts on the campus of Princeton University at 5:15 and 8 P.M. The concerts were not open to the public, the occasion being the twenty-fifth anniversary of the class of 1904, that of John Philip Sousa Jr. That afternoon the band led a procession, traditionally known as the "P-rade," to the baseball stadium for the Princeton-Yale game.

REQUIREMENTS FOR MEMBERSHIP

Membership in Sousa's Band was a matter of considerable pride, and the more years of service, the greater the pride. As Elvin L. Freeman, a tubist, said, "Those of us who were privileged to play under the baton of John Philip Sousa now know that a bit of star dust fell on our heads."[8] Some literally took their pride to the grave; saxophonist Rudolph Becker was buried in his Sousa Band uniform sixty-four years after leaving the group.

Few players of wind or percussion instruments of that period could not say they once wished they could play with Sousa's Band. Ed Chennette, a composer, observed, "Undoubtedly the best band men in the world are with Sousa. Some who are not with him will not agree with me, but I am quite willing to bet that Sousa could have any man in the United States if he only asked for him. And many a musician owes his reputation to the fact that he had been with Sousa. . . . And I'll wager further that he could get a thousand musicians tomorrow, who would play for nothing and pay all their own expenses for the reputation of having been a season with Sousa."[9] New members knew they would be joining a select group. To glance at the band's all-time roster is to view a "Who Was Who in American Music" (Appendix II).

Being a fine musician was by no means the only requirement for membership in the band; one also had to be a "regular fellow." That meant being able to get along with fellow musicians under all circumstances. They performed together, they ate together, and they lived together.

The personnel managers, such as Jay Sims and Herbert L. Clarke, were Sousa's chief talent scouts and considered recommendations from alumni or present members as well as from other notable musicians with whom they had contact. They did not hesitate to inquire about a candidate's background. "Is he congenial?" they would ask. "Does he have a pleasant personality from the standpoint of an audience? Would he make a good trouper? Could he possibly turn into a malcontent or a grouch?" Thus a candidate's personality was almost as important as his playing ability. It was well understood by the personnel manager that Sousa wanted no man whose moral standards were questionable; he expected every member of the band to live a life without blemish.

Religious preference mattered not. The band knew that religious intolerance was an abomination to Sousa. He once, for example, called a musician into his office and asked if he had referred to another member of the band as a "dirty Jew." When the man admitted that he had, Sousa politely discharged him, provided three weeks' severance, and informed him that he should never ask to return to the band.[10] Nationality was also unimportant as far as Sousa was concerned. He promoted Americanism in music and longed for an all-American band, but that did not happen until the very end of his

The Sousa Band was a close-knit group. Because they lived and worked together for long periods, all potential members were carefully screened to make sure they had high moral standards and the ability to get along well with colleagues. Among the "regular fellows" shown here on the 1921–22 tour are several Freemasons. (Author's Collection)

career. Until that time there were always foreign-born musicians in the band. When the group was formed in 1892 few American-born musicians could compete with the fine musicians who had emigrated from Europe.

There was no retirement policy for the band. Sousa let it be known that he did not intend to retire and any musician was free to play in the band so long as he was physically able and uncompromised in professional ability. Until the late 1920s almost all players were auditioned by Sousa, the personnel manager, and/or section leaders. By that time reliable background information could be found on nearly any musician in the country, and many were accepted into the band without audition.

MUTUAL RESPECT

If a single word could describe John Philip Sousa it would be *gentleman*. He expected musicians to be gentlemen too—courteous, kindly, and unselfish. He commanded the utmost respect from his men because he respected them. He did not, for example, reprimand musicians for making mistakes, whether in rehearsals or in concerts. If at a concert, he would pretend not to hear a playing error. When the same passage was correctly played at a later concert he would perhaps look at the errant musician and place his hand over his heart to let him know that he was now happy. If the same error was made a second time he would mutter quietly to himself, something like "Christ Almighty—twice in the same place!" and go on.

In one instance when a musician was making repeated mistakes Sousa called him to his office. Rather than chastise him, Sousa asked how things were with his family back home. It turned out that the musician's wife was seriously ill. Sousa said he knew something had been bothering the man, gave him a week's pay, and told him to take

8. *Sousa Band Fraternal Society News,* Nov. 1972, 9.
9. "Sousa's Band," *Musical Messenger,* Dec. 1920, 1.
10. Author interview with Louis Morris, 1963.

a week off to care for his wife.[11] Such incidents endeared Sousa to the musicians; his reputation as a kindly leader was one reason that many left other fine orchestras or bands to play with him.

The mutual respect between Sousa and musicians was something they brought up for the remainder of their lives. Sousa was not "one of the boys," as has often been surmised; his relation with the men was similar to the relationship between officers and enlisted men in the military. He did not have opportunity to fraternize because the public demanded his attention wherever he went. When he was available, however, he was always approachable and congenial. In his last years, when he was conducting a band of young men, the dynamic became one of father and son. It was said that he "meets kings and emperors with quiet dignity but shows the same courtesy to a bootblack . . . always quiet, modest and unassuming."[12] To that description should be added "honorable." In the words of his traveling manager, William Schneider, "In the years I knew Mr. Sousa, he impressed me as being the man who tried to be the most honorable person who ever walked the face of this earth."[13]

LIFE IN THE SOUSA BAND

For musicians, the decision to tour with the band was a difficult one. It meant being away from home for several months. Wives very seldom traveled with the band because doing so would double the musician's expenses. Pay was considered good for the times, however, especially for instrumental soloists and first-chair men (Appendix III). Minimum pay for section players ranged from $35 per week in the early 1890s to $74 per week in the late 1920s. Vocal and violin soloists were paid on a different scale, depending upon their renown. As a general rule, musicians could only speculate about the amounts others in the band were receiving because salary figures were kept confidential by the management and not known until many years after Sousa's death. Women soloists were the highest paid; soprano Marjorie Moody's 1928 salary, for example, was $250 a week.

Transportation between cities was paid by the band, but hotel expenses and meals were not. A nightly rate at an acceptable hotel was $2, and most of the band saved money by doubling up. By the same token, restaurant meals were much less expensive than they now are.

Band members were required to supply their own uniforms. The only exception came during the first year of the band, when uniforms were of a distinctive design and musicians had the option of renting them. The expense was not as great as one might imagine, however, because the men saved on civilian clothing. Uniforms were to be worn at all times other than off-days. The black or navy blue military-style uniforms were similar to those many other bands used, so those who left Sousa's Band could likely still find use for the garments. On tour,

the men were required to keep their uniforms cleaned and pressed, which would have been difficult had it not been for hotel overnight laundry services.

The uniforms were made of good-quality wool. The fact that wool made working in cool auditoriums more bearable was offset on hot summer days long before air conditioning. Various companies made the uniforms. Bandsmen were given a preferred manufacturer's address, but it was sometimes possible to choose another company. Group photographs reveal slight differences in uniform style, usually because garments were made over different years. Some dark navy uniforms mixed with the solid black ones during the years the band was making the transition from navy to black.

Musicians furnished their own instruments and nickel-plated music stands except for those who played large percussion instruments and sousaphones.[14] Sousa preferred C. G. Conn instruments

Most pictures of the band show the musicians in their traditional black uniforms. For the first year of the band's operation, however, the uniforms were flashier. They were sky blue with gold braid and insignia, and the trousers had red stripes. This photograph of clarinetist William Langan was taken on October 21, 1893. He later played three European tours with the band. (Author's Collection, courtesy of Osmund Varela)

11. Ibid.
12. Peterson, "The Human Side of Sousa," 3–4.
13. Author interview with William Schneider, 1968.

14. During the 1920s the band also furnished the bass saxophone used in the saxophone octet.

whenever possible because he felt that doing so gave a section a more blended, or matched, sound. Besides, Conn furnished free instruments to most of the soloists in exchange for advertising. Sousa claimed not to have personally received fees for endorsing Conn instruments.

Players were given printed route schedules that were updated as necessary so there would be absolutely no question about the times and places of concerts. These also informed relatives back home where to send mail. Sousa insisted that every concert start at the precise time it was advertised. This was often an absolute necessity because the band usually had a limited amount of time to pack up and catch a train to the next town. Every musician was to be in his seat, ready to play, at the appointed time.

One bandsman was often designated to pick up and distribute incoming mail and for doing so be paid a nominal fee, for example, ten cents per week, by the others. Mail was sent to post offices or concert halls where they were playing but not to cities where the band would play on a Sunday.

Someone else was often appointed to negotiate group hotel rates, a valuable service well worth another nominal fee. Seldom was there a slip-up on hotel arrangements, but there were a few times when rooms could not be found. In those instances it was necessary to go to a police station for help, go from door to door asking to be put up for the night (the uniform helped), or catch a train to a neighboring town.

Generally speaking, most musicians did not choose the most expensive hotels. Sousa, however, did because he met with so many dignitaries. His daughter, Helen, loved to tell of her mother, Jane, meeting him in Atlanta. When she could not remember the name of the hotel she told the cab driver to take her to the best one in town— and there he was.

An unwritten rule in Sousa's Band was that bandsmen should not associate with female soloists. Occasionally the women would accompany a group of them for sightseeing on a day off, but at all other times they were expected to distance themselves. Sousa wanted, at all cost, to avoid rumors of fraternization, and to help enforce that policy he asked the women to eat their meals in public with him.[15] That meant either two or three, a soprano soloist, a violin soloist (between 1893–1924), and the harpist (1920–30). He paid for their meals and complained that they "ate up one side of a menu and down the other." The women also sat away from the men when on the train. They always rode in the same car with Sousa, seated next to him or in an adjacent compartment. When they did have occasion to pass down the aisles in the men's areas they were always treated with the utmost respect.

One of the group's two passenger cars was normally for those who did not smoke, and the other for smokers. The former was sometimes referred to as the "gentleman's car" and the latter the "roughneck's car," where one or more poker games were usually in progress.

The group might have missed their families, but they were often made to feel they were part of a larger fraternity. Wherever they traveled they were welcomed warmly by local musicians. Sometimes they were met at a station and escorted to the concert hall, and often they were serenaded. Quite often the greeters would be a youth band, and, of course, Sousa would be asked to conduct one of his marches. He was greatly pleased by the children's bands and lavish in his praise. Their presence reinforced his belief that the future of music in America was in good hands.

WILLOW GROVE, A HOME AWAY FROM HOME

Sousa's Band was based in New York City, but Willow Grove Park, just fourteen miles north of downtown Philadelphia, where the band played 2,751 concerts, could be called its home away from home. The band played there every summer from 1901 through 1926 with the exception of 1911, the year of the world tour. Engagements lasted from nine days to eleven weeks, with four forty-five-minute concerts daily that usually lasted up to an hour because of encores. One additional visit, for three concerts only, was made on August 12, 1928.

Willow Grove was then called the "summer music capital of the nation" because of the many famous orchestras and bands performing there. The park opened in 1896, when electric lights were new to many, and by 1901 was well established. Only the music organizations in great demand were engaged. Once they played there Sousa and the band became the main attraction and consistently drew the largest crowds, making their fee consistently higher than for other musical organizations. Among the leading groups that performed at Willow Grove were the Victor Herbert Orchestra, New York Symphony Orchestra, Chicago Symphony Orchestra, Theodore Thomas Orchestra, and Russian Symphony Orchestra. Bands were the most popular attractions, among them those of Arthur Pryor, Giuseppe Creatore, Patrick Conway, Thomas Preston Brooke, Oreste Vessella, and Frederick Neil Innes.

Willow Grove was once a farmland and wooded area with a population of barely one hundred. With the coming of electric streetcars, however, traction companies (which eventually evolved into the Philadelphia Rapid Transit Company) extended their lines to the suburbs, and Willow Grove quickly became an attractive amusement park. For 30 cents or less it was possible to ride decorated and illuminated trolleys from Philadelphia through the pleasant countryside and then enjoy fine entertainment at the park. People also came from all directions by horse and buggy. There was no admission charge until the mid-1920s.

From its beginning, Willow Grove was known as a park with morals and had an atmosphere of refinement, distinguishing it from places like Coney Island (often called "Sodom by the sea"). Men were required to wear suits and ties, and women and children dressed in their finest. Alcohol was strictly forbidden. Guards kept people off the grass, where sheep grazed, and couples were even discouraged

---

15. The one case of "fraternization" (violin soloist Nicoline Zedeler married tubist Emil Mix) took place after the couple left the band.

Many famous symphony orchestras and bands performed at Willow Grove Park, where some visitors enjoyed renting boats and listening to concerts from the lake next to the music pavilion. (U.S. Marine Band, top; Author's Collection, bottom)

from holding hands. Serious offenders of these rules were jailed, and lesser offenders were asked to leave the premises.

The band shell was part of an enclosed pavilion seating four thousand, and surrounding the pavilion benches seated an additional five thousand. Crowds were larger on excursion days and for events such as Sunday school outings, Children's Day, or Grand Army of the Republic Day. The last day of a Sousa Band stay was always well attended, with as many as fifty thousand people crowded in and around the pavilion for the final concert. The pavilion accommodated musicians with ample dressing rooms and offices in the back. Sousa used a private office on the second floor above the dressing rooms, and people knew that was where requests for music were to be taken.

Beside the pavilion was a lake, where boaters could row close to shore and listen to concerts. In the middle of the lake was an electric fountain, its water shooting forty feet into the air and illuminated with revolving colored lights, thus giving the impression of dancing lights. In 1934 it was named the Sousa Fountain. A tradition developed at the pavilion that lasted for many years. Above the bandstand was a large wooden American flag with rows of red, white, and blue lights that were turned on when a band or orchestra played "The Stars and Stripes Forever."

Willow Grove provided a welcome change from the routine of boarding a train after a concert and moving on to the next town. A few preferred to keep on the move, but most enjoyed sleeping in the same bed night after night and not having to hunt for restaurants before or after a concert or worrying about getting to a station on time.

At Willow Grove most musicians stayed at nearby boarding houses, mixing with local people. Sousa usually stayed at the Huntingdon Valley Country Club so he could do business more conveniently and enjoy a daily horseback ride. Some musicians would send for their families so they could enjoy a vacation while the band worked the four daily concerts. There were always interesting pastimes for families, whether a wide variety of rides such as the roller coaster, the shoot-the-chute (water slide), or a giant merry-go-round and picnic and swimming areas. The park's staff often organized baseball games with local teams for band members.

Long stays at Willow Grove provided opportunities for families to get acquainted, and many lasting friendships developed. Lengthy engagements were a test of endurance, however, for the band's librarian, whose task it was to prepare folders for four completely different concerts each day. He started to work on these immediately after the last concert each evening and worked well past midnight. The next morning he arose early and finished the job so musicians could come backstage and study the new music for the concerts that afternoon and evening.

Because the band received $1,000 a day for the Willow Grove concerts everyone put their best foot forward to make each concert as perfect as possible. Sousa would schedule any music he thought would present difficulties or was new for Monday programs when audiences were smallest. Once the band had gained familiarity with an especially troublesome piece he would usually repeat it at a later date when the audience was larger. Perennial favorites and pieces showcasing the band's virtuosity were programmed on weekends.

Weekly "All-Sousa" concerts were begun in 1913. On Thursdays it became customary to present all four concerts with nearly all selections by Sousa. These were well received, so one concert of a similar nature was also given on a Saturday or Sunday. Many people, in fact, came just to see Sousa, so he felt obligated to conduct every concert. When his mother died during the 1908 engagement he and the family arranged the timing of the funeral in Washington so it would not be necessary for him to miss any of the concerts. He left for Washington on a late train after the last concert of the day, caught a late-morning train back the next day immediately after the funeral, and arrived just before the first concert. Few knew of the hurried trip until newspapers reported it the following day.

Willow Grove also provided an extended audition period for certain members of the band, and outstanding newcomers found themselves featured as soloists. That afforded Sousa the opportunity to judge the caliber of new musicians and determine whether they could become regular soloists on tour. He also wanted to know exactly who the logical choices for back-up men would be in the event a regular soloist took ill and a last-minute substitute was needed.

Willow Grove Park's importance to American music history was perhaps summed up best by Arthur Pryor in a 1909 interview: "I am a firm believer in the uplifting power of good music. It is chiefly on account of this kind of musical development observed at Willow Grove that the music of Bach and Beethoven, Wagner and Chopin, Schubert, Mendelssohn, Liszt, Rossini, Verdi, Mozart, and the great masters who sway the musical world, has become a favorite in American households where twenty years ago the work of these musicians was unknown and unappreciated."[16]

SPORTS

The band had its own baseball team, but it was brought together only occasionally during long engagements such as Willow Grove. The team was likely formed in 1899 or 1900; one press account states that band members defeated a team of the American Guard in 1900 while playing at the Paris Exposition. Pryor's Band played the Sousa Band team several times, games that were not true grudge matches, although according to a story handed down by members of Sousa's Band he once wanted to avenge a lopsided loss to the Pryor players and secretly hired a professional pitcher and catcher from the Philadelphia Athletics. The Sousa Band won the next game handily.

Sousa had been a good baseball player as a youth, and he usually pitched the first inning when the band played a local team of renown and there was the possibility of capitalizing on the publicity. He continued the practice until at least 1904, when he was fifty, and even made a token appearance at a charity game against Pryor's Band in 1916. When possible, well-known public officials were enticed to umpire.

The band club won most of its games, usually against city or military teams and sometimes against semiprofessionals. As the band grew larger during the 1920s, however, the team ceased playing outside teams and formed two teams within the band—woodwinds

The band's baseball team won most of its games against local teams. Sousa, a baseball player in his youth, usually pitched the first inning. When Sousa composed his march "The National Game" in 1925, he had many fond memories from which to draw. The ringer in this 1904 photo was John Philip Sousa Jr., wearing the Nassau jersey, first baseman of the Princeton University team. (Author's Collection, courtesy of Osmund Varela)

16. Arthur Pryor quoted in the *Old York Road Historical Bulletin* 56 (1966): 17.

In the 1920s the band had not one ball team but two, one for brass players and the other for woodwinds (reeds). According to the scoreboard in this game at Willow Grove in the summer of 1924 the reeds were beating the brass 10–2 at the end of the sixth inning. (Barry Owen Furrer Collection)

versus brass. Sousa loved to watch those games. Musicians said they never saw him laugh as hard as the day tuba player Jack Richardson split the seat of his trousers while fielding a ball at first base.

The band also fielded a basketball team during the 1920s, although it was not as successful as the early baseball team, perhaps because basketball requires more endurance. One newspaper account of a 1923 game against a Yakima, Washington, team reported, "The game started with the musicians caging the ball in such rapid succession that it appeared that they would win easily. Their rotundity began to tell on them in the waning moments of the first session, as indicated by the high rise and low fall of bosoms."

WHEN SOUSA WAS INDISPOSED

When William Schneider described Sousa as the "whole show," he meant that people came to concerts primarily to see the March King in action. Despite his strict adherence to "the show must go on" tradition, there were times when Sousa was unable to do so. Attendance did indeed drop off when people knew that in advance. By 1898 the band had been in existence long enough to have gained considerable popularity; it otherwise might have folded had Sousa been absent for any appreciable period. The press books provide a running example of an occurrence just as the Spanish-American War was coming to an end in November of that year.[17]

Sousa became afflicted with a recurrence of the malaria he had suffered earlier, greatly complicated by typhoid fever. As the tour continued, traveling south through Wisconsin, he felt the effects of what he first thought to be a severe cold. Arthur Pryor took over in Sheboygan on the evening of November 20, but Sousa made a valiant effort to conduct in Milwaukee the following afternoon against a physician's orders. He became so weak, however, that he had to leave the stage after the third number; Pryor conducted for the next twelve days. A few days thereafter word of Sousa's absence apparently had not been communicated to a theater manager in Chillicothe, Ohio. When the

news did finally reach him he sought a lawyer and sued the band for damages. The band showed its mettle, however, by offering to present the concert at no charge. The manager accepted the offer, and the band parted amid rousing cheers. In Philadelphia on December 3 Sousa attempted another concert but lasted only through the first number. The concert on December 4 in New York turned out to be the final one of the tour. Six weeks of concerts were canceled. Sousa's condition did not improve, and he later revealed that he had been near death.

On another occasion near the end of the lengthy European tour of 1903, Sousa became ill in St. Leonards, England, and again had to turn the baton over to Pryor for five days of concerts between June 26 and July 2. Sousa was hospitalized, and the illness was reported as a "chill on the liver." As expected, attendance dropped.

Ptomaine poisoning was the cause of another forced absence, in 1907. Sousa had apparently eaten some tainted prairie chicken in Milwaukee and could lead only half the concert. Pryor was no longer with the band, so Herbert L. Clarke took over. Thinking he was well enough to return to the podium, Sousa conducted the following evening in Madison but had to leave halfway through the evening. He was more seriously ill than he realized. The tour continued until Albany, New York, on December 14, and then the remainder (an undetermined number of cities) was canceled.

Sousa's malaria recurred just before the 1911 world tour, nearly causing financial disaster. A short warm-up tour began in New York and took the band up through the New England states and back again to New York before departing for England on the first leg of the world tour. Sousa felt the attack coming on as the band played in three cities in Connecticut. On November 8 at Yale University in New Haven he became so ill that he was carried from the stage on a stretcher and taken to a nearby hospital. Clarke again assumed the conducting duties, this time until November 21, when Sousa was able to continue in Montreal. Despite Clarke's poised conducting, attendance was lower than normal. "Sousa's Band without Sousa is like an egg without salt" was one comment.[18]

Another short-lived absence in Australia, on June 23, 1911, was typical of a few other times when Sousa was only temporarily indisposed. Because of something reported as "a chill" he missed two performances in Ballerat on June 23, and Clarke again conducted. The absence with the most serious consequence took place in 1921 when Sousa was thrown from a horse, cracking vertebrae in his neck (chapter 2).

Sousa's final serious illness on tour conveniently came at the end of the 1929 tour. He was suffering from bronchitis as the band pulled into Syracuse, New York, on September 27, so Clarence J. Russell conducted. Askin wasted no time canceling the remainder of the tour, which included stops in Binghamton, New York, and Scranton, Pennsylvania, and Sousa was transported to his home on Long Island.

17. Sousa was to have been commissioned a captain in the U.S. Army to organize regimental bands as soon as the tour was completed.

18. Quoted in *New York Dramatic Mirror,* Nov. 23, 1911.

THE MUSIC LIBRARY

Because the band played so many different pieces over the course of any given year its music library was one of the largest assembled. Much was used for only a short period or not at all. Sousa had standard orders with several publishers for new editions and more came gratis from others, but he disposed of music quickly if he thought the public would be indifferent toward it.

All music was stored in New York warehouses, and from them several trunks would be shipped to places such as Willow Grove, where there were many different programs. Only about three hundred pieces were taken along on regular tours. Music for each concert was kept in folders, one for each stand. The encore book, also on each stand, included as many as 125 pieces to be used for quick encores, and more than half were usually Sousa marches. Over the years there were five sets of encore books, and the older sets would be cannibalized to make new ones.[19]

When Sousa lost the library to the Blakely family in 1901 he started anew with a fresh set of compositions. By the time a member of the Blakely family sold the old library back to Sousa in 1924 the most usable pieces had been replaced, so a selling price of approximately $500, according to Sousa's road secretary, saxophonist J. Fred Campbell, was negotiated. Much of the old music was then mixed with the current library and tested on audiences for the next two years. A large portion was given to Victor J. Grabel, a close friend of Sousa's who had served as one of his assistants at the Great Lakes Naval Training Station during World War I. The most valuable part of the library Sousa bought back was a cache of his own handwritten manuscripts, on which he apparently did not place much value at the time because many were among the music given to Grabel.

The story of the old library (1892–1901) and the later (1901–32) library is complicated and, for the most part, beyond the scope of this book. Grabel's part of the old library, mixed with other music amassed during his career, ended in two places: the United States Marine Band Library and the Library of Congress. The later library, with the exception of the last set of encore books, was donated to the University of Illinois Band Department shortly after Sousa's death. A final set of encore books ended at the Marine Band library, and some of the earlier green encore books are in scattered locations. At rough estimate, 74 percent of the band's music library is in the Sousa Archives and Center for American Music at the University of Illinois at Urbana-Champaign, 24 percent is in the Marine Band Library, and 1 percent is located in the Library of Congress.

INSTRUMENTATION AND SEATING

For decades musicians have debated the merits of Sousa's choices of instruments and the seating arrangement he used with the band.

He made practically no changes in the types of instruments used, just the numbers of each instrument (Appendix III). He made quite a departure from the instrumentation used by Gilmore's Band, and the strength of his choices is demonstrated by the fact that concert bands in the United States and many other countries continue to use, more than a century later, what is essentially Sousa's instrumentation. The only major difference is that most contemporary bands use trumpets instead of cornets, yielding a brighter, less mellow sound.

Sousa campaigned for the international standardization of instrumentation, which would have resulted in universal music publishing practices. His efforts were somewhat successful, although some countries, such as Italy and France, had long traditions and never made the change. This means that adaptations must be made if bands in one country want to use the music of another.[20]

The seating arrangement Sousa used, also the subject of much discussion, has changed very little over the years. Members of the brass family were always on the conductor's right, blowing across the stage rather than toward the audience; woodwinds were on the conductor's left, facing the brass; and in the middle, in front of the conductor, was the harp.

There were at least three basic reasons for that arrangement. First, woodwind and brass players could hear one another better, resulting in better precision and balance. The harp, in the middle, often acted as liaison between the brass and woodwinds in softer passages and helped maintain a constant pitch. Second, it was much easier for brass players, seated in a general cluster near the apron, to step to the front of the stage for the grand finale of a march. Third, having the brass not face the audience gave a smoother, less bright overall sound.

The stages in some theaters were not very deep, which often caused difficulties in seating, but the general arrangement of the band was not altered except under extreme circumstances. The stage setup was defined by requirements, as described in a typical instruction sheet, and those needs were sent well in advance of a concert to avoid last-minute changes that might affect a performance.

STAGE DIRECTIONS AND PROPERTY PLOT

1. FULL STAGE, with bare floor.
2. When stage is large enough, we require full width and thirty feet from footlights in depth, with boxed in set, side, and center doors.
3. When stage is limited in size, do not make set, but wait for arrival of baggage in charge of stage manager before making set. If crowded, can use back drop and wings.
4. Band baggage is kept off stage, each side.
5. CURTAIN IS USED. Must be down when house is opened, and raised at beginning of each concert. No other movements necessary.
6. LIGHTS. Stage (excepting footlights) and house lights full during entire performance. Footlights for lady soloists only.
7. PROPS. Three dressing rooms and sixty chairs on stage. Solid chairs preferred.

---

19. The first three sets of encore books were green. The final set was both red and black; it is not known whether the earlier set was red or black.

20. The way in which instrumentation varies from country to country appears in Rehrig, *The Heritage Encyclopedia of Band Music*, Appendix V.

The Sousa Band's seating arrangement, from behind, in the summer of 1930, playing one of its four daily concerts on the far end of the Steel Pier in Atlantic City. (U.S. Marine Band)

In 1924 Sousa put together a small jazz band as an experiment, and in 1925 he wrote a fantasie called "Jazz America." (Author's Collection, courtesy of Leonard B. Smith)

The sextet from Donizetti's opera *Lucia de Lammermoor* was always a favorite with audiences. The soloists for 1915, left to right, were Herbert L. Clarke, John Perfetto, Ralph Corey, Edward Williams, Frank Simon, and Clarence Russell. (U.S. Marine Band)

Throughout the history of the band, Sousa used only three percussionists to play this variety of instruments. When one considers that most large bands today use five or more percussionists to play the same instruments, it could be concluded that (left to right) George Carey, Howard Goulden, and August Helmecke stayed busy. (Author's Collection, courtesy of Leonard B. Smith)

THE SOLIDARISM

The solidarism, a tuba wrapped in a different manner, produces sounds in the same register as a tuba. It winds around the body of the player like its predecessor, the headnotes-style tuba, but the bell points either straight up ("bell up"), first built by the J. W. Pepper Company of Philadelphia, apparently in 1895, or to the front ("bell front"). It was Sousa's theory that sound would "mushroom over the band like frosting on a cake" if the bell pointed straight up.

The sousaphone, Sousa's invention, came about as a result of a request he made to J. W. Pepper around 1893.[21] At that time some band members were endorsing Pepper instruments, although many later endorsed C. G. Conn instruments. Pepper craftsmen modified one of their largest model BB-flat helicon tubas and fit it with a removable upright bell.[22] Sousa's face was engraved on the bell of Pepper's sousaphone accompanied by an inscription:

> Highest
> Medal & Diploma
> Chicago 1893
> Premier
> J. W. Pepper
> Maker
> Philadelphia
> and
> Chicago
> No. 8800

In 1898 C. G. Conn also built a sousaphone, the one eventually put into production, and all sousaphones used after that time were Conns. Others were added to the mix of regular tubas until such time Sousa decided to use sousaphones exclusively. He did not approve of the bell-front sousaphone's directional sound and permitted its use only during times when a new player was endeavoring to find a suitable bell-up horn or was having one manufactured.

THE SOUSA BAND FRATERNAL SOCIETY

Among the many tributes to famous conductors, the touching tribute to John Philip Sousa seen in the formation of the Sousa Band Fraternal Society stands out. Twelve years after Sousa died, former members of the band created a fraternal organization that met each year in New York City on the anniversary of his birth, a practice that

John (Jack) Richardson with a later Conn sousaphone. Richardson was with the band longer than any other tuba player, from 1903 to 1931. (Author's Collection)

continued so long as they were physically able. Chapters were also formed in Philadelphia and Los Angeles.[23]

Membership in the society was limited to those who had made at least one tour with the band. Several motions were made to include children and grandchildren of Sousa Band members, but these were consistently voted down. The motions were made by older members of the band who remembered the days when Sousa's Band was the most popular musical organization in America. They thought that perhaps the country would remember the glory days of the band and continue to hold it in high esteem. Younger members, more numerous, noted however that many changes had occurred in the entertainment industry and attempting to perpetuate the fraternity through descendants was unrealistic. Thus the society became a tontine, a "last man's club." Theoretically, the final surviving member was to travel to New York by himself and have dinner in Sousa's honor. The concept was abandoned, however, as members grew older and were unable to travel; the last dinner was held by the Los Angeles chapter on June 29, 1972.

The idea of forming a society had been discussed in the spring of 1944 at a meeting in the home of William Gretsch, a manufac-

---

21. In an article in the August 30, 1922, issue of the *Christian Science Monitor,* Sousa told of having made his request to Pepper "some thirty years ago," therefore in 1892 or 1893. The first sousaphone was apparently used only for a short time for reasons not mentioned in any of Sousa's writings. The use of such an instrument would surely have been mentioned in reviews of concerts, and it is also reasonable to assume that such accounts would have been added to the band's press books. The only extant press book for 1893, however, includes concert programs; several other press books for that era are missing.

22. An advertisement for Pepper shows a photograph of tuba player Herman Conrad and the sousaphone and adds that it was "used daily in Sousa's Peerless Concert Band." According to George B. Class of the Pepper Company, the advertisement was inserted as a circular in an issue of the *J. W. Pepper Musical Times and Band Journal.* In the photograph Conrad wears a uniform in the style of 1894 and 1895. Serial numbers of Pepper instruments indicate that the company's only known sousaphone was made around 1895.

23. It was determined that Saturday meetings would be more practical than weekday meetings so gatherings were held on the Saturday nearest November 6. The Philadelphia and Los Angeles chapters did not always meet on that weekend.

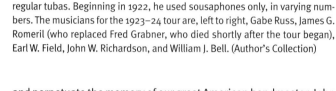

Sousa used only one sousaphone, with a mix of regular tubas, through the 1918 tour. For part of the 1919–20 season he used two sousaphones in addition to regular tubas. Beginning in 1922, he used sousaphones only, in varying numbers. The musicians for the 1923–24 tour are, left to right, Gabe Russ, James G. Romeril (who replaced Fred Grabner, who died shortly after the tour began), Earl W. Field, John W. Richardson, and William J. Bell. (Author's Collection)

What is probably the original J. W. Pepper sousaphone was located in Reading, Pennsylvania, and has been reconditioned. Pepper advertising claimed that it was "used daily" in Sousa's Band, but if so that was for only a short period. The Pepper company had financial difficulties during the 1890s, perhaps explaining why their sousaphone was not put into production. It is assumed that they built just this one sousaphone, although the possibility that they built more than one must not be ruled out. (Author's Collection, courtesy of George B. Class, photo retouched)

turer of percussion instruments, in Forest Hills, New York. The seven founders (former Sousa players who were present) were William Bell, Howard Bronson, August Helmecke, Eugene LaBarre, William Paulson, Sherley Thompson, and Francis Sutherland. Four other meetings took place, and then a formal organizational meeting was held in New York's Steinway Hall on September 13, 1944. The constitution was dated October 6, and the first dinner was held in New York on November 6, with seventy-seven members present. The constitution laid out the organization's purpose: "To unite the former members of the Sousa Band in the same spirit of friendship that existed throughout the band's entire career and to promote a reunion once a year on November 6th to commemorate the birthday

and perpetuate the memory of our great American bandmaster, John Philip Sousa."

Word of the society reached most of the band's alumni, widely scattered in America and abroad, and membership swelled to 242 by 1950. Once the society began, members kept in touch through their own newsletter, the *Sousa Band Fraternal Society News,* and the membership lists it published. By design it was sent out "every now and then," and fifty-one issues were printed between 1944 and 1990. The last few were issued by the Detroit Concert Band as part of its own newsletter, *Band Fan.*

The *News* had three editors: Sherley Thompson (1944–49), Eugene Slick (1949–65), and Edmund C. Wall (1967–84). The membership lists were also helpful to nonmembers seeking information. Few institutions or individuals have complete runs of the publication, but those that do exist document the history of the organization.

Members submitted information about themselves and other members and, of course, stories about adventures during their times with the band. Many previously unpublished photographs were included, material unavailable in any other publication. After only a few years the practice of printing obituaries was dropped, succeeded by "In Memoriam" notices because it pained members to learn that a comrade had fallen.

It came as no surprise that the colorful and witty bass drummer August (Gus) Helmecke, the central figure in so many of the stories about the band's adventures, was elected the first president. Succeeding him were Howard Bronson, William Gens, Eugene Slick, John (Jack) Bell, Meredith Willson, and Carl Rundquist.

The society's first project was to place a wreath on Sousa's grave in Washington each year on his birthday. The first ceremony took place on November 6, 1945, and for many years society members in the Washington area played taps at the event.

Meeting of the Sousa Band Fraternal Society, New York City, 1947. (Author's Collection)

A number of former Sousa Band members settled in California, and a Los Angeles branch of the Sousa Band Fraternal Society was formed. (Author's Collection)

Still another branch of the Sousa Band Fraternal Society was formed in Philadelphia. Clarinetist Louis Morris (left, front row) was also the band's copyist; Rudolph Becker (center, seated) was a member of the original band in 1892; and Albert Knecht (seated, second from right) kept the diary of the 1911 world tour that is reprinted in chapter 7. (Author's Collection)

conductors of any period in American history have been honored in such a sincere manner so many years after their death. The Sousa Band Fraternal Society truly was a "last man's club," unique in many ways. Their collective spirit lives on in the countless thousands of other musicians whom they inspired.

The society's meetings were grand reunions, with members reminiscing and making the acquaintances of others who had played before or after their time. It was a tradition for members to tell of their most memorable experiences in the band. Very few left the organization because they considered it an honor to be associated with so many distinguished members of their profession. Sousa's practice of isolating women soloists from the band members was abandoned, and several joined and made special efforts to attend. Moreover, Sousa's two daughters, both New York residents, were frequent guests and were made honorary members.

For the centennial of Sousa's birth in 1954, member Charles A. Wall asked several prominent band composers to write commemorative marches and guaranteed they would be published. Four responded, Peter Buys with "Sousa Band Fraternal March"; William Fletcher with "John Philip Sousa Centennial March"; Leonard B. Smith with "The March King"; and Charles O'Neill with "March Nonpareil." Buys and Fletcher were members of the society. The four marches were published by Associated Music Publishers in a set that also included ten of Sousa's marches.

Society members were always eager to assist people doing research on Sousa or Sousa's Band, and several individuals were invited to annual meetings and asked to tell of their work.[24] Very few

---

24. I attended three of the New York meetings, and a special meeting was convened in St. Petersburg in 1964 when I was in Florida conducting research on the Sousa alumni who had retired in that area. Much of the information in my other books is the result of contact with the fifty society members I have interviewed around the country. For more information on membership of the society, see Bierley, *Sousa Band Fraternal Society News Index.*

CHAPTER FOUR

Stars and Staff

All who were ever associated with Sousa's Band were considered "stars," particularly in the communities of their origin, but this chapter is limited to a list of prominent individuals who distinguished themselves on a much broader scale. Each helped develop the band's enviable reputation, either through artistry or by virtue of long service with the band. Some were famous before joining the Sousa organization. Others achieved fame after their careers with the band, which contributed to the legend that many of the finest musicians of the era performed with Sousa at one time or another. Additional information about each individual appears in Appendix II.

HARRY ASKIN

Harry Askin was the band's general manager longer than any other, from 1919 to 1932. He assumed that position at a critical time, just as Sousa had considered halting the band's tours because of diminishing profits.

Askin had a background in theater management and had known Sousa for many years. He convinced him that a theater manager could arrange more effective tours than the concert managers who had planned tours in the past. He was correct. Tours soon became more profitable and continued until the 1930s, when a variety of conditions made lengthy tours impractical.

Askin began his career in Philadelphia and New York. He was then a producer and theater manager in Chicago, Boston, and again in New York. He met with Sousa in 1915 in San Francisco and persuaded him to engage the band for nine months of the *Hip! Hip! Hooray!* extravaganza at the New York Hippodrome Theatre. Before working with Sousa he managed several other prominent artists, such as George Gershwin and Lillian Russell. After Sousa's death, Askin briefly managed the Goldman Band before becoming manager of the Paul Whiteman Orchestra.

Harry Askin. (Author's collection, artwork courtesy of Kari E. Kovach)

WINIFRED BAMBRICK

Canadian-born Winnie Bambrick, the only female member of the band except for the vocal and violin soloists, replaced veteran harpist Joseph Marthage in 1920 and was with the band for nearly every engagement until the end of the 1930 tours. In addition to playing regular concert numbers, she performed solos on several tours and accompanied vocal and violin soloists on encore selections.

Bambrick made her professional debut in New York at the age of twelve and went on to become one of America's finest harpists. She

Winifred Bambrick. (Barry Owen Furrer Collection)

William J. Bell. (Author's collection, courtesy of Winston Morris)

had an extensive repertoire and specialized in the classics. Between Sousa Band tours and after Sousa's death she toured with other artists, presented recitals, and was soloist with symphony orchestras. Bambrick's talents were not limited to music. She was also an author. Her novel *Keller's Continental Review* (1946) was well received.

WILLIAM J. BELL

A legendary tubist, Bill Bell joined the band at the age of eighteen in 1921 and became such a virtuoso that he occupied first chair on the 1923–24 tour. Although that was his last tour with the band he later played for several short engagements.

Bell was a giant in the world of tuba players, often referred to as "Mr. Tuba" or the "king of the tuba players." He was largely self-taught and played with three major American orchestras (the Cincinnati Symphony Orchestra, New York Philharmonic, and NBC Symphony) after his career with Sousa. He also played with many of the nation's finest bands, such as the Goldman Band, the Cities Service Band of America, Bachman's Million Dollar Band, Fillmore's Band, and the Armco Band.

Bell served on the faculties of the Cincinnati Conservatory of Music, the Juilliard School of Music, Indiana University, and several other institutions. Many of his students have held prominent positions in American musical organizations.

HERMAN BELLSTEDT

Herman Bellstedt gained national recognition as a member of Sousa's Band in 1904 and 1905. He was cornet soloist at the 1904 World's Fair in St. Louis, sharing honors with Herbert L. Clarke and Walter B. Rogers. Before his period with Sousa he was cornet soloist with Gilmore's Band and cornet soloist/assistant conductor of the Innes Band.

Bellstedt also gained renown as a composer, arranger, conductor, and music educator. He composed or arranged many works for band and others for piano, violin, and orchestra. His light-hearted nature is seen in his humoresques for band, most of which were created at Sousa's request, and his original cornet solos became staples of many noted soloists.

He was also a fine violinist, as evidenced by his "Variations on Dixie," which incorporated Paganini-like technical difficulties and was a showpiece for virtuoso violinists.

Much of Bellstedt's life was spent in Cincinnati, where he was principal trumpeter of the Cincinnati Symphony Orchestra and a professor of music at the Cincinnati Conservatory of Music. He also conducted his own group there, the Bellstedt-Ballenger Band, as well as the Syrian Temple Shrine Band. For a short time he was conductor of the Denver Municipal Band.

Herman Bellstedt. (Author's Collection)

David Blakely. (Author's Collection)

DAVID BLAKELY

Had it not been for David Blakely's realization of Sousa's potential, Sousa might never have had an illustrious career as a civilian bandmaster. It is also possible that he might never have gained great wealth as a composer had Blakely not taken negotiations with publishers out of his hands. Blakely's vision of creating an American concert band without peer provided Sousa with the incentive to become its guiding light.

Blakely's background in music, artist management, publishing, and printing was unique. Before becoming associated with Sousa, he was regarded as America's premier artist manager. After studying at Vermont College, he moved to Minnesota, where he became chief clerk in the House of Representatives and the secretary of state and superintendent of public instruction at the early age of twenty-seven.

While in Minneapolis he conducted the Mendelssohn Choir and the Philharmonic Choral Society, trained several male choruses, and sponsored a festival featuring the Theodore Thomas Orchestra. A perfectionist, he referred to himself as a "musical crank." He continued in concert management with the Theodore Thomas Orchestra and the American tour of the [Eduard] Strauss Vienna Orchestra. Before creating Sousa's Band, he managed Gilmore's Band for six years and the first two tours of the U.S. Marine Band while Sousa was leader.

Blakely was also editor and owner of various Minnesota newspapers, including the *Rochester City Post, Bancroft Pioneer, Mower County Mirror, Minneapolis Morning Tribune, Minneapolis Evening Journal,* and *St. Paul Pioneer,* in addition to the *Chicago Evening Post.* Yet another interest was the Blakely Printing Company of Chicago, also a bindery.

It is easy to see how much of the early success of Sousa's Band can be attributed to this brilliant man. The publicity machine he created for the band was a marvel. Blakely died suddenly of a heart attack in 1896 at age sixty-three. A bicycle accident just days before his death might have been a contributing factor.

GEORGE J. CAREY

Sousa Band publicity writers proclaimed George Carey to be the world's greatest xylophonist. He was featured as a soloist for most of the tours between 1920 and 1926 and because of his dashing style was called upon to perform many encores. The xylophone he used, reportedly twelve feet long, was built specifically for Sousa at a cost of $15,000, according to band publicity.

Carey spent much of his early life in Boston and Rochester, New York, and before joining Sousa he served as leader of the Eleventh Marine Band in France during World War I. At other times he was a percussionist with the Metropolitan Opera Orchestra, the Cincinnati Symphony Orchestra, Victor Herbert's Orchestra, the Black Hussar Band in Chicago, and the Ellis Band.

He composed several of his own solos, including ones entitled "The March Wind" and "Andree," and arranged numerous others from classical, popular, and jazz literature. In January 1958 he col-

George J. Carey. (Author's Collection)

Edwin G. Clarke. (Author's Collection)

lapsed and died onstage during a concert with the Cincinnati Symphony Orchestra.

EDWIN G. CLARKE

The versatile Edwin G. Clarke served the band in many capacities. He performed on cornet (and sometimes flugelhorn) from 1893 to 1910, worked in several lower-echelon management positions from 1906 to 1910, and was general manager from 1910 to 1919. On the world tour of 1911 he also doubled as band treasurer. Even while manager he was sometimes called upon to fill in for an ailing cornetist.

In 1907 he conducted the band for his younger brother Herbert's solos when Herbert served as both conductor and solo cornetist when Sousa was incapacitated. He also conducted some of the Victor recording sessions in 1910 and 1911. At various times during his career Clarke directed several theater and hotel orchestras and led the U.S. Army Twenty-first Infantry Band. After leaving Sousa's Band he taught music privately.

HERBERT L. CLARKE

Music historians generally agree that Herbert L. Clarke was the finest cornetist of all time, and thousands of budding young cornetists attended Sousa Band concerts just to hear him play. After achieving fame with Gilmore's Band he was with Sousa from 1893 to 1917, except for brief periods when he appeared with other famous bands. He was also cornet soloist on three of the four European tours and the world tour of 1911.

Herbert L. Clarke. (U.S. Marine Band)

Clarke was known for amazing endurance; he played the first-cornet part during concerts and performed solos as well. He was also assistant conductor for brief periods when Sousa was ill. He conducted many of the recordings of Sousa's Band for the Victor Talking Machine Company. In the early years he also served as the band's personnel manager and librarian.

He was a versatile composer and arranger, composing many of his own solos and arranging numerous other works for use with the band. Most of his compositions and arrangements are in the Herbert L. Clarke Music and Personal Papers in the Sousa Archives and Center for American Music at the University of Illinois at Urbana-Champaign. His cornet solos, pyrotechnic in nature but still very lyrical, have challenged several generations of soloists. Clarke wrote several books on pedagogy, an autobiography, and a series of articles about the 1911 world tour.

During his lengthy career, he was associated with many organizations, such as the New York Philharmonic, the Metropolitan Opera Orchestra, the Innes Band, and Victor Herbert's Twenty-second Regiment Band. As a conductor, he led several prominent bands, including the Long Beach Municipal Band, the Anglo-American Leather Company Band in Huntsville, Ontario, and several other Canadian orchestras and bands.

Unassuming and mild-mannered, Clarke was loved by even his staunchest rivals. He died in Long Beach at seventy-seven and is buried in Congressional Cemetery in Washington, D.C., a few feet from the grave of John Philip Sousa.

HERMAN C. CONRAD

Herman C. Conrad achieved fame as the musician who played the first upright-bell sousaphone manufactured by the J. W. Pepper Company in 1893 and also the first upright sousaphone manufactured by the C. G. Conn Company in 1898.

Conrad came to America from Germany in 1888 after serving in the German army and played tuba with Gilmore's Band until Gilmore died in 1892. He then signed on with Sousa and was with the band until 1903, a period when the band made its first three European tours.

After leaving Sousa's Band, Conrad was a studio artist with the Victor Talking Machine Company and may be heard on many recordings of the Victor Symphony Orchestra and the Victor Military Band. It is likely that he returned to Germany during the 1920s.

RALPH COREY

Boston native Ralph Corey became a member of the band for the third tour of 1906 and played nearly all tours and other engagements until 1920, including the 1911 world tour. At the time he joined he was the band's youngest member.

Corey succeeded Leo Zimmerman as soloist in 1908 and was a featured soloist from that time on. After his career with Sousa he held numerous positions in New York–area theater orchestras.

Herman C. Conrad. (Author's Collection, courtesy of Osmund Varela)

Ralph Corey. (Author's Collection)

JOSEPH O. DE LUCA

Italian-born Joe De Luca, graduate of the Perugia, Italy, Conservatory of Music, was well established as an artist with orchestras and bands before immigrating to America. Proficient on both trombone and euphonium, it was with the latter instrument that he made his mark on American band history.

He was with the band from 1921 to 1928 and soloed on almost all the tours. In addition to his career with Sousa, he was also a member of the Philadelphia Orchestra, Victor Herbert's Orchestra, and the bands of Giuseppe Creatore, Patrick Conway, and Frederick Neil Innes. He directed the Tucson Symphony Orchestra and bands at Arizona State University for many years.

De Luca composed more than two hundred works, most of them for band, and many of the solos he performed with Sousa's Band were his own. His "Beautiful Colorado," originally a euphonium solo, has been a band repertoire piece for several decades. His march "The American Gentleman" (1926) was dedicated to Sousa.

JOHN DOLAN

John Dolan ranks with the finest cornet soloists of all time, and it is the opinion of numerous band historians that he was without peer during his years with Sousa. He got his start in the music world as a U.S. Army musician and was soloist with Patrick Conway's Band before joining Sousa's. He was with the band from 1920 to 1928 and then a prominent theater musician in the New York area.

Joseph O. De Luca. (Barry Owen Furrer Collection)

John Dolan. (Author's Collection)

Dolan was a reliable first-chair player. As a soloist, audiences always demanded encores. Sousa Band programs reveal that he had an unusually large repertoire.

NORA FAUCHALD

Sometimes billed as the "Norwegian nightingale," soprano soloist Nora Fauchald was born in Norway while her mother was visiting her homeland, but they returned to North Dakota a few months later. She studied voice in both America and Norway after initially considering a career as a violinist.

Sousa was impressed by Fauchald's singing while she was a student in New York City and engaged her for tours beginning in 1923. She was with the band until 1927, alternating with Marjorie Moody. After leaving Sousa she had an illustrious career in opera, as a recitalist, and as a soloist in Europe and America. She married her accompanist, George H. Morgan. Later in her career she taught at the Juilliard School of Music. Her gracious personality endeared her to

Nora Fauchald. (Author's Collection)

Howard N. Goulden. (Author's Collection)

the band, and she often attended meetings of the Sousa Band Fraternal Society.

HOWARD N. GOULDEN

Howard Goulden, percussionist, was with the band for most of the tours and other engagements from 1920 to 1931. He was featured as a xylophone soloist, sometimes playing duets with George Carey on an oversized xylophone. When Sousa had a small group of players perform jazz numbers Goulden was leader.

Between band tours he began to build a career with theater and radio studio orchestras and was proprietor of a drum shop in Bridgeport, Connecticut. After Sousa's death Goulden performed as a theater and studio musician in New York, Chicago, and several other American cities.

FRANZ HELLE

When his band played in San Francisco at the Mid-Winter Exposition of 1894 Sousa was impressed with the artistry of Franz Helle, who was appearing as flugelhorn soloist of the famed Vienna Prater Orchestra. It was probably no coincidence that Helle was playing with Sousa's Band two years later. He remained with the band until 1905, a period when the group made four tours of Europe.

Helle was an outstanding trumpeter and cornetist, but he specialized on the flugelhorn and received much praise from music critics for his beautiful tone and interpretation of classics and simple melodies alike. After the period with Sousa he became a member of the Philadelphia Orchestra. He was also a soloist in the San Diego area, particularly with the Coronado Tent City Band.

Franz Helle. (Author's Collection)

AUGUST HELLEBERG SR.

The *Musical Trade* magazine of April 21, 1900, stated, "Every musician in New York knows the genial Gus Helleberg, the greatest bass player that ever blew breath into a tuba." If that and similar accounts are accurate, he ranked among the finest tuba players of his era.

The Danish-born Helleberg was a member of the Tenth Regiment Army Band before immigrating to America. He was a member of Sousa's Band from 1898 to 1903 and along on the European tours of 1900, 1901, and 1903. Among the other organizations with which he was associated were the New York Philharmonic, Metropolitan Opera Orchestra, and Chicago Symphony Orchestra.

According to legend, Helleberg could play four notes simultaneously, but that was a stunt and not used at concerts. Replica mouthpieces bearing his name are still in use. He is shown here with his two sons, August Junior and John, both of whom played with Sousa's Band at later dates.

AUGUST HELMECKE

In publicity issued by his band's office, Sousa was quoted as saying that Helmecke was the world's finest bass drummer and had the soul of a great artist. Judging from the opinions of colleagues, Sousa was not overstating. Helmecke's playing was artistic as well as sensitive.

Helmecke was with the band longer than any other percussionist, from 1916 through 1931. Before that he played in vaudeville houses and briefly with the New York Philharmonic. After Sousa's death he played with the Metropolitan Opera Orchestra, the Goldman Band, and several other premier musical organizations. Helmecke was the first president of the Sousa Band Fraternal Society and later voted honorary life president. Something of a prankster, he was the central figure in numerous stories told by Sousa musicians.

August Helmecke. (U.S. Marine Band)

ALBERT A. KNECHT

Although not a soloist, Knecht made an important contribution by documenting an important part of the band's history through the diary he kept of the 1911 world tour (chapter 7). He also kept a daybook to chronicle Sousa Band activities in several other years, and his collection of photographs provided further documentation.

Knecht was a member of the band from 1905 to 1919, other than in 1906 and 1909 and for a few other short periods. At various times in his career he was associated with the Philadelphia Orchestra, the American Saxophone Quartet, and numerous other organizations. With former Sousa Band saxophonist H. Benne Henton he operated the highly regarded Henton-Knecht music store in Philadelphia.

BOHUMIR KRYL

Bohumir Kryl was a cornet soloist with the band in 1898 and reportedly with the band for several other short periods during the 1890s (rosters and Sousa Band press book accounts for the 1890s are incomplete). He played for other famous bands, notably the Innes Band, before forming his own band and orchestra. Kryl's Band and his Women's Symphony Orchestra toured America for thirty-five consecutive years.

Kryl was a man of many talents. Before joining Sousa, he had been a sculptor and an acrobat. He also composed several band pieces, notably cornet solos, and collected art. In his later years Kryl was affiliated with several banks in the Chicago area. He died in his eighties, leaving a sizable estate.

August Helleberg Sr. (Author's Collection)

Albert A. Knecht. (Author's Collection)

ESTELLE LIEBLING

Lyric soprano Estelle Liebling made her mark in the music world not only with Sousa but also with the Metropolitan Opera in New York and several opera houses in Europe. She performed with Sousa for nine tours between 1902 and 1905 and numerous off-tour concerts, singing an estimated 1,600 concerts.

After her career with Sousa she toured America as conductor of the Liebling Singers, as well as a recitalist, concert artist, and lecturer. She also composed and arranged music. During the latter half of her career she became a renowned teacher, with Amelita Galli-Curci and Beverly Sills among her students. She also taught at the Curtis Institute of Music and was one of the few Sousa Band alumni to receive an honorary doctorate.

Estelle Liebling. (U.S. Marine Band)

Bohumir Kryl. (Author's Collection, courtesy of Oliver Graham)

Marcella Lindh. (Author's Collection)

MARCELLA LINDH

Marcella Lindh was the stage name of Rosalind Marcella Jacobson (Jellinek), who had the distinction of being the first soprano soloist with the band when it was formed in 1892. She was with the group for tours and engagements in 1892, 1893, and 1894.

Lindh also sang with the Metropolitan Opera in New York and later with opera companies in Hungary, Germany, Russia, and Portugal. After the death of her husband in Budapest, she returned to the United States, settling in Detroit. She lived until the age of ninety-nine and was able to provide valuable information on the Sousa Band's early history.

MARCUS C. LYON

Trombonist Marc Lyon was a charter member of the band and remained with it for twenty-five years. Although not a soloist, he performed in countless trios, quartets, and other brass ensembles and was also the reliable baggage master of the band for nearly twenty years. He made many recordings with the band on the Victor label.

Little is known of Lyon's early life other than that he was reportedly born in England and came to America via India, running away from his abusive father.

Marcus C. Lyon. (Author's Collection)

SIMONE MANTIA

Because of his extraordinary technique, euphonium solos recorded by Italian-born Simone Mantia are much sought after by record collectors. Some authorities on brass instrumentalists maintain that he was without equal in technical ability. He replaced his teacher, Joseph Michele Raffayolo, as euphonium soloist of the band in 1895 and was with the group until 1903, leaving with Arthur Pryor when Pryor organized his own band. With Pryor's Band he was also assistant conductor.

During his lengthy career Mantia also performed as a virtuoso trombonist with the New York Philharmonic, the NBC Symphony, the Metropolitan Opera Orchestra, and Victor Herbert's Orchestra. He was active as a euphonium player and soloist with various organizations until late in his seventies. He also composed and arranged many of his own solos, "Priscilla" being dedicated to Sousa's daughter.

Simone Mantia. (Author's Collection, courtesy of Osmund Varela)

Jean H. B. Moeremans. (Author's Collection, courtesy of Osmund Varela)

JEAN H. B. MOEREMANS

Even before he immigrated to Canada from Belgium Jean H. B. Moeremans was recognized as a saxophone artist and had been a member of the Belgian Guards Band. Patrick Gilmore, who heard him play in Canada, enlisted him as a soloist with his band. Later Moeremans joined Sousa's Band in the same capacity.

Moeremans was a pioneer saxophone soloist and thrilled audiences with his technique and expressive playing. With Sousa from 1894 to 1905 except for two overseas tours, Moeremans also gained fame as a teacher. Among his students were celebrated saxophone virtuosi such as Sousa Band soloist Harold B. Stephens.

MARJORIE MOODY

When the band was playing in Boston in 1916, cornetist Frank Simon happened to hear a remarkable soprano voice coming from a second-story window. He informed Sousa, and an audition was arranged. Marjorie Moody was engaged as a soloist briefly for that season and was with the band until 1931, sometimes sharing the spotlight with other sopranos. She sang approximately 2,500 solos.

Moody's clarity, range, and power, combined with her charm, brought outstanding reviews. She was called upon to sing as many

Marjorie Moody. (Author's Collection)

as five encores at a concert. Sousa dedicated two songs, "There's a Merry Brown Thrush" and "Love's Radiant Hour," to her. After her career with Sousa, Moody soloed with numerous symphony orchestras and sang opera in North America, South America, and Europe.

JOSEPH NORRITO

The genial Norrito had the distinction of being with Sousa's Band longer than anyone except Sousa himself. He was a member of the original band in 1892 and continued until 1922. He worked his way up through the section to principal clarinetist and was soloist on many occasions.

Born in Italy, Norrito had made a name for himself in Boston before he joined Sousa's Band. After his career with Sousa he returned to Italy. His brother Giacomo (Jack) also played with the band for many years.

JOHN J. PERFETTO

"Of all the musicians who have used my instruments in the past, I have regarded you as the squarest and best," said C. G. Conn in an October 25, 1913, letter to euphonium soloist John Perfetto. Perfetto joined Sousa's Band in 1904, replacing Simone Mantia as soloist, and was with the group until 1920. He was born in Italy and came to America in 1887.

Perfetto was also an accomplished trombonist. After he left Sousa he was a member of the New York Symphony Orchestra, the New York Philharmonic, the Metropolitan Opera Orchestra, and several other fine bands such as those of Arthur Pryor and Patrick Conway.

John J. Perfetto. (Author's Collection, courtesy of Antoinette Cendali)

Maud Powell. (U.S. Marine Band)

Joseph Norrito. (Author's Collection, courtesy of Leonard B. Smith)

He was elected to the Trombone Hall of Fame in 1922. Shortly after Sousa's death in 1932, Perfetto commissioned a portrait of Sousa that for many years hung in the musicians' union office in New York City and is now in the possession of the Ocean Grove, New Jersey, Historical Society.

MAUD POWELL

Maud Powell ranked with the world's greatest violinists of her era. She made European tours with Sousa's Band in 1903 and 1905, experiences that provided a step toward becoming America's premier violin soloist.

Powell's extensive and eclectic repertoire is evidenced by the many Victor "Red Seal" recordings that document her artistry. She is also remembered through CD reissues of those recordings, Karen Shaffer and Neva Greenwood's *Maude Powell: Pioneer American Violinist* (1988), and the efforts of the Maud Powell Society. Powell, a champion of American music, was once described as being "as American as 'The Stars and Stripes Forever.'" An ardent patriot, she performed for the Armed Forces in American hospitals and training camps during World War I.

ARTHUR W. PRYOR

Many who have studied the recordings and performance history of Arthur Pryor declare that he was the greatest trombonist of all time. He drew wide attention in the United States and abroad, especially for his performances on the European tours of 1900, 1901, and 1903. When the band played in Leipzig, Germany, in 1900, members of the Gewandhaus Symphony Orchestra came backstage and requested that he disassemble his instrument so they could see if he was concealing a trick device to enable him to exhibit such phenomenal technique.

After leaving Sousa in 1903, Pryor continued his illustrious career. His band toured for many years and also played lengthy engagements, including twenty seasons at Asbury Park in New Jersey and nine seasons in Miami. Pryor was a renowned recording artist, not only as a soloist but also as a conductor, being an assistant conductor of Sousa's Band. He conducted the majority of the Victor recording sessions of the band and hundreds of others with his own band and orchestra.

JOHN W. RICHARDSON

John W. Richardson was with the band longer than any other tuba player. He joined for the second tour of 1903 and continued with few interruptions through the 1931 tour. He also played most of the radio broadcasts starting in 1929.

Except for periods with Thomas Preston Brooke's Chicago Marine Band and Mayhew L. Lake's Symphony of Gold, most of Richardson's professional playing career was spent with Sousa's Band. Much publicity centered around him because he was the tallest in the band and played the largest sousaphone. The "long and the short" of the band pictured Richardson and Winifred Bambrick.

Arthur W. Pryor. (Author's Collection, courtesy of Osmund Varela)

John W. Richardson with Winifred Bambrek. (Author's Collection)

WALTER B. ROGERS

Of all the noted cornet soloists Herbert L. Clarke observed during his climb to fame, he claimed to have learned the most from Walter Rogers. He and Rogers eventually became side partners in Sousa's Band and shared solo duties. Each was quick to praise the other's playing.

Rogers performed with or conducted several other bands and orchestras before and after his years with Sousa. He then had a successful career in the recording industry as a studio conductor and executive. He was associated with at least seven different recording companies, including Victor and Columbia.

VIRGINIA ROOT

Virginia Root, a lyric soprano, endeared herself to Sousa by introducing many of his songs. She was also much loved by the band because of her charm and outgoing manner. She rose from being a singer in a Baptist church to attain considerable renown through her association with Sousa's Band. She was with the band from 1909 to 1917, longer than any soprano except Marjorie Moody.

After her career with Sousa she toured as a recitalist and soloist with symphony orchestras and sang with the National Opera Company of New York. She was a great-niece of American composer George Frederick Root. The only portion of her music library that has been found is now in the Sousa Archives and Center for American Music at the University of Illinois at Urbana-Champaign.

CLARENCE J. RUSSELL

Sousa's righthand man, whether on the road or between tours, was cornetist Clarence Russell, known affectionately as "Buss." As band librarian he was charged with such duties as seeing that musicians had the correct music in their folders and in the right order, making sure they were ready to play all encores, and checking seating arrangements at concerts. It was a big responsibility, particularly when the band was playing four completely different concerts a day at such engagements as Willow Grove Park.

The amiable Russell was with the band from 1910 to 1932. He made audience announcements when necessary, such as introducing the groups of instruments in Sousa's humoresque "Showing Off Before Company." He also conducted the band on a few occasions when Sousa was ill.

Russell was one of the few in the band with a college education. In order to play with Sousa he left his position as superintendent of schools in Pittsfield, Massachusetts, and a part-time job with the New York Symphony Orchestra. After Sousa's death in 1932 he cataloged and prepared the band's music library for shipment to the University of Illinois.

Walter B. Rogers. (Author's Collection, computer enhancement by Betty Holling)

Virginia Root. (U.S. Marine Band)

Clarence J. Russell. (Barry Owen Furrer Collection)

William Schneider. (Author's Collection)

WILLIAM SCHNEIDER

One of the most important individuals in the Sousa Band organization was the young Willie Schneider, a management member who traveled with the band from 1919 to 1929.

It was he who collected the receipts from concerts, checked the number of tickets, and was accountable for all money to Sousa and the band's general manager in New York. He also acted as paymaster, seeing that band members received their salaries every Saturday.

JOHN P. SCHUELER

John Schueler was last on the band's long list of distinguished trombone soloists. He was an assistant bandmaster in a U.S. Army band during World War I and then was with Sousa from 1920 to 1931 except for the three short tours of 1930.

After leaving the Sousa Band he played with the Walter Damrosch Orchestra, the Metropolitan Opera Orchestra, Pryor's Band, and numerous other bands and orchestras. Later he became a music

John P. Schueler. (Author's Collection)

educator, serving on the faculty of Syracuse University and directing several high school bands in the state of New York.

Two of Schueler's brothers were also members of the band during the 1920s: Henry A. on cornet and William P. on clarinet. William P. Schueler was director of the Daytona Beach Municipal Band for many years.

FRANK SIMON

Frank Simon was a cornet soloist with the band from 1914 to 1920, and after Herbert L. Clarke retired in 1917 he assumed the assistant conductor's position. Before he was with Sousa, he was with the Cincinnati Symphony Orchestra and Weber's Prize Band of America. On the recommendation of former cornet soloist Herman Bellstedt he was accepted into Sousa's Band without audition. Simon was an emotional man, and this quality was reflected in his artistry.

After leaving the band in 1920 he founded and conducted an industrial band for the American Rolling Mills Company (Armco) in Middletown, Ohio. The Armco Band started as a band of amateurs and grew to a fully professional band with weekly network radio broadcasts.

Simon then turned to music education. He taught at the Cincinnati Conservatory of Music and the University of Arizona and was mentor to several students who eventually rose to the top of their profession. He was one of the first men elected to the prestigious American Bandmasters Association and later served as its president.

JAY G. SIMS

A seasoned trouper, Jay Sims joined the band in 1919 after having been a trombonist with Pryor's Band, Conway's Band, Buffalo Bill's Wild West Show, and numerous other bands and orchestras. He had also served as a U.S. Army bugler during the Spanish-American War. He remained with the band until Sousa's death in 1932.

In addition to playing bass trombone Sims was the personnel manager, responsible for hiring musicians and seeing that they behaved at all times. Being older and more experienced than most players, he had their respect.

Sims was a charter member of the Sousa Band Fraternal Society, attending the annual New York meetings as long as he was able. He was elected to the Trombone Hall of Fame in 1922 along with veteran Sousa bandsman John Perfetto.

EUGENE SLICK

Most of Gene Slick's notoriety as a member of the Sousa Band came not while a member but in later years through his many activities on behalf of the Sousa Band Fraternal Society. He was editor of the society's newsletter for fourteen years, encouraging members to document their experiences in an informative, behind-the-scenes history of the band. He also served as president of the organization.

Frank Simon. (Author's Collection)

Jay G. Sims. (Author's Collection)

Eugene Slick. (Author's Collection)

Maurice Van Praag. (Author's Collection)

Slick played saxophone on the 1928 tour and clarinet on the 1929 outing and was also a member of the saxophone octet. Before his period with Sousa he was with several circus bands and other traveling shows. In his post-Sousa days he was proprietor of Slick's Music House in Anderson, Indiana. He was a master instrument repairman and also taught music. For several years he represented the C. G. Conn Instrument Manufacturing Company. He was also a consultant for the Frank Holton Company and designed one of their most popular saxophones.

MAURICE VAN PRAAG

Becoming a great French horn player was not Maurice Van Praag's ambition. He had first trained to become a concert pianist or violinist, but an accident to his right hand forced him to take up an instrument that could be fingered with the left hand. The horn became his passion.

Van Praag came to America from the Netherlands. After playing with the Chicago Symphony Orchestra and being principal horn of the St. Paul Symphony Orchestra, he joined Sousa's Band as principal horn and was with the group from 1914 to 1918. Sousa, impressed by his extraordinary talent, used Van Praag as a soloist on part of the 1915, 1917, and 1918 tours. The remainder of his career was spent with the New York Philharmonic, where he was personnel manager for thirty-six years.

Benjamin Vereecken. (Author's Collection)

BENJAMIN VEREECKEN

Belgian saxophonist Ben Vereecken played with the circus band of Barnum and Bailey in Europe before coming to America. He was a member of several American bands, including a stint as flute soloist with Pryor's Band, before he joined the Sousa organization. He was with the Sousa Band for an estimated five tours starting in 1910, including the world tour of 1911.

Vereecken, one of Sousa's finest arrangers, excelled in accompaniments for vocal or violin solos. He made at least seventy-eight special arrangements for Sousa.

FRANK W. WADSWORTH

Frank W. Wadsworth distinguished himself as a leading musician in military service and with theater orchestras in England before immigrating to America in the 1880s. He was flute soloist with Gilmore's Band until Gilmore died in 1892, and in 1893 he was named principal flutist with Sousa's Band. He remained with the band until 1899 and during that period was regarded as one of America's finest flutists.

Critics of Sousa Band concerts often commented on the lyricism of Wadsworth's obbligatos for the sopranos' solos. Sousa also featured him as a soloist on flute and occasionally on the piccolo.

EDMUND C. WALL

It was Sousa's practice to have one or more of the nation's finest woodwind players in his band, a tradition maintained with Edmund C. Wall, solo principal clarinetist from 1926 to 1931 except for part of the 1929 tour. His brother, Charles A., was also with the band for part of the same period. Edmund A., their father, was with the group earlier and wrote a poem about the world tour (chapter 7).

Wall had a distinguished career after Sousa's death, performing with the New York City Ballet or the Metropolitan Opera Orchestra

Edmund C. Wall. (Author's Collection)

during their regular seasons and with the Goldman Band or Pryor's Band during the summer months.

A charter member of the Sousa Band Fraternal Society, he edited and published the newsletter for seventeen years, providing information on the band's history and musicians' activities.

MEREDITH WILLSON

Frank Simon was surprised by the artistry of a young flutist named Meredith Willson whom he had heard in Mason City, Iowa. He recommended him to Sousa, and from 1921 to 1924 Willson was a star of the band. His period with Sousa proved to be a stepping stone; he went on to become one of the biggest names in American music.

Willson became well known in New York circles as a flutist with the New York Philharmonic and in theater orchestras. He then became involved with radio productions. He was music director of network programs before creating the popular *Meredith Willson Show*. During World War II he enlisted in the U.S. Army and was director of Armed Forces Radio.

Willson is remembered as the composer of one of the finest Broadway musicals of all time, *The Music Man*. His *The Unsinkable Molly Brown* and two symphonies were among his other works, and his book, *And There I Stood with My Piccolo,* is a testament to his wit.

The friendships he cultivated as a member of Sousa's Band were lasting ones. He was president of the Sousa Band Fraternal Society

Frank W. Wadsworth. (Author's Collection, courtesy of Osmund Varela)

from 1976 until his death in 1984. American Legion Post 777 in Denver was named after him, and the Meredith Willson Museum is located in Mason City.

NICOLINE ZEDELER

Violin soloist Nicoline Zedeler studied and concertized in her native Sweden and several other European countries before immigrating to America. She was only twenty in 1910, the year she toured twice with Sousa's Band. She was then selected from a hundred applicants to make the 1911 world tour and remained with the band for the 1912 season.

After leaving Sousa, she had a dual career as soloist with leading symphony orchestras and as a music educator at the Chicago Music College and the Chatham Square Music School. She married Sousa Band tubist Emil Mix, who later managed several American symphony orchestras.

When Zedeler reported for the world tour with fourteen trunks, she was shocked when Sousa told her she could take but one—and, he joked, she should pick a flat one in the event she had to sleep on it.

Nicoline Zedeler. (Author's Collection)

Meredith Willson. (Author's Collection)

CHAPTER FIVE

Sousa and Recording

STAYING AWAY FROM RECORDING STUDIOS

It usually shocks people when they learn that John Philip Sousa served as the conductor for only eight of the 1,770 pieces issued on commercial recordings under the name "Sousa's Band." He did, however, conduct two additional pieces with another band.

Sousa had a distinct distaste for the scratchy, tinny sound of early acoustic recordings, which were a far cry from the concert hall sound. Moreover, he preferred playing to live audiences, and personal communication with listeners was completely lacking in the cramped quarters of recording studios. In general he had an aversion to most forms of mechanically reproduced music.

It was not until the mid-1920s, when microphones were used to produce more realistic electrical recordings, that he was partially won over to the recording media. Even so he missed live audiences. Of all the commercial recordings bearing the Sousa Band name, Sousa actually conducted only three sessions.[1] Two others were done at a separate session with the Philadelphia Rapid Transit Company Band: "March of the Mitten Men" (later entitled "Power and Glory") and "The Thunderer." In addition to those five sessions, he also conducted a reading of "The Stars and Stripes Forever" that was prerecorded for use on a Thanksgiving Day 1929 radio broadcast over the NBC network. It is also remotely possible that he recorded one or more pieces on May 14, 1929, presumably in New York City.[2]

Sousa's Band plays for *you*

Sousa generally left the conducting on recordings to others. Arthur Pryor, his trombonist and assistant conductor, directed a majority of the sessions. This drawing appeared in a 1922 Victrola advertisement. (Author's Collection)

GROWING UP WITH THE RECORDING INDUSTRY

Before the days of radio and sound films there was high demand for recordings of the music that Sousa's Band was presenting in person. Despite thousands of concerts around the country, many people—especially in towns not served by railroads—could experience the music live only occasionally. If a person wanted to hear more of the band its music was available only on cylinders or 78–rpm records. Recordings were plentiful, and playing devices were sold in even the most remote regions of the country.

Because the band was so widely known it created its own market for records. In general, band music was the recording industry's greatest moneymaker at the time.[3] To appreciate the impact of Sousa

---

1. Eight pieces, seven of which were Sousa marches, were recorded in three sessions for Victor. "Sabre and Spurs" and "Solid Men to the Front" were recorded on September 6, 1917; "The Star Spangled Banner" (not released), "The Liberty Loan, America First" (not released), and "The U.S. Field Artillery" were recorded on December 21, 1917; and "Nobles of the Mystic Shrine" and "The Dauntless Battalion" were recorded on March 29, 1923.
2. Checks were drawn, evidently for a recording session, on this date. No other details, such as the name of the conductor, are known.

3. Author discussions with Frederick P. Williams, a discographer and authority on early Victor recordings.

and his band on the American recording industry, one has merely to glance over the vast number of singles that the group recorded (Appendix VI). The band began recording while the industry was in its infancy and continued to grow with it.

Sousa's Band was a major factor in the rapid development of the Victor Talking Machine Company, even the recording industry in general. Before Victor's highly successful classical Red Seal series of discs, the popular market produced most of the revenue, with Sousa Band releases leading the way.[4] Between 1900 and 1903 Victor catalogs listed 260 Sousa Band numbers, 202 by tenor Harry Macdonough, and 192 by a studio group known as the Metropolitan Orchestra.[5] Sousa's name was, of course, a household word, whereas Macdonough and the studio orchestra were known only through recordings. By 1904 the band had performed more than five thousand concerts and played in all forty-five states plus several territories as well as fourteen foreign countries.

Marches had the advantage of being short, thus meeting the time constraints (sometimes by omitting repeats) of the early recordings. They were especially popular in the early 1900s, and Sousa's were responsible for the sale of millions of records on many different labels. It is particularly significant that "The Stars and Stripes Forever" probably has been recorded more often than any other piece of music ever written.[6] Walter Mitziga's *The Sound of Sousa,* published in 1986, a year before the piece was designated America's official march, lists nearly a thousand recordings of the work. Many more have been recorded since that time.

Individual members of Sousa's Band were also important to the recording industry. A number of them established reputations as both recording artists and studio conductors. Arthur Pryor, for example, the celebrated trombone soloist and one of Sousa's assistant conductors, conducted thousands of recording sessions, including the majority of the Sousa Band sessions. Pryor worked first with the Berliner Gramophone Company, then with the Columbia Phonograph Company, and finally with the Victor Talking Machine Company. His trombone solos on the Berliner and Victor labels have become collectors' items. Pryor's own band (and orchestra) made more recordings than Sousa's, and for nearly all the sessions he employed many Sousa musicians because their proficiency had been amply demonstrated.

Herbert L. Clarke, a Sousa soloist and assistant conductor, also made a mark on the industry. His cornet solos have become collectors' items as well and been reissued on modern recordings. Clarke was a studio conductor, first with Edison (the National Phonograph Com-

pany) and then with Victor. In keeping with the practice set by Pryor, he engaged many Sousa musicians.

Another Sousa Band cornet soloist who recorded was Walter B. Rogers, who also became a studio conductor, first with Victor, leading Sousa Band recording sessions. He was later a studio conductor with the Brunswick, Emerson, Paramount, and Par-O-Ket companies and continued to employ numerous Sousa musicians while with companies other than Victor.

Henry Higgins, yet another Sousa cornet soloist, conducted Sousa Band recording sessions. He led the band on several of the Berliner discs and probably on some of the earlier Columbia cylinders (Appendix VI).

Bohumir Kryl, cornetist with the band for a short period in the 1890s, recorded on the Columbia, Edison, Victor, and Zonophone labels, mostly with his own band and sometimes as cornet soloist.

Still another Sousa cornetist, and later the band's manager, was Edwin G. Clarke, who, it is believed, worked exclusively with Victor. Like his brother, Herbert, he employed mostly Sousa musicians, taking advantage of friendships developed during his association with the band.

Another aspect of the band's influence on the recording industry was evident in the number of former members who recorded with various recording companies throughout the years. Their reputations enabled them to acquire positions in the industry, even many years after the Sousa Band era. Concert band music began to diminish in relative popularity with the coming of the dance music craze during and after World War I. Dozens of new "pops" record companies sprang up, issuing dance music exclusively and almost completely replacing band recordings. The Sousa Band was still popular in the concert hall, but changing public taste was reflected in record sales.

The band's influence on the recording industry has faded into the distant past, but Sousa's influence is still very much in evidence. Record albums devoted exclusively to the music of "band" composers are rare, but a number of all-Sousa albums have continued to be, for various instrumental and vocal groups, produced in recent years.

A DISCOGRAPHY

All known commercial Sousa Band recordings for release in the United States are listed in Appendix VI, a discography. The titles reflect the popular music that people preferred to hear. The repertory of Sousa's concert programs was more extensive and serious, but the music on the recordings was that which brought people to his concerts. Various companies have produced several re-releases of Sousa marches proclaiming "as conducted by Sousa," but only rarely do they feature selections conducted by Sousa himself.

PRIMITIVE RECORDINGS

Listening time on the first recordings, which were wax cylinders, was limited to approximately two minutes, so many compositions were necessarily shortened. The first cylinders produced were unique—each

---

4. Some Red Seal collectors suggest that Enrico Caruso popularized Victor, but the Sousa Band recordings started the trend two years earlier. Red Seal records were more expensive and therefore more prestigious, catering to an elite clientele. Enrico Caruso was followed by numerous other artists of the concert stage, giving Victor an initial advantage over other companies in the classical market. The Sousa Band's role in Victor's rapid growth is discussed at length in discographer Frederick P. Williams's article in the 1972 issue of the *Association for Recorded Sound Collectors Journal.*

5. Data compiled by discographer Paul Charosh.

6. My postulation is based on conversations with Frederick Williams; that does not necessarily mean that more recordings have been sold.

was, that is, an original—because a way to mass-produce cylinders had not yet been developed.[7] In order to produce three hundred cylinders, for example, musicians had to cram themselves in front of a battery of ten amplifying horns, each of which was attached to a wax cylinder cutter, and play a piece thirty times. As might be expected, each cylinder had a slightly different sound.[8] Because of their brittleness, few of those early "brown wax" cylinders are still in existence.

Recording sessions were tedious affairs for the participants. Stellar artists were discouraged at the thought of repeating a piece of music over and over again. That tedium, in addition to Sousa's objection to the recordings' primitive sound and his preference for live audiences, accounts for his absence from recording studios.

SOUSA'S U.S. MARINE BAND AS A PIONEER RECORDING GROUP

Thomas Edison invented the phonograph in 1877, but it was not until the last decade of the nineteenth century that using it to reproduce music was thought to be practical. The phonograph was, in fact, initially regarded as a toy. It also enabled music and the human voice to be preserved for the first time in history. The new technology quickly became immensely popular.

Among the first music cylinders produced for sale were those manufactured by the Columbia Phonograph Company of Washington, D.C. Brass and woodwind instruments reproduced better than string instruments because they could play louder and be heard above the surface noise of the records. Thus bands were preferred over orches-

tras for recording purposes. Because America's most prominent military band, the U.S. Marine Band, was located in Washington, where many of the early recordings were made, several of its musicians were hired to make recordings in a makeshift studio just across the street from the Marine Barracks. Sousa, the leader of the Marine Band at the time, would have no part in those recordings. He did not, however, prohibit his men from participating. He felt strongly that

The Berliner Gramophone Company was the first to record Sousa's Band on discs. They were seven inches in diameter. Beginning late in 1900, all Sousa Band disc recordings were made by the Victor Talking Machine Company. Victor's early discs were also seven inches in diameter, but ten- and twelve-inch discs became the most popular. A few eight-inch discs were made in 1906. Until 1908 all discs were single-sided, but double-sided discs became the standard. Discs eventually won out over cylinders, primarily because they took up less space. (Author's Collection, courtesy of Frederick P. Williams)

The first recordings of Sousa's Band were cylinders made of wax. Edison (the National Phonograph Company) later introduced cylinders that had even longer playing time and for which better fidelity was claimed. All Sousa Band cylinders were acoustic (made before the use of microphones). (Author's Collection, courtesy of Frederick P. Williams)

In one of the earliest phonograph music recording sessions in history, around 1890, members of the U.S. Marine Band recorded for the Columbia Phonograph Company in Washington, D.C. Sousa was leader of the band at the time, but for artistic reasons he declined to participate. In this "studio," sixteen musicians played in front of an array of recording devices. (Library of Congress)

---

7. Discs, however, could be mass-produced by a stamping process.
8. All horns could not be in the most desirable location. Single, large horns were later built into specialized recording studios.

the musicians were underpaid and encouraged them to find outside employment.

SOUSA AND RECORDED MUSIC

Because of early recording studios' spatial limitations only about a third of Sousa's musicians could be used in the recording process; the horns, or funnels, that collected sound could pick it up effectively from only a few feet away. The result was an acoustic sound as opposed to the later electrical recordings made with microphones. As such, the sound on earlier recordings was a far cry from the actual sound of Sousa's band, and he saw the futility of reaching large numbers of people with the new invention.

The process of recording was, for Sousa, an abomination. Indeed, he never set foot in the Columbia recording "studio," a room large enough to accommodate players representing most instrumental parts in addition to multiple recording machines and technicians to operate them.[9] Sousa disliked recordings for another reason as well—he was not paid for the use of his music. This was a minor irritation at first because cylinders were produced in low quantities. That number grew, however, with development of a new type of entertainment, the "nickel-in-a-slot" parlor, where several patrons could listen to a cylinder through earphones. Disc recordings soon ensued, and along with them came technology that brought mass production of both discs and cylinders. Sousa found that he was not being paid for the widespread use of his music even though it was copyrighted. With the advent of mass production, Sousa was one of numerous creators not compensated for the use of their music, and it was his opinion that if manufacturers were making money from a composer's art, then composers were entitled to part of it.

It could be argued that an indirect benefit might come because increased interest in music would result in greater sales of sheet music. Sousa, however, would soon point out that recordings made it possible for amateur musicians to enjoy well-played music without having to make the effort of acquiring the skill of making it themselves, in which case less sheet music would be sold. Some time after Sousa's civilian band was organized in 1892 contracts were drawn up between the band's management and phonograph manufacturers. Under those contracts Sousa was paid a presumably small percentage for the use of his name, but the free use of his music still aggravated him.

WAS IT REALLY SOUSA'S BAND?

The question of using the Sousa Band name on recording labels and in catalogs without all members of the band being present raised the question of justification for use of the name. David Blakely, Sousa's manager, thought doing so was ethically acceptable because Sousa Band musicians were, during the time he was manager, apparently being used exclusively.

Recording sessions were carefully planned to fall at the end of a tour, just before a tour began, or when the band had an engagement in the city of a recording studio. Examples of the latter were recordings made in Philadelphia or Camden, New Jersey, when the band was playing at Willow Grove Park just north of Philadelphia. There, selected musicians could work mornings at the recording studio and get back to play the afternoon and evening concerts at Willow Grove. New York sessions were held while the band had extended engagements at such places as the Metropolitan Opera House, the New York Hippodrome, or Manhattan Beach.

In some instances after World War I, however, a few sessions were held while the band was touring many miles away. Logs of the Victor Talking Machine Company indicate that several former Sousa Band members were employed but in some cases Pryor's Band or the Victor Band was substituted. The conductor for most of those sessions was Arthur Pryor or another conductor well versed in Sousa's style, and numerous former Sousa musicians were members of Pryor's own band or Victor's permanent recording staff. Sousa himself apparently had to approve the test pressings.[10]

CROSSOVER

During the time early recordings were being made the distinction between symphony orchestra and professional band employment practices in America was not as pronounced as it now is. Of necessity, brass, woodwind, and percussion players moved from one field to the other. Symphony and opera orchestras had much shorter operating seasons than they now do, requiring musicians to seek other employment for months at a time. Bands often helped them pick up the slack. Many Sousa musicians also played with symphony, opera, and theater orchestras (Appendix II).

They also found employment in recording studios. In Camden, for example, some Victor studio musicians were also members of the Philadelphia Orchestra. The artistic background of an individual wind or percussion musician was not critical to recording companies because that individual likely had both band and orchestra experience.

AN AMERICAN PRESIDENT SPEAKS OUT

Shortly after the turn of the twentieth century, President Theodore Roosevelt proposed that the American copyright law be revised to give composers and authors more equity in the rewards for their creations. Before then, as Sousa well knew, composers were not paid for the mechanical reproduction of their music. Manufacturers of phonograph machines, piano rolls, and other mechanical devices

---

9. As stated in arguments concerning S. 6330 and H.R. 19853 before the Committee on Patents, U.S. Senate and U.S. House of Representatives, June 6–9, 1906.

10. I discovered two boxes of these test pressings, one of which had never been opened, along with a few production records, in basement archives at Sousa's Long Island estate in 1964. At the request of Sousa's daughter, Helen Sousa Abert, I delivered both boxes to the Music Division of the Library of Congress.

joined forces to fight the threat of legislation, whereas support among composers was practically nonexistent until Victor Herbert and Sousa entered the picture. Both men gave strong testimony at congressional hearings, and the battle became less one-sided. Not all composers were as vocal, but because of the popularity of their music Herbert and Sousa had more to lose.

SOUSA AND THE PRESS

Not content with the prospect of Congress automatically rectifying matters after hearing both sides of the argument, given the powerful manufacturers' lobby, Sousa enlisted public help. His first effort was in the form of "The Menace of Mechanical Music," an article in the September 1906 issue of *Appleton's Magazine*. In it, he attacked "canned music" (borrowing a phrase coined by his friend Mark Twain) and declared that when a mechanical system of gears and megaphones substituted for human skill and soul it defeated nature itself. Records, he warned, could lead to the deterioration of musical taste and would put many musicians out of work. Moreover, the desire to study music would be diminished, and future Mozarts and Wagners would lose their incentive to create new work.

How, Sousa asked, could corporations be so blind about the moral and ethical questions involved as to take an artist's work, reproduce it a thousandfold and then deny the artist all participation in the financial returns? It was piracy pure and simple. Moreover, composers' exclusive right to the use of their creations was guaran-

teed by the Constitution. It was unfair that the devices of phonograph manufacturers were protected by patents while the creators who made their industry possible had no protection against the wholesale use of their music.

Following the *Appleton's* article was another in New York's *Town Topics* on December 6, 1906. This time Sousa was at his satirical best. He described a fictitious concert of classical music played by a stage full of phonographs conducted by a "Professor Punk" and told of a performance of *Faust* by an all-star cast at the home of the "Automated Opera." The event ushered in a new era, he stated, in which mechanical devices would completely replace obsolete instruments such as the violin, flute, clarinet, and trombone.

A third article, "My Contention," appeared in the Christmas 1906 issue of *Musical Trades*. He used the occasion to reinforce his posi-

" 'There is a man in there playing the piano with his hands!' "

A cartoon accompanying Sousa's satire in the September 1906 issue of *Appleton's Magazine* demonstrated his disdain for early phonograph recordings. (Author's Collection)

Sousa, whose music had no small impact on the recording industry, and Thomas Alva Edison (right), inventor of the device that had made the musician's art immortal. Edison's invention had alienated Sousa a quarter of a century earlier, but this meeting, arranged by the editor of *Etude* magazine and described in an October 1923 article entitled "A Momentous Musical Meeting," produced only a few anxious moments and ended amicably. (Edison National Historic Site)

tion on the copyright situation and explain that the wording of the existing copyright law was ambiguous and being interpreted by record producers to their advantage.

JUSTICE SERVED

The result of the congressional copyright deliberations was passage of new legislation in 1909 requiring that composers be compensated for the mechanical reproduction of their music. With the battle won, Sousa's relationship with the recording industry from that time forward was much less antagonistic. He began a series of long-term contracts with the Victor Talking Machine Company, largely because their representatives had been sympathetic toward his position during the hearings. He severed connections with Columbia, however, whose representatives had taken an adversarial position at the hearings. Ironically, Sousa never benefited financially from the sale of recordings of many of his most popular marches such as "The Stars and Stripes Forever." The 1909 legislation applied only to work published after enactment of the legislation, and many Sousa marches had been composed before 1909.

A DEGREE OF RECONCILIATION

In the decade before Sousa's death he came to realize that phonographs made it possible to preserve at least some degree of the art of great performers. Recordings are, in effect, historical documents. Despite their shortcomings, the recordings of Sousa's Band and numerous other bands are significant because they preserve the era in which touring bands were an important part of the American scene and also provide a rough index of the recording industry. The recordings maintain the memory of what was once one of America's most revered musical organizations, the band of John Philip Sousa.[11]

---

11. An authentic compact disc set of the recordings of Sousa's marches as recorded by Sousa's Band was made possible by the extraordinary efforts of Frederick P. Williams. In 2000 it was produced as a set of three discs by Crystal Records (CD461–3), *Sousa Marches Played by the Sousa Band*. Because the original recordings had not all been cut at the standard 78.26–rpm speed, pitch adjustments were made to bring each selection to the proper keys.

CHAPTER SIX

Sousa and Radio

A TOKEN IMPACT

The influence of Sousa's Band on the radio industry in America was minimal when compared to the influence of many other musical organizations that broadcast over much longer periods. The band made only thirty-five live broadcasts and three prerecorded ones, all within a period of three years. Its contribution must not be disregarded, however, because the band was so well known and the broadcasts were nationwide.

The broadcasts were made long before the advent of television, beginning in 1929 and ending when Sousa died in 1932. How popular the programs might have become had he lived longer is subject to speculation. One might also wonder if the band would have become an important media attraction had it still existed after the introduction of television.

AN EXCITING NEW MEDIUM

Today, radio is taken for granted. It is difficult to imagine that the first pre-advertised broadcast, on KDKA in Pittsburgh, was not made until 1920. In 1921 there were only thirty-one stations in the entire United States. It is also difficult to imagine that the first significant network broadcasts did not take place until 1926, and then with only twenty-one stations on the network, the National Broadcasting Company.

Radios available today are a far cry from the bulky receivers of the 1920s, which had expensive vacuum tubes, separate speakers, two tuning knobs (before the invention of the superheterodyne receiver), and outside antennas. Conflicting broadcast frequencies and limited broadcast hours of the few stations on the air also created confusion during the 1920s. Static-free frequency modulation (FM) was still in the distant future.

SOUSA'S RESISTANCE TO RADIO

John Philip Sousa viewed the early stages of radio broadcasting with indifference, thinking it would have little effect on either him or the band. He felt that the rapport between performers and audiences could not be duplicated in functional, sound-dampened broadcasting studios.[1] Moreover, he believed that attendance at live concerts would be greatly diminished. He preferred not to broadcast because "radio kills it [the effect]."[2] The band's manager, Harry Askin, felt even stronger about the subject, as Sousa once indicated in a letter to a woman who requested that the band go on radio:

January 23, 1924
Mrs. J. C. Wall,
57 North Michigan Avenue,
Pasadena, California.
My dear Madam:
    My manager some time ago told one of the Broadcasting Companies that he would allow the Band to broadcast for a certain number of days, for $110,000, and he would not allow me, under any condition, to broadcast for less than $5,000 a performance.
    You can readily see how utterly impossible it is for me to accede to your wishes.
    With every good wish, believe me
    John Philip Sousa

He could not, however, isolate himself from the effects of radio. Income from sales of his sheet music had dropped considerably because the music was now widely available over the airwaves. In 1924 Senator Clarence Dill introduced a bill to exempt broadcasters from paying royalties on copyrighted music, a proposal that further aroused Sousa's ire. Many composers and lyricists would have felt the effect

---

1. Author interviews with Helen Sousa Abert, 1963.
2. *Cleveland Plain Dealer,* June 9, 1927.

of this bill had it passed. Irving Berlin, Victor Herbert, and Sousa, along with other influential members of the American Society of Composers, Authors and Publishers (ASCAP), appeared before a Senate committee on April 24 to state their case. The radio industry's attempt alarmed those whose livelihood was threatened, and their apprehensions were compounded by the rapid growth of the new medium.

Sousa's testimony before the committee was blunt. His position was similar to the position he took on recordings: If the radio industry (i.e., broadcasters and radio manufacturers) were making money from a creator's product, the creator should also be compensated. In his opinion, widespread broadcasting of copyrighted music without paying for it amounted to unregulated piracy. Victor Herbert testified that one of his recent tunes, "A Kiss in the Dark," was being broadcast many times each day although he did not receive a penny for it. Moreover, he said, the music had been jammed into the ears of listeners so often they were sick of it, and no one would think of buying the sheet music.[3]

A second bill, the Johnson-Newton bill, was soon introduced to Congress. This time, on May 6, 1924, fifty ASCAP members assembled in Washington to protest the new legislation. Like Dill's bill, the new one did not pass. The music creators had won their battle, thanks largely to the untiring efforts of Victor Herbert, truly a champion of composers' (and authors' and publishers') rights. Herbert died two weeks later, and Sousa took his place as vice president of ASCAP.

MEETING THE MICROPHONE

Sousa's concerts had always been performed without amplification, so he never had occasion to use a microphone, a relatively new inven-

tion. It was a new experience for him when he was asked to make brief personal appearances on local radio stations where the band traveled. He did not know how to act in front of a microphone. For the first time, he could not enjoy the reaction of his audiences or know how many people might be listening.

When the band was in Milwaukee for a concert in 1927, Sousa was invited to speak on WTJM on Sunday, November 6, his birthday. His question to the program manager on how he should commence his talk was unintentionally humorous ("Am I supposed to lead with the Lord's Prayer?") and picked up by newspapers across the country. When appearing on local stations Sousa would typically begin by telling stories about his experiences and go well beyond his allotted time. Band members loved to tell of how he once kept talking to a microphone for fifteen minutes after he was off the air.

FACING REALITY

Sousa eventually realized that radio was here to stay. The band was still filling concert halls, but how much longer could it last? Why should people undergo the inconvenience of dressing up, traveling to a crowded concert hall, and paying admission when they could listen to a variety of entertainments in the comfort of their own homes? Radio, along with movies, no longer silent, was forcing Sousa's competitors out of business one by one.

By 1929 he had received more than ten thousand requests to bring the band to radio. One request that particularly caught his attention was from General Motors, which wanted the band for a weekly hour-long program on NBC starting in the spring of 1929. The band would not be on tour at the time, so Sousa accepted the company's

ASCAP members not only testified before Congress in April 1924 but also appealed to President Calvin Coolidge. Here, in front of the White House, Sousa is on the far left, and Victor Herbert, ASCAP vice president, is on the far right. Next to Herbert is Gene Buck, president of ASCAP, Irving Berlin, and Jerome Kern. (U.S. Marine Band)

3. *Washington Herald,* April 28, 1924.

offer of $5,000 per broadcast.[4] He also finally issued a statement to the press: "I have, therefore, finally concluded that people want to hear us and that it would be foolish to fail to utilize this great modern invention which makes it possible for millions instead of a few thousand to listen to a concert. I am happy in the decision and am looking forward with enthusiasm to what I believe will be another thrilling adventure."[5] That meant people around the country would be able to hear the band when it was not on tour. The timing was right. The Great Depression was only a few months away and would seriously limit the extent of the band's tours.

THE FIRST BROADCAST

The first NBC network broadcast of Sousa's Band, on the evening of May 6, 1929, was one of the most ambitious such efforts of the time. Before the program ended NBC received congratulatory telegrams from nearly every state in the union. Thousands of letters and telegrams continued to pour in. Sousa was overwhelmed by the response. No

Sousa and his band (including several substitute musicians) were heard on thirty-eight radio broadcasts, beginning in 1929 and ending with his death in 1932. The programs were broadcast over the NBC network, except for two over CBS. Sousa also made a few earlier speaking appearances on local stations where the band traveled but was uncomfortable in front of a microphone. (Author's Collection)

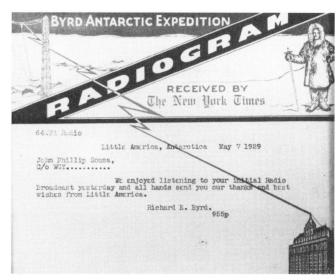

It took more than ten thousand personal requests to convince Sousa to put his band on the radio, but the response to the first broadcast was overwhelming. Admiral Richard E. Byrd, hearing the broadcast from the South Pole, sent a congratulatory radiogram. (U.S. Marine Band)

doubt Sousa then began to consider broadcasting as a possible substitute for lengthy tours because he had not made plans for a tour later in 1929.[6]

THIRTY-EIGHT BROADCASTS

The Sousa Band broadcasts provided in Table 3 were reconstructed primarily from radio schedules printed in the *New York Times*. Performances were live other than the Thanksgiving broadcast of 1929, of which the Sousa Band was a part, and the two programs for Standard Oil of Indiana, all of which were transcribed in New York for later broadcast. All programs were evening broadcasts except for the Thanksgiving program of 1929, which aired at various times during the afternoon.

THE THANKSGIVING 1929 BROADCAST

The 1929 NBC broadcast on Thanksgiving Day was a landmark in radio history, transmitted over forty-one stations in twenty-eight states. Using music prerecorded specifically for the occasion, it was the first international broadcast of that magnitude and the first time a program of European music was broadcast in America. The program's sponsor, the General Baking Company (Bond Bakers), was also proud of "firsts," having been the first to advertise its bread nationally and claiming to be the first American bakery to deliver fresh bread two times daily.

Creating the two-hour program was a major undertaking. These were the days before tape recorders, and portable recording equipment was cumbersome and impractical. During the first three decades of the twentieth century recordings were made by cutting discs (or cylinders), and the machinery to do so was massive. The Bond

4. Author interview with Frank Simon, Sousa's former solo cornetist and assistant conductor, Nov. 13, 1966. That amount was apparently paid until after the Great Depression, when the programs were reduced to thirty minutes under another sponsor. Payrolls located in the library of the U.S. Marine Band show 1931 and 1932 payments of $1,250 per broadcast.
5. *Boston Herald,* April 8, 1929.

6. Author interview with William Schneider, the band's traveling manager, Sept. 15, 1968.

Table 3. Dates of Sousa Band Radio Broadcasts, 1929–32

Date	Program	Time*	Network	Features
Mon., 6 May 1929	General Motors Family Party	9:30–10:30	NBC	Martha Atwood, soprano; male chorus on "U.S. Field Artillery March"
Mon., 13 May 1929	"	"	"	Marjorie Moody, soprano; Everett Marchall, baritone, Howard Goulden, xylophone
Mon., 20 May 1929	"	"	"	Aida Dominelli, soprano
Mon., 27 May 1929	"	"	"	Merle Alcock, contralto
Mon., 3 June 1929	"	"	"	William Tong, cornet; Howard Goulden, xylophone
Mon., 10 June 1929	"	"	"	Edward Heney, saxophone
Mon., 17 June 1929	"	"	"	Winifred Bambrick, harp
Mon., 24 June 1929	"	"	"	
Mon., 1 July 1929	"	"	"	
Mon., 7 Oct. 1929	"	"	"	Cornet solo
Mon., 14 Oct. 1929	"	"	"	Merle Alcock, contralto
Mon., 21 Oct. 1929	"	"	"	Cornet trio; xylophone solo
Mon., 28 Oct. 1929	"	"	"	
Mon., 4 Nov. 1929	"	"	"	
Mon., 25 Nov. 1929	"	"	"	Olive Kline, soprano; Allen McQuhae, tenor
Thurs., 29 Nov. 1929	Bond Bakers	Afternoon	"	Several bands and orchestras (prerecorded)
Wed., 12 Mar. 1930	Standard Oil of Indiana	9:00–10:00	CBS	Will Rogers; Louise Homer; vocalist (prerecorded)
Thurs., 9 Apr. 1931	"	"	"	(Prerecorded)
Sat., 31 Oct. 1931	Goodyear Hour	9:00–10:00	NBC	Revelers Quartet
Tues., 3 Nov. 1931	"	8:30–9:00	"	Revelers Quartet; orchestra with vocal interludes
Tues., 10 Nov. 1931	"	"	"	Revelers Quartet
Tues., 17 Nov. 1931	"	"	"	" "
Tues., 24 Nov. 1931	"	"	"	Revelers Quartet; orchestra with vocal interludes
Tues., 1 Dec. 1931	"	"	"	
Tues., 8 Dec. 1931	"	"	"	Revelers Quartet
Wed., 16 Dec. 1931	"	"	"	Revelers Quartet; orchestra with vocal interludes
Wed., 23 Dec. 1931	"	"	"	" " "
Wed., 30 Dec. 1931	"	"	"	
Wed., 6 Jan. 1932	"	"	"	Revelers Quartet
Wed., 13 Jan. 1932	"	"	"	Revelers Quartet; orchestra
Wed., 20 Jan. 1932	"	"	"	
Wed., 27 Jan. 1932	"	"	"	
Wed., 3 Feb. 1932	"	"	"	
Wed., 10 Feb. 1932	"	"	"	Revelers Quartet; orchestra with vocal interludes
Wed., 17 Feb. 1932	"	"	"	" " "
Wed., 24 Feb. 1932	"	"	"	" " "
Wed., 2 Mar. 1932	"	"	"	" " "
Wed., 9 Mar. 1932	"	"	"	Revelers Quartet; Arthur Pryor, conductor

* Eastern Standard Time except for the two Standard Oil of Indiana broadcasts, which were Central Standard Time, and the Thanksgiving 1929 program, which was broadcast in several time zones.

Bakers' project required forty-four trunks of recording apparatus, and each recording was made on location by music critic William Pier, his wife, Mary, and two recording engineers.[7] The following bands and orchestras performed: the Band of His Majesty's Royal Air Force (England); Pipes of His Majesty's Scot Guards (Scotland); Milan Symphony Orchestra (Italy); Irish Regimental Band (Ireland); Viennese Schrammel Quartet (Vienna); Budapest Gypsy Orchestra (Hungary); Swisslander Alpine Band (Switzerland); Musique de la Garde Républicaine (France); National Band of Germany; St. Germain Chamber Orchestra (France); and Sousa's Band (the United States). Five other European groups were recorded but not included on the broadcast.

Deems Taylor, the popular radio personality, composer, and music critic, was narrator for the program. Sousa's Band provided the finale, playing his own "The Stars and Stripes Forever" and "The Thunderer" and Victor Herbert's "American Fantasy." Inasmuch as there are so few recordings of Sousa's voice, it is fitting that his comments be given:

Thank you, Mr. Taylor. This is John Philip Sousa, and I'm very glad to be here with my band, representing my own country, America, on this international program. When the Bond Bakers asked me to transcribe my voice and my band for this unique occasion, I was greatly honored because I realize, as Mr. Taylor has said, that some of the finest bands in the world have been engaged to play for you. I hope, however, that you will enjoy hearing me again as much as I always enjoy playing for you. I've been asked to begin with a march that is an old favorite of mine. Maybe you will recognize it.

"The Stars and Stripes Forever" followed.

7. "Music of European Bands Crosses the Sea on Discs," New York Times, Nov. 24, 1929.

In the *New York Times* of September 22, 1929, Sousa is quoted as saying, "I had never heard a radio concert up to the time I played over it [with his band] myself." (Author's Collection)

DIFFERENT CONDITIONS

Sousa quickly discovered that performing in a radio studio with only technicians and officials present was vastly different from performing in a concert hall with the warm touch of an audience. In the first place, he could not use his regular touring musicians because they came from many different parts of the country, and although a few exceptions were made at Sousa's request, Local 802 of the American Federation of Musicians had a "six-month wait" rule before outsiders could perform in New York. Many musicians were freelancers and had irregular schedules so a different group would perform every week.[8] The result prompted one former Sousa Band member to comment after hearing the Thanksgiving Day recording many years later, "Oh— the boys were having a bad day!"[9]

Sousa was also surprised to learn that he had no control over the broadcast format. The choice of selections had to be approved each week by a network committee. After writing his own list of selections on the studio blackboard, he would usually find some were erased, shortened, or switched around by the advertising representative to allow for an introduction, commercial messages, a sign-off, and special announcements. The advertising representative for the first series of programs was Arthur Pryor Jr., son of Sousa's famous trombone soloist of many years earlier.

Even the seating arrangement had to be different from that the band used for nearly four decades, which was not optimum for microphone response. What disappointed Sousa most, however, was that he could not honor hundreds of requests or insert the quick encores that were his trademark.

A LEGACY LOST

It is tragic that none of the more than fifteen thousand concerts performed by Sousa's Band has been preserved for posterity. The closest one can come to capturing the actual sound of the band with Sousa conducting is the Thanksgiving 1929 broadcast recording, the only occasion on which he conducted his band and a microphone was used. The group, however, was not his regular band.

Collectors have never located any original disks of the Thanksgiving broadcast except for a single copy of "The Stars and Stripes Forever." Although transcriptions were sent out to approximately forty stations, by contract they had to be returned uncopied or "scored" (destroyed) by each. All copies were presumably destroyed, meaning that a link to the history of Sousa's Band is lost forever.

8. Verified by a study of payrolls in U.S. Marine Band library.
9. Author interview with saxophonist Eugene Slick, July 10, 1965.

CHAPTER SEVEN

Around the World in 1911

A RECORD VOYAGE

The Sousa Band's 352–day tour around the world in 1911 was at the time the most extensive tour undertaken by a musical organization of that size. There were fifty-six musicians, including Sousa and the two women soloists. Long before the days of air travel, the unit traveled by train and steamer for a total of 47,346 miles. The venture was a major financial risk for Sousa, who could have lost a fortune, especially if connections were missed at points where there were long periods—months—between steamer departure times. Amazingly, the tour proved profitable.

Overseas arrangements were made under the management of the Quinlan International Agency, which had offices in London, New York, and Melbourne, Australia. The Quinlan staff did quite well financially in Britain but lost money on the part of the tour extending from South Africa through New Zealand. The agency was philosophical about the loss, however, and stated they did not regret it because the tour offered premium entertainment never before available to several parts of the British Empire.

Albert A. Knecht, tenor saxophonist of the band, kept a tour diary with day-by-day entries, noting such details as incremental time changes, miles traveled between stops, and concert attendance. That remarkable documentary is reproduced through the permission of his daughter, Betty McCloskey, and other than minor corrections and rearrangements for the sake of consistency appears in this chapter as he recorded it.

Knecht's observations reveal what life was like outside the boundaries of the United States in the early part of the twentieth century, as well as the hardships the hardy musicians endured. Among the many inconveniences were extremes of temperatures at concerts, highly inadequate hotel accommodations, and lengthy sea passages on ships with no stabilization systems.

OTHER CONTRIBUTORS

Knecht was not the only one to write about the world tour, and I have added excerpts from other accounts where appropriate. Sousa's comments were extracted from his autobiography, *Marching Along*. The comments of solo cornetist Herbert L. Clarke came from his series of twelve articles, "A World's Tour with Sousa," which were published in monthly issues of the *Musical Messenger* between July 1918 and May 1919, a series revised and reprinted as "Around the World with Sousa" in *Jacobs' Band Monthly* between January 1934 and September 1935. Other comments were taken from cornetist (and later librarian) Clarence J. Russell's series of eight articles entitled "Around the World with Sousa" in *Musical America* between February 4, 1911, and November 18, 1911. Finally, at the end of the chapter is a set of verses by clarinetist Edmund A. Wall that provides a nostalgic commentary about individual members of the band. The first three pages of the diary are autographs in ink of the following names:

John Philip Sousa
Virginia Root, 227 West 13th St., New York (soprano soloist)
Nicoline Zedeler, Helmstedherst 9, Berlin W. (violin soloist)
Herbert L. Clarke, Reading, Mass. (cornet)
Edwin G. Clarke, New York (manager, substitute cornet)
J. Cameron Simmons, Victoria Road, Kilburn, London (not a band member)
Ross Millhouse, 33 E. 84th St., New York (cornet)
Guy G. Gaugler, Musician's Club, Washington, D.C. (cornet)
C. J. Russell, Pittsfield, Mass. (cornet)
Victor Welte, New York (trumpet)
Harry Freeman, New York, c/o Mr. Mrs. P.N., 210 E. 86th St. (trumpet)
J. Spindler, 144 E. 86th, New York (flute/piccolo)

Paul J. Senno, 225 Connecticut St., Buffalo, N.Y. (flute/piccolo)

Geo. Ahlborn, Strawberry Hill Ave., Norwalk, Conn. (flute/piccolo)

Arthur L. Berry, 210–E-86 St., New York (B♭ clarinet)

Hermann Hand, New York (horn)

Clarence H. Smith, Lancaster, Pa. (horn)

Arthur H. Kunze, New York (horn)

Wm. E. Laendner, 144 E. 86th St., New York (horn)

John J. Perfetto, 2029 Hughes Ave., New York (euphonium)

A. J. Garing, Box P.O., Boston, Mass., 23 Sunnyside St., Greenville, S.C. (euphonium)

Ralph Corey, 44 Cortes St., Boston (trombone)

George Lucas, New York (trombone)

Marc C. Lyon, c/o Sousa's Band, c/o Quinlan Mus. Agency, 1 West 34th St., New York (trombone, baggage handler)

Edward A. Williams, Local 161 A.F. of M., Washington, D.C. (trombone)

Arthur E. Storch, 515 W. 135th St., New York (tuba)

A. L. Griswold, 210 E. 86 St., New York (tuba)

E. Mix, Y.M.C.A., E. 86 St., New York (tuba)

A. Helleberg, 214 Dodd St., Station I, Hoboken, N.J. (tuba)

Ben Vereecken, 112 Land Courverstr, Kiel, Antwerp, Belgium (saxophone)

Albert A. Knecht, Conshohocken, Pa. (saxophone)

Stanley Lawton, c/o "Musicians Union," c/o "Magee" the Hatter, 629 S. Spring St., Los Angeles, Calif. (saxophone)

Joseph Norrito, 232 Summit Ave., Hagerstown, Md. (B♭ clarinet)

Ernest C. Gatley, Newbury, Vt. (B♭ clarinet)

Irving Davis, 9 East 101 St., New York (B♭ clarinet)

William J. Robinson, 11 Crescent Ave., Buffalo, N.Y. (B♭ clarinet)

Jim Lawnham, 146 E. 86 St., New York (B♭ clarinet)

Harry Baldwin, 402 East 1st Ave., Mitchell, S.D. (B♭ clarinet)

George C. Kampke, 2155–86th St., Brooklyn, N.Y. (B♭ clarinet)

J. S. Lomas, 253 N. James St., Hamilton, Ont. (B♭ clarinet)

W. E. Sheaffer, Palmyra, N.Y. (B♭ clarinet)

Wm. H. Culley, Chicago, Ill. (B♭ clarinet)

C. R. Livingston, Marathon, N.Y. (B♭ clarinet)

Edmund A. Wall, 1307 College Ave., New York (B♭ clarinet)

Walter D. Collins, 708 E. Fayette St., Syracuse, N.Y. (B♭ clarinet)

Sol. Eckstein, 2323 N. 13th St., Philadelphia (B♭ clarinet)

Joseph Kapralek, 1709 E. Eager St., Baltimore (E♭ clarinet)

Rene Magnant, St. Jerome, Que. (alto clarinet)

Carl Schroeder, 1042 First Ave., New York (bass clarinet, librarian)

P. Lephilibert, 112 E. 32nd St., New York (oboe)

Joseph Gerard, Local 310, New York (oboe)

O. Modess, 146 E. 86. St., New York (bassoon)

W. H. Decker, 367 S. Washington St., Tiffin Ohio (bassoon)

G. H. Cunnington, 1816 Dayton Ave., St. Paul (bassoon)

J. L. Marthage, 103 Joiner St., Rochester, N.Y. (harp)

M. F. Haynes, 183 Campbell Ave., Revere, Mass. (percussion)

William Lowe, 37 Ridge Ave., Rutherford, N.J. (percussion, physician)

Frank A. Snow, Park Theatre, Boston (percussion)

Louis Friedrich, 60 Essex Ave., Bloomfield, N.J. (not a band member)

Missing from the autographs is James Hewson, Sousa's valet, who traveled with the band as far as England. Nonmusicians accompanying the tour included Jane Sousa; the two Sousa daughters, Jane Priscilla and Helen; Mrs. Root, mother of the soprano soloist Virginia Root, who may have acted as chaperone for the two single women soloists; and the wives of band members A. J. Garing, Lyon Marc, and Victor Welte.

The Diary of Albert A. Knecht

Dec. 24th, Saturday. 1910.

Left Conshohocken at 7:08 Changing at Columbia Ave. Station in Philda. taking the 8 o'clock train over the P.&R.R.R. for New York. A fog hanging over the Hudson River caused 20 minutes delay to the Ferry in crossing to New York. Arrived at 23rd St. at 10:30. Boarded the steamer "Baltic" White Star Line at 10:40. Dock 60 foot of 19th St. Owing to a rain the band did not play when leaving the wharf as has been the custom when leaving the country.

The boat sailed at 12:10 during the rain storm which continued all day. Sea is rather smooth but at that there was motion enough to send some of the boys to the rail feeding the fish.

I felt a bit queer at times but passed the day without becoming seasick. The list of passengers on the boat is very light owing I suppose to the holiday season. Guy Gaugler is my cabin mate. Cabin 195. Turned in early about 8:30 p.m.

Clock set ahead 31 minutes at midnight.

Mileage Conshohocken to New York City 103.

Dec. 25th (Christmas), Sunday.

Arose at 7:30 feeling fine. Day is very dull with a cold wind blowing. No rain but very heavy clouds hanging low make Christmas Day look anything but cheerful. The sea is very choppy causing a lot of seasickness. The dining tables are beginning to show vacant chairs. Ship sailed 330 miles, the mileage being taken on all boats at 12 o'clock noon. I lost in the first pool fixed up by Mark Lyon. We have but 104 passengers in the cabin list. J. B. Ransom is Commander of the "Baltic." I attended service in the cabin held by the Chaplain at 10. a.m. Had a grand and glorious dinner at 6 p.m. The heavy clouds passed away, and now at 7 p.m. everything is clear, permitting a walk on deck. Deck games will no doubt start tomorrow, as we expect a fine day. Six meals are served here daily. Mr. & Mrs. Sousa passed around a box of cigars and a basket of fruit as their Christmas present to the boys. Retired at 11 o'clock well tired out.

Clock moved forward 32 minutes at midnight.

Mileage 330.

Dec. 26th, Monday.

Awake and out at 7:30 a.m. feeling good. The sky is again cloudy, but no rain, while a fine spring-like breeze made the deck promenade enjoyable. The deck-games are all full handed and working overtime.

The sea has calmed down considerable, and there is scarcely any noticeable motion to the boat. No seasickness today. Sun peeped thro the clouds at noon, and I am able to take a couple pictures with the camera.

At about 3 p.m. it turned very cold, making overcoats necessary. Oiled the springs of my saxophone, which I took from the trunk in the hold. I lost in the pool today.

At 11:15 p.m. we sighted the steamer "Oceanic" bound for New York. The two steamers exchanged signal rockets.

Clock moved forward 33 minutes at midnight.

Mileage 390.

Dec. 27th, Tuesday.

Arose at 7:30, and after breakfast spent 2 hours at the deck games. The ocean is very quiet almost like a mill-pond. A cold breeze is blowing making overcoats again necessary. The boys have their instruments out doing some practice. I lost in two pools today. We have been sailing on the banks of Newfoundland all day, running into no fog until tonight at 10 o'clock, when the fog horn sounded at intervals of one minute. Wind has changed from the N.E. to the S.W. and a heavy blow is expected. Marconi wireless reported to be in communication with the steamer "Cedric" 600 miles to the East.

Clock moved forward 33 minutes at midnight.

Mileage 392.

Dec. 28th, Wednesday.

Arose at 7:30. Weather is moderate. Partly cloudy, with a fine spring-like breeze blowing from the S.W. The sea is about like yesterday, causing no motion to the boat noticeable. The expected storm didn't materialize, much to the disappointment of a good many people making their first ocean trip and who are anxious to see a storm at sea. I would like to see one myself, as this continued good weather is growing monotonous. A sudden squall came up at 10:45 a.m. and lasted about 5 minutes. I had opened the porthole, and the 5 minutes of the squall was significant to mess up things in our cabin and get everything wet. A good strong wind followed up the squall, but the sun came out and dried up the wet on deck. After lunch we had an hour playing hand ball on deck, and it was the best workout I have had on the trip so far. I lost in three pools today, including one I made myself. We have a 10:30 rehearsal called for tomorrow morning in preparation of the concert to be given on the boat Friday evening. An orchestra of 5 men on the boat gives concerts every morning and evening, and they play very well. Spent the evening playing cards and managed to turn in at 11.

Clock set forward 36 minutes at midnight.

Mileage 384.

Dec. 29th, Thursday.

The bath steward got me out at 7 o'clock to take a hot sea water bath. I felt anything like getting up, as I put in a strenuous day yesterday playing all the games aboard. The bath fixed me up fine, as it helped take out the kinks in my muscles. The weather today is cloudy, and a S. East breeze is blowing. Sea is moderate just about like the two previous days. Wearing an overcoat while walking on deck would start a perspiration. I lost in two pools. Luck is against me, but my turn will come yet. Our rehearsal of the band lasted an hour and a half, from 10:30 till 12. I had another good workout this afternoon with the hand ball for an hour. Time passes quickly on a trip of this kind, and it doesn't seem possible that we have been on the boat nearly six days. The passengers are a congenial set, and that helps some. Our trip so far has been pleasant, and I believe a good many people will hate to leave when we land at Liverpool.

Clock moved ahead 40 minutes at midnight.

Mileage 392.

Dec. 30th, Friday.

Arose at the usual hour 7:30 and after breakfast took a half hour's walk on deck. Weather about the same. Cloudy with a mild breeze from the South. No overcoats necessary. The sea is calm, and the boat is making good time sailing as if we were on a lake. Everyone is on hand for their meals, while seasickness seems to be a lost art with this crowd. Rehearsal from 10:30 to 11:30. I lost in two pools. The pleasure was mine to meet Mr. Gilbert Balfour the Marconi wireless operator on this boat. Ernest Gately introduced me, and we three had a very interesting conversation. Mr. Balfour explained the Wireless System to us, which seems to be very simple in its construction. The "Baltic" is the boat that went to the rescue of the ill-fated steamer "Republic" of which Jack Binns was the accredited hero and who afterward cleaned up in vaudeville. While all the honors were showered on Binns for his work at that time, my idea is that this man Balfour, a modest unassuming person, is a greater hero than Binns. Balfour was at that time the junior operator on the boat, and he found his chief asleep while on duty when he should have been awake and on the job. The machine flashed the frantic appeals for aid received from Binns an hour while the chief sat sleeping before Balfour came into the room. Upon being awakened, the Chief collapsed knowing well the disgrace he bore and was of no use for work. Balfour then went to work on the tedious job of locating the "Republic" by wireless, as the terrible fog prevented the deck officers from seeing anything. The work of transferring the passengers was tedious as a sea was running from 20 to 30 feet high, but it was accomplished successfully, and they were taken into New York. Balfour being at the machine all the while or about 53 hours. The steamer "Florida" is the boat that rammed the "Republic."

Very few people have heard of what this man Balfour did simply because he is not of a very showy nature.

For his work during that accident his reward was a gold medal, a piece of parchment, and the position as chief operator on this boat. He is considered one of the best men in the employ of the Marconi Company and has refused the position as chief operator on the steamer "Lusitania." He likes this boat, "Baltic." Mr. Balfour explained very plainly the Marconi System, and it is wonderful in its simplicity.

The afternoon was spent in another workout on deck playing ball. Tonight at 9 o'clock the band concert was given in the First Saloon. A collection of $125.00 was taken for the aid of the Seamen's Charities Liverpool and New York. Considering the number of passengers, not more than 170, the benefit was a success. Gen. Frederick W. Benson K.C.B. acted as toastmaster.

Clock moved forward 41 minutes at midnight.

Mileage 397.

Dec. 31st, Saturday.

Arose at 9:30 having overslept myself and also breakfast. Weather today is the finest we have had on the voyage. I lost in two pools again. Boat made 389 miles. Clock moved forward 53 minutes at 2:30 p.m. Land sighted at 1:30 p.m. Coast of Ireland. We passed the Fastnet Light-House at 5:05 with 60 miles to go before we reach Queenstown. There are 4,000 bags of mail to go off there, and the men have been working since 8 o'clock this morning taking it out of the hold. Arrived at Queenstown 9 o'clock. We stopped in the Harbor, and a lighter came alongside, taking off passengers and mail. Stop of 20 minutes was made. At midnight, a lot of the boys with instruments made a parade all over the ship celebrating the arrival of the New Year. The Captain was serenaded. After that was over, I went down into the glory hold where the stewards were having a celebration all to themselves. They put over a regular vaudeville show that was very good. I finally went to bed at 1:30 a.m.

Mileage 389.

Jan. 1st, Saturday. 1911.

Weather cloudy with a moderate sea. We had 133 miles to make from yesterday noon until we stopped at Queenstown. Arrived Liverpool at 11:15. Disembarked at 12:05.

Hand baggage and trunks were examined by customs, and we left by the London and Great Western R.R. at 12:55, arriving at the Euston Station at 5 o'clock. The equipment of trains here is so much different to the American trains that they looked like a great big joke to me. The engines are smaller and built on different lines than on our own roads, and the coaches are also different. The cars are built into compartments with doors on the side leading to a running board on the outside. But the train made very good time from Liverpool to London. This piece of track is considered the best in England, and I must say it was very good. Had lunch on the train in the dining car. On arriving in London, I took a taxi to the Central Hotel, located on Percy Street off Tottenham Court Road W. I have a nice room with electric light, but no heat except the open fire place, which is as good as nothing to me.

Went to the Alhambra in the evening and heard a concert by the Coldstream Guards Band. Conductor Lieut. J. Mackenzie-Rogan. They played well in their style and I enjoyed a very pleasant evening. After the concert, I was invited to the London Motor Club by a Mr. Morrison, and together with about 8 more of our boys we had a good time. Turned in at 11:15 after spending my first six hours in London very pleasantly.

Mileage Boat 3,092. Train Liverpool to London 201.

U.S. miles New York to Liverpool 3,309.

Jan. 2nd, Monday. London.

We had a rehearsal at 11 o'clock at Queen's Hall, which was as cold as everything else I have seen in England.

Matinee at 3, and evening concert at 8 to fair houses. But what was lacking in number made up in the way we were received.

[Clarke]: They [band members] were told to report the next morning for rehearsal at Queen's Hall, where we were to play a week's engagement; and when the time arrived, and all the men present, the first playing sounded rather strange, after the sea voyage, during which time there was very little practice of any kind, and especially those of the band who were not good sailors seemed weak, but so glad to get on land once more. However, it did not take long to brush up, and as every one of us was anxious to do his best at the first performance, which was to be that same evening, we got down to work and forgot that the voyage had weakened our "embouchures," although our work was mighty hard for the first few days on account of the rest.[1]

They were most generous in applause, and we handed over two rattling good concerts. The day is dull and damp, while a rain set in towards evening. I had lunch at the Black Horse Cafe and dinner at Pinolis on Waldour St. 17. I turned in at 12 o'clock well tired out.

Jan. 3rd, Tuesday. London.

The sun made valiant attempts to get thro the clouds and fog this morning, but the best it could do was to show a very pretty red globe like a red painted circle in the sky. I went to Rudall Carte Co. and purchased pads and felt for Jos. Small, also some flute solos which I had sent direct to him from the house. I then did some shopping along Oxford St., buying cutlery etc. Stopped in to see Alfred Hayes on Old Bond St. about having my saxophone repaired. I bought a set of pads and a set of springs there.

Matinee at 3 to a fair house. Had dinner at Paganis Italian Restaurant on Great Portland Street. Concert at 8.

Business doesn't seem to improve, but at that it isn't bad. The people go almost crazy over our music. Some of the boys are complaining of feeling homesick. This terrible cold that goes right thro to the bone has something to do with it.

Turned in at 12 o'clock.

Jan. 4th, Wednesday. London.

Started for Alfred Hayes Co. after breakfast with my saxophone to have it repaired. From there, I took a bus to Rudall Carte's and received the goods I ordered yesterday. They showed me a trumpet which I tried out. I was invited to make their place my headquarters while in London. At 2 o'clock, my saxophone was ready for me at Hayes' place, and I was in time for the matinee.

Business much better at today's concerts. Weather cold and damp. A light rain started this evening making walking bad. A few of we boys, six in all, Marthage, Senno, Gately, Decker, Schaeffer and myself decided to form a club. Dues to be paid weekly and a banquet given on our return to American soil.

Jan. 5th, Thursday. London.

After breakfast, I started out with Mix, Laendner and Lawton on my first sight-seeing trip of London. We first visited the St. Paul's Cathedral, the second largest in the world. Passed the Mansion House Lord Mayor's home, then the Bank of England, a feature being their method used formerly of sinking the vault containing the currency each night in water. We passed thro Cheapside on our way to the London Tower. One shilling admission is charged to the London Tower Grounds. Our first interesting sight was the Traitor's Gate, thro which prisoners were brought into the Tower. Water from the Thames was let in, permitting the entrance of prisoners by boat. Then we walked thro the Jewel House, where I saw a most beautiful collection of old and modern gems and gold ornaments. It is all the property of the Government and very carefully guarded. One piece called The Stars of Africa was presented to King Edward VII by the Transvaal Gov. The large diamond in this piece weighs 516½ carats. Not very large well I guess. Coming out of the Jewel House, we had a look at the Thames River and the Tower Bridge. Upon entering the Tower Armouries at the foot of the spiral stairway, an inscription tells of the tradition connected with the stairs. The bones of Edward the 5th and his brother were supposed to have been found under the stairs. They were removed to the Westminster Abbey.

At the top of the stairs, we entered the St. Paul's Chapel. We then passed into the chamber containing the instruments of torture used long ago, including the Heading axe used in 1679. I ran my fingers over the blade edge. Lord Lovat was beheaded with this axe on April 9th, 1747. I saw the blanket that Gen. Wolfe died in at Quebec. The Coronation robes of the late King Edward and his Queen Alexandra Aug. 9th, 1902 were exhibited in a glass case. Walked up another stairway to the Horse Armouries, where we saw all kinds of ancient armour. King Henry VIII armour on exhibition weighs over 100 lbs. That finished our look at

---

1. Herbert L. Clarke, "A World's Tour with Sousa," *Musical Messenger,* July 1918, 4.

the Tower. Coming out I stood on the site of the scaffold on which was executed Queen Anne Boleyn May 19th, 1536. In the Beauchamp Tower, an interesting thing is the markings made on the walls by the prisoners. We then walked slowly out of the grounds and rode back to the hotel well tired out.

Matinee at 3. Evening at 8.

Business continues to improve.

Jan. 6th, Friday. London.

Arose at 9 o'clock, and the day is dull with a fog threatening. After breakfast, Arthur Kunze, Jos. Gerard and I started out to find White Hall, where the British Regulars have guard-mount at 10:30. In asking directions, Kunze inquired the way to White Chapel. It was a blunder on his part and upon arriving at the part of the City called White Chapel, we found ourselves in a very tough portion of the town, and near the scene of the recent riots and fight between two anarchists vs. the police and soldiers. Thro the mistake we missed guard mount but took a motor bus to the Westminster Abbey, passing Parliament House on the way. Services were being held in the Abbey when we arrived there, and I was fortunate in hearing a very excellent male choir and a fine pipe organ. Several boy sopranos were exceptionally good. After the services, we took a hurried look about the most wonderful Church I was ever in. They have buried right in the building the remains of former kings, queens and noblemen of England together with the most prominent and illustrious people of the country in years gone by. Wonderful works of sculpture are here in commemoration of great men and women. The different sights were many, too much in fact to fully realize its magnitude during my short visit of about 45 minutes.

The following are just a few of the tombs of former great and historic men that I can remember on my hurried glance while walking. Richard III, the two princes nephews of Richard III, whom he killed in the London Tower, hiding their bodies beneath the foot of the stairway. The bodies were found about 200 years after by workmen making repairs and then transferred to the Abbey. Mary Queen of Scots who was beheaded. Queen Elizabeth and Anne. The Duke of Buckingham. Oliver Cromwell was buried here for 2 years when his body was taken out. Handel, Shakespeare and Henry Irving are buried here with countless other brilliant men of their day. I saw the coronation chair on which all Kings of England are crowned. Under the seat rests a stone from Pharoah's tomb and called the "stone of destiny."

A heavy downpour of rain began at 11:30 and continued during the day.

Concerts at 3 and 8 to good business.

The Club which was spoken of on Wednesday was finally started tonight. Gately was elected President, and I was elected Secretary and Treasurer. We have six members to start with. A name for the club is to be decided later. A social session followed the meeting. I turned in at 1:45 a.m.

Jan. 7th, Saturday. London.

The weather today is the best since our arrival in London. The mist and fog is less intense, and the sun has had half a chance. Guy Gaugler and I visited the Parliament Bldgs, taking a look at the House of Lords and the House of Commons Chamber, Whitehall parade grounds and Trafalgar Square. I took a picture of Gaugler standing in front of a tramcar from Westminster Bridge, also one of the two horse-guards mounted standing in front of Whitehall. Route sheets were distributed for our English tour.

Matinee at 3 and evening concert at 8. The band was received very well at both performances.

Sousa and Thomas Quinlan of the Quinlan International Agency. (Author's Collection, courtesy of Betty McCloskey)

[Clarke]: We played twice daily during the first week to crowded houses, and our house receipts amounted to some forty-five hundred pounds sterling, or approximately $22,500. Not bad for the first week. . . . The band was received with great enthusiasm at each concert, and before the end of the week every house was sold out long before we started to play; and I remember one night, besides the ten programmed numbers, I counted just thirty-seven! So many encores were demanded.

[Russell]: Mr. Sousa presented a different program each day and on Friday, by request, played an entire program of his own compositions, which proved to be the most popular program of the week. Needless to say, encore after encore was demanded and granted throughout the week.[2]

We held another meeting of the club and a social session after adjourning at 1:35.

Jan. 8th, Sunday. London.

Attended High Mass at the Westminster Cathedral. The Cathedral is one of the most wonderful Catholic churches I have yet visited in all my travels.

Our club met at 1 o'clock to see London by auto. The first stop was at Hyde Park, across which we walked, stopping at the Albert Memorial Monument. We visited the Albert Victorian "Museum," where I saw the original score of "Hear My Prayer" by Mendelssohn, written in 1871. We passed a monument erected to Cardinal Newman on our way back standing in front of the Brompton Oratory. Beggars are scarce on the London streets, but today I ran across one a woman blind but assisted by a trained fox terrier. As I dropped a coin in the tin cup the dog licked my hand as if thanking me for the donation.

The day is miserable, so we returned to the hotel early. We six had dinner at the Hotel Bedford Head in Tottenham Court Road. Turned in early to rest up thoroughly for travel that commences tomorrow. I have spent one week in London and will say that outside of miserable weather I enjoyed myself very much.

Jan. 9th, Monday. Hastings.

Called at 6:30. Left London at 9 o'clock (Victoria Station) on the London Brighton and So. Coast R.R. Arrived in Hastings at 11:30. The club

2. Herbert L. Clarke, "A World's Tour with Sousa," *Musical Messenger,* Aug. 8, 1918, 1; Clarence J. Russell, "Around the World with Sousa," *Musical American,* Feb. 4, 1911, 15.

occupied a compartment and tried to sing the popular songs of the day. Oh! what a headache. I am stopping at the Provincial Hotel, which is right good. The day is fierce a heavy rain having set in. Concerts at 3 & 8 in the Royal Concert Hall. Hastings is a sea-coast town and at one time one of the most prosperous seashore resorts on the English coast, but time has worked its changes, so the Hastings is on the downward slide of its career. Tonight I became initiated into the candle circuit hotels and I must say that it is not a bit pleasant going to bed in a cold room by candle light.

Mileage London to Hastings 76.

Jan. 10th, Tuesday. Eastbourne.

Had a good rest and was up at 9:45. Train left at 11:30 for Eastbourne over the L.B.&.S.C.R.R., arriving at 12:50. The day is fine, and traveling was more enjoyable.

Concerts at 3 and 8 at Floral Hall to very big houses. The audiences were composed of very aristocratic people. The Floral Hall, located in Devonshire Park, is very pretty, and in fact the whole city is beautiful, being about the finest resort in England on the sea-coast. I am stopping at the Bijou Hotel. After our night concert, three of we boys stopped in a theatre and saw the last act of "The Merry Widow." There were no medals on the production.

Mileage Hastings to Eastbourne 20.

Jan. 11th, Wednesday. Brighton.

Awake at 8:30 and the room felt like an ice-box positively the coldest proposition I was ever up against. Left Eastbourne at 11 o'clock, arriving in Brighton at 12:15. Stopping with Thos. Stabbins, clarinetist with the Brighton Orchestra. 35 Middle St. This house was built by the Duke of Cumberland brother of King George 4th. The two cellars under it were used as prisons. It was built in 1770.

Concert to good business at 3 & 8 in the Dome. The Dome was built and used as a riding school by King George 4th. Brighton is another swell seashore resort. The rainy weather prevented me from having a look at the fine beach front. The club held a meeting tonight.

Mileage Eastbourne to Brighton 23.

Jan. 12th, Thursday. Portsmouth.

The day is damp and rainy. A heavy wind is blowing, and on the spot where we boys were standing awaiting a train car for the station a minute after boarding the car, a heavy tree was snapped off by the wind and crashed to the ground. A very narrow escape for the club members. We left Brighton at 10:15 on the L.B.&.S.C.R.R., arriving in Portsmouth at 12:10 over 20 minutes late. The club located in very nice quarters at the Royal Hotel on Commercial Road. The weather cleared, and it has turned extremely cold.

The Portland Hall, where we played concerts at 3 & 8 to good business, is located in South-Sea. The hall was very cold, and it was painful to work on our cold instruments as the fingers would almost freeze. At the night concert the temperature of the hall was a little better, as the management decided to put in a couple oil heaters. Mark Lyon made a hit carrying off the stage a hot stove right before the concert. Portsmouth is a great sea-port town. The British battleships make this harbor their principal port.

Mileage Brighton to Portsmouth 45.

Jan. 13th, Friday. Southampton.

The day is fine and suited to take a couple pictures before the train pulled out. We left Portsmouth at 11:10, arriving in Southampton at 12:30. The club is stopping at the Bannister Hotel. My room is only fairly good and faces Queen's Park.

We played a matinee at the Palace Theatre to a big house. At night we played in the Hartley Hall to a fair sized audience.

Hartley Hall is very small, and we boys were sitting almost on top of one another on the small stage. I bought a woolen vest here, paying 10/6 a half guinea for it. A heavy vest is very necessary in this weather. After the night concert, we were invited to the Palace Theatre to see what they call here a pantomime entitled "Babes in the Woods." The meaning of pantomime is different from our idea of the word at home. This show was a regular musical extravaganza as we know them by having their comedians, singers, dancers etc. But the show was far from being up to the standard of our American productions. But they had about 12 men in the orchestra never the less considering that the theatre is small and not a real first-class house. Upon making inquiry, I learned that the salary of the orchestra boys average from 30 to 40 shillings a week. After the show, Marthage, Senno, Decker and myself had some very fine stout, after which I had some fun. Went to my refrigerator cold storage room at 12:30.

Mileage Portsmouth to Southampton 30.

Jan. 14th, Saturday. Bournemouth.

The day opened bright, sunny and cold. Our train left Southampton at 11:55, arriving in Bournemouth over the London and So. Western R.R. at 1:15. We made a 10-minute stop at Lyndhurst Inc., where passengers for Isle of Wight change trains. We had a game of handball on the station platform, which put a little heat into my body and overcoming the chill I had been sitting in all morning. Stopping at the Macey Hotel. As is customary here, I have given my order for tomorrow morning's breakfast. I don't know whether I will feel like having what I had ordered tomorrow morning but it doesn't matter. It's up to me.

We played at the Winter Gardens, about a mile from my hotel, giving concerts at 3 and 8 to very big business. Dan Godfrey Jr. was in the audience at the matinee. Ed Clarke our manager held over our salaries, giving for his reason that some of the men were playing dice. We will shortly have a Sunday School band here, altho it will be a hard proposition for Clarke with men like Griswold, Modess, Kunze to reform. This town is the most beautiful we have yet visited, and I am sorry our engagement here is not of longer duration.

Mileage Southampton to Bournemouth 28.

Jan. 15th, Sunday. London.

Train left at 8:03 over the L.&S.W.R.R. Therefore I was up at 7 o'clock. The cold was intense, but a nice pitcher of hot water helped out considerably. Owing to a heavy fog, the train was late in arriving. 11:30 instead of 10:30. We took a motor bus over to the Central Hotel and having a look into our trunks which we left there for the week. The principal news was the account of a wild auto ride by Lawton and Cunnington, who missed the train at Bournemouth. They left the town at 10:25 to make the 124 miles into London before matinee time at 3:30. It was a long cold drive, but they managed to pull up to the stage door of the Palladium at 3:05 in time for the concert. The trip cost them £3 apiece.

The Palladium just opened and brand new is the finest house we have yet played, and the building was packed. We had barely time to eat supper before the night concert at 7 o'clock in the Queen's Hall. Restaurants close during certain hours on Sunday and only open at 6 o'clock.

Business big at the evening concert.

Mileage Bournemouth to London 123.

Jan. 16th, Monday. Mat. Torquay. Eve. Exeter

Called at 5:30, and after a struggle with the cold managed to get up and have breakfast at 6:15. About 20 of us chartered a big sight-seeing auto to take us to the station, but at the appointed time the car didn't put in its appearance. We then all made our way to the Paddington Station as best we could. Decker, Marthage, Gately and myself took a hansom and made the train at the far distant station. Three of the boys missed the train, which left at 7:30 over the Great Western R.R., arriving in Torquay at 1:45.

We played to a packed house in the Bath Saloons, leaving by special train "immediately after" at 5:55, arriving in Exeter at 7:32. Walter Schaeffer engaged rooms for us at the Elmfield Hotel, where we ate supper in a hurry and quickly made our way to the New Queen's Hall, where we started our concert at 8:22, playing to a packed house. The proprietor of the hotel refused to put a fire in our rooms, being afraid that we might be a crowd of loafers and perhaps sit up all night and play cards, which might disturb the other guests. Anyone that travels like we do thank their stars to be able to turn in after the concert. Our club meeting called for tonight was postponed, because we are dainty creatures, and in these rooms our toes might be frost bitten were we to sit about.

Mileage London to Torquay 200. Torquay to Exeter 26. Total 226.

Jan. 17th, Tuesday. Plymouth.

Train pulled out at 10:45 on the Great Western R.R., arriving in Plymouth at 12:10. We are stopping at the Dingler Hotel. Preceding the violin solo number at the concert this afternoon, Mr. Russell announced that Miss Zedeler was suffering from an attack of gastrutis and would be unable to appear. At the night concert, John Perfetto was substituted with a euphonium solo.

[Clarke]: After the concert was over we learned that both of our lady soloists had been overcome by escaping gas in their dressing room, and when their door was forced open both ladies were found in an unconscious state, and it took some time to resuscitate them. This almost proved fatal to Miss Zedeler, who was placed under the care of a physician at the hotel; and neither of the soloists were able to appear for the evening's concert, nor were they in good condition for some days after. But we were all glad that, through the timely breaking in of their door, opening the windows and getting them out of the hall, their lives were saved.[3]

Concerts at 3 & 8 in the Guild Hall to packed houses. This town is quite historical, but owing to lack of time I was unable to go sightseeing. Club meeting tonight.

Mileage Exeter to Plymouth 52.

Jan. 18th, Wednesday. Mat. Bath. Eve. Bristol.

We left Plymouth at 8:30, arriving in Bath at 12:30. The day is fine, and I took advantage of an hour to spare before the matinee to take a look at the Old Roman Baths. They were built in the year 40 A.D. by the Romans during their invasion of England, being in possession of the country for 3 or 4 centuries. As time wore on, the baths were filled in and finally forgotten. It has only been 28 years ago that traces of the Roman Architecture was discovered, which eventually led to the digging out of the baths. The water that supplies the bath comes out naturally hot from the only hot spring in England with a temperature of 120 degrees. The Old Roman Baths are not used, but a modern bath house is unequalled in its appointments. A guide escorted we boys about the place, the most interesting feature being the different ideas used by the Romans in construction. Mix took pictures of the boys standing in different places. On one picture the boys climbed up on the pedestals

that formerly supported statues around the bath pool. We played the Palace Theatre to good business at the matinee. Train left Bath at 5:51, arriving in Bristol at 6:10. Stopping at a regular "Jolly Robbers" Hotel called the Royal Victoria.

Concert this evening at the Coliseum to a packed house of about 6,000 people. Miss Zedeler received a great reception from the boys when she came back on the job tonight. After the concert tonight, Gus Helleberg and myself lost our way, but we took a taxi back to the hotel and all was well.

Mileage Plymouth to Bath 142. Bath to Bristol 11. Total 153.

Jan. 19th, Thursday. Mat. Aberdare. Eve. Merthyr Tydfil.

Left Bristol at 9:34 on the G.W.R.R. and traveled thro a very dense fog. It was impossible at times to see the fence at the side of the railroad. We passed thro the Severn Tunnel built under the Severn River and the longest tunnel in England, about four miles long. Arrived in Aberdare at 12:19. We are now in Wales, and a marked difference I find in everything from England. The audience, for instance, which packed the Market Hall at the matinee, was much more music loving than in England. During the "Welsh Rhapsody," the people went almost frantic with enthusiasm. The day is cold and disagreeable. Our steward of the club "Mons" Decker put in a supply of food for supper during our trip to Merthyr Tydfil. We arrived at 7:25, and the concert went on at 8:22 at the Drill Hall.

An accident which might have resulted seriously to someone happened here. The stage in the Drill Hall being too small to accommodate the whole band was enlarged by an extension erected in front. It was a frail looking affair, and about 22 of the men were seated on it together with Mr. Sousa. When the six trombones went to the front during "The Fairest of the Fair" march, the platform collapsed and dropped nearly 5 feet to the floor. The platform split in half, and only the brass side went down. That caused Mr. Sousa to fall all the way to the ground with the music rack and trunk to fall after him. Mr. Sousa struck the floor on his back and Millhouse, Hand and Smith prevented the trunk and rack from striking him, which would have caused a serious injury. In the mix up Mr. Sousa was concerned mostly over his glasses. It certainly was a mess to look at musicians, instruments, music, music stands and boards all jumbled together, and it was a miracle that Mr. Sousa escaped being hurt beyond a few bruises. The only accident of more consequence was a sprained thumb to Mr. Garing. We learned afterwards that the contractor who built the stage has a double business, carpenter and undertaker. Never again will he build a platform for Sousa's Band.

[Sousa]: My conducting stand collapsed and I was buried seven feet beneath it. It was a breath-snatching sensation to fall seven feet below the floor with nothing to catch on to. I went down in a cloud of dust and debris and the prima donna, Miss Root, on hearing the crash, believed I had been killed and rushed out on the stage, screaming. I quickly righted myself, however, crawled up out of the depths, bowed to the audience, and said, "We will now continue." Calmly, we finished the programme.

[Clarke]: I noticed several cracks underneath me several times during the concert, but paid little attention to these sounds. . . . There was a crash as the men walked out in front of the new structure on the brass side, one-half of the new addition coming down and burying Mr. Sousa, with about ten of us heavy men, beneath the broken timbers. Fortunately, no one was injured seriously, except Mr. Sousa, who fell on his shoulder, and could not extricate himself without help. After he was placed upon his feet, and his eyeglasses recovered from the wreckage,

3. Herbert L. Clarke, "A World's Tour with Sousa," *Musical Messenger,* Sept. 1918, 1.

the concert was resumed, and finished as usual without a flaw, most of the men on the stage proper and others below with the ruins.[4]

Ed Williams went on to Swansea to fix and engage rooms for the boys, but the club decided to look for our own place. We left Merthyr Tydfil after the night concert at 10:35, arriving in Swansea at 12:20 only to find the City locked tight all hotels closed and our chances to get rooms very bad. Luck was with us and we found a man that took us to the Royal Hotel, where I have the best room so far in England. Turned in at 1:30 after a very hard day, as we were in four towns, played two concerts besides having plenty of excitement.

Mileage Bristol to Aberdare 66. Aberdare to Merthyr Tydfil 8. Merthyr Tydfil to Swansea 30. Total 114.

Jan. 20th, Friday. Swansea.

Awake at 11 o'clock when Ed Wall gave me a bunch of American mail to distribute to the boys stopping here. The extreme cold moderated somewhat today. Matinee at 3 in the Albert Hall after which we had a rehearsal on the Sunday program for London.

Evening concert at 8 o'clock. Business good.

Jan. 21st, Saturday. Mat. Cardiff. Eve. Newport.

We left Swansea at 10:15, arriving in Cardiff at 11:40. A light rain made walking miserable, but a party of the boys went into the Cardiff Castle, which was built in the 12th Century. We had a look into the famous dungeon. Mix took a couple pictures, one as we were standing on the steps leading to the last stronghold, a sort of fort which is erected in the center of the grounds and which in event of an enemy capturing the outer defenses a good stronghold would be relied upon to put up a last fight. It was surrounded by a moat with drawbridges and all the other necessary arrangements. It is the most interesting thing I have visited since leaving London.

We played to good business at the Palace Theatre at 3 o'clock.

Caught the 5:45 train to Newport, arriving at 6:20. I am stopping at Morrich's Hotel, which is very good.

Concert at Stow Hill Rink at 8 o'clock to good business.

Mileage Swansea to Cardiff 45. Cardiff to Newport 11. Total 56.

Jan. 22nd, Sunday. London.

Called at 6 o'clock and caught the 6:45 train on the G.W.R.R. Had breakfast on the train, arriving in London at 9:15 Paddington Station. Took the Metropolitan Underground train to Euston Road Station and walked from there to the Central Hotel. A heavy yellow fog was hanging at 10:30 when Decker and I took a bus to the Brompton Oratory, hearing high mass. The choir in this Church is by far the finest I have ever heard in my life. Memories of that choir will, I hope, remain with me for years. At 2 o'clock, when I started for the Palladium, (where we gave concerts at 3 & 7) the fog turned from yellow to black and it was as dark as any night. Street lights were lit, and it felt strange to be going to a matinee at 2 o'clock in the afternoon with darkness upon you. Luckily the black fog remained overhead and didn't lower to the surface or else it would have been impossible to navigate in the streets.

We did very big business having packed houses at both concerts.

Mileage Newport to London 133.

Jan. 23rd, Monday. Mat. Leamington. Eve. Northampton.

Train left Euston Station, over the London and North Western R.R. at 10 o'clock, arriving in Leamington at 12:20. The heavy fog cleared as we pulled away from London and at Leamington. The weather was fine. I used my camera, taking snaps of the saxophone section that turned out bad. We are now just about 12 miles from Stratford-on-Avon, Shakespeare's home.

Concert at 3 in the Winter Garden to good business.

We left Leamington at 5:50, arriving in Northampton at 7:35. Four of we boys chased around this town trying to find quarters until 8:15, finally locating at the Hotel Bell, Jim McLean proprietor. Without supper, I started the concert with the band at 8:35 given in the Corn Exchange. Mark Lyon was taken sick here.

Mileage London to Leamington 88. Leamington to Northampton 34. Total 122.

Jan. 24th, Tuesday. Mat. Cheltenham. Eve. Gloucester.

Called at 7 o'clock, leaving Northampton at 8:34, arriving in Cheltenham at 11:50. Rode up to town on a tram-car and took a picture of the boys riding on the top of the car. Cheltenham has been called the garden spot of England, and even from its beautiful appearance now in the dead of winter it can be rightly called the garden spot.

Business good at the matinee at 3 in the Town Hall. The auditorium of the Town Hall is a dream. We left Cheltenham at 5:40, arriving in Gloucester at 5:53. I am stopping at Constants Hotel.

Concert at 8 o'clock in Shire Hall to a fair house. Ed Wall taken sick and sent home at the intermission.

Mileage Northampton to Cheltenham 80. Cheltenham to Gloucester 6. Total 86.

Jan. 25th, Wednesday. Birmingham.

Left Gloucester at 11:32 arriving in Birmingham at 12:43. I felt bum with a headache, so a hotel near the station suited me real well. Schaftesbury Hotel did the trick.

Concerts at 3 and 8 in the Town Hall to packed houses.

After the concert at night, four of the Club, Schaeffer, Decker, Marthage, and I met an American dentist, Dr. Fyles from Toledo Ohio. We proceeded to paint the town red, stopping first at the Cosmopolitan Club of Birmingham, where we met some of the most prominent men of the city. This club consists of men in all walks of life and of different nationalities. When they closed the place up, we went over to the Press Club and had one good time playing pool until about 2 o'clock. Then I hit up some ragtime on the piano, and we all went home, well fixed at about 4 a.m. Met the editors of several papers, and all told had a fine time. Rode home in a taxi, not that we couldn't walk, but because we were about 2 miles away from our hotel. Bill Culley was off today with a touch of the grippe.

Mileage Gloucester to Birmingham. Midland R.R.

Jan. 26th, Thursday. Mat. Malvern. Eve. Worcester.

Out at 9:30 feeling good. Train left at 10:55, arriving in Malvern at 1:05. Malvern is a very pretty town, situated on the slope of a mountain, and its high altitude makes it a very desirable place to live. Retired people are here in good numbers. From the summit of the Malvern Peak, an excellent view can be obtained of the valley for miles about.

We played to a fair house in the Assembly Rooms at 3. The weather has moderated from last week's bitter cold, and everybody is happy. Train left at 6:05, arriving in Worcester at 6:24. Stopping at the Central Hotel, which is quite modern with electric lights etc. Off the candle circuit tonight.

Concert at 8 in the Town Hall to standing room.

Mileage Birmingham to Malvern 35. Malvern to Worcester 8.

---

4. Sousa, *Marching Along*, rev. ed., 65; Herbert L. Clarke, "A World's Tour with Sousa," *Musical Messenger*, Aug. 1918, 4.

Jan. 27th, Friday. Derby.

Left Worcester at 10:15 on the Midland R.R., arriving in Derby at 12:38. We had 30 minutes lay-over at Birmingham, where I had a chat with Mr. Sousa, and he gave me in detail our plans for the coming trips. Stopping at the Waverley Hotel, which is very good.

We played two concerts here in Drill Hall to fair business.

Weather gradually getting colder.

Mileage Worcester to Derby 65.

Jan. 28th, Saturday. Nottingham.

Left Derby at 12:05 over the Midland R.R., arriving in Nottingham at 12:38. Played two concerts to big business in the Mechanics' Large Hall.

Stopping at the Granby Hotel, which is very good. On my way to the Mechanics' Hall in a tram-car, I passed the Public Market Square, where for two blocks the entire space is covered with portable tents where the merchants display their goods. A person can buy almost anything there from a grand piano to a basket of potatoes. Nottingham is a very busy place, the chief industry being the manufacture of lace.

Mileage Derby to Nottingham 17.

Jan. 29th, Sunday. Eve. Burton-on-Trent.

My alarm clock awakened me at 9:45. After breakfast, some of we boys attended Mass at the St. Barnabas Cathedral. The proprietor of the Granby Hotel caught us napping and overcharged on our bill. Train left at 2:05, arriving in Burton-on-Trent at 3:05. We had no matinee, so Doc Lowe and I took a walk across the River Trent and into the fine residential section. The city proper is a quaint place and very interesting. Mix, the band photographer, took a picture of the boys standing at the main business corner of the town. Had dinner at the Queen's Hotel.

Concert at 7:45. Burton-on-Trent is the home of Bass Ale Brewery, which is the main industry of the town. They have 18 miles of rail on their premises, with 11 engines to handle the traffic. The total out-put of the brewery averages about two miles and a half of cars per day.

Left for Sheffield after the concert at 11:05 arriving 12:25.

Mileage Nottingham to Burton 23. Burton to Sheffield 47.

Jan. 30th, Monday. Sheffield.

Stopping at the Norfolk Hotel and had a good nights rest. I met Jos. Marthage and Paul Senno, and we went to the cutlery works of Colquhoun and Cadmann on Arundel St., where I bought an assortment of razors and cutlery.

Our personal trunks were brought up to the Victoria Hall today where we played two concerts to fair business.

After the matinee, Mr. Sousa called a rehearsal after which he made a few remarks to the men making it plain to every one what to expect on this trip. He told us that the band had about 12 months yet to go on this trip. Mr. Sousa also assured us that everything would be done that is possible for our comfort while on the water.

Jan. 31st, Tuesday. Manchester.

After breakfast I went over to Geo. Wostenholm factory and bought a dozen knives and forks, also a couple pocket knives. Their cutlery looked better to me than any I have yet seen. Train left at 11:05, and on the way to Manchester I cut my thumb on a trick knife Corey brought around. Doc Lowe fixed me up. We arrived in Manchester at 1:30, and after about an hour's walk located at the Bay Horse Hotel. Gately and myself shared a room. Marthage and Senno are also here.

We played two concerts at the Free Trade Hall to good business. I

spoke to Mr. Sousa about my damaged finger and was told to take it easy during the concert. Weather much colder.

Mileage Sheffield to Manchester 41.

Feb. 1st, Wednesday. Mat. Southport. Eve. Lancaster.

It is very cold this morning. Caught the 10:15 train for Southport over the Lancashire and Yorkshire R.R. arriving in Southport at 11:40. Gave Ed Clarke instructions concerning filling out checks to be sent home. Had a look at the beach front and the pier, which is one mile long. The beach is fixed up-to-date with all sorts of amusements.

Concert at 2:30 in Cambridge Hall to fair business.

Train left at 6:05, arriving in Lancaster at 7:25 about 15 minutes late. Stopping at the "Palatine" Temperance Hotel. Concert at 8:15 in the Town Hall, a very beautiful building. This night is the coldest we have experienced on the trip, and a strange coincidence it is, because the hottest day we had with the band was on Monday afternoon concert in Lancaster, Penna., U.S.A. last September.

Gately and I warmed up on some ale, but getting in my cold bed at night was a terrible proposition.

Mileage Southport from Manchester 34. Southport to Lancaster 35. Total 69.

Feb. 2nd, Thursday. Mat. Blackburn. Eve. Preston.

Left Lancaster at 9:48, arriving in Blackburn at 11:15. Weather very cold, and how we escaped freezing on the train I can't explain. Matinee at 2:30 in the Palace Theatre. Stopped in the Star and Garter Hotel after the concert for a warmth producer. Train left Blackburn at 5:35, arriving in Preston at 6:06.

Concert at 8 to fair business at the Public Hall.

Mileage Lancaster to Blackburn 32. Blackburn to Preston 11.

Feb. 3rd, Friday. Mat. Huddersfield. Eve. Rochdale.

Left Preston at 9:30 in a very heavy fog, arriving in Huddersfield at 12:45. Matinee in the Palace Theatre at 3 to a small house.

I bought a couple pair of Dent's gloves here today. Train left at 5:58, arriving in Rochdale at 7:15. While boarding the train at Huddersfield, I was unfortunate enough to catch the third finger of my left hand in the door, with the result that I crushed and tore the nail clean out of place. The trip to Rochdale seemed an age. Doc. Lowe bandaged up the finger, and a Doctor at Rochdale told me that I was fortunate not to have crushed the bone but that the finger was in very bad condition and needed careful attention. After reporting to Mr. Sousa my condition, I caught the 8:53 train to Manchester. I had engaged a room at the Bay Horse Hotel, so I had no trouble getting located. The bleeding of the finger didn't stop, so at 11 o'clock the proprietor Jones, a mighty good fellow, dressed the finger for me using boracic acid powder. The boys came in at 11:55, Gately taking my suitcase here for me from the train.

Mileage Preston to Huddersfield 51. Huddersfield to Rochdale 29. Rochdale to Manchester 11.

Feb. 4th, Saturday.

I decided to remain here in Manchester a few days, perhaps until Tuesday, as the band is back here again for the night. My finger is not so painful, but it is very badly swollen, and it would be impossible for me to work. A few days rest will help it a great deal. The boys caught the 11 o'clock train for Liverpool. Mr. Jones dressed my finger after breakfast, and he told me of a great game of football that was to be played this afternoon. The two best teams in England are to play, and I decided to see it. On my way to the grounds, I met a young fellow who told me that it was impossible to procure grandstand seats, as they are all booked in advance. Therefore, I acted on his advice and accompanied him to the 6d. stands. On the inside of the gates, I saw a sight never to be forgotten, and I was immediately swallowed up as it were by the mass of people who swarmed over everything in their endeavor to get a point of vantage. I was pushed here and pulled there until I scarcely knew that I was alive. I have been in huge crowds, but never before have I had so little room to exist, and this world so large. They were packed tighter than sardines in a box and when anyone in the rear started to push the whole crowd would go forward and then swing back again like waves on the ocean. The massive stands are built entirely around the field, and at today's game the attendance was about 80,000 people. The opposing teams were the Manchester United and the Birmingham Aston Villa's team, the cracks of Great Britain. The result was in favor of the Manchester, score 2 to 1. I was glad to get out of the crowd, but never-the-less my experience at that game, with the spectators growing wildly excited as the play progresses, was worth all the discomforts I had. Contented myself in the evening to a walk about Manchester taking in the sights.

Mileage Manchester to Liverpool 30.

Feb. 5th, Sunday.

Called at 9:30 and after breakfast went to Mass at St. Chad's Church. After Mass I met the Rector the Rev. Father Sheehan, as well as the Choir Master, who explained his method of organizing his male choir. He said that he worked 12 months with the boys on one Mass alone. The boys are easy to handle and are awarded prizes at the end of each year for attendance etc. Tenors and bass singers are scarce. The finger feels better today after being dressed. Jones and I had a chat all afternoon, and he put me wise to the law in England controlling hotel. On Sunday for instance the bar is open from 12 to 2:30 in the afternoon and from 6 to 10 in the evening. I had tea with Mr. & Mrs. Jones. Very fine people. Finished the evening writing. I am going to join the band tomorrow, as this loafing gets on my nerves.

Mileage Liverpool to Blackpool 37.

Feb. 6th, Monday. Mat. Warrington. Eve. St. Helens.

After breakfast, Jones fixed my finger and I caught the 10:45 train for Warrington, arriving about 11:20. Walked to the Palace Theatre and heard the last part of the vaudeville show rehearsal playing here this week. 12 men in the Orchestra.

The band came in at about 12, and I felt better to be back with the boys once more. Mr. Sousa inquired about my finger, and I told him that I would take a chance with it. I managed to get thro the program somehow. Lawton was glad to see me back on the job, as he said there was a big hole made in the section with the tenor saxophone missing. We left Warrington at 5:30, arriving at St. Helens at 6:15. Concert in the Town Hall at 8. We took the 10:25 train to Manchester, arriving at 11:43.

Mileage Manchester to Warrington 18. Warrington to St. Helens 7. St. Helens to Manchester 20. Total 45.

Feb. 7th, Tuesday. Mat. + Eve. Oldham.

My finger is slowly improving, and Jones was on the job again and dressed it. We took the 11:30 train for Oldham, arriving 11:50. I bought a small pair of wooden shoes made for a baby. Oldham is the center of the wooden shoe district of England, and all working people wear them. The shoe maker guarantees each pair for a period of four years and the price of shoes is regulated according to size, the larger the shoe the higher the price. We played the Empire Theatre here. Concerts at 3 and 8. I figured up our mileage since leaving New York City, and it amounts to 5470. Mr. Sousa inquired for the mileage this far and I am

the only man that thought to take it. We caught the 10:18 train to Manchester, arriving at 10:50.

Mileage Manchester to Oldham and return 16 miles.

Feb. 8th, Wednesday. Mat. Bolton. Eve. Chorley.

Left Manchester at 11:20, arriving in Bolton at 11:39. My finger is in better condition today. Mr. and Mrs. Jones came here this afternoon and enjoyed our concert.

We played in the Theatre Royal at 2:30 to fair business.

After the matinee, the party of us including the Joneses went to a hotel and had tea. Train left from Bolton at 6:19, arriving in Chorley at 6:40. Fair business at the night concert given in Town Hall at 8 o'clock. Caught the 10:06 train for Manchester, arriving at 10:40 o'clock.

Mileage Manchester to Bolton 11. Bolton to Chorley 11. Chorley to Manchester 22. Total 44.

Feb. 9th, Thursday. Mat. + Eve. Bradford.

All the boys that stopped with Jones at the Bay Horse Hotel were sorry to leave this morning. Jones, I guess, was just as sorry to see us go. I have a very enjoyable time in Manchester, even tho my finger caused me so much annoyance. We took the 10:25 train, arriving in Bradford at 11:37. I located at the Central Hotel.

Business very good at both concerts, given in St. George's Hall.

Bradford is a dirty looking town and I can't say that I like it, even tho I had a good time. On my way home, I stopped in the Theatre Royal and saw the last three scenes of "Sinbad the Sailor," a pantomime. The shows start here at 7:15 and rings down at 10:45. The show tonight was the best of its kind I have seen here. Mark Lyon joined the band and received a good reception.

Mileage Manchester to Bradford 40.

Feb. 10th, Friday. Mat. + Eve. Leeds.

I dressed my finger today, which shows improvement after one week's treatment. At the rate of progress, it will be at least six weeks more before the finger will be in good condition. We caught the 1 o'clock train, arriving in Leeds at 1:17. This town looks better to me than Bradford.

The afternoon concert was fairly well attended at the Town Hall, which is a very beautiful structure, containing one of the finest organs in England. Calabash pipes are made here, and the boys invested heavily in them.

Concert at night to a packed house. The city square is very pretty at night with bronze statues of women holding lights, presenting a fine sight in comparison to the surroundings which are old and old looking like everything else in England. We are stopping at the West Riding Hotel, and it is very fine. Yesterday, I started to clear up an attack of rash.

Mileage Bradford to Leeds 9.

Feb. 11th, Saturday. Mat. Halifax. Eve. Burnley.

Train left at 11:10 over the Great Northern R.R., arriving in Halifax at 11:40. Today's weather is the finest since our arrival in England.

Matinee at 3 in the Palace Theatre to a big house.

Marthage and I had a run for the train being late buying lunch for our trip tomorrow. We left at 5:44, arriving in Burnley at 6:40. I am stopping at Barker's Hotel.

Concert at 8 in the Mechanics' Institute to only a fair house.

Mileage Leeds to Halifax 14. Halifax to Burnley 23. Total 37.

Feb. 12th, Sunday.

Left Burnley at 8:20 in a very heavy fog and pulled into Manchester at 9:35, a little late. We left Manchester at 10 o'clock by special train, making fast time. At 11 o'clock the fog had cleared, giving us an ideal day to do our hardest day's traveling since we started in England. Our journey from Manchester to Holyhead carried us thro a very beautiful part of Wales. Northern Wales being by far the most interesting to me. The country is rugged in appearance with a bright sunshine glistening on snow capped mountains, presenting a spectacle similar to our wonderful Rockies. Numerous old castles were passed, chief among which was the ancient Conway Castle built by Edward I in 1284. His object in building this Castle being to keep the troublesome Welsh in those days in check. It is by far the most beautiful ruins in Wales, containing dungeons, the most noted being built under the King's tower. We then came across the Menai Suspension Bridge built in 1819 by Telford. Seven year's work being required to put it up. A very noticeable thing as we traveled along was the neat appearance of the Welsh farm houses, whitewashed from top to bottom and looking as neat and clean as a pin. We arrived in Holyhead at 1:05 and boarded the steamer "Munster," a boat of 3000 tons, modern in every respect and a very speedy ship, making about 24 knots. The Irish Channel appeared calm today, much different from its regular behavior. On the rocks about a mile distant from our dock, we could see the ill-fated steamer "Bushmill" driven on the rocks only six weeks ago by a severe gale. The London Salvage Corps, after working for weeks, abandoned her, a total loss to smash to pieces. No one was lost during the wreck, as the men were taken off by the life guards stationed here.

Our voyage across the channel was very good, and we arrived at Kingston Pier at 4:45. Took a train to Dublin, arriving at 5:30. The band management arranged to stay in Dublin over night, but a party of we boys (13) secured our tickets to come on to Cork with the intention of visiting Blarney Castle. I had dinner in the Ross Hotel and we started again on our way to Cork at 8:35. It was a long tiresome ride, but we finally arrived in Cork at 2:50 a.m. A bus from the Imperial Hotel met our party at the station, and it was 3:30 before I got to bed after a very long day.

Mileage Burnley to Manchester 28. Manchester to Holyhead 130. Holyhead to Kingston Pier 57. Pier to Dublin 9. Dublin to Cork 167. Total 391.

Feb. 13th, Monday. Mat. + Eve. Cork.

Called at 9 o'clock but felt like sleeping till 12. Our party took jaunting cars, four men on each, and started for Blarney Castle at 10:25. Our ride to the Castle was fine, as we passed thro lovely country, where real Irish life, including sights of extreme-poverty were seen. The thatched roofed houses made a hit with me. The Castle finally came into view, and it was a stately appearing object surrounding by most beautiful country. The day was a trifle dull, but our sightseeing spirit wasn't dampened a bit. We climbed the stone spiral stairway, and at the top landing we saw the object of our trip, the famous Blarney Castle. Cameras began clicking, and Mix set his moving picture machine in position to take the boys as they kissed the stone. It is a very difficult operation to kiss the stone, and it requires a bit of nerve to go thro with it, but nevertheless the boys were on the job and went at it. I was greatly handicapped with my crushed finger, as I have no strength in that hand so I passed up kissing the stone to the more fortunate. It was with a feeling of regret that I came away without kissing the stone but under the conditions I had no other alternative.

[Clarke]: This was quite a feat to accomplish as the stone is outside the wall many feet from the ground. In order to successfully do this trick, you must be held by the feet by some one on the ledge and hang down head first to kiss the stone.

[Russell]: Miss Root's and Miss Zedeler's courage failed them and the stone was left untouched by feminine lips in so far as the Sousa party was concerned.[5]

We were back in Cork at 1:40 after a most delightful trip, which well repaid us for the awful traveling I did to get to this City.

Concerts at 3 & 8 in the Assembly rooms to good business.

Feb. 14th, Tuesday. Mat. + Eve. Limerick.

Left Cork at 9:30, and after a long journey, during which we had a rainstorm, the first in a long time, we arrived in Limerick at 1:30. I booked a room at 34 Henry St. The Royal Theatre, where we played, is the most tumbled down affair I was ever in during my experience.

It has been condemned, and anyone would do the community a favor by touching a match to it. It is cold and damp, while ordinary sanitary conditions are unknown.

Business was good and our audience very enthusiastic.

A very fine class of people attended the night concert, despite the vile surroundings. "Reminiscences of Ireland" was played instead of the "Slavonic Rhapsody" at this night Concert. The River Shannon a small stream runs thro the city. Limerick, with its 38,000 people, put up a miserable appearance today partly due to heavy rains. I suppose Lace making is the principal industry.

Mileage Cork to Limerick 61.

Feb. 15th, Wednesday. Mat. + Eve. Dublin.

Our walk to the station this morning was made thro mud of the sticky kind. One step forward might result in sliding back two steps. Train left from the Great Southern and Western Sta. at 8:15, and after a cold ride arrived at the Dublin King's Bridge Sta. at 12:30. I passed the Guinness Brewery on our way to the Provincial Hotel where I located. The Liffey River runs directly in front of the hotel and thro the center of the town.

We gave concerts to good business at Rathmines Rink.

After the matinee, the boys all went to the Peterson pipe factory and made a clean-up on pipes. I met Mr. Peterson, a very fine old fellow, and he treated us loyally. I bought four pipes.

Dublin is the finest town in Ireland that I have visited. In fact, I like it better than any commercial town in England that we have played. The lovely seashore towns are of course different and in a class by themselves. They surpass anything in the States as real places of beauty. Very sorry that we are not playing here for a longer period, as they have many things for a traveler to see.

Mileage Limerick to Dublin 124.

Feb. 16th, Thursday. Mat. + Eve. Bellfast.

Train left at 9 o'clock over the G.N.I. Station, arriving in Bellfast at 12:55. Our trip brought us to a very historical spot. We stopped at Drogheda Station, and a few hundred yards further on we crossed the famous Boyne River. I saw the monument erected to commemorate the Battle of Boyne. Belfast is a fine city and ranks second to Dublin.

Business fair at the concerts in Ulster Hall.

The boys bought a quantity of linen from the Robinson and Cleaver store after the matinee. I am stopping at the Union Hotel opposite the City Hall, which is a beauty.

Mileage Dublin to Belfast 113.

5. Herbert L. Clarke, "A World's Tour with Sousa," *Musical Messenger,* Aug. 1918, 5; Clarence J. Russell, "Around the World with Sousa," *Musical American,* May 6, 1911, 9.

Feb. 17th, Friday. Mat. + Eve. Londonderry.

Breakfast at 7, after which four of us took a jaunting car to the Midland Station and caught the 8 o'clock train for Londonderry, arriving at 11 a.m. The station we came in on is situated on the opposite side of the Foyle River from the town, so I took the trip across the river on a small boat called the "Victoria," used as a ferry and capable of holding 60 people. To cross the Carlisle Bridge would have been a very long trip to the St. Columb's Hall. Londonderry, originally called Derry, is a very historical City and the center of hostilities during the Irish Revolution, made famous by one of the world's greatest sieges. I walked around the city wall, taking about 25 minutes to do the trick. I saw the Walker Monument, Cathedral, Roaring Meg, the old gun and many more interesting things.

Concerts well attended. We boarded the Laird Line steamer "Rose" after the night concert on our way to Glasgow. The weather has been bad so we expect a very rough trip. This boat, altho the best in the Company's service, is too small to accommodate the passengers properly, so some of the boys were in very uncomfortable quarters.

Mileage Belfast to Londonderry 95.

Feb. 18th, Saturday. Mat. + Eve. Glasgow.

Day opened very dark and cheerless, while a heavy rain beat the ship's decks. The sea was rather calm, and our trip was better than we expected and we reached dock 45 minutes ahead of scheduled time. The trip up the Clyde River would have been great only that the heavy rain spoiled our view. We passed the monument erected to Henry Bell and the Dunbarton Rocks. The extensive ship building plants along the river is a wonderful sight. I saw about 50 boats in the course of construction, but that doesn't give the faintest idea of what it looks like. People who know told me that they are about 20 year's back on orders for vessels and they can't possibly build them faster than they are going. We arrived at the Glasgow dock at 12:30. Located the George Hotel in a heavy rain.

Matinee to big business at the St. Georges Hall. Mr. Thos. MacFarlane came to see Bill Schensley and was very much disappointed that he isn't with the band. It has been 19 years since the two last saw each other, but MacFarlane is still there with the friendship thing. He heard the matinee and then invited me to his home tomorrow.

Good house at night.

Mileage Londonderry to Glasgow 140.

Feb. 19th, Sunday.

Bright and sunshiny this morning, and I attended High-Mass at St. Aloysius Church, still under course of operation. It will be a beauty when completed and built of brick and concrete resembling the Westminster Cathedral on the interior. Mr. MacFarlane came to my hotel at 1 o'clock, and we strolled about seeing some of the interesting sights. I had my camera and took snaps of MacFarlane, the Cathedral (Church of Scotland) and the oldest house in Glasgow, built in 1070. I then took a picture of Bill Schensley's old home while in Glasgow 19 years ago, 237 Duke Street, across from the cattle market. From there, we went to MacFarlane's present home at 167 Graeme Street and had a great time the balance of the day. Mrs. MacFarlane was so pleased to see me that nothing was too good. The main topic of conversation was Schensley and all about him. One of the daughters named Jeanie, who Bill nursed, is now a good looking girl of 20 years. They have a large family about 7 or 8 children, the youngest being about 8 years of age. I was given a horse shoe upon leaving, as the Scotch are very superstitious. All told, I had a fine day.

Feb. 20th, Monday. Mat. + Eve. Aberdeen.

Left from the Buchanan St. Station at 10 o'clock, and the train was very fast over the Caledonian R.R., arriving in Aberdeen at 1:55. The country we went thro was fine, and the snow flurries put a little touch to the trip out of the ordinary. It was the first snow we have seen since arriving on this side except what we could see on the top of the Welsh Mountains. We passed the Grampian Nits and the Sterling Castle this morning.

Stopping at the Forsythe Hotel here.

Business light at both concerts given in the Music Hall.

Mileage Glasgow to Aberdeen 152.

Feb. 21st, Tuesday. Mat. + Eve. Dundee.

Rain came down in torrents when I walked to the North British R.R. station this morning. Train left at 9:28, arriving in Dundee at 11:16. Ernest Gately wrote a letter in French to Evette and Schaeffer Paris for their prices on reeds.

Business poor at both concerts given in Kinnaird's Hall. The weather was bad.

Mileage Aberdeen to Dundee 71.

Feb. 22nd, Wednesday. Mat. + Eve. Edinburgh.

Train left at 11:22, arriving in Edinburgh at 12:45. We crossed the Firth of Forth this morning on the longest cantilever bridge in the world. The day opened fine, but as we neared Edinburgh a terrific hail storm came up. A very spectacular sight. Edinburgh is the most beautiful city we have yet visited, and there is so much to it that any description I could give would be a joke.

The Waverley Market Hall, where we played two concerts to very big business, was no joke tho. Positively the coldest barn I have ever sat two hours and a half in. After the matinee, we boys, about 8 of us, walked up to the Edinburgh Castle, but it was then after closing time, so we looked at it from the outside. Stopping at the Cockburn Hotel. The Club held a meeting after the night concert.

Mileage Dundee to Edinburgh 51.

Feb. 23rd, Thursday. Mat. + Eve. Newcastle-on-Tyne.

Left Edinburgh at 10 o'clock Waverly Station over the N. British R.R., arriving in Newcastle-on-Tyne at 12:45. Back again in England. Stopping at the Crown Hotel.

Concerts fairly attended, mostly the society people at the Town Hall. Weather very bad.

Mrs. Welte left for home today. Jimmy Hewson, Sousa's valet, went back to his old job as bugler on the steamer "Baltic."

Mileage Edinburgh to Newcastle-on-Tyne 124.

Feb. 24th, Friday. Mat. Darlington. Eve. Middlesboro.

Left Newcastle at 10:05 over the North Eastern R.R., arriving in Darlington at 11:50. We traveled in American style cars on this trip. The poverty stricken condition of the lower class of England was very much in evidence here today.

Bad business at the Assembly Hall.

Left Darlington at 6:12 from the Bank Top Sta., arriving in Middlesboro at 6:50. Stopping at the Albany Hotel, where I ran into the candle circuit again after a lay off.

Business good at the concert given in the Town Hall.

Mileage Newcastle to Darlington 39. Darlington to Middlesboro 15.

Feb. 25th, Saturday. Mat. + Eve. Sunderland.

Left Middlesboro at 10:16, arriving in Sunderland at 12 o'clock. Received only 4 bad exposures of the film of 6 that I left in Aberdeen to be developed. The pictures were taken in Glasgow.

Business good at concerts given in the Victoria Hall.

Ben Vereecken wrote an order to Evette and Schaeffer for reeds for me after the matinee. Stopping at the Manor Hotel.

Mileage Middlesboro to Sunderland 46.

Feb. 26th, Sunday. Eve. Scarborough.

Awoke to see sun streaming in my window, a very decided novelty. Left Sunderland by special train at 10:42. Arrived in Scarborough at 1:30. The trip was fine. Upon arriving at the N.E. Station, we found all the doors and exits locked, and we were like so many prisoners. No one on duty about the big station to let us out, but finally one of the boys found an unfastened window thru which we all climbed.

[Russell]: The musicians found themselves locked in the station, but soon escaped through an insecurely fastened window, meeting the station-master leisurely walking down the street to "open up shop."[6]

Mr. Sousa and party later found an open gateway at the far end of the station by which to get out and saving him the effort of crawling thru the window. Stopping at the Matson Hotel. After getting located, a party of the boys started out to see the city, which proved to be the prettiest sea coast resort we have yet visited. A walk along the drive back of the sea-wall was pretty, while waves dashed over the wall, and a strong breeze blew the spray over the side walk and drive. We climbed up the 300 feet to the old Castle built in the 12th Century and destroyed by Cromwell after its famous siege. An old well, excavated to a depth of 175 feet, brought out all sorts of relics of past years, including pottery, human bones etc. While exploring the dungeon of the castle they found the skeleton of a prisoner wearing an iron bar twisted about its neck, being put there while the iron was red hot. The view from the castle today was great, and the boys took many pictures.

Concert at 8:15 to fair business in the Olympia on the sea front.

Mileage Sunderland to Scarboro 98.

Feb. 27th, Monday. Mat. York. Eve. Hull.

Train left at 10:35, arriving in York at 11:49. Rain spoiled hopes of a big sight seeing trip, but never-the-less I visited the York Cathedral, the third largest Cathedral in the world. They started building the church in 1220 and worked on it 200 years. Parts of the church show signs of decay. Glass in the windows is crumbling and rotting away. The famous "Five Sisters" windows are here. Considering its age, this church is a beautiful structure and by far the largest I have ever visited. This city of York is very old and dates back as one of the oldest in England's history. The city walls are still here, altho broken in places to allow for modern improvements.

We played a matinee to a fair house in the Exhibition Hall, which certainly was cold.

Left by special train at 4:55, arriving in Hull at 6:05. Booked a room at Harmons Hotel. We played our concert tonight at the City Hall, which is one of the prettiest and most comfortable we have yet performed in. It is finished in white marble, and the effect is very pretty.

Our audience was very big, packed to the doors, and comprised the best set of people in the city. The janitor of this place looked like the king of something covered with medals. They gave him his medals for service in the army.

Mileage Scarborough to York 42. York to Hull 42.

---

6. Clarence J. Rusell, "Around the World with Sousa," *Musical American,* May 6, 1911, 9.

Feb. 28th, Tuesday. Mat. Grimsby. Eve. Lincoln.

Steamer "Doncaster" sailed away from the Corporation Pier with Sousa's Band aboard at 9:15, crossing the Humber River to New Holland, taking a train from there to Grimsby, arriving at 11:30. A heavy rain prevented me from looking over the famous fish market here, the largest in the world. It was a few miles out of this port that a Russian battleship fired on some English trawlers (fishing boats) during the Russian-Japanese War.

Business good in the City Hall.

Made the trip to Lincoln by special train, arriving at 6:30. Located at the Central Hotel. After the concert given in the New Central Hall, the proprietor of our hotel had a pet monkey do some tricks.

Mileage Hull to New Holland 3½. New Holland to Grimsby 21. Grimsby to Lincoln 40. Total 64½.

Mar. 1st, Wednesday. Mat. + Eve. Oxford.

Train left at 7:23, arriving in Oxford at 12:15. We traveled pretty fast this morning, and our coaches certainly rocked some. At times we didn't know whether we were on or off the rails. Stopping at the Oxford Apartments. This is the great college town of England and is a very ancient looking town.

Concerts in the Town Hall to fair business.

Mileage Lincoln to Oxford 121.

Mar. 2nd Thursday. Mat. Crystal Palace. Eve. Alexandra Palace.

Train at 9:35 from Oxford, arriving at the Crystal Palace, London at 12:04. I had a look over the whole Crystal Palace buildings and grounds, which are fine.

Business fair at the matinee given in the Crystal Palace Theatre.

The band took motor busses after the matinee and had a fine ride across London to the Alexandra Palace. Concert started at 8:30 to a packed house, some 10,000 people. We were scheduled to start the concert at 8 o'clock and the delay caused a lot of uneasiness among the audience, and when Mr. Sousa appeared he was hooted and hissed. The concert went great. Caught a train from the Wood Green Station to King's Cross Station. Booked a room at the Waverley Hotel.

Mileage Oxford to Crystal Palace 65. Crystal Palace to Alexandra Palace 15. Alexandra Palace to King's Cross 5. Total 85.

Mar. 3rd, Friday. Mat. Bristol.

Left London (Paddington Sta) at 11 o'clock. Arrived in Bristol at 1:05. Played to a fair house at the Coliseum. This was our last concert in England, and every one in the band appeared well pleased. Train left at 6:33, arriving in Plymouth at 10:20. Stopping at the Waverley Hotel.

Mileage Bristol to Plymouth 128. London to Bristol 117½. Total 245½.

Total Mileage of the British tour 4,360.

Total receipts of the British tour $87,000.

Mileage Conshohocken to Bristol en Route 7,772.

Mar. 4th, Saturday. Streamer "Tainui."

After breakfast, I did some necessary shopping and started for the dock loaded down with parcels. Most all the other boys bought a lot of necessities, and it was a queer looking Sousa's Band, more like a convention of peddlers.

The tender "Sir. Francis Drake" transferred us from the wharf to the steamer "Tainui," which lay out in the harbor. Boarded the "Tainui" at 12:45, and our stateroom is fine. I am sharing it with Ben Vereecken and Joe Kapralec. We steamed out of the Harbor at 1:52. Watches put back 32 minutes after leaving Plymouth. Moffat is the Captain of the boat, which is not equipped with wireless but up-to-date in all other respects. Very clean and in fine condition.

The dimensions of the boat are as follows: 375 feet long, 64 feet wide, and 9,957 tons, with a speed of between 14 & 15 knots. Weather is bad, a cold rain falling, while the sea is rough and choppy. Many of the boys became seasick during the day.

Mar. 5th, Sunday. Streamer "Tainui."

Breakfast at 8 o'clock. We are now in the much-dreaded Bay of Biscay, and the boat is rolling some. The hand ball game started today and with the excellent deck space makes a good game. Weather has become a lot warmer, and it is a relief after 8 weeks of freezing in England. Spent most of the day on deck, while pinochle occupied the evening. We are off the coast of France.

Clock moved back 26 minutes.

Mileage 291 till twelve noon from yesterday time of sailing.

Mar. 6th, Monday. Steamer "Tainui."

Called at 6:45, and after a sea-water hot bath which I have ordered at the same time every day, a game of hand-ball fixed up an appetite for breakfast.

We have our first touch of spring like weather today, but the sea is rough, tossing the boat about.

I started making pools on the ship's run today, the time being from noon of one day till noon the next.

Spent the evening playing piano and then cards.

Mileage 327.

Mar. 7th, Tuesday. Steamer "Tainui."

A woman was reported to have died of heart failure in the steerage, but it was contradicted later in the day.

Made pools and lost on them. The sea is quieting down.

Mileage 326.

Mar. 8th, Wednesday. Steamer "Tainui."

Bath and handball every morning before breakfast. We are sailing below the Mediterranean Sea now and expect to arrive in Tenerife this evening. Orders from Mr. Sousa to take our instruments out of the trunks. Weather partly cloudy with a light sea running.

We came in sight of the Tenerife light at 9 o'clock, arriving and casting anchor at 11:07 in the Santa Cruz Bay. A heavy rain and wind storm lasted during the night.

Mar. 9th, Thursday. Santa Cruz de Tenerife on Canary Islands.

Passed a bad night with one of the men sharing the stateroom being unable to behave himself with a gag. Santa Cruz lay like a beautiful picture this morning at the base of the mountains.

The deck was swarmed with hotel runners and agents selling tickets for a trip about town. Other Spaniards had laces, silks and other fabrics for sale. It was a hard proposition to get thru them to walk on deck. A ticket, for which I paid 3/-, entitled me to the motor boat ashore and an hour's ride about town in a carriage. We started the trip after breakfast. Occasional showers came up, and a person never knew when they would get soaking wet, as the weather was peculiar. One minute, then sunshine, and the next a heavy shower. Mr. and Mrs. Garing, Ben Vereecken and myself formed our party for the carriage, and our first stop was at the bull pen, where three times a year bull fights are held. Capacity of this place is 10,000 and a very interesting place.

We then went to the City Market and bought some fruit very reasonable. The Cathedral was next on the list. The guide called our attention to a solid silver altar.

The city is old and truly Spanish, with their milk women leading a flock of goats, distributing positively fresh milk, because she milks the goats before your eyes when given an order. The natives use burros almost entirely for their wagons or carts. Beggars are plentiful, and they use many different schemes to draw the pennies from your pocket. The city squares are all pretty, containing palms and generally water fountains where the women come for their water, carrying it in jugs upon their head. We returned to the "Tainui" at 1 o'clock, and I received a good ducking getting aboard. During the wait before sailing, a crowd of boys amused us by some very fine diving for money thrown into the water. They certainly handle themselves like ducks and never lose a piece of money. One young fellow dove and swam under our ship, and this boat draws about 30 feet of water.

One of their stunts was to climb up on the ship to the highest deck and dive a distance of 40 feet and bring up a silver coin thrown by a passenger. A cablegram sent to New York from here costs $4.00 a word.

The band played several marches and the national anthems of England, America & Spain as we sailed out of the harbor. Mt. Tenerife 12,000 feet high looked pretty from the bay.

Mileage 160.

Mar. 10th, Friday. Steamer "Tainui."

Real warm weather today, and the deck awnings were put up while the people started shedding heavy clothing. 3 pools were made up today and I won in one of them. A cricket match was played today between the 1st and 2nd cabin our team losing.

Our club long neglected held a meeting tonight, and a little life was put into the affair.

Mileage 298. Miss Zedeler's birthday.

Mar. 11th, Saturday. Steamer "Tainui."

Hand ball is still one of our main pastimes. Three pools again, and I lost. Started fixing and cleaning my saxophone today, and it needed it. The fire drill and lowering of the life boats by the crew was interesting. Miss Zedeler had a rehearsal on a violin solo composed by Herman Hand. The night is fine with a very bright moon almost directly overhead. I signed a paper today dealing with the immigration laws of So. Africa.

Mileage 338.

Mar. 12th, Sunday. Steamer "Tainui."

Religious service held in the First Saloon at 11 o'clock. The sea is as calm as a lake, scarcely a breeze blowing, while the heat is intense. Finished work on my instrument this afternoon. Three pools and I lost. Mark Lyon had a birthday party tonight but refused to tell his age. Several of the boys guessed anywhere between 90 and a 100.

Mileage 332.

Mar. 13th, Monday. Steamer "Tainui."

The heat was fierce this morning at 8 o'clock, with no wind to help out. Three pools again and I lost. Hand ball in the afternoon. After dinner, the Washy Hose Band made a parade around the decks and gave a concert, amusing the passengers, I hope. George Cunnington sang a song containing about a million verses. Mrs. Sousa asked me to play piano for a little dancing party they started after the band stopped.

Mileage 332.

Mar. 14th, Tuesday. Steamer "Tainui."

Spent a restless night, owing to the heat. The Equator is near and no mistake. Rehearsal of the band at 11 o'clock on deck. The sea presented a peculiar appearance just like a huge plate of glass. Not a ripple except those caused by the ship. We are in a dead calm, but a light breeze came up later in the day.

Three pools again and I lost. The third class men challenged the 2nd class to a tug of war. The third class had the husky boys, all right, but our team won, and very decisively too, in the first two pulls in less than 30 seconds each. Spent the afternoon playing cricket, in which Mr. Sousa made good with the bat. A celebration was held in the evening in honor of crossing the Equator. Ed Wall wore a costume to represent Father Neptune, while Geo. Cunnington represented Neptune's Prime Minister. The boys all dressed up in a grotesque manner and made a parade all over the ship. The ceremonies in the first saloon were funny and we were there about 15 minutes. Captain Moffat granted a request to keep the 2nd saloon bar open an hour longer than usual. Mix took a snap shot of the crowd in their make up with the Captain and Sousa family in the front. Went to sleep on deck tonight with the gang. We crossed the Equator at 4 a.m. Wednesday morning, Mar. 15th.

Mileage 331.

Mar. 15th, Wednesday. Steamer. "Tainui."

A sharp whistle woke up the boys sleeping on deck at 6 o'clock, as the decks are washed with a hose every morning. The boys put on their make up that they used last night, and Mix took some pictures.

Harry Freeman was the goat playing deck billiards this morning, and he bought us a few drinks at the conclusion of the games. The third class have been given all kinds of sporting events. One game, called tilting the bucket, is a peach. The 2nd mate invited Harry Baldwin to his stateroom on the bridge deck, and we had quite a little chat, principally about things concerning this ship. He spoke about the life boats being always in readiness for service with a supply of fresh water and biscuits, also the different signal lights while a mast and sail as well as a pair of oars go to complete the outfit. Each boat to contain 50 people.

Walking on deck we saw any amount of flying fish, and the sky presented a typical tropical scene. We could see three different showers on the horizon, and a dog rainbow looked pretty. The sunset tonight was beautiful and of the kind only seen about the equator. Used the deck again tonight, bringing the mattress up from my cabin. A heavy rain shower came up about 3 o'clock and drove us all to our staterooms.

Mileage 319.

Mar. 16th, Thurdsay. Steamer "Tainui."

We had a band rehearsal on deck at 11 o'clock this morning. Three pools again today and I lost.

One of the boys fixed a team to pull the 3rd class tug-of-war and had me on his list. I preferred to play cricket, and the other boys thought the same, with the result that the tug-of-war was off. Had a workout with the medicine ball before dinner. We held a club meeting tonight.

Mileage 324.

Mar. 17th, Friday. Steamer "Tainui."

One of the male passengers in the third class jumped overboard during the night and was lost. A coat and hat with his will in a pocket of his coat they found on a chair.

[Clarke]: It seems that he had acted queerly during the entire trip, and became demented, possibly through being seasick nearly all the time he was on board.[7]

Three pools again today. Cricket in the afternoon. About 25 of the men, Ross Millhouse conducting, gave a concert to the 3rd class, and they thoroughly enjoyed it, cheering themselves hoarse at the conclusion.

Mileage 313.

Mar. 18th, Saturday. Steamer "Tainui."

Spent the night in our cabin, as it is gradually becoming cooler the farther South we get. The ladies played a cricket match against the men in the first cabin, winning the game. I have been raising a moustache since boarding the boat, and now I look nearly like a human being.

Mileage 313.

Mar. 19th, Sunday. Steamer "Tainui."

Religious services held in the first saloon at 10:30. The weather today is rather dismal, clouds obscuring the sun for the first time in over a week. Nothing of interest today. Even the playing of games is not permitted on Sunday. Beautiful sunset this evening, and a peculiar thing about this portion of the globe is the absence of very much twilight.

Mileage 324.

Mar. 20th, Monday. Steamer "Tainui."

Band rehearsal this morning on deck at 11 o'clock. While playing medicine ball this afternoon, Doc. Lowe threw the ball overboard.

Mileage 323.

Because the ocean voyages were lengthy, several rehearsals en route were necessary. Weather permitting, they were held on deck. (Author's Collection, courtesy of Betty McCloskey)

A ceremony, complete with King Neptune, was held for the benefit of those crossing the equator for the first time. (Author's Collection)

7. Herbert L. Clarke, "A World's Tour with Sousa," *Musical Messenger*, Oct. 1918, 4.

Mar. 21st, Tuesday. Steamer "Tainui."

It is cooler this morning, partly cloudy, and an occasional shower comes up. During the afternoon, a heavy sea began rolling us about. The boat pitched badly, and the old seasickness came on to the regulars. Our Washy Hose band played a couple numbers for an informal social gathering of the Masons on board.

Mileage 311.

Mar. 22nd, Wednesday. Steamer "Tainui."

Passed a very rough night, and the boat rolled and pitched badly. The storm continued all thro the day.

Mileage 251.

Mar. 23rd, Thursday. Steamer "Tainui."

We were due to arrive in Cape Town this morning, but the weather delayed us. Packed our trunks this afternoon down in the forward hatch in a very crowded place. Weather is better than on the two previous days. The light-house at Cape Town was sighted at 8 o'clock, and our trip into the harbor, with the countless lights of Cape Town's streets shining brightly and with the mountains for a background, made a very pretty sight. The anchor was cast 12 o'clock. We were all happy to see land once more.

Mileage 238.

Mar. 24th, Friday. Cape Town, So. Africa.

Called at 5 o'clock to be passed by the quarantine health officer of the port. Went back to bed again and was called at 7 o'clock. Cape Town looked pretty this morning to eyes only accustomed to looking at the horizon, water and a few seagulls. After breakfast, we disembarked at about 9 o'clock and were given a reception and a carriage drive up to the Town Hall. Stopping at the Central Hotel. This town is a beauty, and the City Hall on the same calibre.

Small house at the matinee today.

The weather is hot, and this is the fall of the Year. Negroes are very plentiful here.

Mileage 133 from noon yesterday into this port. Mileage Plymouth to Cape Town 5,908. Nautical U.S. Miles Plymouth to Cape Town 6,499.

Mar. 25th, Saturday. Mat. + Eve. Cape Town.

Clarence Livingston, Ben Vereecken and I took a trip to Cecil Rhodes estate. The grounds are a treat, and they contain a small zoo. I took a picture of a couple ostriches. Coming back to town on the tram-car, we passed the Market place where the natives (colored) have their goods for sale.

After lunch, Livingston and I made the trip to Camps Bay, a seashore resort returning by a mountain route around the Lion's Head peak. All the shops close at 12 o'clock today, half holiday.

Matinee on the Pageant Grounds to a fair audience.

A band stand was erected in the open air with no protection from the hot blazing sun, and we almost perished.

Evening concert at 8:15 to good business. Matinee at 4 o'clock.

A hot land breeze blew all during the evening concert, parching our throats.

Mar. 26th, Sunday. Traveling.

We left Cape Town by special train at 11 o'clock over the Cape Government R.R. The trip brought us thru a very mountainous country, very much similar to the American Rockies. The native Kaffirs were interesting standing in groups as our train sped by. Grapes are plentiful, delicious and cheap. We passed many sheep and goat ranches. The dining car service was excellent and hard to beat any place, and we were given a very reasonable rate. But the sleeping car accommodations are bad and not a bit like our Pullman coaches.

Mar. 27th, Monday. Eve. Kimberley.

Passed a comfortable night, which became very cool towards morning. We passed many ostrich farms, and the plumed birds are very plentiful throughout this section. We made a stop at Deal Fontein, and I had an opportunity of taking a snap-shot of the site where the Imperial Yeomanry Hospital stood during the Boer War. The Hospital was built of tents generally, and below its site is the burial ground of the unfortunate English killed in the battles around here. The surrounding country is barren and deserted, very much like a desert.

We passed thru many battlefields and historical places of the Boer War. Block houses used to protect the railroad are very plentiful. The weather warmed up a bit as the day progressed, and when we arrived in Kimberley at 4:30 the heat was oppressive. I am stopping at the Central Hotel.

The band opened here tonight at the City Hall to poor business. An American in the audience requested "Dixie." It was played.

Mileage Cape Town to Kimberley 647.

Mar. 28th, Tuesday. Mat. Kimberley. Traveling.

Breakfast at 8:30. The band met by appointment at 10 o'clock in the Grand Hotel to visit the diamond mines. The De Beers Company had a special train of small cars waiting for us on their property. Mix took a moving picture of us as we left for the mines. The company owns over 15,000 acres of land, on which they have five mines, all in operation. We first visited the washing machines where all the earth is dumped after it has been thoroughly dried in the sun for 12 months.

In the drying process, the diamonds become loosened and when put into the washing machine easily find their way to the bottom, being heavier than other substances.

We then saw the pulsator, where the actual finding of the gems is done. They use crude vaseline in which all the stones drop, but only the diamonds stick there, as continual running water carries off the stuff they don't want. We all registered at the main office as visitors, and we saw the output of yesterday's work. About a pail full of diamonds lay on the table ready to be weighed and shipped. We then went over to one of the mines, and about 12 of us put on coats and caps and took a look about the bottom of the mine. The drop in the shaft was 750 feet and we were at the bottom in less than 25 seconds.

Conditions in the mine were better than I expected, as the air was good, and water, which is generally plentiful in most mines, was scarce. I saw the boiler and machine shops and noticed that all the machinery was American manufacture. We saw the great hole, one of the wonders of the modern world, which before the De Beers Co bought it was worked by individual persons.

Mr. Adams, a man from Wilkes-Barre Pa., is the general manager of this mine, and it was thro his courtesy that we boys were enabled to see everything.

Matinee at 3 o'clock to a very poor house.

After the matinee, a few of we boys took a swim in the pool of the De Beers Club.

Train left at 7:15 for Johannesburg.

Mar. 29th, Wednesday. Mat. + Eve. Johannesburg.

We arrived in Johannesburg (Joburg) at 9:30. The Police Band was at the station to welcome us. I met Mr. Clark, assistant conductor of the band, who invited me to stay at his home during our engagement in

The most discussed part of the world tour was the time spent in South Africa, where the musicians visited the diamond mines in Kimberley. (Author's Collection, courtesy of Antoinette Cendali)

this city, and I accepted. He and his wife live alone in a very pretty cottage, and I felt right at home with them.

We opened this afternoon to fair business at the Wanderer's Grounds, playing in the open air.

Big attendance at night. Johannesburg is more like a real live American city than any town in So. Africa that we have played. The cost of living is high, and everything else in general is very expensive. This is the gold center of the country, and money is plentiful.

Mileage Kimberley to Joburg 309.

Mar. 30th, Thursday. Mat. + Eve. Joburg.

Passed a sleepless night due to several flocks of mosquitoes singing lullabies about my ears all night. Jersey mosquitoes were never like these. Our baseball team held its first practice this morning, and a game with the Joburg Wanderer's to finish up with. We were beaten 9 to 4. Bought a bundle of mosquito netting and hope to have a comfortable sleep tonight.

Business light in the afternoon and good at night.

Mar. 31st, Friday. Mat. + Eve. Joburg.

Passed a fairly comfortable night, but those mosquitoes are some wise gents. Baseball practice this morning, on the Wanderer's Grounds. Shower baths and all athletic conveniences are here for us. A local photographer took several pictures of the band with good results.

Business the same as yesterday.

April 1st, Saturday. Mat. + Eve. Joburg.

Two teams from the band played a game of ball today. Regulars beat the Youngans. Score 12 to 9. Business good.

April 2nd, Sunday. Mat. Boksburg. Eve. Joburg.

We left Joburg at 8:45, arriving at the Vogelfontein Station at 9:30, where we were met by the Mgr. of the Cinderella Gold Mine compound. At the compound, they arranged especially for us a Kaffir dance and it was the greatest thing ever. About 1500 black fellows went thro their dance, all of them half naked, but what few rags they did wear, were of the most flashy colors and design. We all had our cameras along and took many fine pictures of the natives, Kaffirs and Zulus in their original dances.

[Sousa]: The various tribes that work in the mines were to perform their traditional dances in the compound. Each tribe seemed to keep

aloof from the others and to avoid interference in any way with the dances of another tribe. One of their musical instruments must have been the great-great-grandfather of the xylophone. It had no definite scale and consisted only of four or five pieces of wood grouped in such a way that hammering on them produced an indefinable sound not worthy of the name of music![8]

The mine company gave the natives a feast for their efforts a roast oxen and plenty Kaffir beer, a substance that looked like soap-suds but which contains a high percentage of alcohol. It is interesting to know under what conditions the natives are handled by the mine company, so to gain the information I consulted the compound keeper who is by the way always ready to use a .44 gun in case of necessity. The blacks are brought here from the interior of Africa under a 6 months contract for a pay which averages from 1/6 to 3/- per day. They are provided with all the necessities of life by the Company, and their simple luxuries they buy from the Compound store out of their wages.

But they must live in the compound, an enclosure more like a prison yard surrounded with small cell-like rooms, and they don't get out until their 6 months expire. Great and desperate men are to be found among them with quite a few murderers, some of whom have worked in the mine for years. But the majority of the 6-month men collect their pay at the expiration of their time and go back to the wilds—and buy a few wives, who keep them for the balance of their lives.

Fights are frequent in the compound between the different tribesmen, and the hospital is generally full of patients suffering from broken heads, arms etc.

We were entertained royally by the company and they had a fine lunch ready for us at 12 o'clock. Walter Kelley, the Virginia Judge, a vaudeville star, was in our party and the real cause of our being here. A heavy hail and rain storm came up about noon, and the remainder of the day was cold and miserable.

Afternoon concert at 3:15 in the Krosk Park, Boksburg with about a 100 people standing about in the cold rain in attendance. It was one chilly day.

Train left at 5:50, arriving in Joburg at 6:35.

Concert this evening in the Wanderer's Club Gymnasium to fair business.

Mileage Johannesburg to Vogelfontein and return 30 miles.

April 3rd, Monday. Mat. + Eve. Pretoria.

Left Joburg at 9 o'clock, arriving in Pretoria at 11:30. Raining hard, and the streets are mud puddles. Located at the International Hotel.

Matinee in the Opera House at 3 o'clock to a very poor house. Evening concert at the Capitol Rink to fair business.

I canvassed the band for orders from the boys for pictures of the band.

Mileage Joburg to Pretoria 45.

April 4th, Tuesday. Mat. + Eve. Pretoria.

I visited the Zoo this morning, which has some very fine birds and a good collection of animals. A big hippo went thro a few stunts and nearly caught a little colored boy that was working about the cage. I saw Paul Kruger's homestead.

Matinee at the Opera House to bad business. Good house at the Capitol Rink in the evening.

---

8. Sousa, *Marching Along*, 268–69.

The band posed without instruments in Johannesburg. Knecht is seated at the left on the rug; the Quinlan representative (wearing a straw hat) is behind him. (U.S. Marine Band)

April 5th, Wednesday. Mat. Joburg. Eve. Krugersdorf.

Left Pretoria at 9:45, arriving in Joburg at 11:45. I gave the photographer an order for 58 pictures he took of the band.

Matinee at the Wanderer's gymnasium at 3 o'clock to bad business.

Train left at 6 o'clock, arriving in Krugersdorf at 7. A local band gave us a reception and escorted us to the Wanderer's Park, where we played a concert in the open air to a big audience at 8:40. A heavy mist was falling, and we played wearing our overcoats. We used the sleeping cars tonight standing on a side track.

Mileage Pretoria to Joburg 45. Joburg to Krugersdorf 21.

April 6th, Thursday. Mat. + Eve. Joburg.

Had breakfast in the dining car on our train. Left Krugersdorf at 11:30, arriving in Joburg at 12:30. The folks at the house didn't expect me until tomorrow, but our route was changed only recently.

Concerts at the Wanderer's Gymnasium to poor business.

Senno is sick and goes to the hospital for treatment.

Mileage Krugersdorf to Joburg 21.

April 7th, Friday. Mat. + Eve. Germiston.

Visited Senno at the hospital and he is doing nicely. Train left at 11:30, arriving in Germiston at 11:50. This is a gold mining center, and surrounding the Driehock Grounds where we played two concerts to very bad business are mines in full operation. It was cold enough to wear overcoats at the evening concert.

Left Germiston at 11:10, arriving in Joburg at 11:40.

Mileage Joburg to Germiston and return 18 miles.

April 8th, Saturday. Mat. + Eve. Joburg.

Our baseball team met defeat in a game with Doc Brennan's Joburg team. Score 11 to 8. Went to the hospital to see Senno, but he put over a trick on me as he was discharged a half hour before I got there.

Concerts in the Gymnasium fairly attended.

April 9th, Sunday. Mat. Benoni. Eve. Joburg.

We took the 10 o'clock train for Benoni, arriving at about 11:10. I took a cab for Kleinfontein, where we played the afternoon concert on the athletic field to a big audience. I had lunch at a mine boarding house, and it was very good. We were compelled to walk the 2 miles back to the station, as our cabs were not in sight. Train left at 6, arriving in Joburg at 6:55.

Concert on the Wanderer's Grounds to good business.

Mileage Joburg to Benoni and return 42 miles.

April 10th, Monday. Traveling.

Sorry to leave Joburg, as my stay was made very pleasant by Mr. & Mrs. Clark, with whom I lived. Weather pleasant today for traveling. Left Joburg at 8:40 a.m. with very poor accommodations on our train. This thing of sleeping on a shelf covered with only a blanket and no mattress doesn't make a hit with me.

April 11th, Tuesday. Mat. + Eve. Pieter-Maritzburg.

I woke up at 8 o'clock and we were in Maritzburg. We had no water or towels on our cars this morning. Oh! fine. I rushed up to the Horse Shoe Hotel and brushed up. This town contains many thousands of Hindoos and East Indians and therefore looks very much different from other So. African cities. Their women do a lot of peddling and also all kinds of hard work. They wear all manner of jewelry stuck all over them, rings on their toes, ankles, in their nose and ears, but a very clean appearing race of people. The Rickshaw boys are plentiful, and the excellent streets afford a good going for them.

[Clarke]: Instead of cabs and autos for passenger service around town, we were carried around in "rickshaws," drawn by immense Zulus, all decorated with horns on their heads, and bodies painted up like our one-time Indians. Their clothing consists of a girdle about the waist only, and, with the different colored decorations upon their ivory black skin, made them look fierce, although grotesque. My opinion of the Zulu race is that they are about the finest specimens of strongly built men in the world, none being less than six feet tall, and many over seven feet, and they can run like deer, as we found out, by offering them prizes for the fastest runner, when leaving the hotel to reach the pier, a distance of a mile or more, and we certainly flew along in these rickshaws.[9]

Maritzburg is a whole lot different from Joburg and the absence of that commercial hustle is very noticeable and agreeable.

Business poor at the matinee but good at the night concert held at the Town Hall.

Mileage Joburg to Maritzburg 411.

April 12th, Wednesday. Mat. + Eve. Durban.

Train left at 7:45, and our trip to Durban was thru the most picturesque country of So. Africa. We passed many orange groves, banana,

Band members were amazed at the speed of natives who pulled rickshaws around South African cities. Trombonist/baggagemaster Marcus Lyon was one of many who had a picture taken for postcards to be sent home. (Author's Collection)

bamboo and palm trees and in fact everything that grows in a tropical climate. It was a mountainous country, but the earth was one mass of green vegetation and a sight for the eyes. Durban was the prettiest spot in all So. Africa and is on the sea coast.

We played two concerts here today to good business at the Town Hall, which is one of the finest constructed buildings we have played in on the whole trip. The auditorium where we played contains a fine pipe organ and couldn't be improved on. The manager of the Waverly Hotel where I stopped had the Stars and Stripes flying from the flagpole in our honor. West Street, the principle business street, greatly resembles Atlantic Ave. Atlantic City leading down to the ocean front.

Mileage Maritzburg to Durban 71.

The club held a meeting tonight, and I was appointed chairman of a committee to put on a minstrel show to be given on the steamer "Ionic" going to Australia.

April 13th, Thursday. Mat. Durban.

After breakfast, Ben Vereecken and I walked to the beach and had a dip in the Indian Ocean. The Municipal owns and controls all public conveniences, bath houses, trams etc. The ocean here is infested with man-eating sharks, and numerous accidents have happened to bathers here until a cage like arrangement was built to keep out all sharks. The cage extends out into the water several hundred feet. The water was warm and we had a fine swim.

We played a matinee to a fair house, after which I took a rickshaw to the Union Castle Line Dock and boarded the steamer "Laxon." The "Laxon" has a tonnage of 12,385 and can make 18 knots. The harbor is a beauty, and we are sorry that our stay was so short. The quarters on this boat are fine, but the food very ordinary. Sea is calm, and we are going along smoothly.

April 14th, "Good Friday." Mat. + Eve. East London.

The boat anchored in the East London harbor at 7 o'clock this morning. After breakfast, we were transferred to the tender "Stork" in a basket, another novel experience. We landed on the wharf at 10 o'clock, and I took a cab up to town and located at the Phoenix Hotel. This town appeared dead this morning, as the streets were deserted.

Concert at 3 in the Recreation Park to very poor business. Not one encore was given and Mr. Sousa rushed the concert as much as possible. This fact of not playing an encore is perhaps the first time it has happened in the history of the band.

Night concert to a poor house in the Town Hall.

Mileage Durban to East London 252.

April 15th, Saturday. Mat. + Eve. King Williamstown.

Train left East London at 8:15, arriving at King Williamstown at 11 o'clock. Two bands were at the Station to receive us. We were to make a parade up into town, but this band can't see anything like that, so the boys beat it to hotels as quick as they could. I am stopping at the Commercial Hotel. Vereecken and I took a walk thru a Kaffir Kraal and saw the natives in their home life. One tribe, called the red blanket tribe, is particularly interesting. The women wear only a bunch of paint on their faces using red white and yellow clay for paint and their red blankets. They look like American Indians to a certain degree.

Matinee at the Recreation Park at 3 to small business. Night concert poorly attended at the Town Hall.

I asked Mr. Sousa to write words to the number from "Three Quotations Suite," "In Darkest Africa," to be used in our minstrel show.

Mileage East London to King Williamstown 42.

9. Herbert L. Clarke, "A World's Tour with Sousa," *Musical Messenger,* Oct. 1918, 5.

April 16th, Easter Sunday. Traveling.

Attended Mass at the Church of the Sacred Heart, a building about the size of St. Matthew's at home. The day is beautiful, not a cloud in the sky. We left King Williamstown at 11:50. A badly managed contract between Major Ward the local manager of the band and the railroad company resulted in not having enough accommodation on the train for the band. After holding the train for nearly an hour, the station master put on another car, which he might have done in the first place and avoided a lot of discussion and loss of time. No dining car on this train, and we boys spent Easter Sunday living on ham sandwiches we were lucky enough to carry from King Williamstown. Our route brought us thru a wild portion of the country dotted with native Kraals. Kaffir boys half starved, naked and fleet of foot, ran along with the train calling for bread and pennies which the passengers tossed to them from the car windows. A wild scramble ensued between the boys when anything was thrown to them.

We had no bedding provided for the seats on which we tried to sleep, so we passed the night as best we could under the conditions. A spectacular lightning storm with rain came up in the evening and continued thru the night.

April 17th, Monday. Mat. + Eve. Grahamstown.

Arrived in Grahamstown at 6:30. Rain all day.

Business bad at both concerts here in the City Hall. Everybody is away from town during the Easter Holidays, and the town, tho quite

In Sousa's autobiography he tells of being alarmed by the attention of natives when recordings of his marches were played in his presence: "One by one those natives stole up, felt my coat, and salaamed until their noses nearly touched the ground." (Author's Collection, courtesy of Antoinette Cendali)

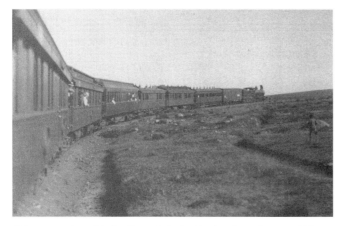

Africans ran alongside the Sousa train, hoping band members would throw coins to them. (Barry Owen Furrer Collection)

pretty made an unfavorable impression with me. Mr. Sousa gave me the words and music of the song for our minstrel show.

Mileage King Williamstown to Grahamstown 222.

April 18th, Tuesday. Eve. Port Elizabeth.

I bought a bunch of pineapples at a penny apiece, and they were delicious. Train left for Port Elizabeth at 9:30, arriving at 4 o'clock. The boys bought a lot of ostrich plumes here, as this town is the center for that business. We played to one of the largest audiences of our trip in So. Africa tonight at the Feather Market. Train left at 11:25 for Cape Town.

Mileage Grahamstown to Port Elizabeth 104.

April 19th, Wednesday. Traveling.

Spent the day cooking up material for the minstrel show.

April 20th, Thursday. Eve. Cape Town.

Still traveling and quite comfortable, as the weather is ideal. Arrived in Cape Town at 6:05. p.m. Located at the Central Hotel.

Concert to bad business at the City Hall.

Mileage Port Elizabeth to Cape Town 838.

April 21st, Friday. Mat. + Eve. Cape Town.

I bought a few ostrich plumes this morning, also some music and supplies for the show.

Business bad at both concerts. We were instructed to report at the City Hall tomorrow morning at 9:15 to receive instructions about the steamer "Ionic."

Total So. African Mileage 3,118.

April 22nd, Saturday. Steamer "Ionic."

Instructed to go aboard the "Ionic" at 1:30 this afternoon. Schroeder, Vereecken and I took a taxi to the Pier Head Dock. The "Ionic" lay out in the harbor, flying a yellow flag, meaning that some contagious disease is aboard. Small-pox is reported as being the disease. It was rumored that the band would take another boat to Australia, but at 2 o'clock the tender "Sir Charles Elliot" steamed away from the dock with all on board, Mr. Sousa being assured that the small-pox rumor was just a slight heat rash that broke out on the boat while crossing the Equator.

The "Ionic" steamed out of the Cape Town Harbor at 5:45, the weather being fine. At six o'clock, I witnessed the burial at sea of a baby, which had died this morning of dysentery. The body was sewed in a canvas bag, weighted, and as it lay on the burial plank it was covered over with the British Flag and services held before it was dropped into the Ocean. All the ships officers were present and as the body dropped the ship was stopped a few minutes.

Clock moved forward 38 minutes at midnight.

April 23rd, Sunday. Steamer "Ionic."

All the regulars are again seasick, as the sea is choppy.

[Clarke]: As one of the men remarked after the first day out, he thought he was going to die, and being more seasick the second day, wished he would die.[10]

Boat made 228 miles at 12 o'clock. Our accommodations on this boat are not as nice as on the steamer "Tainui," as deck space is

10. Herbert L. Clarke, "A World's Tour with Sousa," *Musical Messenger,* Nov. 1918, 4.

scarce, and for that reason our trip may not be as nice as former voyages.

Clock moved forward 23 minutes.
Mileage 228.

April 24th, Monday. Steamer "Ionic."

Miss Zedeler is interested in our minstrel show and will help us as much as she can. Ed Clarke distributed 2/6, the money the management didn't pay the So. African R.R. for not supplying bedding for us last Sunday night. Rehearsal of the show this afternoon. Marc Lyon taken sick with ptomaine poisoning. Bert Clarke will arrange my song for the show.

Clock moved forward 23 minutes at midnight. Heavy seas all day.
Mileage 272.

April 25th, Tuesday. Steamer "Ionic."

Cloudy weather rain and heavy sea. Rehearsals both afternoon & morning for the show. We played with the medicine ball late in the afternoon. A heavy gale sprang up towards evening, with a heavy sea rolling.

Clock moved forward 25 minutes.
Mileage 321.

April 26th, Wednesday. Steamer "Ionic."

Our personal and instrument trunks were taken on deck for our use this morning. Miss Zedeler secured permission from the Captain for we boys to use the upper 1st Class deck for our games from 3 till 5:30. Mrs. Garing and Lyon are very sick. Mr. Simmons told me that the show could use the First Saloon for our minstrel show rehearsals.

Clock moved forward 27 minutes at midnight.
Mileage 309.

April 27th, Thursday. Steamer "Ionic."

Weather bad, and it is turning cold. 48 degrees at noon. Medicine ball this afternoon, and we worked hard to keep warm. Minstrel show rehearsals.

Clock moved forward 27 minutes.
Mileage 285.

April 28th, Friday. Steamer "Ionic."

Sun shining faintly, and it is the best morning we have had so far. The 1st and 2nd cabin played a game of deck cricket this afternoon. We bundled up good and played the game, our team losing. Score 65 to 27 runs. The purser made 50 runs for the first cabin before he quit, as our bowlers were out of form. Mr. Sousa, Simmons and the other first class team were easy outs. I made the 27 runs scored by the second class. Rehearsal tonight at 7:30.

Clock moved forward 27 minutes.
Mileage 283.

April 29th, Saturday. Steamer "Ionic."

We struck a heavy gale tonight, but the boat stood the storm well. Rehearsal in the morning and medicine ball in the afternoon.

Clock moved forward 28 minutes.
Mileage 300.

April 30th, Sunday. Steamer "Ionic."

The weather is the same as the past few days, with a good stiff gale blowing dull and dreary. Church services at 10:30. No rehearsals today except for the end men.

Clock moved forward 26 minutes.
Mileage 296.

May 1st, Monday. Steamer "Ionic."

A rehearsal of the orchestra and songs this morning at 10:30, and everything went well, to the surprise of all. The weather is getting colder all the time as we go farther South. Medicine ball this afternoon.

Clock moved forward 27 minutes.
Mileage 325.

May 2nd, Tuesday. Steamer "Ionic."

The Ship's doctor, a very much overworked man, was taken sick today, and our rehearsal was called off. The Doctor has had a great amount of sickness to attend too besides the vaccination of the entire steerage, altho nothing has been heard of the small-pox.

[Clarke]: Fortunately, we always carried a doctor with us, in case of accidents, who played tympani in the band, and he was called upon to care for the ship's doctor, eventually given the position of ship doctor by the captain. He soon brought the doctor around (he was unconscious for three days and unable to get out of bed for the remainder of the voyage). . . . Dr. Willie Lowe was certainly a wonder and we all felt proud of him.[11]

Mr. Greenwood the Purser allowed the rehearsal to take place in the 1st Class smoke room this afternoon. Mr. Sousa attended the rehearsal. Mix, our photographer, gave me a practical lesson on developing films.

Clock moved forward 29 minutes.
Mileage 304.

May 3rd, Wednesday. Steamer "Ionic."

Weather very cold today. After a talk with Mr. Simmons, we decided to postpone the minstrel show until next Monday night, as the Doctor's condition is such that no noise is allowed not even the 12 o'clock whistle goes and the weather is dead against us. I gave the ship's printer the program to fix up. Medicine ball in the afternoon.

Clock moved forward 29 minutes.
Mileage 298.

May 4th, Thursday. Steamer "Ionic."

A storm followed all thro the day by similar ones came up after breakfast. They were of the kind customary to the Indian Ocean of about 10 or 15 minutes duration, with a heavy gale and snow with sleet. At 8 o'clock, the temperature was 38 degrees. The frequent squalls started a very heavy sea, with the result that the fiddles [racks put around the tops of tables to keep things from falling off] were put on the saloon tables at meal time. Since leaving New York, today is our roughest.

[Clarke]: This boat seemed to have a regular corkscrew motion, caused from the high stern seas. Sometimes the bow of the ship would rise sixty or seventy feet in the air, then plunge downward beneath the waves, which would break over the forward decks. With this plunge there was also a side roll, when the decks were sometimes on an angle of nearly forty-five degrees. I saw this happen one day by watching a gauge or pendulum on the under deck amidships, which marked the forty-five-degree point. Thus you can

11. Ibid., 5.

imagine the difficulty in walking up along a steep roof, only the roof was always moving and never stationary. When sleeping in the berths we had to be strapped in or wedged against the wall to keep from falling out.[12]

Many accidents happened to passengers from falling about, and one particularly high sea caused the ship to go over so far that for the time I didn't expect she would right herself. I was on the top deck when it happened. Mrs. Root fell at that time, and Dr. Lowe of the band put several stitches in her nose.

[Clarke]: The mother of our soprano soloist also met with a serious accident at the close of our noon meal one day. As she arose from her chair the ship gave an unusual lurch, throwing Mrs. Root across the entire dining saloon, where she struck her head against a steam radiator, knocking her senseless. When she was picked up and carried to her stateroom it was found that there was a deep gash about two inches long on her nose. Our Dr. Lowe put several stitches in it, washed and bandaged it up carefully in such a splendid manner that when the cut healed up it did not even show the sign of scar. He was all right![13]

Dishes fell all over the place, and a half cooked dinner spread itself all over the floor of the kitchen, meaning a whole new dinner for the cooks to prepare.
Clock moved forward 26 minutes.
Mileage 285.

May 5th, Friday. Steamer "Ionic."

We passed thro a very rough night, with our steamer trunks flying all about the cabin, but I slept all thro it. We certainly had a fine night picked for our show last night, the worst we have had on the whole trip. It is very cold, and the decks are being continually washed with huge waves dashing over. The gale is still with us, with an occasional squall to enliven things. We are now about half way around the world, a few hours after midnight this morning.
Clock moved forward 26 minutes.
Mileage 275.

May 6th, Saturday. Steamer "Ionic."

This is a dismal day, with rain and not even a heavy sea to look at. The band held a meeting this afternoon, the object being to give a banquet at the close of the present tour. Wm. Robinson presided, and after about an hour's work the whole scheme fell thro. Our club held a meeting tonight and named it the Globe Trotters.
Clock moved forward 27 minutes.
Mileage 296.

May 7th, Sunday. Steamer "Ionic."

It had been snowing all night, but the salt air soon melted what was laying on the deck. Services at 10:30. Weather very rough, and the fiddles were again put on the tables. The weather has been behind us, and the heavy gale has helped to drive us on all the way from Cape Town. All shipping travel this same way as the trade winds blow the one direction all the while. So far, we neither sighted a boat nor has the wireless picked up a communication with any other boat.
Clock moved forward 29 minutes.
Mileage 310.

May 8th, Monday. Steamer "Ionic."

Band rehearsal at 11 o'clock in the 1st Saloon. The ship doctor has improved greatly under Dr. Lowe's care, which permitted the rehearsal. We decided to give the minstrel show this coming Wednesday night, weather permitting.
Clock moved forward 30 minutes.
Mileage 300.

May 9th, Tuesday. Steamer "Ionic."

Band rehearsal this morning at 11 o'clock. Minstrel show tickets sold rapidly. Medicine ball this afternoon.
Clock moved forward 28 minutes.
Mileage 299.

May 10th, Wednesday. Steamer "Ionic."

Band rehearsal at 11 o'clock. Minstrel show rehearsal at 3 o'clock. The deck steward and the electrician, with a squad of sailors, started work on the deck for the show tonight, and they made one grand sight of it with flags and bunting in abundance. Foot lights, border and bunch lights were all fixed beside a curtain. At 6:30, I started making up the boys, and at 8 I finished 9, including myself. Bill Decker, the orchestra leader, started the overture at 8:25, and at 8:35 the curtain went aside to a packed audience that filled every available inch of deck space. Ben Vereecken made a good job arranging the music, and the boys on the stage all on the job resulted in a good first part. 15 men on the stage, with 14 in the orchestra, including Miss Zedeler playing violin. After an intermission the olio [medley of musical numbers] went on, the big hits being Irving Davis in a monologue and the two Sousa girls in a Spanish dance. Herman Hand female impersonator, Arthur Kunze and Frank Snow completed the bill with an act by Emil Mix concluding the show. It was a mechanical musical act in which Kunze, Smith, Lawton and Eckstein were the actors. Everybody appreciated the show and spoke kindly of it.

[Russell]: The most interesting event of the voyage was a minstrel show given by members of the band under the general direction of Albert Knecht, whose enthusiasm was very contagious. Of course no music could be purchased, so several favorite songs of the minstrel stage were scored from memory and new songs were composed for the occasion by members of the band. The ship's purser arranged an attractive stage setting and light effects on the saloon deck and the audience that assembled was so large that it caused the ship to list to port. An old-time first part was put on with songs, choruses and good-natured roasts on all present. Miss Zedeler assisted in the minstrel orchestra, but she refused to black up. She said she was afraid it might not come off and wasn't going to take any chances. An olio followed, consisting of several stunts by the band members and an original song and dance by the Misses Sousa.[14]

I was all in after the show and retired early.
Clock moved forward 27 minutes.
Mileage 308.

May 11th, Thursday. Steamer "Ionic."

Spent the morning clearing up the financial part of our show. Net proceeds amounted to £9, 5/-. Expenses taken out show a balance of £6, 3/- to go to the Sailor's, Widow's and Orphan's Home. Land sighted at 2:30, and it was welcome after our long perilous trip from Cape Town.

---

12. Ibid., 4–5.
13. Ibid., 5.

14. Clarence J. Russell, "Around the World with Sousa," *Musical American*, Aug. 5, 1918, 19.

We anchored in the Hobart Harbor at 11:30 p.m.
Mileage 311 till 12 noon. 135 to Port. Total 446.
Cape Town to Hobart 5,740 nautical miles.
Cape Town to Hobart 6,413 U.S. Miles.
Mileage. En Route Conshohocken to Hobart 23,703.

May 12th, Friday. Eve. Launceston, Tasmania.

We passed the Port health officer very easily this morning. Landed on the dock at 7:45 and took a cab to the Tasmanian R.R. Station. Scheduled to leave at 9:30, but a poor transfer of our baggage from the "Ionic" delayed us until 12 o'clock. By special train Hobart to Launceston, arriving at 5:10. We were booked to play Hobart last night, but the boat arrived too late. Stopping at the National Hotel. Business very big in the Albert Hall.

Mr. Edwards, former leader of the band here, is proprietor of the National.

[Clarke]: We were happy and jolly, ready for our first concert, at Launceston, which we reached in the afternoon; and, as we disembarked from the train, created much excitement among the inhabitants, being the first American musical organization to ever visit Tasmania.[15]

Mileage Hobart to Launceston 133.

May 13th, Saturday. Steamer "Rotomohana."

I visited the famous Launceston Gorge this morning and the Suspension Bridge swinging across it. We boarded the steamer "Rotomohana" at 2 o'clock for Melbourne. This boat is the first steel boat built for the Australian waters in 1879. It made 17 knots, and in comparison to the slow 12 knot "Ionic" we seemed to fairly fly across the water. Our trip was fine and the weather perfect.

May 14th, Sunday. Traveling, Melbourne to Sydney.

Arrived in Melbourne at 9 o'clock and took a walk about the business part of the city, and it looks good very much like an American town in appearance. Everything is closed here today. No cigars to be had or anything else. Tram-cars are not run during the church hour. We took a train out at 12 o'clock, making fast time and traveling thro a very pretty country.

Mileage Launceston to Melbourne 250 American miles.

May 15th, Monday. Mat. + Eve. Sydney.

Arrived in Sydney at 8:03. We had no sleeping car accommodations, but I passed a comfortable night in a first class compartment. Hotels seemed scarce, and I finally located at the Wynyard Hotel, cor. Erskine & Clarence St. At 11 o'clock, the Sydney people gave us a grand reception, the biggest this band has ever had accorded to it. At the Town Hall, Mr. Sousa was welcomed by the Mayor and made a reply.

[Clarke]: An immense crowd congregated at the depot to greet us; all Sydney seemed to have turned out to salute the March King and his famous band, and the parade started, headed by an immense band, made up of all the musicians in Sydney and the surrounding towns. Mr. Sousa, his family, the soloists and staff riding in luxuriant carriages, and the bandmen following, seated in large vans, all decorated with British and American flags, each van drawn by six horses, upon which were seated the drivers in full costume. This parade extended through the main streets of Sydney, which were jammed on both sides by the populace, cheering, as we rode on to the town hall,

and a great reception was accorded us by the mayor, council and citizens, who crowded into the immense hall to its fullest capacity.[16]

In the afternoon, the Sydney Musicians gave us a reception, but I didn't attend, enjoying a good nap instead.
We opened at the Town Hall tonight to a big house.

[Sousa]: It isn't every fellow who comes thousands of miles with his band, and is met by a band of a thousand, a rattling good one too, and then, entering a hall, hears another band play his own music faithfully and beautifully.[17]

Mileage Melbourne to Sydney 582.

May 16th, Tuesday. Eve. Sydney.

Worked all morning with my personal trunk. No matinee.
Business good at the night concert.
An invitation was received by the band from the Sydney professional musicians to go on a trip around the Sydney Harbor, one of the finest in the world.
Sydney is a great city, full of life and hustle, and compares in most respects to American cities.

May 17th, Wednesday. Mat. + Eve. Sydney.

Business good at both concerts.

May 18th, Thursday. Eve. Sydney.

We had a very hard rehearsal this morning, from 11 to 1. A few of our ball team went out to the Sydney University to play a practice game. We arrived there late and could do nothing. Arranged a game for some day next week.
Business very big at the night concert.

May 19th, Friday. Eve. Sydney.

The band assembled at 2 o'clock at the Fort McQuarie Pier and boarded the Government launch "Premier."
Mr. Sousa made the trip around the Sydney Harbor with us, and we all enjoyed the hospitality of the musicians immensely. We were back at 5:30 after one of the prettiest trips I have ever made. We passed the "Makura," the ship we are to go home on.
Business improves every day.

May 20th, Saturday. Mat. + Eve. Sydney.

Saturday being a national half holiday, all shops closed at 12 noon. The people take life easy here, and nobody really kills themselves by overwork.
Business great at both concerts.

May 21st, Sunday. Sydney.

This is a beautiful day, and after church I took a trip to Manley, the finest sea-side resort about Sydney. A ride of a half an hour across the Bay brought us to the resort. I had a fine trip and enjoyed myself. Street cars stop running during the church hours, from 11 till 12 and from 7 to 8 in the evening. No concerts today.

May 22nd, Monday. Eve. Sydney.

Rehearsal at 11 o'clock. Evening concert to a big house. Boarded the steamer "Namoi" at 11:15 p.m. for Newcastle. The boat is a side wheel-

15. Herbert L. Clarke, "A World's Tour with Sousa," *Musical Messenger*, Dec. 1918, 4.

16. Ibid., 5.
17. Sousa, *Marching Along*, 270.

er and the dirtiest ship I was ever on. Our berths were fierce, nothing more than a plank covered with a sheet. Fleas and other insects enjoyed themselves at our expense.

May 23rd, Tuesday. Mat. + Eve. Maitland.

The stewards gave us about 10 minutes to get off the boat after docking at Newcastle. We caught the 6:47 train for Maitland, arriving at 7:40. I located at Barry's Commercial Hotel and enjoyed a sleep until 1 o'clock. The boys held a meeting and placed the experience we had last night to Mr. Sousa, who promised that we would go back to Sydney by train instead of the boat.

Business fair at both concerts at the Adelphi Theatre.

Mileage Sydney to Newcastle by boat 67. Newcastle to Maitland by rail 20. Total 87. New Zealand

May 24th, Wednesday. Mat. + Eve. Newcastle.

Mrs. Barry, proprietress of the hotel, certainly put one over on us this morning. Her rate increased over night because it was 5 shillings a day yesterday, and to get out we paid 10 shillings this morning. Some class to that lady, and 18 wise guys took the count and fell for the 10 shillings thing. Train left at 10:05, arriving in Newcastle at 11:10.

Business fair at the Central Mission Hall both concerts. Stopping at the Shortland Hotel.

Mileage Maitland to Newcastle 20.

May 25th, Thursday. Mat. + Eve. Sydney.

Train left Newcastle at 7:50 arriving in Sydney at 11:10. I am living with people by the name of Black here in Sydney.

Big business both concerts at the City Hall.

Mileage Newcastle to Sydney 104.

May 26th, Friday. Eve. Sydney.

Rehearsal at 11 o'clock, and Mr. Sousa was very strict with the men.

Business big at night.

May 27th, Saturday. Mat. + Eve. Sydney.

It rained all day and is the most miserable weather we have had since our arrival here in Australia.

Matinee at the Adelphi Theatre to a packed house.

Evening at the Town Hall to a packed house.

May 28th, Sunday.

Nothing doing today except to keep warm after the drop in temperature after yesterday's rain and to take a few pictures of the lovely lawns surrounding this house I am living at.

May 29th, Monday. Eve. Sydney.

Rehearsal at 10:30. Three of the boys are laid up with heavy colds. The baseball games arranged for Tuesday and Friday of this week are off, as we play matinees every day except today.

Business good at the evening concert.

May 30th, Tuesday. Mat. + Eve. Sydney.

I made an appointment with Bain, a vaudeville agent, for tomorrow thru Mr. Gilbey concerning a musical act.

Business big at both concerts.

May 31st, Wednesday. Mat. + Eve. Sydney.

Had a very interesting talk to Mr. Bain, who would handle an act for me here in Australia to cover the Tex Ricard houses.

Business good at both concerts.

June 1st, Thursday. Mat. + Eve. Sydney.

Rehearsal this morning at 10:30, and all were present except Lephilibert, the first oboe. He refused to make the rehearsal, claiming to have a sore lip resulting from overwork. A rehearsal and two concerts a day is too much for Philly's health.

Concerts to good business. The Governor of N.S.W. attended the evening concert with his wife and staff.

June 2nd, Friday. Mat. + Eve. Sydney.

Six of the band were invited by the Sydney Musicians to take an auto ride about the surrounding country, and today is the eventful date. We left town at 10:30, crossing the ferry to North Sydney. Trouble started as soon as we struck the first hill, as the fuse burned out on the car. The same trouble followed us all thru the day. It took us until 3:30 to get to Paramatta, a distance of about 25 miles. That car landed in ditches and every other thing along the road, resulting in some good snapshots for the camera fiends. We pushed the car up hills, etc, but thru it all we had a good time as we were a good natured crowd. We had dinner at the Paramatta Park Gates Hotel at 3:40 and started the return trip at 4:30 taking a shorter route.

The machine worked good on the home stretch, and we made the 15 miles in less than an hour.

Big business at the night concert.

June 3rd, Saturday. Mat. + Eve. Sydney.

Packed trunk this morning.

Packed houses at both concerts. Mr. Sousa was compelled to make a speech after the long 2 hour and 35 minute program at the night concert.

[Sousa]: On the closing night in Sydney I made probably the shortest speech on record. As we finished Auld Lang Syne there were cheers and pleas for a speech. I bowed and backed off but the applause continued, so I advanced to the front of the platform and when I had obtained silence I called out, "Can everybody hear me?" "Yes!" came from all parts of the house. With a broad smile I shouted back. "Good night" and scampered off the stage.[18]

The folks at the house gave us a farewell supper. Some lobster salad.

June 4th, Sunday. Traveling.

Spent the day having a good time on the lawn taking pictures and having an all day feast.

Mr. Bradley at the house gave we boys stopping there a glass tube containing all kinds of minerals, which he had dug in Tasmania while touring thru there with the Jeffries-Johnson fight pictures.

I took the first section leaving for Melbourne at 7:25. The train was splendid and the trip good. We had sleeping cars this time.

June 5th, Monday. Mat. + Eve. Melbourne.

Called at 7 o'clock, and it was cold getting up this morning, as the difference in climate going South is certainly noticeable. Had breakfast at Albury.

We changed R.R. here at Albury, as every state in Australia has a different railway gauge.

At Melbourne we had the greatest reception given us by the citizens that the band ever received, completely putting the Sydney reception in the shade.

Fifteen bands massed played at the station and escorted us up town.

---

18. Ibid., 274–75.

We rode in carriages, and the line of march was up Little Collins Street to the Town Hall. About 300,000 people would be a safe estimate were standing by. The police were unable to control the crowds in places, and we were simply crowded out. It is impossible to explain the affair except if it is in the words of the Sup't of Police. He said that we had more people turn out to welcome us than would be on hand to see the Gov. General of the Province.

We opened at the Glaciarium to good business this afternoon. I am stopping private at 29 MacKenzie Street.

Business good at night.

Mileage Sydney to Melbourne 582.

June 6th, Tuesday. Eve. Melbourne.

Arthur Storch received news of the death of his baby on April 15th. That is the third death in the immediate families of any of the boys. A brother of Walter Collins and the wife of Arthur Berry being the other two.

Business poor the evening concert.

June 7th, Wednesday. Mat. + Eve. Melbourne.

The weather has been cold and unsettled all week with rain every day.

[Clarke]: The climate is never severe, but quite chilly, at this time of the year, and there is no artificial heating in this country, nor steam heat in hotels, Theatres, trains nor stores, and, although the temperature seldom falls below 40 degrees, we found it uncomfortable, the cold penetrating every fiber of one's body, especially while sitting for a two hours' concert. My fingers were so numb while playing solos I could hardly move them at times, and often sat on my right hand to keep it warm just before my solo number.[19]

Business fair at both concerts. The Glaciarium is a very cold building, and the heating apparatus is not adequate enough to push sufficient heat into the hall, with the result that people won't come as they should.

June 8th, Thursday. Eve. Melbourne.

I ordered a picture from a local photographer of our reception here on arrival.

Business improving slightly.

June 9th, Friday. Eve. Melbourne.

Spent the day sticking hotel labels on my trunk.

Business good at the night concert.

June 10th, Saturday. Mat. + Eve. Melbourne.

This is a miserable day, a cold rain falling and a biting wind.

We had good business at both concerts. A flash light photo of the band was taken tonight.

June 11th, Sunday.

Another bum day, just about like yesterday.

It cleared a bit by noon, and I took a cable car out to St. Kilda, from which place I went to Brighton by electric car. Brighton is a summer resort and has a beautiful beach. Another heavy shower came up while I was on the beach, and I made a quick break for the car.

June 12th, Monday. Eve. Melbourne.

Rehearsal this morning at 10:30. No matinee, so Helleberg and I

19. Herbert L. Clarke, "A World's Tour with Sousa," *Musical Messenger,* Dec. 1918, 5.

went over to the Melbourne Athletic Club and saw a few fighters do some stunts exercising.

Business fair tonight. Ernest Gately taken to a hospital.

June 13th, Tuesday. Mat. + Eve. Melbourne.

Dull and rainy today.

Fair business at both concerts.

June 14th, Wednesday. Mat. + Eve. Melbourne.

I had a rehearsal with Jos. Norrito on some clarinet solos he is to play.

Business fair at both concerts. Rehearsal in Collins room at the Union Club Hotel.

June 15th, Thursday. Mat. + Eve. Melbourne.

Weather bad again today. I rehearsed a violin solo with Miss Zedeler ("Romeo & Juliet") at the Grand Hotel after the matinee.

Business good at both concerts.

June 16th, Friday. Mat. + Eve. Melbourne.

Helleberg and I visited Ernest Gatley at the Garlick's Hospital today, and he shows signs of improvement. He has an attack of pneumonia.

Business fair at both concerts.

June 17th, Saturday. Mat. + Eve. Melbourne.

Rehearsal at 11 o'clock. The weather cleared for a few hours today. Big business today.

June 18th, Sunday.

Attended Mass at the Church of the Sacred Heart at 11 o'clock. Women still sing in the choirs here, the same as at the St. Mary's Church Sydney. The day is fine, and Helleberg and I took a five-mile walk thru the Botanical Gardens, a very beautiful place. The band attended a show in the new J. D. William's Melba Theatre this evening.

June 19th, Monday. Mat. + Eve. Melbourne.

Rehearsal at 10:30. Mr. Sousa asked me to get mutes for the alto and tenor saxophones for a certain passage in the Dvorak "New World Symphony" number.

Bad house at the matinee. Big business at night.

June 20th, Tuesday. Mat. + Eve. Melbourne.

I cut out patterns for the saxophone mutes and had them made out of a light cloth.

Matinee to bad business. Fair at night. The saxophone mutes were used tonight.

June 21st, Wednesday. Mat. + Eve. Melbourne.

Rain all day.

Fair business at both concerts.

June 22nd, Thursday. Mat. + Eve. Melbourne.

The coronation of King George and Queen Mary today in London makes a national holiday for the whole British Empire. A monster parade was held here this afternoon, while other ceremonies took place about the City.

Business was big at the matinee. The electrical display at night, when all the public bldgs. were illuminated, was pretty.

Business fair at the night concert. The Australian management is behind in the receipts of the band so far, especially the present Melbourne season. Weather was against us here very much.

June 23rd, Friday. Mat. + Eve. Ballarat.

We left Melbourne this morning at 7:40, arriving in Ballarat at 11:10. This city is situated in a very high altitude, and the weather is correspondingly cold. We all suffered greatly with it. Mr. Sousa suffered a chill, which prevented him from conducting the concerts here. Herbert Clarke conducted the band while Doc Lowe attended Mr. Sousa at his hotel.

[Clarke]: I remember that, after conducting the overture and an encore, my solo came next on the program, and, picking up my cornet from the director's stand, I began to play, after the introduction by the band. Found that, on account of the extreme cold (no heat in the Coliseum), my first note was just half a tone flat! Horrors! How it did sound! But, luckily, the solo started with a long cadenza, and by the time I had finished and ready for the band to come in, my cornet heated up a little from my breath, and soon was in tune. While playing I could see the steam come out of the bell of the cornet. The men all played with their overcoats on.[20]

We played two concerts to fair business at the Coliseum, a building without heating apparatus, and it was cold. We wore our overcoats and caps at both concerts. A local band gave us a farewell at the station upon leaving on sleepers at 10:40. We had a brand new equipment of cars on this special train, and the trip to Adelaide was fine.

Mileage Melbourne to Ballarat 78.

June 24th, Saturday. Mat. + Eve. Adelaide.

We arrived in Adelaide at 12:22. All the local bands, about 8 or 10 in number, escorted Mr. Sousa from his hotel to the Exhibition Bldg., where we played two concerts to big business. I am stopping private in very comfortable quarters. Adelaide, a residential sort of town, is very pretty, surrounded by picturesque mountains and contains many pretty parks.

It is also called the Church City being noted for its numerous churches. The weather is lovely and much better than the cold Ballarat weather. We are now six months away from New York City.

Mileage. Ballarat to Adelaide 405.

June 25th, Sunday. Adelaide Australia.

Visited the Cathedral. The day is dull and threatening. At noon it

Eight bands and a huge crowd welcomed the band at the train station in Adelaide, Australia. The reception in Sydney was even greater, with fifteen bands and an estimated three hundred thousand people. (Barry Owen Furrer Collection)

cleared, affording Helleberg and I to take a walk thru the Botanical Gardens here and we saw a strange sight. Scattered in different parts of the park were preachers, stump speakers, and religious fanatics, each surrounded by their followers.

The Salvation Army were the strongest, having a brass band of 35. Then there were faith healers, Israelites, Socialists and others. One fellow wearing red whiskers, a faith healer, seemed to be the fall guy, as he was the target for all kinds of ridicule. The crowd put an end to his speech by mobbing him, which I learned happened regularly to him every Sunday. We then walked thru the Zoo, which contains a very fine collection of animals. This town is poorly lighted by gas except on King William's Street, which has electric light.

June 26th, Monday. Mat. + Eve. Adelaide.

Today is another of the many holidays observed by the Australians. This is the Prince of Wales Birthday. I took a trip out of the City this morning, about six miles, and the view of the town was great from a slight elevation.

Concerts to very big business.

Mr. Sousa has a return attack of malaria and is very sick. Mr. Clarke conducts part of the concerts.

June 27th, Tuesday. Mat. + Eve. Adelaide.

The weather is ideal. A fine bright warm sun and cool nights. Adelaide is the prettiest town in Australia.

The baseball team played on the athletic field back of the Exhibition Bldg. Mr. Sousa conducted only a part of the concerts today.

Business big.

June 28th, Wednesday. Mat. + Eve. Adelaide.

I bought an outfit to develop and print my own pictures. Mr. Sousa is slowly improving.

Good business today.

June 29th, Thursday. Mat. + Eve. Adelaide.

Thru the courtesy of Mr. John Reid, a local liveryman, the band made a fine trip about the mountains in coaches furnished by him. We drove past orange orchards and many pretty scenes while on the 18-mile trip to the Scenic Hotel, nearly 2,000 feet high.

About 40 of the boys made the trip.

Business good at both concerts.

Miss Zedeler was taken ill and unable to play today. Paul Senno took her place on the program.

June 30th, Friday. Mat. Adelaide.

I bought a quantity of opals from a jeweler, W. R. Snow, 43 Rundle Street, this morning. Eckstein and Helleberg also invested.

Business big at the afternoon concert. No evening concert.

We took a train at 6:40 for Melbourne, using the same cars we had coming into this town from Ballarat.

July 1st, Saturday. Mat. + Eve. Melbourne.

Arrived in Melbourne at 11:40. The sun was shining when we got here, and it was a novelty to see the sun in Melbourne for us. Concerts at the Exhibition Bldg., an enormous place, and very cold. Prices are reduced.

Stopping at the Mackenzie Street house.

Mileage Adelaide to Melbourne 483.

July 2nd, Sunday.

Temperature this morning below 45 degrees, not much like the July

20. Ibid.

weather I am accustomed to having. Enjoyed a trip to Toorak this afternoon. Toorak is the fashionable part of Melbourne.

July 3rd, Monday. Mat. + Eve. Melbourne.

I bought some new material to make pictures today. As a photographer, I have showed little promise so far and must consider myself a frost.

Business bad at the matinee and good at night.

The boys are suffering very much from the cold in the Exhibition Bldg.

Three of the boys had a mix-up over a very trivial matter this evening. Freeman took a pass from Wall, and when they were through Arthur Berry was forced into the affray, and a well-placed uppercut decorated Wall's eye for the 4th of July.

July 4th, Tuesday. Mat. + Eve. Melbourne.

The day opened bright and cold with a sharp wind blowing. The boys celebrated Independence Day in different ways, each having their own ideas about it.

The band played American music at both concerts, which seemed to be very well enjoyed by the good sized audiences. American flags were in evidence, and the boys decorated their instruments and music stands with them. It was a very strange Fourth of July.

July 5th, Wednesday. Mat. + Eve. Bendigo.

It was very cold this morning, with a heavy frost, and ice formed in the gutters. Special train left at 8:15, arriving in Bendigo at 11:30. Located at the Court House Hotel. This city looks good to me with its wide well-kept streets and the electric trains.

Matinee and evening concerts at the Drill Hall to big business.

I witnessed a part of an English Rugby football match after the matinee.

Mileage Melbourne to Bendigo 100.

July 6th, Thursday. Mat. + Eve. Melbourne.

Special train left at 8:15, arriving in Melbourne at 11:30.

Concerts to good business at the Exhibition Hall.

Route sheets were distributed today. "Shorty" Griswold invited all the boys to bet on "Central Green," a sure winner in the Grand National Steeple chase, to be run over the Flemington Race Track. The boys fell for the tip.

Mileage Bendigo to Melbourne 100.

July 7th, Friday. Mat. + Eve, Ballarat.

Train left at 7:40, with Helleberg and I just about making it by one minute. Arrived in Ballarat at 11:30. Stopping at Carlyon's Hotel. The weather is better than on our last visit here to this city.

I took a trip to the Gardens and saw some very fine statuary mostly from the hand of Charles Summers, an English born sculptor. Lusana was the finest piece in which the life-like eyes alone are worth about £2,000. It required six months work on the eyes alone.

Matinee & evening at the Coliseum to good business.

Mileage Melbourne to Ballarat 78.

July 8th, Saturday. Mat. + Eve. Melbourne.

Special train leaving Ballarat at 8:45. Arrived in Melbourne at 11:30. Very cold weather at Melbourne today. Hotel trunks are not to be taken to Sydney or Brisbane.

Matinee fair business. Night packed house the third largest on this trip.

Mileage Ballarat to Melbourne 78.

July 9th, Sunday. Traveling.

Left the Spencer Street Station at 11 o'clock for Sydney. Changed trains at Albury to sleeping cars at 8 o'clock.

July 10th, Monday. Mat. + Eve. Sydney.

Arrived in Sydney at 5:40 and got up at 8 o'clock. Stopping with the Blacks and glad to get back to this town.

Business poor at both concerts at the Town Hall.

Mileage Melbourne to Sydney 582.

July 11th, Tuesday. Mat. + Eve. Sydney.

Nothing happened today except rain and bad business.

July 12th, Wednesday. Mat. + Eve. Sydney.

Rehearsal at 11 o'clock. Mr. Sousa, in a reprimand to the men, said that they were losing their artistic temperament and playing like any ordinary band.

1,000 school children attended the matinee, and they were a noisy bunch.

Business bad at night.

July 13th, Thursday. Mat. + Eve. Sydney.

Bad weather is following us, as it has been miserable and cold all week.

2,500 children at the Matinee.

[Russell]: Recognizing the value of these concerts from an educational standpoint, the school authorities in Sydney made arrangements to have all the public school pupils hear them.[21]

Bad house at night.

July 14th, Friday. Mat. + Eve. Sydney.

Spent the morning buying spaghetti, cheese etc., as we expect some lay-out after the matinee. We had another bunch of children at the matinee.

I was chef at the spaghetti lay-out, and it was the goods.

Business light at the evening concert.

July 15th, Saturday. Mat. + Eve. Sydney.

Matinee at the Adelphi Theatre to a packed house.

Evening at the Town Hall to a packed house.

The folks at the house gave us another farewell supper after the concert.

July 16th, Sunday.

Train left at 5:10 p.m. for Toowoomba. We had sleeping cars, and they were fine, regular Pullman coaches nearly. About 30 miles out, one of the cars started a hot-box. Of course it happened to be the car I was on and at Newcastle they took the coach off and put on an ordinary car and the trip was spoiled. We had to sleep on the seats, about two feet wide, and it was some trick to stay off the floor.

July 17th, Monday. Eve. Toowoomba.

Arrived in Toowoomba at 4:50 p.m., and were given a reception by the local band. Stopping at the Harp of Erin Hotel.

We did good business at the evening concert.

Mileage Sydney to Toowoomba 693.

21. Clarence J. Russell, "Around the World with Sousa," *Musical American*, Sept. 9, 1911, 19.

July 18th, Tuesday. Eve. Brisbane.

I felt like having boiled eggs this morning, but the only two eggs in the Harp of Erin Hotel were being served to one of the other boys.

Train left at 7:20, arriving in Brisbane at 12:28. Stopping at the People's Palace Hotel, a brand new up-to-date place owned by the Salvation Army.

A reception that amounted to nothing greeted us here.

Evening concert at the Exhibition Bldg., situated on the outskirts of the town, to light business.

Mileage Toowoomba to Brisbane 101.

July 19th, Wednesday. Mat. + Eve. Brisbane.

Weather here is perfect and very enjoyable after the terrible Melbourne weather.

Business poor at both concerts.

July 20th, Thursday. Mat. + Eve. Brisbane.

Brisbane is right in the heart of the Australian fruit country, but this is the wrong season for fruit, so we are left.

Business bad at the matinee and fair at night.

July 21st, Friday. Mat. + Eve. Brisbane.

About 20 of the boys accepted an invitation from Cook's Picture House and witnessed a show there at 11 o'clock. It was the finest picture show I ever saw.

Business fair.

July 22nd, Saturday. Mat. + Eve. Brisbane.

Concerts at 3 and 8 to packed houses.

July 23rd, Sunday. Traveling.

The hotel people fixed up packets of sandwiches for our long trip. We left Brisbane at 7:40. Sorry to leave on account of the beautiful weather. The only bad feature about Brisbane is the poor sanitation, while the water is very bad. We rode over the Queensland R.R. on coaches built like trolley cars with seats along the side.

At Wallangara at 5:30. We had supper and changed railroads this time, taking the New South Wales R.R. and leaving on sleepers at 6:10. Storch, Eckstein, Decker and I played pinochle over 13 hours today.

July 24th, Monday. Mat. Sydney.

We arrived in Sydney at 10:50, and the Blacks gave us a lovely reception. It is raining hard today.

Evening concerts drew larger crowds than afternoon concerts in both Australia and New Zealand. Often an overflow crowd would be seated around the band onstage, as here in Brisbane. (Barry Owen Furrer Collection)

Matinee to a big house at the Adelphi Theatre.
Train left at 7:25 for Melbourne.
Mileage Brisbane to Sydney 794.

July 25th, Tuesday.

Arrived at Albury at 7:30, changing over to the Victoria R.R. and arriving in Melbourne at 12:50. We had a lay-over until 5 o'clock, when we boarded the steamer "Rotamohana" for Launceston, Tasmania. A large gathering of friends was at the dock to see us off, and we were sorry to leave Australia after having 11 weeks in the Country. Australia is a beautiful Country. Sydney is the wide awake City. Adelaide is the prettiest town we visited, while Melbourne is the best laid out city of the lot. Our finest weather we had in Brisbane.

Mileage Sydney to Melbourne 582.

Total Tasmanian and Australian Mileage 6,215.

July 26th, Wednesday. Mat. + Eve. Launceston.

We had a fine voyage across the Bass Straits and arrived here in Launceston at 12:30. Stopping at the National Hotel.

Big business at the concerts given in the Albert Hall.

Mileage Melbourne to Launceston 250.

July 27th, Thursday. Mat. + Eve. Hobart.

Special train left at 7:40 over the Tasmanian R.R. and our trip to Hobart was the worst I ever made. I was nearly train sick. Arrived in Hobart at 1:20.

Located at the Old Commodore Hotel.

Big business at the King's Hall.

Mileage Launceston to Hobart 133.

July 28th, Friday. Aboard Steamer "Ulimaroa."

Boarded the Huddart-Parker steamer "Ulimaroa" and sailed at 5:20 for New Zealand. This boat is over 6,000 tons, fitted with wireless, and all told is a splendid ship. A large amount of cargo is being carried.

July 29th, Saturday. Aboard Steamer "Ulimaroa."

Weather is fine and the sea moderate. Club Meeting tonight.
Clock moved forward 29 minutes at Midnight.
Mileage: At 12 noon, we made 260 miles.

July 30th, Sunday. Aboard Steamer "Ulimaroa."

Contrary to expectations, this trip is fine. Officers on the boat say that this is one of the finest voyages on record, as the weather is usually very stormy.

Clock moved forward 23 minutes at midnight.
Mileage 340.

July 31st, Monday. Mat. + Eve. Invercargill, N.Z.

Land sighted this morning, and sailing thru the Toveaux Strait the snow clad mountain made a very pretty picture. We passed medical examination and landed at Bluff, New Zealand at 12 o'clock.

Mileage 334 on the day.

At Bluff we boarded a train at the most Southern Railroad Station in the world and arrived in Invercargill at 1 o'clock, where the local bands gave us a reception.

Stopping at the Criterion Hotel. Marc Lyon left Mix's tuba trunk and the trombone trunk on the boat.

[Clarke]: Our baggageman, Mark Lyon, who was responsible for all the baggage, nearly collapsed, his trombone also being in the missing trunk; but, being equal to the occasion, he immediately went to

the depot and arranged for a special engine and truck to run back to the Bluffs and see if the missing trunks had been left on the steamer. Of course, there was no time to wait until these trunks could be brought back in order to start the concert at 8 o'clock, as the large audience were already impatient for the band to start, and Mr. Sousa is a man who is the essence of punctuality and told the men he would start on time, even without the missing instruments. Our trombone players were non-plussed, and did not know what they were going to do, knowing how important the trombone parts were in the opening overture; but some local musicians, who were at the back of the stage talking with our boys, came to the rescue, and offered the use of their instruments, which is characteristic of that people, and after returning hurriedly from their home, bringing the necessary number of trombones, these were found to be high pitch! However, "Yankee gumption" cropped up, and our men drew the tuning slides out to the limit, and used some rubber tape to keep the crooks from dropping out; but these local instruments were of a small bore and bell, and our men could not use their own mouthpieces. Still, after sounding a few notes, the concert began on time, was given in its entirety, as usual, without the audience being any the wiser.[22]

Business good at both concerts at the New Town Hall Theatre. I enjoyed a plate of New Zealand oysters after the concert.

Mileage Hobart to Bluff 934 nautical miles. U.S. miles 997. Bluff to Invercargill 17 miles.

Aug. 1st, Tuesday. Eve. Dunedin.

Called at 5:30. Gus Helleberg was the big comedian this morning. Train left at 6:15 over the New Zealand Government Railroad, arriving at Dunedin in 11 o'clock. Owing to an agricultural exhibition it was hard to secure hotel accommodations. We were given a reception on our arrival. By a lucky chance, Helleberg, Eckstein and myself located at a private house with people named McKinnon on 4 Maitland Street.

Night concert to a fair house in Garrison Hall

Mileage Invercargill to Dunedin 138.

Aug. 2nd, Wednesday. Mat. + Eve. Dunedin.

Rain all day.

Business poor at the matinee and big in the evening.

I stopped in the King's Theatre a vaudeville house after our night concert and saw one act.

Aug. 3rd, Thursday. Mat. + Eve. Dunedin.

Today was shopping day, and I walked about in a heavy rain. Green stone, beads, novelties, etc. and a Mosgiel rug were among my purchases. The Mosgiel rugs have a world-wide reputation and have won first prizes at all exhibitions whenever shown. Most all the boys bought rugs.

Matinee bad house. Evening good business. People here are not accustomed to matinees.

Aug. 4th, Friday. Mat + Eve. Dunedin.

Helleberg and I took a tram-car to St. Cloud and had a look at the beautiful beach. We started to walk to St. Kilda but came across the Forbury Racing Park, so we stopped to see it. We learned that the Coursing Club was holding races, and we were invited by the Club steward to stay and see a couple. I took pictures of dogs named Polar Star and Cross-boy. Cross-boy finished second on the day's events. It is very interesting to see the fleetness of both hares and dogs.

Matinee fair. Evening packed house.

I visited the Shamrock Hotel where Mix is stopping and had a lesson from him in developing films. I had a peculiar experience at the Hotel as the proprietor disobeyed one of the New Zealand laws in allowing me inside the hotel after 10 o'clock. A person found on the premises after 10 o'clock not residing there is liable to a £2 fine. I took a chance and got away with it.

Aug. 5th, Saturday. Mat. + Eve. Dunedin.

By appointment, I met Miss Zedeler at the Grand Hotel at 11 o'clock, and one of the Brothers of the St. Dominic Priory brought us there, where we entertained the Sisters, violin and piano. The Mother gave me a letter from Miss Anna Walker Weightman of Philadelphia. We were well treated and shown about the Convent and it is one swell place.

Concerts at 3 and 8 to big business.

Mrs. McKinnon gave each of we boys stopping here a handkerchief as a remembrance. We have been treated better at our home in Dunedin than at any place on our whole trip.

Aug. 6th, Sunday.

After breakfast and church, Eckstein, Mr. McKinnon, Mr. Anderson and myself took a walk up the hill back of our house, obtaining a wonderful view of Dunedin. Spent the balance of the day fooling with photographs.

Aug. 7th, Monday. Eve. Christchurch.

Train left at 8 o'clock, and I was sorry to leave Dunedin. The scenery was great this morning, as the snow clad mountains on the western coast of New Zealand with the Pacific Ocean on our right were fine. Arrived in Christchurch at 5:30 and were relieved to know that we were given no reception. I located at Jas. Geddes Rotherfield Hotel. A big racing meet is on here this week, and the City is crowded.

Concert at 8 in the King Edward's Barracks to poor business. The hall is very large and without heat. We sat thru the concert freezing.

[Clarke]: Arrived at Christchurch at about 7:30 p.m., and commenced a week's series of concerts that same evening at the King Edward's Barracks, a tremendous-sized armory, where it was, without a doubt, the coldest playing I ever experienced, as the roof of the armory was above the walls and space between the two without any shelter, so it was like playing out of doors. The audience was comfortably wrapped in rugs and shawls, and did not seem to mind in the least, but when I blew into my cornet my breath, coming through the instrument, extended a foot or two from the bell in steam, and I expected to see flakes of snow drop from this vapor.[23]

Mileage Dunedin to Christchurch 230.

Aug. 8th, Tuesday. Mat. + Eve. Christchurch.

I lost a Peterson pipe on the train coming into this town, and the Lost and Found Dep't. of the railroad knew nothing of it.

Business poor today.

Aug. 9th, Wednesday. Mat. + Eve. Christchurch.

Helleberg and I went out to the Metropolitan Trotting Track to see the races. We made several bets on the Totalisator and broke even. No book makers are allowed here, and betting is all done under government supervision, 10% going to the gov't.

Business bad at both concerts.

22. Herbert L. Clarke, "A World's Tour with Sousa," *Musical Messenger*, March 1919, 4.

23. Ibid.

Aug. 10th, Thursday. Mat. + Eve. Christchurch.

We visited the Canterbury Jockey club today, and I saw my first stee-plechase and won on Flamingo. Several falls happened, and one jockey was nearly killed. This town is crazy over horse racing, and horse talk is all you hear.

Business fair today.

The management placed a few gas heaters in the King Edward Barrack's today.

Aug. 11th, Friday. Mat. + Eve. Christchurch.

Business good at both concerts.

Aug. 12th, Saturday. Mat. + Eve. Christchurch.

Sol Eckstein had a couple dandy tips on today's races. Thru the usual luck, we didn't back the horses at the right time, or we may have been wealthy men now. Czar Kolohol was the horse. Ran twice. We backed him on the first race and he finished 7th. We didn't back him in the next race and the dividend paid was at £13,13/-. Some of the boys made money this week on the races.

Concerts to big business.

Train left at 11 o'clock for Lyttleton. We boarded the steamer "Tar-rawera" of the Union Line. Tonnage 1,269. This boat is another lemon, second to the despised steamer "Namoi." Rat traps are scattered about the staterooms. We steamed out at 11:50. Calm Sea.

Mileage Christchurch to Lyttelton 7.

Aug. 13th, Sunday. Steamer "Tarrawera."

A beautiful day, and we are sailing in sight of land all the time. A school of dolphins were having sport about the bow of our ship, diving about and swimming with remarkable speed ahead of the boat. They appeared to be pilots like the famous Polorous Jack guiding our boat. Wellington looked fine coming into the harbor. We landed at 2:45. Stopping at the Peoples Palace Hotel. Took a walk about town, and it looks better than any New Zealand City.

Mileage Lyttelton to Wellington 175.

Aug. 14th, Monday. Eve. Wellington.

Showers all day. Concert in the evening to good business, and we were well received. Concert in the Town Hall.

Aug. 15th, Tuesday. Mat. + Eve. Wellington.

We had about 175 people at the matinee.

Big house at night.

Aug. 16th, Wednesday. Mat. + Eve. Wellington.

Visited an interesting Maori Museum this morning. I saw two Maoris greeting each other. They place their foreheads together and rub nos-es. The Maori women have markings on their chin, denoting their class. Some of their girls are real pretty.

Business poor at the matinee and good at night.

Aug. 17th, Thursday.

Fair business at both concerts.

Aug. 18th, Friday. Mat. + Eve. Wellington.

I rode out to the beautiful Island Bay this morning. At the matinee we had the entire "Jack and the Beanstalk" company in our audience.

Good house at night.

I saw the last part of the "Beanstalk" show at the Opera House after our concert tonight.

Aug. 19th, Saturday. Mat. + Eve. Wellington.

Big business today. The Governor and staff of New Zealand attended the night concert and remained seated while we played "The Star Spangled Banner."

Aug. 20th, Sunday.

Attended Mass at the St. Joseph's Church. Met a Mr. Cotterill, who suggested a trip this afternoon. We went to Day's Landing and had a fine time. Coming back on the boat, one chap fell overboard, but he was rescued. Heard the Wellington Professional Orchestra in the Town Hall at night.

Aug. 21st, Monday. Mat. + Eve. Palmerston.

Train left at 7:45, arriving in Palmerston at 11:30. Stopping at the Masonic Hotel. Business fair at the concert in the Opera House.

Palmerston is called the Chicago of New Zealand.

Mileage Wellington to Palmerston 87.

Aug. 22nd, Tuesday. Mat. + Eve. Wanganui.

Left Palmerston at 7:10, arriving in Wanganui at 11 o'clock. Located at the Metropolitan Hotel.

Concerts to poor business at the Municipal Opera House. After the matinee, I took a trip by carriage to the Maori village close to this town. The Temple contains many pieces of carving dating back many years. We had pictures taken standing in front of the Temple. Left on sleepers by special train for Hamilton.

[Clarke]: The sleeping-car accommodations of New Zealand are quite primitive, there being but four sleepers in the country; we occupied three of them. They are corridor cars, and one is compelled to dress and undress in the passageway, as the staterooms are so small one can hardly turn around in them.[24]

Mileage Palmerston to Wanganui 63.

Aug. 23rd, Wednesday. Mat. Hamilton. Eve. Auckland.

Arrived in Hamilton at 12 o'clock.

Concert at 1 that filled the small Opera House.

We played only 7 program numbers. Train left at 3:20, arriving in Auckland at 6:30. Stopping at the Grande Vue House situated on the hill overlooking the Auckland Harbor.

Concert at 8:15 in the Fuller's Opera House to big business.

Mileage Wanganui to Hamilton 261. Hamilton to Auckland 86.

Aug. 24th, Thursday. Mat. + Eve. Auckland.

People in this Country are not accustomed to matinees, thus the poor attendance.

Business poor at matinee. Big at night.

Aug. 25th, Friday. Mat. + Eve. Auckland.

A heavy wind and rain storm continued all day.

Business the same as yesterday. I saw the last act of "The Arcadi-ans" at the Her Majesty's Theatre tonight.

Aug. 26th, Saturday.

Visited the Maori Museum this morning.

Business good.

24. Ibid., 5.

Aug. 27th, Sunday.

A party of our boys were invited on a fishing trip about the Auckland Harbor, but the boat could only take 8. The boys that were left chartered a boat, and we had a fine trip about the harbor, which comes second to the Sydney Harbor. We had 8 with us, and of the eight five climbed the Rangitoto Mt., about 2,500 feet high. Mt. Rangitoto is an extinct volcano, and it was interesting to see the lava formation surrounding the bowl like crater and sides. The volcano was in eruption only 30 years ago. We arrived home at 4:30. The boat we were on was named "The Scout."

Aug. 28th, Monday. Mat. + Eve. Auckland.

While shopping this morning my greatest difficulty was in finding lisle socks.

Concerts to good business.

Aug. 29th, Tuesday. Mat. + Eve. Auckland.

A party of 9 went out on a fishing trip this morning on the "Scout." Mr. Miller, a son of the Minister of New Zealand R.R., went along as our guest. Fishing was bad, only nine being caught, while the honors went to me for making the highest catch, 3. Mix with his moving picture machine made a good film, taking we boys saving Bill Culley from drowning. After the picture taking, one of the ropes became caught in the propeller. Mix swam under the boat and unwound the rope some job.

Business good at both concerts.

Aug. 30th, Wednesday.

Good business today at concerts.

Aug. 31st, Thursday. Mat. + Eve. Auckland.

Business good at both concerts. On our New Zealand tour Auckland is the only town that we made money in. Australia, to my opinion, is the better country of the two, while both are bound to be wonderful countries in the future. New Zealand is a working man's paradise, as their laws are great for that class of men. We were given a farewell reception at our last concert tonight.

New Zealand Mileage total. 1,064 miles.

Mileage Conshohocken to Auckland en Route 31,916.

Sept. 1st, Friday. Steamer "Makura."

Boarded the steamer "Makura" at 12 o'clock. A large crowd was at the dock to see us off, and we sailed for America at 2:20, amid frantic cheering. Gus Helleberg and I are sharing one stateroom, and we are fixed very good. John Gibb is commander of the "Makura." Speed 18 knots.

Sept. 2nd, Saturday. Steamer "Makura."

Sea is very choppy, and the boat is rolling heavy. The food on this boat is not up to expectations, altho Budweiser beer that was stocked especially for us tasted mighty good. Arthur Kunze started making book on the first man to get full. Sweet pipe Joe of Baltimore won easily.

Mileage 327.

Sept. 3rd, Sunday. Steamer "Makura."

The boys are most all seasick today. I escaped again. Ambition seems to be nill concerning a minstrel show, as the boys are all too sick to think of anything.

Mileage 377.

Sept. 4th, Monday. Steamer "Makura."

Mr. Sousa sent for me this morning and gave me an opening for the minstrel show. Seasickness is slowly passing away, as the people are getting accustomed to the ship. Mt. Washington on the Kandaru Island was sighted and passed this afternoon. We docked at Suza, Fiji Islands at 6 o'clock. After dinner, Helleberg and I took a walk thru the town. It is very hot, and all the white population (1,200) dress in white. The natives don't worry much about dress at all. It was too hot to walk much, so after drinking a cup of kava, the native drink, which at first doesn't taste good being somewhat the flavor of absinthe and a brownish color non alcoholic, I went back to the boat and did a little fishing from the stern.

Mileage 358. 83 miles from noon to Suza.

Sept. 5th, Tuesday. Suza, Fiji Islands.

The loading of 900 tons of raw sugar continued all thru the night by the natives, who knew how to shout and keep everybody awake. After breakfast, I took a walk thru the town and saw many queer sights. Some few of the Islands in the Fijian group are still inhabited by cannibals, and to look at some of the specimens here on the streets would lead a person to think that they are also man eaters.

[Clarke]: Some of the boys were induced by the natives to hire carriages for a drive into the back woods, but were terribly frightened after going a mile or so, by a lot of black people who came out of the brush and rushed towards them in a seemingly unfriendly manner. Maybe there was not a scurrying of horses and carriages pointing for the town, the boys remembering a warning not to go beyond the limits of the city, and that these islands still contained cannibals! Civilization has progressed wonderfully during the past thirty years in these South Sea Islands. Up to and before these years, cannibal outrages and devilish cruelty and torture existed in such forms as the victims being brained before they were cooked, also being compelled to build their own ovens, and then to arrange themselves therein, in a convenient posture for roasting![25]

The ship was loaded at 2 o'clock, and we sailed at 2:15, leaving a very beautiful spot behind where a person could spend a week looking over the numerous interesting things. We sighted about 20 Islands on our way thru the Fiji group. A strong trade wind from the N.E. helped to keep the temperature down.

Clock moved forward 18 minutes at midnight.

Sept. 5th, Tuesday. Steamer "Makura."

By crossing the International Date Line, we lose a day going East, therefore the two Tuesdays dated the same.

[Clarke]: When crossing the 180th parallel, which divides the days, we retired on Tuesday night, and awakened the next morning on Tuesday! A day of forty-eight hours. This is why Australia is one day ahead of America. The amusing part of this incident was caused by a new member of the band demanding an extra day's pay from Mr. Sousa, (as all the members of his band were paid a certain amount of salary when on the ocean). This bandsman was a real "union musician," who played music by the "foot or yard," but was not ever serious to give twelve inches to the foot, nor three feet to the yard. He did not realize the fact, when leaving New York nearly a year before, traveling east continually, that there were not quite twenty-four hours

25. Herbert L. Clarke, "A World's Tour with Sousa," *Musical Messenger*, April 1919, 5.

in a day, although he had been paid up to this time for a full day, and when he did reach New York at the close of the tour, the hours in each day would be properly equalized. So there was a debate held in the captain's cabin one day, the captain acting as judge. . . . This decision did not satisfy our "worthy" member, who later on, brought the matter up before the Los Angeles Local A.F. of M. when we reached that city five weeks later, whose Board of Directors reprimanded him for his ignorance. This man was released from his contract with Mr. Sousa in Los Angeles, not on account of his argument, but that his work during the trip was not equal to 100 cents to the dollar, as every musician should and easily can do.[26]

The boys finally decided to put on a minstrel show, and our first rehearsal occurred today. I met Mr. Honey, the chap that arranged for sports in the First Saloon, and we decided on Sept. 16th as the date for the show.
Clock moved forward 16 minutes at midnight.
Mileage 322.

Sept. 6th, Wednesday. Steamer "Makura."

The trade wind is still with us, offering some relief from the heat. Rehearsal of the show with good results. Three of us boys used the upper deck as sleeping quarters tonight.
Clock moved forward 15 minutes at midnight.
Mileage 351.

Sept. 7th, Thursday. Steamer "Makura."

Minstrel rehearsal this morning. The Washy Hose Band gave a concert on deck tonight when Decker won a lady's bag auctioned off by Perfetto. Used the deck again tonight as sleeping quarters.
Clock moved forward 4 minutes at midnight.
Mileage 359.

Sept. 8th, Friday. Steamer "Makura."

We crossed the Equator at about 7 o'clock this morning with no ceremonies. Minstrel show rehearsal today.
Clock moved forward 17 minutes at midnight.
Mileage 368.

Sept. 9th, Saturday. Steamer "Makura."

Very hot today, with the temperature about 114 in the shade. We have the sun about overhead. Several rain storms failed to cool it off. Rehearsals for the show today. Washy Hose Band again on deck, and Kunze took up a collection to improve the funds of the Syndicate.
The boys hit them hard lately on the ship's mileage. This has been the longest week I ever spent in my life.
Clock moved forward 15 minutes at midnight.
Mileage 367.

Sept. 10th, Sunday. Steamer "Makura."

Services were held at 10 o'clock in the First Saloon. Twenty-five of the men gave a concert on the deck this evening, conducted by Ross Millhouse.
Clock moved forward 16 minutes at midnight
Mileage 380.

Sept. 11th, Monday. Steamer "Makura."

A totalizator was started today, and the boys played heavy on the ship's run. Minstrel rehearsal this afternoon.

26. Ibid., 6.

Clock moved forward 14 minutes.
Mileage 366.

Sept. 12th, Tuesday. Mat. + Eve. Honolulu.

Passed the quarantine doctor's inspection at 7:30, and the boat docked at the Alakea Wharf Honolulu Hawaii Islands at 8 o'clock. Four of we boys made a dash into the City—and into a Baltimore Lunch having a regular breakfast. I changed a little money at the bank, and we started out to see the town. Visited the Crater and the Aquarium, which contains a most interesting collection of fish taken from waters of the surrounding Islands. The interesting thing about the fish is that they are of all colors and shapes very uncommon. Honolulu is the prettiest town of its kind that I have ever been in, and we were given royal treatment such as only Americans can give. Coconut, banana and palm trees are plentifully distributed along the streets, and the City is beautiful. The American flag flying made the town look much better of course, but I can state that regardless of the flag this is the prettiest town we have visited on our whole tour so far. The "Makura" was held over 6 hours to enable us to play two concerts here.
Business was very good at the Bijou Theatre. Boat sailed at 10:45. The Hawaiian Band under the leadership of Mr. Berger played us off.
Clock moved forward 13 minutes at midnight.
Mileage 286.

Sept. 13th, Wednesday. Steamer "Makura."

Rehearsal of the show in the morning. Ed Clarke gave us the route of the American tour up until Nov. 16th.
Clock moved forward 14 minutes at midnight.
Mileage 192.

Sept. 14th, Thursday. Steamer "Makura."

Rehearsal today. The band gave a concert in the First Saloon this evening. A collection amounting to £26 was taken to be donated to the "Yougala Relief Fund." We started at 9 o'clock, and Captain Gibb and passengers were well pleased.
Clock moved forward 9 minutes at midnight.
Mileage 374.

Sept. 15th, Friday. Steamer "Makura."

It is gradually getting cooler as we keep going north. I have been very unsuccessful playing the totalisator. Rehearsal today. Paul Senno had two piccolos and a flute stolen from his cabin. Small articles such as watches etc. have also disappeared lately. A search was made, and two fellows, one a stoker and the other a stowaway from Honolulu and a deserter from the American Navy there, were found to have several watches in their possession belonging to passengers. They were placed in irons.
The captain and the whole crew of officers assisted in the search, but Senno's instruments couldn't be found. They were perhaps thrown overboard by the thief to escape detection.
Clock moved forward 18 minutes at midnight
Mileage 387.

Sept. 16th, Saturday. Steamer "Makura."

The 11:45 parade of the Sousa-Makura Minstrel Company made a hit marching about the decks. The crew on the boat made a wonderful job in turning one of the hatches into a regular stage, besides turning the after deck into a regular looking theatre. Full rehearsal on the show this afternoon. I made up the boys after dinner this evening for the show, which was better than our last Sousa-Ionic Minstrels. 19 men sat in the circle with 6 end men. The Olio was good, as we had Mr. Benlow a baritone singer. Misses Min Black and Robin White, Mr. & Mrs. Matin A. Hagan and Jack Hagan, all professional people, Arthur Kunze's Washy Hose Band en route to the Zulu King went big. Show started at 8:30 and was over at 10:50. The proceeds amounting to £18, 11/9 with deductions for expenses turned over to the Yongala Relief Fund. £14, 8/3 being the sum. Everybody on the ship was in attendance.

Clock moved forward 16 minutes at midnight.

Mileage 380.

Sept. 17th, Sunday. Steamer "Makura."

It is quite cool this morning—quite different from the lovely night we had for our show last evening. I settled up the financial part of the show this morning. A few birds the first on this voyage are following the boat today.

Clock moved forward 13 minutes.

Mileage 378.

Sept. 18th, Monday. Steamer "Makura."

Making preparations for disembarking.

We held an informal dance on deck this evening. Light houses our first sign of anything American were sighted after dark.

Clock moved forward 12 minutes at midnight.

Mileage 380 till noon. 251 from noon to Victoria B.C. Mileage Auckland to Victoria 6,203 nautical miles. U.S. Miles 6,823. Mileage Conshohocken to Victoria en Route 38,739 miles.

Sept. 19th, Tuesday.

Passed the health quarantine inspection at 6:30. Landed in Victoria at 9 o'clock. I located at the St. Francis Hotel, after which I visited the U.S. immigration office and vouched as to my citizenship of the country. The boys of the band non-citizens, including the men that have their first papers, are compelled to pay $4.00 head tax to enter the United States.

Saw a vaudeville show this evening at the Sullivan and Considine's Empress Theatre.

Sept. 20th, Wednesday. Eve. Victoria, B.C.

Rehearsal of the band at 10:30. Mr. Sousa gave me a check in exchanging some money today. Rain all day. Concert in the Victoria Theatre to a packed house.

[Sousa]: When we reached Victoria, we found the Canadian elections going at high pitch. One politician named Kelly seemed to be the storm center of the day, but of course my thoughts were more on the concert than on any election. I was delighted to play to a packed house. In my journey around the world I had often played as a popular number the song, "Has Anybody Here Seen Kelly?" On election night in Victoria, I played it as a matter of course. Now just before we struck up that piece the information was passed out that Kelly had been "snowed under" in the election. Apparently my audience rejoiced in the tidings, for the moment the boy put up the sign, announcing the title, "Has Anybody Here Seen Kelly?" and the band swung into the melody, a loud yell arose that shook the rafters. At the end of the concert a number of people surged backstage to congratulate me, believing that I had written the piece for the occasion.[27]

Met Mr. Nagle, leader of the Empress Theatre orchestra, and we visited the Turn Verein.

Sept. 21st, Thursday. Eve. Vancouver.

We left Victoria on the steamer "Princess Charlotte" at 2:15, and after a beautiful trip up the Puget Sound we arrived in Vancouver at 6:45. Stopping at the Winters Hotel. This is election day in Canada, and Vancouver is full of excitement, as the returns are coming in. The City has made wonderful strides in the past few years and I notice a big improvement in the last two years since I was here on my last visit.

Concert at 8:30 to a packed house in the Vancouver Opera House.

Met Fred Winlow after the show and had a good old chat.

Mileage Victoria to Vancouver 86.

Sept. 22nd, Friday. Eve. Bellingham, Wash., U.S.A.

Left Vancouver at 10 o'clock over the Great Northern R.R., and it felt like home to again ride in large comfortable coaches. We crossed the line and into the United States at 11:40, stopping at Blaine, Wash., the first American town we came to, and the boys set up a cheer. The customs held some of the boys up for duty on foreign articles found in their trunks. The inspector found nothing in my trunk.

Located at the Victor House in Bellingham.

Big house at the evening concert in the Beck Theatre.

Mileage Vancouver to Bellingham 59.

Sept. 23rd, Saturday. Mat. + Eve. Seattle.

This is my birthday, but nothing doing on a celebration. Caught the 7:30 train and arrived in Seattle at 11:45. Stopping at the 4th Ave. Hotel. This town certainly looks good.

Concerts to big business at the Seattle Theatre.

We were given a reception here on our arrival by the professional musicians playing "Home Sweet Home." Some reception.

Mileage Bellingham to Seattle 97.

Sept. 24th, Sunday. Mat. Tacoma.

Train left at 8 o'clock, arriving in Tacoma at 9:30. Stopping with the Stines at the Rossmore Hotel.

Matinee only today at the Tacoma Theatre to a poor house.

The whole band attended the performance of the "Missouri Girl" at the Tacoma Theatre in the evening, and they had a packed house. The show was so good that I came out after the first act.

Mileage Seattle to Tacoma 41.

Sept. 25th, Monday. Eve. Tacoma.

Rehearsal of the band at 11 o'clock, spoiling a fishing trip I had planned for the day.

Good house tonight.

Sept. 26th, Tuesday. Mat. + Eve. Aberdeen, Wash.

Left Tacoma at 9 o'clock, arriving in Aberdeen at 1:35.

Concerts to fair business at the Opera House.

This town is a great lumber center of the North-West and is built in style typical of a lumber town. We took sleepers after the night concert at 12:05 for Portland.

Mileage Tacoma to Aberdeen 92.

Sept. 27th, Wednesday. Mat. + Eve. Portland, Ore.

Arrived in Portland at 7:10. Located at the Rainier Hotel. I made the trip to the Summit of Portland Heights, where a grand view is obtained of the surrounding valley and snow clad mountains, Mt. Hood, Rainier etc. Portland, called the Rose City, is one of the best towns on the Pacific Coast.

Business big at both concerts at the Baker Theatre.

Mileage Aberdeen to Portland 147.

27. Sousa, *Marching Along*, 287–88.

Sept. 28th, Thursday. Eve. Eugene, Ore.

Left Portland at 8:30, and the very slow train arrived in Eugene at 2 o'clock. This is a very pretty town, and our weather is fine.

Evening concert to a packed house at the Eugene Theatre.

We left Eugene on sleepers and special train at 11:55 for Chico.

Mileage Portland to Eugene 123.

Sept. 29th, Friday. Eve. Chico, Cal.

We are traveling over the Shasta Sunset Route, and the scenery equals anything on the trip. Mt. Shasta, about 14,000 feet high, came into view at 11:20 a.m., and at 2 o'clock we were 12 miles from its base, the nearest point we got to it, and then the huge mountain appeared not more than two or three miles away. It is snow clad the year around and is a very pretty sight. We had no time for a stop at the famous Shasta Springs, where water, naturally charged, gushes forth from the earth clear and sparkling. Arrived in Chico at 6:45. Stopping at the Western Hotel.

Business fair tonight at the Majestic Theatre.

Mileage Eugene to Chico 462.

Sept. 30th, Saturday. Mat. + Eve. Sacramento, Cal.

Train left Chico at 6:48, arriving in Sacramento at 10:10. Stopping at the Colonial Hotel and treated well. Met Walter Smith and the whole Pantages Theatre bunch after our night concert and had a great session in the Schlitz Cafe. Tod Lanborn, Gus Lewin and Greer leader of the California State Band were all in the party.

Business fair at the Chime Theatre.

Mileage Chico to Sacramento 96.

Oct. 1st, Sunday. Mat. + Eve. San Francisco, Cal.

Train left at 8:20, arriving in San Francisco at 11:30. Located at the Grand Hotel.

Business fair at both concerts in the Dreamland Rink.

Mileage Sacramento to San Francisco 90.

Oct. 2nd, Monday. Mat. + Eve. San Francisco.

I moved to the Herald Hotel this morning a newer and finer house.

Business about like that of yesterday.

Oct. 3rd, Tuesday. Mat. + Eve. San Francisco.

Weather is very fine.

Business improving.

Oct. 4th, Wednesday. Mat. + Eve. San Francisco.

On our last day here to play, the house was fair at the matinee and capacity at night.

Oct. 5th, Thursday. Mat. + Eve. Berkeley.

Made the trip to Berkeley over the Key Route and played to big business at the Greek Theatre. Over 5,000 people at the night concert. The Greek Theatre is a very pretty open air structure, and the acoustics are perfect.

Mileage Frisco to Greek Theatre Berkeley 12 miles return.

Oct. 6th, Friday. Eve. Palo Alto.

We left Frisco from the 3rd and Townsend St. Station at 3 o'clock over the So. Pacific R.R., arriving in Palo Alto at 3:54.

Concert at 8:15 to a fair house in the Stanford University Auditorium. Concert finished at 10:42, and our train left at 11:02, and the station over a mile away. We caught the train, but it was by a very close mar-

The last leg of the world tour took the band across the United States from west to east, with concerts in seventeen states, including an appearance at the Greek Theatre in Berkeley, California. (Barry Owen Furrer Collection)

gin. Arrived in San Jose at 11:35 and located at the Montgomery Hotel. Mileage Frisco to Palo Alto 34. Palo Alto to San Jose 17. Total 51.

Oct. 7th, Saturday. Mat. + Eve. San Jose.

Concerts to fair business at the Victory Theatre. Our evening concert is very long and runs about 2½ hours.

Oct. 8th, Sunday. Mat. + Eve. Stockton.

Train left San Jose at 9:10, arriving in Stockton at 1:30. Located at the Grand Central Hotel.

This town looks good, altho our business was poor at both concerts at the Yosemite Theatre.

Mileage San Jose to Stockton 92.

Oct. 9th, Monday. Mat. + Eve. Fresno.

We left Stockton at 7:23, arriving in Fresno at 11:50. Stopping at the Berkeley House.

Business bad at the matinee and good at the night concert at the Barton Opera House. About 12 of we boys took a look thru the Japanese and Chinese quarters tonight after the concert.

Mileage Stockton to Fresno 144.

Oct. 10th, Tuesday. Mat. Coalinga. Eve. Hanford.

Left Fresno at 9:15 by special train, arriving in Coalinga at 12 o'clock. This is an oil town, just five years old, and some town. Dust up to your ankles all the while.

Matinee at the Liberty Theatre to bad business.

We left this town by special train at 5:15 and glad to escape, arriving in Hanford at 6:40.

Hanford has it on Coalinga by a shade, and at the Hanford Opera House our business was fair. Located at the Ezrey Annex.

Mileage Fresno to Coalinga 99. Coalinga to Hanford 43. Total 142.

Oct. 11th, Wednesday. Mat. + Eve. Bakersfield.

Train left Hanford at 9:40, arriving in Bakersfield at (Kern Station) 12:15.

Matinee to less than 100 people. I enjoyed a bicycle ride about town after the matinee.

Business bad at night.

Left Bakersfield by special train on sleepers at 12 o'clock.
Mileage Hanford to Bakersfield 100.

Oct. 12th, Thursday. Mat. + Eve. Pasadena.

Arrived in Los Angeles at 7:30. Had a lay-over until 11:20, when we left for Pasadena, arriving at 12 noon. Located at the Glenwood Apts. A gentleman invited a party of four to take an auto ride about town. We met Miss Zedeler on the way, and she jumped in with us. We visited the Adolph Busch Gardens, and they are very pretty. Pasadena's residential section will long be remembered by its beauty. We stopped and picked oranges from the trees, and they were delicious.

Big business at both concerts at the Chime Theatre.
Mileage Bakersfield to Pasadena 182.

Oct. 13th, Friday. Mat. Pomona. Eve. Riverside.

Left Pasadena at 9:10, arriving in Pomona at 10:15. The heat is intense, and I stayed out of the sun as much as possible.
Concert to fair business at the Opera House.
Train left at 5:05, arriving in Riverside at 7:05. Business fair at the Lorimer Theatre. A few bets were made on the World Series baseball games between the Athletics and the N.Y. Giants. Riverside is a very pretty town.
Mileage Pasadena to Pomona 47. Pomona to Riverside 32. Total 79.

Oct. 14th, Saturday. Mat. Redlands. Eve. San Bernardino.

Left Riverside at 9:35 over the Santa Fe, arriving in Redlands at 10:50. It is very hot in the sun. We are now in the heart of the orange growing country of California.
Matinee at the Opera House to fair business.
Train left at 5:25, arriving in San Bernardino at 5:50. Located at the St. Bernard Hotel.
Fair business at the Opera House.
Mileage Riverside to Redlands 20. Redlands to San Bernardino 8. Total 28.

Oct. 15th, Sunday. Mat. + Eve. Long Beach.

Left San Bernardino at 9:40, arriving in Los Angeles at 12 noon. We had a special car over the Long Beach Electric R.R., leaving Los Angeles at 12:20 and arriving in Long Beach at 1 o'clock. A party of we boys took a dip in the Pacific Ocean before the matinee. Mr. Sousa arrived here late owing to a break down to an auto he was making the trip here in.
Concerts at 3:15 and at 8:15 in the Auditorium to fair business. We had a special car back to Los Angeles after the night concert. Stopping in Los Angeles at the Munn Hotel.
Mileage San Bernardino to Long Beach 82. Long Beach to Los Angeles 20. Total 102.

Oct. 16th, Monday. Mat. + Eve. Los Angeles.

A committee of Globe Trotters, Marthage, Lomas and myself made arrangements to hold the club banquet at the Roma Restaurant in the King Edward Hotel Bld'g. President Taft is in town, and I managed to catch a glimpse of his big, round, fat smiling face as he was being escorted from the station to the Auditorium.
We opened here this afternoon at the Auditorium, doing poor business at both concerts.

Oct. 17th, Tuesday. Mat. + Eve. Los Angeles.

I had a look at the baseball scoreboard when the Athletics beat the Giants in 11 innings score 3 to 2. Met Espinoso, at one time saxophone in this band.
Business poor at both concerts today.

Oct. 18th, Wednesday. Mat. + Eve. Los Angeles.

Weather very warm.
Business improving.

Oct. 19th, Thursday. Mat. + Eve. Los Angeles.

Business good today. The banquet celebrating our return to the United States given by the Globe Trotter's Club at the Roma Restaurant after the night concert was one grand success. Souvenir pins were given, and the boys had a great time. We adjourned at 2:30 a.m. President Walter Sheaffer was toastmaster, and all the members had something to say.

Oct. 20th, Friday. Mat. + Eve. Los Angeles.

The least said about my headache this morning the better, but I had a peach.
We played to packed houses today.

Oct. 21st, Saturday. Mat. + Eve. Los Angeles.

Big business today. I bought Stanley Lawton's trunk for the saxophones today. Lawton, Cunnington, Berry and Culley closed here with the band tonight.

Oct. 22nd, Sunday. Traveling.

We had Pullman cars out of Los Angeles, leaving at 1:50 for Phoenix Ariz. Made a stop at Yuma, where Indian squaws had all sorts of Indian stuff for sale.

Oct. 23rd, Monday. Mat. + Eve. Phoenix, Ariz.

Arrived in Phoenix at 7:30. Located at the Denver Apts. This town is booming at present and will be a regular city very soon. An Indian School is located here.
Poor matinee at the Elk's Theatre. Packed house at night including about one third Indians.
Mileage Los Angeles to Phoenix 449.

Oct. 24th, Tuesday. Eve. Tucson, Ariz.

Left Phoenix at 12:40 arriving in Tucson at 5:15. Met Rob't Dale a local jeweler formerly from Lancaster. He knew Clarence Smith of the band and we three had a look about town. The old part of town is very interesting and it is one of the oldest towns in the Country. Band left on sleepers after the night concert to good business in the Tucson Opera House.
Mileage Phoenix to Tucson 122.

Oct. 25th, Wednesday. Mat. + Eve. El Paso, Texas.

Arrived in El Paso at 12:20. Located at the St. Louis Hotel.
Matinee in the El Paso Theatre to poor business.
After the matinee, virtually the whole band made the trip over the Rio Grande River to Ciudad Juarez, Mexico. It is a very interesting town and shows the effects of the late war to a very noticeable degree. The burned court house and the Catholic church, shot-ridden, are examples of how the Insurrectos fought. The Liberals had a body of sharpshooters hidden behind a wall on top of the church doing excellent work shooting down the Insurrectos until a Texas cowboy loving adventure happened along, and with a Winchester picked off the sharpshooters one at a time. Almost every building in town shows marks of the insurrection. This town is somewhat similar to Tenerife except that Tenerife is much cleaner. The bull pen here is used every Sunday. Cock fighting is the other favorite pastime with the Mexicans. We passed the customs officials of both Countries.
Concert to good business at night.
Mileage Tucson to El Paso 312.

Oct. 26th, Thursday. Traveling.

Train left El Paso at 10:35 and we had Pullman cars. News of the deciding game of the World Series we received at Valentine, Texas.

Oct. 27th, Friday. Mat. + Eve. San Antonio, Texas.

Arrived in San Antonio at 12:30.

Concerts at the Opera House to fair business at the matinee, and a packed house at night.

Visited the Alamo after the matinee.

We left on sleepers after the night concert at 11:30 for Galveston.

Mileage El Paso to San Antonio 620.

Oct. 28th, Saturday. Mat. + Eve. Galveston.

Arrived in Galveston at 1:05. Located at the San Antonio Hotel.

Concerts to fair houses at the Opera House.

Mileage San Antonio to Galveston 268.

Oct. 29th, Sunday. Mat. + Eve. Houston.

We left Galveston at 7:20, arriving in Houston at 9 o'clock. Located at the Wood's Hotel. I saw a round-up of cattle today numbering about 2,000 head.

Business fair at both concerts at the Prince Theatre.

Walter Collins went to the Baptist Hospital here, and we boys visited him after the matinee.

Mileage Galveston to Houston 58.

Oct. 30th, Monday. Eve. Austin.

Left Houston at 9:15, arriving in Austin at 4:30. Stopping at the Hancock Hotel. The principal thing about Austin today was mud, and we had plenty of that.

Concert to a poor house at the Hancock Theatre.

Mileage Houston to Austin 166.

Oct. 31st, Tuesday. Mat. Waco. Eve. Fort Worth.

Left Austin by special train at 8 o'clock, arriving in Waco at 12:10.

Concert at 1:15 at the Auditorium to a poor house.

Special train at 4 o'clock, arriving at Fort Worth at 7:30.

Concert at the Beyer's Opera House at 8:40 to fair business.

Located at the Terminal Hotel.

Mileage Austin to Waco 115. Waco to Fort Worth 98.

Nov. 1st, Wednesday. Mat. + Eve. Dallas.

Left Fort Worth at 9:15, arriving in Dallas at 10:50. Stopping at the Aetna Hotel.

Concerts to fair business at the Grand Opera House.

Herman Hand and Julius Spindler pulled off a little comedy for the boys after tonight's concert.

Mileage Fort Worth to Dallas 32.

Nov. 2nd, Thursday. Mat. Sherman. Eve. Dennison.

Left Dallas at 8:40, arriving in Sherman at 12 o'clock. Enjoyed the use of the Y.M.C.A. gymnasium and swimming pool before the matinee.

Poor house at the Opera House.

Left Sherman at 5:20 by special train, arriving in Dennison at 6:30.

Concert to poor business at the Opera House.

Left on sleepers over the M.K.&T.R.R. at 11:30 for Oklahoma City.

Mileage Dallas to Sherman 60. Sherman to Dennison 11. Total 71.

Nov. 3rd, Friday. Mat. + Eve. Oklahoma City, Okla.

Arrived in Oklahoma City at 7:30.

Played the Overholser Theatre two concerts to fair business.

When this town turned prohibition, the government officials poured 28,000 barrels of beer into the gutters. The people then distinguished themselves by using dippers and drinking as much of the beer as they could. We left on sleepers on the Rock Island Road for Muskogee at 12:40.

Mileage Dennison to Oklahoma City 184.

Nov. 4th, Saturday. Mat. + Eve. Muskogee, Okla.

We changed railroads at McAllister, taking the M.K.&T.R.R. at 10:45, arriving in Muskogee at 1:15.

Business bad today at the Hinton Opera House.

Mileage Oklahoma City to Muskogee 182.

Nov. 5th, Sunday. Mat. + Eve. Tulsa, Okla.

Left Muskogee at 9:15, arriving in Tulsa at 12:30. I became soaking wet in the heavy rain while walking to the Robinson Hotel.

It rained all day, and our business was bad at the Grand Theatre.

Mileage Muskogee to Tulsa 51.

Nov. 6th, Monday. Mat. Bartlesville, Okla. Eve. Parsons, Kansas.

Walter Collins put in his appearance this morning, looking well after his week in the hospital in Houston. Train left at 8:15 over the Rock Island Rail Road, arriving in Bartlesville at 10:30.

Matinee to a packed house at the Oklahoma Theatre.

Left Bartlesville over the M.K.&T.R.R. at 5:05, arriving in Parsons, Kansas at 7:30.

Concert to a fair house at the Ellis' Theatre. Located at the Mathewson Hotel.

Mileage Tulsa to Bartlesville 50. Bartlesville to Parsons 61. Total 111.

Nov. 7th, Tuesday. Mat. Pittsburg, Kan. Eve. Carthage, Mo.

Left Parsons at 8:40 over the Frisco System, arriving in Pittsburg at 11:20.

Concert at the La Belle Theatre to a poor house. We had a game of hand ball while waiting for the train, which left at 5:40, arriving in Carthage at 7:15. Located at the Carthage Hotel.

Poor business at the Opera House.

Mileage Parsons to Pittsburg 54. Pittsburg to Carthage 49. Total 103.

Nov. 8th, Wednesday. Mat. Aurora. Eve. Springfield.

Left Carthage at 8:03 arriving in Aurora at 11:30.

Fair business at the Grand Opera House.

Left Aurora at 5:35, arriving in Springfield at 7:30. Located at the Traveler's Inn.

Business good at the Lander's Theatre.

Mileage Carthage to Aurora 49. Aurora to Springfield 30. Total 79.

Nov. 9th, Thursday. Mat. + Eve. Joplin, Mo.

Left Springfield at 7:45, arriving in Joplin at 12 noon. Had lunch and dinner at the Forney Hotel.

Poor houses at the matinee and night concert at the New Club Theatre.

We left on sleepers at 11:30 for Kansas City.

Mileage Springfield to Joplin 93.

Nov. 10th, Friday. Mat. Kansas City. Eve. Fort Leavenworth.

Arrived in Kansas City at 7:05. Located at the Sexton Hotel.

Matinee at the Willis Wood Theatre to a poor house. The Eddie Foy company was in our audience.

Left Kansas City at 5:20, arriving at Fort Leavenworth, Kansas at 6:30.

Poor business at the Peoples Theatre.

Wm. "Mons" Decker closed tonight, going to the San Francisco Opera Co. We left on sleepers at 12:30 for Lincoln, Neb.

Mileage Joplin to Kansas City 179. Kansas City to Fort Leavenworth 25. Total 204.

Nov. 11th, Saturday. Mat. + Eve. Lincoln, Neb.

Arrived in Lincoln at 10:30. A very sudden change in the weather made us sit up and take notice. The temperature last night in Fort Leavenworth was about 60 degrees. This morning, the temperature was about 20 degrees above zero with a light-snow falling. Located at the New Lindell Hotel.

Concerts at the Auditorium to poor business.

I saw the after-piece of Geo. Evans Honey Boy Minstrels this afternoon. Temperature tonight 8 degrees above zero.

Mileage Fort Leavenworth to Lincoln 225.

Nov. 12th, Sunday. Mat. + Eve. Omaha, Neb.

The regular 9:40 train we were to take being over two hours late. Ed Clarke fixed up a special leaving at 10:25, arriving in Omaha at 12:05. Located at the Hotel Boquet. The Honey Boy Minstrel Co. listened to our concert this afternoon.

Business good at the Boyd Theatre.

Time changes here one hour earlier.

Mileage Lincoln to Omaha 58.

Nov. 13th, Monday. Mat. + Eve. Des Moines, Iowa.

Left Omaha at 7 o'clock. Russell, our minute man, made a hundred yard dash and caught the rear car on the fly. We arrived in Des Moines at 12:20. I located at the Royal Hotel.

Business very bad at both concerts in the Coliseum.

The Coliseum has a seating capacity of over 7,000, and our 300 patrons at the matinee and 500 at night were hardly noticeable.

Mileage Omaha to Des Moines 145.

Nov. 14th, Tuesday. Mat. Grinnell. Eve. Marshalltown, Iowa.

Left Des Moines at 12:05 over the Rock Island R.R., arriving in Grinnell at 1:35.

Matinee to a fair house at the Opera House.

A special train over the Iowa Central R.R. at 5:30 brought us to Marshalltown at 6:30. Located at the Danley Hotel.

Concert at the New Odeon Theatre to fair business.

Mileage Des Moines to Grinnell 55. Grinnell to Marshalltown 25. Total 80.

Nov. 15th, Wednesday. Mat. Waterloo. Eve. Cedar Rapids.

Left Marshalltown at 11:50 and arrived in Waterloo at 2:05.

Played the Waterloo Opera House to a poor house.

Train left Waterloo at 5:40, arriving in Cedar Rapids at 7 o'clock. Located at the De Lavan Hotel.

Business good at Greene's Opera House.

Stopped in at the T.M.A. rooms tonight. Weather perfect.

Mileage Marshalltown to Waterloo 48. Waterloo to Cedar Rapids 53. Total 101.

Nov. 16th, Thursday. Mat. Muscatine. Eve. Davenport.

Left Cedar Rapids at 10:15, arriving in Muscatine at 1:15. Concert to fair business at the Opera House.

Left Muscatine at 6 o'clock, arriving in Davenport at 7. Located at the St. James Hotel.

Business good at the Burtis Theatre. I walked to my hotel in a heavy rain tonight.

Mileage Cedar Rapids to Muscatine 62. Muscatine to Davenport 27. Total 89.

Total Mileage Conshohocken to Davenport via "around the world en tour with Sousa's Band" 44,798 miles.

Mileage Victoria B.C. to Davenport Iowa 6,059.

Nov. 17th, Friday. Mat. Clinton. Eve. Dubuque.

Left Davenport over the Burlington Route at 11:45, arriving in Clinton at 12:50. A combination of rain and snow made the day miserable.

Concert to a fair house at the Clinton Opera House.

Left Clinton by special train, arriving in Dubuque at 7:15. Ed Ott and Arch McCarr, my old partners, met me at the station, and we then walked over to the Page Hotel, where I registered. I fixed the boys with tickets for our concert at the Opera House, where we did bad business. I met Eddie Klein after our concert, as he came over from Chicago on the train, arriving here at 9:30. The boys have a few days lay-off here, opening Sunday at the Majestic Theatre. A general good time happened after our concert in Ed Ott's room with Millhouse, Lucas and Helleberg filling out the party, which lasted as long as the boys could stand it or about 3:30. We had one pleasant time.

Mileage Davenport to Clinton 35. Clinton to Dubuque 48. Total 83.

Nov. 18th, Saturday. Mat. Beloit, Wis. Eve. Janesville, Wis.

I had three hours sleep and got up at 6:45. Train left at 7:45, arriving in Beloit at 12:50. Sheaffer fixed a pool on the football games today on the train.

Matinee to a poor house at the Wilson Opera House.

Left Beloit at 5:45 arriving in Janesville at 7:05. Located at the Grand Hotel.

Business poor at the Myers Opera House. Weather very cold.

Mileage Dubuque to Beloit 116. Beloit to Janesville 17. Total 133.

Nov. 19th, Sunday. Mat. Milwaukee.

Train left Janesville at 7:30, arriving in Milwaukee at 10:30. Located at the Blatz Hotel.

Concert this afternoon at the Shubert Theatre to good business.

The band, including Mr. Sousa, attended the performance of Mr. Holbrooke Blinn in the "Boss" at the Shubert in the evening. A good show. I paid a visit to my old friend Gallagher at the Wayside Inn after the show. An inch of snow fell this evening.

Mileage Janesville to Milwaukee 71.

Nov. 20th, Monday. Eve. Sheboygan, Wis.

Left Milwaukee at 2 p.m., arriving in Sheboygan at 4:10. Located at the Grand Hotel.

Packed house at the Opera House. The odor from a nearby tannery made the atmosphere offensive throughout the town.

Mileage Milwaukee to Sheboygan 52.

Nov. 21st, Tuesday. Mat. Fond du Lac. Eve. Oshkosh.

Left Sheboygan at 10 o'clock by special train on the C.M. & St. Paul R.R., arriving in Fond du Lac 11:40.

Matinee to a fair house at the Boyle Theatre.

Special train at 5:30 arriving in Oshkosh at 6:05.

Concert to poor business at the Opera House.

We were to leave over the Soo Line at 11:41, but the engine ran off the track while running on a side track to get our baggage car, with the result that we came over by special train, leaving at 4 o'clock on sleepers.

Mileage Sheboygan to Fond du Lac 44. Fond du Lac to Oshkosh 18. Total 62.

Nov. 22nd, Wednesday. Mat. Minneapolis, Minn. Eve. St. Paul.

Arrived in Minneapolis at 10:40. Plenty of snow here.

Concert at the Auditorium to good business. We had about 200 old soldiers at the Matinee.

I took a trolley car over to St. Paul and located at the Boardman Hotel.

Concert at the beautiful Auditorium to big business.

Mileage Oshkosh to Minneapolis 298. Minneapolis to St. Paul 10. Total 308.

Nov. 23rd, Thursday. Mat. Winona, Minn. Eve. La Crosse, Wis.

Left St. Paul at 7:20, arriving in Winona at 10:30. It is snowing today and very cold.

Business fair at the Opera House.

Special train leaving at 5:35. Arrived in La Crosse at 6:25. Located at the North Western Hotel.

Business good at the La Crosse Theatre.

Mileage St. Paul to Winona 103. Winona to La Crosse 26. Total 129.

Nov. 24th, Friday. Mat. + Eve. Madison, Wis.

Left La Crosse at 7:55, arriving in Madison at 12:50. Located at the Hotel Madison.

Concerts at the Opera House to poor business.

Mileage La Crosse to Madison 133.

Nov. 25th, Saturday. Mat. Kenosha. Eve. Racine.

Train left Madison at 8:05, arriving in Kenosha at 12:45. A big football pool was arranged today by Walter Sheaffer, with twenty-five colleges represented. I made several bets on the games, won two and tied two.

Matinee small at the Rhoades Opera House. Train left at 5:25, arriving in Racine at 6 o'clock. Registered at the Belvedere Hotel.

Concert at the Racine Theatre to a small house.

After the concert, I changed from the Belvedere Hotel to the Racine Hotel.

Mileage Madison to Kenosha 115. Kenosha to Racine 10. Total 125.

Nov. 26th, Sunday. Mat. + Eve. Chicago, Ill.

Left Racine at 8:35, arriving in Chicago at 10:15. Located at the Saratoga Hotel.

Concerts to big business at the Auditorium Theatre.

Simone Mantia borrowed my extra uniform coat at the matinee and played trombone in the "Stars & Stripes" march down front. Mr. Sousa thought it the best joke ever. Had lunch after the night concert at the Berghof Cafe.

Mileage Racine to Chicago 61.

Nov. 27th, Monday. Mat. Dowagiac, Mich. Eve. Kalamazoo.

Left Chicago at 9:05 over the Michigan Central R.R., arriving in Dowagiac at 11:50.

Matinee to a good house in the Beckwith Memorial Theatre.

Train left at 6:15, arriving in Kalamazoo at 7:30. Located at Ehrman's Hotel.

Business good at the Academy of Music. The early calls day after day, long jumps, two towns a day, etc. is certainly hard work, and we boys are feeling the effects of all this.

Mileage Chicago to Dowagiac 105. Dowagiac to Kalamazoo 36. Total 141.

Nov. 28th, Tuesday. Mat. + Eve. Grand Rapids.

Train left at 7:45, arriving in Grand Rapids at 10:20. Stopping at the Morton Hotel.

Concerts at the Powers Opera House to good business.

500 school children sang the "Stars and Stripes," standing on the stage, accompanied by the band and directed by their lady teacher. Snow storm in the evening. The local newsboy's band attended the night concert.

Mileage Kalamazoo to Grand Rapids 49.

Nov. 29th, Wednesday. Mat. Jackson. Eve. Lansing.

Left Grand Rapids at 11:15, arriving in Jackson at 2:10.

Matinee to good business at the Atheneum.

Special train at 5:15 arriving in Lansing at 6:30. Located at the Butler Hotel.

Concert at the Gladner Theatre to big business.

Mileage Grand Rapids to Jackson 95. Jackson to Lansing 37. Total 132.

Nov. 30th, Thursday, Thanksgiving. Mat. + Eve. Saginaw.

Train left Lansing over the Michigan Central 30 minutes late at 8:28, arriving in Saginaw at 11 o'clock. Located at the Vincent Hotel and enjoyed a fine turkey dinner.

Concerts at the Auditorium to fair business.

Won a couple bets on the University of Pennsylvania playing Cornell at football.

Mileage Lansing to Saginaw 63.

Dec. 1st, Friday. Mat. Bay City. Eve. Flint.

Left Saginaw at 11 o'clock, one hour late, arriving in Bay City at 11:40. Concert to a poor house in the Lyric Theatre.

Left Bay City at 5:55 over the Pierre Marquette R.R., arriving in Flint at 7:35. Located at the Sherman House.

Business fair at the Stone Opera House.

Mileage Saginaw to Bay City 12. Bay City to Flint 46. Total 58.

Dec. 2nd, Saturday. Mat. + Eve. Toledo, Ohio.

Left Flint at 9:30, arriving in Toledo at 1:35. Located at the Wayne Hotel.

Business fair at both concerts given in the Valentine Theatre.

Mileage Flint to Toledo 101.

Dec. 3rd, Sunday. Mat. + Eve. Cleveland.

Left Toledo at 9:05, arriving in Cleveland at 11:50. A severe snow storm continued throughout the afternoon.

Business very big at both concerts at the Hippodrome.

Left Cleveland at 1:35 on sleepers for Auburn over the Lake Shore R.R.

Mileage Toledo to Cleveland 108.

Dec. 4th, Monday. Mat. + Eve. Auburn, N.Y.

Arrived in Rochester 35 minutes late, where we changed to the New York Central R.R. Arrived in Auburn at 1:10. Located at the Cayuga Hotel, where our first meal today tasted good.

Concerts to fair business at the Burtiss Auditorium.

Met Gardner and Vincent, a vaudeville act. Also Will Gardner working in the act. After our evening concert, the boys were invited to see moving pictures at the Exchange Hotel. The New York Up State boys gave a banquet tonight at the Osbourne Hotel.

Mileage Cleveland to Auburn 327.

Dec. 5th, Tuesday. Mat. + Eve. Ithaca.

Left Auburn at 11:35 over the Leheigh Valley R.R., arriving in Ithaca at 1:15. Had lunch at the Office Hotel.

Matinee to a fair house in Sibley Hall, Cornell College.

Supper at the college restaurant.

Big house at night. Left on sleepers at 11:45.

Mileage Auburn to Ithaca 42.

Dec. 6th, Wednesday. Mat. + Eve. Albany.

Arrived in Albany at 9:35. Located at the Keeler's Hotel. Saw the arrival of eight Western Governors at 10:30.

Matinee to fair business at the Hermanus Bleecker Hall.

Mr. Sousa called a rehearsal after the matinee, and in a neat little speech thanked the men for their services during this tour. He spoke of receiving a letter from Branscombe, the Australian manager of the band, who said that while they lost 1,600 pounds on the African, Australian and New Zealand tour of this band, they were not sorry, because we gave those countries a musical treat such as they have never had before.

Mr. Sousa told us that the receipts abroad, figuring every day we played, amounted to $1,300 a day.

Business big at the night concert.

Mileage Ithaca to Albany 216.

Dec. 7th, Thursday. Mat. Newburgh. Eve. Poughkeepsie.

Left Albany at 9:40, arriving in Newburgh at 1:20. This is Walter Collins' home, and it was in a very muddy condition.

Business good at the Armory.

Took the Newburgh and Peekskill Ferry at 5:08. Train left Peekskill over the New York Central R.R. at 6:15, arriving in Poughkeepsie at 7:30.

Located with Chas. Mandel.

Business good at the Collingswood Theatre.

Mileage Albany to Newburgh 85. Newburgh to Poughkeepsie 16. Total 101.

Dec. 8th, Friday. Mat. + Eve. Yonkers.

We left Poughkeepsie at 8:30, arriving in Yonkers at 10:40. A heavy fall of snow recently made the streets miserable for walking.

We played concerts to fair business at the Armory.

I took a street car after the evening concert, making the change to the subway arriving at 50th St. New York at 11:30. Located at the Hotel Van Cortlandt, where a party of we boys are stopping. I was fortunate in getting a room with bath on the 10th floor at a dollar a day rate. Hotel Van Cortlandt is situated at 142 E. 49th St.

Mileage Poughkeepsie to Yonkers 58. Yonkers to New York 15. Total 73.

Dec. 9th, Saturday. Mat. + Eve. Newark, N.J.

Visited Conn's New York store this morning but didn't see Benny Henton, and the place wasn't the same. Did a little shopping at Sach's. Left for Newark at 12:50, arriving at 1:30.

Concerts at the Symphony Auditorium to good business. The Auditorium is a new building and a very fine one. Arrived back in New York at 11:15. We traveled over the Central Railroad of New Jersey.

Mileage New York to Newark and return 20 miles.

Dec. 10th, 1911. Sunday. Eve. New York City.

I checked my trunk to Conshohocken at about 1 o'clock and then visited the Curtiss' Rehearsal at the Hippodrome at 3 o'clock. Met Bill Schensley, who came over to New York to see the boys. We two had dinners at the Marie Cafe on 41st St.

We played the Hippodrome to a packed house. Mr. Sousa was presented with a huge horse-shoe of flowers. The floral piece stood over six feet high. A general all around handshake occurred after the concert, and the band closed the world's tour very quietly.

Dec. 11th, Monday. Conshohocken.

I brought my saxophone to Carl Fischer's for repairs. Left New York from the new Pennsylvania R.R. Station at 33rd & 7th Ave. at 9:30, arriving in Broad St. Station Philda. at 11:46. My father met me in Philda. at the station. Caught the 12:28 train over the P.R.R., arriving in Conshohocken at 1:10. Everybody glad to see me at home.

Mileage New York to Conshohocken 103.

Total Mileage of our trip "around the world."	
Conshohocken to New York	103 U.S. miles
Steamer "Baltic" N.Y. to Liverpool	3,309 U.S. miles
English Tour	4,360 U.S. miles
Steamer "Tainui"	6,499 U.S. miles
So. African Tour	3,118 U.S. miles
Steamer "Ionic"	6,314 U.S. miles
Tasmanian and Australian Tours	6,215 U.S. miles
Steamer "Ulimaroa"	997 U.S. miles
New Zealand Tour	1,064 U.S. miles
Steamer "Makura"	6,823 U.S. miles
American Tour	8,647 U.S. miles
New York to Conshohocken	103 U.S. miles
	47,552 U.S. miles

Around the world New York to New York 47,346 miles.

[Clarke]: This tour was certainly a wonderful undertaking for one man, involving over $600,000, and I doubt if there is such a financier in all the world as John Philip Sousa, who would have the nerve, single-handed, to do this, paying American salaries to the best musicians who were available in all the world to the last penny. I have heard that the profits netted Mr. Sousa $60,000, which must have been gratifying, even though he stood to lose many hundred thousands of dollars.[28]

AROUND THE WORLD WITH SOUSA:
A Memento of the Tour
Edmund A. Wall

When this our glorious Sousa's Band
Made its world's tour from land to land
And sea to sea, by rail and ship,
All previous records to eclipse;
Now that the closing time draws near
Returning with the waning year,
We think that some memento meet
Should signalize the tour, complete.

In after years when time has fled,
And once again these rhymes are read,
The mind returning to the scene
Will ever keep the memories green;
Each scene and incident recall,
Connected with the members all.

28. Herbert L. Clarke, "A World's Tour with Sousa," *Musical Messenger,* May 1919, 5.

and very decisively too in the first two pulls in
less than 30 seconds each. Spent the afternoon playing
cricket in which Mr. Sousa made good with the bat.
A celebration was held in the evening in honor of the
crossing the Equator. Ed. Wall wore a costume to
represent Father Neptune while Geo. Cunnington represented
Neptunes Prime Minister. The boys all dressed up in a
grotesque manner and made a parade all over the
ship. The ceremonies in the first saloon were funny
and we were there about 15 minutes. Captain Moffat
granted a request to keep the 2nd saloon bar open
an hour longer than usual. Mix took a snap shot
of the crowd in their make up with the Captain and
Sousa family in the front. Went to sleep on deck tonight
with the gang. We crossed the Equator at 4 A.M.
Wednesday morning Mar. 15th
Mileage 331.

Mar. 15th, Wednesday.   Str. Tainui.
A sharp whistle woke up the boys sleeping on deck at
6 OClock as the decks are washed with a hose every morning

A page (actual size) of Albert A. Knecht's diary of the 1911 world tour, published here through the courtesy of his daughter, Betty McCloskey. Knecht played alto saxophone with Sousa's Band from 1905 to 1920, although not continuously. He and a fellow saxophonist, H. Benne Henton, later established a popular music store in Philadelphia.

And therefore, with this end in view,
We'll try and say a thing or two
About the members, as they pass,
And show as in a looking glass
As facts, to which we can attest
The many qualities possessed.

It has been said, and truly, too;
"That if you search the whole world through,
Some work for good you'll surely find
In the most abject of mankind."
The faults and foibles that you see
As with "Great Caesar," buried be:
And now with sentiments like these,
We'll cease all animosities.
And therefore, without more ado
We will proceed the roster through.

Paul **Senno** here must head the list,
His piccolo we will insist
Has made a hit in every land,
As soloist, with Sousa's Band.

The next our Flutist **Spindler** see,
An artist he of high degree,
Renowned for purity of tone,
And phrasing too, he stands alone.

Our oboist **Lephilibert,**
Cannot be beaten anywhere,
One of the greatest hits is Phillie
In "Anybody here seen Kelly?"

Now, **Joe Gerard,** your oboe true
Is all the part requires of you,
In solo parts you are not daunted,
Your voice is heard wherever wanted.

Kapralek, E-flat clarinet,
"Til Eulenspiegel," is his pet,
For men may come and men may go,
Still he'll be known as "Sweet Pipe Joe."

Now **Joe Norrito,** grand old Joe,
As solo clar. his equal show.
A friend sincere in heart and hand,
A credit to his native land.

And **Ernest Gatley,** Boston's pride;
The solo clarinet sits beside,
A helper he, both strong and steady,
For an emergency he's ready.

Now see our **Davis Isador,**
He always keeps us in a roar
Of laughter, with his many jokes,
His merry tricks our mirth provokes.

The next see **Willie Robinson,**
Who has our admiration won;
Altho' rheumatics pain his feet,
He sticks it out, the tour complete.

Jim Lawnham from the Emerald Isle,
Who always greets you with a smile,
Finds relatives in every land,
While on the tour with Sousa's Band.

And **Harry Baldwin,** handsome Harry,
Whom we infer will shortly marry,
May all their innings prove home runs,
Their troubles, "only little ones."

George Kampe has a stand alone,
His partner from his side has flown;
It makes no matter, George don't care,
He'll hold his part down anywhere.

Walt. Sheaffer comes from up the state,
In California, met his fate,
He will not bother hunting jobs,
But settle down to raising squabs.

Joe Lomas, known as quiet Joe,
He plays his part and saves his dough;
Of Canada he is a son,
His native home is Hamilton.

The next is **Clarence Livingston,**
As "Livy" he is sometimes known;
And when this lengthy tour is done,
He will return to Binghampton.

The next, the mail man, **E. A. Wall,**
Who letters bring for one and all.
He, cuttings saves, and programmes, too,
Pastes them in books the whole tour through.

Now, **Walter Collins** next you see,
A very good musician he;
His earned degree could be no greater
From Syracuse, his alma mater.

Behold **Sol Eckstein,** good old Solly,
Good natured ever, always jolly;
He's up to date where'er we go,
From Philadelphia, he's not slow.

Now **Magnant,** he's all right you bet,
He plays the alto clarinet;
He minds his business, plays his part
With all the acumen of art.

Carl Schroeder, our librarian,
Has proved a very useful man;
He keeps the parts, there's no mistakes,
All owing to the care he takes.

Now, **Oscar Modess,** first bassoon,
Is heard in many a funny tune;
He makes folks la **Oscar Modess,** ugh until they cry,
In "Kelley with the Green Necktie."

And there's **Will Decker,** "Deck" as known,
Has skill as a bassoonist shown;
He thinks he'll quit the music game,
In California he'll raise cane.

And next, our alto saxophone,
Ben Vereeken, a musician known,
Arranges parts the whole day long;
They are correct; you'll find none wrong.

There's **Al. Knecht:** "Beeman," you know;
Who always runs our "Minstrel Show."
Both he and Ben are hits 'tis true
In the "Two Little Girls in Blue."

Our solo cornet, **H. L. Clarke,**
In every land has made his mark;
He plays the parts, and solos too,
And plays them as none else can do.

Ross Millhouse fills the second chair,
And when he's needed, always there;
When Bert was called to lead the band,
He played the part, met each demand.

Guy Gaugler, "Washy," known is he,
Not "Washey Hose," the reason see;
Because he hails from Washington,
Where he'll return, when we are done.

And **Bishop Russell,** nicknamed "Buss,"
Was never known to make a fuss;
When he returns, his school he'll teach—
You ought to hear "Buss" make a speech.

Our first trumpet, **Victor Welte,**
Although he's thin, is very healthy;
He makes no breaks, his tones are true,
Knows all about the rail roads, too.

When **Harry Freeman** joined the band,
'Twas with a purpose he had planned
Again to journey o'er the sea,
With home and friends once more to be.

Our solo horn is **Herman Hand,**
One of the finest in the land;
His lip is sure, makes no mistakes,
"The Siegfried Call," he never breaks.

Our second horn, is **Clarence Smith;**
True, as reported, 'tis no myth;
His hobby is baseball to play
With **Mix,** is partner day by day.

Now, **Arthur Kunze,** he's the man,
A natural comedian;
With **Modess** as his running mate,
Much laughter caused the syndicate.

Now **Laendner,** he's all right, you bet,
'Tis he completes the horn quartette;
You'll find the proposition chilly
To try and fool our little Willie.

Here's **John Perfetto,** dandy John,
He plays the first euphonium,
And looks as neat as neat can be,
An artist, every inch is he.

And **A. J. Garing** called "Garingo,"
Good-natured man is he, by jingo;
And Mrs. G., was with him too,
Remained with us the whole tour through.

Ralph Corey plays the first trombone,
And much ability he's shown;
Another "Beantown" product he,
A good white boy, you'll all agree.

George Lucas close beside Ralph sits,
And well the combination fits;
George also plays on the trombone,
And plays it well, you'll surely own.

Mark Lyon is the baggage man;
You'll always find him in the van;
With toil and trouble everywhere,
Poor Mark has had the "Lyon's" share.

And now **Ed Williams,** trombone bass,
Whose name deserves a special place;
Accommodating, good and kind,
A better friend you'll seldom find.

Now **Arthur Storch,** in him you see
Our tuba, first; nor can there be
A finer tone in any case,
It sounds just like a big string bass.

Here's **Griswold,** best as "Shorty" known,
Who plays the giant Sousaphone;
A very nimble wit has he
And always full of repartee.

Now **Emil Mix,** known near and far
As artist, of the camera;
His moving pictures are a treat,
He has them of the tour, complete.

Gus Helleberg, a tuba, too,
And he can surely play a few;
The girls in Melbourne surely did
Say "Gussy was the Candy Kid."

Our tympanist, is **Doctor Lowe,**
And many things to him we owe;
Advice, he always renders free,
Altho' a graduate M.D.

Frank Haynes, he hails from Boston town,
The place of beans of great renown;
No other lands he cares to see,
Says "Boston's good enough for me."

Frank Snow, he beats the big bass drum,
He has the wallop, he is some;
From day to day, the tour complete
You'll never find him off the beat.

Joe Marthage, "Roly Poly Joe,"
He plays the golden harp, you know;
To please the ladies, has the knack,
He charms them in "The Band Came Back."

Berry, Cully, Lawton, Cunnington,
Were with us when the tour begun;
But when we reached our native shore
Our number was reduced by four.

But still they made the tour around
The world; and therefore, we are bound
To place their names where all may be;
So that the list complete may be.

Our vocalist, **Virginia Root;**
Soprano, she, of high repute;
Her audiences never weary;
Brings down the house, with "Annie Laurie."

Miss Zedeler, solo violin;
And much applause, her numbers win;
She is our pride, a little queen,
Our dainty, little **Nicoline.**

Now, **E. G. Clarke,** our business man,
Much has he to contrive and plan;
On salary day, where'er we go,
Ed's always ready with the dough.

E'er we conclude, a final name
That stands "colossal" in its fame,
John Philip Sousa, "March King" he,
Whose fame extends o'er land and sea.

In Europe's highways "Sousa's Band"
Is known as in its native land;
Among its people, such his fame
As "King" in music, they acclaim.

But not content with fields like these
He sought the far Antipodes
E'en as the Argonauts of old;
"Who sailed, to find the fleece of gold."

"Land of the Golden Fleece," have we
Reached in our great itiner'y,
Where "Looking Upward," we descry
"Beneath the Southern Cross," we lie.

The multitudes, both far and near
Have joined to greet, and welcome here,
As though a king, to claim his own,
And place him firmly on his throne.

His throne their hearts, voices and hands,
And so, preceded by massed bands
The cortege passed from street to street;
While countless thousands cheer and greet.

The town "en fete," named hold aloof
But wave from window and from roof;
The city's dignitaries all
Await him, at the Grand Town Hall.

With many a flowery speech is he
Welcomed by the community;
While the massed bands raise the refrain,
The "Stars and Stripes," his magic strain.

And ever thus, the whole world o'er
Until we reached our native shore;
And even then, a triumph earned,
As victor from the wars returned.

But now returned; content to be
"Dwellers of the Western World," are we;
And so, to every promise true
John Philip; here's our love to you.

CHAPTER EIGHT

Some Lighter Moments

In the process of presenting more than fifteen thousand concerts around the world, much anecdotal material about Sousa's Band and its members was generated. At least a small part of it should be preserved, especially because all former members of the band are now deceased. My intent in providing a few stories, some humorous and others serious, is to present a more intimate look into the everyday life of a Sousa band member. Most of the stories were told to me over a forty-year period, during personal interviews with former members of the band. Additional ones were gleaned from news clippings in Sousa Band press books; a few others came from the band's alumni newsletter, the *Sousa Band Fraternal Society News,* and other sources.

A large number of early band members had died before my research began in 1963, so accounts of many events dating back to the early 1890s are probably lost forever, although it is likely that some remain in private hands, whether in diaries, journals, or letters to loved ones. It is my hope that more of this material will be unearthed so future scholars can weave a broader tapestry from experiences of those privileged to be part of the incredible band of John Philip Sousa.

YES, MR. SOUSA IS AMERICAN

Was Mr. Sousa Italian? English? German? This was asked of Sousa Band musicians wherever they traveled. The question was a natural one and asked even more frequently after 1897 because of clever rumors concerning the origin of the Sousa name.

As one version went, Sousa was supposed to have been an Italian named John Philipso, and when he came to the United States his trunk was marked with his name and destination: "JOHN PHILIPSO U.S.A." The last two blocks of letters were somewhat jumbled on the immigration papers, and he became "John Philip Sousa." Other versions had him as English ("JOHN PHILIP SO.") or a German, Siegfried Ochs, thus "S.O. U.S.A," to which he deliberately added "John Philip."

The truth is that his name really was John Philip Sousa. "Sousa" is a venerable old Portuguese name. His father, Antonio Sousa, was born in Spain of Portuguese parents, and the names *John* and *Philip* appear in the family trees of both parents.

George Frederick Hinton of the band's management staff is often blamed for originating the original rumor of the Sousa surname, but he did not. In the *New York Evening Telegram* of June 7, 1897, Hinton debunked the story—although reluctantly because it was "so pretty." When the band first went to Europe in 1900, however, Hinton apparently did little to dispel the rumor. He did not play it down because it gave Sousa and the band a considerable amount of free publicity.

By the time Hinton left the band in 1903 speculation that Sousa was not the original family name had grown, and reporters were constantly asking Sousa whether it was true. He stated many times that he had been called upon to deny it "in every country on the face of the earth." Sousa Band press books contain dozens of interviews in which Sousa was compelled to deny the rumors, and he mentioned it numerous times in his own writing. Yet the myth persists. On several occasions, for example, well-meaning individuals informed me that my research was lacking. "I suppose you've heard that Sousa's name really wasn't Sousa," was a typical comment. "You see, when he came to this country. . . ."

PROHIBITING PROHIBITION

Clarinetist Eddie Wall, a source of many Sousa Band anecdotes, liked to tell about the time he and several other band members found beer in a Wisconsin college town (he would never say which one) during Prohibition.

On the long 1928 tour the band was playing matinee and evening concerts in the town. Eddie and the others, looking for a restaurant after the matinee, asked a man on the street where they could find a "suitable" place. That meant, they hinted, a spot that could possibly provide beer. The man quietly told of such a place, and they had a pleasant meal there. The next morning on their way to the depot they passed the same man—this time in a uniform. He was the chief of police.

ALL ABOARD FOR OLD HEIDELBERG

The band began a tour in the summer of 1924 with an eleven-week engagement at Willow Grove Park near Philadelphia. There were traditionally no rehearsals for Willow Grove engagements, so there would be no rehearsals for the tour that followed. Sousa solved the problem by strategically scheduling tour numbers on programs so that the band would have them polished by the time it took to the road. Starting a season without rehearsals would be risky under any circumstances, and in 1924 the band had several new members. The musicians were all seasoned professionals, however, and things went smoothly. One of the new members was percussionist Paul Diercks, who was temporarily substituting for George Carey.

There was a problem in that Carey was the band's star xylophone soloist, and Sousa had scheduled him for solos on the first day, Sunday, August 14. Diercks, a fine percussionist, was not known as a xylophone soloist so Sousa deleted the xylophone solo from the program and substituted a regular concert number. He chose a fantasie by Theodore Moses Tobani, "Old Heidelberg."

Although "Old Heidelberg" had been in the band's music library since 1903, band members recount that it was used infrequently after the 1924 performance. Eager to make good in his role as a rookie Sousa band member, Diercks studied the music before the concert. He had a question about "Old Heidelberg" and consulted the band's veteran bass drummer, Gus Helmecke, who knew the repertoire. He also knew how to play sly pranks and had a reputation for doing just that. Helmecke, usually deadpan, could dispense humor with a straight face.

The piece, Diercks noted, began with a slow introduction followed by a G.P. (grand pause) and then went into a brisk waltz. "Mr. Helmecke," he asked, "is there any special effect that goes here in the G.P.?"

"Oh yes, young man," Helmecke replied without hesitation. "Didn't you know? That's where you grab this megaphone here and shout out to the audience, 'All aboard for Old Heidelberg.'"

Diercks and Sousa were strangers; there had been no time for the new band members to be introduced. He was about to make his own introduction, however, and in a manner that would become legendary in Sousa Band history. The piece was begun, and the slow introduction went uneventfully. Then came the G.P. Suddenly, up came the megaphone, and Diercks shouted in Sousa's direction, and at the top of his voice, "ALL ABOARD FOR OLD HEIDELBERG!!!"

Sousa was visibly shocked. Musicians in the first row of the band, recalling the event, mused that they thought he would fall off the podium and into the audience. He quickly regained his composure,

however, and went on as though nothing had happened. Helmecke stared innocently at his music.

The men knew that only one person would dare to pull such a prank, and after the concert they remained to see what would happen. Although they also knew that Sousa had a keen sense of humor, as might be expected of a man who had composed fifteen comic operettas, the event must have tried his patience.

All eyes were upon him as he walked around behind the percussion section to where Helmecke stood, guiltless and unconcerned. "Well, Mr. Helmecke," Sousa said sarcastically. "I see you're up to your old tricks again." He continued on the way to his dressing room.

"HELMECKIZED"

Helmecke, who had a part in many other humorous stories, was legendary for his numerous practical jokes and witty remarks.

One day, on a piece calling for no percussion, he stepped behind the curtain. The stage was small, and the musicians were backed up against a very dirty curtain. Helmecke peered through a hole in the curtain and spied the ear of a bassoonist. He then plucked a feather from a duster and stuck it through the hole, tickling the bassoonist, who was so startled that he swung his instrument backward and gave the dirty curtain a good whack. The portion of the band nearest him was covered in a shower of dust.

Helmecke was also known for adding unlikely effects in the parts of unsuspecting new percussionists, as in the "Old Heidelberg" incident. On yet another occasion he added a cuckoo whistle, which a new percussionist unceremoniously added to the end of a piccolo player's cadenza.

The tale about the day Helmecke and xylophone soloist Howard Goulden missed their early morning train in Albuquerque, New Mexico, is classic. Both explained that they had overslept because the hotel clerk neglected to give them a wake-up call. The train was well on its way eastward when other band members realized that the two had been left behind.

In inquiring about ways to get to the next stop, Clovis, New Mexico, Helmecke and Goulden lost hope upon learning that few trains went in that direction. Moreover, the Sousa train had been contracted as a special. They were desperate. Someone told them about a pilot whose three-seat, open-cockpit biplane was housed at the local airport, so they rushed there and pleaded with him to fly them in the direction of Clovis. Navigation was by "iron compass" (the railroad tracks).

Fortunately, the train stopped in Vaughn, New Mexico, for a meal break, and the pilot managed to land in a nearby field. Helmecke and Goulden hopped out and raced with their suitcases to the restaurant. The band gathered around them, and saxophone soloist Ed Heney greeted them with, "Three cheers for the Flying Dutchman!"—Wagner's *Overture to the Flying Dutchman* being part of the repertory that year. Helmecke's reply, it is said, was definitely not fit for print. He had won $50 playing a punchboard game in Albuquerque but barely broke even by the time he paid for the "chartered" flight.

DOLANIZED

John Dolan, the band's cornet soloist during the 1920s, thrilled audiences with his virtuosity. He did not wish to mix with them, however. Being gracious was not one of his virtues. Indeed, other band members were of the opinion that he was downright unsociable. After a concert Dolan would often walk briskly away from the stage and pretend not to hear his name. That was not always possible. One night a man cornered him, shook his hand, and said, "Do you remember me? I met you two years ago in Wheeling, West Virginia, and. . . ." Dolan pulled his hand away and retorted, "So you are he!" Then he turned on his heel and walked away.

On another occasion he was in a dressing room before a matinee and overheard a young boy looking for him, hoping to take a lesson. Dolan crouched in a dark corner. When the boy got close he sprang up, distorted his face, and growled, "You want to see me?!" The boy was so frightened that he whirled around, ran out of the dressing room, and flew up the stairs and out of the theater.

The question most frequently asked at concerts was, "Where do you go from here?" Dolan became so annoyed by this that he would sometimes answer, "Shanghai. Yes, Shanghai, China. We are going ahead by dirigible balloon."

The comment that brought him to his indignant best was when a concert patron rushed up to him and said, "So you are the great Herbert L. Clarke!" Dolan, thoroughly insulted, glanced upward and rushed off in a huff. Band members joked afterward that his chin stuck out so far that "three pigeons could roost on it."

Fellow band members seldom attempted to socialize with Dolan, who was a loner and would pick his own friends if he felt so inclined. He sat by himself on train trips, but one day a new member of the band had the audacity to seat himself next to Dolan and attempt a conversation. Dolan pretended not to hear and then suddenly blurted, "Young man, do you have a soul? Have you ever seen one? Do you know anybody who has ever seen one?!" The newcomer quickly removed himself—exactly what Dolan wanted.

No doubt Dolan could have been with the band until its very end had his odd disposition not stood in the way. He engaged in a heated argument with Sousa on the train while traveling through the Midwest in September of 1928. The incident shocked the musicians who witnessed it, who had never seen Sousa angry or heard him use foul language. Dolan resigned on the spot. As the train pulled away, the band last saw him as they lined up along the windows, gawking at him standing alone on the depot platform with his cornet and wardrobe trunk.

DE LUCIZED

Joe De Luca was Sousa's fine euphonium soloist during the 1920s. He was good-natured and had a keen sense of humor, and perhaps because of that he was the butt of several jokes. Bill Bell, the youngest sousaphone player and a virtuoso in his own right, was good-natured as well and also had a good sense of humor. He tried De Luca's patience many times on the 1923–24 tour while warming up backstage or in dressing rooms. Bell would place himself near De Luca and repeat his warm-up routine note for note but an octave lower. Several times it drove Joe to exclaim, as the society's newsletter reported, "Somea day I'm-a gonna killa that kid!"

De Luca could play very loudly when necessary—too loudly, some say. One day he received a note that read, "Mr. De Luca, you play too damn loud." The message had been delivered by one of the band, along with information that it was a request from the audience. Several musicians swore that Sousa himself had been the author.

One day De Luca came to Sousa to ask if he could play his solo at an afternoon concert rather than at the evening concert because his girlfriend could be there only in the afternoon. Sousa said he was not sure he could rearrange the program, which had been made up months earlier. De Luca's face reflected great sadness until Sousa chuckled and said he would be glad to make the switch.

Graydon Lower was second-chair euphonium one season when an attractive young woman asked him what instrument he played. Before he could reply, De Luca thumped his chest and said, according to the same newsletter, "He'sa only the seconda euphonium. I'ma Joseph De Luca, the greatesta euphonium player ina the whole world!"

The most embarrassing prank played on De Luca came in 1927 when the band was in Bozeman, Montana, giving concerts in a school. When clarinetist Warren (Snorky) Williams found a yellow wooden duck in the kindergarten room where they warmed up, he smuggled it onstage. During one cadenza in De Luca's solo he would play a series of three-note chords and sway back and forth and close his eyes, producing an effect, some bandsmen quipped, that resembled a waddling duck. When De Luca closed his eyes—the moment for which Williams waited—he quietly placed the duck on the floor beside De Luca. When he finished the cadenza there was great laughter instead of the usual applause. When he looked down and saw what the crowd was laughing at, De Luca's face grew red, and he kicked the duck off the stage. "Please, Mr. Sousa," he complained, "I'ma insulted!" Sousa saw the humor of the incident but issued an order saying there would be no more pranks played on Mr. De Luca—at least while he was playing his solos.

TRAINING PROBLEMS

Being in uniform most of the time meant that band members were sometimes mistaken for bellhops or elevator operators. In an Atlanta train station, one woman noticed "SOUSA" on their caps and was heard to ask, "Where does *that* line run?" Another once inquired, "Since when did the railroads start advertising their conductors?" when she saw "SOUSA, CONDUCTOR" on a poster.

Sousa did not escape mistaken identity either. On one occasion a woman approached him in a train station and asked about a departure time. "I'm sorry, madam," he said, "but I don't know." "Then why don't you know?" she said indignantly. "You are a conductor, aren't you?" "Yes," he replied, "but of a brass band."

KIDDING THE KID FROM BOHEMIA

Before Bohumir Kryl became a member of the band he had worked as a sculptor and an acrobat before deciding on a career in music. The young man from Bohemia had seen little of the United States when he joined Sousa and was thrilled at the prospect of viewing Niagara Falls when the band played in Buffalo. Arthur Pryor and some of the others, however, decided to have fun at Kryl's expense by telling him that the concert fell on a Sunday, a day when the falls were turned off. Kryl believed them, but Pryor explained that he could perhaps see the falls anyway. The mayor of Buffalo, Pryor said, a personal friend, might consider turning on the falls for a short period to impress the new cornet soloist of Sousa's Band. Kryl saw the falls and was grateful to Pryor for making special arrangements on his behalf.

Kryl was a rising star in the music world, but his career with Sousa was a very short one. There were those in the band who maintained that he was dismissed for secretly copying some of Sousa's special arrangements to use in the event he would someday have a band of his own. He did, in fact, soon form his own band and was one of Sousa's competitors for many years.

SOUSA'S PRIVATE JOKE

A high percentage of the audience at matinees was sometimes children, who could become inattentive and noisy. On rare occasions, and nearly always in remote areas where concert etiquette had not been taught, even more mature audiences would misbehave in the same manner. One afternoon in the late 1920s Sousa was particularly annoyed by such a crowd, and when the situation did not improve as the program progressed he did not call for a scheduled encore. "All right, boys," he said, "if they're going to act like children we'll give them children's music. Get up 'Mother Goose.'" The band then played his "Mother Goose March," number thirteen in the encore books. The musicians remembered Sousa's subtle joke with fondness. Thereafter, whenever they encountered a rude audience they would nudge one another and whisper, "Uh-oh. The old man's about ready to give 'em 'Mother Goose'!"

A MARCHING ORDER

Howard Rowell, trumpet player on the 1921 tour, recalled two rowdy boys who created a disturbance in the front row at a matinee. Their behavior greatly annoyed Sousa, who pointed at them when the number concluded and shouted, "You two boys! Attention!" Startled, they stood up. "Right face," Sousa continued. "Forward, march!" The two noisemakers marched to the end of the aisle, up the main aisle, and out of the auditorium.

A SECOND OPINION

It was a big moment in the lives of Sousa's Band members when they played one of his new marches for the first time. That usually occurred before tours began, to see whether alterations were needed before the compositions were sent off to a publisher.

A new march was passed out at rehearsal one morning in the late 1920s. The musicians studied the piece, its title unknown, briefly and were eager to begin. The baton came down, but Sousa's reaction was unusual. He seemed indifferent from the first bar. As the piece progressed he appeared puzzled. The last note sounded, and for what seemed like an eternity there was total silence. All waited patiently to hear if the March King would comment on the new march. He lay down his baton and spoke softly but emphatically: "Christ Almighty! Did *I* write that?"

The musicians sat motionless through another long silence broken only by a woman's voice from the back of the theater. "Philip, that was marvelous." A look of profound astonishment came over his face, and he turned to discover that his wife, Jane, had slipped unnoticed into the theater. He turned slowly back to the band and in his most satirical voice announced, "That's what it is—it's marrr-velll-ousss."

THE DAY KELLY DISAPPEARED

When Sousa was in need of a funny story to put an interviewer at ease, one of his favorites was how the performance of "Has Anybody Here Seen Kelly?" brought down the house in Victoria, B.C. The band had just finished the Pacific leg of the 1911 world tour and was giving its first concert on the way back to New York.

A patron borrowed the band's encore card for this snapshot following the "Has Anybody Here Seen Kelly?" incident. (Author's Collection)

"Kelly," a type of composition he called a "humoresque," was used to add levity to concerts. It was a popular tune of the day, and the arrangement passed the melody from instrument to instrument in a clever way, much to the delight of audiences. It had been especially well received in England, home of its composer, Will Letters.

The band was using it as a regular encore feature on the tour. When the encore card announcing the piece was held up in Victoria on September 20, the audience shouted and roared with laughter. Sousa and the musicians were startled, and they did not learn the reason for the response until after the concert.

As it happened, it was a local election day, and a candidate named Kelly had just lost by a huge margin. Several people rushed backstage to congratulate Sousa for his astute showmanship, some believing he had hurriedly arranged the piece for the occasion. He said nothing because, as he remarked many times, "I hate to kill a good story."

A ONE-ARMED CLARINETIST?

Sousa instructed Jay Sims, the personnel manager of the band, to have one of the clarinetists report to him at the end of a concert. He had noticed the musician periodically playing his instrument with only one hand and concluded that he was not performing his duties to the full extent of his ability. When the man explained that certain passages could be played with just one hand, Sousa paused and then stated that he had just been inspired to compose a concerto for a one-armed clarinet player. The concerto evidently was never written because no such Sousa manuscript is known to exist and there are no accounts of a performance in Sousa Band programs or in concert reviews in the band's press books.

FRITSCHE'S GRAND DETOUR

While playing in Germany on the European tour of 1900 Sousa learned that Robert Vollstedt, a German composer, would be in the audience one evening. Although none of Vollstedt's compositions was on the programs for that part of the tour, Sousa decided to add one for the occasion. There was no time to rehearse the new number, but that was nothing new for Sousa's seasoned musicians. There was a problem, however, in a clarinet cadenza when solo clarinetist Otto Fritsche took it upon himself to improve on Vollstedt's written cadenza by adding material of his own.

Fritsche launched into the cadenza with great aplomb, but in the process of adding his own material he somehow became lost and ended in the wrong key. He then began to improvise by playing arpeggios and scales in various keys. Sousa was astonished. He stared at his score, not believing what he was hearing. The frantic improvisation continued until Fritsche devised a way out of his self-created maze by going into a long, ascending chromatic scale, ending on a shrieking high note, and then finishing the cadenza as written. Sousa breathed a sigh of relief and whispered softly, "Welcome home, Mr. Fritsche." Vollstedt's opinion was not made known, but he may have been as baffled as Sousa.

FOLLOW THE LEADER

Sousa found out how super-attentive musicians could be while playing one September day between races at the 1901 Indiana State Fair in Indianapolis. One race began while the band was still playing, and several musicians, Sousa noticed, were catching glances at the track while playing from memory. An ardent horseman himself, he could not resist looking around to see what the attraction was. Whatever it was he saw caused him to freeze at the top of the upbeat, his arm held high. The band stopped playing—immediately. On several occasions he stated that he had once vowed never to mix business with pleasure. After this incident he announced he was renewing that vow.

NO REVIEWS FOR THESE CONCERTS

After a concert in Raleigh, North Carolina, on January 4, 1899, a report of the event appeared in a local newspaper: "An account of Sousa's concert at the Academy of Music last night is unnecessary, for everybody in Raleigh seems to have been present."

Yet another report was published in a Greensboro, North Carolina, periodical after a March 4, 1924, appearance in that city: "Sousa's Band played at the National Theatre last night before what was probably the largest audience that ever attempted to visit a concert in the city of Greensboro. Not only were all seats sold, but not even newspaper passes were honored for seats, and it is, therefore, impossible to report on the quality of the concert."

A SINCERE MUSICAL STATEMENT

Before organizing his band John Philip Sousa had developed special relationships with presidents of the United States during his twelve-year tenure as leader of the U.S. Marine Band—the "President's Own." In particular he felt a deep loss when James A. Garfield was assassinated in 1881. Garfield, like Sousa, was a Mason.

William McKinley's assassination in 1901 was also a blow. Rather than make a statement to the press, Sousa responded with a musical tribute at concerts immediately after McKinley's death. His action is perhaps best described in a poignant account that appeared in the *Columbus* (Ohio) *Dispatch* on September 21:

> One of the most graceful and beautiful acts John Philip Sousa has ever performed in Columbus was done Friday night at the concert at the Great Southern [Theatre]. The last number before the intermission had just been played and the magnificent finale of Giordano's grand scene and ensemble, "Andrea Chenier," had barely died away when the world's greatest bandmaster again raised his baton.
>
> Instantly a profound hush fell upon the audience, for something not on the program was coming. No one knew what. Then softly in strains sweeter than Apollo's lute, in harmony that seemed to have its source in realms celestial, there stole upon the ear that wondrous creation of the Christian hymnology, "Nearer, My God to Thee."

The audience hardly breathed, for with one wave of the master-hand they were suddenly lifted from the midst of the grandest band concert ever given in the Ohio capital and set down beside the catafalque of the dead president.

Tears welled in nearly every eye as that divine hymn was played. It seemed as if its matchless beauty had never been fully realized before. And midst the solemn breathing sound, faint as the distant echo from some sacred shrine, there came the tolling of the funeral bell.

No words can picture the effect. The eyes of strong men blurred as the tide of an irrepressible emotion welled within, and heads were bowed in grief.

If Sousa had never done anything else to make him the idol of the public, that simple, soulful unheralded tribute to the fallen chieftain should lift him to the pinnacle. It was as a song without words, but words were never so eloquent as the heavenly music of that incomparable band.

A STEAK DINNER CHALLENGE

Clarinetist Lou Morris of Philadelphia knew all about the artistic snobbery that symphony orchestra musicians sometimes demonstrate against band musicians; he had played in both the Philadelphia Orchestra and Sousa's Band. While he was with Sousa the band passed through Philadelphia for a series of concerts. Several orchestra musicians and band members happened to meet one morning, and the subject of bands versus orchestras became a lively debate. The orchestra musicians suggested that bands were inherently inferior to orchestras and should not play orchestral literature. Band members bristled and issued a challenge. One of the features of the band's tour that year was Richard Strauss's "Till Eulenspiegel's Merry Pranks," and Sousa's masterful interpretation of it had drawn favorable reviews.

The Sousa band challenged the orchestra to come to the concert, furnished them with complimentary tickets, and made a bet. If the band did not play the Strauss piece better than the orchestra had, the band members would buy the orchestra steak dinners. The orchestra would buy if the reverse was true. After the concert the Philadelphia Orchestra musicians bought the steak dinners.

FOLLOW THE SWALLOW

Sousa and the band played numerous engagements at the old Methodist Camp Ground at Ocean Grove, New Jersey, but wore out their welcome at a concert there on July 10, 1926.

Although Methodists were staunch Prohibitionists, Sousa was featuring his latest humoresque, "The Mingling of the Wets and the Drys," on the 1926 tour and planned to play it at Ocean Grove. The comical piece poked fun at Prohibition, depicting a "wet" and a "dry" drinking tea and water while longing for the days before Prohibition. The band might have played the piece with a minimum of objection had it not been for a publicity poster fashioned in the shape of a whiskey bottle. This caught the attention of members of the Ocean Grove Camp Meeting Association, who reasoned that a performance of the piece would not be in their best interest.

The Rev. Charles M. Boswell, the association's president, was indignant and urged people not to attend the concert if Sousa insisted on playing "The Mingling of the Wets and the Drys." The protest puzzled Sousa, but he agreed to play something else. Perhaps he was being contrary when he substituted another of his humoresques, "Follow the Swallow," which had nothing to do with drinking and was based on themes suggestive of a swallow's flight from north to south. Its title likely seemed appropriate.

The association was not amused and never again engaged Sousa. The following year, when reporters asked the association why the band was not invited back to Ocean Grove, which neighboring communities often referred to as "Ocean Grave," the reply was that it was the association's policy not to have the same attractions year after year. Policy or not, Sousa's Band had appeared there in successive years from 1921 through 1924. Whatever the reason, one of the favorite stories among former Sousa musicians concerned how their esteemed conductor, not a Prohibition supporter, lost business because of a politically incorrect decision.

A BLAST FROM THE BACK ROW

Jack Richardson, the band's first tuba player for many years, misunderstood the sequence of pieces on a program one day. One piece was to begin very softly, but Richardson thought it was a Sousa march and had a rousing beginning. The baton came down, and he responded with a solid fortissimo—in the wrong key. When time came to play the same piece the following day Sousa paused, looked at the back row, and carefully raised his palm in Richardson's direction before giving the downbeat.

AVOIDING DISASTER

Sousa had enough experience in understanding the temperament of audiences to be ready for nearly any situation arising during a concert. For example, he avoided calamity when the lights went out one night, leaving both audience and band in total darkness. He quickly announced "Oh Dear, What Can the Matter Be?" which the band played from memory. This was followed by "Wait 'til the Clouds Roll By," and when the lights came back on he was greeted by laughter and applause.

A much more serious situation arose in Kansas City, Missouri, on the afternoon of February 22, 1899. A crowd of twelve thousand was on hand to dedicate the new Convention Center. As the concert was about to end a man in the balcony wanted to hear a trombone solo by Arthur Pryor, a native of nearby St. Joseph. Although he shouted "Pryor!" many in the audience misunderstood him to say "fire!" A stampede toward the exits began. Sousa instantly shouted to the band, "'Dixie'! 'Dixie'!" He calmly turned toward the audience, and before the band had played the tune through three times people had returned to their seats. No doubt many lives were saved by Sousa's quick thinking. Newspapers across the country wrote about the incident, but whether he granted the request from the balcony was not mentioned.

HANDS ACROSS THE ROYALTIES

The Sousa daughters, Priscilla and Helen, often repeated the story of how their father had entered one of his pieces in a march contest in 1899. It won second prize, the first prize going to a Baptist minister. Sousa's march was published by John Church, but neither daughter could recall the name of the minister, the title, or what company published the first-place march.

A year later Sousa had a chance meeting with the minister at a concert and inquired about the prize-winning composition. The modest reply was that only thirty or forty copies had been sold. The minister then asked Sousa how *his* march was coming along. "You heard it just before intermission," Sousa replied. The band had just played "Hands across the Sea," which had quickly become a big seller and is still being played by bands.

ALL PRESENT OR ACCOUNTED FOR

School children are not the only ones who play hooky. Even members of prestigious government law-making bodies do so, as the band learned one afternoon in 1901 when playing in Olympia, Washington.

Between numbers a man standing at the side of the auditorium was creating a disturbance by peering into the audience as though looking for someone. Sousa sent him a polite request to stand where he could not be seen. The man came backstage during the intermission and explained what he was doing. "I beg your pardon, Mr. Sousa, but I'm the sergeant-at-arms of the legislature and we couldn't transact any business because we lacked a quorum. I've been hunting all over town for the members. When I came here, I was able to count in your audience the legislators of both houses, almost to a man."

A DEGREE OF HASTE

Honorary doctorates were conferred more sparingly in the early twentieth century than they are today, and when Sousa received word from Milwaukee that Marquette University wished to confer an honorary doctor of music degree upon him, he made an extraordinary effort to be present for the ceremony on November 16, 1923.

There was a serious problem, however. The band was on tour at the time and not scheduled to be in Milwaukee until the day after the ceremony. There were two concerts in Akron, Ohio, the day before the ceremony, and two concerts in Hammond, Indiana, the same day as the ceremony. With clever planning, however, as well as with luck and considerable expense, the "governor" received his degree.

The distance from Akron to Hammond was approximately 350 miles by rail, so it was necessary for the band to board a special sleeper train immediately after the evening concert in Akron in order to be in Hammond in time for the matinee the next day. It would not seem possible for Sousa to travel the extra hundred miles northward to Milwaukee,

attend the morning award ceremony, and then travel another hundred miles back down to Hammond in time for the matinee there. But Willie Schneider, the road manager, came up with a daring plan.

He met with railroad officials and made arrangements for a sleeper train, powered by four engines, to whisk Sousa to Milwaukee so he could be at the 10:30 a.m. ceremony at the university. After the evening concert in Akron, Sousa boarded his special train with Schneider and his road secretary/valet, Donald Snyder, while band members boarded their own train. Sousa's section sped ahead, averaging seventy-five miles per hour, and the railroad cooperated by clearing the tracks in its path.

The morning ceremony in Milwaukee was to begin the minute Sousa arrived. Dean Liborius Semmann of the College of Music met him at the rail station, and they rushed to campus by automobile. After several brief speeches of high praise, Father Albert C. Fox, president of the university, presented Sousa with his diploma. Pictures were then taken, and he was rushed back to the train station.

The grand rush now began in earnest. Even with the most expedient means of transportation available at the time it would have taken a miracle to get Sousa to Hammond by the time the concert was scheduled to begin. However, Schneider and Sousa knew how to handle the situation—they instructed the band to commence with a Sousa piece, "Showing Off before Company," a humoresque designed to introduce the various instruments of the band to young musicians. It could last from twenty to thirty-five minutes, depending upon the situation. Musicians came onstage singly or in small groups, each playing short passages to demonstrate the sound of their instruments, which a narrator from the band described. After everyone was in place the band would strike up the last few measures of one of Sousa's most familiar marches, and he would strut onstage just in time to conduct the last few notes.

Minus Sousa (who had instructed them to "stretch it out"), the band began "Showing Off before Company" as their conductor sped toward Hammond; Schneider had even arranged for a police escort to meet him and clear the way. About three-fourths of the way through "Showing Off" the audience heard sirens approaching the concert hall, unaware this signaled the approach of the man they had come to hear. The band, knowing "the governor" was at hand, resumed its normal pace. After all instrumentalists had "shown off" they launched into the last few bars of Sousa's "Liberty Bell March." On came Sousa, baton in hand, to conduct the final few notes. The audience was none the wiser.

PUNCTUALITY

"Punctuality is the politeness of kings." That philosophy drove Sousa to begin his concerts exactly on time and is described elsewhere in this book. For a band member to be late for a performance was unthinkable, but occasionally it happened. Usually there were extenuating circumstances and the player was forgiven. In the summer of 1899, for example, a third of the band did not arrive for an extended engagement at Manhattan Beach in New York. Their train had been involved in an accident. Some of the newer men thought Sousa would surely not begin the concert without them; the more senior musicians, however, were well aware of his obsession with punctuality.

When the late-comers arrived the band was in the middle of a selection that had a march as an encore. At the beginning of the encore they marched onstage, single-file and playing their instruments. Sousa was astonished. The audience, much to his surprise, loved it. Ever willing to please audiences, he had the band repeat the impromptu piece the next night. The musicians all kept their jobs.

A LITERAL MANHATTAN BEACH

Leo Zimmerman (Zimmy) succeeded Arthur Pryor as principal trombonist of the band and was soloist on several tours in the early part of the twentieth century. He was also known as a practical joker. A prank he pulled at an engagement at the Corn Palace in Mitchell, South Dakota, caused Zimmerman to be remembered fondly for decades by band alumni.

A vaudeville act was playing at the Corn Palace as well, and as part of the routine an actor would pull a rope that released a trap door, allowing some two hundred hats to rain down onto the stage. Zimmerman discovered that the rope hung next to his seat at the end of the trombone section. It would liven their grueling tour, he thought, if part of the band could be showered with the hats during a concert.

Fittingly, it was during the "Manhattan Beach" march that he took action. As Sousa recalled in his autobiography, apparently unaware that one of his musicians had been the instigator, "We were the most surprised lot of men you ever saw when a shower of hats descended upon us. In the bells of the sousaphones they were piled nearly three feet deep. The laughter that overwhelmed the audience was so tremendous that you couldn't hear the band play at all, although they valiantly continued to play!" According to John J. Perfetto, another soloist, Sousa also had a hearty laugh.

SWEET REVENGE

Zimmerman was himself the victim of a few pranks. Not everyone in the band knew he wore a toupee, but flutist Julius Spindler did, and he devised a scheme to get even for pranks Zimmerman had pulled on him.

Just before the curtain went up one day, Spindler tied a fishhook to a piece of string, slipped up behind Zimmerman, and carefully embedded the hook in his toupee. Spindler tied the other end of the string to the curtain, and when it went up, so did Zimmerman's hairpiece. It swung back and forth, leaving those in the front rows wondering about the symbolic meaning of a scalp dangling in front of the band. It remained there until intermission, when Zimmerman returned to full dress.

A SITUATION IN HAND

French hornist Hermann Hand learned the hard way that the practice of loving and forgetting could be expensive. His plight began while on the 1911 world tour, aboard the steamship *Ionic* between South Africa and Tasmania. Louisa Nutter, who was English, later claimed that he courted her aboard the ship but then abandoned her. She tracked him to Australia, then to New Zealand, then to the Fiji Islands, and on to America. She caught up with him in New York three years later and sued him for $10,000, claiming breach of promise.

Hand had, Nutter claimed, been kind to her, wooed her, and eventually asked for her hand in marriage. She could not keep pace with the band on its grueling tour through several countries but followed behind as much as her financial situation would allow. She had, she told the jury, been forced to work as a kitchen maid in order to earn enough money to continue her pursuit.

Hand told a much different story. Nutter, he said, had become enamored of him after he saved her life by preventing her from jumping overboard. Once she reached America, he claimed, she made his life miserable by constant telephoning and was "about to ruin me and drive me to the cemetery." Hand's testimony was dramatic. "For three years," he shouted, "I have waited to clear my honor!" It was only the money she wanted, he added.

Hand left the Sousa Band after the world tour and came to be regarded as one of the world's finest French horn players, but it was doubtful that he could have managed $10,000. The jury took into consideration that there was no proof of a marriage contract but reasoned that some compensation might be appropriate. They could not agree after five hours of deliberation, however, so the judge dismissed them. Many years later former Sousa Band members seldom spoke of Hand's predicament and could not recall what became of Louisa Nutter.

ANOTHER CLAIM TO FAME

Hermann Hand figured in still another Sousa Band story, this one concerning a "back door" audition of one of his French horn students. Hand was reputed to be a fine teacher, and one of his standout students was Benjamin Hudish, nineteen. At one lesson he played a very difficult passage so well that Hand telephoned John Philip Sousa and asked Hudish to play the passage again, this time for him. Sousa was so impressed that he promised to engage Hudish for the next tour, which was in 1912. Hudish became the youngest member of the band, eventually its principal hornist, and had the distinction of being the only member of the Sousa Band to be hired by auditioning over the telephone.

AN OFFER HE COULD REFUSE

Sousa was generous in granting requests for music to be played at his concerts and always looking for new selections that would be appreciated by audiences. One suggestion came in the form of a note, which he liked to quote verbatim:

Dear Sir:
    Have a Hot quick step that I have tried to erange can not mook it. What Royalty will you take to erange it for Band Mandolin Orchestra and Piano. Evry one is stuck on it.
        Yours
        Leader of opry House Orchestor

ONE SUIT AHEAD OF THE LAW

John Brennan, the naturopath who traveled with the band and treated Sousa during the period when he was recuperating from the injury suffered in falling from a horse in 1921, was involved in a clandestine incident with a band member.

As told by Brennan's younger brother, Edward, one musician was behind in alimony payments, and his former wife sent legal papers to the sheriff in a town where the band was scheduled to play. The musician somehow learned that the sheriff had a warrant for his arrest and would be seeking him. He prevailed upon Brennan to trade clothing with him so the sheriff could find no one by his name in a Sousa Band uniform. Whether the law caught up with the offending musician in a later town—or whether he quickly made alimony payments—is not recorded.

"LET 'EM HAVE IT, JOHNNY!"

Tchaikovsky's symphonic ballad *Le Voyvode* poses a challenge for symphony orchestras. It is even more difficult for bands to play because clarinets and saxophones must negotiate its intricate string parts. It is a programmatic piece that sets to music a poem by the Russian poet Alexander Pushkin. The climax, a stormy section that bandsmen termed a "dogfight," leads to a pistol shot to mark the moment when the *voyvode* (warrior) is killed. The work then ends with a mournful section depicting sorrow.

Although bands perform the work infrequently, Sousa's Band did so successfully on the 1926 world tour until one night when everything went wrong. The trombones made their bold thematic entry at the wrong time; other sections picked up on the wrong entry, confusing others; and all of a sudden the band was lost. Some repeated phrases, and some skipped ahead. Chaos resulted. Sousaphone player Jack Richardson came to the rescue. He turned around to the percussion section and yelled, "Let 'em have it, Johnny!" John Heney then fired his blank pistol. The band stopped, instinctively picked up on the soft passage, and finished the piece. *Le Voyvode* was an unfamiliar work at the time, so it is possible that most of the audience thought Tchaikovsky had written it that way. One thing was certain. The night in 1926 when the band fell apart was an experience no one in the group forgot.

THE SHOW MUST GO ON

Sousa made extraordinary efforts to present every concert precisely at the designated time, even in the face of considerable difficulty. One of the most difficult times was when he felt obligated to conduct just three hours after his beloved mother was buried in the family plot in Washington, D.C. She had died on August 23, 1908, after a three-month struggle with Bright's disease.

At the time, the band was playing a three-week engagement at Willow Grove Park north of Philadelphia. There were the usual four concerts per day, the first starting at 2 p.m. When Sousa received word of his mother's death, band members assumed that Herbert L. Clarke would be conducting the band while Sousa went down to Washington to be with the family. Not so.

His straightforward reason for not missing a single concert was typically Sousa. His mother, he explained, would have wanted it that way. "My mother always told me that under no consideration must I disappoint the people who had come to hear my band. She always said that a man must do his duty before he should attend to anything personal. She always considered that my duty was to play for the public, and I am following her wishes."

He took a late train from Philadelphia to Washington after the last concert of the evening; the funeral had been arranged to be held at 9 the following morning. Immediately thereafter he took a return train to Philadelphia, arriving in time for the 2 o'clock concert.

Some three thousand people in attendance at the park's pavilion were surprised to see Sousa on the podium. As a Philadelphia newspaper reported, however, "He bowed and smiled, but the smiles were not so broad nor the bows so deep and graceful as customary. . . . The nonchalance always noticeable in Sousa was missing. He kept his attention upon the musicians, and, although striving hard to swing the baton with the grace and careless freedom of old, he failed. . . . It was easy to note that every man was striving to do his best and thereby relieve the leader of any worries other than those which already weighed heavily on them."

A DEAD END

Sousa had a great love for many longer works of classical composers. Because his avowed mission in music was to raise the level of America's appreciation, he longed to present some of these longer pieces to the public. He knew, however, that the audiences to which his band appealed would not tolerate lengthy works. They were accustomed to his style of presenting a large variety of shorter pieces. Sousa was sensitive to the criticism of those abroad who thought America existed in a cultural void, however, and realized that if the American public was ever to gain a level of appreciation approaching that of European audiences it would have to be exposed to longer masterworks, one way or another.

The solution was to present works with judicious cuts, leaving only highlights, that is, including only the more interesting passages and eliminating what Sousa sometimes referred to as "padding." One such piece was a tone poem by the German composer Richard Strauss, *Death and Transfiguration*. Performances by symphony orchestras typically lasted twenty-five minutes. With cuts, Sousa's presentation was considerably shorter. As the band traveled deeper into the southern states, where audiences of the era were often less sophisticated than elsewhere, he found it necessary to keep increasing the number of cuts. That led to a joke among the band. Referring to the individual described in the tone poem, a frail artist who eventually dies and is ushered into the afterlife, the musicians quipped, "We had him dead and buried in less than eight minutes!"

ONE HELLE OF A NOTE

It is unlikely that Franz Helle, Sousa's virtuoso flugelhorn player, took a suggestion of Sousa's to heart. According to a story appearing in newspapers around the country, a hotel employee in Washington, D.C., commented on Helle's curious name. Sousa replied that he had jokingly advised Helle to consider naming his children What The and Go To.

"IS THERE A BAND IN HEAVEN?" (ADAPTED FROM AN OLD BASEBALL JOKE)

Willie and Looie, former members of Sousa's Band, were of the belief that there surely would be a band in heaven, because bands are so wonderful. Their belief was reinforced when hearing, upon the death of a prominent band member, that he "joined the Grand Band in the Sky." They made a pact: Whoever died first would find a way to return to tell the other about the "Grand Band in the Sky."

Willie died first. While sitting in his studio one day Looie heard a voice. "Looie! This is Willie. Wake up! I have news for you. I have some good news and some bad news. Yes, there is a band in heaven, and what a band! I never heard such a sound in my life. Mr. Sousa and Pat Gilmore are the permanent co-conductors.

"In the cornet and trumpet section I see Herbert L. Clarke, Herman Bellstedt, Frank Simon, Del Staigers, and John Dolan. And would you believe, this season Mr. Sousa added something new—women. In the cornet section he has Helen May Butler and Alice Raymond.

"In the French horn section are Maurice Van Praag, Hermann Hand, Ben Hudish, and Pete Biroschak. The trombone section features Arthur Pryor, Leo Zimmerman, Ralph Corey, Ed Williams, Marc Lyon, and Jay Sims. Playing euphonium are Joe Raffoyolo, Simone Mantia, and Johnny Perfetto.

"Back in the percussion section are Gus Helmecke, Johnny Heney, Frank Holt, Howard Goulden, Lou Mehling, and Doc Lowe.

"Playing flute are Frank Wadsworth, Meredith Willson, and Jack Bell. The clarinet section includes Dad Norrito, Eddie Wall, and behind them are Eddie's dad and brother. In the saxophone section are E. A. Lefebre, Rudy Becker, Harold Stephens, and Ed Heney."

Looie said, "This is all great news. But you said there was bad news, too. What's the bad news?

"The bad news, Looie," Willie responded, "is that you're on for a solo at the matinee tomorrow."

APPENDIX I

WHERE THE BAND PLAYED

Scope

This appendix is a compilation of dates and locations of the 15,623 Sousa Band performances that took place over a period of forty years (see Table 1 in Chapter 1). It is the culmination of a research project that also took place over a period of forty years.

Sources

Of all the sources employed, the most productive was a far-from-complete collection of the band office's printed itineraries that had been furnished to the author by former band members. Since there were seventy-nine individual tours plus many engagements in the home base of New York City, it should come as no surprise that there were huge gaps in the recorded coverage.

Of great importance were the eighty-five Sousa Band press books. These contain thousands upon thousands of clippings of concert reviews, preconcert publicity, fragments of tour schedules, and other pertinent information.

Although most Sousa Band financial records were destroyed in the 1970s, the few that survived proved to be immensely helpful. Among those records, the most fruitful were weekly concert receipt sheets, a few theater contracts, railroad schedules, hotel receipts, and publicity releases. The papers of David Blakely, Sousa's first manager, also provided valuable data.

Other sources included preliminary tour routes that were usually sent out with "call sheets" to the band members. These communications often describe the tours and provide details such as rehearsal times, information on uniform makers, and essentials needed for travel.

Since more than 1,200 people were associated with the band, one would think there would be many diaries or memoirs revealing detailed accounts of all the band's travels. Such was not the case, however; only a half dozen were located. These were extremely useful, even though each covers only a short timespan. The diaries and day books of saxophonist Albert A. Knecht and cornetist Clarence J. Russell were of inestimable help.

Several collections of the personal papers of individual musicians were studied in detail, but each collection typically covers only the short period when the individual was with the band. Group photographs of the band, as well as individual and section photographs, were useful in linking dates and places.

Occasionally, fragments of band schedules would appear in music journals such as the *Musical Courier* and *Metronome*. The same is true of issues of the *Sousa Band Fraternal Society News*. A few partial tour itineraries were also printed in Sousa Band programs. Confirmations of several dates were found in Sousa's autobiography, *Marching Along*.

Among additional sources were holdings in libraries and private collections.

Reconstructing Tours

Reconstructing parts of some tours was made possible by systematically studying accounts submitted by theater managers or owners for publication in the *New York Dramatic Mirror* and the *New York Clipper*. These journals reported on the entertainment activities of major theaters of the country. Locating and sorting through these was a tedious process, always beginning with the "shotgun" method of searching.

In the end, it became necessary to write several thousand letters to libraries, historical societies, and museums in cities along the railroad routes in use at the time. Armed with the knowledge that the band was traveling in a general area at a given time, I was eventually able to complete final documentation of the tours.

Missing Dates

Small gaps of a day or two on this listing might indicate that the band management was unable to book concerts for those times or that there were cancellations. If a date fell on a Sunday, it usually meant that blue laws were in effect in an area, meaning that entertainments such as concerts were not permitted on Sundays.

A gap of a day or two might also mean that the distance was great between two cities so that the time was needed for travel. This was particularly true in western states. Still other gaps, although rare, were caused by accidents or extremes of weather.

Telling a Story

The outreach of Sousa's Band should be obvious with even a cursory examination of this appendix. It should also be obvious that the band was the most successful organization of its kind in the history of entertainment. In the process of crossing cultural boundaries, Sousa and his band exemplified the spirit and energy of America.

During the four decades of what Sousa described as his "mission in music," he became a wealthy man. He must have been doing something right. Very right.

1ST 1892 TOUR

Soloists: Marcella Lindh, soprano; [Mr.] Bologua & Antonio Galassi, baritone; Arthur Smith, cornet; Joseph Michele Raffayolo, euphonium; John S. Cox, flute; C.L. Staats & Gustave Stengler, clarinet.

SEPTEMBER

26	Mon.	Eve.	Plainfield, NJ	Stillman Music Hall
27	Tue.	Eve.	Trenton, NJ	Taylor's Opera House
28	Wed.	Mat.	York, PA	York Opera House
28	Wed.	Eve.	Harrisburg, PA	Grand Opera House
29	Thu.	Mat.	Danville, PA	Opera House
29	Thu.	Eve.	Williamsport, PA	Lycoming Opera House
30	Fri.	Mat.	Corning, NY	Opera House
30	Fri.	Eve.	Elmira, NY	Opera House

OCTOBER

1	Sat.	Mat.	Towanda, PA	Hale's Opera House
1	Sat.	Eve.	Ithaca, NY	Wilgus Opera House
2	Sun.	Eve.	Buffalo, NY	Music Hall
3	Mon.	Eve.	Detroit, MI	Lyceum Thea.
4	Tue.	Mat.	Ann Arbor, MI	Grand Opera House
4	Tue.	Eve.	Jackson, MI	Hibbard Opera House
5	Wed.	Mat.	Owoso, MI	Salisbury's Opera House
5	Wed.	Eve.	Saginaw, MI	Academy of Music
6	Thu.	Mat.	Flint, MI	Music Hall
6	Thu.	Eve.	Lansing, MI	Baird's Opera House
7	Fri.	Mat.	Battle Creek, MI	Hamblin's Opera House
7	Fri.	Eve.	Kalamazoo, MI	Academy of Music
8	Sat.	M/E	Muskegon, MI	Muskegon Opera House
9	Sun.	Eve.	Grand Rapids, MI	Hartman's Hall
10	Mon.	Eve.	Chicago, IL	Auditorium
11	Tue.	Eve.	Chicago, IL	Auditorium
12	Wed.	M/E	Chicago, IL	Auditorium
13	Thu.	Eve.	Chicago, IL	Auditorium
14	Fri.	Eve.	Chicago, IL	Auditorium
15	Sat.	M/E	Chicago, IL	Auditorium
16	Sun.	Mat.	Racine, WI	Belle City Opera House
17	Mon.	Eve.	Chicago, IL	Auditorium
18	Tue.	Mat.	Beloit, WI	Opera House
18	Tue.	Eve.	Rockford, IL	Opera House
19	Wed.	Eve.	Chicago, IL	Auditorium (Inaugural ball)
20	Thu.	Day	Chicago, IL	World's Fair (parade 12:30)
21	Fri.	Day	Chicago, IL	World's Fair (building dedication)
21	Fri.	Eve.	Chicago, IL	Auditorium
22	Sat.	Day	Chicago, IL	World's Fair (building dedication)
23	Sun.	Eve.	Lima, OH	Faurot Opera House
24	Mon.	Mat.	Ada, OH	Ada Opera House
24	Mon.	Eve.	Fort Wayne, IN	Masonic Temple
25	Tue.	Mat.	Bucyrus, OH	Bucyrus Opera House
25	Tue.	Eve.	Mansfield, OH	Memorial Opera House
26	Wed.	Mat.	Johnstown, PA	Adair's Opera House
26	Wed.	Eve.	Altoona, PA	11th Ave. Opera House
27	Thu.	Mat.	Washington, DC	Metzerott Music Hall
27	Thu.	Eve.	Wilmington, DE	Grand Opera House
28	Fri.	M/E	Washington, DC	Metzerott Music Hall
29	Sat.	M/E	Philadelphia, PA	Academy of Music
30	Sun.	Eve.	New York, NY	Broadway Thea.

[End of 1st 1892 tour]

2ND 1892 TOUR

Soloists: Marcella Lindh, soprano; Antonio Galassi, baritone; Alessandro Liberati & Arthur Smith, cornet; Arthur Pryor, trombone; John S. Cox, flute; Gustave Stengler, clarinet.

NOVEMBER

13	Sun.	Eve.	New York, NY	Broadway Thea.
14	Mon.	Mat.	Bridgeport, CT	Bunnell's Thea.
14	Mon.	Eve.	Meriden, CT	Opera House
15	Tue.	Mat.	New Britain, CT	Opera House
15	Tue.	Eve.	New Haven, CT	Hyperion Thea.
16	Wed.	Mat.	Middletown, CT	Middlesex Thea.
16	Wed.	Eve.	Hartford, CT	Foot Guard Armory
17	Thu.	Mat.	Woonsocket, RI	Woonsocket Opera House
17	Thu.	Eve.	Providence, RI	Music Hall
18	Fri.	Mat.	Amesbury, MA	Amesbury Opera House
18	Fri.	Eve.	Haverhill, MA	Academy of Music
19	Sat.	Mat.	Exeter, NH	Exeter Opera House
19	Sat.	Eve.	Dover, NH	Opera House
20	Sun.	Eve.	Boston, MA	Music Hall
21	Mon.	Eve.	Lowell, MA	Lowell Opera House
22	Tue.	Mat.	Brunswick, ME	Town Hall
22	Tue.	Eve.	Lewiston, ME	City Hall
23	Wed.	M/E	Bangor, ME	Bangor Opera House
24	Thu.	Mat.	Skowhegan, ME	Coburn Hall
24	Thu.	Eve.	Augusta, ME	Grand Opera House
25	Fri.	Mat.	Bath, ME	Almeda Opera House
25	Fri.	Eve.	Rockland, ME	Farwell Opera House
26	Sat.	M/E	Portland, ME	City Hall
27	Sun.	Eve.	Boston, MA	Music Hall
28	Mon.	Eve.	Salem, MA	Cadet Armory
29	Tue.	Mat.	Marlborough, MA	Marlboro Thea.
29	Tue.	Eve.	Worcester, MA	Mechanics' Hall
30	Wed.	Mat.	Northampton, MA	Academy of Music
30	Wed.	Eve.	Springfield, MA	City Hall

DECEMBER

1	Thu.	Mat.	Schenectady, NY	Centre Street Opera House
1	Thu.	Eve.	Gloversville, NY	Kasson Opera House
2	Fri.	Mat.	Little Falls, NY	Skinner Opera House
2	Fri.	Eve.	Utica, NY	Utica Opera House
3	Sat.	Mat.	Oneida, NY	Monroe Opera House
3	Sat.	Eve.	Rome, NY	Washington Street Opera House
4	Sun.	M/E	Rochester, NY	Lyceum Thea.
5	Mon.	Mat.	Geneva, NY	Linden Opera House
5	Mon.	Eve.	Auburn, NY	Burtis Opera House
6	Tue.	M/E	Syracuse, NY	Alhambra Thea.
7	Wed.	M/E	Scranton, PA	Academy of Music
8	Thu.	M/E	Wilkes-Barre, PA	Armory
9	Fri.	M/E	Allentown, PA	Music Hall
10	Sat.	Mat.	Pottstown, PA	Grand Opera House
10	Sat.	Eve.	Philadelphia, PA	Academy of Music

[End of 2nd 1892 tour]

1893 OFF-TOUR CONCERTS

JANUARY

23	Mon.	Eve.	New York, NY	Carnegie Hall

Soloists: Marcella Lindh, soprano; Katherine Fleming, contralto; Antonio Galassi, baritone; Edward O'Mahoney, basso; Joseph Michele Raffayolo, euphonium.

APRIL

16	Sun.	Eve.	New York, NY	Carnegie Hall

No soloists with band.

1ST 1893 TOUR

Soloists: Emmy Fursch-Madi & Marie Van Cautern, soprano; Minne Zehnee, contralto; Albert Guille, Italo Campanini, & William Foran, tenor; William Mertens, baritone; Ludovico Viviani & [Mr.] Christori, basso; Leonora Von Stosch, violin; Herbert L. Clarke & Albert Bode, cornet; Michele Raffayolo, euphonium; Petro D'Onofrio, bassoon.

APRIL

30	Sun.	Eve.	New York, NY	Grand Central Palace

MAY

1	Mon.	Mat.	Trenton, NJ	Association Hall
1	Mon.	Eve.	Philadelphia, PA	Academy of Music
2	Tue.	Eve.	Philadelphia, PA	Academy of Music
3	Wed.	Mat.	South Norwalk, CT	Music Hall
3	Wed.	Eve.	Bridgeport, CT	Bunnell's Thea.

Thu., 4th through Sun. 7th (4 days), Boston, MA, Mechanics' Hall. 2 concerts per day except eve. only on 4th.

8	Mon.	M/E	Syracuse, NY	Alhambra Thea.
9	Tue.	M/E	Buffalo, NY	Music Hall
10	Wed.	M/E	Detroit, MI	Auditorium
11	Thu.	M/E	Louisville, KY	Auditorium
12	Fri.	Eve.	St. Louis, MO	Grand Music Hall
13	Sat.	M/E	St. Louis, MO	Grand Music Hall
14	Sun.	M/E	Kansas City, MO	Auditorium
15	Mon.	M/E	Omaha, NE	Exposition Music Hall
16	Tue.	M/E	Des Moines, IA	Calvary Msn. Tabernacle
17	Wed.	Eve.	Minneapolis, MN	Exposition Hall

145

18	Thu.	M/E	Minneapolis, MN	Exposition Hall
19	Fri.	M/E	Duluth, MN	Lyceum Thea.
20	Sat.	M/E	St. Paul, MN	Auditorium
21	Sun.	M/E	Milwaukee, WI	Schlitz Park Thea.

MAY–JUNE

Sun., 22 May through Wed., 28 June (38 days), Chicago, World's Fair (Columbian Exposition). Two concerts per day except extra morning concert on Tue., 27 June.

Soloists: Frank Wadsworth, flute; Giacomo Norrito, piccolo; A.P. Cercillo-Stengler, clarinet; E.A. Lefebre, saxophone; Herbert L. Clarke & Albert Bode, cornet; Joseph Michele Raffayolo & August Hasse, euphonium; Arthur Pryor, trombone; Charles P. Lowe, xylophone; Elden Baker, tuba.

JUNE

| 29 | Thu. | M/E | Pittsburgh, PA | Silver Lake Grove |
| 30 | Fri. | M/E | Lancaster, PA | Conestoga Park |

[End of 1ˢᵗ 1893 tour]

JULY–SEPTEMBER

Sat., 1 July through Mon., 4 Sept. (66 days), Manhattan Beach, Brooklyn, NY, 2 or 3 concerts per day.

Soloists: Camille d'Arville, Marcella Lindh, Nice Moreska, Lilly Post, & Ella Wernig, soprano; Jennie Dickerson, Rosa Linde, & Gertrude Stein, contralto; Marie Tavary, vocalist; Victor Clodio, Fernando Michelena, & E.C. Towne, tenor; De Wolf Hopper, Graham Reed, & [Mr.] Sartori, baritone; Conrad Behrens, Eugene Cowles, & Ludovico Viviani, basso; Marie Tavary, [Mr.] Lucet, & [Mr.] Manton, other vocalists; Albert Bode, Herbert L. Clarke, & Frank Seltzer, cornet; Joseph Michele Raffayolo, euphonium; Arthur Pryor, trombone; Henry Koch, horn; Frank Wadsworth, flute; Giacomo Norrito, piccolo; August Cercillo-Stengler, Joseph Lacalle, & Joseph Norrito, clarinet; Robert Messenger, oboe; E.A. Lefebre, saxophone; A. Pagliani, bassoon; Charles Lowe, xylophone.

2ᴺᴰ 1893 TOUR

SEPTEMBER – OCTOBER

Wed., 6 Sept. through Sun., 22 Oct. (47 days), St. Louis Exposition. 4 concerts per day nearly all days.

Soloists: Lillian Blauvelt, Marcella Lindh, Nice Moreska, & Mrs. S.B. Sale, soprano; Maria Kern & Sophia Schalchi, contralto; Hermann Barosch & Percy B. Weston, tenor; Giuseppe Campanari, Antonio Galassi, & Salvatore Leonori, baritone; George P. Thomas, basso; Josie Ludwig, [Ms] Yaeger, & [Mr.] Rohan, other vocalists; Leonora von Stosch, violin; Albert Bode, Herbert L. Clarke, & Alice Raymond, cornet; Joseph Michele Raffayolo, euphonium; Arthur Pryor, trombone; Frank Wadsworth, flute; Giacomo Norrito, piccolo; Edward A. Lefebre, saxophone; Charles P. Lowe, xylophone; Inez Carusi, harp; Lettie E. Crowl, whistler.

Soloists for remainder of tour: Nice Moreska, soprano; Leonora von Stosch, violin; Arthur Pryor, trombone.

OCTOBER

23	Mon.	M/E	Indianapolis, IN	Tomlinson Hall
24	Tue.	Mat.	London, OH	High Street Thea.
24	Tue.	Eve.	Delaware, OH	Gray Chapel
25	Wed.	M/E	Columbus, OH	Board of Trade Auditorium
26	Thu.	Eve.	Cleveland, OH	Music Hall
27	Fri.	Mat.	Warren, OH	Warren Opera House
27	Fri.	Eve.	New Castle, PA	Opera House
29	Sun.	Eve.	Washington, DC	Albaugh's Grand Opera House
30	Mon.	Mat.	Baltimore, MD	Albaugh's Lyceum Thea.
30	Mon.	Eve.	Wilmington, DE	Grand Opera House
31	Tue.	Eve.	Philadelphia, PA	Academy of Music

NOVEMBER

1	Wed.	M/E	Harrisburg, PA	Grand Opera House
2	Thu.	Mat.	Batavia, NY	Dellinger Opera House
2	Thu.	Eve.	Buffalo, NY	Music Hall
3	Fri.	Mat.	Hamilton, ONT/Canada	Grand Opera House

Mon., 6ᵗʰ thru Sun., 19ᵗʰ (13 days), Chicago, Trocadero. 2 concerts per day.

20	Mon.	Eve.	Detroit, MI	Lyceum Thea.
21	Tue.	Mat.	Woodstock, ONT/Canada	Opera House
21	Tue.	Eve.	Hamilton, ONT/Canada	Grand Opera House
22	Wed.	M/E	Syracuse, NY	Bastable Thea.

[End of 2ⁿᵈ 1893 tour]

1893 OFF-TOUR CONCERTS

NOVEMBER

| 26 | Sun. | Eve. | Brooklyn, NY | Amphion Thea. |

Soloists: Albert Bode, cornet; Arthur Pryor, trombone.

DECEMBER

| 3 | Sun. | Eve. | Brooklyn, NY | Columbia Thea. |

Soloists: Annie Walker, soprano; Arthur Pryor, Trombone; E.A. Lefebre, saxophone.

| 10 | Sun. | Eve. | Brooklyn, NY | Columbia Thea. |

No soloists with band.

| 17 | Sun. | Eve. | New York, NY | Broadway Thea. |

No soloists with band.

1894 OFF-TOUR CONCERTS

JANUARY

| 14 | Sun. | Eve. | Brooklyn, NY | Amphion Thea. |

Soloists: Nina Bertini-Humphreys, soprano; Robert J. Webb, tenor.

| 18 | Thu. | Mat. | New York, NY | Metropolitan Opera House |

Soloists: Giuseppe Campanari, baritone; Eugene Cowles, basso.

| 18 | Thu. | Eve. | Brooklyn, NY | Academy of Music |

Soloists: Nina Bertini-Humphreys, soprano; Laura B. Phelps, violin; E.A. Lefebre, saxophone.

| 21 | Sun. | Eve. | Brooklyn, NY | Columbia Thea. |

Soloists: Nina Bertini-Humphreys, soprano; Robert J. Webb, tenor; Joseph Michele Raffayolo, euphonium.

| 28 | Sun. | Eve. | Brooklyn, NY | Columbia Thea. |

Soloists: Matilda Ackerman & Linyard Sweetser, soprano; Albert Bode & Frank Martin, cornet.

FEBRUARY

| 24 | Sat. | Eve. | Brooklyn, NY | 23ʳᵈ Regt. Armory |

Soloists: Albert Bode, cornet; Arthur Pryor, trombone.

| 25 | Sun. | Eve. | Brooklyn, NY | Park Thea. |

Soloists: Robert J. Webb, tenor; Albert Bode, cornet; Joseph Michele Raffayolo, euphonium.

FEBRUARY–MARCH

Mon. 26 Feb. to Sat., 3 March (6 days), New York, NY, Madison Square Garden, International Wine & Tobacco Exposition. 2 concerts per day except eve. only on Wed., 28 Feb. & matinee only last day.

Soloists not known but probably Albert Bode, cornet; Joseph Michele Raffayolo, euphonium; Arthur Pryor, trombone.

1ˢᵀ 1894 TOUR

Soloists on way to San Francisco Mid-Winter Exposition: Inez Mecusker, soprano; Albert Bode, cornet; Arthur Pryor, trombone.

MARCH

4	Sun.	Eve.	Washington, DC	National Thea.
5	Mon.	Mat.	Martinsburg, WV	Central Opera House
5	Mon.	Eve.	Cumberland, MD	Academy of Music
6	Tue.	Mat.	Columbus, OH	Grand Opera House
6	Tue.	Eve.	Springfield, OH	Grand Opera House
7	Wed.	Mat.	Hamilton, OH	Globe Opera House
7	Wed.	Eve.	Cincinnati, OH	Pike Street Thea.
8	Thu.	Mat.	Paris, KY	Grand Opera House
8	Thu.	Eve.	Lexington, KY	Lexington Opera House
9	Fri.	Mat.	Columbus, IN	Crump's Thea.
9	Fri.	Eve.	Indianapolis, IN	Tomlinson Hall
10	Sat.	M/E	St. Louis, MO	Exposition Music Hall
11	Sun.	Eve.	Kansas City, MO	Coates Opera House
12	Mon.	Eve.	Denver, CO	Broadway Thea.
13	Tue.	Mat.	Denver, CO	Broadway Thea.
13	Tue.	Eve.	Colorado Springs, CO	Opera House
14	Wed.	M/E	Pueblo, CO	Grand Opera House
15	Thu.	Mat.	Leadville, CO	Opera House
16	Fri.	Mat.	Provo, UT	Provo Opera House
16	Fri.	Eve.	Salt Lake City, UT	Salt Lake Thea.

MARCH–APRIL

Sun., 18 Mar. thru Sun., 22 Apr. (36 days), San Francisco, for Mid-Winter Exposition, with runouts on 12ᵗʰ & 20ᵗʰ (as below). 2 concerts per day except 3 on Sat., 14 April & 1 on Sat., 21 Apr. & 1 on Sun., 22 Apr.

Soloists for Mid-Winter Exposition: Albert Bode, William Griffin, & Frank Martin, cornet; Henry Koch, horn; August Haase & Joseph Michele Raffayolo, euphonium; Arthur Pryor, trombone; Frank W. Wadsworth, flute; Giacomo Norrito, piccolo; Robert Messenger, oboe; Henry Toedte, bassoon; Joseph Lacalle, E-flat clarinet; August Cercillo-Stengler & William Foerster, B-flat clarinet; Jean H.B. Moeremans, saxophone.

Soloists for remainder of 1st 1894 tour: Inez Mecusker, soprano; Arthur Pryor, trombone.

APRIL

12	Thu.	Eve.	San Jose, CA	Auditorium
20	Fri.	Eve.	Oakland, CA	Macdonough Thea.
23	Mon.	Mat.	Pasadena, CA	Grand Opera House
23	Mon.	Eve.	Los Angeles, CA	Hazard's Pavilion
24	Tue.	Mat.	Riverside, CA	Loring Thea.
24	Tue.	Eve.	San Bernardino, CA	Grand Opera House
25	Wed.	Eve.	San Diego, CA	Fisher Opera House
26	Thu.	M/E	Los Angeles, CA	Hazard's Pavilion
27	Fri.	Eve.	Fresno, CA	Barton Opera House
28	Sat.	M/E	Stockton, CA	Pavilion
29	Sun.	M/E	Sacramento, CA	Pavilion

MAY

1	Tue.	Eve.	Salt Lake City, UT	Tabernacle
2	Wed.	Eve.	Leadville, CO	Opera House
3	Thu.	M/E	Denver, CO	Broadway Thea.
4	Fri.	Mat.	Lincoln, NE	Lansing Thea.
4	Fri.	Eve.	Omaha, NE	Exposition Music Hall
5	Sat.	M/E	Des Moines, IA	Grand Opera House
6	Sun.	M/E	Chicago, IL	Haymarket Thea.
7	Mon.	M/E	Indianapolis, IN	Tomlinson Hall
8	Tue.	Mat.	Steubenville, OH	Grand Opera House
8	Tue.	Eve.	Wheeling, WV	Opera House
9	Wed.	M/E	Harrisburg, PA	Grand Opera House
10	Thu.	Mat.	Lancaster, PA	Fulton Opera House
10	Thu.	Eve.	West Chester, PA	Assembly Hall
11	Fri.	Mat.	Camden, NJ	Temple Thea.
11	Fri.	Eve.	Atlantic City, NJ	Ocean Pier
12	Sat.	M/E	Philadelphia, PA	Academy of Music

[End of 1st 1894 tour]

MAY-JUNE, 1894

Sun., 13 May through Sun., 17 June (36 days), Madison Square Garden, promenade concerts. 1 or 2 concerts per day.

Soloists: Frances Guthrie-Moyer, Ida Klein, Marcella Lindh, Inez Mecusker, Zippora Montieth, & Carola Riegg, soprano; Anton Schott, tenor; Arturo Mareschalchi & Lewis Williams, baritone; Conrad Behrens & A. Dahm Peterson, basso; Henrietta Dreyer, [Mr.] F.W. Elliott, & [Mr.] Pasquale, other vocalists; Joseph Michele Raffayolo, euphonium; Arthur Pryor, trombone; Frank W. Wadsworth, flute; Jean H.B. Moeremans, saxophone.

2ND 1894 TOUR

Soloists: Francesca Guthrie-Moyer, soprano; Anton Schott, tenor; Arthur Pryor, trombone.

JUNE

18	Mon.	Mat.	Rutland, VT	City Hall
18	Mon.	Eve.	Burlington, VT	Howard Opera House
19	Tue.	Mat.	Plattsburgh, NY	Plattsburgh Thea.
19	Tue.	Eve.	Montreal, QUE/Canada	Queen's Thea.
20	Wed.	M/E	Montreal, QUE/Canada	Queen's Thea.
21	Thu.	M/E	Ottawa, ONT/Canada	Rideau Rink
22	Fri.	Mat.	Peterborough, ONT/Canada	Bradburn's Opera House
22	Fri.	Eve.	Toronto, ONT/Canada	Massey Music Hall
23	Sat.	M/E	Toronto, ONT/Canada	Massey Music Hall
24	Sun.	Mat.	Niagara Falls, NY	Orpheus Park Thea.
24	Sun.	Eve.	Buffalo, NY	Music Hall
25	Mon.	Mat.	Chatham, ONT/Canada	Grand Opera House
25	Mon.	Eve.	Detroit, MI	Auditorium
26	Tue.	M/E	Cleveland, OH	Sangerfest Hall
27	Wed.	M/E	Pittsburgh, PA	Silver Lake Grove
28	Thu.	Mat.	Lancaster, PA	Fulton Opera House
28	Thu.	Eve.	Philadelphia, PA	Academy of Music
29	Fri.	Mat.	Trenton, NJ	Inter-State Fair Grounds
29	Fri.	Eve.	Newark, NJ	Krueger Auditorium

[End of 2nd 1894 tour]

JUNE-SEPTEMBER, 1894

Sat., 30 June through Mon., 3 Sept. (66 days), Manhattan Beach, Brooklyn, NY, 2 or 3 concerts per day.

Soloists: Laura Bellini, Louise Natali, Adele Ritchie, Lillian Riva, & Bertha Walzinger, soprano; Mary Foley & Rosa Linde, contralto; Albert Guille & Anton Schott, tenor; De Wolf Hopper, baritone; Conrad Behrens & Eugene Cowles, basso; Julia Aramenti, Louise Beaudet, Estella Mann, Lucille Sanders, Cora Tanner, & Nellie Zelma, Harry Foresman, William Pruette, Arthur Seaton, & J. Marshall Williams, other vocalists; Arthur Hartman, violin; Albert Bode,& Frank Martin, cornet; Henry Koch, horn; August Haase & Joseph Michele Raffayolo, euphonium; Arthur Pryor, trombone; Robert Messenger, oboe; Henry Toedt, bassoon; Frank Wadsworth, flute; Giacomo Norrito, piccolo; August Cercillo Stengler, clarinet; & Jean H.B. Moeremans, saxophone.

3RD 1894 TOUR

SEPTEMBER-OCTOBER

Wed., 5 Sept. through Sat., 20 Oct. (46 days), St. Louis Exposition, 4 concerts per day except 3 on 3 October.

Soloists for St. Louis Exposition: Marie Kern, Selma Kört-Kronold, Mrs. S.B. Sale, & L. Sutter, soprano; N. Dodson, contralto; G. Baron, Herman Barosche, & Percy B. Weston, tenor; Louis Bauer, Alex J. Joel, W.M. Porteous, & Arthur Weld, basso; Thomas Haines, other vocalist; Albert Bode and Frank Martin, cornet; Henry Koch, horn; August Haase & Michele Raffayolo, euphonium; Arthur Pryor, trombone; Herman Conrad, tuba; Frank W. Wadsworth, flute; Giacomo Norrito, piccolo; August Cercillo-Stengler, clarinet; & Jean H.B. Moeremans, saxophone.

Soloists for remainder of tour: Francesca Guthrie-Moyer, soprano; Charles W. Strine, baritone [note: also member of Sousa Band management staff]; Arthur Pryor, trombone; & Jean H.B. Moeremans, saxophone.

OCTOBER

21	Sun.	Eve.	Springfield, MO	Baldwin's Thea.
22	Mon.	Mat.	Little Rock, AR	Sherwood Park
22	Mon.	Eve.	Little Rock, AR	Pavilion
23	Tue.	Eve.	Memphis, TN	Auditorium
24	Wed.	M/E	Memphis, TN	Auditorium
25	Thu.	M/E	Nashville, TN	Tabernacle
26	Fri.	M/E	Louisville, KY	Auditorium
27	Sat.	Mat.	Columbus, IN	Crump's Thea.
27	Sat.	Eve.	Indianapolis, IN	English Opera House
28	Sun.	Mat.	Logansport, IN	Dolan's Opera House
28	Sun.	Eve.	Lafayette, IN	Grand Opera House
29	Mon.	Eve.	Chicago, IL	Auditorium
30	Tue.	Eve.	Chicago, IL	Auditorium
31	Wed.	M/E	Chicago, IL	Auditorium

NOVEMBER

1	Thu.	Mat.	Dowagiac, MI	Beckwith Memorial Thea.
1	Thu.	Eve.	Kalamazoo, MI	Academy of Music
2	Fri.	Mat.	Battle Creek, MI	Hamblin's Opera House
2	Fri.	Eve.	Grand Rapids, MI	Lockerby Hall
3	Sat.	Mat.	Bay City, MI	Opera House
3	Sat.	Eve.	Saginaw, MI	Academy of Music
4	Sun.	Eve.	Detroit, MI	Lyceum Thea.
5	Mon.	Mat.	Adrian, MI	Croswell Opera House
5	Mon.	Eve.	Toledo, OH	Memorial Hall
6	Tue.	M/E	Cleveland, OH	Lyceum Thea.
7	Wed.	Mat.	Ashtabula, OH	Haskell or Bussir Hall
7	Wed.	Eve.	Erie, PA	Park Opera House
8	Thu.	Mat.	Warren, PA	Library Thea.
8	Thu.	Eve.	Jamestown, NY	Institute Hall
9	Fri.	M/E	Buffalo, NY	Music Hall
10	Sat.	M/E	Buffalo, NY	Music Hall
11	Sun.	Mat.	Batavia, NY	Dellinger Opera House
11	Sun.	Eve.	Rochester, NY	Lyceum Thea.
12	Mon.	Mat.	Newark, NY	Sherman Opera House
12	Mon.	Eve.	Syracuse, NY	Wieting Opera House
13	Tue.	Mat.	Rome, NY	Washington St. Op. House
13	Tue.	Eve.	Herkimer, NY	Grand Opera House
14	Wed.	Mat.	Schenectady, NY	Van Curler Opera House
14	Wed.	Eve.	Albany, NY	Harmanus Bleeker Hall
15	Thu.	Mat.	Hudson, NY	Opera House
15	Thu.	Eve.	Poughkeepsie, NY	Collingwood Opera House
16	Fri.	Mat.	Pittsfield, MA	Academy of Music
16	Fri.	Eve.	Springfield, MA	Court Square Thea.
17	Sat.	M/E	Worcester, MA	Mechanics' Hall
18	Sun.	Eve.	Boston, MA	Boston Thea.
19	Mon.	Mat.	Amesbury, MA	Amesbury Opera House

19	Mon.	Eve.	Salem, MA	Cadet Armory
20	Tue.	Eve.	Lawrence, MA	Opera House
21	Wed.	Mat.	Exeter, NH	Exeter Opera House
21	Wed.	Eve.	Haverhill, MA	Academy of Music
22	Thu.	Mat.	Brunswick, ME	Town Hall
22	Thu.	Eve.	Lewiston, ME	City Hall
23	Fri.	Mat.	Bath, ME	Almeda Opera House
23	Fri.	Eve.	Rockland, ME	Farwell Opera House
24	Sat.	M/E	Portland, ME	City Hall
25	Sun.	M/E	Boston, MA	Boston Thea.
26	Mon.	Eve.	Boston, MA	People's Thea.
27	Tue.	Mat.	Woonsocket, RI	Woonsocket Opera House
27	Tue.	Eve.	Taunton, MA	Taunton Thea.
28	Wed.	Eve.	Boston, MA	Mechanics' Hall
29	Thu.	M/E	Providence, RI	Infantry Hall
30	Fri.	Mat.	Meriden, CT	Opera House
30	Fri.	Eve.	Hartford, CT	Foot Guard Armory
DECEMBER				
1	Sat.	Mat.	Middletown, CT	Middlesex Thea.
1	Sat.	Eve.	New Haven, CT	Hyperion Thea.
2	Sun.	Eve.	Bridgeport, CT	Park City Thea.
3	Mon.	Mat.	South Norwalk, CT	Music Hall
3	Mon.	Eve.	Newark, NJ	Krueger Auditorium
4	Tue.	Eve.	Elizabeth, NJ	Lyceum Thea.
5	Wed.	Eve.	Jersey City, NJ	1st Tabernacle Congregational Church
6	Thu.	Eve.	Orange, NJ	Orange Athletic Club
7	Fri.	Eve.	New Brunswick, NJ	Opera House
8	Sat.	M/E	Brooklyn, NY	Rink
9	Sun.	Eve.	Brooklyn, NY	Columbia Thea.
10	Mon.	Mat.	Pottstown, PA	Grand Opera House
10	Mon.	Eve.	Reading, PA	Academy of Music
11	Tue.	Mat.	Lancaster, PA	Fulton Opera House
11	Tue.	Eve.	York, PA	Fulton Opera House
12	Wed.	M/E	Washington, DC	Metzerott Music Hall
13	Thu.	M/E	Baltimore, MD	Music Hall
14	Fri.	Mat.	Wilmington, DE	Grand Opera House
14	Fri.	Eve.	Philadelphia, PA	Academy of Music
15	Sat.	M/E	Philadelphia, PA	Academy of Music
16	Sun.	Eve.	Brooklyn, NY	Columbia Thea.
17	Mon.	Eve.	Trenton, NJ	Taylor Opera House
18	Tue.	Eve.	Easton, PA	Able Opera House

[End of 3rd 1894 tour]

1895 OFF-TOUR CONCERT

JANUARY

10	Thu.	Eve.	Paterson, NJ	Opera House

Soloists: not known.

1ST 1895 TOUR

Soloists: Myrta French, soprano; Currie Duke, violin; Frank Wadsworth, flute; Robert Messenger, oboe; Gustave Stengler, clarinet.

JANUARY

20	Sun.	Eve.	Washington, DC	Allen's Grand Opera House
21	Mon.	Eve.	Norfolk, VA	Academy of Music
22	Tue.	M/E	Richmond, VA	Academy of Music
23	Wed.	M/E	Baltimore, MD	Music Hall
24	Thu.	Mat.	Hagerstown, MD	Academy of Music
24	Thu.	Eve.	Chambersburg, PA	Opera House
25	Fri.	M/E	Harrisburg, PA	Grand Opera House
26	Sat.	M/E	Philadelphia, PA	Academy of Music
27	Sun.	Eve.	New York, NY	Herald Square Thea.

[End of 1st 1895 tour]

2ND 1895 TOUR

Soloists: Myrta French & Maria Barnard, soprano; Currie Duke, violin.

FEBRUARY

9	Sat.	Mat.	Putnam, CT	Opera House
9	Sat.	Eve.	Woonsocket, RI	Woonsocket Opera House
10	Sun.	Eve.	Boston, MA	Boston Thea.
11	Mon.	Mat.	Middleboro, MA	City Hall
11	Mon.	Eve.	Taunton, MA	Taunton Thea.
12	Tue.	Mat.	Nashua, NH	Nashua Thea.

12	Tue.	Eve.	Manchester, NH	Manchester Opera House
13	Wed.	Mat.	Marlborough, MA	Marlboro Thea.
13	Wed.	Eve.	Waltham, MA	Park Thea.
14	Thu.	M/E	Providence, RI	Infantry Hall
15	Fri.	Eve.	Fall River, MA	Academy of Music
16	Sat.	M/E	Lowell, MA	Lowell Opera House
17	Sun.	Mat.	Brockton, MA	Opera House
17	Sun.	Eve.	Boston, MA	Boston Thea.
18	Mon.	Mat.	Gloucester, MA	City Hall
19	Tue.	Eve.	Salem, MA	Cadet Armory
20	Wed.	Mat.	New Britain, CT	Russwin Lyceum
20	Wed.	Eve.	Hartford, CT	Foot Guard Armory
21	Thu.	M/E	Bridgeport, CT	Park City Thea.
22	Fri.	M/E	Brooklyn, NY	Academy of Music

[End of 2nd 1895 tour]

3RD 1895 TOUR

Soloists: Marie Barnard, soprano; Currie Duke, violin; Albert Bode, cornet; Joseph Michele Raffayolo, euphonium; Arthur Pryor, trombone; Frank W. Wadsworth, flute; Robert Messenger, oboe; Gustave Stengler, clarinet; Jean H.B. Moeremans, saxophone.

MARCH

8	Fri.	Eve.	Baltimore, MD	Ford's Grand Opera House
9	Sat.	Mat.	Baltimore, MD	Ford's Grand Opera House
9	Sat.	Eve.	Frederick, MD	City Opera House
10	Sun.	Eve.	Washington, DC	Albaugh's Grand Opera House
11	Mon.	Mat.	Allentown, PA	Academy of Music
11	Mon.	Eve.	Easton, PA	Able Opera House
12	Tue.	Eve.	Scranton, PA	Academy of Music
13	Wed.	M/E	Wilkes-Barre, PA	Armory
14	Thu.	Mat.	Pottsville, PA	Academy of Music
14	Thu.	Eve.	Reading, PA	Academy of Music
15	Fri.	Mat.	South Bethlehem, PA	Fountain Hill Opera House
15	Fri.	Eve.	Philadelphia, PA	Academy of Music
16	Sat.	M/E	Philadelphia, PA	Academy of Music
17	Sun.	M/E	Brooklyn, NY	Columbia Thea.
18	Mon.	Eve.	Troy, NY	Music Hall
19	Tue.	Eve.	Cohoes, NY	Armory
20	Wed.	Eve.	Albany, NY	Harmanus Bleeker Hall
21	Thu.	Mat.	Johnstown, NY	Grand Opera House
21	Thu.	Eve.	Gloversville, NY	Kasson Opera House
22	Fri.	Mat.	Little Falls, NY	Skinner Opera House
22	Fri.	Eve.	Utica, NY	Utica Opera House
23	Sat.	M/E	Rochester, NY	Lyceum Thea.
24	Sun.	Eve.	Rochester, NY	Lyceum Thea.
25	Mon.	Eve.	Toronto, ONT/Canada	Massey Music Hall
26	Tue.	M/E	Toronto, ONT/Canada	Massey Music Hall
27	Wed.	Eve.	Buffalo, NY	Music Hall
28	Thu.	M/E	Buffalo, NY	Music Hall
29	Fri.	Eve.	Cleveland, OH	Music Hall
30	Sat.	M/E	Cleveland, OH	Music Hall
31	Sun.	Eve.	Detroit, MI	Detroit Opera House
APRIL				
1	Mon.	Mat.	Adrian, MI	Croswell Opera House
1	Mon.	Eve.	Toledo, OH	Memorial Hall
2	Tue.	Mat.	Findlay, OH	Marvin Opera House
2	Tue.	Eve.	Fostoria, OH	Andes' Opera House
3	Wed.	Mat.	Urbana, OH	Market Square Thea.
3	Wed.	Eve.	Springfield, OH	Grand Opera House
4	Thu.	Mat.	Xenia, OH	Opera House
4	Thu.	Eve.	Dayton, OH	Grand Opera House
5	Fri.	Mat.	Hamilton, OH	Globe Opera House
5	Fri.	Eve.	Cincinnati, OH	Pike Street Thea.
6	Sat.	Mat.	Richmond, IN	Grand Opera House
6	Sat.	Eve.	Indianapolis, IN	English Opera House
7	Sun.	Eve.	Lafayette, IN	Grand Opera House
8	Mon.	Mat.	Wabash, IN	Harter's Opera House
8	Mon.	Eve.	Fort Wayne, IN	Masonic Temple
9	Tue.	Mat.	Peru, IN	Emerick's Opera House
9	Tue.	Eve.	Logansport, IN	Dolan's Opera House
10	Wed.	Mat.	Crawfordsville, IN	Music Hall
10	Wed.	Eve.	Terre Haute, IN	Naylor's Opera House
11	Thu.	Mat.	Mattoon, IL	Dole Opera House

11	Thu.	Eve.	Decatur, IL	Powers' Grand Op. House
12	Fri.	Mat.	Springfield, IL	Olympic Thea.
12	Fri.	Eve.	Jacksonville, IL	Grand Opera House
13	Sat.	M/E	St. Louis, MO	Exposition Music Hall
14	Sun.	M/E	St. Louis, MO	Exposition Music Hall
15	Mon.	Eve.	Evansville, IN	Grand Opera House
16	Tue.	Eve.	Louisville, KY	Auditorium
17	Wed.	M/E	Nashville, TN	Vendome Thea.
18	Thu.	M/E	Chattanooga, TN	Chattanooga Opera House
19	Fri.	Eve.	Atlanta, GA	Grand Opera House
20	Sat.	Eve.	Atlanta, GA	Grand Opera House
21	Sun.	M/E	Atlanta, GA	Grand Opera House
22	Mon.	M/E	Augusta, GA	Grand Opera House
23	Tue.	M/E	Macon, GA	Academy of Music
24	Wed.	M/E	Montgomery, AL	Montgomery Thea.
25	Thu.	M/E	Mobile, AL	Mobile Thea.
26	Fri.	Eve.	New Orleans, LA	Academy of Music
27	Sat.	M/E	New Orleans, LA	Academy of Music
28	Sun.	Eve.	New Orleans, LA	Academy of Music
29	Mon.	Eve.	Vicksburg, MS	Vicksburg Opera House
30	Tue.	Eve.	Memphis, TN	Auditorium
MAY				
1	Wed.	M/E	Memphis, TN	Auditorium
2	Thu.	M/E	Little Rock, AR	Glenwood Park
3	Fri.	M/E	Dallas, TX	Tabernacle
4	Sat.	M/E	Waco, TX	Blake Building
5	Sun.	M/E	San Antonio, TX	Grand Opera House
6	Mon.	M/E	Austin, TX	Millett's Opera House
7	Tue.	M/E	Houston, TX	Auditorium
8	Wed.	M/E	Fort Worth, TX	Auditorium
9	Thu.	M/E	Wichita, KS	Civic Auditorium
10	Fri.	Mat.	Emporia, KS	Whitley's Opera House
10	Fri.	Eve.	Topeka, KS	Hamilton Hall
11	Sat.	M/E	Kansas City, MO	Auditorium
12	Sun.	Mat.	Atchison, KS	Atchison Thea.
12	Sun.	Eve.	Leavenworth, KS	Music Hall
13	Mon.	Eve.	St. Joseph, MO	Tootle Thea.
14	Tue.	M/E	Omaha, NE	Boyd's Thea.
15	Wed.	Eve.	Des Moines, IA	Foster Opera House
16	Thu.	M/E	Davenport, IA	Burtis Opera House
17	Fri.	Eve.	Peoria, IL	Tabernacle
18	Sat.	M/E	Peoria, IL	Tabernacle
19	Sun.	Eve.	Racine, WI	Belle City Opera House

Mon., 20th through Sat., 25th (6 days), Chicago, IL, Auditorium. Evening concerts each day except M/E on Wed. 22nd.

26	Sun.	M/E	Milwaukee, WI	Schlitz Park
27	Mon.	Mat.	Muskegon, MI	Muskegon Opera House
27	Mon.	Eve.	Grand Rapids, MI	Lockerby Hall
28	Tue.	M/E	London, ONT/Canada	Princess Rink
29	Wed.	M/E	Toronto, ONT/Canada	Massey Music Hall
30	Thu.	M/E	Buffalo, NY	Music Hall
31	Fri.	M/E	Ottawa, ONT/Canada	Rideau Rink
JUNE				
1	Sat.	M/E	Montreal, QUE/Canada	Drill Hall
2	Sun.	M/E	Montreal, QUE/Canada	Drill Hall
3	Mon.	Eve.	Quebec, QUE/Canada	Quebec Rink
4	Tue.	Eve.	St. John, NB/Canada	St. Andrew's Rink
5	Wed.	M/E	St. John, NB/Canada	St. Andrew's Rink
6	Thu.	Eve.	Halifax, NS/Canada	Exhibition Building
7	Fri.	M/E	Halifax, NS/Canada	Exhibition Building
8	Sat.	Mat.	Moncton, NB/Canada	Victoria Rink
9	Sun.	Eve.	Bangor, ME	City Hall
10	Mon.	Eve.	Boston, MA	Boston Thea.
11	Tue.	M/E	Holyoke, MA	Holyoke Opera House

[End of 3rd 1895 tour]

JUNE-SEPTEMBER, 1895
Sat., 15 June through Mon., 2 Sept. (80 days), Manhattan Beach, Brooklyn, NY. 2 concerts per day.
Soloists: Marie Barnard, Theresa Vaughn, Sidonia Trenkman, Hattie Norton, Frances Miller, Grace Haskell, & [Ms] Todd-Deimer, soprano; Rosa Linde, Belle Cole, & Clara Aline Jewell, Katherine Fleming, & Fielding Roselle, contralto; Alfred Guile & Manzione de Pasquale, tenor; DeWolf Hopper, Perry Averill, Charles W. Strine, & Giuseppe Tagliapetra, baritone; Conrad Behrens, basso; Albert Bode & Henry Higgins,

cornet; Bernhardt Baumgartel, horn; Arthur Pryor, trombone; Giacomo Norrito, piccolo; Jean Moeremans, saxophone.*

4TH 1895 TOUR

SEPTEMBER-OCTOBER
Mon., 4 Sept. through Sat., 19 Oct. (46 days), St. Louis Exposition.
4 concerts per day except 3 on 3 Oct. and 2 on 4 & 5 Oct.
Soloists: Jessie Foster, soprano; Bertha Waechter, contralto; Martha Koenigsman & Jessie Womach, other vocalists; Albert Bode & Henry Higgins, cornet; Hans Wunderlich, trumpet; Simone Mantia & August Haase, euphonium; Arthur Pryor, trombone; Frank Wadsworth, flute; Giacomo Norrito, piccolo; Jean Moeremans, saxophone.
OCTOBER

20	Sun.	M/E	Little Rock, AR	Glenwood Park

OCTOBER-NOVEMBER
Mon., 21 Oct. through Sun., 3 Nov. (14 days), Dallas, TX, Texas State Fair. 2 concerts per day.
*Soloists: not known
Soloists for remainder of tour except for Atlanta/Cotton States Exposition: Myrta French, soprano; Dr. Robert O. Owens, baritone; Currie Duke, violin;*
NOVEMBER

4	Mon.	M/E	Houston, TX	Auditorium
5	Tue.	M/E	New Orleans, LA	Artillery Hall
6	Wed.	M/E	Mobile, AL	Mobile Thea.
7	Thu.	Mat.	Selma, AL	Academy of Music
7	Thu.	Eve.	Montgomery, AL	Montgomery Thea.
8	Fri.	M/E	Birmingham, AL	O'Brien's Opera House
9	Sat.	M/E	Memphis, TN	Auditorium
11	Mon.	M/E	Nashville, TN	Vendome Thea.
12	Tue.	M/E	Evansville, IN	Grand Opera House
13	Wed.	Mat.	Terre Haute, IN	Naylor's Opera House
13	Wed.	Eve.	Indianapolis, IN	Tomlinson Hall
14	Thu.	M/E	Louisville, KY	Macauley's Thea.
15	Fri.	Mat.	Paris, KY	Grand Opera House
15	Fri.	Eve.	Lexington, KY	Lexington Opera House
16	Sat.	M/E	Knoxville, TN	Staub's Thea.

NOVEMBER-DECEMBER
Mon., 18 Nov. through Sat., 7 Dec. (20 days), Atlanta, GA, Cotton States and International Exposition (20 days). 2, 3, or 4 concerts per day. (See also 1 Dec. below.)
Soloists: Inez Mekusker & Luzy Gartrell, soprano; [Mr.] Campobello, baritone; Albert Bode & Henry Higgins, cornet; August Grosskurth, trumpet; Bernhardt Baumgartel, horn; Simone Mantia, euphonium; Arthur Pryor, trombone; Frederick Lars Walen, tuba; Frank Wadsworth, flute; Giacomo Norrito, piccolo; August Cercillo-Stengler, clarinet; Jean Moeremans, saxophone.
DECEMBER

1	Sun.	M/E	Atlanta, GA	Grand Opera House
8	Sun.	M/E	Atlanta, GA	Grand Opera House
9	Mon.	Eve.	Spartanburg, SC	Converse College
10	Tue.	Mat.	Charlotte, NC	Charlotte Opera House
11	Wed.	Mat.	Danville, VA	Academy of Music
11	Wed.	Eve.	Lynchburg, VA	Opera House
12	Thu.	Eve.	Petersburg, VA	Academy of Music
13	Fri.	M/E	Norfolk, VA	Academy of Music
14	Sat.	M/E	Richmond, VA	Academy of Music

[End of 4th 1895 tour]

1ST 1896 TOUR

Soloists: Myrta French, soprano; Currie Duke, violin; Arthur Pryor, trombone.
JANUARY

1	Wed.	Eve.	Washington, DC	Lafayette Square Opera House
5	Sun.	Eve.	Washington, DC	Lafayette Square Opera House
6	Mon.	Eve.	Baltimore, MD	Music Hall
7	Tue.	Eve.	Baltimore, MD	Music Hall
8	Wed.	Mat.	York, PA	York Opera House
8	Wed.	Eve.	Lancaster, PA	Fulton Opera House
9	Thu.	Mat.	Pottsville, PA	Academy of Music
9	Thu.	Eve.	Reading, PA	Academy of Music

10	Fri.	Eve.	Philadelphia, PA	Academy of Music
11	Sat.	M/E	Philadelphia, PA	Academy of Music
12	Sun.	Eve.	Brooklyn, NY	Montault Thea.
13	Mon.	Eve.	Orange, NJ	Orange Athletic Club
14	Tue.	Mat.	Peekskill, NY	Depew Opera House
14	Tue.	Eve.	Poughkeepsie, NY	Collingwood Opera House
15	We	M/E	Albany, NY	Harmanus Bleeker Hall
16	Thu.	M/E	Troy, NY	Music Hall
17	Fri.	Mat.	Johnstown, NY	Grand Opera House
17	Fri.	Eve.	Utica, NY	Utica Opera House
18	Sat.	M/E	Rochester, NY	Lyceum Thea.
19	Sun.	M/E	Rochester, NY	Lyceum Thea.
20	Mon.	Eve.	Toronto, ONT/Canada	Massey Music Hall
21	Tue.	M/E	Toronto, ONT/Canada	Massey Music Hall
22	Wed.	Eve.	Buffalo, NY	Music Hall
23	Thu.	M/E	Buffalo, NY	Music Hall
24	Fri.	Eve.	Cleveland, OH	Music Hall
25	Sat.	M/E	Cleveland, OH	Music Hall
26	Sun.	Eve.	Detroit, MI	Detroit Opera House
27	Mon.	Mat.	Battle Creek, MI	Hamblin's Opera House
27	Mon.	Eve.	Kalamazoo, MI	Academy of Music
28	Tue.	Mat.	Niles, MI	Opera House
28	Tue.	Eve.	Benton Harbor, MI	Opera House
29	Wed.	Mat.	La Porte, IN	Opera House
29	Wed.	Eve.	Chicago, IL	Auditorium
30	Thu.	Eve.	Chicago, IL	Auditorium
31	Fri.	Mat.	Beloit, WI	Opera House
31	Fri.	Eve.	Rockford, IL	Grand Opera House
FEBRUARY				
1	Sat.	Mat.	Milwaukee, WI	Meyers Opera House
1	Sat.	Eve.	Milwaukee, WI	Pabst Thea.
2	Sun.	Mat.	Chicago, IL	Haymarket Thea.
2	Sun.	Eve.	Chicago, IL	Hooley's Thea.
3	Mon.	Mat.	Janesville, WI	Myers Grand Opera House
3	Mon.	Eve.	Madison, WI	University Hall
4	Tue.	M/E	Minneapolis, MN	Lyceum Thea.
5	Wed.	M/E	Duluth, MN	Lyceum Thea.
6	Thu.	M/E	St. Paul, MN	Grand Opera House
7	Fri.	M/E	Fargo, ND	Fargo Opera House
9	Sun.	Mat.	Anaconda, MT	Evans' Grand Opera House
9	Sun.	Eve.	Butte, MT	Maguire's Opera House
10	Mon.	M/E	Helena, MT	Auditorium
11	Tue.	M/E	Spokane, WA	Auditorium
12	Wed.	Eve.	Tacoma, WA	Tacoma Thea.
13	Thu.	M/E	Seattle, WA	Seattle Thea.
14	Fri.	M/E	Victoria, BC/Canada	Victoria Thea.
15	Sat.	Mat.	Olympia, WA	Opera House
15	Sat.	Eve.	Tacoma, WA	Tacoma Thea.
16	Sun.	Eve.	Seattle, WA	Seattle Thea.
17	Mon.	Eve.	Portland, OR	Armory
18	Tue.	M/E	Portland, OR	Armory
19	Wed.	Eve.	Salem, OR	Reed's Opera House
21	Fri.	Eve.	Fresno, CA	Barton Opera House
22	Sat.	M/E	Los Angeles, CA	Hazard's Pavilion
23	Sun.	M/E	San Diego, CA	Fisher Opera House
24	Mon.	Eve.	Los Angeles, CA	Hazard's Pavilion
25	Tue.	M/E	Santa Barbara, CA	Opera House
26	Wed.	Mat.	Bakersfield, CA	Niederaur's Armory Hall
26	Wed.	Eve.	Tulare, CA	Old Skating Rink
27	Thu.	M/E	San Jose, CA	Auditorium
28	Fri.	Eve.	San Francisco, CA	Pavilion
29	Fri.	M/E	San Francisco, CA	Pavilion
MARCH				
1	Sun.	Mat.	San Francisco, CA	Auditorium
1	Sun.	Eve.	San Francisco, CA	Pavilion
2	Mon.	Eve.	Stockton, CA	Yosemite Thea.
3	Tue.	M/E	Sacramento, CA	Metropolitan Opera House
4	Wed.	Mat.	Virginia City, NV	Opera House
4	Wed.	Eve.	Reno, NV	McKissick Opera House
5	Thu.	Eve.	Ogden, UT	Grand Opera House
6	Fri.	Eve.	Salt Lake City, UT	Tabernacle
7	Sat.	Mat.	Salt Lake City, UT	Tabernacle
7	Sat.	Eve.	Provo, UT	Tabernacle
8	Sun.	M/E	Leadville, CO	Weston Opera House
9	Mon.	Eve.	Denver, CO	Broadway Thea.

10	Tue.	M/E	Denver, CO	Broadway Thea.
11	Wed.	Mat.	Colorado Springs, CO	Opera House
11	Wed.	Eve.	Pueblo, CO	Grand Opera House
12	Thu.	Mat.	Hutchinson, KS	Opera House
12	Thu.	Eve.	Wichita, KS	Civic Auditorium
13	Fri.	Mat.	Kansas City, MO	Auditorium
13	Fri.	Eve.	St. Joseph, MO	Tootle Thea.
14	Sat.	M/E	Omaha, NE	Boyd's Thea.
15	Sun.	Mat.	Chicago, IL	Haymarket Thea.
15	Sun.	Eve.	Chicago, IL	Columbia Thea.
16	Mon.	M/E	Cincinnati, OH	Pike Street Thea.
17	Tue.	Mat.	Xenia, OH	Opera House
17	Tue.	Eve.	Dayton, OH	Grand Opera House
18	Wed.	Mat.	Springfield, OH	Grand Opera House
18	Wed.	Eve.	Columbus, OH	High Street Thea.
19	Thu.	Eve.	Pittsburgh, PA	Carnegie Music Hall
20	Fri.	Eve.	Philadelphia, PA	Academy of Music
21	Sat.	M/E	Philadelphia, PA	Academy of Music
22	Sun.	Eve.	Washington, DC	Lafayette Square Opera House
23	Mon.	Eve.	Baltimore, MD	Music Hall
24	Tue.	Mat.	Hagerstown, MD	Opera House
24	Tue.	Eve.	Chambersburg, PA	Opera House
25	Wed.	Mat.	Carlisle, PA	Sentinel Opera House
25	Wed.	Eve.	Harrisburg, PA	Grand Opera House
26	Thu.	Mat.	Shamokin, PA	G.A.R. Opera House
26	Thu.	Eve.	Hazleton, PA	Grand Opera House
27	Fri.	Mat.	Pittston, PA	Music Hall
27	Fri.	Eve.	Scranton, PA	Frothingham Thea.
28	Sat.	Mat.	Bethlehem, PA	Opera House
28	Sat.	Eve.	Allentown, PA	Academy of Music
29	Sun.	Eve.	Brooklyn, NY	Montauk Thea.
30	Mon.	M/E	Paterson, NJ	Armory

[End of 1st 1896 tour]

1896 OFF-TOUR CONCERT

APRIL

5	Sun.	M/E	Brooklyn, NY	Montauk Thea.

Soloists not known.

2ND 1896 TOUR

Soloists: Minnie Tracy & Myrta French, soprano; Arthur Pryor, trombone.

APRIL

24	Fri.	Mat.	New Britain, CT	Lyceum Thea.
24	Fri.	Eve.	Hartford, CT	Foot Guard Armory
25	Sat.	Mat.	Northampton, MA	Academy of Music
25	Sat.	Eve.	Springfield, MA	Court Square Thea.
26	Sun.	Eve.	Boston, MA	Boston Thea.
27	Mon.	M/E	Boston, MA	Tremont Temple
28	Tue.	Mat.	Gloucester, MA	City Hall
28	Tue.	Eve.	Lynn, MA	Lynn Thea.
29	Wed.	Mat.	Concord, NH	Opera House
29	Wed.	Eve.	Manchester, NH	Manchester Opera House
30	Thu.	Mat.	Exeter, NH	Exeter Opera House
30	Thu.	Eve.	Haverhill, MA	Academy of Music
MAY				
1	Fri.	Mat.	Lowell, MA	Lowell Opera House
1	Fri.	Eve.	Nashua, NH	City Hall
2	Sat.	Mat.	South Framingham, MA	Elmwood Opera House
2	Sat.	Eve.	Worcester, MA	Mechanics' Hall
3	Sun.	Eve.	Boston, MA	Boston Thea.
4	Mon.	Eve.	Lawrence, MA	Opera House
5	Tue.	Mat.	Newburyport, MA	City Hall
5	Tue.	Eve.	Salem, MA	Cadet Armory
6	Wed.	Mat.	Biddeford, ME	City Opera House
6	Wed.	Eve.	Lewiston, ME	City Hall
7	Thu.	Mat.	Waterville, ME	City Hall
7	Thu.	Eve.	Bangor, ME	Bangor Opera House
8	Fri.	Mat.	Bath, ME	Columbia Thea.
8	Fri.	Eve.	Rockland, ME	Farwell Opera House
9	Sat.	M/E	Portland, ME	City Hall
10	Sun.	Eve.	Boston, MA	Boston Thea.
11	Mon.	Mat.	Taunton, MA	Taunton Thea.

11	Mon.	Eve.	Brockton, MA	City Thea.
12	Tue.	Mat.	Middleboro, MA	City Hall
12	Tue.	Eve.	Fall River, MA	Academy of Music
13	Wed.	M/E	Providence, RI	Infantry Hall
14	Thu.	Mat.	Middletown, CT	Middlesex Thea.
14	Thu.	Eve.	New Haven, CT	Hyperion Thea.
15	Fri.	Eve.	Philadelphia, PA	Academy of Music
16	Sat.	M/E	Philadelphia, PA	Academy of Music
17	Sun.	Mat.	Atlantic City, NJ	Ocean Pier
17	Sun.	Eve.	Atlantic City, NJ	Academy of Music
18	Mon.	Mat.	Chester, PA	Grand Opera House
18	Mon.	Eve.	West Chester, PA	Assembly Hall
19	Tue.	Mat.	Mauch Chunk, PA	Mauch Chunk Opera House
19	Tue.	Eve.	Wilkes-Barre, PA	Grand Opera House
20	Wed.	Mat.	Mt. Carmel, PA	Opera House
20	Wed.	Eve.	Shenandoah, PA	Ferguson's Thea.
21	Thu.	Mat.	Sunbury, PA	Lyon's Opera House
21	Thu.	Eve.	Williamsport, PA	Lycoming Opera House
22	Fri.	Eve.	Baltimore, MD	Ford's Grand Opera House
23	Sat.	M/E	Baltimore, MD	Ford's Grand Opera House
24	Sun.	Eve.	Washington, DC	Lafayette Square Opera House
25	Mon.	Mat.	Martinsburg, WV	Opera House
25	Mon.	Eve.	Cumberland, MD	Academy of Music
26	Tue.	Mat.	Connellsville, PA	Newmyer's Opera House
26	Tue.	Eve.	Pittsburgh, PA	Carnegie Music Hall
27	Wed.	Mat.	Franklin, PA	Opera House
27	Wed.	Eve.	Oil City, PA	Opera House
28	Thu.	Mat.	Meadville, PA	Academy of Music
28	Thu.	Eve.	Erie, PA	Park Opera House
29	Fri.	Mat.	Dunkirk, NY	Nelson Opera House
29	Fri.	Eve.	Buffalo, NY	Music Hall
30	Sat.	M/E	Buffalo, NY	Music Hall
31	Sun.	Eve.	Rochester, NY	Lyceum Thea.
JUNE				
1	Mon.	Mat.	Syracuse, NY	Wieting Opera House
1	Mon.	Eve.	Oswego, NY	Richardson Thea.
2	Tue.	Mat.	Watertown, NY	City Opera House
2	Tue.	Eve.	Ogdensburg, NY	Opera House
3	Tue.	Mat.	Belleville, ONT/Canada	Carman Opera House
3	Tue.	Eve.	Kingston, ONT/Canada	Martin's Opera House
4	Thu.	Eve.	Ottawa, ONT/Canada	Rideau Rink
5	Fri.	Eve.	Montreal, QUE/Canada	Victoria Rink
6	Sat.	M/E	Montreal, QUE/Canada	Victoria Rink
7	Sun.	Mat.	Plattsburgh, NY	Plattsburgh Thea.
8	Mon.	Mat.	Burlington, VT	Howard Opera House
8	Mon.	Eve.	Montpelier, VT	Armory

[End of 2nd 1896 tour]

1896 OFF-TOUR CONCERTS

JUNE
Thu., 11th (evening), New York, NY, Broadway Thea., band plays in grand march finales of *El Capitan* operetta.
JUNE-SEPTEMBER
Sun., 14 June through Mon., 7 Sept. (86 days), Manhattan Beach, Brooklyn, NY. 2 concerts per day except 1 mat. last day.
   Soloists: Minnie Tracy, Ethel Stewart, Marie Glover, Frances Rosseau, Elizabeth Northrup, Frances Miller, Grace Rutledge, Martha Garrison Miner, Marian Von Duyn, Katherine Rose, Jessamine Hallenback, Camille D'Arville, Shannah Coming Jones, Cherida Simpson, Fielding Roselle, & [Ms] Holding, soprano; Viola Pratt & Mary Louise Clary, contralto; Ellison Van Hoose, Henry Martin, & Arthur Adamini, tenor; George Schute, Basil Tetson, & Walter Bruce, baritone; Marie Von Wegern, Herman Gerold, & Henry Cook, other vocalists; Martina Johnstone, violin; Albert Bode, Henry Higgins, William Griffin, & Walter Smith, cornet; Franz Helle, flugelhorn; Arthur Pryor, trombone; Frank Wadsworth & Giacomo Norrito, flute; Robert Messenger, oboe; Joseph Norrito & August Cercillo-Stengler, clarinet; Jean Moeremans, saxophone.
SEPTEMBER
Mon., 7th through Sun., 13th (7 evenings), New York, NY, Hammerstein's Olympia. Soloists not known.

1896-97 TOUR

Soloists: Elizabeth Northrop, soprano; Zora Gladys Horlocker, contralto; Forrest Dabney, basso; Martina Johnstone, violin; Leontine Gaertner, cello; Franz Helle, flugelhorn; Simone Mantia, euphonium; Arthur Pryor, trombone; Jean Moeremans, saxophone.

DECEMBER 1896				
27	Sun.	Eve.	New York, NY	Carnegie Hall
28	Mon.	Mat.	Fishkill, NY	Peatie's Academy of Music
28	Mon.	Eve.	Peekskill, NY	Depew Opera House
29	Tue.	Mat.	Trenton, NJ	Taylor Opera House
29	Tue.	Eve.	New Brunswick, NJ	Columbia Hall
30	Wed.	Eve.	Newark, NJ	Krueger Auditorium
31	Thu.	Eve.	Brooklyn, NY	not known
JANUARY 1897				
1	Fri.	M/E	Philadelphia, PA	Academy of Music
2	Sat.	M/E	Philadelphia, PA	Academy of Music
3	Sun.	Eve.	Washington, DC	Lafayette Square Opera House
4	Mon.	Eve.	Baltimore, MD	Music Hall
5	Tue.	Mat.	Charlottesville, VA	Levy Opera House
5	Tue.	Eve.	Richmond, VA	Academy of Music
6	Wed.	M/E	Norfolk, VA	Academy of Music
7	Thu.	Mat.	Goldsboro, NC	Messenger Opera House
7	Thu.	Eve.	Wilmington, NC	Opera House
8	Fri.	M/E	Charleston, SC	Academy of Music
9	Sat.	M/E	Savannah, GA	Savannah Thea.
10	Sun.	Eve.	Jacksonville, FL	Park Thea.
11	Mon.	Eve.	Atlanta, GA	Grand Opera House
12	Tue.	M/E	Atlanta, GA	Grand Opera House
13	Wed.	Eve.	Montgomery, AL	Montgomery Thea.
14	Thu.	Eve.	New Orleans, LA	St. Charles Thea.
15	Fri.	Eve.	New Orleans, LA	St. Charles Thea.
16	Sat.	M/E	New Orleans, LA	St. Charles Thea.
17	Sun.	Mat.	New Orleans, LA	St. Charles Thea.
18	Mon.	Eve.	Natchez, MS	Temple Opera House
19	Tue.	Eve.	Vicksburg, MS	Vicksburg Opera House
20	Wed.	Mat.	Helena, AR	Opera House
20	Wed.	Eve.	Memphis, TN	Grand Opera House
21	Thu.	Mat.	Fulton, KY	Vendome Opera House
21	Thu.	Eve.	Cairo, IL	Cairo Opera House
22	Fri.	Eve.	St. Louis, MO	Exposition Music Hall
23	Sat.	Mat.	Evansville, IN	Grand Opera House
23	Sat.	Eve.	Owensboro, KY	Temple Thea.
24	Sun.	Eve.	Louisville, KY	Grand Opera House
25	Mon.	Mat.	Paris, KY	Grand Opera House
25	Mon.	Eve.	Lexington, KY	Lexington Opera House
26	Tue.	Eve.	Cincinnati, OH	Music Hall
27	Wed.	Mat.	Washington Ct. House, OH	Opera House
27	Wed.	Eve.	Columbus, OH	High Street Thea.
28	Thu.	Mat.	Urbana, OH	Market Square Thea.
28	Thu.	Eve.	Springfield, OH	Grand Opera House
29	Fri.	Mat.	Xenia, OH	Opera House
29	Fri.	Eve.	Dayton, OH	Grand Opera House
30	Sat.	Mat.	Anderson, IN	Grand Opera House
30	Sat.	Eve.	Indianapolis, IN	Tomlinson Hall
31	Sun.	Mat.	Logansport, IN	Dolan's Opera House
31	Sun.	Eve.	Lafayette, IN	Grand Opera House
FEBRUARY				
1	Mon.	Eve.	Chicago, IL	Auditorium
2	Tue.	Eve.	Chicago, IL	Auditorium
3	Wed.	M/E	Chicago, IL	Auditorium
4	Thu.	Mat.	Freeport, IL	Germania Opera House
4	Thu.	Eve.	Dubuque, IA	Grand Opera House
5	Fri.	Mat.	Clinton, IA	Davis Opera House
5	Fri.	Eve.	Cedar Rapids, IA	Greene's Opera House
6	Sat.	M/E	Sioux City, IA	Grand Opera House
7	Sun.	M/E	Omaha, NE	Boyd's Thea.
8	Mon.	Eve.	St. Joseph, MO	Crawford Thea.
9	Tue.	Mat.	Leavenworth, KS	Crawford Opera House
9	Tue.	Eve.	Kansas City, MO	Auditorium
10	Wed.	Mat.	Topeka, KS	Grand Opera House
10	Wed.	Eve.	Emporia, KS	Whitley's Opera House
11	Thu.	Eve.	Wichita, KS	Civic Auditorium
12	Fri.	Eve.	Denver, CO	Broadway Thea.

13	Sat.	M/E	Denver, CO	Broadway Thea.
14	Sun.	Eve.	Denver, CO	Broadway Thea.
15	Mon.	Mat.	Colorado Springs, CO	Opera House
15	Mon.	Eve.	Pueblo, CO	Grand Opera House
16	Tue.	Eve.	Trinidad, CO	Jaffe Opera House
17	Wed.	Eve.	Albuquerque, NM	Grant's Opera House
19	Fri.	Mat.	San Bernardino, CA	Grand Opera House
19	Fri.	Eve.	Riverside, CA	Loring Thea.
20	Sat.	M/E	Los Angeles, CA	Hazard's Pavilion
21	Sun.	M/E	San Diego, CA	Fisher Opera House
22	Mon.	M/E	Los Angeles, CA	Hazard's Pavilion
23	Tue.	Eve.	Oakland, CA	Macdonough Thea.
24	Wed.	M/E	San Jose, CA	Auditorium

Thu., 25th through Sun., 28th (4 days), San Francisco, California Thea.
2 concerts per day except eve. only 1st day.

MARCH

2	Tue.	Eve.	Portland, OR	Armory
3	Wed.	M/E	Portland, OR	Armory
4	Thu.	M/E	Seattle, WA	Seattle Thea.
5	Fri.	M/E	Spokane, WA	Auditorium
6	Sat.	Mat.	Missoula, MT	Bennett Opera House
6	Sat.	Eve.	Anaconda, MT	Evans' Grand Opera House
7	Sun.	M/E	Butte, MT	Murray Opera House
8	Mon.	M/E	Helena, MT	Auditorium
10	Wed.	M/E	Fargo, ND	Fargo Opera House
11	Thu.	M/E	St. Paul, MN	Metropolitan Opera House
12	Fri.	M/E	Duluth, MN	Lyceum Thea.
13	Sat.	M/E	Minneapolis, MN	Lyceum Thea.
14	Sun.	Mat.	Minneapolis, MN	Metropolitan Opera House
14	Sun.	Eve.	St. Paul, MN	Metropolitan Opera House
15	Mon.	Eve.	Milwaukee, WI	Pabst Thea.
16	Tue.	M/E	Milwaukee, WI	Pabst Thea.
17	Wed.	Mat.	Goshen, IN	Irwin Thea.
17	Wed.	Eve.	Elkhart, IN	Bucklen Opera House
18	Thu.	Mat.	Coldwater, MI	Tibbitts Opera House
18	Thu.	Eve.	Jackson, MI	First M.E. Church
19	Fri.	Eve.	Grand Rapids, MI	Lockerby Hall
20	Sat.	Mat.	Bay City, MI	Wood's Opera House
20	Sat.	Eve.	Saginaw, MI	Academy of Music
21	Sun.	Mat.	Detroit, MI	Lyceum Thea.
21	Sun.	Eve.	Toledo, OH	Valentine Thea.
22	Mon.	Mat.	Norwalk, OH	Gardiner's Music Hall
22	Mon.	Eve.	Cleveland, OH	Music Hall
23	Tue.	M/E	Cleveland, OH	Music Hall
24	Wed.	Mat.	Meadville, PA	Academy of Music
24	Wed.	Eve.	Oil City, PA	Opera House
25	Thu.	Mat.	Warren, PA	Library Thea.
25	Thu.	Eve.	Erie, PA	Park Opera House
26	Fri.	Eve.	Buffalo, NY	Music Hall
27	Sat.	M/E	Buffalo, NY	Music Hall
28	Sun.	Eve.	Rochester, NY	Lyceum Thea.
29	Mon.	Mat.	Corning, NY	Opera House
29	Mon.	Eve.	Elmira, NY	Lyceum Thea.
30	Tue.	Mat.	Owego, NY	Wilson Opera House
30	Tue.	Eve.	Ithaca, NY	Lyceum Thea.
31	Wed.	Mat.	Cortland, NY	Cortland Opera House
31	Wed.	Eve.	Binghamton, NY	Stone Opera House

APRIL

1	Thu.	Mat.	Rome, NY	Washington St. Op. House
1	Thu.	Eve.	Utica, NY	Utica Opera House
2	Fri.	Mat.	Schenectady, NY	Van Curler Opera House
2	Fri.	Eve.	Albany, NY	Harmanus Bleeker Hall
3	Sat.	M/E	Troy, NY	Music Hall
4	Sun.	Eve.	New York, NY	Broadway Thea.
8	Thu.	Mat.	Bethlehem, PA	Opera House
8	Thu.	Eve.	Allentown, PA	Academy of Music
9	Fri.	Eve.	Philadelphia, PA	Academy of Music
10	Sat.	M/E	Philadelphia, PA	Academy of Music
11	Sun.	Eve.	Washington, DC	Lafayette Square Opera House
12	Mon.	Eve.	Baltimore, MD	Music Hall
13	Tue.	Mat.	Hagerstown, MD	Academy of Music
13	Tue.	Eve.	Chambersburg, PA	Opera House
14	Wed.	Mat.	Lebanon, PA	Fisher Opera House
14	Wed.	Eve.	Reading, PA	Academy of Music

15	Thu.	Mat.	Pottsville, PA	Academy of Music
15	Thu.	Eve.	Hazleton, PA	Grand Opera House
16	Fri.	Mat.	Mahoney City, PA	Kair's Opera House
16	Fri.	Eve.	Wilkes-Barre, PA	Grand Opera House
17	Sat.	Mat.	Pittston, PA	Music Hall
17	Sat.	Eve.	Scranton, PA	Frothingham Thea.
18	Sun.	Eve.	New York, NY	Broadway Thea.
19	Mon.	Mat.	South Norwalk, CT	Hoyt's Thea.
19	Mon.	Eve.	New Haven, CT	Hyperion Thea.
20	Tue.	Mat.	Winsted, CT	Winsted Opera House
20	Tue.	Eve.	Waterbury, CT	City Hall Auditorium
21	Wed.	Mat.	New Britain, CT	Lyceum Thea.
21	Wed.	Eve.	Hartford, CT	Foot Guard Armory
22	Thu.	Eve.	Springfield, MA	Court Square Thea.
23	Fri.	Eve.	Holyoke, MA	Holyoke Opera House
24	Sat.	Mat.	Fitchburg, MA	City Hall
24	Sat.	Eve.	Worcester, MA	Mechanics' Hall
25	Sun.	Eve.	Boston, MA	Boston Thea.
26	Mon.	M/E	Boston, MA	Tremont Temple
27	Tue.	Eve.	Lynn, MA	Lynn Thea.
28	Wed.	Mat.	Saco, ME	City Hall
28	Wed.	Eve.	Portland, ME	City Hall
29	Thu.	Mat.	Waterville, ME	City Hall
29	Thu.	Eve.	Bangor, ME	City Hall
30	Fri.	Mat.	Belfast, ME	Opera House
30	Fri.	Eve.	Rockland, ME	Farwell Opera House

MAY

1	Sat.	Mat.	Augusta, ME	City Hall
1	Sat.	Eve.	Lewiston, ME	City Hall
2	Sun.	Eve.	Boston, MA	Boston Thea.
3	Mon.	Mat.	Plymouth, MA	Davis Opera House
3	Mon.	Eve.	Brockton, MA	City Thea.
4	Tue.	Eve.	Salem, MA	Cadet Armory
5	Wed.	M/E	Manchester, NH	Manchester Opera House
6	Thu.	M/E	Haverhill, MA	Academy of Music
7	Fri.	M/E	Lowell, MA	Lowell Opera House
8	Sat.	M/E	New Bedford, MA	Grand Opera House
9	Sun.	Eve.	Boston, MA	Boston Thea.
10	Mon.	Eve.	Lawrence, MA	Opera House
11	Tue.	Mat.	Middleboro, MA	City Hall
11	Tue.	Eve.	Fall River, MA	Academy of Music
12	Wed.	M/E	Providence, RI	Infantry Hall
13	Thu.	Mat.	New London, CT	Lyceum Thea.
13	Thu.	Eve.	Norwich, CT	Broadway Thea.
14	Fri.	Eve.	Philadelphia, PA	Academy of Music
15	Sat.	M/E	Philadelphia, PA	Academy of Music
16	Sun.	Eve.	Washington, DC	Lafayette Square Opera House
17	Mon.	M/E	Baltimore, MD	Music Hall
18	Tue.	Eve.	Harrisburg, PA	Grand Opera House
19	Wed.	Mat.	Tyrone, PA	Academy of Music
19	Wed.	Eve.	Altoona, PA	11th Ave. Opera House
20	Thu.	Mat.	Johnstown, PA	Cambria Thea.
20	Thu.	Eve.	Pittsburgh, PA	Alvin Thea.
21	Fri.	M/E	Pittsburgh, PA	Alvin Thea.
22	Sat.	M/E	Buffalo, NY	Music Hall
23	Sun.	Eve.	Rochester, NY	Lyceum Thea.
24	Mon.	Mat.	Woodstock, ONT/Canada	Opera House
24	Mon.	Eve.	London, ONT/Canada	Princess Rink
25	Tue.	Mat.	Guelph, ONT/Canada	Royal Opera House
25	Tue.	Eve.	Toronto, ONT/Canada	Massey Music Hall
26	Wed.	Mat.	Peterborough, ONT/Canada	Bradburn's Opera House
26	Wed.	Eve.	Belleville, ONT/Canada	Carman Opera House
27	Thu.	Mat.	Ogdensburg, NY	Opera House
27	Thu.	Eve.	Hamilton, ONT/Canada	Grand Opera House
28	Fri.	Mat.	Brockville, ONT/Canada	Grand Opera House
28	Fri.	Eve.	Ottawa, ONT/Canada	Rideau Rink
29	Sat.	M/E	Montreal, QUE/Canada	Victoria Rink
30	Sun.	Eve.	Quebec, QUE/Canada	Drill Hall
31	Mon.	Mat.	Newport, VT	Lane's Opera House
31	Mon.	Eve.	St. Johnsbury, VT	Music Hall

JUNE

2	Wed.	M/E	St. Stephen, NB/Canada	Curling Rink
3	Thu.	Eve.	Fredericton, NB/Canada	City Hall
4	Fri.	M/E	St. John, NB/Canada	Opera House

5	Sat.	Mat.	Amherst, NS/Canada	Aberdeen Rink
5	Sat.	Eve.	Moncton, NB/Canada	Victoria Rink
7	Mon.	Eve.	Charlottetown, PEI/Canada	Exhibition Building
8	Tue.	Mat.	Pictou, NS/Canada	Exhibition Hall
8	Tue.	Eve.	New Glasgow, NS/Canada	New Glasgow Skating Rink
9	Wed.	Mat.	Truro, NS/Canada	Curling Rink
9	Wed.	Eve.	Halifax, NS/Canada	Academy of Music
10	Thu.	M/E	Halifax, NS/Canada	Academy of Music
11	Fri.	Eve.	Kentville, NS/Canada	Exhibition Building
12	Wed.	Mat.	Yarmouth, NS/Canada	Agricultural Building
13	Sun.	Eve.	Boston, MA	Boston Thea.
14	Mon.	Mat.	Pawtucket, RI	Pawtucket Opera House
14	Mon.	Eve.	Newport, RI	Opera House

[End of 1896-97 tour]

JUNE-SEPTEMBER, 1897
Sat., 19 June through Mon., 6 Sept. (80 days), Brooklyn, NY, Manhattan Beach. 2 concerts per day first two days, then one matinee per day thereafter.

Soloists: Maude Reese Davies, Lillian Van Liew, Nedda Morrison, Elizabeth Northrop, Ida Klein, Hilda Clark, Nella Bergan, Bertha Waltzinger, Mary Helen Howe, Rene Fabrice, & Martha G. Minor, soprano; Fielding Roselle, contralto; Lloyd Rand, Dante Del Papa, & Thomas McQueen, tenor; DeWolf Hopper, Achille Alberti, Lewis Williams, Frank Osborn, & Gwyllim Miles, baritone; Eugene Cowles, basso; Isidore Luckstone & Alfred Klein, other vocalists; Albert Bode & Henry Higgins, cornet; Franz Helle, flugelhorn; Simone Mantia, euphonium; Arthur Pryor, trombone; Frank Wadsworth & Giacomo Norrito, flute/piccolo; Robert Messinger, oboe; August Cercillo-Stengler, clarinet; Jean Moeremans, saxophone.

1897 OFF-TOUR CONCERTS

SEPTEMBER
Tues. 7th through Fri., 10th (4 days), New York, NY, Hammerstein's Olympia. Evening concerts only.

Soloists: Rachel Walker & Marie Brandis, vocalists; Franz Helle, flugelhorn; Simone Mantia, euphonium; Arthur Pryor, trombone; Jean Moeremans, saxophone.

1897 TOUR

Soloists before Pittsburgh Exposition: Maud Reese Davies & Saidee Estelle Kaiser, soprano; Franz Helle, flugelhorn; Simone Mantia, euphonium; Arthur Pryor, trombone; Frank W. Wadsworth & Giacomo Norrito, piccolo; Jean Moeremans, saxophone.

OCTOBER
4	Mon.	Eve.	Scranton, PA	Lyceum Thea.
5	Tue.	Eve.	Wilkes-Barre, PA	Grand Opera House
6	Wed.	Mat.	Danville, PA	Opera House
6	Wed.	Eve.	Williamsport, PA	Lycoming Opera House
7	Thu.	Mat.	Wellsboro, PA	Bache Auditorium
7	Thu.	Eve.	Elmira, NY	Lyceum Thea.
8	Fri.	Mat.	Corning, NY	Opera House
8	Fri.	Eve.	Hornell, NY	Shattuck Opera House
9	Sat.	Mat.	Olean, NY	Olean Opera House
9	Sat.	Eve.	Bradford, PA	Wagner Opera House
10	Sun.	Eve.	Buffalo, NY	Music Hall

Mon., 11th through Sat., 16th (6 days), Pittsburgh Expo. 4 concerts per day.
Soloists: Franz Helle, flugelhorn; Simone Mantia, euphonium; Arthur Pryor, trombone; Frank Wadsworth & Giacomo Norrito, piccolo.

17	Sun.	Eve.	Washington, DC	Lafayette Square Opera House
18	Mon.	Eve.	Baltimore, MD	Music Hall
19	Tue.	Mat.	Frederick, MD	City Opera House
19	Wed.	Eve.	York, PA	York Opera House
20	Wed.	Mat.	Lebanon, PA	Fisher Opera House
20	Wed.	Eve.	Harrisburg, PA	Grand Opera House
21	Thu.	Mat.	Chester, PA	Grand Opera House
21	Thu.	Eve.	West Chester, PA	Assembly Hall
22	Fri.	Eve.	Philadelphia, PA	Academy of Music
23	Sat.	M/E	Philadelphia, PA	Academy of Music
24	Sun.	Eve.	New York, NY	Broadway Thea.

Mon., 25th through Sat., 30th (6 days), Boston, MA, Boston Food Fair. 2 concerts per day.

Soloists: Franz Helle, flugelhorn; Simone Mantia, euphonium; Arthur Pryor, trombone; Jean Moeremans, saxophone.

31	Sun.	Eve.	New York, NY	Broadway Thea.

Soloists: Bertha Waltzinger, soprano; Gwyllim Miles, baritone.

[End of 1897 tour]

1ST 1898 TOUR

Soloists: Maude Reese Davies, Marcella Powell, & Sadie Estelle Kaiser, soprano; Jennie Hoyle, violin; Florie Van Den Hende, cello; Franz Helle, flugelhorn; Arthur Pryor, trombone; possibly others.

JANUARY
7	Fri.	Eve.	Newark, NJ	Krueger Auditorium
8	Sat.	Eve.	New York, NY	Broadway Thea.
9	Sun.	Eve.	New York, NY	Harlem Opera House
10	Mon.	Mat.	Peekskill, NY	Depew Opera House
10	Mon.	Eve.	Poughkeepsie, NY	Collingwood Opera House
11	Tue.	Eve.	Utica, NY	Utica Opera House
12	Wed.	Mat.	Watertown, NY	City Opera House
12	Wed.	Eve.	Syracuse, NY	Wieting Opera House
13	Thu.	Mat.	Amsterdam, NY	Opera House
13	Thu.	Eve.	Albany, NY	Harmanus Bleeker Hall
14	Fri.	M/E	Troy, NY	Music Hall
15	Sat.	M/E	Brooklyn, NY	Academy of Music
16	Sun.	Eve.	Washington, DC	Lafayette Square Opera House
17	Mon.	Mat.	Staunton, VA	Opera House
17	Mon.	Eve.	Charlottesville, VA	Jefferson Auditorium
18	Tue.	M/E	Norfolk, VA	Academy of Music
19	Wed.	Mat.	Petersburg, VA	Academy of Music
19	Wed.	Eve.	Richmond, VA	Academy of Music
20	Thu.	Mat.	Washington, DC	Lafayette Square Opera House
20	Thu.	Eve.	Baltimore, MD	Music Hall
21	Fri.	Mat.	Wilmington, DE	Grand Opera House
21	Fri.	Eve.	Philadelphia, PA	Academy of Music
22	Sat.	M/E	Philadelphia, PA	Academy of Music
23	Sun.	Eve.	New York, NY	Broadway Thea.
24	Mon.	Mat.	Pottstown, PA	Grand Opera House
24	Mon.	Eve.	Lancaster, PA	Fulton Opera House
25	Tue.	Mat.	Pottsville, PA	Academy of Music
25	Tue.	Eve.	Reading, PA	Academy of Music
26	Wed.	Mat.	Tyrone, PA	Academy of Music
26	Wed.	Eve.	Altoona, PA	11th Ave. Opera House
27	Thu.	Mat.	Beaver Falls, PA	Thea.
27	Thu.	Eve.	Youngstown, OH	Opera House
28	Fri.	Mat.	Salem, OH	Grand Opera House
28	Fri.	Eve.	Canton, OH	Grand Opera House
29	Sat.	Mat.	Bucyrus, OH	Bucyrus Opera House
29	Sat.	Eve.	Marion, OH	Grand Opera House
30	Sun.	Eve.	Columbus, OH	Great Southern Thea.
31	Mon.	Mat.	Hamilton, OH	Globe Opera House
31	Mon.	Eve.	Middletown, OH	Sorg Opera House

FEBRUARY
1	Tue.	Eve.	Cincinnati, OH	Music Hall
2	Wed.	Mat.	Columbus, IN	Crump's Thea.
2	Wed.	Eve.	Indianapolis, IN	Tomlinson Hall
3	Thu.	Mat.	Crawfordsville, IN	Music Hall
4	Fri.	Mat.	Danville, IL	Grand Opera House
4	Fri.	Eve.	Chicago, IL	Auditorium
5	Sat.	M/E	Chicago, IL	Auditorium
6	Sun.	M/E	St. Louis, MO	Olympic Thea.
7	Mon.	Mat.	Jacksonville, IL	Grand Opera House
7	Mon.	Eve.	Springfield, IL	Chatterton's Opera House
8	Tue.	Mat.	Decatur, IL	Powers' Grand Op. House
8	Tue.	Eve.	Bloomington, IL	Grand Opera House
9	Wed.	Mat.	Lincoln, IL	Broadway Thea.
9	Wed.	Eve.	Peoria, IL	Grand Opera House
10	Thu.	Mat.	Canton, IL	Opera House
10	Thu.	Eve.	Galesburg, IL	Auditorium
11	Fri.	Mat.	Princeton, IL	Apollo Hall
11	Fri.	Eve.	Aurora, IL	Sherwood Opera House
12	Sat.	Mat.	Joliet, IL	Joliet Thea.
12	Sat.	Eve.	Ottawa, IL	Sherwood Opera House
13	Sun.	Eve.	Davenport, IA	Burtis Opera House

14	Mon.	Mat.	Washington, IA	Grand Opera House
14	Mon.	Eve.	Burlington, IA	Grand Opera House
15	Tue.	Mat.	Oskaloosa, IA	Masonic Opera House
15	Tue.	Eve.	Ottumwa, IA	Grand Opera House
16	Wed.	Mat.	Iowa City, IA	Opera House
16	Wed.	Eve.	Cedar Rapids, IA	Greene's Opera House
17	Thu.	Eve.	Dubuque, IA	Grand Opera House
18	Fri.	Mat.	Freeport, IL	Germania Opera House
18	Fri.	Eve.	Rockford, IL	Grand Opera House
19	Sat.	Mat.	Janesville, WI	Myers Grand Opera House
19	Sat.	Eve.	Madison, WI	Fuller Opera House
20	Sun.	Eve.	Milwaukee, WI	Davidson Thea
22	Tue.	Mat.	Valparaiso, IN	Memorial Opera House
22	Tue.	Eve.	South Bend, IN	Oliver Opera House
23	Wed.	Mat.	Huntington, IN	Huntington Thea.
23	Wed.	Eve.	Fort Wayne, IN	Masonic Temple
24	Thu.	Mat.	Hartford City, IN	Van Cleve Thea.
24	Thu.	Eve.	Muncie, IN	Wysor's Grand Op. House
25	Fri.	Mat.	Portland, IN	Auditorium
25	Fri.	Eve.	Lima, OH	Faurot Opera House
26	Sat.	Mat.	Adrian, MI	Croswell Opera House
26	Sat.	Eve.	Ann Arbor, MI	University Hall
27	Sun.	Mat.	Detroit, MI	Lyceum Thea.
27	Sun.	Eve.	Toledo, OH	Valentine Thea.
28	Mon.	Mat.	Fremont, OH	Opera House
28	Mon.	Eve.	Sandusky, OH	Nielson Opera House

MARCH

1	Tue.	M/E	Cleveland, OH	Grays' Armory
2	Wed.	Eve.	Buffalo, NY	Music Hall
3	Tue.	M/E	Rochester, NY	Lyceum Thea.
4	Fri.	Mat.	Geneva, NY	Smith Opera House
4	Fri.	Eve.	Ithaca, NY	Lyceum Thea.
5	Sat.	Mat.	Binghamton, NY	Stone Opera House
5	Sat.	Eve.	Cortland, NY	Cortland Opera House
6	Sun.	Eve.	Syracuse, NY	Wieting Opera House
7	Mon.	Mat.	Gloversville, NY	Kasson Opera House
7	Mon.	Eve.	Johnstown, NY	Grand Opera House
8	Tue.	Mat.	North Adams, MA	Columbia Opera House
8	Tue.	Eve.	Pittsfield, MA	Academy of Music
9	Wed.	Mat.	Greenfield, MA	Opera House
9	Wed.	Eve.	Holyoke, MA	Holyoke Opera House
10	Thu.	Mat.	Athol, MA	Academy of Music
10	Thu.	Eve.	Gardner, MA	Opera House
11	Fri.	Mat.	Brattleboro, VT	Greenfield Opera House
11	Fri.	Eve.	Bellows Falls, VT	Opera House
12	Sat.	Mat.	Keene, NH	Opera House
12	Sat.	Eve.	Fitchburg, MA	City Hall
13	Sun.	Eve.	Boston, MA	Boston Thea.
14	Mon.	Mat.	Middleboro, MA	City Hall
14	Mon.	Eve.	Brockton, MA	City Thea.
15	Tue.	Eve.	Salem, MA	Cadet Armory
17	Thu.	M/E	Providence, RI	Infantry Hall
18	Fri.	Mat.	Boston, MA	Boston Thea.
18	Fri.	Eve.	Fall River, MA	Academy of Music
19	Sat.	M/E	Worcester, MA	Mechanics' Hall
20	Sun.	Eve.	Boston, MA	Boston Thea.
21	Mon.	Mat.	Lawrence, MA	Opera House
22	Tue.	Mat.	Springfield, MA	Court Square Thea.
22	Tue.	Eve.	Hartford, CT	Foot Guard Armory
23	Wed.	Mat.	Winsted, CT	Winsted Opera House
23	Wed.	Eve.	Waterbury, CT	Jacques Auditorium
24	Thu.	Mat.	Meriden, CT	Opera House
24	Thu.	Eve.	New Haven, CT	Hyperion Thea.
25	Fri.	Eve.	Philadelphia, PA	Academy of Music
26	Sat.	M/E	Philadelphia, PA	Academy of Music
27	Sun.	Eve.	New York, NY	Metropolitan Opera House

[End of 1st 1898 tour]

1898 OFF-TOUR CONCERTS

APRIL
* Denotes performance of *The Trooping of the Colors* pageant

3	Sun.	Eve.	New York, NY	*Metropolitan Opera House

Soloists: Marcella Powell, soprano; Flavie Van Den Hende, cello

10	Sun.	Eve.	New York, NY	Metropolitan Opera House

Soloist: DeWolf Hopper, baritone.

2ND 1898 TOUR

Soloists: Louise M. Brehany & Nella Bergen, soprano; Ada May Benzing, contralto; Basil Tetson & William Pruette, baritone; Jenny Hoyle, violin; Emil Kenecke, cornet; Franz Helle, flugelhorn; Simone Mantia, euphonium; Arthur Pryor, trombone.

* Denotes performance of *The Trooping of the Colors* pageant

APRIL

13	Wed.	Eve.	Pittsburgh, PA	*Carnegie Music Hall
14	Thu.	M/E	Pittsburgh, PA	*Carnegie Music Hall
15	Fri.	Eve.	Cincinnati, OH	*Music Hall
16	Sat.	M/E	Cincinnati, OH	*Music Hall
17	Sun.	Eve.	Toledo, OH	Valentine Thea.
18	Mon.	Eve.	Dayton, OH	*Grand Opera House
19	Tue.	M/E	Dayton, OH	*Grand Opera House
20	Wed.	Mat.	Indianapolis, IN	*Tomlinson Hall
21	Thu.	M/E	Indianapolis, IN	*Tomlinson Hall
22	Fri.	Eve.	Louisville, KY	*Auditorium
23	Sat.	M/E	Louisville, KY	*Auditorium
24	Sun.	Eve.	Terre Haute, IN	Grand Opera House
25	Mon.	Eve.	Chicago, IL	*Auditorium
26	Tue.	M/E	Chicago, IL	*Auditorium
27	Wed.	M/E	Chicago, IL	*Auditorium
28	Thu.	M/E	Chicago, IL	*Auditorium
29	Fri.	Eve.	Detroit, MI	*Light Guard Armory
30	Sat.	Eve.	Detroit, MI	*Light Guard Armory

MAY

1	Sun.	Eve.	Detroit, MI	*Light Guard Armory
2	Mon.	Eve.	Columbus, OH	*Great Southern Thea.
3	Tue.	M/E	Columbus, OH	*Great Southern Thea.
4	Wed.	Eve.	Cleveland, OH	*Grays' Armory
5	Wed.	a.m.	Cleveland, OH	Escorted troops in parade
5	Thu.	M/E	Cleveland, OH	*Grays' Armory
6	Fri.	Eve.	Buffalo, NY	*Music Hall
7	Sat.	M/E	Buffalo, NY	*Music Hall
8	Sun.	M/E	Rochester, NY	Lyceum Thea.
9	Mon.	Eve.	Baltimore, MD	*Ford's Grand Op. House
10	Tue.	M/E	Baltimore, MD	*Ford's Grand Op. House
11	Wed.	Eve.	Washington, DC	*Lafayette Square Opera House
12	Thu.	M/E	Washington, DC	*Lafayette Square Opera House
13	Fri.	Eve.	Philadelphia, PA	*Academy of Music
14	Sat.	M/E	Philadelphia, PA	*Academy of Music
15	Sun.	Eve.	New York, NY	Metropolitan Opera House
16	Mon.	Eve.	Boston, MA	place not known
17	Tue.	M/E	Boston, MA	place not known
18	Wed.	M/E	Boston, MA	place not known
19	Thu.	Eve.	Portland, ME	City Hall
20	Fri.	Eve.	Providence, RI	Providence Opera House
21	Sat.	M/E	Worcester, MA	Mechanics' Hall
22	Sun.	Eve.	New York, NY	Columbus Thea.
24	Tue.	Eve.	New York, NY	*Metropolitan Opera House
25	Wed.	Eve.	New York, NY	*Metropolitan Opera House
26	Thu.	Eve.	New York, NY	*Metropolitan Opera House
27	Fri.	Eve.	New York, NY	*Metropolitan Opera House
28	Sat.	M/E	New York, NY	*Metropolitan Opera House
29	Sun.	Eve.	New York, NY	*Metropolitan Opera House
30	Mon.	M/E	New York, NY	*Metropolitan Opera House

[End of 2nd 1898 tour]

3RD 1898 TOUR

SEPTEMBER
Wed., 7th through Tues., 13th except for Sun. 11th (6 days), Pittsburgh Exposition. 4 concerts per day. Escorted troops in parade on Sun., 11th.

Soloists: Emile Kenecke, cornet; Franz Helle, flugelhorn; Simone Mantia, euphonium; Arthur Pryor, trombone; Frank Wadsworth & Giacomo Norrito, piccolo; Jean Moeremans, saxophone.

SEPTEMBER-OCTOBER
Wed., 14 Sept. through Sat., 29 Oct. (46 days), St. Louis Exposition. 4 concerts per day.

Soloists: Wayman McCreery, tenor; Emil Kenecke & Otto Mesloh, cornet; Franz Helle, flugelhorn; Simone Mantia, euphonium; Arthur Pryor, trombone; Frank Wadsworth & Giacomo Norrito, piccolo; Jean Moeremans, saxophone.

Soloists for remainder of tour: Maud Reese Davies, soprano; Dorothy Hoyle, violin; Emil Kenecke, cornet; Arthur Pryor, trombone.

OCTOBER

| 30 | Sun. | M/E | Kansas City, MO | Coates Opera House |
| 31 | Mon. | Eve. | St. Joseph, MO | Tootle Thea. |

NOVEMBER

1	Tue.	Eve.	Sedalia, MO	Wood's Opera House
2	Wed.	Mat.	Hannibal, MO	Park Thea.
2	Wed.	Eve.	Quincy, IL	Empire Thea.
3	Thu.	Mat.	Keokuk, IA	Keokuk Opera House
3	Thu.	Eve.	Burlington, IA	Grand Opera House
4	Fri.	Mat.	Fort Madison, IA	Ebinger Grand
4	Fri.	Eve.	Galesburg, IL	Auditorium
5	Sat.	Eve.	Peoria, IL	Grand Opera House
6	Sun.	Mat.	Clinton, IA	Economic Thea.
6	Sun.	Eve.	Davenport, IA	Burtis Opera House
7	Mon.	Eve.	Cedar Rapids, IA	Greene's Opera House
8	Tue.	Mat.	Oskaloosa, IA	Masonic Opera House
8	Tue.	Eve.	Ottumwa, IA	Grand Opera House
9	Wed.	Mat.	Marshalltown, IA	Odeon Thea.
9	Wed.	Eve.	Des Moines, IA	Foster Opera House
10	Thu.	Eve.	Sioux City, IA	Grand Opera House
11	Fri.	Eve.	Mankato, MN	Mankato Thea.
12	Sat.	M/E	Minneapolis, MN	Lyceum Thea.
13	Sun.	M/E	St. Paul, MN	Metropolitan Opera House
14	Mon.	Eve.	Eau Claire, WI	Grand Opera House
15	Tue.	Mat.	Winona, MN	Winona Opera House
15	Tue.	Eve.	La Crosse, WI	La Crosse Thea.
16	Wed.	Mat.	Baraboo, WI	The Grande
16	Wed.	Eve.	Madison, WI	Fuller Opera House
17	Thu.	Mat.	Fond du Lac, WI	Crescent Opera House
17	Thu.	Eve.	Oshkosh, WI	Grand Opera House
18	Fri.	Mat.	Appleton, WI	Appleton Opera House
18	Fri.	Eve.	Green Bay, WI	Turner's Opera House
20	Sun.	Eve.	Sheboygan, WI	Opera House
21	Mon.	Mat.	Milwaukee, WI	Davidson Thea.
21	Mon.	Eve.	Racine, WI	Belle City Opera House
22	Tue.	Mat.	Freeport, IL	Germania Opera House
22	Tue.	Eve.	Rockford, IL	Grand Opera House
23	Wed.	Mat.	Beloit, WI	Opera House
23	Wed.	Eve.	Elgin, IL	Eglin Opera House
24	Thu.	M/E	Elkhart, IN	Bucklen Opera House
25	Fri.	Mat.	Wabash, IN	Harter's Opera House
25	Fri.	Eve.	Marion, IN	Grand Opera House
26	Sat.	Eve.	Indianapolis, IN	Tomlinson Hall
27	Sun.	Eve.	Columbus, OH	Great Southern Thea.
28	Mon.	Mat.	Chillicothe, OH	Masonic Opera House
28	Mon.	Eve.	Portsmouth, OH	Grand Opera House
29	Tue.	Mat.	Parkersburg, WV	Auditorium
29	Tue.	Eve.	Marietta, OH	Auditorium
30	Wed.	Eve.	Cumberland, MD	Academy of Music

DECEMBER

1	Thu.	Mat.	Washington, DC	Lafayette Square Opera House
1	Thu.	Eve.	Baltimore, MD	Music Hall
2	Fri.	Eve.	Philadelphia, PA	Academy of Music
3	Sat.	M/E	Philadelphia, PA	Academy of Music
4	Sun.	Eve.	New York, NY	Harlem Opera House

[End of 3rd 1898 tour]

1ST 1899 TOUR

Soloists: Maud Reese Davies & Juliette Corden, soprano; Bessie Bonsall, contralto; George Moore, tenor; Leland Langey, basso; Dorothy Hoyle, violin; Sada, violin; Herbert L. Clarke, cornet; Franz Helle, flugelhorn; Arthur Pryor, trombone.

JANUARY

16	Mon.	Eve.	Newark, NJ	Krueger Auditorium
17	Tue.	M/E	Norfolk, VA	Academy of Music
18	Wed.	Eve.	Philadelphia, PA	Academy of Music
19	Thu.	Mat.	Lebanon, PA	Academy of Music
19	Thu.	Eve.	Reading, PA	Academy of Music
20	Fri.	Mat.	Wilmington, DE	Grand Opera House
20	Fri.	Eve.	Baltimore, MD	Music Hall
21	Sat.	Eve.	Philadelphia, PA	Academy of Music
22	Sun.	Eve.	Washington, DC	Lafayette Square Opera House
23	Mon.	M/E	Richmond, VA	Academy of Music
24	Tue.	M/E	Norfolk, VA	Academy of Music
25	Wed.	Mat.	Goldsboro, NC	Messenger Opera House
25	Wed.	Eve.	Raleigh, NC	Academy of Music
26	Thu.	Mat.	Charlotte, NC	Charlotte Opera House
26	Thu.	Eve.	Spartanburg, SC	Converse College
27	Fri.	Mat.	Columbia, SC	Opera House
27	Fri.	Eve.	Augusta, GA	Grand Opera House
28	Sat.	M/E	Charleston, SC	Academy of Music
29	Sun.	Mat.	St. Augustine, FL	Opera House
29	Sun.	Eve.	Jacksonville, FL	Park Thea.
30	Mon.	M/E	Savannah, GA	Genovar's Opera House
31	Tue.	Mat.	Thomasville, GA	Opera House
31	Tue.	Eve.	Albany, GA	Auditorium

FEBRUARY

1	Wed.	Mat.	Macon, GA	Academy of Music
1	Wed.	Eve.	Atlanta, GA	Grand Opera House
2	Thu.	M/E	Atlanta, GA	Grand Opera House
3	Fri.	M/E	Montgomery, AL	Montgomery Thea.
4	Sat.	Eve.	Pensacola, FL	Opera House
5	Sun.	M/E	New Orleans, LA	Crescent Thea.
6	Mon.	M/E	Galveston, TX	Grand Opera House
7	Tue.	M/E	Houston, TX	Sweeny & Combs Opera House
8	Wed.	Mat.	San Antonio, TX	Grand Opera House
8	Wed.	Eve.	Austin, TX	Hancock Opera House
9	Thu.	Mat.	Fort Worth, TX	Greenwall's Opera House
9	Thu.	Eve.	Dallas, TX	Opera House
10	Fri.	Mat.	Marshall, TX	Opera House
10	Fri.	Eve.	Shreveport, LA	Grand Opera House
11	Sat.	Eve.	Hot Springs, AR	Opera House
12	Sun.	M/E	Little Rock, AR	Capital Thea.
13	Mon.	M/E	Memphis, TN	Grand Opera House
14	Tue.	M/E	Nashville, TN	Vendome Thea.
15	Wed.	M/E	Louisville, KY	Auditorium
16	Thu.	Mat.	Lexington, KY	Lexington Opera House
16	Thu.	Eve.	Cincinnati, OH	Music Hall
17	Fri.	M/E	Dayton, OH	Grand Opera House
18	Sat.	Mat.	Vincennes, IN	McJimsey's Thea.
18	Sat.	Eve.	Evansville, IN	Grand Opera House
19	Sun.	Eve.	Terre Haute, IN	Grand Opera House
20	Mon.	Mat.	Champaign, IL	Walker Opera House
20	Mon.	Eve.	Bloomington, IN	Grand Opera House
21	Tue.	Mat.	Decatur, IL	Powers' Grand Op. House
21	Tue.	Eve.	Springfield, IL	Chatterton's Opera House
22	Wed.	M/E	Kansas City, MO	Convention Hall
22	Wed.	Eve.	Kansas City, MO	Convention Hall Ballroom (late concert)
23	Thu.	Mat.	Lawrence, KS	Bowersock's Opera House
23	Thu.	Eve.	Topeka, KS	Grand Opera House
24	Fri.	Mat.	Beatrice, NE	Paddock Opera House
24	Fri.	Eve.	Lincoln, NE	Oliver Thea.
25	Sat.	M/E	Denver, CO	Broadway Thea.
26	Sun.	M/E	Denver, CO	Broadway Thea.
27	Mon.	Mat.	Colorado Springs, CO	Opera House
27	Mon.	Eve.	Pueblo, CO	Grand Opera House
28	Tue.	Eve.	Grand Junction, CO	Park Opera House

MARCH

1	Wed.	M/E	Salt Lake City, UT	Salt Lake Thea.
3	Fri.	Eve.	San Francisco, CA	Alhambra Thea.
4	Sat.	Eve.	San Francisco, CA	Alhambra Thea.
5	Sun.	M/E	San Francisco, CA	Alhambra Thea.
6	Mon.	Mat.	Vallejo, CA	Farragut Hall
6	Mon.	Eve.	Santa Rosa, CA	Antheneaum
7	Tue.	M/E	Oakland, CA	Macdonough Thea.
9	Thu.	M/E	San Jose, CA	Victory Thea.
10	Fri.	Eve.	San Francisco, CA	California Thea.
11	Sat.	M/E	San Francisco, CA	California Thea.
12	Sun.	Eve.	Fresno, CA	Barton Opera House

13	Mon.	Mat.	Ventura, CA	Ventura Opera House
13	Mon.	Eve.	Santa Barbara, CA	Opera House
14	Tue.	M/E	Los Angeles, CA	Simpson Tabernacle
15	Wed.	M/E	San Diego, CA	Fisher Opera House
16	Thu.	M/E	Los Angeles, CA	Simpson Tabernacle
17	Fri.	Eve.	Stockton, CA	Yosemite Thea.
18	Sat.	M/E	Sacramento, CA	Clunie Thea.
20	Mon.	Eve.	Portland, OR	Armory
21	Tue.	M/E	Portland, OR	Armory
22	Wed.	Eve.	Tacoma, WA	Tacoma Thea.
23	Thu.	M/E	Seattle, WA	Seattle Thea.
24	Fri.	M/E	Spokane, WA	Auditorium
25	Sat.	M/E	Helena, MT	Auditorium
26	Sun.	M/E	Butte, MT	Grand Opera House
28	Tue.	Mat.	Crookston, MN	Grand Opera House
28	Tue.	Eve.	Grand Forks, ND	Metropolitan Opera House
29	Wed.	Eve.	Winnipeg, MAN/Canada	Winnipeg Thea.
30	Thu.	M/E	Winnipeg, MAN/Canada	Winnipeg Thea.
31	Fri.	M/E	Fargo, ND	Fargo Opera House

APRIL

1	Sat.	M/E	Minneapolis, MN	Lyceum Thea.
2	Sun.	M/E	St. Paul, MN	Metropolitan Opera House
3	Mon.	Eve.	Chicago, IL	Auditorium
4	Tue.	Eve.	Chicago, IL	Auditorium
5	Wed.	M/E	Chicago, IL	Auditorium
6	Thu.	Mat.	Dowagiac, MI	Beckwith Memorial Thea.
6	Thu.	Eve.	Kalamazoo, MI	Academy of Music
7	Fri.	Mat.	Lansing, MI	Auditorium
7	Fri.	Eve.	Grand Rapids, MI	Auditorium
8	Sat.	Mat.	Jackson, MI	Anthenaeum
8	Sat.	Eve.	Ann Arbor, MI	University Hall
9	Sun.	M/E	Detroit, MI	Lyceum Thea.
10	Mon.	Eve.	Toledo, OH	Valentine Thea.
11	Tue.	Mat.	Wooster, OH	City Opera House
11	Tue.	Eve.	Akron, OH	Grand Opera House
12	Wed.	M/E	Cleveland, OH	Grays' Armory
13	Thu.	Mat.	Ashtabula, OH	Auditorium
13	Thu.	Eve.	Erie, PA	Park Opera House
14	Fri.	M/E	Buffalo, NY	Music Hall
15	Sat.	M/E	Toronto, ONT/Canada	Massey Music Hall
16	Sun.	Eve.	Rochester, NY	Lyceum Thea.
17	Mon.	Mat.	Binghamton, NY	Stone Opera House
17	Mon.	Eve.	Scranton, PA	Lyceum Thea.
18	Tue.	Eve.	Wilkes-Barre, PA	Nesbitt Thea.
19	Wed.	Mat.	Bethlehem, PA	Opera House
19	Wed.	Eve.	Easton, PA	Able Opera House
20	Thu.	Mat.	Washington, DC	Lafayette Square Opera House
20	Thu.	Eve.	Baltimore, MD	Music Hall
21	Fri.	Mat.	Wilmington, DE	Grand Opera House
21	Fri.	Eve.	Philadelphia, PA	Academy of Music
22	Sat.	M/E	Philadelphia, PA	Academy of Music
23	Sun.	Eve.	New York, NY	Metropolitan Opera House

[End of 1ˢᵗ 1899 tour]

2ND 1899 TOUR

Soloists: Maud Reese Davies, soprano; Dorothy Hoyle, violin; Herbert L. Clarke, cornet; Arthur Pryor, trombone.

APRIL

| 30 | Sun. | Eve. | Brooklyn, NY | Montauk Thea. |

MAY

1	Mon.	Mat.	New Britain, CT	Lyceum Thea.
1	Mon.	Eve.	Waterbury, CT	Poli's Thea.
2	Tue.	Mat.	Bridgeport, CT	Park City Thea.
2	Tue.	Eve.	New Haven, CT	Hyperion Thea.
3	Wed.	Mat.	Winsted, CT	Winsted Opera House
3	Wed.	Eve.	Hartford, CT	Foot Guard Armory
4	Thu.	Mat.	New London, CT	Lyceum Thea.
4	Thu.	Eve.	Norwich, CT	Broadway Thea.
5	Fri.	M/E	Providence, RI	Infantry Hall
6	Sat.	Mat.	Pawtucket, RI	Pawtucket Opera House
6	Sat.	Eve.	Woonsocket, RI	Woonsocket Opera House
7	Sun.	Eve.	Boston, MA	Boston Thea.
8	Mon.	M/E	Boston, MA	Tremont Temple
9	Tue.	Mat.	Athol, MA	Academy of Music

9	Tue.	Eve.	Gardner, MA	Opera House
10	Wed.	Mat.	Westfield, MA	Westfield Opera House
10	Wed.	Eve.	Springfield, MA	Court Square Thea.
11	Thu.	Mat.	Brattleboro, VT	Auditorium
11	Thu.	Eve.	Bellows Falls, VT	Opera House
12	Fri.	Mat.	Keene, NH	City Hall
12	Fri.	Eve.	Fitchburg, MA	City Hall
13	Sat.	M/E	Worcester, MA	Mechanics' Hall
14	Sun.	Eve.	Boston, MA	Boston Thea.
15	Mon.	Mat.	Newport, RI	Opera House
15	Mon.	Eve.	Fall River, MA	Academy of Music
16	Tue.	Mat.	Gloucester, MA	City Hall
16	Tue.	Eve.	Salem, MA	Cadet Armory
17	Wed.	Mat.	Greenfield, MA	Opera House
17	Wed.	Eve.	Northampton, MA	Academy of Music
18	Thu.	Mat.	Newburyport, MA	City Hall
18	Thu.	Eve.	Haverhill, MA	Academy of Music
19	Fri.	Mat.	Laconia, NH	Moulton Opera House
19	Fri.	Eve.	Manchester, NH	Manchester Opera House
20	Sat.	Mat.	Concord, NH	Opera House
20	Sat.	Eve.	Lawrence, MA	Opera House
21	Sun.	Eve.	Boston, MA	Boston Thea.
22	Mon.	Eve.	Lewiston, ME	City Hall
23	Tue.	M/E	Portland, ME	City Hall
24	Wed.	Mat.	Newport, VT	Lane's Opera House
24	Wed.	Eve.	St. Johnsbury, VT	Music Hall
25	Thu.	M/E	Montreal, QUE/Canada	Her Majesty's Thea.
26	Fri.	M/E	Ottawa, ONT/Canada	Russell Thea.
27	Sat.	Mat.	Watertown, NY	City Opera House
27	Sat.	Eve.	Oswego, NY	Richardson Thea.
28	Sun.	Eve.	Syracuse, NY	Wieting Opera House
29	Mon.	Mat.	Ilion, NY	Ilion Opera House
29	Mon.	Eve.	Utica, NY	Utica Opera House
30	Tue.	Mat.	Cohoes, NY	Opera House
30	Tue.	Eve.	Troy, NY	Music Hall
31	Wed.	M/E	Albany, NY	Empire Thea.

JUNE

| 1 | Thu. | Mat. | Kingston, NY | Kingston Opera House |
| 1 | Thu. | Eve. | Newburgh, NY | Academy of Music |

[End of 2ⁿᵈ 1899 tour]

JUNE-SEPTEMBER, 1899

Sat., 17 June through Mon., 4 Sept. (81 days), Manhattan Beach, Brooklyn, NY. 2 concerts per day except mat. only on last day.

Soloists: Frances Lee, Grace Lee Carroll, Clara Douglas Carroll, Bertha Waltzinger, & Mary Helen Howe, soprano; Belle Newport, contralto; Kate Dewey Hanford, vocalist; Herbert L. Clarke, Henry Higgins, & Otto Mesloh, cornet; Franz Helle, flugelhorn; Henry Koch, horn; Arthur Pryor, trombone; Frank Wadsworth, flute; Giacomo Norrito, piccolo.

3RD 1899 TOUR

SEPTEMBER

Weds., 6ᵗʰ through Tues., 19ᵗʰ (12 days), Pittsburgh Exposition. 4 concerts per day except 2 on 1ˢᵗ day & no concerts Sun. 10ᵗʰ & Sun. 17ᵗʰ.

Soloists: Herbert L. Clarke, Henry Higgins, & Emil Kenecke, cornet; Simone Mantia, euphonium; Arthur Pryor, trombone; Joseph Norrito, clarinet; Jean Moeremans, saxophone.

Soloists for remainder of tour: Louis Duches, vocalist; Herbert L. Clarke & Emil Kenecke, cornet; Franz Helle, flugelhorn; Arthur Pryor, trombone.

20	Wed.	M/E	Indianapolis, IN	Indiana State Fair
21	Thu.	M/E	Indianapolis, IN	Indiana State Fair
22	Wed.	Mat.	Dayton, OH	Victoria Thea.
22	Wed.	Eve.	Springfield, OH	Grand Opera House
23	Sat.	Mat.	Newark, OH	Auditorium
23	Sat.	Eve.	Zanesville, OH	Schultz Opera House
24	Sun.	M/E	Wheeling, WV	Wheeling Park Casino

Mon., 25ᵗʰ through Fri., 29ᵗʰ (5 days), 1ˢᵗ segment (of 2) of Philadelphia National Export Exposition. 3 concerts per day.

| 30 | Sat. | a.m. | New York, NY | Dewey Parade |

[End of 3ʳᵈ 1899 tour]

4TH 1899 TOUR

OCTOBER
Mon. 16th through Sat., 21st (6 days), Boston Food Fair. 2 concerts per day.
Soloists: Emil Kenecke, Walter Rogers, Henry Higgins, & Otto Mesloh, cornet; Franz Helle, flugelhorn; Simone Mantia, euphonium; Arthur Pryor, trombone.
[End of 4th 1899 tour]

5TH 1899 TOUR

OCTOBER-NOVEMBER
Mon., 30 Oct. through Sat., 4 Nov. (6 days), 2nd segment (of 2) of Philadelphia National Export Exposition. 4 concerts per day.
Soloists: Emil Kenecke & Walter Rogers, cornet; Franz Helle, flugelhorn; Simone Mantia, euphonium; Arthur Pryor, trombone.
[End of 5th 1899 tour]

1ST 1900 TOUR

Soloists: Blanche Duffield & Maud Reese Davies, soprano; Bertha Bucklin, violin; Herbert L. Clarke, Emil Kenecke, & Walter Rogers, cornet; Franz Helle, flugelhorn; Arthur Pryor, trombone.

JANUARY

31	Wed.	Eve.	Newark, NJ	Krueger Auditorium

FEBRUARY

1	Thu.	Mat.	Washington, DC	National Thea.
1	Thu.	Eve.	Baltimore, MD	Music Hall
2	Fri.	Eve.	Philadelphia, PA	Academy of Music
3	Sat.	M/E	Philadelphia, PA	Academy of Music
4	Sun.	Eve.	Brooklyn, NY	Montauk Thea.
5	Mon.	Mat.	Meriden, CT	Opera House
5	Mon.	Eve.	New Haven, CT	Hyperion Thea.
6	Tue.	Mat.	Middletown, CT	Middlesex Thea.
6	Tue.	Eve.	Hartford, CT	Foot Guard Armory
7	Wed.	Mat.	Rockland, MA	Rockland Opera House
7	Wed.	Eve.	Fall River, MA	Academy of Music
8	Thu.	M/E	Providence, RI	Infantry Hall
9	Fri.	Mat.	Holyoke, MA	Holyoke Opera House
9	Fri.	Eve.	Springfield, MA	City Hall
10	Sat.	M/E	Worcester, MA	Mechanics' Hall
11	Sun.	M/E	Boston, MA	Boston Thea.
12	Mon.	Mat.	Pittsfield, MA	Academy of Music
12	Mon.	Eve.	Troy, NY	Music Hall
13	Tue.	Mat.	Gloversville, NY	Kasson Opera House
13	Tue.	Eve.	Utica, NY	Utica Opera House
14	Wed.	Mat.	Cortland, NY	Cortland Opera House
14	Wed.	Eve.	Syracuse, NY	Wieting Opera House
15	Thu.	M/E	Rochester, NY	Lyceum Thea.
16	Fri.	Eve.	Buffalo, NY	Convention Hall
17	Sat.	M/E	Cleveland, OH	Grays' Armory
18	Sun.	M/E	Detroit, MI	Detroit Opera House
19	Mon.	Eve.	Saginaw, MI	Academy of Music
20	Tue.	Mat.	Pontiac, MI	Eagle Thea. [probably]
20	Tue.	Eve.	Ann Arbor, MI	University Hall
21	Wed.	Mat.	Lansing, MI	Baird's Opera House
21	Wed.	Eve.	Grand Rapids, MI	Powers' Thea.
22	Thu.	Mat.	Coldwater, MI	Tibbits Opera House
22	Thu.	Eve.	South Bend, IN	Auditorium
23	Fri.	M/E	Chicago, IL	Grand Opera House
24	Sat.	Mat.	Chicago, IL	Auditorium
24	Sat.	Eve.	Elgin, IL	Elgin Opera House
25	Sun.	M/E	Chicago, IL	Grand Opera House
26	Mon.	Mat.	Galesburg, IL	Auditorium
26	Mon.	Eve.	Kewanee, IL	McClure's Opera House
27	Tue.	Mat.	Sterling, IL	Academy of Music
27	Tue.	Eve.	Davenport, IA	Burtis Opera House
28	Wed.	Mat.	Peoria, IL	Grand Opera House
28	Wed.	Eve.	Monmouth, IL	Pattee Opera House

MARCH

1	Thu.	Mat.	Macomb, IL	Opera House
1	Thu.	Eve.	Quincy, IL	Empire Thea.
2	Fri.	Mat.	Chillicothe, MO	Luella Thea.
2	Fri.	Eve.	St. Joseph, MO	Tootle Thea.
3	Sat.	Mat.	Lawrence, KS	Bowersock's Opera House
3	Sat.	Eve.	Topeka, KS	Grand Opera House

4	Sun.	M/E	Kansas City, MO	Convention Hall
5	Mon.	Mat.	Nebraska City, NE	Overland
5	Mon.	Eve.	Lincoln, NE	Oliver Thea.
6	Tue.	M/E	Omaha, NE	Boyd's Thea.
7	Wed.	Eve.	Sioux City, IA	Grand Opera House
8	Thu.	Mat.	Boone, IA	Aires' Opera House
8	Thu.	Eve.	Des Moines, IA	Auditorium
9	Fri.	Mat.	Iowa City, IA	Opera House
9	Fri.	Eve.	Cedar Rapids, IA	Greene's Opera House
10	Sat.	Mat.	Waterloo, IA	Brown's Opera House
10	Sat.	Eve.	Iowa Falls, IA	Metropolitan Opera House
11	Sun.	M/E	St. Paul, MN	Metropolitan Opera House
12	Mon.	M/E	Minneapolis, MN	Lyceum Thea.
13	Tue.	Mat.	Winona, MN	Winona Opera House
13	Tue.	Eve.	La Crosse, WI	La Crosse Thea.
14	Wed.	M/E	Milwaukee, WI	Davidson Thea.
15	Thu.	Mat.	Paris, IL	Schoaff's Opera House
15	Thu.	Eve.	Terre Haute, IN	Grand Opera House
16	Fri.	Mat.	Greencastle, IN	Opera House
16	Fri.	Eve.	Bloomington, IN	Indiana University Gymnasium
17	Sat.	M/E	Louisville, KY	Auditorium
18	Sun.	M/E	Cincinnati, OH	Music Hall
19	Mon.	Mat.	Chillicothe, OH	Rink
19	Mon.	Eve.	Columbus, OH	Great Southern Thea.
20	Tue.	Mat.	Marietta, OH	Auditorium
20	Tue.	Eve.	Parkersburg, WV	Auditorium
21	Wed.	Mat.	Huntington, WV	Davis Thea.
21	Wed.	Eve.	Charleston, WV	Burlew Opera House
22	Thu.	Mat.	Charlottesville, VA	Jefferson Auditorium
22	Thu.	Eve.	Staunton, VA	Opera House
23	Fri.	M/E	Norfolk, VA	Academy of Music
24	Sat.	M/E	Richmond, VA	Academy of Music
25	Sun.	M/E	Washington, DC	National Thea.
26	Mon.	Eve.	Baltimore, MD	Music Hall
27	Tue.	Mat.	Frederick, MD	City Opera House
27	Tue.	Eve.	York, PA	York Opera House
28	Wed.	Mat.	Lancaster, PA	Fulton Opera House
28	Wed.	Eve.	Lebanon, PA	Academy of Music
29	Thu.	Mat.	Pottsville, PA	Academy of Music
29	Thu.	Eve.	Reading, PA	Academy of Music
30	Fri.	Mat.	Allentown, PA	Lyric Thea
30	Fri.	Eve.	Philadelphia, PA	Academy of Music
31	Sat.	M/E	Philadelphia, PA	Academy of Music

APRIL

1	Sun.	Eve.	New York, NY	Harlem Opera House
2	Mon.	Eve.	Paterson, NJ	Armory
3	Tue.	Mat.	Hudson, NY	Opera House
3	Tue.	Eve.	Albany, NY	Jacobs' Lyceum
4	Wed.	Mat.	Plattsburgh, NY	Plattsburgh Thea.
4	Wed.	Eve.	Montreal, QUE/Canada	Her Majesty's Thea.
5	Thu.	M/E	Montreal, QUE/Canada	Her Majesty's Thea.
6	Fri.	Eve.	Watertown, NY	City Opera House
7	Sat.	Mat.	Kingston, NY	Kingston Opera House
7	Sat.	Eve.	Newburgh, NY	Academy of Music

[End of 1st 1900 tour]

1900 OFF-TOUR CONCERT

APRIL

22	Sun.	Eve.	New York, NY	Metropolitan Opera House

Soloists: Blanche Duffield, soprano; Bertha Bucklin, violin; Arthur Pryor, trombone.

2ND 1900 TOUR (Europe)

Soloists: Herbert L. Clarke, Walter B. Rogers, & Holly Wilder, cornet; Franz Helle, flugelhorn; Simone Mantia, euphonium; Arthur Pryor, trombone. [Also, for one concert only, Minne Tracy, soprano.]

APRIL

30	Mon.	Eve.	*U.S.M.S. St. Paul* [at sea]	Saloon [relief concert]

[Begin 1st segment of engagement (11 days) at Paris Exposition as official American Band]

MAY

5	Sat.	Mat.	Paris, France	Palais des Beaux Arts
6	Sun.	Mat.	Paris, France	Champ de Mars

157

7	Mon.	Mat.	Paris, France	Champ de Mars
8	Tue.	Mat.	Paris, France	Esplanade de Invalides
9	Wed.	Mat.	Paris, France	Esplanade de Invalides
10	Thu.	Mat.	Paris, France	place not known
11	Fri.	Mat.	Paris, France	place not known
12	Sat.	Mat.	Paris, France	Rue des Nations
13	Sun.	Mat.	Paris, France	place not known
14	Mon.	Mat.	Paris, France	Esplanade de Invalides
14	Mon.	Eve.	Paris, France	Ritz Hotel (dinner party)
15	Tue.	Aft.	Paris, France	a) Amer. Machinery Bldg.
				b) German Pavilion

[End 1st segment of engagement at Paris Exposition]

16	Wed.	Eve.	Brussels, Belgium	Theatre de l'Alhambra
17	Thu.	M/E	Brussels, Belgium	Theatre de l'Alhambra
18	Fri.	Eve.	Liege, Belgium	Jardin d'Acclamation
19	Sat.	Eve.	Paris, France	Ritz Hotel (private party)

Sun., 20th through Sun., 27th (8 days), Berlin, Germany. Royal Opera House and Kroll's Gardens. 2 concerts per day.
MAY-JUNE
Mon., 28 May through Mon., 4 June (8 days), Hamburg, Germany, Concerthaus. 2 concerts per day.
JUNE

5	Tue.	Eve.	Bremen, Germany	Burger Park
6	Wed.	Eve.	Bremen, Germany	Burger Park
7	Thu.	Eve.	Hannover, Germany	Tivoli
8	Fri.	Eve.	Hannover, Germany	Tivoli
9	Sat.	Eve.	Halle, Germany	Wintergarten

JUNE
Sun., 10th through Wed., 13th (4 days), Leipzig, Germany, Palm Garden. 2 concerts per day.
Thu., 14th through Sun., 17th (4 days), Dresden, Germany, Bergkeller. 2 concerts per day.

| 18 | Mon. | unk. | Nuremburg, Germany | Stadt Park |

Tue., 19th through Fri., 22nd (4 days), Munich, Germany, Kindl Keller. 2 concerts per day.

| 23 | Sat. | M/E | Wurzburg, Germany | Huttenschler Garten |
| 24 | Sun. | M/E | Bad Nauheim, Germany | Kurpark |

Mon., 25th through Wed., 27th (3 days), Frankfurt am Main, Germany, Austellungsplatz. 2 concerts per day.

| 28 | Thu. | M/E | Wiesbaden, Germany | Kurpark |

JUNE-JULY
Fri., 29 June through Sun., 1 July (3 days), Cologne, Germany, Flora Garden. 2 concerts per day.
JULY

| 2 | Mon. | Mat. | Aix-la-Chapelle, Germany | Zoological Garden |
| 2 | Mon. | Eve. | Aix-la-Chapelle, Germany | Bernhardt's Theatre |

[Begin 2nd segment of engagement (17 days) at Paris Exposition]

3	Tue.	a.m.	Paris, France	Washington Monument
3	Tue.	Mat.	Paris, France (2 concerts)	Esplanade des Invalides
4	Wed.	a.m.	Paris, France	a) Lafayette Statue
				b) Parade
4	Wed.	Mat.	Paris, France	Esplanade de Invalides
4	Wed.	Eve.	Paris, France	Place de l'Opera

Thu., 5th through Mon., 9th (5 days), Esplanade de Invalides. Daily afternoon concerts.

| 9 | Mon. | Eve. | Paris, France | Private dinner |

Tue., 10th through Thu., 19th (10 days), Esplanade de Invalides. Daily afternoon concerts

[End 2nd segment of engagement at Paris Exposition. Total 28 days at 1900 Paris Exposition.]

21	Sat.	Eve.	Heidelberg, Germany	Schloss Garden
22	Sun.	M/E	Strassburg, Germany	Orangerie
23	Mon.	M/E	Mayence, Germany	Stadthalle
24	Tue.	M/E	Stuttgart, Germany	Liederhalle
25	Wed.	M/E	Stuttgart, Germany	Liederhalle
26	Thu.	M/E	Baden Baden, Germany	Kurpark
27	Fri.	M/E	Frankfurt am Main, Germ.	Ausstellungsplatz

JULY-AUGUST
Sat., 28 July through Sun., 5 Aug. (9 days), Berlin, Germany, Royal Opera House and Kroll's Gardens. 2 concerts per day.
AUGUST

| 6 | Mon. | Eve. | Magdeburg, Germany | Concerthaus |
| 7 | Tue. | Eve. | Cassel, Germany | Stadt Park |

Wed., 8th through Sun., 12th (5 days), Frankfurt am Main, Germany, Ausstellungsplatz. 2 concerts per day.

| 13 | Mon. | Eve. | Dusseldorf, Germany | Tonhall Garden |

Tues., 14th through Thu., 16th (3 days), Cologne, Germany, Flora Garden. 2 concerts per day.

17	Fri.	Eve.	Amsterdam, Holland	Paleis voor Volksvlyt
18	Sat.	Eve.	Hague, Holland	Dierentuin
19	Sun.	Mat.	Amsterdam, Holland	Paleis voor Volksvlyt
19	Sun.	Eve.	Haarlem, Holland	Vereeniging
20	Mon.	Eve.	Breda, Holland	Concordia
21	Tue.	Eve.	Hague, Holland	Dierentuin
22	Wed.	Mat.	Nymwegen, Holland	Vereeniging
22	Wed.	Eve.	Arnheim, Holland	Musis Sacrum
23	Thu.	Eve.	Amsterdam, Holland	Paleis voor Volksvlyt
24	Fri.	Eve.	Utrecht, Holland	Tivoli
25	Sat.	Eve.	Hague, Holland	Dierentuin
26	Sun.	M/E	Amsterdam, Holland	Paleis voor Volksvlyt

SEPTEMBER

| 7 | Fri. | Eve. | *U.S.M.S. St. Louis* [at sea] | Second Cabin Saloon |

[End 1st 1900 tour (Europe)]

3RD 1900 TOUR

Soloists: Blanche Duffield, soprano; Bertha Bucklin, violin; Herbert L. Clarke & Walter B. Rogers, cornet; Franz Helle, flugelhorn; Simone Mantia, euphonium; Arthur Pryor, trombone.
SEPTEMBER

| 23 | Sun. | Eve. | New York, NY | Metropolitan Opera House |

Mon., 24th through Sat., 29th (6 days), 1st segment (of 2) of Pittsburgh Exposition. 4 concerts per day.

| 30 | Sun. | Eve. | New York, NY | Metropolitan Opera House |

[End of 3rd 1900 tour]

4TH 1900 TOUR

Soloists: Same as for 3rd 1900 tour except Louise M. Brehany for 1 concert in Oct.
OCTOBER

| 7 | Sun. | Eve. | New York, NY | Metropolitan Opera House |

Mon., 8th through Sat., 13th (6 days), Boston, 1st segment (of 2) of Merchants and Manufacturers Exposition. 2 concerts per day.

| 14 | Sun. | Eve. | New York, NY | Metropolitan Opera House |

Mon., 15th through Sat., 20th (6 days), 2nd segment (of 2) of Pittsburgh Exposition. 4 concerts per day.

| 21 | Sun. | Eve. | Brooklyn, NY | Montauk Thea. |

Mon., 22nd through Sat., 27th, (6 days), Boston, 2nd segment (of 2) of Merchants and Manufacturers Exposition. 2 concerts per day.

| 28 | Sun. | Eve. | New York, NY | Metropolitan Opera House |

[End of 4th 1900 tour]

1900 OFF-TOUR CONCERT

DECEMBER

| 30 | Sun. | Eve. | New York, NY | Metropolitan Opera House |

1ST 1901 TOUR

Soloists: Blanche Duffield, soprano; Bertha Bucklin, violin; Herbert L. Clarke & Walter B. Rogers, cornet; Franz Helle, flugelhorn; Simone Mantia, euphonium; Arthur Pryor, trombone.
JANUARY

3	Thu.	M/E	Brooklyn, NY	Academy of Music
4	Fri.	Eve.	Newark, NJ	Krueger Auditorium
5	Sat.	M/E	New York, NY	Carnegie Hall
6	Sun.	Eve.	New York, NY	Carnegie Hall
7	Mon.	Mat.	Bethlehem, PA	Opera House
7	Mon.	Eve.	Reading, PA	Academy of Music
8	Tue.	Mat.	Mauch Chunk, PA	Mauch Chunk Opera House
8	Tue.	Eve.	Wilkes-Barre, PA	Nesbitt Thea.
9	Wed.	M/E	Scranton, PA	Lyceum Thea.
10	Thu.	Mat.	Hazleton, PA	Grand Opera House
10	Thu.	Eve.	Shamokin, PA	G.A.R. Opera House
11	Fri.	Mat.	York, PA	York Opera House
11	Fri.	Eve.	Baltimore, MD	Music Hall
12	Sat.	M/E	Philadelphia, PA	Academy of Music
13	Sun.	Eve.	Washington, DC	National Thea.
14	Mon.	M/E	Richmond, VA	Academy of Music
15	Tue.	Mat.	Newport News, VA	Academy of Music

15	Tue.	Eve.	Norfolk, VA	Academy of Music
16	Wed.	Mat.	Durham, NC	Opera House
16	Wed.	Eve.	Raleigh, NC	Academy of Music
17	Thu.	Mat.	Spartanburg, SC	Converse College
17	Thu.	Eve.	Asheville, NC	Grand Opera House
18	Fri.	Mat.	Bristol, TN	Harmeling Thea.
18	Fri.	Eve.	Knoxville, TN	Staub's Thea.
19	Sat.	M/E	Chattanooga, TN	Chattanooga Opera House
21	Mon.	Mat.	Rome, GA	Opera House
21	Mon.	Eve.	Anniston, AL	Noble Street Opera House
22	Tue.	M/E	Birmingham, AL	Jefferson Thea.
23	Wed.	Mat.	Columbia, TN	Grand Opera House
23	Wed.	Eve.	Nashville, TN	Vendome Thea.
24	Thu.	M/E	Memphis, TN	Lyceum Thea.
25	Fri.	Mat.	Springfield, MO	Baldwin Thea.
25	Fri.	Eve.	Carthage, MO	Opera House
26	Sat.	Mat.	Joplin, MO	Club Thea.
26	Sat.	Eve.	Pittsburg, KS	Opera House
27	Sun.	M/E	Kansas City, MO	Convention Hall
28	Mon.	Mat.	Richmond, MO	Farris Thea.
28	Mon.	Eve.	St. Joseph, MO	Tootle Thea.
29	Tue.	M/E	Des Moines, IA	Auditorium
30	Wed.	M/E	Omaha, NE	Boyd's Thea.
31	Thu.	Mat.	Fremont, NE	Love's Thea.
31	Thu.	Eve.	Lincoln, NE	Oliver Thea.

FEBRUARY

1	Fri.	Mat.	York, NE	Auditorium
1	Fri.	Eve.	Hastings, NE	Kerr Opera House
2	Sat.	Mat.	Grand Island, NE	Bartenbach's Opera House
2	Sat.	Eve.	Kearney, NE	Kearney Opera House
3	Sun.	M/E	Denver, CO	Broadway Thea.
4	Mon.	M/E	Denver, CO	Broadway Thea.
5	Tue.	Mat.	Colorado Springs, CO	Opera House
5	Tue.	Eve.	Pueblo, CO	Grand Opera House
6	Wed.	Mat.	Canon City, CO	Canon City Opera House
6	Wed.	Eve.	Cripple Creek, CO	Grand Opera House
7	Thu.	Mat.	Glenwood Springs, CO	Opera House
7	Thu.	Eve.	Grand Junction, CO	Park Opera House
8	Fri.	M/E	Salt Lake City, UT	Tabernacle
10	Sun.	Eve.	San Francisco, CA	Alhambra Thea.
11	Mon.	M/E	San Jose, CA	Victory Thea.
12	Tue.	M/E	Oakland, CA	Macdonough Thea.

Wed., 13th thru Sat., 16th (4 days), San Francisco, CA, Alhambra Thea.
2 concerts per day.

17	Sun.	Eve.	Oakland, CA	Macdonough Thea.
18	Mon.	Eve.	Fresno, CA	Barton Opera House
19	Tue.	Mat.	Ventura, CA	Ventura Opera House
19	Tue.	Eve.	Santa Barbara, CA	Opera House
20	Wed.	Mat.	Redlands, CA	Academy of Music
20	Wed.	Eve.	Riverside, CA	Loring Thea.
21	Thu.	Mat.	Santa Ana, CA	Grand Opera House
21	Thu.	Eve.	Los Angeles, CA	Hazard's Pavilion
22	Fri.	M/E	Los Angeles, CA	Hazard's Pavilion
23	Sat.	M/E	Los Angeles, CA	Hazard's Pavilion
24	Sun.	Eve.	Sacramento, CA	Clunie Thea.
26	Tue.	M/E	Portland, OR	Marquam Grand
27	Wed.	Mat.	Olympia, WA	Olympia Thea.
27	Wed.	Eve.	Tacoma, WA	Tacoma Thea.
28	Thu.	M/E	Seattle, WA	Seattle Thea.

MARCH

1	Fri.	M/E	Spokane, WA	Auditorium
2	Sat.	M/E	Butte, MT	Grand Opera House
4	Mon.	Mat.	Crookston, MN	Grand Opera House
4	Mon.	Eve.	Grand Forks, ND	Metropolitan Opera House
5	Tue.	M/E	Winnipeg, MAN/Canada	Winnipeg Thea.
6	Wed.	M/E	Fargo, ND	Fargo Opera House
7	Thu.	Mat.	Little Falls, MN	Grand Opera House
7	Thu.	Eve.	St. Cloud, MN	Davidson Opera House
8	Fri.	Mat.	West Superior, WI	Grand Opera House
8	Fri.	Eve.	Duluth, MN	Lyceum Thea.
9	Sat.	M/E	Minneapolis, MN	Lyceum Thea.
10	Sun.	M/E	St. Paul, MN	Metropolitan Opera House
11	Mon.	Mat.	Austin, MN	Opera House
11	Mon.	Eve.	Albert Lea, MN	Albert Lea Opera House
12	Tue.	Mat.	Marshalltown, IA	Odeon Thea.

12	Tue.	Eve.	Cedar Rapids, IA	Greene's Opera House
13	Wed.	Mat.	Muscatine, IA	Grand Opera House
13	Wed.	Eve.	Davenport, IA	Burtis Opera House
14	Thu.	Mat.	Freeport, IL	Grand Opera House
14	Thu.	Eve.	Rockford, IL	Grand Opera House
15	Fri.	Eve.	Chicago, IL	Auditorium
16	Sat.	M/E	Chicago, IL	Auditorium
17	Sun.	M/E	Milwaukee, WI	Davidson Thea.
18	Mon.	Mat.	Lafayette, IN	Grand Opera House
18	Mon.	Eve.	Indianapolis, IN	Tomlinson Hall
19	Tue.	M/E	Louisville, KY	Auditorium
20	Wed.	Mat.	Greensburg, IN	Grand Opera House
20	Wed.	Eve.	Cincinnati, OH	Music Hall
21	Thu.	Mat.	Muncie, IN	Wysor's Grand Op. House
21	Thu.	Eve.	Fort Wayne, IN	Masonic Temple
22	Fri.	Mat.	Kalamazoo, MI	Academy of Music
22	Fri.	Eve.	Grand Rapids, MI	Powers' Thea.
23	Sat.	Mat.	Battle Creek, MI	Hamblin's Opera House
23	Sat.	Eve.	Ann Arbor, MI	University Hall
24	Sun.	Mat.	Detroit, MI	Lyceum Thea.
24	Sun.	Eve.	Toledo, OH	Lyceum Thea.
25	Mon.	Eve.	Buffalo, NY	Convention Hall
26	Tue.	M/E	Buffalo, NY	Convention Hall
27	Wed.	M/E	Cleveland, OH	Grays' Armory
28	Thu.	M/E	Rochester, NY	Lyceum Thea.
29	Fri.	Mat.	Washington, DC	National Thea.
29	Fri.	Eve.	Baltimore, MD	Music Hall
30	Sat.	M/E	Philadelphia, PA	Academy of Music
31	Sun.	Eve.	New York, NY	Metropolitan Opera House

[End of 1st 1901 tour]

2ND 1901 TOUR

Soloists: Before Willow Grove engagement, same as for 1st 1900 tour.

APRIL

7	Sun.	Eve.	New York, NY	Metropolitan Opera House
8	Mon.	Mat.	Albany, NY	Odd Fellows Hall
8	Mon.	Eve.	Troy, NY	Music Hall
9	Tue.	Mat.	Bennington, VT	Bennington Opera House
9	Tue.	Eve.	North Adams, MA	Richmond Thea.
10	Wed.	Mat.	Leominster, MA	Leominster Opera House
10	Wed.	Eve.	Fitchburg, MA	Cumings' Thea.
11	Thu.	Mat.	Clinton, MA	Town Hall
11	Thu.	Eve.	Lawrence, MA	Grand Opera House
12	Fri.	Mat.	Lynn, MA	Lynn Thea.
12	Fri.	Eve.	Boston, MA	Symphony Hall
13	Sat.	M/E	Worcester, MA	Mechanics' Hall
14	Sun.	Eve.	Boston, MA	Symphony Hall
15	Mon.	Eve.	Lewiston, ME	City Hall
16	Tue.	M/E	Portland, ME	Jefferson Thea.
17	Wed.	Mat.	Newburyport, MA	City Hall
17	Wed.	Eve.	Boston, MA	Symphony Hall
18	Thu.	M/E	Providence, RI	Infantry Hall
19	Fri.	M/E	Hartford, CT	Foot Guard Armory
20	Sat.	M/E	New Haven, CT	Hyperion Thea.
21	Sun.	Eve.	New York, NY	Metropolitan Opera House
22	Mon.	Eve.	Paterson, NJ	Armory
23	Tue.	Mat.	Willimantic, CT	Loomer Opera House
23	Tue.	Eve.	Putnam, CT	Bradley Thea.
24	Wed.	Mat.	New London, CT	Lyceum Thea.
24	Wed.	Eve.	Norwich, CT	Broadway Thea.
25	Thu.	Mat.	Middleboro, MA	City Hall
25	Thu.	Eve.	Fall River, MA	Academy of Music
26	Fri.	Mat.	Attleboro, MA	Bates Opera House
26	Fri.	Eve.	Taunton, MA	Taunton Thea.
27	Sat.	Mat.	Boston, MA	Symphony Hall
27	Sat.	Eve.	Brockton, MA	City Opera House
28	Sun.	Eve.	Boston, MA	Symphony Hall
29	Mon.	Mat.	Rockland, MA	Rockland Opera House
29	Mon.	Eve.	New Bedford, MA	New Bedford Thea.
30	Tue.	Mat.	Salem, MA	Salem Thea.
30	Tue.	Eve.	Boston, MA	Symphony Hall

MAY

| 1 | Wed. | Mat. | Lebanon, NH | Opera House |
| 1 | Wed. | Eve. | St. Johnsbury, VT | Music Hall |

2	Thu.	Mat.	Montpelier, VT	Blanchard Opera House
2	Thu.	Eve.	Burlington, VT	Howard Opera House
3	Fri.	M/E	Montreal, QUE/Canada	Arena
4	Sat.	Mat.	Ogdensburg, NY	Opera House
4	Sat.	Eve.	Watertown, NY	City Opera House
5	Sun.	Eve.	Rochester, NY	Lyceum Thea.
6	Mon.	Mat.	Jamestown, NY	Samuels Opera House
6	Mon.	Eve.	Meadville, PA	Academy of Music
7	Tue.	Mat.	New Castle, PA	Opera House
7	Tue.	Eve.	Sharon, PA	Morgan Grand Opera House
8	Wed.	M/E	Cleveland, OH	Grays' Armory
9	Thu.	Mat.	Marion, OH	Grand Opera House
9	Thu.	Eve.	Lima, OH	Faurot Opera House
10	Fri.	Eve.	Chicago, IL	Auditorium
11	Sat.	M/E	Chicago, IL	Auditorium
12	Sun.	Eve.	Chicago, IL	Auditorium
13	Mon.	Mat.	Luddington, MI	Luddington Opera House
13	Mon.	Eve.	Manistee, MI	Opera House
14	Tue.	Mat.	Big Rapids, MI	Opera House
14	Tue.	Eve.	Muskegon, MI	Muskegon Opera House
15	Wed.	Mat.	Grand Rapids, MI	Powers' Thea.
15	Wed.	Eve.	Lansing, MI	Baird's Opera House
16	Thu.	Mat.	Flint, MI	Stone's Opera House
16	Thu.	Eve.	Port Huron, MI	City Opera House
17	Fri.	Mat.	Stratford, ONT/Canada	Albert Thea.
17	Fri.	Eve.	Guelph, ONT/Canada	Guelph Opera House
18	Sat.	M/E	Toronto, ONT/Canada	Massey Music Hall
19	Sun.	Eve.	Buffalo, NY	Teck Thea.
20	Mon.	Mat.	Warren, PA	Library Thea.
20	Mon.	Eve.	Bradford, PA	Wagner Opera House
21	Tue.	Mat.	Ridgway, PA	Ridgway Thea.
21	Tue.	Eve.	Du Bois, PA	Fuller Opera House
22	Wed.	M/E	Pittsburgh, PA	Duquesne Garden
23	Thu.	Mat.	Johnstown, PA	Cambria Thea.
23	Thu.	Eve.	Altoona, PA	11th Ave. Opera House
24	Fri.	Mat.	Harrisburg, PA	Grand Opera House
24	Fri.	Eve.	Lancaster, PA	Fulton Opera House

MAY-JUNE

Sat., 25 May through Sun., 9 June (16 days), Willow Grove (PA) Park. 4 concerts per day.

Soloists: Herbert L. Clarke & Walter B. Rogers, cornet; Franz Helle, flugelhorn; Simone Mantia, euphonium; Arthur Pryor, trombone; Marshall P. Lufsky, piccolo.

JUNE-JULY

Mon., 10 June through Sat., 6 July (27 days), Buffalo, NY, Pan-American Exposition. 2 concerts per day.

Soloists: Herbert L. Clarke & Walter B. Rogers, cornet; Franz Helle, flugelhorn; Simone Mantia, euphonium; Arthur Pryor, trombone.

[End of 2nd 1901 tour]

JULY-SEPTEMBER, 1901

Sun., 7 July through Mon., 2 Sept. (58 days), Brooklyn, NY, Manhattan Beach. 2 concerts per day.

Soloists: Herbert L. Clarke, Walter B. Rogers, & Henry Higgins, cornet; Franz Helle, flugelhorn; Simone Mantia, euphonium; Arthur Pryor, trombone; Marshall P. Lufsky, piccolo; Joseph Norrito & Louis Christie, clarinet.

3RD 1901 TOUR

SEPTEMBER

3	Tue.	Eve.	Huntingdon, PA	Opera House

Wed., 4th through Tue., 17th (12 days), Pittsburgh Exposition. 4 concerts per day except no concerts on Sun., 8th & Sun., 15th.

Soloists: Soloists: Herbert L. Clarke & Walter B. Rogers, cornet; Franz Helle, flugelhorn; Bernhardt Baumgartel, horn; Simone Mantia, euphonium; Arthur Pryor, trombone; Marshall P. Lufsky, piccolo.

Soloists for remainder of tour: Blanche Duffield, soprano; Herbert L. Clarke & Walter B. Rogers, cornet; Franz Helle, flugelhorn; Arthur Pryor, trombone; Marshall P. Lufsky, piccolo.

SEPTEMBER

18	Wed.	M/E	Indianapolis, IN	Indiana State Fair
19	Thu.	M/E	Indianapolis, IN	Indiana State Fair
20	Fri.	Mat.	Xenia, OH	Opera House
20	Fri.	Eve.	Columbus, OH	Great Southern Thea.
21	Sat.	M/E	Wheeling, WV	West Virginia State Fair
22	Sun.	Eve.	New York, NY	Metropolitan Opera House

[End of 3rd 1901 tour]

4TH 1901 TOUR (England and Scotland)

Soloists: Minnie Tracy & Maud Reese Davies, soprano; Dorothy Hoyle, violin; Arthur Pryor, trombone.

SEPTEMBER

30	Mon.	Eve.	U.S.M.S. St. Louis [at sea]	Main Saloon

OCTOBER

4	Fri.	Eve.	London, England	Albert Hall
5	Sat.	M/E	London, England	Albert Hall

OCTOBER-NOVEMBER

Mon., 7 Oct. through Sat., 2 Nov. (27 days), Glasgow, Scotland, Glasgow Exhibition. 2 concerts per day.

NOVEMBER

3	Sun.	Eve.	Middlesborough, England	Town Hall
4	Mon.	Mat.	Middlesborough, England	Town Hall
4	Mon.	Eve.	Tynemouth, England	Tynemouth Palace
5	Tue.	M/E	Newcastle-on-Tyne, Engl.	Town Hall
6	Wed.	M/E	Halifax, England	Victoria Hall
7	Thu.	M/E	Huddersfield, England	Town Hall
8	Fri.	M/E	Leeds, England	Victoria Hall
9	Sat.	M/E	Liverpool, England	Philharmonic Hall
11	Mon.	Mat.	Southport, England	Cambridge Hall
11	Mon.	Eve.	Preston, England	Public Hall
12	Tue.	M/E	Blackpool, England	Winter Gardens
13	Wed.	M/E	Sheffield, England	Albert Hall
14	Thu.	M/E	Bradford, England	St. George's Hall
15	Fri.	Eve.	Manchester, England	Free Trade Hall
16	Sat.	M/E	Manchester, England	Free Trade Hall
18	Mon.	M/E	Nottingham, England	Albert Hall
19	Tue.	M/E	Wolverhampton, England	Agricultural Hall
20	Wed.	M/E	Birmingham, England	Town Hall
21	Thu.	Mat.	Oxford, England	Town Hall
21	Thu.	Eve.	Bath, England	Assembly Rooms
22	Fri.	M/E	Bristol, England	Colston Hall

Sat., 23 Nov. through Sat., 7 Dec. (14 days), London, England. Afternoon concerts at Empire Thea. and evening concerts at Covent Garden except for eve. of Sun., 1 Dec. for command performance at Sandringham Castle in Sandringham, England.

DECEMBER

9	Mon.	M/E	London, England	Crystal Palace
10	Tue.	M/E	Brighton, England	Brighton Dome
11	Wed.	M/E	Bournemouth, England	Winter Gardens
12	Thu.	M/E	Cheltenham, England	Winter Gardens
13	Fri.	M/E	Southampton, England	Philharmonic Hall

[End of 4th 1901 tour]

1901 OFF-TOUR CONCERT

DECEMBER

22	Sun.	Eve.	New York, NY	Herald Square Thea.

Soloists: Maud Reese Davies, soprano; Dorothy Hoyle, violin; Arthur Pryor, trombone.

1ST 1902 TOUR

Soloists: Maud Reese Davies & Blondelle Ver Trees, soprano; Dorothy Hoyle & Ruby Gerard-Braun, violin; Walter B. Rogers, cornet; Arthur Pryor, trombone; Marshall P. Lufsky, piccolo.

JANUARY

11	Sat.	Eve.	New York, NY	22nd Regiment Armory
12	Sun.	Eve.	New York, NY	Herald Square Thea.
13	Mon.	Mat.	Albany, NY	Empire Thea.
13	Mon.	Eve.	Troy, NY	Music Hall
14	Tue.	Mat.	Greenfield, MA	Opera House
14	Tue.	Eve.	Northampton, MA	Academy of Music
15	Wed.	Mat.	Brattleboro, VT	Auditorium
15	Wed.	Eve.	Bellows Falls, VT	Opera House
16	Thu.	Mat.	Lebanon, NH	Opera House
16	Thu.	Eve.	St. Johnsbury, VT	Howe Opera House
17	Fri.	Mat.	Keene, NH	Opera House
17	Fri.	Eve.	Fitchburg, MA	Cumings' Thea.
18	Sat.	M/E	Worcester, MA	Mechanics' Hall

19	Sun.	Eve.	Boston, MA	Symphony Hall
20	Mon.	Eve.	Lewiston, ME	City Hall
21	Tue.	M/E	Portland, ME	Jefferson Thea.
22	Wed.	M/E	Boston, MA	Symphony Hall
23	Thu.	M/E	Providence, RI	Infantry Hall
24	Fri.	M/E	Hartford, CT	Foot Guard Armory
25	Sat.	Mat.	Meriden, CT	Opera House
25	Sat.	Eve.	New Haven, CT	Hyperion Thea.
26	Sun.	Mat.	New York, NY	Star Thea.
26	Sun.	Eve.	New York, NY	Herald Square Thea.
27	Mon.	Unk.	New York, NY	Private engagement
28	Tue.	M/E	Scranton, PA	Armory
29	Wed.	Mat.	Elizabeth, NJ	Jacobs Thea.
29	Wed.	Eve.	Trenton, NJ	Taylor Opera House
30	Thu.	M/E	Baltimore, MD	Music Hall
31	Fri.	Eve.	Philadelphia, PA	Academy of Music

FEBRUARY

1	Sat.	Mat.	Philadelphia, PA	Academy of Music
1	Sat.	Eve.	Wilmington, DE	Grand Opera House
2	Sun.	Eve.	Washington, DC	Columbia Thea.
3	Mon.	Mat.	Fredericksburg, VA	Opera House
3	Mon.	Eve.	Richmond, VA	Academy of Music
4	Tue.	Mat.	Newport News, VA	Academy of Music
4	Tue.	Eve.	Norfolk, VA	Academy of Music
5	Wed.	Mat.	Lynchburg, VA	Opera House
5	Wed.	Eve.	Roanoke, VA	Academy of Music
6	Thu.	Mat.	Greensboro, NC	Grand Opera House
6	Thu.	Eve.	Raleigh, NC	Academy of Music
7	Fri.	Mat.	Fayetteville, NC	Opera House
7	Fri.	Eve.	Wilmington, NC	Opera House
8	Sat.	Mat.	Columbia, SC	Columbia Thea.
8	Sat.	Eve.	Augusta, GA	Grand Opera House
10	Mon.	Eve.	Charleston, SC	Academy of Music
11	Tue.	M/E	Savannah, GA	Savannah Thea.
12	Wed.	Mat.	Milledgeville, GA	Opera House
12	Wed.	Eve.	Macon, GA	Academy of Music
13	Thu.	Mat.	Athens, GA	Opera House
13	Thu.	Eve.	Atlanta, GA	Grand Opera House
14	Fri.	Mat.	Anniston, AL	Noble Street Opera House
14	Fri.	Eve.	Birmingham, AL	Jefferson Thea.
15	Sat.	M/E	Mobile, AL	Mobile Thea.
16	Sun.	Eve.	New Orleans, LA	Tulane Thea.
17	Mon.	Mat.	Jackson, MS	Century Thea.
17	Mon.	Eve.	Yazoo City, MS	Citizens' Opera House
18	Tue.	Mat.	Greenwood, MS	Opera House
18	Tue.	Eve.	Greenville, MS	Grand Opera House
19	Wed.	Mat.	Helena, AR	Opera House
19	Wed.	Eve.	Memphis, TN	Lyceum Thea.
20	Thu.	Mat.	Texarkana, TX	Grand Opera House
20	Thu.	Eve.	Shreveport, LA	Grand Opera House
21	Fri.	M/E	Beaumont, TX	Kyle Thea.
22	Sat.	Mat.	Galveston, TX	Grand Opera House
22	Sat.	Eve.	Houston, TX	Sweeny & Combs Opera House
23	Sun.	Eve.	San Antonio, TX	Grand Opera House
24	Mon.	Eve.	Austin, TX	Hancock Opera House
25	Tue.	Mat.	Temple, TX	Exchange Opera House
25	Tue.	Eve.	Waco, TX	Auditorium
26	Wed.	Mat.	Fort Worth, TX	Greenwall's Opera House
26	Wed.	Eve.	Dallas, TX	Opera House
27	Thu.	Mat.	Greenville, TX	Opera House
27	Thu.	Eve.	Denison, TX	Opera House
28	Fri.	Mat.	Galena, KS	Sapp's Opera House
28	Fri.	Eve.	Joplin, MO	Club Thea.

MARCH

1	Sat.	Mat.	Nevada, MO	Moore's Opera House
1	Sat.	Eve.	Fort Scott, KS	Auditorium
2	Sun.	M/E	Kansas City, MO	Convention Hall
3	Mon.	Mat.	Beatrice, NE	Paddock Opera House
3	Mon.	Eve.	Lincoln, NE	Oliver Thea.
4	Tue.	M/E	Omaha, NE	Boyd's Thea.
5	Wed.	Mat.	Norfolk, NE	Auditorium
5	Wed.	Eve.	Sioux City, IA	Grand Opera House
6	Thu.	Mat.	Fort Dodge, IA	Midland Opera House
6	Thu.	Eve.	Des Moines, IA	Auditorium

7	Fri.	Eve.	Chicago, IL	Auditorium
8	Sat.	M/E	Chicago, IL	Auditorium
9	Sun.	Eve.	Chicago, IL	Auditorium
10	Mon.	Mat.	Watertown, WI	Turner Opera House
10	Mon.	Eve.	Fond du Lac, WI	Crescent Opera House
11	Tue.	Mat.	Berlin, WI	Waverly Hall
11	Tue.	Eve.	Oshkosh, WI	Grand Opera House
12	Wed.	Mat.	Appleton, WI	Congregational Church
12	Wed.	Eve.	Green Bay, WI	Green Bay Thea.
13	Thu.	Mat.	Oconto, WI	Turner Opera House
13	Thu.	Eve.	Marinette, WI	Scott Thea.
14	Fri.	Mat.	Escanaba, MI	Peterson Opera House
14	Fri.	Eve.	Marquette, MI	Marquette Opera House
15	Sat.	M/E	Calumet, MI	Calumet Thea.
16	Sun.	Eve.	Ashland, WI	Grand Opera House
17	Mon.	Mat.	West Superior, WI	Grand Opera House
17	Mon.	Eve.	Duluth, MN	Lyceum Thea.
18	Tue.	Mat.	St. Paul, MN	Metropolitan Opera House
18	Tue.	Eve.	Minneapolis, MN	Lyceum Thea.
19	Wed.	Mat.	Stillwater, MN	Grand Opera House
19	Wed.	Eve.	Eau Claire, WI	Grand Opera House
20	Thu.	Mat.	Stevens Point, WI	Opera House
20	Thu.	Eve.	Wausau, WI	Grand Opera House
21	Fri.	Mat.	Portage, WI	Portage Opera House
21	Fri.	Eve.	Madison, WI	Fuller Opera House
22	Sat.	M/E	Milwaukee, WI	Davidson Thea.
23	Sun.	Mat.	Bloomington, IL	Grand Opera House
23	Sun.	Eve.	Decatur, IL	Powers' Grand Op. House
24	Mon.	M/E	St. Louis, MO	Odeon Thea.
25	Tue.	Mat.	Vincennes, IN	McJimsey's Thea.
25	Tue.	Eve.	Evansville, IN	Grand Opera House
26	Wed.	M/E	Louisville, KY	Macauley's Thea.
27	Thu.	Mat.	Frankfort, KY	Capital Thea.
27	Thu.	Eve.	Lexington, KY	Lexington Opera House
28	Fri.	Mat.	Cincinnati, OH	Music Hall
28	Fri.	Eve.	Maysville, KY	Washington Opera House
29	Sat.	Mat.	Huntington, WV	Huntington Thea.
29	Sat.	Eve.	Charleston, WV	Burlew Opera House
30	Sun.	Eve.	Washington, DC	National Thea.
31	Mon.	Eve.	Baltimore, MD	Music Hall

APRIL

1	Tue.	Eve.	Brooklyn, NY	Academy of Music
2	Wed.	Mat.	Middletown, NY	Armory
2	Wed.	Eve.	Newark, NJ	Krueger Auditorium

[End of 1st 1902 tour]

1902 OFF-TOUR CONCERTS

APRIL

6	Sun.	Mat.	New York, NY	Star Thea.

Soloists: Blondelle Vertreese, soprano; Ruby Gerard-Braun, violin; Arthur Pryor, trombone.

6	Sun.	Eve.	New York, NY	Metropolitan Opera House

Soloists same as for matinee.

2ND 1902 TOUR

Soloists before Willow Grove engagement: Lucille Jocelyn, soprano; Marguerite de Fritsch, violin; Arthur Pryor, trombone.

MAY

11	Sun.	Mat.	New York, NY	Metropolis Thea.
11	Sun.	Eve.	New York, NY	Metropolitan Opera House
12	Mon.	Mat.	Utica, NY	Majestic Thea.
12	Mon.	Eve.	Syracuse, NY	Wieting Opera House
13	Tue.	Mat.	Auburn, NY	Burtis Opera House
13	Tue.	Eve.	Rochester, NY	Lyceum Thea.
14	Wed.	M/E	Buffalo, NY	Convention Hall
15	Thu.	Mat.	Dunkirk, NY	Nelson Opera House
15	Thu.	Eve.	Erie, PA	Park Opera House
16	Fri.	Mat.	Youngstown, OH	Opera House
16	Fri.	Eve.	Akron, OH	Colonial Thea.
17	Sat.	M/E	Cleveland, OH	Grays' Armory
18	Sun.	M/E	Detroit, MI	Lyceum Thea.
19	Mon.	Mat.	Chatham, ONT/Canada	Grand Opera House
19	Mon.	Eve.	London, ONT/Canada	Grand Opera House
20	Tue.	Mat.	Woodstock, ONT/Canada	Opera House

20	Tue.	Eve.	Brantford, ONT/Canada	Drill Hall
21	Wed.	Mat.	Hamilton, ONT/Canada	Drill Hall
21	Wed.	Eve.	Toronto, ONT/Canada	Massey Music Hall
22	Thu.	Mat.	Belleville, ONT/Canada	Carman Opera House
22	Thu.	Eve.	Kingston, ONT/Canada	Rink
23	Fri.	Mat.	Brockville, ONT/Canada	Grand Opera House
23	Fri.	Eve.	Ottawa, ONT/Canada	Rideau Rink
24	Sat.	M/E	Montreal, QUE/Canada	Arena
25	Sun.	Eve.	Three Rivers, QUE/Canada	Rink
26	Mon.	M/E	Quebec, QUE/Canada	Quebec Rink
27	Tue.	Mat.	Claremont, NH	Opera House
27	Tue.	Eve.	Concord, NH	Opera House
28	Wed.	Mat.	Franklin, NH	Franklin Opera House
28	Wed.	Eve.	Manchester, NH	Manchester Opera House
29	Thu.	Mat.	Athol, MA	Academy of Music
29	Thu.	Eve.	Springfield, MA	City Hall

MAY-JUNE

Fri., 30 May through Sun., 15 June (17 days), Willow Grove (PA) Park. 4 concerts per day.

Soloists: Lucille Jocelyn, soprano; Marguerite de Fritsch, violin; Walter B. Rogers & Emil Kenecke, cornet; Franz Helle, flugelhorn; Simone Mantia, euphonium; Arthur Pryor & Arthur Bauer, trombone; Darius Lyons, flute; Giacomo Norrito, piccolo; A. Bertram, oboe; Jean H.B. Moeremans, saxophone.

[End of 2nd 1902 tour]

3RD 1902 TOUR

JUNE-AUGUST

Sat., 28 June through Sun., 31 Aug. (85 days), Atlantic City, NJ, Steel Pier. 4 concerts per day.

Soloists: Lucille Jocelyn, Blanche Duffield, Estelle Liebling, Nettie Vester, & Ruby Powell, soprano; T. Vassey, tenor; Karl Stall, baritone; Marguerite de Fritsch & Grace Jenkins, violin; Walter B. Rogers & Emil Kenecke, cornet; Franz Helle, flugelhorn; R. Crasz, horn; Simone Mantia, euphonium; Arthur Pryor, trombone; Darius Lyons, flute; Marshall P. Lufsky, piccolo; Joseph Norrito, clarinet; Jean H.B. Moeremans, saxophone.

SEPTEMBER

| 2 | Tue. | Mat. | Hagerstown, MD | Academy of Music |
| 2 | Tue. | Eve. | Winchester, VA | Auditorium |

Wed., 3rd through Tue., 16th, Pittsburgh Exposition. 4 concerts per day except 2 on opening day and no concerts on Sun. 7th & Sun. 14th.

Soloists: Estelle Liebling, soprano; Grace Courtney Jenkins, violin; Walter B. Rogers & Emil Kenecke, cornet; Franz Helle, flugelhorn; Arthur Pryor, trombone.

Soloists for remainder of tour same as Pittsburgh Exposition.

SEPTEMBER

17	Wed.	M/E	Indianapolis, IN	Indiana State Fair
18	Thu.	Mat.	Indianapolis, IN	Indiana State Fair
18	Thu.	Eve.	Indianapolis, IN	Tomlinson Hall
19	Fri.	Mat.	Bloomington, IL	Grand Opera House
19	Fri.	Eve.	Peoria, IL	Coliseum
20	Sat.	M/E	Peoria, IL	Coliseum
21	Sun.	Eve.	Peoria, IL	Coliseum
22	Mon.	Mat.	Abingdon, IL	Illinois Opera House
22	Mon.	Eve.	Galesburg, IL	Auditorium
23	Tue.	Mat.	Streator, IL	Plumb Opera House
23	Tue.	Eve.	Joliet, IL	Joliet Thea.
24	Wed.	Mat.	Ottawa, IL	Farrell's Thea.
24	Wed.	Eve.	Aurora, IL	Grand Opera House
25	Thu.	M/E	Milwaukee, WI	Davidson Thea.
26	Fri.	Eve.	Chicago, IL	Auditorium
27	Sat.	M/E	Chicago, IL	Auditorium
28	Sun.	Eve.	Chicago, IL	Auditorium
29	Mon.	Mat.	Clinton, IA	Economic Thea.
29	Mon.	Eve.	Dubuque, IA	Grand Opera House
30	Tue.	Mat.	Prairie du Chien, WI	Metropolitan Thea.
30	Tue.	Eve.	La Crosse, WI	La Crosse Thea.

OCTOBER

1	Wed.	M/E	St. Paul, MN	Auditorium
2	Thu.	M/E	Minneapolis, MN	Lyceum Thea.
3	Fri.	Mat.	Jamestown, ND	Opera House
3	Fri.	Eve.	Bismarck, ND	Anthenaeum
4	Sat.	Mat.	Billings, MT	Opera House

4	Sat.	Eve.	Livingston, MT	Hefferlin Opera House
5	Sun.	Mat.	Bozeman, MT	Bozeman Opera House
5	Sun.	Eve.	Helena, MT	Helena Thea.
6	Mon.	M/E	Butte, MT	Sutton's Broadway Thea.
7	Tue.	M/E	Spokane, WA	Auditorium
8	Wed.	M/E	Tacoma, WA	Tacoma Thea.
9	Thu.	M/E	Seattle, WA	Grand Opera House
10	Fri.	M/E	Portland, OR	Marquam Grand
11	Sat.	Mat.	Albany, OR	Albany Opera House
11	Sat.	Eve.	Salem, OR	Grand Opera House
13	Mon.	Mat.	Marysville, CA	Marysville Thea.
13	Mon.	Eve.	Sacramento, CA	Clunie Thea.
14	Tue.	Mat.	Sacramento, CA	Clunie Thea.
14	Tue.	Eve.	Stockton, CA	Yosemite Thea.
15	Wed.	M/E	Oakland, CA	MacDonough Thea.
16	Thu.	M/E	San Jose, CA	Victory Thea.

Fri., 17th through Sun. 19th (3 days), San Francisco, CA, Alhambra Thea. 2 concerts per day.

20	Mon.	Eve.	San Luis Obispo, CA	Pavilion Thea.
21	Tue.	Mat.	Ventura, CA	Ventura Opera House
21	Tue.	Eve.	Santa Barbara, CA	Opera House
22	Wed.	Mat.	Redlands, CA	Armory
22	Wed.	Eve.	Riverside, CA	Loring Thea.
23	Thu.	Mat.	Santa Ana, CA	Grand Opera House
23	Thu.	Eve.	Los Angeles, CA	Hazard's Pavilion
24	Fri.	M/E	Los Angeles, CA	Hazard's Pavilion
25	Sat.	M/E	Los Angeles, CA	Hazard's Pavilion
27	Mon.	M/E	Phoenix, AZ	Dorris Thea.
28	Tue.	M/E	Tucson, AZ	Tucson Opera House
29	Wed.	M/E	El Paso, TX	Myar Opera House
30	Thu.	Mat.	Albuquerque, NM	Colombo Hall
30	Thu.	Eve.	Santa Fe, NM	Loretta Hall
31	Fri.	Mat.	Trinidad, CO	Jaffe Opera House
31	Fri.	Eve.	La Junta, CO	La Junta Thea.

NOVEMBER

1	Sat.	M/E	Denver, CO	Broadway Thea.
2	Sun.	M/E	Denver, CO	Broadway Thea.
3	Mon.	Mat.	Victor, CO	Victor Opera House
3	Mon.	Eve.	Cripple Creek, CO	Grand Opera House
4	Tue.	M/E	Colorado Springs, CO	Opera House
5	Wed.	Mat.	Canon City, CO	Canon City Opera House
5	Wed.	Eve.	Pueblo, CO	Grand Opera House
6	Thu.	Mat.	Hutchinson, KS	Home Thea.
6	Thu.	Eve.	Wichita, KS	Toler Auditorium
7	Fri.	Mat.	Strong City, KS	Strong City Auditorium
7	Fri.	Eve.	Topeka, KS	City Auditorium
8	Sat.	Mat.	Lawrence, KS	Bowersock's Opera House
8	Sat.	Eve.	Ottawa, KS	Rohrbaugh Thea.
9	Sun.	M/E	Kansas City, MO	Willis Wood Thea.
10	Mon.	Mat.	Richmond, MO	Dougherty Auditorium
10	Mon.	Eve.	St. Joseph, MO	Tootle Thea.
11	Tue.	Mat.	Osceola, IA	Touet Opera House
11	Tue.	Eve.	Des Moines, IA	Auditorium
12	Wed.	Mat.	Oskaloosa, IA	Masonic Opera House
12	Wed.	Eve.	Ottumwa, IA	Market Street Thea.
13	Thu.	Mat.	Washington, IA	Graham Thea.
13	Thu.	Eve.	Rock Island, IL	Illinois Thea.
14	Fri.	Mat.	Monmouth, IL	Pattee Opera House
14	Fri.	Eve.	Burlington, IA	Grand Opera House
15	Sat.	Mat.	Keokuk, IA	Keokuk Opera House
15	Sat.	Eve.	Quincy, IL	Empire Thea.
16	Sun.	Mat.	Springfield, IL	Chatterton's Opera House
16	Sun.	Eve.	Decatur, IL	Powers' Grand Op. House
17	Mon.	Mat.	Anna, IL	Opera House
17	Mon.	Eve.	Cairo, IL	Cairo Opera House
18	Tue.	Mat.	Fulton, KY	Vendome Opera House
18	Tue.	Eve.	Paducah, KY	Kentucky Thea.
19	Wed.	M/E	Louisville, KY	Auditorium
20	Thu.	Mat.	Cincinnati, OH	Pike Street Thea.
20	Thu.	Eve.	Dayton, OH	Victoria Thea.
21	Fri.	Mat.	Springfield, OH	Grand Opera House
21	Fri.	Eve.	Columbus, OH	Great Southern Thea.
22	Sat.	M/E	Cleveland, OH	Grays' Armory
23	Sun.	Eve.	Buffalo, NY	Teck Thea.
24	Mon.	Mat.	Lockport, NY	Hodge Opera House

24	Mon.	Eve.	Rochester, NY	Lyceum Thea.
25	Tue.	Mat.	Penn Yan, NY	Yates Lyceum
25	Tue.	Eve.	Elmira, NY	Lyceum Thea.
26	Wed.	Mat.	Lock Haven, PA	Lock Haven Opera House
26	Wed.	Eve.	Williamsport, PA	Lycoming Opera House
27	Thu.	M/E	Baltimore, MD	Fifth Regiment Armory
28	Fri.	Eve.	Washington, DC	Convention Hall
29	Sat.	Mat.	Elizabeth, NJ	Jacobs Thea.
29	Sat.	Eve.	Orange, NJ	Music Hall
30	Sun.	Mat.	New York, NY	West End Thea.
30	Sun.	Eve.	New York, NY	Herald Square Thea.

DECEMBER

1	Mon.	Mat.	Princeton, NJ	Alexander Hall
1	Mon.	Eve.	Paterson, NJ	Armory
2	Tue.	Mat.	Poughkeepsie, NY	Collingwood Opera House
2	Tue.	Eve.	Troy, NY	Music Hall
3	Wed.	Mat.	Pittsfield, MA	Casino Opera House
3	Wed.	Eve.	Springfield, MA	City Hall
4	Thu.	Mat.	Athol, MA	Opera House
4	Thu.	Eve.	Fitchburg, MA	Cumings' Thea.
5	Fri.	M/E	Providence, RI	Infantry Hall
6	Sat.	M/E	Worcester, MA	Mechanics' Hall
7	Sun.	Eve.	Boston, MA	Symphony Hall
8	Mon.	Mat.	Boston, MA	Tremont Temple
8	Mon.	Eve.	Lowell, MA	Huntington Hall
9	Tue.	Mat.	Boston, MA	Tremont Temple
9	Tue.	Eve.	Malden, MA	Auditorium
10	Wed.	M/E	Boston, MA	Tremont Temple
11	Thu.	M/E	Hartford, CT	Foot Guard Armory
12	Fri.	Mat.	Meriden, CT	Opera House
12	Fri.	Eve.	Waterbury, CT	Auditorium
13	Sat.	M/E	New Haven, CT	Yale University
14	Sun.	Eve.	New York, NY	Casino Thea.

[End of 3rd 1892 tour]

1902 OFF-TOUR CONCERTS

DECEMBER

| 21 | Sun. | Mat. | Mt. Vernon, NY | Orpheum Thea. |

Soloists: Estelle Liebling, soprano; Anna E. Otten, violin.

| 21 | Sun. | Eve. | New York, NY | Casino Thea. |

Soloists same as for matinee.

1ST 1903 TOUR (Europe)

JANUARY

Soloists: Estelle Liebling & Caroline Montefiore, soprano; Maud Powell, violin; Walter Rogers & Emil Kenecke, cornet; Franz Helle, flugelhorn; Simone Mantia, euphonium; Arthur Pryor, trombone; Marshall P. Lufsky, flute; Jean H.B. Moeremans, saxophone.
Friday, 2nd through Sat., 10th (8 days), London, England, Queen's Hall. 2 concerts per day except no concerts Sun. 4th & eve. only on first & last days.

11	Sun.	Mat.	London, England	Alhambra Thea.
11	Sun.	Eve.	London, England	Queen's Hall
12	Mon.	M/E	Brighton, England	Brighton Dome
13	Tue.	Mat.	Reading, England	County Thea.
13	Tue.	Eve.	Swindon, England	Baths
14	Wed.	M/E	Newport, Wales	Lyceum Thea.
15	Thu.	M/E	Cardiff, Wales	Park Hall
16	Fri.	M/E	Cheltenham, England	Winter Gardens
17	Sat.	Mat.	Stratford-on-Avon, Engl.	Memorial Thea.
17	Sat.	Eve.	Leamington, England	Winter Hall
17	Sat.	Eve.	Warwick, England	Warwick Castle – extra concert for royalty
18	Sun.	M/E	London, England	Alhambra Thea.
19	Mon.	M/E	Birmingham, England	Town Hall
20	Tue.	Mat.	Stafford, England	Borough Hall
20	Tue.	Eve.	Walsall, England	Imperial Hall
21	Wed.	Mat.	Buxton, England	Town Hall
21	Wed.	Eve.	Derby, England	Drill Hall
22	Thu.	M/E	Nottingham, England	Albert Hall
23	Fri.	Mat.	Buxton, England	Pavilion
23	Fri.	Eve.	Stockport, England	Stockport Armoury
24	Sat.	M/E	Liverpool, England	Philharmonic Hall
26	Mon.	M/E	Blackpool, England	Winter Gardens

27	Tue.	M/E	Southport, England	Cambridge Hall
28	Wed.	M/E	Preston, England	Public Hall
29	Thu.	M/E	Bolton, England	Temperance Hall
30	Fri.	M/E	Sheffield, England	Albert Hall
31	Sat.	Eve.	Windsor, England	Windsor Castle command performance

FEBRUARY

2	Mon.	Mat.	Dublin, Ireland	Opera House
3	Tue.	Eve.	Dublin, Ireland	Dublin Castle
4	Wed.	M/E	Belfast, Ireland	Ulster Hall
5	Thu.	Mat.	Dublin, Ireland	Royal Thea.
5	Thu.	Eve.	Dublin, Ireland	Rotunda
6	Fri.	M/E	Glasgow, Scotland	St. Andrew's Hall
7	Sat.	M/E	Perth, Scotland	City Hall
9	Mon.	M/E	Aberdeen, Scotland	Music Hall
10	Tue.	M/E	Falkirk, Scotland	Town Hall
11	Wed.	M/E	Kirkcaldy, Scotland	Adam Smith Hall
12	Thu.	M/E	Dundee, Scotland	Kinnaird's Hall
13	Fri.	M/E	Edinburgh, Scotland	Synod Hall
14	Sat.	M/E	Edinburgh, Scotland	Synod Hall
16	Mon.	Mat.	Berwick-on-Tweed, Engl.	Corn Exchange
16	Mon.	Eve.	Newcastle-on-Tyne, Engl.	Town Hall
17	Tue.	M/E	Sunderland, England	Victoria Hall
18	Wed.	M/E	Newcastle-on-Tyne, Engl.	Town Hall
19	Thu.	M/E	West Hartlepool, England	Town Hall
20	Fri.	Mat.	Middlesborough, England	Royal Thea.
20	Fri.	Eve.	Darlington, England	Assembly Rooms
21	Sat.	Mat.	York, England	Festival Concert Hall
21	Sat.	Eve.	Hull, England	Assembly Rooms
23	Mon.	Mat.	Harrogate, England	Grand Opera House
23	Mon.	Eve.	Leeds, England	Town Hall
24	Tue.	M/E	Leeds, England	Town Hall
25	Wed.	M/E	Bradford, England	St. George's Hall
26	Thu.	Mat.	Halifax, England	Victoria Hall
26	Thu.	Eve.	Huddersfield, England	Town Hall
27	Fri.	Mat.	Chester, England	Music Hall
27	Fri.	Eve.	Liverpool, England	Philharmonic Hall
28	Sat.	M/E	Liverpool, England	Philharmonic Hall

MARCH

2	Mon.	M/E	Manchester, England	Free Trade Hall
3	Tue.	M/E	Manchester, England	Free Trade Hall
4	Wed.	Mat.	Wigan, England	Court Thea.
4	Wed.	Eve.	Warrington, England	Parr Hall
5	Thu.	M/E	Burnley, England	Mechanics' Institute
6	Fri.	M/E	Bolton, England	Victoria Hall
7	Sat.	M/E	Southport, England	Cambridge Hall
9	Mon.	Mat.	Accrington, England	Town Hall
9	Mon.	Eve.	Bury, England	Athenaeum Hall
10	Tue.	M/E	Blackburn, England	Blackburn Exchange Hall
11	Wed.	M/E	Rochdale, England	Town Hall
12	Thu.	M/E	Nottingham, England	Albert Hall
13	Fri.	M/E	Nottingham, England	Albert Hall
14	Sat.	M/E	Derby, England	Drill Hall
16	Mon.	M/E	Sheffield, England	Albert Hall
17	Tue.	M/E	Sheffield, England	Albert Hall
18	Tue.	M/E	Birmingham, England	Town Hall
19	Thu.	M/E	Northampton, England	Corn Exchange
20	Fri.	Mat.	Banbury, England	Exchange Hall
20	Fri.	Eve.	Bedford, England	Exchange Hall
21	Sat.	Mat.	Chelmsford, England	Corn Exchange
21	Sat.	Eve.	Colchester, England	Corn Exchange
23	Mon.	M/E	Norwich, England	St. Andrew's Hall
24	Tue.	M/E	Leicester, England	Temperance Hall
25	Wed.	Mat.	Rugby, England	Royal Thea.
25	Wed.	Eve.	Coventry, England	Corn Exchange
26	Thu.	M/E	Wolverhampton, England	Agricultural Hall
27	Fri.	M/E	Hanley, England	Town Hall
28	Sat.	M/E	Hanley, England	Town Hall
30	Mon.	M/E	Hereford, England	Shire Hall
31	Tue.	M/E	Bath, England	Assembly Rooms

APRIL

1	Wed.	M/E	Bristol, England	Victoria Rooms
2	Thu.	M/E	Bristol, England	Victoria Rooms
3	Fri.	M/E	Merthyr Tydfil, Wales	Drill Hall
4	Sat.	M/E	Swansea, Wales	Albert Hall

6	Mon.	M/E	Cardiff, Wales	Park Hall
7	Tue.	M/E	Cardiff, Wales	Park Hall
8	Wed.	Mat.	Taunton, England	Assembly Rooms
8	Wed.	Eve.	Exeter, England	Victoria Hall
9	Thu.	M/E	Plymouth, England	Guild Hall
10	Fri.	Eve.	London, England	Alexandra Palace

Sat., 11th through Sat., 18th (7 days), London, England, Queen's Hall. 2 concerts per day except no concerts on Sun. 12th.

Sun., 19th through Wed., 29th (11 days), Paris, France, Noveau Thea. 2 concerts per day except eve. only 1st day.

APRIL

30	Thu.	M/E	Lille, France	Hippodrome

MAY

1	Fri.	M/E	Lille, France	Hippodrome

Sat., 2nd through Mon., 4th (3 days), Brussels, Belgium, Theatre de l'Ahambra. 2 concerts per day.

5	Tue.	M/E	Ghent, Belgium	Grand Thea.
6	Wed.	M/E	Antwerp, Belgium	Royal Thea.
7	Thu.	M/E	Liege, Belgium	Cirque Variete
8	Fri.	M/E	Cologne, Germany	Gurzenich

Sat., 9th through Wed., 13th (5 days), Berlin, Germany, Philharmonie. 2 concerts per day except eve. only 1st day.

MAY

14	Thu.	M/E	Konigsberg, Germany	Thiergarten

Sat., 16th through Wed., 20th (5 days), St. Petersburg, Russia, Cirque Ciniselli. 2 concerts per day except eve. only 1st day.

MAY

22	Fri.	M/E	Warsaw, Poland	Filharmonija Warszawskiej

Sat., 23rd through Tue., 26th (4 days), Vienna, Austria, Englischer Garten. 2 concerts per day.

27	Wed.	Eve.	Prague, Bohemia	Rudolfinum
28	Thu.	M/E	Dresden, Germany	Zoological Garten
29	Fri.	M/E	Dresden, Germany	Zoological Garten
30	Sat.	M/E	Leipzig, Germany	Zoological Garten
31	Sun.	Eve.	Hamburg, Germany	Hansa-Theater

JUNE

1	Mon.	M/E	Hamburg, Germany	Hansa-Theatre
2	Tue.	M/E	Hamburg, Germany	Hansa-Theatre
3	Wed.	Eve.	Copenhagen, Denmark	Concertpalaeet
4	Thu.	M/E	Copenhagen, Denmark	Concertpalaeet
5	Fri.	M/E	Kiel, Germany	Wriedt's Etab'ment
6	Sat.	Eve.	Dortmund, Germany	Fredenbaum
7	Sun.	Mat.	Amsterdam, Holland	Paleis voor Volksvlyt
7	Sun.	Eve.	Hague, Holland	Dierentiun
8	Mon.	M/E	Richmond, England	Prince of Wales Thea.
9	Tue.	Mat.	Kennington, England	Kennington Thea.
9	Tue.	Eve.	Bromley, England	Grand Hall
10	Wed.	Mat.	Balham, England	Duchess Palace
10	Wed.	Eve.	Islington, England	Grand Thea.
11	Thu.	M/E	Wood Green, England	Alexandra Palace
12	Fri.	Mat.	Woolwich, England	Grand Thea.
12	Fri.	Eve.	Gravesend, England	Public Hall
13	Sat.	M/E	Crouch End, England	Opera House
15	Mon.	M/E	Sydenham, England	Crystal Palace
16	Tue.	Mat.	Stroke Newington, England	Alexandra Thea.
16	Tue.	Eve.	Windsor, England	Royal Albert Institute
17	Wed.	Mat.	Aldershot, England	Royal Thea.
17	Wed.	Eve.	Guildford, England	Drill Hall
18	Thu.	M/E	New Cross, England	Broadway Thea.
19	Fri.	Mat.	Peckham, England	Crown Thea.
19	Fri.	Eve.	Reading, England	County Thea.
20	Sat.	M/E	Oxford, England	Town Hall
22	Mon.	M/E	Tunbridge Wells, England	Opera House
23	Tue.	M/E	Margate, England	Grand Thea.
24	Wed.	Mat.	Sittingbourne, England	Bowes Park
24	Wed.	Eve.	Chatham, England	Town Hall
25	Thu.	M/E	Folkstone, England	Victoria Pier
26	Fri.	M/E	St. Leonards, England	Royal Concert Hall
27	Sat.	M/E	Eastbourne, England	Devonshire Park Thea.
29	Mon.	M/E	Brighton, England	Brighton Dome
30	Tue.	M/E	Southsea, England	Portland Hall

JULY

1	Wed.	M/E	Southsea, England	Portland Hall
2	Thu.	M/E	Southampton, England	Philharmonic Hall
3	Fri.	M/E	Weymouth, England	Royal Jubilee Hall

4	Sat.	M/E	Bournemouth, England	Winter Gardens
6	Mon.	M/E	Bristol, England	Victoria Rooms
7	Tue.	M/E	Newport, England	Tredegar Hall
8	Wed.	Mat.	Gloucester, England	Shire Hall
8	Wed.	Eve.	Cheltenham, England	Winter Gardens
9	Thu.	Mat.	Malvern, England	Assembly Rooms
9	Thu.	Eve.	Worcester, England	Town Hall
10	Fri.	M/E	Chester, England	Music Hall

Sat., 11th through Mon., 13th (3 days), Morecambe, England, Winter Gardens. 2 concerts per day.

Tue., 14th through Thu., 16th (3 days), Douglas, Isle of Man, England, at Palace. 2 concerts per day.

JULY

17	Fri.	M/E	Belfast, Ireland	Grand Opera House
18	Sat.	Mat.	Newry, Ireland	Town Hall
18	Sat.	Eve.	Belfast, Ireland	Grand Opera House
20	Mon.	M/E	Dublin, Ireland	Rotunda
21	Tue.	M/E	Dublin, Ireland	Rotunda
22	Wed.	M/E	Cork, Ireland	Palace Thea.
23	Thu.	M/E	Cork, Ireland	Palace Thea.
24	Fri.	M/E	Carnavon, Wales	Pavilion
25	Sat.	M/E	Carnavon, Wales	Pavilion
27	Mon.	M/E	Llandudno, Wales	Hippodrome
28	Tue.	M/E	Llandudno, Wales	Hippodrome
29	Wed.	M/E	Blackpool, England	Hippodrome
30	Thu.	M/E	Blackpool, England	Hippodrome

AUGUST

7	Fri.	Eve.	S.S. Cedric, [At sea]	Place on ship not known

[End of 1st 1903 tour]

2ND 1903 TOUR

AUGUST-SEPTEMBER

Sun., 30 Aug. through Sun., 6 Sept. (9 days), Willow Grove (PA) Park. 4 concerts per day.

Soloists: Estelle Liebling, soprano; Anna E. Otten, violin; Walter B. Rogers & Emil Kenecke, cornet; Franz Helle, flugelhorn; Simone Mantia, euphonium; Marshall P. Lufsky, piccolo; A. Bertram, oboe; Jean H.B. Moeremans, saxophone.

Soloists for remainder of tour, including Pittsburgh Exposition: Estelle Liebling, soprano; Anna E. Otten, violin; Walter B. Rogers & Emil Kenecke, cornet; Franz Helle, flugelhorn; Simone Mantia, euphonium; Leo Zimmerman, trombone; Marshall P. Lufsky, piccolo; A. Bertram, oboe; Jean H.B. Moeremans, saxophone.

SEPTEMBER

8	Tue.	Mat.	Martinsburg, WV	Opera House
8	Tue.	Eve.	Cumberland, MD	Academy of Music
9	Wed.	Mat.	Grafton, WV	Brinkman's Opera House
9	Wed.	Eve.	Fairmont, WV	Grand Opera House
10	Thu.	Mat.	New Martinsville, WV	Grand Opera House
10	Thu.	Eve.	Sistersville, WV	Auditorium
11	Fri.	Mat.	Parkersburg, WV	Camden Thea.
11	Fri.	Eve.	Marietta, OH	Auditorium
12	Sat.	Mat.	Athens, OH	Opera House
12	Sat.	Eve.	Chillicothe, OH	Masonic Opera House

Sun., 13th through Tue., 15th (3 days), Cincinnati, OH, Fall Festival. 2 concerts per day.

16	Wed.	Mat.	Indianapolis, IN	Indiana State Fair
16	Wed.	Eve.	Indianapolis, IN	Tomlinson Hall
17	Thu.	Mat.	Indianapolis, IN	Indiana State Fair
17	Thu.	Eve.	Indianapolis, IN	Tomlinson Hall
18	Fri.	Eve.	Chicago, IL	Auditorium
19	Sat.	M/E	Chicago, IL	Auditorium
20	Sun.	Eve.	Chicago, IL	Auditorium
21	Mon.	Mat.	Defiance, OH	Citizens Opera House
22	Tue.	Eve.	Tiffin, OH	Noble's Opera House
23	Wed.	Mat.	Fremont, OH	Opera House
23	Wed.	Eve.	Findlay, OH	Marvin Opera House
24	Thu.	Mat.	Upper Sandusky, OH	Auditorium
24	Thu.	Eve.	Mansfield, OH	Memorial Opera House
25	Fri.	Mat.	Massillon, OH	Armory
25	Fri.	Eve.	New Philadelphia, OH	Union Opera House
26	Sat.	Mat.	Cambridge, OH	Colonial Thea.
26	Sat.	Eve.	Bellaire, OH	Columbia Thea.
27	Sun.	Eve.	Wheeling, WV	Court Thea.

SEPTEMBER-OCTOBER
Mon., 28 Sept. through Sat., 3 Oct. (6 days), Pittsburgh Exposition.
4 concerts per day.
Soloists: Estelle Liebling, soprano; Anna Otten, violin; Walter B. Rogers & Emil Kenecke, cornet; Franz Helle, flugelhorn; Simone Mantia, euphonium; Leo Zimmerman, trombone; Marshall P. Lufsky, piccolo; Jean H.B. Moeremans, saxophone.
OCTOBER

| 4 | Sun. | Eve. | New York, NY | Carnegie Hall |

[End of 2ⁿᵈ 1903 tour]

1ˢᵀ 1904 TOUR

Soloists before St. Louis Exposition: Estelle Liebling, soprano; Jessie Straus, violin; Herbert L. Clarke, cornet; Jean H.B. Moeremans, saxophone.
APRIL

2	Sat.	Mat.	Asbury Park, NJ	Pavilion
2	Sat.	Eve.	Red Bank, NJ	Opera House
3	Sun.	Eve.	New York, NY	Metropolitan Opera House
4	Mon.	Mat.	Meriden, CT	Meriden Thea.
4	Mon.	Eve.	New Haven, CT	Hyperion Thea.
5	Tue.	Mat.	Waterbury, CT	Poli's Thea.
5	Tue.	Eve.	Hartford, CT	Parsons' Thea.
6	Wed.	M/E	Providence, RI	Infantry Hall
7	Thu.	M/E	Boston, MA	Symphony Hall
8	Fri.	M/E	Portland, ME	Jefferson Thea.
9	Sat.	M/E	Worcester, MA	Mechanics' Hall
10	Sun.	Eve.	New York, NY	Metropolitan Opera House
11	Mon.	Mat.	Princeton, NJ	Alexander Hall
11	Mon.	Eve.	Jersey City, NJ	Elks' Hall
12	Tue.	Mat.	Elizabeth, NJ	Jacobs Thea.
12	Tue.	Eve.	Newark, NJ	Krueger Auditorium
13	Wed.	Mat.	Norristown, PA	Grand Opera House
13	Wed.	Eve.	Wilmington, DE	Grand Opera House
14	Thu.	Mat.	Salem, NJ	Salem Opera House
14	Thu.	Eve.	Bridgeton, NJ	Criterion Thea.
15	Fri.	Mat.	Washington, DC	National Thea.
15	Fri.	Eve.	Baltimore, MD	Lyric Thea.
16	Sat.	M/E	Baltimore, MD	Lyric Thea.
17	Sun.	M/E	Buffalo, NY	Teck Thea.
18	Mon.	Mat.	Ashtabula, OH	Auditorium
18	Mon.	Eve.	Cleveland, OH	Grays' Armory
19	Tue.	Mat.	Toledo, OH	Valentine Thea.
19	Tue.	Eve.	Detroit, MI	Light Guard Armory
20	Wed.	Mat.	Lansing, MI	Baird's Opera House
20	Wed.	Eve.	Grand Rapids, MI	Powers' Thea.
21	Thu.	Mat.	Benton Harbor, MI	Bell Opera House
21	Thu.	Eve.	La Porte, IN	Hall's Opera House
22	Fri.	Eve.	Chicago, IL	Auditorium
23	Sat.	Mat.	Chicago, IL	Auditorium
23	Sat.	Eve.	Valparaiso, IN	Memorial Opera House
24	Sun.	M/E	Chicago, IL	Auditorium
25	Mon.	Eve.	Fort Wayne, IN	Masonic Temple
26	Tue.	Mat.	Springfield, OH	Grand Opera House
26	Tue.	Eve.	Columbus, OH	Great Southern Thea.
27	Wed.	Mat.	Dayton, OH	Victoria Thea.
27	Wed.	Eve.	Cincinnati, OH	Music Hall
28	Thu.	M/E	Louisville, KY	Auditorium

APRIL-JUNE
Sat., 30 Apr. through Sat., 4 June (36 days), St. Louis, World's Fair (Louisiana Purchase Exposition). 2 or 4 concerts per day.
Soloists: Herbert L. Clarke, Walter B. Rogers, & Herman Bellstedt, cornet; Franz Helle & Leon Prevost, flugelhorn; John J. Perfetto, euphonium; Leo Zimmerman, trombone; Marshall P. Lufsky, piccolo; Jean H.B. Moeremans, saxophone; Martin Schlig, xylophone.
[End of 1ˢᵗ 1904 tour]

2ⁿᵈ 1904 TOUR

AUGUST-SEPTEMBER
Sun., 28 Aug. through Mon., 5 Sept. (9 days), Willow Grove (PA) Park.
4 concerts per day.
Soloists: Herbert L. Clarke & Herman Bellstedt, cornet; Franz Helle, flugelhorn; John J. Perfetto, euphonium; Leo Zimmerman, trombone; Marshall P. Lufsky, piccolo; Jean H.B. Moeremans, saxophone.

SEPTEMBER

| 6 | Tue. | Mat. | Lebanon, PA | Academy of Music |

Soloists: Herbert L. Clarke, cornet; Franz Helle, flugelhorn; Leo Zimmerman, trombone; Jean H.B. Moeremans, saxophone.

| 6 | Tue. | Eve. | Harrisburg, PA | Lyceum Thea. |

Soloists same as for matinee.
Wed., 7ᵗʰ through Sat., 17ᵗʰ (10 days), Pittsburgh Exposition. 2 concerts per day except none on Sun. 11ᵗʰ.
Soloists: Estelle Liebling, soprano; Jessie Straus, violin; Herbert L. Clarke & Herman Bellstedt, cornet; Franz Helle, flugelhorn; John J. Perfetto, euphonium; Leo Zimmerman, trombone; Marshall P. Lufsky, piccolo; Jean H.B. Moeremans, saxophone.
Soloists for tour between Pittsburgh Exposition & Mitchell/Corn Palace same as for Pittsburgh Exposition.
SEPTEMBER

18	Sun.	Eve.	Akron, OH	Colonial Thea.
19	Mon.	Mat.	Warren, OH	Warren Opera House
19	Mon.	Eve.	Youngstown, OH	Opera House
20	Tue.	Mat.	Massillon, OH	Armory
20	Tue.	Eve.	Wooster, OH	Memorial Chapel
21	Wed.	Mat.	Bucyrus, OH	Bucyrus Opera House
21	Wed.	Eve.	Mansfield, OH	Memorial Opera House
22	Thu.	Mat.	St. Marys, OH	Grand Opera House
22	Thu.	Eve.	Muncie, IN	Wysor's Grand Opera House
23	Fri.	M/E	Richmond, IN	Coliseum
24	Sat.	M/E	Chicago, IL	Auditorium
25	Sun.	M/E	Chicago, IL	Auditorium

SEPTEMBER-OCTOBER
Mon., 26 Sept. through Sat., 1 Oct. (6 days), Mitchell, SD, Corn Palace. 2 or 3 concerts per day.
Soloists same as for Pittsburgh Exposition.
Soloists for remainder of tour: Estelle Liebling, soprano; Jessie Straus, violin; Herbert L. Clarke, cornet.
OCTOBER

2	Sun.	M/E	Sioux City, IA	Grand Opera House
3	Mon.	Mat.	Council Bluffs, IA	New Thea.
3	Mon.	Eve.	Omaha, NE	Auditorium
4	Tue.	Eve.	Lincoln, NE	Oliver Thea.
5	Wed.	Mat.	Manhattan, KS	Wareham's Opera House
5	Wed.	Eve.	Topeka, KS	City Auditorium
6	Thu.	M/E	Kansas City, MO	Convention Hall
7	Fri.	Mat.	Junction City, KS	Opera House
7	Fri.	Eve.	Salina, KS	Opera House
8	Sat.	M/E	Pueblo, CO	Grand Opera House
9	Sun.	M/E	Denver, CO	Broadway Thea.
10	Mon.	Eve.	Boulder, CO	Chautauqua
11	Tue.	Mat.	Fort Collins, CO	Fort Collins Opera House
11	Tue.	Eve.	Greeley, CO	Opera House
12	Wed.	Mat.	Cheyenne, WY	Turner Hall
12	Wed.	Eve.	Laramie, WY	Opera House
13	Thu.	Mat.	Rawlins, WY	Opera House
13	Thu.	Eve.	Rock Springs, WY	Union Opera House
14	Fri.	Eve.	Ogden, UT	Grand Opera House
16	Sun.	Eve.	San Francisco, CA	Alhambra Thea.
17	Mon.	Eve.	San Francisco, CA	Alhambra Thea.
18	Tue.	M/E	San Francisco, CA	Alhambra Thea.
19	Wed.	Eve.	San Francisco, CA	Alhambra Thea.
20	Thu.	M/E	San Francisco, CA	Alhambra Thea.
21	Fri.	Mat.	Berkeley, CA	Greek Thea.
21	Fri.	Eve.	San Francisco, CA	Alhambra Thea.
22	Sat.	M/E	San Francisco, CA	Alhambra Thea.
23	Sun.	M/E	San Francisco, CA	Alhambra Thea.
24	Mon.	M/E	San Jose, CA	Victory Thea.
25	Tue.	Eve.	San Luis Obispo, CA	Pavilion Thea.
26	Wed.	Eve.	Santa Barbara, CA	Opera House

Thu., 27ᵗʰ through Sun., 30ᵗʰ (4 days), Los Angeles, CA, Hazard's Pavilion. 2 concerts per day except mat. only Thu., 27ᵗʰ.

| 31 | Mon. | Mat. | Pomona, CA | Fraternal Aid Assn. Hall |
| 31 | Mon. | Eve. | Riverside, CA | Loring Thea. |

NOVEMBER

1	Tue.	Mat.	San Bernardino, CA.	Grand Opera House
1	Tue.	Eve.	Santa Ana, CA	Grand Opera House
2	Wed.	M/E	Bakersfield, CA	Scribner's Opera House
3	Thu.	Mat.	Hanford, CA	Hanford Opera House

3	Thu.	Eve.	Fresno, CA	Barton Opera House
4	Fri.	M/E	Oakland, CA	Macdonough Thea.
5	Sat.	Eve.	Santa Rosa, CA	Anthenaeum
6	Sun.	Mat.	Napa, CA	Napa Opera House
6	Sun.	Eve.	Vallejo, CA	Farragut Hall
7	Mon.	Mat.	Stockton, CA	Yosemite Thea.
7	Mon.	Eve.	Sacramento, CA	Clunie Thea.
8	Tue.	Eve.	Grass Valley, CA	Auditorium
9	Wed.	Mat.	Carson City, NV	Carson City Opera House
9	Wed.	Eve.	Reno, NV	McKissick's Opera House
10	Thu.	Eve.	Salt Lake City, UT	Tabernacle
11	Fri.	M/E	Salt Lake City, UT	Tabernacle
12	Sat.	M/E	Leadville, CO	Opera House
13	Sun.	M/E	Cripple Creek, CO	Grand Opera House
14	Mon.	M/E	Colorado Springs, CO	Opera House
15	Tue.	Mat.	Rocky Ford, CO	Grand Opera House
15	Tue.	Eve.	La Junta, CO	La Junta Thea.
16	Wed.	Eve.	Hutchinson, KS	Home Thea.
17	Thu.	Mat.	Newton, KS	Ragsdale Opera House
17	Thu.	Eve.	Wichita, KS	Toler Auditorium
18	Fri.	Mat.	Wellington, KS	Wood's Opera House
18	Fri.	Eve.	Arkansas City, KS	Fifth Avenue Opera House
19	Sat.	Mat.	Winfield, KS	Grand Opera House
19	Sat.	Eve.	Perry, OK	Grand Opera House
20	Sun.	M/E	Guthrie, OK	Brook's Opera House
21	Mon.	Mat.	Enid, OK	not known
21	Mon.	Eve.	Reno City, OK	McKissick's Opera House
22	Tue.	Mat.	El Reno, OK	Opera House
22	Tue.	Eve.	Chickasha, OK	Opera House
23	Wed.	M/E	Oklahoma City, OK	Overholser Thea.
24	Thu.	Mat.	South McAlester, OK	Langsdale Opera House
24	Thu.	Eve.	Muskogee, OK	Gavigan's Opera House
25	Fri.	Mat.	Parsons, KS	Edward's Opera House
25	Fri.	Eve.	Independence, KS	Auditorium
26	Sat.	Mat.	Pittsburg, KS	La Belle Thea.
26	Sat.	Eve.	Iola, KS	Grand Thea.
27	Sun.	M/E	Kansas City, MO	Convention Hall
28	Mon.	Mat.	Creston, IA	Temple Grand Thea.
28	Mon.	Eve.	Des Moines, IA	Auditorium
29	Tue.	Mat.	Iowa City, IA	Opera House
29	Tue.	Eve.	Davenport, IA	Burtis Opera House
30	Wed.	Eve.	Milwaukee, WI	Davidson Thea.
DECEMBER				
1	Thu.	Eve.	Kalamazoo, MI	Academy of Music
2	Fri.	Eve.	Ann Arbor, MI	University Hall
3	Sat.	M/E	Cleveland, OH	Grays' Armory
4	Sun.	Eve.	New York, NY	Carnegie Hall
5	Mon.	Eve.	Newark, NJ	Krueger Auditorium

[End of 2nd 1904 tour]

1904 OFF-TOUR CONCERTS

DECEMBER

Soloists for these 3 NY concerts: Estelle Liebling, soprano; Jessie Straus, violin; Herbert L. Clarke & Herman Bellstedt, cornet; Marshall P. Lufsky, piccolo.

25	Sun.	Eve.	New York, NY	Carnegie Hall
26	Mon.	Eve.	New York, NY	Carnegie Hall
27	Tue.	Eve.	New York, NY	Carnegie Hall

1ST 1905 TOUR (Britain)

Soloists: Estelle Liebling, soprano; Maud Powell, violin; Pearl Bryer, cello; Herbert L. Clarke, cornet; Franz Helle, flugelhorn; Leo Zimmerman, trombone; Marshall P. Lufsky, flute & piccolo.

JANUARY

3	Tue.	Eve.	*R.M.S. Baltic* [at sea]	Dining Saloon
6	Fri.	Eve.	Liverpool, England	Philharmonic Hall
8	Sun.	M/E	Liverpool, England	Philharmonic Hall

Mon., 9th through Sat., 14th (6 days), London, England, Queen's Hall. 2 concerts per day.

15	Sun.	M/E	Southend, England	Kursaal

Mon., 16th through Fri., 20th (5 days), London, England, Queen's Hall. 2 concerts per day.

21	Sat.	Mat.	London, England	Alexandra Palace
21	Sat.	Eve.	London, England	Queen's Hall

22	Sun.	M/E	London, England	Alhambra Thea.
23	Mon.	Mat.	New Cross, England	Broadway Thea.
23	Mon.	Eve.	Chatham, England	Town Hall
24	Tue.	M/E	St. Leonards, England	Royal Concert Hall
25	Wed.	M/E	Brighton, England	Brighton Dome
26	Thu.	M/E	Southsea, England	Portland Hall
27	Fri.	Mat.	Southampton, England	Palace of Varieties
27	Fri.	Eve.	Salisbury, England	County Hall
28	Sat.	M/E	Bournemouth, England	Winter Gardens
30	Mon.	M/E	Bristol, England	Victoria Rooms
31	Tue.	M/E	Cardiff, Wales	Park Hall
FEBRUARY				
1	Wed.	M/E	Swansea, Wales	Albert Hall
2	Thu.	Mat.	Cheltenham, England	Winter Gardens
3	Fri.	M/E	Bath, England	Assembly Rooms
4	Sat.	M/E	Oxford, England	Town Hall
6	Mon.	Mat.	Holloway, England	Marlborough Thea.
6	Mon.	Eve.	Forest Gate, England	Public Hall
7	Tue.	Mat.	Woolwich, England	Grand Thea.
7	Tue.	Eve.	Guilford, England	Large Hall
8	Wed.	Mat.	Worthing, England	Royal Thea.
8	Wed.	Eve.	Eastbourne, England	Devonshire Park Thea.
9	Thu.	Mat.	Tunbridge Wells, Engl.	Opera House
9	Thu.	Eve.	Maidstone, England	Corn Exchange
10	Fri.	Mat.	Maidenhead, England	Grand Thea.
10	Fri.	Eve.	Reading, England	Large Town Hall
11	Sat.	Mat.	Croydon, England	Grand Thea.
11	Sat.	Eve.	Queen's Road, England	not known
13	Mon.	M/E	Northampton, England	Corn Exchange
14	Tue.	Mat.	Bedford, England	Royal County Thea.
14	Tue.	Eve.	Kettering, England	Victoria Hall
15	Wed.	Mat.	Leicester, England	Leicester Palace
15	Wed.	Eve.	Nuneaton, England	Prince of Wales Thea.
16	Thu.	M/E	Wolverhampton, Engl.	Agricultural Hall
17	Fri.	Mat.	Walsall, England	Her Majesty's Thea.
17	Fri.	Eve.	Stratford-on-Avon, Engl.	Borough Hall
18	Sat.	M/E	Henley, England	Victoria Hall
20	Mon.	M/E	Birmingham, England	Town Hall
21	Tue.	M/E	Nottingham, England	Albert Hall
22	Wed.	M/E	Sheffield, England	Albert Hall
23	Thu.	Mat.	Buxton, England	Opera House
23	Thu.	Eve.	Macclesfield, England	Drill Hall
24	Fri.	M/E	Chester, England	Music Hall
25	Sat.	Mat.	Shrewsbury, England	Royal Thea.
25	Sat.	Eve.	Crewe, England	Co-operative Hall
26	Sun.	M/E	Oldham, England	Unity Hall
27	Mon.	M/E	Bolton, England	Victoria Hall
28	Tue.	M/E	Manchester, England	Free Trade Hall
MARCH				
1	Wed.	M/E	Manchester, England	Free Trade Hall
2	Thu.	M/E	Blackburn, England	Blackburn Exchange Hall
3	Fri.	Mat.	Rochdale, England	Town Hall
3	Fri.	Eve.	Stockport, England	Stockport Armoury
4	Sat.	M/E	Warrington, England	Parr Hall
6	Mon.	M/E	Huddersfield, England	Town Hall
7	Tue.	M/E	Halifax, England	Victoria Hall
8	Wed.	M/E	Bradford, England	St. George's Hall
9	Thu.	M/E	Preston, England	Public Hall
10	Fri.	M/E	Carlisle, England	Drill Hall
11	Sat.	Mat.	Kendal, England	St. George's Hall
11	Sat.	Eve.	Lancaster, England	Palatine Hall
13	Mon.	M/E	Blackpool, England	Winter Gardens
14	Tue.	Mat.	Dublin, Ireland	Royal Thea.
14	Tue.	Eve.	Kingstown, Ireland	Kingstown Pavilion
15	Wed.	Mat.	Dublin, Ireland	Royal Thea.
15	Wed.	Eve.	Dundalk, Ireland	Town Hall
16	Thu.	M/E	Belfast, Ireland	Ulster Hall
17	Fri.	Mat.	Hamilton, Scotland	Town Hall
17	Fri.	Eve.	Coatbridge, Scotland	Town Hall
18	Sat.	M/E	Glasgow, Scotland	St. Andrew's Hall
20	Mon.	Mat.	Stirling, Scotland	Albert Hall
20	Mon.	Eve.	Edinburgh, Scotland	Waverley Market Hall
21	Tue.	Mat.	Dundee, Scotland	Her Majesty's Thea.
21	Tue.	Eve.	Edinburgh, Scotland	Waverley Market Hall
22	Wed.	Mat.	Berwick-on-Tweed, Engl.	Corn Exchange

22	Wed.	Eve.	Alnwick, England	Corn Exchange
23	Thu.	M/E	Newcastle-on-Tyne, Engl.	Exhibition Hall
24	Fri.	M/E	Middlesborough, England	Theatre Royal
25	Sat.	Mat.	Tynemouth, England	Tynemouth Palace
25	Sat.	Eve.	South Shields, England	Royal Assembly Hall
26	Sun.	M/E	Blythe, England	Theatre Royal
27	Mon.	Mat.	Durham, England	Durham Drill Hall
27	Mon.	Eve.	West Hartlepool, England	not known
28	Tue.	Mat.	Whitby, England	Temperance Hall
28	Tue.	Eve.	Scarborough, England	Londesborough Thea.
29	Wed.	Mat.	York, England	Festival Concert Hall
29	Wed.	Eve.	Harrogate, England	Kursall
30	Thu.	M/E	Leeds, England	Town Hall
31	Fri.	M/E	Leeds, England	Town Hall
APRIL				
1	Sat.	M/E	Hull, England	Assembly Rooms
2	Sun.	M/E	Grimsby, England	Prince of Wales Thea.
3	Mon.	M/E	Hull, England	Assembly Rooms
4	Tue.	Mat.	Sheffield, England	Theatre Royal
4	Tue.	Eve.	Doncaster, England	Corn Exchange
5	Wed.	Mat.	Nottingham, England	Theatre Royal
5	Wed.	Eve.	Derby, England	Drill Hall
6	Tue.	Mat.	Leamington, England	Winter Hall
6	Tue.	Eve.	Market Harborough, Engl.	Assembly Rooms
7	Fri.	Mat.	Peterborough, England	Theatre Royal
7	Fri.	Eve.	Lynn, England	New Royal Thea.
8	Sat.	Mat.	Norwich, England	St. Andrew's Hall
8	Sat.	Eve.	Lowestoft, England	Marina Thea.
9	Sun.	M/E	Yarmouth, England	Britannia Pier
10	Mon.	Mat.	Ipswich, England	Public Hall
10	Mon.	Eve.	Colchester, England	Corn Exchange
11	Tue.	Mat.	Canterbury, England	Canterbury Theatre Royal
11	Tue.	Eve.	Ramsgate, England	Royal Victoria Pavilion
12	Wed.	Mat.	Folkstone, England	Pleasure Gardens Thea.
12	Wed.	Eve.	Ashford, England	Corn Exchange
13	Thu.	Mat.	St. Leonards, England	Royal Concert Hall
13	Thu.	Eve.	Eastbourne, England	Devonshire Park Thea.
14	Fri.	M/E	Southampton, England	Philharmonic Hall
15	Sat.	M/E	Bournemouth, England	Winter Gardens
16	Sun.	M/E	Weymouth, England	Royal Victoria Jubilee Hall
17	Mon.	M/E	Ryde, England	Theatre Royal
18	Tue.	M/E	Portsmouth, England	Town Hall
19	Wed.	Mat.	Worthing, England	The Theatre
19	Wed.	Eve.	Tunbridge Wells, England	Opera House
20	Thu.	M/E	Sydenham, England	Crystal Palace
21	Fri.	Eve.	London, England	Alexandra Palace
22	Sat.	M/E	Brighton, England	Brighton Dome
23	Sun.	Mat.	London, England	Alhambra Thea.
23	Sun.	Eve.	London, England	Queen's Hall

Mon., 24th through Sat., 29th (6 days), London, England, Queen's Hall.
2 concerts per day.

30	Sun.	M/E	London, England	Alhambra Thea.
MAY				
1	Mon.	Eve.	Gravesend, England	Public Hall
2	Tue.	Mat.	Watford, England	Clarendon Hall
2	Tue.	Eve.	Wycombe, England	Town Hall
3	Wed.	Mat.	city not known, England	Coronet Thea.
3	Wed.	Eve.	Bromley, England	Lyric Thea.
4	Thu.	Mat.	city not known, England	Camden Thea.
4	Thu.	Eve.	Highbury, England	Anthenaeum
5	Fri.	Mat.	city not known, England	King's Thea.
6	Sat.	Eve.	London, England	Queen's Hall
8	Mon.	unk.	city not known	not known
9	Tue.	M/E	Liverpool, England	Philharmonic Hall
16	Tue.	Eve.	*R.M.S. Baltic* [at sea]	Dining saloon
21	Sun.	Eve.	New York, NY	Metropolitan Opera House

[End of 1st 1905 tour]

2ND 1905 TOUR

Sat., 27 May through Sat., 10 June (15 days), Willow Grove (PA) Park, 1st (of 2) engagements. 4 concerts per day.

Soloists: Ada Chambers, soprano; Jessie Straus, violin; Herbert L. Clarke & Ira Holland, cornet; John J. Perfetto, euphonium; Leo Zimmerman, trombone; Charles P. Lowe, xylophone.

JUNE
| 11 | Sun. | Eve. | New York, NY | Hippodrome |

Soloists: Estelle Liebling, soprano; Herman Bellstedt, cornet.

[End of 2nd 1905 tour]

1905 OFF-TOUR CONCERT

JUNE
| 18 | Sun. | Eve. | New York, NY | Hippodrome |

Soloists: Estelle Liebling, soprano; Herbert L. Clarke, cornet.

3RD 1905 TOUR

AUGUST
| 25 | Fri. | M/E | Asbury Park, NJ | Casino |

Soloists: Ada Chambers, soprano; Jessie Straus, violin; Herbert L. Clarke, cornet.

AUGUST-SEPTEMBER
Sat., 26 Aug. through Mon. 4 Sept. (10 days), Willow Grove (PA) Park, 2nd (of 2) engagements. 4 concerts per day.

Soloists: Ada Chambers, soprano; Herbert L. Clarke & Herman Bellstedt, cornet; Franz Helle, flugelhorn; John J. Perfetto, euphonium; Leo Zimmerman, trombone; Marshall P. Lufsky, piccolo; Jean H.B. Moeremans, saxophone.

[End of 3rd 1905 tour]

4TH 1905 TOUR

SEPTEMBER
| 10 | Sun. | Eve. | New York, NY | Hippodrome |

Soloists: Ada Chambers, soprano; Jessie Straus, violin; Herbert L. Clarke, cornet; Franz Helle, flugelhorn.

Mon. 11th through Sat., 16th (6 days), 1st (of 2) engagements at Pittsburgh Exposition. 4 concerts per day.

Soloists: Ada Chambers, soprano; Jessie Straus, violin; Herbert L. Clarke & Ira Holland, cornet; Franz Helle, flugelhorn; John J. Perfetto, euphonium; Charles P. Lowe, xylophone.

| 17 | Sun. | Eve. | New York, NY | Hippodrome |

Soloists: Ada Chambers, soprano; Jessie Straus, violin. Soloists for remainder of tour, including Pittsburgh Exposition: Elizabeth Schiller, soprano; Jessie Straus, violin; Herbert L. Clarke, cornet; Leo Zimmerman, trombone; Charles P. Lowe, xylophone.

18	Mon.	Mat.	Utica, NY	Majestic Thea.
18	Mon.	Eve.	Syracuse, NY	Wieting Opera House
19	Tue.	M/E	Buffalo, NY	Convention Hall
20	Wed.	Mat.	Ashtabula, OH	Auditorium
20	Wed.	Eve.	Youngstown, OH	Opera House
21	Thu.	Mat.	Norwalk, OH	Gilger Thea.
21	Thu.	Eve.	Toledo, OH	Valentine Thea.
22	Fri.	Mat.	Coldwater, MI	Tibbits Opera House
22	Fri.	Eve.	South Bend, IN	Auditorium
23	Sat.	M/E	Chicago, IL	Auditorium
24	Sun.	M/E	Chicago, IL	Auditorium
25	Mon.	Mat.	DeKalb, IL	Chronical Hall
25	Mon.	Eve.	Belvidere, IL	Derthick Opera House
26	Tue.	Mat.	Dixon, IL	Dixon Opera House
26	Tue.	Eve.	Sterling, IL	Academy of Music
27	Wed.	Mat.	Freeport, IL	Grand Opera House
27	Wed.	Eve.	Dubuque, IA	Grand Opera House
28	Thu.	Mat.	Independence, IA	Gedney Opera House
28	Thu.	Eve.	Waterloo, IA	Brown's Opera House
29	Fri.	Mat.	Iowa Falls, IA	Metropolitan Opera House
29	Fri.	Eve.	Fort Dodge, IA	Midland Opera House
30	Sat.	Mat.	Le Mars, IA	Le Mars Opera House
30	Sat.	Eve.	Sioux City, IA	Grand Opera House
OCTOBER				
1	Sun.	Eve.	Omaha, NE	Auditorium

Mon., 2nd through Sat., 7th (6 days), Kansas City, MO, Convention Hall. 2 concerts per day.

8	Sun.	Mat.	Mattoon, IL	Mattoon Thea.
8	Sun.	Eve.	Terre Haute, IN	Grand Opera House
9	Mon.	Mat.	Crawfordsville, IN	Music Hall
9	Mon.	Eve.	Lafayette, IN	Grand Opera House
10	Tue.	Mat.	Frankfort, IN	Blinn Thea.
10	Tue.	Eve.	Marion, IN	Indiana Thea.
11	Wed.	Mat.	Greenville, OH	Trainor's Opera House
11	Wed.	Eve.	Piqua, OH	May's Opera House

167

12	Thu.	Mat.	Urbana, OH	Clifford Thea.
12	Thu.	Eve.	Columbus, OH	Great Southern Thea.
13	Fri.	Mat.	Canal Dover, OH	Hardesty Thea.
13	Fri.	Eve.	Canton, OH	Canton Thea.
14	Sat.	M/E	Cleveland, OH	Grays' Armory
15	Sun.	Mat.	Elyria, OH	Elyria Thea.
15	Sun.	Eve.	Akron, OH	Colonial Thea.

Mon., 16ᵗʰ through Sat., 21ˢᵗ (6 days), 2ⁿᵈ (of 2) engagements at Pittsburgh Exposition. 2 concerts per day.

| 22 | Sun. | Eve. | New York, NY | Hippodrome |

[End of 4ᵗʰ 1905 tour]

1905 OFF-TOUR CONCERT

OCTOBER

| 29 | Sun. | Eve. | New York, NY | Hippodrome |

Soloists: Elizabeth Schiller, soprano; Giuseppe Tagliapietra, baritone; Jessie Straus, violin;

1ˢᵀ 1906 TOUR

Soloists: Elizabeth Schiller, soprano; Jeannette Powers, violin; Herbert L. Clarke & Ross Millhouse, cornet; Leo Zimmerman, trombone.

JANUARY

7	Sun.	Eve.	New York, NY	Hippodrome
8	Mon.	Mat.	Naugatuck, CT	Gem Opera House
8	Mon.	Eve.	New Haven, CT	Hyperion Thea.
9	Tue.	M/E	Worcester, MA	Mechanics' Hall
10	Wed.	M/E	Boston, MA	Symphony Hall
11	Thu.	Mat.	New Bedford, MA	New Bedford Thea.
11	Thu.	Eve.	Fall River, MA	Academy of Music
12	Fri.	M/E	Providence, RI	Infantry Hall
13	Sat.	M/E	Hartford, CT	Foot Guard Armory
14	Sun.	Eve.	New York, NY	Hippodrome
15	Mon.	M/E	Newark, NJ	Krueger Auditorium
16	Tue.	Mat.	Mauch Chunk, PA	Mauch Chunk Opera House
16	Wed.	Eve.	Pottsville, PA	Academy of Music
17	Wed.	Mat.	Sunbury, PA	Chestnut St. Opera House
17	Wed.	Eve.	Shamokin, PA	G.A.R. Opera House
18	Thu.	Mat.	Shenandoah, PA	O'Hara Thea.
18	Thu.	Eve.	Reading, PA	Academy of Music
19	Fri.	Mat.	Lancaster, PA	Fulton Opera House
19	Fri.	Eve.	York, PA	York Opera House
20	Sat.	M/E	Baltimore, MD	Lyric Thea.
21	Sun.	Eve.	Washington, DC	Columbia Thea.
22	Mon.	Mat.	Fredericksburg, VA	Opera House
22	Mon.	Eve.	Richmond, VA	Academy of Music
23	Tue.	Mat.	Newport News, VA	Academy of Music
23	Tue.	Eve.	Norfolk, VA	Academy of Music
24	Wed.	Mat.	Durham, NC	Academy of Music
24	Wed.	Eve.	Raleigh, NC	Academy of Music
25	Thu.	Mat.	Winston-Salem, NC	Elks' Auditorium
25	Thu.	Eve.	Greensboro, NC	Grand Opera House
26	Fri.	Mat.	Salisbury, NC	Meroney's Thea.
26	Fri.	Eve.	Charlotte, NC	Academy of Music
27	Sat.	Mat.	Spartanburg, SC	Converse College
27	Sat.	Eve.	Asheville, NC	Auditorium
29	Mon.	Mat.	Morristown, TN	Susong Building
29	Mon.	Eve.	Knoxville, TN	Staub's Thea.
30	Tue.	Mat.	Cleveland, TN	Craigmiles' Opera House
30	Tue.	Eve.	Chattanooga, TN	Chattanooga Opera House
31	Wed.	Mat.	Dalton, GA	Dalton Opera House
31	Wed.	Eve.	Rome, GA	Opera House

FEBRUARY

1	Thu.	Mat.	Anniston, AL	Noble Street Thea.
1	Thu.	Eve.	Birmingham, AL	Jefferson Thea.
2	Fri.	M/E	Atlanta, GA	Grand Opera House
3	Sat.	Mat.	Augusta, GA	Genovar's Opera House
3	Sat.	Eve.	Columbia, SC	Columbia Thea.
4	Sun.	Mat.	St. Augustine, FL	Opera House
4	Sun.	Eve.	Jacksonville, FL	Duval Thea.
5	Mon.	Mat.	Waycross, GA	Bailey Thea.
5	Mon.	Eve.	Brunswick, GA	Brunswick Opera House
6	Tue.	M/E	Savannah, GA	Savannah Thea.
7	Wed.	Mat.	Milledgeville, GA	Opera House
7	Wed.	Eve.	Macon, GA	Grand Opera House

8	Thu.	Mat.	Americus, GA	Glover's Opera House
8	Thu.	Eve.	Columbus, GA	Springer Opera House
9	Fri.	Mat.	Montgomery, AL	Bijou Thea.
9	Fri.	Eve.	Selma, AL	Academy of Music
10	Sat.	Mat.	Starkville, MS	A&M College
10	Sat.	Eve.	Columbus, MS	Industrial Institute College
11	Sun.	M/E	New Orleans, LA	Tulane Thea.
12	Mon.	Eve.	Natchez, MS	Baker Grand Thea.
13	Tue.	Mat.	Jackson, MS	Century Thea.
13	Tue.	Eve.	Vicksburg, MS	Walnut Street Thea.
14	Wed.	M/E	Shreveport, LA	Grand Opera House
15	Thu.	Mat.	Lake Charles, LA	Opera House
15	Thu.	Eve.	Beaumont, TX	Kyle Thea.
16	Fri.	M/E	Galveston, TX	Grand Opera House
17	Sat.	M/E	Houston, TX	Houston Thea.
18	Sun.	Mat.	San Antonio, TX	Grand Opera House
18	Sun.	Eve.	Austin, TX	Hancock Opera House
19	Mon.	Mat.	Temple, TX	Exchange Opera House
19	Mon.	Eve.	Waco, TX	Brown's Opera House
20	Tue.	Mat.	Cleburne, TX	Brown's Opera House
20	Tue.	Eve.	Fort Worth, TX	Greenwall's Opera House
21	Wed.	Mat.	Gainesville, TX	Brown's Opera House
21	Wed.	Eve.	Sherman, TX	Opera House
22	Thu.	M/E	Dallas, TX	Dallas Opera House
23	Fri.	Mat.	McKinney, TX	Opera House
23	Fri.	Eve.	Greenville, TX	Play House
24	Sat.	Mat.	Paris, TX	Peterson's Thea.
24	Sat.	Eve.	Texarkana, TX	Grand Opera House
25	Sun.	Mat.	Hot Springs, AR	Auditorium
26	Mon.	M/E	Little Rock, AR	Capital Thea.
27	Tue.	M/E	Memphis, TN	Lyceum Thea.
28	Wed.	Mat.	Humboldt, TN	Lyric Thea.
28	Wed.	Eve.	Jackson, TN	Marlowe Thea.

MARCH

1	Thu.	Mat.	Paris, TN	Crete Opera House
1	Thu.	Eve.	Paducah, KY	Kentucky Thea.
2	Fri.	Mat.	Clarksville, TN	Elder's Opera House
2	Fri.	Eve.	Hopkinsville, KY	Tabernacle
3	Sat.	Mat.	Henderson, KY	Park Thea.
3	Sat.	Eve.	Owensboro, KY	The Grand
4	Sun.	M/E	Louisville, KY	Macauley's Thea.
5	Mon.	Mat.	Washington, IN	Spink Opera House
5	Mon.	Eve.	Evansville, IN	Grand Opera House
6	Tue.	Mat.	Pana, IL	Grand Opera House
6	Tue.	Eve.	Decatur, IL	Powers' Grand Op. House
7	Wed.	Mat.	Jacksonville, IL	Grand Opera House
7	Wed.	Eve.	Springfield, IL	Chatterton's Opera House
8	Thu.	Mat.	Lincoln, IL	Broadway Thea.
8	Thu.	Eve.	Bloomington, IL	Grand Opera House
9	Fri.	M/E	Peoria, IL	Coliseum
10	Sat.	Mat.	Chicago, IL	Orchestra Hall
10	Sat.	Eve.	Joliet, IL	Joliet Thea.
11	Sun.	M/E	Chicago, IL	Orchestra Hall
12	Mon.	M/E	Milwaukee, WI	Pabst Thea.
13	Tue.	Mat.	Sheboygan, WI	Opera House
13	Tue.	Eve.	Oshkosh, WI	Grand Opera House
14	Wed.	Mat.	Appleton, WI	Appleton Thea.
14	Wed.	Eve.	Green Bay, WI	Green Bay Thea.
15	Thu.	Mat.	Marinette, WI	Scott Thea.
15	Thu.	Eve.	Escanaba, MI	Peterson Opera House
16	Fri.	Mat.	Marquette, MI	Marquette Opera House
16	Fri.	Eve.	Ishpeming, MI	Ishpeming Thea.
17	Sat.	Mat.	Hancock, MI	Kerredge Thea.
17	Sat.	Eve.	Calumet, MI	Calumet Thea.
18	Sun.	Mat.	West Superior, WI	Grand Opera House
18	Sun.	Eve.	Duluth, MN	Lyceum Thea.
19	Mon.	M/E	Minneapolis, MN	Auditorium
20	Tue.	Mat.	Red Wing, MN	Auditorium
20	Tue.	Eve.	Rochester, MN	Metropolitan Thea.
21	Wed.	Mat.	La Crosse, WI	La Crosse Thea.
21	Wed.	Eve.	Winona, MN	Winona Opera House
22	Thu.	Mat.	Owatonna, MN	Metropolitan Opera House
22	Thu.	Eve.	Faribault, MN	Faribault Opera House
23	Fri.	Mat.	Mankato, MN	Mankato Thea.
23	Fri.	Eve.	Albert Lea, MN	Broadway Thea.

24	Sat.	Mat.	Charles City, IA	Hildreth Opera House
24	Sat.	Eve.	Mason City, IA	Wilson Opera House
25	Sun.	M/E	Des Moines, IA	Auditorium
26	Mon.	Mat.	What Cheer, IA	Masonic Opera House
26	Mon.	Eve.	Cedar Rapids, IA	Greene's Opera House
27	Tue.	Mat.	Maquoketa, IA	Rice's Grand Opera House
27	Tue.	Eve.	Clinton, IA	Clinton Opera House
28	Wed.	Mat.	Goshen, IN	Jefferson Thea.
28	Wed.	Eve.	Battle Creek, MI	Post Thea.
29	Thu.	Mat.	Bay City, MI	Washington Thea.
29	Thu.	Eve.	Saginaw, MI	Academy of Music
30	Fri.	Mat.	Detroit, MI	Lyceum Thea.
30	Fri.	Eve.	Ann Arbor, MI	University Hall
31	Sat.	M/E	Toronto, ONT/Canada	Massey Music Hall

APRIL

1	Sun.	Mat.	Niagara Falls, NY	International Thea.
1	Sun.	Eve.	Buffalo, NY	Shea's Thea.
2	Mon.	Mat.	Batavia, NY	Dellinger Opera House
2	Mon.	Eve.	Rochester, NY	Lyceum Thea.
3	Tue.	Mat.	Geneva, NY	Smith Opera House
3	Tue.	Eve.	Auburn, NY	Burtis Opera House
4	Wed.	Mat.	Penn Yan, NY	Yates Lyceum
4	Wed.	Eve.	Elmira, NY	Lyceum Thea.
5	Thu.	Mat.	Waverly, NY	Loomis Opera House
5	Thu.	Eve.	Ithaca, NY	Lyceum Thea.
6	Fri.	Mat.	Towanda, PA	Hale's Opera House
6	Fri.	Eve.	Wilkes-Barre, PA	Nesbitt Thea.
7	Sat.	M/E	Scranton, PA	Lyceum Thea.
8	Sun.	Eve.	New York, NY	Hippodrome

[End of 1ˢᵗ 1906 tour]

2ᴺᴰ 1906 TOUR

APRIL

15 Sun. Eve. New York, NY Hippodrome

Soloists: Elizabeth Schiller, soprano; Jeannette Powers, violin; Herbert L. Clarke, cornet.

Soloists for remainder of tour: Elizabeth Schiller, soprano; Jeannette Powers, violin; Herbert L. Clarke & Ross Millhouse, cornet; Leo Zimmerman, trombone.

17	Tue.	Mat.	Plattsburgh, NY	Plattsburgh Thea.
17	Tue.	Eve.	Burlington, VT	Strong Thea.
18	Wed.	M/E	Montreal, QUE/Canada	Arena
19	Thu.	Mat.	Newport, VT	Lane's Opera House
19	Thu.	Eve.	St. Johnsbury, VT	Music Hall
20	Fri.	Mat.	Claremont, NH	Opera House
20	Fri.	Eve.	Concord, NH	Opera House
21	Sat.	Mat.	Franklin, NH	Franklin Opera House
21	Sat.	Eve.	Manchester, NH	Manchester Opera House
22	Sun.	Mat.	Lynn, MA	Lynn Thea.
22	Sun.	Eve.	Boston, MA	Boston Thea.
23	Mon.	Mat.	Newburyport, MA	City Hall
23	Mon.	Eve.	Portsmouth, NH	Music Hall
24	Tue.	Mat.	Haverhill, MA	Academy of Music
24	Tue.	Eve.	Dover, NH	Opera House
25	Wed.	Mat.	Biddeford, ME	City Opera House
25	Wed.	Eve.	Portland, ME	Jefferson Thea.
26	Thu.	Mat.	Bath, ME	Columbia Thea.
26	Thu.	Eve.	Rockland, ME	Farwell Opera House
27	Fri.	Mat.	Augusta, ME	Grand Opera House
27	Fri.	Eve.	Lewiston, ME	Empire Thea.
28	Sat.	Mat.	Salem, MA	Salem Thea.
28	Sat.	Eve.	Lawrence, MA	New Opera House
29	Sun.	Mat.	Lowell, MA	Associate Hall
29	Sun.	Eve.	Boston, MA	Boston Thea.
30	Mon.	Mat.	Nashua, NH	Nashua Thea.
30	Mon.	Eve.	Fitchburg, MA	Cumings' Thea.

MAY

1	Tue.	Mat.	Keene, NH	City Hall
1	Tue.	Eve.	Bellows Falls, VT	Opera House
2	Wed.	Mat.	Greenfield, MA	Washington Hall
2	Wed.	Eve.	Northampton, MA	Academy of Music
3	Thu.	Mat.	North Adams, MA	Empire Thea.
3	Thu.	Eve.	Pittsfield, MA	Colonial Thea.
4	Fri.	Mat.	Saratoga Springs, NY	Town Hall

4	Fri.	Eve.	Troy, NY	Rand Opera House
5	Sat.	M/E	Albany, NY	Harmanus Bleeker Hall
6	Sun.	Eve.	New York, NY	Hippodrome

[End of 2ⁿᵈ 1906 tour]

3ᴿᴰ 1906 TOUR

AUGUST

11 Sat. M/E Asbury Park, NJ Casino

Soloists: Estelle Liebling, soprano; Jeannette Powers, violin; Herbert L. Clarke, cornet.

AUGUST-SEPTEMBER

Sun., 12 Aug. through Mon., 3 Sept. (23 days), Willow Grove (PA) Park. 4 concerts per day.

Soloists: Estelle Liebling, Ada Chambers, Ethel Crane, & Lucy Anne Allen, soprano; Jeannette Powers, violin; Herbert L. Clarke, cornet; John J. Perfetto, euphonium; Leo Zimmerman, trombone; Joseph Norrito, clarinet.

[End of 3ʳᵈ 1906 tour]

4ᵀᴴ 1906 TOUR

SEPTEMBER

16 Sun. Eve. Cumberland, MD Academy of Music

Soloists: Ada Chambers, soprano; Jeannette Powers, violin; Herbert L. Clarke, cornet.

Mon., 17ᵗʰ thru Sat., 22ⁿᵈ (6 days), Pittsburgh Exposition. 4 concerts per day.

Soloists: Ada Chambers, soprano; Jeannette Powers, violin; Herbert L. Clarke & Ross Millhouse, cornet; H. LeBarbier, trumpet; Leo Zimmerman, trombone; Giacomo Norrito, piccolo; Joseph Norrito, clarinet; William Schensley, saxophone.

Soloists for tour up until Springfield/Illinois Music Festival: Ada Chambers, soprano; Jeannette Powers, violin; Herbert L. Clarke, cornet.

SEPTEMBER

23	Sun.	Eve.	Akron, OH	Colonial Thea.
24	Mon.	Mat.	Massillon, OH	Armory
24	Mon.	Eve.	Alliance, OH	Craven's Opera House
25	Tue.	Mat.	Warren, OH	Warren Opera House
25	Tue.	Eve.	Youngstown, OH	Park Thea.
26	Wed.	Mat.	Cambridge, OH	Colonial Thea.
26	Wed.	Eve.	Marietta, OH	Auditorium
27	Thu.	Mat.	Bellefontaine, OH	Grand Opera House
27	Thu.	Eve.	Dayton, OH	Victoria Thea.
28	Fri.	Mat.	Xenia, OH	Opera House
28	Fri.	Eve.	Hamilton, OH	Jefferson Thea.
29	Sat.	M/E	Indianapolis, IN	English Opera House

OCTOBER

Mon., 1ˢᵗ through Sat., 6ᵗʰ (6 days), Illinois Music Festival at Illinois State Armory in Springfield. 2 concerts each evening Mon. through Fri. and matinee on Sat., 6th.

Soloists: Ada Chambers, soprano; Jeannette Powers, violin; Herbert L. Clarke, Ross Millhouse, & Henry Higgins, cornet; John J. Perfetto, euphonium; Leo Zimmerman, trombone; Joseph Norrito, clarinet.

Soloists until Boston Food Fair: Ada Chambers, soprano; Jeannette Powers, violin; Herbert L. Clarke, cornet.

OCTOBER

6	Sat.	Eve.	Decatur, IL	Powers' Opera House
7	Sun.	Mat.	Danville, IL	Grand Opera House
7	Sun.	Eve.	Bloomington, IL	Grand Opera House
8	Mon.	Mat.	Logansport, IN	Dowling Thea.
8	Mon.	Eve.	Wabash, IN	Eagles' Thea.
9	Tue.	Mat.	Defiance, OH	Citizens Opera House
9	Tue.	Eve.	Tiffin, OH	Auditorium
10	Wed.	Mat.	Urbana, OH	Clifford Thea.
10	Wed.	Eve.	Delaware, OH	Gray Chapel
11	Thu.	Mat.	Dunkirk, NY	Nelson Opera House
11	Thu.	Eve.	Jamestown, NY	Samuels Opera House
12	Fri.	Mat.	Hornell, NY	Shattuck Opera House
12	Fri.	Eve.	Corning, NY	Opera House
13	Sat.	Mat.	Port Jervis, NY	Casino
13	Sat.	Eve.	Middletown, NY	Armory
14	Sun.	Eve.	New York, NY	Hippodrome

Mon., 15ᵗʰ through Sat., 27ᵗʰ (12 days), Boston Food Fair. 2 concerts per day except none on Sun., 21ˢᵗ.

Soloists: Ada Chambers & Lucy Anne Allen, soprano; Jeannette Powers, violin; Herbert L. Clarke & Ross Millhouse, cornet; H. LeBarbier, trumpet; John J. Perfetto, euphonium; Leo Zimmerman, trombone; Giacomo Norrito, piccolo.
OCTOBER

| 28 | Sun. | Eve. | New York, NY | Hippodrome |

Soloists: Ada Chambers & Estelle Liebling, soprano; Jeannette Powers, violin; Herbert L. Clarke, cornet.
[End of 4ᵗʰ 1906 tour]

1907 TOUR

AUGUST

| 8 | Thu. | M/E | Asbury Park, NJ | Casino |

Soloists: Lucy Allen, soprano; Jeannette Powers, violin; Herbert L. Clarke, cornet.
AUGUST-SEPTEMBER
Sat., 10 Aug. through Mon., 2 Sept. (24 days), Willow Grove (PA), Park. 4 concerts per day.

Soloists: Estelle Liebling, Ada Chambers, & Lucy Anne Allen, soprano; Jeannette Powers, violin; Herbert L. Clarke & Ross Millhouse, cornet; John J. Perfetto, euphonium; Leo Zimmerman, trombone; Giacomo Norrito, flute/piccolo; Joseph Norrito, clarinet; Charles P. Lowe, xylophone.
SEPTEMBER

3	Tue.	Eve.	Easton, PA	Able Opera House
4	Wed.	Eve.	Lancaster, PA	Fulton Opera House
5	Thu.	Eve.	Sunbury, PA	Chestnut St. Opera House
6	Fri.	Eve.	Clearfield, PA	Opera House
7	Sat.	M/E	Altoona, PA	Mishler Thea.

Mon., 9ᵗʰ through Fri., 20ᵗʰ (12 days), Pittsburgh Exposition. 2 concerts per day except no concerts on Sun., 15ᵗʰ.

Soloists: Lucy Anne Allen, soprano; Jeannette Powers, violin; Herbert L. Clarke, cornet; Leo Zimmerman, trombone; Julius Spindler, flute; Joseph Norrito, clarinet.

| 21 | Sat. | Eve. | Valparaiso, IN | Memorial Opera House |
| 22 | Sun. | Eve. | Fort Dodge, IA | Midland Opera House |

Mon., 23ʳᵈ through Sat., 28ᵗʰ (6 days), Mitchell, SD, Corn Palace. 2 concerts per day.

Soloists: Lucy Anne Allen, soprano; Jeannette Powers, violin; Herbert L. Clarke & Ross Millhouse, cornet; John J. Perfetto, euphonium; Leo Zimmerman, trombone; Julius Spindler, flute; Joseph Norrito, clarinet.

Soloists for remainder of tour: Lucy Anne Allen, soprano; Jeannette Powers, violin; Herbert L. Clarke, cornet; John J. Perfetto, euphonium; Leo Zimmerman, trombone; Joseph Norrito, clarinet.

| 30 | Mon. | Mat. | Brainerd, MN | Opera House |
| 30 | Mon. | Eve. | St. Cloud, MN | Davidson Opera House |

OCTOBER

1	Tue.	Eve.	Fargo, ND	Fargo Opera House
2	Wed.	Mat.	Jamestown, ND	Opera House
2	Wed.	Eve.	Bismarck, ND	Anthenaeum
3	Thu.	Eve.	Billings, MT	Coliseum Rink
4	Fri.	M/E	Helena, MT	Helena Thea.
5	Sat.	M/E	Great Falls, MT	Grand Thea.
6	Sun.	M/E	Butte, MT	Auditorium
7	Mon.	M/E	Spokane, WA	Spokane Thea.
8	Tue.	Mat.	Yakima, WA	Yakima Thea.
8	Tue.	Eve.	Ellensburg, WA	Opera House
9	Wed.	Eve.	Tacoma, WA	Tacoma Thea.
10	Thu.	Eve.	Tacoma, WA	Tacoma Thea.
11	Fri.	Eve.	Seattle, WA	Dreamland Rink
12	Sat.	M/E	Seattle, WA	Dreamland Rink
13	Sun.	M/E	Seattle, WA	Dreamland Rink
14	Mon.	Eve.	Vancouver, BC/Canada	Opera House
15	Tue.	M/E	Bellingham, WA	Beck Thea.
16	Wed.	M/E	Everett, WA	Everett Thea.
17	Thu.	Eve.	Olympia, WA	Olympia Thea.
18	Fri.	Eve.	Portland, OR	Armory
19	Sat.	M/E	Portland, OR	Armory
21	Mon.	M/E	San Jose, CA	Victory Thea.
22	Tue.	Eve.	Sacramento, CA	Clunie Thea.
23	Wed.	Eve.	Berkeley, CA	Greek Thea.
24	Thu.	Eve.	Fresno, CA	Barton Opera House
25	Fri.	M/E	Los Angeles, CA	Auditorium
26	Sat.	M/E	Los Angeles, CA	Auditorium
27	Sun.	M/E	Long Beach, CA	Municipal Auditorium

Tue., 29ᵗʰ through Thu., 31ˢᵗ (3 days), San Francisco, Dreamland Park. 2 concerts per day.
NOVEMBER

1	Fri.	M/E	Stockton, CA	Yosemite Thea.
2	Sat.	Eve.	Auburn, CA	Auburn Opera House
4	Mon.	M/E	Salt Lake City, UT	Tabernacle
5	Tue.	M/E	Salt Lake City, UT	Tabernacle
6	Wed.	Eve.	Rock Springs, WY	Union Opera House
7	Thu.	Eve.	Cheyenne, WY	Capitol Avenue Thea.
8	Fri.	M/E	Pueblo, CO	Grand Opera House
9	Sat.	M/E	Colorado Springs, CO	Opera House
10	Sun.	M/E	Denver, CO	Broadway Thea.
11	Mon.	Eve.	La Junta, CO	La Junta Thea.
12	Tue.	Mat.	Kingman, KS	Grand Opera House
12	Tue.	Eve.	Hutchinson, KS	Home Thea.
13	Wed.	M/E	Wichita, KS	Toler Auditorium
14	Thu.	M/E	Topeka, KS	Auditorium
15	Fri.	Eve.	Atchison, KS	Atchison Thea.
16	Sat.	M/E	Lincoln, NE	Oliver Thea.
17	Sun.	M/E	Omaha, NE	Auditorium
18	Mon.	M/E	Des Moines, IA	Auditorium
19	Tue.	Mat.	Iowa Falls, IA	Metropolitan Opera House
19	Tue.	Eve.	Mason City, IA	Wilson Opera House
20	Wed.	Eve.	Faribault, MN	Faribault Opera House
21	Thu.	M/E	St. Paul, MN	Auditorium
22	Fri.	M/E	Minneapolis, MN	Auditorium
23	Sat.	M/E	Superior, WI	Superior Grand Opera House
24	Sun.	M/E	Duluth, MN	Lyceum Thea.
25	Mon.	Eve.	Eau Claire, WI	Grand Opera House
26	Tue.	M/E	Milwaukee, WI	Pabst Thea.
27	Wed.	Eve.	Madison, WI	University Armory
28	Thu.	Eve.	Chicago, IL	Orchestra Hall
29	Fri.	Eve.	Chicago, IL	Orchestra Hall
30	Sat.	M/E	Peoria, IL	Coliseum

DECEMBER

1	Sun.	Eve.	Peoria, IL	Coliseum
2	Mon.	Mat.	Burlington, IA	Grand Opera House
2	Mon.	Eve.	Galesburg, IL	Auditorium
3	Tue.	M/E	Kawanee, IL	Armory
4	Wed.	Mat.	Aurora, IL	Grand Opera House
4	Wed.	Eve.	Joliet, IL	Joliet Thea.
5	Thu.	Eve.	Mansfield, OH	Memorial Opera House
6	Fri.	Eve.	Canton, OH	Auditorium
7	Sat.	M/E	Cleveland, OH	Grays' Armory
8	Sun.	Mat.	Elyria, OH	Elyria Thea.
8	Sun.	Eve.	Sandusky, OH	Grand Opera House
9	Mon.	Eve.	Ann Arbor, MI	University Hall
10	Tue.	M/E	Detroit, MI	Light Guard Armory
11	Wed.	M/E	Buffalo, NY	Convention Hall
12	Thu.	M/E	Toronto, ONT/Canada	Massey Music Hall
13	Fri.	M/E	Rochester, NY	Lyceum Thea.
14	Sat.	M/E	Albany, NY	Armory

[End of 1907 tour]

1ˢᵀ 1908 TOUR

Soloists: Lucy Allen, soprano; Jeannette Powers, violin; Herbert L. Clarke, cornet; Joseph Norrito, clarinet.
JANUARY

5	Sun.	Eve.	New York, NY	Hippodrome
7	Tue.	M/E	Providence, RI	Infantry Hall
8	Wed.	M/E	Boston, MA	Symphony Hall
9	Thu.	M/E	Worcester, MA	Mechanics' Hall
10	Fri.	M/E	Hartford, CT	Foot Guard Armory
11	Sat.	M/E	New Haven, CT	Hyperion Thea.
12	Sun.	Eve.	New York, NY	Hippodrome
13	Mon.	Eve.	Reading, PA	Academy of Music
14	Tue.	M/E	Richmond, VA	Academy of Music
15	Wed.	Mat.	Charlottesville, VA	Cabell Hall
15	Wed.	Eve.	Lynchburg, VA	Academy of Music
16	Thu.	Mat.	Goldsboro, NC	Messenger Opera House
16	Thu.	Eve.	Wilmington, NC	Academy of Music
17	Fri.	Mat.	Florence, SC	Florence Auditorium

17	Fri.	Eve.	Columbia, SC	Columbia Thea.	
18	Sat.	M/E	Charleston, SC	Academy of Music	
19	Sun.	M/E	Jacksonville, FL	Dixie Thea.	
20	Mon.	M/E	Savannah, GA	Savannah Thea.	
21	Tue.	M/E	Augusta, GA	Grand Opera House	
22	Wed.	M/E	Barnesville, GA	Auditorium	
23	Thu.	M/E	Macon, GA	Grand Opera House	
24	Fri.	M/E	Birmingham, AL	Jefferson Thea.	
25	Sat.	Eve.	Huntsville, AL	Elks' Thea.	
26	Sun.	Eve.	Decatur, AL	Lyceum Thea.	
27	Mon.	Mat.	Anniston, AL	not known	
28	Tue.	M/E	Chattanooga, TN	Chattanooga Opera House	
29	Wed.	M/E	Nashville, TN	Ryman Auditorium	
30	Thu.	M/E	Memphis, TN	Lyceum Thea.	
31	Fri.	Mat.	Holly Springs, MS	Opera House	
31	Fri.	Eve.	Covington, TN	Opera House	

FEBRUARY

1	Sat.	M/E	Hot Springs, AR	Auditorium
2	Sun.	M/E	St. Louis, MO	Olympic Thea.
3	Mon.	Mat.	Belleville, IL	Lyric Thea.
3	Mon.	Eve.	Centralia, IL	Pittenger Grand Opera House
4	Tue.	Mat.	Alton, IL	Temple Thea.
4	Tue.	Eve.	St. Louis, MO	Odeon Thea.
5	Wed.	M/E	St. Louis, MO	Odeon Thea.
6	Thu.	Mat.	Lincoln, IL	Broadway Thea.
6	Thu.	Eve.	Bloomington, IL	Grand Opera House
7	Fri.	Eve.	Decatur, IL	Powers' Grand Op. House
8	Sat.	M/E	Urbana, IL	University of Illinois
9	Sun.	Eve.	Terre Haute, IN	Grand Opera House
10	Mon.	Eve.	Richmond, IN	Coliseum
11	Tue.	Eve.	Maysville, KY	Washington Opera House
12	Wed.	M/E	Lexington, KY	Auditorium
13	Thu.	M/E	Cincinnati, OH	Music Hall
14	Fri.	M/E	Columbus, OH	Memorial Hall
15	Sat.	M/E	Charleston, WV	Burlew Thea.
16	Sun.	Eve.	Washington, DC	National Thea.
17	Mon.	M/E	Baltimore, MD	Lyric Thea.
18	Tue.	Mat.	Carlisle, PA	Carlisle Opera House
18	Tue.	Eve.	York, PA	York Opera House
19	Wed.	Mat.	Coatsville, PA	Opera House
19	Wed.	Eve.	Allentown, PA	Lyric Thea.
20	Thu.	M/E	New Brunswick, NJ	Opera House
21	Fri.	Mat.	Peekskill, NY	Colonial Thea.
21	Fri.	Eve.	Yonkers, NY	Blaney's Thea.
22	Sat.	M/E	Newark, NJ	Krueger Auditorium
23	Sun.	Eve.	New York, NY	Hippodrome
24	Mon.	Mat.	Northampton, MA	Academy of Music
24	Mon.	Eve.	Springfield, MA	Court Square Thea.
25	Tue.	Mat.	New Bedford, MA	New Bedford Thea.
25	Tue.	Eve.	Brockton, MA	City Thea.
26	Wed.	M/E	Fall River, MA	Academy of Music
27	Thu.	M/E	Worcester, MA	Mechanics' Hall
28	Fri.	Mat.	Lowell, MA	Lowell Opera House
28	Fri.	Eve.	Manchester, NH	Mechanics' Hall
29	Sat.	Mat.	Portsmouth, NH	Mechanics' Hall
29	Sat.	Eve.	Dover, NH	Opera House

MARCH

1	Sun.	Mat.	Lynn, MA	Lynn Thea.
1	Sun.	Eve.	Boston, MA	Colonial Thea.
2	Mon.	Mat.	Attleboro, MA	Bates Opera House
2	Mon.	Eve.	Taunton, MA	Taunton Thea.
3	Tue.	M/E	Providence, RI	Infantry Hall

[End of 1ˢᵗ 1908 tour]

1908 OFF-TOUR CONCERT

AUGUST

11	Tue.	M/E	Asbury Park, NJ	Casino

Soloists not known.

2ᴺᴰ 1908 TOUR

AUGUST-SEPTEMBER

Sun., 16 Aug. through Mon., 7 Sept. (23 days), Willow Grove (PA) Park. 4 concerts per day.

Soloists: Estelle Liebling, Lucy Anne Allen, soprano; Giacinta della Rocca & Rose Reichard, violin; Herbert L. Clarke & Ross Millhouse, cornet; John J. Perfetto, euphonium; Ralph Corey, trombone; Julius Spindler, flute; Paul J. Senno, piccolo; Joseph Norrito, clarinet.

SEPTEMBER

8	Tue.	Mat.	Huntingdon, PA	Huntingdon Opera House
8	Tue.	Eve.	Altoona, PA	Mishler Thea.

Wed., 9ᵗʰ through Sat., 19ᵗʰ (10 days), Pittsburgh Exposition. 2 concerts per day except no concerts Sun. 13ᵗʰ.

Soloists: Lucy Anne Allen, soprano; Rose Richard, violin; Herbert L. Clarke & Ross Millhouse, cornet; Paul J. Senno, piccolo.

Soloists between Pittsburgh Exposition & Boston Food Fair: Lucy Allen, soprano; Rose Reichard, violin; Herbert L. Clarke & Ross Millhouse, cornet; Paul J. Senno, piccolo.

20	Sun.	Eve.	Marietta, OH	Auditorium
21	Mon.	Eve.	Clarksburg, WV	Grand Opera House
22	Tue.	Mat.	Grafton, WV	Brinkman's Opera House
22	Tue.	Eve.	Fairmont, WV	Grand Opera House
23	Wed.	Mat.	Piedmont, WV	Opera House
23	Wed.	Eve.	Cumberland, MD	Maryland Thea.
24	Thu.	Mat.	Martinsburg, WV	Opera House
24	Thu.	Eve.	Winchester, VA	Auditorium
25	Fri.	Mat.	Frederick, MD	City Opera House
25	Fri.	Eve.	Hagerstown, MD	Academy of Music
26	Sat.	Eve.	Plainfield, NJ	Plainfield Thea.
27	Sun.	Eve.	New York, NY	Hippodrome

SEPTEMBER-OCTOBER

Mon., 28 Sept. through Sat., 17 Oct. (19 days), Boston Food Fair. 2 concerts per day except no concerts on Sundays.

Soloists: Lucy Anne Allen & Louise Ormsby, soprano; Rose Reichard & Giacinta della Rocca, violin; Herbert L. Clarke & Ross Millhouse, cornet; John J. Perfetto, euphonium; Ralph Corey, trombone.

OCTOBER

18	Sun.	Eve.	New York, NY	Hippodrome

Soloists: Louise Ormsby, soprano; Giacinta della Rocca, violin; Herbert L. Clarke, cornet.

[End of 2ⁿᵈ 1908 tour]

1908 OFF-TOUR CONCERT

NOVEMBER

1	Sun.	Eve.	New York, NY	Metropolitan Opera House

Soloists: Estelle Liebling, soprano; Giacinta della Rocca, violin; Herbert L. Clarke, cornet.

1909 OFF-TOUR CONCERT

FEBRUARY

7	Thu.	Eve.	New York, NY	Casino Thea.

Soloists: Helen Noldi, soprano; John J. Perfetto, euphonium; Alice Dean, violin; Edoardo Boccalari, guest conductor.

1909 TOUR

AUGUST-SEPTEMBER

Sun., 15 Aug. through Mon., 6 Sept. (23 days), Willow Grove (PA) Park. 4 concerts per day.

Soloists: Virginia Root, Helen Crennan, Francis Hoyt, & Grace Hoyt, soprano; Giacinta della Rocca, Rose Ford, & Florence Hardeman, violin; Herbert L. Clarke & Ross Millhouse, cornet; John J. Perfetto, euphonium; Ralph Corey, trombone; Paul J. Senno & Marshall P. Lufsky, piccolo.

Soloists between Willow Grove & Pittsburgh Exposition: Ada Chambers & Elizabeth Schiller, soprano; Jessie Straus, violin; Herbert L. Clarke, cornet; Leo Zimmerman, trombone.

SEPTEMBER

7	Tue.	Eve.	Hartford, CT	Foot Guard Armory
8	Wed.	M/E	Hartford, CT	Foot Guard Armory
9	Thu.	Mat.	Rockville, CT	Town Hall
9	Thu.	Eve.	Putnam, CT	Bradley Thea.
10	Fri.	Mat.	Woonsocket, RI	Woonsocket Opera House
10	Fri.	Eve.	Attleboro, MA	Bates Opera House
11	Sat.	Mat.	Newport, RI	Opera House
11	Sat.	Eve.	Brockton, MA	City Thea.
12	Sun.	Eve.	Boston, MA	Boston Thea.
13	Mon.	Mat.	Lowell, MA	Lowell Opera House
13	Mon.	Eve.	Manchester, NH	Mechanics' Hall
14	Tue.	Mat.	Portsmouth, NH	Portsmouth Thea.

14	Tue.	Eve.	Dover, NH	Opera House
15	Wed.	Mat.	Portland, ME	Jefferson Thea.
15	Wed.	Eve.	Lewiston, ME	Empire Thea.
16	Thu.	Eve.	Sherbrooke, QUE/Canada	Clement Thea.
17	Fri.	M/E	Quebec, QUE/Canada	Bennett's Auditorium
18	Sat.	M/E	Montreal, QUE/Canada	Arena
19	Sun.	M/E	St. Johns, QUE/Canada	Exhibition Grounds
20	Mon.	M/E	Montreal, QUE/Canada	Arena
21	Tue.	a.m.	Ottawa, ONT/Canada	Dey's Arena
21	Tue.	Mat.	Ottawa, ONT/Canada	Dey's Arena
22	Wed.	Mat.	St. Albans, VT	Waugh Opera House
22	Wed.	Eve.	Burlington, VT	Strong Thea.
23	Thu.	Mat.	Rutland, VT	Opera House
23	Thu.	Eve.	Bennington, VT	Bennington Opera House
24	Fri.	Mat.	Oneonta, NY	Oneonta Thea.
24	Fri.	Eve.	Binghamton, NY	Armory
25	Sat.	Mat.	Wellsville, NY	Baldwin's Thea.
25	Sat.	Eve.	Olean, NY	Olean Opera House
26	Sun.	Mat.	Du Bois, PA	Avenue Thea.

SEPTEMBER-OCTOBER
Mon., 27 Sept. through Sat., 2 Oct. (6 days), Pittsburgh Exposition.
2 concerts per day.
Soloists: Ada Chambers, soprano; Jessie Straus, violin; Herbert L. Clarke & Ira Holland, cornet; John J. Perfetto, euphonium; Leo Zimmerman, trombone.

Soloists for remainder of tour: Francis Hoyt & Grace Hoyt, soprano; Florence Hardeman, violin; Herbert L. Clarke, cornet; John J. Perfetto, euphonium; Paul J. Senno, piccolo.

OCTOBER
3	Sun.	Eve.	Akron, OH	Colonial Thea.
4	Mon.	M/E	Columbus, OH	Memorial Hall
5	Tue.	Mat.	Springfield, OH	Fairbanks Thea.
5	Tue.	Eve.	Dayton, OH	Victoria Thea.
6	Wed.	M/E	Cincinnati, OH	Music Hall
7	Thu.	Eve.	Alton, IL	Temple Thea.
8	Fri.	Mat.	Hannibal, MO	Park Thea.
8	Fri.	Eve.	Quincy, IL	Empire Thea.
9	Sat.	Mat.	Macon, MO	Logan's Thea.
9	Sat.	Eve.	Chillicothe, MO	Luella Thea.
10	Sun.	Eve.	St. Joseph, MO	Tootle Thea.
11	Mon.	Mat.	Lawrence, KS	Bowersock's Opera House
11	Mon.	Eve.	Topeka, KS	Grand Opera House
12	Tue.	Mat.	Ottawa, KS	Rohrbaugh Thea.
12	Tue.	Eve.	Emporia, KS	Whitley's Opera House
13	Wed.	Mat.	Newton, KS	Ragsdale Opera House
13	Wed.	Eve.	Wichita, KS	Crawford Thea.
14	Thu.	Mat.	Kingman, KS	Grand Opera House
14	Thu.	Eve.	Hutchinson, KS	Home Thea.
15	Fri.	Mat.	La Junta, CO	La Junta Thea.
16	Sat.	M/E	Colorado Springs, CO	Opera House
17	Sun.	M/E	Denver, CO	Broadway Thea.
18	Mon.	Mat.	Trinidad, CO	West Thea.
18	Mon.	Eve.	Raton, NM	Coliseum
19	Tue.	Mat.	Santa Fe, NM	Elks' Thea.
19	Tue.	Eve.	Albuquerque, NM	Elks' Thea.
20	Wed.	Eve.	Prescott, AZ	Elks' Thea.
21	Thu.	M/E	Phoenix, AZ	Elks' Thea.
22	Fri.	Mat.	Needles, CA	Santa Fe Park
23	Sat.	Mat.	Redlands, CA	Wyatt Opera House
23	Sat.	Eve.	San Bernardino, CA	Grand Opera House
24	Sun.	M/E	San Diego, CA	Garrick Thea.

Mon., 25th through Sat., 30th (6 days), Los Angeles, CA, Temple Auditorium. 2 concerts per day.
31	Sun.	M/E	Long Beach, CA	Municipal Auditorium

NOVEMBER
1	Mon.	Mat.	Hanford, CA	Hanford Opera House
1	Mon.	Eve.	Bakersfield, CA	Bakersfield Opera House
2	Tue.	Eve.	Fresno, CA	Barton Opera House
3	Wed.	M/E	Stockton, CA	Yosemite Thea.

Thu., 4th through Sun., 7th (4 days), San Francisco, CA, Dreamland Park. 2 concerts per day.
8	Mon.	Mat.	Berkeley, CA	Harmon Thea.
8	Mon.	Eve.	Berkeley, CA	Greek Thea.
9	Tue.	M/E	San Jose, CA	Victory Thea.
10	Wed.	Mat.	Watsonville, CA	Opera House

10	Wed.	Eve.	Palo Alto, CA	Stanford University
11	Thu.	M/E	Woodland, CA	Opera House
12	Fri.	Mat.	Chico, CA	Majestic Thea.
12	Fri.	Eve.	Marysville, CA	Marysville Thea.
13	Sat.	M/E	Sacramento, CA	Clunie Thea.
14	Sun.	M/E	Reno, NV	Wheelman Thea.
15	Mon.	Eve.	Ogden, UT	Tabernacle
16	Tue.	M/E	Salt Lake City, UT	Tabernacle
18	Thu.	Eve.	Cheyenne, WY	Capitol Avenue Thea.
19	Fri.	Mat.	York, NE	York Opera House
19	Fri.	Eve.	Lincoln, NE	Oliver Thea.
20	Sat.	M/E	Omaha, NE	Auditorium
21	Sun.	M/E	Kansas City, MO	Convention Hall
22	Mon.	Eve.	Galesburg, IL	Auditorium
23	Tue.	Mat.	Joliet, IL	Plumb Opera House
23	Tue.	Eve.	Streator, IL	Plumb Opera House
24	Wed.	M/E	Chicago, IL	Orchestra Hall
25	Wed.	M/E	Chicago, IL	Orchestra Hall
26	Fri.	Mat.	Bloomington, IL	Coliseum
26	Fri.	Eve.	Springfield, IL	Chatterton's Opera House
27	Sat.	M/E	St. Louis, MO	Coliseum
28	Sun.	M/E	St. Louis, MO	Coliseum
29	Mon.	Mat.	Taylorville, IL	Elks' Thea.
29	Mon.	Eve.	Decatur, IL	Powers' Grand Op. House
30	Tue.	M/E	Urbana, IL	University of Illinois

DECEMBER
1	Wed.	Mat.	South Bend, IN	Auditorium
1	Wed.	Eve.	Goshen, IN	Jefferson Thea.
2	Thu.	Mat.	Kalamazoo, MI	Fuller Thea.
2	Thu.	Eve.	Battle Creek, MI	Post Thea.
3	Fri.	M/E	Detroit, MI	Light Guard Armory
4	Sat.	M/E	Toledo, OH	Valentine Thea.
5	Sun.	M/E	Cleveland, OH	Hippodrome
6	Mon.	M/E	Buffalo, NY	Convention Hall
7	Tue.	M/E	Toronto, ONT/Canada	Massey Music Hall
8	Wed.	M/E	Rochester, NY	Lyceum Thea.
9	Thu.	Mat.	Newark, NY	Sherman Opera House
9	Thu.	Eve.	Syracuse, NY	Wieting Opera House
10	Fri.	M/E	Schenectady, NY	Armory
11	Sat.	M/E	Albany, NY	Harmanus Bleeker Hall
12	Sun.	Eve.	New York, NY	Hippodrome
13	Mon.	Mat.	Walden, NY	Opera House
13	Mon.	Eve.	Middletown, NY	State Armory
14	Tue.	Mat.	Danbury, CT	Taylor Opera House
14	Tue.	Eve.	Winsted, CT	Winsted Opera House
15	Wed.	Mat.	New Britain, CT	Lyceum Thea.
15	Wed.	Eve.	Middletown, CT	Middlesex Thea.
16	Thu.	Mat.	New London, CT	Lyceum Thea.
16	Thu.	Eve.	Norwich, CT	Broadway Thea.
17	Fri.	M/E	Worcester, MA	Mechanics' Hall
18	Sat.	M/E	Providence, RI	Infantry Hall
19	Sun.	Eve.	Boston, MA	Boston Thea.
20	Mon.	Mat.	Northampton, MA	Academy of Music
20	Mon.	Eve.	Springfield, MA	Court Square Thea.
21	Tue.	Mat.	Waterbury, CT	Poli's Thea.
21	Tue.	Eve.	Bridgeport, CT	Jackson's Thea.

[End of 1909 tour]

1909 OFF-TOUR CONCERT

26	Sun.	Eve.	New York, NY	Hippodrome

Soloists: Virginia Root, soprano; Florence Hardeman, violin; Herbert L. Clarke, cornet.

1910 OFF-TOUR CONCERTS

Soloists: Virginia Root, soprano; Florence Hardeman, violin; Herbert L. Clarke, cornet; John J. Perfetto, euphonium.
2	Sun.	Eve.	New York, NY	Hippodrome
9	Sun.	Eve.	New York, NY	Hippodrome

1ST 1910 TOUR

AUGUST
13	Sat.	M/E	Ocean Grove, NJ	Great Auditorium

Soloists: Virginia Root, soprano; Florence Hardeman, violin; Herbert L. Clarke, cornet.

AUGUST-SEPTEMBER
Sun., 14 Aug. through Mon., 5 Sept. (23 days), Willow Grove (PA) Park.
4 concerts per day.
Soloists: Virginia Root & Beatrice Bowman, soprano; Florence Hardeman & Nicoline Zedeler, violin; Herbert L. Clarke & Ross Millhouse, cornet; Paul J. Senno & Marshall P. Lufsky, piccolo.

Soloists between Willow Grove & Pittsburgh Exposition: Virginia Root, soprano; Nicoline Zedeler, violin; Herbert L. Clarke.

SEPTEMBER

6	Tue.	M/E	Lancaster, PA	Rocky Springs Park
7	Wed.	Mat.	Lebanon, PA	Academy of Music
7	Wed.	Eve.	Reading, PA	Academy of Music
8	Thu.	Mat.	South Bethlehem, PA	Opera House
8	Thu.	Eve.	Allentown, PA	Lyric Thea.
9	Fri.	Mat.	Mauch Chunk, PA	Mauch Chunk Opera House
9	Fri.	Eve.	Wilkes-Barre, PA	Irem Temple
10	Sat.	M/E	Scranton, PA	Town Hall
11	Sun.	M/E	Syracuse, NY	Wieting Opera House
12	Mon.	M/E	Utica, NY	Armory
13	Tue.	Mat.	Amsterdam, NY	State Armory
13	Tue.	Eve.	Gloversville, NY	State Armory
14	Wed.	M/E	Schenectady, NY	Armory
15	Wed.	Mat.	Oneonta, NY	Oneonta Thea.
15	Thu.	Eve.	Binghamton, NY	Stone Opera House
16	Fri.	Mat.	Canton, PA	Lewis Opera House
16	Fri.	Eve.	Lock Haven, PA	Lock Haven Opera House
17	Sat.	M/E	Altoona, PA	Lyric Thea.

Mon., 19th thru Sat., 24th (6 days), Pittsburgh Exposition. 4 concerts per day.
Soloists: Virginia Root, soprano; Nicoline Zedeler, violin; Herbert L. Clarke & Ross Millhouse, cornet; John J. Perfetto, euphonium; Ralph Corey, trombone; Paul J. Senno & Marshall P. Lufsky, piccolo.
[End 1st 1910 tour]

2ND 1910 TOUR

Soloists before NY Cement Exposition: Virginia Root, soprano; Nicoline Zedeler & [Ms] Feldman, violin; Herbert L. Clarke, cornet.

NOVEMBER

6	Sun.	Eve.	New York, NY	Metropolitan Opera House
7	Mon.	Mat.	Danbury, CT	Taylor Opera House
7	Mon.	Eve.	Waterbury, CT	Poli's Thea.
8	Tue.	Mat.	Middletown, CT	Middlesex Thea.
8	Tue.	Eve.	New Haven, CT	Yale University
9	Wed.	Mat.	Willimantic, CT	Loomer Opera House
9	Wed.	Eve.	Springfield, MA	City Hall
10	Thu.	Mat.	Rockville, CT	Town Hall
10	Thu.	Eve.	Hartford, CT	Parsons' Thea.
11	Fri.	M/E	Providence, RI	Infantry Hall
12	Sat.	Mat.	Worcester, MA	Worcester Thea.
12	Sat.	Eve.	Fitchburg, MA	City Hall
13	Sun.	Mat.	Lowell, MA	Lowell Opera House
13	Sun.	Eve.	Boston, MA	Boston Thea.
14	Mon.	Mat.	Keene, NH	Opera House
14	Mon.	Eve.	Brattleboro, VT	Auditorium
15	Tue.	Mat.	Springfield, VT	Springfield Opera House
15	Tue.	Eve.	Bellows Falls, VT	Opera House
16	Wed.	Mat.	Newport, NH	Newport Opera House
16	Wed.	Eve.	Claremont, NH	Opera House
17	Thu.	Mat.	Lebanon, NH	Town Hall
17	Thu.	Eve.	White River Junction, VT	Junction House
18	Fri.	Mat.	Randolph, VT	Chandler Music Hall
18	Fri.	Eve.	Barre, VT	Barre Opera House
19	Sat.	Mat.	Montpelier, VT	Armory
19	Sat.	Eve.	St. Johnsbury, VT	Colonial Thea.
21	Mon.	M/E	Montreal, QUE/Canada	Arena
22	Tue.	Mat.	Kingston, ONT/Canada	Opera House
22	Tue.	Eve.	Peterborough, ONT/Canada	Bradburn's Opera House
23	Wed.	Mat.	Brantford, ONT/Canada	Opera House
23	Wed.	Eve.	Hamilton, ONT/Canada	Grand Opera House
24	Thu.	M/E	Buffalo, NY	Convention Hall
25	Fri.	Mat.	Detroit, MI	Detroit Opera House
25	Fri.	Eve.	Ann Arbor, MI	University Hall
26	Sat.	M/E	Grand Rapids, MI	Powers' Thea.
27	Sun.	M/E	Cleveland, OH	Hippodrome

28	Mon.	Mat.	Elyria, OH	Elyria Thea.
28	Mon.	Eve.	Canton, OH	Auditorium
29	Tue.	Mat.	Mansfield, OH	Memorial Opera House
29	Tue.	Eve.	Marion, OH	Grand Opera House
30	Wed.	Mat.	Delaware, OH	City Opera House
30	Wed.	Eve.	Columbus, OH	Memorial Hall

DECEMBER

1	Thu.	Mat.	Columbus, OH	Memorial Hall
1	Thu.	Eve.	Dayton, OH	Memorial Hall
2	Fri.	Mat.	Paris, KY	Grand Opera House
2	Fri.	Eve.	Lexington, KY	Lexington Opera House
3	Sat.	M/E	Knoxville, TN	Staub's Thea.
4	Sun.	M/E	Morristown, TN	Read's Thea.
5	Mon.	M/E	Asheville, NC	Auditorium
6	Tue.	M/E	Columbia, SC	Columbia Thea.
7	Wed.	M/E	Charlotte, NC	Academy of Music
8	Thu.	Mat.	Greensboro, NC	Opera House
8	Thu.	Eve.	Winston-Salem, NC	Elks' Auditorium
9	Fri.	Eve.	Wilmington, NC	Academy of Music
10	Sat.	Mat.	Durham, NC	Academy of Music
11	Sun.	M/E	Washington, DC	National Thea.
12	Mon.	Mat.	Hagerstown, MD	Academy of Music
12	Mon.	Eve.	Carlisle, PA	Carlisle Opera House
13	Tue.	Mat.	Hanover, PA	Opera House
13	Tue.	Eve.	York, PA	York Opera House

Wed., 14th through Tue., 20th (7 days), New York, NY, Madison Square Garden, Cement Exposition. 2 concerts per day except eve. only 1st day.
Soloists: Herbert L. Clarke & Ross Millhouse, cornet; John J. Perfetto, euphonium; Ralph Corey, trombone; Paul J. Senno, piccolo.
[End 2nd 1910 tour]

1910-11 WORLD TOUR

Soloists: Virginia Root, soprano; Nicoline Zedeler, violin; Herbert L. Clarke, cornet; John J. Perfetto, euphonium; Ralph Corey, trombone; Paul J. Senno, piccolo; Joseph Norrito, clarinet; Joseph Marthage, harp.

DECEMBER, 1910

30	Fri.	Eve.	*S.S. Baltic*, [At sea]	First Saloon

JANUARY, 1911
Mon., 2nd, through Sat., 7th (6 days), London, England, Queen's Hall.
2 concerts per day.

9	Mon.	M/E	Hastings, England	Royal Concert Hall
10	Tue.	M/E	Eastbourne, England	Floral Hall
11	Wed.	M/E	Brighton, England	Brighton Dome
12	Thu.	M/E	Portsmouth, England	Portland Hall
13	Fri.	Mat.	Southampton, England	Palace Thea.
13	Fri.	Eve.	Southampton, England	Hartley Hall
14	Sat.	M/E	Bournemouth, England	Winter Gardens
15	Sun.	Mat.	London, England	Palladium
15	Sun.	Eve.	London, England	Queen's Hall
16	Mon.	Mat.	Torquay, England	Bath Saloons
16	Mon.	Eve.	Exeter, England	Queens Hall
17	Tue.	M/E	Plymouth, England	Guild Hall
18	Wed.	Mat.	Bath, England	Palace Thea.
18	Wed.	Eve.	Bristol, England	Coliseum
19	Thu.	Mat.	Aberdare, Wales	Market Hall
19	Thu.	Eve.	Merthyr Tydfil, Wales	Drill Hall
20	Fri.	M/E	Swansea, Wales	Albert Hall
21	Sat.	Mat.	Cardiff, Wales	Palace Thea.
21	Sat.	Eve.	Newport, Wales	Stow Hill Rink
22	Sun.	M/E	London, England	Palladium
23	Mon.	Mat.	Leamington, England	Winter Hall
23	Mon.	Eve.	Northampton, England	Corn Exchange
24	Tue.	Mat.	Cheltenham, England	Town Hall
24	Tue.	Eve.	Gloucester, England	Shire Hall
25	Wed.	M/E	Birmingham, England	Town Hall
26	Thu.	Mat.	Malvern, England	Assembly Rooms
26	Thu.	Eve.	Worcester, England	Town Hall
27	Fri.	M/E	Derby, England	Drill Hall
28	Sat.	M/E	Nottingham, England	Mechanics' Hall
29	Sun.	Eve.	Burton-on-Trent, England	Opera House
30	Mon.	M/E	Sheffield, England	Victoria Hall
31	Tue.	M/E	Manchester, England	Free Trade Hall

FEBRUARY

1	Wed.	Mat.	Southport, England	Cambridge hall

1	Wed.	Eve.	Lancaster, England	Town Hall
2	Thu.	Mat.	Blackburn, England	Palace Thea.
2	Thu.	Eve.	Preston, England	Public Hall
3	Fri.	Mat.	Huddersfield, England	Palace Thea.
3	Fri.	Eve.	Rochdale, England	Town Hall
4	Sat.	M/E	Liverpool, England	Philharmonic Hall
5	Sun.	M/E	Blackpool, England	Winter Gardens
6	Mon.	Mat.	Warrington, England	Palace Thea.
6	Mon.	Eve.	St. Helens, England	Town Hall
7	Tue.	M/E	Oldham, England	Empire Thea.
8	Wed.	Mat.	Bolton, England	Royal Thea.
8	Wed.	Eve.	Chorley, England	Town Hall
9	Thu.	M/E	Bradford, England	St. George's Hall
10	Fri.	M/E	Leeds, England	Town Hall
11	Sat.	Mat.	Halifax, England	Palace Thea.
11	Sat.	Eve.	Burnley, England	Mechanics' Institute
13	Mon.	M/E	Cork, Ireland	Assembly Rooms
14	Tue.	M/E	Limerick, Ireland	Royal Thea.
15	Wed.	M/E	Dublin, Ireland	Rathmine's Rink
16	Thu.	M/E	Belfast, Ireland	Ulster Hall
17	Fri.	M/E	Londonderry, Ireland	St. Columb's Hall
18	Sat.	M/E	Glasgow, Scotland	St. George's Hall
20	Mon.	M/E	Aberdeen, Scotland	Music Hall
21	Tue.	M/E	Dundee, Scotland	Kinnaird's Hall
22	Wed.	M/E	Edinburgh, Scotland	Waverley Market Hall
23	Thu.	M/E	Newcastle-on-Tyne, Engl.	Town Hall
24	Fri.	Mat.	Darlington, England	Town Hall
24	Fri.	Eve.	Middlesborough, Engl.	Town Hall
25	Sat.	M/E	Sunderland, England	Victoria Hall
26	Sun.	Eve.	Scarborough, England	Olympia
27	Mon.	Mat.	York, England	Exhibition Hall
27	Mon.	Eve.	Hull, England	City Hall
28	Tue.	Mat.	Grimsby, England	Town Hall
28	Tue.	Eve.	Lincoln, England	New Central Hall

MARCH

1	Wed.	M/E	Oxford, England	Town Hall
2	Thu.	Mat.	London, England	Crystal Palace
2	Thu.	Eve.	London, England	Alexandra Palace
3	Fri.	Mat.	Bristol, England	Coliseum
9	Thu.	Mat.	*R.M.S. Tainui* [at sea]	on deck
19	Sun.	a.m.	*R.M.S. Tainui* [at sea]	Church service
24	Fri.	M/E	Cape Town, So. Africa	City Hall
25	Sat.	M/E	Cape Town, So. Africa	Pageant Grounds
27	Mon.	Eve.	Kimberly, So. Africa	Town Hall
28	Tue.	M/E	Kimberly, So. Africa	Town Hall

MARCH-APRIL

Wed.., 29 Mar. through Sat., 1 Apr. (4 days), Johannesburg, So. Africa, Wanderer's Park. 2 concerts per day.

APRIL

2	Sun.	Mat.	Boksburg, So. Africa	Kiosk Park
2	Sun.	Eve.	Johannesburg, So. Africa	Wanderer's Park
3	Mon.	Mat.	Pretoria, So. Africa	Opera House
3	Mon.	Eve.	Pretoria, So. Africa	Capitol Rink
4	Tue.	Mat.	Pretoria, So. Africa	Opera House
4	Tue.	Eve.	Pretoria, So. Africa	Capitol Rink
5	Wed.	Mat.	Johannesburg, So. Africa	Wanderer's Park
5	Wed.	Eve.	Krugersdorp, So. Africa	Wanderer's Park
6	Thu.	M/E	Johannesburg, So. Africa	Wanderer's Gymnasium
7	Fri.	M/E	Germiston, So. Africa	Driehoek Grounds
8	Sat.	M/E	Johannesburg, So. Africa	Wanderer's Park
9	Sun.	Mat.	Benoni, So. Africa	Athletic Field
9	Sun.	Eve.	Johannesburg, So. Africa	Wanderer's Park
11	Tue.	M/E	Maritzburg, So. Africa	Town Hall
12	Wed.	M/E	Durban, So. Africa	Town Hall
13	Thu.	Mat.	Durban, So. Africa	Town Hall
14	Fri.	Mat.	East London, So. Africa	Recreation Park
14	Fri.	Eve.	East London, So. Africa	Town Hall
15	Sat.	Mat.	Kingwilliamstown, So. Afr.	Recreation Park
15	Sat.	Eve.	Kingwilliamstown, So. Afr.	Town Hall
17	Mon.	M/E	Grahamstown, So. Africa	City Hall
18	Tue.	Eve.	Port Elizabeth, So. Africa	Feather Market
20	Thu.	Eve.	Cape Town, So. Africa	City Hall
21	Fri.	M/E	Cape Town, So. Africa	City Hall

MAY

12	Fri.	Eve.	Launceston, Tasmania	Albert Hall

Mon., 15th through Mon., 22nd (7 days), Sydney, Australia, Town Hall. Evening concerts daily except M/E concerts on Wed., 17th & Sat., 20th, and none on Sun., 21st.

23	Tue.	M/E	Maitland, Australia	Adelphi Thea.
24	Wed.	M/E	Newcastle, Australia	Central Mission Hall

MAY-JUNE

Thu., 25 May through Sat., 3 June (9 days), Sydney, Australia. 2 concerts per day except eve. only on Fri., 26th & Mon., 29th and none on Sun., 28th. All concerts at Town Hall except mat. on Sat., 27th at Adelphi Thea.

JUNE

Mon., 5th through Thu., 22nd (16 days), Melbourne, Australia, Glaciarium. 2 concerts per day except eve. only on Tue., 6th, Thu., 8th, & Fri., 9th, and none on Sun., 11th & Sun., 18th.

23	Fri.	M/E	Ballarat, Australia	Coliseum

Sat., 24th through Fri., 30th (5 days), Adelaide, Australia, Exhibition Building. 2 concerts per day except none on Sun. 25th & matinee only on Fri., 30th.

JULY

Sat., 1st, through Tues. 4th (3 days), Melbourne, Australia, Exhibition Building. 2 concerts per day except none on Sun., 2nd.

5	Wed.	M/E	Bendigo, Australia	Drill Hall
6	Thu.	M/E	Melbourne, Australia	Exhibition Building
7	Fri.	M/E	Ballarat, Australia	Coliseum
8	Sat.	M/E	Melbourne, Australia	Exhibition Building

Mon., 10th through Sat., 15th (6 days), Sydney, Australia. 2 concerts per day. Concerts at Town Hall except mat. on Sat., 15th at Adelphi Thea.

17	Mon.	Eve.	Toowoomba, Australia	Astral Hall

Tue., 18th through Sat., 22nd (5 days), Brisbane, Australia, Exhibition Building. 2 concerts per day except eve. only on Tue., 18th.

24	Mon.	Mat.	Sydney, Australia	Adelphi Thea.
26	Wed.	M/E	Launceston, Tasmania	Albert Hall
27	Thu.	M/E	Hobart, Tasmania	Kings Hall
31	Mon.	M/E	Invercargill, New Zealand	Municipal Thea.

AUGUST

Tue., 1st through Sat., 5th (5 days), Dunedin, New Zealand, Garrison Hall. 2 concerts per day.

7	Mon.	Mat.	Timaru, New Zealand	Olympia Hall

Mon., 7th through Sat., 12th (6 days), Christchurch, New Zealand, King Edward's Barracks. 2 concerts per day except eve. only on Mon., 7th.

Mon., 14th through Sat., 19th (6 days), Wellington, New Zealand, Town Hall. 2 concerts per day except eve. only on Mon. 14th.

21	Mon.	M/E	Palmerston, New Zealand	Municipal Opera House
22	Tue.	M/E	Wanganui, New Zealand	Opera House
23	Wed.	Mat.	Hamilton, New Zealand	Opera House

Wed., 23rd through Thu., 31st (8 days), Auckland, New Zealand, Fuller's Opera House. 2 concerts per day except eve. only on Wed., 23rd & none on Sun., 27th.

SEPTEMBER

10	Sun.	Eve.	*S.S. Makura* [At sea]	On deck; 25 men only
12	Tue.	M/E	Honolulu, Hawaii	Bijou Thea.
14	Thu.	Eve.	*S.S. Makura* [At sea]	First Saloon
20	Wed.	Eve.	Victoria, BC/Canada	Victoria Thea.
21	Thu.	M/E	Vancouver, BC/Canada	Vancouver Opera House
22	Fri.	Eve.	Bellingham, WA	Beck Thea.
23	Sat.	M/E	Seattle, WA	Seattle Thea.
24	Sun.	Mat.	Tacoma, WA	Tacoma Thea.
25	Mon.	Eve.	Tacoma, WA	Tacoma Thea.
26	Tue.	M/E	Aberdeen, WA	Opera House
27	Wed.	M/E	Portland, OR	Baker Thea.
28	Thu.	Eve.	Eugene, OR	Eugene Thea.
29	Fri.	Eve.	Chico, CA	Majestic Thea.
30	Sat.	M/E	Sacramento, CA	Clunie Thea.

OCTOBER

Sun., 1st through Wed., 4th (4 days), San Francisco, CA, Dreamland Park. 2 concerts per day.

5	Thu.	M/E	Berkeley, CA	Greek Thea.
6	Fri.	Eve.	Palo Alto, CA	Stanford University
7	Sat.	M/E	San Jose, CA	Victory Thea.
8	Sun.	M/E	Stockton, CA	Yosemite Thea.
9	Mon.	M/E	Fresno, CA	Barton Opera House
10	Tue.	Mat.	Coalinga, CA	Liberty Thea.
10	Tue.	Eve.	Hanford, CA	Hanford Opera House
11	Wed.	M/E	Bakersfield, CA	Bakersfield Opera House
12	Thu.	M/E	Pasadena, CA	Chime Thea.
13	Fri.	Mat.	Pomona, CA	Opera House

13	Fri.	Eve.	Riverside, CA	Lorimer Thea.
14	Sat.	Mat.	Redlands, CA	Wyatt Opera House
14	Sat.	Eve.	San Bernardino, CA	Grand Opera House
15	Sun.	M/E	Long Beach, CA	Municipal Auditorium

Mon., 16th through Sat., 21st (6 days), Los Angeles, CA, Auditorium.
2 concerts per day.

23	Mon.	M/E	Phoenix, AZ	Elks' Thea.
24	Tue.	Eve.	Tucson, AZ	Tucson Opera House
25	Wed.	M/E	El Paso, TX	El Paso Thea.
27	Fri.	M/E	San Antonio, TX	Grand Opera House
28	Sat.	M/E	Galveston, TX	Grand Opera House
29	Sun.	M/E	Houston, TX	Prince Thea.
30	Mon.	Eve.	Austin, TX	Hancock Opera House
31	Tue.	Mat.	Waco, TX	Auditorium
31	Tue.	Eve.	Fort Worth, TX	Beyer's Opera House

NOVEMBER

1	Wed.	M/E	Dallas, TX	Grand Opera House
2	Thu.	Mat.	Sherman, TX	Opera House
2	Thu.	Eve.	Denison, TX	Opera House
3	Fri.	M/E	Oklahoma City, OK	Overholser Opera House
4	Sat.	M/E	Muskogee, OK	Hinton Opera House
5	Sun.	M/E	Tulsa, OK	Grand Thea.
6	Mon.	Mat.	Bartlesville, OK	Oklahoma Thea.
6	Mon.	Eve.	Parsons, KS	Ellis Thea.
7	Tue.	Mat.	Pittsburg, KS	La Belle Thea.
7	Tue.	Eve.	Carthage, MO	Opera House
8	Wed.	Mat.	Aurora, MO	Grand Opera House
8	Wed.	Eve.	Springfield, MO	Lander's Thea.
9	Thu.	M/E	Joplin, MO	Club Thea.
10	Fri.	Mat.	Kansas City, MO	Willis Wood Thea.
10	Fri.	Eve.	Leavenworth, KS	People's Thea.
11	Sat.	M/E	Lincoln, NE	Auditorium
12	Sun.	M/E	Omaha, NE	Boyd's Thea.
13	Mon.	M/E	Des Moines, IA	Coliseum
14	Tue.	Mat.	Grinnel, IA	Opera House
14	Tue.	Eve.	Marshalltown, IA	Odeon Thea.
15	Wed.	Mat.	Waterloo, IA	Waterloo Opera House
15	Wed.	Eve.	Cedar Rapids, IA	Greene's Opera House
16	Thu.	Mat.	Muscatine, IA	Opera House
16	Thu.	Eve.	Davenport, IA	Burtis Opera House
17	Fri.	Mat.	Clinton, IA	Clinton Opera House
17	Fri.	Eve.	Dubuque, IA	Grand Opera House
18	Sat.	Mat.	Beloit, WI	Opera House
18	Sat.	Eve.	Janesville, WI	Myers Grand Opera House
19	Sun.	Mat.	Milwaukee, WI	Shubert Thea.
20	Mon.	Eve.	Sheboygan, WI	Opera House
21	Tue.	Mat.	Fond du Lac, WI	Boyle Thea.
21	Tue.	Eve.	Oshkosh, WI	Grand Opera House
22	Wed.	Mat.	Minneapolis, MN	Auditorium
22	Wed.	Eve.	St. Paul, MN	Auditorium
23	Thu.	Mat.	Winona, MN	Winona Opera House
23	Thu.	Eve.	La Crosse, WI	La Crosse Thea.
24	Fri.	M/E	Madison, WI	Fuller Opera House
25	Sat.	Mat.	Kenosha, WI	Rhoades Opera House
25	Sat.	Eve.	Racine, WI	Racine Thea.
26	Sun.	M/E	Chicago, IL	Auditorium
27	Mon.	Mat.	Dowagiac, MI	Beckwith Memorial Thea.
27	Mon.	Eve.	Kalamazoo, MI	Academy of Music
28	Tue.	M/E	Grand Rapids, MI	Powers' Thea.
29	Wed.	Mat.	Jackson, MI	Anthenaeum
29	Wed.	Eve.	Lansing, MI	Gladmer Thea.
30	Thu.	M/E	Saginaw, MI	Auditorium

DECEMBER

1	Fri.	Mat.	Bay City, MI	Lyric Thea.
1	Fri.	Eve.	Flint, MI	Stone's Opera House
2	Sat.	M/E	Toledo, OH	Valentine Thea.
3	Sun.	M/E	Cleveland, OH	Hippodrome
4	Mon.	M/E	Auburn, NY	Burtis Opera House
5	Tue.	M/E	Ithaca, NY	Sibley Dome
6	Wed.	M/E	Albany, NY	Harmanus Bleeker Hall
7	Thu.	Mat.	Newburgh, NY	Armory
7	Thu.	Eve.	Poughkeepsie, NY	Collingwood Opera House
8	Fri.	M/E	Yonkers, NY	Armory
9	Sat.	M/E	Newark, NJ	Symphony Auditorium

| 10 | Sun. | Eve. | New York, NY | Hippodrome |

[End of 1910–11 world tour]

1912 TOUR

Soloists from beginning of tour through Willow Grove: Virginia Root, soprano; Nicoline Zedeler, violin; Herbert L. Clarke, cornet.

AUGUST

16	Fri.	M/E	Boston, MA	Prides Crossing
18	Sun.	M/E	Allentown, PA	Central Park
19	Mon.	M/E	Ocean Grove, NJ	Great Auditorium
20	Tue.	Mat.	Washington, NJ	Skalla Park
20	Tue.	Eve.	Delaware Water Gap, PA	Castle Inn Music Hall
21	Wed.	M/E	Easton, PA	Island Park
22	Thu.	M/E	Hazleton, PA	Hazle Park
23	Fri.	M/E	Harrisburg, PA	Paxtang Park
24	Sat.	Mat.	Lancaster, PA	Rocky Springs Park

AUGUST–SEPTEMBER

Sun., 25 Aug. through Sun., 8 Sept. (15 days), Willow Grove (PA) Park.
4 concerts per day.
Mon., 9th through Sat., 21st (12 days), Pittsburgh Exposition. 4 concerts per day except none on Sun., 15th.

Soloists: Virginia Root, soprano; Nicoline Zedeler, violin; Herbert L. Clarke, cornet; John J. Perfetto, euphonium; Ralph Corey, trombone; Paul J. Senno, piccolo.

Soloists for remainder of tour: Virginia Root, soprano; Nicoline Zedeler, violin; Herbert L. Clarke & Clarence J. Russell, cornet.

SEPTEMBER

22	Sun.	M/E	Columbus, OH	Great Southern Thea.
23	Mon.	Mat.	Newark, OH	Auditorium
23	Mon.	Eve.	Zanesville, OH	Schultz Opera House
24	Tue.	Mat.	Cambridge, OH	Colonial Thea.
24	Tue.	Eve.	New Philadelphia, OH	Union Opera House
25	Wed.	Mat.	Wooster, OH	City Opera House
25	Wed.	Eve.	Mansfield, OH	Memorial Opera House
26	Thu.	Mat.	Upper Sandusky, OH	Auditorium
26	Thu.	Eve.	Lima, OH	Memorial Hall
27	Fri.	Mat.	Bellefontaine, OH	Grand Opera House
27	Fri.	Eve.	Piqua, OH	May's Opera House
28	Sat.	Mat.	Springfield, OH	Fairbanks Thea.
28	Sat.	Eve.	Dayton, OH	Victoria Thea.
29	Sun.	M/E	Cincinnati, OH	Grand Opera House
30	Mon.	M/E	Richmond, IN	Gennett Thea.

OCTOBER

1	Tue.	Mat.	Anderson, IN	Grand Opera House
1	Tue.	Eve.	Indianapolis, IN	English Opera House
2	Wed.	Mat.	Brazil, IN	Sourwine Thea.
2	Wed.	Eve.	Terre Haute, IN	Grand Opera House
3	Thu.	Mat.	Danville, IL	Grand Opera House
3	Thu.	Eve.	Urbana, IL	Illinois Thea.
4	Fri.	Mat.	Effingham, IL	Austin Opera House
4	Fri.	Eve.	Centralia, IL	Pittenger Grand Op. House
5	Sat.	Mat.	Belleville, IL	Lyric Thea.
5	Sat.	Eve.	Alton, IL	Temple Thea.
6	Sun.	Mat.	St. Louis, MO	Shubert Thea.
7	Mon.	Mat.	Jacksonville, IL	Grand Opera House
7	Mon.	Eve.	Springfield, IL	Chatterton's Opera House
8	Tue.	Mat.	Pana, IL	Grand Opera House
8	Tue.	Eve.	Decatur, IL	Powers' Grand Op. House
9	Wed.	Mat.	Normal, IL	Normal School Hall
9	Wed.	Eve.	Bloomington, IL	Chatterton Opera House
10	Thu.	Mat.	Pekin, IL	Standard Thea.
10	Thu.	Eve.	Peoria, IL	Majestic Thea.
11	Fri.	Mat.	Galesburg, IL	Auditorium
11	Fri.	Eve.	Moline, IL	Barrymore Thea.
12	Sat.	M/E	Rockford, IL	Grand Opera House
13	Sun.	Mat.	Chicago, IL	Auditorium
14	Mon.	Mat.	Janesville, WI	Myers Grand Opera House
14	Mon.	Eve.	Madison, WI	Fuller Opera House
15	Tue.	Mat.	La Crosse, WI	La Crosse Thea.
15	Tue.	Eve.	Winona, MN	Winona Opera House
16	Wed.	Mat.	Rochester, MN	Metropolitan Thea.
16	Wed.	Eve.	Red Wing, MN	Auditorium
17	Thu.	M/E	Minneapolis, MN	Auditorium
18	Fri.	M/E	St. Paul, MN	Auditorium

19	Sat.	M/E	Eau Claire, WI	Grand Opera House
20	Sun.	M/E	Duluth, MN	Lyceum Thea.
21	Mon.	M/E	Hancock, MI	Kerredge Thea.
22	Tue.	M/E	Calumet, MI	Calumet Thea.
23	Wed.	Mat.	Ishpeming, MI	Ishpeming Thea.
23	Wed.	Eve.	Marquette, MI	Marquette Opera House
24	Thu.	Mat.	Escanaba, MI	Peterson Opera House
24	Thu.	Eve.	Menominee, MI	Menominee Thea.
25	Fri.	Mat.	Appleton, WI	Appleton Thea.
25	Fri.	Eve.	Fond du Lac, WI	Boyle Thea.
26	Sat.	M/E	Milwaukee, WI	Pabst Thea.
27	Sun	Mat.	Chicago, IL	Auditorium
28	Mon.	Mat.	La Porte, IN	Hall's Opera House
28	Tue.	Eve.	South Bend, IN	Oliver Opera House
29	Tue.	Mat.	Benton Harbor, MI	Bell Opera House
29	Mon.	Eve.	Elkhart, IN	Bucklen Thea.
30	Wed.	Mat.	Kalamazoo, MI	Fuller Thea.
30	Wed.	Eve.	Battle Creek, MI	Post Thea.
31	Thu.	M/E	Grand Rapids, MI	Powers' Thea.

NOVEMBER

1	Fri.	Mat.	Coldwater, MI	Tibbits Opera House
1	Fri.	Eve.	Jackson, MI	Anthenaeum
2	Sat.	Mat.	Norwalk, OH	Gilger Thea.
2	Sat.	Eve.	Lorain, OH	Majestic Thea.
3	Sun.	M/E	Cleveland, OH	Hippodrome
4	Mon.	Mat.	Alliance, OH	Columbia Thea.
4	Mon.	Eve.	Canton, OH	Auditorium
5	Tue.	Mat.	Conneaut, OH	Republic Thea.
5	Tue.	Eve.	Erie, PA	Majestic Thea.
6	Wed.	M/E	Buffalo, NY	Broadway Arsenal
7	Thu.	Mat.	Oneida, NY	Madison Thea.
7	Thu.	Eve.	Rome, NY	Lyric Thea.
8	Fri.	M/E	Utica, NY	Majestic Thea.
9	Sat.	M/E	Syracuse, NY	Wieting Opera House
10	Sun.	Eve.	New York, NY	Hippodrome
11	Mon.	Mat.	Middletown, CT	Middlesex Thea.
11	Mon.	Eve.	New Haven, CT	Woolsey Hall
12	Tue.	M/E	Great Barrington, MA	Mohaiwe Thea.
13	Wed.	M/E	Pittsfield, MA	Majestic Thea.
14	Thu.	Mat.	Amsterdam, NY	Opera House
14	Thu.	Eve.	Schenectady, NY	Van Curler Opera House
15	Fri.	M/E	Albany, NY	Harmanus Bleeker Hall
16	Sat.	Mat.	Gardner, MA	Gardner Thea.
16	Sat.	Eve.	Fitchburg, MA	City Hall
17	Sun.	Mat.	Lowell, MA	Lowell Opera House
17	Sun.	Eve.	Boston, MA	Mechanics' Hall
18	Mon.	Mat.	Newport, RI	Opera House
18	Mon.	Eve.	Fall River, MA	Savoy Thea.
19	Tue.	Mat.	New Bedford, MA	New Bedford Thea.
19	Tue.	Eve.	Brockton, MA	City Thea.
20	Wed.	Mat.	Portsmouth, NH	Music Hall
20	Wed.	Eve.	Dover, NH	Opera House
21	Thu.	M/E	Portland, ME	Jefferson Thea.
22	Fri.	Mat.	Brunswick, ME	Columbia Thea.
22	Fri.	Eve.	Augusta, ME	Grand Opera House
23	Sat.	M/E	Worcester, MA	Worcester Thea.
24	Sun.	Mat.	Malden, MA	Auditorium
24	Sun.	Eve.	Boston, MA	Mechanics' Hall
25	Mon.	Mat.	Greenfield, MA	Bijou Thea.
25	Mon.	Eve.	Brattleboro, VT	Auditorium
26	Tue.	Mat.	Ludlow, VT	Opera House
26	Tue.	Eve.	Bellows Falls, VT	Opera House
27	Wed.	Mat.	Windsor, VT	Opera House
27	Wed.	Eve.	Randolph, VT	Chandler Music Hall
28	Thu.	Mat.	Montpelier, VT	City Hall
28	Thu.	Eve.	Barre, VT	Barre Opera House
29	Fri.	Mat.	Woodsville, NH	Opera House
29	Fri.	Eve.	Newport, VT	Lane's Opera House
30	Sat.	Mat.	Enosburg Falls, VT	Opera House
30	Sat.	Eve.	St. Albans, VT	Waugh Opera House

DECEMBER

1	Sun.	Mat.	Burlington, VT	Strong Thea.
2	Mon.	Mat.	St. Johnsbury, VT	Colonial Thea
2	Mon.	Eve.	Littleton, NH	Opera House
3	Tue.	Mat.	Lisbon, NH	Opera House

3	Tue.	Eve.	Lancaster, NH	Opera House
4	Wed.	Mat.	White River Junction, VT	Opera House
4	Wed.	Eve.	Hanover, NH	Webster Hall
5	Thu.	Mat.	Newport, NH	Newport Opera House
5	Thu.	Eve.	Claremont, NH	Opera House
6	Fri.	Mat.	Springfield, VT	Springfield Opera House
6	Fri.	Eve.	Keene, NH	Opera House
7	Sat.	Mat.	Rutland, VT	Opera House
7	Sat.	Eve.	Bennington, VT	Bennington Opera House
8	Sun.	Eve.	New York, NY	Hippodrome
9	Mon.	M/E	Newark, NJ	Symphony Auditorium

[End of 1912 tour]

1913 TOUR

Soloists up to Willow Grove Park: Virginia Root, soprano; Margel Gluck, violin; Herbert L. Clarke, cornet.

AUGUST

10	Sun.	M/E	Allentown, PA	Central Park
11	Mon.	M/E	Ocean Grove, NJ	Great Auditorium
12	Tue.	Mat.	Dover, NJ	Baker Thea.
12	Tue.	Eve.	Delaware Water Gap, PA	Castle Inn Music Hall
13	Wed.	M/E	Pottsville, PA	Academy of Music
14	Thu.	M/E	Shamokin, PA	G.A.R. Opera House
15	Fri.	M/E	Harrisburg, PA	Paxtang Park
16	Sat.	M/E	Harrisburg, PA	Paxtang Park

AUGUST-SEPTEMBER

Sun., 17 Aug. through Sun., 7 Sept. (22 days), Willow Grove (PA) Park. 4 concerts per day.

Soloists: Virginia Root, soprano; Margel Gluck, violin; Herbert L. Clarke, cornet; John J. Perfetto, euphonium.

SEPTEMBER

Mon., 8th through Sat., 20th (13 days), Pittsburgh Exposition. 4 concerts per day except none on Sun., 14th.

Soloists: Virginia Root, soprano; Margel Gluck, violin; Herbert L. Clarke, cornet; R. Lindenhahn, horn; John J. Perfetto, euphonium; Ralph Corey, trombone; Louis P. Fritze, flute; Joseph Norrito, clarinet; William F. Schensley, saxophone; Joseph Marthage, harp.

Soloists between Pittsburgh Exposition & Atlanta Automobile Show: Virginia Root, soprano; Margel Gluck, violin; Herbert L. Clarke, cornet; Joseph Marthage, harp.

SEPTEMBER

21	Sun.	M/E	Columbus, OH	Great Southern Thea.
22	Mon.	Mat.	Delaware, OH	City Opera House
22	Mon.	Eve.	Marion, OH	Chautauqua Pavilion
23	Tue.	Mat.	Findlay, OH	Majestic Thea.
23	Tue.	Eve.	Lima, OH	Faurot Opera House
24	Wed.	M/E	Indianapolis, IN	Murat Thea.
25	Thu.	Mat.	Huntington, IN	Huntington Thea.
25	Thu.	Eve.	Fort Wayne, IN	Majestic Thea.
26	Fri.	Mat.	Goshen, IN	Jefferson Thea.
26	Fri.	Eve.	Elkhart, IN	Bucklen Thea.
27	Sat.	M/E	Kalamazoo, MI	Fuller Thea.
28	Sun.	M/E	Detroit, MI	Detroit Opera House
29	Mon.	Mat.	Port Huron, MI	Majestic Thea.
29	Mon.	Eve.	Mt. Clemens, MI	Bijou Thea.
30	Tue.	Mat.	Pontiac, MI	Howland Thea.
30	Tue.	Eve.	Flint, MI	Stone's Opera House

OCTOBER

1	Wed.	Mat.	Bay City, MI	Washington Thea.
1	Wed.	Eve.	Saginaw, MI	Academy of Music
2	Thu.	Mat.	Owosso, MI	Owosso Opera House
2	Thu.	Eve.	Lansing, MI	Gladmer Thea.
3	Fri.	Mat.	Adrian, MI	Croswell Opera House
3	Fri.	Eve.	Ann Arbor, MI	Whitney Thea.
4	Sat.	M/E	Toledo, OH	Valentine Thea.
5	Sun.	M/E	Cleveland, OH	Hippodrome
6	Mon.	M/E	Akron, OH	Grand Opera House
7	Tue.	Mat.	Sharon, PA	Morgan Grand Op. House
7	Tue.	Eve.	Youngstown, OH	Grand Opera House
8	Wed.	Mat.	Corry, PA	Library Thea.
8	Wed.	Eve.	Jamestown, NY	Samuels Opera House
9	Thu.	M/E	Buffalo, NY	Elmwood Music Hall
10	Fri.	Mat.	Lockport, NY	Temple Thea.
10	Fri.	Eve.	Buffalo, NY	Elmwood Music Hall

11	Sat.	M/E	Rochester, NY	Schubert Thea.
12	Sun.	M/E	Syracuse, NY	Wieting Opera House
13	Mon.	Mat.	Oneida, NY	Madison Thea.
13	Mon.	Eve.	Utica, NY	Majestic Thea.
14	Tue.	Mat.	Amsterdam, NY	Opera House
14	Tue.	Eve.	Schenectady, NY	Van Curler Opera House
15	Wed.	M/E	Albany, NY	Harmanus Bleeker Hall
16	Thu.	Mat.	Hudson, NY	Playhouse
16	Thu.	Eve.	Poughkeepsie, NY	Collingwood Opera House
17	Fri.	Mat.	Great Barrington, MA	Mohaiwe Thea.
17	Fri.	Eve.	Pittsfield, MA	Colonial Thea.
18	Sat.	M/E	Worcester, MA	Mechanics' Hall
19	Sun.	Mat.	Malden, MA	Auditorium
19	Sun.	Eve.	Boston, MA	Colonial Thea.
20	Mon.	M/E	Portland, ME	City Hall
21	Tue.	Mat.	Augusta, ME	Grand Opera House
21	Tue.	Eve.	Waterville, ME	City Opera House
22	Wed.	M/E	Bangor, ME	Bangor Opera House
23	Thu.	Mat.	Brunswick, ME	Cumberland Thea.
23	Thu.	Eve.	Lewiston, ME	Empire Thea.
24	Fri.	Mat.	Portsmouth, NH	Music Hall
24	Fri.	Eve.	Dover, NH	Opera House
25	Sat.	M/E	Manchester, NH	Franklin Street Church
26	Sun.	Mat.	Malden, MA	Auditorium
26	Sun.	Eve.	Boston, MA	Colonial Thea.
27	Mon.	M/E	Fall River, MA	Savoy Thea.
28	Tue.	Mat.	Attleboro, MA	Bates Opera House
28	Tue.	Eve.	Milford, MA	Opera House
29	Wed.	M/E	Providence, RI	Infantry Hall
30	Thu.	M/E	Springfield, MA	Court Square Thea.
31	Fri.	Mat.	Derby, CT	Sterling Thea.
31	Fri.	Eve.	Middletown, CT	Middlesex Thea.

NOVEMBER

1	Sat.	M/E	New Haven, CT	Woolsey Hall
2	Sun.	M/E	Troy, NY	Rand Opera House
3	Mon.	Mat.	Saratoga Springs, NY	Broadway Thea.
3	Mon.	Eve.	Glens Falls, NY	Empire Thea.
4	Tue.	Mat.	Oneonta, NY	Oneonta Thea.
4	Tue.	Eve.	Binghamton, NY	Stone Opera House
5	Wed.	Mat.	Waverly, NY	Loomis Opera House
5	Wed.	Eve.	Elmira, NY	Lyceum Thea.
6	Thu.	Mat.	Lock Haven, PA	Martin Thea.
6	Thu.	Eve.	Williamsport, PA	Lycoming Opera House
7	Fri.	M/E	Wilkes-Barre, PA	Grand Opera House
8	Sat.	M/E	Scranton, PA	Lyceum Thea.
9	Sun.	Eve.	New York, NY	Hippodrome

Tue., 11th through Sat., 15th (5 days), Atlanta, GA, Southern Auto Show. 4 concerts per day.

Soloists: Virginia Root, soprano; Margel Gluck, soprano; Herbert L. Clarke, cornet; John J. Perfetto, euphonium; Ralph Corey, trombone; Kelsey Mackey, flute; Joseph Norrito, clarinet.

15	Sat.	a.m.	Atlanta, GA	Penitentiary

Soloists for remainder of tour: Virginia Root, soprano; Margel Gluck, violin; Herbert L. Clarke, cornet; Joseph Marthage, harp.

17	Mon.	Mat.	Winston-Salem, NC	Elks' Auditorium
17	Mon.	Eve.	Greensboro, NC	Grand Opera House
18	Tue.	Mat.	Durham, NC	Academy of Music
18	Tue.	Eve.	Raleigh, NC	Academy of Music
19	Wed.	M/E	Norfolk, VA	Wells Thea.
20	Thu.	Eve.	Newport News, VA	Academy of Music
21	Fri.	M/E	Richmond, VA	Academy of Music
22	Sat.	M/E	Baltimore, MD	Lyric Thea.
23	Sun.	M/E	Washington, DC	National Thea.

[End of 1913 tour]

MAY 1914

Note regarding activities during the last part of May 1914: Sousa, with about 28 or 30 musicians, made a short tour of several American cities between Chicago and Boston as part of a traveling "Lambs' gambol." This was a minstrel show presented by the Lambs Club, an actors' guild. It is believed that several of the musicians were current or past members of Sousa's Band. The minstrel band should not be considered the regular Sousa Band, if for no reason other than its size, even though newspapers sometimes referred to it as "Sousa and his band."

1914 TOUR

Soloists for 1914 tour before Willow Grove engagement: Grace Hoffman & Gertrude Van Deinse, soprano; Susan Tompkins, violin; Herbert L. Clarke, cornet; Ralph Corey, trombone; Joseph Norrito, clarinet.

AUGUST

Sat., 15th through Mon., 17th (3 days), Brooklyn, NY, Coney Island/Luna Park. 2 concerts per day.

17	Mon.	M/E	Lancaster, PA	Rocky Springs Park
18	Tue.	M/E	Harrisburg, PA	Paxtang Park
19	Wed.	M/E	Brooklyn, NY	Coney Island/Luna Park
20	Thu.	M/E	Stamford, CT	Alhambra Thea.
21	Fri.	M/E	Ocean Grove, NJ	Great Auditorium
22	Sat.	M/E	Ocean Grove, NJ	Great Auditorium

AUGUST-SEPTEMBER

Sun., 23 Aug. through Sun., 13 September (22 days), Willow Grove (PA) Park. 4 concerts per day.

Soloists: Virginia Root, Grace Hoffman, & Odette LeFontenay, soprano; Susan Tompkins & Dorothy Hoyle, violin; Herbert L. Clarke, Frank Simon, & Richard McCann, cornet; Joseph Norrito, clarinet.

SEPTEMBER

Mon., 14th through Sat. 26th (12 days), Pittsburgh Exposition. 4 concerts per day except none on Sun., 20th.

Soloists: Virginia Root & Grace Hoffman, soprano; Susan Tompkins & Margel Gluck, violin; Herbert L. Clarke, cornet; Ralph Corey, trombone; Joseph Norrito, clarinet.

Soloists for remainder of tour: Virginia Root, soprano; Margel Gluck, violin; Herbert L. Clarke & Richard McCann, cornet.

28	Mon.	Mat.	Cambridge, OH	Colonial Thea.
28	Mon.	Eve.	Zanesville, OH	Schultz Opera House
29	Tue.	Mat.	Wooster, OH	City Opera House
29	Tue.	Eve.	Canton, OH	Auditorium
30	Wed.	Mat.	New Philadelphia, OH	Union Opera House
30	Wed.	Eve.	Coshocton, OH	Sixth Street Thea.

OCTOBER

1	Thu.	Mat.	Marietta, OH	Auditorium
1	Thu.	Eve.	Parkersburg, WV	Camden Thea.
2	Fri.	M/E	Charleston, WV	Armory
3	Sat.	M/E	Huntington, WV	Huntington Thea.
4	Sun.	M/E	Columbus, OH	Great Southern Thea.
5	Mon.	Mat.	Xenia, OH	Xenia Opera House
5	Mon.	Eve.	Dayton, OH	Victoria Thea.
6	Tue.	Mat.	Urbana, OH	Clifford Thea.
6	Tue.	Eve.	Springfield, OH	Fairbanks Thea.
7	Wed.	M/E	Fort Wayne, IN	Majestic Thea.
8	Thu.	Mat.	Valparaiso, IN	Memorial Opera House
8	Thu.	Eve.	Gary, IN	Gary Thea.
9	Fri.	M/E	South Bend, IN	Oliver Opera House
10	Sat.	M/E	Grand Rapids, MI	Powers' Thea.
11	Sun.	M/E	Detroit, MI	Detroit Opera House
12	Mon.	Mat.	Coldwater, MI	Tibbits Opera House
12	Mon.	Eve.	Goshen, IN	Jefferson Thea.
13	Tue.	Mat.	La Porte, IN	Madison Thea.
13	Tue.	Eve.	Michigan City, IN	Orpheum Thea.
14	Wed.	Mat.	Kankakee, IL	Remington Thea.
14	Wed.	Eve.	Streator, IL	Plumb Opera House
15	Thu.	M/E	Peoria, IL	Majestic Thea.
16	Fri.	Mat.	Urbana, IL	Illinois Thea.
16	Fri.	Eve.	Danville, IL	Fischer Thea.
17	Sat.	Mat.	Paris, IL	Schoaff's Opera House
17	Sat.	Eve.	Terre Haute, IN	Grand Opera House
18	Sun.	M/E	Indianapolis, IN	Murat Thea.
19	Mon.	Mat.	Anderson, IN	Grand Opera House
19	Mon.	Eve.	Marion, IN	Indiana Thea.
20	Tue.	Mat.	Elwood, IN	Grand Thea.
20	Tue.	Eve.	Muncie, IN	Wysor's Grand Op. House
21	Wed.	Mat.	Peru, IN	Wallace Thea.
21	Wed.	Eve.	Logansport, IN	Nelson Thea.
22	Thu.	M/E	Toledo, OH	Auditorium
23	Fri.	Mat.	Tiffin, OH	The Grand
23	Fri.	Eve.	Findlay, OH	Majestic Thea.
24	Sat.	Mat.	Fremont, OH	Opera House
24	Sat.	Eve.	Sandusky, OH	Sandusky Thea.
25	Sun.	M/E	Cleveland, OH	Hippodrome

26	Mon.	Mat.	Warren, OH	Warren Opera House
26	Mon.	Eve.	Akron, OH	Grand Opera House
27	Tue.	Mat.	Sharon, PA	Morgan Grand Opera House
27	Tue.	Eve.	New Castle, PA	Opera House
28	Wed.	Mat.	Franklin, PA	Opera House
28	Wed.	Eve.	Oil City, PA	Opera House
29	Thu.	Mat.	Titusville, PA	Grand Thea.
29	Thu.	Eve.	Warren, PA	Library Thea.
30	Fri.	Mat.	Kane, PA	Temple Thea.
30	Fri.	Eve.	Bradford, PA	Bradford Thea.
31	Sat.	M/E	Niagara Falls, NY	International Thea.

NOVEMBER

1	Sun.	M/E	Buffalo, NY	Tech Thea.
2	Mon.	M/E	Lockport, NY	Temple Thea.
3	Tue.	Mat.	Batavia, NY	Dellinger Opera House
3	Tue.	Eve.	Geneva, NY	Smith Opera House
4	Wed.	M/E	Rochester, NY	Lyceum Thea.
5	Thu.	M/E	Syracuse, NY	Wieting Opera House
6	Fri.	M/E	Binghamton, NY	Stone Opera House
7	Sat.	Mat.	Middletown, NY	Stratton Thea.
7	Sat.	Eve.	Newburgh, NY	Academy of Music
8	Sun.	Eve.	New York, NY	Hippodrome
9	Mon.	Mat.	New Canaan, CT	Nicholas Opera House
9	Mon.	Eve.	Stamford, CT	Stamford Thea.
10	Tue.	M/E	New Haven, CT	Woolsey Hall
11	Wed.	M/E	Providence, RI	Infantry Hall
12	Thu.	M/E	Haverhill, MA	Colonial Thea.
13	Fri.	Mat.	Brunswick, ME	Cumberland Thea.
13	Fri.	Eve.	Bath, ME	Bath Opera House
14	Sat.	M/E	Portland, ME	Jefferson Thea.
15	Sun.	Mat.	Salem, MA	Auditorium
15	Sun.	Eve.	Boston, MA	Colonial Thea.
16	Mon.	M/E	Fall River, MA	Casino Thea.
17	Tue.	M/E	Boston, MA	Symphony Hall
18	Wed.	Mat.	Norwich, CT	Auditorium
18	Wed.	Eve.	Westerly, RI	Bliven Opera House

[End of 1914 tour]

1915 TOUR

Soloists until San Francisco/Panama-Pacific Exposition: Virginia Root & Grace Hoffman, soprano; Margel Gluck, violin; Herbert L. Clarke, cornet.

APRIL

5	Mon.	M/E	Newark, NJ	Armory
6	Tue.	M/E	Paterson, NJ	Armory
7	Wed.	M/E	Trenton, NJ	Armory
8	Thu.	M/E	Wilmington, DE	Playhouse
9	Fri.	M/E	Lancaster, PA	Fulton Opera House
10	Sat.	Mat.	Chambersburg, PA	Orpheum Thea.
10	Sat.	Eve.	Martinsburg, WV	Opera House
11	Sun.	M/E	Washington, DC	National Thea.
12	Mon.	M/E	Baltimore, MD	Lyric Thea.
13	Tue.	Mat.	Hanover, PA	Opera House
13	Tue.	Eve.	York, PA	Orpheum Thea.
14	Wed.	Mat.	Lebanon, PA	Academy of Music
14	Wed.	Eve.	Harrisburg, PA	Majestic Thea.
15	Thu.	M/E	Altoona, PA	Mishler Thea.
16	Fri.	M/E	Johnstown, PA	Cambria Thea.
17	Sat.	M/E	Columbus, OH	Memorial Hall
18	Sun.	M/E	Cincinnati, OH	Lyric Thea.
19	Mon.	Mat.	Oxford, OH	Miami Auditorium
19	Mon.	Eve.	Hamilton, OH	Jefferson Thea.
20	Tue.	Mat.	Bellefontaine, OH	Grand Opera House
20	Tue.	Eve.	Delaware, OH	City Opera House
21	Wed.	M/E	Mansfield, OH	Memorial Opera House
22	Thu.	M/E	Toledo, OH	Auditorium
23	Fri.	Mat.	Jackson, MI	Antheraeum
23	Fri.	Eve.	Lansing, MI	Gladmer Thea.
24	Sat.	M/E	Battle Creek, MI	Post Thea.
25	Sun.	M/E	Kalamazoo, MI	Fuller Thea.
26	Mon.	Eve.	Chicago, IL	Medinah Temple
27	Tue.	Mat.	Kenosha, WI	Rhoades Opera House
27	Tue.	Eve.	Chicago, IL	Medinah Temple

28	Wed.	M/E	Chicago, IL	Medinah Temple
29	Thu.	Mat.	Aurora, IL	Grand Opera House
29	Thu.	Eve.	Chicago, IL	Medinah Temple
30	Fri.	Eve.	Chicago, IL	Medinah Temple

MAY

1	Sat.	M/E	Chicago, IL	Medinah Temple
2	Sun.	M/E	Milwaukee, WI	Auditorium
3	Mon.	M/E	Clinton, IA	Coliseum
4	Tue.	M/E	Cedar Rapids, IA	Greene's Opera House
5	Wed.	M/E	Waterloo, IA	Chautauqua Auditorium
6	Thu.	M/E	Sioux City, IA	Auditorium
7	Fri.	M/E	Des Moines, IA	Coliseum
8	Sat.	M/E	Des Moines, IA	Coliseum
9	Sun.	M/E	Omaha, NE	Auditorium
10	Mon.	M/E	Lincoln, NE	Auditorium
11	Tue.	M/E	St. Joseph, MO	Auditorium
12	Wed.	M/E	Topeka, KS	Grand Opera House
13	Thu.	M/E	Wichita, KS	Crawford Thea.
14	Fri.	M/E	Pueblo, CO	Mineral Palace
15	Sat.	M/E	Colorado Springs, CO	Burns Thea.
16	Sun.	M/E	Denver, CO	Auditorium
17	Mon.	Mat.	Greeley, CO	Sterling Thea.
17	Mon.	Eve.	Cheyenne, WY	Capitol Avenue Thea.
18	Tue.	M/E	Salt Lake City, UT	Tabernacle
19	Wed.	M/E	Salt Lake City, UT	Tabernacle
20	Thu.	M/E	Ogden, UT	Tabernacle

MAY-JULY

Sat., 22 May through Fri., 23 July (63 days), San Francisco, CA, Panama-Pacific Exposition. 2 concerts per day except 1, 3, or 4 concerts some days.

Soloists: Virginia Root & Louise M. Brehany, soprano; Margel Gluck & Susan Tompkins, violin; Herbert L. Clarke, Frank Simon, & Richard McCann, cornet; Maurice van Praag, horn; Ralph Corey, trombone; Louis P. Fritze, flute; Joseph Norrito, clarinet.

Soloists until Spokane/Natatorium Park: Grace Hoffman, soprano; Florence Hardeman, violin; Herbert L. Clarke, cornet.

25	Sat.	M/E	Portland, OR	Oaks Park
26	Mon.	M/E	Portland, OR	Oaks Park
27	Tue.	Eve.	Tacoma, WA	Stadium
28	Wed.	Eve.	Tacoma, WA	Stadium

Thu., 29th through Sat., 31st (3 days), Seattle, WA, Metropolitan Thea. 2 concerts per day.

AUGUST

Sun., 1st through Sun., 8th (8 days), Spokane, WA, Natatorium Park. 2 concerts per day.

11	Wed.	M/E	Minneapolis, MN	Metropolitan Opera House
12	Thu.	M/E	St. Paul, MN	Auditorium

Soloists: Virginia Root, soprano; Susan Tompkins, violin; Herbert L. Clarke & Frank Simon, cornet; John J. Perfetto & Athol J. Garing, euphonium; Ralph Corey, trombone; Louis P. Fritze, flute; Joseph Norrito, clarinet.

Soloists until Willow Grove: Grace Hoffman, soprano; Florence Hardeman, violin; Herbert L. Clarke, cornet.

AUGUST-SEPTEMBER

Sun., 15 Aug. through Sun., 12 Sept. (29 days), Willow Grove (PA) Park. 4 concerts per day.

Soloists: Virginia Root & Grace Hoffman, soprano; Frank Croxton, basso; Susan Tompkins, Florence Hardeman, & Helen D. Jacobs, violin; Lucille Orrell, cello; Herbert L. Clarke & Frank Simon, cornet; John J. Perfetto, euphonium; Ralph Corey, trombone; Louis P. Fritze, flute.

SEPTEMBER

Mon., 13th through Sun., 26th (14 days), Pittsburgh Exposition. 4 concerts per day except none on Sun., 19th.

Soloists: Grace Hoffman, soprano; Susan Tompkins, violin; Lucille Orrell, cello; Herbert L. Clarke & Frank Simon, cornet; Maurice Van Praag, horn; Ralph Corey, trombone; Louis P. Fritze, flute; Ugo Savolini, bassoon; Joseph Marthage, harp.

[End of 1915 tour]

1915-16 NEW YORK HIPPODROME ENGAGEMENT

SEPTEMBER, 1915 – JUNE, 1916

Between Thu., 30 Sept. 1915 and Sat., 3 June 1916 (30 weeks), the band performed at the New York Hippodrome, furnishing music for the *Hip! Hip! Hooray!* extravaganza. The band accompanied two shows per day except for Sundays. On Sunday evenings, except for 30 Apr. 1916 and the final 3 weeks, the band presented regular concerts. The Sunday concerts are listed below.

OCTOBER, 1915

3   Sun.   Eve.   New York, NY   Hippodrome
    Soloists: Grace Hoffman, soprano; Florence Hardeman, violin.
10 Sun.   Eve.   New York, NY   Hippodrome
    Soloists: Grace Hoffman, soprano; Florence Hardeman, violin; Herbert L. Clarke, cornet.
17 Sun.   Eve.   New York, NY   Hippodrome
    Soloists: Virginia Root & Belle Storey, soprano; Orville Harrold, tenor; Nat Wills, comedy singer.
24 Sun.   Eve.   New York, NY   Hippodrome
    Soloists: Belle Storey, soprano; Orville Harrold, tenor; Nat Wills, comedy singer.
31 Sun.   Eve.   New York, NY   Hippodrome
    Soloists: Belle Storey & Sidone Spero, soprano; Nat Wills, comedy singer.

NOVEMBER

7   Sun.   Eve.   New York, NY   Hippodrome
    Soloist: Nat Wills, comedy singer.
14 Sun.   Eve.   New York, NY   Hippodrome
    Soloists: Belle Storey, soprano; Nat Wills, comedy singer.
21 Sun.   Eve.   New York, NY   Hippodrome
    Soloists: Ruth McTammany, soprano; Orville Harrold, tenor; Susan Tompkins, violin.
28 Sun.   Eve.   New York, NY   Hippodrome
    Soloists: Alice Nielson, soprano; Susan Tompkins, violin.

DECEMBER

5   Sun.   Eve.   New York, NY   Hippodrome
    Soloists: Belle Storey, soprano; Orville Harrold, tenor.
12 Sun.   Eve.   New York, NY   Hippodrome
    Soloists: Emmy Destinn, soprano; Helen Jacobs, violin.
19 Sun.   Eve.   New York, NY   Hippodrome
    No soloists with band.
26 Sun.   Eve.   New York, NY   Hippodrome
    Soloists: Tamake Miura, soprano; Orville Harrold, tenor; George Baklanoff, baritone; Jose Mardones, basso.
31 Fri.   Eve.   New York, NY   Plaza Hotel (New Year's party)

JANUARY, 1916

2   Sun.   Eve.   New York, NY   Hippodrome
    Soloists: Nellie Melba, soprano; Gaston Sergent, basso; Beatrice Harrison, cello.
9   Sun.   Eve.   New York, NY   Hippodrome
    Soloists: Tamake Miura, soprano; Giuseppi Gaudenzi, tenor; Jose Mardones, basso.
16 Sun.   Eve.   New York, NY   Hippodrome
    Soloists: Luisa Villani, soprano; Riccardo Martin, tenor; Thomas Chalmers, baritone.
23 Sun.   Eve.   New York, NY   Hippodrome
    Soloists: Julia Culp, soprano; Kathleen Parlow, violin.
30 Sun.   Eve.   New York, NY   Hippodrome
    Soloists: Maggie Teyte, soprano; Giuliano Romani, tenor.

FEBRUARY

6   Sun.   Eve.   New York, NY   Hippodrome
    Soloists: Belle Storey, soprano; Orville Harrold, tenor; David Bispham, baritone; Nat Wills, comedy singer.
13 Sun.   Eve.   New York, NY   Hippodrome
    No soloists with band.
20 Sun.   Eve.   New York, NY   Hippodrome
    Soloists: Battina Freeman, soprano; Lee Ornstein, piano.
27 Sun.   Eve.   New York, NY   Hippodrome
    No soloists with band.

MARCH

5   Sun.   Eve.   New York, NY   Hippodrome
    No soloists with band.
12 Sun.   Eve.   New York, NY   Hippodrome
    Soloists: Olive Fremstad, soprano; Ernest Schelling, piano; David Hockstein, violin.
19 Sun.   Eve.   New York, NY   Hippodrome
    Soloists: Arthur Aldridge & John O'Malley, tenor; Maggie Cline & William Harrigan, vocalists.
26 Sun.   Eve.   New York, NY   Hippodrome
    Soloists: Sybil Vane, soprano; J. Humbrid Duffey, baritone.

APRIL

2   Sun.   Eve.   New York, NY   Hippodrome
    Soloists: Margerethe Ober, soprano; Olte Goritz, baritone; Herma Menth, piano; Mary Zentan, violin.
9   Sun.   Eve.   New York, NY   Hippodrome
    Soloists: Pauline Donalda, soprano; Evelyn Starr, violin.
12 Wed.   a.m.   New York, NY   Hippodrome parade
16 Sun.   Eve.   New York, NY   Hippodrome
    Soloist: Ada Androva, soprano.
23 Sun.   M/E   New York, NY   Hippodrome
    Soloists: Ada Androva & Karuki Onuku, soprano; Robert Martland, baritone.

MAY

7   Sun.   Eve.   New York, NY   Hippodrome
    Soloists: Julia Hill & Karuki Onuku, soprano.

[End 1915-16 New York Hippodrome engagement on Sat., 3 June; total 425 performances]

1916 TOUR

AUGUST

18 Fri.   M/E   Ocean Grove, NJ   Great Auditorium
19 Sat.   M/E   Ocean Grove, NJ   Great Auditorium
    Soloists for 18th & 19th: Grace Hoffman, soprano; Mary Gailey, violin; Herbert L. Clarke, cornet.

AUGUST-SEPTEMBER

Sun., 20 Aug. through Sun., 10 Sept. (23 days), Willow Grove (PA) Park. 4 concerts per day.

[End 1916 tour]

1916-17 *HIP! HIP! HOORAY!* ROAD TOUR

** denotes regular concert between *Hip! Hip! Hooray!* shows.

OCTOBER

6   Fri.   M/E   New York, NY   New York Hippodrome
7   Sat.   M/E   New York, NY   New York Hippodrome

Sat., 14th through Sat., 21st (6 days), 1st segment (of 4) of *Hip! Hip! Hooray!* engagement in Philadelphia, Metropolitan Opera House. 2 shows per day.

22 Sun.   M/E   **Washington, DC   National Thea.
    Soloists: Karuki Onuku & Leslie Leigh, soprano; Harry Westford & Howard Marsh, tenor; Herbert L. Clarke & Frank Simon, cornet; John J. Perfetto, euphonium; Louis P. Fritze, flute; Joseph Norrito, clarinet.

Mon., 23rd through Sat., 28th (6 days), 2nd segment (of 4) of *Hip! Hip! Hooray!* engagement in Philadelphia, Metropolitan Opera House. 2 shows per day.

29 Sun.   M/E   **Atlantic City, NJ   Nixon Thea.
    Soloists: Karuki Onuku & Leslie Leigh, soprano; Harry Westford & Howard Marsh, tenor; Herbert L. Clarke & Frank Simon, cornet; John J. Perfetto, euphonium; Louis P. Fritze, flute; Joseph Norrito, clarinet.

OCTOBER-NOVEMBER

Mon., 30 Oct. through Sat., 4 Nov. (6 days), 3rd segment (of 4) of *Hip! Hip! Hooray!* engagement in Philadelphia, Metropolitan Opera House. 2 shows per day.

NOVEMBER

5   Sun.   M/E   **Newark, NJ   Broad Street Thea.
    Soloists: Karuki Onuku & Leslie Leigh, soprano; Harry Westford & Howard Marsh, tenor; Herbert L. Clarke & Frank Simon, cornet; John J. Perfetto, euphonium; Louis P. Fritze, flute; Joseph Norrito, clarinet.

Mon., 6th through Sat., 11th (6 days), 4th segment (of 4) of *Hip! Hip! Hooray!* Engagement in Philadelphia, Metropolitan Opera House. 2 shows per day.

12 Sun.   M/E   **Providence, RI   Providence Opera House
    Soloist: Marjorie Moody, soprano.

Mon., 13th through Sat., 18th (6 days), 1st segment (of 5) of *Hip! Hip! Hooray!* engagement in Boston, Boston Opera House. 2 shows per day except eve. only on Mon., 13th.

19 Sun.   Eve.   **Boston, MA   Boston Opera House
    Soloists: Marjorie Moody, soprano; Nat Wills, comedy singer.

Mon., 20th through Sat., 25th (6 days), 2nd segment (of 5) of *Hip! Hip! Hooray!* engagement in Boston, Boston Opera House. 2 shows per day.

26 Sun.   Eve.   **Boston, MA   Boston Opera House
    Soloists: Charlotte Williams Hill, soprano; Harry Griffeths, baritone; William Harrigan, character singer.

NOVEMBER-DECEMBER
Mon., 27 Nov. through Sat., 2 December (6 days), 3rd segment (of 5) of *Hip! Hip! Hooray!* engagement in Boston, Boston Opera House. 2 shows per day.

DECEMBER

| 3 | Sun. | Eve. | **Boston, MA | Boston Opera House |

Soloists: Diamond Donner & Marjorie Moody, soprano.
Mon., 4th through Sat. 9th (6 days), 4th segment (of 5) of *Hip! Hip! Hooray!* engagement in Boston, Boston Opera House. 2 shows per day.

| 10 | Sun. | Mat. | **Springfield, MA | Auditorium |

Soloist(s) not known.

| 10 | Sun. | Eve. | **Worcester, MA | Mechanics' Hall |

Soloist: Leonora Simonsen, soprano
Mon., 11th through Sat., 16th (6 days), 5th segment (of 5) of *Hip! Hooray!* engagement in Boston, Boston Opera House. 2 shows per day.

Soloists for Sun., 17th through Sat., 23rd: Diamond Donner & Marjorie Moody, soprano; Herbert L. Clarke, Frank Simon, and Clarence J. Russell, cornet; Louis P. Fritze, flute; Joseph Norrito, clarinet; Joseph Marthage, harp.

17	Sun.	Mat.	**Salem, MA	Federal Thea.
17	Sun.	Eve.	**Lynn, MA	Auditorium
18	Mon.	Mat.	**Westfield, MA	Westfield Opera House
18	Mon.	Eve.	**Pittsfield, MA	Colonial Thea.
19	Tue.	M/E	**Albany, NY	Harmanus Bleeker Hall
20	Wed.	Mat.	**Rome, NY	Morris Family Thea.
20	Wed.	Eve.	**Utica, NY	Colonial Thea.
21	Thu.	M/E	**Syracuse, NY	Empire Thea.
22	Fri.	Mat.	**Erie, PA	Park Opera House
22	Fri.	Eve.	**Ashtabula, OH	Majestic Thea.
23	Sat.	M/E	**Toledo, OH	Valentine Thea.

Sun., 24th through Sat., 30th (7 days), Cincinnati, OH, Music Hall, *Hip! Hip! Hooray!* engagement. 2 shows per day except eve. only on Sun., 24th.

| 31 | Sun. | M/E | **Indianapolis, IN | Murat Thea. |

Soloists: Leonora Simonsen, soprano; Herbert L. Clarke, cornet; Louis P. Fritze, flute; Joseph Marthage, harp.

JANUARY, 1917
Mon., 1st through Sat., 6th (6 days), St. Louis, MO, Coliseum, *Hip! Hip! Hooray!* engagement. 2 shows per day.

| 7 | Sun. | M/E | **St. Joseph, MO | Auditorium |

Soloists: Leonora Simonsen, soprano; Nat Wills, comedy singer; Herbert L. Clarke, cornet; Louis P. Fritze, flute; Joseph Marthage, harp.
Mon., 8th through Sat., 13th (6 days), Kansas City, MO, Convention Hall, *Hip! Hip! Hooray!* engagement. 2 shows per day.

| 14 | Sun. | M/E | **Des Moines, IA | Coliseum |

Soloists: Leonora Simonsen, soprano; Howard Marsh, tenor; Nat Wills, comedy singer: Herbert L. Clarke & Frank Simon, cornet; Joseph Marthage, harp.
Mon., 15th through Sun., 21st (7 days), St. Paul, MN, Auditorium, *Hip! Hip! Hooray!* engagement. 2 shows per day except eve. only on Mon. 15th.

| 22 | Mon. | M/E | **St. Paul, MN | Auditorium |

Soloists: Leonora Simonsen, soprano; Howard Marsh, tenor; Nat Wills, comedy singer; possibly others.

JANUARY-MARCH
Tue., 23 Jan. through Sat., 3 Mar. (39 days), Chicago, Auditorium, *Hip! Hip! Hooray!* engagement. 2 shows per day except eve. only on Tue., 23 Jan.

MARCH
Mon., 5th through Sat., 10th (6 days), Cleveland, OH, Hippodrome, *Hip! Hip! Hooray!* engagement. 2 shows per day except eve. only on Mon., 5th.

Soloists for remainder of 1916-17 Hip! Hip! Hooray! road tour: Leonora Simonsen, Diamond Donner, & Leslie Leigh, soprano; Howard Marsh, tenor; Herbert L. Clarke & Frank Simon, cornet; Louis P. Fritze, flute; Joseph Marthage, harp.

11	Sun.	Mat.	**Newark, OH	Auditorium
11	Sun.	Eve.	**Columbus, OH	Hartman Thea.
12	Mon.	Mat.	**Parkersburg, WV	Auditorium
12	Mon.	Eve.	**Wheeling, WV	Court Thea.
13	Tue.	Mat.	**Clarksburg, WV	Robinson's Grand Thea.
13	Tue.	Eve.	**Uniontown, PA	West End Thea.
14	Wed.	Mat.	**Connellsville, PA	Armory
14	Wed.	Eve.	**Cumberland, MD	Maryland Thea.
15	Thu.	Mat.	**Hagerstown, MD	Academy of Music
15	Thu.	Eve.	**York, PA	Orpheum Thea.
16	Fri.	Mat.	**Lancaster, PA	Fulton Opera House
16	Fri.	Eve.	**Reading, PA	Academy of Music
17	Sat.	M/E	**Easton, PA	Orpheum Thea.
18	Sun.	Eve.	**New York, NY	Hippodrome

[End of 1916-17 Hip! Hip! Hooray! road tour]

1917 OFF-TOUR ENGAGEMENTS:

MARCH

| 22 | Thu. | Eve. | New York, NY | Madison Square Garden |

No soloists; patriotic rally

APRIL

| 12 | Thu. | a.m. | New York, NY | NY Hippodrome parade |

JUNE

| 7 | Thu. | Eve. | New York, NY | Hippodrome |

Soloist: Frances Alda, soprano

| 30 | Sat. | Mat. | Brooklyn, NY | Prospect Park |

Soloist: Anna Case, soprano

1ST 1917 TOUR

JULY
Sat., 14th through Sun., 29th (16 days), Montreal, QUE/Canada, Dominion Park. 2 concerts per day.

Soloists: Virginia Root, soprano; Percy Hemus, baritone; Herbert L. Clarke & Frank Simon, cornet: John J. Perfetto, euphonium; Ralph Corey, trombone; Arthur Geithe, horn; Louis P. Fritze, flute; Joseph Plantamura, piccolo; Joseph Norrito, clarinet.
Also while in Montreal:

| 23 | Mon. | a.m. | Montreal, QUE/Canada | Grey Nuns' Convalescent Home |

JULY-AUGUST
Mon., 30 July through Sun., 5 Aug. (7 days), Toronto, ONT/Canada, Hanlan's Point. 2 concerts per day.

Soloists: Virginia Root, soprano; Percy Hemus, baritone; Herbert L. Clarke & Frank Simon, cornet; Louis P. Fritze, flute.

Soloists for remainder of 1st 1917 tour: Virginia Root, soprano; Percy Hemus, baritone; Herbert L. Clarke & Frank Simon, cornet; Louis P. Fritze, flute; Joseph Marthage, harp.

AUGUST

6	Mon.	Mat.	Niagara Falls, NY	St. Mary's Lyceum
6	Mon.	Eve.	Buffalo, NY	Elmwood Music Hall
7	Tue.	Mat.	Batavia, NY	Dellinger Opera House
7	Tue.	Eve.	Rochester, NY	Convention Hall
8	Wed.	Mat.	Geneva, NY	Smith Opera House
8	Wed.	Eve.	Auburn, NY	Auditorium
9	Thu.	Mat.	Cohoes, NY	Opera House
9	Thu.	Eve.	Saratoga Springs, NY	Convention Hall
10	Fri.	Mat.	Johnstown, NY	Grand Thea.
10	Fri.	Eve.	Amsterdam, NY	Rialto Thea.
11	Sat.	Mat.	Oneonta, NY	Oneonta Thea.
11	Sat.	Eve.	Norwich, NY	Colonia Thea.
12	Sun.	Mat.	Johnson City, NY	Johnson Field
12	Sun.	Eve.	Endicott, NY	Ideal Park

[End of 1st 1917 tour]

2ND 1917 TOUR

Sun., 19 Aug. through Sun., 9 Sept. (22 days), Willow Grove (PA) Park. 4 concerts per day.

Soloists: Marjorie Moody & Alice Eversman, soprano; Percy Hemus, baritone; Susan Tompkins & Mary Gailey, violin; Herbert L. Clarke & Frank Simon, cornet; John J. Perfetto, euphonium; Ralph Corey, trombone; Joseph Norrito, clarinet; Ralph Lick, saxophone; Louis P. Fritze, flute; Joseph Plantamura, piccolo; Joseph Green, xylophone.
[End of 2nd 1917 tour]

1918 TOUR

Soloists before Montreal/Dominion Park engagement: Odette le Fontenay, soprano; Ruby Helder, contralto; Frank Simon, cornet.

JUNE

26	Wed.	Mat.	Poughkeepsie, NY	Collingwood Opera House
26	Wed.	Eve.	Hudson, NY	Playhouse
27	Thu.	Mat.	Mechanicville, NY	Park Thea.
27	Thu.	Eve.	Glens Falls, NY	Empire Thea.
28	Fri.	Mat.	Plattsburgh, NY	Plattsburgh Thea.
28	Fri.	Eve.	Burlington, VT	Strong Thea.

Sat., 29 June through Sun., 14 July (16 days), Montreal, QUE/Canada, Dominion Park. 2 concerts per day.

Soloists: Odette le Fontenay & Ruby Helder, soprano; Bert Brown, cornet; Maurice van Praag, horn; Louis P. Fritze, flute.

Also while in Montreal:
JULY
10	Wed.	a.m.	Montreal, QUE/Canada	Gray Nun's Conv. Home
11	Thu.	a.m.	Montreal, QUE/Canada	Khaki Club Garden

Mon., 15th through Sun., 21st (7 days), Toronto, ONT/Canada, Hanlan's Point. 2 concerts per day.

Soloists: Marjorie Moody & Ruby Helder, soprano; Bert Brown, cornet; Maurice van Praag, horn; Louis P. Fritze, flute.

22	Mon.	Mat.	St. Catherines, ONT/Canada	Grand Opera House
22	Mon.	Eve.	Hamilton, ONT/Canada	Grand Opera House
23	Tue.	Eve.	London, ONT/Canada	Grand Opera House
24	Wed.	Mat.	Mt. Clemens, MI	Bijou Thea.
24	Wed.	Eve.	Pontiac, MI	Oakland Thea.
25	Thu.	Mat.	Ypsilanti, MI	Pease Auditorium
25	Thu.	Eve.	Ann Arbor, MI	Hill Auditorium
26	Fri.	M/E	Toledo, OH	Coliseum
27	Sat.	M/E	Akron, OH	Armory
28	Sun.	M/E	Youngstown, OH	Idora Park
29	Mon.	M/E	Detroit, MI	Clark Park
30	Tue.	M/E	Detroit, MI	Northwestern Park
31	Wed.	M/E	Detroit, MI	Pingree Park

AUGUST
1	Thu.	M/E	Detroit, MI	Belle Isle
2	Fri.	M/E	Detroit, MI	Pingree Park
3	Sat.	M/E	Detroit, MI	Belle Isle
4	Sun.	M/E	Detroit, MI	Belle Isle
5	Mon.	Mat.	Mansfield, OH	Memorial Opera House
5	Mon.	Eve.	Canton, OH	Grand Opera House
6	Tue.	M/E	Pittsburgh, PA	Syria Mosque
7	Wed.	M/E	Johnstown, PA	Cambria Thea.
8	Thu.	Mat.	Huntingdon, PA	Grand Thea.
8	Thu.	Eve.	Altoona, PA	Mishler Thea.
9	Fri.	Eve.	Williamsport, PA	Majestic Thea.
10	Sat.	Mat.	Sayre, PA	Sayre Thea.
10	Sat.	Eve.	Ithaca, NY	Bailey Hall
11	Sun.	Mat.	Johnson City, NY	Johnson Field
11	Sun.	Eve.	Endicott, NY	Ideal Park
12	Mon.	Mat.	Towanda, PA	Keystone Opera House
12	Mon.	Eve.	Elmira, NY	Mozart Thea.
13	Tue.	Mat.	Mauch Chunk, PA	Mauch Chunk Opera House
13	Tue.	Eve.	Wilkes-Barre, PA	Irem Temple
14	Wed.	M/E	Scranton, PA	Armory
15	Thu.	M/E	Hazleton, PA	Feeley Thea.
16	Fri.	Mat.	Mt. Carmel, PA	G.A.R. Opera House
16	Fri.	Eve.	Shamokin, PA	G.A.R. Opera House
17	Sat.	M/E	Pottsville, PA	Hippodrome Thea.

AUGUST-SEPTEMBER
Sun., 18 Aug. through Sun., 8 Sept. (22 days), Willow Grove (PA) Park. 4 concerts per day.

Soloists: Marjorie Moody, Alice Eversman, Florence French, & Ruby Helder, soprano; Florence Hardeman, Susan Tompkins, & Mary Gailey, violin; Frank Simon & Bert Brown, cornet; Maurice van Praag, horn; John J. Perfetto, euphonium; Ralph Corey, trombone; Louis P. Fritze, flute; Joseph Plantamura, piccolo; Joseph Green, xylophone.
[End of 1918 tour]

1919-20 TOUR
Soloists before Calgary/Fair Grounds engagement: May Stone & Mary Baker, soprano; Frank Simon, cornet.
JUNE
14	Sat.	M/E	Brooklyn, NY	Academy of Music
15	Sun.	M/E	Newark, NJ	Olympia Park
16	Mon.	Mat.	Dover, NJ	Baker Thea.
16	Mon.	Eve.	Morristown, NJ	Lyons Thea.
17	Tue.	Mat.	Owego, NY	Tioga Thea.
17	Tue.	Eve.	Ithaca, NY	Lyceum Thea.
18	Wed.	Mat.	Cortland, NY	Cortland Thea.
18	Wed.	Eve.	Syracuse, NY	Wieting Opera House
19	Thu.	Mat.	Lockport, NY	Auditorium
19	Thu.	Eve.	Buffalo, NY	Elmwood Music Hall
20	Fri.	M/E	Saginaw, MI	Auditorium

21	Sat.	M/E	Sault Ste. Marie, MI	High School
22	Sun.	Eve.	Ishpeming, MI	Ishpeming Thea.
23	Mon.	M/E	Ironwood, MI	Rialto Thea.
24	Tue.	M/E	Ashland, WI	Royal Thea.
25	Wed.	Eve.	Duluth, MN	Armory
26	Thu.	Eve.	Glenwood, MN	Lakeside Pavilion
27	Fri.	Mat.	Valley City, ND	Fair Grounds
28	Sat.	M/E	Minot, ND	High School

JUNE-JULY
Mon., 30 June through Sat., 5 July (6 days), Calgary, ALB/Canada, Fair Grounds. 2 concerts per day.

Soloists: May Stone & Mary Baker, soprano; Frank Simon, Del Staigers, & Eugene LaBarre, cornet; John J. Perfetto, euphonium; Ralph Corey, trombone; Louis P. Fritze, flute; G.A. Smith, piccolo; H. Benne Henton, saxophone; Joseph Green, xylophone.
JULY
Mon., 7th through Sat., 12th (6 days), Edmonton, ALB/Canada, Fair Grounds. 2 concerts per day.
Soloists same as for Calgary.
Mon., 14th through Sat., 19th (6 days), Saskatoon, SAS/Canada, Fair Grounds. 2 concerts per day.
Soloists same as for Calgary.
Mon., 21st through Thu., 24th (4 days), Winnipeg, MAN/Canada, Fair Grounds. 2 concerts per day.
Soloists same as for Calgary.
Fri., 25th & Sat., 26th (2 days), Brandon, MAN/Canada, Fair Grounds. 2 concerts per day.
Soloists same as for Calgary.
JULY-AUGUST
Sun., 27 July through Sat., 2 Aug. (7 days), Regina, SAS/Canada, Fair Grounds. 2 concerts per day.
Soloists same as for Calgary.
AUGUST
4	Mon.	M/E	Fort William, ONT/Canada	Orpheum Thea.
5	Tue.	M/E	Sudbury, ONT/Canada	Grand Opera House
6	Wed.	M/E	North Bay, ONT/Canada	Royal Thea.
7	Thu.	M/E	Ottawa, ONT/Canada	Russell Thea.

Fri., 8th through Sun., 10th (3 days), Montreal, QUE/Canada, Dominion Park. 2 concerts per day.
Soloists same as for Calgary.
11	Mon.	M/E	Saranac Lake, NY	Pontiac Thea.
12	Tue.	Eve.	Utica, NY	Lumberg Thea.
13	Wed.	Mat.	Batavia, NY	Dellinger Opera House
13	Wed.	Eve.	Rochester, NY	Convention Hall
14	Thu.	Mat.	Geneva, NY	Smith Opera House
14	Thu.	Eve.	Auburn, NY	Auditorium
15	Fri.	Eve.	Johnstown, NY	Grand Opera House
16	Sat.	M/E	Ocean Grove, NJ	Great Auditorium

AUGUST-SEPTEMBER
Sun., 17 Aug. through Sun., 14 Sept. (29 days), Willow Grove (PA) Park. 4 concerts per day.

Soloists: Marjorie Moody, Mae Stone, & Mary Baker, soprano; Betty Gray, contralto; Florence Hardeman & Jeannette Powers, violin; Frank Simon, Del Staigers, & Eugene LaBarre, cornet; John J. Perfetto, euphonium; Ralph Corey, trombone; Louis P. Fritze, flute; G.A. Smith, piccolo; Joseph Norrito, clarinet; H. Benne Henton, saxophone; Joseph Green, xylophone.

Soloists for remainder of tour: Mary Baker, soprano; Florence Hardeman, violin; Frank Simon, cornet; H. Benne Henton & Jascha Gurewitz, saxophone; Joseph Green, xylophone.
SEPTEMBER
15	Mon.	M/E	Springfield, MA	Court Square Thea.
16	Tue.	M/E	Hartford, CT	Foot Guard Armory
17	Wed.	M/E	Bridgeport, CT	Casino Thea.
18	Thu.	M/E	New Haven, CT	Woolsey Hall
19	Fri.	M/E	Providence, RI	Infantry Hall
20	Sat.	Mat.	Manchester, NH	The Academy
20	Sat.	Eve.	Lawrence, MA	Armory
21	Sun.	ME.	Boston, MA	Symphony Hall
22	Mon.	Mat.	Plainfield, NJ	Plainfield Thea.
22	Mon.	Eve.	Trenton, NJ	Trenton Thea.
23	Tue.	Mat.	Wilmington, DE	Playhouse
23	Tue.	Eve.	Baltimore, MD	Lyric Thea.
24	Wed.	Mat.	Mount Union, PA	Shapiro Thea.
24	Wed.	Eve.	Altoona, PA	Mishler Thea.

25	Thu.	M/E	Johnstown, PA	Cambria Thea.
26	Fri.	Mat.	Pittsburgh, PA	Nixon Thea.
26	Fri.	Eve.	Pittsburgh, PA	Syria Mosque
27	Sat.	M/E	Wheeling, WV	Court Thea.
28	Sun.	Mat.	Newark, OH	Auditorium
28	Sun.	Eve.	Columbus, OH	Hartman Thea.
29	Mon.	M/E	Springfield, OH	Memorial Hall
30	Tue.	Eve.	Dayton, OH	Memorial Hall

OCTOBER

1	Wed.	Eve.	Cincinnati, OH	Music Hall
2	Thu.	Eve.	Hamilton, OH	High School
3	Fri.	M/E	Middletown, OH	Sorg Opera House
4	Sat.	Mat.	Richmond, IN	Murray Thea.
4	Sat.	Eve.	Anderson, IN	Grand Opera House
5	Sun.	M/E	Indianapolis, IN	English Opera House
6	Mon.	Mat.	Frankfort, IN	Blinn Thea.
6	Mon.	Eve.	Logansport, IN	Nelson Thea.
7	Tue.	Eve.	Lima, OH	Memorial Hall
8	Wed.	M/E	Akron, OH	Armory
9	Thu.	M/E	Canton, OH	Auditorium
10	Fri.	M/E	Canton, OH	Auditorium
11	Sat.	M/E	Cleveland, OH	Masonic Auditorium
12	Sun.	M/E	Detroit, MI	Adena Gardens Auditorium
13	Mon.	Mat.	Flint, MI	Masonic Temple
13	Mon.	Eve.	Lansing, MI	Prudden Auditorium
14	Tue.	Mat.	Jackson, MI	West Intermediate School
14	Tue.	Eve.	Battle Creek, MI	Post Thea.
15	Wed.	Eve.	Grand Rapids, MI	Armory
16	Thu.	Eve.	Kalamazoo, MI	Armory
17	Fri.	Mat.	Racine, WI	Orpheum Thea.
17	Fri.	Eve.	Kenosha, WI	Coliseum
18	Sat.	M/E	Milwaukee, WI	Auditorium
19	Sun.	M/E	Milwaukee, WI	Auditorium
20	Mon.	Mat.	Kohler, WI	Nature Thea.
20	Mon.	Eve.	Kohler, WI	Kohler Engineering Bldg.
21	Tue.	M/E	Rockford, IL	Shrine Temple
22	Wed.	M/E	Dubuque, IA	Majestic Thea.
23	Thu.	M/E	Iowa City, IA	Armory
24	Fri.	M/E	Oskaloosa, IA	Chautauqua Auditorium
25	Sat.	Mat.	Waterloo, IA	Waterloo Thea.
25	Sat.	Eve.	Marshalltown, IA	Odeon Thea.
26	Sun.	M/E	Mason City, IA	Armory
27	Mon.	M/E	St. Paul, MN	Auditorium
28	Tue.	M/E	Minneapolis, MN	Auditorium
29	Wed.	M/E	St. Cloud, MN	Miner Thea.
30	Thu.	Mat.	Crookston, MN	Armory
30	Thu.	Eve.	Grand Forks, ND	City Auditorium
31	Fri.	M/E	Fargo, ND	Fargo Auditorium

NOVEMBER

1	Sat.	M/E	Bismarck, ND	City Auditorium
3	Mon.	Eve.	Miles City, MT	Auditorium
4	Tue.	M/E	Billings, MT	Babcock Thea.
5	Wed.	M/E	Butte, MT	Broadway Thea.
6	Thu.	M/E	Missoula, MT	Liberty Thea.
7	Fri.	M/E	Spokane, WA	Auditorium
8	Sat.	M/E	Walla Walla, WA	Keylor Grand Thea.
9	Sun.	Eve.	Yakima, WA	Armory
10	Mon.	M/E	Seattle, WA	Arena
11	Tue.	M/E	Vancouver, BC/Canada	Arena
12	Wed.	M/E	Bellingham, WA	Armory
13	Thu.	M/E	Tacoma, WA	Armory
14	Fri.	M/E	Portland, OR	Municipal Auditorium
15	Sat.	M/E	Albany, OR	Armory
16	Sun.	Mat.	Ashland, OR	Armory
17	Mon.	Eve.	Chico, CA	Majestic Thea.
18	Tue.	M/E	San Jose, CA	Victory Thea.
19	Wed.	M/E	Berkeley, CA	Greek Thea.
20	Thu.	M/E	Oakland, CA	Auditorium
21	Fri.	Eve.	San Francisco, CA	Exposition Auditorium
22	Sat.	M/E	San Francisco, CA	Exposition Auditorium
23	Sun.	M/E	San Francisco, CA	Exposition Auditorium
24	Mon.	Mat.	Visalia, CA	Municipal Auditorium
24	Mon.	Eve.	Fresno, CA	White Thea.
25	Tue.	M/E	Los Angeles, CA	Shrine Auditorium
26	Thu.	Mat.	Pomona, CA	Greek Thea.

26	Wed.	Eve.	Riverside, CA	Orpheum Thea.
27	Thu.	Mat.	Pomona, CA	Greek Thea.
27	Thu.	Eve.	Long Beach, CA	Municipal Auditorium
28	Fri.	Eve.	Santa Barbara, CA	Potter Thea.
29	Sat.	M/E	Sacramento, CA	Clunie Thea.
30	Sun.	M/E	Reno, NV	Rialto Thea.

DECEMBER

1	Mon.	Eve.	Ogden, UT	Tabernacle
2	Tue.	M/E	Salt Lake City, UT	Tabernacle
3	Wed.	M/E	Grand Junction, CO	Armory
4	Thu.	Eve.	Pueblo, CO	City Auditorium
5	Fri.	Mat.	Fort Collins, CO	Colorado Agricultural College
5	Fri.	Eve.	Greeley, CO	Sterling Thea.
6	Sat.	Mat.	Boulder, CO	Macky Auditorium
6	Sat.	Eve.	Denver, CO	Auditorium
7	Sun.	M/E	Cheyenne, WY	Princess Thea.
8	Mon.	Mat.	Holdrege, NE	Holdrege Auditorium
9	Tue.	M/E	Grand Island, NE	Liederkranz Hall
12	Fri.	M/E	Red Oak, IA	Beardsley Thea.
14	Sun.	M/E	Kansas City, MO	Convention Hall
15	Mon.	Mat.	Lawrence, KS	Univ. of Kansas
15	Mon.	Eve.	Topeka, KS	City Auditorium
16	Tue.	M/E	Hutchinson, KS	Convention Hall
17	Wed.	M/E	Wichita, KS	Forum
18	Thu.	M/E	Enid, OK	Tabernacle
19	Fri.	M/E	Tulsa, OK	Convention Hall
20	Sat.	M/E	Oklahoma City, OK	Overholser Opera House
21	Sun.	Eve.	Ardmore, OK	Princess Thea.
22	Mon.	Mat.	Durant, OK	Liberty Thea.
22	Mon.	Eve.	Denison, TX	High School
23	Tue.	M/E	Cleburne, TX	High School
24	Wed.	M/E	Fort Worth, TX	Chamber of Commerce Auditorium
25	Thu.	M/E	Dallas, TX	Fair Park Coliseum
26	Fri.	M/E	Austin, TX	TX House of Representatives
27	Sat.	M/E	San Antonio, TX	Beethoven Hall
28	Sun.	M/E	Houston, TX	Houston Auditorium
29	Mon.	Mat.	Orange, TX	Liberty Thea.
29	Mon.	Eve.	Beaumont, TX	Kyle Thea.
30	Tue.	M/E	Lake Charles, LA	Arcade Thea.
31	Wed.	M/E	Shreveport, LA	Coliseum

JANUARY, 1920

1	Thu.	M/E	Texarkana, TX	Grand Opera House
2	Fri.	M/E	Memphis, TN	Goodwyn Institute
3	Sat.	M/E	Nashville, TN	Ryman Auditorium
5	Mon.	M/E	Winston-Salem, NC	Reynolds Auditorium
6	Tue.	Mat.	Durham, NC	Academy of Music
6	Tue.	Eve.	Raleigh, NC	Auditorium
7	Wed.	Mat.	Danville, VA	Majestic Thea.
7	Wed.	Eve.	Lynchburg, VA	City Auditorium
8	Thu.	M/E	Norfolk, VA	Colonial Thea.
9	Fri.	M/E	Newport News, VA	Academy of Music
10	Sat.	M/E	Richmond, VA	City Auditorium

[End of 1919-20 tour]

1920 TOUR

Soloists before Willow Grove: Marjorie Moody, soprano; John Dolan, cornet; George Carey, xylophone; Winifred Bambrick, harp.

JULY

31	Sat.	M/E	Norwalk, CT	Regent Thea.

AUGUST

1	Sun.	M/E	Springfield, MA	Riverside Park
2	Mon.	Mat.	North Adams, MA	Drury High School
2	Mon.	Eve.	Pittsfield, MA	Majestic Thea.
3	Tue.	Eve.	Northampton, MA	John McGreene Hall
4	Wed.	Mat.	Middletown, CT	Middlesex Thea
4	Wed.	Eve.	Meriden, CT	Auditorium
5	Thu.	Mat.	Willimantic, CT	Loomer Opera House
5	Thu.	Eve.	Waterbury, CT	American Brass Park
6	Fri.	Mat.	Fall River, MA	Academy of Music
6	Fri.	Eve.	Taunton, MA	Park Thea.
7	Sat.	M/E	New Bedford, MA	New Bedford Thea.

8	Sun.	Mat.	Boston, MA	Fenway Park
9	Mon.	M/E	Portland, ME	City Hall
10	Tue.	Mat.	Brunswick, ME	Town Hall
10	Tue.	Eve.	Lewiston, ME	City Hall
11	Wed.	M/E	Bangor, ME	Auditorium
12	Thu.	Mat.	Portsmouth, NH	Colonial Thea.
12	Thu.	Eve.	Salem, MA	Empire Thea.
13	Fri.	M/E	Lowell, MA	Keith's Thea.
14	Sat.	M/E	Fitchburg, MA	Whalom Park

AUGUST-SEPTEMBER

Sun., 15 Aug. through Sun., 12 Sept. (29 days), Willow Grove (PA) Park. 4 concerts per day.

Soloists: Marjorie Moody, Mary Baker, & Leonora Ferrari, soprano; Betty Gray, contralto; Florence Hardeman, violin; John Dolan & Richard Stross, cornet; John P. Schueler, Charles Gussikoff, & Manuel Yingling, trombone; Ellis McDiarmid, flute; Lee H. Davis & Jose R. Acosta, piccolo; Joseph Norrito, clarinet; Jascha Gurewich, saxophone; George J. Carey, xylophone.

Soloists for remainder of tour: Mary Baker, soprano; Florence Hardeman, violin; John Dolan, cornet; George J. Carey, xylophone; Winifred Bambrick, harp.

SEPTEMBER

13	Mon.	Eve.	Trenton, NJ	Armory
14	Tue.	Mat.	Lebanon, PA	Academy of Music
14	Tue.	Eve.	Harrisburg, PA	Orpheum Thea.
15	Wed.	Mat.	Sunbury, PA	Strand Thea.
15	Wed.	Eve.	Williamsport, PA	Majestic Thea.
16	Thu.	Mat.	Berwick, PA	Park Dance Hall
16	Thu.	Eve.	Wilkes-Barre, PA	Irem Temple
17	Fri.	Mat.	Pittston, PA	Strand Thea.
17	Fri.	Eve.	Scranton, PA	Town Hall
18	Sat.	M/E	Binghamton, NY	Kalurab Temple
19	Sun.	M/E	Syracuse, NY	Empire Thea.
20	Mon.	Eve.	Auburn, NY	Auditorium
21	Tue.	Mat.	Geneva, NY	Smith Opera House
21	Tue.	Eve.	Rochester, NY	Convention Hall
22	Wed.	Mat.	Oneida, NY	Madison Thea.
22	Wed.	Eve.	Utica, NY	Park Thea.
23	Thu.	Mat.	Amsterdam, NY	Amsterdam Thea.
23	Thu.	Eve.	Schenectady, NY	Armory
24	Fri.	Mat.	Glens Falls, NY	Rialto Thea.
24	Fri.	Eve.	Troy, NY	Music Hall
25	Sat.	Mat.	Kingston, NY	Kingston Opera House
25	Sat.	Eve.	Poughkeepsie, NY	Collingwood Opera House
26	Sun.	Eve.	New York, NY	Hippodrome
27	Mon.	Mat.	Allentown, PA	Lyric Thea.
27	Mon.	Eve.	Reading, PA	Rajah Temple
28	Tue.	Mat.	Washington, DC	National Thea.
29	Wed.	Eve.	Baltimore, MD	Lyric Thea.
30	Thu.	Mat.	Lewistown, PA	Temple Opera House
30	Thu.	Eve.	Altoona, PA	Mishler Thea.

OCTOBER

1	Fri.	Mat.	Greensburg, PA	High School
1	Fri.	Eve.	Uniontown, PA	Penn Thea.
2	Sat.	M/E	Pittsburgh, PA	Syria Mosque
3	Sun.	Mat.	Newark, OH	Auditorium
3	Sun.	Eve.	Columbus, OH	Hartman Thea.
4	Mon.	Eve.	Parkersburg, WV	Camden Thea.
5	Tue.	M/E	Clarksburg, WV	Grand Opera House
6	Wed.	M/E	Morgantown, WV	Stroud Thea.
7	Thu.	Mat.	New Castle, PA	Opera House
7	Thu.	Eve.	Youngstown, OH	Park Thea.
8	Fri.	M/E	Akron, OH	Armory
9	Sat.	M/E	Cleveland, OH	Masonic Auditorium
10	Sun.	M/E	Detroit, MI	Orchestra Hall
11	Mon.	Mat.	Sandusky, OH	Sandusky Thea.
11	Mon.	Eve.	Toledo, OH	Coliseum
12	Tue.	Mat.	Marion, OH	Grand Opera House
12	Tue.	Eve.	Lima, OH	Memorial Hall
13	Wed.	Mat.	Mansfield, OH	Memorial Opera House
13	Wed.	Eve.	Canton, OH	Auditorium
14	Thu.	Eve.	Dayton, OH	Memorial Hall
15	Fri.	M/E	Cincinnati, OH	Music Hall
16	Sat.	M/E	Louisville, KY	Jefferson County Armory
17	Sun.	M/E	Evansville, IN	Coliseum

18	Mon.	M/E	Terre Haute, IN	Grand Opera House
19	Tue.	M/E	St. Louis, MO	Odeon Thea.
20	Wed.	Mat.	Hannibal, MO	Park Thea.
20	Wed.	Eve.	Quincy, IL	Empire Thea.
21	Thu.	Mat.	Decatur, IL	Lincoln Square Thea.
21	Thu.	Eve.	Urbana, IL	University of Illinois
22	Fri.	Mat.	Bloomington, IL	Chatterton Opera House
22	Fri.	Eve.	Peoria, IL	Majestic Thea.
23	Sat.	M/E	Springfield, IL	State Arsenal
24	Sun.	Mat.	Chicago, IL	Auditorium
25	Mon.	Mat.	Janesville, WI	Myers Grand Opera House
25	Mon.	Eve.	Madison, WI	Fuller Opera House
26	Tue.	Eve.	Kenosha, WI	Coliseum
27	Wed.	Eve.	Milwaukee, WI	Auditorium
28	Thu.	Eve.	Waukesha, WI	Colonial Thea.
29	Fri.	Eve.	Milwaukee, WI	Auditorium
30	Sat.	M/E	Milwaukee, WI	Auditorium
31	Sun.	M/E	Milwaukee, WI	Auditorium

NOVEMBER

1	Mon.	M/E	Green Bay, WI	Enna School of Music
2	Tue.	M/E	Eau Claire, WI	Auditorium
3	Wed.	M/E	St. Paul, MN	Auditorium
4	Thu.	M/E	Minneapolis, MN	Auditorium
5	Fri.	M/E	Hibbing, MN	Armory
6	Sat.	M/E	Duluth, MN	Armory
7	Sun.	M/E	Mankato, MN	Mankota Thea.
8	Mon.	M/E	Sioux City, IA	Auditorium
9	Tue.	Eve.	Lincoln, NE	Lincoln Auditorium
10	Wed.	M/E	Omaha, NE	Auditorium
11	Thu.	Mat.	Ames, IA	Gymnasium
11	Thu.	Eve.	Des Moines, IA	Coliseum
12	Fri.	Mat.	Iowa City, IA	Iowa State University
12	Fri.	Eve.	Davenport, IA	Coliseum
13	Sat.	Mat.	Elkhart, IN	Bucklen Thea.
13	Sat.	Eve.	South Bend, IN	Coliseum
14	Sun.	Eve.	Indianapolis, IN	English Opera House
15	Mon.	Mat.	Norwalk, OH	Gilger Thea.
15	Mon.	Eve.	Elyria, OH	Rialto Thea.
16	Tue.	M/E	Erie, PA	Academy High School
17	Wed.	Mat.	Niagara Falls, NY	International Thea.
17	Wed.	Eve.	Buffalo, NY	Broadway Auditorium
18	Thu.	Mat.	Warren, PA	Library Thea.
18	Thu.	Eve.	Jamestown, NY	Shca's Opera House
19	Fri.	Mat.	Bradford, PA	High School
19	Fri.	Eve.	Olean, NY	Palace Thea.
20	Sat.	Mat.	Corning, NY	Opera House
20	Sat.	Eve.	Elmira, NY	State Armory

[End of 1920 tour]

1921 TOUR

Soloists before Montreal/Dominion Park: Marjorie Moody, soprano; John Dolan, cornet; George Carey, xylophone; Winifred Bambrick, harp.

JULY

14	Thu.	M/E	North Adams, MA	Drury High School
15	Fri.	Mat.	Rutland, VT	Armory
15	Fri.	Eve.	Bennington, VT	Bennington Opera House

Sat., 16th through Sun., 24th (9 days), Montreal, QUE/Canada, Dominion Park. 2 concerts per day.

Soloists: Marjorie Moody, soprano; John Dolan & Henry A. Schueler, cornet; Joseph DeLuca, euphonium; John P. Schueler, trombone; Ellis McDiarmid, flute; William W. Kunkel, piccolo; Joseph Norrito, clarinet; Jascha Gurewitz, saxophone; George J. Carey, xylophone.

Soloists between Montreal & Willow Grove: Marjorie Moody, soprano; John Dolan, cornet; George J. Carey, xylophone; Winifred Bambrick, harp.

Also while in Montreal:

22	Fri.	a.m.	Children's Memorial Hospital	
25	Mon.	Eve.	Ottawa, ONT/Canada	Dey's Arena
26	Tue.	Mat.	Ogdensburg, NY	Strand Thea.
26	Tue.	Mat.	Malone, NY	Armory
27	Wed.	M/E	Saranac Lake, NY	Pontiac Thea.
28	Thu.	Mat.	Plattsburgh, NY	Plattsburgh Thea.
28	Thu.	Eve.	Burlington, VT	University of Vermont
29	Fri.	Mat.	Glens Falls, NY	Rialto Thea.

29	Fri.	Eve.	Schenectady, NY	Armory
30	Sat.	Mat.	Little Falls, NY	Linton Thea.
30	Sat.	Eve.	Rome, NY	Morris Family Thea.
31	Sun.	M/E	Watertown, NY	Olympic Thea.

AUGUST

1	Mon.	Eve.	Rochester, NY	Convention Hall
2	Tue.	Mat.	Herkimer, NY	Liberty Thea.
2	Tue.	Eve.	Utica, NY	Gaiety Thea.
3	Wed.	Eve.	Gloversville, NY	Armory
4	Thu.	Eve.	Catskill, NY	Community Thea.
5	Fri.	Mat.	Newburgh, NY	Academy of Music
5	Fri.	Eve.	Middletown, NY	Stratton Thea.
6	Sat.	M/E	Ocean Grove, NJ	Great Auditorium

AUGUST-SEPTEMBER

Sun., 7 Aug. through Sun., 11 Sept. (36 days), Willow Grove (PA) Park. 4 concerts per day.

Soloists: Marjorie Moody, Mary Baker, & Thelma Melrose, soprano; Betty Gray & Ruth Lloyd Kinney, contralto; Helen Jacobs, violin; John Dolan, Henry A. Schueler, & Arthur Danner, cornet; William N. Pierce, horn; Joseph DeLuca, euphonium; John P. Schueler, trombone; Ellis McDiarmid & Meredith Willson, flute; William W. Kunkel, piccolo; Joseph Norrito, clarinet; Jascha Gurewich & Anthony d'Ortenzo, saxophone; William J. Bell, tuba; George J. Carey, xylophone; Winifred Bambrick, harp.

Soloists for remainder of 1921 tour: Mary Baker, soprano; Florence Hardeman, violin; John Dolan, cornet; Ellis McDiarmid, flute; George J. Carey, xylophone.

SEPTEMBER

12	Mon.	M/E	Bridgeport, CT	Casino Thea.
13	Tue.	M/E	New Haven, CT	Woolsey Hall
14	Wed.	Mat.	Danbury, CT	Empress Thea.
14	Wed.	Eve.	Waterbury, CT	Buckingham Hall
15	Thu.	M/E	Hartford, CT	Foot Guard Armory
16	Fri.	M/E	Pittsfield, MA	Majestic Thea.
17	Sat.	M/E	Springfield, MA	Auditorium
18	Sun.	M/E	Boston, MA	Symphony Hall
19	Mon.	Mat.	Fitchburg, MA	City Hall
19	Mon.	Eve.	Worcester, MA	Mechanics' Hall
20	Tue.	Mat.	Augusta, ME	City Hall
20	Tue.	Eve.	Lewiston, ME	City Hall
21	Wed.	M/E	Portland, ME	City Hall
22	Thu.	Mat.	Manchester, NH	Strand Thea.
22	Thu.	Eve.	Nashua, NH	High School
23	Fri.	Mat	Newport, RI	Opera House
23	Fri.	Eve.	New Bedford, MA	Elm Rink
24	Sat.	M/E	Brockton, MA	High School
25	Sun.	Mat.	Fall River, MA	Empire Thea.
25	Sun.	Eve.	Providence, RI	Majestic Thea.

[End of 1921 tour]

1921-22 TOUR

Soloists: Mary Baker, soprano; Florence Hardeman & Jeanette Powers, violin; John Dolan, cornet; Joseph DeLuca, euphonium; George J. Carey, xylophone; Winifred Bambrick, harp.

NOVEMBER

21	Mon.	Mat.	Canton, OH	McKinley High School
21	Mon.	Eve.	Canton, OH	City Auditorium
22	Tue.	M/E	Fort Wayne, IN	Palace Thea.
23	Wed.	M/E	Milwaukee, WI	Auditorium
24	Thu.	M/E	Minneapolis, MN	Auditorium
25	Fri.	M/E	St. Paul, MN	Auditorium
26	Sat.	Mat.	Mitchell, SD	Corn Palace
26	Sat.	Eve.	Sioux Falls, SD	Coliseum
27	Sun.	M/E	Omaha, NE	Auditorium
28	Mon.	M/E	Sioux City, IA	Auditorium
29	Tue.	M/E	Council Bluffs, IA	Auditorium
30	Wed.	M/E	Lincoln, NE	Auditorium

DECEMBER

1	Thu.	Eve.	Grand Island, NE	Liederkranz Hall
2	Fri.	M/E	Holdrege, NE	Auditorium
3	Sat.	Mat.	Boulder, CO	Macky Auditorium
3	Sat.	Eve.	Denver, CO	Auditorium
4	Sun.	Mat.	Denver, CO	Auditorium
4	Sun.	Eve.	Cheyenne, WY	Princess Thea.

5	Mon.	M/E	Rock Springs, WY	Rialto Thea.
6	Tue.	M/E	Salt Lake City, UT	Tabernacle
7	Wed.	M/E	Idaho Falls, ID	Colonial Thea.
8	Thu.	M/E	Butte, MT	Broadway Thea.
9	Fri.	M/E	Great Falls, MT	Grand Opera House
10	Sat.	M/E	Helena, MT	Shrine Temple
11	Sun.	M/E	Missoula, MT	Liberty Thea.
12	Mon.	M/E	Spokane, WA	Lewis & Clark High School
13	Tue.	M/E	Walla Walla, WA	Keylor Grand Thea.
14	Wed.	M/E	Yakima, WA	Capitol Thea.
15	Thu.	M/E	Bellingham, WA	American Thea.
16	Fri.	M/E	Seattle, WA	Masonic Temple
17	Sat.	M/E	Portland, OR	Municipal Auditorium
18	Sun.	M/E	Portland, OR	Municipal Auditorium
19	Mon.	Eve.	Tacoma, WA	Tacoma Thea.
20	Tue.	Eve.	Eugene, OR	Armory
21	Wed.	M/E	Medford, OR	Page Thea.
22	Thu.	Mat.	Chico, CA	Majestic Thea.
22	Thu.	Eve.	Marysville, CA	Atkins Thea.
23	Fri.	M/E	Sacramento, CA	Armory
24	Sat.	M/E	Oakland, CA	Auditorium
25	Sun.	M/E	San Francisco, CA	Exposition Auditorium
26	Mon.	M/E	San Francisco, CA	Exposition Auditorium
27	Tue.	M/E	San Francisco, CA	Exposition Auditorium
28	Wed.	Eve.	San Jose, CA	Victory Thea.
29	Thu.	M/E	Stockton, CA	T & D Thea.
30	Fri.	M/E	Fresno, CA	Civic Auditorium
31	Sat.	M/E	Bakersfield, CA	Bakersfield Thea.

JANUARY, 1922

1	Sun.	Mat.	Long Beach, CA	Municipal Auditorium

Sun., 1st through Wed., 4th (4 days), Los Angeles, CA, at Philharmonic Auditorium. 2 concerts per day except eve. only on Sun., 1st.

5	Thu.	Mat.	Ontario, CA	Chaffey Union High School
5	Thu.	Eve.	Santa Ana, CA	High School
6	Fri.	Eve.	San Diego, CA	Spreckles Thea.
7	Sat.	M/E	San Diego, CA	Spreckles Thea.
8	Sun.	M/E	Yuma, AZ	Gondolfo Thea.
9	Mon.	M/E	Phoenix, AZ	El Zaribah Temple
10	Tue.	M/E	Tucson, AZ	Armory
11	Wed.	M/E	El Paso, TX	Liberty Hall
13	Fri.	M/E	San Antonio, TX	Beethoven Hall
14	Sat.	M/E	Houston, TX	Auditorium
15	Sun.	M/E	Galveston, TX	City Auditorium
16	Mon.	M/E	Austin, TX	Junior High School
17	Tue.	Eve.	Waco, TX	Cotton Palace
18	Wed.	M/E	Fort Worth, TX	First Baptist Church
19	Thu.	M/E	Dallas, TX	Fair Park Coliseum
20	Fri.	Eve.	Okmulgee, OK	Hippodrome Thea.
21	Sat.	M/E	Oklahoma City, OK	Coliseum
22	Sun.	Mat.	Muskogee, OK	Convention Hall
22	Sun.	Eve.	Tulsa, OK	Convention Hall
23	Mon.	Eve.	McAlester, OK	Busby Thea.
24	Tue.	M/E	Texarkana, TX	Grand Opera House
25	Wed.	M/E	Shreveport, LA	Coliseum
26	Thu.	M/E	Port Arthur, TX	Auditorium
27	Fri.	M/E	Beaumont, TX	Kyle Thea.
28	Sat.	Eve.	New Orleans, LA	Anthenaeum
29	Sun.	M/E	New Orleans, LA	Anthenaeum
30	Mon.	Mat.	New Orleans, LA	Anthenaeum
30	Mon.	Eve.	Gulfport, MS	Strand Thea.
31	Tue.	M/E	Pensacola, FL	High School

FEBRUARY

1	Wed.	M/E	Tallahassee, FL	Leon High School
2	Thu.	M/E	Jacksonville, FL	Armory
3	Fri.	M/E	Tampa, FL	Tampa Bay Casino
4	Sat.	M/E	St. Petersburg, FL	Plaza Thea.
7	Tue.	Eve.	Havana, Cuba	National Thea.
8	Wed.	Mat.	Havana, Cuba	National Thea.
9	Thu.	Eve.	Havana, Cuba	National Thea.
10	Fri.	Eve.	Havana, Cuba	National Thea.
11	Sat.	Eve.	Havana, Cuba	National Thea.
12	Sun.	M/E	Havana, Cuba	National Thea.
13	Mon.	Eve.	Key West, FL	Strand Thea.
14	Tue.	M/E	Miami, FL	Central School
15	Wed.	M/E	Daytona Beach, FL	Auditorium

16	Thu.	M/E	Savannah, GA	Municipal Auditorium
17	Fri.	Mat.	Macon, GA	Grand Thea.
17	Fri.	Eve.	Columbus, GA	Springer Opera House
18	Sat.	M/E	Birmingham, AL	Jefferson Thea.
19	Sun.	M/E	Montgomery, AL	Municipal Auditorium
20	Mon.	M/E	Atlanta, GA	Armory
21	Tue.	M/E	Greenville, SC	Textile Hall
22	Wed.	M/E	Spartanburg, SC	Converse College
23	Thu.	M/E	Asheville, NC	Auditorium
24	Fri.	M/E	Columbia, SC	Columbia Thea.
25	Sat.	M/E	Charlotte, NC	Auditorium
27	Mon.	Mat.	Durham, NC	Academy of Music
27	Mon.	Eve.	Raleigh, NC	Auditorium
28	Tue.	Mat.	Greensboro, NC	National Thea.
28	Tue.	Eve.	Winston-Salem, NC	Reynolds Auditorium

MARCH

1	Wed.	Mat.	Danville, VA	Majestic Thea.
1	Wed.	Eve.	Lynchburg, VA	Academy of Music
2	Thu.	M/E	Norfolk, VA	Colonial Thea.
3	Fri.	M/E	Norfolk, VA	Colonial Thea.
4	Sat.	M/E	Richmond, VA	City Auditorium
5	Sun.	Eve.	New York, NY	Hippodrome
6	Mon.	Eve.	Philadelphia, PA	Metropolitan Opera House
7	Tue.	Eve.	Scranton, PA	Armory
8	Wed.	M/E	Wilkes-Barre, PA	Irem Temple
9	Thu.	M/E	New Brunswick, NJ	Reade's State Thea.
10	Fri.	Eve.	Elizabeth, NJ	Armory
11	Sat.	M/E	Brooklyn, NY	Academy of Music
12	Sun.	Eve.	New York, NY	Bronx Armory
13	Mon.	Mat.	Washington, DC	National Thea.
14	Tue.	Eve.	Baltimore, MD	Lyric Thea.
15	Wed.	Mat.	Hagerstown, MD	Maryland Thea.
15	Wed.	Eve.	Cumberland, MD	Maryland Thea.
16	Thu.	M/E	Clarksburg, WV	Grand Opera House
17	Fri.	M/E	Youngstown, OH	Park Thea.
18	Sat.	M/E	Chicago, IL	Auditorium
19	Sun.	Mat.	Cincinnati, OH	East High School
19	Sun.	Eve.	Cincinnati, OH	Music Hall
20	Mon.	M/E	Charleston, WV	Tabernacle
21	Tue.	M/E	Huntington, WV	Auditorium
22	Wed.	M/E	Louisville, KY	Macauley's Thea.
23	Thu.	M/E	Lexington, KY	Auditorium
24	Fri.	M/E	Springfield, OH	Memorial Hall
25	Sat.	M/E	Pittsburgh, PA	Syria Mosque
26	Sun.	Mat.	Newark, OH	Auditorium
26	Sun.	Eve.	Columbus, OH	Hartman Thea.
27	Mon.	Eve.	Toledo, OH	Coliseum
28	Tue.	Mat.	Elyria, OH	Rialto Thea.
28	Tue.	Eve.	Sandusky, OH	Sandusky Thea.
29	Wed.	M/E	Akron, OH	Armory
30	Thu.	M/E	Washington, PA	Capitol Thea.
31	Fri.	M/E	Altoona, PA	Mishler Thea.

APRIL

1	Sat.	M/E	Harrisburg, PA	Orpheum Thea.

[End of 1921-22 tour]

1922 TOUR

Soloists before Montreal/Dominion Park: Marjorie Moody, soprano; John Dolan, cornet; Meredith Willson & William W. Kunkel, piccolo; George J. Carey, xylophone; Winifred Bambrick soprano.

JULY

19	Wed.	M/E	Albany, NY	Harmanus Bleeker Hall
20	Thu.	Mat.	Glens Falls, NY	Rialto Thea.
20	Thu.	Eve.	Rutland, VT	Armory
21	Fri.	Mat.	Montpelier, VT	City Hall
21	Fri.	Eve.	Burlington, VT	University of Vermont

Sat., 22nd through Sun., 30th (9 days), Montreal, QUE/Canada, Dominion Park. 2 concerts per day.

Soloists: Marjorie Moody, soprano; John Dolan, cornet; William Pierce, horn; Joseph DeLuca, euphonium; John P. Schueler, trombone; Meredith Willson & William W. Kunkel, piccolo; Joseph Norrito, clarinet; George J. Carey, xylophone.

31	Mon.	Eve.	Ottawa, ONT/Canada	Dey's Arena

AUGUST

1	Tue.	M/E	Watertown, NY	Olympic Thea.
2	Wed.	Mat.	Canandaigua, NY	Mayhouse Thea.
2	Wed.	Eve.	Rochester, NY	Convention Hall
3	Thu.	Eve.	Syracuse, NY	Armory
4	Fri.	Eve.	Utica, NY	Gaiety Thea.
5	Sat.	M/E	Ocean Grove, NJ	Great Auditorium

AUGUST-SEPTEMBER

Sun., 6 Aug. through Sun., 10 Sept. (36 days), Willow Grove (PA) Park. 4 concerts per day.

Soloists: Marjorie Moody & Mary Baker, soprano; John Dolan, Paul Blagg, Henry P. Schueler, & Arthur Danner, cornet; Joseph DeLuca, euphonium; John P. Schueler, trombone; William J. Bell, tuba; Meredith Willson, flute; William W. Kunkel, piccolo; Joseph Norrito, clarinet; George J. Carey, xylophone; Winifred Bambrick, harp.

Soloists after Willow Grove: Marjorie Moody, soprano; Caroline Thomas, violin; John Dolan, cornet; Meredith Willson & William W. Kunkel, piccolo; Jascha Gurewich, saxophone; George J. Carey, xylophone; Winifred Bambrick, harp.

SEPTEMBER

11	Mon.	M/E	South Norwalk, CT	Armory
12	Tue.	Mat.	Danbury, CT	Empress Thea.
12	Tue.	Eve.	Bridgeport, CT	High School
13	Wed.	M/E	New Haven, CT	Woolsey Hall
14	Thu.	Mat.	Middletown, CT	Middlesex Thea.
14	Thu.	Eve.	Meriden, CT	Auditorium
15	Fri.	Mat.	Rockville, CT	Town Hall
15	Fri.	Eve.	Hartford, CT	Foot Guard Armory
16	Sat.	M/E	Springfield, MA	Auditorium
17	Sun.	M/E	Boston, MA	Symphony Hall
18	Mon.	M/E	Worcester, MA	Mechanics' Hall
19	Tue.	M/E	Lowell, MA	Auditorium
20	Wed.	Mat.	Concord, NH	City Hall
20	Wed.	Eve.	Manchester, NH	Strand Thea.
21	Thu.	Mat.	Dover, NH	Opera House
21	Thu.	Eve.	Portland, ME	Auditorium
22	Fri.	Mat.	Waterville, ME	City Hall
22	Fri.	Eve.	Bangor, ME	Auditorium
23	Sat.	Mat.	Haverhill, MA	Colonial Thea.
23	Sat.	Eve.	Lynn, MA	Waldorf Thea.
24	Sun.	Mat.	New Bedford, MA	Olympia Thea.
24	Sun.	Eve.	Providence, RI	Majestic Thea.
25	Mon.	Mat.	Northampton, MA	Academy of Music
25	Mon.	Eve.	Greenfield, MA	Lawlor Thea.
26	Tue.	M/E	Troy, NY	Music Hall
27	Wed.	Eve.	Auburn, NY	Auditorium
28	Thu.	M/E	Buffalo, NY	Elmwood Music Hall
29	Fri.	M/E	Erie, PA	Academy High School
30	Sat.	M/E	Cleveland, OH	Public Auditorium

OCTOBER

1	Sun.	M/E	Detroit, MI	Orchestra Hall
2	Mon.	Mat.	Ypsilanti, MI	Pease Auditorium
2	Mon.	Eve.	Ann Arbor, MI	Whitney Thea.
3	Tue.	Mat.	Jackson, MI	West Intermediate School
3	Tue.	Eve.	Lansing, MI	Prudden Auditorium
4	Wed.	Eve.	Battle Creek, MI	Post Thea.
5	Thu.	M/E	Fort Wayne, IN	Palace Thea.
6	Fri.	Eve.	Grand Rapids, MI	Armory
7	Sat.	Mat.	Elkhart, IN	Bucklen Thea.
7	Sat.	Eve.	South Bend, IN	High School
8	Sun.	M/E	Chicago, IL	Auditorium
9	Mon.	M/E	Rochester, MN	Armory
10	Tue.	M/E	St. Paul, MN	Auditorium
11	Wed.	M/E	Minneapolis, MN	Auditorium
12	Thu.	M/E	Virginia, MN	High School
13	Fri.	M/E	Duluth, MN	Armory
14	Sat.	M/E	Eau Claire, WI	Auditorium
15	Sun.	M/E	Milwaukee, WI	Auditorium
16	Mon.	M/E	Madison, WI	Parkway Thea.
17	Tue.	Mat.	Janesville, WI	Myers Grand Opera House
17	Tue.	Eve.	Rockford, IL	Shrine Temple
18	Wed.	Eve.	Des Moines, IA	Coliseum
19	Thu.	Mat.	Iowa City, IA	University of Iowa
19	Thu.	Eve.	Davenport, IA	Coliseum
20	Fri.	M/E	Peoria, IL	Shrine Temple

21	Sat.	M/E	Springfield, IL	State Arsenal
22	Sun.	M/E	St. Louis, MO	Odeon Thea.
23	Mon.	Mat.	Decatur, IL	Lincoln Square Thea.
23	Mon.	Eve.	Urbana, IL	University of Illinois
24	Tue.	M/E	Terre Haute, IN	Grand Opera House
25	Wed.	Eve.	Indianapolis, IN	Cadle Tabernacle
26	Thu.	Mat.	Vincennes, IN	Pantheon Thea.
26	Thu.	Eve.	Evansville, IN	High School
27	Fri.	M/E	Nashville, TN	Ryman Auditorium
28	Sat.	M/E	Chattanooga, TN	Wyatt High School
30	Mon.	M/E	Knoxville, TN	Bijou Thea.
31	Tue.	M/E	Johnson City, TN	Auditorium

NOVEMBER

1	Wed.	M/E	Roanoke, VA	City Auditorium
2	Thu.	M/E	Washington, DC	President's Thea.
3	Fri.	Eve.	Baltimore, MD	Lyric Thea.
4	Sat.	M/E	Kennett Square, PA	Longwood Gardens
5	Sun.	Eve.	New York, NY	Hippodrome
6	Mon.	M/E	Morristown, NJ	High School
7	Tue.	M/E	Shenandoah, PA	Strand Thea.
8	Wed.	M/E	Pottsville, PA	Hippodrome Thea.
9	Thu.	M/E	Reading, PA	Orpheum Thea.
10	Fri.	Eve.	Shamokin, PA	Strand Thea.
11	Sat.	M/E	Elmira, NY	Lyceum Thea.
12	Sun.	M/E	Binghamton, NY	Binghamton Thea.
13	Mon.	Mat.	Norwich, NY	Colonia Thea.
13	Mon.	Eve.	Cortland, NY	Cortland Thea.
14	Tue.	Mat.	Towanda, PA	Keystone Opera House
14	Tue.	Eve.	Wilkes-Barre, PA	Irem Temple
15	Wed.	Eve.	Scranton, PA	Town Hall
16	Thu.	Eve.	Newark, NJ	Armory
17	Fri.	Eve.	Yonkers, NY	Armory
18	Sat.	M/E	Brooklyn, NY	Academy of Music

[End of 1922 tour]

1923-24 TOUR

Soloists before Willow Grove: Marjorie Moody, soprano; John Dolan, cornet; Joseph DeLuca, euphonium; Meredith Willson & William W. Kunkel, piccolo; George J. Carey, xylophone; Winifred Bambrick, harp.

JULY

21	Sat.	M/E	Kennett Square, PA	Longwood Gardens
22	Sun.	M/E	Newark, NJ	Olympic Park
23	Mon.	Eve.	Patchogue, NY	Patchogue Thea.
24	Tue.	M/E	Stroudsburg, PA	Stroud Thea.
25	Wed.	M/E	Pottsville, PA	Schuylkill Park
26	Thu.	M/E	Pottsville, PA	Schuylkill Park
27	Fri.	Mat.	Oneonta, NY	Oneonta Thea.
27	Fri.	Eve.	Schenectady, NY	State Thea.
28	Sat.	M/E	Lake Placid, NY	Lake Placid Club
29	Sun.	M/E	Watertown, NY	Avon Thea.
30	Mon.	M/E	Utica, NY	Colonial Thea.
31	Tue.	Eve.	Syracuse, NY	Armory

AUGUST

1	Wed.	Eve.	Rochester, NY	Eastman Thea.
2	Thu.	M/E	Albany, NY	Harmanus Bleeker Hall
3	Fri.	M/E	Catskill, NY	Community Thea.
4	Sat.	M/E	Ocean Grove, NJ	Great Auditorium

AUGUST-SEPTEMBER

Sun., 5 Aug. through Sat., 15 Sept. (42 days), Willow Grove (PA) Park. 4 concerts per day.

Soloists: Marjorie Moody & Nora Fauchald, soprano; Rachel Senior, violin; John Dolan, Dana M. Garrett, & Arthur Danner, cornet; Joseph DeLuca, euphonium; John P. Schueler, trombone; William J. Bell, tuba; Meredith Willson, flute; William W. Kunkel, piccolo; George J. Carey, xylophone; Winifred Bambrick, harp.

Soloists for remainder of tour: Marjorie Moody & Nora Fauchald, soprano; Rachel Senior, violin; John Dolan, cornet; Meredith Willson, flute; George J. Carey, xylophone; Winifred Bambrick, harp.

SEPTEMBER

16	Sun.	M/E	Boston, MA	Symphony Hall
17	Mon.	M/E	Lowell, MA	Memorial Hall
18	Tue.	M/E	Portland, ME	City Hall
19	Wed.	M/E	Bangor, ME	Auditorium
20	Thu.	Mat.	Augusta, ME	City Hall

20	Thu.	Eve.	Lewiston, ME	City Hall
21	Fri.	Mat.	Lawrence, MA	Colonial Thea.
21	Fri.	Eve.	Manchester, NH	Strand Thea.
22	Sat.	M/E	Worcester, MA	Mechanics' Hall
23	Sun.	Mat.	New Bedford, MA	Olympia Thea.
23	Sun.	Eve.	Providence, RI	Albee Thea.
24	Mon.	M/E	Brockton, MA	High School
25	Tue.	Mat.	New London, CT	Capitol Thea.
25	Tue.	Eve.	Norwich, CT	Armory
26	Wed.	M/E	New Haven, CT	Woolsey Hall
27	Thu.	M/E	Hartford, CT	Foot Guard Armory
28	Fri.	Mat.	North Adams, MA	Drury High School
28	Fri.	Eve.	Pittsfield, MA	Armory
29	Sat.	M/E	Springfield, MA	Auditorium
30	Sun.	Mat.	Bridgeport, CT	Poli's Palace Thea.
30	Sun.	Eve.	Waterbury, CT	Armory

OCTOBER

1	Mon.	M/E	Poughkeepsie, NY	Bardavon Thea.
2	Tue.	Mat.	Newburgh, NY	Academy of Music
2	Tue.	Eve.	Middletown, NY	Stratton Thea.
3	Wed.	M/E	Easton, PA	Orpheum Thea.
4	Thu.	Mat.	Lebanon, PA	Academy of Music
4	Thu.	Eve.	Harrisburg, PA	Orpheum Thea.
5	Fri.	M/E	York, PA	High School
6	Sat.	M/E	Lancaster, PA	Lancaster Athletic Club
7	Sun.	Eve.	New York, NY	Madison Square Garden
8	Mon.	Mat.	Scranton, PA	Central High School
8	Mon.	Eve.	Scranton, PA	Armory
9	Tue.	Eve.	Wilkes-Barre, PA	Irem Temple
10	Wed.	M/E	Williamsport, PA	Majestic Thea.
11	Thu.	M/E	State College, PA	Auditorium
12	Fri.	M/E	Altoona, PA	Mishler Thea.
13	Sat.	M/E	Pittsburgh, PA	Syria Mosque
14	Sun.	Eve.	Olean, NY	Palace Thea.
15	Mon.	Mat.	Corning, NY	State Thea.
15	Mon.	Eve.	Hornell, NY	Shattuck Thea.
16	Tue.	Mat.	Warren, PA	Library Thea.
16	Tue.	Eve.	Jamestown, NY	Palace Thea.
17	Wed.	M/E	Meadville, PA	Park Thea.
18	Thu.	M/E	Niagara Falls, NY	Cataract Thea.
19	Fri.	M/E	Buffalo, NY	Elmwood Music Hall
20	Sat.	M/E	Cleveland, OH	Public Auditorium
21	Sun.	M/E	Detroit, MI	Orchestra Hall
22	Mon.	Mat.	Ypsilanti, MI	Auditorium
22	Mon.	Eve.	Ann Arbor, MI	Hill Auditorium
23	Tue.	Eve.	Toledo, OH	Coliseum
24	Wed.	Mat.	Findlay, OH	Majestic Thea.
24	Wed.	Eve.	Lima, OH	Memorial Hall
25	Thu.	M/E	Springfield, OH	Memorial Hall
26	Fri.	M/E	Dayton, OH	Memorial Hall
27	Sat.	M/E	Indianapolis, IN	Cadle Tabernacle
28	Sun.	M/E	Chicago, IL	Auditorium
29	Mon.	M/E	West Lafayette, IN	Purdue University Armory
30	Tue.	M/E	Danville, IL	Palace Thea.
31	Wed.	M/E	Peoria, IL	Shrine Temple

NOVEMBER

1	Thu.	Eve.	St. Louis, MO	Coliseum
2	Fri.	M/E	Bowling Green, KY	Auditorium
3	Sat.	M/E	Louisville, KY	Armory
4	Sun.	M/E	Cincinnati, OH	Emery Auditorium
5	Mon.	Eve.	Lexington, KY	Woodland Auditorium
6	Tue.	M/E	Huntington, WV	Auditorium
7	Wed.	M/E	Clarksburg, WV	Carmichael Auditorium
8	Thu.	M/E	Fairmont, WV	Fairmont Thea.
9	Fri.	M/E	Johnstown, PA	Cambria Thea.
10	Sat.	M/E	Wheeling, WV	Court Thea.
11	Sun.	Mat.	Newark, OH	Auditorium
11	Sun.	Eve.	Coshocton, OH	Sixth Street Thea.
12	Mon.	M/E	Columbus, OH	Memorial Hall
13	Tue.	M/E	Canton, OH	McKinley High School
14	Wed.	M/E	Youngstown, OH	Park Thea.
15	Thu.	M/E	Akron, OH	Armory
16	Fri.	M/E	Hammond, IN	Parthenon Thea.
17	Sat.	M/E	Milwaukee, WI	Auditorium
18	Sun.	M/E	Milwaukee, WI	Auditorium

19	Mon.	Mat.	Winona, MN	Winona Opera House
19	Mon.	Eve.	Rochester, MN	Armory
20	Tue.	M/E	St. Paul, MN	Auditorium
21	Wed.	M/E	Minneapolis, MN	Auditorium
22	Thu.	M/E	Mankato, MN	Armory
23	Fri.	M/E	Sioux City, IA	Auditorium
24	Sat.	M/E	Omaha, NE	Auditorium
25	Sun.	M/E	Grand Island, NE	Liederkranz Hall
26	Mon.	M/E	Holdrege, NE	Auditorium
27	Tue.	Eve.	Lincoln, NE	Auditorium
28	Wed.	M/E	Council Bluffs, IA	Auditorium
29	Thu.	M/E	Des Moines, IA	Coliseum
30	Fri.	Mat.	Oskaloosa, IA	Masonic Opera House
30	Fri.	Eve.	Ottumwa, IA	Grand Opera House

DECEMBER

1	Sat.	M/E	St. Joseph, MO	Auditorium
2	Sun.	M/E	Kansas City, MO	Convention Hall
3	Mon.	Mat.	Lawrence, KS	University of Kansas
3	Mon.	Eve.	Topeka, KS	City Auditorium
4	Tue.	M/E	Emporia, KS	Normal School
5	Wed.	M/E	Wichita, KS	Forum
6	Thu.	M/E	Hutchinson, KS	Convention Hall
7	Fri.	M/E	Pueblo, CO	City Auditorium
8	Sat.	M/E	Denver, CO	Auditorium
9	Sun.	Mat.	Cheyenne, WY	Princess Thea.
10	Mon.	Mat.	Fort Collins, CO	Colorado Agr. College
10	Mon.	Eve.	Greeley, CO	Teachers College
11	Tue.	M/E	Colorado Springs, CO	Auditorium
12	Wed.	M/E	Grand Junction, CO	Avalon Thea.
13	Thu.	M/E	Salt Lake City, UT	Tabernacle
14	Fri.	M/E	Ogden, UT	Alhambra Thea.
15	Sat.	M/E	Pocatello, ID	Idaho Technical Institute
16	Sun.	Eve.	Butte, MT	Broadway Thea.
17	Mon.	M/E	Great Falls, MT	Grand Opera House
18	Tue.	M/E	Helena, MT	Shrine Temple
19	Wed.	M/E	Missoula, MT	Wilma Thea.
20	Thu.	Mat.	Moscow, ID	Univ. of Idaho
20	Thu.	Eve.	Pullman, WA	College
21	Fri.	M/E	Spokane, WA	Lewis & Clark High School
25	Tue.	M/E	Yakima, WA	Capitol Thea.
26	Wed.	M/E	Seattle, WA	Metropolitan Thea.
27	Thu.	M/E	Seattle, WA	Metropolitan Thea.
28	Fri.	M/E	Port Angeles, WA	Mack Thea.
29	Sat.	M/E	Victoria, BC/Canada	Victoria Thea.
30	Sun.	M/E	Vancouver, BC/Canada	Capital Thea.
31	Mon.	M/E	Tacoma, WA	Tacoma Thea.

JANUARY, 1924

1	Tue.	M/E	Portland, OR	Municipal Auditorium
2	Wed.	M/E	Portland, OR	Municipal Auditorium
4	Fri.	Eve.	San Francisco, CA	Exposition Auditorium
5	Sat.	M/E	San Francisco, CA	Exposition Auditorium
6	Sun.	M/E	San Francisco, CA	Exposition Auditorium
7	Mon.	M/E	Oakland, CA	Auditorium
8	Tue.	M/E	Sacramento, CA	Armory
9	Wed.	M/E	Modesto, CA	Strand Thea.
10	Thu.	M/E	Fresno, CA	High School
11	Fri.	M/E	Long Beach, CA	Municipal Auditorium
12	Sat.	M/E	San Diego, CA	Spreckles Thea.
13	Sun.	M/E	San Diego, CA	Spreckles Thea.

Mon., 14th through Wed., 16th (3 days), Los Angeles, CA, Philharmonic Auditorium. 2 concerts per day.

17	Thu.	M/E	Phoenix, AZ	El Zaribah Temple
18	Fri.	M/E	Tucson, AZ	Armory
19	Sat.	M/E	El Paso, TX	Liberty Hall
21	Mon.	M/E	San Antonio, TX	Beethoven Hall
22	Tue.	M/E	Beaumont, TX	Kyle Thea.
23	Wed.	Eve.	Galveston, TX	Auditorium
24	Thu.	M/E	Houston, TX	Auditorium
25	Fri.	M/E	Austin, TX	University
26	Sat.	Eve.	Waco, TX	Cotton Palace
28	Mon.	M/E	Fort Worth, TX	First Baptist Church
29	Tue.	M/E	Wichita Falls, TX	Palace Thea.
30	Wed.	M/E	Dallas, TX	Fair Park Coliseum
31	Thu.	M/E	Okmulgee, OK	Hippodrome Thea.

FEBRUARY

1	Fri.	M/E	Tulsa, OK	Convention Hall
2	Sat.	M/E	Oklahoma City, OK	High School
3	Sun.	M/E	Ponca City, OK	Municipal Auditorium
4	Mon.	M/E	Independence, KS	Memorial Hall
5	Tue.	M/E	Springfield, MO	Shrine Mosque
6	Wed.	Mat.	Fayetteville, AR	University
6	Wed.	Eve.	Fort Smith, AR	New Thea.
7	Thu.	Mat.	Little Rock, AR	Kempner Thea.
7	Thu.	Eve.	Hot Springs, AR	Auditorium
8	Fri.	M/E	Shreveport, LA	Coliseum
9	Sat.	M/E	New Orleans, LA	Jerusalem Temple
10	Sun.	M/E	New Orleans, LA	Jerusalem Temple
11	Mon.	M/E	Mobile, AL	Bijou Thea.
12	Tue.	M/E	Pensacola, FL	High School
13	Wed.	M/E	Tallahassee, FL	Leon High School
14	Thu.	M/E	Jacksonville, FL	Armory
15	Fri.	M/E	St. Petersburg, FL	Plaza Thea.
16	Sat.	M/E	Tampa, FL	Tampa Bay Casino
17	Sun.	M/E	Lakeland, FL	Auditorium
18	Mon.	M/E	Daytona Beach, FL	Auditorium
19	Tue.	M/E	Savannah, GA	Municipal Auditorium
20	Wed.	M/E	Columbia, SC	Columbia Thea.
21	Thu.	Mat.	Augusta, GA	Imperial Thea.
21	Thu.	Eve.	Athens, GA	Moss Auditorium
22	Fri.	M/E	Rome, GA	Municipal Auditorium
23	Sat.	M/E	Birmingham, AL	Masonic Auditorium
24	Sun.	M/E	Montgomery, AL	Municipal Auditorium
25	Mon.	Mat.	Americus, GA	Rylander Thea.
25	Mon.	Eve.	Columbus, GA	Springer Opera House
26	Tue.	M/E	Macon, GA	Grand Opera House
27	Wed.	M/E	Atlanta, GA	Armory
28	Thu.	M/E	Greenville, SC	Textile Hall
29	Fri.	M/E	Spartanburg, SC	Converse College

MARCH

1	Sat.	M/E	Charlotte, NC	Auditorium
3	Mon.	Mat.	Lexington, NC	Lexington Opera House
3	Mon.	Eve.	Greensboro, NC	National Thea.
4	Tue.	Mat.	Durham, NC	High School
4	Tue.	Eve.	Raleigh, NC	Auditorium
5	Wed.	M/E	Norfolk, VA	Academy of Music
6	Thu.	M/E	Richmond, VA	City Auditorium
7	Fri.	Mat.	Washington, DC	National Thea.
8	Sat.	M/E	Baltimore, MD	Lyric Thea.

[End of 1923-24 tour]

1924 TOUR

Soloists before Willow Grove: Marjorie Moody, cornet; John Dolan, cornet; Joseph DeLuca, euphonium; John P. Schueler, trombone; John W. Bell, piccolo; Howard Goulden, xylophone; Winifred Bambrick, harp.

JUNE

21	Sat.	M/E	Kennett Square, PA	Longwood Gardens
22	Sun.	M/E	Newark, NJ	Olympic Park
23	Mon.	M/E	Patchogue, NY	Patchogue Thea.
24	Tue.	Eve.	Amsterdam, NY	Rialto Thea.
25	Wed.	Mat.	Brattleboro, VT	Auditorium
25	Wed.	Eve.	Keene, NH	City Hall
26	Thu.	Mat.	Rutland, MA	Playhouse
26	Thu.	Eve.	Glens Falls, NY	K of C Auditorium
27	Fri.	Eve.	White Plains, NY	Armory
28	Sat.	M/E	Ocean Grove, NJ	Great Auditorium

JUNE-SEPTEMBER

Sun., 29 June through Sun. 14 Sept. (76 days), Willow Grove (PA) Park. 4 concerts per day.

Soloists: Marjorie Moody, Nora Fauchald, & Rachel Jane Hamilton, soprano; Florence Goulden, contralto; John Dolan, Dana M. Garrett, William Tong, & Jacob Knuttenen, cornet; Joseph DeLuca & Noble Howard, euphonium; John P. Schueler, trombone; R.E. Williams, flute; John W. Bell & Edward Hall, piccolo; Roy Schmidt, clarinet; Edward J. Heney, saxophone; Howard Goulden, xylophone.

Soloists for remainder of tour: Marjorie Moody & Nora Fauchald, soprano; John Dolan, cornet; Robert Gooding, saxophone; George J. Carey & Howard Goulden, xylophone.

SEPTEMBER

15	Mon.	M/E	Plainfield, NJ	High School
16	Tue.	M/E	Stamford, CT	Stamford Thea.
17	Wed.	Mat.	Danbury, CT	Empress Thea.
17	Wed.	Eve.	Bridgeport, CT	Lyric Thea.
18	Thu.	M/E	New Haven, CT	Woolsey Hall
19	Fri.	Mat.	New Britain, CT	Lyceum Thea.
19	Fri.	Eve.	Hartford, CT	Foot Guard Armory
20	Sat.	M/E	Springfield, MA	Auditorium
21	Sun.	M/E	Boston, MA	Symphony Hall
22	Mon.	Mat.	Lynn, MA	Waldorf Thea.
22	Mon.	Eve.	Lowell, MA	Auditorium
23	Tue.	Mat.	Portsmouth, NH	Portsmouth Thea.
23	Tue.	Eve.	Portland, ME	City Hall
24	Wed.	M/E	Bangor, ME	Auditorium
25	Thu.	Mat.	Rumford, ME	City Hall
25	Thu.	Eve.	Lewiston, ME	Armory
26	Fri.	Mat.	Laconia, NH	Colonial Thea.
26	Fri.	Eve.	Manchester, NH	Practical Arts High School
27	Sat.	M/E	Worcester, MA	Mechanics' Hall
28	Sun.	Mat.	Pawtucket, RI	Strand Thea.
28	Sun.	Eve.	Providence, RI	Albee Thea.
29	Mon.	Mat.	Woonsocket, RI	Park Thea.
29	Mon.	Eve.	Fall River, MA	Casino Thea.
30	Tue.	Mat.	Ansonia, CT	Capitol Thea.
30	Tue.	Eve.	Meriden, CT	Poli's Thea.

OCTOBER

1	Wed.	M/E	Utica, NY	Colonial Thea.
2	Thu.	M/E	Rochester, NY	Eastman Thea.
3	Fri.	Mat.	Ridgway, PA	Strand Thea.
3	Fri.	Eve.	Punxsutawney, PA	Jefferson Thea.
4	Sat.	M/E	Pittsburgh, PA	Syria Mosque
5	Sun.	Mat.	Cambridge, OH	Colonial Thea.
5	Sun.	Eve.	Columbus, OH	Memorial Hall
6	Mon.	M/E	Athens, OH	Ohio University
7	Tue.	M/E	Clarksburg, WV	Carmichael Auditorium
8	Wed.	M/E	Uniontown, PA	State Thea.
9	Thu.	M/E	New Castle, PA	Benjamin Franklin Jr. HS
10	Fri.	Eve.	Youngstown, OH	Reyan Wood Auditorium
11	Sat.	M/E	Akron, OH	Armory
12	Sun.	M/E	Cincinnati, OH	Emery Auditorium
13	Mon.	M/E	Middlesboro, KY	Manring Thea.
14	Tue.	M/E	Knoxville, TN	Bijou Thea.
15	Wed.	M/E	Asheville, NC	Auditorium
16	Thu.	M/E	Chattanooga, TN	Memorial Auditorium
17	Fri.	M/E	Memphis, TN	Municipal Auditorium
18	Sat.	M/E	Nashville, TN	Ryman Auditorium
19	Sun.	Mat.	Vincennes, IN	Pantheon Thea.
19	Sun.	Eve.	Terre Haute, IN	Grand Opera House
20	Mon.	Mat.	Clinton, IA	Clinton Opera House
20	Mon.	Eve.	Davenport, IA	Masonic Temple
21	Tue.	Mat.	Iowa City, IA	University of Iowa
21	Tue.	Eve.	Cedar Rapids, IA	Majestic Thea.
22	Wed.	M/E	Waterloo, IA	Dairy Cattle Congress Hippodrome
23	Thu.	M/E	Minneapolis, MN	Kenwood Armory
24	Fri.	M/E	St. Paul, MN	Auditorium
25	Sat.	M/E	Duluth, MN	Armory
26	Sun.	M/E	Ashland, WI	Royal Thea.
27	Mon.	M/E	Hibbing, MN	High School
28	Tue.	M/E	Bemidji, MN	High School
29	Wed.	M/E	Grand Forks, ND	City Auditorium
30	Thu.	M/E	Fargo, ND	Fargo Auditorium
31	Fri.	M/E	Valley City, ND	State Teachers College

NOVEMBER

1	Sat.	M/E	Eau Claire, WI	Auditorium
2	Sun.	M/E	Chicago, IL	Auditorium
3	Mon.	Mat.	Bloomington, IL	Illini Thea.
3	Mon.	Eve.	Springfield, IL	Elks' Auditorium
4	Tue.	M/E	St. Louis, MO	Odeon Thea.
5	Wed.	Mat.	Decatur, IL	High School
5	Wed.	Eve.	Urbana, IL	University of Illinois
6	Thu.	M/E	Madison, WI	Parkway Thea.
7	Fri.	M/E	Appleton, WI	Lawrence Memorial Chapel
8	Sat.	M/E	Milwaukee, WI	Auditorium

9	Sun.	M/E	Milwaukee, WI	Auditorium
10	Mon.	Mat.	Michigan City, IN	Tivoli Thea.
10	Mon.	Eve.	Kalamazoo, MI	Fuller Thea.
11	Tue.	Eve.	Grand Rapids, MI	Armory
12	Wed.	M/E	Detroit, MI	Orchestra Hall
13	Thu.	Mat.	Ypsilanti, MI	Mich. St. Normal College
13	Thu.	Eve.	Ann Arbor, MI	Hill Auditorium
14	Fri.	Eve.	Toledo, OH	Coliseum
15	Sat.	M/E	Cleveland, OH	Public Auditorium
16	Sun.	Mat.	Brooklyn, NY	Academy of Music
16	Sun.	Eve.	New York, NY	Manhattan Opera House

[End of 1924 tour]

1925-26 TOUR

Soloists before Willow Grove: Marjorie Moody, soprano; John Dolan, cornet; Joseph DeLuca, euphonium; John P. Schueler, trombone; George J. Carey & Howard Goulden, xylophone; Winifred Bambrick, harp.

JULY

4	Sat.	M/E	Hershey, PA	Convention Hall
5	Sun.	M/E	Hershey, PA	Convention Hall
6	Mon.	M/E	Pottsville, PA	Hippodrome Thea.
7	Tue.	M/E	Trenton, NJ	Woodlawn Park
8	Wed.	M/E	Cedarhurst, NY	Central Thea.
9	Thu.	Mat.	Newburgh, NY	Cohen's Thea.
9	Thu.	Eve.	Middletown, NY	State Thea.
10	Fri.	Mat.	Norwich, NY	Colonia Thea.
10	Fri.	Eve.	Syracuse, NY	Keith's Thea.

Sat., 11th through Wed., 15th (5 days), Springfield, MA, Riverside Park. 2 concerts per day.

16	Thu.	Mat.	Newark, NY	High School
16	Thu.	Eve.	Rochester, NY	Eastman Thea.
17	Fri.	M/E	Chautauqua, NY	Amphitheater
18	Sat.	M/E	Winona Lake, IN	Tabernacle
19	Sun.	M/E	Kohler, WI	Nature Thea.
20	Mon.	Mat.	Bay City, MI	Central High School
20	Mon.	Eve.	Saginaw, MI	Auditorium
21	Tue.	M/E	Sault Ste. Marie, MI	High School
22	Wed.	M/E	Hancock, MI	Kerredge Thea.
23	Thu.	M/E	Duluth, MN	Duluth Exposition
24	Fri.	M/E	Crookston, MN	Armory
25	Sat.	M/E	Devils Lake, ND	Grand Thea.

JULY-AUGUST

Mon., 27 July through Sat., 1 Aug. (6 days), Regina, SAS/Canada, Fair Grounds. 2 concerts per day.

Soloists probably same as for earlier part of tour, plus others.

AUGUST

3	Mon.	M/E	Winnipeg, MAN/Canada	Walker Thea.
4	Tue.	M/E	Winnipeg, MAN/Canada	Walker Thea.
5	Wed.	Eve.	Fort William, ONT/Canada	Prince of Wales Rink
6	Thu.	Eve.	Sudbury, ONT/Canada	Palace Rink
7	Fri.	M/E	Ottawa, ONT/Canada	Keith's Thea.
8	Sat.	M/E	Lake Placid, NY	Club Agora

AUGUST-SEPTEMBER

Sun., 9 Aug. through Sun., 13 Sept. (36 days), Willow Grove (PA) Park. 4 concerts per day.

Soloists: Marjorie Moody & Nora Fauchald, soprano; Florence Goulden, contralto; John Dolan, William Tong, Harold O. Stambaugh, & Albertus Meyers, cornet; Joseph DeLuca, euphonium; John P. Schueler, trombone; R.E. Williams, flute; Edward Hall, piccolo; Harold B. Stephens & Edward J. Heney, saxophone; George J. Carey, xylophone.

Soloists for remainder of tour: Marjorie Moody, soprano; John Dolan & William Tong, cornet; Joseph DeLuca, euphonium; Harold B. Stephens, saxophone; George J. Carey & Howard Goulden, xylophone; Winifred Bambrick, harp.

SEPTEMBER

14	Mon.	M/E	Kennett Square, PA	Longwood Gardens
15	Tue.	Mat.	Sunbury, PA	Chestnut Street Thea.
15	Tue.	Eve.	Williamsport, PA	Majestic Thea.
16	Wed.	M/E	Elmira, NY	Lyceum Thea.
17	Thu.	Mat.	Batavia, NY	New Family Thea.
17	Thu.	Eve.	Buffalo, NY	Elmwood Music Hall
18	Fri.	Mat.	Hamilton, ONT/Canada	Capitol Thea.
18	Fri.	Eve.	London, ONT/Canada	Arena
19	Sat.	M/E	Toronto, ONT/Canada	Massey Music Hall

Date	Day	Time	City	Venue
20	Sun.	Mat.	Niagara Falls, NY	Armory
20	Sun.	Eve.	Lockport, NY	Palace Thea.
21	Mon.	Mat.	Geneva, NY	Smith Opera House
21	Mon.	Eve.	Ithaca, NY	Bailey Hall
22	Tue.	Mat.	Oswego, NY	Richardson Thea.
22	Tue.	Eve.	Watertown, NY	Olympic Thea.
23	Wed.	M/E	Utica, NY	Colonial Thea.
24	Thu.	M/E	Schenectady, NY	State Thea.
25	Fri.	M/E	Albany, NY	Armory
26	Sat.	M/E	New Haven, CT	Woolsey Hall
27	Sun.	M/E	Boston, MA	Symphony Hall
28	Mon.	Mat.	Cambridge, MA	Sanders Thea.
28	Mon.	Eve.	Haverhill, MA	Academy of Music
29	Tue.	Mat.	Rochester, NH	City Hall
29	Tue.	Eve.	Portland, ME	City Hall
30	Wed.	Mat.	Augusta, ME	City Hall
30	Wed.	Eve.	Lewiston, ME	Armory

OCTOBER

Date	Day	Time	City	Venue
1	Thu.	M/E	Salem, MA	Cadet Armory
2	Fri.	Mat.	Concord, NH	Auditorium
2	Fri.	Eve.	Manchester, NH	Practical Arts High School
3	Sat.	M/E	Worcester, MA	Mechanics' Hall
4	Sun.	Mat.	Woonsocket, RI	Park Thea.
4	Sun.	Eve.	Providence, RI	Albee Thea.
5	Mon.	Mat.	New London, CT	Capitol Thea.
5	Mon.	Eve.	Norwich, CT	Palace Thea.
6	Tue.	M/E	Brooklyn, NY	Academy of Music
7	Wed.	M/E	Washington, DC	Washington Auditorium
8	Thu.	M/E	Charlottesville, VA	Memorial Gymnasium
9	Fri.	M/E	Roanoke, VA	City Auditorium
10	Sat.	M/E	Baltimore, MD	Lyric Thea.
11	Sun.	Eve.	New York, NY	Mecca Temple
12	Mon.	Eve.	Scranton, PA	Armory
13	Tue.	Mat.	Lewistown, PA	Armory
13	Tue.	Eve.	Altoona, PA	Mishler Thea.
14	Wed.	M/E	Johnstown, PA	Cambria Thea.
15	Thu.	M/E	Indiana, PA	Ritz Thea.
16	Fri.	Mat.	Pittsburgh, PA	Nixon Thea.
16	Fri.	Eve.	Pittsburgh, PA	Syria Mosque
17	Sat.	M/E	Cleveland, OH	Public Auditorium
18	Sun.	M/E	Detroit, MI	Orchestra Hall
19	Mon.	Mat.	Fremont, OH	Fremont Thea.
19	Mon.	Eve.	Toledo, OH	Coliseum
20	Tue.	M/E	Akron, OH	Armory
21	Wed.	M/E	Youngstown, OH	Park Thea.
22	Thu.	M/E	Wheeling, WV	Court Thea.
23	Fri.	M/E	Alliance, OH	High School
24	Sat.	M/E	Canton, OH	Auditorium
25	Sun.	M/E	Chicago, IL	Auditorium
26	Mon.	M/E	Joliet, IL	High School
27	Tue.	Mat.	La Porte, IN	La Porte Thea.
27	Tue.	Eve.	South Bend, IN	Palais Royale
28	Wed.	Mat.	Kalamazoo, MI	Fuller Thea.
28	Wed.	Eve.	Battle Creek, MI	Post Thea.
29	Thu.	M/E	Lansing, MI	Prudden Auditorium
30	Fri.	M/E	Fort Wayne, IN	South Side High School
31	Sat.	M/E	Cincinnati, OH	Music Hall

NOVEMBER

Date	Day	Time	City	Venue
1	Sun.	M/E	Indianapolis, IN	Murat Thea.
2	Mon.	M/E	Louisville, KY	Brown Thea.
3	Tue.	M/E	Bloomington, IN	Indiana University
4	Wed.	M/E	Lafayette, IN	Purdue University
5	Thu.	M/E	Urbana, IL	University of Illinois
6	Fri.	M/E	Peoria, IL	Shrine Temple
7	Sat.	Mat.	Belvidere, IL	Apollo Thea.
7	Sat.	Eve.	Rockford, IL	Shrine Temple
8	Sun.	M/E	Milwaukee, WI	Auditorium
9	Mon.	M/E	Oshkosh, WI	Grand Opera House
10	Tue.	M/E	Green Bay, WI	Auditorium
11	Wed.	M/E	La Crosse, WI	La Crosse Thea.
12	Thu.	M/E	Keokuk, IA	Grand Thea.
13	Fri.	Eve.	Des Moines, IA	Coliseum
14	Sat.	M/E	Fort Dodge, IA	High School
15	Sun.	Mat.	Mason City, IA	Armory
15	Sun.	Eve.	Faribault, MN	Grand Thea.
16	Mon.	M/E	St. Paul, MN	Auditorium
17	Tue.	M/E	Minneapolis, MN	Kenwood Armory
18	Wed.	M/E	Aberdeen, SD	Normal State Technical College
19	Thu.	M/E	Huron, SD	Huron College
20	Fri.	M/E	Mitchell, SD	Corn Palace
21	Sat.	M/E	Sioux Falls, SD	Coliseum
22	Sun.	M/E	Sioux City, IA	Auditorium
23	Mon.	M/E	Omaha, NE	Auditorium
24	Tue.	M/E	Grand Island, NE	Liederkranz Hall
25	Wed.	M/E	Holdrege, NE	Auditorium
26	Thu.	M/E	Denver, CO	Auditorium
27	Fri.	M/E	Colorado Springs, CO	Auditorium
28	Sat.	M/E	Pueblo, CO	City Auditorium
29	Sun.	M/E	Trinidad, CO	West Thea.
30	Mon.	M/E	Albuquerque, NM	Armory

DECEMBER

Date	Day	Time	City	Venue
1	Tue.	M/E	Amarillo, TX	Municipal Auditorium
2	Wed.	M/E	Wichita Falls, TX	Palace Thea.
3	Thu.	M/E	Fort Worth, TX	First Baptist Church
4	Fri.	M/E	Dallas, TX	Fair Park Coliseum
5	Sat.	Mat.	Okmulgee, OK	Hippodrome Thea.
5	Sat.	Eve.	Muskogee, OK	Orpheum Thea.
6	Sun.	M/E	Tulsa, OK	Convention Hall
7	Mon.	M/E	Bartlesville, OK	Civic Center
8	Tue.	M/E	Oklahoma City, OK	Shrine Auditorium
9	Wed.	M/E	Enid, OK	Convention Hall
10	Thu.	M/E	Wichita, KS	Forum
11	Fri.	Eve.	Hays, KS	State Teachers College
12	Sat.	M/E	Salina, KS	Memorial Hall
13	Sun.	M/E	Kansas City, MO	Convention Hall
14	Mon.	Mat.	Lawrence, KS	Univ. of Kansas
14	Mon.	Eve.	Topeka, KS	City Auditorium
15	Tue.	M/E	Manhattan, KS	State Agricultural College
16	Wed.	M/E	Pittsburg, KS	Carney Hall
16	Wed.	Eve.	Joplin, MO	Joplin Thea.
17	Thu.	M/E	Fort Smith, AR	Joie Thea.
18	Fri.	Mat.	Little Rock, AR	Kempner Thea.
18	Fri.	Eve.	Hot Springs, AR	Auditorium
19	Sat.	M/E	Pine Bluff, AR	Saenger Thea.
20	Sun.	M/E	Shreveport, LA	Strand Thea.
21	Mon.	M/E	El Dorado, AR	High School
22	Tue.	M/E	Monroe, LA	Saenger Thea.
23	Wed.	M/E	Alexandria, LA	Rapides Thea.
24	Thu.	M/E	Baton Rouge, LA	Columbia Thea.
25	Fri.	M/E	New Orleans, LA	Jerusalem Temple
26	Sat.	M/E	Lake Charles, LA	Arcade Thea.
27	Sun.	M/E	Houston, TX	Auditorium
28	Mon.	M/E	Corsicana, TX	High School
29	Tue.	M/E	Austin, TX	Hancock Opera House
30	Wed.	M/E	San Antonio, TX	Beethoven Hall

JANUARY, 1926

Date	Day	Time	City	Venue
1	Fri.	M/E	El Paso, TX	Liberty Hall
2	Sat.	M/E	Douglas, AZ	Grand Thea.
3	Sun.	Mat.	Tucson, AZ	High School
3	Sun.	Eve.	Phoenix, AZ	El Zaribah Temple
4	Mon.	M/E	San Bernardino, CA	Municipal Auditorium
5	Tue.	Mat.	Pomona, CA	High School
5	Tue.	Eve.	Pasadena, CA	High School
6	Wed.	M/E	Hollywood, CA	Hollywood High School

Thu., 7th through Sat., 9th (3 days), Los Angeles, CA, Philharmonic Auditorium. 2 concerts per day.

Date	Day	Time	City	Venue
10	Sun.	M/E	San Diego, CA	Spreckles Thea.
11	Mon.	M/E	Long Beach, CA	Municipal Auditorium
12	Tue.	Mat.	Hanford, CA	Civic Auditorium
12	Tue.	Eve.	Fresno, CA	High School
13	Wed.	M/E	Modesto, CA	Strand Thea.
14	Thu.	M/E	Oakland, CA	Auditorium
15	Fri.	Eve.	San Francisco, CA	Exposition Auditorium
16	Sat.	M/E	San Francisco, CA	Exposition Auditorium
17	Sun.	M/E	San Francisco, CA	Exposition Auditorium
18	Mon.	M/E	Stockton, CA	Stockton High School
19	Tue.	M/E	Sacramento, CA	State Thea.
20	Wed.	M/E	Medford, OR	Medford Armory
21	Thu.	M/E	Eugene, OR	State Armory

22	Fri.	M/E	Salem, OR	Armory
23	Sat.	M/E	Portland, OR	Municipal Auditorium
24	Sun.	M/E	Portland, OR	Municipal Auditorium
25	Mon.	M/E	Longview, WA	Columbia Thea.
26	Tue.	M/E	Seattle, WA	Metropolitan Thea.
27	Wed.	M/E	Seattle, WA	Metropolitan Thea.
28	Thu.	M/E	Yakima, WA	Capitol Thea.
29	Fri.	M/E	Spokane, WA	Lewis & Clark High School
30	Sat.	Mat.	Lewiston, ID	Lewiston State Normal School
30	Sat.	Eve.	Pullman, WA	State College
31	Sun.	M/E	Baker, OR	Clarick Thea.

FEBRUARY

1	Mon.	M/E	Boise, ID	High School
2	Tue.	M/E	Pocatello, ID	Idaho Technical Institute
3	Wed.	M/E	Salt Lake City, UT	Tabernacle
4	Thu.	M/E	Rock Springs, WY	Rialto Thea.
5	Fri.	Eve.	Boulder, CO	Macky Auditorium
6	Sat.	M/E	Hastings, NE	Auditorium
7	Sun.	M/E	St. Joseph, MO	Lyceum Thea.
8	Mon.	Eve.	Kirksville, MO	Kirk Auditorium
9	Tue.	M/E	Columbia, MO	Columbia Thea.
10	Wed.	Mat.	East St. Louis, IL	East St. Louis High School
10	Wed.	Eve.	St. Louis, MO	Odeon Thea.
11	Thu.	M/E	Memphis, TN	Municipal Auditorium
12	Fri.	M/E	Jackson, MS	Auditorium
13	Sat.	M/E	Birmingham, AL	Municipal Auditorium
14	Sun.	M/E	Montgomery, AL	Municipal Auditorium
15	Mon.	Mat.	Tuskegee, AL	Tuskegee Chapel
15	Mon.	Eve.	La Grange, GA	John Brown Tabernacle
16	Tue.	M/E	Albany, GA	Auditorium
17	Wed.	M/E	Jacksonville, FL	Duval County Armory
18	Thu.	M/E	Gainesville, FL	University
19	Fri.	M/E	Tampa, FL	Victory Thea.
20	Sat.	M/E	St. Petersburg, FL	First Congregational Chur.
22	Mon.	M/E	Orlando, FL	Beachman Thea.
23	Tue.	M/E	Daytona Beach, FL	Auditorium
24	Wed.	M/E	Savannah, GA	Municipal Auditorium
25	Thu.	M/E	Augusta, GA	Imperial Thea.
26	Fri.	M/E	Atlanta, GA	Atlanta Thea.
27	Sat.	M/E	Atlanta, GA	Atlanta Thea.

MARCH

1	Mon.	M/E	Spartanburg, SC	Converse College
2	Tue.	Mat.	Rock Hill, SC	Winthrop College
2	Tue.	Eve.	Gastonia, NC	High School
3	Wed.	Mat.	Salisbury, NC	New Capitol Thea.
3	Wed.	Eve.	Greensboro, NC	National Thea.
4	Thu.	M/E	Winston-Salem, NC	Reynolds Auditorium
5	Fri.	M/E	Norfolk, VA	Academy of Music
6	Sat.	M/E	Richmond, VA	City Auditorium

[End of 1926-26 tour]

1926 TOUR

Soloists before Atlantic City/Steel Pier: Marjorie Moody, soprano;
John Dolan, cornet; Roy Schmidt, clarinet; Edward J. Heney, saxophone;
Howard Goulden, xylophone.

JULY

4	Sun.	M/E	Hershey, PA	Hershey Park
5	Mon.	M/E	Hershey, PA	Hershey Park
6	Tue.	M/E	Chautauqua, NY	Amphitheater
7	Wed.	M/E	Chautauqua, NY	Amphitheater
8	Thu.	Mat.	Canandaigua, NY	Playhouse
8	Thu.	Eve.	Rochester, NY	Eastman Thea.
9	Fri.	Mat.	Sidney, NY	Smalley's Thea.
9	Fri.	Eve.	Oneonta, NY	Oneonta Thea.
10	Sat.	M/E	Ocean Grove, NJ	Great Auditorium

Sun., 11th through Sat., 17th (7 days), Atlantic City, NJ, Steel Pier. 4
concerts per day.

Soloists: Marjorie Moody, soprano; John Dolan, cornet; R.E.
Williams, flute; John W. Bell, piccolo; Roy Schmidt, clarinet; Edward J.
Heney, saxophone; Howard Goulden, xylophone.

JULY-SEPTEMBER

Sun., 18 July through Sun., 12 Sept. (57 days), Willow Grove (PA) Park.
4 concerts per day.

Soloists: Marjorie Moody, Nora Fauchald, & Winifred Ridge,
soprano; Betty Gray, contralto; John Dolan, William Tong, Harold
Stambaugh, & Jacob Knutunen, cornet; Joseph DeLuca & Noble P.
Howard, euphonium; John P. Schueler, trombone; R.E. Williams, flute;
John W. Bell & Edward Hall, piccolo; Edward J. Heney, saxophone;
Howard Goulden, xylophone.

SEPTEMBER

13	Mon.	M/E	Kennett Square, PA	Longwood Gardens
14	Tue.	M/E	Reading, PA	Rajah Temple
15	Wed.	M/E	Hartford, CT	Foot Guard Armory
16	Thu.	M/E	New Haven, CT	Woolsey Hall
17	Fri.	M/E	Haverhill, MA	Academy of Music
18	Sat.	M/E	Lawrence, MA	Colonial Thea.
19	Sun.	M/E	Boston, MA	Symphony Hall
20	Mon.	Mat.	Waterville, ME	City Hall
20	Mon.	Eve.	Bangor, ME	Auditorium
21	Tue.	M/E	Moncton, NB/Canada	Brae Rink
22	Wed.	M/E	Halifax, NS/Canada	Arena Rink
23	Thu.	M/E	St. John, NB/Canada	Imperial Thea.
24	Fri.	M/E	Portland, ME	City Hall
25	Sat.	M/E	Worcester, MA	Mechanics' Hall
26	Sun.	Mat.	Woonsocket, RI	Park Thea.
26	Sun.	Eve.	Providence, RI	Rhode Island Auditorium
27	Mon.	Mat.	Melrose, MA	City Auditorium
27	Mon.	Eve.	Lowell, MA	Memorial Hall
28	Tue.	Mat.	Concord, NH	Auditorium
28	Tue.	Eve.	Manchester, NH	Practical Arts High School
29	Wed.	Mat.	Taunton, MA	Park Thea.
29	Wed.	Eve.	Fall River, MA	Capitol Thea.
30	Thu.	Mat.	Leominster, MA	City Hall
30	Thu.	Eve.	Athol, MA	Memorial Auditorium

OCTOBER

1	Fri.	Mat.	White River Junction, VT	Yates Opera House
1	Fri.	Eve.	Montpelier, VT	City Hall
2	Sat.	M/E	Burlington, VT	University of Vermont
3	Sun.	Mat.	Fort Plain, NY	Smalley's Thea.
3	Sun.	Eve.	Gloversville, NY	Gloversville Thea.
4	Mon.	M/E	Erie, PA	Academy High School
5	Tue.	M/E	Butler, PA	High School
6	Wed.	M/E	New Castle, PA	Benjamin Franklin Jr. HS
7	Thu.	M/E	Sandusky, OH	Sandusky Thea.
8	Fri.	Mat.	Findlay, OH	Majestic Thea.
8	Fri.	Eve.	Lima, OH	Memorial Hall
9	Sat.	M/E	Toledo, OH	Coliseum
10	Sun.	M/E	Detroit, MI	Orchestra Hall
11	Mon.	M/E	Flint, MI	High School
12	Tue.	M/E	Grand Rapids, MI	Armory
13	Wed.	M/E	Kenosha, WI	Central High School
14	Thu.	M/E	Appleton, WI	Lawrence Memorial Chapel
15	Fri.	M/E	Fond du Lac, WI	Fisher Thea.
16	Sat.	M/E	Mankato, MN	Armory
17	Sun.	M/E	St. Paul, MN	Auditorium
18	Mon.	M/E	Minneapolis, MN	Lyceum Thea.
19	Tue.	M/E	Fergus Falls, MN	High School
20	Wed.	M/E	Grand Forks, ND	City Auditorium
21	Thu.	M/E	Minot, ND	High School
22	Fri.	M/E	Jamestown, ND	Junior High School
23	Sat.	Mat.	Redfield, SD	High School
23	Sat.	Eve.	Huron, SD	Huron College Auditorium
24	Sun.	M/E	Miller, SD	Miller Auditorium
25	Mon.	M/E	Watertown, SD	Methodist Church
26	Tue.	Mat.	Yankton, SD	Dakota Thea.
26	Tue.	Eve.	Vermillion, SD	University
27	Wed.	M/E	Waterloo, IA	Dairy Cattle Congress Hippodrome
28	Thu.	M/E	Cedar Rapids, IA	Majestic Thea.
29	Fri.	M/E	Davenport, IA	Masonic Temple
30	Sat.	M/E	Dubuque, IA	Columbia College
31	Sun.	M/E	Clinton, IA	Coliseum

NOVEMBER

1	Mon.	M/E	Monmouth, IL	Tabernacle
2	Tue.	Mat.	Hannibal, MO	Orpheum Thea.
2	Tue.	Eve.	Quincy, IL	Quincy College
3	Wed.	Mat.	East St. Louis, IL	East St. Louis High School
3	Wed.	Eve.	St. Louis, MO	Odeon Thea.

4	Thu.	M/E	Elgin, IL	Masonic Temple
5	Fri.	Mat.	Janesville, WI	Franklin Gardens
5	Fri.	Eve.	Madison, WI	Central High School
6	Sat.	M/E	Milwaukee, WI	Auditorium
7	Sun.	M/E	Chicago, IL	Auditorium
8	Mon.	Mat.	Vincennes, IN	Pantheon Thea.
8	Mon.	Eve.	Evansville, IN	Coliseum
9	Tue.	M/E	Hopkinsville, KY	Auditorium
10	Wed.	M/E	Nashville, TN	Ryman Auditorium
11	Thu.	M/E	Chattanooga, TN	Memorial Auditorium
12	Fri.	M/E	Knoxville, TN	Lyric Thea.
13	Sat.	M/E	Asheville, NC	Auditorium
15	Mon.	M/E	Bluefield, WV	Colonial Thea.
16	Tue.	M/E	Charleston, WV	High School
17	Wed.	Mat.	McKeesport, PA	Junior High School
17	Wed.	Eve.	Pittsburgh, PA	Syria Mosque
18	Thu.	M/E	Lancaster, PA	Fulton Opera House
19	Fri.	M/E	Washington, DC	Washington Auditorium
20	Sat.	M/E	Baltimore, MD	Lyric Thea.

[End of 1926 tour]

1ST 1927 "MOVIE" TOUR

This tour was unusual in that concerts were combined with showings of motion pictures. There were week-long engagements in 6 cities. Four or five times each day, the band would play a concert of approximately forty minutes duration, and this would be followed by the showing of a movie. In addition to the Sousa Band concerts and the movies, there would often be other entertainment, such as a local orchestra, chorus, organist, or soloist. Between the cities with the concert/movie format, concerts of regular length, without the movies, were presented in two cities, as noted by **.

Soloists for the entire tour were Marjorie Moody, soprano, John Dolan, cornet, and Howard Goulden, xylophone.
MARCH-APRIL
Sat., 26 Mar. through Fri., 1 Apr. (7 days), New York, NY., Paramount Thea.
Movie: Fashion Shows for Women.
APRIL
Sat., 2nd through Fri., 8th (7 days), Brooklyn, NY, Strand Thea.
Movie: *Hills of Kentucky.*
Sat., 9th through Fri., 15th (7 days), Boston, MA, Metropolitan Thea.
Movie: *Blind Alley.*

| 16 | Sat. | Eve. | **Springfield, MA | Auditorium |

Sun., 17th through Sat., 23rd (7 days), Buffalo, NY, Shea's Thea.
Movie: *Orchids and Ermine.*
Sun., 24th through Sat., 30th (7 days), Detroit, MI, Michigan Thea.
Movie: *Wolf's Clothing.*
MAY

| 1 | Sun. | M/E | **Fort Wayne, IN | Paramount Thea. |

Mon., 2nd through Sun. 8th (7 days), Chicago, IL, Chicago Thea.
Movie: *Evening Clothes*
[End of 1st 1927 "movie tour"]

2ND 1927 TOUR

A regular concert tour except that the "movie" tour format, as used on the 1st 1927 tour, was again used for the last month. Regular concerts were presented in between cities with the concert/movie format, again denoted by **.

Soloists before Atlantic City/Steel Pier: Marjorie Moody, soprano; John Dolan, cornet; Edward J. Heney, saxophone; Howard Goulden, xylophone.
JULY

14	Thu.	Eve.	Great Neck, NY	Playhouse
15	Fri.	Eve.	Mineola, NY	Mineola Thea.
16	Sat.	Eve.	White Plains, NY	Armory

Sun., 17 July through Sat., 13 Aug. (28 days), Atlantic City, Steel Pier. 4 concerts per day.
Soloists: Marjorie Moody & Nora Fauchald, soprano; Betty Gray, contralto; John Dolan & William Tong, cornet; Joseph DeLuca, euphonium; John P. Schueler, trombone; John W. Bell, piccolo; Edmund C. Wall, clarinet; Edward J. Heney, saxophone; Howard Goulden, xylophone; Winifred Bambrick, harp.

AUGUST
Sat., 14th through Thu., 25th (12 days), Cleveland, OH, Cleveland Industrial Exposition. 4 concerts per day.

| 26 | Fri. | Eve. | Chicago, IL | Grant Park |

AUGUST-SEPTEMBER
Sat., 27 Aug. through Fri., 2 Sept. (7 days), Des Moines, IA, Iowa State Fair. 3 concerts per day.
Soloists: Marjorie Moody, soprano; John Dolan, cornet; Joseph DeLuca, euphonium; John W. Bell, piccolo; Edward J. Heney, saxophone; Howard Goulden, xylophone.
SEPTEMBER
Sat., 3rd through Fri., 9th (7 days), St. Paul, MN, Minnesota State Fair. 3 concerts per day.
Soloists: Marjorie Moody, soprano; John Dolan & William Tong, cornet; Joseph DeLuca, euphonium; John W. Bell, piccolo; Edward J. Heney, saxophone; Howard Goulden, xylophone.
Soloists for remainder of tour, including concert/movie segment of the tour: Marjorie Moody, soprano; John Dolan & William Tong, cornet; Edmund C. Wall, clarinet; Edward J. Heney, saxophone; Howard Goulden, xylophone; Winifred Bambrick, harp.

10	Sat.	M/E	Duluth, MN	Armory
11	Sun.	M/E	Ashland, WI	Royal Thea.
12	Mon.	M/E	Hibbing, MN	High School
13	Tue.	M/E	International Falls, MN	High School
14	Wed.	M/E	Winnipeg, MAN/Canada	Amphitheatre
15	Thu.	Eve.	Regina, SAS/Canada	Stadium
16	Fri.	M/E	Saskatoon, SAS/Canada	Rink
17	Sat.	Eve.	No. Battleford, SAS/Canada	Rink
19	Mon.	M/E	Edmonton, ALB/Canada	Fair Grounds
20	Tue.	M/E	Calgary, ALB/Canada	Fair Grounds
21	Wed.	M/E	Great Falls, MT	Liberty Thea.
22	Thu.	M/E	Billings, MT	Midland Empire Fair Audit.
23	Fri.	M/E	Bozeman, MT	State College
24	Sat.	M/E	Helena, MT	Shrine Temple
25	Sun.	M/E	Missoula, MT	Wilma Thea.
26	Mon.	M/E	Spokane, WA	Lewis & Clark High School
27	Tue.	Mat.	Moscow, ID	University of Idaho
27	Tue.	Eve.	Pullman, WA	College
28	Wed.	M/E	Lewiston, ID	Lewiston State Normal School
29	Thu.	M/E	Yakima, WA	Capitol Thea.
30	Fri.	M/E	Seattle, WA	Metropolitan Thea.

OCTOBER

1	Sat.	M/E	Seattle, WA	Metropolitan Thea.
2	Sun.	M/E	Port Angeles, WA	Olympian Thea.
3	Mon.	M/E	Victoria, BC/Canada	Arena
4	Tue.	M/E	Vancouver, BC/Canada	Arena
5	Wed.	M/E	Bellingham, WA	Auditorium
6	Thu.	M/E	Aberdeen, WA	Grand Thea.
7	Fri.	M/E	Longview, WA	Columbia Thea.
8	Sat.	M/E	Portland, OR	Municipal Auditorium
9	Sun.	M/E	Portland, OR	Municipal Auditorium
10	Mon.	M/E	Eugene, OR	State Armory
11	Tue.	M/E	Salem, OR	Elsinore Thea.
12	Wed.	M/E	Walla Walla, WA	Capitol Thea.
13	Thu.	M/E	Boise, ID	High School
14	Fri.	M/E	Twin Falls, ID	Orpheum Thea.
15	Sat.	M/E	Pocatello, ID	Frazier Hall
16	Sun.	M/E	Idaho Falls, ID	Colonial Thea.
17	Mon.	M/E	Logan, UT	Capitol Thea.
18	Tue.	M/E	Salt Lake City, UT	Tabernacle
19	Wed.	Mat.	Laramie, WY	University of Wyoming
19	Wed.	Eve.	Cheyenne, WY	Lincoln Thea.
20	Thu.	M/E	Colorado Springs, CO	Burns Thea.
21	Fri.	Mat.	Fort Collins, CO	Colorado Agricultural Coll.
21	Fri.	Eve.	Boulder, CO	Macky Auditorium
22	Sat.	M/E	Denver, CO	Auditorium
24	Mon.	M/E	Hays, KS	Sheridan Coliseum
25	Tue.	M/E	Wichita, KS	Forum
26	Wed.	M/E	Pittsburg, KS	Kansas State Teachers College
27	Thu.	Mat.	Lawrence, KS	Univ. of Kansas
27	Thu.	Eve.	Topeka, KS	City Auditorium
28	Fri.	M/E	Emporia, KS	Kansas State Teachers College

29	Sat.	M/E	Salina, KS	Shrine Auditorium
30	Sun.	M/E	Grand Island, NE	Liederkranz Hall
31	Mon.	M/E	Holdrege, NE	Auditorium

NOVEMBER

1	Tue.	M/E	Lincoln, NE	Univ. of Nebraska
2	Wed.	M/E	Norfolk, NE	Norfolk High School
3	Thu.	M/E	Sioux City, IA	Auditorium
4	Fri.	M/E	Rochester, MN	Chateau Dodge Thea.
5	Sat.	M/E	Wausau, WI	Wausau High School
6	Sun.	M/E	Milwaukee, WI	Auditorium
7	Mon.	M/E	Galesburg, IL	Armory
8	Tue.	M/E	Peoria, IL	Shrine Temple
9	Wed.	M/E	Lafayette, IN	State Arsenal
10	Thu.	M/E	Springfield, IL	State Arsenal
11	Fri.	M/E	Bloomington, IL	Illini Thea.

[Begin concert/movie section of tour]
Sat., 12th through Fri., 18th (7 days), Kansas City, MO, Midland Thea.
Movie: *The Woman on Trial*.
Sat., 19th through Fri., 25th (7 days), St. Louis, MO., State Thea.
Movie: *Body and Soul*.

26	Sat.	M/E	**Columbus, OH	Memorial Hall
27	Sun..	Mat.	**Newark, OH	Auditorium
27	Sat.	Eve.	**Zanesville, OH	Weller Thea.

NOVEMBER-DECEMBER
Mon., 28 Nov. through Sat., 3 Dec. (7 days), Pittsburgh, PA, Penn Thea.
Movie: *Topsy and Eva*.

DECEMBER
Mon, 5th through Sat., 10th (6 days), Baltimore, MD, Century Thea.
Movie: *Topsy and Eva*.

[End of concert/movie section of tour; end of 2nd 1927 tour]

1928 "GOLDEN JUBILEE" TOUR

A tour of regular concerts except for the first week (Rochester, NY) and the final week (Chicago), when the concert/movie format was used again.

Soloists until the Atlantic City/Steel Pier engagement were Marjorie Moody, soprano; John Dolan, William Tong, Jacob O. Knuttunen, & Ralph Ostrom, cornet; Noble Howard, euphonium; Edmund C. Wall, clarinet; Edward J. Heney, saxophone; Howard Goulden, xylophone.

JULY

| 19 | Thu. | M/E | Schenectady, NY | Wedgeway Thea. |
| 20 | Fri. | M/E | Utica, NY | Forest Park |

Sat., 21st through Fri., 27th (7 days), Rochester, NY, Eastman Thea.
Movie: *Walking Back*.

| 28 | Sat. | M/E | Kennett Square, PA | Longwood Gardens |

Sun., 29 July through Sat., 11 Aug. (14 days), Atlantic City, NJ, Steel Pier. 4 concerts per day.

Soloists: Marjorie Moody & Mina Delores, soprano; John Dolan, William Tong, Jacob O. Knuttunen, & Ralph Ostrom, cornet; Noble P. Howard, euphonium; John Fisher, flute; Edmund C. Wall, clarinet; Edward J. Heney, saxophone; Howard Goulden, xylophone.

Soloists for remainder of 1928 tour: Marjorie Moody, soprano; John Dolan [left band in Sept.], William Tong, & Ralph Ostrom, cornet; Noble P. Howard, euphonium; Edmund C. Wall, clarinet; Edward J. Heney, saxophone; Howard Goulden, xylophone.

AUGUST

| 12 | Sun. | M/E* | Willow Grove, PA | Willow Grove Park |

* 3 concerts this day

13	Mon.	Mat.	New London, CT	Garde Thea.
13	Mon.	Eve.	Providence, RI	Carleton Thea.
14	Tue.	Mat.	Putnam, CT	Bradley Thea.
14	Tue.	Eve.	Worcester, MA	Mechanics' Hall
15	Wed.	Mat.	Dover, NH	Opera House
15	Wed.	Eve.	Portland, ME	City Hall
16	Thu.	Mat.	Augusta, ME	Colonial Thea.
16	Thu.	Eve.	Lewiston, ME	Armory
17	Fri.	Mat.	Portsmouth, NH	Colonial Thea.
17	Fri.	Eve.	Manchester, NH	Practical Arts High School
18	Sat.	Mat.	Concord, NH	Auditorium
18	Sat.	Eve.	Laconia, NH	Colonial Thea.
19	Sun.	Mat.	Boston, MA	Symphony Hall
20	Mon.	Mat.	Gloucester, MA	North Shore Thea.
20	Mon.	Eve.	Salem, MA	Federal Thea.
21	Tue.	Mat.	New Bedford, MA	Olympia Thea.
21	Tue.	Eve.	Plymouth, MA	Memorial Thea.

22	Wed.	Mat.	Framingham, MA	Memorial Auditorium
22	Wed.	Eve.	Athol, MA	Memorial Auditorium
23	Thu.	Mat.	Bellows Falls, VT	Opera House
23	Thu.	Eve.	Brattleboro, VT	Community Hall
24	Fri.	Mat.	Bennington, VT	Armory
24	Fri.	Eve.	Troy, NY	Music Hall
25	Sat.	M/E	Chautauqua, NY	Amphitheater

Sun., 26 Aug. through Sat., 1 Sept. (7 days), Columbus, OH, Ohio State Fair. 3 concerts per day except only 2 concerts 1st day.

SEPTEMBER
Sun., 2nd through Sat., 8th (7 days), Detroit, MI, Michigan State Fair. 2 concerts per day.

9	Sun.	M/E	Saginaw, MI	Auditorium
10	Mon.	M/E	Sault Ste. Marie, MI	High School
11	Tue.	M/E	Marquette, MI	Delft Thea.
12	Wed.	M/E	Hancock, MI	Kerredge Thea.
13	Thu.	M/E	Escanaba, MI	Delft Thea.
14	Fri.	M/E	Marinette, WI	High School
15	Sat.	M/E	Manitowoc, WI	Capitol Thea.
16	Sun.	M/E	Green Bay, WI	Columbus Auditorium
17	Mon.	M/E	Oshkosh, WI	Fischer Thea.
18	Tue.	M/E	Racine, WI	Memorial Hall
19	Wed.	M/E	St. Charles, IL	Arcadia Thea.
20	Thu.	M/E	Urbana, IL	University of Illinois
21	Fri.	M/E	Joliet, IL	High School
22	Sat.	M/E	Evanston, IL	University
23	Sun.	M/E	Chicago, IL	Auditorium
24	Mon.	M/E	Ripon, WI	Ripon College
25	Tue.	Mat.	Winona, MN	Winona Opera House
25	Tue.	Eve.	Red Wing, MN	T.B. Sheldon Memorial
26	Wed.	M/E	Minneapolis, MN	Auditorium
27	Thu.	M/E	Fargo, ND	Fargo Auditorium
28	Fri.	M/E	Minot, ND	High School
29	Sat.	M/E	Williston, ND	Grand Thea.
30	Sun.	Mat.	Glendive, MT	Garage

OCTOBER

1	Mon.	Mat.	Dickinson, ND	State Normal School Auditorium
1	Mon.	Eve.	Bismarck, ND	City Auditorium
2	Tue.	M/E	Aberdeen, SD	Stafford Hall
3	Wed.	M/E	Brookings, SD	College
4	Thu.	M/E	Sioux Falls, SD	Coliseum
5	Fri.	M/E	Des Moines, IA	Drake University
6	Sat.	M/E	Cedar Rapids, IA	Shrine Temple
7	Sun.	Mat.	Davenport, IA	Masonic Temple
8	Mon.	M/E	Omaha, NE	Technical High School
9	Tue.	Mat.	Kearney, NE	Junior High School
9	Tue.	Eve.	Kearney, NE	State Teachers College
10	Wed.	M/E	Manhattan, KS	College
11	Thu.	M/E	Hutchinson, KS	Convention Hall
12	Fri.	M/E	Ponca City, OK	Municipal Auditorium
13	Sat.	M/E	Tulsa, OK	Convention Hall
14	Sun.	M/E	Shawnee, OK	Criterion Thea.
15	Mon.	M/E	Oklahoma City, OK	Shrine Auditorium
16	Tue.	M/E	Enid, OK	Convention Hall
17	Wed.	M/E	Wichita Falls, TX	Memorial Auditorium
18	Thu.	M/E	Abilene, TX	Simmons University
19	Fri.	M/E	Denton, TX	College of Industrial Arts
20	Sat.	M/E	Beaumont, TX	Auditorium
21	Sun.	M/E	Houston, TX	Auditorium
22	Mon.	M/E	Corpus Christi, TX	Palace Thea.
23	Tue.	M/E	Harlingen, TX	Municipal Auditorium
24	Wed.	M/E	Austin, TX	Hancock Opera House
25	Thu.	M/E	San Antonio, TX	Municipal Auditorium
26	Fri.	Eve.	El Paso, TX	Liberty Hall
27	Sat.	Mat.	Douglas, AZ	Grand Thea.
27	Sat.	Eve.	Tucson, AZ	Temple of Music
28	Sun.	M/E	San Diego, CA	Spreckles Thea.
29	Mon.	M/E	Pasadena, CA	Raymond Thea.
30	Tue.	M/E	Long Beach, CA	Municipal Auditorium
31	Wed.	Mat.	Hanford, CA	Auditorium
31	Wed.	Eve.	Fresno, CA	High School

NOVEMBER

| 1 | Thu. | M/E | Modesto, CA | Strand Thea. |
| 2 | Fri. | M/E | Sacramento, CA | Memorial Auditorium |

3	Sat.	M/E	Oakland, CA	Auditorium
4	Sun.	M/E	San Francisco, CA	Dreamland Park
5	Mon.	M/E	San Francisco, CA	Dreamland Park
6	Tue.	M/E	Palo Alto, CA	Stanford University
7	Wed.	Mat.	Santa Barbara, CA	Grenada Thea.
7	Wed.	Eve.	Santa Cruz, CA	not known
8	Thu.	Mat.	Santa Ana, CA	High School
8	Thu.	Eve.	Pomona, CA	High School
9	Fri.	M/E	Los Angeles, CA	Shrine Civic Auditorium
10	Sat.	M/E	Los Angeles, CA	Shrine Civic Auditorium
11	Sun.	M/E	Phoenix, AZ	El Zaribah Temple
12	Mon.	M/E	Flagstaff, AZ	Amhurst Auditorium
13	Tue.	M/E	Albuquerque, NM	Univ. of New Mexico
14	Wed.	M/E	Clovis, NM	Lyceum Thea.
15	Thu.	M/E	Lubbock, TX	Texas Technical College
16	Fri.	M/E	Brownwood, TX	Memorial Hall
17	Sat.	M/E	Commerce, TX	Eastern Texas Teachers College
18	Sun.	M/E	Waco, TX	Cotton Palace
19	Mon.	M/E	Fort Worth, TX	First Baptist Church
20	Tue.	M/E	Denison, TX	High School
21	Wed.	M/E	Springfield, MO	Shrine Mosque
22	Thu.	Mat.	East St. Louis, IL	East St. Louis High School
22	Thu.	Eve.	East St. Louis, IL	Coliseum
23	Fri.	M/E	Indianapolis, IN	Cadle Tabernacle
24	Sat.	M/E	Louisville, KY	Columbia Auditorium
25	Sun.	M/E	Cincinnati, OH	Emery Auditorium
26	Mon.	Mat.	Wilmington, OH	Murphy Thea.
26	Mon.	Eve.	Dayton, OH	Memorial Hall
27	Tue.	M/E	Muncie, IN	Armory
28	Wed.	M/E	Youngstown, OH	Stambaugh Auditorium
29	Thu.	M/E	Cleveland, OH	Music Hall
30	Fri.	M/E	Canton, OH	Auditorium

DECEMBER

1	Sat.	M/E	Akron, OH	Armory
2	Sun.	M/E	Milwaukee, WI	Auditorium
3	Mon.	M/E	Gary, IN	Memorial Auditorium
4	Tue.	M/E	South Bend, IN	Notre Dame University
5	Wed.	M/E	Grand Rapids, MI	Armory
6	Thu.	Eve.	Battle Creek, MI	Battle Creek Sanitarium
7	Fri.	M/E	Lansing, MI	Prudden Auditorium

Sat., 8th through Fri., 14th (7 days), Chicago, Chicago Thea.
Movie: not known

15	Sat.	M/E	Freeport, IL	Consistory Auditorium

[End of 1928 tour]

1929 OFF-TOUR CONCERTS
JUNE

15	Sat.	M/E*	Princeton, NJ	Princeton University

*Parade preceded matinee concert

1929 TOUR
Soloists: Marjorie Moody, soprano; Jacob O. Knuttunen, cornet; Edmund C. Wall, clarinet; Edward J. Heney, saxophone; Howard Goulden, xylophone.
AUGUST

24	Sat.	M/E	Atlantic City, NJ	Steel Pier
25	Sun.	M/E	Atlantic City, NJ	Steel Pier
26	Mon.	M/E	New Kensington, PA	Community Auditorium
27	Tue.	M/E	Chautauqua, NY	Amphitheater
28	Wed.	M/E	Winona Lake, IN	Tabernacle

AUGUST-SEPTEMBER
Thu., 29 Aug. through Sun., 1 Sept., Minneapolis, MN (4 days). Afternoon concert Thu., & 2 concerts per day on Fri. & Sat. at Auditorium; afternoon concert Sun. on Foshay Tower Observational Balcony.
SEPTEMBER

2	Mon.	M/E	Sioux City, IA	Auditorium
3	Tue.	M/E	Hastings, NE	Municipal Auditorium
4	Wed.	M/E	McCook, NE	World Thea.
5	Thu.	M/E	Sterling, CO	Blair Hall
6	Fri.	M/E	Colorado Springs, CO	Auditorium
7	Sat.	M/E	Denver, CO	Auditorium
8	Sun.	M/E	Pueblo, CO	City Auditorium
9	Mon.	Eve.	Trinidad, CO	West Thea.

10	Tue.	M/E	Dodge City, KS	Senior High School
11	Wed.	M/E	Independence, KS	Memorial Hall
12	Thu.	M/E	Joplin, MO	Memorial Hall
13	Fri.	M/E	Eureka Springs, AR	Auditorium
14	Sat.	M/E	Cape Girardeau, MO	State Teachers College
16	Mon.	M/E	Decatur, IL	Masonic Temple
17	Tue.	M/E	Bloomington, IL	High School
18	Wed.	M/E	Peoria, IL	Shrine Temple
19	Thu.	M/E	Urbana, IL	University of Illinois
20	Fri.	M/E	Rockford, IL	Shrine Temple
21	Sat.	M/E	Milwaukee, WI	Auditorium
22	Sun.	M/E	Chicago, IL	Orchestra Hall
23	Mon.	M/E	Elkhart, IN	High School
24	Tue.	M/E	Erie, PA	Academy High School
25	Wed.	M/E	Buffalo, NY	Edmond Music Hall
26	Thu.	Mat.	Batavia, NY	High School
26	Thu.	Eve.	Rochester, NY	Convention Hall
27	Fri.	M/E	Syracuse, NY	Armory

[End of 1929 tour]

1ST 1930 TOUR
Soloists before Atlantic City/Steel Pier: Marjorie Moody, soprano; Leo Zimmerman, trombone; Howard Goulden, xylophone.
AUGUST

24	Sun.	M/E	Newark, NJ	Olympic Park
25	Mon.	M/E	Lancaster, PA	Fulton Opera House
26	Tue.	M/E	Kennett Square, PA	Longwood Gardens

AUGUST-SEPTEMBER
Wed., 27 Aug. through Tue., 2 Sept. (7 days), Atlantic City, NJ, Steel Pier. 4 concerts per day.
Soloists: Marjorie Moody, soprano; William Tong, cornet; Leo Zimmerman, trombone; Edward J. Heney, saxophone; Howard Goulden, xylophone.
[End of 1st 1930 tour]

2ND 1930 TOUR
Soloists: Marjorie Moody, soprano; Edward J. Heney, saxophone; Howard Goulden & William T. Paulson, xylophone.
SEPTEMBER

14	Sun.	M/E	Springfield, MA	Fair Grounds Coliseum
15	Mon.	Mat.	Lebanon, NH	Opera House
15	Mon.	Eve.	St. Johnsbury, VT	Star Thea.
16	Tue.	Mat.	Montpelier, VT	Opera House
16	Tue.	Eve.	Burlington, VT	Memorial Auditorium
17	Wed.	M/E	Montreal, QUE/Canada	Forum
18	Thu.	M/E	Ottawa, ONT/Canada	Auditorium
19	Fri.	M/E	Malone, NY	Armory
20	Sat.	M/E	Albany, NY	Capitol Thea.

[End of 2nd 1930 tour]

3RD 1930 TOUR
Soloists: Marjorie Moody, soprano; William Tong, cornet; Edward J. Heney, saxophone; Howard Goulden & William T. Paulson, xylophone.
OCTOBER

6	Mon.	Eve.	Ridgefield Park, NJ	Washington High School
7	Tue.	M/E	Montclair, NJ	Montclair High School
8	Wed.	M/E	Scranton, PA	Masonic Temple
9	Thu.	Mat.	Ypsilanti, MI	Mich. St. Normal College
9	Thu.	Eve.	Jackson, MI	High School
10	Fri.	M/E	Flint, MI	I.M.A. Auditorium
11	Sat.	M/E	Muskegon, MI	Central Campus
12	Sun.	M/E	Chicago, IL	Civic Opera House
13	Mon.	M/E	St. Charles, IL	Arcadia Thea.
14	Tue.	M/E	Urbana, IL	University of Illinois
15	Wed.	M/E	Carbondale, IL	So. Illinois State Normal University
16	Thu.	Mat.	Cairo, IL	Cairo High School
16	Thu.	Eve.	Paducah, KY	Orpheum Thea.
17	Fri.	M/E	Jackson, TN	High School
18	Sat.	M/E	Memphis, TN	Municipal Auditorium
20	Mon.	M/E	Greenwood, MS	High School
21	Tue.	Mat.	College Station, MS	A&M College
21	Tue.	Eve.	Columbus, MS	Whitfield Auditorium
22	Wed.	M/E	Jackson, MS	City Auditorium

23	Thu.	M/E	Hattiesburg, MS	State Teachers College
24	Fri.	M/E	Selma, AL	Junior High School
25	Sat.	M/E	Pensacola, FL	High School
27	Mon.	M/E	Macon, GA	Municipal Auditorium
28	Tue.	M/E	Atlanta, GA	Armory
29	Wed.	M/E	Rome, GA	Municipal Auditorium
30	Thu.	M/E	Birmingham, AL	Municipal Auditorium
31	Fri.	M/E	Nashville, TN	Ryman Auditorium

NOVEMBER

1	Sat.	M/E	Huntsville, AL	Huntsville High School
3	Mon.	Mat.	Chattanooga, TN	Chattanooga High School
3	Mon.	Eve.	Chattanooga, TN	Memorial Auditorium
4	Tue.	M/E	Knoxville, TN	Lyric Thea.
5	Wed.	M/E	Johnson City, TN	Capitol Thea.
6	Thu.	M/E	Greenville, SC	Textile Hall
7	Fri.	M/E	Augusta, GA	Richmond Academy
8	Sat.	M/E	Charleston, SC	Victory Thea.
10	Mon.	M/E	Florence, SC	Florence High School
11	Tue.	M/E	Columbia, SC	Auditorium
12	Wed.	M/E	Charlotte, NC	Armory
13	Thu.	Mat.	Salisbury, NC	Boyden High School
13	Thu.	Eve.	Greensboro, NC	North Carolina College for Women
14	Fri.	M/E	Raleigh, NC	Broughton High School
15	Sat.	M/E	Kinston, NC	Grainger High School
17	Mon.	M/E	Norfolk, VA	City Auditorium
18	Tue.	Mat.	Hampton, VA	Robert C. Ogden Hall
18	Tue.	Eve.	Newport News, VA	High School
19	Wed.	M/E	Richmond, VA	Mosque Auditorium
20	Thu.	M/E	Washington, DC	D.A.R. Auditorium
21	Fri.	Eve.	Philadelphia, PA	Academy of Music
22	Sat.	M/E	New York, NY	Columbia University

[End of 3rd 1930 tour]

1931 TOUR

Soloists: Marjorie Moody, soprano; Oscar Short, cornet; John J. Heney, xylophone.

AUGUST

29	Sat.	M/E	Chautauqua, NY	Amphitheater
30	Sun.	Mat.	Binghamton, NY	Recreation Park
30	Sun.	Eve.	Endicott, NY	En-Joie Health Park
31	Mon.	M/E	Wilkes-Barre, PA	Elmer L. Meyers High School

SEPTEMBER

1	Tue.	M/E	Phoenixville, PA	Memorial Jr. High School

Wed., 2nd through Tue., 8th (7 days), Atlantic City, NJ, Steel Pier.
4 concerts per day.

[End of 1931 tour; last Sousa Band live concerts except for broadcasts]

Historical Registry

This roster is an all-inclusive register of individuals who were associated with Sousa's Band during its forty years of existence. Included in the entry for each individual, where possible, are:

1. His/her instrument(s) and/or other duties
2. His/her periods of service (see Appendix I for definitions of tours)
3. Special notation if featured as a soloist
4. Mentions of other career activities
5. Vital statistics (if available)
6. Affiliation with the Sousa Band Fraternal Society
7. Sources of the author's information

Accuracy

It is not claimed that the roster is 100 percent complete. However, it was painstakingly compiled over a period of four decades from an unusually large number of sources, including personal interviews with sixty-five former members of Sousa's Band. Numerous research techniques were developed along the way.

All extant payrolls and personnel lists were studied in great detail. The resulting roster could have been even more comprehensive except that financial records dating from 1897-1919 (and almost all later ones, as well) are known to have been destroyed. Those records would have included payrolls, the most important source of personnel information. Most of the payrolls before 1897 are unaccounted for.

The reader will note many references to the Sousa Band Fraternal Society and its newsletter, the *Sousa Band Fraternal Society News*. An index of all entries in that newsletter is presented in the book, *Sousa Band Fraternal Society News Index*. Membership in the fraternal society was accepted as sufficient proof that the person was with the band for at least one tour (or a lengthy

engagement), because that was a condition of society membership.

Scope

The musicians listed in this register are those who actually performed with the band; it does not include other performers who appeared on Sousa Band programs with their own accompaniment. An example of this would be a singer who had his or her own piano accompaniment or who sang without accompaniment.

Of the 1,209 individuals listed here, 1,169 were musicians. The other forty were staff members. The staff included members of the management team, secretaries, Sousa's personal valets, and a few stage setup men who were not hired on a regular basis.

The stage setup men were called by various names, such as "carpenter," and it is believed that the baggage handlers, who were members of the band, performed this duty much of the time. In some years the librarian who passed out the music was also responsible for arranging the stage or supervising local stagehands.

Also included in this roster is Dr. John Paul Brennan, who attended to Sousa on the 1921-22 tour following Sousa's riding injury.

Accounting for all of the staff members presented an insurmountable difficulty; their names seldom appeared on known rosters or other personnel records. No doubt some are missing from this roster, especially the advance men. Most of the advance men were also associated with other touring groups and were hired only before a tour to travel ahead of the band and make arrangements with local authorities.

Outside arrangers and copyists are not included. They did not travel with the band and were not hired for any appreciable length of time. For the most part, arrangers and copyists were regular members of the touring band. A few, such as solo cornetist Herman Bellstedt, continued to make special arrangements for Sousa after leaving the band.

Criteria

Every effort was made to include the names of all individuals who were ever part of the Sousa Band organization. Since the band's impact on the American music scene is of considerable historical significance, those associated with the band deserve to be recognized.

On the other hand, it would not be prudent to include those for whom documentation is lacking. At the end of this appendix is a section entitled "Documentation Lacking" which lists the names of individuals whose association with the band has not been definitively established. The criteria for establishing membership is explained in that section.

Terms Used

Explanations for the use of certain terms and expressions is in order:

Cornet/trumpet means a musician could have played either cornet or trumpet, but the majority played cornet. A few actually played both, but probably not on the same tour. The cornet/trumpet section typically consisted of four or six cornets and two trumpets. It should be noted that until 1902, the cornet/trumpet section often included one or two flugelhorns that played the lower cornet parts in lieu of cornets.

Tuba means either an upright tuba or a sousaphone, both being members of the tuba family of instruments and sounding in the same range. Some players played both instruments, but on different tours.

Vocalist indicates that the category of an individual (i.e., soprano, contralto, etc.) is not known.

(vocal) was added after the names of singers who were tenors or baritones so as to avoid confusion with the musical instruments known as tenors or baritones.

Partial indicates that a musician was not with the band for a complete tour or engagement. "Partial" was not used, however, in denoting those musicians who performed for the radio broadcasts of 1929-31. Since only a few payrolls for these broadcasts have survived, and because so many different musicians were used, it was impractical to attempt to distinguish between those who played most of the broadcasts and those who played only a few.

Probably and **possibly** means that the extent of an individual's service on a tour or engagement is in question. The use of one term or the other reflects the author's judgment, taking into consideration a knowledge of the conditions and trends of band employment practices at the time and a specific musician's employment history. Complete rosters do not exist for a majority of the tours and engagements.

Recorded for means the musician participated in recordings made for the labels specified. Some were soloists, whereas others were members of recording ensembles. Since assembling data on recording dates, titles, and companies is the domain of discographers, no attempt was made to catalog the collective contributions of each artist.

Photos refers to those (a) in the author's collection, (b) in various museums or libraries, (c) in private collections, or (d) those found in the Sousa Band press books or other collections of clippings.

Berger roster. Band historian Kenneth Berger's register of over four hundred names was the first serious attempt to compile an all-time Sousa Band roster. It was included as an appendix to his book *The March King and His Band*, published in 1957.

Pruyn roster. Berger's alphabetical roster was later sorted according to instrumentation (with a few additions) by another band historian, William Pruyn. Although the roster of this appendix was compiled independently of the Berger roster and the later Pruyn roster, the historical contribution of both Berger and Pruyn are gratefully acknowledged. Their lists were consulted regularly and served as a nucleus for this study.

References in **SBFS News** means that an individual is mentioned in issues of the *Sousa Band Fraternal Society News*.

Other Factors

Information about some Sousa Band personnel, particularly those who served in the early years, was often extremely difficult to find. Detailed genealogical and career path searches were beyond the scope of this book.

When noting other career positions held by Sousa Band personnel, only rarely could exact dates be determined. Available sources do not always state whether the positions were held before or after Sousa Band membership.

Where page numbers of various sources are not given (many clippings lacking identification and/or dates were examined) it is either because they are not known or because they are too numerous to mention. It was deemed unnecessary to give page numbers of encyclopedic volumes because such volumes are alphabetical in nature.

Citations

For details of book, periodical, and collection citations, see the bibliography.

Abbreviations

*	Not regular member of Sousa Band organization
b.	Born
d.	Died
MB	Manhattan Beach [amusement park] (New York)
PBk	Sousa Band press book(s)
SB	Sousa Band
SBFS	Sousa Band Fraternal Society
StPr	Steel Pier (Atlantic City, NJ)
Varela	Photograph collection of Osmund Varela, Sousa's grand-nephew
WG	Willow Grove Park (Philadelphia)

ABEEL, GEORGE A., *oboe*
1920 WG; 1921-22 tour; 1922 tour; 1923-24 tour (partial). Member, SBFS.
Sources: Roster in 1920 WG programs; 1921 SB photo; 1921-22 SB roster; 1923 SB photo; 1923-24 group photos; references in SBFS News.

*ACKERMAN, MATILDA, *soprano*
Soloist, 28 Jan 1894, Brooklyn, NY. Other position: Metropolitan Opera Co.
Source: Advertisement in PBk 3, p. 52.

ACOSTA (COSTA), JOSE R., *flute/piccolo*
1920 tour. 1920 WG (**soloist**). Other positions: Broncale Opera Co. (Havana, Cuba); Conway's Band; various theater orchestras; 62nd U.S. Army Coast Artillery Band; 28th Infantry Band; conductor of symphony orchestras in Buffalo, Cleveland, Detroit, Hamilton (ONT), & Schenectady (NY). b. Cuba.
Sources: SB programs; references in PBks 54 & 55; autographed photo & unidentified clipping in George Ford Collection.

ADAMS, RAY, *B-flat clarinet*
Briefly, probably late 1920s, possibly WG only. Other position: Allentown (PA) Band.
Source: Allentown Band Archives.

ADELMANN, JOSEPH, *percussion*
Date(s) of SB service uncertain, but briefly during 1890s.
Source: Clippings in PBk 9 (1900) refer to Adelmann as "late of Sousa's Band."

AHLBORN, C., *saxophone*
1907 tour.
Source: Roster in New York Dramatic Mirror, 7 Sep 1907.

AHLBORN, GEORGE, *flute/piccolo*
Probably all tours, 1907-17. b. 1872, Germany.
Sources: 1909 SB photo; signature on 1914 birthday card from band to Sousa (refers to first year with SB as 1907); roster in Musical Courier, 9 Jun 1915; 1915 Tuxedo tobacco advertisement with SB musicians' signatures; roster in Dec, 1916 New York Musician and Knocker; International Who Is Who in Music (edition not noted); references in SBFS News.

*ALBERTI, ACHILLE, *baritone (vocal)*
Soloist. 1897 MB (partial).
Source: SB program in PBk 5, p. 62.

ALBRECHT, GUSTAV, *horn*
Possibly one or both 1904 tours; 1st 1905 tour (Britain); 1907 tour; 2nd 1908 tour.
Sources: S.S. Baltic ship's list, 19 May 1905; rosters in New York Dramatic Mirror, 7 Sep 1907 & 1 Sep 1908; PBk 22, p. 39.

ALBRECHT, JOHN H., *B-flat clarinet*
1921-22 tour; 1922 tour.
Sources: 1921 SB photo; 1921-22 SB roster; "In Memoriam" list, SBFS organizational booklet (1945).

ALBRECHT, W., *horn*
1908 WG; possibly 1908 tour.
Source: Roster in New York Dramatic Mirror, 1 Sep 1908.

*ALCOCK, MERLE., *contralto*
Soloist. 1929 radio broadcasts. Recorded for Columbia & Victor.
Source: Newspaper radio schedules; author's correspondence with Frederick P. Williams, discographer.

*ALDRIDGE, ARTHUR, *tenor (vocal)*
Soloist, 19 Mar 1916, 11 Mar 1917, & 18 Mar 1918, New York.
Source: Clarence J. Russell's diary.

ALLEN, JULIE, *management?*
Secretary, 1897, and possibly earlier and later.
Source: Metronome, Jan, 1897, p. 16.

*ALLEN, LUCY ANNE, *soprano*
Soloist. 3rd 1906 tour; 4th 1906 tour, Boston Food Fair only; 1st 1907 tour; 1st 1908 tour; 2nd 1908 tour. Married name Havilland.
Sources: SB programs; Metronome, Dec, 1907, p. 29; references in PBks 27, 28, & 29.

ALTAMONT, G., *flute/piccolo*
1907 tour.
Source: Roster in New York Dramatic Mirror, 7 Sep 1907.

ANDREWS, ____, *clarinet*
1919-20 tour (partial).
Source: Handwritten addition to 1919-20 SB roster.

ANDROVA, ADA, see CHAMBERS, ADA

*ARAMENTI, JULIA, *vocalist*
Soloist. 1894 MB (partial).
Source: References in PBk 3.

ARNOLD, MAXWELL F. (Chick), *cornet/trumpet*
1926 tour; 1st 1927 tour. Member, SBFS. d. 20 Feb 1956.
Sources: SB photo, Jul, 1926; SBFS organizational booklet (1945); references in SBFS News.

ASKIN, HARRY, *management*
General manager, 1919-32. Other positions: managed tours for Paul Whiteman, Lillian Russell, George Gershwin, Viola Aller, and others; also managed theaters and produced shows in New York, Philadelphia, and Chicago. b. ca. 1867; d. 30 Sep 1934, New York.
Sources: SB programs; SB financial papers; SB office correspondence with band members; references in PBks; Variety, 2 Oct 1934 [obituary].

*ATWOOD, MARTHA, *soprano*
Soloist, 6 May 1929 radio broadcast. Recorded for Victor.
Source: Newspaper radio schedules; author's correspondence with Frederick P. Williams, discographer.

AUSTIN, JAMES C., *B-flat clarinet*
1st 1927 tour; 1928 tour; one or more of 1930 tours. Other positions: Pryor's Band; Ringling Bros. and Barnum & Bailey Circus Band; Bachman's Million Dollar Band; Royal Scotch Highlanders Band. Member, SBFS.

Sources: SB payrolls, rosters, programs, & photos; Eugene Slick's 1928 autograph book; references in SBFS News; author's correspondence with Austin & interviews with Kenneth B. Slater, bandmaster.

BABCOCK, HAROLD J., *B-flat clarinet*
1925-26 tour (partial).
Sources: 11 Jul 1925 SB payroll; roster in Jacobs' Band Monthly, *Aug, 1925.*

BAEHR, JEROME, *saxophone*
1923-24 tour (partial).
Source: 1923-24 saxophone section photo.

BAGLEY, HENRY LUTHER, *B-flat clarinet
Sat in with SB on two occasions in Denver, CO, dates unknown. Other position: Denver Symphony Orchestra.
Source: Author's correspondence with James C. Dutton, researcher.

BAKER, ELDON, *tuba*
Possibly 1st & 2nd 1892 tours; 1st 1893 tour (**soloist** at Columbian Exposition); 2nd 1893 tour. Other position: Gilmore's Band.
Sources: Partial roster in Metronome, *Apr, 1893, p. 10; J.W. Pepper Musical Times and Band Journal, Spring, 1895 & May, 1898; 1892 Gilmore's Band roster.*

BAKER, MARY, *soprano*
Soloist. 1919-20 tour; 1920 tour, starting with WG; 1921 tour; 1921-22 tour.
Sources: SB rosters & programs.

BAKLANOFF, GEORGE, *baritone (vocal)
Soloist, 26 Dec 1915, New York. Recorded for Columbia & HMV.
Source: Clarence J. Russell's Diary; author's correspondence with Frederick P. Williams, discographer.

BALDWIN, HARRY, *B-flat clarinet*
Majority of tours, 1907-15, including 1911 world tour. Charter member, SBFS.
Sources: SB photos; roster in New York Dramatic Mirror, *7 Sep 1907; roster in Albert A. Knecht's world tour diary; Edmund A. Wall's world tour poem; roster in* Musical Courier, *9 Jun 1915; 1915 Tuxedo tobacco advertisement with SB musicians' signatures; references in SBFS News.*

BAMBRICK, WINIFRED (Winnie), *harp*
1920-30, nearly all engagements; 1929 radio broadcasts; 12 Mar 1931 recording; occasional **soloist**; often accompanied vocal or violin soloists on encore numbers. Other positions: various symphony orchestras & bands in North America and Europe; recitalist; toured with revue company in Europe. Novelist. b. 1892, Ottawa, Canada; d. 1969, Montreal.
Sources: SB payrolls, rosters, photos, & programs; numerous photos & feature articles in PBks; The Feminist Companion to Literature in English; *references in SBFS News.*

BAND, JULIUS, *B-flat clarinet*
1925-26 tour (partial).
Sources: 1925-26 SB hotel assignment list; SBFS News, May, 1983, p. 31.

BARBERIS, ____ (male), *vocalist
Soloist, 3 Jun 1894, New York.
Source: Advertisement in New York World, *3 Jan 1894, p. 12.*

BARBOUR, GEORGE A., *tuba*
3rd 1894 tour; 4th 1895 tour; probably other engagements in 1896 and/or 1897.
Sources: Composite 1895-96 SB photo; advertisement in J.W. Pepper Musical Times and Band Journal, *May, 1898.*

BARCLAY, CHESTER A., *flute/piccolo*
1921-22 tour; 1922 tour; possibly early part of 1923-24 tour. Other positions: Radio City Music Hall Orchestra (New York); Goldman Band. Member, SBFS. b. 25 May 1902; d. Jul, 1975, Port Murray, NJ.
Sources: 1921-22 SB roster; 1921 SB photo; references in SBFS News; Social Security Death Index.

BARNARD (BARNA), MARIE, *soprano*
Stage name Marie Barna. Soloist. 3rd 1895 tour; possibly single engagements in 1896. Other positions: sang with opera companies and symphony orchestras in Italy, France, Germany, & U.S.A.; Haydn Oratorio Soc.
Sources: SB programs; composite 1895-96 SB photo; references in PBk 5; National Cyclopedia of American Biography.

BARNES, JAMES R., *management*
General manager, 1902-1910 & treasurer for undetermined period. Other positions: manager of Henrietta Crosman, Minnie Maddern Fisk, Richard

Walton Tully, Mr. & Mrs. Charles Coburn, & Henry W. Savage Attractions. b. ca. 1894; d. 15 May 1942, Staten Island, NY.
Sources: SB programs; references in PBks; Variety, *20 May 1942 [obituary].*

BARON, GEORGE A., *tenor (vocal)
Soloist. 1894 St. Louis Exposition (partial).
Source: SB program in St. Louis Post-Dispatch, *9 Sep 1894.*

BARONE, CLEMENT, *piccolo
Not SB member. Made two recordings as piccolo **soloist** with SB on Victor label.
Sources: Victor 78 rpm record # 4455 (in 1905) & #17134 (in 1912); The Sousa Band A Discography.

BARONNE, VINCENT, *cornet/trumpet*
1st 1892 tour; possibly 2nd 1892 tour.
Sources: 1892 C.G. Conn advertisement; author's correspondence with Barry Owen Furrer, band historian.

BAROSCHE, HERMAN, *tenor (vocal)
Soloist. 1893 & 1894 St. Louis Expositions.
Sources: St. Louis Post-Dispatch, 13 Sep 1893; also 14 & 15 Oct 1894.

BARRON, HENRI J., *B-flat clarinet*
Possibly part of 1920 tour; 1921 tour; 1921-22 tour; 1922 tour; 1923-24 tour (partial). Charter member, SBFS.
Sources: SB rosters; 1921 SB photo; Fillmore clarinet advertisement in Musical Messenger, *Dec, 1922, p. 22; references in SBFS News.*

BARTOW, WILLIAM N. (Billy), *cornet/trumpet*
Probably 1912 tour only. Other positions: New York Symphony Orchestra; Goldman Band; [Mayhew L. Lake's] Symphony of Gold; conductor of Standard Oil Band (Bayonne, NJ) & Westfield (NJ) Band & Liberty Band (Elizabeth, NJ) & Elks Band (Elizabeth, NJ). Recorded for Brunswick, Columbia, Edison, Emerson, Pathe, & Victor. Composer. Elected to American Bandmasters Assn., 1932. b. 9 May 1869, Clover Hill, NJ, Berkeley Heights, NJ; d. 14 Oct 1958.
Source: Supplement to The Heritage Encyclopedia of Band Music; *author's correspondence with Thomas Bardwell, band historian, with Charles Greaves, researcher; & with Frederick P. Williams, discographer.*

BASKIND, HARRY W., *B-flat clarinet*
Either 1928 or 1929 tour (partial). Other positions: Ballet Russe de Monte Carlo; theater orchestras. Member, SBFS.
Sources: References in SBFS News; Berger roster.

BASSETT, DON, *B-flat clarinet*
1919-20 tour; possibly parts of tour(s) in 1921 and/or 1922. Other positions: John C. Weber's Band (Cincinnati); National Military Home Band; Pryor's Band; Armco Band; conductor of Dayton (OH) Municipal Band & Antioch Temple Shrine Band (Dayton). Member, SBFS.
Sources: Various 1919-20 rosters; Dayton Daily News, 18 Aug 1973, p. 3; International Musician, Mar, 1975; references in SBFS News; author's interviews and correspondence with Bassett.

BAUER, ARTHUR WILLARD, *trombone*
1st 1902 tour; 2nd 1902 tour; probably 1905 WG (played on SB baseball team). Composer.
Sources: SB programs; references in PBks 16 & 19; The Heritage Encyclopedia of Band Music.

BAUER, LOUIS, *basso
Soloist. 1894 St. Louis Exposition (partial).
Sources: St. Louis Post-Dispatch, 16 & 18 Sep 1894.

BAUMGARTEL, BERNHARDT, *horn*
3rd 1895 tour; 1895 MB; 1st 1896 tour; 2nd 1896 tour; 1896 MB; 1896-97 tour; 1897 tour; possibly 2nd 1897 tour & other tours in 1898-1901; 4th 1901 tour (Britain). Native of Germany.
Sources: SB payrolls & programs; hotel registration, Adrian, MI, 1 Apr 1895; composite 1895/96 SB photo; SB/Grenadier Guards banquet seating chart of 17 Oct 1901; references in SBFS News; advertisements in J.W. Pepper Musical Times and Band Journal, *Spring, 1895 & May, 1898.*

BAXTER, HARRY, *B-flat clarinet*
Either 2nd 1927 tour or 1928 tour (partial). Other positions: Pryor's Band; Goldman Band; St. Petersburg (FL) Municipal Band; Ballet Russe de Monte Carlo. Member, SBFS.
Sources: Author's correspondence with Baxter; references in SBFS News.

BAYERS, FREDERICK W., *saxophone*
1923-24 tour (**soloist** at WG). Other positions: conductor of several bands. Member, SBFS. d. 8 Jan 1975.

Sources: SB programs; A Study of the Saxophone Soloists Performing with the John Philip Sousa Band: 1893-1930; *references in* SBFS News; *Berger roster; author's interview with Bayers.*

BEARMAN, EDWIN R., *tuba*
1928 tour.
Sources: 1928 SB payrolls.

*BEAUDET, LOUISE, *vocalist*
Soloist. 1894 MB (partial). Other positions: actress and singer in theater, operetta, and vaudeville productions; headed own troupe, the Louise Beaudet Opera Co.; McCaull Opera Co.; Maurice Grau Opera Productions (London). b. ca. 1861; d. 31 Dec 1947, New York.
Sources: References in PBk 3, p. 57; Variety, 7 Jan 1948 [obituary].

BECKER, FREDERICK EDWARD RUDOLPH (Rudy, Rudybaker), *saxophone*
1st 1892 tour; 2nd 1904 tour; 1st 1905 tour (Britain); 2nd 1908 tour; 1914 tour; 1915 tour; 1916-17 tour. Other positions: 7th Infantry Regt. Band (Germany); Giannini's Royal Marine Band (Italy); Victor Herbert's Orchestra; Philadelphia Orchestra; Meyer Davis Band (Philadelphia); Mackey's Municipal Band (Philadelphia); American Saxophone Quartet; Wannamaker Band (Philadelphia). Author of music instruction books and compiler of ensemble books. b. Oldisleben, Thuringia, Germany, 15 Sep 1865; d. 25 Sep 1981, Philadelphia, PA. Member, SBFS.
Sources: S.S. Baltic *ship's list, 19 May 1905; roster in* New York Dramatic Mirror, *1 Sep 1908; references in PBk 21; signature on 6 Nov 1914 birthday card from band members to Sousa (refers to 1st year with band as 1892); roster in* Musical Courier, *9 Jun 1915; 1915 Tuxedo tobacco advertisement with SB musicians' signatures; roster in Dec, 1916* New York Musician and Knocker; *author's correspondence with Walter Kaville, band historian; references in* SBFS News; *Berger roster.*

BECKER, JOHN U., *B-flat clarinet*
1914 tour; 1915 tour; possibly 1916 tour; 1916-17 tour. Other positions: Pryor's Band; Kryl's Band; National Theatre Orchestra. Member, SBFS.
Sources: Signature on 6 Nov 1914 birthday card from band to Sousa (refers to 1st year with band as 1914); roster in Musical Courier, *9 Jun 1915; 1915 Tuxedo tobacco advertisement with SB members' signatures; roster in Dec, 1916* New York Musician and Knocker; *references in* SBFS News; *Berger roster.*

BEHNEE, HARRIET MINNE (Minnie), *contralto*
Soloist. 1st 1893 tour. Other positions: Opera companies in Germany & U.S.A. b. 1873; d. 1963, New York, NY.
Sources: SB programs; Metronome, *Apr, 1893, p. 10; references in PBk 21.*

BEHRENS, CONRAD, *basso*
Soloist. 1st 1893 tour; 1893 MB; 1894 MB; 2nd 1894 Madison Square Garden engagement (partial). Other position: Metropolitan Opera Co.
Sources: SB programs; references in PBks 2, 3; Metronome, *Sep, 1894, p. 7.*

*BELL, DOROTHY, *harp*
Soloist, 9 Apr 1931 radio broadcast.
Source: Newspaper radio schedule.

BELL, JOHN WESTON (Jack), *flute/piccolo, saxophone*
1923-24 tour; 1924 tour; 1926 tour; 1st & 2nd 1927 tours; 12 Mar 1930 radio broadcast; 12 Mar 1931 recording; 9 Apr 1931 radio broadcast; late 1931 radio broadcasts. Soloist, 1924 tour & several engagements in 1926 & 1927. Other positions: U.S. Navy Band; Bachman's Million Dollar Band; NBC Symphony Orchestra; New York theater, radio, & television orchestras; Paul Whiteman's Orchestra; Phil Spitalny's Orchestra; Goldman Band; 7th Regt. Band (New York). Charter member, SBFS (President, 1964-76). b. 21 Jun 1901; d. Feb, 1976, Elmhurst, NY.
Sources: SB payrolls, rosters, programs, & photos; references in PBks; references in SBFS News; *author's interviews with Bell; Social Security Death Index.*

BELL, WILLIAM JOHN (Bill), *tuba*
1921 tour; 1921-22 tour; 1922 tour; 1923-24 tour. Also other brief engagements. Soloist, 1921 WG, 1922 WG, & 1923 WG. Other positions: New York Philharmonic; NBC Symphony Orchestra; Cincinnati Symphony Orchestra; Bachman's Million Dollar Band; Goldman Band; Cities Service Band of America; Armco Band; Henry Fillmore's Band; Ringling Bros. and Barnum & Bailey Circus Band; Asbury Park Municipal Band; W.W. Norton Band; music faculty, Cincinnati Conservatory of Music, Juilliard School of Music, New York University, Columbia Teachers College, Manhattan School of Music, & Indiana University.

Composer. Author of tuba instruction books. Recorded for Columbia, Golden Crest, Sonora, & Victor. Co-founder, SBFS. b. 25 Dec 1902, Creston, IA; d. 7 Aug 1971, Perry, IA.
Sources: SB programs; rosters and photos; research by Harvey J. Phillips; interviews with the author (Bell's tuba student); references in SBFS News; *Berger roster;* International Musician, *Oct, 1971;* Getzen Gazette, *Oct, 1971, p. 6; author's interviews and correspondence with Bell; author's correspondence with Frederick P. Williams, discographer.*

*BELLINI, LAURA, *soprano*
Soloist. 1894 MB (partial).
Sources: Metronome, *Sep, 1894, p. 7; references in PBk 3.*

BELLSTEDT, HERMAN, *cornet/trumpet; arranger*
1st 1904 tour; 2nd 1904 tour; 1st 1905 tour (Britain); 2nd 1905 tour; possibly 3rd & 4th 1905 tours. Soloist at 1904 St. Louis Exposition, 1904 WG, 1904 Pittsburgh Exposition, 1904 & 1905 off-tour concerts, & 1905 WG. Other positions: Gilmore's Band; Red Hussar Band; Innes' Band; Cincinnati Orchestra Reed Band; conductor of Denver Municipal Band & Herman Bellstedt's Concert Band (Cincinnati) & Bellstedt-Ballenburg Military Band; music faculty, Cincinnati Conservatory of Music. Composer and arranger (numerous humoresques, novelties, and arrangements for SB, many after leaving band). Recorded for Victor. b. 21 Feb 1858, Bremen, Germany; d. 8 Jun 1926, San Francisco.
Sources: SB payrolls; S.S. Baltic *ship's list, 19 May 1905; references in PBks 18-21;* The Heritage Encyclopedia of Band Music; *Supplement to the Heritage Encyclopedia of Band Music;* Pioneers in Brass; *Bands of America;* The New Grove Dictionary of American Music; *The Sousa Band A Discography;* Musical Messenger, *May, 1922, pp. 1-4;* American Musician, *28 Feb 1907.*

BENDER, WALTER H., *B-flat clarinet*
2nd 1927 tour; 1928 tour; 1929 tour; one or more of 1930 tours. Other position: Allentown (PA) Band. Member, SBFS. d. ca. 1970.
Sources: SB payrolls; 1927 SB hotel assignment list;1928 SB roster; 1930 SB photo; Morning Call *(Allentown), 25 Feb 1975, p. 6; references in* SBFS News; *Berger roster; author's interview with Bender.*

BENZING, ADA MAY, *contralto*
Soloist. 2nd 1898 tour.
Sources: Programs in Pittsburgh Times, *13 Apr 1898; references in PBk 5.*

BERGEN, NELLA, *vocalist*
Soloist. 1896 MB (partial); 1897 MB (partial); last week of 2nd 1898 tour in New York. Other positions: sang in several Sousa operettas; other musical theater productions, mostly in New York. 4th wife of DeWolf Hopper. d. 25 Apr 1919, Freeport, NY.
Sources: SB programs; references in PBks; Variety, *2 May 1919 [obituary].*

BERNALFO, GIUSEPPE, *horn*
One or both 1892 tours.
Source: 1892 C.G. Conn advertisement.

BERRY, ARTHUR L., *B-flat clarinet*
1911 world tour (left band on final segment of tour in California).
Sources: Roster in Albert A. Knecht's world tour diary; Edmund A. Wall's world tour poem.

*BERTINI-HUMPHRIES, NINA, *soprano*
Soloist, 14, 18, & 21 Jan 1894, Brooklyn, NY.
Source: SB program.

BERTRAM, ADOLPH A., *oboe*
Probably some engagements in 1900; 2nd 1902 tour; probably 3rd 1902 tour; 1st 1903 tour (Europe); 2nd 1903 tour; 1914 tour; 1916-17 tour. Possibly other tours. Soloist at 1902 WG & 1903 WG. Other position: Metropolitan Opera Orchestra.
Sources: SB programs; 6 Nov 1914 birthday card from band to Sousa (refers to 1st year with band as 1900); Musical America, *22 Aug 1914; roster Dec, 1916* New York Musician and Knocker; *references in PBk 40.*

BETTONEY, F., *bassoon*
1916-17 tour.
Source: Roster in Dec, 1916 New York Musician and Knocker.

BIANCO, EMELIO, *tuba*
1919-20 tour. Other positions: Russian Symphony Orchestra; Pryor's Band; Conway's Band. Recorded for Victor.
Sources: Various 1919-20 tour rosters; photo in Musical Truth, *Oct, 1923.*

BIROSCHAK, PETER J. (Pete), *horn*
1923-24 tour; 1924 tour (**soloist** at WG) 1925-26 tour; 1926 tour; 1st & 2nd 1927 tours; 1928 tour. Other position: New York Symphony Orchestra.
Sources: SB payrolls, programs, & photos; roster in Jacobs' Band Monthly, *Aug, 1925; 1925-26 & 1927 SB hotel assignment lists; references in PBks; references in SBFS News.*

BISHOF, GEORGE, *B-flat clarinet*
1919-20 tour.
Sources: Various 1919-20 tour rosters.

BISHOP, EUGENE J., *cornet/trumpet*
1919-20 tour. Member, SBFS.
Sources: Various 1919-20 tour rosters; Holton advertisement in Musical Messenger, *Oct, 1919, p. 2; references in SBFS News; Berger roster.*

*BISPHAM, DAVID, *baritone (vocal)*
Soloist, 6 Feb 1916, New York. Other positions: Metropolitan Opera Co.; Royal Opera House (London); concert artist. Author. Recorded for Columbia & Victor. b. 5 Jan 1857, Philadelphia; d. 2 Oct 1921, New York.
Sources: Clarence J. Russell's diary. Baker's Biographical Dictionary of Musicians; Portraits of the World's Best-Known Musicians; *author's correspondence with Frederick P. Williams, discographer.*

BLADET, ROBERT, *flute/piccolo*
1931 tour.
Source: 1931 SB payrolls.

BLAGG, PAUL G., *cornet/trumpet*
1922 tour (**soloist** at WG). Other positions: Pryor's Band; Dayton (OH) Philharmonic; conductor of Antioch Shrine Band (Dayton); private music teacher. Recorded for Victor. Charter member, SBFS. b. 29 Jun 1902, Muncie, IN; d. 3 Dec 1992, Dayton.
Sources: SB programs; references in PBk 56; references in SBFS News; author's correspondence Blagg, with family & with Frederick P. Williams, discographer.

BLAKELY, DAVID, *management*
General manager, 1892-1896. Other positions: managed 1891 & 1892 tours of U.S. Marine Band when Sousa was leader; managed Gilmore's Band and American tour of the [Eduard] Strauss Vienna Orchestra; choral conductor; owned and/or edited newspapers in Minneapolis, St. Paul, & Chicago; co-owner of Blakely Printing Co. (Chicago). b. 1833, Binghamton, NY; d. 7 Nov 1896, New York.
Sources: SB programs; SB promotional material; Blakely Papers at the New York Public Library; Barry Owen Furrer Collection; Perspectives on John Philip Sousa, *pp. 120-133;* John Philip Sousa, American Phenomenon, *pp. 54-64;* Musical Courier, *1 Feb 1893;* New York Times, *8 Nov 1896, p. 5; references in SBFS News; Berger roster. See also Chapters 1 & 2.*

BLAUERT, _____, *instrument?*
1st 1892 tour.
Source: Blakely papers.

*BLAUVET, LILLIAN EVANS, *soprano*
Soloist. 1893 St. Louis Exposition (partial). Sang opera in America and Europe (received Coronation Medal from King Edward VII of England). Recorded for Columbia & Victor. b. 16 Mar 1874, Brooklyn, NY; d. 29 Aug 1947, Chicago.
Sources: St. Louis Post-Dispatch, *3-7 Oct 1893; author's correspondence with Frederick P. Williams, discographer.*

*BLOCK, FREDRICK, *piano*
Soloist, 8 Nov 1927, Peoria, IL. This boy pianist, a student of former SB violinist Jeanette Powers, was inserted as a feature into Sousa's *Showing Off Before Company* fantasie.
Source: Peoria (IL) Star, *9 Nov 1927.*

BLODGETT, FRED, *trombone*
Probably part of 1918 tour. Recorded for Zonophone.
Sources: Berger roster; author's interviews with Kenneth B. Slater, bandmaster; author's correspondence with Frederick P. Williams, discographer.

BOCCAVECCHIA (BOCCA), GIUSEPPE (JOSEPH), *alto clarinet, arranger, copyist*
Possibly 1st 1893 tour; 2nd 1893 tour; probably other tours in 1894 & 1895; 1st 1896 tour; 1896-97 tour; possibly 1897 tour; possibly 1st & 2nd 1898 tours; 3rd 1898 tour; 2nd 1900 tour (Europe).

Sources: SB payrolls & photos; seating chart in Philadelphia Press, *7 May 1897; signatures & dates (as late as 1913) on manuscripts in SB library at University of Illinois.*

BODE, ALBERT, *cornet/trumpet*
Apparently all engagements from May, 1893 to Sep, 1897. Cornet **soloist**, often sharing duties with Herbert L. Clarke, Frank Seltzer, Walter F. Smith, William Griffin, or Henry Higgins. Other position: Gilmore's Band. Recorded for Columbia & Victor.
Sources: SB payrolls, programs, & photographs; references in PBks; references in various music journals; author's correspondence with Frederick P. Williams, discographer

BOLLE, JULES, *cornet/trumpet*
1928 tour; off-tour concert, 15 Jun 1929, Princeton, NJ; 1929 tour; 1929 radio broadcasts; 12 Mar 1931 recording; 9 Apr 1931 radio broadcast; late 1931 radio broadcasts. Member, SBFS. d. ca. 1961.
Sources: SB payrolls; references in SBFS News.

*BOLOGUA, _____, *baritone (vocal)*
Soloist, 26 Sep 1892, Plainfield, NJ (substituted for Antonio Galassi at first Sousa Band concert).
Source: PBk 1, p. 1.

BONSALL, BESSIE, *contralto*
Sang in quartet, 1st 1899 tour (partial). Other position: D'Oyly Carte Co. (London). Married name Mrs. George Barron. b. 1871, Canada; d. 15 Dec 1963, Paris, ONT.
Sources: References in PBks 8 & 12; Variety, *25 Dec 1963 [obituary].*

BOOTH, CLARENCE, *bassoon*
2nd 1927 tour; 1928 tour; 1929 tour; one or more of 1930 tours. Other positions: Minneapolis Symphony Orchestra; St. Petersburg (FL) Municipal Band; Anglo-Canadian Leather Company Band. Member, SBFS.
Sources: SB payrolls & rosters; references in SBFS News; author's correspondence with Booth.

BORRELLI, JAMES G. (Jimmy), *B-flat clarinet*
Apparently all engagements 1919-22. Other positions: U.S. Army bandmaster in Europe during World War I; Conway's Band; conductor of Duquesne University bands & high school and junior high bands in Lebanon, PA & several theater orchestras. Member, SBFS; b. ca. 1898; d. 8 Apr 1973.
Sources: SB rosters and photos; author's correspondence with Borrelli; references in SBFS News; International Musician, Jun, 1973.

BORST, ROBERT, *cornet/trumpet*
1929 radio broadcasts.
Source: 1 Jul 1929 payroll.

BORTMAN, WILLIAM T. (Bill), *B-flat clarinet*
1916-1917 tour; 1929 & 1930 radio broadcasts; 12 Mar 1931 recording; 9 Apr 1931 radio broadcast; late 1931 radio broadcasts. Other positions: Ballet Russe de Monte Carlo; New York theater orchestras. Charter member, SBFS. d. ca. 1975.
Sources: SB payrolls; roster in Dec, 1916 New York Musician and Knocker; *references in SBFS News.*

BOSCHECK, CHARLES, *B-flat clarinet*
1925-26 tour (partial). Member, SBFS.
Sources: 1925-26 SB hotel assignment list; references in SBFS News.

BOURDON, ROSARIO, *studio conductor*
Conducted SB in Victor studio for at least 10 recordings in 1919, 1929, & 1930. Composer.
Sources: ASCAP Biographical Dictionary; Discographic data from Frederick P. Williams.

*BOWMAN, BEATRICE, *soprano*
Soloist. 1910 WG (partial). Other positions: concert and opera singer; private music teacher. b. ca. 1878; d. 3 Jan 1943, Berkeley, CA.
Sources: SB programs; Variety, *13 Jan 1943 [obituary].*

BRABROOK, ARTHUR NELSON (Nick), *cornet/trumpet*
1921 tour; 1921-22 tour; one or more of 1930 tours. Member, SBFS.
Sources: SB rosters & photos; references in SBFS News. d. 30 May 1953.

BRANDENBURG, WILLIAM G., *B-flat clarinet*
1921 tour (partial); 1921-22 tour; 1923-24 tour. Charter member, SBFS.
Sources: 1921-22 SB roster; 1923 SB payrolls; SB photos; "In Memoriam" list, SBFS organizational booklet (1945).

*BRANDIS, MARIE, *contralto*
Soloist at concerts 7-10 Sep, 1897 (New York).
Source: PBk 4, pp. 96-98.

BRANT, FRED G., *B-flat clarinet, saxophone*
1919-20 tour; 1920 WG; 1921 tour; 12 Mar 1930 radio broadcast. Member, SBFS. d. 1980.
Sources: SB rosters; SB payroll 12 Mar 1930; references in SBFS News.

BRANTHAM, J. HOWARD, *saxophone*
1921-22 tour (partial).
Sources: 1921 SB photo.

BRAUN, CLIFFORD B. (Cliff), *trombone*
1926 tour; 2nd 1927 tour; 1928 tour; 1929 tour; one or more of 1930 tours; 1931 tour. Member, SBFS.
Sources: SB payrolls, rosters, & photos; SB expense sheet, Nov, 1926; 1925-26 & 1927 SB hotel assignment lists; references in SBFS News.

BREHANY, LOUISE M., *soprano*
Soloist. 2nd 1898 tour; one or more concerts in Oct, 1900 (New York); 1915 Panama-Pacific Exposition.
Sources: SB program, 5 Jul 1915; PBk 5, p. 228; PBk 10, p. 226.

*BRENNAN, DR. JOHN PAUL, *physician*
Sousa's personal physician on 1921-22 tour.
Sources: 1921-22 SB roster; 1921 SB photo; SBFS News, Vol. 1, No. 1 (1945), p. 1; author's correspondence with family.

BRISBIN (BRISBANE), CLAUDE D. (Doc), *trombone*
1921 tour; 1924 WG. Other positions: St. Petersburg (FL) Municipal Band. Member, SBFS.
Sources: 1921 SB roster; advertisement in Conn Musical Truth, Oct, 1921 (Sousa Edition); references in SBFS News.

BRISSETTE, FRED J., *B-flat clarinet*
1st 1903 tour (Europe); 1st 1905 tour (Britain); off-tour concert 15 Jun 1929, Princeton, NJ; 1929 radio broadcasts; 1st 1930 tour; 12 Mar 1931 recording; 9 Apr 1931 radio broadcast; late 1931 radio broadcasts.
Sources: SB payrolls; SB publicity for 1st 1893 tour; S.S. Baltic ship's list, 19 May 1905; 1930 SB photo; "In Memoriam" list, SBFS organizational booklet (1945).

BRONSON, CHET, *E-flat clarinet*
2nd 1893 tour; possibly other tours. Other positions: clarinetist and bandmaster with Barnum and Bailey Circus; founder and conductor of Kalamazoo (MI) Symphony Orchestra. b. ca. 1857; d. 29 Sep 1857.
Sources: 1893 SB photo; Varela photo; research by Charles Conrad, band historian.

BRONSON, HOWARD C., *B-flat clarinet*
Most engagements 1923-28. Other positions: North Dakota National Guard Band; U.S. Navy Yard Band (Bremerton, WA); U.S. Army bandmaster during World War I; conductor of 129th Infantry National Guard Band & 137th Cavalry Band & 51st Artillery Band & Tebala Shrine Band (Mount Morris, IL) & Kable Bros. Band & Aberdeen (SC) Municipal Band; supervisor, U.S. Army band program & music advisor, War Dept. during World War II. Elected to American Bandmasters Assn., 1932. Co-founder, SBFS (Vice President, 1944-47; Honorary Life Member, 1951; President 1947-52). b. 7 Nov 1889, Algona, IA; d. 23 Jan 1960, Richmond, VA.
Sources: SB payrolls, rosters, & photos; Band Encyclopedia; The Heritage Encyclopedia of Band Music; Bandmen; American Bandmasters Association Newsletter, 8 Feb 1960; references and photos in SBFS News.

BROWN, HERBERT FULLER (Bert), *cornet/trumpet*
1915-16 New York Hippodrome; **soloist,** 1918 tour. Other positions: Chicago Symphony Orchestra; Pryor's Band; Boos' Band; 1893 World's Fair Band [Chicago]; Weldon's Chicago Band; Brooke's Chicago Marine Band; 2nd Regt. Band (Chicago); Innes' Band; theater orchestras in Chicago, Pittsburgh, & Cleveland; John Duss Band (Pittsburgh); Bellstedt's Band (Cincinnati); Fanciulli's Band (New York); Bachman's Million Dollar Band; conductor of Dockstader & Thomas Minstrels. Recorded for Victor. Member, SBFS. b. 28 Jan 1869, Orland, IN; d. 21 Feb 1959, Miami, FL.
Sources: SB programs; Pioneers in Brass; Musical Messenger, Jan, 1919, pp. 1-4; Berger roster; author's correspondence with Frederick P. Williams, discographer.

BROWN, RALPH W., *horn*
1923-24 tour (partial); 1929 radio broadcasts; 12 Mar 1931 recording; 9 Apr 1931 radio broadcast; late 1931 radio broadcasts. Charter member, SBFS.
Sources: SB payrolls; references in SBFS News.

BROWNING, JOSEPH R., *cornet/trumpet*
1st 1927 tour. Other position: Ringling Bros. and Barnum & Bailey Circus Band; Royal Scotch Highlanders Band. Member, SBFS.
Sources: References in SBFS News; Berger roster; author's interview with Browning.

*BRUCE, WALTER, *baritone (vocal)*
Soloist. 1896 MB.
Source: SB program in PBk 4, p. 44.

BRYER, PEARL EVELYN, *cello*
Soloist. 1st 1905 tour (partial, in Britain).
Source: References in PBk 23.

BUCKLIN, BERTHA, *violin*
Soloist. 1st, 3rd, & 4th (Britain) 1900 tours. 1st 1901 tour; off-tour concert 22 Apr 1900. Other positions: Metropolitan Opera Co.; toured in Europe as concert artist.
Sources: SB programs; references in PBks 9, 14, & 18.

BUONOCORE, E., *B-flat clarinet*
1907 tour; 2nd 1908 tour.
Sources: Roster in New York Dramatic Mirror, 7 Sep 1907 & 1 Sep 1908.

BURANT, EDWARD, *tuba*
1921 tour.
Source: 1921 SB roster.

BURKE, THOMAS M., *B-flat clarinet*
Probably 4th 1895 tour; 1st 1896 tour; 1896-97 tour; probably other tours in 1897.
Sources: SB payrolls & photos; seating chart in Philadelphia Press, 7 May 1897.

BURNELL, FRANK, *cornet/trumpet*
2nd 1927 tour; off-tour concert 15 Jun 1929, Princeton, NJ. Composer.
Sources: SB payrolls; 1925-26 hotel assignment list; references in SBFS News; Berger roster.

BURNHAM, WILLIAM R., *horn*
1924 tour; 1925-26 tour.
Sources: SB payroll 11 Dec 1925; roster in Jacobs' Band Monthly, Aug, 1925; 1925-26 SB hotel assignment list

BUSCHER, PHILIP, *saxophone*
1st 1903 tour (Europe).
Source: SB publicity for 1st 1903 tour.

BUXLEY, THOMAS, *oboe*
1919-20 tour.
Source: Various 1919-20 tour rosters.

BUYS, PETER, *E-flat clarinet; arranger; copyist*
1st 1917 tour; 1917 WG. Other positions: U.S. Military Academy Band (West Point); music faculty, Juniata College; conductor of Hagerstown (MD) Municipal Band. Honorary doctorate, Dana Musical Institute. Composer & arranger (numerous arrangements for Sousa after leaving band); author. Elected to American Bandmasters Assn., 1929 (president, 1939-40). Member, SBFS. b. 11 Aug 1881, Amsterdam, Holland; d. 5 Mar 1964.
Sources: Program Notes for Band, pp. 101-102; Who Is Who in Music, 5th Edition; Bandmen; references in SBFS News; signatures & dates on manuscripts in SB library at University of Illinois.

BYRA, STANLEY, *B-flat clarinet*
1923-24 tour; 1924 tour; 1925-26 tour (partial); 2nd 1927 tour; off-tour concert 15 Jun 1929, Princeton, NJ; one or more of 1930 tours. Member, SBFS.
Sources: SB payrolls; roster in Jacobs' Band Monthly, Aug, 1925; references in SBFS News.

BYRNE, GERALD R., *horn*
1920 WG; 1921 tour; 1921-22 tour; 1922 tour; 1923-24 tour. Charter member, SBFS.
Sources: SB payrolls, programs, & photos; references in PBk 58; references in SBFS News.

CAMERON, WALTER H., *cornet/trumpet*
1925-26 tour (partial); 1926 tour; 1929 tour; one or more of 1930 tours; 1931 tour (partial). Other positions: 111th U.S. Army E.F. Band during World War I; conductor of Carnegie, PA, school bands. Member, SBFS. d. Nov, 1972.
Sources: SB payrolls & photos; references in SBFS News.

*CAMPANARI, GIUSEPPE, *baritone (vocal)*
Soloist. 2nd 1893 tour (St. Louis Exposition only). Other positions: Metropolitan Opera Co.; earlier, cellist with Boston Symphony Orchestra and Hinrich's Opera Co. (New York). Recorded for Columbia & Victor. b. 17 Nov 1855, Venice, Italy; d. 31 May 1927, Milan, Italy.
Sources: Programs of Sep & Oct, 1893 in issues of St. Louis Post-Dispatch; Baker's Biographical Dictionary of Musicians; *author's correspondence with Frederick P. Williams, discographer.*

CAMPANINI, ITALO, *tenor (vocal)*
Soloist. 1st part of 1st 1893 tour; 18 Jan 1894 (New York). Other positions: Metropolitan Opera Co.; sang opera in America, Italy, & England. Served in Italian Army. b. 30 Jun 1845, Parma, Italy; d. 14 Nov 1896, Parma.
Sources: SB programs; SB publicity for 1st 1893 tour; Baker's Biographical Dictionary of Musicians.

CAMPBELL, W. FRED (Freddie), *flute/piccolo*
1924 tour. Sousa's secretary during WG engagement (took dictation for articles in 1925 *Saturday Evening Post* that served as basis for later book, *Marching Along*). Other positions: Fred Waring's Pennsylvanians; St. Petersburg (FL) Symphony Orchestra; Tampa Symphony Orchestra. Charter member, SBFS. b. 4 Mar 1901; d. 13 Apr 1993, Ft. Lauderdale, FL.
Sources: SB payrolls & photos; Ft. Lauderdale Sun Sentinel, *16 Apr 1993; references in* SBFS News; *author's interview & correspondence with Campbell & with family.*

*CAMPOBELLO, ____, *baritone (vocal)*
Soloist, 24 Nov 1895, Atlanta.
Source: Atlanta Constitution, *24 Nov 1895.*

CAREY, GEORGE J., *percussion*
1920 tour; 1921 tour; 1921-22 tour; 1923-24 tour; 1924 tour; 1925-26 tour; xylophone **soloist** on most tours. Other positions: Cincinnati Symphony Orchestra, Metropolitan Opera Orchestra; Victor Herbert's Orchestra; Black Hussar Band (Chicago); Frank Ellis Band (Chicago); asst. conductor of 11th Regt. Marine Band in Europe during World War I. Composer & arranger. Member, SBFS. b. ca. 1894; d. 28 Jan 1958, Cincinnati, OH.
Sources: SB payrolls, rosters, & photos; Leedy Drum Topics, *15 Jun 1924, 15 Oct 1923, Feb, 1926, Dec, 1928, & Oct, 1939; references in PBks; references in* SBFS News; *author's correspondence with Russ Girsberger, music librarian.*

CARNEY, JOHN, *B-flat clarinet*
1920 WG.
Source: Roster in 1920 WG programs.

CARNS, EARL J., *trombone*
1922 WG. Member, SBFS. d. ca. 1960.
Sources: 1922 WG programs (listing Carns in brass sextet); references in SBFS News.

CARR, JOHN CAROLL (Johnny, Hank), *B-flat clarinet*
1923-24 tour; 1924 tour; 1925-26 tour; 1929 & 1930 radio broadcasts. Other positions: Pryor's Band; Conway's Band; New York theater orchestras; Fairmont (WV) Symphony Orchestra; music faculty, University of West Virginia; conductor of bands and orchestras in Morgantown & Fairmont, WV public schools. Charter member, SBFS.
Sources: SB payrolls, rosters, & photos; roster in Jacob's Band Monthly, *Aug, 1925; references in PBks 61 & 63; references in* SBFS News.

*CARROLL, CLARA DOUGLAS, *soprano*
Soloist. 1899 MB (partial).
Source: PBk 9, pp. 27 & 28.

*CARROLL, GRACE LEE, *vocalist*
Soloist. 1899 MB.
Sources: PBk 9, pp. 27 & 28.

CARROLL, STEPHEN L., *B-flat clarinet*
1920 WG; 1921 tour. Member, SBFS.
Sources: SB rosters & photos; advertisement in Conn Musical Truth, *Oct, 1921 (Sousa Edition); references in* SBFS News.

CARUSI, INEZ, *harp*
Soloist. 2nd 1893 tour (St. Louis Exposition only).
Sources: References in St. Louis Post-Dispatch, 19-23 Sep 1893.

*CASE, ANNA, *soprano*
Soloist, 30 Jun 1917, Brooklyn, NY. Other positions: Metropolitan Opera Co.; recitalist & concert artist in America and Europe. Composer. Recorded for Columbia & Victor. Married name Mrs. Clarence MacKay. b. 1889, Clinton, NJ.
Sources: References in PBk 45; New Encyclopedia of Music and Musicians; Portraits of the World's Best-Known Musicians; Musical Courier, *5 Jul 1917; author's correspondence with Frederick P. Williams, discographer.*

CASTELLUCCI, LOUIS, *trombone*
Date(s) of SB service uncertain, but apparently part of one tour in mid-1920s. Composer. b. 26 Oct 1897, Naples, Italy.
Sources: Who Is Who in Music, *1951 Edition;* The Heritage Encyclopedia of Band Music.

CASTER, LESLIE D., *B-flat clarinet*
1921 tour; 1921-22 tour. Other position: Pryor's Band. d. 26 Sep 1926.
Sources: SB rosters; advertisement in Conn Musical Truth, *Oct, 1921 (Sousa Edition);* Musical Messenger, *Jul, 1922, p. 19; research by Charles Conrad, band historian.*

CESKY, MATTHIAS, *tuba*
1st 1892 tour; possibly 2nd 1892 tour. Other positions: Fahrbach's Band (Vienna).
Sources: SB publicity for 1st 1893 tour; 1892 C.G. Conn advertisement; Pruyn roster.

CHALIFF, LOUIS, *B-flat clarinet*
1921 tour (partial).
Source: 1921 SB roster.

*CHALMERS, THOMAS, *baritone (vocal)*
Soloist, 16 Jan 1916 New York. Other positions: Metropolitan Opera Co.; Boston Opera Co.; Century Opera Co. (New York). Also writer, conductor, producer, & music critic. Recorded for Edison. b. 20 Oct 1884, New York; d. 1966.
Source: Clarence J. Russell's Diary. The Biographical Encyclopedia and Who's Who of the American Theatre; *references in PBk 42; author's correspondence with Frederick P. Williams, discographer.*

CHAMBERS, ADA, *soprano*
Soloist. Stage name Ada Androva (adopted in 1912). 3rd & 4th 1905 tours; 3rd & 4th 1906 tours; 1st part of 1907 tour; 16 Apr 1916 (New York); 1916 WG (partial).
Sources: SB programs; references in PBks.

CHAPMAN, CHRISTOPHER JOSEPH (Chris), *percussion*
2nd 1900 tour (Europe); 3rd 1901 tour; possibly 1st & 2nd 1902 tours; 3rd 1902 tour; 1st 1903 tour (Europe). Recorded for Perfect & Victor.
Sources: SB rosters & photos; PBk 14, p. 212; advertisement in Leedy Drum Topics, *Aug, 1934; references in* SBFS News; *SBFS organizational booklet (1945); author's correspondence with Frederick P. Williams, discographer & with Russ Girsberger, music librarian.*

CHAPMAN, ROSS, *trombone*
2nd 1900 tour (Europe).
Sources: 1900 SB programs listing Chapman in brass sextet; roster in SB program of 22 Apr 1900.

CHASE, WILLIAM A., *harp*
1st 1906 tour; 1907 tour; probably 1st 1908 tour; 2nd 1908 tour.
Sources: Daily Olympian (Olympia, WA), 16 Oct 1907; rosters in New York Dramatic Mirror, *7 Sep 1907 & 1 Sep 1917; references in PBk 25.*

CHENEY, JOSEPH J., *B-flat clarinet, bass clarinet*
1915 tour; 1916 tour; 1915-16 Hip! Hip! Hooray! engagement. 1916-17 tour; 1919-20 tour; 1925-26 tour (partial); 1926 tour; 1st 1927 tour; 1929 radio broadcasts; one or more of 1930 tours; 12 Mar 1931 recording; 9 Apr 1931 radio broadcast; 1931 tour (partial); late 1931 radio broadcasts. Other position: assistant conductor of U.S. Army Aviation Band (Fairfield, OH).
Sources: SB rosters, payrolls, & photos; roster in Musical Courier, *9 Jun 1915; 1915 Tuxedo tobacco advertisement with SB musicians' signatures; roster in Dec, 1916 New York Musician and Knocker;* Metronome, *Sep, 1936; SB payroll 11 Jul 1925; PBk 44, p. 66; references in* SBFS News.

CHIAFARELLI, ALBERT C., *B-flat clarinet*
Probably 1st or 2nd 1904 tour. Other positions: Metropolitan Opera Orchestra; theater & radio orchestras, New York; Goldman Band; New York World's Fair Band (1939). Composer. Recorded for Columbia. Charter member, SBFS. b. 5 Feb 1884, Prata, Italy; d. 31 Oct 1945, New York.
Sources: References in SBFS News; *author's correspondence with Frederick P. Williams, discographer.*

CHICK, ARNOLD (ANTON) LAMONT, *cornet/trumpet*
1919-20 tour; 1925-26 tour (partial). Other positions: U.S. Army (European) band during World War I; director of music at Watertown (MA) High School; conductor of own band in York Beach, ME & Watertown American Legion Band. Member, SBFS. b. ca. 1890, Haverhill, MA; d. 20 Feb 1956, Watertown.
Sources: SB rosters & payrolls; advertisement in Musical Enterprise, *Feb, 1920; 1925-26 SB hotel assignment list; C.G. Conn advertisement, Feb, 1926;*

CHRISTENSEN, PAUL OTTO, *saxophone*
1922 tour. Other positions: Helen Hughes and Her Orchestra (Davenport, IA); conductor of Huron (SD) Municipal Band & Huron Jr./Sr. High School Bands & high school bands in Alpena, Tulare, & Wessington Springs, SD. Composer. Honorary doctorate (posthumous), Huron College, 1962. Elected to American School Band Directors Assn., 1955, & American Bandmasters Assn., 1962. Member, SBFS. b. 1899, Copenhagen, Denmark; d. 8 Mar 1962, Huron, SD.
Sources: Who's Who in South Dakota, *1951 Edition;* Band Encyclopedia; *references in SBFS News; author's correspondence with family.*

CHRISTIAN, A.J., *horn*
1921 tour. Member, SBFS.
Sources: 1921 SB roster; 1921 SB horn section photo; advertisement in Conn Musical Truth, *Oct, 1921 (Sousa Edition); references in SBFS News.*

CHRISTIANER, FRANK, *management*
On management staff as general manager (1897), assistant manager, business manager, or advance man, 1892-1906; laid out most tours while with band. Other position: management staff, Gilmore's Band.
Sources: SB publicity and office papers; references in New York Dramatic Mirror; *references in PBks; references in SBFS News.*

CHRISTIE, LOUIS H., *B-flat clarinet*
3rd 1898 tour; 2nd 1900 tour (Europe); 1st, 2nd, & 3rd 1901 tours; possibly 4th 1901 tour (Britain); possibly some tours in 1902; 1st 1903 tour (Europe); possibly other tours. Other positions: Pryor's Band; conductor of Morgan Park Boys' Band, Duluth, MN. Recorded for Victor. Charter member, SBFS.
Sources: SB rosters & photos; Pioneers in Brass; *references in SBFS News; author's correspondence with Frederick P. Williams, discographer.*

CHRISTMAN, C., *B-flat clarinet*
2nd 1908 tour.
Sources: Roster in New York Dramatic Mirror, *1 Sep 1908; PBk 21, p. 134.*

CHRISTMAN, HENRY, *B-flat clarinet*
1929 radio broadcasts.
Source: SB payroll 7 Oct 1929.

CHRISTOPHER, REI, *horn*
1920 WG. Other positions: Director of Music in Pueblo, CO, public schools; music faculty, Western State College. Member, SBFS. d. Jul, 1970.
Sources: Roster in 1920 WG programs; references in SBFS News.

CHRISTORI, ____, *basso*
1st part of 1st 1893 tour (in vocal sextet).
Sources: SB programs, May, 1893.

CICCONE, ____, *B-flat clarinet*
2nd 1893 tour; possibly other tours.
Source: Program in St. Louis Post-Dispatch, *17 Oct 1893.*

CILIBERTI, CARMELLO, *cornet/trumpet*
One WG engagement between 1915-1925.
Source: Author's correspondence with Alfred N. Ricciardi, researcher.

CIMERA, JAMES, *trombone*
1915 tour. Composer. Brother of Jaraslav Cimera. Member, SBFS. d. ca. 1967.

Sources: Roster in Musical Courier, *9 Jun 1915; 1915 Tuxedo tobacco advertisement with musicians' signatures;* Heritage Encyclopedia of Band Music; *references in SBFS News.*

CIMERA, JAROSLAV (Jerry), *trombone*
1913 tour. Other positions: Kryl's Band; Innes' Band; Weldon's 2nd Regiment Band; radio studio orchestras in Chicago; conductor of Czechoslovak Band (Chicago) & Cimera Concert Band (Chicago); music faculty, Northwestern University & Chicago Conservatory of Music. Recorded for Cimera Records, Okeh, Rainbow, Victor, & Zonophone. Honorary doctorate, Coe College. Composer. Author of trombone & tuba instruction books. Brother of James Cimera. Member, SBFS. b. 7 Jul 1885, Pilsen, Bohemia; d. Apr, 1972, Chicago.
Sources: SB programs; Who Is Who in Music; *The Heritage Encyclopedia of Band Music;* Bandmen; *references in SBFS News; Social Security Death Index; author's correspondence with Cimera & with Frederick P. Williams, discographer.*

*CLARK, HILDA, *soprano*
Soloist. 1897 MB (partial). Other positions: Singer/actor in light opera and musicals in America. b. 1881; d. 1955.
Sources: PBk 5, p. 73. Index to Women of the World from Ancient to Modern Times.

CLARK, WILLIAM COBURN, *cornet/trumpet*
One or more of 1930 tours; 1931 tour (partial). Other positions: Fred Waring's Pennsylvanians; New York theater orchestras; NBC Radio staff musician; Cities Service Band of America; Cesar La Monica's Band (Miami, FL); music faculty, Miami University. Also xylophone soloist but not with SB. Member, SBFS.
Sources: Jay Sims' 1930 tour roster; references in SBFS News; Berger roster.

CLARKE, EDWIN GAGE, *flugelhorn, cornet/trumpet, & management*
Instrumentalist on most tours, 1893-1910 except 1901-03; also some engagements in 1914 & 1915. General Manager, 1910-19; various other management capacities, 1906-1910. Conducted SB in Herbert L. Clarke's solos when Sousa was incapacitated in 1907. Other positions: Queen's Own Rifle Regt. Band (Toronto); Grand Opera House Orchestra (Toronto); New York theater orchestras. Conductor of 21st U.S. Army Infantry Band & Bijou Orchestra & Symphony Orchestra (Indianapolis). Composer. Brother of Ernest H. Clarke and Herbert L. Clarke. Member, SBFS. b. 23 Feb 1864.
Sources: SB payrolls, rosters, photos, & office papers; signature on 6 Nov 1914 birthday card from band to Sousa [refers to 1st year with band as 1893]; 1915 Tuxedo tobacco advertisement with SB musicians' signatures; The Sousa Band A Discography; references in PBks; references in SBFS News.

CLARKE, ERNEST HORATIO (Ern), *trombone*
1914 tour (partial); 1915-16 New York Hippodrome. Other positions: New York Symphony Orchestra; Victor Herbert's Orchestra; Cappa's Band; Gilmore's Band; Innes' Band; Ellis Brooke Band; Queen's Own Rifle Regt. Band (Toronto); Neyer's 7th Regt. Band (New York); Miles Standish Band (Boston); music faculty, Columbia University & Juilliard School of Music. Author of trombone instruction books. Recorded for Victor. b. 9 Oct 1865, Woburn, MA; d. 16 Sep 1947, New York. Brother of Edwin G. Clarke & Herbert L. Clarke. Member, SBFS.
Sources: Band Encyclopedia; Bandmen; Pioneers in Brass; *Conn Musical Truth, May, 1915, p. 3; references in SBFS News; author's correspondence with Frederick P. Williams, discographer.*

CLARKE, HERBERT LINCOLN (Herb, Bert), *cornet/trumpet*
1st, 2nd, & 3rd 1893 tours; 1893 MB; all other tours & engagements, 1900-1917. **Soloist** for most tours & engagements. Assistant conductor after 1903. Librarian in 1893, possibly later. Personnel manager at times. Other positions: Queens Own Rifle Regt. Band & other bands & orchestras in Canada; several orchestras (on viola or violin); Gilmore's Band; Victor Herbert's 22d Regiment Band; Miles Standish Band (Boston); When Band (Indianapolis); Brook's Orchestra (St. Augustine); New York Philharmonic; Metropolitan Opera Orchestra; Innes' Band; other bands and orchestras. Conductor American Band of Providence (RI) [later Clarke's Providence Band] & Anglo-Canadian Leather Co. Band & Heintzman Piano Co. Band & Taylor Safe Works Band & Long Beach (CA) Municipal Band; cornet tester C.G. Conn Co.; music faculty, Toronto College & Great Lakes Naval Training Station (World War I); private music teacher. Recorded for Berliner, Brunswick, Columbia, Edison, Odeon & Victor (conducted numerous recording sessions of SB for Victor, 1904-15).

Honorary doctorate, Phillips University; Composer. Author. Brother of Edwin G. Clarke & Ernest H. Clarke. Member, SBFS; b. 12 Sep 1867, Woburn, MA; d. 30 Jan 1945, Long Beach, CA.

Sources: SB rosters, programs, & photos; The Life and Works of Herbert H. Clarke (1867-1945); How I Became a Cornetist (autobiography); Pioneers in Brass; The Heritage Encyclopedia of Band Music; Supplement to the Heritage Encyclopedia of Band Music; Bands of America; Band Encyclopedia; Bandmen; The New Grove Dictionary of American Music, Vol. 1, p. 451; The Sousa Band A Discography; "Herbert L. Clarke, Cornet Soloist of the Sousa Band" (Crystal Records CD #450); numerous entries in reference books & music journals; references in PBks; references in SBFS News; Author's interviews with SB musicians; author's correspondence with Frederick P. Williams, discographer.

*CLARY, MARY LOUISE, *contralto*
Soloist. 1896 MB (partial).
Sources: PBk 4, pp. 48, 49.

CLIFFORD, PAUL E., *B-flat clarinet*
Possibly one or more tours between 1894-1900. 4th 1901 tour (Britain); 3rd 1902 tour; 1st 1903 tour (Europe); 1905 WG. Charter member, SBFS. d. ca. 1951.
Sources: SB rosters & photos; references in SBFS News.

*CLINE, MAGGIE, *vocalist*
Soloist, 19 Mar 1916, New York. Other positions: Singer/comedienne in musical comedy, revue, and vaudeville, mostly in New York. b. 1 Jan 1857, Haverhill, MA; d. 11 Jun 1934, Fair Haven, NJ.
Sources: Clarence J. Russell's Diary; The Encyclopedia of Vaudeville; The Oxford Companion to the American Theatre.

*CLODIO, VICTOR, *tenor (vocal)*
Soloist. 1893 MB (partial).
Sources: PBk 3, pp. 13, 14.

COBURN, WILLIAM, *cornet/trumpet*
One or more of 1930 tours.
Source: Jay Sims' 1930 tour roster.

COE, ROGER, *horn*
1923-24 tour. Other positions: Conductor of Packard Band (Warren, OH).
Sources: Photos of 1923-24 SB horn section; Instrumentalist, Apr, 1997, p. 82.

COLBY, LOUIS, *B-flat clarinet*
1925-26 tour (partial).
Source: 1925-26 SB hotel assignment list.

COLE, WILLIAM, *instrument?*
Evidently 1st 1905 tour (Britain).
Source: S.S. Baltic ship's list, 19 May 1905, New York.

COLEMAN, HERBERT L., *bassoon*
1925-26 tour. Other positions: New York theater orchestras. Charter member, SBFS.
Sources: SB payroll 11 Jul 1925; roster in Jacob's Band Monthly, Aug, 1925; 1925-26 SB hotel assignment list; references in SBFS News.

COLLINS, JOHN, *flute/piccolo*
1926 tour; 2nd 1927 tour (partial); 1928 tour (partial); 1929 & 1930 radio broadcasts; 12 Mar 1931 recording; 9 Apr 1931 radio broadcast. Other position: Anglo-Canadian Leather Co. Band.
Sources: SB payrolls; 1928 SB programs listing Collins in flute sextet.

COLLINS, WALTER D., *B-flat clarinet*
1911 world tour; possibly 1912 tour.
Sources: SB photos; roster in Albert A. Knecht's world tour diary; Edmund A. Wall's world tour poem; "In Memoriam" list, SBFS organizational booklet (1945).

CONKLIN, BENJAMIN, *saxophone*
1925-26 tour (partial); 1926 tour; 1st 1927 tour; 1929 radio broadcasts. Member, SBFS.
Sources: SB payrolls, photos, & programs; roster in Jacobs' Band Monthly, Aug, 1925; 1925-26 SB hotel assignment list; references in SBFS News.

CONRAD, HERMAN C., *tuba*
Probably all tours, 1892-1903. Other positions: Gilmore's Band; Barnum and Bailey's Circus Band (string bass). Recorded for Edison & Victor. b. Germany.
Sources: SB payrolls, rosters, photos, & programs; The Sousa Band A Discography; J.W. Pepper advertisement, 1898; references in PBks; references in SBFS News; author's correspondence with family, with

Frederick P. Williams, discographer, with Lloyd Farrar, band historian, with Charles Conrad, band historian, & with George B. Class, J.W. Pepper Co.

CONRAD, WILLIAM, *instrument?*
Date(s) of SB service uncertain.
Source: "In Memoriam" list, SBFS organizational booklet (1945).

COPELAND, EDWARD V. (Eddie), *saxophone*
1923-24 tour except WG. Other positions: Music faculty, Bradbury School of Music; theater orchestras. Charter member, SBFS. d. ca. 1961.
Sources: 1923-24 saxophone section photos; references in SBFS News; undated photo in PBk 66.

*CORDAY, CHARLOTTE, *vocalist*
Soloist. 1894 MB (partial).
Source: PBk 3, p. 67.

CORDEN, JULIETTE, *soprano*
2nd 1899 tour (in vocal quartet; later soloist).
Sources: References in PBk 8, pp. 171-179.

COREY, RALPH H., *trombone*
3rd & 4th 1906 tours; 1907 tour; 2nd 1908 tour (succeeded Leo Zimmerman as principal trombonist); 2nd 1908 tour; 1st part of 1909 tour; 1st & 2nd 1910 tours; 1911 world tour; 1912 tour; last part of 1913 tour; 1914 tour; 1915 tour; probably 1915-16 New York Hippodrome; 1916 tour; 1916-17 tour; 1917 tour; WG part of 1918 tour; 1919-20 tour. Soloist on most tours. Other positions: theater orchestras.
Sources: SB rosters, programs, & photos; various other rosters; Musical Messenger, Nov, 1926, p. 15; references in PBks; references in SBFS News; author's interview & correspondence with family.

CORRADO, FRANK, *horn*
9 Apr 1931 radio broadcast; late 1931 radio broadcasts.
Source: SB payroll 9 Apr 1931.

COSTA, *see* ACOSTA, JOSE R.

COTT, OSCAR R., *tuba*
1910 tour; 1914 tour; 1915 tour; 1916-17 tour; 1919 WG; possibly other tours.
Sources: SB rosters & photos; signature on 1914 birthday card from band to Sousa (refers to first year with SB as 1910); roster in Musical Courier, 9 Jun 1915; 1915 Tuxedo tobacco advertisement with SB musicians' signatures; roster in Dec, 1916 New York Musician and Knocker; references in PBk 44; references in SBFS News.

COURTNEY, GRACE, *see* JENKINS, GRACE COURTNEY

*COWLES, EUGENE, *basso*
Soloist. 1893MB (partial); 18 Jan 1894 (New York); 1894 MB (partial); 1897 MB (partial). Other positions: Sang operetta in American theaters; private music teacher. Composer. Recorded for Victor. b. 17 Jan 1860, Quebec; d. 22 Sep 1948, Boston.
Sources: SB programs; references in PBks 2, 3, & 5; The New Grove Dictionary of American Music; The Heritage Encyclopedia of Band Music; Portraits of the World's Best-Known Musicians; author's correspondence with Frederick P. Williams, discographer.

COX, JOHN S., *flute/piccolo*
1st 1892 tour (occasional flute soloist); possibly 2nd 1892 tour; possibly 1st & 2nd 1893 tours; possibly 1st & 2nd 1894 tours; 1894 MB. Other positions: Gilmore's Band; Philadelphia theater orchestras. Composer. b. Scotland.
Sources: The Heritage Encyclopedia of Band Music; Supplement to the Heritage Encyclopedia of Band Music; Marching Along, pp. 65-66, 334; 1892 C.G. Conn advertisement; Metronome, Sep, 1892, p. 16 & Apr, 1893; references in PBks 1,2,3.

CRAGER, GEORGE C., *management*
Business manager, 2nd 1900 tour (Europe).
Source: Musical Courier, 13 Jun 1900, p. 5.

*CRANE, ETHEL, *soprano*
1906 WG (partial). Other position: New York Oratorio Society. d. 25 Dec 1962, South Nyack, NY.
Sources: SB programs; Variety, 6 Jan 1963 [obituary].

CRASZ, R., *horn*
2nd 1902 tour; 3rd 1902 tour (soloist at StPr); 1st 1903 tour (Europe); 1920 WG.
Sources: SB programs; roster in 1920 WG programs.

CRAWFORD, FRANCIS MARION (Frank), *B-flat clarinet*
1923-24 tour (all except end). Other positions: Shrine bands in San Antonio, TX. Member, SBFS (editor of late issues of *SBFS News*).

Sources: SB clarinet section photos; references in PBk 62; references in SBFS News; Bastrop Advertiser and County News (San Antonio, TX), 31 Dec 1987; author's correspondence with Crawford & with Leonard B. Smith, composer.

*CRENNAN, HELEN, soprano
Soloist. 1909 WG (partial).
Sources: SB programs; references in PBks 29, 31, & 45.

CROMER, R. S., B-flat clarinet
1928 tour.
Sources: 1928 SB payrolls; 1928 SB roster; Eugene Slick's 1928 autograph book; references in SBFS News.

*CROWL, LETTIE E., whistler
Soloist. 1893 St. Louis Exposition (partial)
Sources: References in St. Louis Post Dispatch, 13, 14, & 21 Oct 1893.

*CROXTON, FRANK, basso
Soloist. 1915 WG (partial). Recorded for Victor.
Sources: SB programs; Clarence J. Russell's diary; author's correspondence with Frederick P. Williams, discographer.

CULLEY, WILLIAM H., B-flat clarinet
1911 world tour (left band on final segment of tour in California).
Sources: Roster in Albert A. Knecht's world tour diary; Edmund A. Wall's world tour poem; references in SBFS News.

*CULP, JULIA, soprano
Soloist, 23 Jan 1916, New York. Other positions: Concert artist in America & Europe. Recorded for Odeon & Victor. b. 6 Oct 1880, Groningen, Holland; d. 13 Oct 1970, Amsterdam.
Sources: Clarence J. Russell's diary; Baker's Biographical Dictionary of Musicians; PBk 42, p. 95; author's correspondence with Frederick P. Williams, discographer.

CUNNINGTON, G. H., bassoon
1911 world tour (left band on final segment of tour in California).
Sources: Roster in Albert A. Knecht's world tour diary; Edmund A. Wall's world tour poem; references in SBFS News.

CUSUMANO, CHARLES, trombone
Apparently played with SB for a short period, ca. 1918, in New York. Other positions: Pryor's Band; Conway's Band; Nahan Franko's Orchestra. Recorded for Edison. b. 23 Aug 1883, Santa Margherita, Italy; d. 26 Sep 1925, New York.
Sources: Pioneers in Brass; advertisement in Conn Musical Truth, Oct, 1921 (Sousa Edition); author's correspondence with Frederick P. Williams, discographer.

*DABNEY, FOREST, basso
Soloist, 18 Apr 1897, New York.
Source: PBk 5, p. 24.

DAMMEYER, CHARLES, saxophone
1929 radio broadcasts.
Source: SB payroll for 4 Nov 1929.

D'ANA, LEONARD, euphonium
1920 tour.
Sources: Roster in 1920 WG programs; PBk 55, p. 65 (in brass sextet).

DANIELS, EDWIN L. (Ed), flute/piccolo
1922 WG. Member, SBFS.
Sources: SB program 28 Aug 1922 (in piccolo quartet); PBk 33, p. 30; references in SBFS News.

DANNER, ARTHUR, cornet/trumpet
1919-20 tour after WG; 1920 tour; 1921 tour (cornet **soloist** at WG); 1921-22 tour (cornet **soloist** at WG & Dominion Park [ONT]); 1923-24 tour (cornet **soloist** at WG); off-tour concert, 15 Jun 1929, Princeton, NJ; 1929 & 1930 radio broadcasts; 12 Mar 1931 recording; 9 Apr 1931 radio broadcast; 1931 tour; late 1931 radio broadcasts. Charter member, SBFS.
Sources: SB payrolls, rosters, programs, & photos; references in SBFS News.

*D'ARVILLE, CAMILLE, soprano
Soloist. 1893 MB (partial); 1896 MB (partial). Other positions: Singer/actress in opera, comic opera, & vaudeville in America and England. Recorded for Berliner. b. 1863, Holland; d. 9 Sep 1932.
Sources: SB programs; references in PBks 3 & 4; The Oxford Companion to American Theatre; Who Was Who in America, Vol. 1; author's correspondence with Frederick P. Williams, discographer.

DAVENPORT, ARTHUR D., tuba
1925-26 tour (partial). Composer.

Sources: SB payroll 11 Jul 1925; 1925-26 SB hotel assignment list; The Heritage Encyclopedia of Band Music.

DAVIDSON, MAXWELL, saxophone
2nd 1900 tour (Europe); 4th 1901 tour (Britain); possibly other tours.
Sources: SB rosters & photos; SBFS News, May, 1951, p. 7; author's correspondence with Donald Callahan, researcher.

DAVIES, MAUD REESE, soprano
Soloist. 1897 MB (partial); 1897 tour; 1st 1898 tour; last part of 3rd 1898 tour; 1st & 2nd 1899 tours; last part of 1st 1900 tour; 4th 1901 tour (Britain); 1st 1902 tour. Recorded for Victor.
Sources: References in PBks 8 & 9; SBFS News, May, 1951, p. 8.

DAVIS, ARTHUR C., bass clarinet
1915 tour; 1919-20 tour; 1920 tour; 1921 tour; 1921-22 tour; 1922 tour; possibly other tours. Other position: Conway's Band. Brother of Lee H. Davis.
Sources: SB rosters & photos; Bands of America, p. 280; roster in Musical Courier, 9 Jun 1915; 1915 Tuxedo tobacco advertisement with SB musicians' signatures; PBk 54, p. 63.

DAVIS, ISADORE (IRVING) (Izzy), B-flat clarinet
1907 tour; 2nd 1908 tour; 1909 tour; 1911 world tour; 1929 radio broadcasts.
Sources: 1911 SB photos; rosters in New York Dramatic Mirror, 7 Sep 1907 & 1 Sep 1908; roster in Albert A. Knecht's 1911 world tour diary; Edmund C. Wall's world tour poem; references in SBFS News.

DAVIS, LEE H., flute/piccolo
1920 tour (**soloist** at WG); one or more of 1930 tours. Brother of Arthur C. Davis.
Sources: Roster in 1920 WG programs; Jay Sims' 1930 tour roster; references in PBks 53, 54, & 55.

DAVIS, PAUL S., horn
1928 tour; off-tour concert, 15 Jun 1929, Princeton, NJ; one or more of 1930 tours. Other position: Ringling Bros. and Barnum & Bailey Circus Band.
Sources: SB payrolls; Eugene Slick's 1928 autograph book; references in SBFS News.

DAVIS, ROBIN W. (Doc), B-flat clarinet
1928 tour. Other positions: Los Angeles Symphonic Band; Los Angeles County Band; Los Angeles Senior Citizen Symphony; Lockheed Band (Los Angeles). Charter member, SBFS.
Sources: 1928 SB payrolls; The Sousa Oral History Project; references in SBFS News; author's interview & correspondence with Davis.

*DEAN, ALICE, violin
Soloist, 7 Feb 1909, New York.
Source: PBk 31, p. 13.

DeBLASI, PHILLIP, cornet/trumpet
1st 1904 tour. Member, SBFS.
Sources: Conn Musical Truth, May, 1904; references in SBFS News; author's correspondence with Keith Clark, researcher.

DeBLEYE, JOSEPH, horn
3rd 1895 tour; possibly other 1895 tours; 1st 1896 tour; 1896 MB (in horn quartet); 1896-97 tour; 2nd 1898 tour; 4th 1901 tour (Britain); 1st 1903 tour (Europe); 1907 tour; 2nd 1908 tour; possibly other tours between 1901 and 1908.
Sources: SB payrolls; 1895 & 1896 J.W. Pepper advertisements; seating chart in Philadelphia Press, 7 May 1897; J.W. Pepper Musical Times and Band Journal, May, 1898; SB/Grenadier Guards banquet seating chart of 17 Oct 1901; roster in New York Dramatic Mirror, 1 Sep 1908.

DeBUERIS, JOHN, alto clarinet
12 Mar 1930 radio broadcast; 12 Mar 1931 recording; 9 Apr 1931 radio broadcast; late 1931 radio broadcasts.
Sources: SB payrolls

DECKER, WILLIAM H. (Will; Deck), bassoon
1911 world tour; also several earlier tours. Other positions: Victor Herbert's Orchestra; San Francisco Symphony Orchestra. d. Aug, 1914, Ogden, Utah.
Sources: Roster in Albert A. Knecht's world tour diary; Edmund A. Wall's world tour poem; references in SBFS News; author's interview with family.

deFRITSCH, MARGUERITE, violin
Soloist. 1902 WG (partial); 2nd 1902 tour.
Sources: SB programs; references in PBks 16 & 18.

*de GOGORZA, EMELIO, *baritone*
Made 2 recordings with SB on Victor label (#1452 & #1453, both in 1902). Also recorded for Berliner, Bettini, Climax, Edison, Globe, and Zonophone. Other position: music teacher. b. 28 May 1894, Brooklyn, NY; d. 10 May 1914, New York.
Sources: The Encyclopedic Discography of Victor Recordings, Pre-Matrix Series; The Sousa Band A Discography; *correspondence with Frederick P. Williams, discographer, & Cameron-Graham Memorial Band Museum.*

DeKAY, GARRET L. (Deke), *trombone*
1st 1927 tour; one or more of 1930 tours. Other position: Long Beach (CA) Municipal Band. Member, SBFS.
Sources: Jay Sims' 1930 tour roster; references in SBFS News.

DeLIO, GIUSEPPE (JOSEPH), *B-flat clarinet*
4th 1901 tour (Britain); 3rd 1902 tour; 1st 1903 tour (Europe); 1907 tour; probably other tours.
Sources: SB rosters; SB/Grenadier Guards banquet seating chart of 17 Oct 1901; rosters in New York Dramatic Mirror, *6 Sep 1902 & 7 Sep 1907.*

De LUCA, JOSEPH O. (Joe), *euphonium*
All tours, 1921-28. **Soloist** on most tours. Other positions: Italian Grand Opera Co.; several Italian bands; Creatore's Band; Liberati's Grand Military Band; Innes' Band; Conway's Band; Philadelphia Orchestra; Victor Herbert's Orchestra; conductor of Pipateatina (Italy) Municipal Band & bands at University of Arizona. Composer. Recorded for Columbia, Edison, & Victor. Elected to Society of Others (Italy). b. 26 Mar 1890, Rome, Italy; d. 22 Oct 1935, Tucson, AZ.
Sources: SB payrolls, rosters, programs, & photos; The Heritage Encyclopedia of Band Music; Supplement to the Heritage Encyclopedia of Band Music; Bands of America, *pp. 273 & 279; references in PBks; references in* SBFS News; *De Luca career scrapbook; author's correspondence with Frederick P. Williams, discographer.*

De SANTOS, _____ , *harp*
Believed to have played with SB for a very short period, possibly the 2nd or 3rd 1930 tour.
Source: Jay Sims handwritten financial papers.

DEL NEGRO, ANTHONY (Tony), *oboe*
1919-20 tour (partial). Other positions: Conway's Band; theater orchestras. Member, SBFS.
Sources: Various 1919-20 tour rosters; references in SBFS News.

DEL NEGRO, LUCA A., (Luke), *tuba*
Probably all tours, 1900-08. 1929 radio broadcasts. Other positions: Innes' Band; Conway's Band; New York theater orchestras.
Sources: SB payrolls, rosters, & photos; initials & dates on music in SB library at University of Illinois; SB/Grenadier Guards banquet seating chart of 17 Oct 1901; rosters in New York Dramatic Mirror, *7 Sep 1907 & 1 Sep 1908; references in* SBFS News.

*DEL PAPA, DANTE, *tenor (vocal)*
1897 MB. Recorded for Bettini.
Sources: PBk 5, pp. 63 & 80; author's correspondence with Frederick P. Williams, discographer.

della ROCCA, GIACINTA, *violin*
Soloist. 2nd 1908 tour; 1 Nov 1908, New York; 1st part of 1909 tour.
Sources: SB programs; references in PBks 30 & 31.

DESIMONE, JERRY G., *horn*
1919-20 tour. Other positions: New York theater orchestras. Charter member, SBFS.
Sources: Various 1919-20 tour rosters; references in SBFS News.

DESMOND, PAUL A., *saxophone*
2nd 1927 tour; 1928 tour; 1929 tour. Other positions: Staff arranger, radio station KDKA (Pittsburgh); theater orchestra. Member, SBFS.
Sources: SB payrolls, rosters, programs, & photos; Hartford (CT) Times, *18 Jul 1927.*

*DESTINN, EMMY, *soprano*
Soloist, 12 Dec 1916, New York. Other positions: Metropolitan Opera Co.; Berlin Opera; Covent Garden (London). Recorded for Columbia, Deutsche Gramophone, & Victor. b. 26 Feb 1878, Prague, Bohemia; d. 28 Jan 1930, Budejovice, Czechoslovakia.
Sources: PBk 42, pp. 42 & 43; Clarence J. Russell's diary; Baker's Biographical Dictionary of Musicians; *author's correspondence with Frederick P. Williams, discographer.*

*de VASSEY, T., *tenor (vocal)*
Soloist. 1902 WG (partial).
Sources: SB programs; PBk 18, p. 175.

De VAUX, EUGENE (Jene), *oboe*
2nd 1900 tour (Europe); 1st 1903 tour (Europe).
Sources: SB rosters & photos; references in SBFS News.

*DICKERSON, JENNIE, *contralto*
Soloist. 1893 MB (partial). Other positions: Theater & movie actress; sang opera, mostly in New York. b. 1855, Newburgh, NY; d. 14 Aug 1943, Philadelphia.
Sources: References in PBks 2 & 3; Who Was Who on Screen.

DICKINSON, HOMER W., *saxophone*
2nd 1900 tour (Europe).
Sources: Roster in SB program of 22 Apr 1900; SB photo, 30 May 1900; SBFS News, *May, 1951, p. 7.*

DIERKS, PAUL, *percussion*
1924 WG.
Sources: References in SBFS News.

*DOCHES, LOUIS, *vocalist*
Soloist. 1899 Indiana State Fair (partial); 1st Philadelphia National Export Exposition (1899) (partial).
Sources: PBk 9, pp. 11, 13, 31.

*DODSON, MRS. N., *contralto*
Soloist. 1893 St. Louis Exposition (partial).
Source: St. Louis Post-Dispatch, *21 Oct 1893.*

DOLAN, JOHN F., *cornet/trumpet*
Most all engagements, May, 1920 – Sep, 1928; cornet **soloist** on all tours. Other positions: U.S. Army bands during & after Spanish-American War; Conway's Band; Barrere Little Symphony; New York theater orchestras. b. 27 Jan 1875, Schuler Falls, NY; d. 8 Apr 1942, Staten Island, NY.
Sources: SB payrolls, rosters, programs, & photos; Pioneers in Brass; *references in PBks; references in* SBFS News; *author's interviews with SB members.*

*DOLORES, MINA, *soprano*
Soloist. 1928 StPr.
Sources: SB program of 12 Aug 1928.

*DOMINELLI, AIDA, *soprano*
Soloist, 20 May 1929 radio broadcast.
Sources: Radio schedules in New York Times & New York Civic Commercial Tribune.

*DONALDA, PAULINE, *soprano*
Soloist 9 Apr 1916 (New York). Other positions: Metropolitan Opera Co.; Manhattan Opera Co. (New York); Opera-Comique (Paris); sang opera in England & Belgium. Recorded for HMV. b. 5 Mar 1882, Montreal [birth name Pauline Lightstone]; d. 22 Oct 1970, Montreal.
Source: Clarence J. Russell's diary; Baker's Biographical Dictionary of Musicians; The New Grove Dictionary of Music and Musicians; *author's correspondence with Frederick P. Williams, discographer.*

DONATI, A., *bass clarinet*
2nd 1900 tour (Europe). Composer.
Sources: Roster in SB program of 22 Apr 1900; SB photo, 30 May 1900.

*DONNER, DIAMOND, *soprano*
Soloist, 3 Dec 1916 & 17-23 Dec 1916 & 1-23 Jan 1917, New York.
Source: Clarence J. Russell's diary.

D'ONOFRIO, PETRO, *bassoon*
1st 1893 tour (occasional **soloist**).
Sources: SB publicity for 1st 1893 tour; Metronome, *Apr, 1893.*

DORNHEIM, HELMAR, *E-flat clarinet*
2nd 1900 tour (Europe).
Sources: Roster in SB program of 22 Apr 1900; SB photo, 30 May 1900.

D'ORTENZIO, ANTHONY, *saxophone*
1920 WG; 1921 tour; 1921-22 tour (**soloist** at 1921 WG); 1922 tour. Member, SBFS.
Sources: SB rosters & programs; 1921 SB photo; A Study of the Saxophone Soloists Performing with the John Philip Sousa Band: 1893-1930; *advertisement in* Conn Musical Truth, *ca. 1922; references in PBk 58; references in* SBFS News.

DOUCET, A., *oboe/English horn*
1907 tour.
Source: Roster in New York Dramatic Mirror, *7 Sep 1907.*

DOUGHERTY, WILLIAM, *B-flat clarinet*
Probably most tours, 1892-1897.
    Sources: SB payrolls & photos; SB publicity for 1ˢᵗ 1893 tour; 1892 C.G. Conn advertisement; seating chart in Philadelphia Press, *7 May 1897.*

*DREYER, HENRIETTA LOUISE, *vocalist*
Soloist. 2ⁿᵈ 1894 Madison Square Garden engagement (partial). Other positions: Drama in America. b. 3 Aug 1863, Brooklyn, NY.
    Sources: Woman's Who's Who of America; New York World, *3 Jun 1894, p. 12.*

DRUCKER, SAM, *cornet/trumpet*
1920 WG.
    Source: Roster in 1920 WG programs.

DUBLE, ANNA, *see OTTEN, ANNA*

*DUFFEY, J. HUMBRID, *baritone (vocal)*
Soloist, 26 Mar 1916, New York.
    Source: Clarence J. Russell's diary.

DUFFIELD, BLANCHE, *soprano*
Soloist. All but last part of 1ˢᵗ 1900 tour; off-tour concert, 22 Apr 1900, New York; 3ʳᵈ & 4ᵗʰ 1900 tours; 1ˢᵗ & 2ⁿᵈ 1901 tours; 3ʳᵈ 1901 tour after Pittsburgh Exposition; 1902 StPr. Other positions: Sang opera & operetta in New York; Victor Herbert's Orchestra.
    Sources: SB programs; references in PBks; Musical Courier, *18 Sep 1901, p. 23; SBFS News, May, 1951, pp. 4 & 5.*

DUKE, CURRIE, *violin*
Soloist. 1ˢᵗ, 2ⁿᵈ, & 3ʳᵈ 1895 tours; last part of 4ᵗʰ 1895 tour; 1ˢᵗ 1896 tour.
    Sources: SB payrolls, programs, & photos; Blakely Papers, New York Public Library; Colorado Springs (CO) Gazette, 12 Mar 1896; references in PBk 12.

DUNCAN, WILLIAM EARL, *cornet/trumpet*
1928 tour; 1929 tour; one or more of 1930 tours; 1931 tour (partial). Charter member, SBFS. d. Oct, 1980.
    Sources: SB payrolls; Jay Sims' 1930 tour roster; 1931 SB roster; references in SBFS News; author's correspondence with Duncan.

DUTSCHKE, HERMAN, SR., *instrument?*
Date(s) of SB service uncertain.
    Source: "In Memoriam" list, SBFS organizational booklet (1945).

DUTSCHKE, HERMAN, JR., *horn*
1914 tour. Member, SBFS.
    Sources: signature on 6 Nov 1914 birthday card from band to Sousa [refers to 1ˢᵗ year with band as 1914]. References in SBFS News.

*DWYER, EDNA, *contralto*
Soloist, 19 May 1915, New York.
    Source: Clarence J. Russell's diary.

EAU CLAIRE, FELIX, *saxophone*
2ⁿᵈ 1927 tour; 1928 tour; 1929 tour; one or more of 1930 tours; 1931 tour. Other positions: U.S. Marine Band. Member, SBFS. d. ca. 1982.
    Sources: SB payrolls, rosters, programs, & photos; references in PBks; references in SBFS News.

ECKSTEIN, SOL (Solly), *B-flat clarinet*
1909 tour; probably 1910 tour; 1911 world tour; probably 1912 & 1913 tours; 1914 tour.
    Sources: Roster in Albert A. Knecht's world tour diary; Edmund A. Wall's world tour poem; signature on 6 Nov 1914 birthday card from band members to Sousa (refers to first year with band as 1909); references in SBFS News.

ELEHMOR, W. *instrument?*
Believed to have played with SB for a very short period, possibly the 2ⁿᵈ or 3ʳᵈ 1930 tour.
    Source: Jay Sims handwritten financial papers.

ELLIOTT, EDWARD E., *B-flat clarinet*
1924 tour; 1925-26 tour (partial); 1926 tour.
    Sources: SB payrolls & photos; roster in Jacob's Band Monthly, *Aug, 1925; 1925-26 SB hotel assignment list. SBFS, May, 1983, p. 31.*

*ELLIOTT, F.W., *vocalist*
Soloist. 2ⁿᵈ 1894 Madison Square Garden engagement (partial); 1894 MB (partial).
    Source: New York Times, *28 May 1894.*

ENGBERG (ENGERQUASST), LORENZO A. (Lew), *B-flat clarinet*
1914 tour; 1915 tour; 1916 tour; 1916-17 tour; probably 1918 tour; 1919-20 tour; 1921-22 tour; 1922 tour; 1923-24 tour; 1924 tour; 1925-26 tour; 1926 tour; 1ˢᵗ & 2ⁿᵈ 1927 tours. Member, SBFS.

    Sources: SB payrolls, rosters, & photos; signature on 6 Nov 1914 birthday card from band members to Sousa (refers to first year with band as 1900); roster in Musical Courier, *9 Jun 1915; 1915 Tuxedo tobacco advertisement with SB musicians' signatures; roster in Dec, 1916 New York Musician and Knocker; various 1919-20 tour rosters; roster in* Jacobs' Band Journal, *Aug, 1925; 1925-26 SB hotel assignment list; 1927 hotel assignment list; references in SBFS News.*

ENGBERG, R., *B-flat clarinet*
2nd 1900 tour (Europe).
    Sources: Roster in SB program of 22 Apr 1900; SB photo, 30 May 1900.

*ENSIGN, HORACE, *basso*
Soloist, 19 May 1915, Salt Lake City, UT.
    Sources: Clarence J. Russell's diary.

ESPINOSA, ____, *saxophone*
One or more tours before 1911.
    Sources: Albert Knecht's world tour diary; SBFS News, Jul 1952, p. 22.

EVANS, ALFRED, *saxophone*
Off-tour concert, 15 Jun 1929, Princeton, NJ; 1929 & 1930 radio broadcasts; 9 Apr 1931 radio broadcast; late 1931 radio broadcasts.
    Sources: SB payrolls.

EVANS, ERIC J. *flute/piccolo*
1928 tour; off-tour concert, 15 Jun 1929, Princeton, NJ; 1929 tour.
    Sources: SB payrolls & photos; references in SBFS News.

EVANS, REUBEN CLINTON (Johnny), *tuba*
1928 tour; 1929 tour. Other positions: John Robinson Circus Band; Lee Bros. Circus Band; Ringling Bros. and Barnum & Bailey Circus Band; staff musician for NBC & CBS radio orchestras, Chicago; Guy Lombardo Orchestra; Paul Whiteman's Orchestra. d. Aug, 1992.
    Sources: SB payrolls, rosters, & photos; Instrumentalist, *Jan, 1991, pp. 21-28 & Oct, 1992, p. 2; T.U.B.A. Journal, Fall, 1997, pp. 48-51; references in SBFS News; author's interview with Evans.*

*EVERSMAN, ALICE, *soprano*
Soloist. 1917 WG (partial); 1918 WG (partial). Other positions: Metropolitan Opera Co.; Chicago Opera Co.; Montreal Opera Co.; Century Opera Co.; San Carlo Opera Co. (New York); toured with other opera companies in Cuba & British West Indies; Victor Herbert's Orchestra; toured in Europe as concert artist; later music editor & critic, *Washington Star.* b. Effingham, IL; d. 1974.
    Sources: SB programs; references in PBk 46; Who Was Who in America, *Vol. VI.*

EVERSON, ____, *horn*
1ˢᵗ 1894 tour; possibly other tours.
    Source: Program in San Francisco Chronicle, *26 Mar 1894.*

*FABRICE, RENE, *soprano*
Soloist. 1897 MB (partial).
    Source: PBk 5, p. 71.

FABRIZIO, JOHN, *flute/piccolo*
1929 radio broadcasts.
    Source: SB payroll for 1 Jul 1929.

FAGAN, GEORGE W., *cornet/trumpet*
Date(s) of SB service uncertain but ca. 1919.
    Source: Undated advertisement in Musical Messenger, *ca. 1919; "In Memoriam" list, SBFS organizational booklet (1945).*

FAIR, REX ALTON, *flute/piccolo*
1925-26 tour (partial); 1926 tour. Other positions: Pryor's Band; Bachman's Million Dollar Band; traveling theater orchestras; music faculty, University of Colorado at Boulder; instrument repairman. Author. Member, SBFS. b. York, Nebraska; d. ca. 1957.
    Sources: 1925-26 SB payroll; Who Is Who in Music, *1951 Edition; references in SBFS News.*

FALCO, A., *saxophone*
1907 tour.
    Source: Roster in New York Dramatic Mirror, *7 Sep 1907.*

FANTILLI, A., *instrument?*
Believed to have played with SB for a very short period, possibly the 2ⁿᵈ or 3ʳᵈ 1930 tour.
    Source: Jay Sims handwritten financial papers.

FASANELLOR, P., *instrument?*
Believed to have played with SB for a very short period, possibly the 2ⁿᵈ or 3ʳᵈ 1930 tour.
    Source: Jay Sims handwritten financial papers.

FAUCHALD, NORA, *soprano*
Soloist. 1923 WG (partial); 1923-24 tour (partial); 1924 tour (partial); 1925 WG (partial); 1926 WG (partial); 2nd 1927 tour (partial). Other positions: sang opera and recitals in Europe and U.S.A. & soloed with numerous American orchestras; music faculty, Juilliard School of Music. Elected to North Dakota Hall of Fame. Member, SBFS. Married name Mrs. George H. Morgan. b. 25 Jan 1898, Norway; d. 10 Dec 1971, Waterbury, CT.
Sources: SB rosters, programs, & photos. Sunday Republican (Waterbury, CT), 26 Feb 1967; references in PBks. References in SBFS News; author's interviews and correspondence with Fauchald & with family.

FEE, GEORGE, *cornet/trumpet*
1st & 2nd 1927 tours; 1928 tour; one or more of 1930 tours. Other positions: Paul Whiteman's Orchestra; Pryor's Band; Goldman Band; U.S. Navy Band; Ringling Bros. and Barnum & Bailey's Circus Band. Member, SBFS.
Sources: SB payrolls, rosters, & photos; 1927 SB hotel assignment list; Eugene Slick's 1928 autograph book; references in SBFS News.

*FELDMAN, ____, *violin*
Soloist, 7 Dec 1909, Toronto.
Source: PBk 31, p. 102.

FERRARA, NICOLA (Nick), *tuba*
1921 tour; 1921-22 tour; 1922 tour. Charter member, SBFS.
Sources: SB rosters & photos; references in SBFS News.

*FERRATA, LEONORA, *soprano*
Soloist. 1920 WG (partial). Other positions: Chicago English Opera Co.; Ravinia Opera Co.
Sources: SB programs; references in PBks 54 & 55.

FIELD, EARL W., *tuba*
1921-22 tour; 1922 tour; 1923-24 tour except WG. Other positions: Seattle Symphony Orchestra; Kryl's Band; Burtnell-Miller Orchestra (Los Angeles). Member, SBFS. d. 1952.
Sources: SB rosters & photos; advertisement in Conn Musical Truth, Mar, 1925; references in SBFS News.

FINEGAN, LILLIAN J., *secretary*
Secretary in New York office, probably continuously from 1916-1932. b. 22 Jun 1894; d. Aug, 1968, Brooklyn, NY.
Sources: SB payrolls & rosters; author's interview and correspondence with Finegan; Social Security Death Index.

FINK, LEO, *B-flat clarinet*
1st 1905 tour (Britain).
Source: S.S. Baltic ship's list, 19 May 1905, New York.

FINNIE, ALEX A., *trombone*
Probably one or more tours, 1895 or 1896; also possibly 14 Nov 1914, New York. Composer.
Sources: The Heritage Encyclopedia of Band Music; Supplement to the Heritage Encyclopedia of Band Music; advertisement in J.W. Pepper Musical Times and Band Journal, May, 1898; Musical Courier, 18 Nov 1915; PBk 42, p. 28.

FISHER, JOHN A., *flute/piccolo*
1928 tour (partial) (flute **soloist** StPr).
Source: SB program for 12 Aug 1928.

*FITCHHORN, ELVER J., (E.J.) *horn*
23 Jan – 10 Mar 1917. Other positions: U.S. Army bandmaster in Europe during World War I; Redpath Chautauqua Circuit Orchestra; school band director in Delaware, Kenton, & Mt. Gilead, OH. Named one of 10 best high school band conductors in America by *School Musician* magazine, 1936. Inventor of saxette [a song flute].
Sources: Columbus (OH) Dispatch, 17 Aug 1969; other clippings in family collection; author's interview with Fitchhorn & correspondence with family.

FLASTER, MAX, *E-flat clarinet*
1915 tour; 1916-17 tour. Other positions: Pryor's Band; Conway's Band. b. Hungary.
Sources: SB rosters & photos; roster in Musical Courier, 9 Jun 1915; 1915 Tuxedo tobacco advertisement with SB musicians' signatures; roster in Dec, 1916 New York Musician and Knocker; advertisements in Musical Messenger, Jul & Dec, 1922; references in SBFS News.

*FLEMING, KATHERINE, *contralto*
Soloist. 1894 MB (partial).
Source: PBk 3, p. 5

FLEMING, ROBERT, *B-flat clarinet*
2nd 1893 tour; possibly 1st, 2nd, & 3rd 1894 tours; 3rd 1895 tour; possibly 4th 1895 tour; 1st 1896 tour; possibly 2nd 1896 tour; 1896-97 tour; 1897 tour.
Sources: SB payrolls, programs, & photos; hotel registration, Adrian, MI, 1 Apr 1895.

FLETCHER, JOHN, *cornet/trumpet*
One or more tours in 1904; 1st 1905 tour (Britain); 2nd 1905 tour (cornet **soloist** at WG); 2nd 1908 tour; possibly other tours. Recorded for Indestructible Cylinders. Member, SBFS.
Sources: SB programs; Conn Musical Truth, May, 1904; roster in New York Dramatic Mirror, 1 Sep 1908; advertisement in Conn Musical Truth, Oct, 1921 (Sousa Edition); SBFS News, Feb, 1955, p. 14; author's correspondence with Keith Clark, researcher & with Frederick P. Williams, discographer.

FLETCHER, WILLIAM, *B-flat clarinet*
One tour in 1904; 1st 1905 tour (Britain). Other positions: Victor Herbert's Orchestra; Philadelphia Chamber Symphony Orchestra; Innes' Band; conductor of Fletcher concert Band & Fletcher Woodwind Symphonette; music faculty, Girard College and Hamilton School of Music; conductor of Princeton (NJ) High School Band. Composer of *J.P.S. Centennial March* & others). Member, SBFS.
Sources: S.S. Baltic ship's list, 10 May 1905; The Heritage Encyclopedia of Band Music; Bands of America, p. 155; references in SBFS News.

FOERSTER, WILLIAM, *alto clarinet, B-flat clarinet*
1st 1894 tour (occasional **soloist** on B-flat clarinet); 1st 1899 tour; possibly 2nd, 3rd, & 4th 1899 tours; possibly 1st 1900 tour; 2nd 1900 tour (Europe).
Sources: SB rosters & programs; photo in Sousa's personal 1899/1900 photo album.

*FOLEY, MARY DELORES, *contralto*
Soloist. 1894 MB (partial).
Sources: PBk 3, pp. 72 & 73.

FOLTS, LLOYD H., *trombone*
1928 tour. Other position: U.S. Marine Band. Member, SBFS. d. 2 Jun 1974.
Sources: SB payrolls; references in SBFS News.

FONTANELLA, FERD, *B-flat clarinet*
1929 radio broadcasts.
Sources: SB payrolls.

FONZO, JOSEPH, *saxophone*
12 Mar 1930 radio broadcast; 12 Mar 1931 recording; 9 Apr 1931 radio broadcast; 1931 tour; late 1931 radio broadcasts.
Sources: SB payrolls.

FOOTE, EARL VAN WYCK, *B-flat clarinet, saxophone*
1921-22 tour; 1922 tour; 1923-24 tour; 1924 tour; 1925-26 tour (partial); 1926 WG; off-tour concert, 15 Jun 1929, Princeton, NJ; 1929 tour (partial); one or more of 1930 tours; 1931 tour; 1932 radio broadcasts. Other positions: Pryor's Band; private music teacher. In later years, was piano accompanist to former SB sopranos Marjorie Moody and Nora Fauchald. Charter member, SBFS. b. ca. 1898; d. Apr, 1973.
Sources: SB payrolls, rosters, & photos; roster in Jacobs' Band Monthly, Aug, 1925; author's interview and correspondence with Foote; references in SBFS News.

*FORAN, WILLIAM, *tenor (vocal)*
Soloist. 1893 tour (partial). Other positions: Vaudeville performer and actor. b. ca. 1879; d. 9 Mar 1954, New York.
Sources: Variety, 17 Mar 1954, p. 63 [obituary]; PBk 30, pp. 32 & 33.

FORD, GEORGE FRANK, *flute/piccolo*
1920 WG; 1921 tour; 1921-22 tour; 1922 tour; 1926 tour (partial); one or more of 1930 tours. Other positions: Paul Whiteman's Orchestra; 1940 World's Fair Band (New York); Shep Fields "New Music" Band; New York theater orchestras. Charter member, SBFS. b. 6 Nov 1895, Naugatuck, CT; d. 6 Jan 1975.
Sources: SB payrolls, rosters, and photos; author's interview & correspondence with Ford; references in SBFS News.

FORD, HENRY C. (Wick), *trombone*
1923-24 tour (partial); 1924 tour; 1925-26 tour (**soloist** at WG).
Sources: SB payroll 11 Jul 1925; SB programs; 1925-26 SB hotel assignment list; PBk 67, p. 14.

*FORD, ROSE, *violin*
Soloist. 1909 WG (partial).
Sources: SB programs.

*FORESMAN, HARRY, *vocalist*
Soloist. 1894 MB (partial).
Source: PBk 21, p. 60.

FORSTER, HERMAN, *percussion, librarian*
Probably all tours, 1892-94 & 1898-1909. Other positions: Saro's
Prussian Guards.
*Sources: SB rosters & photos; 1892 C.G. Conn advertisement; various
other rosters; copyist's manuscripts in SB library at University of Illinois;
references in SBFS News.*

*FOSTER, JESSIE, *soprano*
Soloist. 1895 St. Louis Exposition (partial)
Sources: Programs in St. Louis Post-Dispatch.

FRANK, FRITZ, *percussion*
1926 StPr.
Source: 1926 SB photo.

FRANKEL, JOSEPH, *B-flat clarinet*
1st and/or 2nd 1904 tour. Other positions: Victor Herbert's Band; conductor
of military and municipal bands in Philadelphia & 108th Pennsylvania
National Guard Field Artillery Band. Member, SBFS. b. 1883; d. 12 Jul
1956, Philadelphia.
*Sources: Band Encyclopedia; Berger roster; Pruyn roster; SBFS News,
Oct, 1950, p. 3.*

FRANKLIN, EDWIN (Teddy), *flute/piccolo*
1924 tour (flute **soloist** at WG). Other positions: U.S. Marine Band; Innes'
Band; Boston Opera Co. Orchestra; Commissioner of Music, City of
Boston.
*Sources: SB payroll & programs; photo in Philadelphia Public Ledger,
ca. Aug, 1924; SBFS News, Feb, 1955, p. 6.*

FRANTZ, ARTHUR L., *horn*
1st & 2nd 1927 tours; 1928 tour. Other positions: Pryor's Band; Moses'
Band (St. Petersburg, FL). Member, SBFS.
*Sources: SB payrolls; 1927 SB hotel assignment list; references in SBFS
News; author's interview & correspondence with Frantz.*

FRANZL, JOSEPH, *horn*
Off-tour concert, 15 Jun 1929, Princeton, NJ; 1929 radio broadcasts; 12
Mar 1931 recording.
Sources: SB payrolls.

*FREEMAN, BATTINA, *soprano*
Soloist, 20 Feb 1916, New York. Recorded for Columbia.
*Source: Clarence J. Russell's diary; author's correspondence with
Frederick P. Williams, discographer.*

FREEMAN, ELVIN L. (Jake), *tuba*
2nd 1927 tour; 1928 tour; off-tour concert, 15 Jun 1929, Princeton, NJ.
Other positions: Pryor's Band; U.S. Military Academy Band (West Point);
President, NY State School Music Assn.; conductor of Syracuse University
Band; public school music teacher, Syracuse, NY, area. Author of music
instruction books. Member, SBFS. b. 25 Oct 1901, Brudete, WV; d. May,
1983.
*Sources: SB payrolls, rosters, & photos; Eugene Slick's 1928 autograph
book; Band Encyclopedia; Who Is Who in Music, 1951 Edition; Woodwind, Brass & Percussion, Sep, 1976; references in SBFS News; author's
correspondence with Freeman.*

FREEMAN, HARRY, *cornet/trumpet*
1911 world tour. Other positions: Sydney (Australia) Philharmonic
Orchestra; Grenadier Guards Band (England). Composer. b. 1883,
England.
*Sources: Roster in Albert A. Knecht's world tour diary; Edmund A.
Wall's world tour poem; The Heritage Encyclopedia of Band Music;
Supplement to the Heritage Encyclopedia of Band Music; Metronome,
Mar, 1913, p. 19; advertisement in Conn Musical Truth, Oct, 1921 (Sousa
Edition); references in SBFS News; PBk 34, p. 20;.*

*FREMSTAD, OLIVE, *soprano*
Soloist, 12 Mar 1916, New York. Other positions: Metropolitan Opera
Co.; Manhattan Opera Co. (New York); Boston Opera Co.; Chicago Opera
Co.; Royal Bavarian Opera (Munich); Covent Garden (London); also
concert pianist. Decorated as Officer of the Academy and Officer of
Public Instruction by French government. Recorded for Columbia. b. 14
Mar 1871, Stockholm, Sweden; d. 21 Apr 1951, Irvington-on-Hudson,
NY.
*Sources: Clarence J. Russell's diary; Woman's Who's Who in America;
Baker's Biographical Dictionary of Musicians; Who Was Who in*

America, *Vol. 3; author's correspondence with Frederick P. Williams,
discographer.*

FRENCH, MYRTA FLORENCE (Myrta), *soprano*
Soloist. 1st 1895 tour; probably other tours in 1895; 1st 1896 tour; 1918
WG (partial).
Sources: SB payrolls, programs, & photos; references in PBk 5.

FRICKE, HARRY A., *horn*
Most tours and engagements, 1893-1898.
*Sources: SB payrolls, rosters, programs, & photos; hotel registration,
Adrian, MI, 1 Apr 1895; signature in Lester Levy's autograph book, Nov,
1895; seating chart in Philadelphia Press, 7 May 1897; advertisement in
J.W. Pepper Musical Times and Band Journal, Spring, 1895; references in
PBks.*

FRICKE, WALTER, *horn*
1929 radio broadcasts.
Source: SB payroll 4 Nov 1929.

FRIGGA, EINAR, *B-flat clarinet*
1921 tour; 1921-22 tour; 1922 tour; 1923-24 tour; 1924 tour; 1925-26 tour;
1926 tour; 1928 tour; off-tour concert, 15 Jun 1929, Princeton, NJ; 1929
radio broadcasts; one or more of 1930 tours. Member, SBFS.
b. Denmark.
*Sources: SB payrolls, rosters, & photos; roster in Jacobs' Band
Monthly, Aug 1925; 1925-26 SB hotel assignment list; advertisement in
Conn Musical Truth, Oct, 1923; Jay Sims' 1930 tour roster; references in
SFBS News.*

FRITSCHE, OTTO, *B-flat clarinet*
3rd 1898 tour; 2nd 1900 tour (Europe); possibly other tours.
*Sources: Seating chart in St. Louis Post-Dispatch, 25 Sep 1898; Roster
in SB program of 22 Apr 1900; SB photo, 30 May 1900; PBk 67, p. 29.*

FRITZ, EDWARD, *cornet/trumpet*
1st 1892 tour; possibly 2nd 1892 tour; possibly tours in 1893. Other
positions: Allentown (PA) Band.
*Sources: Advertisement in J.W. Pepper Musical Times and Band
Journal, May, 1898; Morning Call (Allentown), 25 Feb 1975, p. 6; SBFS
News, Sep, 1975, p. 10.*

FRITZE, LOUIS P., *flute/piccolo*
All tours, 1913 to 1919-20 tour. Flute **soloist** frequently, particularly at
WG. Other positions: Philadelphia Orchestra; concert tours with Amelita
Galli-Curci. Recorded for Columbia & Indestructible Cylinders.
*Sources: SB rosters, programs, & photos; roster in Musical Courier,
9 Jun 1915; 1915 Tuxedo tobacco advertisement with SB musicians'
signatures; roster in Dec, 1916 New York Musician and Knocker; various
1919-20 tour rosters; references in PBks; author's correspondence with
family and with Frederick P. Williams, discographer.*

FULGHUM, RALPH, *valet & encore card boy*
Sousa's personal valet & holder of encore cards ("card boy") at concerts,
2nd 1927 tour & 1928 tour.
*SB payrolls; Otto Kraushaar's autobiography; references in SBFS
News.*

FULLER, ARBOR L. ROBERT (Bob), *tuba*
1928 tour; 1929 tour; one or more of 1930 tours. Member, SBFS. d.
1969.
*Sources: SB payrolls & photos; Eugene Slick's 1928 autograph book;
Jay Sims' 1930 tour roster; references in SBFS News.*

FULTZ, JOHANN HAROLD, *trombone*
Date(s) of SB service uncertain, but probably briefly in late 1920s. Other
position: U.S. Navy Band. Composer. Member, SBFS.
*Sources: The Heritage Encyclopedia of Band Music; SBFS News, Jan,
1953, p. 15; author's interviews with Kenneth B. Slater, bandmaster.*

FUNARO, PASQUALE CHARLES, *euphonium, trombone*
2nd 1904 tour (in trombone ensemble, Pittsburgh Exposition); 1st 1905
tour (Britain). Other positions: Metropolitan Opera Orchestra; Kryl's Band;
Conway's Band; John Duss Band (Pittsburgh) (also assistant conductor).
*Sources: SB programs; S.S. Baltic ship's list, 19 May 1905; Bands of
America, p. 273; PBk 21, p. 24; author's correspondence with family.*

FURSH-MADI, EMMY, *soprano*
Soloist. 1st part of 1893 tour. Other positions: Sang opera in France,
England, and U.S.A. b. 1847, Bayonne, France; d. 20 Sep 1894, Warrens-
ville, NJ.
*Sources: SB programs; Baker's Biographical Dictionary of Musicians;
Metronome, Apr, 1893; references in PBk 2.*

GAETNER, LEONTINE, *cello*
1897 tour (partial).
Source: PBk 5, p. 16.

GAILEY, MARY, *violin*
Soloist. 1916 tour (partial); 1917 WG (partial); 1918 WG (partial).
Sources: SB programs; Instrumentalist, Feb, 1972, p. 70; Grand Rapids Press, 5 Jan 1971; Clarence J. Russell's diary; references in PBk 44; author's correspondence with Harold Geerdes, researcher.

GALASSI, ANTONIO, *baritone (vocal)*
Soloist. 1st & 2nd 1892 tours; 1893 St. Louis Exposition (partial); possibly other tours in 1893.
Sources: SB programs; SB incidental receipts signed by Galassi; references in PBk 1.

GALLUCHI, NICOLA, *euphonium*
1929 radio broadcasts. Other positions: Goldman Band; Cities Service Band of America.
Source: SB payroll 6 May 1929; correspondence with Loras J. Schissel, music historian.

GARDNER, BIRLEY, *cornet/trumpet*
1928 tour; off-tour concert, 15 Jun 1929, Princeton, NJ. Other positions: Pryor's Band; U.S. Navy Band; U.S. Naval Academy Band; Long Beach (CA) Municipal Band; conductor of Navajo Indian Band (Window Rock, AZ). Member, SBFS. b. 27 Mar 1898; d. 3 Jun 1978, Long Beach, CA.
Sources: SB payrolls & photos; references in SBFS News; author's interview and correspondence with Gardner.

GARDNER, DONALD C., *tuba*
1921-22 tour; 1922 tour; 1925-26 tour (partial). Other Positions: Pryor's Band; Thaviu's Band; Conway's Band; Bachman's Million Dollar Band; Indianapolis, IN, theater orchestras. Recorded for Columbia & Emerson. Member, SBFS. b. 7 Feb 1882; d. Dec, 1974, Liberty, IN.
Sources: SB rosters & payrolls; roster in Jacobs' Band Monthly, Aug, 1925; references in SBFS News; author's interview and correspondence with Gardner; Social Security Death Index.

GARING, ATHOL JOHN, (A. J.) *euphonium*
1909 tour; possibly both 1910 tours; 1911 world tour; probably 1912 tour; 1913 tour (**soloist** at Pittsburgh Exposition); 1914 tour; 1915 tour; 1915-16 New York Hippodrome; possibly 1916 tour; 1916-17 tour. Arranger/copyist; sometimes business manager. Other positions: Conductor of orchestra at some New York Hippodrome shows; conductor of Furman University Band & Georgia Tech University Band & Shrine Band in Greenville, SC; contractor for American Federation of Musicians. Composer. Member, SBFS.
Sources: SB rosters & photos; roster in Albert A. Knecht's world tour diary; Edmund A. Wall's world tour poem; signature on 6 Nov 1914 birthday card from band members to Sousa (refers to first year with band as 1909); roster in Musical Courier, 9 Jun 1915; 1915 Tuxedo tobacco advertisement with SB musicians' signatures; roster in Dec, 1916 New York Musician and Knocker; Supplement to the Heritage Encyclopedia of Band Music; advertisement in Conn Musical Truth, Feb, 1926; references in SBFS News; references in PBks 38, 42, 44, & 54; Clarence J. Russell's diary.

GARRETT, DANA M., *cornet/trumpet*
1923-24 tour (cornet **soloist** at WG); 1924 tour (**soloist** at WG); 1925-26 tour; possibly 1926 WG. Member, SBFS.
Sources: SB payrolls, programs, & photos; roster in Jacobs' Band Monthly, Aug, 1925; 1925-26 SB hotel assignment list; references in SBFS News.

GARRETT, PAUL, *B-flat clarinet*
With SB for short period sometime between 1919 & 1926. Other positions: National Symphony Orchestra; Almas Temple Shrine Band (Washington, DC).
Source: Author's interviews with Kenneth B. Slater, bandmaster.

*GARRISON, MARTHA, *soprano*
Soloist. 1896 MB (partial).
Source: PBk 4, pp. 62 & 63.

*GARTRELL, LUZY, *soprano*
Soloist. 1895 Cotton State Exposition (partial).
Source: Programs in Atlanta Constitution.

GATLEY, ERNEST C., *B-flat clarinet*
1911 world tour. b. 1876, Portland, ME.
Sources: Roster in Albert A. Knecht's world tour diary; Edmund A. Wall's world tour poem; SBFS News, Dec, 1951, p. 19.

*GAUDENZI, GIUSEPPI, *tenor (vocal)*
Soloist, 9 Jan 1916, New York.
Source: Clarence J. Russell's diary.

GAUGLER, GUY GEORGE (Washy Hose), *cornet/trumpet, librarian*
One or both 1910 tours; 1911 world tour; probably 1912 & 1913 tours; 1914 tour; 1915 tour; probably 1915-16 New York Hippodrome; 1916-17 tour; probably 1917 & 1918 tours; 1919-20 tour; 1923-24 tour; 1924 tour; 1925-26 tour; 1926 StPr. Served in U.S. Army in Cuba during Spanish-American War. Other positions: Calhoun Military Band; Pryor's Band; New York Hippodrome Orchestra; Washington, D.C. theater orchestras; music faculty, Washington (DC) College of Music. Member, SBFS. d. 12 Jun 1953, Philadelphia, PA.
Sources: SB payrolls, rosters, programs, & photos; signature on 6 Nov 1914 birthday card from band members to Sousa (refers to first year with band as 1910); roster in Albert A. Knecht's world tour diary; Edmund A. Wall's world tour poem; roster in Musical Courier, 9 Jun 1915; 1915 Tuxedo tobacco advertisement with SB musicians' signatures; roster in Dec, 1916 New York Musician and Knocker; handwritten 1919 roster, presumably by SB member; roster in Jacobs' Band Monthly, Aug, 1925; 1925-26 SB hotel assignment list; references in SBFS News; author's correspondence with family.

GAVIN, EVERT A., *B-flat clarinet*
1925-26 tour (partial); 1926 WG. Other position: Ringling Bros. and Barnum & Bailey Circus Band.
Sources: SB payroll 11 Jul 1925; roster in Jacobs' Band Monthly, Aug, 1925.

GEBHART, WILLIAM C., *horn*
Date(s) of SB service uncertain. Member, SBFS.
Sources: References in SBFS News.

GEISE, HENRY, *B-flat clarinet*
Possibly both 1892 tours; possibly 1st 1893 tour; 2nd 1893 tour; probably some tours in 1894, 1895, & 1896; 1896-97 tour.
Sources: Composite 1895/96 SB photo; program of 17 Oct 1893 in St. Louis Post Dispatch; seating chart in Philadelphia Press, 7 May 1897.

GEITHE, ARTHUR, *horn*
1st 1917 tour (**soloist** at Dominion Park [Quebec]); possibly 2nd 1917 tour.
Sources: SB programs for Jul, 1917.

GENS, WILLIAM C. (Bill), *tuba*
Apparently in band for a short period in 1922, 1923, or 1924. Other positions: Bay State Orchestra; 1st Massachusetts Regt. Band during World War I; 71st New York Regt. Band; Pryor's Band; Aleppo Temple Shrine Band (Boston); Salaam Temple Shrine Band (Newark, NJ); Sphinx Temple Shrine Band (Hartford, CT). Member, SBFS (Vice President, 1951-52; President, 1952-58).
Sources: References in SBFS News.

GENTILE, AMERICO, *B-flat clarinet, bass clarinet*
Probably one or more tours in 1906; 1907 tour; possibly other tours between 1909-1913. Other positions: Goldman Band; conductor of 69th New York Regt. Band. Charter member, SBFS. d. 13 Dec 1945, New York.
Sources: Roster in New York Dramatic Mirror, 7 Sep 1907; references in PBks 53 & 55; references in SBFS News.

GENTILE, ERNEST E., *trombone*
1916-17 tour; 1st 1917 tour. Other positions: New York theater orchestras; assistant conductor of a U.S. Marine Corps band during World War I; assistant conductor, 307th U.S. Infantry Regt. Band; conductor of Edenton (NC) High School Band. Charter member, SBFS. d. ca. 1962.
Sources: SB programs 14-29 Jul, 1917; roster in Dec, 1916 New York Musician and Knocker; PBk 44, pp. 51 & 58; references in SBFS News.

GENTILE, PIRRO, *bass clarinet*
1st part of 1919-20 tour.
Sources: Various 1919-20 tour rosters; Berger roster.

GEOFFRINE, _____, *instrument?*
1st 1892 tour.
Source: Blakely papers.

GERARD, see GUERARD

*GERARD-BRAUN, RUBY, *violin*
Soloist, 6 Apr 1902, New York.
Sources: PBk 18, p. 124; PBk 19, p. 158.

GERHARDT, PAUL OSCAR, *oboe*
Possibly 1912 and/or 1913 tours; 1915 tour; possibly other tours between 1916 & 1918; 1920 tour; 1921 tour; 1921-22 tour; 1922 tour; 1923-24

tour; 1924 tour; 1925-26 tour; 1926 tour; 1929 radio broadcasts; one or more of 1930 tours; 9 Apr 1931 radio broadcast; 1932 radio broadcasts. Charter member, SBFS. d. 26 Mar 1952.

Sources: SB payrolls, rosters, & photos; roster in Musical Courier, *9 Jun 1915; 1915 Tuxedo tobacco advertisement with SB musicians' signatures; roster in* Jacob's Band Monthly, *Aug, 1925; 1925-26 SB hotel assignment list; references in SBFS News.*

GERICKE, CHARLES, *percussion*
1st 1892 tour; possibly 2nd 1892 tour; 1st 1893 tour; possibly all 1894 & 1895 tours; 1st 1896 tour; possibly 2nd 1896 tour; 1896-97 tour; possibly later tours. Other positions: Cappa's 7th Regt. New York Band. Brother of Oscar Gericke.

Sources: SB payrolls and photos; advertisement in J.W. Pepper Musical Times and Band Journal, Spring, 1895; seating chart in Philadelphia Press, *7 May 1897; advertisement in* Leedy Drum Topics, *Aug, 1934; author's correspondence with Russ Girsberger, music librarian.*

GERICKE, OSCAR, *percussion*
1st 1892 tour; possibly 2nd 1892 tour; possibly 1st 1893 tour; 2nd 1893 tour; probably other tours in 1894; possibly 1st, 2nd, and 3rd 1895 tours; 4th 1895 tour; 1st 1896 tour; possibly 1896-97 tour; possibly other tours between 1898-1901; 4th 1901 tour (Britain). Brother of Charles Gericke.

Sources: SB payrolls & photos; advertisement in J.W. Pepper Musical Times and Band Journal, Spring, 1895; signature in Lester Levy's autograph book, Nov 1895; SB/Grenadier Guards banquet seating chart of 17 Oct 1901; advertisement in Leedy Drum Topics, *Aug, 1934; author's correspondence with Russ Girsberger, music librarian.*

GERMOND, GEORGE H., *B-flat clarinet*
2nd 1927 tour; 1928 tour. Other positions: Anglo-Canadian Leather Co. Band. Member, SBFS.

Sources: SB payrolls & photos; 1927 SB hotel assignment list; Eugene Slick's 1928 autograph book; references in SBFS News.

GERSTENBERGER, EMIL, *B-flat clarinet*
Possibly 1st, 2nd, & 3rd 1895 tours; 4th 1895 tour; 1st 1896 tour; possibly other tours in 1896; 1896-97 tour; probably 1897 tour; possibly 1st & 2nd 1898 tours; 3rd 1898 tour. Other position: Gilmore's Band.

Sources: SB payrolls & photos; signature in Lester Levy's autograph book, Nov, 1895; seating chart in St. Louis Post-Dispatch, *25 Sep 1898.*

GERTH, FRANK, *management*
Evidently SB treasurer for a short period; a receipt of $1,754.00 for band salaries, dated 3 Dec 1892, was received from Gerth by Thomas F. Shannon, SB personnel manager.

Source: Blakely papers.

GIACHETTI, WILLIAM, *percussion*
Probably 3rd 1898 tour; possibly other tours in late 1890s.

Source: SBFS News, Jul, 1954, p. 19.

GIANDONATO, see GINDONATO, P.

GIBBS, ARTHUR ERNEST, *trombone*
1921-22 tour.

Sources: 1921 SB photo; 1921-22 SB roster.

GILL, GEORGE, *bassoon*
4th 1901 tour (Britain); 3rd 1902 tour; 1st 1903 tour (Europe); 1907 tour; 2nd 1908 tour; possibly other tours between 1901 & 1909.

Sources: SB payrolls, rosters, & photos; rosters in New York Dramatic Mirror, *7 Sep 1907 & 1 Sep 1908; "In Memoriam" list, SBFS organizational booklet (1945).*

GILLESPIE, EARL H., *horn*
Possibly 1st 1927 tour; 2nd 1927 tour.

Sources: SB payroll 16 Jul 1927; 1927 SB hotel assignment list; references in SBFS News.

GILLILAND, BRADFORD D., *cornet/trumpet*
1st 1905 tour (Britain); possibly other tours between 1901-04. Other positions: Baker Opera Orchestra; C.G. Philips Uncle Tom Co. Orchestra; Prouty Famous Orchestra (Nassau, Bohme Islands); U.S. Marine Band; Brooke's Chicago Marine Band; theater orchestras; conductor of Kilties Band (Canada) & Boston Lyric Opera Co. Orchestra & Warren (OH) Black Hussar Band; music faculty, Warren (OH) Military Band School. Composer.

Sources: S.S. Baltic ship's list, 19 May 1905; The Heritage Encyclopedia of Band Music; Conn Musical Truth, May, 1904 & May, 1915; Musical Messenger, Apr & Jul, 1918; publicity brochure in PBk 21, p. 294.

GINDONATO, P., *horn*
1921 tour.

Sources: 1921 SB roster; advertisement in Conn Musical Truth, *Oct, 1921 (Sousa Edition); SBFS News, Feb, 1955, p. 15.*

GIONONNE, E., *euphonium*
1st 1896 tour; possibly 2nd 1896 tour & MB; 1896-97 tour; possibly later tours. Other positions: Liberati's Grand Military Band.

Sources: SB payrolls; seating chart in Philadelphia Press, *7 May 1897.* Bands of America, p. 273.

GIONNONE, G., *B-flat clarinet*
3rd 1898 tour; possibly other tours in late 1890s.

Source: Seating chart in St. Louis Post-Dispatch, *25 Sep 1898.*

GIORDANO, FRANK R., *B-flat clarinet*
2nd 1908 tour; possibly other tours.

Sources: Roster in New York Dramatic Mirror, *1 Sep 1908; 1904 New York musicians' union directory.*

GIOVANNONE, TOMASO, *tuba*
3rd 1894 tour; 1st 1896 tour; 1896-97 tour; possibly other tours between 1893-97.

Sources: 1896 SB payrolls; 11 Oct 1896 program in St. Louis Post-Dispatch *(in tuba/trombone quartet); composite 1895/96 SB photo; seating chart in* Philadelphia Press, *7 May, 1897.*

GLEASON, AMBROSE NEIL (Matt), *trombone*
1925-26 tour (partial). Member, SBFS.

Sources: SB payroll 11 Jul 1925; roster in Jacobs' Band Monthly, *Aug, 1925; 1925-26 SB hotel assignment list; references in SBFS News.*

*GLENUM, ARTHUR R. (Waxie), *oboe*
Substituted for short periods between 1920-24, probably at WG. Other positions: Almas Temple Shrine Band (Washington, DC).

Source: Author's interviews with Glenum & with Kenneth B. Slater, bandmaster.

GLINES, see MOODY, MARJORIE

*GLOVER, MARIE, *soprano*
Soloist. 1896 MB (partial).

Sources: SB programs in PBk 4, pp. 20, 21.

GLUCK, MARGEL, *violin*
Soloist. 1913 tour; 1914 tour (Pittsburgh Exposition & last half of tour); 1915 tour (1st half of tour).

Sources: SB programs; references in PBks; Clarence J. Russell's diary.

GOBLE, WALTER, *tuba*
1920 WG. Possibly remainder of 1920 tour.

Source: Roster in 1920 WG programs.

*GODBOLD, IRA M., *contralto*
Soloist, 3 Dec 1893, Brooklyn, NY.

Source: SB program in PBk 3, p. 47.

GOEDERTIER, G., *horn*
1916-17 tour.

Source: Roster in New York Musician and Knocker, *Dec, 1916.*

GOETTLER, CHARLES, *management*
Advance man for 1st 1917 tour and possibly others.

Source: Variety, 10 Aug 1917.

GONZALES, GUILLERMO, *studio conductor*
Conducted SB in Victor studio for at least one recording in 1919.

Source: Discographic data from Frederick P. Williams.

GONZALES, JOSE, *cornet/trumpet*
1st 1895 tour; possibly other tours.

Sources: Metronome, Jan, 1895.

GOODING, G. ROBERT, *saxophone*
1924 tour (**soloist**). Other positions: Portland (OR) Symphony Orchestra (as oboist); conductor of 90th Winnipeg Rifles Band & Dallas City Temple Saxophone Band & British cavalry band (in Honolulu). Served with British Army in India, South Africa, and Egypt; served with U.S. Army before World War I.

Sources: SB payroll 27 Nov 1924; SB programs; The Saxophone Symposium, Vol. 23 (1998); photos & articles in PBks 64 & 66.

GOODMAN, WILBUR, *saxophone*
1929 radio broadcast; 9 Apr 1931 radio broadcast; late 1931 radio broadcasts.

Sources: SB payrolls.

GOODRICH, GERALD E., *saxophone*
1924 tour; 1925-26 tour (partial). Other positions: Karl Rhode Orchestra (Boston); theater orchestras; directed own dance orchestra; private music teacher. Member, SBFS. b. 31 Oct 1899, Brentwood, NH; d. 25 Aug 1965, Bradford, NH.
Sources: SB payrolls, programs, & photos; 1925-26 SB hotel assignment list; Conn Musical Truth, Feb, 1926; references in SBFS News.

GORODNER, A., *instrument?*
Believed to have played with SB for a very short period, possibly the 2nd or 3rd 1930 tour.
Source: Jay Sims handwritten financial papers.

*GOULDEN, FLORENCE, *contralto*
Soloist. 1924 WG (partial); 1925 WG (partial).
Sources: SB programs; photos & articles in PBks 67 & 68.

GOULDEN, HOWARD N., *percussion*
Xylophone **soloist.** 1920 tour; 1921 tour; 1921-22 tour; 1922 tour; 1923-24 tour; 1924 tour; 1925-26 tour; 1926 tour; 1st & 2nd 1927 tours; 1928 tour; 1929 radio broadcasts; 1929 tour; 12 Mar 1930 radio broadcast; one or more of 1930 tours; 12 Mar 1931 recording; 9 Apr 1931 radio broadcast; late 1931 radio broadcasts; was leader of "jazz band" ensemble of the SB during the 1920s. Other positions: Pryor's Band; theater orchestras in New York, Chicago, Minneapolis, & Kansas City; radio studio orchestras; Raymond Paige Orchestra; bandsman in U.S. Navy during World War I. Charter member, SBFS.
Sources: SB payrolls, rosters, programs, & photos; Leedy Drum Topics, 15 Jun 1923, 15 Oct 1924, 30 Jul 1925, Mar, 1928, Dec, 1928, & Oct, 1939; references in PBks; references in SBFS News; author's correspondence with family & with Russ Girsberger, music librarian.

GRABNER, FRED D., *tuba*
1923-24 tour (partial). b. ca. 1888; d. 23 Jul 1923, Pottsville, PA, while on tour with SB.
Sources: 1923-24 SB payrolls; references in PBks 61 & 62; "In Memoriam" list, SBFS organizational booklet (1945).

*GRAHAM, FRED, *tenor (vocal)*
Soloist, 19 May 1915, Salt Lake City, UT.
Source: Clarence J. Russell's diary.

GRAHAM, JOHN, *management*
Management staff, approx. 1904-10, probably as advance man.
Sources: PBk 34, p. 124; PBk 44, pp. 64 & 67; Bridgeport (CT) Daily Standard, 22 Dec 1909.

GRANT, EDWARD E., *horn*
One or more of 1930 tours; 1931 tour. Member, SBFS.
Sources: Jay Sims' 1930 tour roster & handwritten checklist for 1931 tour; references in SBFS News.

GRANT, THEODORE R., *B-flat clarinet*
Date(s) of SB service uncertain. Member, SBFS.
Sources: References in SBFS News.

GRANTHAM, J. HOWARD, *saxophone*
1921-22 tour (partial).
Sources: 1921 SB photo; 1921-22 SB roster.

GRAY, BETTY, *contralto*
Soloist. 1919 WG (partial); 1920 WG (partial); 1921 WG (partial); 1926 WG (partial); 2nd 1927 tour (partial).
Sources: SB programs; references in PBks; references in SBFS News.

GRAY, LESTER M., *trombone*
1923-24 tour; 1924 tour; 1926 tour. Charter member, SBFS (Vice President, 1958-63). d. ca. 1962.
Sources: SB payrolls & photos; references in SBFS News; author's interview with Gray.

GREEN, JOSEPH (Joe), *percussion*
1917 WG (xylophone **soloist**); possibly remainder of 1917 tour; 1918 tour (xylophone **soloist**); 1919-20 tour. Other positions: Kryl's Band; theater & hotel orchestras; house drummer at Victor recording studio; NBC radio staff drummer. Recorded for Columbia & Victor. Composer and author.
Sources: Various 1919-20 tour rosters; advertisement in Conn Musical Truth, Oct, 1921 (Sousa Edition); Leedy Drum Topics, 15 Jul 1924, Jul, 1927 & Jan, 1939; references in PBks; SBFS News, Feb, 1955, p. 12; author's correspondence with Frederick P. Williams, discographer & with Russ Girsberger, music librarian.

GREYBACK, JOSEPH P. (Joe), *B-flat clarinet*
1928 tour.
Sources: 1928 SB payrolls; references in SBFS News.

GRIEVE, WILLIAM L., *trombone*
Date(s) of SB service uncertain but probably part of one tour in 1921, 1922, or 1923. Member, SBFS. d. ca. 1950, Rochester, NY.
Sources: Short all-time SB roster in the Constitution and By-Laws of the Sousa Band Fraternal Society, dated May, 1945; references in SBFS News.

*GRIFFETHS, HARRY, *baritone (vocal)*
Soloist, 26 Nov 1916, Boston.
Source: Boston Herald, 26 Nov 1916.

GRIFFIN, WILLIAM, *cornet/trumpet*
1st 1893 tour; 2nd 1893 tour; 1st 1894 tour; 2nd 1894 Madison Square Garden engagement (**soloist**); 1894 MB; 4th 1895 tour; 1st 1896 tour; possibly other tours between 1892-1896. Other positions: Cappa's 7th Regt. Band (New York).
Sources: SB payrolls; signature in Lester Levy's autograph book, Nov, 1895; references in PBks.

GRISWOLD, ARTHUR L. (Shorty), *tuba*
1911 world tour; 1912 tour; possibly other tours.
Sources: 1912 SB photo; roster in Albert A. Knecht's world tour diary; Edmund A. Wall's world tour poem; references in SBFS News; signatures & dates on music in SB library at University of Illinois.

GROSSKURTH, AUGUST, *cornet/trumpet*
Probably all tours & engagements between 1895-1908; copyist. Other positions: U.S. Marine Band (before SB). Recorded for Columbia.
Sources: SB payrolls, rosters, programs, & photos; various other rosters; advertisements in music journals. Association of Recorded Sound Collection Journal, 1979; references in PBks; references in SBFS News; author's correspondence with Frederick P. Williams, discographer.

*GRYCE, ELAINE, *soprano*
Soloist, 25 Feb 1894, New York.
Source: Program in PBk 3, p. 54.

GUERARD (GERARD), JOSEPH (Joe), *oboe*
[Apparently changed name from Gerard to Guerard during period with SB]
One or both 1910 tours; 1911 world tour; possibly 1912 & 1913 tours; 1914 tour; 1915 tour; 1916-17 tour.
Sources: Roster in Albert A. Knecht's world tour diary; Edmund A. Wall's world tour poem; signature on 6 Nov 1914 birthday card from band members to Sousa (refers to first year with band as 1910); 1915 Tuxedo tobacco advertisement with SB musicians' signatures; roster in Dec, 1916 New York Musician and Knocker.

GUILLE, ALBERT L., *tenor (vocal)*
Soloist. 1st 1893 tour; 1894 MB (partial). Other positions: Concert artist in Europe; Metropolitan Opera Co. Knighted by King of Portugal. b. Avignon, France.
Sources: Metropolitan Opera Annuls; Marching Along, p. 135; Metronome, Apr, 1893 & Sep, 1894; references in PBk 3.

GUREWITZ, JASCHA (Jack), *saxophone*
1919-20 tour (partial) (**soloist**); 1921 tour (**soloist**). Other positions: Thaviu's Band; theater & vaudeville orchestras. Composer. Served in U.S. Army during World War I. b. 4 Jul 1896, Russia; d. 1940.
References: SB programs, rosters, and photos; A Study of the Saxophone Soloists of the John Philip Sousa Band, 1893-1930; data from Harold B. Stephens, SB saxophonist.

GUSIKOFF, CHARLES, *trombone*
1920 tour (**soloist** at WG). Other position: Philadelphia Orchestra. Member, SBFS.
Sources: Roster in 1920 WG programs; advertisement in Conn Musical Truth, Oct, 1921 (Sousa Edition); references in PBks 54 & 55; references in SBFS News.

GUTHRIE-MOYER, FRANCESCA, *soprano*
Soloist. 2nd 1894 Madison Square Garden engagement (partial); 28 Jun 1894 (Philadelphia); last half of 1894 tour.
Sources: SB programs; Metronome, Jan, 1895; references in PBks.

HAAS, HOWARD, *euphonium*
Possibly 1918 tour; 1921-22 tour (partial). Other position: Allentown (PA) Band.
Sources: 1921-22 SB roster; Morning Call (Allentown), 25 Feb 1975, p. 6; SBFS News, Sep, 1975, p. 10.

HAASE, AUGUST, *euphonium*
1st & 2nd 1892 tours; 1st 1893 tour (**soloist** at Chicago World's Fair); 2nd 1893 tour; probably 3rd 1893 tour; probably 1st & 2nd 1894 tours (**soloist** at Mid-Winter Exposition); 1894 MB (**soloist**); 3rd 1894 tour; probably 1st &

2nd 1895 tours; 3rd 1895 tour (**soloist**); 4th 1895 tour; probably other tours in 1895 & 1897. Composer.

Sources: SB photos, programs, & rosters; The Heritage Encyclopedia of Band Music; 1893 C.G. Conn advertisement; Metronome, Apr, 1893 & Jan, 1895; St. Louis Post-Dispatch, 7, 10, & 14 Oct 1894; advertisement in J.W. Pepper's Musical Times and Band Journal, Spring, 1895 & May, 1898; Lester Levy's autograph book, Nov, 1895.

HACKERT, HENRY L.A., *B-flat clarinet*
2nd 1908 tour; possibly other tours. Composer.
Sources: The Heritage Encyclopedia of Band Music; roster in New York Dramatic Mirror, 1 Sep 1908.

HAGER, JAMES A., *percussion*
1929 radio broadcasts; off-tour concert, 15 Jun 1929, Princeton, NJ; 12 Mar 1931 recording.
Source: SB payrolls.

HAINES, LEROY (Roy), *trombone*
Date(s) of SB service uncertain. Other position: Innes' Band.
Source: "In Memoriam" list, SBFS organizational booklet (1945); Bands of America, p. 241.

***HAINES, THOMAS,** *vocalist*
Soloist. 1894 St. Louis Exposition (partial).
Source: St. Louis Post-Dispatch, 12 Oct 1894.

HALL, CLYDE L., *B-flat clarinet*
1926 tour. Other positions: U.S. Marine Band; Royal Scotch Highlanders Band; Lancaster (PA) City Band; New Holland (PA) Band; Nickel Mine Band. Member, SBFS. b. 5 Aug 1900; d. Jul, 1977, Bird-in-Hand, PA.
Sources: SB payroll for Nov, 1926; 1926 SB photo; author's interview & correspondence with Hall & with Carole Nowicke, band historian; Social Security Death Index.

HALL, EDWARD C. (Eddie), *flute/piccolo*
1925-26 tour; 1926 tour; possibly 1st 1927 tour; 1928 tour.
Sources: SB payrolls & photos; roster in Jacobs' Band Monthly, Aug, 1925; 1925-26 SB hotel assignment list; Eugene Slick's 1928 autograph book; references in SBFS News.

***HALLENBECK, JESSAMINE,** *soprano*
Soloist. 1896 MB (partial)
Sources: Programs in PBk 4.

HALLOWAY, JACK, *euphonium*
Off-tour concert, 15 Jun 1929 Princeton, NJ.
Source: SB payroll 15 Jun 1929.

HAMANN, RICHARD, *flute/piccolo*
2nd 1908 tour; possibly other tours.
Source: Roster in New York Dramatic Mirror, 1 Sep 1908.

***HAMILTON, CAROLINE,** *soprano*
Soloist. 1893 MB (partial).
Sources: PBk 2, pp. 49 & 53.

***HAMILTON, RACHEL JANE,** *soprano*
Soloist. 1924 WG (partial).
Sources: SB programs; publicity in Philadelphia newspapers (PBks).

HAND, HERMANN, *horn*
1911 world tour; possibly other tours of that period; arranger & copyist. Other positions: symphony and opera orchestras in New York.
Sources: Roster in Albert A. Knecht's world tour diary; Edmund A. Wall's world tour poem; references in PBks 34 & 40; references in SBFS News; correspondence with Loras J. Schissel, music historian.

***HANFORD, KATE DEWEY,** *soprano*
1899 MB (partial).
Sources: SB programs in PBk 9, pp. 35-41.

HANKINS, ROSS, *flute/piccolo*
1929 radio broadcasts.
Sources: SB payrolls.

HARDEMAN, FLORENCE, *violin*
Soloist. 1909 tour; off-tour concerts, 26 Dec 1909, 2 & 9 Jan 1910, & 13-14 Aug 1910; 1910 WG (partial); 3 Oct 1915, New York; 1916 WG (partial); 1918 WG (partial); 1919 WG (partial); 1919-20 tour; 1920 tour starting with WG; 1921 tour after WG; 1921-22 tour. Other position: Toured with contralto Ernestine Schumann-Heink. b. Covington, KY.
Sources: SB rosters, programs, & photos; Clarence J. Russell's diary; Portraits of the World's Best-Known Musicians; references in PBks.

HARPER, J. ERNEST, *B-flat clarinet*
1920 WG; 1921 tour. Member, SBFS.

Sources: SB rosters & photos; advertisement in Conn Musical Truth, Oct, 1921 (Sousa Edition); references in SBFS News; author's correspondence with Harper.

***HARRIGAN, WILLIAM,** *tenor (vocal)*
Soloist, 19 Mar 1916, 26 Nov 1916, & 11-18 Mar 1917, New York (as character singer). Other positions: Actor in theater in America. b. ca. 1894; d. 1 Feb 1966, New York.
Sources: Clarence J. Russell's diary; Variety, 9 Feb 1966, p. 54 [obituary]; PBk 44, p. 56.

HARRINGTON, JAMES N., *percussion*
1914 tour.
Sources: Signature on 6 Nov 1914 birthday card from band members to Sousa (refers to first year with band as 1914; advertisement in Leedy Drum Topics, Aug, 1934; author's correspondence with Russ Girsberger, music librarian.

HARRIS, AARON, *euphonium*
Probably 1st or 2nd 1917 tour; possibly 1918 tour; 1919-20 tour; one or more of 1930 tours. Member, SBFS.
Sources: Advertisement in Conn Musical Truth, Oct, 1921 (Sousa Edition); 1930 SB photo; references in SBFS News; partial roster in George Ford Collection.

HARRIS, CHARLES W. (Cy), *trombone*
1919-20 tour (partial); off-tour concert, 15 Jun 1929, Princeton, NJ; 12 Mar 1930 radio broadcast; 12 Mar 1931 recording; 9 Apr 1931 radio broadcast; late 1931 radio broadcasts. Other positions: Vaudeville & theater orchestras. Charter member, SBFS (Board of Governors, 1944-48). d. Jul, 1962.
Sources: SB payrolls; various 1919-20 tour rosters; advertisement in Conn Musical Truth, Oct, 1921 (Sousa Edition); references in SBFS News.

HARRIS, SAMUEL (Sam, Sammie), *B-flat clarinet*
1912 tour; probably 1913 tour; 1914 tour; 1915 tour; 1915-16 *Hip! Hip! Hooray!* engagement; 1916-17 tour; probably 1918 tour; 1919-20 tour; collected clippings for SB PBks some years. Other position: John C. Weber's Prize Band of America (Cincinnati). Member, SBFS.
Sources: SB rosters & photos; signature on 6 Nov 1914 birthday card from band members to Sousa (refers to first year with band as 1912); roster in Musical Courier, 9 Jun 1915; 1915 Tuxedo tobacco advertisement with SB musicians' signatures; roster in Dec, 1916 New York Musician and Knocker; various 1919-20 tour rosters; Gras Clarinet Co. advertisements in Musical Messenger, Mar, 1921 & Jan, 1922; PBk 44, pp. 11 & 66; references in SBFS News.

HARRIS, WALTER B., JR., *B-flat clarinet*
2nd 1927 tour; 1928 tour; off-tour concert, 15 Jun 1929, Princeton, NJ; 1929 & 1930 radio broadcasts; one or more of 1930 tours; Charter member, SBFS.
Sources: SB payrolls, rosters, & photos; 1927 SB hotel assignment list; references in SBFS News.

***HARRISON, BEATRICE,** *cello*
Soloist, 2 Jan 1916, New York Hippodrome. Other position: Concert artist in England. Recorded for HMV & Victor. b. Roorkee, India.
Sources: Clarence J. Russell's diary; PBk 42, pp. 68 & 70; author's correspondence with Frederick P. Williams, discographer.

***HARROLD, ORVILLE,** *tenor (vocal)*
Several concerts Oct, 1915-Feb, 1916, New York. Other positions: Metropolitan Opera Co.; London Opera House; toured as concert artist; sang in vaudeville and light opera. Recorded for Victor & Columbia. b. Delaware County, IN, 1878; d. 23 Oct 1933, Darien, CT.
Sources: Clarence J. Russell's diary; Metropolitan Opera Annuls; Who Was Who in America, Vol. 1; Portraits of the World's Best-Known Musicians; references in PBk 42.

***HARRYMAN, MRS. AMOS,** *soprano*
Soloist, 26 Mar 1900, Baltimore (substituted for Blanche Duffield).
Source: PBk 9, p. 71.

***HARTMANN, ARTHUR,** *violin*
Soloist. 1894 MB (partial). Other positions: Toured in America and Europe as concert artist; music faculty, Eastman School of Music; private music teacher. Composer and transcriber. Author. b. 23 Jul 1881, Maté Szalka, Hungary.
Sources: SB programs; Baker's Biographical Dictionary of Musicians; The New Grove Dictionary of American Music; references in PBk 3.

HARVEY, H.S., *cornet/trumpet*
Apparently with SB briefly sometime before 1921. Other positions: Snedeker's Band (New York); recording studio musician.
Source: Advertisement in Conn Musical Truth, *Oct, 1921 (Sousa Edition).*

HAUSER, ERIC, *horn*
1929 & 1930 radio broadcasts; 12 Mar 1931 recording; 9 Apr 1931 radio broadcast; late 1931 radio broadcasts.
Sources: SB payrolls.

HAVENS, see HOWARD, M.B.

HAVILLAND, see ALLEN, LUCY

HAYNES, M. FRANCIS (Frank), *percussion*
Probably 1909 tour; possibly both 1910 tours; 1911 world tour; possibly 1912 & 1913 tours; 1914 tour; 1915 tour; 1916-17 tour. Member, SBFS. d. ca. 1949.
Sources: Albert A. Knecht's world tour diary; Edmund A. Wall's world tour poem; signature on 6 Nov 1914 birthday card from band members to Sousa (refers to first year with band as 1909); roster in Musical Courier, *9 Jun 1915; 1915 Tuxedo tobacco advertisement with SB musicians' signatures; roster in Dec, 1916* New York Musician and Knocker; *PBk 44, p. 66; advertisement in* Leedy Drum Topics, *Aug, 1934; references in SBFS News; author's correspondence with Russ Girsberger, music librarian.*

HAZEL, JOHN T. *cornet/trumpet*
Probably part of one tour, early 1900s. Other positions: Hadley's American Band of Providence; Gilmore's Band; Buffalo Bill's Cowboy Band; Boston Festival Orchestra; conductor, Repasz Band (Williamsport, PA), 1910-1941. Recorded for Columbia, Edison, U.S. Everlasting Cylinders, & Zonophone. b. 28 Sep 1865, Bellefonte, PA; d. 26 Jun 1948, Williamsport, PA
Sources: The Heritage Encyclopedia of Band Music; Supplement to the Heritage Encyclopedia of Band Music; Metronome, *Jul, 1910, p. 47; author's correspondence with John Hunsinger, Hazel's biographer, & with Frederick P. Williams, discographer.*

HEATER, EARL F., *cornet/trumpet*
2nd 1927 tour; one or more of 1930 tours; 1931 tour. Other positions: Ringgold Band (Reading, PA); Allentown (PA) Band.
Sources: SB payrolls; 1927 SB hotel assignment list; Jay Sims' 1930 tour roster & 1931 handwritten checklist; clippings in the Allentown Band archives; Morning Call *(Allentown), 25 Feb 1975, p. 6; references in SBFS News; correspondence with Loras J. Schissel, music historian.*

HEGNER, WALTER, *saxophone*
12 Mar 1931 recording; 9 Apr 1931 radio broadcast; late 1931 radio broadcasts.
Source: SB payrolls.

HEIDELBERG, HENRY N., *flute/piccolo*
Possibly 1st 1900 tour; 2nd & 3rd 1902 tours; 1st 1903 tour (Europe); possibly other tours between 1904 & 1913; 1914 tour (**soloist** at WG); 1915 tour. Other position: Goldman Band (also personnel manager). Recorded for Columbia.
Sources: 1902 SB programs; roster in New York Dramatic Mirror, *6 Sep 1902; 1903 SB European tour publicity; signature on 6 Nov 1914 birthday card from band members to Sousa (refers to first year with band as 1900); roster in* Musical Courier, *9 Jun 1915; 1915 Tuxedo tobacco advertisement with SB musicians' signatures; author's correspondence with Loras J. Schissel, music historian, & with Frederick P. Williams, discographer.*

HEINRICH, WILLIAM H. (Bill), *flute/piccolo*
Probably 1915-16 New York Hippodrome. Member, SBFS.
Sources: References in SBFS News.

HELD, EARL D., *flute/piccolo*
1st & 2nd 1927 tours; off-tour concert, 15 Jun 1929, Princeton, NJ; 1929 tour; possibly one or more of 1930 tours; 1931 tour. Other positions: Allentown (PA) Band; conductor of Earl Held's All-Girl Band, Easton, PA. Member, SBFS. b. 31 May 1899; d. 17 Feb 1975, Easton, PA.
Sources: SB payrolls; 1927 SB hotel assignment list; Jay Sim's 1930 tour list list; Morning Call *(Allentown), 25 Feb 1975, p. 6; references in SBFS News; Social Security Death Index.*

HELDER, RUBY, *vocalist*
Soloist. 1918 tour. Recorded for Columbia.
Sources: SB programs; author's correspondence with Frederick P. Williams, discographer.

HELLE (HELL), FRANZ (Frank), *flugelhorn*
Probably all tours and engagements between Jun, 1896 & Jun, 1905. Soloist on most. Other positions: Vienna Prater Orchestra; Philadelphia Orchestra; Ohlmeyer Band (San Diego, CA); Coronado Tent City Concert Band (San Diego). Recorded for Victor.
Sources: SB payrolls, rosters, programs, & photos. S.S. Baltic *ship's list, 19 May 1905; Coronado Tent City Concert Band publicity, ca. Jun, 1908; references in PBks; references in SBFS News; author's correspondence with Frederick P. Williams, discographer.*

HELLEBERG, AUGUST, SR. (Gus), *tuba*
Probably all tours & engagements between 3rd 1898 tour & 1st 1903 tour (Europe). Other positions: Chicago Symphony Orchestra; Metropolitan Opera Orchestra; New York Philharmonic; 10th Regiment Band (Denmark); Liberati's Grand Military Band; New York Military Band; Goldman Band; Goldman's Metropolitan Sextette (New York); Conway's Band; private music teacher. Recorded for Brunswick. Father of August Helleberg, Jr. & John Helleberg. b. Jylland, Denmark, 7 Mar 1861.
Sources: SB payrolls, rosters, & photos; roster in St. Louis Post-Dispatch, *25 Sep 1898; SB/Grenadier Guards banquet seating chart, 17 Oct 1901;* Bands of America; Conn Musical Truth, *Sep, 1910, p. 1;* T.U.B.A. Journal, *Summer, 1982, p. 2; references in PBks 6 & 9; references in SBFS News; author's correspondence with John M. Taylor, music historian, with Frederick P. Williams, discographer, and with Jorgen Voigt Arnsted, researcher.*

HELLEBERG, AUGUST, JR. (Gus), *tuba*
1911 world tour; 1915-16 New York Hippodrome; off-tour concert, 15 Jun 1929, Princeton, NJ. Son of August Helleberg, Sr. & brother of John H. Helleberg. b. 1892.
Sources: SB payroll for 15 Jun 1929; SB photos; roster in Albert A. Knecht's world tour diary; Edmund A. Wall's world tour poem.

HELLEBERG, HONUS, *instrument?*
Date(s) of SB service uncertain.
Source: "In Memoriam" list, SBFS organizational booklet (1945).

HELLEBERG, JOHN, *contrabassoon*
2nd 1900 tour (Europe). Other position: Pryor's Band.
Sources: Roster in SB program of 22 Apr 1900; SB photo, 30 May 1900; author's interviews with Kenneth B. Slater, bandmaster.

HELLEBERG, JOHN HENRY, *tuba*
Possibly 2nd 1904 tour; 1st 1905 tour (Europe); 2nd 1905 tour; possibly 3rd & 4th 1905 tours; possibly all 4 tours in 1906; 1907 tour; possibly 1st 1908 tour; 2nd 1908 tour. Son of August Helleberg, Sr. & brother of August Helleberg, Jr. Charter member, SBFS. b. 18 Jun 1886; d. Feb, 1973, Roslyn, NY.
Sources: SB photos; S.S. Baltic *ship's list, 19 May 1905; rosters in* New York Dramatic Mirror *7 Sep 1907 & 1 Sep 1908; references in SBFS News; Social Security Death Index.*

HELMECKE, AUGUST, JR. (Gus), *percussion*
1916-17 tour; most all other tours and engagements, 1919-1931, including radio broadcasts. Other positions: Metropolitan Opera Orchestra; New York Philharmonic; Goldman Band; Bachman's Million Dollar Band; Conway's Band. Recorded for Columbia & Victor. Co-founder, SBFS (President, 1944-47); d. 26 Feb 1954.
Sources: SB payrolls, rosters, programs, & photos; various other rosters; various advertisements in Leedy Drum Topics; *feature articles, photos, & other references in PBks; references in SBFS News; author's correspondence with Frederick P. Williams, discographer, with Martin Snitzer, researcher, & with Russ Girsberger, music librarian.*

HEMUS, PERCY, *baritone (vocal)*
Soloist. 1st & 2nd 1917 tours. Other positions: Comic opera and concert singer; radio actor. Recorded for Victor. b. ca. 1878, Auckland, New Zealand; d. 22 Dec 1943, New York.
Sources: SB programs; Clarence J. Russell's diary; Variety, *29 Dec 1943, p. 39 [obituary]; references in PBk 46; author's correspondence with Frederick P. Williams, discographer.*

HENEY, EDWARD J., *saxophone*
1924 tour; 1925-26 tour; 1926 tour; 1st & 2nd 1927 tours; 1928 tour (**soloist**); 1929 tour (**soloist**); 1929 radio broadcasts; one or more of 1930 tours (**soloist**). Other positions: Scotch Highlanders Band; St. Petersburg (FL) Municipal Band; conductor of Florida Military Academy Band. Brother of John Joseph Heney & William P. Heney. Member, SBFS (Vice President, 1980-85). b. 4 Jul 1901, San Francisco, CA; d. 19 Feb, 1989, Ukiah, CA.

Sources: SB payrolls, rosters, programs, & photos; A Study of the Saxophone Soloists of the John Philip Sousa Band, 1893-1930. St. Petersburg (FL) Times, 26 Jan 1944 & 9 Mar 1989; references in SBFS News; author's interview and correspondence with Heney.

HENEY, JOHN JOSEPH (Johnny), *percussion, other*
1926 tour; 1931 tour (xylophone **soloist**). Percussionist, but on 1926 tour also played saxophone in the saxophone octet and clarinet in a clarinet trio. Other positions: Ringling Bros. and Barnum & Bailey Circus Band; Sells-Floto Circus Band; Hagenback & Wallace Circus Band; Royal Scotch Highlanders Band; McDonald's Highlanders Band; Daytona Beach (FL) Municipal Band and Eddie's Dixie Aces (Daytona Beach); conductor of Stetson University Band & DeLand (FL) school bands & Ketterlinus High School Band (St. Augustine, FL). Composer. Author. Elected to American Bandmasters Assn., 1940. Elected to Florida Bandmasters Assn. Hall of Fame, 1992 (honorary life president). Brother of Edward J. Heney & William P. Heney. Member SBFS (Vice Pres., 1971-78). b. 1902, San Francisco, CA; d. 1 Sep 1978, DeLand, FL.
Sources: SB payrolls, rosters, programs & photos; Bandmen; numerous articles in music journals; references in SBFS News; author's interviews & correspondence with Heney & correspondence with Russ Girsberger, music librarian.

HENEY, WILLIAM P., *valet & encore card boy*
Sousa's valet on 1929 and 1931 tours and possibly one or more of 1930 tours. Also served as "card boy," or holder of the encore cards during concerts. Brother of Edward J. Heney and John Joseph Heney. Member, SBFS.
Sources: 1929 & 1931 SB payrolls; SB photos; references in SBFS; author's correspondence with Heney & with family.

HENNEGAR, RUSSELL D., *cornet/trumpet*
1924 tour. Other positions: Conway's Band; Fred Waring's Orchestra; theater & radio orchestras; conductor of Sioux Falls (SD) Municipal Band & Elks Band (Sioux Falls) & El Riad Shrine Band (Sioux Falls); private music teacher. Elected to American Bandmasters Assn., 1940. Charter member, SBFS. b. 9 Sep 1897, Chamberlain, SD; d. Mar, 1968, Sioux Falls, SD.
Sources: SB payroll 27 Nov 1924; Who Is Who in Music, 1951 edition; advertisement in Conn Musical Truth, Mar, 1925; references in SBFS News; PBK 63, p. 131.

HENTON, H. BENNE (Benny), *saxophone*
1919-20 tour (**soloist**) (partial). Other positions: Weldon's Band; Kryl's Band; Conway's Band. Composer. Recorded for Edison & Victor. b. 23 Oct 1880, Shelbyville, Illinois; d. Philadelphia, PA, 9 Jul 1938.
Sources: SB rosters, programs, & photos; A Study of the Saxophone Soloists of the John Philip Sousa Band, 1893-1930; Portraits of the World's Best-Known Musicians; Jacob's Band Monthly, May, 1923, p. 74, & Jun, 1924, p. 50, & Aug, 1925, p. 61. Metronome, Oct, 1917, p. 52, & Jun, 1927, p. 35; various 1919-20 rosters; Conn Musical Truth, Oct, 1923; author's correspondence with Frederick P. Williams, discographer.

HEPPNER, F., *cornet/trumpet*
1st & 2nd 1893 tours; possibly other tours or engagements. Other position: Innes' Band.
Sources: 1893 SB photo; Varela photo.

HERB, WILLIAM, *tuba*
1924 tour; 1925-26 tour; 1926 tour; 1929 tour; one or more of 1930 tours; 1931 tour. Other positions: Allentown (PA) Band; Ringgold Band (Reading, PA); theater orchestras.
Sources: SB payrolls; roster in Jacobs' Band Monthly, 26 Dec 1925; 1925-26 SB hotel assignment list; Jay Sims' 1931 handwritten checklist; author's interview & correspondence with family; Morning Call, (Allentown), 25 Feb 1975, p. 6.

*HESSELBERG, EDOUARD, *piano*
Soloist, 29 Jan 1908, Nashville, TN. Composer. b. 3 May 1870, Riga, Latvia; d. 12 Jun 1935, Los Angeles, CA.
Sources: The Heritage Encyclopedia of Band Music; Supplement to the Heritage Encyclopedia of Band Music; references in PBks.

HEUSE, F., *B-flat clarinet*
2nd 1900 tour (Europe).
Sources: Roster in SB program of 22 Apr 1900; SB photo, 30 May 1900.

HEWSON, JIMMY, *valet*
Sousa's valet on 1911 world tour.
Sources: Roster in Albert A. Knecht's world tour diary; references in SBFS News.

HEYER, JOHN F., *horn*
Date(s) of SB service uncertain, but probably ca. 1906. Other positions: New York theater orchestras. Charter member, SBFS.
Source: References in SBFS News.

HICKEY, JOHN (Jack), *B-flat clarinet*
2nd 1900 tour (Europe); 4th 1901 tour (Britain); possibly other tours in 1900 & 1901; possibly other tours between 1902 & 1913; 1915 tour.
Sources: SB rosters & photos; SB/Grenadier Guards banquet seating chart of 17 Oct 1901; roster in Musical Courier, 9 Jun 1915; 1915 Tuxedo tobacco advertisement with SB musicians' signatures; references in SBFS News.

HIGGINS, CONRAD, *instrument?*
Date(s) of SB service uncertain.
Source: "In Memoriam" list, SBFS organizational booklet (1945).

HIGGINS, HENRY A., *cornet/trumpet*
Practically all tours & engagements between 4th 1895 tour & 1st 1906 tour; possibly 1907 tour; 2nd 1908 tour; **soloist** on most tours. Recorded for Berliner & Victor (conducted SB on Berliner recordings, 1897-99 & possibly Columbia recordings, 1895).
Sources: SB payrolls, rosters, programs, & photos; Lester Levy's autograph book, Nov, 1895; The Sousa Band A Discography; advertisement in J.W. Pepper's Musical Times and Band Journal, May, 1898; various other rosters; PBk 15, p. 246; author's correspondence with Frederick P. Williams, discographer, & with Keith Clark, researcher.

HIGGINS, THOMAS (Tom), *B-flat clarinet*
1st & 2nd 1906 tour; possibly 1907 tour. Other position: Gilmore's Band.
Sources: Hartford (CT) Evening Post, 15 Jan 1906; Metronome, Feb, 1906.

HILDENBRANDT, CHRISTIAN, *bassoon*
1st & 2nd 1892 tours. Other position: Heinrich's American Opera Orchestra.
Sources: Partial roster in C.G. Conn advertisement, Dec, 1892; Pruyn roster.

*HILL, JULIA, *soprano*
Soloist, 7 May 1916, New York.
Source: Clarence J. Russell's diary.

*HILLS, CHARLOTTE WILLIAM, *soprano*
Soloist, 26 Nov 1916, Boston.
Source: PBk 44, p. 50.

HILTENSMITH, ALBERT J. (Al), *cornet/trumpet*
Probably with SB for a short period before 1921; 1923-24 tour; 1929 radio broadcasts; off-tour concert, 15 Jun 1929, Princeton, NJ; 1929 tour; 12 Mar 1931 recording; 9 Apr 1931 radio broadcast; 1931 tour; late 1931 radio broadcasts. Other positions: Goldman Band; Ringling Bros. and Barnum & Bailey Circus Band. Member, SBFS. d. ca. 1961.
Sources: SB payrolls; advertisement in Conn Musical Truth, Oct, 1921 (Sousa Edition); Jay Sims' handwritten checklist for 1931 tour; references in SBFS News; author's interviews with Kenneth B. Slater, bandmaster.

HINTON, GEORGE FREDERICK, *management*
1897-1903; served as secretary, advance agent, press agent, road manager, assistant manager, business manager, and general manager, not necessarily in that order; was general manager on European tour of 1900. Other positions: Newspaper reporter/editor for Boise (ID) Statesman & New York World; theater manager in New York and England; manager, Manhattan Grand Opera Co.; agent for numerous entertainment figures in England and America, including DeWolf Hopper, Blanche Ring, Lillian Russell, and Fred Astaire. Served in U.S. Army during World War I. b. 5 Dec 1863, New York; d. 19 Nov 1934, Sawtelle, CA.
Sources: SB rosters, programs, & photos; Marching Along, p. 157; Variety, 27 Nov 1934, p. 62 [obituary]; references in PBks & other music journals; references in SBFS News.

*HIRSCHFIELD, AMELIA, *vocalist*
Soloist. 2nd 1894 Madison Square Garden engagement (partial); 1894 MB (partial).
Sources: SB programs in PBk 3.

HOCHSTEIN, DAVID, *violin*
Soloist, 12 Mar 1916, New York. b. 16 Feb 1892, Rochester, NY; d. 12 Oct 1918, Belleau Wood, France.
Sources: Clarence J. Russell's diary; references in PBk 42.

HOFFMAN, GRACE, *soprano*
Soloist. 1st half of 1914 tour; 1915 tour except for Panama-Pacific Exposition in San Francisco; 1916 WG (partial); 2 & 10 Oct 1915, New York; 1916 tour. Other position: Goldman Band. Recorded for Victor.
Sources: SB programs; Clarence J. Russell's diary; Musical America, 30 Sep 1915; references in PBk 40; author's correspondence with Frederick P. Williams, discographer.

HOFMANN, SENTA, *harp*
1931 tour.
Sources: SB payrolls; Jay Sims' handwritten checklist for 1931 tour; author's interview & correspondence with Hoffman & with Loras J. Schissel, music historian.

*HOLDING, ____ , *soprano*
Soloist. 1896 MB (partial).
Source: SB program.

HOLL, WILLIAM BENJAMIN (Bill), *B-flat clarinet*
Possibly part of 1921-22 tour; 1924 tour. Other positions: New York theater orchestras; Boyd Raeburn's Dance Orchestra; music faculty, University of Illinois Band Dept.; conductor of Danville (IL) High School Band; private music teacher. Served in U.S. Army during World War I. Member, SBFS. b. 28 Jul 1895; d. 26 Feb 1985, Danville, IL.
Sources: SB payroll 27 Nov 1924; research by Phyllis Danner, Sousa Archives for Band Research, University of Illinois; references in SBFS News; obituary in Danville newspaper, 27 Feb 1985; author's correspondence with family; Social Security Death Index.

HOLLAND, IRA F., *cornet/trumpet*
3rd 1905 tour (**soloist** at WG); 4th 1905 tour (**soloist** at Pittsburgh Exposition); possibly 1912 tour. Other positions: Reeves' American Band; Clark's Providence (RI) Band.
Sources: SB programs; references in PBks 21 and 24; Berger roster.

HOLMES, W. BURR, *horn*
1928 tour; off-tour concert, 15 Jun 1929, Princeton, NJ; one or more of 1930 tours. Other position: Pryor's Band.
Sources: SB payrolls; Eugene Slick's 1928 autograph book.

HOLT, FRANK, *percussion.*
1st & 2nd 1927 tours; 1928 tour; 1929 tour; one or more of 1930 tours; 1931 tour. Other positions: Ringling Bros. and Barnum & Bailey Circus Band; theater orchestras in Massachusetts, New Hampshire, & Maine; Aleppo Temple Shrine Band (Haverhill, MA); Haverhill Community Band; owner of drum shop in Haverhill; private music teacher. Author. Member, SBFS. b. 12 Sep 1891, Haverhill, MA; d. 20 Jan 1968, Haverhill.
Sources: SB payrolls; Eugene Slick's 1928 autograph book; Jay Sims' 1930 tour roster & handwritten checklist for 1931 tour; references in Leedy Drum Topics, 1927-1932; Holt's diary of 1928 tour in Jacobs' Band Monthly, May, Jun, Jul, & Aug, 1929; Haverhill Gazette, 22 Jan 1968 [obituary]; author's correspondence with family & with Russ Girsberger, music librarian.

HOLT, G. DANA, *cornet/trumpet*
3rd 1894 tour (partial). Other positions: Boston Symphony Orchestra; conductor of Frank L. Callahan's Original Columbian Minstrels Orchestra & Baldwin's Cadet Band & other bands and orchestras in Maine, Connecticut, New Hampshire, & North Carolina. Composer. Recorded for Edison. b. 2 Mar 1874, Dixfield, ME; d. 24 Jul 1950, Dixfield.
Sources: The Heritage Encyclopedia of Band Music; Supplement to the Heritage Encyclopedia of Band Music; Metronome, Oct, 1894, p. 10; Metronome, Jan, 1895, p. 1; author's correspondence with Frederick P. Williams, discographer.

HOLT, WALFRED T. (Wally), *B-flat clarinet*
1928 tour; 1929 tour. Member, SBFS. d. 21 Oct 1962, Houston, TX.
Sources: SB payrolls & photos; Eugene Slick's 1928 autograph book; references in SBFS News.

HOLTON, FRANK, *trombone*
1st 1892 tour; probably 2nd 1892 tour; 1st 1893 tour. Other positions: Ellis Brooks Band; 2nd Regt. Band (Chicago); Hi Henry Minstrels Orchestra; theater & hotel orchestras; founder/operator of Frank Holton Band Instrument Manufacturing Co., Elkhorn, WI. b. 10 Mar 1858, Allegan, MI; d. 17 Apr 1942, Elkhorn, WI.
Sources: Pioneers in Brass; Musical Messenger, Jan, 1917, pp. 1-2; 1892 C.G. Conn advertisement; author's correspondence with Raoul F. Camus, band historian.

HOOKHAM, GEORGE, *tuba*
1920 tour.
Source: Roster in 1920 WG programs.

HOPPE, ROBERT, *horn*
1st & 2nd 1892 tours. b. ca. 1849; d. 1917.
Sources: 1892 C.G. Conn advertisement; Jacobs' Band Monthly, Jul, 1917.

*HOPPER, DeWOLF, *baritone-basso*
Soloist. 1893 MB (partial); 1894 MB (partial); 1897 MB (partial). Other positions: sang in several Sousa operettas (and others) in America and Europe; McCall Opera Co.; Weber and Fields Music Hall Co. Recorded for Victor. b. ca. 1858, New York; d. 22 Sep 1935, Kansas City, MO.
Sources: SB programs; Reminiscences of DeWolf Hopper; Variety, 25 Sep 1935, p. 79 [obituary]; references in PBks; author's correspondence with Frederick P. Williams, discographer.

HORLOCKER, ZORA GLADYS, *contralto*
Soloist. Last part of 1896-97 tour.
Sources: References in PBk 5.

HORNER, ANTON, *horn*
Possibly part of one tour before 1900; 1st & 2nd (Europe) tours; tour 3rd or 4th 1900 tour; 2nd 1901 tour (partial). Other positions: Philadelphia Orchestra; Wassili Leps Symphony Orchestra; Pittsburgh Symphony Orchestra; Philadelphia theater orchestras; Innes' Band; Conway's Band; music faculty, Curtis Institute of Music. Recorded for Victor. Member, SBFS. b. 21 Jun 1877, Grossengrun, Austria; d. 4 Dec 1971, Philadelphia.
Sources: Roster in SB program of 22 Apr 1900; SB photos; The International Musician, Feb, 1972 [obituary]; references in SBFS News; author's interviews & correspondence with Walter I. Kaville, band historian, with Kenneth B. Slater, bandmaster, & with Frederick P. Williams, discographer; Social Security Death Index.

*HOULDING, ____ , *soprano*
Soloist. 1896 MB (partial).
Source: SB program in PBk 4, p. 44.

HOWARD, M. B. (Mose), *saxophone, personnel manager*
Stage name M.B. Howard; given name Moses Bertrand Howard Havens. 1915 tour; 1916-17 tour; possibly 1918 tour; 1919-20 tour (personnel manager). Member, SBFS. d. 1947, San Francisco, CA.
Sources: Clarence J. Russell's diary; roster in Musical Courier, 9 Jun 1915; 1915 Tuxedo tobacco advertisement with SB musicians' signatures; roster in Dec, 1916 New York Musician and Knocker; various 1919-20 tour rosters; author's correspondence with family; references in SBFS News.

HOWARD, NOBLE P., *euphonium*
1926 tour (**soloist** at StPr); possibly 1st 1927 tour; 1928 tour; 1929 tour; one or more of 1930 tours (partial). Other positions: Indianapolis Symphony Orchestra; Ringling Bros. and Barnum & Bailey Circus Band. Member, SBFS. b. 8 Nov 1883; d. May, 1976.
Sources: SB payrolls; references in SBFS News; author's interviews & correspondence with Howard & with Kenneth B. Slater, bandmaster.

*HOWARD, ORVILLE, *tenor (vocal)*
Soloist, 6 & 21 Nov 1915 and 5 & 21 Dec 1915 and 6 Feb 1916, New York.
Sources: Clarence J. Russell's diary; references in PBk 42.

*HOWE, MARY HELEN, *soprano*
Soloist. 1897 MB (partial); 1899 MB (partial).
Sources: SB programs; references in PBks 5 & 9.

HOWLAND, PAUL ESTEY, *B-flat clarinet*
1925-26 tour (partial); 1931 tour. Charter member, SBFS. d. ca. 1967.
Sources: SB payrolls; roster in Jacobs' Band Monthly, Aug, 1925; 1925-26 SB hotel assignment list; references in SBFS News; author interview.

HOXIE, BURTON, *oboe*
1920 tour.
Source: Roster in 1920 WG programs.

HOYLE, DOROTHY (Jennie), *violin*
Name changed from Jennie to Dorothy ca. 1898. **Soloist**. 1st 1898 tour; 2nd 1898 tour (partial); 3rd 1898 tour (partial); 1st & 2nd 1899 tours; last part of 1st 1900 tour; 4th 1901 tour (Britain); off-tour concert 22 Dec 1901 (New York); 1st 1902 tour; 1914 WG (partial). Recorded for Victor. b. Acrington, England.
Sources: SB programs; The Sousa Band A Discography; references in PBks; SBFS News, May, 1951, p. 8.

HOYT, FRANCES and GRACE, *sopranos*
Soloists. 1909 tour. Other positions: Toured in America and England.
Sources: SB programs; references in PBks 31 & 47; publicity booklet, "The Misses Hoyt"; research by Barry Owen Furrer, band historian.

HUBLEY, CLAUDE F., *horn*
1924 tour; 1925-26 tour; 1926 tour; 1931 tour. Other positions: Cincinnati Symphony Orchestra; Utica (NY) Municipal Band. Member, SBFS.
Sources: SB payrolls; roster in Jacobs' Band Monthly, Aug, 1925; 1925-26 SB hotel assignment list; Jay Sims' handwritten checklist for 1931 tour; references in PBk 66; references in SBFS News.

HUDISH, BENJAMIN (Ben, Benny), *horn*
1912 tour; 1913 tour. Other positions: Metropolitan Opera Orchestra; New York Symphony Orchestra; Detroit Symphony Orchestra; Radio City Music Hall Orchestra (New York); New York theater orchestras; 7th Regiment Band (New York); with a U.S. Army band during World War I. Member, SBFS. b. 4 May 1892, Kubilnik, Russia; d. 25 Oct 1991, Brooklyn, NY.
Sources: Instrumentalist, Nov, 1986, p. 10; New York Times, 15 Apr 1986; Bay News (Brooklyn, NY), 4 Jun 1990, pp. 5-6; program of testimonial [to Hudish] banquet, 15 Apr 1986, New York; The Sousa Oral History Project; references in SBFS News; author's correspondence with Hudish, with Raoul F. Camus, band historian, & with Leonard B. Smith, composer; Social Security Death Index.

HUDSON, CARL H., *B-flat clarinet*
1919-20 tour; 1929 radio broadcasts; off-tour concert 15 Jun 1929, Princeton, NJ; 12 Mar 1931 recording; 9 Apr 1931 radio broadcast; late 1931 radio broadcasts. Member, SBFS.
Sources: SB payrolls; roster in Ft. Williams (ONT) Daily Times-Journal, 15 Aug 1919; references in SBFS News.

HUFFMAN, C. GERALD (Jerry), *cornet/trumpet*
2nd 1927 tour; 1928 tour. Other positions: Chicago Symphony Orchestra; Chicago Civic Orchestra; U.S. Navy Band; U.S. Naval Academy Band; Anglo-Canadian Leather Co. Band. Member, SBFS. d. Dec, 1981.
Sources: SB payrolls & photos; 1927 SB hotel assignment list; Eugene Slick's 1928 autograph book; references in SBFS News.

HUGHES, THOMAS A. (Tommy), *B-flat clarinet*
Possibly some 1897 tours; possibly 1st, 2nd, & 3rd 1898 tours; possibly some 1899 tours; possibly 1st 1900 tour; 2nd 1900 tour (Europe); 1915 tour; 1929 radio broadcasts; 12 Mar 1931 recording; 9 Apr 1931 radio broadcast; late 1931 radio broadcasts. Recorded for Columbia. Charter member, SBFS.
Sources: SB payrolls & photos; seating chart in St. Louis Post-Dispatch, 25 Sep 1898; photo in Sousa's personal 1899/1900 photo album; roster in Musical Courier, 9 Jun 1915; 1915 Tuxedo tobacco advertisement with SB musicians' signatures; references in SBFS News; author's correspondence with Frederick P. Williams, discographer.

HUNGERFORD, CHARLES G., *property man*
Listed variously as property man, stagehand, or baggage handler; 1928 tour; one or more of 1930 tours.
Sources: SB payrolls; Eugene Slick's 1928 autograph book; Jay Sims' 1930 tour roster; references in SBFS News; author's correspondence with Loras J. Schissel, music historian.

HUTCHINGS, CARL B., *flute/piccolo*
1922 tour; 1923-24 tour.
Sources: SB payrolls & photos; "In Memoriam" list, SBFS organizational booklet (1945); SBFS News, May, 1983, p. 32.

INGALLS, LEWIS, *percussion*
1st 1892 tour.
Source: Advertisement in Leedy Drum Topics, Aug, 1934; author's correspondence with Russ Girsberger, music librarian.

*INGMAN, RUTH, *soprano*
Sang in quartet with SB on 19 May 1915 at Salt Lake City, UT.
Source: Clarence J. Russell's diary

JABON, FERDINAND, *bassoon*
1st 1892 tour; possibly other tours. Other position: Brussels Grand Opera Orchestra.
Source: Roster in SB promotional booklet, Sep, 1892.

JACOB, OTTO, (Mike), *B-flat clarinet*
1921 tour; 1921-22 tour; 1925-26 tour (partial); 1926 tour; 1st & 2nd 1927 tours. Also copyist.
Sources: SB payrolls and photos; 1925-26 & 1927 SB hotel assignment lists; invoice for music copywork dated 19 Nov 1926; roster in Jacobs'

Band Monthly, *26 Dec 1925;* Bridgeport (CT) Herald, *10 Sep 1922; references in SBFS News.*

*JACOBI, HATTIE, *vocalist*
Soloist. 1901 MB (partial).
Sources: SB programs; references in PBks 16 & 18.

JACOBS, HARRY L., *cornet/trumpet*
Probably 1st 1892 tour (**soloist** in Chicago). Other positions: Brookes' Chicago Marine Band; Chicago theater orchestras. b. Staunton, IL.
Sources: Undated article in Musical Messenger, entitled "Harry L. Jacobs," ca. Mar, 1919.

*JACOBS, HELEN De WITT, *violin*
Soloist. 1915 WG (partial); 12 Dec 1915, New York; 1921 WG (partial). Other position: Concert artist in America.
Sources: SB programs; Clarence J. Russell's diary; Musical Courier, 26 Aug 1915 & 23 Dec 1915; references in PBks 41 & 42.

JACOBSON, ANDREW A. (Andy), *saxophone*
1919-20 tour after WG. Other position: Own dance band in Boston. Member, SBFS.
Sources: Various 1919-20 tour rosters; incomplete roster in George Ford Collection; references in SBFS News.

JACQUES, C.C., *B-flat clarinet*
1925-26 tour (partial).
Source: 1925-26 SB hotel assignment list.

JAEGER, BERNHARD, *trombone*
Date(s) of SB service uncertain, but ca. 1899. Other position: George Thatcher's Minstrels.
Source: New York Clipper, 27 Jan 1906.

JAHN, PAUL, *B-flat clarinet*
Possibly 1st 1892 tour; 2nd 1892 tour; 1st 1893 tour; 2nd 1893 tour; probably tours in 1894; probably 1st & 2nd 1895 tours; 3rd 1895 tour; probably 4th 1895 tour; possibly 1st 1896 tour.
Sources: SB photos; 1892 C.G. Conn advertisement; SB publicity for 1st 1893 tour; Varela photo, 21 Oct 1893; hotel registration, Adrian, MI, 1 Apr 1895.

JANKINS, FRANK N., *bassoon*
1919-20 tour.
Source: Various 1919-20 tour rosters.

JANOVSKY, ERNST, *instrument?*
1st 1905 tour (Britain).
Source: S.S. Baltic ship's list, 19 May 1905.

JANSSEN, CURTIS W. *cornet/trumpet*
Date(s) of SB service uncertain, but probably part of one tour in 1920 or 1921.
Source: Correspondence with George Brozak, researcher.

JEFFERY, JOHN (Jeff), *valet*
Sousa's valet on 1924 tour after WG and on part or all of 1925-26 tour. Also assistant librarian.
Sources: SB payrolls; SB "breakfast" payroll for 10 Oct 1925; SBFS News, Jul, 1973, p. 17.

JENKINS, GEORGE M., *bass clarinet, B-flat clarinet*
1923-24 tour after WG; 1925-26 tour. Member, SBFS.
Sources: SB payrolls & photos; roster in Jacobs' Band Monthly, Aug, 1925; 1925-26 SB hotel assignment list.

JENKINS, GRACE COURTNEY, *violin*
Soloist. 3rd 1902 tour (partial).
Sources: SB programs; New York Dramatic Mirror, 6 Sep 1902; references in PBk 19.

JESCHKA, WILLIAM A., *B-flat clarinet*
1st 1892 tour; 2nd 1893 tour; possibly other tours between 1893 & 1904; 1st 1905 tour (Britain).
Sources: SB photo, Sep/Oct, 1893; Varela photo, 1 Dec 1893; S.S. Baltic ship's list, 19 May 1905.

JOCELYN, LUCILLE, *soprano*
Soloist. 2nd 1902 tour.
Sources: SB programs; references in PBk 16.

*JOEL, ALEX J., *basso*
Soloist. 1894 St. Louis Exposition (partial)
Source: St. Louis Post-Dispatch, 11 Sep 1894.

JOHNSON, CLARENCE M., *saxophone*
1925-26 tour. Member, SBFS.

Sources: SB payrolls, programs, & photos; roster in Jacobs' Band Monthly, *Aug, 1925; 1925-26 SB hotel assignment list; advertisement in* Conn Musical Truth, *Feb, 1926; references in* SBFS News.

JOHNSON, EDWARD D. (Ed), *B-flat clarinet*
1921 tour; 1921-22 tour; 1928 tour; 1929 tour; one or more of 1930 tours; 1931 tour.
Sources: SB payrolls & photos; advertisement in Musical Messenger, *Jan, 1922; Jay Sims' handwritten checklist for 1931 tour; references in* SBFS News.

JOHNSON, HERMAN R., *bass clarinet*
1921 tour; 1921-22 tour; possibly 1922 tour; 1923-24 tour; 1924 tour. Other positions: Liberati's Band; Allentown (PA) Band. Member, SBFS. d. Nov, 1979.
Sources: SB payrolls, rosters, & photos; references in SBFS News; *author's interview & correspondence with Johnson & with family;* Morning Call *(Allentown), 25 Feb 1975, p. 6.*

JOHNSON, SAMUEL, *percussion*
Date(s) of SB service uncertain but probably one tour in late 1890s.
Source: SBFS News, *Jul, 1954, p. 19.*

JOHNSTONE, MARTINA, *violin*
Soloist. 1896 MB (partial); 1896-97 tour; 1897 MB. b. Sweden.
Sources: 1897 SB payroll; SB programs; references in PBks 5 & 10.

*JONES, SHANNAH CUMMING, *soprano*
Soloist. 1896 MB (partial).
Source: SB programs in PBk 4.

*JORDAN, JULES, *tenor (vocal)*
Soloist, 30 Jun 1893, Lancaster, PA. b. 10 Nov 1850, Willimatic, CT; d. 5 Mar 1927.
Sources: Portraits of the World's Best-Known Musicians; *PBk 2, pp. 45 & 77.*

*JOSLAR, MRS. L., *vocalist*
Soloist, 24 Oct 1895, Dallas, TX.
Source: Dallas Morning News, *24 Oct 1895, p. 2.*

JOSTE, FRED, *B-flat clarinet*
1921 tour (partial).
Source: George Ford's 1921 roster.

KAISER, SADIE ESTELLE, *soprano*
Soloist. 1897 tour (partial); 1898 tour (partial).
Sources: References in PBks 5 & 22.

KALMBACH, HERBERT A., *B-flat clarinet*
1919-20 tour except WG; 1922 tour except WG. Other positions: Pfeiffer's Orchestra (Wildwood, NJ); Philadelphia theater orchestras. Charter member, SBFS.
Sources: Correspondence between Kalmbach and Jay Sims, SB personnel manager; various 1919-20 tour rosters; references in SBFS News.

KAMPE (KAMPKE), GEORGE C., *B-flat clarinet*
2nd 1900 tour (Europe); 1907 tour; 1911 world tour; 1914 tour; 1915 tour; 1916-17 tour; 1919-20 tour; 1923-24 tour; 1924 tour; 1925-26 tour; 1926 tour; 1928 tour; 1929 radio broadcast; 1929 tour; one or more of 1930 tours; 12 Mar 1931 recording; 9 Apr 1931 radio broadcast; late 1931 radio broadcasts.
Sources: SB payrolls & photos; roster in Albert A. Knecht's world tour diary; Edmund A. Wall's world tour poem; roster in Musical Courier, *9 Jun 1915; 1915 Tuxedo tobacco advertisement with SB musicians' signatures; various other rosters.*

KAPRALEK, FRANK JOSEPH, *E-flat clarinet*
1st 1905 tour (Britain); 1907 tour; 2nd 1908 tour; 1911 world tour; 1915 tour. Other position: U.S. Marine Band.
Sources: S.S. Baltic ship's list, 19 May 1905; roster in New York Dramatic Mirror, *1 Sep 1908; roster in Albert A. Knecht's world tour diary; Edmund A. Wall's world tour poem; roster in* Musical Courier, *9 Jun 1915; 1915 Tuxedo tobacco advertisement with SB musicians' signatures; author's correspondence with family.*

KARA, JOSEPH, *trombone*
1906 tour; 2nd 1908 tour. Possibly also played euphonium.
Sources: Roster in New York Dramatic Mirror, *1 Sep 1908; PBk 26, pp. 108 & 109.*

KARDASEN, CHARLES M., *B-flat clarinet*
1925-26 tour (partial); 1926 tour; 2nd 1927 tour. Charter member, SBFS.

Sources: SB payrolls & photos; roster in Jacobs' Band Monthly, *Aug, 1925; 1925-26 & 1927 SB hotel assignment lists; references in* SBFS News.

KARNS, EARL, *trombone*
Date(s) of SB service uncertain, but ca. 1923. Member, SBFS. d. ca. 1961.
Sources: References in SBFS News; *Berger roster.*

KEHM, ROBERT, *horn*
Date(s) of SB service uncertain, but ca. 1921 and also 1st 1927 tour. Other position: Allentown (PA) Band.
Sources: Morning Call *(Allentown), 25 Feb 1975, p. 6.* SBFS News, *Sep, 1975, p. 10.*

KEINKE, WALTER, *B-flat clarinet*
1923-24 tour (partial).
Sources: 1923 SB payrolls.

KELLER, EARL, *tuba.*
1925-26 tour (partial). Other positions: Reading (PA) Philharmonic Band; Geigertown (PA) Cornet Band; assistant conductor of a U.S. Army band during World War I;
Sources: SB payroll 11 Jul 1925; roster in Jacobs' Band Monthly, *Aug, 1925; unidentified clipping from a Reading (PA) newspaper dated Sep, 1925; author's correspondence with family.*

KEMPER, GEORGE, *instrument?*
1907 tour.
Source: Undated article from Detroit News, *reporting on SB train wreck of 9 Dec 1907, listing Kemper among those injured [PBk 29, p. 25].*

KENECKE (KOENECKE), EMIL, *cornet/trumpet*
2nd & 3rd 1898 tours; 3rd & 4th 1899 tours; 1st 1900 tour; 2nd & 3rd 1902 tours; 1st 1903 tour; 2nd 1903 tour (cornet **soloist** on all). Other positions: Pryor's Band; Innes' Band; Stewart's Band (Boston); various bands & orchestras in New York; Victor Brass Quartet. Composer. Recorded for Columbia & Victor. b. 7 Apr 1866, Magdeburg, Germany; d. 1930, Camden, NJ.
Sources: SB rosters, programs, & photos; various other rosters; Pioneers in Brass; The Heritage Encyclopedia of Band Music; Bands of America, *p. 240;* The Sousa Band A Discography; *"In Memoriam" list, SBFS organizational booklet (1945); author's interviews with Kenneth B. Slater, bandmaster; correspondence with Patricia Backhaus, band historian, & with Frederick P. Williams, discographer.*

KENN, DANIEL, *percussion*
4th 1901 tour (Britain); 2nd 1902 tour; 1st 1903 tour (Europe); possibly 1st & 2nd 1904 tours; 1st 1905 tour (Britain); 2nd 1905 tour; 2nd 1906 tour; 1907 tour; possibly 1st 1908 tour; 2nd 1908 tour.
Sources: SB payrolls, rosters, & photos; SB/Grenadier Guards banquet seating chart of 17 Oct 1901; S.S. Baltic ship's list, 19 May 1905; rosters in New York Dramatic Mirror, *7 Sep 1907 & 1 Sep 1908; "In Memoriam" list, SBFS organizational booklet (1945).*

*KENNEDY, H.H., *basso*
Soloist. 1894 MB (partial); 1896 MB (partial).
Sources: SB programs in PBks 3 & 4.

KENSINGER, VANE H. (Swipes), *B-flat clarinet*
1923-24 tour; 1925-26 tour (partial); 1926 tour; 1929 tour. Other positions: Kilties Band (Canada); Detroit Concert Band; various other bands and orchestras in Midwestern states; Moslem Temple Shrine Band (Detroit); served in U.S. Army during World War I. Member, SBFS. b. 30 Aug 1885; d. 16 Jul 1968, Ferndale, MI.
Sources: SB payrolls & photos; roster in Jacobs' Band Monthly, *Aug, 1925; references in* SBFS News; *author's interviews and correspondence with Kensinger.*

KENT, LOREN EARL, *tuba*
1926 tour (partial); 1st & 2nd 1927 tours. Other positions: Served in Great Lakes Naval Training Station Band under Sousa during World War I; Navy band aboard *U.S.S. Pennsylvania;* Cummins Municipal Band (Olney, IL). Member, SBFS. b. 3 Nov 1895; d. 28 Nov 1977, Olney, IL.
Sources: SB payrolls & photos; Otto Kraushaar's autobiography, p. 54; undated obituary in Olney newspaper; references in SBFS News.

KENT, RICHARD EUGENE (Dick), *saxophone*
1921-22 tour; 1922 tour. Other positions: Chautauqua bands; assistant conductor of Urbana (IL) High School Orchestra; arranger for M. Witmark & Sons, Southern Music, and other publishers. Charter member, SBFS. b. 25 Sep 1899, Jacksonville, IL; d. 19 Mar 1996, Urbana, IL.

Sources: 1921-22 SB roster; SB contract for 1922; The Saxophone Symposium, Vol. 23 (1998); references in SBFS News; research by Phyllis Danner, Sousa Archives for Band Research, University of Illinois; author's interview and correspondence with Kent.

*KERKER, VERNA, *violin*
Apparently **soloist** with SB on one or more occasions when band was in Decatur, IL. Other positions: Director of Music, Millikin University & Townsend School of Music; private music teacher. Married name Townsend. b. 31 Mar 1887, Tolono, IL; d. 8 Mar 1979, Urbana, IL.
Sources: Data from Sousa Archives for Band Research, University of Illinois; Champaign-Urbana News-Gazette, 9 Mar 1979 [obituary].

*KERN, MARIE, *soprano*
Soloist. 1894 St. Louis Exposition (partial).
Source: St. Louis Post-Dispatch, 11 Oct 1894.

KERNS, JACK WILLIAM, *bass clarinet*
1920 WG; possibly remainder of 1920 tour. Possibly also played saxophone. Member, SBFS.
Sources: Roster in 1920 WG programs; references in SBFS News.

KILGOUR, EARL D., *B-flat clarinet*
1923-24 tour; 1924 tour; 1925-26 tour (partial); 1926 tour; 1st & 2nd 1927 tours. Other positions: Armco Band; music teacher, Evansville (IN) schools; instrument repairman. Member, SBFS. b. 15 Aug 1899; d. 20 May 1889, Evansville.
Sources: SB payrolls & photos; roster in Jacobs' Band Monthly, Aug, 1925; 1925-26 & 1927 SB hotel assignment lists; references in SBFS News; Social Security Death Index.

KILSON, WILMER, *valet*
Sousa's valet on 1915 tour. Also assistant librarian.
Source: Roster in Musical Courier, 9 Jun 1915; 1915 Tuxedo tobacco advertisement with SB musicians' signatures.

KINCAID, OWEN D. (Gilhooley), *saxophone*
1926 tour; 1st & 2nd 1927 tours; 1928 tour; one or more of 1930 tours; 1931 tour (soloist). Member, SBFS. b. 19 Aug 1906, Youngstown, OH; d. 21 Sep 1996, Warren, OH.
Sources: SB rosters, programs, & photos; Owen Kincaid Collection; 1927 SB hotel assignment list; Jay Sims' 1930 tour roster & handwritten checklist for 1931 tour; author's interviews and correspondence with Kincaid.

KINNEY, RUTH LLOYD, *contralto*
Soloist. 1921 WG (partial).
Sources: SB programs.

KIRSHNER, MAURICE, *bassoon*
1918 tour; 1919-20 tour. Other position: Cleveland Orchestra.
Source: Jay Sims' 1919-20 tour roster.

KIRSHNER, PHILIP, *oboe*
1919-20 tour; 1929 radio broadcasts.
Sources: SB payrolls; PBk 49, p. 73.

KIVLAN, EDWIN G., *B-flat clarinet*
1929 radio broadcasts; 12 Mar 1931 recording; 9 Apr 1931 radio broadcast; late 1931 radio broadcasts.
Sources: SB payrolls.

*KLEIN, ALFRED, *vocalist*
Soloist. 1896 MB (partial); 1897 MB (partial). Other position: DeWolf Hopper Opera Co.
Sources: SB programs in PBk 4; PBk 5, p. 81.

*KLEINE, IDA, *soprano*
Soloist. 2nd 1894 Madison Square Garden engagement (partial); 1894 MB (partial); 1897 MB (partial).
Sources: SB programs in PBk 3; PBk 5, pp. 63 & 81.

KLEMOLA, WILLIAM M., *B-flat clarinet*
1928 tour.
Sources: SB payrolls & photos; Eugene Slick's 1928 autograph book.

KLUMP, ROLLAND (Signor), *flute/piccolo*
2nd 1927 tour.
Sources: SB payroll 16 Jul 1927; 1927 SB hotel assignment list; references in SBFS News.

KNECHT, ALBERT A., *saxophone*
3rd & 4th 1905 tours; 1st, 2nd, 3rd, & 4th 1906 tours; 1st & 2nd 1908 tours; 1st & 2nd 1910 tours; 1911 world tour; 1912 tour; 1st part of 1913 tour through WG; 1914 tour; 1915 tour; 1919-20 tour. Other positions: Philadelphia Orchestra; Pryor's Band; Buffalo Bill's Wild West Show; W. Paris

Chambers' Band; American Saxophone Quartet; co-owner of Henton-Knecht Music Co. (Philadelphia). Charter member, SBFS. b. 23 Sep 1882; d. 4 Dec 1954.
Sources: Knecht's day book; Knecht's world tour diary; Knecht's personal correspondence & photo albums; Edmund A. Wall's world tour poem; signature on 6 Nov 1914 birthday card from band members to Sousa (refers to first year with band as 1905); roster in Musical Courier, 9 Jun 1915; 1915 Tuxedo tobacco advertisement with SB musicians' signatures; Jay Sims' 1919-20 tour roster; advertisements in Conn Musical Truth, Oct, 1921 & Oct, 1923; author's interviews & correspondence with family & with William H. Rehrig, band historian.

KNIGHT, HARRY, *B-flat clarinet*
Date(s) of SB service uncertain, but probably for a short period in late 1920s. Other position: Allentown (PA) Band.
Source: Allentown Band archives.

KNISS, PAUL, *tuba*
1925-26 tour (partial).
Sources: 1925-26 SB hotel assignment list; SBFS News, May, 1983, p. 31.

KNITTLE, LOUIS, *saxophone*
2nd 1900 tour (Europe).
Sources: Roster in SB program of 22 Apr 1900; SB photo, 30 May 1900.

KNUTTUNEN, GEORGE J., *B-flat clarinet*
1928 tour; 1929 tour; one or more of 1930 tours; 1931 tour. Brother of Jacob O. Knuttunen.
Sources: SB payrolls; Jay Sims' 1930 tour roster & handwritten checklist for 1931 tour; references in SBFS News.

KNUTTUNEN, JACOB O., *cornet/trumpet*
1926 tour (cornet **soloist** at StPr); 2nd 1927 tour; 1928 tour; 1929 tour. Other positions: Boston Theater orchestras. Brother of George J. Knuttunen. Member, SBFS.
Sources: SB payrolls, programs, & photos; 1927 SB hotel assignment list; Eugene Slick's 1928 autograph book; references in SBFS News.

KOCH, HENRY D., *horn*
1st 1892 tour; probably 2nd 1892 tour; 1st & 2nd 1893 tours; 1893 MB; 1st 1894 tour (**soloist** at Mid-Winter Expositions); probably 2nd 1894 tour; 1894 MB; possibly 3rd 1894 tour; 2nd & 3rd 1898 tours; 1899 MB (**soloist**); 1st 1905 tour (Britain). Other position: Hinrich's American Grand Opera Orchestra. Composer. Recorded for Berliner. d. 7 Jun 1917.
Sources: SB programs; manuscripts in Sousa Archives for Band Research, University of Illinois; 1892 C.G. Conn advertisement; SB photo, Sep/Oct, 1893; 1893 Varela photo; SB publicity for 1st 1893 tour; Jacobs' Band Monthly, 2 Jul 1917 [obituary]; advertisement in J.W. Pepper's Musical Times and Band Journal, May, 1898; seating chart in St. Louis Post-Dispatch, 25 Sep 1898; S.S. Baltic ship's list, 19 May 1905; references in PBks; references in SBFS News; author's correspondence with Frederick P. Williams, discographer.

KOCH, _____, *trombone*
1893 MB (in trombone quartet); 2nd 1893 tour.
Sources: Programs in PBk 3.

KOENECKE, see KENECKE, EMIL

*KOENIGSMANN, MARTHA, *vocalist*
Soloist. 1895 St. Louis Exposition (partial).
Sources: 1895 SB programs.

KOPPITZ, CHARLES O., *cornet/trumpet*
1920 tour; 1921 tour; 1921-22 tour.
Sources: SB rosters; "In Memoriam" list, SBFS organizational booklet (1945).

KRAUSHAAR, OTTO J., *bassoon*
1926 tour; 1st 1927 tour, 1 engagement only on 1 May; 2nd 1927 tour; 1928 tour; 1st 2 weeks of 1929 tour. Other positions: Served in Great Lakes Naval Training Station Band under Sousa during World War I; Navy band aboard U.S.S. Pennsylvania; Kilties Band (Canada); Chicago Concert Band; representative of C.G. Conn Co.; conductor of high school bands in Waupun, WI, Lake Wales, FL, & Miami, FL; conductor, university summer music camps in FL. Elected to American Bandmasters Assn., 1933 (president, 1961). Elected to Florida Music Education Assn. Hall of Fame, 1969. Member, SBFS. b. 1896, Sturgis, MI; d. 4 Dec 1979, Miami, FL.
Sources: Otto Kraushaar's autobiography; Bandmen; Instrumentalist, Apr, 1962, p. 82; School Musician, Aug-Sep, 1973, p. 12; references in

SBFS News; *author's interviews & correspondence with Kraushaar and family.*

KROCEK, HUGO, *saxophone*
1921 tour (partial).
Sources: 1921 SB roster; SBFS News, Feb, 1955, p. 12; advertisement in Conn Musical Truth, *Oct, 1921 (Sousa Edition).*

KROEDER, B., *B-flat clarinet*
2nd 1900 tour (Europe).
Sources: Roster in SB program of 22 Apr 1900; SB photo, 30 May 1900.

*KRONOLD, SELMA, *soprano*
Soloist. 1894 St. Louis Exposition (partial). Other positions: Metropolitan Opera Co.; Berlin Royal Opera; Gustav Hinrich's Opera Co. (U.S.A.); toured Europe with Angelo Neumann Opera Co. b. 1866, Krakow, Poland; d. 9 Oct 1920, New York.
Sources: SB programs in 1894 St. Louis Post-Dispatch; Index to Women of the World from Ancient to Modern Times; The New Encyclopedia of the Opera.

KROUSE, HARRY SYLVESTER, *instrument?*
Date(s) of SB service uncertain but probably one tour ca. 1899. Composer.
Source: PBk 9, p. 47.

KRUGER, CHARLES WILLIAM, *saxophone, librarian*
Probably all tours & engagements from 2nd 1893 tour to 2nd 1902 tour; 3rd 1902 tour; possibly other tours. Copyist. Other position: U.S. Marine Band. b. ca. Apr, 1863, Hamburg, Germany; d. 18 Nov 1903.
Sources: SB payrolls & photos; Varela photo, 15 Oct 1893; librarian's notation on p. 1 of PBk 4; hotel registration, Adrian, MI, 1 Apr 1895; Lester Levy's autograph book, Nov, 1895; seating chart in Philadelphia Press, *7 May 1897; seating chart in St. Louis Post-Dispatch, 25 Sep 1898; Cuthbert (GA) Leader, 21 Sep 1899 [letter to the editor by Kruger]; Washington Star, 19 Nov 1902 [obituary]; references in PBks; author's correspondence with Carole Nowicke, band historian.*

KRUGER, E., *bassoon*
1st 1903 tour (Europe).
Source: SB publicity for 1st 1893 tour.

KRUSE, WILLIAM (Bill), *bassoon*
1926 tour (partial); 1st & 2nd 1927 tours; 1929 tour (partial). Other positions: Served in U.S. Naval Training Station Band under Sousa during World War I; Navy band aboard *U.S.S. Pennsylvania.*
Sources: SB payrolls & photos; Otto Kraushaar's autobiography; 1927 SB hotel assignment list; references in SBFS News.

KRYL, BOHUMIR, *cornet/trumpet*
Date(s) of SB service uncertain, but between 1894-1898 (**soloist** at some concerts in 1898). Other positions: theater orchestras [also played string bass and saxophone]; When Band (Indianapolis, IN); soloist & assistant conductor with Innes' Band; Brooke's Chicago Marine Band; John Duss Band (Pittsburgh). Founder/conductor of Kryl's Band & Kryl's Orchestra & Women's Symphony Orchestra. Recorded for Berliner, Columbia, Edison, Pathe, Norcross, Victor, & Zonophone. Composer. Member, SBFS. Served in Bohemian Army. b. 2 May 1877, Horice, Bohemia; d. 7 Aug 1961, Wilmington, NY.
Sources: An Orchestra Musician's Odyssey, *pp. 120-155 & 185-202;* Pioneers in Brass; Bands of America; The Heritage Encyclopedia of Band Music; Supplement to the Heritage Encyclopedia of Band Music; The New Grove Dictionary of American Music; Musical Messenger, Mar, 1917, pp. 1-2; Band Fan, Summer, 1995, p. 4; references in PBks; references in SBFS News; author's correspondence with Frederick P. Williams, discographer.*

KUHN, JOHN M. (Chief Red Cloud), *tuba*
1915 tour; possibly tours in 1917 & 1918; 1919-20 tour; 1920 tour. Other positions: Kryl's Band; Conway's Band; Isham Jones' Orchestra; Chicago radio staff orchestras. Member, SBFS. d. ca. Jul, 1962.
Sources: SB photos; Roster in Musical Courier, *9 Jun 1915; 1915 Tuxedo tobacco advertisement with SB musicians' signatures; various 1919-20 tour rosters; roster in 1920 WG programs; references in PBks; references in SBFS News; author's interviews & correspondence with Glenn D. Bridges, band historian; Social Security Death Index.*

KUHN, MATHIAS J., *horn*
1921-22 tour; 1926 tour; possibly other brief periods in 1920s. Other position: Cincinnati Symphony Orchestra. Member, SBFS. b. 10 Jul 1892, Gyertyamos, Hungary; d. 9 Mar 1996, Cincinnati, OH.

Sources: 1921-22 SB roster; 1921 SB photo; Western Hills *(Cincinnati)* Press, *12 Apr 1995; PBk 54, p. 2; author's interview with Kuhn.*

KUNKEL, WILLIAM M., *flute/piccolo*
1921 tour (**soloist** at WG); 1921-22 tour (**soloist** at WG); 1922 tour (**soloist** at WG); 1923-24 tour (partial) (**soloist** at WG). Other positions: Conductor of University of New Mexico Band & Ballut Alyad Shrine Band (Albuquerque, NM) & Albuquerque Civic Symphony & Albuquerque Municipal Band. Member, SBFS. Elected to American Bandmasters Assn., 1939.
Sources: SB rosters, programs, & photos. Waterbury *(CT)* Democrat, *29 Sep 1923; references in SBFS News.*

KUNZE, ARTHUR H., *horn*
1st 1892 tour; at least one other tour in 1892 or 1893; 1911 world tour; 1912 tour.
Sources: roster in Albert A. Knecht's world tour diary; roster in J.W. Pepper Musical Times and Band Journal, May, 1898; Edmund A. Wall's world tour poem; Clarence J. Russell Papers (handwritten note on route sheet for 26 Sep 1912 indicates that Kunze was a member of the original Sousa Band in 1892); references in SBFS News.

LaBARRE, EUGENE G. (Gene), *cornet/trumpet*
1919-20 tour (**soloist**, WG); 1931 tour. Other positions: Pryor's Band; Conway's Band; Liberati's Grand Concert Band; Innes' Band; Groton (NY) Band; 8th U.S. Cavalry Band; Moslem Temple Shrine Band (Detroit); conductor of Peoria (IL) Municipal Band & New York Police Dept. Band & Long Beach (CA) Municipal Band & 1940 World's Fair Band (New York) & Dodge Bros. Motor Co. Band (Detroit) & Detroit Elks Band & Detroit Fire Dept. Band. Composer. Co-founder, SBFS. b. 3 Oct 1888, Groton, NY; d. 19 Oct 1956, Long Beach, CA.
Sources: SB payrolls, programs, & photos; various 1919-20 tour rosters; The Heritage Encyclopedia of Band Music; Supplement to the Heritage Encyclopedia of Band Music; Bandmen; advertisement for Virtuoso Cornet School (Buffalo, NY) in Jacobs' Band Monthly, Apr, 1917, p. 75; advertisement in Conn Musical Truth, Oct, 1921 (Sousa Edition); Jay Sims' handwritten checklist for 1931 tour; PBk 30, p. 17; references in SBFS News; author's correspondence with Edmund C. Wall, SB clarinetist & with Lynn Sams, band historian.

LABATE, BRUNO, *oboe*
Date(s) of SB service uncertain but probably 1909 or 1910. Other position: New York Philharmonic.
Sources: References in SBFS News; correspondence with Stephen Secan, orchestra historian.

LACALLE, JOSEPH M., *B-flat clarinet, E-flat clarinet*
1st 1893 tour; possibly other tours in 1893; 1st 1894 tour (**soloist** on E-flat clarinet at Mid-Winter Exposition) 1894 MB; possibly other tours in 1894; some tours in late 1895 or early 1896; 1896-97 tour. Possibly also played flute/piccolo. Other positions: 7th Regt. Band (New York); Gilmore's Band; conductor of Columbia Spanish Band (New York) & Lacalle Band & 23rd Regt. Band (New York) & Hoadley Musical Society Amateur Orchestra (New York). Composer. Recorded for Columbia, Indestructible Cylinders, & Lakeside Cylinders. b. 17 Nov 1859, Spain; d. 11 Jun 1937, Brooklyn, NY.
Sources: SB photos & programs; SB publicity for 1st 1893 tour; The Heritage Encyclopedia of Band Music; Supplement to the Heritage Encyclopedia of Band Music; Metronome, Apr, 1893; seating chart in Philadelphia Press, 7 May 1897; SBFS News, May, 1956, p. 12; author's correspondence with Frederick P. Williams, discographer.

LaCROIX, WILLIAM, *instrument?*
Date(s) of SB service uncertain but sometime between 1915-20. Other positions: Metropolitan Opera Orchestra; New York Symphony Orchestra.
Sources: C.G. Conn's Musical Truth, May, 1915, p. 23 & Oct, 1921.

LAENDNER, WILLIAM (Willie), *horn*
1909 tour; possibly 1st & 2nd 1910 tours; 1911 world tour.
Sources: Roster in Albert A. Knecht's world tour diary; Edmund A. Wall's world tour poem; references in SBFS News.

LAING, FANNIE, *vocalist*
Soloist, 26 Oct 1895, Dallas, TX.
Source: Dallas Morning News, 26 Oct 1895, p. 2.

LAMMERS, HYRUM (Hy), *trombone*
1920 tour; 1921 tour (partial). Other positions: Warner Bros. studio orchestra (movies). Member, SBFS.
Sources: SB rosters; PBk 55, p. 65; references in SBFS News.

LAMMERS, JOHN, *flute/piccolo*
1929 tour.
Source: SB payroll 7 Sep 1929.

LANGAN, WILLIAM H. (Billy), *B-flat clarinet*
1st 1892 tour; 2nd 1893 tour; 4th 1895 tour; 1st 1896 tour; possibly 2nd 1896 tour; 1896-97 tour; 3rd 1898 tour; 2nd 1900 tour (Europe); 4th 1901 tour (Britain); 1st 1903 tour (Europe); 2nd 1908 tour; possibly other tours between 1893-1913; 1915 tour; 1929 & 1930 radio broadcasts. Charter member, SBFS. b. England; d. 6 Jul 1945.
Sources: SB payrolls, rosters, programs, & photos; partial roster in 1892 C.G. Conn advertisement; SB publicity for 1st 1893 tour; 1893 Varela photo; article in St. Louis Post-Dispatch, 7 Oct 1893 entitled "One of Band Held On"; program for 17 Oct 1893 in St. Louis Post-Dispatch; SB/Grenadier Guards banquet seating chart of 17 Oct 1901; SB publicity for 1st 1903 tour; roster in New York Dramatic Mirror, 1 Sep 1908; roster in Musical Courier, 9 Jun 1915; 1915 Tuxedo tobacco advertisement with SB musicians' signatures; references in PBks; references in SBFS News.

LANGE, WILLIAM R., *horn*
1st 1896 tour; 1896 MB; 1896-97 tour; 3rd 1898 tour; 2nd 1900 tour (Europe); 4th 1901 tour (Britain); 1st 1903 tour (Europe).
Sources: SB payrolls, rosters, programs, & photos; seating chart in Philadelphia Press, 7 May, 1897; seating chart in St. Louis Post-Dispatch, 25 Sep 1898; photo in Sousa's personal 1899/1900 photo album; references in PBks; SBFS News, May, 1951, p. 7.

LANGENUS, GUSTAV JEAN, *B-flat clarinet*
Possibly 3rd 1902 tour; 1st 1903 tour (Europe). Other positions: Queen's Hall Orchestra (London); Duke of Devonshire's Orchestra (Eastbourne, England); New York Symphony Orchestra; New York Philharmonic; music faculty, Juilliard School of Music, Dalcroze School of Music, Teacher's College of Columbia University, Institute of Musical Arts, & Oberlin Conservatory of Music; co-founder of New York Chamber Music Soc.; private music teacher. Composer. Author. Member, SBFS. b. 6 Aug 1883, Malines, Belgium; d. 30 Jan, 1957, New York.
Sources: SB publicity for 1st 1893 tour; Who Is Who in Music, 1951 Edition; The Heritage Encyclopedia of Band Music; Musical Messenger, Jul, 1918, pp. 1-4; Selmer advertisement in Musical Messenger, May, 1922; references in SBFS News.

LANGEY, LELAND H., *basso*
1st 1899 tour (in vocal quartet).
Sources: PBk 8, pp. 171-179.

*LaPEARL, ROY, *vocalist*
Soloist, 27 Feb 1916, New York.
Sources: PBk 42, pp. 122 & 128.

LAPITINO, FRANCIS, *harp*
Date(s) of SB service uncertain, but briefly ca. early 1920s, probably WG only.
Source: Author's interview with SB oboist Arthur Glenum.

LAURENDEAU, ALEXANDER, *saxophone*
2nd 1900 tour (Europe).
Sources: Roster in SB program of 22 Apr 1900; SB photo, 30 May 1900; author's correspondence with family.

LAWBOR, RICHARD, *carpenter*
1926 tour.
Source: 1926 SB roster.

LAWNHAM, JAMES (Jim), *B-flat clarinet*
One or more tours in 1905 but not 1st; 1907 tour; 2nd 1908 tour; 1909 tour; possibly 2nd 1910 tour; 1911 world tour; 1914 tour; 1916-17 tour.
Sources: Rosters in New York Dramatic Mirror, 7 Sep 1907 & 1 Sep 1908; roster in Albert A. Knecht's world tour diary; Edmund A. Wall's world tour poem; signature on 6 Nov 1914 birthday card from band members to Sousa (refers to first year with band as 1905); roster in Dec, 1916 New York Musician and Knocker; references in PBks 21 & 24; references in SBFS News.

LAWTON, STANLEY, *saxophone*
2nd 1893 tour; 3rd & 4th 1895 tours; 1st 1896 tour; 1896-97 tour; 3rd 1898 tour; 3rd 1899 tour; 2nd 1900 tour (Europe); 4th 1901 tour (Britain); 1st 1903 tour (Europe); 1907 tour; 1922 world tour; probably other tours. Other position: U.S. Marine Band.
Sources: SB payrolls, rosters, & photos; SB publicity for 1st 1893 tour; Lester Levy's autograph book, Nov, 1895; seating chart in Philadelphia Press, 7 May 1897; seating chart in St. Louis Post-Dispatch, 25 Sep 1898; photo in Sousa's personal 1899/1900 photo album; SB/Grenadier Guards

banquet seating chart of 17 Oct 1901; roster in New York Dramatic Mirror, 7 Sep 1907.

LEAVITT, VERNE M., *euphonium*
1919-20 tour (partial).
Source: Various 1919-20 tour rosters.

LeBARBIER, E., *cornet/trumpet*
4th 1906 tour (trumpet **soloist** at Pittsburgh Exposition & Boston Food Fair); 2nd 1908 tour.
Sources: New York Dramatic Mirror, 1 Sep 1908; PBk 26, pp. 85 & 181.

*LEE, FRANCES, *soprano*
Soloist. 1899 MB (partial).
Sources: PBk 8, p. 249; PBk 9, pp. 1, 4, & 5.

LEFEBRE, EDOUARD (EDWARD) A., *saxophone*
1st 1892 tour; 2nd 1893 tour (**soloist** at Chicago World's Fair); 1893 MB (**soloist**); 2nd 1893 tour (**soloist**); off-tour concert, 3 Dec 1893, Brooklyn, NY (**soloist**); off-tour concert, 18 Jan 1894, Brooklyn; 1894 MB. Other positions: Jullien's Orchestra (New York); Gilmore's Band; designed saxophones for C.G. Conn Co. Recorded for Berliner.
Sources: SB photos; A Study of the Saxophone Soloists with the John Philip Sousa Band: 1893-1930; author's correspondence with Frederick P. Williams, discographer.

LeFONTENAY, ODETTE, *soprano*
Soloist. 1914 WG (partial); 1918 tour (partial). Recorded for Edison.
Sources: SB programs; author's correspondence with Frederick P. Williams, discographer.

LEFTER, JOSEPH GROVE (Joe), *flute/piccolo*
One or more of 1930 tours. Other positions: Conductor of St. Petersburg (FL) Municipal Band; owner of music store in St. Petersburg. Bandstand in St. Petersburg named for Lefter. Member, SBFS. b. Daleville, IN, 28 Apr 1909; d. 24 May 1982, St. Petersburg, FL.
Sources: Jay Sims' 1930 tour roster; The Sousa Oral History Project; International Musician, Jul, 1982 [obituary]; undated article in St. Petersburg Times; references in SBFS News; author's interview & correspondence with Lefter; Social Security Death Index.

LEIBY, CHARLES A., *B-flat clarinet*
1925-26 tour (partial); 1926 tour; 1929 tour; one or more of 1930 tours. Member, SBFS.
Sources: SB payrolls & photos; roster in Jacobs' Band Monthly, Aug, 1925; 1925-26 SB hotel assignment list; Jay Sims' 1930 tour roster; references in SBFS News.

LEICK, JOHN S., *cornet/trumpet*
Date(s) of SB service uncertain, but ca. 1909. Other positions: The Military Octette (vaudeville); Denver (CO) Municipal Band; conductor of Kilties Band (Canada) & El Jebel Shrine Band (Denver) & Highlander Boys' Band (Denver).
Sources: Handwritten letter from Sousa to Leick dated 4 Sep 1929; article, with photo of Sousa & Leick, in Denver Post, ca. 7 Sep 1929; author's correspondence with family

LEIGH, LESLIE, *soprano*
Soloist. 1916-17 tour (partial).
Sources: Clarence J. Russell's diary; PBk 44, pp. 9, 34, & 43.

LEIGL, JOHN S., *B-flat clarinet*
1921-22 tour; possibly 1922 tour; 1923-24 tour; off-tour concert, 29 Jun 1929 Princeton, NJ; 1929 tour. Other positions: U.S. Navy Band; U.S. Naval Training Station Band (San Diego, CA); Danner Municipal Band; made European tours with wife Mabel, also a cornetist and known as the "Sousa Girl;" vaudeville orchestras; conductor of Shrine band in Denver, CO; Member, SBFS.
Sources: SB payrolls, rosters, & photos; author's correspondence with family; references in SBFS News.

LEMCKE, HANS J., *cornet/trumpet*
1923-24 tour (partial). Other position: Supervisor of instrumental music in Webster Groves, MO.
Source: St. Louis Post-Dispatch, 26 Sep 1968.

*LEONORI, SALVATORE, *baritone (vocal)*
Soloist. 1893 St. Louis Exposition (partial).
Sources: Programs in St. Louis Post-Dispatch, Sep, 1893.

LEPHILIBERT, P., *oboe*
1907 tour; 2nd 1908 tour; possibly tours in 1909 & 1910; 1911 world tour.

Sources: SB photos; roster in New York Dramatic Mirror, *1 Sep 1908; roster in Albert A. Knecht's world tour diary; Edmund A. Wall's world tour poem; SBFS News, Dec, 1951, p. 19.*

LeROUX, ANTON, *bassoon*
1896-97 tour; one or more tours in 1897; possibly 1st & 2nd 1898 tours; 3rd 1898 tour; possibly tours in 1899 & 1st 1900 tour; 2nd 1900 tour (Europe).

Sources: 1897 SB tour payroll; seating chart in Philadelphia Press, *7 May 1897; seating chart in* St. Louis Post-Dispatch, *25 Sep 1898; roster in SB program of 22 Apr 1900; SB photo, 30 May 1900; references in PBk 5; references in SBFS News.*

LEROY, H.L., *B-flat clarinet*
1931 tour (partial).
Source: SB payrolls.

LEVY, ABRAHAM (Abe), *B-flat clarinet*
One or more tours in 1899; 2nd 1900 tour (Europe); 1st 1901 tour; 4th 1901 tour (Britain); 3rd 1902 tour; 3rd 1903 tour; 2nd 1905 tour; probably several other tours between 1899 & 1905. Brother of Theodore Levy. b. 1875; d. 1929.

Sources: Roster in SB program of 22 Apr 1900; SB photos; photo in Sousa's personal 1899/1900 photo album; SB/Grenadier Guards banquet seating chart of 17 Oct 1901; roster in New York Dramatic Mirror, *6 Sep 1902; Levy family photos; PBk 14, p. 21; PBk 19, p. ii; references in SBFS News; author's correspondence with family.*

LEVY, THEODORE, *cornet/trumpet*
4th 1901 tour (Britain); 3rd 1902 tour; 1st 1903 tour (Europe); probably 2nd 1905 tour; possibly other tours between 1901 & 1905. Brother of Abraham Levy. b. 1876; d. 1924.

Sources: SB photos; SB/Grenadier Guards banquet seating chart of 17 Oct 1901; roster in New York Dramatic Mirror, *6 Sep 1902; SB publicity for 1st 1903 tour; Levy family photos; PBk 14, p. 21; PBk 19, p. ii; "In Memoriam" list, SBFS organizational booklet (1945); author's correspondence with family.*

LEWIS, WAYNE, *euphonium*
(Name at birth Harry; legally changed to Wayne). 1926 StPr; probably remainder of 1926 tour; possibly 1st & 2nd 1927 tours; one or more of 1930 tours; 1931 tour. Other positions: Goldman Band; numerous other bands in New York area. Charter member, SBFS. b. 4 Oct 1899; d. 4 Mar 1995, St. Petersburg, FL.

Sources: SB payrolls; 1927 SB hotel assignment list; Jay Sims' handwritten checklist for 1931 tour; 1948 advertisement for Holton Band Instrument Co.; references in SBFS News; author's interviews & correspondence with Lewis, with Kenneth B. Slater, bandmaster, & with Donald Callahan, researcher; Social Security Death Index.

LIBERATI, ALESSANDRO (ALEXANDER), *cornet/trumpet*
1st 1892 tour; 2nd 1892 tour (cornet **soloist**). Other positions: First Cacciatori Band (Rome); Gilmore's Band; Dodworth's Band (New York); C.D. Hess Grand Opera Orchestra; Baldwin Cadet Band (Boston); free-lance soloist with numerous other bands; New York Philharmonic; founder/conductor of Liberati's Grand Military Band & Liberati Grand Opera Co. Conductor of several Canadian artillery bands & Dodge Bros. Motor Co. Band (Detroit) & Michigan National Guard Light Guard Band & 71st Regt. Band (New York); private music teacher. Composer. Recorded for Edison. Member, SBFS. b. 24 Aug 1847, Frescati, Italy; d. 6 Nov 1927, New York.

Sources: SB programs; receipt for salary received 3 Dec 1892; Bands of America; The Heritage Encyclopedia of Band Music; Supplement to the Heritage Encyclopedia of Band Music; PBk 3, pp. 3 & 5; SBFS News, Oct, 1973, p. 12; author's interviews & correspondence with Raoul F. Camus, band historian, with Loras J. Schissel, music historian, with Frederick P. Williams, discographer, & Kenneth B. Slater, bandmaster.

LIBERATI, ANTHONY, *euphonium, trombone*
1919-20 tour. Member, SBFS.

Sources: Various 1919-20 tour rosters; SB program, 11 Nov 1919; references in SBFS News.

LICK, RALPH L., *saxophone*
1917 WG (**soloist**).

Sources: SB programs; A Study of the Saxophone Soloists of the John Philip Sousa Band, 1893-1930; Lick's letter-to-the-editor, Jacobs' Band Monthly, *Jan, 1918; author's correspondence with Russ Girsberger, music librarian.*

LIEBLING, ESTELLE, *soprano*
Soloist. 3rd 1902 tour; 1st 1903 tour (Europe); 2nd 1903 tour; 1st 1904 tour before St. Louis Exposition; 2nd 1904 tour except WG; 3 off-tour concerts,

Dec, 1904, New York; 1st 1905 tour (Britain); 3rd 1906 tour (partial); 1907 WG (partial); 1908 WG (partial); off-tour concert, 1 Nov 1908 (New York). Other positions: Dresden Royal Opera; Stuttgart Opera; Opera Comique (Paris); Metropolitan Opera Co.; founder/conductor of Liebling Singers; music faculty, Curtis Institute of Music; private music teacher. Composer, arranger, author. Honorary doctorate, Farleigh Dickinson Univ. Member, SBFS. b. 21 Apr 1880, New York, NY; d. 25 Sep 1970, NY.

Sources: SB rosters, programs, & photos; The New Grove Dictionary of American Music; Who Is Who in Music, 1951 edition; S.S. Baltic ship's list, 19 May 1905; references in PBks; references in SBFS News; author's interviews & correspondence with Liebling & with Beverly Sills, Liebling's student.

LILLIBACH, WALTER D., *trombone*
Date(s) of SB service uncertain, but before 1921.

Source: Advertisement in Conn Musical Truth, *Oct, 1921 ("Sousa Edition").*

LINDE, JOHN T., *bassoon*
1921 tour; 1921-22 tour; possibly 1922 tour; 1923-24 tour; 1924 tour.

Sources: SB payrolls, rosters, & photos; references in SBFS News.

*LINDE, ROSA, *contralto*
Soloist. 1893 MB (partial); 1894 (partial).

Sources: SB programs; references in PBks.

LINDENHAHN, RICHARD, *horn*
1913 tour. Other position: Minneapolis Symphony Orchestra.

Sources: SB programs in PBk 38, pp. 14 & 16; undated C.G. Conn Co. post card advertisement.

LINDH, MARCELLA, *soprano*
Soloist. 1st & 2nd 1892 tours; 1893 MB; 2nd 1893 tour; 2nd 1894 Madison Square Garden engagement (partial). Other positions: Metropolitan Opera Co.; Royal Opera (Budapest); also sang opera and concerts in Italy, Germany, Russia, & Portugal. Birth name Rosalind Marcella Jacobson; married name Jellinek. b. 1867, Kalamazoo, MI; d. Aug, 1966, Detroit.

Sources: Undated receipt for SB salary ca. 3 Dec 1892; Musical Courier, 9 Dec 1920, p. 9; Detroit Free Press, 11 Jul 1963; references in PBk 1; references in SBFS News; author's interview & correspondence with Lindh, with family, & with Leonard B. Smith, composer.

LINDSAY, C.M.O., *management*
Treasurer. Date(s) of SB service uncertain except for 1908.

Source: Roster in New York Dramatic Mirror, *1 Sep 1908.*

LITKE, H., *bassoon*
1907 tour.

Source: Roster in New York Dramatic Mirror, *7 Sep 1907.*

LIVINGSTON, CLARENCE R. (Livvy), *B-flat clarinet*
2nd 1906 tour; 1907 tour; 2nd 1908 tour; 1909 tour; probably other tours between 1906-1911; 1911 world tour; 1923-24 tour. Other positions: Ithaca (NY) Band; piano tuner. Member, SBFS.

Sources: SB payrolls; roster in New York Dramatic Mirror, *7 Sep 1907; roster in Albert A. Knecht's world tour diary; Edmund A. Wall's world tour poem; references in PBks; references in SBFS News.*

LIVINGSTON, FREDERICK, *B-flat clarinet*
Date(s) of SB service uncertain. Other positions: Conway's Band; various bands in Marathon, NY. b. ca. 1873; d. 12 Feb 1945, Marathon.

Sources: References in SBFS News.

LOBBER, CHARLES, *saxophone*
1921-22 tour (partial).

Source: 1921-22 SB roster.

LOCHMYER, A., *E-flat clarinet*
2nd 1900 tour (Europe).

Sources: Roster in SB program of 22 Apr 1900.

LOCKE, EDWARD E., *B-flat clarinet, saxophone*
2nd 1900 tour (Europe); 4th 1901 tour (Britain); 1st 1903 tour (Europe).

Sources: Roster in SB program of 22 Apr 1900; SB photos; SB salary list, Oct-Dec, 1901; SB/Grenadier Guards banquet seating chart of 17 Oct 1901; roster in New York Dramatic Mirror, *6 Sep 1902; SB publicity for 1st 1903 tour; SBFS News, May, 1951, p. 7.*

LOEHMANN, CHARLES, *bassoon*
1921 tour; 1921-22 tour.

Sources: SB rosters; 1921 SB photo; "In Memoriam" list, SBFS organizational booklet (1945).

LOFFINI, M., *euphonium*
1920 tour.

Source: Roster in 1920 WG programs.

LOMAS, JOSEPH (Joe), *B-flat clarinet*
1911 world tour; 1st part of 1919-20 tour. Other positions: Kilties Band (Canada); Anglo-Canadian Leather Co. Band; Conway's Band; Brockville (ONT) Citizens Band; conductor of Brockville Collegiate Institute Band & McIntyre Mine Band (Timmins, ONT) & Brockville Rifles Band. Member, SBFS. b. ca. 1880, Dundas, ONT; d. May, 1966, Brockville.
Sources: Roster in Albert A. Knecht's world tour diary; Edmund A. Wall's world tour poem; various 1919-20 tour rosters; Ottawa Journal, 16 May 1966; clipping from undated Brockville newspaper; references in SBFS News; author's interview with Lomas.

LOOMIS, GEORGE N., *management*
Member of management staff ca. 1892-1913, evidently specializing as advance agent and/or tour manager. Other positions: Business manager of Gilmore's Band; manager of soprano Emma Abbott and others.
Sources: 1897 SB payroll; references in PBks; references in New York Dramatic Mirror & New York Clipper.

LORENZ, R.R., *clarinet*
1921 tour.
Source: 1921 SB roster.

LORENZ, ROBERT J., *B-flat clarinet*
1921 tour; 1921-22 tour.
Sources: SB rosters; photos in Lorenz family collection; author's correspondence with family.

LORETTO, _____, *instrument?*
1st 1905 WG engagement.
Source: Unidentified clipping, ca., Jun, 1905 [PBk 21, p. 22].

LOTZ, JOHN, *B-flat clarinet*
2nd 1901 tour; possibly other tours in 1904 and 1908. Member, SBFS.
Sources: SB photo, 30 May 1900; references in SBFS News.

LOTZ, PHILIP, *horn*
1st 1893 tour; 2nd 1900 tour (Europe). Other position: Gilmore's Band.
Sources: Roster in SB program of 22 Apr 1900; SB photo, 30 May 1900; PBk 2, p. 36.

LOVERIDGE, CLARENCE A., *flute/piccolo*
1921 tour. Member, SBFS. d. 25 Jun 1948.
Sources: 1921 SB payroll; references in SBFS News.

LOWE, CHARLES P., *percussion*
1st 1893 tour; 1893 MB; 2nd 1893 tour (xylophone **soloist**); 3rd & 4th 1905 tours (xylophone **soloist**); 2nd 1906 tour; 1907 tour (partial) (xylophone **soloist**). Other positions: Gilmore's Band; Henry Savage Musical Shows. Recorded for Berliner & Columbia.
Sources: SB publicity for 1st 1893 tour; advertisement in Leedy Drum Topics, Aug, 1934; references in PBks; "In Memoriam" list, SBFS organizational booklet (1945); author's correspondence with Frederick P. Williams, discographer, & with Russ Girsberger, music librarian.

LOWE, WILHELMENA, *harp (probably)*
1st 1905 tour (Britain).
Source: S.S. Baltic ship's list, 19 May 1905.

LOWE, [Dr.] WILLIAM (Willie), *percussion*
1st 1893 tour (partial); 1907 tour; 1911 world tour (also served as band's physician on this tour).
Sources: Roster in New York Dramatic Mirror, 7 Sep 1907; roster in Albert A. Knecht's world tour diary; Edmund A. Wall's world tour poem; advertisement in Leedy Drum Topics, Aug, 1934; references in SBFS News; author's correspondence with Russ Girsberger, music librarian.

LOWER, GRAYDON C., *euphonium*
1925-26 tour (partial); one or more of 1930 tours. Other positions: Pryor's Band; Bachman's Million Dollar Band; 5th Regt. U.S. Army Band; 304th Cavalry U.S. Army Band. Brother of Nathan C. Lower. b. 26 Feb 1895, Minier, IL; d. 17 Sep 1962, Indianapolis, IN.
Sources: Jay Sims' 1930 tour roster; Indianapolis Times, 19 Sep 1962 [obituary]; Pekin (IL) Times, 22 Sep 1962 [obituary]; Pruyn roster; SBFS News, Aug, 1978, p. 19; author's correspondence with family & with William R. Miller, researcher; Social Security Death Index.

LOWER, NATHAN C. (Nat, Nate), *tuba*
1925-26 tour (partial); 1928 tour; one or more of 1930 tours. Other positions: Chicago Symphony Orchestra; Pryor's Band; Bachman's Million Dollar Band. Brother of Graydon C. Lower. Member, SBFS. b. 26 May 1904, Minier, IL; d. 27 Jan 1963, Tucson, AZ.
Sources: SB payrolls & photos; roster in Jacobs' Band Monthly, Aug, 1925; 1925-26 SB hotel assignment list; Eugene Slick's 1928 autograph book; family genealogy; Pekin (IL) Times, 30 Jan 1963 [obituary];

references in SBFS News; author's correspondence with family & with William R. Miller, researcher.

LUBIS, THEODORE, *B-flat clarinet*
1921-22 tour; 1923-24 tour; 1924 tour; off-tour concert, 15 Jun 1929, Princeton, NJ; 1929 tour; one or more of 1930 tours; 1931 tour. Other positions: Lebanon (PA) Municipal Band. Charter member, SBFS.
b. 6 Jan 1890; d. ca. 1972, Shamokin, PA.
Sources: SB payrolls, rosters, & photos; Jay Sims' 1930 tour roster; references in SBFS News; Social Security Death Index.

LUCAS, GEORGE, *trombone*
Possibly 1st & 2nd 1910 tours; 1911 world tour. Other positions: New York Philharmonic; Metropolitan Opera Orchestra; Volpe Symphony Orchestra; Goldman Band; St. Petersburg (FL) Municipal Band. Recorded for Edison. Charter member, SBFS. b. 1 Jan 1886, England; d. 30 Jan 1981.
Sources: Roster in Albert A. Knecht's world tour diary; Edmund A. Wall's world tour poem; St. Petersburg Times, 31 Jan 1981; Conn Musical Truth, May, 1915, p. 23; references in SBFS News; author's interview & correspondence with Lucas & with Donald Callahan, researcher.

*LUCET, _____ (male), *vocalist*
Soloist. 1893, MB (partial).
Source: PBk 2, p. 70.

*LUCKSTONE, ISIDORE (Henry, Harry), *baritone (vocal)*
Soloist. 1896 MB (partial); 1897 MB (partial). Other positions: Metropolitan Opera Co.; music faculty, New York University; also accompanist [piano] to Enrico Caruso, Fritz Kreisler, & Lillian Nordica. b. 29 Jan 1861, Baltimore, MD; d. 12 Mar 1941, New York.
Sources: SB programs in PBk 4; Baker's Biographical Dictionary of Musicians; Current Biography Yearbook, 1941; The Grand Opera Singers of To-Day.

*LUDWIG, JOSIE, *vocalist*
Soloist. 1893 St. Louis Exposition (partial).
Source: Announcement in St. Louis Post-Dispatch, 21 Oct 1893.

LUFSKY, MARSHALL P. (Jimmy), *flute/piccolo*
Most all tours & engagements from 2nd 1900 tour to 2nd 1910 tour (piccolo or flute **soloist** on most of these tours); off-tour concert, 25 Jun 1929, Princeton, NJ; 1929 radio broadcasts. Other positions: New York Philharmonic; Metropolitan Opera Orchestra; Victor Herbert's Orchestra; Wisconsin Symphony Orchestra; Christoph Bach's Orchestra (Milwaukee); Pryor's Band; Innes' Band. Recorded for Brunswick, Columbia, D&R, Harmony, Oxford, & Victor. b. 4 Oct 1878, Milwaukee, WI; d. 11 Dec 1948, Milwaukee.
Sources: SB payrolls, rosters, programs & photos; various other rosters; S.S. Baltic ship's list, 19 May 1905; Flutist, Apr, 1928, pp. 100-102; Hobbies, Feb, 1949 [obituary]; Milwaukee Journal, 18 Jan 1940; references in PBks; The Sousa Band A Discography; SBFS News, May, 1951, p. 6; author's correspondence with Frederick P. Williams, discographer.

LUNDGREN, JORAM, *B-flat clarinet*
1923-24 tour; 1924 tour; 1925-26 tour; 1929 radio broadcasts.
Sources: SB payrolls & photos; roster in Jacobs' Band Monthly, Aug, 1925.

LYON, MARCUS CHARLES (Marc), *trombone*
Evidently all engagements from 1st 1892 tour to 1916-17 tour except for a few off-tour concerts in New York; often member of trombone quartet or other brass ensembles; also baggage handler. Recorded for Berliner, Columbia, & Victor. Given name Michael Charles Lyon. b. 12 Mar 1852; d. 7 Jun 1927, Camden, NJ.
Sources: SB payrolls, rosters, programs, & photos; various other rosters; roster in Albert A. Knecht's world tour diary; Edmund A. Wall's world tour poem; The Sousa Band A Discography; advertisements for Holton, J.W. Pepper, & H.N. White in music journals; family photo collection; references in PBks; references in SBFS News; author's interviews & correspondence with family; author's correspondence with Andre Smith, music historian.

LYONS, DARIUS A., *flute/piccolo*
2nd 1900 tour (Europe); 1st 1900 tour; 4th 1901 tour (Britain); 2nd & 3rd 1902 tours; probably other tours in 1900, 1901, & 1902; often flute or piccolo **soloist**. Recorded for Victor. b. St. Paul, MN, ca. 1878; d. Washington County, MN, 14 Jul 1911.
Sources: SB rosters, programs, & photos; roster in SB program of 22 Apr 1900; The Sousa Band A Discography; correspondence with Susan Nelson, discographer; references in SBFS News.

MacADAM, see ROOT, VIRGINIA

MACHNER, AUGUST, *saxophone*
1925-26 tour (partial); 1926 WG.
Sources: SB payroll 11 Jul 1925; Jay Sims' 1925-26 tour roster; SB programs; roster in Jacobs' Band Monthly, *Aug, 1925; references in PBks.*

MACK, CHARLES R., *tuba*
1920 WG; probably remainder of 1920 tour.
Sources: Roster in 1920 WG programs; advertisement in undated Conn Musical Truth.

MACK, WARREN B., *instrument?*
1st 1905 tour (Britain).
Source: S.S. Baltic ship's list, 19 May 1905.

MacKAY, see CASE, ANNA

MACKEY, C. STANLEY, *tuba*
1st 1905 tour (Britain). Other positions: Philadelphia Orchestra; conductor of Philadelphia Band & Philadelphia Municipal Band. d. 26 Sep 1915, Philadelphia.
Sources: S.S. Baltic ship's list, 19 May 1905; New York Tribune, *27 Sep 1915;* Philadelphia Public Ledger, *27 Sep 1915.*

MACKEY, KELSEY, *flute/piccolo*
1913 tour (**Soloist**, Atlanta Auto Show); 1916-17 tour.
Sources: Roster in Dec, 1916 New York Musician and Knocker; *PBk 38, p. 74.*

*MacTAMMANY, RUTH, *soprano*
Soloist, 21 Nov & 19 Dec, 1915, New York.
Sources: Clarence J. Russell's diary; unidentified New York newspaper dated 22 Nov 1915 [PBk 42, p. 26].

MADDEN, ALBERT O. (Bert), *saxophone*
1925-26 tour (partial); 1926 tour; 1st & 2nd 1927 tours.
Sources: SB payrolls, programs, & photos; 1927 SB hotel assignment list; references in SBFS News.

MAGNANT, RENE, *alto clarinet, E-flat clarinet*
2nd 1904 tour; 1907 tour; possibly other tours between 1904-07; 2nd 1908 tour; 1911 world tour; 1914 tour; 1915 tour; 1916-17 tour. Evidently E-flat clarinet on 2nd 1904 tour & alto clarinet on other tours.
Sources: SB photos; roster in New York Dramatic Mirror, *7 Sep 1907; roster in Albert A. Knecht's world tour diary; Edmund A. Wall's world tour poem; signature on 6 Nov 1914 birthday card from band members to Sousa (refers to first year with band as 1904); roster in* Musical Courier, *9 Jun 1915; 1915 Tuxedo tobacco advertisement with SB musicians' signatures; roster in Dec, 1916* New York Musician and Knocker; *SBFS News, Dec, 1951, p. 20.*

MAITLAND, ROBERT, *baritone (vocal)*
Soloist. 1916 WG (partial).
Sources: SB programs; Clarence J. Russell's diary.

MAJOR, U. H., *B-flat clarinet*
1928 tour.
Sources: SB payrolls; Eugene Slick's 1928 autograph book; Otto Kraushaar's autobiography, p. 54; references in SBFS News.

MALY, ANTHONY (ANTON) N. (Tony), *oboe*
1921 tour; 1921-22 tour (partial); probably 1922 tour; 1923-24 tour; 1924 tour; 1925-26 tour (partial); 1926 tour; 1st 1927 tour. Other positions: Prague Philharmonic; Pryor's Band; Radio City Music Hall Orchestra; New York radio studio orchestras; music faculty, Manhattan School of Music, Columbia University, & Newton (NJ) High School. Charter member, SBFS. b. Poland; d. ca. 1962
Sources: SB payrolls, rosters, & photos; roster in Jacobs' Band Monthly, *Aug, 1925; 1925-26 SB hotel assignment list; references in SBFS News; author's interviews with Kenneth B. Slater, bandmaster.*

MANCINELLI, LUIGI, *instrument?*
1st 1899 tour.
Source: Photo in Sousa's personal 1899/1900 photo album.

MANCINI, FRANK, *B-flat clarinet*
1915 tour (partial); probably other tours. Other positions: Paris Opera Orchestra; Chicago Opera Orchestra; Philadelphia Opera Orchestra; Lombardi Grand Opera Orchestra; New York Symphony Orchestra; Conway's Band; Ellery's Band; Thaviu's Band; Golden State Band; Weber's Band (Cincinnati); conductor of Modesto (CA) Civic Band & Modesto Jr. College Band & Modesto High School Band. Elected to American Bandmasters Assn., 1940. b. 13 Jan 1886, Serramonacesca, Italy; d. 15 Nov, 1964, Modesto, California.

Sources: SB photo, 1915; Band Encyclopedia; *author's correspondence with composer Roger Nixon, student of Mancini;* Social Security Death Index.

MANN, CHARLES, *flute/piccolo*
1921-22 tour (partial).
Source: 1921-22 SB roster.

*MANN, ESTELLA LOUISE, *soprano*
Soloist. 1894 MB (partial). Other positions: Mantelli Grand Opera Co.; Lyric Trio (comic opera & vaudeville, mostly in New York). Recorded for Berliner, Lyric, Talking Machine Co. & Zonophone; Owner of Lyric Phonograph Co. (New York). b. 1 Nov 1871, Nashville, TN; d. 24 Aug 1947.
Sources: SB programs in PBk 3; Hobbies, *Apr, 1952, pp. 24-35.*

MANTIA, SIMONE, *euphonium, trombone*
Most all tours & engagements from 4th 1895 tour through 2nd 1903 tour; off-tour concert, 15 Jun 1929, Princeton, NJ; 1929 radio broadcasts; euphonium **soloist** on most; 12 Mar 1931 recording. Other positions: [played trombone for orchestral work] Pryor's Band (also assistant conductor); Metropolitan Opera Orchestra (also personnel manager); New York Philharmonic; Philadelphia Grand Opera Orchestra; Chicago Grand Opera Orchestra; Brooklyn Grand Opera Orchestra; Russian Symphony Orchestra; Victor Herbert's Orchestra; Cities Service Band of America; 1940 World's Fair Band (New York); founder/conductor of Mantia's Orchestra (Asbury Park, NJ). Composer. Author. Recorded for Berliner, Edison, & Zonophone. Co-founder, SBFS. b. 6 Feb 1873, Palermo, Italy; d. 25 Jun 1951, New York.
Sources: SB payrolls, rosters, programs, & photos; various other rosters; Pioneers in Brass; Bands of America; The Heritage Encyclopedia of Band Music; Supplement to the Heritage Encyclopedia of Band Music; Band Encyclopedia; Bandmen; The Sousa Band A Discography; *Asbury Park (NJ) Press, 9 Jan 1944; advertisements in various issues of* Conn Musical Truth; *references in PBks; references in SBFS News; author's correspondence with Raoul F. Camus, band historian, & with Frederick P. Williams, discographer.*

MANTON, _____ (male), *vocalist*
1893 MB; 2nd 1893 tour (member of vocal sextet).
Sources: SB programs; references in PBks 2 & 3.

*MARASCHALCHI, ARTURO, *baritone (vocal)*
Soloist. 1893 MB (partial) (in vocal trio); 2nd 1894 Madison Square Garden engagement (partial).
Sources: References in PBk 3; New York World, *3 Jun 1894, p. 12.*

MARCHESE, PASQUALE, *B-flat clarinet*
1st 1893 tour; 2nd 1893 tour; probably 1893 MB; 1st 1896 tour; 1896-97 tour; possibly 1897 tour; 3rd 1898 tour; 2nd 1900 tour (Europe); 4th 1901 tour (Britain); 3rd 1902 tour; 1st 1903 tour (Europe); possibly other tours between 1892-1904. Other position: Municipal Band of Milan, Italy. b. Italy.
Sources: SB payrolls, rosters, & photos; SB publicity for 1st 1893 tour; program in St. Louis Post-Dispatch, *17 Oct 1893; seating chart in* Philadelphia Press, *7 May 1897; seating chart in* St. Louis Post-Dispatch, *25 Sep 1898; SB/Grenadier Guards banquet seating chart of 17 Oct 1901; roster in* New York Dramatic Mirror, *6 Sep 1902;* SBFS News, *May, 1951, p. 7.*

*MARDONES, JOSÉ, *basso*
Soloist, 26 Dec 1915 & 9 Jan 1916, New York. Other positions: Metropolitan Opera Co.; Boston Opera Co.; sang opera with other companies in South America, Spain, & Portugal. Recorded for Columbia & Victor. b. 1869, Fontecha, Spain; d. 4 May, 1932, Madrid.
Sources: Clarence J. Russell's diary; The Grand Opera Singers of To-Day; The Metropolitan Opera Encyclopedia; *PBk 42, p. 44.*

MARKERT, DANIEL J., *tuba*
1921 tour; 1921-22 tour.
Sources: SB rosters; "In Memoriam" list, SBFS organizational booklet (1945).

MARSH, ALBERT A., *oboe*
Off-tour concert, 15 Jun 1929, Princeton, NJ; 1929 radio broadcasts.
Sources: SB payrolls.

*MARSH, HOWARD, *tenor (vocal)*
Soloist, 29 Oct 1916, Atlantic City, NJ & 5 Nov 1916, Newark, NJ, & 1-23 Jan 1917, New York. Other positions: Singer/actor in operettas & Broadway musicals, mostly in New York. b. 16 Aug 1888, Bluffton, IN; d. 7 Aug 1969, Long Beach, NJ.

Sources: Clarence J. Russell's diary; Encyclopedia of the Musical Theatre; The Oxford Companion to American Theatre; Social Security Death Index.

MARSHALL, FREDERICK STANLEY, *saxophone*
1920 WG; probably remainder of 1920 tour. Member, SBFS. d. ca. 1950.
Sources: Roster in 1920 WG programs; references in SBFS News.

MARTHAGE, JOSEPH L., *harp*
One or both 1910 tours; 1911 world tour; 1912 tour; 1913 tour; 1914 tour; 1915 tour; 1915-16 New York Hippodrome; 1916-17 tour; probably 1918 tour; 1919-20 tour; occasional **soloist**. Other position: Susan Tompkins Orchestra (Rochester, NY). Member, SBFS; d. ca. 1957.
Sources: SB programs & photos; roster in Albert A. Knecht's world tour diary; Edmund A. Wall's world tour poem; signature on 6 Nov 1914 birthday card from band members to Sousa (refers to first year with band as 1910); roster in Musical Courier, 9 Jun 1915; 1915 Tuxedo tobacco advertisement with SB musicians' signatures; roster in Dec, 1916 New York Musician and Knocker; undated clipping Rochester Times [PBk 35, p. 50]; various 1919-20 tour rosters; references in PBks and in SBFS News; author's interviews with Louis Morris, SB clarinetist & copyist.

MARTIN, CARROLL F., *trombone*
Date(s) of SB service uncertain. Other positions: St. Paul Symphony Orchestra; Chicago Symphony Orchestra; NBC radio staff orchestra (Chicago); Innes' Band; Weldon's 2nd Regiment Band (Chicago); Benson Orchestra (Chicago). Composer. Recorded for Brunswick. b. 8 Apr 1867, Kingswood, WV; d. 16 Sep 1939, Racine, WI.
Source: Pioneers in Brass.

MARTIN, FRANK, *cornet/trumpet*
2nd 1893 tour; off-tour concert, 28 Jan 1894, Brooklyn, NY; 1st 1894 tour (**soloist** at Mid-Winter Exposition); 2nd 1894 Madison Square Garden engagement (**soloist**); 1894 MB (**soloist**); 3rd 1894 tour.
Sources: References in PBks 3 & 25.

*MARTIN, HENRY D., *tenor (vocal)*
Soloist. 1896 MB (partial).
Sources: SB programs in PBk 4.

*MARTIN, RICCARDO, *tenor (vocal)*
Soloist, 16 Jan 1916, New York. Other positions: Metropolitan Opera Orchestra; Chicago Opera. Recorded for Victor. b. 18 Nov 1878, Hopkinsville, KY.
Sources: Clarence J. Russell's diary; PBk 42, p. 85; author's correspondence with Frederick P. Williams, discographer.

MATTHES, OSCAR, *B-flat clarinet, E-flat clarinet*
1913 tour; 1914 tour; 1915 tour; probably 1915-16 New York Hippodrome; 1916-17 tour; probably 1918 tour; 1919-20 tour. E-flat clarinet probably on 1919-20 tour only.
Sources: Signature on 6 Nov 1914 birthday card from band members to Sousa (refers to first year with band as 1913); roster in Musical Courier, 9 Jun 1915; 1915 Tuxedo tobacco advertisement with SB musicians' signatures; roster in Dec, 1916 New York Musician and Knocker; various 1919-20 tour rosters; references in SBFS News.

MAURER, GEORGE H., *percussion*
1915 tour. Member, SBFS.
Sources: SB photos; roster in Musical Courier, 9 Jun 1915; 1915 Tuxedo tobacco advertisement with SB musicians' signatures; advertisement in Leedy Drum Topics, Aug, 1934; references in SBFS News.

*MAXON, D.N., *baritone (vocal)*
1894 MB (as member of vocal quartet). [Note: also 1896 MB as member of vocal quartet but not with band].
Sources: SB programs in PBks 3 & 4.

MAYER, ROBERT, *oboe*
One or more of 1930 tours (partial). Other positions: Chicago Symphony Orchestra (& Woodwind Quintet); music faculty, Northwestern University. Author. Served in U.S. Army during World War II. Member, SBFS. b. 26 Aug 1910; d. 9 Mar 1994, Clearwater, FL.
Sources: Jay Sims' 1930 tour roster; Intermezzo (Chicago Federation of Musicians), May-Jun, 1994, p. 14 [obituary]; references in SBFS News; author's interview with Mayer, with Keith Brion, conductor of the New Sousa Band, & with Donald Callahan, researcher; Social Security Death Index.

MAYER, see also STRAUS, JESSIE

McCANN, RICHARD, *cornet/trumpet*
1914 tour (cornet **soloist**); 1915 tour; 1929 radio broadcasts; off-tour concert, 15 Jun 1929, Princeton, NJ; 12 Mar 1930 radio broadcast; 12 Mar

1931 recording; 9 Apr 1931 radio broadcast; late 1931 radio broadcasts. Recorded for Columbia. Charter member, SBFS. b. Sharon, PA; d. ca. 1961.
Sources: SB programs & dates; signature on 6 Nov 1914 birthday card from band members to Sousa (refers to first year with band as 1914); roster in Musical Courier, 9 Jun 1915; 1915 Tuxedo tobacco advertisement with SB musicians' signatures; references in PBks 39 & 40 and in SBFS News; correspondence with Frederick P. Williams, discographer.

McCRARY, DAWSON, *carpenter*
Listed as "carpenter" but probably meant baggage handler/stage manager. 1st 4 weeks of 1923-24 tour.
Sources: 1923 SB payrolls.

*McCREEY, WAYMAN, *tenor (vocal)*
Soloist. 1898 St. Louis Exposition (partial).
Source: PBk 7, p. 28.

McDIARMID, ELLIS, *flute/piccolo*
1920 tour (**soloist** at WG); 1921 tour; 1929 radio broadcasts. Other positions: Cincinnati Symphony Orchestra; Cleveland Symphony Orchestra; NBC Radio Orchestra. Recorded for Victor. Author. b. 3 Aug 1894, Cincinnati, OH.
Sources: SB payrolls, rosters, & programs; The Story of the Flute and How to Play It; references in PBks 52, 53, & 54; "In Memoriam" list, SBFS organizational booklet (1945).

McDONNELL, H., *B-flat clarinet*
1919-20 tour.
Source: Handwritten 1919 roster, presumably by SB member.

McGIBNEY, C.G. (Doc), *B-flat clarinet*
1st 1905 tour (Britain); 1929 & 1930 radio broadcasts; 12 Mar 1931 recording; 9 Apr 1931 radio broadcast; late 1931 radio broadcasts;. Charter member, SBFS; d. 26 Dec 1947.
Sources: SB payrolls; S.S. Baltic ship's list, 19 May 1905; references in SBFS News.

McGRATH, JOHN, *management*
Advance man for early part of 1923-24 tour.
Sources: 1923 SB payrolls.

McKAY, R.C., *oboe*
1919-20 tour (partial).
Source: Roster in Ft. Williams (ONT) Daily Times-Journal, 15 Aug 1919.

McKNIGHT, CHAUNCEY P., *flute/piccolo*
1st 1896 tour; 1896-97 tour; possibly one or both 1897 tours.
Sources: SB payrolls; composite 1895/96 SB photo; seating chart in Philadelphia Press, 7 May 1897; Kenneth Berger's correspondence with McKnight family [Kenneth Berger Collection].

McLAUGHLIN, WILLIAM, *B-flat clarinet*
1915 tour (partial).
Sources: SBFS News, Jan, 1954, p. 21, with 1915 photo of clarinet section.

*McQUEEN, THOMAS, *tenor (vocal)*
Soloist. 1897 MB (partial).
Source: PBk 5, p. 66.

McRITCHIE, G. ROWE, *bassoon*
1929 tour (partial); one or more of 1930 tours; 1931 tour (partial). Member, SBFS. d. Jul, 1968.
Sources: 1929 SB payrolls & photos; Jay Sims' handwritten checklist for 1931 tour; references in SBFS News; author's interview with McRitchie and correspondence with Barry Owen Furrer, band historian.

McTAMMANY, see MacTAMMANY

MEAD, WILLIAM B., *management*
Date(s) of SB service uncertain; listed as treasurer in Jun, 1899.
Source: Clipping from Newburgh (NY) newspaper dated 2 Jun 1899 [PBk 8, p. 232].

MEAGHER, SEELYE (Red), *horn*
Possibly 1st 1927 tour; 2nd 1927 tour; 1929 tour; one or more of 1930 tours.
Sources: SB payroll 28 Sep 1929; Jay Sims' 1930 tour roster; SB photos; references in SBFS News.

MEAR, SAMUEL E. (Sid) *cornet/trumpet*
Date(s) of SB service uncertain, but probably late 1920s. Other positions: Conductor of Whitewater (WI) High School Band & Whitewater Municipal Band. Elected to American Bandmasters Assn., 1932. Composer. Served in U.S. Army during Korean War. d. 1974.

Sources: Band Encyclopedia; Lest We Forget; references in SBFS News.

MECUSKER, INEZ, *soprano*
Soloist. 1st 1894 tour; 2nd 1894 Madison Square Garden engagement (partial); possibly 1894 MB (partial); Cotton States Exposition (Atlanta), 1895 (partial). Other positions: Schubert Quartet; sang with various opera companies; toured on Keith's vaudeville circuit & Redpath Chautauqua circuit; private music teacher. Married names Van Osten & Booth.
b. 4 Jul 1868, East Branch, Pa; d. 20 Apr 1941, Corry, PA.
Sources: SB programs; New York Clipper, 1 Jun 1895; advertisements in New York Dramatic Mirror, 10 Feb & 1 Apr 1894; undated advertising circular for A Trial Run, *featuring Inez Mecusker & George Abbott; references in PBks 3 & 9; author's correspondence with Sabina Freeman, researcher, & with Barry Owen Furrer, band historian.*

MEDROW, see TOMPKINS, SUSAN

MEHL, HENRY J., *B-flat clarinet*
Date(s) of SB service uncertain, but briefly ca. 1922. Member, SBFS.
Sources: "In Memoriam" list, SBFS organizational booklet (1945); references in George Ford Collection.

MEHLING, LOUIS (Lou, Louie), *percussion*
Probably 1st 1895 tour; 4th 1895 tour; 1905 WG; possibly other tours between 1896 & 1914; 1920 WG; 1921 tour (partial); numerous off-tour engagements in New York. Other positions: U.S. Marine Band when Sousa was leader; Gilmore's Band; Victor Herbert's Orchestra; Metropolitan Opera Orchestra; New York Philharmonic; Wagnerian Opera Co.; Pryor's Band; New York theater orchestras. Charter member, SBFS. d. 1955.
Sources: Roster in 1920 WG programs; 1921 SB roster; SB photos; U.S. Marine Band photo, ca. 1888; advertisement in Leedy Drum Topics, 15 Oct 1924, p. 5; references in SBFS News; author's correspondence with family.

*MELBA, NELLIE, *soprano*
Soloist, 2 Jan 1916, New York. Other positions: Sang opera in America and abroad. Recorded for Victor. b. 19 May 1861, Melbourne, Australia; d. 23 Feb 1931, Sydney, Australia.
Sources: New York Times, 2 Jan 1916, p. 8; author's correspondence with Frederick P. Williams, discographer.

MELODY, C., *encore card boy & presumably Sousa's valet*
1919-20 tour (partial).
Source: Handwritten 1919 roster, presumably by SB member.

*MELROSE, THELMA, *soprano*
Soloist. 1921 WG (partial).
Sources: SB programs.

*MENTH, HERMA, *piano*
Soloist, 2 Apr 1916, New York. Other positions: Recitalist in New York.
b. 1891, Vienna, Austria; d. 25 Feb 1968, New York.
Sources: Clarence J. Russell's diary; New York Telegraph, 30 Mar 1916; New York Times, 1 Mar 1968 [obituary].

MERRILL, LYNN TIM, *cornet/trumpet*
1923-24 tour.
Sources: SB payrolls & photos; SBFS News, Feb, 1947, p. 8.

MERTINS, WILLIAM, *baritone (vocal)*
1st 1893 tour (member of vocal trio & sextet) (partial). Other position: Boston Opera Co. b. Konigsburg, Prussia.
Sources: SB programs; SB publicity for 1st 1893 tour; references in PBks 2 & 3.

MERVILLE, R.B., *tuba*
One or more of 1930 tours.
Source: 1930 SB photo.

MESLOH, OTTO, *cornet/trumpet*
3rd 1898 tour; one or more tours in 1899; 1899 MB (cornet **soloist**). Recorded for Columbia.
Sources: SB programs; seating chart in St. Louis Post-Dispatch, 25 Sep 1898; photo in Sousa's personal 1899/1900 photo album; references in PBks 7 & 9; author's correspondence with Frederick P. Williams, discographer.

MESSINGER, ROBERT, *oboe*
Full name Erinner von Roe Messinger. Probably all tours & engagements between 1892-99 (occasional **soloist**); 4th 1901 tour (Britain); 1st 1903 tour (Europe); possibly other tours between 1900-1903. Arranger & copyist. Other position: Hinrich's American Grand Opera Orchestra.

Sources: SB payrolls, rosters, programs, & photos; 1892 C.G. Conn advertisement; SB publicity for 1st 1893 tour; 1894 Varela photo; hotel registration, Adrian, MI, 1 Apr 1895; signature in Lester Levy's autograph book, Nov, 1895; seating chart in Philadelphia Press, 7 May 1897; seating chart in St. Louis Post-Dispatch, 25 Sep 1898; photo in Sousa's personal 1899/1900 photo album; SB/Grenadier Guards banquet seating chart of 17 Oct 1901; references in PBks; author's correspondence with Loras J. Schissel, music historian.

METZGER, EDGAR (Ed), *horn*
Probably 1923-24 tour (partial); 1926 tour (partial). Other position: Allentown (PA) Band; Member, SBFS.
Sources: SB payroll 20 Nov 1926; unidentified clipping in Allentown Band Archives; Morning Call (Allentown), 25 Feb 1975, p. 6; references in SBFS News.

MEYERS, ALBERTUS LEVI (Bert), *cornet/trumpet*
1925-26 tour (1st half of tour, leaving after WG) (**soloist**, WG). Other positions: Liberati's Grand Military Band; Pryor's Band; Conway's Band; Victor Herbert's Orchestra; Allentown, PA., theater orchestras; founder/conductor of Allentown High School Band; conductor of Allentown Band & Lehigh University Concert Band & bands at Muhlenburg College. Elected to American Bandmasters Assn., 1930. Composer. Bridge in Allentown named in his honor. Honorary doctorate from Muhlenburg College. Member, SBFS. b. 7 Sep 1890, Allentown; d. 15 May 1979, Allentown.
Sources: SB payroll 11 Jul 1925; roster in Jacobs Band Monthly, Aug, 1925; SB programs & photos; The Heritage Encyclopedia of Band Music; Supplement to the Heritage Encyclopedia of Band Music; Band Encyclopedia; Allentown Band Archives; author's interviews & correspondence with Meyers, with Ron Demkee, conductor of Allentown Band, with Warren Wilson, business manager of Allentown Band, & with Kenneth B. Slater, bandmaster; Morning Call (Allentown), 24 Feb 1975, pp 5-6 & 25 Feb 1975, p. 6.

MEYERS, HAROLD, *B-flat clarinet*
1929 tour; one or more of 1930 tours. Other position: Allentown (PA) Band.
Sources: Allentown Band Archives; author's correspondence with Warren Willson, business manager of Allentown Band.

*MICHELENA, FERNANDO, *tenor (vocal)*
Soloist. 1893 MB (partial).
Sources: PBk 2, p. 70; programs in PBk 3.

MIEL, HEINRICH, *horn*
One or more tours in 1894; one or more tours in 1895 or 1896.
Sources: 1894 Varela photo; composite 1895/96 SB photo.

*MILES, GWYLIM, *baritone (vocal)*
Soloist. 1893 St. Louis Exposition (partial); 1897 MB (partial).
Sources: PBk 5, pp. 72 & 82; PBk 21, p. 36; reporter's interview with Sousa in unidentified newspaper (PBk 22, p. 1).

*MILLAR, JESSIE [Miss], *cornet/trumpet*
Cornet **soloist**, apparently in Dec, 1894, New York.
Source: New York Dramatic Mirror, 29 Dec 1894, p. 686.

*MILLER, FRANCES, *soprano*
Soloist. 1896 MB.
Sources: PBk 4, pp. 41 & 42.

MILLER, RALPH J., *saxophone*
1921 tour (partial). Member, SBFS.
Source: 1921 SB roster.

MILLER, ROY M., *B-flat clarinet*
1920 tour (partial); 1924 tour; 1926 tour (partial). Other positions: Conductor of 112th U.S. Army Infantry Band during World War I & National Transit Band (Oil City, PA) & New Castle (PA) Cathedral Band & Bessemer Railroad Band (Greenville, PA) & Aut Mori Grotto Band (Youngstown, OH). Assistant conductor of Cass Technical High School Band (Detroit) & Wayne State University Band. Author. Member, SBFS. d. Jan, 1970.
Sources: SB payroll 27 Nov 1924; SB photos; Band Encyclopedia; PBk 69, p. 242; references in SBFS News; author's interview & correspondence with Miller & with family.

MILLHOUSE, ROSS, *cornet/trumpet*
2nd 1904 tour; possibly 3rd 1906 tour; 4th 1906 tour; 1907 tour (cornet **soloist**); possibly 1st 1908 tour; 2nd 1908 tour (**soloist**); 1909 tour (**soloist** at WG); 1st & 2nd 1910 tours; 1911 world tour. Other positions: Goldman

Band; Ithaca (NY) Municipal Band. Member, SBFS. Recorded for Victor.

Sources: SB programs; various rosters; roster in Albert A. Knecht's world tour diary; Edmund A. Wall's world tour poem; The Sousa Band A Discography; references in SBFS News; author's interviews with Kenneth B. Slater, bandmaster.

MILLS, THOMAS, *percussion*
2nd 1900 tour (Europe). Recorded for Columbia.
Sources: Roster in SB program of 22 Apr 1900; SB photo, 30 May 1900; references in SBFS News; author's correspondence with Frederick P. Williams, discographer.

*MILTON, GRACE, *soprano*
Soloist. 1896 MB (partial).
Sources: SB programs.

*MINER, MARTHA GARRISON, *soprano*
Soloist. 1897 MB (partial).
Source: PBk 5, p. 72.

MIRENDA, DOMENICO, *tuba*
3rd 1898 tour.
Sources: Seating chart in St. Louis Post-Dispatch, 25 Sep 1898; "In Memoriam" list, SBFS organizational booklet (1945); author's correspondence with Raoul F. Camus, band historian.

*MIURA, TAMAKA, *soprano*
Soloist, 26 Dec 1915 & 9 Jan 1916, New York. Other positions: Metropolitan Opera Co.; Boston National Opera Co.; Chicago Opera Co.; sang opera in Germany and England; operatic singer and concert artist in Japan. Recorded for Columbia. b. 22 Feb 1884, Tokyo; d. 26 May 1946, Tokyo.
Sources: Clarence J. Russell's diary; Portraits of the World's Best-Known Musicians; references in PBk 42; author's correspondence with Kozo Suzuki & Seiichiro Takahashi, Japan Sousa Society.

MIX, EMIL, *tuba*
Possibly 1st & 2nd 1910 tours; 1911 world tour. Other positions: New York Symphony Orchestra (also manager); New York Philharmonic; Metropolitan Opera Orchestra (also manager); Philadelphia Orchestra; NBC Symphony Orchestra; CBS Orchestra; Morton Gould's Orchestra; Pryor's Band; Goldman Band; Innes' Band; manager of Chicago Symphony Orchestra, Cleveland Orchestra, Milwaukee Symphony Orchestra, Minneapolis Symphony Orchestra, Richmond (VA) Symphony Orchestra, American Symphony (New York), New York Chamber Music Orchestra, & Young Peoples Symphony (New York). Charter member, SBFS. Married Nicoline Zedeler, soprano soloist of SB. b. Scotland, SD; d. 18 Dec 1954, New York.
Sources: SB photos; roster in Albert A. Knecht's world tour diary; Edmund A. Wall's world tour poem; references in SBFS News; author's correspondence with David H. Stanon, author.

MIX, see also ZEDELER, NICOLINE

MODESS, OSKAR, *bassoon*
Possibly 1st & 2nd 1910 tours; 1911 world tour; off-tour concert 15 Jun 1929, Princeton, NJ; 1929 radio broadcasts; 12 Mar 1931 recording; 9 Apr 1931 radio broadcast; 1931 tour; late 1931 radio broadcasts.
Sources: SB payrolls & photos; roster in Albert A. Knecht's world tour diary; Edmund A. Wall's world tour poem; Jay Sims' handwritten checklist for 1931 tour; references in SBFS News.

MOEREMANS, JEAN H.B., *saxophone*
1st 1894 tour; probably 2nd 1894 tour; 1894 Madison Square Garden; 1894 MB; 3rd 1894 tour; possibly 1st & 2nd 1895 tours; 3rd 1895 tour; 1895 MB; 4th 1895 tour; 1st 1896 tour; possibly 2nd 1896 tour; 1896 MB; 1896-97 tour (partial); 1897 MB; 1897 tour; 3rd 1898 tour; 1899 MB; 3rd 1899 tour; 2nd & 3rd 1902 tours; 1st 1903 tour (Europe); 2nd 1903 tour; 1st & 2nd 1904 tours; 1st 1905 tour (Britain); 2nd 1905 tour; 1st 1905 WG; **soloist** on nearly all tours & engagements. Other positions: Royal Belgium Guards; Gilmore's Band; conductor of Maxwell-Briscoe Band (New Castle, PA); music faculty, Warren (OH) Military Band School; private music teacher. Composer. Recorded for Berliner & Victor. b. ca. 1866, Belgium; d. ca. 1938, Belgium.
Sources: SB payrolls, rosters, programs, & photos. A Study of the Saxophone Soloists Performing with the John Philip Sousa Band: 1893-1930; 1894 Varela photo; hotel registration, Adrian, MI, 1 Apr 1895; signature in Lester Levy's autograph book, Nov, 1895; seating chart in Philadelphia Press, 7 May 1897; roster in St. Louis Post-Dispatch, 25 Sep 1898; American Musician, 28 Mar 1914; references in PBks; references in SBFS News; author's interviews & correspondence with Harold B.

Stephens, SB saxophone soloist & student of Moeremans; author's correspondence with Frederick P. Williams, discographer.

MOHLES, PAUL, *oboe*
2nd 1900 tour (Europe); 4th 1901 tour (Britain); possibly other tours in 1900 & 1901.
Sources: Roster in SB program of 22 Apr 1900; SB photos; SB/Grenadier Guards banquet seating chart of 17 Oct 1901.

MONROE, FRED K. (Hoopie), *saxophone*
1924 tour; 1925-26 tour; 1926 tour; 1st & 2nd 1927 tours; 1928 tour; 1929 tour; 1929 radio broadcasts; one or more of 1930 tours (partial). Member, SBFS. d. ca. 1961.
Sources: SB payrolls, programs, & photos; 1925-26 & 1927 hotel assignment lists; Eugene Slick's 1928 autograph book; Jay Sims' 1930 tour roster; references in SBFS News.

*MONTEFIORE, CAROLINE, *soprano*
Soloist. 1st 1903 tour (Europe) (London concerts only).
Sources: SB programs; SB publicity for; Musical Courier, 21 Jan 1903, p. 6; references in PBk 19.

*MONTIETH, ZIPPORA, *soprano*
Soloist. 2nd 1894 Madison Square Garden engagement (partial). Other position: Concert artist in Europe.
Source: SB program; correspondence file of David Blakely.

*MOODY, LEO W., *B-flat clarinet*
1914 tour (substitute briefly in Chicago). Served in Great Lakes Naval Training Station Band under Sousa during World War I.
Sources: Scotts Bluff (NE) Star-Herald, 6 May 1937; author's correspondence with Keith Brion, conductor of the New Sousa Band.

MOODY, MARJORIE, *soprano*
Soloist. 1916-17 tour (partial); 1917 WG (partial); 1918 tour; 1919 WG (partial); 1st half of 1920 tour (left after WG); 1921 tour; 1922 tour (after WG); 1923-24 tour (partial); 1924 tour; 1925-26 tour; 1926 tour; 1st & 2nd 1927 tours; 1928 tour; 1929 tour; 13 May 1929 radio broadcast; off-tour concert 15 Jun 1929, Princeton, NJ; one or more of 1930 tours; 1931 tour. Other positions: Sang opera in Europe, South America, & U.S.A.; Chicago Civic Opera; sang with numerous American symphony orchestras; People's Choral Union (Boston); radio story reader. Recorded for Victor. Member, SBFS. Married name Mrs. Everett Glines; b. 23 1896, Lynn, MA; d. 10 Jul 1974, Albany, NY.
Sources: SB payrolls, rosters, programs, & photos; various other rosters; John Philip Sousa, American Phenomenon; Moody publicity in Musical Courier, 19 Mar 1925; references in PBks; references in SBFS News; news clippings in Owen D. Kincaid Collection; author's interviews & correspondence with Moody; author's correspondence with Virginia B. Bowers, Albany City Historian.

MOORE, FRED C., *B-flat clarinet*
1926 tour; 1st & 2nd 1927 tours. Other position: Anglo-Canadian Leather Co. Band. Member, SBFS. d. ca. 1951.
Sources: SB payrolls; 1927 SB hotel assignment list; references in SBFS News.

*MOORE, GEORGE LEON, *tenor*
1st 1899 tour (member of vocal quartet).
Sources: PBk 8, pp. 171-179.

MORAN, KATE, *vocalist*
Soloist. 3rd 1893 tour (partial; before Chicago World's Fair).
Sources: PBk 2, pp. 29 & 31; SBFS News, Jul, 1954, p. 13.

MORESKA, NICE, *soprano*
Soloist. 2nd 1893 tour (partial); 1893 MB (partial); 2nd 1893 tour (St. Louis Exposition only, partial).
Sources: Program in St. Louis Post-Dispatch, 22 Oct 1893; references in PBks 2 & 3.

MORRIS, LOUIS (Lou), *B-flat clarinet*
Also copyist and arranger. Possibly part of 1907 tour; apparently all tours & engagements from 1908 tour (partial) through 1920 tour except 1911 world tour. Other positions: Philadelphia Orchestra; Philadelphia theater orchestras; Victor Herbert's Band; Conway's Band; Philco Band; founder/conductor of Morris and His High Society Orchestra. Recorded for Victor. Member, SBFS. b. 27 Nov 1885, Vienna, Austria; d. Nov, 1970, Philadelphia.
Sources: SB rosters & photos; manuscripts at Sousa Archives for Band Research, University of Illinois; signature on 6 Nov 1914 birthday card from band members to Sousa (refers to first year with band as 1908); roster in Musical Courier, 9 Jun 1915; 1915 Tuxedo tobacco advertise-

ment with SB musicians' signatures; roster in Dec, 1916 New York Musician and Knocker; *History of My Life as a Musician; author's interviews & correspondence with Morris and other SB members; references in PBks; references in* SBFS News.

*MORRISON, NEDDA, soprano
Soloist. 1897 MB (partial).
Source: PBk 5, p. 62.

MOSES, EVERETT ALLYN, cornet/trumpet
Date(s) of SB service uncertain, but probably briefly in early 1920s. Other positions: Pryor's Band; Scotch Highlanders Band; conductor of Daytona Beach (FL) Municipal Band & Daytona Beach Symphony Orchestra & Moses and His Band & Kem Shrine Band (Grand Forks, ND) & several theater orchestras in U.S.A. Elected to American Bandmasters Assn., 1931. Composer. b. 17 Jan 1893, Tangent, OR; d. 7 Jun 1965.
Sources: Who Is Who in Music, *1951 edition;* Band Encyclopedia; The Heritage Encyclopedia of Band Music; Lest We Forget.

MOTT, BERNARD L., horn
1929 tour; one or more of 1930 tours.
Source: SB payroll 28 Sep 1929; 1930 SB photo.

MOUNTZ, JOHN J., horn
1923-24 tour.
Sources: SB payrolls & photos; SBFS News, Feb, 1951, p. 4.

MOWA, JOHN, instrument?
1907 tour.
Source: Report in undated St. Cloud (MN) Press *about Mowa being injured, apparently on train en route to St. Cloud.*

MUELBE, WILLIAM, horn
1929 tour. Member, SBFS.
Sources: SB payroll 28 Sep 1929; references in SBFS News.

MUELLER, O. ERNST, percussion
One or both 1893 tours. Other position: Gilmore's Band.
Sources: Metronome, Apr, 1893; *author's correspondence with Donald Callahan, researcher.*

MUELLER, FLORIAN FREDERICK, oboe
1929 tour (partial; joined band in Minneapolis). Other positions: Chicago Symphony Orchestra; music faculty, University of Michigan; private music teacher. Composer. b. 15 Jun 1904, Bay City, MI; d. Mar, 1983, St. Petersburg, FL.
Sources: SB payroll 28 Sep 1929; The Sousa Oral History Project; The Heritage Encyclopedia of Band Music; *references in* SBFS News.

MULLENIX, CARLOS W., oboe
1928 tour; off-tour concert, 15 Jun 1929, Princeton, NJ; 1929 & 1930 radio broadcasts; one or more of 1930 tours; 12 Mar 1931 recording; 9 Apr 1931 radio broadcast; 1931 tour. Other position: Conductor of San Diego Teachers College Band. Member, SBFS. d. ca. 1964.
Sources: SB payrolls; Eugene Slick's 1928 autograph book; 1930 SB photo; Jay Sims' handwritten checklist for 1931 tour.

MURDOCH, JOHN C., B-flat clarinet
Date(s) of SB service uncertain, but probably part of 1922 tour. Other position: Long Beach (CA) Municipal Band. Member, SBFS. d. ca. 1959.
Sources: References in SBFS News.

MURPHY, EDWARD A., horn
1931 tour.
Sources: SB payrolls; Jay Sims' handwritten checklist for 1931 tour.

MYSEH, JOHN G., oboe
1924 tour.
Source: SB payroll 17 Nov 1924.

NAEVY, H., E-flat clarinet
3rd 1898 tour; possibly other tours.
Source: Seating chart in St. Louis Post-Dispatch, 25 Sep 1898.

NAPOLELLE, FRANCIS, instrument?
Date(s) of SB service uncertain, but probably one WG engagement between 1920-24.
Source: Author's interview with SB oboist Arthur Glenum.

NAROTSKY, H., horn
1893 MB; 2nd 1893 tour.
Sources: PBk 2, p. 53; author's correspondence with Raoul F. Camus, band historian.

*NATALI, LOUISE, soprano
Soloist. 1894 MB (partial).
Source: PBk 3, p. 56.

NAVA, LUCINO, horn
1929 radio broadcasts; 12 Mar 1930 radio broadcast; one or more of 1930 tours (partial); 12 Mar 1931 recording; 9 Apr 1931 radio broadcast; late 1931 radio broadcasts;
Sources: SB payrolls.

NELSON, HENRY (Hal), B-flat clarinet
2nd 1900 tour (Europe); 4th 1901 tour (Britain); possibly 1st & 2nd 1902 tours; 3rd 1902 tour; 1st 1903 tour (Europe).
Sources: Roster in SB program of 22 Apr 1900; SB photo, 30 May 1900; SB roster for 4th 1901 tour (Britain); SB/Grenadier Guards banquet seating chart of 17 Oct 1901; roster in New York Dramatic Mirror, 6 Sep 1902; *SB publicity for 1st 1903 tour;* SBFS News, May, 1951, p. 7.

NEUBAUER, HERMAN, horn
4th 1901 tour (Britain); possibly 1st & 2nd 1902 tours; 3rd 1902 tour; 1st 1903 tour (Europe); 1916-17 tour.
Sources: SB/Grenadier Guards banquet seating chart of 17 Oct 1901; SB roster for 4th 1901 tour (Britain); roster in New York Dramatic Mirror, 6 Sep 1902; *SB publicity for 1st 1903 tour; roster in Dec, 1916* New York Musician and Knocker.

NEUMANN, ARTHUR J., B-flat clarinet
Possibly 1912 and 1913 tours; 1915 tour; 1916-17 tour. Other position: Metropolitan Opera Orchestra. Member, SBFS.
Sources: Roster in Musical Courier, 9 Jun 1915; *1915 Tuxedo tobacco advertisement with SB musicians' signatures; roster in Dec, 1916* New York Musician and Knocker; *SBFS organizational booklet (1945).*

NEWCOMB, EDWIN E. (Eddie), cornet/trumpet
1920 tour; 1921 tour; 1921-22 tour. Member, SBFS.
Sources: SB rosters, photos, & programs; advertisement in Conn Musical Truth, Oct, 1921 (Sousa Edition); *1921 SB photo; references in* SBFS News.

*NEWPORT, BELLE, contralto
Soloist. 1899 MB (partial).
Sources: SB programs in PBk 9; undated article & photo in Musical Courier.

NICKELETTO, FRANK, instrument?
Date(s) of SB service uncertain, but probably one WG engagement between 1920-24.
Source: Author's interview with SB oboist Arthur Glenum.

NICKELL (NICKOL), MAX, percussion
3rd 1898 tour; one or more tours in 1899.
Sources: Seating chart in St. Louis Post-Dispatch, 25 Sep 1898; *photo in Sousa's personal 1899/1900 photo album; advertisement in* Leedy Drum Topics, Aug, 1934; *author's correspondence with Russ Girsberger, music librarian; PBk 8, p. 10.*

*NIELSEN, ALICE, soprano
Soloist, 28 Nov & 14 Dec 1915, New York. Other positions: Metropolitan Opera Co.; Boston Opera Co.; Pike Opera Co. (Oakland, CA); Tivoli Opera Co. (San Francisco); Bostonians Co.; also sang opera in Europe. Recorded for Berliner, Columbia, & Victor. b. 7 Jun 1869, Nashville, TN; d. 8 Mar 1943, New York.
Sources: Clarence J. Russell's diary; The New Grove Dictionary of Music and Musicians; Portraits of the World's Best-Known Musicians; New York Clipper, 5 Mar 1898, p. 1; *references in PBk 42; author's correspondence with Frederick P. Williams, discographer.*

NIELSEN, PETER, cornet/trumpet
2nd 1900 tour (Europe); possibly 3rd 1900 tour; possibly 1st, 2nd, & 3rd 1901 tours; 4th 1901 tour (Britain); probably 1st & 2nd 1902 tours; 1st 1903 tour (Europe).
Sources: Roster in SB program of 22 Apr 1900; SB photo, 30 May 1900; SB roster for 4th 1901 tour (Britain); SB/Grenadier Guards banquet seating chart of 17 Oct 1901; roster in New York Dramatic Mirror, 6 Sep 1902; *SB publicity for 1st 1903 tour; references in* SBFS News.

NILSSEN, KARL, cornet/trumpet
1919-20 tour.
Sources: Roster in Ft. Williams (ONT) Daily Times-Journal, 15 Aug 1919; *handwritten 1919 roster, presumably by SB member; clipping from unidentified Trenton (NJ) newspaper dated 21 Sep 1919 [PBk 53, p. 40].*

*NOLDI, HELEN, soprano
Soloist, 7 Feb 1909, New York. Recorded for Edison.
Sources: PBk 31, p. 13; author's correspondence with Frederick P. Williams, discographer.

NOME, ROBERT, *saxophone*
12 Mar 1930 radio broadcast; one or more of 1930 tours. Member, SBFS. d. ca. 1948.
Sources: 1930 SB photo; listed in instrumental roster of SBFS membership directory dated 1 May 1945; references in SBFS News.

NORRITO, GIACOMO (Jack), *flute/piccolo*
Possibly all tours & engagements from 1893-1907; occasional piccolo **soloist** or member of a flute ensemble. Composer. Brother of Joseph Norrito.
Sources: SB payrolls, rosters, programs, & photos; various other rosters; The Heritage Encyclopedia of Band Music; Supplement to the Heritage Encyclopedia of Band Music; references in SBFS News.

NORRITO, JOSEPH (Joe, Dad), *B-flat clarinet*
Possibly all engagements, 1892-1922. With SB longer than any other musician. Often **soloist** at WG, fairs, and expositions; **soloist** on 1907 tour and part of both 1908 tours. Brother of Giacomo Norrito. b. Italy; d. Italy.
Sources: SB payrolls, rosters, programs, & photos; various other rosters; advertisements in various music journals; roster in Albert A. Knecht's world tour diary; Edmund A. Wall's world tour poem; roster in Musical Courier, 9 Jun 1915; 1915 Tuxedo tobacco advertisement with SB musicians' signatures; references in PBks; references in SBFS News.

NORTHROP, ELIZABETH, *soprano*
Soloist. 1896 MB (partial); 1896-97 tour; 1897 MB (partial).
Sources: SB programs; 1897 SB payroll; references in PBks 4 & 5.

NOVAK, LOUIS, *B-flat clarinet*
1923-24 tour.
Sources: SB payrolls & photos.

NOYES, H.F., *B-flat clarinet*
1st 1892 tour; probably 2nd 1892 tour; probably 1st 1893 tour; 2nd 1893 tour. Other position: Gilmore's Band.
Sources: 1892 C.G. Conn advertisement; program in St. Louis Post-Dispatch, 17 Oct 1893; SB publicity for 1st 1893 tour.

NUTTER, OSCAR L., *trombone*
1921 tour; 1921-22 tour; possibly 1922 tour. Other positions: Morrow Concert Band (Brighton, PA); Erie (PA) Philharmonic; Pittsburgh & Erie theater orchestras; music faculty, Erie Conservatory of Music; director of music, Erie public schools. Member, SBFS. b. 24 Apr 1890, Newburg, PA; d. 6 Sep 1971, Erie, PA.
Sources: SB rosters & photos; International Musician, Nov, 1971 [obituary]; references in SBFS News; author's correspondence with Nutter; Social Security Death Index.

NUTTICK, CHARLES S., *oboe*
2nd 1927 tour; 1928 tour. Other positions: U.S. Navy Band; music faculty, Stetson University. Member, SBFS.
Sources: SB payrolls; 1927 SB hotel assignment list; Eugene Slick's 1928 autograph book; references in SBFS News.

NUTZE, FRANK T., *cornet/trumpet, management*
1915 tour (partial); advance man for part of 1915 tour.
Sources: Plainfield (NJ) Courier News, 26 Mar 1915; roster in Musical Courier, 9 Jun 1915; 1915 Tuxedo tobacco advertisement with SB musicians' signatures; advertisement in Conn Musical Truth, Oct, 1921 (Sousa Edition); SBFS News, Feb, 1955, p. 16.

O'BRIEN, JAMES (Jimmy), *carpenter*
Listed as carpenter but probably meant baggage handler/stage manager. 1923-24 tour (partial); 1924 tour; 1925-26 tour (partial).
Source: 1923 SB payrolls.

O'CONNOR, MARTIN J. (Marty), *tuba*
1924 tour. Other position: Ringling Bros. and Barnum & Bailey Circus Band. Member, SBFS.
Sources: SB payroll 27 Nov 1924; references in SBFS News.

OECONAMACOS, NICHOLAS, *B-flat clarinet*
1st 1903 tour (Europe). Other position: Opera Comique Orchestra (Paris).
Sources: SB publicity for 1st 1903 tour; PBk 21, p. 289.

O'GORMAN, WILLIAM D., *saxophone*
1929 & 1930 radio broadcasts; 12 Mar 1931 recording; 9 Apr 1931 radio broadcast; late 1931 radio broadcasts.
Sources: SB payrolls.

O'LEARY, EUGENE, *E-flat clarinet*
1918 tour. Member, SBFS.
Source: SBFS organizational booklet (1945).

*O'MAHONEY, EDWARD, *basso*
Soloist. 1893 MB (partial).

Source: Program in PBk 3, p. 5.

*O'MALLEY, JOHN, *tenor (vocal)*
Soloist, 19 Mar 1916, New York.
Sources: Clarence J. Russell's diary; references in PBk 42.

*ONUKU, KARUKI, *soprano*
Soloist, 7 May 1916, New York; 22 Oct 1916, Philadelphia; 5 Nov 1916, Newark, NJ. b. Japan.
Sources: Clarence J. Russell's diary; PBk 44, pp. 20, 43, & 97.

ORMSBY, LOUISE, *soprano*
Soloist. 2nd 1908 tour (partial).
Sources: SB programs; references in PBk 30.

*ORNSTEIN, LEO, *piano*
Soloist, 20 Feb (possibly also 13 Feb) 1916, New York. b. 11 Dec 1895, Krementchug, Russia.
Sources: Clarence J. Russell's diary; Portraits of the World's Best-Known Musicians; PBk 42, p. 116.

OROSKY, JOHN J., *flute/piccolo*
2nd 1927 tour; 1928 tour (partial); 1929; one or more of 1930 tours; 1931 tour. Member, SBFS.
Sources: SB payrolls, programs, & photos; 1927 SB hotel assignment list; Jay Sims' handwritten checklist for 1931 tour; references in SBFS News.

ORRELL, LUCILLE, *cello*
Soloist. 1915 WG (partial); 1915 Pittsburgh Exposition (partial).
Sources: Clarence J. Russell's diary; PBk 41, pp. 63 & 66.

*OSBORN, FRANK HOUGH, *baritone (vocal)*
Soloist. 1897 MB (partial).
Source: PBk 5, p. 71.

OSTEN, CLARA M., *secretary*
1902 & 1903; possibly other years.
Source: SB roster in New York Dramatic Mirror, 6 Sep 1902; SB publicity for 1st 1903 tour lists Osten as secretary on executive staff.

OSTROM, RALPH K., *cornet/trumpet*
2nd 1927 tour; 1928 tour (cornet soloist at StPr); one or more of 1930 tours. Other positions: U.S. Navy Band; U.S. Army Band. b. 9 Mar 1908; d. Dec, 1984, Marion, NC.
Sources: SB payrolls, programs, & photos; Eugene Slick's 1928 autograph book; Musical Messenger, Nov, 1922, p. 17; author's interviews & correspondence with Patricia Backhaus, band historian, & with Kenneth B. Slater, bandmaster; Social Security Death Index.

OTTEN, ANNA, *violin*
Soloist. 2nd 1903 tour. Given name Duble; stage name Anna Otten.
Sources: SB programs; references in PBks 18 & 19.

OTTO, CHARLES, *B-flat clarinet*
2nd 1900 tour (Europe); possibly 1st, 2nd, & 3rd 1901 tours; 4th 1901 tour (Britain); possibly 1st, 2nd, & 3rd 1902 tours; 1st 1903 tour (Europe). Also assistant librarian.
Sources: Roster in SB program of 22 Apr 1900; SB photo, 30 May 1900; SB roster for 4th 1901 tour (Britain); SB/Grenadier Guards banquet seating chart of 17 Oct 1901; SB publicity for 1st 1903 tour; SBFS News, May, 1951, p. 7.

*OWEN, (Dr.) ROBERT OTWAY, *baritone (vocal)*
Soloist, 11 Dec 1895, Lynchburg, VA. Physician in Lynchburg. b. 23 Apr 1964, Lynchburg; d. 18 Jan 1903, San Bernardino, Ca.
Sources: Lynchburg News, 12 Dec 1895, p. 6; author's correspondence with Lewis H. Averette, Jones Memorial Library, Lynchburg.

PAGE, CLARENCE W. (Doc), *saxophone, B-flat clarinet*
1923-24 tour; 1924 tour; 1925-26 tour (partial).
Sources: SB payrolls, programs, & photos; roster in Jacobs' Band Monthly, Aug, 1925; references in PBks 58, 67, & 68; references in SBFS News.

PAGLIANI, A., *bassoon*
2nd 1893 tour; 1893 MB (soloist).
Sources: SB photo, Sep, 1893; program in PBk 3, p. 16.

PALMER, LESTER, *trombone*
1919-20 tour (partial).
Source: Various 1919-20 tour rosters.

PAONE, BIAGIO, *euphonium*
1907 tour; substituted briefly in 1916; 1929 & 1930 radio broadcasts; 9 Apr 1931 radio broadcast; late 1931 radio broadcasts.
Sources: SB payrolls; roster in New York Dramatic Mirror, 7 Sep 1907.

PAQUAY, ARMAND, *horn*
1916-17 tour.
Source: Roster in Dec, 1916 New York Musician and Knocker; unidentified article and photo (probably Nov, 1916) in PBk 44, p. 88.

PARDEE, KIRBY C., *management*
Date(s) of SB service uncertain, but on management staff in Apr, 1898.
Sources: Article in Louisville (KY) Post, Mar or Apr, 1898 [PBk 5; placements of articles rearranged but now on p. 215].

PARELLA, PASQUELLA, *trombone*
Date(s) of SB service uncertain, but prior to 1921. Other position: Metropolitan Opera Orchestra.
Source: Advertisement in Conn Musical Truth, Oct, 1921 (Sousa Edition).

PARK, ROBERT A., *B-flat clarinet*
1925-26 tour (partial).
Sources: SB payroll 11 Jul 1925; roster in Jacobs' Band Monthly, Aug, 1925; 1925-26 SB hotel assignment list.

PARKER, WILLIAM E., *trombone*
1921-22 tour (partial).
Sources: 1921 SB photo; 1921-22 SB roster; article & photo from a Seattle (WA) newspaper dated 19 Dec 1921 [PBk 54, p. 101].

*PARLOW, KATHLEEN, *violin*
Soloist, 23 Jan 1916 (New York). Other positions: Toured as concert artist with symphony orchestras in America & Europe; music faculty at Mills College; private music teacher. Recorded for Columbia. b. 20 Sep 1890, Calgary, ALB; d. 16 Aug 1963, Oakville, ONT.
Sources: Clarence J. Russell's diary; The New Grove Dictionary of American Music; Portraits of the World's Best-Known Musicians; New York Evening Mail, 24 Jan 1916; author's correspondence with Frederick P. Williams, discographer.

PAS, *see* **PONS, ALBERT A.**

*PASCHEDAG, THEODORE (Ted, Pasch), *flute/piccolo*
Substituted for 3 weeks, starting 1 Nov 1923, on 1923-24 tour. Other positions: Representative of C.G. Conn Co.; conductor of bands and orchestras in West Frankfort, IL public schools & Southern Illinois Concert Band. Composer. b. 10 Aug 1905, St. Louis, MO.
Sources: Who's Who in American Music, 1951 edition; The Heritage Encyclopedia of Band Music; author's interview with Paschedag.

*PASQUALE, _____ (male), *vocalist*
Soloist. 2nd 1894 Madison Square Garden engagement (partial). Recorded for Columbia.
Source: New York World, 3 Jun 1894, p. 12.

PASQUALE, see MARCHESE, PASQUALE
[Note: In SB publicity for 1893 tour, Marchese's name is incorrectly listed as Marchese Pasquale.]

PASTERNACK, JOSEPH, *studio conductor*
Conducted SB in Victor studio for at least 11 recordings in 1919-22 & 1925. Composer.
Source: Discographic data from Frederick P. Williams.

PAUL, FERDINAND (Ferd), *saxophone*
Possibly 1st & 2nd 1904 tours; 1st 1905 tour (Britain). Other position: American Saxophone Quartet.
Sources: S.S. Baltic ship's list, 19 May 1905; PBk 22, p. 39; author's interview with SB oboist Arthur Glenum.

PAULSEN, ERNEST J., *instrument?*
1925-26 tour (partial).
Source: SB payroll 6 Mar 1926.

PAULSON, WILLIAM T. (Billy), *percussion*
One or more of 1930 tours (xylophone **soloist**); 12 Mar 1930 radio broadcast; 9 Apr 1931 radio broadcast; late 1931 radio broadcasts. Co-founder, SBFS. Other positions: Pryor's Band; Bachman's Million Dollar Band.
Sources: Jay Sims' 1930 tour roster; unidentified clipping in Owen Kincaid Collection; references in PBk 75; author's interviews with Kenneth B. Slater, bandmaster.

PAYER, JOE, *B-flat clarinet*
1907 tour; 2nd 1908 tour; possibly other tours.
Sources: Rosters in New York Dramatic Mirror, 7 Sep 1907 & 1 Sep 1908; author's interview with Frank Mader, associate of Payer's.

PECHIN, ERNEST, *cornet/trumpet*
1912 tour; 1913 tour. Other positions: Kryl's Band; Innes' Band; Rochester (NY) Municipal Band; Conway's Band; WGN Radio Orchestra (Chicago); also conductor); conductor of Anglo-Canadian Leather Co. Band. Recorded for Edison. b. 18 Nov 1891, Seymour, IA; d. 23 Sep 1946, Oakland, FL.
Sources: Pioneers in Brass; advertisements in Musical Messenger, Feb, 1920, Mar, 1925, & Nov, 1926; references in SBFS News; author's interviews with Kenneth B. Slater, bandmaster, & with Frederick P. Williams, discographer.

PECHMANN, LEO, *oboe*
2nd 1892 tour; 1st 1893 tour; possibly other tours. Other position: Richard Wagner Theatre Orchestra (Beyreuth, Germany).
Sources: 1892 C.G. Conn advertisement; SB publicity for 1st 1893 tour.

PELLETIER, ALLPHONE, *horn*
Date(s) of SB service uncertain.
Source: Author's interviews with Kenneth B. Slater, bandmaster.

PERFETTO, JOHN JAMES (Johnny), *euphonium*
Also played trombone on occasion. Nearly all tours and engagements, 1904-1917 (euphonium **soloist** on most); last half of 1918 tour; 1919-20 tour. Other positions: Gilmore's Band; Pryor's Band; Conway's Band; Luciano Centerno's Band; Slafer's Band; 9th, 23rd, & 71st Regiment Bands (New York); trombonist with New York Philharmonic, New York Symphony Orchestra; Metropolitan Opera Orchestra, theater & radio orchestras in New York; music faculty, Community Center Conservatory of Music (New York). Elected to Trombone Hall of Fame, 1922. Recorded for Victor, Columbia, Domino, & Hager. Composer. Charter member, SBFS. b. 28 Mar 1876, Boiano, Campobasso, Italy; d. 21 May 1953, Rockville Centre, NY.
Sources: SB programs & photos; S.S. Baltic ship's list, 19 May 1905; roster in New York Dramatic Mirror, 1 Sep 1908; roster in Albert A. Knecht's world tour diary; Edmund A. Wall's world tour poem; signature on 6 Nov 1914 birthday card from band members to Sousa (refers to first year with band as 1904); roster in Musical Courier, 9 Jun 1915; 1915 Tuxedo tobacco advertisement with SB musicians' signatures; roster in Dec, 1916 New York Musician and Knocker; various 1919-20 rosters; feature articles & other references in PBks; references in SBFS News; author's interviews and correspondence with family.

PERRIER, PIERRE, *B-flat clarinet, saxophone(?)*
3rd 1901 tour (clarinet); 4th 1900 tour (Britain) (clarinet) possibly one or more tours in 1902; 1st 1903 tour (Europe) (clarinet); possibly 1st or 2nd 1904 tour; might have played saxophone on one tour.
Sources: SB/Grenadier Guards banquet seating chart of 17 Oct 1901; SB publicity for 1st 1903 tour; author's correspondence with William H. Rehrig, band historian.

PERRY, CHESTER A., *flute/piccolo*
1923-24 tour (partial); 1924 tour; 1925-26 tour. Other positions: Aberdeen (SD) Municipal Band; Norton Chautauqua Band & Orchestra; school music teacher in Los Angeles; member, SBFS; b. 13 Nov 1900; d. 15 Sep 1984, Fairfax, VA.
Sources: SB payrolls & photos; Harold Stambaugh's 1925-26 hotel assignment list; references in SBFS News; author's correspondence with John S. Burroughs, U.S. Marine Band; author's correspondence with Perry; Social Security Death Index.

PESCHE, _____, *harp*
Believed to have played with SB for a very short period, possibly the 2nd or 3rd 1930 tour.
Source: Jay Sims handwritten financial papers.

PETERS, A.G., *B-flat clarinet*
1st 1892 tour; possibly 2nd 1892 tour.
Source: 1892 C.G. Conn advertisement.

*PETERSEN, A. DAHN, *basso*
Soloist, 26 May 1894, New York.
Source: SB program.

PETERSON, OSCAR S., *tuba*
1915 tour.
Sources: SB photos; roster in Musical Courier, 9 Jun 1915; 1915 Tuxedo tobacco advertisement with SB musicians' signatures.

PETIT, CHARLES, *cornet/trumpet*
1st 1892 tour (cornet **soloist**); possibly 2nd 1892 tour. Other position: Gilmore's Band.

Sources: 1892 C.G. Conn advertisement; advertisement in J.W. Pepper's Musical Times and Band Journal, *May, 1898.*

PETRIE, JOHN C. (Jack), *flute/piccolo*
1925-26 tour; 1926 tour; 1st & 2nd 1927 tours; 1928 tour. Other positions: D'Oyly Carte Opera Orchestra (New York); New York theater orchestras. Charter member, SBFS. d. Oct 1971.
Sources: SB payrolls, rosters, photos & programs; references in SBFS News; *Social Security Death Index.*

PETZSCH, HERMAN, *alto clarinet*
4th 1901 tour (Britain); possibly 1st & 2nd 1902 tours; 3rd 1902 tour; 1st 1903 tour (Europe).
Sources: SB roster for 4th 1901 tour (Britain); SB/Grenadier Guards banquet seating chart of 17 Oct 1901; roster in New York Dramatic Mirror, *6 Sep 1902; SB publicity for 1st 1903 tour.*

PEW, HOWARD, *management*
Various management positions, 1892 to 1897. Other positions: Management staff of David Blakely's organization which managed tours of the U.S. Marine Band in 1891 & 1892 when Sousa was leader; manager of Brooke's Chicago Marine Band, Gilmore's Band, Creatore's Band, Banda Rosa, London Symphony Orchestra, Carlisle Indian Band, and various touring artists; also management staff of Vienna Strauss Orchestra; also bandmaster of note. d. 1917, Jersey City, NJ.
Sources: Band of America, *pp. 188 & 227;* Perspectives on John Philip Sousa, *pp. 121-126; references in PBks & theatrical journals.*

PFAFF, FRED E. (Freddie), *tuba*
1921 tour; possibly 1922 tour; 12 Mar 1930 radio broadcast; 9 Apr 1931 radio broadcast. Other positions: Pryor's Band; Conway's Band; Allentown (PA) Band; Florida Symphony Orchestra (Orlando); New York radio studio orchestras. Recorded for Victor. Charter member, SBFS.
Sources: 1921 SB roster; SB payroll 12 Mar 1930; Morning Call (Allentown), *25 Feb 1975, p. 6; author's interview and correspondence with Pfaff; references in SBFS News.*

PFAFF, GEORGE, *B-flat clarinet*
1925-26 tour (partial).
Sources: SB payroll for Jul-Dec, 1925; 1925-26 SB hotel assignment list.

PHARES, HALE W. (Venus), *flute/piccolo*
1928 tour; 1929 tour; one or more of 1930 tours. d. ca. 1961.
Sources: SB payrolls & programs; Eugene Slick's 1928 autograph book; references in SBFS News.

*PHELPS, LAURA B., *violin*
Soloist, off-tour concert 18 Jan 1894, New York.
Source: Program in PBk 3, p. 51.

PHENEY, J.J., *bass clarinet*
1926 tour (partial?).
Source: SB photo, Jul, 1926.

PHOENIX, WILLIAM H. (Bill), *cornet/trumpet*
1923-24 tour. Other positions: Pryor's Band; St. Petersburg (FL) Municipal Band.
Sources: SB payrolls & photos; St. Petersburg Independent, *1 Feb 1924.*

PIATES, DAVID, *B-flat clarinet*
1919-20 tour (partial). Member, SBFS. b. 27 Dec 1894; d. Aug, 1965, Cincinnati, OH.
Sources: Various 1919-20 tour rosters [name sometimes misspelled as Pinter]; Musical Messenger, *Nov, 1919; Berger roster; references in SBFS News; Social Security Death Index.*

PIERCE, JOHN J. (Jack), *tuba*
1929 & 1930 radio broadcasts; 12 Mar 1931 recording. Other positions: Metropolitan Opera Orchestra; Pryor's Band; Conway's Band.
Sources: SB payrolls; "In Memoriam" list, SBFS organizational booklet (1945).

PIERCE, WILLIAM N. (Bill), *horn*
1920 tour; 1921 tour (**soloist** at WG); 1921-22 tour (**soloist** at Dominion Park [Quebec]). Other position: Long Beach (CA) Municipal Band. Member, SBFS. d. ca. 1948.
Sources: SB rosters; 1921 SB photo; PBk 54, p. 162; references in SBFS News.

PINSCHL, HENRY, *instrument?*
1909 tour; possibly other tours.
Source: 1909 photo in Arthur Storch family collection.

PINTER, see PIATES, DAVID

PLANTAMURA, JOSEPH, *flute/piccolo*
1916-17 tour; 1st & 2nd 1917 tours; 1918 tour; 1919-20 tour (partial); sometimes piccolo **soloist.**
Sources: SB programs; roster in Dec, 1916 New York Musician and Knocker.

POLING, EARLE A., *instrument?*
2 concerts on 6 Nov 1928 (Palo Alto, CA). Other positions: New York Symphony Orchestra; Paul Whiteman's Orchestra.
Sources: SB contract for one day only, letter from Sousa, and other memorabilia in Poling family collection.

*POLLOCK, EMMA, *soprano*
Soloist, 18 Mar 1917 (New York).
Source: Clarence J. Russell's diary.

POMO, ETTORE, *B-flat clarinet*
2nd 1900 tour (Europe); 4th 1901 tour (Britain); possibly other tours in 1900 & 1901.
Sources: Roster in SB program of 22 Apr 1900; SB photo, 30 May 1900; SB roster for 4th 1901 tour (Britain); SB/Grenadier Guards banquet seating chart of 17 Oct 1901.

PONS, ALBERT A., *flute/piccolo*
[Name sometimes misspelled as Pas]. 1919-20 tour; possibly part of one other tour. Other position: Played in a U.S. Army band in Europe during World War I. b. ca. 1890; d. ca. 1962.
Sources: SBFS News, Oct, 1950, p. 3; various 1919-20 tour rosters; author's correspondence with family.

PORLATTO, CAL, *B-flat clarinet*
1926 tour (partial).
Source: SB photo, Jul, 1926.

PORPORA, STEVE, *B-flat clarinet*
1907 tour; 2nd 1908 tour; possibly other tours between 1906-10. Recorded for Victor.
Sources: Rosters in New York Dramatic Mirror, *7 Sep 1907 & 1 Sep 1908; author's correspondence with Frederick P. Williams, discographer.*

*PORTEOUS, WILLIAM M., *basso*
Soloist. 1894 St. Louis Exposition.
Sources: St. Louis Post-Dispatch, 12 Oct 1894; author's correspondence with Missouri Historical Society.

POSSELL, GEORGE, *flute/piccolo*
1929 radio broadcasts; 12 Mar 1931 recording ; 9 Apr 1931 radio broadcast; late 1931 radio broadcasts.
Sources: SB payrolls.

*POST, LILLY, *soprano*
Soloist. 1893 MB (partial).
Sources: Programs & references in PBks 2 & 3.

POVAH, _____, *cornet/trumpet*
Date(s) of SB service uncertain, but ca. 1903.
Source: PBk 20, p. 53.

POWELL, MARCELLA, *soprano*
Soloist. 2nd 1898 tour.
Sources: References in PBks 5 & 9.

POWELL, MAUD, *violin*
Soloist. 1st 1903 tour (Europe); 1st 1905 tour (Britain). Other positions: Concert artist (recitals & with symphony orchestras in America & Europe); Maud Powell Concert Company; before Sousa, toured with New York Arion Society & Gilmore's Band. Recorded for Victor. Author. b. 22 Aug 1867, Peru, IL; d. 8 Jan 1920, Uniontown, PA.
Sources: SB rosters, programs, & photos; Maud Powell, Pioneer American Violinist; The New Grove Dictionary of American Music; Portraits of the World's Best-Known Musicians; *publicity of Maud Powell Foundation;* The Art of Maud Powell *(3 compact discs);* American String Teacher, *Spring, 1980, pp. 32-33;* The Strad, *Aug, 1980, pp. 237-241; references in SBFS News; author's correspondence with Karen A. Shaffer & Neva Garner Greenwood, Powell's biographers.*

*POWELL, RUBY, *soprano*
Soloist. 1902 StPr (partial).
Sources: SB programs; PBk 18, p. 175.

POWERS, JEANETTE AVERY, *violin*
Soloist. Probably all 1906 & 1907 engagements; 1st 1908 tour; 1919 WG (partial); 1921-22 tour (partial). Other positions: Concert artist in America. Married name Mrs. Carl C. Block. b. Decatur, IL; d. 1 Aug 1942, Chicago.

231

Sources: SB programs & photos; references in PBks; research by Phyllis Danner, Sousa Archives for Band Research, University of Illinois.

PREBLE, CARL E., _euphonium_
1921 tour; 1921-22 tour; 1923-24 tour; 1924 tour; 1925-26 tour; 1926 tour. Member, SBFS.

Sources: SB payrolls & photos; Band Encyclopedia; advertisement in Conn Musical Truth, *Oct, 1921 ("Sousa Edition"); roster in* Jacobs' Band Monthly, *Aug, 1925; 1925-26 SB hotel assignment list; references in* SBFS News.

PREISS (later PRICE), EMIL G., _B-flat clarinet_
Probably all tours, 1892-1905; 1929 radio broadcasts.

Sources: SB payrolls, rosters, programs, & photos; various other rosters; 1892 C.G. Conn advertisement; references in SBFS News; author's correspondence with Donald Callahan, researcher.

PREVOST, LEON, _flugelhorn_
1st 1904 tour; possibly other tours.

Sources: SB programs in PBk 18 (refer to flugelhorn duets with Franz Helle).

PRICE, see PREISS, EMIL G.

PROHASKA, FRED B., _alto clarinet_
1920 tour; 1921 tour; 1921-22 tour; probably 1922 tour; 1923-24 tour.
Sources: SB payrolls, rosters, & photos.

PRUETTE, WILLIAM, _baritone (vocal)_
Soloist. 1894 MB (partial); last week of 2nd 1898 tour in New York. Other positions: Vaudeville and concert singer. d. 14 Jul 1918, Liberty, NY.

Sources: Programs in PBk 3; New York Clipper, 4 Jun 1898; Variety, 19 Jul 1918, p. 16 [obituary].

PRYOR, ARTHUR WILLARD, _trombone_
Probably all engagements, 1892-1st 1903 tour (Europe), except briefly to conduct Victor recording sessions in 1901 & 1902. Soloist; also assistant conductor. Other positions: Liberati's Grand Military Band; conductor of Stanley Opera Co.; founder/conductor of Pryor's Band; music director of Victor Phonograph Co. (conducted many SB recording sessions); also recorded for Berliner; private music teacher. Composer. Charter member, American Bandmasters Assn.; charter member, SBFS. Brother of Samuel Pryor and Walter D. Pryor. b. 22 Sep 1870, St. Joseph, MO; d. 17 Jun 1942, Long Branch, NJ.

Sources: SB payrolls, rosters, programs, & photos; Arthur Pryor (1870-1942), American Trombonist, Bandmaster, Composer; *Arthur Pryor;* Pioneers in Brass; *John Philip Sousa, American Phenomenon;* Band Encyclopedia; *The Sousa Band A Discography;* Association of Recorded Sound Collections Journal, *1979; "Arthur Pryor, Trombone Soloist of the Sousa Band" (Crystal Records CD # 451); numerous references in PBks; references in SBFS News; author's interviews & correspondence with former members of Pryor's Band & SB, with Leonard B. Smith, composer, with Kenneth B. Slater, bandmaster, & with Frederick P. Williams, discographer.*

PRYOR, SAMUEL, _percussion_
With SB for short period ca. 1902. Other position: Pryor's Band. Brother of Arthur W. Pryor & Walter D. Pryor.
Sources: Berger roster; SBFS, Sep, 1951, p. 8.

PRYOR, WALTER D., _cornet/trumpet_
With SB for short periods in 1897 & 1898. Other position: Pryor's Band. Recorded for Victor. Brother of Arthur W. Pryor & Samuel Pryor.

Sources: 1897 SB payroll; Varella photo; seating chart in Philadelphia Press, *7 May 1897; advertisement in* J.W. Pepper Musical Times and Band Journal, *May, 1898; SBFS News, Sep, 1951, p. 8; author's interviews & correspondence with Frederick P. Williams, discographer, & with Kenneth B. Slater, bandmaster.*

*PULITI, GIOGRI, _basso_
Soloist, 9 Jan 1916, New York.
Source: SB program.

RAFFAYOLO, JOSEPH MICHELE, _euphonium_
1st & 2nd 1892 tours; off-tour concert 23 Jan 1893, New York; 1st 1893 tour; 1893 MB; 2nd 1893 tour; off-tour concert 21 Jan 1894, Brooklyn, NY; off-tour concert 25 Feb 1894, New York; 1st 1894 tour; 1st & 2nd 1894 Madison Square Garden engagements; 1894 MB; 3rd 1895 tour (soloist on all the above); 4th 1895 tour; possibly other tours. Other position: Gilmore's Band. d. 1896.

Sources: SB programs & photos; publicity for 1st 1893 tour; Bands of America, *pp. 130 & 200; references in various music journals.*

RAGONE, VINCENT, _clarinet_
Probably one or more tours in 1905 and/or 1906. Composer, arranger; made numerous arrangements for SB. Other positions: Innes' Band; Fanciulli's Band; Weil's Band; Phinney's United States Band. b. ca. 1859, Capaccio, Italy; d. 1929.

Sources: Letter of recommendation dated 25 Mar 1907 from Sousa; author's correspondence with family; correspondence with Sousa Archives for Band Research, University of Illinois.

*RAND, LLOYD, _tenor (vocal)_
Soloist. 1897 MB.
Source: PBk 5, p. 62.

RASP, WALTER F. _B-flat clarinet_
2nd 1927 tour. Member, SBFS. b. 22 Apr 1906; d. Jan, 1982, Seattle, WA.
Sources: 1927 SB payroll; 1927 SB hotel assignment list; references in SBFS News; Social Security Death Index.

RATZEKY, ALEX, _oboe_
1st 1896 tour; 1896-97 tour.
Sources: SB payrolls; composite 1895/96 SB photo; seating chart in Philadelphia Press, *7 May 1897.*

*RAYMOND, ALICE, _cornet/trumpet_
Soloist (not SB member). 1893 St. Louis Exposition. Other positions: Brooke's Chicago Marine Band (guest soloist). Recorded for Berliner.
Sources: Programs for 8-21 Oct 1893 in St. Louis Post-Dispatch; Bands of America, *p. 226; author's correspondence with Frederick P. Williams, discographer.*

RAYMOND, ARTHUR, _tuba_
1923-24 tour; 1924 tour.
Sources: SB payrolls; 1924 SB photo; SBFS News, Oct, 1970, p. 4.

*READ, SAM, _percussion_
Evidently with SB as substitute for short periods. 1915 tour (partial); possibly 1917 and/or 1918 tours (partial); possibly 1919-20 tour (partial). Other positions: Twin Cities Symphony (Minneapolis); music faculty, Andrews University; served in U.S. Army during World War II. b. Battle Creek, MI.

Sources: Undated articles in author's collection; author's correspondence with John J. Heney, SB percussionist, & with Music Dept., Andrews University.

*REED, GRAHAM, _baritone (vocal)_
Soloist. 1893 MB (partial). Other positions: Concert artist in England; music faculty, Chicago Music College & DePaul University; private music teacher; management staff, Metropolitan Opera Co. b. 1865, Brooklyn, NY; d. 16 Oct 1952, Brooklyn.

Sources: SB program in PBk 3, p. 35; New York Times, 18 Oct 1952, p. 19.

REICHARD, ROSE, _violin_
Soloist. 2nd 1908 tour. Other positions: Concert tours in America; Waterloo (IA) Symphony Orchestra; music faculty, Drake University and Waterloo public schools. Married name Mrs. Herbert F. Marshall. b. 31 Aug 1879, Mitchellville, IA.

Sources: Who Is Who in Music, 1951 edition; references in PBk 30.

REINES, ABRAHAM (Abe), _bassoon_
1914 tour; 1915 tour; 1916-17 tour; 1921 tour. Other positions: NBC Symphony Orchestra; staff bassoonist, NBC Radio, New York. Member, SBFS. b. 17 Feb 1896; d. Jan, 1970, Hollywood, FL.

Sources: Signature on 6 Nov 1914 birthday card from band members to Sousa (refers to first year with band as 1914); roster in Musical Courier, *9 Jun 1915; 1915 Tuxedo tobacco advertisement with SB musicians' signatures; roster in Dec, 1916* New York Musician and Knocker; *SB rosters for 1921 & 1921-22 tours; references in SBFS News; Social Security Death Index.*

REINES, MORRIS, _bassoon_
1915 tour; 1920 tour.
Sources: Roster in 1920 WG programs; SBFS News, Jun, 1949.

REISE, A., _horn_
1907 tour.
Source: Roster in New York Dramatic Mirror, *7 Sep 1907.*

REISSNER, ANDREW (Andy), _bass clarinet, B-flat clarinet_
1st & 2nd 1927 tours; 1928 tour; off-tour concert 15 Jun 1929, Princeton, NJ; 1929 tour; 1929 & 1931 radio broadcasts; one or more of 1930 tours; 12 Mar 1931 recording; 9 Apr 1931 radio broadcast; 1931 tour (partial). Other positions: Gilmore's Band; Liberati's Grand Concert Band.

Sources: SB payrolls & programs; 1927 SB hotel assignment list; Eugene Slick's 1928 autograph book; references in SBFS News.

REITZ, WILLIAM H., *percussion*
Date(s) of SB service uncertain, but apparently with band for short period ca. World War I. Recorded for Victor. d. 1935.
Sources: Leedy Drum Co. advertisement ca. Aug, 1924; author's correspondence with Frederick P. Williams, discographer.

RENZ, ADOLF, *B-flat clarinet*
1ˢᵗ and/or 2ⁿᵈ 1892 tours. Other position: Peabody's Orchestra (Baltimore).
Source: 1892 C.G. Conn advertisement.

RENZI, PAOLO, *oboe*
2ⁿᵈ 1927 tour (StPr only); 12 Mar 1930 radio broadcast; 1931 tour. Other position: NBC Symphony Orchestra. Member, SBFS.
Sources: SB payrolls; Jay Sims' handwritten checklist for 1931 tour; references in SBFS News; *author's interviews with Kenneth B. Slater, bandmaster.*

RESCHKE, FRANK F., *sarrusophone*
3ʳᵈ 1902 tour; 1ˢᵗ 1903 tour (Europe). [Note: these were probably the only tours where the SB used a sarrusophone.] d. 20 Jul 1914.
Sources: "In Memoriam" list, SBFS organizational booklet (1945); roster in NY Dramatic Mirror, *6 Sep 1902;* Detroit News, *21 Jul 1914.*

REUFFEL, WILLIAM, *bass clarinet*
Probably tours in 1895; 1ˢᵗ 1896 tour; 1896-97 tour; probably later tours.
Sources: SB payrolls; composite 1895/96 SB photo; seating chart in Philadelphia Press, *7 May 1897.*

REYNOLDS, EVERETT R., *management*
General manager, 1897-1900. Other positions: Manager, Long Island Railroad; agent/manager for DeWolf Hopper.
Sources: SB advertising fliers; Marching Along, *p. 165; references in PBks 8, 9, 14, & 21.*

RICCIARDI, EDGARD I., *flute/piccolo*
1919 WG; 1919-20 tour; possibly one earlier tour. Other positions: Creatore's Band; Victor Herbert's Orchestra; John Wanamaker Band. b. Italy; d. 4 Nov 1967, Camden, NJ.
Sources: 1919 SB photo; Camden *(NJ)* Courier-Post, *9 Nov 1967; author's correspondence with family.*

RICE, ED. L., *B-flat clarinet*
3ʳᵈ 1898 tour; possibly other tours in 1898 & 1899.
Source: Seating chart in St. Louis Post-Dispatch, *25 Sep 1898.*

RICHARDSON, JOHN W. (Jack), *tuba*
2ⁿᵈ 1903 tour; probably 1ˢᵗ & 2ⁿᵈ 1904 tours; 1ˢᵗ 1905 tour (Britain); possibly 3ʳᵈ & 4ᵗʰ 1905 tours; 1ˢᵗ & 2ⁿᵈ 1906 tours; possibly 3ʳᵈ & 4ᵗʰ 1906 tours; 1907 tour; 1ˢᵗ & 2ⁿᵈ 1908 tours; possibly tours in 1909 & 1910; 1912 tour; possibly 1913 tours; 1914 tour; 1915 tour; 1916-17 tour; probably 1ˢᵗ 1917 tour; 2ⁿᵈ 1917 tour; 1918 tour; 1923-24 tour; 1924 tour; 1925-26 tour; 1926 tour; 1ˢᵗ & 2ⁿᵈ 1927 tours; 1928 tour; off-tour concert 15 Jun 1929, Princeton, NJ; 1929 tour; 1929 radio broadcasts; 12 Mar 1930 radio broadcast; one or more of 1930 tours; 12 Mar 1931 recording; 9 Apr 1931 radio broadcast; 1931 tour; late 1931 radio broadcasts. Other positions: Brooke's Chicago Marine Band; [Mayhew L. Lake's] Symphony of Gold; Finney's Band; Anglo-Canadian Leather Co. Band; 65ᵗʰ & 74ᵗʰ New York Regiment Bands; Allentown (PA) Band; Lancaster (PA) City Band; Ephrata (PA) Band. Recorded for U.S. Phonograph Co.
Sources: SB payrolls, rosters, & photos; numerous other rosters; "In Memoriam" list, SBFS organizational booklet (1945) & references in SBFS News; *references in PBks.*

RICHART, SANTIAGO, *horn*
1914 tour; 1915 tour; possibly tours in 1917 & 1918; 1929 radio broadcasts. Charter member, SBFS. d. ca. 1948.
Sources: SB payrolls; signature on 6 Nov 1914 birthday card from band members to Sousa (refers to first year with band as 1914); roster in Musical Courier, *9 Jun 1915; 1915 Tuxedo tobacco advertisement with SB musicians' signatures; references in* SBFS News.

RICHTOR, RUDOLPH, *percussion*
Possibly 1ˢᵗ & 2ⁿᵈ 1895 tours; 3ʳᵈ & 4ᵗʰ 1895 tours; 1ˢᵗ 1896 tour; 1896-97 tour; possibly 1897 tour; 3ʳᵈ 1898 tour.
Sources: J.W. Pepper's Musical Times and Band Journal, Spring, 1895; 1896 & 1897 SB payrolls; composite 1895/96 SB photo; seating chart in St. Louis Post-Dispatch, *27 Sep 1898.*

*RIDGE, WINIFRED, *soprano*
Soloist. 1926 WG (partial).
Sources: SB programs.

RIDGLEY, CLIFFORD E., *B-flat clarinet*
12 Mar 1930 radio broadcast.
Source: SB payroll.

*RIEGG, CAROLA, *vocalist*
Soloist. 2ⁿᵈ 1894 Madison Square Garden engagement (partial).
Source: New York Times, *25 May 1894, p. 4.*

*RING, BLANCHE, *soprano*
Soloist, apparently one time only in Kansas City, MO; date uncertain but probably sometime between 1904-1909. Other positions: Actress/singer in vaudeville, musical comedy, and revues. Recorded for Victor. b. 24 Apr 1871, Boston; d. 13 Jan 1961, Santa Monica, CA.
Sources: The New Grove Dictionary of American Music; San Jose *(CA)* Mercury-Herald, *16 Sep 1917;* Variety, *18 Jan 1961, p. 70 [obituary].*

RIPPLE, WALTER E., *cornet/trumpet*
1912 tour; possibly 1913 tour; 1914 tour; 1915 tour (partial); 1916-17 tour. Other positions: Anglo-Canadian Leather Co. Band; St. Petersburg (FL) Grotto Band; several bands in Pennsylvania. Member, SBFS. d. ca. 1959, St. Petersburg.
Sources: signature on 6 Nov 1914 birthday card from band members to Sousa (refers to first year with band as 1912); roster in Musical Courier, *9 Jun 1915; 1915 Tuxedo tobacco advertisement with SB musicians' signatures; roster in Dec, 1916* New York Musician and Knocker; *references in* SBFS News; *author's interviews with Kenneth B. Slater, bandmaster.*

*RITCHIE, ADELE, *soprano*
Soloist. 1894 MB (partial). Other positions: sang opera, musical comedy, and vaudeville, mostly in New York. b. 1874, Philadelphia; d. 24 Apr 1930.
Sources: SB programs in PBk 3; The Oxford Companion to American Theatre; Who Was Who in America, *Vol. 1.*

*RIVA, LILLIAN, *soprano*
Soloist. 1894 MB (partial).
Sources: Programs in PBk 3.

ROBINSON, WILLIAM J. (Willie), *B-flat clarinet*
1907 tour; 2ⁿᵈ 1908 tour; 1911 world tour; 1920 tour; 1929 tour; one or more of 1930 tours; 1931 tour.
Sources: SB payrolls; rosters in New York Dramatic Mirror, *7 Sep 1907 & 1 Sep 1908; roster in Albert A. Knecht's world tour diary; Edmund A. Wall's world tour poem; roster in 1920 WG programs; Jay Sims' 1930 tour roster & handwritten checklist for 1931 tour; references in* SBFS News.

ROCHSTROH, _____, *instrument?*
1ˢᵗ 1892 tour.
Source: Blakely papers.

ROEDER, LOUIS, *cornet/trumpet*
1907 tour; possibly 1ˢᵗ 1908 tour; 2ⁿᵈ 1908 tour; 1929 & 1930 radio broadcasts; 1ˢᵗ 1930 tour.
Sources: SB payrolls & programs; roster in New York Dramatic Mirror, *7 Sep 1907; 1930 SB photo; PBk 27, p. 21.*

ROESCHEL, WILLIAM E., *B-flat clarinet*
Off-tour concert 15 Jun 1929, Princeton, NJ; 1929 & 1930 radio broadcasts; 12 Mar 1931 recording; 9 Apr 1931 radio broadcast; late 1931 radio broadcasts.
Sources: SB payrolls.

ROGERS, WALTER BOWMAN, *cornet/trumpet*
4ᵗʰ & 5ᵗʰ 1899 tours; 1ˢᵗ 1900 tour; 2ⁿᵈ European tour (Europe); 3ʳᵈ & 4ᵗʰ 1900 tours; 1ˢᵗ, 2ⁿᵈ, & 3ʳᵈ 1901 tours; 4ᵗʰ 1901 tour (Britain); 1901 MB; 1ˢᵗ, 2ⁿᵈ, 3ʳᵈ, & 4ᵗʰ 1902 tours; 1ˢᵗ 1903 tour (Europe); 2ⁿᵈ 1903 tour; 1ˢᵗ 1904 tour; cornet **soloist** on all. Other positions: English Opera Co. Orchestra & other theater orchestras in Indianapolis, IN; Indianapolis Municipal Band; Cappa's 7ᵗʰ Regt. Band (New York – later conductor); Anglo-Canadian Leather Co. Band; Phinney's Iowa State Band; Baldwin's Cadet Band (Boston); conductor of Goshen (IN) town bands; Director of Music, Victor Talking Machine Co. (conducted numerous bands, orchestras, and Light Opera Co.; Recording Manager, Paroquette Record Co. (conducted Walter B. Rogers Military Band); Music Director, Paramount Record Co. (conducted Walter B. Rogers Band in dance recordings); Recording Director, Brunswick Co.; also associated with Emerson Record Co. Made cornet solo recordings for Berliner, Brunswick, Columbia, Paroquette, & Victor (including some with Sousa's Band); Composer, arranger. b. 14 Oct 1865, Delphi, IN; d. 24 Dec 1939, Brooklyn, NY.

Sources: SB rosters, programs, & photos; Pioneers in Brass; The Heritage Encyclopedia of Band Music; Supplement to the Heritage Encyclopedia of Band Music; Band Encyclopedia; Bands of America, *pp. 122 & 240;* The Sousa Band A Discography; *Hobbies, Feb, 1959, pp. 34-40; articles & photos in various music journals; articles & photos in PBks; references in SBFS News.*

*ROHAN, _____ (male), *vocalist*
Soloist. 1893 St. Louis Exposition (partial).
Source: St. Louis Post-Dispatch, 21 Oct 1893.

*ROMANI, GIULIANO, *tenor (vocal)*
Soloist, 30 Jan 1916, New York.
Sources: Clarence J. Russell's diary; PBk 42, p. 100.

ROMERIL, JAMES G. (Jack), *tuba*
1923-24 tour (partial); 1924 tour.
Sources: SB payrolls & photos; author's correspondence with Herbert N. Johnston, band historian.

ROOT, ELEANOR VIRGINIA (Virginia), *soprano*
Soloist. 1909 WG; off-tour concerts 26 Dec 1909, 2 Jan 1910, & 9 Jan 1910, New York; 1st 1910 tour; 2nd 1910 tour except last week; 1911 world tour; 1912 tour; 1913 tour; 1914 tour except 1st week; 1915 tour except last 2 weeks; 1916 WG (partial); some Boston Sunday concerts Nov-Dec, 1916; 1st 1917 tour. Other positions: Recitalist; featured soloist with symphony orchestras; toured with Sir Harry Lauder, using the pseudonym Virginia Vervelle. Member, SBFS. Married name Mrs. George T. MacAdam. b. 14 Apr 1884; d. 2 Jun 1980, Springfield, MA.
Sources: SB rosters, programs, & photos; roster in Albert A. Knecht's world tour diary; Edmund A. Wall's world tour poem; Virginia Root Collection; Clarence J. Russell's diary; references in PBks; references in SBFS News; music with marginalia on music at the Sousa Archives for Band Research, University of Illinois; author's correspondence with Phyllis Danner, Sousa Archives for Band Research.

ROSANDER, ARTHUR HAROLD, SR. (Rosey), *saxophone, librarian*
1909 tour; probably 1st & 2nd 1910 tours; 1919-20 tour. Other positions: Pryor's Band; toured with Chautauqua bands and orchestras and theater orchestras; conductor of John Wanamaker Band (Philadelphia). Composer. Charter member, SBFS. d. 23 May 1951.
Sources: Various 1919-20 rosters; references in SBFS News.

ROSANDER, ARTHUR HAROLD, JR., *saxophone*
Possibly 1922 tour; 1923-24 tour; 1924 tour. Charter member, SBFS (Vice President, 1963-71). b. 6 Sep 1901; d. Feb, 1971.
Sources: SB payrolls & photos; Berger roster; references in SBFS News; author's interview with Rosander.

ROSE, EUGENE C., *flute/piccolo, bassoon*
2nd 1900 tour (Europe) (flute/piccolo); possibly other tours in 1900 & 1901; 4th 1901 tour (Britain) (bassoon). Other position: Metropolitan Opera Orchestra. Recorded for Edison. Member, SBFS. b. 26 Jul 1866, Danzig, Poland; d. ca. 1961.
Sources: SB photo, May, 1900; roster in SB program of 22 Apr 1900; SB/Grenadier Guards banquet seating chart of 17 Oct 1901; Bands of America, p. 210; author's interview & correspondence with family.

*ROSE, KATHERINE, *soprano*
Soloist. 1896 MB (partial).
Sources: Programs in PBk 4.

*ROSELLE, FIELDING, *contralto*
Soloist. 1896 MB (partial); 1897 MB (partial).
Sources: Programs in PBks 4 & 5.

*ROSENBLATT, JOSEF, *tenor (vocal)*
Soloist. 1919 WG (partial). Other positions: Concert artist and synagogue cantor. Recorded for Columbia & Victor. d. 19 Jun 1933, Jerusalem, Israel.
Sources: SB programs; PBk 30, p. 28; Variety, 20 Jun 1933, p. 41 [obituary]; author's correspondence with Frederick P. Williams, discographer.

ROSS, ROBERT A. (Bob), *B-flat clarinet*
1921 tour; 1921-22 tour; 1923-24 tour; 1924 tour; 1925-26 tour (partial); 2nd 1927 tour.
Sources: SB payrolls, rosters, & photos; 1926 & 1927 SB hotel assignment lists; PBk 62, p. 50; PBk 72, p. 115; references in SBFS News.

*ROSSEAU, FRANCES, *soprano*
Soloist. 1896 MB (partial).
Sources: Programs in PBk 4.

ROTHWELL, C. IRVING (Irv), *trombone*
1919-20 tour. Member, SBFS. d. ca. 1951, Lynbrook, NY.
Sources: Various 1919-20 tour rosters references in SBFS News.

ROW, FRANK, *flute/piccolo*
1915 tour (partial).
Source: 1915 Tuxedo tobacco advertisement with SB musicians' signatures.

ROWELL, HOWARD L., *cornet/trumpet*
1920 tour; 1921 tour; 1921-22 tour. Other positions: Buffalo Bill's Wild West Show Band; Merrimac Carriage Makers Band; William Sweeney's Cowboy Band; Haverhill (MA) City Band; Salem Cadet Band; Chandler's Band (Portland, ME); Bektesh Temple Shrine Band (Concord, NH); Aleppo Temple Shrine Band (Haverhill); various orchestras; conductor of Rowell's Band (Haverhill); music faculty, Consentino School of Music (Dover, NH). Member, SBFS. b. 17 Jun 1882, Haverhill; d. 28 Aug 1963, Haverhill.
Sources: SB rosters; references in SBFS News; undated obituary, author's collection.

RUBEL, GEORGE, *B-flat clarinet*
1915 tour (partial). Recorded for Edison.
Sources: 1915 clarinet section photo; Clarinet Recordings Vol. 1 (compact disc privately produced by Stan Stanford, discographer); SBFS News, Jan, 1954, p. 21; author's correspondence with Frederick P. Williams, discographer.

RUCKLE, CLIFFORD F., *bassoon*
1925-26 tour; 1926 tour. Member, SBFS. d. 1947.
Sources: SB payrolls; references in SBFS News.

RUMPFF, OTTO, *B-flat clarinet*
2nd 1908 tour.
Sources: Roster in New York Dramatic Mirror, 1 Sep 1908; author's correspondence with Raoul F. Camus, band historian.

RUNDQUIST, CARL T., *B-flat clarinet*
1925-26 tour (partial); 1st & 2nd 1927 tours. Served in Great Lakes Naval Training Station Band under Sousa during World War I; Bachman's Million Dollar Band; Minneapolis theater orchestras; music faculty, Parsons College; operated music store in Fairfield, IA. Member, SBFS (President, 1987-1990). b. Minnesota; d. 19 Sep 1990, Fairfield.
Sources: SB payroll 11 Jul 1925; roster in Jacobs' Band Monthly, Aug, 1925; 1925-26 & 1927 SB hotel assignment lists; references in SBFS News; correspondence between Rundquist and Malcolm Heslip, author; author's correspondence with Rundquist & with Loras Schissel, music historian.

RUNDQUIST, WILLARD, *B-flat clarinet*
1925-26 tour. Member, SBFS. b. 27 Apr 1899; d. Oct, 1967, Minneapolis.
Sources: References in SBFS News; author's correspondence with family; Social Security Death Index.

RUPP, JACOB, *B-flat clarinet*
Date(s) of SB service uncertain, but was with band during 1890s.
Source: PBk 5, p. 173.

RUSCICA, S., *instrument?*
Believed to have played with SB for a very short period, possibly the 2nd or 3rd 1930 tour.
Source: Jay Sims handwritten financial papers.

RUSS, GABE, *tuba*
1923-24 tour; 1924 tour; 1925-26 tour; 1926 tour; 1st & 2nd 1927 tours. Other position: Long Beach (CA) Municipal Band. Member, SBFS.
Sources: SB payrolls & photos; Jay Sims' 1919-20 tour roster; 1925-26 & 1927 SB hotel assignment lists; author's interviews with Kenneth B. Slater, bandmaster.

RUSS, JESS, *tuba*
Possibly 1918 tour; 1919-20 tour. Member, SBFS.
Sources: Various 1919-20 tour rosters; references in SBFS News.

RUSSELL, CLARENCE JOHN (Buss), *cornet/trumpet, librarian*
Evidently all tours, other engagements, & radio broadcasts, 1910-32. Occasional **soloist**. Conducted when Sousa was indisposed on 1929 tour. Narrated at concerts when necessary. Other positions: Russian Symphony Orchestra; Boston Symphony Orchestra; New York Symphony Orchestra; music faculty, Brooklyn School of Music & National High School Band & Orchestra Camp (Interlochen, MI); private music teacher. Author. b. 1875, Pittsfield, MA; d. 23 Jan 1941.

Sources: SB payrolls, rosters, programs, & photos; various other rosters; Metronome, 15 Apr 1925, p. 20; Etude, Oct, 1934, p. 622; roster in Albert A. Knecht's world tour diary; Edmund A. Wall's world tour poem; references in PBks; advertisements in various trade journals; references in SBFS News; author's correspondence with family and with Barry Owen Furrer, band historian.

RUSSO, ENRICO, B-flat clarinet
4th 1901 tour (Britain); 1st 1903 tour (Europe).
Sources: SB/Grenadier Guards banquet seating chart of 17 Oct 1901; SB salary list, Oct-Dec, 1901; SB publicity for 1st 1903 tour.

*RUTLEDGE, GRACE, soprano
Soloist. 1896 MB (partial).
Sources: Programs in PBk 4.

RYBA, WALTER M., horn
1929 tour; one or more of 1930 tours; 1931 tour. Other position: Music faculty, University of Tennessee.
Sources: SB payrolls; Jay Sims' 1930 tour roster & handwritten checklist for 1931 tour; author's correspondence with Owen D. Kincaid, SB saxophonist & with W.J. Julien, associate of Ryba.

SACKETT, MAURICE, flute/piccolo
1923-24 tour; 1926 tour; off-tour concert 15 Jun 1929, Princeton, NJ. Other positions: New York Philharmonic; Barrere Little Symphony; National Chamber Orchestra; American Orchestral Society; Paul Whiteman's Orchestra; Isham Jones Orchestra; served in a U.S. Coast Guard band in World War II. Member, SBFS. b. ca. 1905, Waco, TX.
Sources: References in PBks 61 & 62; references in SBFS News; author's correspondence with Sackett.

*SADA, violin
Soloist. Full name uncertain; performed with SB in New York, Philadelphia, Baltimore, and Washington, D.C. 20-23 Apr on 1st 1899 tour. Reported to be 14 years old at the time.
Sources: References in PBk 86.

*SALE, MRS. S.B., soprano
Soloist. 1894 St. Louis Exposition (partial).
Sources: St. Louis Post-Dispatch, 20 Sep & 17 Oct & 19 Oct 1894; author's correspondence with St. Louis Public Library.

*SARTORI, _____, baritone (vocal)
Soloist. 1893 MB (partial).
Sources: Programs & references in PBks 2 & 3.

SAUM, JOSEPH F., B-flat clarinet
1919-20 tour (partial). Member, SBFS.
Sources: References in SBFS News; various 1919-20 tour rosters.

*SAUNDERS, LUCILLE, vocalist
Soloist. 1894 MB (partial).
Sources: Programs in PBk 3.

SAVENIERS, JOHN, cornet/trumpet
1st 1892 tour; possibly 2nd 1892 tour & 1st 1893 tour. Other position: Belgian Guides Royal Symphonic Band.
Source: Advertisement in J.W. Pepper's Musical Times and Band Journal, May, 1898.

SAVOLINI, UGO, bassoon
1915 tour.
Sources: Roster in Musical Courier, 9 Jun 1915; 1915 Tuxedo tobacco advertisement with SB musicians' signatures.

SCHAERGES, CHARLES, horn
1st & 2nd 1927 tours.
Sources: 1927 SB hotel assignment list; Philadelphia Record, 31 Jul 1927; references in SBFS News.

SCHAICH, SAMUEL (SAUL), B-flat clarinet, saxophone
Might have played saxophone in 1892; otherwise clarinet. 1st 1892 tour; possibly 2nd 1892 tour; 2nd 1893 tour; 3rd 1893 tour; 1st 1896 tour; 1896-97 tour; 1897 tour; 3rd 1898 tour; possibly 1st & 2nd 1904 tours; 1st 1905 tour (Britain); 4th 1906 tour; 2nd 1908 tour; 1912 tour; 1914 tour; 1915 tour; 1916-17 tour; probably other tours and engagements. Other position: American Saxophone Quartet.
Sources: SB payrolls, programs, & photos; 1892 C.G. Conn advertisement; seating chart in Philadelphia Press, 7 May 1897; seating chart in St. Louis Post-Dispatch, 27 Sep 1898; S.S. Baltic ship's list, 19 May 1905; roster in New York Dramatic Mirror, 1 Sep 1908; Lancaster (PA) Intelligencer, 26 Aug 1912; signature on 6 Nov 1914 birthday card from band members to Sousa (refers to first year with band as 1892); roster in Musical Courier, 9 Jun 1915; 1915 Tuxedo tobacco advertisement with SB

musicians' signatures; references in PBks 21, 22, 26, 36, & 44; "The Last Days of Sousa" (unpublished paper of Eugene Wiedner, conductor of Ringgold Band (Reading, PA).

*SCHALCHI, SOPHIA, contralto
Soloist. 1893 St. Louis Exposition (partial).
Sources: Programs & refs in St. Louis Post-Dispatch, Sep & Oct 1893.

*SCHELLING, ERNEST, piano
Soloist, 12 Mar 1916, New York. Other positions: Concert pianist and symphony orchestra conductor. Composer. b. 26 Jul 1876, Belvidere, NJ; d. 8 Dec 1939, New York.
Sources: Clarence J. Russell's diary; ASCAP Biographical Dictionary, 4th Edition; The New Grove Dictionary of American Music; Portraits of the World's Best-Known Musicians; references in PBk 41.

SCHENES, J., flute/piccolo
1907 tour.
Source: Roster in New York Dramatic Mirror, 7 Sep 1907.

SCHENSLEY, WILLIAM F., saxophone
1st or 2nd 1904 tour; 1st 1905 tour (Britain); 4th 1906 tour (soloist at Pittsburgh Exposition & Boston Food Fair); 2nd 1908 tour; 1913 tour (soloist at Pittsburgh Exposition); 1914 tour; 1915 tour; 1916-17 tour; 1921-22 tour (partial); probably other tours and engagements. Other position: American Saxophone Quartet.
Sources: SB programs & photos; S.S. Baltic ship's list, 19 May 1905; roster in New York Dramatic Mirror, 1 Sep 1908; signature on 6 Nov 1914 birthday card from band members to Sousa (refers to first year with band as 1904]; roster in Musical Courier, 9 Jun 1915; 1915 Tuxedo tobacco advertisement with SB musicians' signatures; references in PBks 21, 22, 39, 44; "In Memoriam" list, SBFS organizational booklet (1945); references in SBFS News.

SCHENTZE, F., B-flat clarinet
3rd 1898 tour.
Source: Seating chart in St. Louis Post-Dispatch, 25 Sep 1898.

SCHILLER, ELIZABETH, soprano
Soloist. 4th 1905 tour (partial); off-tour concert 9 Oct 1905, New York; 1st 1906 tour; 2nd 1906 tour; off-tour concert 15 Apr 1906, New York.
Sources: SB programs; references in PBks 21, 24, & 25.

SCHLANZ, JAMES, saxophone
1926 tour; 1st & 2nd 1927 tours; 1928 tour; off-tour concert 15 Jun 1929, Princeton, NJ; 1929 tour; 1929 radio broadcasts; one or more 1930 tours; Member, SBFS.
Sources: SB payrolls, programs, & photos; 1927 SB hotel assignment list; Eugene Slick's 1928 autograph book; Jay Sims' 1930 tour roster; references in SBFS News.

SCHLIG, MARTIN, percussion
1st 1904 tour (xylophone soloist at St. Louis World's Fair). Recorded for Columbia.
Sources: References in PBk 18.

SCHLOTTERBECK, G., management
Advance agent, 1906-08 & possibly other years.
Sources: New York Dramatic Mirror, 7 Sep 1907 & 1 Sep 1908; PBk 39, p. 34.

SCHMIDT, HERMAN F. (Hermie), saxophone
1921 tour; 1921-22 tour; 1923-24 tour. Member, SBFS. b. 2 May 1896; d. Nov, 1966, Corpus Christi, TX.
Sources: SB payrolls, rosters, & photos; references in SBFS News; author's interview & correspondence with Schmidt & with family; Social Security Death Index.

SCHMIDT, LOUIS, trombone
1916-17 tour; 1st 1917 tour (soloist at Dominion Park [Quebec]); 1929 radio broadcasts; 9 Apr 1931 radio broadcast; late 1931 radio broadcasts. Other position: New York Symphony Orchestra.
Sources: SB payrolls; Clarence J. Russell's diary; undated advertisement in Conn Musical Truth; SBFS News, May, 1956, p. 27.

SCHMIDT, ROY, B-flat clarinet
1925 WG; 1926 tour (partial) (soloist at StPr & WG); possibly 1st 1927 tour; 2nd 1927 tour.
Sources: SB programs & photos; references in PBks 69, 70, & 72.

SCHNEIDER, WILLIAM (Willie), management
Road manager and paymaster, 1919-1929.
Sources: SB payrolls, rosters, & photos. Various other rosters; references in PBks; references in SBFS News; author's interview and correspondence with Schneider.

SCHOENTHAL, CHARLES, *flute/piccolo*
1st 1892 tour; possibly 2nd 1892 tour; one or more tours in 1893.
Source: 1892 C.G. Conn advertisement.

SCHOOF, LAMBERT A. (Papa), *oboe*
2nd 1908 tour. Other position: Metropolitan Opera Orchestra.
Source: Roster in New York Dramatic Mirror, 1 Sep 1908.

SCHOTT, ANTON, *tenor (vocal)*
Soloist. 2nd 1894 Madison Square Garden engagement (partial); 2nd 1894 tour; 1894 MB (partial). Other positions: Metropolitan Opera Company; Berlin Opera; Munich Opera; also sang opera in England and Italy. Served in Prussian Army. b. 24 Jun 1846, Castle Staufeneck, Germany; d. 6 Jan 1913, Stuttgart, Germany.
Sources: SB programs in PBk 3; Baker's Biographical Dictionary of Musicians.

SCHROECK, ALBERT, *B-flat clarinet*
1920 tour.
Source: Roster in 1920 WG programs.

SCHROEDER, CARL, *bass clarinet, librarian*
One or more tours in 1898; probably all other tours and engagements from 1899-1917. Succeeded as librarian by Clarence J. Russell.
Sources: SB rosters & photos; numerous other rosters; roster in Albert A. Knecht's world tour diary; Edmund A. Wall's world tour poem; "In Memoriam" list, SBFS organizational booklet (1945); references in SBFS News; author's interviews with Louis Morris, SB clarinetist & copyist.

SCHROEDER, FRED, *trombone*
Date(s) of SB service uncertain.
Source: "In Memoriam" list, SBFS organizational booklet (1945); author's interviews with Louis Morris, SB clarinetist & copyist.

SCHUELER, HENRY A., *cornet/trumpet*
1921 tour (soloist at WG); 1921-22 tour; 1922 tour (soloist at WG); one or more of 1930 tours; 1931 tour. Other positions: McDonald's Scotch Highlanders Band (St. Augustine, FL); Utica (NY) Civic Band and Orchestra; theater and vaudeville orchestras; Ziyara Shrine Band and other bands in Utica area; conductor of school bands in Utica area; private music teacher. Brother of John Paul Schueler & William P. Schueler. Member, SBFS. b. 5 Feb 1888; d. 25 Aug 1974.
Sources: SB rosters, payrolls, programs, & photos; references in SBFS News; author's correspondence with Schueler & with family.

SCHUELER, JOHN PAUL, *trombone*
1920-29, possibly all engagements; 1929 radio broadcasts; 1931 tour. Soloist 1920-1927. Other positions: Metropolitan Opera Orchestra; Walter Damrosch Orchestra; Pryor's Band; Ellis Brooks Band ; Conway's Band; Bachman's Million Dollar Band; U.S. Army band at Ft. Thomas, KY; U.S. Military Academy Band; Everett Moses' Band (St. Petersburg, FL); theater and vaudeville orchestras; Ziyara Shrine Band (Utica, NY); conductor of high school bands in Syracuse, NY, area; music faculty, Syracuse University; conductor of Utica Civic Band and Orchestra; private music teacher. Brother of Henry A. Schueler & William P. Schueler. Charter member, SBFS. b. 4 Jul 1892, Utica; d. 15 Jul 1964, Utica.
Sources: Addendum to Pioneers in Brass; SB rosters, payrolls, programs, & photos; Utica Daily Press, 16 Jul 1964 [obituary]; author's correspondence with family; references in SBFS News.

SCHUELER, WILLIAM P. (BILL), *B-flat clarinet*
1920-29, most engagements; one or more of 1930 tours; 1931 tour. Other positions: New York Symphony Orchestra; Everett Moses' Band (St. Petersburg, FL); McDonald's Scotch Highlanders Band (St. Augustine, FL); radio and theater orchestras; conductor of Utica (NY) Civic Band & Orchestra; conductor of Daytona Beach (FL) Municipal Band; taught music in Utica area schools; private music teacher. Brother of Henry A. Schueler & John P. Schueler. Charter member, SBFS. d. 2 Jul 1978, Daytona Beach.
Sources: SB rosters, payrolls, & photos; Daytona Beach Morning Journal, 2 Jul 1978 [obituary]; author's interviews with Schueler & with the family; references in SBFS News.

SCHUETZ, FRANZ, *B-flat clarinet*
2nd 1893 tour; probably other tours in 1894 & 1895; 1st 1896 tour; probably other tours between 1896-1899; 2nd 1900 tour (Europe). Other positions: Gilmore's Band; Metropolitan Opera Orchestra.
Sources: 1896 SB payrolls; SB photos; advertisement in Musical Messenger, Jan, 1922, p. 19.

SCHULZE, ADOLF, *horn*
Off-tour concert, 15 Jun 1929, Princeton, NJ; 1929 & 1930 radio broadcasts.
Sources: SB payrolls.

SCHULZE, ROBERT H. (Bob), *horn*
1915 tour; 1929 & 1930 radio broadcasts. Other position: New York Philharmonic. Member, SBFS.
Sources: Roster in Musical Courier, 9 Jun 1915; 1915 Tuxedo tobacco advertisement with SB musicians' signatures; references in SBFS News.

SCHUMAKER, F., *flute/piccolo*
1928 tour (partial).
Sources: SB programs; PBk 76, p. 2; author's correspondence with Raoul F. Camus, band historian.

SCHUMANN, CARL, *horn*
1919-20 tour.
Sources: Various 1919-20 tour rosters; PBk 50, p. 37; PBk 51, p. 4.

SCHUNK, A., *instrument?*
Believed to have played with SB for a very short period, possibly the 2nd or 3rd 1930 tour.
Source: Jay Sims handwritten financial papers.

SCHUTTER, _____, *instrument?*
2nd 1893 tour.
Source: Program for 17 Oct 1893 in St. Louis Post-Dispatch.

*SCHUTZ, GEORGE, *baritone (vocal)*
1896 MB (partial).
Source: Programs in PBk 4.

SCHWANER, ARTHUR C., *flute/piccolo*
1923-24 tour; 1924 tour (piccolo soloist at WG); 1925-26 tour; 1926 tour. Member, SBFS.
Sources: SB payrolls & photos; roster in Jacobs' Band Monthly, Aug, 1925; 1925-26 SB hotel assignment list; author's correspondence with Schwaner.

SCHWARTZ, CHARLES F.A. (Charlee), *B-flat clarinet, saxophone*
1920 tour (saxophone); 1921 tour (clarinet); 1921-22 tour (clarinet). Charter member, SBFS.
Sources: SB rosters; 1921 SB photo; references in SBFS News.

SCHWARTZ, SCHOFIELD (Schof), *B-flat clarinet*
1926 tour; 1st & 2nd 1927 tours. Other position: Anglo-Canadian Leather Co. Band. Member, SBFS. d. ca. 1958.
Sources: SB payrolls & photos; 1927 SB hotel assignment list; references in SBFS News.

SCOTT, E., *instrument?*
1907 tour.
Source: PBk 29, p. 25.

SCOTT, RAYMOND F., *B-flat clarinet*
1925-26 tour (partial). Other position: Goldman Band. Member, SBFS. d. ca. 1974.
Sources: SB payrolls; 1925 SB hotel assignment list; references in SBFS News.

*SEATON, ARTHUR, *vocalist*
Soloist. 1894 MB (partial).
Sources: SB programs in PBk 3.

SEAVEY, HORACE P. (Hod), *tuba*
3rd 1898 tour; possibly tours in 1899; possibly 1st 1900 tour; 2nd 1900 tour (Europe); 4th 1901 tour (Britain); possibly tours in 1902; 1st 1903 tour (Europe).
Sources: Seating chart in St. Louis Post-Dispatch, 25 Sep 1898; roster in SB program of 22 Apr 1900; SB photo, 30 May 1900; SB/Grenadier Guards banquet seating chart of 17 Oct 1901; SB publicity for 1st 1903 tour; "In Memoriam" list, SBFS organizational booklet (1945); references in SBFS News.

SEIGFRIED, *see* **SEYFRIED, HENRY**

SELTZER, FRANK, *cornet/trumpet*
1st 1892 tour; possibly 2nd 1892 tour; possibly 1st 1893 tour; 1893 MB; 2nd 1893 tour; 1st 1894 tour; probably 2nd & 3rd 1894 tours; 1894 MB. Other positions: Philadelphia Orchestra; Gilmore's Band; Conway's Band; 1st Regiment Band (Philadelphia); 69th Regiment Band (New York); Municipal Band of Philadelphia; conductor of Pope's Band (Hartford, CT). Recorded for Columbia, Edison (also conductor of Edison Band), & Victor. Composer, arranger. b. 21 Dec 1863, Philadelphia; d. 1924.

Sources: SB photo, Sep/Oct, 1893; SB publicity for 1st 1893 tour; The Heritage Encyclopedia of Band Music; Supplement to the Heritage Encyclopedia of Band Music; undated photo in Leonard B. Smith Collection; author's correspondence with Frederick P. Williams, discographer.

SENIOR, RACHEL, *violin*
Soloist. 1923-24 tour. Other position: Concert artist in America.
Sources: SB payrolls, programs, & photos; references in SBFS News.

SENNA, NICK, *instrument?*
Date(s) of SB service uncertain.
Source: "In Memoriam" list, SBFS organizational booklet (1945).

SENNO, PAUL J., *flute/piccolo*
2nd 1908 tour (piccolo **soloist** at WG); 1909 tour (piccolo **soloist** at WG); probably 1st 1910 tour; 2nd 1910 tour (piccolo **soloist**); 1911 world tour.
Sources: 1912 SB photo; roster in Albert A. Knecht's world tour diary; Edmund A. Wall's world tour poem; references in PBks; "In Memoriam" list, SBFS organizational booklet (1945); references in SBFS News.

*SERGENT, GASTON, *basso*
Soloist, 2 Jan 1916, New York.
Sources: Clarence J. Russell's diary; New York Sun, 3 Jan 1916.

SEXAUER, PAUL C., *horn*
1923-24 tour (partial). Other position: Pryor's Band. Served in U.S. Army during World War I. Charter member, SBFS. d. ca. 1961.
Sources: References in SBFS News; author's correspondence with family.

SEYFRIED (SEIGFRIED), HENRY, *B-flat clarinet, baggage handler*
1919-20 tour; 1920 tour; 1921 tour; 1921-22 tour; probably 1922 tour; 1923-24 tour; 1924 tour.
Sources: SB payrolls, rosters & photos; SBFS News, Feb, 1955, p. 11.

SHANNON, R., *baggage handler*
1919-20 tour.
Source: Handwritten 1919 roster, presumably by SB member.

SHANNON, THOMAS F., *saxophone, clarinet, management*
Probably all tours and engagements from 2nd 1892 tour to 1896-97 tour. Possibly played clarinet in 1892. Personnel manager of band. Billed as treasurer in 1896. Other positions: Liberati's Grand Military Band; 1st Regiment Band of Philadelphia; Gilmore's Band; conductor of 23rd New York Infantry Band (Brooklyn). Composer. b. 22 Jun 1859, Mount Holly, NJ.
Sources: SB payrolls & programs; 1892 C.G. Conn advertisement; SB publicity for 1st 1893 tour; SB photo, Sep/Oct 1893; hotel registration, Adrian, MI, 1 Apr 1895; signature in Lester Levy's autograph book, Nov, 1895; composite 1895-96 SB photo; advertisements in J.W. Pepper's Musical Times and Band Journal, Spring, 1895 & May, 1898; Supplement to the Heritage Encyclopedia of Band Music; Perspectives on John Philip Sousa, p. 103; PBk 2, p. 28.

SHEAFFER, WALTER E. (Walt), *B-flat clarinet*
1911 world tour.
Sources: Roster in Albert A. Knecht's world tour diary; Edmund A. Wall's world tour poem; photo in Arthur E. Storch family scrapbook; references in SBFS News.

SHEPARD, JAMES W., *B-flat clarinet*
1919-20 tour; 1920 tour; 1921 tour; 1921-22 tour.
Sources: SB rosters & photos; advertisement in Conn Musical Truth, Oct, 1921 (Sousa Edition); SBFS News, Feb, 1955, p. 11.

SHERIDAN, JOHN, *B-flat clarinet*
3rd 1898 tour; probably several tours in 1899; possibly 1st 1900 tour.
Sources: Seating chart in St. Louis Post-Dispatch, 25 Sep 1898; photo in Sousa's personal 1899/1900 photo album; author's correspondence with Raoul F. Camus, band historian.

SHILKRET, NATHANIEL (Nat), *studio conductor*
Conducted SB in Victor studio for at least 24 recordings in 1923-25. Probably played clarinet with the band in some recording sessions. Composer.
Sources: The New Grove Dictionary of American Music; ASCAP Biographical Dictionary; discographic data from Frederick P. Williams.

SHOOF, see SCHOOF, LAMBERT A.

SHORT, OSCAR BYRON, *cornet/trumpet*
1929 radio broadcasts; 12 Mar 1931 recording; 9 Apr 1931 radio broadcast; 1931 tour (cornet **soloist**); late 1931 radio broadcasts. Other positions: Boston Pops Orchestra; New York theater orchestras; U.S. Navy

Band; Boston Navy Yard Band; Pryor's Band; Goldman Band; St. Petersburg (FL) Municipal Band. Charter member, SBFS.
Sources: SB payrolls & programs; advertisements in issues of Conn Musical Truth; Jay Sims' handwritten checklist for 1931 tour; Owen D. Kincaid's scrapbook; references in SBFS News; author's interviews with Kenneth B. Slater, bandmaster; author's correspondence with Gregory Laing, researcher.

SIEBENEICHEN, PAUL, *flute/piccolo*
1926 tour (partial). Member, SBFS.
Sources: SB photo, Jul, 1926; references in SBFS News.

SIETZ, J. FRED, *percussion*
2nd 1908 tour; possibly other tours. Other positions: Concordia Orchestra (Hamburg, Germany); Metropolitan Opera Orchestra; Philadelphia-Chicago Grand Opera Orchestra; Theodore Thomas Orchestra (Chicago); New York Symphony Orchestra; Russian Symphonic Society; 1st Regiment Band (Chicago); Boston Band. Author.
Sources: Roster in New York Dramatic Mirror, 1 Sep 1908; Seitz's Modern School of Tympani Playing; Leedy Drum Topics, 15 Jun 1923; author's correspondence with Russ Girsberger, music librarian.

SILBACH, JOHN, *alto clarinet, saxophone*
Saxophone 1921-24; alto clarinet thereafter. 1921-22 tour; 1923-24 tour; 1924 tour; 1925-26 tour; 1926 tour; 1st & 2nd 1927 tours; 1928 tour; off-tour concert 15 Jun 1929, Princeton, NJ; 1929 tour; 1929 radio broadcasts; one or more of 1930 tours; 1931 tour. Member, SBFS.
Sources: SB payrolls & photos; 1921-22 SB roster; roster in Jacobs' Band Monthly, Aug, 1925; 1925-26 SB hotel assignment list; SB photo, Jul, 1926; Eugene Slick's 1928 autograph book; Jay Sims' 1930 tour roster; references in SBFS News.

SIMON, FRANK, *cornet/trumpet*
Most all tours and engagements from 1914 tour to 1919-20 tour. Cornet **soloist** on all. Other positions: Cincinnati Symphony Orchestra; Kopp's Military Band (Cincinnati); Weber's Prize Band of America (Cincinnati); Sorg's Opera House Orchestra (Middletown, OH); conductor of U.S. Aviation School Band (Dayton, OH) during World War I; founder/conductor of Armco Band; music faculty, Cincinnati Conservatory of Music & University of Arizona; guest conductor; lecturer. Honorary doctorate, Capital University. Composer. Charter member, American Bandmasters Assn. (president, 1935-36; honorary life president). Recorded for Gennett. Member, SBFS. b. 26 Nov 1889, Cincinnati; d. 28 Jan 1967, Cincinnati.
Sources: SB rosters, programs, & photos; numerous other rosters; Music Man; The Heritage Encyclopedia of Band Music; Portraits of the World's Best-Known Musicians; Who Is Who in Music, 1951 edition; Band Encyclopedia; advertisements in various trade journals; references in PBks; references in SBFS News; author's interviews & correspondence with Simon, with family, & with Louis Morris, SB clarinetist & copyist.

SIMONE, J.D., *horn*
1919-20 tour.
Source: Various 1919-20 tour rosters.

SIMONS, GARDELL, *trombone*
1st and/or 2nd 1910 tour. Other positions: Philadelphia Orchestra; NBC Symphony Orchestra; Cincinnati Symphony Orchestra; Cleveland Orchestra; Detroit Symphony Orchestra; Pryor's Band; Conway's Band; Duss Band (New York); several bands & orchestras in Chicago. Composer. Recorded for Zonophone. b. 16 Aug 1878, Alleyan, MI; d. 22 Mar 1945, Miami, FL.
Sources: Pioneers in Brass; The Heritage Encyclopedia of Band Music; Bands of America, pp. 229 & 278; author's interviews with Kenneth B. Slater, bandmaster; author's correspondence with Frederick P. Williams, discographer.

SIMONSEN, LEONORA, *soprano*
Soloist. 1916-17 tour (partial).
Sources: PBk 44, pp. 70 & 71.

*SIMPSON, CHERIDAH, *soprano*
Soloist. 1894 MB (partial).
Sources: Notable Names in the American Theatre; programs in PBk 4.

SIMS, JAY GILMORE, *trombone, personnel manager*
All tours and engagements, 1919-32. Other positions: B.A. Rolfe's Musical Acts (road manager); Peters Comedy Co. Orchestra; Atlanta theater orchestras; Pryor's Band; Conway's Band; [Mayhew L. Lake's] Symphony of Gold; Buffalo Bill's Wild West Show; 1st North Carolina Volunteer Infantry Band during Spanish-American War. Elected to

Trombone Hall of Fame, 1969. Charter member, SBFS. b. 7 Feb 1876, Cabarrus County, NC; d. 9 Jun 1965, Durham, NC.

Sources: SB payrolls, rosters, programs, & photos; various other rosters; Jacobs' Orchestra Monthly, Jul, 1922; Concord (NC) Tribune, 3 Dec 1965; references in PBks; references in SBFS News; research by Phyllis Danner, Sousa Archives for Band Research, University of Illinois; author's interviews with Sims & with family.

SLICK, EUGENE, *B-flat clarinet, saxophone*
1928 tour; 1929 tour. Other positions: Leggett & Brown Shows; Gentry Bros. Circus Band; John Robinson Circus Band; Cole Bros. Circus Band; conductor of several bands in Midwest; chief engineer for Frank Holton Band Instrument Mfg. Co.; field representative for C.G. Conn Co.; instrument repairman. Member, SBFS (Vice President, 1952-58; President, 1958-64; editor of *SBFS News*, 1949-65). b. 8 Jun 1898, Middletown, IN; d. 19 Mar 1971, Anderson, IN.

Sources: SB payrolls & photos; International Musician, Jul, 1971 [obituary]; references in SBFS News; author's interviews and correspondence with Slick & with family; Social Security Death Index.

SMITH, A., *B-flat clarinet*
2nd 1900 tour (Europe).

Sources: Roster in SB program of 22 Apr 1900; SB photo, 30 May 1900.

SMITH, ARTHUR HARRY, *cornet/trumpet*
1st & 2nd 1892 tours (cornet **soloist**). Other positions: Covent Gardens Orchestra (London); Coldstream Guards Band (London).

Sources: SB programs; Marching Along, p. 334; 1892 C.G. Conn advertisement; PBk 1, p. 13; author's correspondence with Barry Owen Furrer, band historian.

SMITH, BURT H., *trombone*
Date(s) of SB service uncertain, but probably one or more tours in 1893 and/or 1894. Other positions: New York Symphony Orchestra; New York recording studios. Charter member, SBFS.

Sources: J.W. Pepper's Musical Times and Band Journal, May, 1898; undated C.G. Conn advertisement in SBFS News, Feb, 1955, p. 16; other references in SBFS News.

SMITH, CARL, *valet, road secretary*
1926 tour; 2nd 1927 tour.

Sources: SB photo, Jul, 1926; SB payroll for 16 Jul 1927; 1927 SB hotel assignment list; references in SBFS News.

SMITH, CLARENCE H., *horn*
2nd 1910 tour; 1911 world tour. Member, SBFS.

Sources: Roster in Albert A. Knecht's world tour diary; Edmund A. Wall's world tour poem; references in PBks; references in SBFS News.

SMITH, FRED M., *B-flat clarinet*
1914 tour.

Source: Signature on 6 Nov 1914 birthday card from band members to Sousa (refers to first year with band as 1914).

SMITH, G. ADOLPH, *flute/piccolo*
1919-20 tour (piccolo **soloist** at WG and occasionally elsewhere).

Sources: SB programs; various 1919-20 tour rosters; PBk 50, p. 23.

SMITH, HAROLD J., *flute/piccolo*
1928 tour.

Sources: SB payrolls; references in SBFS News.

SMITH, J.E., *B-flat clarinet*
1896-97 tour.

Source: Seating chart in Philadelphia Press 7 May 1897.

SMITH, WALTER F., *cornet/trumpet*
All tours & engagements between Apr, 1893-May, 1898. **Soloist** on occasion. Other positions: Before SB with Constantine Band (MI), Roger Goshen Band (IN), & U.S. Marine Band under Sousa; after SB with U.S. Marine Band (second leader); instrument tester for Frank Holton & Co. b. 5 Jun 1859, Vernon County, MO; d. 21 May 1937, Washington, D.C.

Sources: SB payrolls, rosters, & photos; SB publicity for 1893 tour; Walter F. Smith Collections at U.S. Marine Band & Western Michigan University Archives; Jacobs' Orchestra Journal, Mar, 1922, pp. 19-21; Musical Messenger, 1 Oct 1923; research by Carole Nowicke, band historian.

SNEDEKER, L., *cornet/trumpet*
Marched with augmented SB in Dewey Parade, 30 Sep 1899; probably 4th 1899 tour; possibly 5th 1899 tour and/or 1st 1900 tour; 1928 StPr (**soloist**).

Sources: SB programs; Staten Islander (New York), 7 Oct 1899 [PB 9, p. 72].

SNOW, SCOTT, *cornet/trumpet*
Probably one or more tours ca. 1897. Other position: 9th Regiment Band (New York). Composer, arranger. b. Belfast, NY, ca. 1857.

Source: Conn Musical Truth, Dec., 1897, p. 8.

SNOW, FRANK A., *percussion*
1st and/or 2nd 1910 tour; 1911 world tour; possibly 1912 & 1913 tours; 1914 tour; 1915 tour; 1916-17 tour; probably 1917 tour; 1918 tour; 1919-20 tour. Other positions: Boston Symphony Orchestra; Chicago and New York theater orchestras; Middle Western Co. Orchestra; Long Beach (CA) Municipal Band. Member, SBFS. b. ca. 1900; d. 20 Aug 1950, Long Beach.

Sources: Roster in Albert A. Knecht's world tour diary; Edmund A. Wall's world tour poem; signature on 6 Nov 1914 birthday card from band members to Sousa (refers to first year with band as 1910); roster in Musical Courier, 9 Jun 1915; 1915 Tuxedo tobacco advertisement with SB musicians' signatures; various 1919-20 tour rosters; Frank Holt's diary; Leedy Drum Topics, 15 Jun 1923, 15 Oct 1924, Feb, 1926, & Aug, 1934; PBk 44, pp. 66 & 88; references in SBFS News.

SNYDER, DONALD, *valet & road secretary*
1921-22 tour (partial); 1923 tour; 1923-24 tour. Member, SBFS.

Sources: SB payrolls; 1921 SB photo; references in SBFS News; author's correspondence with Snyder.

SNYDER, WILLARD A., *valet & road secretary*
1921 tour; 1921-22 tour (partial).

Sources: SB rosters; 1921 SB photo.

SODOHL, EHRLING A. (Earl), *saxophone*
1921-22 tour. Member, SBFS.

Sources: 1921-22 SB roster; SB photo, Dec, 1921; references in SBFS News.

SOMMER, HUGO, *euphonium*
Date(s) of SB service uncertain. Other position: Indianapolis Symphony Orchestra; Weber's Band. b. ca. 1874; d. Oct, 1950.

Source: SBFS News, Oct, 1950, p. 4.

SON, JAMES E. (Jimmy), *saxophone*
1923-24 tour; 1924 tour. Other position: Long Beach (CA) Municipal Band. Composer. Member, SBFS. b. 5 Nov 1883; d. Apr, 1974, Long Beach.

Sources: SB payrolls & photos; The Heritage Encyclopedia of Band Music; references in SBFS News; Social Security Death Index.

SORDILLO, FORTUNATO F., *euphonium*
Date(s) of SB service uncertain, but probably 1912 & 1913 tours. Other positions: Boston Symphony Orchestra (trombone); Boston Opera Co. Orchestra (trombone); Pryor's Band; conductor of Boston Fire Dept. Band & Boston Consolidated Gas Co. Band & Alexander Graham Bell Post 299 American Legion Band (Boston); private music teacher. Composer, author, inventor. Member, SBFS. b. 4 Jul 1885, Mentifalione, Italy; d. 21 Dec 1952, Brighton, MA.

Sources: Berger roster; The Heritage Encyclopedia of Band Music; Supplement to the Heritage Encyclopedia of Band Music.

SPALTI, LEO, *saxophone*
1926 tour.

Sources: SB payroll for 20 Nov 1926; SB programs; 1926 SB photo; SBFS News, May, 1983, p. 14; PBk 69, pp. 248 & 273; PBk 70, p. 24.

SPEINSON, MORRIS, *horn*
1919-20 tour.

Source: Various 1919-20 tour rosters.

SPENCER, JOHN HENRY, *B-flat clarinet*
1926 tour (partial); 1928 tour; 1929 tour (partial). Other positions: Conway's Band; 151st U.S. Field Artillery Regiment Band; Jalma's Band; theater orchestras; school music teacher in Balsam Lake, WI & Centuria, WI & St. Croix Falls, WI & Red Wing, MN. Composer. b. 25 Jul 1891, Renville, MN; d. 21 Aug 1977, Balsam Lake, WI.

Sources: SB payrolls; Eugene Slick's 1928 autograph book; J. Henry Spencer: His Life and Selected Band Works; The Heritage Encyclopedia of Band Music; author's interview & correspondence with Spencer & with family.

*SPERO, SIDONE, *soprano*
Soloist, 31 Oct & 8 Nov 1915, New York.

Sources: Clarence J. Russell's diary; references in PBk 42.

SPINDLER, JULIUS, *flute/piccolo*
1907 tour (occasional **soloist**); probably 1st 1908 tour; 2nd 1908 tour (occasional **soloist**); probably tours in 1909 & 1910; 1911 world tour. Recorded for Edison.
Sources: SB programs; roster in New York Dramatic Mirror, *1 Sep 1908; roster in Albert A. Knecht's world tour diary; Edmund A. Wall's world tour poem; references in PBks 21, 28, & 30; references in SBFS News; author's correspondence with Frederick P. Williams, discographer.*

SPITZNER, BERTHOLD, *cornet/trumpet*
1896-97 tour; possibly 1897 tour.
Sources: 1897 SB payroll; seating chart in Philadelphia Press, *7 May 1897; advertisement in J.W. Pepper Musical Times and Band Journal, May, 1898.*

STAATS, C.L., *B-flat clarinet*
1st 1892 tour (occasional **soloist**); possibly 2nd 1892 tour; possibly tours in 1893 & 1894; 1894 MB.
Sources: References in PBks 1 & 3.

STAIGERS, CHARLES DELAWARE (Del), *cornet/trumpet*
(Some sources give name as Clarence Adelbert Staigers.) 1919-20 tour (occasional **soloist**); 12 Mar 1931 recording. Other position: Pryor's Band; Goldman Band; 1940 World's Fair Band (New York); Radio City Music Hall Orchestra (New York); Victor Salon Orchestra; radio network orchestras & theater orchestras in New York; MGM studio orchestra (Hollywood); private music teacher. Composer. Recorded for Victor. Member, SBFS. b. 20 Aug 1899, Muncie, IN; d. 12 Jul 1950, Los Angeles.
Sources: SB photos; various 1919-20 tour rosters; Pioneers in Brass; The Heritage Encyclopedia of Band Music; Band Encyclopedia; *author's interviews with Kenneth B. Slater, bandmaster.*

***STALL, KARL,** *baritone (vocal)*
1902 WG (partial). Other positions: Character actor, mostly in musicals; Murray-Lane Opera Co. (New Orleans). b. ca. 1873, Cincinnati, OH; d. 14 Jun 1947, New York.
Sources: SB programs; Variety, *18 Jul 1947, p. 49 [obituary]; PBk 18, p. 173.*

STAMBAUGH, HAROLD O., *cornet/trumpet*
1924 tour; 1925-26 tour (**soloist** at WG); 1926 tour (**soloist** at WG); 1st & 2nd 1927 tours; one or more of 1930 tours. Other positions: Pryor's Band; 7th Regiment Band (New York); 1940 World's Fair Band (New York); Long Beach (CA) Municipal Band; representative for C.G. Conn Co.; taught music in public & private schools in state of New York. Charter member, SBFS. b. 8 Apr 1886; d. 9 Mar 1976, Newburgh, NY.
Sources: SB payrolls & photos; International Musician, *Oct, 1976 [obituary]; Harold Stambaugh's 1925-26 & 1927 hotel assignment lists; Jay Sims' 1930 tour roster; undated advertisement of Virtuoso Music School (Buffalo, NY); author's interview & correspondence with Stambaugh; Social Security Death Index.*

***STARR, EVELYN,** *violin*
Soloist, 9 Apr 1916, New York.
Source: Clarence J. Russell's diary.

***STEIN, GERTRUDE,** *contralto*
Soloist, 1893 MB (partial). Other positions: Author, librettist, & lecturer. b. ca. 1874, Allegheny, PA; d. 27 Jul 1946, Nevilly, France.
Sources: Programs in PBk 3; Variety, *31 Jul 1946, p. 54 [obituary].*

STEINERT, LEOPOLD, *B-flat clarinet*
1920 WG. Composer.
Sources: Roster in 1920 WG programs; The Heritage Encyclopedia of Band Music; *author's correspondence with Steinert.*

STENGLER, AUGUST (GUSTAVE) P. CERCELLO, *B-flat clarinet*
Possibly 1st & 2nd 1893 tours; probably all other tours and engagements, 1893-1898 (occasional **soloist**). Other position: Gilmore's Band. Composer. Recorded for Berliner.
Sources: SB payrolls, programs, & photos; SB publicity for 1st 1893 tour; hotel registration, Adrian, MI, 1 Apr 1895; seating chart in Philadelphia Press, *7 May 1897;* Bands of America; The Heritage Encyclopedia of Band Music; *Clarinet Recordings Vol. 1 (compact disc privately produced by Stan Stanford, discographer); 1892 C.G. Conn advertisement; J.W. Pepper Musical Times and Band Journal, Spring, 1895 & May, 1898; references in other music journals; SBFS News, May, 1951, p. 20; references in PBks 1-5; author's correspondence with Frederick P. Williams, discographer.*

STEPHENS, HAROLD BARNETT, *saxophone*
1925-26 tour (**soloist**). Other positions: Latina Brothers Wild West Show Band; John H. Sparks Circus Band; 1st U.S. Cavalry Band; Long Beach (CA) Municipal Band; Ringling Bros. and Barnum & Bailey Circus Band. Composer. Member, SBFS. b. 22 Jul 1897, Circleville, OH; d. 13 Mar 1983, Long Beach.
Sources: A Study of the Saxophone Soloists of the John Philip Sousa Band, 1893-1930; Long Beach Legionnaire, Apr, 1968, p. 3; Harold B. Stephens' career scrapbooks; author's interviews & correspondence with Stephens & with family.

***STEPHENSON, MABEL,** *soprano*
Soloist. 1894 MB (partial).
Source: PBk 3, p. 47.

STERN, HENRY P. (Hank), *tuba*
1919-20 tour. Member, SBFS.
Sources: Various 1919-20 tour rosters; references in SBFS News.

***STEWART, ETHEL IRENE,** *soprano*
Soloist. 1896 MB (partial).
Sources: SB programs in PBk 4.

STEWART, WILLIAM W., *duties?*
1st 1905 tour (Europe); 1907 tour; 2nd 1908 tour. Name at end of rosters indicates valet, secretary, encore card holder, etc.
Sources: S.S. Baltic ship's list, 19 May 1905 [name spelled Stewart]; rosters in New York Dramatic Mirror, *7 Sep 1907 & 1 Sep 1908 [name spelled Stuart].*

STONE, HARRY, *percussion*
1st 1893 tour.
Source: Advertisement in Leedy Drum Topics, *Aug, 1934 (quoting Frank A. Snow, former SB percussionist).*

STONE, MAY, *soprano*
Soloist. 1st 3 months of 1919-20 tour, including WG. Other position: Boston Opera Co.
Sources: SB programs; references in PBks 50, 51, & 53.

STORCH, ARTHUR E., *tuba*
1909 tour; probably 1st 1910 tour; 2nd 1910 tour; 1911 world tour; 1914 tour; 1915 tour; possibly 1915-16 *Hip! Hip! Hooray!* engagement; 1916-17 tour. Other positions: New York Philharmonic; San Francisco Symph. Orchestra; Pryor's Band; Conway's Band; played string bass with Stuttgart Royal Opera House (Germany), New York Symphony & Castle Square Garden Opera Orchestra (Boston); music faculty, Francisco State College. Member, SBFS. b. Germany, 11 Aug 1877; d. Sep, 1968, San Francisco.
Sources: SB photos; roster in Albert A. Knecht's world tour diary; Edmund A. Wall's world tour poem; autographs on music at Sousa Archives for Band Research, University of Illinois; signature on 6 Nov 1914 birthday card from band members to Sousa (refers to first year with band as 1909); roster in Musical Courier, 9 Jun 1915; 1915 Tuxedo tobacco advertisement with SB musicians' signatures; undated C.G. Conn advertisements; author's correspondence with family & with Harold B. Stephens, SB saxophone soloist; Social Security Death Index.

***STOREY, BELLE,** *soprano*
Soloist, 8 concerts in Oct, Nov, & Dec, 1915, and Feb, 1916, New York.
Sources: Clarence J. Russell's diary; references in PBk 42.

STORM, CHARLES W., *cornet/trumpet*
Date(s) of SB service uncertain, but probably part of 1919-20 tour.
Source: Advertisement for Harry L. Jacob mouthpieces in Musical Enterprise, *Feb, 1920.*

STRAUS, JESSIE, *violin*
Soloist. 1st 1904 tour except St. Louis Exposition; 2nd 1904 tour except WG; off-tour concerts 25-27 Dec 1904, New York; off-tour concert 21 May 1905, New York; 3rd & 4th 1905 tours; off-tour concert 29 Oct 1905, New York. Other position: Concert artist in America. Married name Mrs. Eli Mayer.
Sources: SB programs; references in PBks.

STRETZ, FRANK, *B-flat clarinet*
3rd 1898 tour; possibly other tours. Member, SBFS.
Sources: Seating chart in St. Louis Post-Dispatch, *25 Sep 1898; references in SBFS News.*

STRINE, CHARLES W., *baritone (vocal), management*
Soloist, 1894 MB (partial). Press agent, 1895-97; general manager briefly in 1897; other positions on management staff, 1897-?. Other positions: Newspaper reporter and editor of *Philadelphia Press;* manager of

Metropolitan Opera Co., Melba Opera Co. (Boston), & Tivoli Opera House (San Francisco). d. 6 Apr 1907, Boston.

Sources: SB programs; New York Clipper, 22 Dec 1894 & 19 Jan 1895; references in PBk 5; Philadelphia Press, 7 Apr 1907.

STROSS, RICHARD, *cornet/trumpet*
1920 tour (cornet **soloist** at WG).

Sources: SB programs; roster in 1920 WG programs; references in PBks 54 & 55; SBFS News, Feb, 1955, p. 16.

STROTHKAMP, CHARLES C., Jr., *B-flat clarinet*
1926 tour; probably 1st & 2nd 1927 tours; 1928 tour; off-tour concert 15 Jun 1929, Princeton, NJ; 1929 tour; 1929 & 1930 radio broadcasts; one or more of 1930 tours; 12 Mar 1931 recording; 9 Apr 1931 radio broadcast; 1931 tour. Member, SBFS.

Sources: SB payrolls & photos; Harold Stambaugh's 1927 hotel assignment list; Eugene Slick's 1928 autograph book; Jay Sims' 1930 tour roster; Otto Kraushaar's autobiography, p. 60; references in SBFS News.

STUART, see STEWART, WILLIAM W.

SULLIVAN, FRANK W. (Buddy), *saxophone*
1926 tour; probably 1st & 2nd 1927 tours; 1928 tour; off-tour concert 15 Jun 1929, Princeton, NJ; 1929 tour; one or more of 1930 tours. Other positions: Anglo-Canadian Leather Co. Band; St. Petersburg (FL) Municipal Band; RCAF Central Command Band. Member, SBFS. b. ca. 1908; d. 10 Jun 2000, Peterborough, ONT, Canada.

Sources: SB payrolls & programs; Harold Stambaugh's 1927 hotel assignment list; Jay Sims' 1930 tour roster; references in SBFS News; author's correspondence with Sullivan & with Keith Brion, conductor of the New Sousa Band..

SUTHERLAND, FRANCIS W., *cornet/trumpet*
1916-17 tour. Other positions: 6th U.S. Cavalry Band; 4th U.S. Cavalry Band during Spanish-American War; Haverly's Minstrels; *Wizard of Oz* Troupe Orchestra; conductor of 7th Regiment Band (New York) & 2nd Regiment Massachusetts National Guard Band & Governor's Foot Guard Band (CT) & 104th Field Artillery 27th Division Band & U.S. Army divisional bands in Europe during World War I & Strand Theatre Symphony Orchestra (New York). Recorded for Aeolian & Vocalion. Co-founder, SBFS. d. ca. 1960.

Sources: Band Encyclopedia; references in PBks 29, 45, & 46; references in SBFS News.

*SUTTER, LILLY M., *soprano*
Soloist in *Assembly of the Artisans* at St. Louis Exposition, 1894.

Sources: Programs in St. Louis Post-Dispatch; author's correspondence with St. Louis Historical Society.

SWANN, DAVID, *bassoon*
Off-tour concert 15 Jun 1929, Princeton, NJ; 1929 & 1930 radio broadcasts;

Sources: SB payrolls.

SWEETLAND, WILLIAM W. (Bill), *tuba*
1st 1903 tour (Europe); 1st 1905 tour (Britain); 1916-17 tour.

Sources: SB publicity for 1st 1903 tour; S.S. Baltic ship's list, 19 May 1905; references in SBFS News.

*SWEETSER, CATHERINE LINYARD, *soprano*
Soloist. Off-tour concert, 28 Jan 1894, Brooklyn, NY; 1894 MB (partial).
Sources: Programs in PBk 3.

*TAGLIAPIETRA, GIUSEPPE, *baritone (vocal)*
Soloist. 1896 MB (partial); off-tour concert 29 Oct 1905, New York.
Sources: SB programs in PBk 4; references in PBk 21.

*TANNER, CORA, *vocalist*
Soloist. 1894 MB (partial).
Sources: SB programs in PBk 3.

*TAVARY, MARIE, *vocalist*
Soloist. 1893 MB (partial).
Source: SB program in PBk 3, p. 45.

TAYLOR, E.H., *bassoon*
1920 WG; possibly remainder of 1920 tour.
Source: Roster in 1920 WG programs; 1920 SB photo.

*TEMPEST, MARIE, *vocalist*
Soloist. 1893 MB (partial). Other positions: Actress in theater, movies, and radio in America and Britain. b. ca. 1864, London, England; d. 15 Oct 1942, London.
Sources: Variety, 21 Oct 1942, p. 62; PBk 2, p. 77.

TETSON, BASIL, *baritone (vocal)*
Soloist. 1896 MB (partial); 2nd 1898 tour.
Sources: SB program in PBk 4, p. 27; PBk 5, pp. 223 & 226.

*TEYTE, MAGGIE, *soprano*
Soloist, 30 Dec 1915, New York. Other positions: Chicago Grand Opera; sang opera & operetta in America and abroad. Recorded for Columbia & HMV. b. Wolverhampton, England.
Sources: The New Grove Dictionary of American Music; references in PBk 42.

THETFORD, CHARLES, *B-flat clarinet*
Possibly part of 1908 tour; possibly part of 1915 tour; 1916-17 tour; 1929 radio broadcasts; 12 Mar 1931 recording; 9 Apr 1931 radio broadcast. Other position: Pryor's Band. Charter member, SBFS. b. 3 Jan 1883; d. Jun, 1965, South Orange, NJ.
Sources: Roster in Dec, 1916 New York Musician and Knocker; The Knocker, May, 1917, p. 1; Selmer advertisement in Musical Messenger, May, 1922; PBk 44, p. 88; references in SBFS News; Social Security Death Index.

THIERBACH, MAX, *flute/piccolo*
1st 1903 tour (Europe). Other positions: Conductor of Milwaukee theater orchestras.
Sources: 1903 SB European tour publicity; Milwaukee Journal, 25 Apr 1915 (PBk 41, p. 125).

THOEDE, HENRY, *bassoon, flute/piccolo*
2nd 1893 tour; 1st 1894 tour (**soloist**, Mid-Winter Exposition); 4th 1895 tour (bassoon); 1st 1896 tour (bassoon); possibly other tours and engagements, 1896-1901; 2nd 1900 tour (Europe) (bassoon); 4th 1901 tour (Britain) (flute/piccolo); possibly 1st & 2nd 1902 tours; 3rd 1902 tour (bassoon); 1st 1903 tour (Europe) (bassoon).
Sources: SB payrolls & photos; signature in Lester Levy's autograph book, Nov, 1895; roster in SB program of 22 Apr 1900; roster in New York Dramatic Mirror, 6 Sep 1902; 1903 SB European tour publicity; PBk 3, p. 57; references in SBFS News.

THOMAS, BRUCE, *B-flat clarinet*
1915 tour.
Sources: Roster in Musical Courier, 9 Jun 1915; 1915 Tuxedo tobacco advertisement with SB musicians' signatures.

THOMAS, CAROLINE, *violin*
Soloist. 1922 tour (after WG).
Sources: SB programs; references in PBk 58.

*THOMAS, GEORGE P., *basso*
1893 St. Louis Exposition (partial).
Source: St. Louis Post-Dispatch, 30 Sep 1893.

THOMPSON, ERNEST LEROY, *B-flat clarinet*
1923-24 tour; 1924 tour. Other positions: U.S. Army Band; U.S. Navy Band; New York theater orchestras. Member, SBFS.
Sources: SB payrolls & photos; references in SBFS News; author's correspondence with Thompson.

THOMPSON, HARRY A., *B-flat clarinet, saxophone*
Possibly also played saxophone briefly. 1928 tour; one or more of 1930 tours (partial); 1931 tour. Member, SBFS.
Sources: SB payrolls; 1928 SB roster; Eugene Slick's 1928 autograph book; 1930 SB photo; references in SBFS News.

THOMPSON, LLOYD M., *cornet/trumpet*
Date(s) of SB service uncertain, but probably 1912 tour. Member, SBFS. d. ca. 1951, Detroit, MI.
Sources: References in SBFS News; Berger roster.

THOMPSON, O.J., *B-flat clarinet, saxophone*
Primarily clarinetist; played saxophone briefly. 1926 StPr; possibly remainder of 1926 tour; 1928 tour; 1931 tour. Member, SBFS.
Sources: SB payrolls and photos; Jay Sims' handwritten checklist for 1931 tour; Eugene Slick's 1928 autograph book; references in SBFS News; author's correspondence with Owen D. Kincaid, SB saxophonist.

THOMPSON, SHERLEY (SHIRLEY) C., *bassoon*
1921 tour; 1921-22 tour; probably 1922 tour; 1923-24 tour; 1924 tour. Other positions: New York theater orchestras; Pryor's Band; Long Beach (CA) Municipal Band; Neddermeyer's Band (Columbus, OH). Author. Co-founder, SBFS (editor of *SBFS News,* 1945-49). d. 1967, Long Beach.
Sources: SB payrolls, rosters, & photos; references in PBks; references in SBFS News; author's correspondence with Thompson & with family.

THOMSON, WALDE E., *B-flat clarinet*
1915 tour.
Sources: 1915 Tuxedo tobacco advertisement with SB musicians' signatures; roster in Musical Courier, *9 Jun 1915.*

THORNE, HARRY F., *flute/piccolo*
1924 tour; possibly part of 1929 tour. Other positions: Romberg Concert Orchestra; New York theater orchestras; Anglo-Canadian Leather Co. Band. Brother of Joseph T. Thorne. Charter member, SBFS. b. 13 Oct 1899; d. Feb, 1971, Lecanto, FL.
Sources: References in SBFS News; Pruyn roster; Social Security Death Index.

THORNE, JOSEPH T., *cornet/trumpet*
Possibly part of 1923-24 tour; 1924 tour; possibly part of 1929 tour; 12 Mar 1930 radio broadcast; one or more of 1930 tours (partial). Other positions: Goldman Band; Ringling Bros. & Barnum and Bailey Circus Band; Anglo-Canadian Leather Co. Band; Romberg Concert Orchestra; New York theater orchestras. b. 3 Jul 1902; d. May, 1967, Elmhurst, NY. Brother of Harry F. Thorne. Member, SBFS.
Sources: SB payrolls; references in SBFS News; author's interviews with Kenneth B. Slater, bandmaster; Berger roster.

TOMEI, ALBERTO A., (Tony) **horn**
Date(s) of SB service uncertain, but probably one WG engagement between 1915-20. Other positions: Pryor's Band; Creatore's Band; traveling dance orchestras.
Sources: Author's correspondence with Alfred N. Ricciardi, associate of Tomei; undated obituary in Philadelphia newspaper.

TOMPKINS, GEORGE B., *B-flat clarinet, saxophone*
1st 1927 tour (saxophone?); 2nd 1927 tour (clarinet); one or more of 1930 tours (saxophone); 1931 tour (clarinet). Other positions: Philco Band; conductor of a boys' band in Allentown, PA. Member, SBFS.
Sources: SB payrolls, rosters, & photos; references in SBFS News; author's correspondence with family.

TOMPKINS, SUSAN, *violin*
Soloist. 1st half of 1914 tour (including WG); 1915 Panama-Pacific Exposition (partial); 1915 WG (partial); 1915 Pittsburgh Exposition (partial); 28 November 1915, New York; 1916 WG (partial); 1917 WG (partial); 1918 WG (partial). Other positions: Founder/conductor of Susan Tompkins Orchestra; concert artist in U.S.A. Married name Tedrow.
Sources: SB programs; references in PBks; entries in Clarence J. Russell's diary.

TONG, WILLIAM (Bill, Billy), *cornet/trumpet*
1924 tour (cornet **soloist** at WG); 1925-26 tour (cornet **soloist**); 1926 tour (**soloist**); 1st 1927 tour; 2nd 1927 tour (cornet **soloist**); 1928 tour (cornet **soloist**); off-tour concert 15 Jun 1929, Princeton, NJ; 1929 tour (cornet **soloist**); 1929 & 1930 radio broadcasts; one or more of 1930 tours; 9 Apr 1931 radio broadcast; 1931 tour. Other positions: Pryor's Band; Anglo-Canadian Leather Co. Band; Goldman Band; U.S. Navy Band; Long Beach (CA) Municipal Band; Toronto Symphony Orchestra; New York theater orchestras; music faculty, Carlsbad (CA) Military Academy. d. 1 Feb 1952, Camp Pendleton, CA.
Sources: SB payrolls, rosters, programs, & photos; Pioneers in Brass; Harold Stambaugh's 1925-26 & 1927 hotel assignment lists; references in PBks; references in SBFS News; author's interviews with Kenneth B. Slater, bandmaster.

*TOWNE, E.C., *tenor (vocal)*
Soloist. 1893 MB (partial).
Sources: References in PBk 2; SB programs in PBk 3.

TOWNSEND, see KERKER, VERNA

TOZIER, CECIL E. (Stub), *B-flat clarinet*
2nd 1927 tour; 1928 tour; off-tour concert, 15 Jun 1929, Princeton, NJ; 1929 tour; one or more of 1930 tours. Other positions: Pryor's Band; Conway's Band; Long Beach (CA) Municipal Band; Los Angeles Symphony Band; Kansas City Symphony Orchestra; Hollywood studio orchestras. Member, SBFS. b. 5 Feb 1901; d. 13 Apr 1987, Tucson, AZ.
Sources: SB payrolls, rosters, & photos; Harold Stambaugh's 1927 hotel assignment list; references in SBFS News; correspondence between Tozier & Malcolm Heslip, author.

TRACY, MINNIE, *soprano*
Soloist. 2nd 1896 tour; 1896 MB; 4 Jul 1900, Paris; 1st part of 4th 1901 tour (Britain).
Sources: SB programs; references in PBks.

TREPTE, ARTHUR, *oboe*
3rd 1898 tour; possibly other tours. Recorded for Victor.
Sources: Author's correspondence with Raoul F. Camus, band historian, & with Frederick P. Williams, discographer.

TRITTON, FRANK, *tuba*
2nd 1927 tour. Other position: Kryl's Band. Member, SBFS.
Sources: SB payrolls & photos; Harold Stambaugh's 1927 hotel assignment list; references in SBFS News.

TRUTE, WILLIAM, *bassoon*
1929 & 1930 radio broadcasts; 12 Mar 1931 recording; 9 Apr 1931 radio broadcast; late 1931 radio broadcasts.
Sources: SB payrolls.

TUCKER, COURTNEY S. (Mr. Hooligan), *B-flat clarinet*
1928 tour; 1929 tour (Minneapolis only). Member, SBFS.
Sources: SB payrolls; references in SBFS News.

URBAIN, FRED M., *E-flat clarinet*
1st 1892 tour; possibly 2nd 1892 tour; probably 1st & 2nd 1893 tours. Other position: Gilmore's Band.
Sources: PBk 2, p. 28; C.G. Conn advertisement, ca. Dec, 1892; program in St. Louis Post-Dispatch, *17 October 1893; SB publicity for 1st 1893 tour.*

URBAN, JOHN W., *B-flat clarinet*
1912 tour; probably 1913 tour; 1914 tour; 1915 tour; 1916-17 tour. Other positions: Innes' Band; faculty, U.S. Navy School of Music. Member, SBFS.
Sources: 1912 SB photo; Lancaster (PA) Intelligencer, 26 Oct 1912; 1912 SB photo; signature on 6 Nov 1914 birthday card from band members to Sousa (refers to first year with band as 1912); roster in Musical Courier, *9 Jun 1915; 1915 Tuxedo tobacco advertisement with SB musicians' signatures;* Musical Messenger, *Jul, 1922, p. 19; references in SBFS News.*

VAN AMBERGH, FRED, *B-flat clarinet*
1929 & 1930 radio broadcasts.
Sources: SB payrolls; "In Memoriam" list, SBFS organizational booklet (1945).

VAN CAUTEREN, MARIE, *soprano*
Soloist. 1st 1893 tour; 1893 MB (partial). Other positions: Hinrichs' American Opera Co.; toured with Anton Seidl Orchestra; sang opera in Europe and South America.
Sources: SB publicity for 1st 1893 tour; Metronome, Apr, 1893, p. 10; references in PBks 2 & 3.

VAN DEINSE, GERTRUDE, *soprano*
Soloist. 1914 tour (before WG).
Sources: SB programs; PBk 40, p. 81.

VAN DEN HENDE, FLORIE, *cello*
Soloist. 1st 1898 tour (partial); off-tour concert 3 Apr 1898, New York.
Sources: PBk 5, pp. 217 & 220

VANDER MEERSCHEN, THEODORE, *cornet/trumpet*
3rd 1898 tour; possibly other tours.
Source: Seating arrangement in St. Louis Post-Dispatch, *25 Sep 1898.*

*VAN DUYN, MARIAN, *soprano*
Soloist. 1896 MB (partial).
Sources: SB programs in PBk 4.

*VANE, SYBIL, *soprano*
Soloist, 26 Mar 1916, New York.
Sources: Musical Courier, 30 Mar 1916; Clarence J. Russell's diary.

VAN FOSSEN, JOHN F. (Johnny), *B-flat clarinet*
1925-26 tour (partial); 1926 tour; 1st & 2nd 1927 tours; 1929 tour; one or more of 1930 tours; 1931 tour. Other positions: Leopold Stokowski's Band of Gold; Wanamaker's Band; Conshohocken (PA) Band; Norristown (PA) Band. Member, SBFS. b. 3 Jan 1903; d. 26 May 1994, Olney, PA.
Sources: SB payrolls; Harold Stambaugh's 1925-26 hotel assignment list; If You Knew Sousa, National Public Television program; Philadelphia Inquirer, 17 Dec 1983, 23 Jun 1991, & 29 May 1994 [obituary]; references in SBFS News; author's interview with Van Fossen; Social Security Death Index.

*VAN HOOSE, ELLISON, *tenor (vocal)*
Soloist. 1896 MB (partial). Other positions: Damrosch Opera Co.; Chicago Opera Co.; recitalist in America & Europe. Recorded for Victor. b. 18 Aug 1868, Murfreesboro, TN; d. 24 Mar 1936, Houston, TX.
Sources: SB programs; Baker's Biographical Dictionary of Musicians; Portraits of the World's Best-Known Musicians; PBk 4, pp. 48, 49.

*VAN LIEW, LILLIAN, *soprano*
Soloist. 1897 MB (partial).
Source: References in PBk 5.

VanPOUKE, JACQUES LOUIS, *B-flat clarinet*
1905 tour (Britain) (partial). Other position: U.S. Marine Band. Recorded for Berliner & Columbia.
Source: Author's correspondence with Michael Ressler, U.S. Marine Band, & with Frederick P. Williams, discographer.

VAN PRAAG, MAURICE (Van), *horn*
1914 tour; 1915 tour (**soloist** at Panama-Pacific Exposition); 1917 WG (**soloist**); 1918 tour (**soloist**). Other positions: New York Philharmonic (also personnel manager); Chicago Symphony Orchestra; St. Paul Symphony Orchestra. Charter member, SBFS. b. Amsterdam, Holland, 8 Mar 1886.
Sources: SB programs & photos; signature on 6 Nov 1914 birthday card from band members to Sousa (refers to first year with band as 1914); roster in Musical Courier, 9 Jun 1915; 1915 Tuxedo tobacco advertisement with SB musicians' signatures; references in SBFS News.

*VASSEY, T., *tenor (vocal)*
Soloist. 1902 StPr (partial).
Sources: SB programs.

VEREECKEN, BENJAMIN (Ben), *saxophone*
Also SB arranger & copyist. Possibly 2nd 1910 tour; 1911 world tour; possibly 1912 & 1913 tours; 1915 tour; 1921 tour. Other positions: Pryor's Band; Barnum & Bailey's Circus Band (in Europe); Anglo-Canadian Leather Co. Band; Long Beach (CA) Municipal Band. Composer, author. b. 1872, Tensche, Belgium; d. Feb., 1967.
Sources: Roster in Albert A. Knecht's world tour diary; Edmund A. Wall's world tour poem; roster in Musical Courier, 9 Jun 1915; 1915 Tuxedo tobacco advertisement with SB musicians' signatures; Supplement to the Heritage Encyclopedia of Band Music; A Study of the Saxophone Soloists Performing with the John Philip Sousa Band: 1893-1930; author's correspondence with Barry Owen Furrer, band historian; references in SBFS News.

VERON, WILLIAM, *baritone (vocal)*
Soloist. 1896 MB (partial); 1st 1898 tour (partial).
Sources: SB programs; PBk 5, p. 219.

*VER TREESE, BLONDELLE, *soprano*
Soloist, 6 Apr 1902, New York.
Source: PBk 18, p. 124.

*VESTER, NETTIE, *soprano*
Soloist. 1902 WG (partial).
Sources: SB programs; PBk 18, p. 173.

VIEHM, ROBERT, *horn*
One or more of 1930 tours.
Source: 1930 SB photo.

*VILLANA, LUISA, *soprano*
Soloist, 16 Jan 1916, New York. Other positions: Metropolitan Opera Co.; La Scala Opera. b. Italy.
Sources: Clarence J. Russell's diary; Portraits of the World's Best-Known Musicians.

VINCINGUERRA (VINCI), MICHAEL, *B-flat clarinet*
1920 tour; 1921 tour; 1921-22 tour; probably 1922 tour; 1923-24 tour; 1924 tour; 1925-26 tour; 1926 tour. Other position: Rocchaseau Municipal Band (Italy). Charter member, SBFS.
Sources: SB payrolls, rosters, & photos; roster in Jacobs' Band Monthly, Aug, 1925; Harold Stambaugh's 1925-26 hotel assignment list; author's interview with Vincinguerra; references in SBFS News.

VITOCOLONNA, GIACINTO, *horn*
1919-20 tour. Member, SBFS.
Sources: Various 1919-20 tour rosters; references in SBFS News.

VIVIANI, LUDOVICO, *basso*
Soloist. 1893 tour; 1893 MB (partial). Other positions: Hinrichs' American Opera Co.; toured with Anton Seidl Orchestra. b. Italy.
Sources: SB programs; SB publicity for 1st 1893 tour; Metronome, Apr, 1893; PBk 2, p. 30; PBk 3, p. 6.

VON STOSCH, LEONORA, *violin*
Soloist. 2nd 1893 tour (partial). Other positions: toured as concert artist in America and Europe. Author (won Pulitzer Prize for poetry in 1927). Married name Speyer. b. 7 Nov 1872, Washington, D.C.; d. 14 Aug 1943, Philadelphia.

Sources: SB programs; SB publicity for 1st 1893 tour; World Authors; references in PBk 2.

VOORZANGER, JOSEPH, *trombone*
Date(s) of SB service uncertain, but prior to 1922.
Sources: 1921 C.G. Conn advertisement; SBFS News, Feb, 1955, p. 14.

VOPNI, WILLIAM B., *horn*
1926 tour; probably 1st & 2nd 1927 tours. Other positions: Winnipeg Symphony Orchestra; Toronto Symphony Orchestra; Toronto Symphony Band. Member, SBFS.
Sources: SB financial papers & photos; Winnipeg Globe & Mail, 7 Jul 1966; references in SBFS News.

WADSWORTH, FRANK W., *flute/piccolo*
1st 1893 tour (flute **soloist**); 1893 MB (flute **soloist**); 2nd 1893 tour (flute **soloist**); probably 1st & 2nd 1894 tours (flute **soloist** at Mid-Winter Exposition); 1st & 2nd 1894 Madison Square Garden engagements (**soloist** on 2nd); 1894 MB (flute **soloist**); 3rd 1894 tour (flute **soloist**); 1st 1895 tour (flute **soloist**); probably 2nd 1895 tour; 3rd 1895 tour (flute **soloist**); probably 1895 MB; 4th 1895 tour (flute **soloist**); probably 1st & 2nd 1896 tours; 1896 MB (flute **soloist**); probably 1896-97 tour; 1897 tour (flute & piccolo **soloist**); 3rd 1898 tour (piccolo **soloist**); one or more tours in 1899; 1899 MB (flute (**soloist**). Other position: Gilmore's Band; Levy's Band; Robinson's American Band; New York theater orchestras.
b. Massclesfield, England, 1860.
Sources: SB payrolls, programs, & photos; SB publicity for 1st 1893 tour; Frank W. Wadsworth and Lillian Jane Wadsworth; signature in Lester Levy's autograph book, Nov, 1895; J.W. Pepper's Musical Times and Band Journal, Spring, 1895; review of SB concert in Cedar Rapids, IA, on 16 Feb 1898 by Wadsworth (PBk 5, p. 201); references in PBks 2-7; author's correspondence with family; SBFS News May, 1956, p. 12.

*WAECHTLER, BERTHA, *contralto*
Soloist. 1895 St. Louis Exposition (partial).
Source: SB program for 1 Oct 1895 in St. Louis Post-Dispatch.

WAGNER, AUGUST, *horn*
2nd 1893 tour; 1st 1894 tour; several other tours between 1893-97; 3rd 1898 tour.
Source: Advertisement in J.W. Pepper's Musical Times and Band Journal, May, 1898.

WAGNER, ERNEST F. (Ernie), *flute/piccolo*
1915 tour; possibly 1916-17 tour; 1929 & 1930 radio broadcasts; 12 Mar 1931 recording; 9 Apr 1931 radio broadcast; late 1931 radio broadcasts. Charter member, SBFS.
Sources: SB payrolls; roster in Musical Courier, 9 Jun 1915; references in SBFS News.

WAGNER, GEORGE P., *percussion*
1st 1905 tour (Britain).
Sources: S.S. Baltic ship's list, 19 May 1905; author's correspondence with Raoul F. Camus, band historian.

WALEN, FREDERICK LARS (Fred), *tuba*
Possibly 1st and/or 2nd 1894 tours; 3rd 1894 tour; probably all 1895, 1896, & 1897 tours. Other position: U.S. Marine Band.
Sources: SB payrolls & photos; program in St. Louis Post-Dispatch, 11 Oct 1894; article, "Our Musical Marines" in Washington Star 14 Jun 1890; seating chart in Philadelphia Press, 7 May 1897; data from Michael Ressler, U.S. Marine Band; author's correspondence with family & with Carole Nowicke, band historian.

*WALKER, ANNIE L., *soprano*
Soloist, 10 Dec 1893, Brooklyn, NY.
Source: PBk 3, p. 48.

*WALKER, RACHEL, *vocalist*
Soloist, Sep, 1897, New York.
Sources: PBk 4, pp. 96-98.

WALL, CHARLES A. (Charlie), *B-flat clarinet*
2nd 1927 tour; off-tour concert 15 Jun 1929, Princeton, NJ; 1929 tour; 12 Mar 1930 radio broadcast. Other position: Anglo-Canadian Leather Co. Band. Served in U.S. Army. Son of Edmund A. Wall & brother of Edmund C. Wall. Member, SBFS. b. 17 Sep 1899; d. Dec, 1958.
Sources: SB payrolls & photos; Harold Stambaugh's 1927 hotel assignment list; author's correspondence with family; references in SBFS News; Social Security Death Index.

WALL, EDMUND A., *B-flat clarinet*
Possibly 2nd 1910 tour; 1911 world tour. Father of Charles A. Wall & Edmund C. Wall.

Sources: Roster in Albert A. Knecht's world tour diary; Edmund A. Wall's world tour poem; author's correspondence with family; references in SBFS News.

WALL, EDMUND C., (Eddie), *B-flat clarinet*
1926 tour (partial); 1ˢᵗ 1927 tour; 2ⁿᵈ 1927 tour (**soloist** at StPr); 1928 tour (occasional **soloist**); 1ˢᵗ part of 1929 tour (**soloist** in Minneapolis); 1929 & 1930 radio broadcasts; one or more of 1930 tours; 12 Mar 1931 recording; 9 Apr 1931 radio broadcast; 1931 tour; late 1931 radio broadcasts. Other positions: New York City Ballet Orchestra; Metropolitan Opera Orchestra; New York theater orchestras; Goldman Band; Pryor's Band; Anglo-Canadian Leather Co. Band; 1940 World's Fair Band (New York). Son of Edmund A. Wall & brother of Charles A. Wall. Charter member, SBFS (editor of *SBFS News* 1967-85). b. 28 Jul 1895; d. 24 Jan 1985, New York.
Sources: SB payrolls, programs, & photos; Eugene Slick's 1928 autograph book; H.&A. Selmer advertisement ca. Jul, 1952; author's interviews and correspondence with Wall; Social Security Death Index.

WALT, RUSSELL, *oboe*
1925-26 tour; 1926 tour; 1ˢᵗ & 2ⁿᵈ 1927 tours. Other position: Allentown (PA) Band.
Sources: SB payrolls & photos; roster in Jacobs' Band Monthly, *Aug, 1925; Harold Stambaugh's 1925-26 hotel assignment list; Morning Call (Allentown), 25 Feb 1975, p. 6.*

WALTERS, CLARENCE, *B-flat clarinet*
Date(s) of SB service uncertain but probably 1926 WG. Other position: Allentown (PA) Band.
Sources: Undated clippings in Allentown Band archives; author's correspondence with Warren Wilson, Allentown Band.

*WALTZINGER, BERTHA, *soprano*
Soloist. 1894 MB (partial); 1897 MB (partial); 1899 MB (partial).
Sources: References in PBks 3, 5, & 9.

WARDWELL, ORLANDO EDWARD (Ed, Eddie), *euphonium, trombone*
Mostly euphonium; occasionally trombone. 3ʳᵈ 1898 tour (**soloist**, St. Louis Exposition); probably all 1899 tours; probably 1ˢᵗ 1900 tour; 2ⁿᵈ 1900 tour (Europe); probably 3ʳᵈ & 4ᵗʰ 1900 tours; probably 1ˢᵗ 1901 tour; 2ⁿᵈ 1901 tour (**soloist**); probably 3ʳᵈ 1901 tour; 4ᵗʰ 1901 tour (Britain); probably 1ˢᵗ & 2ⁿᵈ 1902 tours; 3ʳᵈ 1902 tour (**soloist**, Pittsburgh Exposition); 1ˢᵗ 1903 tour (Europe); 2ⁿᵈ 1903 tour (**soloist**, Pittsburgh Exposition). Other positions: Pryor's Band; Turner (ME) Cornet Band; Bubb Comedy Co. Orchestra. Recorded for Victor [including a whistling solo with Sousa's Band, Victor #1168 (in 1902)]. b. 20 Nov 1873, Monmouth, ME.
Sources: SB programs & photos; seating chart in St. Louis Post-Dispatch, *25 Sep 1898; references in PBks;* The Sousa Band A Discography; *references in SBFS News; author's correspondence with family.*

*WARREN, BAILEY, *vocalist (boy)*
Possibly **soloist**, 1 Dec 1925, Amarillo, TX; **soloist**, 28 Oct 1928, San Diego, CA.
Source: PBk 75, p. 91.

WAVREK, BERTHOLD K. (Bert), *flute/piccolo*
1ˢᵗ & 2ⁿᵈ 1927 tours; 1929 tour; one or more of 1930 tours; 1931 tour. Other position: Allentown (PA) Band. Brother of Frederick J. Wavrek. Member, SBFS. b. 26 May 1906; d. Oct, 1968.
Sources: SB payrolls & photos; Harold Stambaugh's 1927 hotel assignment list; Jay Sims' 1930 tour roster & handwritten checklist for 1931 tour; author's correspondence with family & with Warren Wilson, Allentown Band; Morning Call (Allentown), 25 Feb 1975, p. 6; Social Security Death Index.

WAVREK, FREDERICK J. (Fred), *B-flat clarinet*
1929 tour (partial); one or more of 1930 tours; 1931 tour. Other position: Allentown (PA) Band. Brother of Berthold K. Wavrek. Member, SBFS.
Sources: SB payrolls; Jay Sims' 1930 tour roster & handwritten checklist for 1931 tour; Allentown Band Archives; author's interview & correspondence with family; author's correspondence with Warren Wilson, Allentown Band; Morning Call (Allentown), 25 Feb 1975, p. 6; references in SBFS News.

WEAVER, FREDERICK M. (Buck), *B-flat clarinet*
1921 tour (partial); 1921-22 tour; 1923-24 tour; 1924 tour; 1925-26 tour; 1926 tour; 1ˢᵗ & 2ⁿᵈ 1927 tours; 1928 tour; 1929 tour; one or more of 1930 tours. Other positions: Columbus (OH) theater and radio studio orchestras. Member, SBFS. d. 5 Nov 1948, Columbus, Ohio.
Sources: SB payrolls, rosters, & photos; roster in Jacobs' Band Monthly, *Aug, 1925; Harold Stambaugh's 1925-26 & 1927 hotel*

assignment lists; Eugene Slick's 1928 autograph book; Jay Sims' 1930 tour roster; references in SBFS News.

*WEBB, ROBERT J., *tenor (vocal)*
Soloist. 14 Jan, 21 Jan, & 25 Feb 1894, Brooklyn; 1894 MB (partial); 1896 MB (partial).
Sources: SB programs in PBks 3 & 4.

WEBBER, RANDALL B., *B-flat clarinet*
1924 tour. Other position: Santa Barbara (CA) Symphony Orchestra. Member, SBFS.
Sources: Red Wing (MN) Daily Republican, 25 Sep 1928 (PBk 75, p. 62); references in SBFS News.

WEBER, ALBERT L. (Al), *tuba*
1926 tour (partial, after StPr). Other position: Pryor's Band. Member, SBFS.
Sources: 1926 SB payroll; references in SBFS News; author's interview with Weber & with Kenneth B. Slater, bandmaster.

WEBER, CHARLES A., Jr., *saxophone*
1919-20 tour; 1920 tour; 1921 tour; 1921-22 tour (partial). Member, SBFS. d. ca. 1956, Battle Creek, MI.
Sources: SB rosters & photos; 1921 SB photo; 1921 C.G. Conn advertisement; references in SBFS News.

WEBER, EMIL, *tuba*
1915 tour. Off-tour concert 15 Jun 1929, Princeton, NJ. Other position: Pryor's Band.
Sources: Roster in Musical Courier, 9 Jun 1915; 1915 Tuxedo tobacco advertisement with SB musicians' signatures; SB payroll for 15 Jun 1929; "In Memoriam" list, SBFS organizational booklet (1945); author's interviews with Kenneth B. Slater, bandmaster.

WEBER, HENRY, *B-flat clarinet*
1ˢᵗ 1893 tour; possibly other tours. Other positions: Professional bands in Sarasota, FL.
Sources: SB publicity for 1ˢᵗ 1893 tour; SB program for 17 Oct 1893 in St. Louis Post-Dispatch; *author's correspondence with Raoul Camus, band historian; author's interviews with Kenneth B. Slater, bandmaster.*

WEBER, HERBERT E.C., *tuba*
1924 tour; 1926 tour after StPr. Other positions: Pryor's Band; Almas Temple Shrine Band (Washington, D.C.); faculty, U.S. Navy School of Music. Charter member, SBFS. d. ca. 1981, San Diego, CA.
Sources: SB payrolls; references in SBFS News.

WEBSTER, W.V., *tuba*
1919-20 tour (partial).
Sources: Los Angeles Times, 24 Apr 1919; unidentified clipping in PBk 53.

WEIGEL, F.D., *saxophone*
1925-26 tour (partial).
Sources: Harold Stambaugh's 1925-26 hotel assignment list; PBk 67, p. 23; PBk 69, pp. 5-8.

WEIR, LEON E. (Duke), *saxophone*
1920 tour; 1921 tour; 1921-22 tour; probably 1922 tour; 1923-24 tour; 1924 tour; 1925-26 tour; 1926 tour; one or more of 1930 tours (partial). Other positions: Long Beach (CA) Municipal Band; Elks Band (Los Angeles, CA). Member, SBFS. b. 31 Dec 1893; d. Oct, 1976, Long Beach, CA.
Sources: SB payrolls, rosters, programs, & photos; roster in Jacobs' Band Monthly, *Aug, 1925; references in PBks; author's interview & correspondence with Weir; references in SBFS News; Social Security Death Index.*

WEISS, EDSON E., *oboe/English horn*
1928 tour (partial); 1929 tour.
Sources: Receipts for services dated 2 Sep 1928 & 26 Sep 1929.

WEISS, GEORGE E., *bassoon*
Possibly early tours in 1895; 4ᵗʰ 1895 tour; 1ˢᵗ 1896 tour; 1896-97 tour; probably 1897 tour; probably 1ˢᵗ, 2ⁿᵈ, & 3ʳᵈ 1898 tours; 3ʳᵈ 1898 tour; possibly some tours in 1899.
Sources: SB payrolls and photos; signature in Lester Levy's autograph book, Nov, 1895; seating chart in Philadelphia Press, *7 May 1897; seating chart in* St. Louis Post-Dispatch, *25 Sep 1898.*

*WELD, ARTHUR, *basso*
Soloist. 1894 St. Louis Exposition (partial). Other positions: Conductor of New York theater orchestras. Composer. d. 11 Oct 1914, New York.
Sources: References in St. Louis Post-Dispatch, *ca. Sep, 1894; Variety, 17 Oct 1914, p. 13 [obituary].*

WELKER, MAX, *cornet/trumpet*
Date(s) of SB service uncertain.
Source: SBFS News, Jun, 1949, p. 1.

WELLINGHAM, JESSE, *instrument?*
1929 tour.
Sources: SB payroll 28 Sep 1929; PBk 75, pp. 132, 133.

WELTE, VICTOR (Spaff), *cornet/trumpet*
1907 tour; possibly tours in 1908, 1909, & 1910; 1911 world tour; possibly 1912 & 1913 tours; 1914 tour; 1915 tour; 1916 WG; off-tour concert 15 Jun 1929, Princeton, NJ; 1929 tour; 1929 & 1930 radio broadcasts. Member, SBFS.
Sources: SB payrolls & photos; roster in New York Dramatic Mirror, 7 Sep 1907; roster in Albert A. Knecht's world tour diary; Edmund A. Wall's world tour poem; signature on 6 Nov 1914 birthday card from band members to Sousa (refers to first year with band as 1907); roster in Musical Courier, 9 Jun 1915; 1915 Tuxedo tobacco advertisement with SB musicians' signatures; references in SBFS News.

*WERNIG, ELLA, *soprano*
Soloist. 1893 MB (partial).
Sources: PBk 2, pp. 51, 52; PBk 3, pp. 22, 23.

WEST, MAUDE, *secretary*
Date(s) of SB service uncertain but listed as private secretary on list of executive staff for 1st 1903 tour (Europe).
Source: SB publicity for 1st 1903 tour.

*WESTFORD, HARRY, *tenor (vocal)*
Soloist, 24 Oct 1916, Washington, D.C.
Source: Clarence J. Russell's diary.

*WESTON, PERCY B., *tenor (vocal)*
Soloist. 1893 & 1894 St. Louis Expositions (partial, both).
Sources: St. Louis Post-Dispatch, 19 Oct 1893 & undated clipping ca. Sep, 1894.

WHITBY, RICHARD E. (Dick), *trombone*
1914 tour; 1915 tour; off-tour concert 15 Jun 1929, Princeton, NJ; 1929 & 1930 radio broadcasts; 12 Mar 1931 recording.
Sources: SB payrolls, programs, & photos; signature on 6 Nov 1914 birthday card from band members to Sousa (refers to first year with band as 1914); C.G. Conn Musical Truth, May, 1915, p. 23; roster in Musical Courier, 9 Jun 1915; 1915 Tuxedo tobacco advertisement with SB musicians' signatures; 1921 C.G. Conn advertisement; SBFS News, Feb, 1955, p. 14.

WHITCOMB, LAWRENCE, *oboe*
1929 radio broadcasts.
Sources: SB payrolls.

WHITE, ARTHUR, *horn*
1st 1905 tour (Britain); probably some tours in 1906; 1907 tour; probably 1st 1908 tour; 2nd 1908 tour; 1909 tour.
Sources: S.S. Baltic ship's list, 19 May 1905; roster in New York Dramatic Mirror 7 Sep 1907; roster in New York Dramatic Mirror 1 Sep 1908; 1909 SB photo; "In Memoriam" list, SBFS organizational booklet (1945).

WHITTAKER, ADRIAN, *E-flat clarinet*
1st 1895 tour; probably 2nd, 3rd, & 4th 1895 tours; 1st 1896 tour; probably 1896-97 tour; 1897 tour; probably 1st, 2nd, & 3rd 1898 tours; possibly all 5 1899 tours; 4th 1901 tour (Britain); possibly some tours in 1902; 1st 1903 tour (Europe).
Sources: SB payrolls, rosters, & photos; hotel registration, Adrian, MI, 1 Apr 1895; seating chart in Philadelphia Press, 7 May 1897; J.W. Pepper Musical Times and Band Journal, May, 1898; seating chart in St. Louis Post-Dispatch, 25 Sep 1898; SB/Grenadier Guards banquet seating chart of 17 Oct 1901; SB publicity for 1st 1903 tour; "In Memoriam" list, SBFS organizational booklet (1945).

WHITTIER, HARRY, *euphonium*
Date(s) of SB service uncertain but probably 1895 & 1896. Composer.
Sources: J.W. Pepper Musical Times and Band Journal, May, 1898; The Heritage Encyclopedia of Band Music; Supplement to the Heritage Encyclopedia of Band Music; author's correspondence with Leonard B. Smith, composer.

WIENELT, CARL, *horn*
2nd 1900 tour (Europe).
Sources: Roster in SB program of 22 Apr 1900; Metronome, Jun, 1900; SB photo 30 May 1900.

WIGE, RALPH N., *euphonium*
1926 tour (partial); 1928 tour; 1929 tour. Member, SBFS.
Sources: SB payrolls; Eugene Slick's 1928 autograph book; references in SBFS News; author's correspondence with Wige.

WILAT, LESLIE R., *instrument?*
1925-26 tour (partial).
Source: SB payroll 6 Mar 1926.

WILDER, HOLLY, *cornet/trumpet*
2nd 1900 tour (Europe) (occasional cornet **soloist**); possibly other tours. Other position: Gilmore's Band. Recorded for Columbia.
Sources: Roster in SB program of 22 Apr 1900; SB photo 30 May 1900; references in PBks 10 & 11; references in SBFS News; author's correspondence with Raoul F. Camus, band historian, & with Frederick P. Williams, discographer.

WILEY, H.E., *cornet/trumpet*
1919-20 tour (partial).
Source: 1919-20 SB tour roster.

WILHELMS, HERMUT, *horn*
1919-20 tour (partial).
Sources: Jay Sims' 1919-20 tour roster.

WILKINS, WILLIAM, *trombone*
1925-26 tour.
Sources: Harold Stambaugh's 1925-26 hotel assignment list; SBFS News, May, 1983, p. 31.

WILLAMAN, ROBERT G. (Bob), *B-flat clarinet*
1920 WG; 1923-24 tour; 1928 tour (partial); off-tour concert 15 Jun 1929, Princeton, NJ; 1929 tour; 1929 & 1930 radio broadcasts; 12 Mar 1931 recording; 9 Apr 1931 radio broadcast; late 1931 radio broadcasts. Other positions: Victor Herbert's Orchestra; Florida Symphony Orchestra; Duchess County (NY) Symphony Orchestra; New York theater orchestras; theater orchestras & radio studio orchestra in Des Moines, IA; Pryor's Band; Hagenback-Wallace Circus Band; Ringling Bros. Circus Band; U.S. Army Pershing Band; 351st U.S. Infantry Band; Fort Dodge Municipal Band; Illinois State Fair Band; Robert Willaman Clarinet Quartet. Author. Member, SBFS. b. 1 Apr 1893, Monroe, WI; d. 16 Feb 1980, Rochester, MN.
Sources: SB payrolls & photos; Chatfield (MN) Brass Band Newsletter, Mar, 1980; author's interview & correspondence with Willaman.

WILLIAMS, ALEXANDER, *B-flat clarinet*
1929 radio broadcasts.
Sources: SB payrolls.

WILLIAMS, ED (Ping), *clarinet*
1926 tour (partial).
Source: 1926 SB roster.

WILLIAMS, EDWARD A., *trombone*
Apparently all tours and engagements from 1st 1892 tour to 1917 tour. Member of numerous lower brass ensemble features. Other position: Music publisher in Boston. Recorded for Berliner, Columbia, and Victor.
Sources: SB payrolls, rosters, programs, & photos; roster in Albert A. Knecht's world tour diary; numerous other rosters; Edmund A. Wall's world tour poem; The Sousa Band A Discography; advertisements in various music trade journals; references in PBks; references in SBFS News.

WILLIAMS, ERNEST SAMUEL, *cornet/trumpet*
Date(s) of SB service uncertain but probably 2nd 1903 tour. Other positions: Philadelphia Orchestra; State Symphony Orchestra of New York; Liberati's Band; Goldman Band; Innes' Band; Conway's Band; Boston Band; Mace Gay's Martland Band; 158th & 161st Indiana Volunteer Infantry Regiment Bands; conductor of Boston Cadet Band & Lakeside Band (Denver, CO); Founder of Ernest Williams School of Music; music faculty, Juilliard School of Music & Ithaca Military Band School. Composer. Author of music instruction books. Recorded for Columbia. Brother of Jan W. Williams. b. 27 Sep 1881, Washington, IN; d. 8 Feb 1947, Saugerties, NY.
Sources: Pioneers in Brass; The Heritage Encyclopedia of Band Music; Supplement to the Heritage Encyclopedia of Band Music; Band Encyclopedia; undated advertisement for Keefer Trumpets; author's correspondence with Leonard B. Smith, composer, & with Raoul F. Camus, band historian; author's interviews with Kenneth B. Slater, bandmaster.

WILLIAMS, EVAN, *tenor (vocal)*
Soloist. Date(s) of SB service uncertain but apparently part of one tour prior to 1905. Recorded for HMV and Victor.
Source: PBk 22, p. 1.

*WILLIAMS, J. MARSHALL, *vocalist*
Soloist. 1894 MB (partial).
Source: Program in PBk 3, p. 62.

WILLIAMS, JAN A., *B-flat clarinet*
4th 1901 tour (Britain); probably 1st & 2nd 1902 tours; 3rd 1902 tour; 1st 1903 tour (Britain); 1929 & 1930 radio broadcasts; 12 Mar 1931 recording; 9 Apr 1931 radio broadcast; late 1931 radio broadcasts. Other positions: Metropolitan Opera Co. Orchestra; New York Symphony Orchestra; Walter Damrosch's Orchestra; Russian Symphony Orchestra; Victor Herbert's Orchestra; New York radio studio orchestras; conductor of Shrine Band, Erie, PA; music faculty, Juilliard School of Music & Ernest Williams School of Music; private music teacher; clarinet manufacturer. Author. Brother of Ernest S. Williams. Member, SBFS. b. 16 Jun 1884, Fountain City, IN; d. May, 1981, Saugerties, NY.
Sources: SB payrolls; SB/Grenadier Guards banquet seating chart of 17 Oct 1901; roster in New York Dramatic Mirror, 6 Sep 1902; Who Is Who in Music, 1951 Edition; references in SBFS News.

*WILLIAMS, LEWIS, *baritone (vocal)*
2nd 1894 Madison Square Garden engagement (partial); 1894 MB (partial); 1897 MB (partial).
Sources: SB programs in PBks 3 & 5.

WILLIAMS, RAYMOND E. (Lem), *flute/piccolo*
1925-26 tour (**soloist,** WG); 1926 tour (**soloist,** StPr & WG); probably 1st 1927 tour; 2nd 1927 tour. Other position: Accompanist for soprano Amelita Galli-Curci. d. 27 Nov 1947, Lafayette, IN.
Sources: SB payrolls, programs, & photos; roster in Jacobs' Band Monthly, Aug, 1925; Harold Stambaugh's 1925-26 hotel assignment list; references in PBks 69 & 72; references in SBFS News.

WILLIAMS, WARREN (Snorky), *B-flat clarinet*
1925-26 tour (partial); 1926 tour (**soloist**); 1st & 2nd 1927 tours; off-tour concert 15 Jun 1929, Princeton, NJ; one or more of 1930 tours; 1931 tour.
Sources: SB payrolls & photos; Harold Stambaugh's 1925-26 & 1927 hotel assignment lists; references in SBFS News.

WILLINGHAM, JESSE, *carpenter*
Carpenter/stage manager on 1929 tour.
Source: SB payroll.

*WILLS, NAT, *comedy singer, monologist*
Soloist at several New York Hippodrome Sunday series Oct, 1915-Feb, 1916. Recorded for Columbia and Victor.
Sources: Clarence J. Russell's diary; author's correspondence with Frederick P. Williams, discographer.

WILLSON, CEDRIC, *bassoon*
1922 tour. Brother of R.R. Meredith Willson. Member, SBFS. d. 1974, Dallas, TX.
Sources: References in PBk 58; references in SBFS News; author's correspondence with Willson.

WILLSON, ROBERT REINIGER MEREDITH (Meredith, Mer), *flute/piccolo*
1921 tour (**soloist,** WG); 1921-22 tour (**soloist**); 1922 tour (**soloist**); 1923-24 tour (**soloist**); 1929 radio broadcasts. Other positions: New York Philharmonic; New York Chamber Music Soc.; New York theater orchestras; radio producer & director; served in U.S. Army as director of Armed Forces Radio; guest conductor of symphony orchestras & bands. Composer of *The Music Man* & other musicals, 2 symphonies, & other works. Author. The *Music Man* Square in Mason City, IA, and the Meredith Willson Post 777 of American Legion in Arvada, CO, were named in his honor. Brother of Cedric Willson. Member, SBFS (president, 1976-1984). b. 18 May 1902, Mason City, IA; d. 15 Jun 1984, Santa Monica, CA.
Sources: SB payrolls, rosters, programs, & photos; Who Is Who in Music, 1951 Edition; The Heritage Encyclopedia of Band Music; Portraits of the World's Best-Known Musicians; references in PBks; references in SBFS News; author's interviews and correspondence with Willson.

WINGATE, W.F., *clarinet*
1921 tour (partial).
Source: 1921 SB roster.

WINKLER, OTTO, *bassoon*
2nd 1908 tour; possibly other tours.

Sources: Roster in New York Dramatic Mirror, 1 Sep 1908; "In Memoriam" list, SBFS organizational booklet (1945).

WISMAN, LOUIS A., *flute/piccolo*
1925-26 tour (partial).
Source: SB program dated 27 Sep 1925.

WITT, _____, *trombone*
4th 1905 tour.
Sources: 2 clippings in Pittsburgh newspapers in PBk 21, p. 42 list Witt as member of a trombone quintet in an ensemble number.

WOLF, ARTHUR D. (Art), *horn*
1921-22 tour; probably 1922 tour; 1923-24 tour; 1924 tour; 1925-26 tour; 1926 tour. Member, SBFS.
Sources: SB payrolls, rosters, & photos; roster in Jacobs' Band Monthly, Aug, 1925; Harold Stambaugh's 1925-26 hotel assignment list; references in SBFS News.

WOLFSOHN, HENRY, *management*
Date(s) of SB service uncertain but made arrangements in Europe for 3rd 1901 tour & engaged soloists for SB as an independent agent. Other positions: Manager for Fritz Kreisler, Maud Powell, and numerous other artists.
Sources: References in PBks 6 & 9.

*WOMACH, JESSIE, *vocalist*
Soloist. 1895 St. Louis Exposition (partial).
Source: SB program for 4 Oct 1895 in St. Louis Post-Dispatch.

*WOODS, J.T., *tenor (vocal)*
Soloist. 1894 MB (partial); also sang at 1896 MB but as a member of vocal quartet not accompanied by SB.
Sources: SB programs & other references in PBks 3 & 4.

WOOLLEY, GEORGE, *tuba*
One or more of 1930 tours; 12 Mar 1931 recording; 1931 tour; 1931 radio broadcasts.
Sources: SB payrolls; Jay Sims' 1930 tour roster & handwritten checklist for 1931 tour.

WOOLRIDGE, HAROLD I., *B-flat clarinet*
1924 tour; 1925-26 tour (partial); 2nd 1927 tour. Member, SBFS.
Sources: SB payrolls; roster in Jacobs' Band Monthly, Aug, 1925; Harold Stambaugh's 1927 hotel assignment list; references in SBFS News; author's correspondence with Woolridge.

WRIGGINS, ARTHUR M., *flute/piccolo*
1925-26 tour; 1926 tour; 1st part of 1928 tour; off-tour concert 15 Jun 1929, Princeton, NJ; 1929; 12 Mar 1930 radio broadcast; one or more of 1930 tours. Other positions: Ballet Russe Orchestra; Pryor's Band; private music teacher. Member, SBFS. b. 3 Jul 1902; d. Aug, 1953.
Sources: SB payrolls, programs, & photos; roster in Jacobs' Band Monthly, Aug, 1925; Harold Stambaugh's 1925-26 hotel assignment list; references in SBFS News; author's correspondence with family; Social Security Death Index.

WUMMER, JOHN (Johnny), *flute/piccolo*
1927 StPr; 1928 StPr. Other positions: New York Philharmonic; Ringgold Band (Reading, PA); private music teacher. Charter member, SBFS. b. 31 Dec 1899; d. Sep, 1977, New York, NY.
Sources: SB payrolls & programs; Harold Stambaugh's 1927 hotel assignment list; references in SBFS News; Social Security Death Index.

WUNDERLUCH, HANS, *cornet/trumpet*
Evidently most tours & engagements from sometime in 1895 until sometime in 1899 (trumpet **soloist** at 1895 St. Louis Exposition). Other position: U.S. Marine Band. Recorded for Berliner & Victor. Composer. b. 11 Aug 1864, Olsnitz, Saxony; d. 24 Feb 1923, Bremen, Germany.
Sources: SB payrolls & photos; hotel registration, Adrian, MI, 1 Apr 1895; signature in Lester Levy's autograph book, Nov, 1895; seating chart in Philadelphia Press, 7 May 1897; J.W. Pepper's Musical Times and Band Journal, May, 1898; seating chart in St. Louis Post-Dispatch, 25 Sep 1898; author's correspondence with Carole Nowicke, band historian & with Frederick P. Williams, discographer.

*YAEGER, _____, *vocalist (female)*
Soloist. 1893 St. Louis Exposition (partial).
Source: Notice of SB program for 20 Oct 1893 in St. Louis Post-Dispatch.

YENKE, OTTO B., *horn*
1909 tour; possibly 1st and/or 2nd 1910 tour; possibly 1912 and/or 1913 tour; 1914 tour; 1915 tour; probably 1915-16 *Hip! Hip! Hooray!*

engagement; 1916-17 tour. Charter member, SBFS. d. 12 Apr 1946, Lake Ronkonkama, NY.

Sources: Signature on 6 Nov 1914 birthday card from band members to Sousa (refers to first year with band as 1909); roster in Musical Courier, *9 Jun 1915; 1915 Tuxedo tobacco advertisement with SB musicians' signatures; references in* SBFS News.

YINGLING, MANUEL (Manny), *trombone*
1920 WG (**soloist**). Other positions: Theodore Thomas Orchestra; Prouty's Famous Boston Orchestra; Brooks Chicago Marine Band; Conway's Band; Weber's Prize Band of America; Grand Army of the Republic Band (Canton, OH); Royal Scotch Highlanders Band; Neddermeyer's Band (Columbus, OH); Thayer Military Band (Canton, OH); Brand's Cincinnati Band; conductor of Hyperion Band (Newcomerstown, OH); music faculty, Boston Conservatory of Music & Oberlin College. Composer. b. 24 Oct 1892, Newcomerstown; d. 7 Mar 1925, Newcomerstown.

Sources: The Heritage Encyclopedia of Band Music; *several undated articles in* The Band World; St. Petersburg *(FL)* Daily Times, *10 Feb 1918, p. 1; roster in 1920 WG programs; references in* SBFS News; *author's correspondence with family & with Newcomerstown Historical Society.*

ZANGARI, GIOVANNI, *bass clarinet*
1919-20 tour (partial).
Source: SB 1919-20 tour roster.

ZEDELER, NICOLINE, (Nici), *violin*
Soloist. 1st & 2nd 1910 tours; 1911 world tour; 1912 tour. Other positions: Soloist with North American & European symphony orchestras; music faculty, Chicago Music College & Chatham Square Music School. Member, SBFS. Married name Mrs. Emil Mix (tuba player of SB). b. 10 Mar 1890, Stockholm, Sweden; d. 26 Mar 1961, New York, NY.

Sources: SB programs & photos; roster in Albert A. Knecht's world tour diary; Edmund A. Wall's world tour poem; references in PBks; obituary in unidentified newspaper in George Ford Collection.

*ZELMA, NELLIE, *vocalist*
1894 MB (partial).
Source: SB program in PBk 3, p. 60.

*ZENTAN, MARY, *violin*
Soloist, 2 Apr 1916, New York.
Source: Clarence J. Russell's diary.

ZETTLEMANN, JOSEPH, *percussion*
1896-97 tour; possibly other tours.
Sources: Seating chart in Philadelphia Press, *7 May 1897; comments by SB percussionist Frank Snow in* Leedy Drum Topics, *Aug, 1924.*

ZIMMERMAN, LEOPOLD A. (Leo, Zimmy), *trombone*
Most or all engagements, 1903-08; off-tour concert 15 Jun 1929, Princeton, NJ; 1929 radio broadcasts; 12 Mar 1930 radio broadcast; one or more of 1930 tours; 12 Mar 1931 recording; 9 Apr 1931 radio broadcast; 1931 tour; late 1931 radio broadcasts. **Soloist**, 1903-1907 & 1930. Other positions: Grand Army of the Republic Band (Canton, OH); 23rd Regiment Band (NY); 71st Regiment Band (NY); Innes' Band; Goldman Band; Prince's Band; Conway's Band; several symphony orchestras & theater orchestras; 1940 World's Fair Band (New York). Composer. Recorded for Columbia, Edison, Victor, & Zonophone. b. 1 Mar 1866, Canton, OH. d. 18 Dec 1935, Englewood, NJ.

Sources: SB payrolls, rosters & programs; Pioneers in Brass; The Sousa Band A Discography; *various other rosters; references in PBks; references in SBFS News; author's correspondence with family.*

ZIMMERMAN, OSCAR G., *tuba*
1st and/or 2nd 1930 tours. Other positions (on string bass): Philadelphia Orchestra; Philadelphia Grand Opera Orchestra; NBC Symphony Orchestra; Philadelphia area theater orchestras; music faculty, National Music Camp (Interlochen, MI).

Sources: Once More From The Beginning; *Zimmerman's interview with Keith Brion, conductor of the New Sousa Band.*

ZLOTNIK, H. HENRY, *flute/piccolo*
1928 tour; off-tour concert 15 Jun 1929, Princeton, NJ; 1929 tour; 1929 & 1930 radio broadcasts; one or more of 1930 tours; 12 Mar 1931 recording; 9 Apr 1931 radio broadcast; 1931 tour; late 1931 radio broadcasts. Charter member, SBFS. b. 9 Mar 1903; d. Dec, 1983, Astoria, NY.

Sources: SB payrolls & programs; Jay Sims' 1930 tour roster & handwritten checklist for 1931 tour; references in SBFS News; correspondence between Zlotnik & Malcolm Heslip, author; Social Security Death Index.

ZUBER, FRANK J., *B-flat clarinet*
1921 tour; 1921-22 tour; probably 1922 tour; 1923-24 tour; 1924 tour; 1925-26 tour; 1926 tour; 1st & 2nd 1927 tours; 1928 tour; one or more of 1930 tours; 1931 tour.

Sources: SB payrolls, rosters, & photos; roster in Jacobs' Band Monthly, *Aug, 1925; Harold Stambaugh's 1925-26 & 1927 hotel assignment lists; Eugene Slick's 1928 autograph book; Jay Sims' 1930 tour roster; references in* SBFS News.

*ZULUETA, PEDRONE, *basso*
Soloist, 17 Apr 1903, London.
Source: PBk 20, p. 86.

Documentation Lacking

Below is a list of individuals whose presumed membership in Sousa's Band has not been documented. It is possible that a few *did* perform with the band at one time or another, but indisputable evidence is lacking.

Over a period of four decades, contact was made with hundreds of individuals who believed they had knowledge of someone (especially a relative) who played with the band. Each case was investigated, using every resource at the author's disposal. Indeed, some investigations developed into extended musical manhunts.

Verifying the membership of players of the 1890s and the early 1900s was especially troublesome. Beginning in 1963, I personally interviewed over fifty former Sousa musicians and corresponded with many others, but by then most of the players of the 1892-1910 era were no longer living. All former members of Sousa's Band are now deceased.

After examining data from a wide variety of sources, the following criteria for verifying membership was developed:
1. Sousa Band payrolls or other reliable financial records
2. Official Sousa Band rosters or hotel (partner assignment) lists
3. Sousa Band group photographs, with members in uniform
4. Other photographs of individual Sousa Band members in uniform, inscribed with verifiable dates
5. First person accounts in which verifiable performance dates, other band personnel, or itineraries are discussed

It quickly became obvious that newspaper accounts stating that a person "played with Sousa" were not proof that he or she had been a contracted member of Sousa's civilian professional band. This could be interpreted several ways. For example, it could mean they played under Sousa when Sousa was leader of the U.S. Marine Band (1880-92) or they were one of the many U.S. Navy musicians trained under his command at the Great Lakes Naval Training Station during the World War I era (1917-18).

Countless other thousands played under Sousa when he guest-conducted other bands or orchestras, such as high school or youth bands or Shrine Bands. This is obviously not the same as being a member of Sousa's Band. It is understandable how these encounters with Sousa can be misinterpreted after several decades; recall that Sousa died in 1932.

Many newspaper accounts alluding to an individual's membership in Sousa's Band came to my attention, but it must be remembered that newspaper stories are normally written under deadlines.

The same is true of obituaries, which are quite often compiled in haste by grieving relatives without having detailed biographical information at hand. It is only natural to want to glorify the deceased, so mentions of associations with famous people or organizations are understandable.

I want to assure readers that I had no intention of omitting names for which proof of Sousa Band membership might someday be forthcoming.

ABBOTT, LAWRENCE, *saxophone*
ABELMAN, _____
BALDWIN, MATTHEW WILLIAM
BANNER, CHARLES V., *cornet/trumpet*
BATES, WILL E., *cornet/trumpet*
BAUER, C.F., *cornet/trumpet*
BECKER, ANTON
BENT, *cornet/trumpet*
BERNEL, WILLIAM, *cornet/trumpet or percussion*
BEVERLEY, GEORGE, *management*
BEYNAN, CHARLES, *flute/piccolo*
BLEY, WILLIAM, *horn*
BLITZ, ANTON
BLOCK, _____, *cornet/trumpet*
BLUECHER, HENRY
BOISMAN, ERNEST A.
BORDERS, JAMES, *trombone*
BOWYER, W.
BRENZEL, DAVIS L., *trombone*
BRIDGES, LEONARD JAMES, *cornet/trumpet*
BROOKS, W.C., *management*
BROWN, GROVER CLEVELAND
BRYANT (or BURANT), WILLIAM J., *tuba*
BUENEVENTE, M.
CAMPBELL, T., *flute/piccolo*
CENTANINO, D.A.
CHIAFFERELLI (not same as Albert C.)
CINCIONE, PHILIP, *euphonium*
CLARK, TOM, *cornet/trumpet*
COLLINS, W.D., *cornet/trumpet*
COLONNA, JAMES V.
COSMEY, L.E.
CRAMER, WILLIAM, *B-flat clarinet*
DAHM, PAUL JAMES
DEMMS, GEORGE BEAUMONT
DUGAN, _____
DuPERE, JOSEPH N.
ELLISON, E., *B-flat clarinet*
ENGBERG, CLARENCE, *B-flat clarinet*
EPLER, MORTIMER D.
EVANS, A.C.
EVANS, CHARLES, *B-flat clarinet*
FALK, ELMER, *percussion*
FANTILLI, F.
FAUPEL, EDWARD LOUIS
FECHTER, JOHN
FINKELSTEIN, A.
FONZA, JAMES
FOX, NATHAN, *percussion*
FREEMAN, EDWIN T.
FRIBERG, JAMES A., *copyist*
FRIEBEL, ALBERT G.
FRITSCHE, ROL, *copyist*
GEBHARDT, JACOB
GRANDE, _____, *B-flat clarinet*
GREENAWALD, JOHN L.
GRETT, OSCAR CARL
GUIDA, ANTONIO
HAM, HOWARD EARL, *horn*
HARPET, WAINO F.
HARROD, WILLIAM ALVA
HARVEY, WALLACE
HAYMAN, CHARLES PIERCE
HEANLY, PERCY W., *management*

HEIMAN, AL, *saxophone*
HENRY, MERRIL, *cornet/trumpet*
HILL, JOHN MILTON, *B-flat clarinet*
HLADICK, JOHN
HOLROYD, LINCOLN
JONES, T.S.
JOURDAIN, A.
KANDEL, HARRY
KAYSER, CHARLES
KENNEDY, MAUD, *vocalist*
KRATZ, JOHN, *B-flat clarinet*
LANNUTTI, NICHOLAS, *oboe*
LAW, JAMES A.
LAWRIE, WILLIAM ALEXANDER
LAWTON, EDWARD (Teddy)
LENTZ (or LETZ), DONALD A.
LETZ, JOHN
LIBERACE, SALVATORE, *horn*
LIEGL, ERNEST, *flute/piccolo*
LIEHR, HERMAN PAUL
LIVINGSTON, HARRY
MASON, ELDON E.
MAURER, CHARLES, *cornet/trumpet*
McNAMARA, JOSEPH
McNEIL, MARIE, *cornet/trumpet*
MEISWINKEL, MARTIN, *B-flat clarinet*
MEJDRECK, CHARLES, *trombone*
MILLER, VERNE
MIRES, MAYNARD HAROLD, *trombone*
MORELL, J. GEORGE
MORGAN, CARO, *violin*
MORSCHER, SEPP
NICHOLS, ERNEST W.
PADGETT, CARLO
PARISI, P.J., *trombone*
PERKINS, _____, *bass clarinet*
PFARRIS, FRED
PLOTZ, ALBERT, *trombone*
REINES, LEO, *bassoon*
REINES, PHILIP, *bassoon*
RICHARD, _____, *vocalist*
RING, GEORGE
RODBARD, CHARLES
ROELOFSMA, EDMUND
SAGE, OCTAVE
SANTLEMANN, WILLIAM H., *B-flat clarinet*
SAVARINO, GIUSEPPE (JOSEPH), *B-flat clarinet*
SCHAEFFER, AUGUST H., *cornet/trumpet*
SCHECK, EMIL
SCHENK, J. PAUL
SCHMIDT, ADOLPH, *horn*
SCHMIDT, E.
SCHREIBER, OTTO
SCHUET, F.
SCHULZE, KARL
SCHUTTZE, _____
SCHUTZ, _____
SCIOLI, GIUSEPPE
SEEL, LOUIS, *cornet/trumpet*
SHERWOOD, HENRY WALTER
SIMONS, J. CAMERON
SOMERSET, WILLIAM, *B-flat clarinet*
STRATTAN, RULOFF R., *cornet/trumpet*
STUDY, CHARLES
TURNELL, ISAAC AMBROSE
TYRELL, GEORGE FRANCIS
ULIVERE, C.
VISTA, A.
VOLTZ, LOUIS, *clarinet*
WADE, RICHARD F., *cornet/trumpet*
WEGNER, WILLIAM, *tenor (vocal)*
WEISEN, LEON
WINFIELD, REATA, *violin*
WOEST, HERMAN
WOJAHN, FELIX

APPENDIX III

THE MAKEUP OF THE BAND

For the Record

Perhaps publishing every known personnel list of Sousa's Band will put an end to age-old arguments among band historians about the instrumental makeup of the band (i.e., how many instruments of each type were used, who played them, and when). Although personnel and instrumentation varied from season to season, the band was composed of between forty-eight and seventy-six musicians.

Salaries and Positions

Official payroll documents were the most reliable sources of personnel information, but very few payrolls have survived. Most were destroyed by the Sousa family in the 1970s, giving as their reason for doing so that the band was a private business and John Philip Sousa the sole proprietor.

Until several decades after his death only Sousa and a few members of his management staff knew salary amounts. The topic was one of great speculation, because he often paid more than other conductors, above the minimums required by musicians' unions.

Where salaries are shown, a higher amount for a musician does not necessarily mean that person was a soloist or first-chair player; he might have had other duties as well. Cornetist Clarence J. Russell's salary was higher than most others in the section because he was also the band's librarian, and trombonist Jay G. Sims was paid more because he was also personnel manager.

Ranking within sections has been an area of much discussion. Soloists occupied the first chairs, but which musicians played each lower part is not widely known. Where it was

possible to verify seating, it is presented within the individual rosters.

I obtained numerous official band rosters, minus salary figures, from former bandsmen or members of their families; among other valuable sources were several handwritten rosters in the hand of Jay G. Sims. Other sources included personnel lists published in newspapers or music trade journals. These were carefully scrutinized and coordinated with other data to take into account personnel changes while tours were in progress. Personnel turnovers on tour were relatively small, however.

The rosters for individual tours indicate those musicians known not to have completed an entire outing (marked by the notation [partial]). In most cases, the exact dates of these and other personnel changes could not be determined. In general, musicians did not play an entire tour for one of two reasons. Either they were contracted for only a certain period or they had to leave for an emergency or illness, not uncommon given the rigors of the tours.

Sousa's Choices of Instruments

Sousa once explained that he desired a "multiplicity of quartets" in order to produce four-part harmonic structures for colorful effects. According to his theory, a band was thus more versatile than an orchestra because it could create a wider variety of pleasing sounds. He used that theory when he composed and arranged and also when he made adjustments to standard published works.

Among his "quartets" were combinations of woodwind instruments, combinations of brass instruments, and often mixtures of those two families. "Quartet" did not necessarily mean just four instruments, however, and could also refer to four voices, with more than one instrument on each voice.

Audiences and musicians alike recognized that the sound of Sousa's Band was different from other bands, but the differences were so subtle that few could offer an explanation. A detailed study of Sousa's scores helps reveal his secrets.

About the Chart

Explanations of the headings used in the chart, as well as in the individual rosters, are in order.

Flute/piccolo: Musicians normally played both flute and piccolo.

Oboe/English horn: One player in the oboe section doubled on English horn as needed. Sousa usually used two players in the oboe section. It was common to find two oboes and one English horn listed, but usually there were only two players.

Bassoon/contrabassoon: All of the players played bassoon, with one doubling on contrabassoon if necessary. Evidence indicates that the contrabassoon was seldom used except for the first European tour in 1900 and the world tour of 1911.

E-flat clarinet: One of the most significant changes in the band's instrumentation came in the 1920s when Sousa discontinued using the E-flat clarinet in favor of more flutes. The reason for this is debatable, but there might be some validity to comments made by bandsmen who said Sousa had difficulty finding artists with ears keen enough to play this high-voiced instrument in tune.

Sarrusophone: The most unusual instrument used in the band, for one season only (and possibly part of another), was the [contrabass] sarrusophone. This is a hybrid double-reed instrument made of brass with an array of keys similar to the saxophone. The reasons for its omission are more obvious.

The voice was covered sufficiently by saxophones and/or bassoons, and it is rarely used now. It is difficult to play in tune, and to Sousa faulty intonation was an abomination.

Cornet/trumpet: A musician played either cornet or trumpet, but not both. A typical section consisted of four cornets and two trumpets. A few players, such as Harold Stambaugh, played cornet on one tour and trumpet on another. Cornetist Clarence J. Russell was also an exception. On a few occasions he was called upon to move to trumpet when a trumpeter was temporarily absent (one of the other cornets would then cover Russell's part in essential passages). Trumpets were not used on cornet parts, and cornets were not used on trumpet parts.

Flugelhorn: In the early years Sousa used one or two flugelhorns instead of cornets for the lower cornet parts. Both instruments sound in the same register, but the flugelhorn has a richer, more mellow sound. The reason he discontinued the use of the flugelhorn is subject to debate but probably had something to do with the loss of flugelhorn virtuoso Franz Helle. After Helle retired, Sousa did not replace him.

Tuba/sousaphone: The sousaphone is a member of the tuba family, sounding in the same register but shaped differently. It wraps around a player, and those used in the band had upright bells. Later models, still used widely for marching, have bells that point forward. Sousa did not use the bell-front type. Starting in 1898, a mixture of tubas and sousaphones was used until the late 1920s, when sousaphones were used exclusively.

Harp: Sousa used a harp although most other bands did not. He believed it added versatility. Photographs indicate that the harp was almost directly in front of Sousa in the middle of the stage. His reason for this placement, according to Keith Brion, conductor of the New Sousa Band, was that the harp had interplay with the woodwinds on the left and the brass on the right, thus providing an essential coordinating factor and helping stabilize the pitch. The harpist also occasionally performed solos and accompanied vocal and violin soloists on encore selections.

Analyzing Sousa's Instrumentation Practices

It is my intent to show how many instruments of each type were used throughout the history of the band, not to comment on the effectiveness of each instrument within a family of instruments or the ratios of the various families of instruments.

Comparing the instrumentation of Sousa's Band with that of the modern concert band is revealing, an illustration of Sousa's pioneering influence. One might assume that major improvements have been made since his time, but they have not. Other than the numbers of instruments in each section, modern concert bands still use Sousa's basic instrumentation.

Analyses concerning the merits of Sousa's use of various instruments, particularly his mixtures of woodwinds to brass, are left to future scholars. This much, however, must be said of Sousa's formula: it worked.

INSTRUMENTATION OF SOUSA'S BAND, 1892-1921

	1892 (a)	1893 (b)	1896 (c)	1897 (d)	1898 (e)	1900 (f)	1901 (g)	1903 (h)	1905 (i)	1907 (j)	1908 (k)	1911 (l)	1914 (m)	1915 (n)	1916 (o)	1919 (p)	1921 (q)
Oboe/English horn	2	2	2	2	2	2	2	2	2	2	2	2	2	2	2	2	3
Bassoon	2	2	2	2	2	3	2	3	2	2	2	3	2	2	2	2	3
Flute/piccolo	2	2	3	3	2	4	4	4	4	4	3	3	3	4	4	3	4
Eb clarinet	2	2	1	1	2	2	1	1	1	1	1	1	1	2	1	1	0
Bb clarinet	12	14	11	14	14	16	15	15	14	12	14	15	12	18	14	16	18
Alto clarinet	1	1	1	1	1	2	1	1	1	1	1	1	1	1	1	1	1
Bass clarinet	1	1	1	1	1	2	1	1	1	1	1	1	1	1	1	1	1
Saxophone	3	3	4	3	3	5	4	4	5	3	3	3	3	5	4	5	6
Sarrusophone	0	0	0	0	0	0	0	1	0	0	0	0	0	0	0	0	0
Total Woodwinds	**25**	**27**	**25**	**27**	**27**	**36**	**30**	**32**	**30**	**26**	**27**	**29**	**25**	**35**	**29**	**31**	**36**
Cornet/Trumpet	6	6	6	6	6	6	6	6	6	6	6	6	7	8	6	8	8
Flugelhorn	0	0	0	1	1	2	1	0	1	0	0	0	0	0	0	0	0
Horn	4	4	4	4	4	4	4	4	4	4	4	4	4	4	4	4	4
Euphonium	2	2	2	2	2	2	2	2	2	2	2	2	2	2	2	2	2
Trombone	3	3	3	3	3	4	3	3	3	4	4	4	4	5	5	4	4
Tuba/Sousaphone	3	3	3	3	4	4	4	4	4	3	3	4	3	6	4	4	4
Total Brass	**18**	**18**	**18**	**19**	**20**	**22**	**20**	**19**	**20**	**19**	**19**	**20**	**20**	**25**	**21**	**22**	**22**
Percussion	3	3	3	3	3	3	3	3	3	4	3	3	3	3	3	3	3
Harp	0	0	0	0	0	0	0	0	1	1	1	1	1	1	1	1	1
Vocal soloist	2	1	1	1	0	0	1	1	1	1	1	1	1	1	1	1	1
Violin soloist	0	1	1	1	0	0	1	1	1	1	1	1	1	1	0	1	1
Total Musicians (not including Sousa)	**48**	**50**	**48**	**51**	**50**	**61**	**55**	**56**	**56**	**52**	**52**	**55**	**51**	**66**	**55**	**59**	**64**

(a)	Sept. 1892	(g)	Oct. 1901	(m)	Nov. 1914
(b)	Sept. 1893	(h)	Jan.-July 1903	(n)	June 1915
(c)	Jan.-Feb. 1896	(i)	Jan.-May 1905	(o)	Dec. 1916
(d)	May 1897	(j)	Sept. 1907	(p)	1919-1920
(e)	Sept. 1898	(k)	Aug.-Sept. 1908	(q)	Sept. 1921
(f)	May 1900	(l)	Jan.-Dec. 1911		

INSTRUMENTATION OF SOUSA'S BAND 1922-1931

	1922 (r)	1923 (s)	1924 (t)	1925 (u)	1925 (v)	1925 (w)	1926 (x)	1927 (y)	1928 (z)	1929 (aa)	1929 (bb)	1930 (cc)	1930 (dd)	1931 (ee)	1931 (ff)	1931 (gg)
Oboe/english horn	3	3	3	3	3	2	2	2	2	2	3	2	2	2	2	2
Bassoon	3	2	2	2	2	2	2	3	2	2	2	2	2	2	2	2
Flute/piccolo	4	6	6	6	6	6	6	6	6	4	6	4	6	4	5	4
Eb clarinet	0	0	0	0	0	0	0	0	0	0	0	0	0	0	0	0
Bb clarinet	21	24	22	26	25	27	20	23	23	14	19	12	16	14	15	14
Alto clarinet	1	1	1	1	1	1	1	1	1	1	1	1	1	1	1	1
Bass clarinet	2	1	2	1	1	1	1	1	1	1	1	1	1	1	2	1
Saxophone	8	8	7	8	8	8	8	8	8	6	6	6	6	6	4	4
Sarrusophone	0	0	0	0	0	0	0	0	0	0	0	0	0	0	0	0
Total Woodwinds	**42**	**45**	**43**	**47**	**46**	**47**	**40**	**44**	**43**	**30**	**38**	**28**	**34**	**30**	**31**	**28**
Cornet/Trumpet	8	8	8	8	8	8	8	8	10	7	7	7	8	7	9	7
Flugelhorn	0	0	0	0	0	0	0	0	0	0	0	0	0	0	0	0
Horn	4	4	4	4	4	4	4	4	4	4	4	4	4	4	4	4
Euphonium	3	2	2	2	2	2	2	2	2	1	2	1	2	1	1	1
Trombone	5	4	4	4	4	4	4	4	4	3	3	4	3	4	3	4
Tuba/Sousaphone	5	5	5	6	6	6	3	5	6	3	4	3	4	3	3	3
Total Brass	**25**	**23**	**23**	**24**	**24**	**24**	**21**	**23**	**26**	**18**	**20**	**19**	**21**	**19**	**20**	**19**
Percussion	3	3	3	3	3	3	3	3	3	3	3	3	3	3	3	3
Harp	1	1	1	1	1	1	1	1	1	1	1	1	1	1	1	1
Vocal soloist	1	1	1	1	1	1	1	1	1	0	1	0	1	0	1	0
Violin soloist	1	1	0	0	0	0	0	0	0	0	0	0	0	0	0	0
Total Musicians	**73**	**74**	**71**	**76**	**75**	**76**	**66**	**72**	**74**	**52**	**63**	**51**	**60**	**53**	**56**	**51**

(r)	Dec. 1921-Jan. 1922	(x)	July 1926	(cc)	Mar. 12, 1930
(s)	1923-24	(y)	Sep. 1927	(dd)	Aug. 1930
(t)	Nov. 1924	(z)	Sep.-Nov. 1928	(ee)	Transcription Mar. 11, 1930
(u)	July 1925	(aa)	(Radio broadcasts)	(ff)	Radio b'cast Apr. 9, 1931
(v)	Aug.-Sept. 1925		May-Jun. & Oct.-Nov. 1929	(gg)	Aug.-Sept. 1931
(w)	1925-26	(bb)	Sept. 1929		

1892 (2nd 1892 tour)

VOCAL SOLOIST (2)
Galassi, Antonio
Lindh, Marcella

OBOE/ENGLISH HORN (2)
Messinger, Robert
Pechmann, Leo

FLUTE/PICCOLO (2)
Cox, John S.
Schoenthal, Charles

BASSOON (2)
Hildenbrandt, Christian
Jabon, Ferdinand

Eb CLARINET (2)
Urbain, Fred M.
+ 1 other

Bb CLARINET (12)
Dougherty, William
Jahn, Paul
Langan, William H.
Marchesi, Pasquale
Norrito, Joseph
Noyes, H.F.
Peters, A.G.
Preiss, Emil G.
Renz, Adolf
Schaich, Samuel
Staats, C.L.
+ 1 other

ALTO CLARINET (1)
(unknown)

BASS CLARINET (1)
(unknown)

SAXOPHONE (3)
Becker, Frederick E.R.
Kruger, Charles W.
Shannon, Thomas F.

CORNET/TRUMPET (6)
Baronne, Vincent
Fritz, Edward [partial]
Higgins, Henry A. [partial]
Petit, Charles
Saveniers, John
Seltzer, Frank
Smith, Arthur Harry

HORN (4)
Bernalfo, Giuseppe
Hoppe, Robert
Koch, Henry D.
+ 1 other

EUPHONIUM (2)
Haase, August
Raffayolo, Joseph M.
+ 1 other

TROMBONE (3)
Lyon, Marcus C.
Pryor, Arthur W.
Williams, Edward A.

TUBA/SOUSAPHONE (3)
Cesky, Matthias
Jeschka, William A.
+ 1 other

PERCUSSION (3)
Forster, Herman
Ingalls, Lewis
+ 1 other

TOTAL MUSICIANS: 48

Sources: Sousa Band promotional material; *Musical Courier,* Oct. 8, 1892; C.G. Conn advertisement ca. Nov. 1892.

1893 (2nd 1893 tour)

VOCAL SOLOIST (1)
Lindh, Marcella [partial]
Moreska, Nice [partial]

VIOLIN SOLOIST (1)
Von Stosch, Leonora

FLUTE/PICCOLO (2)
Norrito, Giacomo
Wadsworth, Frank W.

OBOE/ENGLISH HORN (2)
Messinger, Robert
+ 1 other

BASSOON (2)
Pagliani, A.
Thoede, Henry

Eb CLARINET (2)
LaCalle, Joseph M.
Urbain, Fred M.

Bb CLARINET (14)
Bronson, Chet
Dougherty, William
Geise, Henry
Jahn, Paul
Langan, William H.
Marchesi, Pasquale
Norrito, Joseph
Preiss, Emil G.
Schaich, Samuel
Schuetz, Franz
Shannon, Thomas F.
Stengler, August P.
+ 2 others

ALTO CLARINET (1)
Boccavecchia, Giuseppe

BASS CLARINET (1)
(unknown)

SAXOPHONE (3)
Kruger, Charles W. (tenor)
Lawton, Stanley (bari.)
Lefebre, Edouard A. (alto)

CORNET/TRUMPET (6)
Bode, Albert
Clarke, Herbert L.
Griffin, William
Heppner, F.
Martin, Frank
Seltzer, Frank

HORN (4)
Fricke, Harry A.
Koch, Henry D.
Narotsky, H.
Wagner, August

EUPHONIUM (2)
Haase, August
Raffayolo, Joseph M.

TROMBONE (3)
Lyon, Marcus C.
Pryor, Arthur W.
Williams, Edward A.

TUBA/SOUSAPHONE (3)
Baker, Eldon
Conrad, Herman C.
Jeschka, William A.

PERCUSSION (3)
Forster, Herman
Lowe, Charles P.
Lowe, (Dr.) William

TOTAL MUSICIANS: 50

Sources: Sousa Band photo, Sept. 1893; individual photos of Sousa Band musicians in Osmund Varela Collection; Sousa Band programs; Sousa Band press books nos. 2 & 3; research by Herbert N. Johnston.

253

1896 (1st 1896 tour) Figures in brackets indicate weekly salaries in dollars.

VOCAL SOLOIST (1)
French, Myrta Florence [100]

VIOLIN SOLOIST (1)
Duke, Currie [200]

FLUTE/PICCOLO (3)
McKnight, Chauncey [40]
Norrito, Giacomo [45]
Wadsworth, Frank W. [45]

OBOE/ENGLISH HORN (2)
Messinger, Robert (1st) [45]
Ratzeky, Alex (2nd) [35]

BASSOON (2)
Thoede, Henry (1st) [45]
Weiss, George E. (2nd) [40]

Eb CLARINET (1)
Whittaker, Adrian [35]

Bb CLARINET (11)
Burke, Thomas M. [35]
Dougherty, William [35]
Fleming, Robert [35]
Gerstenberger, Emil [35]
Langan, William H. [35]
Marchesi, Pasquale [35]
Norrito, Joseph [40]
Preiss, Emil G. [35]
Schaich, Samuel [35]
Schuetz, Franz [40]
Stengler, August P. (1st) [55]

ALTO CLARINET (1)
Boccavecchia, Giuseppe [35]

BASS CLARINET (1)
Reuffel, William [40]

SAXOPHONE (4)
Kruger, Charles W. [35]
Lawton, Stanley [35]
Moeremans, Jean H.B. [45]
Shannon, Thomas F. [40]

CORNET/TRUMPET (6)
Bode, Albert (1st) [55]
Griffin, William [35]
Grosskurth, August [30]
Higgins, Henry A. [35]
Smith, Walter F. [30]
Wunderluch, Hans [35]

HORN (4)
Baumgartel, Bernhardt (1st) [50]
DeBleye, Joseph [35]
Fricke, Harry A. [40]
Lange, William R. [40]

EUPHONIUM (2)
Giononne, E. [35]
Mantia, Simone (1st) [42]

TROMBONE (3)
Lyon, Marcus C. [35]
Pryor, Arthur W. (1st) [50]
Williams, Edward A. [35]

TUBA/SOUSAPHONE (3)
Conrad, Herman C. (1st) [40]
Giovannone, Tomaso [35]
Walen, Frederick Lars [35]

PERCUSSION (3)
Gericke, Charles [40]
Gericke, Oscar [40]
Richtor, Rudolph [30]

TOTAL MUSICIANS: 48

Sources: Six Sousa Band payrolls dating Jan. & Feb. 1896

1897 (1896-97 tour)

VOCAL SOLOIST (1)
Northrop, Elizabeth

VIOLIN SOLOIST (1)
Johnstone, Martina

FLUTE/PICCOLO (3)
McKnight, Chauncey
Norrito, Giacomo
Wadsworth, Frank W.

OBOE/ENGLISH HORN (2)
Messinger, Robert
Ratzeky, Alex

BASSOON (2)
LeRoux, Anton
Weiss, George E.

Eb CLARINET (1)
Whittaker, Adrian

Bb CLARINET (14)
Burke, Thomas M.
Dougherty, William
Fleming, Robert
Geise, Henry
Gerstenberger, Emil
LaCalle, Joseph M.
Langan, William H.
Marchesi, Pasquale
Norrito, Joseph
Preiss, Emil G.
Schaich, Samuel
Schuetz, Franz
Smith, J.E.
Stengler, August P.

ALTO CLARINET (1)
Boccavecchia, Giuseppe

BASS CLARINET (1)
Reuffel, William

SAXOPHONE (3)
Kruger, Charles W.
Lawton, Stanley
Moeremans, Jean H.B.

FLUEGELHORN (1)
Helle, Franz

CORNET/TRUMPET (6)
Bode, Albert
Grosskurth, August
Higgins, Henry A.
Pryor, Walter D.
Spitzner, Berthold
Wunderluch, Hans

HORN (4)
Baumgartel, Bernhardt
DeBleye, Joseph
Fricke, Harry A.
Lange, William R.

EUPHONIUM (2)
Giononne, E.
Mantia, Simone

TROMBONE (3)
Lyon, Marcus C.
Pryor, Arthur W.
Williams, Edward A.

TUBA/SOUSAPHONE (3)
Conrad, Herman C.
Giovannone, Tomaso
Walen, Frederick Lars

PERCUSSION (3)
Gericke, Charles
Richtor, Rudolph
Zettlemann, Joseph

TOTAL MUSICIANS: 51

Sources: Sousa Band payroll; seating chart, *Philadelphia Press*, May 9, 1897.

1898 (3rd 1898 tour)

FLUTE/PICCOLO (2)
Norrito, Giacomo
Wadsworth, Frank W.

OBOE/ENGLISH HORN (2)
Messinger, Robert
Trepte, Arthur

BASSOON (2)
LeRoux, Anton
Weiss, George E.

Eb CLARINET (2)
Naevy, H.
Whittaker, Adrian

Bb CLARINET (14)
Christie, Louis H.
Fritsche, Otto
Gerstenberger, Emil
Gionnone, G.
Hughes, Thomas A.
Langan, William H.
Marchesi, Pasquale
Norrito, Joseph
Preiss, Emil G.
Rice, Ed. L.
Schaich, Samuel
Schuetz, Franz
Sheridan, John
Stretz, Frank

ALTO CLARINET (1)
Boccavecchia, Giuseppe

BASS CLARINET (1)
Schroeder, Carl

SAXOPHONE (3)
Kruger, Charles W.
Lawton, Stanley
Moeremans, Jean H.B.

FLUEGELHORN (1)
Helle, Franz

CORNET/TRUMPET (6)
Grosskurth, August
Higgins, Henry A.
Kenecke, Emil
Mesloh, Otto
Vander Meerschen, Theodore
Wunderluch, Hans

HORN (4)
Fricke, Harry A.
Koch, Henry D.
Lange, William R.
Wagner, August

EUPHONIUM (2)
Mantia, Simone
Wardwell, Orlando E.

TROMBONE (3)
Lyon, Marcus C.
Pryor, Arthur W.
Williams, Edward A.

TUBA/SOUSAPHONE (4)
Conrad, Herman C.
Helleberg, August, Sr.
Mirenda, Domenico
Seavey, Horace P.

PERCUSSION (3)
Forster, Herman
Nickell (Nickol), Max
Richtor, Rudolph

TOTAL MUSICIANS: 50

Source: Seating chart in *St. Louis Post-Dispatch*, Sept. 25, 1898.

1900 (2nd 1900 tour, Europe)

FLUTE/PICCOLO (4)
Lufsky, Marshall P. (3rd)
Lyons, Darius A. (1st)
Norrito, Giacomo (piccolo)
Rose, Eugene C. (2nd)

OBOE/ENGLISH HORN (2)
De Vaux, Eugene (Jene) (1st)
Mohles, Paul (2nd)

BASSOON (3)
Helleberg, John (contra.)
LeRoux, Anton (2nd)
Thoede, Henry (1st)

Eb CLARINET (2)
Dornheim, Helmar
Lochmyer, A.

Bb CLARINET (16)
Christie, Louis H. (1st)
Engberg, R. (2nd)
Fritsche, Otto (solo)
Heuse, F. (1st)
Hickey, John (1st)
Kroeder, B. (1st)
Langan, William H. (1st)
Levy, Abraham (1st)
Locke, Edward E. (3rd)
Marchesi, Pasquale (2nd)
Nelson, Henry (3rd)
Otto, Charles (1st)
Pomo, Ettore (2nd)
Preiss, Emil G. (2nd)
Schuetz, Franz (1st)
Smith, A. (3rd)

ALTO CLARINET (2)
Boccavecchia, Giuseppe
Foerster, William

BASS CLARINET (2)
Donati, A.
Schroeder, Carl

SAXOPHONE (5)
Davidson, Maxwell (tenor)
Dickinson, Homer W. (alto)
Knittle, Louis (tenor)
Laurendeau, Alexander (alto)
Lawton, Stanley (bari.)

FLUEGELHORN (2)
Clarke, Edwin G.
Helle, Franz

CORNET/TRUMPET (6)
Clarke, Herbert L. (solo cor.)
Grosskurth, August (2nd tpt.)
Higgins, Henry A. (2nd cor.)
Nielsen, Peter (1st tpt.)
Rogers, Walter B. (1st cor.)
Wilder, Holly (2nd cor.)

HORN (4)
Horner, Anton (1st)
Lange, William R. (2nd)
Lotz, Philip (3rd)
Wienelt, Carl (4th)

EUPHONIUM (2)
Mantia, Simone (solo)
Wardwell, Orlando E. (2nd)

TROMBONE (4)
Chapman, Ross (1st)
Lyon, Marcus C. (2nd)
Pryor, Arthur W. (solo)
Williams, Edward A. (3rd)

TUBA/SOUSAPHONE (4)
Conrad, Herman C. (sousaphone)
Del Negro, Luca A. (tuba)
Helleberg, August, Sr. (tuba)
Seavey, Horace P. (tuba)

PERCUSSION (3)
Chapman, Christopher J. (drums, etc.)
Forster, Herman (bass drum)
Mills, Thomas (tympani)

TOTAL MUSICIANS: 61

Sources: Sousa Band photo, May 30, 1900, with identifications by Herbert L. Clarke; Metropolitan Opera House program, Apr. 23, 1900; roster in *Metronome*, June 1900; roster in *Musical Courier Trade Extra*, 1900.

1901 (4th 1901 tour, Britain)

VOCAL SOLOIST (1)
Davies, Maud R. [partial]
Tracy, Minnie [partial]

VIOLIN SOLOIST (1)
Hoyle, Dorothy

FLUTE/PICCOLO (4)
Lufsky, Marshall P. (3rd & piccolo)
Lyons, Darius A. (solo)
Norrito, Giacomo (2nd)
Thoede, Henry (4th)

OBOE/ENGLISH HORN (2)
Messinger, Robert (1st)
Mohles, Paul (2nd)

BASSOON (2)
Gill, George (2nd)
Rose, Eugene C. (1st)

Eb CLARINET (1)
Whittaker, Adrian

Bb CLARINET (15)
Christie, Louis H. (1st)
Clifford, Paul E. (1st)
DeLio, Giuseppe (2nd)
Hickey, John (1st)
Langan, William H. (1st)
Levy, Abraham (1st)
Marchesi, Pasquale (2nd)
Nelson, Henry (3rd)
Norrito, Joseph (solo)
Otto, Charles (1st)
Perrier, Pierre (1st)
Pomo, Ettore (2nd)
Preiss, Emil G. (2nd)
Russo, Enrico (1st)
Williams, Jan A. (3rd)

ALTO CLARINET (1)
Petzsch, Herman

BASS CLARINET (1)
Schroeder, Carl

SAXOPHONE (4)
Davidson, Maxwell (tenor)
Lawton, Stanley (bari.)
Locke, Edward E. (alto)
+ 1 other

FLUEGELHORN (1)
Helle, Franz

CORNET/TRUMPET (6)
Clarke, Herbert L. (solo cor.)
Grosskurth, August (2nd tpt.)
Higgins, Henry A. (2nd cor.)
Levy, Theodore (2nd cor.)
Nielsen, Peter (1st tpt.)
Rogers, Walter B. (1st cor.)

HORN (4)
Baumgartel, Bernhardt (1st)
DeBleye, Joseph (4th)
Lange, William R. (2nd)
Neubauer, Herman (3rd)

EUPHONIUM (2)
Mantia, Simone (solo)
Wardwell, Orlando E. (2nd)

TROMBONE (3)
Lyon, Marcus C. (2nd)
Pryor, Arthur W. (solo)
Williams, Edward A. (3rd)

TUBA/SOUSAPHONE (4)
Conrad, Herman C.
Del Negro, Luca A.
Helleberg, August, Sr.
Seavey, Horace P.

PERCUSSION (3)
Forster, Herman (bass drum)
Gericke, Oscar (tympani)
Kenn, Daniel (drums)

TOTAL MUSICIANS: 55

Sources: Sousa Band salary list; banquet seating arrangement for H.M. Grenadier Guards Band/Sousa's Band dinner, Oct. 17, 1901.

1903 (1st 1903 tour, Europe)

VOCAL SOLOIST (1)
Liebling, Estelle
Montefiore, Caroline [partial]

VIOLIN SOLOIST (1)
Powell, Maud

FLUTE/PICCOLO (4)
Heidelberg, Henry N.
Lufsky, Marshall P.
Norrito, Giacomo
Thierbach, Max

OBOE/ENGLISH HORN (2)
De Vaux, Eugene
Messinger, Robert

BASSOON (3)
Gill, George
Kruger, E.
Thoede, Henry

Eb CLARINET (1)
Whittaker, Adrian

Bb CLARINET (15)
Brissette, Fred J.
Christie, Louis H.
Clifford, Paul E.
DeLio, Giuseppe
Langan, William H.
Langenus, Gustav J.
Marchesi, Pasquale
Nelson, Henry
Norrito, Joseph
Oeconamacos, Nicholas
Otto, Charles
Perrier, Pierre
Preiss, Emil G.
Russo, Enrico
Williams, Jan A.

ALTO CLARINET (1)
Petzsch, Herman

BASS CLARINET (1)
Schroeder, Carl

SAXOPHONE (4)
Buscher, Philip
Lawton, Stanley
Locke, Edward E.
Moeremans, Jean H.B.

SARRUSAPHONE (1)
Reschke, Frank F.

CORNET/TRUMPET (6)
Grosskurth, August
Higgins, Henry A.
Kenecke, Emil
Levy, Theodore
Nielsen, Peter
Rogers, Walter B.

HORN (4)
Crasz, R.
DeBleye, Joseph
Lange, William R.
Neubauer, Herman

EUPHONIUM (2)
Mantia, Simone
Wardwell, Orlando E.

TROMBONE (3)
Lyon, Marcus C.
Pryor, Arthur W.
Williams, Edward A.

TUBA/SOUSAPHONE (4)
Conrad, Herman C.
Del Negro, Luca A.
Seavey, Horace P.
Sweetland, William W.

PERCUSSION (3)
Chapman, Christopher J.
Forster, Herman
Kenn, Daniel

TOTAL MUSICIANS: 56

Source: Sousa Band 1903 European tour publicity.

1905 (1st 1905 tour, Britain)

VOCAL SOLOIST (1)
Liebling, Estelle

VIOLIN SOLOIST (1)
Powell, Maud

FLUTE/PICCOLO (4)
Lufsky, Marshall P.
+ 3 others

OBOE/ENGLISH HORN (2)
(unknown)

BASSOON (2)
(unknown)

Eb CLARINET (1)
Kapralek, Frank J.

Bb CLARINET (14)
Fletcher, William

McGibney, C.G.
Norrito, Joseph
Vanpouke, Jacques L. [partial]
+ 10 others

ALTO CLARINET (1)
(unknown)

BASS CLARINET (1)
Schroeder, Carl

SAXOPHONE (5)
Becker, Frederick E.R.
Moeremans, Jean H.B.
Paul, Ferdinand
Schaich, Samuel
Schensley, William F.

FLUEGELHORN (1)
Helle, Franz

CORNET/TRUMPET (6)
Bellstedt, Herman
Clarke, Herbert L.
Fletcher, John
Gilliland, B.D.
Grosskurth, August
Higgins, Henry A.

HORN (4)
Albrecht, Gustav
Koch, Henry D.
White, Arthur
+ 1 other

EUPHONIUM (2)
Funaro, Pasquale C.
Perfetto, John J.

TROMBONE (3)
Lyon, Marcus C.
Williams, Edward A.
Zimmerman, Leopold A.

TUBA/SOUSAPHONE (4)
Helleberg, August, Sr.
Jeschka, William A.
Richardson, John W.
Sweetland, William W.

PERCUSSION (3)
Forster, Herman
Kenn, Daniel
Lowe, (Dr.) William

HARP (1)
Chase, William A.

TOTAL MUSICIANS: 56

Note: Pearl Bryer was cello soloist for several days.

Sources: *U.S.S. Baltic* ship's list, 1905; Sousa Band press book 22.

1907 (1907 tour)

VOCAL SOLOIST (1)
Allen, Lucy Anne [partial]
Chambers, Ada [partial]
Crane, Ethel [partial]
Liebling, Estelle [partial]

VIOLIN SOLOIST (1)
Powers, Jeanette A.

FLUTE/PICCOLO (4)
Altamont, G.
Norrito, Giacomo
Schenes, J.
Spindler, Julius

OBOE/ENGLISH HORN (2)
Lephilibert, P.
Doucet, A.

BASSOON (2)
Gill, George
Litke, H.

Eb CLARINET (1)
Kapralek, Frank J.

Bb CLARINET (12)
Baldwin, Harry
Buonocore, E.
Davis, Isadore
DeLio, Giuseppe
Gentile, Americo
Kampe, George C.
Lawnham, James
Livingston, Clarence R.
Norrito, Joseph
Payer, Joe
Porpora, Steve
Robinson, William J.

ALTO CLARINET (1)
Magnant, Rene

BASS CLARINET (1)
Schroeder, Carl

SAXOPHONE (3)
Ahlborn, C.
Falco, A.
Lawton, Stanley

CORNET/TRUMPET (6)
Clarke, Edwin G.
Clarke, Herbert L.
Grosskurth, August
Millhouse, Ross
Roeder, Louis
Welte, Victor H.

HORN (4)
Albrecht, Gustav
DeBleye, Joseph
Reise, A.
White, Arthur

EUPHONIUM (2)
Paone, Biagio
Perfetto, John J.

TROMBONE (4)
Corey, Ralph H.
Lyon, Marcus C.
Williams, Edward A.
Zimmerman, Leopold A.

TUBA/SOUSAPHONE (3)
Del Negro, Luca A.
Helleberg, August, Sr.
Richardson, John W.

PERCUSSION (4)
Forster, Herman
Kenn, Daniel
Lowe, Charles P.
Lowe, (Dr.) William

HARP (1)
Chase, William A.

OTHER
Stuart, William W. (duties unknown)

TOTAL MUSICIANS: 52

Sources: Roster in *New York Dramatic Mirror*, Sept. 7, 1907; instrumentation list in *Deseret Evening News* (Salt Lake City), Nov. 5, 1907; Sousa Band press books 27 and 28.

1908 (2nd 1908 tour)

VOCAL SOLOIST (1)
Chambers, Ada

VIOLIN SOLOIST (1)
Powers, Jeanette A.

FLUTE/PICCOLO (3)
Hamann, Richard
Norrito, Giacomo
Spindler, Julius

OBOE/ENGLISH HORN (2)
Lephilibert, P.
Schoof, Lambert A.

BASSOON (2)
Gill, George
Winkler, Otto

Eb CLARINET (1)
Kapralek, Frank J.

Bb CLARINET (14)
Buonocore, E.
Christman, C.
Davis, Isadore
Giordano, Frank R.
Hackert, Henry L.A.
Langan, William H.
Lawnham, James
Livingston, Clarence R.
Norrito, Joseph
Payer, Joe
Porpora, Steve
Robinson, William J.
Rumpff, Otto
Schaich, Samuel

ALTO CLARINET (1)
Magnant, Rene

BASS CLARINET (1)
Schroeder, Carl

SAXOPHONE (3)
Becker, Frederick E.R.
Knecht, Albert A.
Schensley, William F.

CORNET/TRUMPET (6)
Clarke, Edwin G.
Clarke, Herbert L.
Fletcher, John
Grosskurth, August
Higgins, Henry A.
LeBarbier, E.

HORN (4)
Albrecht, Gustav
Albrecht, W.
DeBleye, Joseph
White, Arthur

EUPHONIUM (2)
Kara, Joseph
Perfetto, John J.

TROMBONE (4)
Corey, Ralph H.
Lyon, Marcus C.
Williams, Edward A.
Zimmerman, Leopold A.

TUBA/SOUSAPHONE (3)
Del Negro, Luca A.
Helleberg, August, Sr.
Richardson, John W.

PERCUSSION (3)
Forster, Herman
Kenn, Daniel
Sietz, J. Fred

HARP (1)
Chase, William A.

OTHER
Stuart, William W. (duties unknown)

TOTAL MUSICIANS: 52

Source: Roster in *New York Dramatic Mirror*, Sept. 1, 1908.

1911 (1911 world tour)

VOCAL SOLOIST (1)
Root, E. Virginia

VIOLIN SOLOIST (1)
Zedeler, Nicoline

FLUTE/PICCOLO (3)
Ahlborn, George
Senno, Paul J.
Spindler, Julius

OBOE/ENGLISH HORN (2)
Guerard, Joseph
Lephilibert, P.

BASSOON (3)
Cunnington, G.H. *
Decker, William H.
Modess, Oskar

Eb CLARINET (1)
Kapralek, Frank J.

Bb CLARINET (15)
Baldwin, Harry
Berry, Arthur L. *
Collins, Walter D.
Culley, William H. *
Davis, Isadore
Eckstein, Sol
Gatley, Ernest C.
Kampe, George C.
Lawnham, James
Livingston, Clarence R.
Lomas, Joseph
Norrito, Joseph
Robinson, William J.
Shaeffer, Walter E.
Wall, Edmund A.

ALTO CLARINET (1)
Magnant, Rene

BASS CLARINET (1)
Schroeder, Carl

SAXOPHONE (3)
Knecht, Albert A.
Lawton, Stanley *
Vereecken, Benjamin

CORNET/TRUMPET (6)
Clarke, Herbert L.
Freeman, Harry
Gaugler, Guy G.
Millhouse, Ross
Russell, Clarence J.
Welte, Victor H.

HORN (4)
Hand, Hermann
Kunze, Arthur H.
Laendner, William
Smith, Clarence H.

EUPHONIUM (2)
Garing, Athol J.
Perfetto, John J.

TROMBONE (4)
Corey, Ralph H.
Lucas, George
Lyon, Marcus C.
Williams, Edward A.

TUBA/SOUSAPHONE (4)
Griswold, Arthur L. (sousaphone)
Helleberg, August (tuba)
Mix, Emil (tuba)
Storch, Arthur E. Jr. (tuba)

PERCUSSION (3)
Haynes, M. Francis
Lowe, (Dr.), William
Snow, Frank A.

HARP (1)
Marthage, Joseph, L.

TOTAL MUSICIANS: 55

*Left the band in California. It is not known who replaced them.

Notes: Manager, Edwin G. Clarke, substituted on cornet as needed. Jimmie Hewson, Sousa's valet, left band during tour of Britain.

Sources: Albert A. Knecht diary (Chapter 7); Sousa Band group photos and other photos; Edmund A. Wall world tour poem.

1914 (1914 tour) Dates in brackets indicate years the members listed as their first year in the band.

VOCAL SOLOIST (1)
Root, E. Virginia

VIOLIN SOLOIST (1)
Gluck, Margel

FLUTE/PICCOLO (3)
Ahlborn, George [1907]
Fritze, Louis P. [1913]
Heidelberg, Henry N. [1900]

OBOE/ENGLISH HORN (2)
Bertram, Adolph A. [1900]
Guerard, Joseph [1910]

BASSOON (2)
Reines, Abraham [1914]
+ 1 other

Eb CLARINET (1)
(unknown)

Bb CLARINET (12)
Becker, John U. [1914]
Eckstein, Sol [1909]
Engberg, Lorenzo A. [1900]
Harris, Samuel [1912]
Kampe, George C. [1907]
Lawnham, James [1905]
Matthes, Oscar [1913]
Morris, Louis [1908]
Norrito, Joseph [1892]
Schaich, Samuel [1892]
Smith, Fred M. [1914]
Urban, John W. [1912]

ALTO CLARINET (1)
Magnant, Rene [1904]

BASS CLARINET (1)
Schroeder, Carl [1898]

SAXOPHONE (3)
Becker, Frederick E.R. [1892]
Knecht, Albert A. [1905]
Schensley, William F. [1904]

CORNET/TRUMPET (7)
Clarke, Herbert L. (1st cor.) [1893]
Gaugler, Guy G. (cor.) [1910]
McCann, Richard (cor.) [1914]
Ripple, Walter E. (tpt.) [1912]
Russell, Clarence J. (cor.) [1910]
Simon, Frank (cor.) [1914]
Welte, Victor H. (tpt.) [1907]

HORN (4)
Dutschke, Herman, Sr. [1914]
Richart, Santiago [1914]
Van Praag, Maurice [1914]
Yenke, Otto B. [1909]

EUPHONIUM (2)
Garing, Athol J. [1909]

Perfetto, John J. [1904]

TROMBONE (4)
Corey, Ralph H. [1906]
Lyon, Marcus C. [1892]
Whitby, Richard E. [1914]
Williams, Edward A. [1892]

TUBA/SOUSAPHONE (3)
Cott, Oscar R. [1910]
Richardson, John W. [1903]
Storch, Arthur E. [1909]

PERCUSSION (3)
Harrington, James N. [1914]
Haynes, M. Francis [1909]
Snow, Frank A. [1909]

HARP (1)
Marthage, Joseph, L. [1910]

TOTAL MUSICIANS: 51

Source: Birthday card from musicians to Sousa, dated Nov. 6, 1914.

1915

VOCAL SOLOIST (1)
Brchany, Louise M. [partial]
Hoffman, Grace [partial]
Root, E. Virginia [partial]

VIOLIN SOLOIST (1)
Gluck, Margel [partial]
Tompkins, Susan [partial]

FLUTE/PICCOLO (4)
Ahlborn, George
Heidelberg, Henry N.
Row, Frank
Wagner, Ernest F. [partial]

OBOE/ENGLISH HORN (2)
Gerhardt, Paul O.
Guerard, Joseph

BASSOON (2)
Reines, Morris
Savolini, Ugo

Eb CLARINET (2)
Flaster, Max
Kapralek, Frank J.

Bb CLARINET (18)
Baldwin, Harry
Becker, John U.
Cheney, Joseph J.
Davis, Arthur C.
Engberg, Lorenzo A.
Harris, Samuel
Hickey, John
Hughes, Thomas A.
Kampe, George C.
Langan, William H.
Matthes, Oscar
Morris, Louis
Neumann, Arthur J.
Norrito, Joseph
Schaich, Samuel
Thomas, Bruce
Thomson, Walde E.
Urban, John W.

ALTO CLARINET (1)
Magnant, Rene

BASS CLARINET (1)
Schroeder, Carl

SAXOPHONE (5)
Becker, Frederick E.R. (bari.)

Howard, M. Bertrand (tenor)
Knecht, Albert A. (tenor)
Schensley, William F. (alto)
Vereecken, Benjamin (alto)

CORNET/TRUMPET (8)
Clarke, Herbert L. (cor.)
Gaugler, Guy G. (cor.)
McCann, Richard
Nutze, Frank T. (cor.)
Ripple, Walter E. (tpt.)
Russell, Clarence J. (cor.)
Simon, Frank (cor.)
Welte, Victor H. (tpt.)

HORN (4)
Richart, Santiago
Schulze, Robert H.
Van Praag, Maurice (solo)
Yenke, Otto B.

EUPHONIUM (2)
Garing, Athol J.
Perfetto, John J.

TROMBONE (5)
Cimera, James

Corey, Ralph H.
Lyon, Marcus C.
Whitby, Richard E.
Williams, Edward A.

TUBA/SOUSAPHONE (6)
Cott, Oscar R. (tuba)
Kuhn, John M. (sousaphone)
Peterson, Oscar S. (tuba)
Richardson, John W. (sousaphone)
Storch, Arthur E. (tuba)
Weber, Emil (tuba)

PERCUSSION (3)
Haynes, M. Francis (small drum)
Maurer, George H. (bass drum)
Snow, Frank A. (tympani)

HARP (1)
Marthage, Joseph, L.

OTHER
Kilson, Wilmer
(valet/asst. librarian)

TOTAL MUSICIANS: 66

Sources: Musicians' signatures on Tuxedo Tobacco advertisement, Saturday Evening Post, Oct. 23, 1915; roster in *Musical Courier*,
June 9, 1915; roster in *United Musician*, June 1915; Sousa Band group photos.

1916 (1916-17 *Hip! Hip! Hooray!* road tour)

VOCAL SOLOIST (1)
Leigh, Leslie

FLUTE/PICCOLO (4)
Ahlborn, George
Fritze, Louis P.
Mackey, Kelsey
Plantamura, Joseph

OBOE/ENGLISH HORN (2)
Bertram, Adolph A.
Guerard, Joseph

BASSOON (2)
Bettoney, F.
Reines, Abraham

Eb CLARINET (1)
Flaster, Max

Bb CLARINET (14)
Becker, John U.
Bortman, William T.

Cheney, Joseph J.
Engberg, Lorenzo A.
Harris, Samuel
Kampe, George C.
Lawnham, James
Matthes, Oscar
Morris, Louis
Neumann, Arthur J.
Norrito, Joseph
Schaich, Samuel
Thetford, Charles
Urban, John W.

ALTO CLARINET (1)
Magnant, Rene

BASS CLARINET (1)
Schroeder, Carl

SAXOPHONE (4)
Becker, Frederick E.R.
Howard, M. Bertrand

Schensley, William F.
Vereecken, Benjamin

CORNET/TRUMPET (6)
Clarke, Herbert L.
Gaugler, Guy G.
Ripple, Walter E.
Russell, Clarence J.
Simon, Frank
Sutherland, Francis W.

HORN (4)
Goedertier, G.
Neubauer, Herman
Paquay, Armand
Yenke, Otto B.

EUPHONIUM (2)
Garing, Athol J.
Perfetto, John J.

TROMBONE (5)
Corey, Ralph H.
Gentile, Ernest E.
Lyon, Marcus C.
Schmidt, Louis
Williams, Edward A.

TUBA/SOUSAPHONE (4)
Cott, Oscar R.
Richardson, John W.
Storch, Arthur E.
Sweetland, William W.

PERCUSSION (3)
Haynes, M. Francis
Helmecke, August, Jr.
Snow, Frank A.

HARP (1)
Marthage, Joseph, L.

TOTAL MUSICIANS: 55

Note: Cast members of the *Hip! Hip! Hooray!* show often performed with the band on non-show concerts.

Source: Roster in *New York Musician & Knocker,* Dec. 1916.

1919-20 (1919-20 tour)

VOCAL SOLOIST (1)
Baker, Mary

VIOLIN SOLOIST (1)
Hardeman, Florence

FLUTE/PICCOLO (3)
Fritze, Louis P. (1st)
Plantamura, Joseph [partial]
Pons, Albert A. (3rd)
Ricciardi, Edgard I. [partial]
Smith, G. Adolphe (2nd)

OBOE/ENGLISH HORN (2)
Buxley, Thomas [partial]
Del Negro, Anthony (1st) [partial]
Kirshner, Philip [partial]
McKay, R.C. [partial]

BASSOON (2)
Jankins, Frank N. (2nd)
Kirshner, Maurice (1st) [partial]
+ 1 other [partial]

Eb CLARINET (1)
Matthes, Oscar [partial]
+ 1 other [partial]

Bb CLARINET (16)
Andrews, _____ [partial]
Bassett, Don (2nd)
Bishof, George [partial]
Borrelli, James G. (2nd)
Brant, Fred G. (3rd)
Cheney, Joseph J. (1st) [partial]
Engberg, Lorenzo A. (1st)
Harris, Samuel (1st)
Hudson, Carl H. (2nd) [partial]
Kalmbach, Herbert A. [partial]
Kampe, George C. (1st)
Lomas, Joseph (1st)
McDonnell, H. [partial]
Morris, Louis (1st)
Norrito, Joseph (1st)
Piates, David (1st) [partial]
Saum, Joseph F. [partial]
Seyfried, Henry (2nd)
Shepard, James W. [partial]

ALTO CLARINET (1)
Davis, Arthur C. [partial]
+ 1 other [partial]

BASS CLARINET (1)
Gentile, Pirro [partial]
Zangari, Giovanni [partial]

SAXOPHONE (5)
Gurewitz, Jascha (1st alto) [partial]
Henton, H. Benne (1st alto)
Howard, M. Bertrand (1st tenor)
Jacobson, Andrew A. (2nd tenor) [partial]
Knecht, Albert A. (2nd alto)
Rosander, Arthur H., Sr. (bari.)
Weber, Charles A., Jr. [partial]

CORNET/TRUMPET (8)
Bishop, Eugene J. [partial]
Chick, Arnold L. (2nd tpt.) [partial]
Danner, Arthur [partial]
Gaugler, Guy G. (1st tpt.)
LaBarre, Eugene G. (1st cor.) [partial]
Nilssen, Karl [partial]
Russell, Clarence J. (2nd cor.)
Simon, Frank (1st cor.)
Staigers, Charles D. (1st cor.)
Wiley, H.E. (1st cor.) [partial]

HORN (4)
Desimone, Jerry G. (3rd)
Schumann, Carl (1st) [partial]
Speinson, Morris (4th)
Vitocolonna, Giacinto [partial]
Wilhelms, Hermut (2nd)

EUPHONIUM (2)
Harris, Aaron [partial]
Leavitt, Verne M. (2nd) [partial]
Liberati, Anthony (2nd) [partial]
Perfetto, John J. (1st)

TROMBONE (4)
Corey, Ralph H. (1st)
Harris, Charles W. [partial]
Palmer, Lester (3rd) [partial]
Rothwell, C. Irving (1st)
Sims, Jay G. (2nd)

TUBA/SOUSAPHONE (4)
Bianco, Emelio (tuba)
Kuhn, John M. (1st sousaphone)
Russ, Jess (tuba)
Stern, Henry P. (2nd sousaphone)
Webster, W.V. [partial]

PERCUSSION (3)
Green, Joseph (drums)
Helmecke, August, Jr. (bass drum)
Snow, Frank A. (tympani)

HARP (1)
Marthage, Joseph L.

TOTAL MUSICIANS: 59

Sources: Handwritten (possibly by band member) roster; 2 typed rosters with addresses (sources unknown); roster in *Ft. Williams (Ontario) Daily Times-Journal* , Aug. 15, 1919.

1921 (1921 tour*) Figures in brackets indicate weekly salaries in dollars.

VOCAL SOLOIST (1)
Baker, Mary

VIOLIN SOLOIST (1)
Hardeman, Florence

FLUTE/PICCOLO (4)
Ford, George F. (3rd) [60]
Kunkel, William M. (piccolo) [60]
Loveridge, Clarence A.
McDiarmid, Ellis (1st) [90] [partial]
Willson, R. Meredith [60] [partial]

OBOE/ENGLISH HORN (3)
Gerhardt, Paul O. (1st) [85]
Loveridge, Clarence A. (2nd) [60]
Maly, Anthony N. (asst. 1st) [60]
  [partial]

BASSOON (3)
Linde, John T. (2nd) [60]
Loehmann, Charles (asst. 1st) [75]
Reines, Abraham (1st) [100]

Bb CLARINET (18)
Barron, Henri J. (2nd) [60]
Borrelli, James G. (asst. solo) [65]
Brandenburg, William [partial]

Brant, Fred G. [partial]
Carroll, Stephen L. (1st) [60]
Caster, Leslie D.
Chaliff, Louis [partial]
Frigga, Einar (1st) [60]
Harper, J. Ernest (2nd) [60]
Jacob, Otto (3rd) [60]
Johnson, Edward D. (1st) [60]
Joste, Fred [partial]
Lorenz, R. R. (1st) [partial]
Lorenz, Robert J. (1st) [60]
Norrito, Joseph (solo) [85]
Ross, Robert A. (1st) [60]
Schueler, William P. (1st) [60]
Seyfried, Henry (2nd) [75]
Shepard, James W. (2nd) [60]
Vincinguerra, Michael (3rd) [60]
Weaver, Frederick M.
Wingate, W.F. (3rd) [60] [partial]
Zuber, Frank J. (3rd) [60]

ALTO CLARINET (1)
Prohaska, Fred B. [60]

BASS CLARINET (1)
Davis, Arthur C. [75] [partial]
Johnson, Herman R. [partial]

SAXOPHONE (6)
D'ortenzio, Anthony (alto) [75]
Gurewitz, Jascha (alto) [85]
Krocek, Hugo
Miller, Ralph J.
Schmidt, Herman F. (bass) [60]
Schwartz, Charles F.A. (bari.) [60]
Weber, Charles A., Jr. (tenor) [60]
Weir, Leon E. (tenor) [60]

CORNET/TRUMPET (8)
Brabrook, Arthur N. (cor.) [60]
Danner, Arthur (asst. solo cor.) [75]
Dolan, John (solo cor.) [175]
Koppitz, Charles O. (1st tpt.) [75]
Newcomb, Edwin E. (1st cor.) [60]
Rowell, Howard L. (2nd tpt.) [60]
Russell, Clarence J. (2nd cor.) [85]
Schueler, Henry A. (1st cor.) [60]

HORN (4)
Byrne, Gerald R. (2nd)
Christian, A.J. (3rd) [70]
Gindonato, P. (4th) [65]
Pierce, William N. (1st) [90]

EUPHONIUM (2)
De Luca, Joseph O. (1st) [95]
Preble, Carl J. (2nd) [60]

TROMBONE (4)
Brisbin, Claude D. (asst. solo)
Lammers, Hyrum (2nd) [60] [partial]
Nutter, Oscar L. (3rd) [60]
Schueler, John P. (solo) [75]
Sims, Jay G. (2nd) [75]

TUBA/SOUSAPHONE (4)
Bell, William J. (1st tuba) [75]
Burant, Edward (large sousaphone)[60]
Ferrara, Nicola
Markert, Daniel J.
  (small sousaphone) [60]
Pfaff, Fred E. (2nd tuba) [65]

PERCUSSION (3)
Carey, George J. [tymp./xylo.) [85]
Goulden, Howard N. (small drum) [65]
Helmecke, August, Jr. (bass dr.) [partial]
Mehling, Louis (bass drum) [70] [partial]

HARP (1)
Bambrick, Winifred [75]

OTHER
Snyder, Willard A. (valet) [30]

TOTAL MUSICIANS: 64

*Ended on Sept. 25 because of Sousa's riding injury.
Sources: Sousa Band roster with addresses and salaries; handwritten roster with addresses (source unknown); printed roster compiled by flutist George F. Ford.

1922 (1921-22 tour) Figures in brackets indicate weekly salaries in dollars.

VOCAL SOLOIST (1)
Baker, Mary

VIOLIN SOLOIST (1)
Hardeman, Florence [primary]
Powers, Jeanette A. [partial]

FLUTE/PICCOLO (4)
Barclay, Chester A.
Ford, George F.
Kunkel, William M.
Mann, Charles (2nd) [partial]
Willson, R. Meredith

OBOE/ENGLISH HORN (3)
Abeel, George A.
Gerhardt, Paul O.
Maly, Anthony N.

BASSOON (3)
Linde, John T.
Loehmann, Charles
Thompson, Sherley C.

Bb CLARINET (21)
Albrecht, John H.
Barron, Henri J.
Borrelli, James G.

Brandenburg, William
Engberg, Lorenzo A.
Foote, Earl van W.
Frigga, Einar
Jacob, Otto
Johnson, Edward D.
Leigl, John H.
Lorenz, Robert J.
Lubis, Theodore
Norrito, Joseph
Ross, Robert A.
Schueler, William P.
Schwartz, Charles F.A.
Seyfried, Henry
Shepard, James W.
Vincinguerra, Michael
Weaver, Frederick M.
Zuber, Frank J.

ALTO CLARINET (1)
Prohaska, Fred B.

BASS CLARINET (2)
Davis, Arthur C.
Johnson, Herman R.

SAXOPHONE (8)
D'ortenzio, Anthony (alto)

Grantham, J. Howard (bari.)
Kent, Richard E. (alto)
Lobber, Charles (tenor) [partial]
Schmidt, Herman F. (bass)
Silbach, John (tenor)
Sodohl, Ehrling A. (alto)
Weber, Charles A., Jr.(tenor) [partial]
Weir, Leon E. (tenor)

CORNET/TRUMPET (8)
Brabrook, Arthur N. (cor.)
Danner, Arthur (cor.)
Dolan, John (solo cor.)
Koppitz, Charles O. (tpt.)
Newcomb, Edwin E. (cor.)
Rowell, Howard L. (tpt.)
Russell, Clarence J. (cor.)
Schueler, Henry A. (cor.)

HORN (4)
Byrne, Gerald R.
Kuhn, Mathias J.
Pierce, William N.
Wolf, Arthur D.

EUPHONIUM (3)
De Luca, Joseph O.
Haas, Howard [partial]
Preble, Carl J.

TROMBONE (5)
Gibbs, Arthur E.
Nutter, Oscar L.
Parker, William E.
Schueler, John P.
Sims, Jay G.

TUBA/SOUSAPHONE (5)
Bell, William J.
Ferrara, Nicola
Field, Earl W.
Gardner, Donald C.
Markert, Daniel J.

PERCUSSION (3)
Carey, George J. [tymp./drums]
Goulden, Howard N. (drums)
Helmecke, August, Jr. (drums)

HARP (1)
Bambrick, Winifred [75]

OTHER
Brennan, Dr. John Paul
  (Sousa's personal physician)
Snyder, Willard, A.
  (Sousa valet and road secretary)

TOTAL MUSICIANS: 73

Sources: Sousa Band photo, Dec. 1921; Jay Sims's typed roster.

1923 (1923-24 tour) Figures in brackets indicate weekly salaries in dollars.

VOCAL SOLOIST (1)
Fauchald, Nora [100] [partial]
Moody, Marjorie [100] [partial]

VIOLIN SOLOIST (1)
Senior, Rachel [100] [partial]

FLUTE/PICCOLO (6)
Bell, John W. [60]
Hutchings, Carl B. [60]
Kunkel, William M. [70] [partial]
Perry, Chester A. [60] [partial]
Sackett, Maurice [60]
Schwanner, Arthur C. [60]
Willson, R. Meredith [90, 125]

OBOE/ENGLISH HORN (3)
Abeel, George A. [65] [partial]
Gerhardt, Paul O. [105]
Maly, Anthony N. [65]

BASSOON (2)
Linde, John T. [60]
Thompson, Sherley C. [90]

Bb CLARINET (24)
Brandenburg, William [60]
Bronson, Howard C. [60] [partial]
Byra, Stanley [60]
Carr, John C. [80]
Crawford, Francis M. [60]

Engberg, Lorenzo A. [65]
Foote, Earl van W. [60]
Frigga, Einar [60]
Jenkins, George M. [60] [partial]
Kampe, George C. [60]
Keinke, Walter [60]
Kilgour, Earl D. (2nd) [60]
Leigl, John H. [60]
Livingston, Clarence R. [60]
Lubis, Theodore [60]
Lundgren, Joram [60] [partial]
Novak, Louis [60]
Ross, Robert A. [60]
Schueler, William P. [60]
Seyfried, Henry [60]
Thompson, Ernest L. [60]
Vincinguerra, Michael [60]
Weaver, Frederick M. [60]
Willaman, Robert G. [60]
Zuber, Frank J. [60]

ALTO CLARINET (1)
Prohaska, Fred B. [60]

BASS CLARINET (1)
Johnson, Herman R. [70]

SAXOPHONE (8)
Bayers, Frederick W. [75, 86]
Copeland, Edward V. [60] [partial]
Page, Clarence W. [60]

Rosander, Arthur H., Jr. [60] [partial]
Schmidt, Herman F. [65]
Silbach, John [60]
Son, James E. [60]
Weir, Leon E. [65]

CORNET/TRUMPET (8)
Danner, Arthur [75]
Dolan, John [200]
Garrett, Dana M. [60]
Gaugler, Guy G. [75]
Hiltensmith, Albert J. [60]
Merrill, Lynn T. [60]
Phoenix, William H. [60]
Russell, Clarence J. [95]

HORN (4)
Biroschak, Peter J. [100]
Brown, Ralph W. [65] [partial]
Byrne, Gerald R. [65]
Mountz, John J. [65] [partial]
Wolf, Arthur D. [60]

EUPHONIUM (2)
De Luca, Joseph O. [110]
Preble, Carl J. [60]

TROMBONE (4)
Ford, Henry C. [60] [partial]
Gray, Lester M. [60]
Schueler, John P. [75]
Sims, Jay G. [90]

TUBA/SOUSAPHONE (5)
Bell, William J. [85]
Field, Earl W. [70]
Gardner, Donald C. [60]
Grabner, Fred D. [partial; died on road
    July 25, 1923]
Raymond, Arthur [60]
Richardson, John W. [70]
Romeril, James G. [60] [from Aug. 26]

PERCUSSION (3)
Carey, George J. [100]
Goulden, Howard N. [75]
Helmecke, August, Jr. [90]

HARP (1)
Bambrick, Winifred [100]

OTHER
Schneider, William
    (road manager) [100]
Snyder, Donald
    (valet & secretary) [35]
McCrary, Dawson
    (stage mgr.) [67.50] [partial]
O'Brien, James
    (stage mgr.) [75] [partial]
McGrath, John (advance man) [75]

TOTAL MUSICIANS: 74

Sources: Twenty-four Sousa Band payrolls, Jul. 21-Dec. 29, 1923.

1924 (1924 tour)

VOCAL SOLOIST (1)
Fauchald, Nora [partial]
Moody, Marjorie [partial]

FLUTE/PICCOLO (6)
Bell, John W.
Campbell, W. Fred
Franklin, Edwin
Perry, Chester A.
Schwanner, Arthur C.
Thorne, Harry F.

OBOE/ENGLISH HORN (3)
Gerhardt, Paul O.
Maly, Anthony N.
Myseh, John G.

BASSOON (2)
Linde, John T.
Thompson, Sherley C.

Bb CLARINET (22)
Bronson, Howard C.
Byra, Stanley
Carr, John C.
Elliot, Edward E.

Engberg, Lorenzo A.
Foote, Earl van W.
Frigga, Einar
Holl, William B.
Kampe, George C.
Kilgour, Earl D.
Lubis, Theodore
Lundgren, Joram
Miller, Roy M.
Ross, Robert A.
Schueler, William P.
Seyfried, Henry
Thompson, Ernest L.
Vincinguerra, Michael
Weaver, Frederick M.
Webber, Randall B.
Woolridge, Harold I.
Zuber, Frank J.

ALTO CLARINET (1)
Silbach, John

BASS CLARINET (2)
Johnson, Herman R.
Page, Clarence W.

SAXOPHONE (7)
Gooding, G. Robert
Goodrich, Gerald E.
Heney, Edward J.
Monroe, Fred K.
Rosander, Arthur H., Jr.
Son, James E.
Weir, Leon E.

CORNET/TRUMPET (8)
Dolan, John
Garrett, Dana M.
Gaugler, Guy G.
Hennegar, Russell D.
Russell, Clarence J.
Stambaugh, Harold Q.
Thorne, Joseph T.
Tong, William

HORN (4)
Biroschak, Peter J.
Burnham, William R.
Hubley, Claude F.
Wolf, Arthur D.

EUPHONIUM (2)
De Luca, Joseph O.
Preble, Carl J.

TROMBONE (4)
Ford, Henry C.
Gray, Lester M.
Schueler, John P.
Sims, Jay G.

TUBA/SOUSAPHONE (5)
Herb, William
O'Connor, Martin J.
Richardson, John W.
Russ, Gabe
Weber, Herbert E.C.

PERCUSSION (3)
Carey, George J.
Goulden, Howard N.
Helmecke, August, Jr.

HARP (1)
Bambrick, Winifred

OTHER
Schneider, William (road mgr.)
O'Brien, James (stage mgr.)
Jeffrey, John B. (valet)

TOTAL MUSICIANS: 71

Source: Signature sheet for receipt of salaries dated Nov. 17, 1924.

1925 (first part of 1925-26 tour) Figures in brackets indicate weekly salaries in dollars.

VOCAL SOLOIST (1)
Moody, Marjorie

FLUTE/PICCOLO (6)
Hall, Edward C. (piccolo) [60]
Perry, Chester A. [60]
Petrie, John C. [60]
Schwanner, Arthur C. [60]
Williams, Raymond E. (solo) [125]
Wriggins, Arthur M. [60]

OBOE/ENGLISH HORN (3)
Gerhardt, Paul O. (1st) [125]
Maly, Anthony N. (2nd) [70]
Walt, Russell (3rd) [60]

BASSOON (2)
Coleman, Herbert L. (2nd) [60]
Ruckle, Clifford F. (1st) [85]

Bb CLARINET (26)
Babcock, Harold J. (2nd) [60]
Bronson, Howard C. (1st) [60]
Byra, Stanley (3rd) [60]
Carr, John C. (1st) [90]
Cheney, Joseph J. (1st) [60]

Elliot, Edward E. (1st) [60]
Engberg, Lorenzo A. (1st) [65]
Foote, Earl van W. (1st) [60]
Frigga, Einar (1st) [65]
Gavin, Evert A. (1st) [60]
Howland, Paul E. (3rd) [60]
Jacob, Otto (2nd) [60]
Kampe, George C. (1st) [65]
Kardasen, Charles M. (3rd) [60]
Kensinger, Vane H. (3rd) [60]
Kilgour, Earl D. (2nd) [60]
Lundgren, Joram (1st) [60]
Park, Robert A. (2nd) [60]
Rundquist, Carl T. (2nd) [60]
Schueler, William P. (1st) [65]
Scott, Raymond F. (1st) [60]
Van Fossen, John F. (3rd) [60]
Vincinguerra, Michael (3rd) [60]
Weaver, Frederick M. (1st) [65]
Woolridge, Harold I. (2nd) [60]
Zuber, Frank J. (2nd) [60]

ALTO CLARINET (1)
Silbach, John [65]

BASS CLARINET (1)
Jenkins, George M. [70]

SAXOPHONE (8)
Conklin, Benjamin (bari.) [60]
Heney, Edward J. (alto) [60]
Johnson, Clarence M.(alto) [60]
Machner, August (2nd tenor) [60]
Monroe, Fred K. (bass) [60]
Page, Clarence W. (2nd alto) [65]
Stephens, Harold B. (1st alto) [85]
Weir, Leon E. (1st tenor) [65]

CORNET/TRUMPET (8)
Cameron, Walter H. (2nd tpt.) [60]
Dolan, John (solo cor.) [200]
Garrett, Dana M. (solo cor.) [70]
Gaugler, Guy G. (2nd tpt.) [60]
Meyers, Albertus L. (2nd cor.) [60]
Russell, Clarence J. (2nd cor.) [100]
Stambaugh, Harold Q. (1st cor.) [60]
Tong, William (1st cor.) [60]

HORN (4)
Biroschak, Peter J. (1st) [125]
Burnham, William R. [65]
Hubley, Claude F. [60]
Wolf, Arthur D. [60]

EUPHONIUM (2)
De Luca, Joseph O. (1st) [125]
Preble, Carl J. (2nd) [65]

TROMBONE (4)
Ford, Henry C. (1st) [60]
Gleason, Ambrose N. (2nd) [60]
Schueler, John P. (1st) [60]
Sims, Jay G. (bass)

TUBA/SOUSAPHONE (6)
Gardner, Donald C. (3rd desk) [60]
Herb, William (2nd desk) [60]
Keller, Earl (2nd desk) [60]
Lower, Nathan C. (3rd desk) [60]
Richardson, John W. (1st desk) [85]
Russ, Gabe (1st desk) [60]

PERCUSSION (3)
Carey, George J. [100]
Goulden, Howard N. [75]
Helmecke, August, Jr. [90]

HARP (1)
Bambrick, Winifred [100]

OTHER
Jeffery, John B. (valet) [35]

TOTAL MUSICIANS: 76

Source: Handwritten Sousa Band payroll for week ending Jul. 11, 1925.

1925-26 (Willow Grove segment of 1925-26 tour, Aug. 9 – Sept. 13, 1925)

VOCAL SOLOIST (1)
Fauchald, Nora [partial]
Goulden, Florence [partial]
Moody, Marjorie [partial]

FLUTE/PICCOLO (6)
Hall, Edward C. (piccolo soloist)
Perry, Chester A.
Petrie, John C.
Schwanner, Arthur C.
Williams, Raymond E. (flute soloist)
Wriggins, Arthur M.

OBOE/ENGLISH HORN (3)
Gerhardt, Paul O. (1st)
Maly, Anthony N.
Walt, Russell

BASSOON (2)
Coleman, Herbert L.
Ruckle, Clifford F.

Bb CLARINET (25)
Babcock, Harold J.
Bronson, Howard C.
Byra, Stanley
Carr, John C. (solo)
Cheney, Joseph J.
Elliot, Edward E.

Engberg, Lorenzo A.
Foote, Earl van W.
Frigga, Einar
Gavin, Evert A.
Jacob, Otto
Kampe, George C.
Kardasen, Charles M.
Kensinger, Vane H.
Kilgour, Earl D.
Lundgren, Joram
Park, Robert A.
Rundquist, Carl T.
Scott, Raymond F.
Schueler, William P.
Van Fossen, John F.
Vincinguerra, Michael
Weaver, Frederick M.
Woolridge, Harold I.
Zuber, Frank J.

ALTO CLARINET (1)
Silbach, John

BASS CLARINET (1)
Jenkins, George M.

SAXOPHONE (8)
Conklin, Benjamin (bari.)
Heney, Edward J. (alto)

Johnson, Clarence M. (alto)
Machner, August (tenor)
Monroe, Fred K. (bass)
Page, Clarence W. (alto)
Stephens, Harold B. (solo alto)
Weir, Leon E. (tenor)

CORNET/TRUMPET (8)
Cameron, Walter H. (tpt.)
Dolan, John (solo cor.)
Garrett, Dana M. (asst. solo cor.)
Gaugler, Guy G. (tpt.)
Meyers, Albertus L. (2nd cor.)
Russell, Clarence J. (2nd cor.)
Stambaugh, Harold Q. (1st cor.)
Tong, William (1st cor.)

HORN (4)
Biroschak, Peter J.
Burnham, William R.
Hubley, Claude F.
Wolf, Arthur D.

EUPHONIUM (2)
De Luca, Joseph O. (solo)
Preble, Carl J.

TROMBONE (4)
Ford, Henry C. (asst. solo)
Gleason, Ambrose. (2nd)
Schueler, John P. (solo)
Sims, Jay G. (3rd)

TUBA/SOUSAPHONE (6)
Gardner, Donald C. (3rd)
Herb, William (2nd)
Keller, Earl (2nd)
Lower, Nathan C. (3rd)
Richardson, John W. (1st)
Russ, Gabe (1st)

PERCUSSION (3)
Carey, George J.
  (tympani & xylophone soloist)
Goulden, Howard N. (small drums)
Helmecke, August, Jr. (bass drum)

HARP (1)
Bambrick, Winifred

OTHER
Jeffrey, John B. (valet)
O'Brien, James (stage mgr.)

TOTAL MUSICIANS: 75

Souces: Roster in *Jacobs' Band Monthly*, Aug. 1925; Willow Grove concert programs.

1925-26 (1925-26 tour after Willow Grove engagement)

VOCAL SOLOIST (1)
Moody, Marjorie

FLUTE/PICCOLO (6)
Hall, Edward C.
Perry, Chester A.
Petrie, John C.
Schwanner, Arthur C.
Williams, Raymond E.
Wriggins, Arthur M.

OBOE/ENGLISH HORN (2)
Gerhardt, Paul O.
Maly, Anthony N. [partial]
Walt, Russell [partial]

BASSOON (2)
Coleman, Herbert L.
Ruckle, Clifford F.

Bb CLARINET (27)
Babcock, Harold J.
Band, Julius
Boscheck, Charles
Bronson, Howard C.
Carr, John C.
Colby, Louis
Elliot, Edward E.
Engberg, Lorenzo A.

Frigga, Einar
Howland, Paul E.
Jacob, Otto
Jacques, C. C.
Kampe, George C.
Kardasen, Charles M.
Kilgour, Earl D.
Leiby, Charles A.
Park, Robert A.
Pfaff, George
Ross, Robert A.
Rundquist, Carl T.
Schueler, William P.
Scott, Raymond F.
Van Fossen, John F.
Vincinguerra, Michael
Weaver, Frederick M.
Williams, Warren
Zuber, Frank J.

ALTO CLARINET (1)
Silbach, John

BASS CLARINET (1)
Jenkins, George M.

SAXOPHONE (8)
Conklin, Benjamin (bari.)
Goodrich, Gerald E. (alto)

Heney, Edward J. (alto)
Johnson, Clarence M. (alto)
Monroe, Fred K. (bass)
Stephens, Harold B. (alto)
Weigel, F.D.
Weir, Leon E. (tenor)

CORNET/TRUMPET (8)
Cameron, Walter H. (tpt.)
Chick, Arnold, L. (tpt.)
Dolan, John (cor.)
Garrett, Dana M. (cor.)
Gaugler, Guy G. (tpt.)
Russell, Clarence J. (cor.)
Short, Oscar [partial]
Stambaugh, Harold Q. (cor.)
Tong, William (cor.)

HORN (4)
Biroschak, Peter J.
Burnham, William R.
Hubley, Claude F.
Wolf, Arthur D.

EUPHONIUM (2)
De Luca, Joseph O.
Preble, Carl J.

TROMBONE (4)
Braun, Clifford [partial]
Ford, Henry C.
Schueler, John P.
Sims, Jay G.
Wilkins, William [partial]

TUBA/SOUSAPHONE (6)
Davenport, Arthur D.
Herb, William
Kniss, Paul
Lower, Nathan C.
Richardson, John W.
Russ, Gabe

PERCUSSION (3)
Carey, George J.
Goulden, Howard N.
Helmecke, August, Jr.

HARP (1)
Bambrick, Winifred

OTHER
Jeffrey, John B. (valet)
O'Brien, James (stage mgr.) [partial]
Wilat, L.R. (duties unknown)

TOTAL MUSICIANS: 76

Sources: Sousa Band end-of-tour salary sign-off sheet dated March 6, 1926; 1925-26 hotel assignment list; Sousa Band payroll summary for Jul. 4-Dec. 26, 1925; Sousa Band handwritten "breakfast payroll" dated ca. Oct., 1925.

1926 (1926 tour)

VOCAL SOLOIST (1)
Moody, Marjorie

FLUTE/PICCOLO (6 or 7)*
Bell, John W.
Collins, John [partial]
Fair, Rex A. [partial]
Ford, George F. (3rd) [partial]
Petrie, John C. (6th)
Sackett, Maurice (4th)
Siebeneichen, Paul (5th) [partial]
Williams, Raymond E. (solo)[partial]
Wriggins, Arthur M. (2nd)

OBOE/ENGLISH HORN (2)
Gerhardt, Paul O. (1st)
Walt, Russell (2nd)

BASSOON (2)
Kraushaar, Otto J. (2nd)
Kruse, William (1st)

Bb CLARINET (20)
Byra, Stanley (3rd) [partial]
Elliot, Edward E. (1st)
Engberg, Lorenzo A. (solo)
Frigga, Einar (solo)
Hall, Clyde L. (4th)
Jacob, Otto (2nd)

Kampe, George C. (1st)
Kardasen, Charles M. (3rd)
Kilgour, Earl D. (2nd)
Leiby, Charles A. (2nd)
Miller, Roy M. (2nd) [partial]
Moore, Fred C. [partial]
Porlatto, Cal (2nd) [partial]
Schwartz, Schofield [partial]
Schueler, William P. (solo)
Schmidt, Roy (solo) [partial]
Spencer, John H. [partial]
Strothkamp, Charles C., Jr. (4th)
Thompson, O.J. (2nd) [partial]
Van Fossen, John F. (1st)
Wall, Edmund C. [partial]
Weaver, Frederick M. (1st)
Williams, Edward (1st) [partial]
Williams, Warren [partial]
Zuber, Frank J. (1st)

ALTO CLARINET (1)
Silbach, John

BASS CLARINET (1)
Cheney, Joseph J.

SAXOPHONE (8)
Conklin, Benjamin (3rd alto)
Heney, Edward J. (solo alto)

Kincaid, Owen D. (2nd alto)
Madden, Albert O. (2nd tenor)
Monroe, Fred K. (bass)
Schlanz, James (bari.)
Spalti, Leo (4th alto)
Sullivan, Frank W. [partial]
Weir, Leon E. (1st tenor) [partial]

CORNET/TRUMPET (8)
Arnold, Maxwell F. (2nd cor.)
Cameron, Walter H. (2nd tpt.)
Dolan, John (solo cor.)
Gaugler, Guy G. (1st tpt.)
Knuttunen, Jacob O. (1st cor.)
Russell, Clarence J. (2nd cor.)
Stambaugh, Harold Q. (1st cor.)
Tong, William (solo cor.)

HORN (4)
Biroschak, Peter J. (1st)
Hubley, Claude F. (3rd) [partial]
Kuhn, Mathias J. [partial]
Metzger, Edgar
Volpni, William B. (2nd)
Wolf, Arthur D. (4th) [partial]

EUPHONIUM (2)
De Luca, Joseph O. (1st)
Lewis, Wayne (2nd)

TROMBONE (4 or 3)*
Braun, Clifford B. (2nd)
Gray, Lester M. (3rd) [partial]
Schueler, John P. (solo)
Sims, Jay G. (bass)

TUBA/SOUSAPHONE (3 or 5)*
Herb, William (3rd) [partial]
Kent, Loren E. [partial]
Richardson, John W. (1st)
Russ, Gabe (2nd)
Weber, Albert L. [partial]
Weber, Herbert E.C. [partial]

PERCUSSION (3)
Goulden, Howard N.
(tympani/xylophone soloist)
Heney, John J. (small drums)
Helmecke, August, Jr. (bass drum)

HARP (1)
Bambrick, Winifred

OTHER
Smith, Carl (valet)
Lawbor, Richard (stage mgr.)

TOTAL MUSICIANS: 66

* For a short period at the Steel Pier (Atlantic City) seven flutes were used instead of six. Also at Steel Pier, four trombones were used, but only three were used for the remainder of the tour. Also at Steel Pier, three tubas were used but five were used for the remainder of the tour.

Sources: Sousa Band group photo at Atlantic City, July 1926; Sousa Band end-of-tour salary sign-off sheet dated Nov. 20, 1926; handwritten roster with addresses.

1927 (2nd 1927 tour) Figures in brackets indicate weekly salaries in dollars.

VOCAL SOLOIST (1)
Fauchald, Nora (soprano) [partial]
Gray, Betty (contralto) [partial]
Moody, Marjorie (primary) [200]

FLUTE/PICCOLO (6)
Bell, John W. [60]
Collins, John
Held, Earl D. [60]
Klump, Rolland [60]
Orosky, John J. [60]
Wavrek, Berthold K. [60]
Wummer, John [125] [partial]

OBOE/ENGLISH HORN (2)
Nuttick, Charles S. [partial]
Renzi, Paolo [125] [partial]
Walt, Russell [60]

BASSOON (3)
Booth, Clarence [partial]
Kraushaar, Otto J. [60]
Kruse, William [100] [partial]

Bb CLARINET (23)
Bender, Walter H.
Engberg, Lorenzo A. [65]
Germond, George H. [60]
Harris, Walter B., Jr. [60]
Jacob, Otto [60]
Kardasen, Charles M.
Kilgour, Earl D. [60]
Moore, Fred C. [60]
Rasp, Walter F.
Ross, Robert A.
Rundquist, Carl T. [60] [partial]
Schueler, William P. [partial]
Schwartz, Schofield [partial]
Strothkamp, Charles C., Jr. [60]
Tompkins, George B.
Tozier, Cecil E. [60]
Van Fossen, John F. [60]
Wall, Charles A. [60]
Wall, Edmund C. [100]
Weaver, Frederick M. [65]
Williams, Warren [60]
Woolridge, Harold I.
Zuber, Frank J. [60]

ALTO CLARINET (1)
Silbach, John [65]

BASS CLARINET (1)
Reissner, Andrew 80]

SAXOPHONE (8)
Desmond, Paul A. (alto)
Eau Claire, Felix (tenor) [60]
Heney, Edward J. (alto) 85]
Kincaid, Owen D. (alto) [60]
Madden, Albert O. (tenor) [60]
Monroe, Fred K. (bass) [70]
Schlanz, James (bari.) [60]
Sullivan, Frank W. (alto) [partial]

CORNET/TRUMPET (8)
Burnell, Frank (tpt.) [partial]
Dolan, John (cor.) [200]
Fee, George (cor.) [60]
Heater, Earl (cor.)
Huffman, C. Gerald (cor.) [60]
Knuttunen, Jacob O. (tpt.) [60]
Ostrom, Ralph K. (cor.) [partial]
Russell, Clarence J. (cor.) [100]
Stambaugh, Harold Q. (tpt.) [75]
Tong, William (cor.) [125]

HORN (4)
Biroschak, Peter J. [125]
Frantz, Arthur L. [60]
Gillespie, Earl H. [60]
Schaerges, Charles [60]

EUPHONIUM (2)
De Luca, Joseph O. [125]
Lewis, Wayne [60]

TROMBONE (4)
Braun, Clifford B. [60]
Burnell, Frank [partial]
Schueler, John P. [80]
Sims, Jay G. [100]

TUBA/SOUSAPHONE (5)
Freeman, Elvin L. [60]
Kent, Loren E. [60]
Richardson, John W. [100]
Russ, Gabe [60]
Tritton, Frank [partial]

PERCUSSION (3)
Goulden, Howard N. [100]
Helmecke, August, Jr. [100]
Holt, Frank [60]

HARP (1)
Bambrick, Winifred [100]

OTHER
Schneider, William (road mgr.) [150]
Smith, Carl
  (valet, road secretary) [40]
[Name ?] carpenter [110]

TOTAL MUSICIANS: 72

Sources: Jay Sims's handwritten roster, with salaries, dated July 16, 1927; Harold Stambaugh's printed hotel checklist with handwritten amendations in Loren Kent's hand; same checklist printed in *Sousa Band Fraternal Society News* of July 1981, with Eugene Slick's typed amendations.

1928 (1928 tour) Figures in brackets indicate weekly salaries in dollars.

VOCAL SOLOIST (1)
Moody, Marjorie (soprano) [250]

FLUTE/PICCOLO (6)
Evans, Eric J. [99]
Hall, Edward C. [84]
Petrie, John C. [74]
Phares, Hale W. [74]
Smith, Harold J. [74]
Zlotnik, H. Henry [74]

OBOE/ENGLISH HORN (2)
Mullenix, Carlos W. [79]
Nuttick, Charles S. [99]

BASSOON (2)
Booth, Clarence [104]
Kraushaar, Otto J. [74]

Bb CLARINET (23)
Austin, James C. [74]
Bender, Walter H. [74]
Bronson, Howard C. [74]
Cromer, R.S. [74]
Davis, Robin W. [74]
Frigga, Einar [79]
Germond, George H. [74]
Greyback, Joseph P. [74]
Harris, Walter B., Jr. [74]
Holt, Walfred T. [74]
Klemola, William M. [74]
Knuttunen, George J. [74]
Major, U.H. [74]
Schueler, William P. [79]
Spencer, John H. [74]
Strothkamp, Charles C., Jr. [74]
Thompson, Harry A. [74]
Thompson, O.J. [74]
Tozier, Cecil E. [74]
Tucker, Courtney S. [74]
Wall, Edmund C. [114]
Weaver, Frederick M. [84]
Zuber, Frank J. [79]

ALTO CLARINET (1)
Silbach, John [79]

BASS CLARINET (1)
Reissner, Andrew [94]

SAXOPHONE (8)
Desmond, Paul A. [74]
Heney, Edward J. [99]
Kincaid, Owen D. [74]
Monroe, Fred K. [84]
Schlanz, James [74]
Slick, Eugene [74]
Sullivan, Frank W. [74]
Thompson, Harry A.

CORNET/TRUMPET (10)
Bolle, Jules (tpt.) [74]
Dolan, John (cor.) [partial]
Duncan, William E.
Fee, George (cor.) [74]
Gardner, Birley (cor.) [74]
Huffman, C. Gerald (cor.) [74]
Knuttunen, Jacob O. (tpt.) [89]
Ostrom, Ralph K. (cor.) [89]
Russell, Clarence J. (cor.) [114]
Tong, William (cor.) [114]

HORN (4)
Biroschak, Peter J. [125]
Davis, Paul S. [74]
Frantz, Arthur L. [74]
Holmes, W. Burr [74]

EUPHONIUM (2)
Howard, Noble P. [114]
Wige, Ralph N. [74]

TROMBONE (4)
Braun, Clifford B. [74]
Folts, Lloyd H. [74]
Schueler, John P. [94]
Sims, Jay G. [114]

TUBA/SOUSAPHONE (6)
Bearman, Edwin R. [74]
Evans, Reuben C. [74]
Freeman, Elvin L. [74]
Fuller, Arbor L. [74]
Lower, Nathan C. [74]
Richardson, John W. [114]

PERCUSSION (3)
Goulden, Howard N. [114]
Helmecke, August, Jr. [114]
Holt, Frank [74]

HARP (1)
Bambrick, Winifred [124]

OTHER
Fulghum, Ralph
  (valet & encore card boy) [35]
Hungerford, Charles G.
  (stagehand & property mgr.) [95]
Schneider, William
  (road mgr) [160]

TOTAL MUSICIANS: 74

Sources: Eight Sousa Band payrolls, Sept. 28-Nov. 27; Eugene Slick's autograph book for 1928 tour; typed Sousa Band roster with addresses; Jay Sims's handwritten roster with addresses.

1929 (Spring and fall radio broadcasts) Figures in parentheses indicate number of broadcasts played, where known. Figures in brackets indicate salaries per broadcast in dollars, where known

FLUTE/PICCOLO (4)
Collins, John (5) [18,25]
Fabrizio, John (1) [19.50]
Hankins, Ross (5) [19.50, 21]
Lufsky, Marshall P. (4) [19.50]
McDiarmid, Ellis
Possell, George (8) [25, 28]
Wagner, Ernest F. (5) [18, 21]
Willson, R. Meredith
Zlotnik, H. Henry (8) [18, 21]

OBOE/ENGLISH HORN (2)
Gerhardt, Paul O. (5) [23,28]
Kirshner, Philip (4) [26.50]
Marsh, Albert A. (2) [19.50]
Mullenix, Carlos W. (5) [19.50, 28]
Whitcomb, Lawrence (2) [23]

BASSOON (2)
Modess, Oskar (9) [26.50, 28]
Swann, David (4) [12.50, 23]
Trute, William (5) [20, 23]

Bb CLARINET (14)
Bortman, William T. (6) [20, 23]
Brissette, Fred J. (4) [19.50]
Carr, John C. (5) [20, 23]
Cheney, Joseph J. (5) [18, 21]

Christman, Henry (1) [21]
Davis, Isadore
Fontanella, Ferd (2) [19.50]
Frigga, Einar (7) [18, 21.50]
Harris, Walter B., Jr. (3) [19.50]
Hudson, Carl H. (9) [18, 21]
Hughes, Thomas A. (4) [19.50]
Kampe, George C. (9) [18, 21]
Kivlan, Edwin G. (8) [18, 21]
Langan, William H. (5) [18, 21]
Lundgren, Joram (1) [19.50]
McGibney, C.G. (5) [18, 21]
Preiss, Emil G.
Roeschel, William E. (7) [19.50, 21]
Strothkamp, Charles C., Jr.
  (9) [18, 21]
Thetford, Charles (3) [21.50]
Van Ambergh, Fred (8) [18, 21]
Wall, Edmund C. (9) [50, 61.50]
Willaman, Robert G. (9) [20, 23]
Williams, Alexander (2) [19.50]
Williams, Jan A. (5) [18, 21]

ALTO CLARINET (1)
Silbach, John (9) [30, 33]

BASS CLARINET (1)
Reissner, Andrew (9) [19.50, 23]

SAXOPHONE (6)
Conklin, Benjamin (4) [21.50, 24.50]
Dammeyer, Charles (1) [23]
Evans, Alfred (9) [20, 24.50]
Goodman, Wilbur (9) [20, 23]
Heney, Edward J. (8) [50, 61.50]
Monroe, Fred K. (9) [35, 38]
O'Gorman, William (5) [20, 25]
Schlanz, James (9) [35, 38]

CORNET/TRUMPET (7)
Bolle, Jules (8) [19.50, 21]
Borst, Robert (1) [19.50]
Danner, Arthur (9) [19.50, 23]
Hiltensmith, Albert J. (7) [20, 23]
McCann, Richard (9) [20, 23]
Roeder, Louis (2) [19.50]
Russell, Clarence J. (9) [40, 53]
Short, Oscar B.
Tong, William (9) [75, 78]
Welte, Victor H. (9) [20, 26.50]

HORN (4)
Brown, Ralph W. (9) [20, 23]
Franzl, Joseph (4) [26.50]
Fricke, Walter (1) [21]
Hauser, Eric (8) [20, 23]
Nava, Lucino (1) [28]
Richart, Santiago (4) [25, 28]

Schulze, Adolf (5) [21.50, 23]
Schulze, Robert H. (5) [20, 23]

EUPHONIUM (1)
Mantia, Simone (5) [25, 31.50]
Paone, Biagio (4) [15, 28]

TROMBONE (3)
Schueler, John P. (7) [20, 23.50]
Schmidt, Louis (1) [25]
Sims, Jay G. (9) [40, 46]
Whitby, Richard E. (4) [19.50, 21]
Zimmerman, Leopold A. (6) [20, 25]

TUBA/SOUSAPHONE (3)
Del Negro, Luca A. (9) [20, 23]
Pierce, John J. (9) [20, 23]
Richardson, John W. (9) [25, 28]

PERCUSSION (3)
Goulden, Howard N. (9) [25, 53]
Hager, James A. (9) [19.50, 23]
Helmecke, August, Jr. (9) [25, 28]

HARP (1)
Bambrick, Winifred (9) [40, 43]

**TOTAL MUSICIANS
PER BROADCAST: 52**

Sources: Nine Sousa Band payrolls dating from July 10-Nov. 4; Jay Sims's handwritten preliminary personnel list with proposed salaries; author's correspondence with Edmund C. Wall. For more information on broadcasts, see Chapter 6.

1929 (1929 tour) Figures in brackets indicate weekly salaries in dollars.

VOCAL SOLOIST (1)
Moody, Marjorie [300]

FLUTE/PICCOLO (6)
Evans, Eric J. [72]
Held, Earl D. [72]
Mueller, Florian F. [partial]
Orosky, John J. [72]
Phares, Hale W. [82]
Wavrek, Berthold K.
Wriggins, Arthur M. (1st) [97]
Zlotnik, H. Henry [72]

OBOE/ENGLISH HORN (3)
Mueller, Florian F. (1st) [137]
Lammers, John [82]
Weiss, Edson E. [82]

BASSOON (2)
Booth, Clarence (1st) [112]
Kraushaar, Otto J. [partial]
McRitchie, G. Rowe [82]

Bb CLARINET (19)
Bender, Walter H. [77]
Foote, Earl van W. [partial]

Holt, Walfred T. [72]
Johnson, Edward D. [78]
Kampe, George C. [77]
Kensinger, Vane H. [72]
Knuttunen, George J. [72]
Leiby, Charles A. [72]
Leigl, John H. [72]
Lubis, Theodore [72]
Robinson, William J. [72]
Slick, Eugene [72]
Strothkamp, Charles C., Jr. [72]
Tozier, Cecil E. [72]
Van Fossen, John F. [72]
Wall, Charles A. [72]
Wavrek, Frederick J. [72] [partial]
Weaver, Frederick M. [60]
Willaman, Robert G. (1st) [112]

ALTO CLARINET (1)
Silbach, John [77]

BASS CLARINET (1)
Reissner, Andrew [92]

SAXOPHONE (6)
Desmond, Paul A. (tenor) [72]

Eau Claire, Felix (tenor) [72]
Heney, Edward J. (solo alto) [97]
Monroe, Fred K. (bass) [60]
Schlanz, James (bari.) [53]
Sullivan, Frank W. (alto) [60]

CORNET/TRUMPET (7)
Bolle, Jules (tpt.) [72]
Cameron, Walter H. (cor.) [72]
Duncan, William E. (cor.) [72]
Hiltensmith, Albert J. (cor.) [87]
Knuttunen, Jacob O. (1st cor.) [137]
Russell, Clarence J. (cor.) [112]
Welte, Victor H. (tpt.) [87]

HORN (4)
Meagher, Seelye [72]
Mott, Bernard L. [72]
Muelbe, William [137]
Ryba, Walter M. [72]

EUPHONIUM (2)
Howard, Noble P. (1st) [112]
Wige, Ralph N. [72]

TROMBONE (3)
Braun, Clifford B. (2nd) [77]
Schueler, John P. (1st) [92]
Sims, Jay G. (3rd, pers mgr) [112]

TUBA/SOUSAPHONE (4)
Evans, Reuben C. [72]
Fuller, Arbor L. [72]
Herb, William [72]
Richardson, John W. (1st) [112]

PERCUSSION (3)
Goulden, Howard N.
  (xylophone soloist) [112]
Helmecke, August, Jr. (bass drum) [112]
Holt, Frank [72]

HARP (1)
Bambrick, Winifred [112]

OTHER
Finnegan, Lillian (secretary) [50]
Heney, William P. (valet)
Willingham, Jesse Mc. (stage mgr) [100]

TOTAL MUSICIANS: 63

Sources: Sousa Band payrolls for weeks ending Sept. 7 & Sept. 28; railroad pullman berth assignments for Aug. 26, Atlantic City to Pittsburgh.
Note: A preliminary (?) handwritten personnel/salary list of Jay Sims's indicates that the band might have been expanded to 65 players for the off-tour engagement at Princeton University on June 15.

1930 (Radio broadcast March 12) Figures in brackets indicate salaries in dollars.

FLUTE/PICCOLO (4)
Collins, John [23]
Wagner, Ernest F. [25]
Wriggins, Arthur M. [21]
Zlotnik, H. Henry [18]

OBOE/ENGLISH HORN (2)
Mullenix, Carlos W. [23]
Renzi, Paolo [28]

BASSOON (2)
Swann, David [23]
Trute, William [28]

Bb CLARINET (12)
Bortman, William T. [23]
Carr, John C. [21]
Harris, Walter B., Jr. [21]
Langan, William H. [21]
McGibney, C.G. [21]
Ridgley, Clifford [21]
Roeschel, William E. [21]
Strothkamp, Charles C., Jr. [21]
Van Ambergh, Fred [21]
Wall, Edmund C. [53]
Willaman, Robert G. [23]
Williams, Jan A. [23]

ALTO CLARINET (1)
Debueris, John [23]

BASS CLARINET (1)
Reissner, Andrew [23]

SAXOPHONE (6)
Bell, John W. [21]
Brant, Fred G. [21]
Evans, Alfred [21]
Fonzo, Joseph [21]
Nome, Robert [21]
O'Gorman, William [28]

CORNET/TRUMPET (7)
Danner, Arthur [23]
McCann, Richard [23]
Roeder, Louis [23]
Russell, Clarence J. [43]
Thorne, Joseph T. [21]
Tong, William [78]
Welte, Victor H. [23]

HORN (4)
Hauser, Eric [23]
Nava, Lucino [28]
Schulze, Adolf [20]
Schulze, Robert H. [20]

EUPHONIUM (1)
Paone, Biagio [28]

TROMBONE (4)
Harris, Charles W. [21]
Sims, Jay G. [39]

Whitby, Richard E. [21]
Zimmerman, Leopold A. [28]

TUBA/SOUSAPHONE (3)
Pfaff, Fred E. [23]
Pierce, John J. [23]
Richardson, John W. [28]

PERCUSSION (3)
Goulden, Howard N. [28]
Helmecke, August, Jr. [28]
Paulson, William T. [23]

HARP (1)
Bambrick, Winifred [43]

TOTAL MUSICIANS: 51

Source: Sousa Band payroll dated Mar. 12.

1930 (1st 1930 tour) Figures in brackets indicate salaries in dollars.

VOCAL SOLOIST (1)
Moody, Marjorie [300]

FLUTE/PICCOLO (6)
Ford, George F.
Held, Earl D.
Orosky, John J.
Phares, Hale W.
Wavrek, Berthold K.
Zlotnik, H. Henry

OBOE/ENGLISH HORN (2)
Gerhardt, Paul O.
Mullenix, Carlos W.

BASSOON (2)
Booth, Clarence
McRitchie, G. Rowe

Bb CLARINET (16)
Austin, James C.
Bender, Walter H.
Brissette, Fred J.
Byra, Stanley

Cheney, Joseph J.
Frigga, Einar
Harris, Walter B., Jr.
Johnson, Edward D.
Kampe, George C.
Knuttunen, George J.
Leiby, Charles A.
Lubis, Theodore
Robinson, William J.
Schueler, William P.
Strothkamp, Charles C., Jr.
Tompkins, George B.
Tozier, Cecil E.
Van Fossen, John F.
Wall, Edmund C.
Wavrek, Frederick J.
Weaver, Frederick M.
Zuber, Frank J.

ALTO CLARINET (1)
Silbach, John

BASS CLARINET (1)
Reissner, Andrew

SAXOPHONE (6)
Eau Claire, Felix
Foote, Earl van W.
Kincaid, Owen D.
Nome, Robert
Thompson, Harry A.
Weir, Leon E.

CORNET/TRUMPET (8)
Brabrook, Arthur N. [partial]
Cameron, Walter H.
Danner, Arthur
Duncan, William E.
Fee, George [partial]
Heater, Earl [partial]
Hiltensmith, Albert J. [partial]
Roeder, Louis [partial]
Russell, Clarence J.
Thorne, Joseph T.

HORN (4)
Mott, Bernard L.
Nava, Lucino
Ryba, Walter M.
Viehm, Robert

EUPHONIUM (2)
Harris, Aaron
Lewis, Wayne

TROMBONE (3)
Braun, Clifford B.
Sims, Jay G.
Zimmerman, Leopold A.

TUBA/SOUSAPHONE (4)
Herb, William
Merville, R. B.
Richardson, John W.
Woolley, George

PERCUSSION (3)
Goulden, Howard N.
Helmecke, August, Jr.
Holt, Frank

HARP (1)
Bambrick, Winifred

TOTAL MUSICIANS: 60

Source: Sousa Band photo, Aug., with identifications by Herbert N. Johnston.

267

1931 (Radio broadcast April 9) Figures in brackets indicate salaries in dollars.

FLUTE/PICCOLO (4)
Collins, John [18]
Possell, George [25]
Wagner, Ernest F. [18]
Zlotnik, H. Henry [18]

OBOE/ENGLISH HORN (2)
Gerhardt, Paul O. [25]
Mullenix, Carlos W. [20]

BASSOON (2)
Modess, Oskar [25]
Trute, William [20]

Bb CLARINET (14)
Bortman, William T. [20]
Brissette, Fred J. [18]
Cheney, Joseph J. [20]
Hudson, Carl H. [18]
Hughes, Thomas A. [18]
Kampe, George C. [18]

Kilvan, Edwin G. [18]
McGibney, C.G. [18]
Roeschel, William E. [18]
Strothkamp, Charles C., Jr. [18]
Thetford, Charles [20]
Wall, Edmund C. [50]
Willaman, Robert G. [20]
Williams, Jan A. [18]

ALTO CLARINET (1)
Debueris, John

BASS CLARINET (1)
Reissner, Andrew [20]

SAXOPHONE (6)
Bell, John W. [20]
Evans, Alfred [20]
Fonzo, Joseph [20]
Goodman, Wilbur [20]

Hegner, Walter [20]
O'Gorman, William [25]

CORNET/TRUMPET (7)
Bolle, Jules [18]
Danner, Arthur [20]
Hiltensmith, Albert J. [20]
McCann, Richard [25]
Russell, Clarence J. [40]
Short, Oscar B. [20]
Tong, William [50]

HORN (4)
Brown, Ralph W. [20]
Corrado, Frank [25]
Hauser, Eric [20]
Nava, Lucino [20]

EUPHONIUM (1)
Paone, Biagio [25]

TROMBONE (4)
Harris, Charles W.
Schmidt, Louis [18]
Sims, Jay G. [36]
Zimmerman, Leopold A. [25]

TUBA/SOUSAPHONE (3)
Pfaff, Fred E. [20]
Richardson, John W. [25]
Woolley, George [20]

PERCUSSION (3)
Goulden, Howard N. [25]
Helmecke, August, Jr. [25]
Paulson, William T. [20]

HARP (1)
Bell, Dorothy [25]

TOTAL MUSICIANS: 53

Source: Sousa Band payroll for Apr. 9.

1931 (1931 tour) Figures in brackets indicate weekly salaries in dollars.

VOCAL SOLOIST (1)
Moody, Marjorie [300]

FLUTE/PICCOLO (5)
Bladet, Robert (1st) [108]
Held, Earl D.
Orosky, John J. [68]
Wavrek, Berthold K. [68]
Zlotnik, H. Henry [68]

OBOE/ENGLISH HORN (2)
Mullenix, Carlos W. (2nd) [73]
Renzi, Paolo (1st) [108]

BASSOON (2)
McRitchie, G. Rowe (2nd) [68]
Modess, Oskar (1st) [108]

Bb CLARINET (15)
Foote, Earl van W. (2nd) [68]
Howland, Paul E. (1st) [68]
Johnson, Edward D. (1st) [73]
Knuttunen, George J. (3rd) [68]

Leroy, H.L. (1st)
Lubis, Theodore (1st) [68]
Robinson, William J. (1st) [68]
Schueler, William P. (1st) [73]
Strothkamp, Charles C., Jr. (3rd) [68]
Tompkins, George B. (2nd) [68]
Van Fossen, John F. (2nd) [68]
Wall, Edmund C. (1st) [108]
Wavrek, Frederick J. (1st) [68]
Williams, Warren (2nd) [68]
Zuber, Frank J. (1st) [68]

ALTO CLARINET (1)
Silbach, John [73]

BASS CLARINET (2)
Cheney, Joseph J.
Reissner, Andrew [88]

SAXOPHONE (4)
Eau Claire, Felix (tenor) [68]
Fonzo, Joseph (bass) [98]

Kincaid, Owen D. (alto) [93]
Thompson, Harry A. (bari.) [68]

CORNET/TRUMPET (9)
Cameron, Walter H. (3rd cor.)
Danner, Arthur (1st cor.) [83]
Duncan, William E. (3rd cor.) [68]
Heater, Earl (2nd cor.) [68]
Hiltensmith, Albert J. (1st tpt.) [83]
LaBarre, Eugene G. (2nd cor.) [68]
Russell, Clarence J. (3rd cor.) [108]
Schueler, Henry A. (2nd tpt.) [68]
Short, Oscar B. (solo cor.) [158]

HORN (4)
Grant, Edward E. [73]
Hubley, Claude F. [73]
Murphy, Edward A. (1st) [133]
Ryba, Walter M. [68]

EUPHONIUM (1)
Lewis, Wayne [98]

TROMBONE (3)
Braun, Clifford B. (2nd) [73]
Sims, Jay G. (bass) [108]
Zimmerman, Leopold A. (1st) [108]

TUBA/SOUSAPHONE (3)
Herb, William [68]
Richardson, John W. (1st) [108]
Woolley, George [68]

PERCUSSION (3)
Heney, John J. (xylo. soloist) [108]
Helmecke, August, Jr. [108]
Holt, Frank [73]

HARP (1)
Hofmann, Senta [108]

OTHER
Heney, William P.
(valet & encore card boy)

TOTAL MUSICIANS: 56

Sources: Three Sousa Band payrolls for Aug. and Sept.; Sousa Band end-of-tour salary sign-off sheet dated Sept. 8, 1931; Sousa Band group photo at Atlantic City, Sept., 1931.

1931 (Electrical radio transcription March 11) Brackets indicate salaries in dollars.

FLUTE/PICCOLO (4)
Collins, John [35]
Possell, George [35]
Wagner, Ernest F. [35]
Zlotnik, H. Henry [35]

OBOE/ENGLISH HORN (2)
Gerhardt, Paul O. [35]
Mullenix, Carlos W. [35]

BASSOON (2)
Modess, Oskar [35]
Trute, William [35]

Bb CLARINET (14)
Bortman, William T. [35]
Brissette, Fred J. [35]
Cheney, Joseph J. [35]
Hudson, Carl H. [35]
Hughes, Thomas A. [35]

Kampe, George C. [35]
Kilvan, Edwin G. [35]
McGibney, C.G. [35]
Roeschel, William E. [35]
Strothkamp, Charles C., Jr. [35]
Thetford, Charles [35]
Wall, Edmund C. [35]
Willaman, Robert G. [35]
Williams, Jan A. [35]

ALTO CLARINET (1)
Debueris, John [35]

BASS CLARINET (1)
Reissner, Andrew [35]

SAXOPHONE (4)
Bell, John W. [35]
Hegner, Walter [35]
Fonzo, Joseph [35]

O'Gorman, William [35]

CORNET/TRUMPET (7)
Bolle, Jules (tpt.) [35]
Danner, Arthur (cor,) [35]
Hiltensmith, Albert J. (cor.) [35]
McCann, Richard (tpt.) [35]
Russell, Clarence J (cor.) [65]
Short, Oscar B. (cor.) [35]
Staigers, Charles D. (solo cor.) [80]

HORN (4)
Brown, Ralph W. [35]
Franzl, Joseph [35]
Hauser, Eric [35]
Nava, Lucino [35]

EUPHONIUM (1)
Mantia, Simone [35]

TROMBONE (4)
Harris, Charles W. [35]
Sims, Jay G. [70]
Whitby, Richard E. [35]
Zimmerman, Leopold A. [35]

TUBA/SOUSAPHONE (3)
Pierce, John J. [35]
Richardson, John W. [35]
Woolley, George [35]

PERCUSSION (3)
Goulden, Howard N. [35]
Hager, James A. [35]
Helmecke, August, Jr. [35]

HARP (1)
Bambrick, Winifred [35]

TOTAL MUSICIANS: 51

Source: Sousa Band payroll dated Mar. 12. Transcription not used; sponsor unknown.

A Lost Art

Since the death of John Philip Sousa in 1932 there has been much speculation about the actual content of Sousa Band programs. While many of his printed programs have been reproduced, there has never been a collection of his complete programs, i.e., with all the encores.

There is thus a world of difference between the printed programs and what was actually played, because there were usually more encores than regularly scheduled numbers. In two respects, Sousa's unique style of programming was unconventional.

First, encores were played throughout the program rather than at the end, beginning within ten seconds after the end of a scheduled piece – while the audience was still applauding. This tradition was rarely used by other conductors, the main reason being that it severely taxed the musicians' stamina. Were it not for such conductors as Keith Brion, Leonard B. Smith, Loras J. Schissel, and James G. Saied the style might have passed into oblivion.

Second, Sousa unabashedly mixed serious music with lighter music throughout a concert. This custom might be considered outlandish today, but reviews of his concerts attest to the fact that audiences loved it. Because he was such a high-profile entertainer, he could do it with minimal criticism. His audiences were similar to today's pops audiences, not those that would attend formal concerts.

Work for Future Scholars

With publication of this appendix, Sousa's programming techniques are now available for analysis. Detailed analyses are beyond the scope of this book, so it is my hope that scholars will initiate more critical studies of Sousa's innovative programming.

Regular Length and Shorter Concerts

A research associate with Integrity Press, Heather B. Doughty, studied the voluminous Sousa Band press books in great detail. She ferreted out many complete tour programs (showing all of the encores) by examining thousands of reviews of full-length concerts – a burdensome task few scholars would attempt. A few other compete programs were contributed by others. These are presented as Part A of this appendix.

Part B, showing shorter programs, was compiled by the author from percussionist John J. Heney's handwritten marginal notes on printed programs of 1926 Willow Grove Park concerts, where four programs of shorter length without intermission (interval) were performed each day.

The year 1926 was Heney's first year with the band, and he added marginalia to indicate where each encore was played on the programs. Although the band played annual engagements at Willow Grove between 1901 and 1926, Heney's collection is the only known set of the programs showing all the encores. Because Sousa's encores were taken for granted, newspapers did not bother to report them.

Not all of Heney's annotations could be interpreted accurately because he often used nicknames for pieces or shortened the titles. Consequently, only 92 of the 228 Willow Grove programs that season are presented here.

PART (A)
REGULAR-LENGTH CONCERTS

EVENING CONCERT, 11 NOVEMBER 1894
Rochester, New York, at Lyceum Theater

1.	Tannhäuser: Overture	Wagner
	Encore: Plantation Chimes	Hall
	Encore: The Washington Post, march	Sousa
	Encore: Jesus, Lover of My Soul	Marsh
2.	Hungarian Rhapsody No. 2	Liszt
	Encore: Minuet l'Antique	Paderewski
	Encore: The Directorate, march	Sousa
3.	Annie Laurie, air varie	Pryor
	Encore: Love's Old Sweet Song	Molloy
	ARTHUR PRYOR, TROMBONE SOLOIST	
4.	Scenes at a Masquerade	Lacombe
	I Grand March of the Maskers	
	II Ponchiello Family	
	III Columbine Flirtation	
	IV Revelry of the Maskers	
	Encore: Crack Regiment	Haimann
	Encore: Corncracker	Meacham
5.	(a) Serenade Enfantine	Bonnaud
	(b) The Liberty Bell, march	Sousa
	Encore: Manhattan Beach, march	Sousa
6.	O Hail I Greet Thee, from Tannhäuser	Wagner
	Encore: Old Folks at Home	Foster
	FRANCESCA GUTHRIE-MOYER, SOPRANO SOLOIST	
7.	(a) Intermezzo Russe	Franke
	(b) Pasquinade	Gottschalk
	Encore: At the Circus	Dunewaller
	Encore: Bamboula, Negro Dance of Trinidad	Urich
8.	Good-Bye, humoresque	Sousa
	Encore: The High School Cadets, march	Sousa
9.	Prelude to Act I of Lohengrin	Wagner

Note: Placement of interval uncertain

Source: *Rochester Herald*, 12 November 1894

MATINEE CONCERT, 23 MARCH 1895
Rochester, New York, at Lyceum Theater

1.	Festival Overture	Lassen
	Encore: Yazoo Dance	Thompson
2.	Siegfried's Death, from Götterdämmerung	Wagner
	Encore: Manhattan Beach, march	Sousa
	Encore: Spanish Love Song	Joyce
3.	A Shepherd's Life in the Alps, pastoral fantasia	Kling
	Encore: The High School Cadets, march	Sousa
4.	Three Gossips	Hamm
	FRANK W. WADSWORTH, FLUTE; GUSTAV STENGLER, CLARINET;	
	ROBERT MESSENGER, OBOE	
	Encore: Serenade Enfantine	Bonnaud
5.	Enchantress Waltz	Arditi
	Encore: Ben Bolt	Kneass
	MARIE BARNARD, SOPRANO SOLOIST	
6.	Wiener Mad'ln, waltz	Ziehrer
	Encore: The Blending of the Blue and the Gray, fantasie	Dalbey
	Encore: The Washington Post, march	Sousa
7.	(a) Dragoons	Bizet
	(b) The Liberty Bell, march	Sousa
	Encore: The Directorate, march	Sousa
	Encore: The Beau Ideal, march	Sousa
8.	Transcription on Hungarian Themes	Hauser
	Encore: The Swan, from Carnival of the Animals	Saint-Saens
	CURRIE DUKE, VIOLIN SOLOIST	
9.	The King's Lieutenant	Titl

Note: Placement of interval uncertain

Source: *Rochester Herald*, 24 March 1895

EVENING CONCERT, 23 MARCH 1895
Rochester, New York, at Lyceum Theater

1.	Agonies of Tantalus: Overture	Suppe
	Encore: Bamboula	Graud
	Encore: Manhattan Beach, march	Sousa
	Encore: The Blending of the Blue and the Gray, fantasie	Dalbey
2.	Prelude to Hansel and Gretel	Humperdinck
	Encore: Yazoo Dance	Thompson
3.	Norwegian Rhapsody No. 2	Svendsen
4.	Trojan League March	Hamilton
	Encore: Serenade Enfantine	Bonnaud
5.	Theme, Variations and Carnival Tune, from Scenes in Naples	Massenet
	Encore: The High School Cadets, march	Sousa
6.	Enchantress Waltz	Arditi
	Encore: Love Me If I Live	Foote
	MARIE BARNARD, SOPRANO SOLOIST	
7.	(a) Funeral March, from Sonata No. 2 in B-flat	Chopin
	(b) The Directorate, march	Sousa
	Encore: The Liberty Bell, march	Sousa
8.	The Band Came Back, humoresque	Sousa
	Encore: American Patrol	Meacham
	Encore: The Belle of Chicago, march	Sousa
9.	Faust Fantasie	Sarasate
	Encore: Canzonetta, from Concerto No. 1	Godard
	CURRIE DUKE, VIOLIN SOLOIST	
10.	Beautiful Galatea: Overture	Suppe

Note: Placement of interval uncertain

Source: *Rochester Herald*, 24 March 1895

EVENING CONCERT, 24 MARCH 1895
Rochester, New York, at Lyceum Theater

1.	William Tell: Overture	Rossini
	Encore: Plantation Chimes	Hall
	Encore: The High School Cadets, march	Sousa
	Encore: Spanish Love Song	Joyce
2.	Prelude to Act I of Parsifal	Wagner
	Encore: Serenade Enfantine	Bonnaud
	Encore: The Washington Post, march	Sousa
3.	The Carnival of Venice	Paganini
	Encore: Belle of Portland	Anonymous
	JEAN H.B. MOEREMANS, SAXOPHONE SOLOIST	
4.	(a) Parisian Carnival, tone poem	Svendsen
	(b) Sextette, from Lucia di Lammermoor	Donizetti
	Featuring six brass players	
	Encore: The Beau Ideal, march	Sousa
5.	Enchantress Waltz	Arditi
	Encore: Ben Bolt	Kneass
	MARIE BARNARD, SOPRANO SOLOIST	
6.	(a) La Mousme, Japanese mazurka	Ganne
	(b) Manhattan Beach, march	Sousa
	Encore: The Liberty Bell, march	Sousa
7.	Transcription on Hungarian Themes	Hauser
	Encore: Canzonetta, from Concerto No. 1	Godard
	CURRIE DUKE, VIOLIN SOLOIST	
8.	The Band Came Back, humoresque	Sousa
	Encore: Zampa: Overture	Herold
9.	Prelude to Act III of Lohengrin	Wagner

Note: Placement of interval uncertain

Source: *Rochester Herald*, 25 March 1895

MATINEE CONCERT, 18 JANUARY 1896
Rochester, New York, at Lyceum Theater

1. Stradella: Overture — Flotow
   Encore: Kansas Two Step Pryor
   Encore: The Directorate, march — Sousa
   Encore: Whistling Coon — Weldon
2. Kunihild, prelude — Kistler
   Encore: Baby Polka — Bial
   Encore: Honeymoon March — Rosey
3. Hungarian Rhapsody No. 14 — Liszt
   Encore: The Stars and Stripes Forever, march — Sousa
4. Air Americaine — Phillipe
   Encore: Say Au Revoir But Not Good Bye — Kennedy
   SIMONE MANTIA, EUPHONIUM SOLOIST
5. Grand Caprice — Ketterer
6. Melba Valse — Luckstone
   MYRTA FRENCH, SOPRANO SOLOIST
7. Ride of the Valkyries and Magic Fire Music, from Die Walküre — Wagner
8. (a) When You Know the Girl You Love Loves You — Spaulding
   HENRY HIGGINS, CORNET SOLOIST
   (b) Little Nell — Pryor
   JEAN H.B. MOEREMANS, SAXOPHONE SOLOIST
   (c) Only One Girl in the World for Me — Wing
   ARTHUR PRYOR, TROMBONE SOLOIST
   (d) Ben Bolt — English
   Encore: Paradise Alley — Bratton
   ALBERT BODE, CORNET SOLOIST
9. (a) Entr' Acte — Gillet
   (b) King Cotton, march — Sousa
   Encore: The Liberty Bell, march — Sousa
   Encore: The Belle of Chicago, march — Sousa
   Encore: The Thunderer, march — Sousa
10. Zigeunerweisen — Sarasate
    Encore: Dream After the Ball — Czibulka
    CURRIE DUKE, VIOLIN SOLOIST
11. Custer's Last Charge, descriptive piece — Luders
12. Rochester Herald March — Mrs. Millicent R. Clarke

Note: Placement of interval uncertain
Source: Sousa Band press book no. 5, p. 40 (*Rochester Herald*)

EVENING CONCERT, 18 JANUARY 1896
Rochester, New York, at Lyceum Theater

1. Triumphal Overture — Rubinstein
   Encore: Forgetmenot, intermezzo — Macbeth
   Encore: The Directorate, march — Sousa
   Encore: Honeymoon March — Rosey
2. Three Quotations, suite — Sousa
   I   The King of France
   II I, Too, Was Born in Arcadia
   III In Darkest Africa
   Encore: La Paloma — Yradier
   Encore: Manhattan Beach, march — Sousa
   Encore: Spring Song — Mendelssohn
3. Annie Laurie, air varie — Pryor
   Encore: Only One Girl in the World for Me — Wing
   Encore: Say Au Revoir But Not Good Bye — Kennedy
   ARTHUR PRYOR, TROMBONE SOLOIST
4. Siegfried, grand fantasie — Wagner
   Encore: Nightingale Song, from Tyrolean — Masse
5. Delight Valses — Luckstone
   Encore: Sweet Miss Industry, song — Sousa
   MYRTA FRENCH, SOPRANO SOLOIST
6. (a) Water Sprites, caprice — Kunkel
   (b) King Cotton, march — Sousa
   Encore: The Liberty Bell, march — Sousa
   Encore: The Beau Ideal, march — Sousa
7. Zigeunerweisen — Sarasate
   Encore: Dream After the Ball — Czibulka
   CURRIE DUKE, VIOLIN SOLOIST
8. The Band Came Back, humoresque — Sousa

Note: Placement of interval uncertain
Source: Sousa Band press book no. 5, p. 40 (*Rochester Herald*)

MATINEE CONCERT, 19 JANUARY 1896
Rochester, New York, at Lyceum Theater

1. Tannhäuser: Overture — Wagner
   Encore: Swedish Wedding March — Sodermann
   Encore: The Liberty Bell, march — Sousa
   Encore: The Lily Bells, from Our Flirtations — Sousa
2. (a) Butterflies in Sunshine, intermezzo — Gungl
   (b) Molto Pizzicato, Entr' Acte — Thome
   Encore: The Directorate, march — Sousa
   Encore: Serenade Enfantine — Bonnaud
3. Benediction of the Poignards, from Les Huguenots — Meyerbeer
   MESSRS. PRYOR, LYON, AND WILLIAMS, TROMBONISTS
   Encore: Little Marcia Maria — Minnie
4. Scenes from Faust — Gounod
   Encore: Honeymoon March — Rosey
5. (a) Entr' Acte — Gillet
   (b) Moonlight Sonata, Movement I — Beethoven
6. L'Ete   Chaminade
   Encore: Ben Bolt — English
   MYRTA FRENCH, SOPRANO SOLOIST
7. (a) Rigadon de Dardanus — Rameau
   (b) Manhattan Beach, march — Sousa
   Encore: King Cotton, march — Sousa
   Encore: The Belle of Chicago, march — Sousa
   Encore: The Washington Post, march — Sousa
8. Rondo Capriccioso — Saint-Saens
   Encore: Dream After the Ball — Czibulka
   CURRIE DUKE, VIOLIN SOLOIST
9. Wedding Music, from Lohengrin — Wagner

Note: Placement of interval uncertain
Source: *Rochester Herald*, 20 January 1896

EVENING CONCERT, 19 JANUARY 1896
Rochester, New York, at Lyceum Theater

1. Maximillian Robespierre, tone poem — Litolff
   Encore: Bamboula — Graud
   Encore: Manhattan Beach, march — Sousa
   Encore: Plantation Chimes — Hall
2. Prelude to Hansel and Gretel — Humperdinck
   Encore: Lolita — Langey
   Encore: National Fencibles, march — Sousa
   Encore: The Liberty Bell, march — Sousa
3. (a) Intermezzo — Radcliff
   (b) Badinage, morceau — Thome
   Encore: Sextette, from Lucia di Lammermoor — Donizetti
   MESSRS. BODE, GRIFFIN, PRYOR, LYON, WILLIAMS, AND MANTIA
4. My Old Kentucky Home, fantasia — Dalbey
   Encore: Upidee, paraphrase — Tracy
5. (a) Bell Chorus, from I Pagliacci — Leoncavallo
   (b) Water Sprites, caprice — Kunkel
   Encore: The Crusader, march — Sousa
6. Waltz Song, from Romeo and Juliet — Gounod
   Encore: Love Go Hang — Anonymous
   MYRTA FRENCH, SOPRANO SOLOIST
7. (a) Forgetmenot, intermezzo — MacBeth
   (b) The Directorate, march — Sousa
   Encore: King Cotton, march — Sousa
   Encore: The High School Cadets, march — Sousa
   Encore: The Belle of Chicago, march — Sousa
8. Zigeunerweisen — Sarasate
   Encore: Mazurka in G — Zarlaki
   CURRIE DUKE, VIOLIN SOLOIST
9. Variations on Yankee Doodle — Reeves

Note: Placement of interval uncertain
Source: *Rochester Herald*, 20 January 1896

EVENING CONCERT, 31 MAY 1896
Rochester, New York, at Lyceum Theater

1. Maritana: Overture — Wallace
   Encore: Water Sprites, caprice — Kunkel
   Encore: The Directorate, march — Sousa
   Encore: Manhattan Beach, march — Sousa
2. Capriccio Espagnol — Rimsky-Korsakov
   I Albarada
   II Variations
   III Scena e Canto Gitano
   IV Fandango Asturiano
   Encore: Jolly Fellows, waltz — Vollstedt
   Encore: The Liberty Bell, march — Sousa
3. Annie Laurie, air varie — Pryor
   Encore: Say Au Revoir But Not Good Bye — Kennedy
   ARTHUR PRYOR, TROMBONE SOLOIST
4. (a) Indian Reveille — Christein
   (b) Hourida, grand valse — Gillet
   Encore: King Cotton, march — Sousa
5. In a Haunted Forest — MacDowell
6. Stances — Flegier
   Encore: Parla, grand valse — Arditi
   MINNIE TRACY, SOPRANO SOLOIST
7. (a) Narcissus, from Water Scenes — Nevin
   (b) El Capitan, march — Sousa
   Encore: El Capitan, march [portion repeated] — Sousa
8. Ballade and Polonaise — Vieuxtemps
   Encore: Simple Aveu — Thome
   MARTINA JOHNSTONE, VIOLIN SOLOIST
9. Wedding Music, from Lohengrin — Wagner

Note: Placement of interval uncertain
Source: *Rochester Herald*, 1 June 1896

EVENING CONCERT, 28 MARCH 1897
Rochester, New York, at Lyceum Theater

1. Grand Festival Overture — Leutner
   Encore: The Directorate, march — Sousa
   Encore: Happy Days in Dixie — Johnson
   Encore: Pizzicato, from Sylvia — Delibes
2. Prelude to Act I of Lohengrin — Wagner
   Encore: The Liberty Bell, march — Sousa
   Encore: The King of France, from Three Quotations — Sousa
   Encore: La Paloma — Yradier
3. Werner's Farewell — Nessler
   Encore: Don't Be Cross, from Obeisteiger — Zeller
   FRANZ HELLE, FLUGELHORN SOLOIST
4. Robin and Wren, caprice — Kling
   Encore: King Cotton, march — Sousa
   Encore: Water Sprites, caprice — Kunkel
   Encore: My Angeline — Johnson
5. Annie Laurie, air varie — Pryor
   Encore: Sweet Lorena Ray, song — Pryor
   ARTHUR PRYOR, TROMBONE SOLOIST
6. Hungarian Rhapsody No. 1 — Liszt
7. Se Saran Rose — Arditi
   Encore: Comin' Thro' the Rye — Burns
   Encore: I Love and the World Is Mine — John
   ELIZABETH NORTHROP, SOPRANO SOLOIST
8. (a) Prelude and Siciliana, from Cavalleria Rusticana — Mascagni
   (b) El Capitan, march — Sousa
   Encore: El Capitan, march [repeated] — Sousa
9. Hungarian Idylle — Keler-Bela
   Encore: Obertass — Wieniawski
   MARTINA JOHNSTONE, VIOLIN SOLOIST
10. The Cricket on the Hearth, Entr' Acte — Goldmark
    The Star Spangled Banner

Note: Placement of interval uncertain
Source: Sousa Band press book no. 5, p. 24 (*Rochester Herald*)

EVENING CONCERT, 29 MARCH 1897
Elmira, New York, at Lyceum Theater

1. Grand Festival Overture — Leutner
   Encore: The Directorate, march — Sousa
   Encore: Happy Days in Dixie — Johnson
2. Prelude to Act III of Lohengrin — Wagner
   Encore: The Liberty Bell, march — Sousa
   Encore: Manhattan Beach, march — Sousa
3. Werner's Farewell — Nessler
   FRANZ HELLE, FLUGELHORN SOLOIST
4. Robin and Wren, caprice — Kling
   Encore: Water Sprites, caprice — Kunkel
   Encore: King Cotton, march — Sousa
5. Annie Laurie, air varie — Pryor
   Encore: Sweet Lorena Ray, song — Pryor
   ARTHUR PRYOR, TROMBONE SOLOIST
6. Hungarian Rhapsody No. 1 — Liszt
7. Se Saran Rose — Arditi
   Encore: Sweet Miss Industry, song — Sousa
   ELIZABETH NORTHROP, SOPRANO SOLOIST
8. (a) Prelude and Siciliana, from Cavalleria Rusticana — Mascagni
   (b) El Capitan, march — Sousa
   Encore: El Capitan, march [repeated] — Sousa
   Encore: The Belle of Chicago, march — Sousa
9. Hungarian Idylle — Keler-Bela
   Encore: Sample Avue — Thome
   MARTINA JOHNSTONE, VIOLIN SOLOIST
10. The Cricket on the Hearth, Entr' Acte — Goldmark

Note: Placement of interval uncertain
Source: Sousa Band press book no. 5, p. 28 (*Elmira Star-Gazette*)

EVENING CONCERT, 1 APRIL 1897
Utica, New York, at Utica Opera House

1. Grand Festival Overture — Lentner
   Encore: The Directorate, march — Sousa
   Encore: Happy Days in Dixie — Johnson
2. Prelude to Act I of Lohengrin — Wagner
   Encore: The Liberty Bell, march — Sousa
   Encore: Knights of Columbus, march — Fischer
   Encore: Serenade Elgantine — Bonnaud
3. Werner's Farewell — Nessler
   Encore: Don't Be Cross, from Obeisteiger — Zeller
   FRANZ HELLE, FLUGELHORN SOLOIST
4. Robin and Wren, caprice — Kling
   Encore: Water Sprites, caprice — Kunkel
   Encore: My Angeline — Johnson
5. Annie Laurie, air varie — Pryor
   Encore: Sweet Lorena Ray, song — Pryor
   ARTHUR PRYOR, TROMBONE SOLOIST
6. (a) La Siesta de la Señorita, scherzo and habañera — Fumi
   (b) Valse Caprice — Rubinstein
   Encore: King Cotton, march — Sousa
7. Se Saran Rose — Araditi
   Encore: Sweet Miss Industry, song — Sousa
   ELIZABETH NORTHROP, SOPRANO SOLOIST
8. (a) Prelude and Siciliana, from Cavalleria Rusticana — Mascagni
   (b) El Capitan, march — Sousa
   Encore: El Capitan, march [repeated] — Sousa
9. Ballade and Polonaise — Vieuxtemps
   Encore: Simple Aveu — Thome
   MARTINA JOHNSTONE, VIOLIN SOLOIST
10. The Cricket on the Hearth, Entr' Acte — Goldmark
    The Star Spangled Banner

Note: Placement of interval uncertain
Source: Sousa Band press book no. 5, p. 26 (*Utica Herald*)

MATINEE CONCERT, 3 MARCH 1898
Rochester, New York, at Lyceum Theater

1. Promised Bride: Overture — Ponchielli
   Encore: The Directorate, march — Sousa
   Encore: Southern Blossoms — Pryor
2. Bright Star of Hope — Robardi
   Encore: Don't Be Cross, from Obeisteiger — Zeller
   FRANZ HELLE, FLUGELHORN SOLOIST
3. Night Scene, from Tristan and Isolde — Wagner
   Encore: El Capitan, march — Sousa
   Encore: Listen to My Tale of Woe, humoresque — Smith
4. Shadow Song, from Dinorah — Meyerbeer
   Encore: Laughing Song, from Manon Lescaut — Auber
   MAUDE REESE DAVIES, SOPRANO SOLOIST
5. The Last Days of Pompeii, suite — Sousa
   I   In the House of Burbo and Stratonice
   II   Nydia the Blind Girl
   III The Destruction of Pompeii and Nydia's Death
   Encore: The Stars and Stripes Forever, march — Sousa

   The Star Spangled Banner

   * INTERVAL *

6. Transcription on Hungarian Themes — Hauser
   Encore: The Liberty Bell, march — Sousa
   Encore: On the Banks of the Wabash Far Away — Dresser
7. (a) Rondo d'Amour, idyl — Westerhout
   (b) The Bride Elect, march — Sousa
   Encore: The Bride Elect, march [repeated] — Sousa
   Encore: The Bride Elect, march [repeated again] — Sousa
8. Zigeunerweisen — Sarasate
   Encore: Cavatina — Bohm
   JENNIE HOYLE, VIOLIN SOLOIST
9. The Band Came Back, humoresque — Sousa

Source: Sousa Band press book no. 5, p. 210 (*Rochester Herald*)

EVENING CONCERT, 3 MARCH 1898
Rochester, New York, at Lyceum Theater

1. Il Guarany: Overture — Gomez
   Encore: The Directorate, march — Sousa
   Encore: Rondo d'Amour, idyl — Van Westerhout
2. Valse Caprice — Pryor
   Encore: On the Banks of the Wabash Far Away — Dresser
   ARTHUR PRYOR, TROMBONE SOLOIST
3. Pilgrim's Chorus and Evening Star, from Tannhäuser — Wagner
   Encore: El Capitan, march — Sousa
4. Linda di Chamounix — Donizetti
   Encore: May Morning — Denza
   MAUDE REESE DAVIES, SOPRANO SOLOIST
5. Scenes Historical -- Sheridan's Ride — Sousa
   I   Waiting for the Bugle
   II   The Attack
   III The Death of Thoburn
   IV   Coming of Sheridan
   V   Apotheosis
   Encore: The Bride Elect, march — Sousa
   Encore: The Bride Elect, march [repeated] — Sousa

   * INTERVAL *

6. Hungarian Rhapsody No. 2 — Liszt
   Encore: American Patrol — Meacham
   Encore: The Star Spangled Banner
   Encore: The Blending of the Blue and the Gray, fantasie — Dalbey
7. (a) Love in Idleness, intermezzo — MacBeth
   (b) The Stars and Stripes Forever, march — Sousa
   Encore: The Stars and Stripes Forever, march [repeated] — Sousa
8. Gypsy Dances — Nachez
   Encore: Mazurka de Concert — Musin
   JENNIE HOYLE, VIOLIN SOLOIST
9. Over the Footlights in New York, fantasie — Sousa

Source: Sousa Band press book no. 5, p. 210 (*Rochester Herald*)

EVENING CONCERT, 16 APRIL 1899
Rochester, New York, at Lyceum Theater

1. Paragraph III: Overture — Suppe
   Encore: The Stars and Stripes Forever, march — Sousa
   Encore: Georgia Camp Meeting, song — Mills
2. Thoughts of Love — Pryor
   Encore: Just One Girl — Udal
   ARTHUR PRYOR, TROMBONE SOLOIST
3. (a) Carilon de Noel, musette — Smith
   (b) War Time, from Indian Suite — MacDowell
   Encore: Hot Time in the Old Town Tonight, paraphrase — Sousa
   Encore: The Bride Elect, march — Sousa
4. Ah, Fors e Lui, from La Traviata — Verdi
   Encore: Will You Love When the Lilies Are Dead?, from The Charlatan — Sousa
   MAUDE REESE DAVIES, SOPRANO SOLOIST
5. Knights of the Holy Grail, Grand Scene, from Parsifal — Wagner
   Encore: Prelude to Act III of Lohengrin — Wagner

   * INTERVAL *

6. Variations on Jenny Jones, idyl — Godfrey
   Encore: Levee Revels, Afro-American cane hop — O'Hare
   Encore: El Capitan, march — Sousa
   Encore: Ragtime Baby, song — Johnson
7. (a) Serenade Badine — Gabriel-Marie
   (b) The Charlatan, march — Sousa
   Encore: The Charlatan, march [repeated] — Sousa
   Encore: King Cotton, march — Sousa
8. Souvenir de Haydn — Leonard
   Encore: Gypsy Dances — Nachez
   DOROTHY HOYLE, VIOLIN SOLOIST
9. Tarantella, from The Bride Elect — Sousa

Source: Sousa Band press book no. 8, p. 175 (*Rochester Herald*)

EVENING CONCERT, 9 JANUARY 1901
Scranton, Pennsylvania, at Lyceum Theater

1. Isabella: Overture — Suppe
   Encore: The Stars and Stripes Forever, march — Sousa
   Encore: Salome — Laurence
2. The Patriot — Pryor
   Encore: The Tale of a Kangaroo, from Burgomaster — Luders
   ARTHUR PRYOR, TROMBONE SOLOIST
3. The History of Pierrot, ballet suite — Casto
   Encore: A Coon Band Contest, cakewalk — Pryor
   Encore: The Man Behind the Gun, march — Sousa
4. Where Is Love?, from Chris and the Wonderful Lamp — Sousa
   Encore: The Swallows — Cowen
   BLANCHE DUFFIELD, SOPRANO SOLOIST
5. Oh, Fatal Stone, grand scene, from Aida — Verdi
   Encore: Hula, Hula, cakewalk — Van Alstyne
   Encore: Hands Across the Sea, march — Sousa

   * INTERVAL *

6. Invitation a la Valse — Weber
   Encore: Sextette, from Lucia di Lammermoor — Donizetti
   Featuring six brass players
7. In the Soudan, Dervish chorus — Sebek
   Encore, Hail to the Spirit of Liberty, march — Sousa
   Encore: Hail to the Spirit of Liberty, march [repeated] — Sousa
8. Adagio and Moto Perpetum — Ries
   Encore: Molto Stacatto, Entr' Acte — Thome
   BERTHA BUCKLIN, VIOLIN SOLOIST
9. Ritter Pasman, czardas — Strauss

Source: Sousa Band press book no. 14, p. 4 (*Scranton Tribune*)

274

EVENING CONCERT, 18 FEBRUARY 1901
Fresno, California, at Barton Opera House

1. Overture based on Haydn's Emperor's Hymn — Westmeyer
   Encore: The Stars and Stripes Forever, march — Sousa
   Encore: Salome — Lawrence
2. The Patriot — Pryor
   Encore: I Love You, But I Can't Tell Why — Edwards
   Encore: The Tale of a Kangaroo, from Burgomaster — Luders
   ARTHUR PRYOR, TROMBONE SOLOIST
3. Fantasie from Richard Wagner's Operas — Godfrey
   Encore: The Blue and Gray Patrol — Dalbey
   Encore: Owl March — Falkenstein
4. Maid of the Meadow, song — Sousa
   Encore: Spring Is Come — Mendelssohn
   BLANCHE DUFFIELD, SOPRANO SOLOIST
5. Grand Scene and Ensemble, from Andrea Chenier — Giordano
   Encore: The Man Behind the Gun, march — Sousa

* INTERVAL *

6. Invitation a la Valse — Weber
   Encore: Rondo d'Amour, idyl — Van Westerhout
7. (a) In the Soudan, dervish chorus — Sebek
   (b) Hail to the Spirit of Liberty, march — Sousa
   Encore: Hail to the Spirit of Liberty, march [repeated] — Sousa
8. Adagio and Moto Perpetum — Ries
   Encore: Espagnole, serenade — Bizet
   Encore: Elfentanz — Lehar
   BERTHA BUCKLIN, VIOLIN SOLOIST
9. Ritter Pasman, czardas — Strauss

Source: Sousa Band press book no. 14, p. 49 (*Evening Democrat*)

MATINEE CONCERT, 28 MARCH 1901
Rochester, New York, at Lyceum Theater

1. Sakuntala, overture — Goldmark
   Encore: The Stars and Stripes Forever, march — Sousa
2. Arbucklenian Polka — Hartman
   Encore: The Holy City — Adam
   HERBERT L. CLARKE, CORNET SOLOIST
3. History of a Pierot, pantomimic suite — Costa
   Encore: A Coon Band Contest, cakewalk — Pryor
4. Printemps — Stern
   Encore: The Swallows — Cowen
   BLANCHE DUFFIELD, SOPRANO SOLOIST
5. Grand Scene and Death Duet, from Aida — Verdi
   Encore: Sextette, from Lucia di Lammermoor — Donizetti
   MESSRS. CLARKE, HIGGINS, MANTIA, PRYOR, LYON, and WILLIAMS

* INTERVAL *

6. Scene and Soldiers Chorus, from Faust — Gounod
   Encore: Rondo d'Amour, idyl — Van Westerhout
   Encore: La Frangesa! March — Costa
   Trombone ensemble: Messrs. Pryor, Mantia,
   Lyon, Wardwell, and Williams
7. (a) Fesche Frauen, polka caprice — Liebling
   (b) Hail to the Spirit of Liberty, march — Sousa
   Encore: Hail to the Spirit of Liberty [repeated] — Sousa
8. Souvenir de Moscow — Wieniawski
   BERTHA BUCKLIN, VIOLIN SOLOIST
9. Ritter Pasman, czardas — Strauss

Source: Sousa Band press book no. 14, p. 75 (*Rochester Herald*)

EVENING CONCERT, 28 MARCH 1901
Rochester, New York, at Lyceum Theater

1. Isabella: Overture — Suppe
   Encore: The Stars and Stripes Forever, march — Sousa
   Encore: Zamona, Arabian intermezzo — Loraine
2. The Patriot — Pryor

   Encore: I Love You, But I Can't Tell Why — Edwards
   Encore: The Tale of a Kangaroo, from Burgomaster — Luders
   ARTHUR PRYOR, TROMBONE SOLOIST
3. Scandinavian Fantasia — Meyer-Helmund
   Encore: A Coon Band Contest, cakewalk — Pryor
   Encore: The Man Behind the Gun, march — Sousa
4. Where Is Love?, from Chris and the Wonderful Lamp — Sousa
   Encore: The Swallows — Cowen
   BLANCHE DUFFIELD, SOPRANO SOLOIST
5. Grand Scene and Ensemble, from Andrea Chenier — Giordano
   Encore: The Blue and Gray Patrol — Dalbey
   Encore: El Capitan, march — Sousa

* INTERVAL *

6. Invitation a la Valse — Weber
   Encore: Sextette, from Lucia di Lammermoor — Donizetti
   Featuring six brass players
   Encore: Southern Idylle — Turner
7. (a) Serenade Roccoco — Meyer-Hellmund
   (b) Hail to the Spirit of Liberty, march — Sousa
   Encore: Hail to the Spirit of Liberty, march [repeated] — Sousa
8. Polonaise in A Major — Wieniawski
   Encore: Andalusia — Sarasate
   BERTHA BUCKLIN, VIOLIN SOLOIST
9. Hermione, suite — La Rondella

Source: Sousa Band press book no. 14, p. 75 (*Rochester Herald*)

EVENING CONCERT, 5 MAY 1901
Rochester, New York, at Lyceum Theater

1. Aroldo: Overture — Verdi
   Encore: Hands Across the Sea, march — Sousa
   Encore: Rhoda, and Chinese Sojer Man, from San Toy — Monckton
2. Thoughts of Love — Pryor
   Encore: The Palms — Faure
   ARTHUR PRYOR, TROMBONE SOLOIST
3. Excerpts from Carmen — Bizet
   Encore: A Coon Band Contest, cakewalk — Pryor
   Encore: Warblers Serenade — Woods
4. The Pearl of Brazil, aria from the opera — David
   Encore: Bobolink — Bischoff
   BLANCHE DUFFIELD, SOPRANO SOLOIST
   Flute obbligato by Darius A. Lyons
5. In Paradise, prologue, from Mefistofele — Boite
   Encore: The Directorate, march — Sousa

* INTERVAL *

6. The Band Came Back, humoresque — Sousa
   Encore: Rosita, Puerto Rican dance — Missud
7. (a) Zamona, Arabian intermezzo — Loraine
   (b) Hail to the Spirit of Liberty, march — Sousa
   Encore: The Stars and Stripes Forever, march — Sousa
8. a) Nymphalin, reverie — Sousa
   b) Tarantella — Raff
   Encore: Molto Stacatto, Entr' Acte — Thome
   BERTHA BUCKLIN, VIOLIN SOLOIST
9. Zampa: Overture — Herold

Source: Sousa Band press book no. 14, pp. 84-85 (*Rochester Herald*)

275

10:45 p.m. CONCERT, 1 DECEMBER 1901
Command performance before King Edward VII
Sandringham, England, at Sandringham House

God Save the King

The Star Spangled Banner

1.	Three Quotations, suite	Sousa
	I The King of France	
	II I, Too, Was Born in Arcadia	
	III In Darkest Africa	
	Encore: Hands Across the Sea, march	Sousa
2.	El Capitan, march	Sousa
3.	Thoughts of Love	Pryor
	ARTHUR PRYOR, TROMBONE SOLOIST	
4.	Songs of Grace and Songs of Glory, fantasie	Sousa
	Encore: The Washington Post, march	Sousa
	Encore: King Cotton, march	Sousa
5.	Will You Love When the Lilies Are Dead?, from The Charlatan	Sousa
	Encore: Old Folks at Home, song	Foster
	MAUD REESE DAVIES, SOPRANO SOLOIST	
6.	Water Sprites, caprice	Kunkel
7.	The Stars and Stripes Forever, march	Sousa
8.	The Honeysuckle and the Bee, coon song	Penn
	Encore: Dixie	Emmett
9.	Nymphalin, reverie	Sousa
	DOROTHY HOYLE, VIOLIN SOLOIST	
10.	Plantation Songs and Dances	Chambers

The Star Spangled Banner [repeated]

Note: Since there is not a program extant, the precise order shown above might not be entirely correct. From written accounts, however, including Sousa's own, it is known that all of the above selections were played. Possible others were played, since the program was reported to have been two hours in length. There was no mention of an interval in any of the reports.

Sources: Newspaper accounts in Sousa Band press book no. 14; *Marching Along*, pp. 221-23; "Keeping Step" in the *Saturday Evening Post*, 5 December 1925, p. 163

EVENING CONCERT, 24 NOVEMBER 1902
Rochester, New York, at Lyceum Theater

1.	Marche Slav	Tchaikowsky
	Encore: The Stars and Stripes Forever, march	Sousa
	Encore: Warbler's Serenade	Perry
2.	Love's Enchantment	Pryor
	Encore: The Honeysuckle and the Bee	Penn
	Encore: In the Deep Cellar	Fischer
	ARTHUR PRYOR, TROMBONE SOLOIST	
3.	Looking Upward, suite	Sousa
	I By the Light of the Polar Star	
	II Under the Southern Cross	
	III Mars and Venus	
	Encore: The Passing of Ragtime	Pryor
	Encore: El Capitan, march	Sousa
4.	Thou Brilliant Bird, from the Pearl of Brazil	David
	Encore: The Nightingale	Alabieff
	ESTELLE LIEBLING, SOPRANO SOLOIST	
5.	Kamenoi Ostrow, nocturne	Rubinstein
	Encore: Nearer, My God To Thee, hymn	Mason

* INTERVAL *

6.	In the Realm of the Dance, fantasie	Sousa
	Encore: The Philosophic Maid, from The Charlatan	Sousa
	Encore: A Bundle of Mischief	Ziehrer
	Encore: Bumblebee Song, from King Dodo	Luders
7.	(a) Country Dance	Nevin
	(b) Imperial Edward, march	Sousa
	Encore: The Man Behind the Gun, march	Sousa
	Encore: The Invincible Eagle, march	Sousa
	Encore: Hands Across the Sea, march	Sousa
8.	Souvenir de Sorrento	Papini
	Encore: Madrigal	Simonetti
	GRACE JENKINS, VIOLIN SOLOIST	
9.	Chase of the Lion, galop de concert	Kolling

Source: Sousa Band press book no. 19, p. 28 (*Rochester Herald*)

EVENING CONCERT, 27 JANUARY 1903
Southport, England, at Cambridge Hall

1.	Carneval Romaine: Overture	Berlioz
	Encore: Mexican Serenade	Wilson
	Encore: The Stars and Stripes Forever, march	Sousa
2.	Love's Enchantment	Pryor
	Encore: In the Deep Cellar	Fischer
	ARTHUR PRYOR, TROMBONE SOLOIST	
3.	Looking Upward, suite	Sousa
	I By the Light of the Polar Star	
	II Under the Southern Cross	
	III Mars and Venus	
	Encore: The Passing of Ragtime	Pryor
4.	Thou Brilliant Bird, from the Pearl of Brazil	David
	ESTELLE LIEBLING, SOPRANO SOLOIST	
5.	Kamenoi Ostrow, nocturne	Rubinstein
	Encore: Rose, Shamrock, and Thistle, fantasie	Sousa
	Encore: The Washington Post, march	Sousa

* INTERVAL *

6.	Danse Esotica	Mascagni
	Encore: The Philosophic Maid, from The Charlatan	Sousa
	Encore: A Bundle of Mischief	Ziehrer
7.	(a) Country Dance	Nevin
	(b) Imperial Edward, march	Sousa
	Encore: Imperial Edward, march [repeated]	Sousa
	Encore: Imperial Edward, march [repeated again]	Sousa
8.	Violin Concerto	Mendelssohn
	II Andante	
	III Allegro vivace	
	Encore: [unnamed]	
	MAUD POWELL, VIOLIN SOLOIST	
9.	Chase of the Lion, galop de concert	Kolling

Source: Sousa Band press book no. 15, p. 237 (*Southport Guardian*)

10:00 p.m. CONCERT, 31 JANUARY 1903
Command performance before King Edward VII
Windsor, England, at Windsor Castle

God Save the King (as the King and Queen entered the hall)

1.	El Capitan, collocation	Sousa
2.	Love's Enchantment	Pryor
	ARTHUR PRYOR, TROMBONE SOLOIST	
3.	Looking Upward, suite	Sousa
	I By the Light of the Polar Star	
	II Under the Southern Cross	
	III Mars and Venus	
4.	Thou Brilliant Bird, from the Pearl of Brazil	David
	ESTELLE LIEBLING, SOPRANO SOLOIST	
	Flute obbligato by Marshall P. Lufsky	
5.	Badinage Herbert	
6.	(a) In a Clock Store, Idyll	Orth
	(b) The Passing of Rag Time, caprice	Pryor
	(c) Imperial Edward, march	Sousa
7.	Zigeunerweisen	Sarasate
	MAUD POWELL, VIOLIN SOLOIST	
8.	In the Realm of the Dance, fantasie	Sousa
	Encore: The Washington Post, march	Sousa
	Encore: Hands Across the Sea, march	Sousa
	Encore: Way Down South, fantasie	Laurendeau
	Encore: The Stars and Stripes Forever, march	Sousa
	Encore: A Coon Band Contest, cakewalk	Pryor

The Star Spangled Banner

God Save the King

Source: Reconstructed from various clippings in Sousa Band press book no. 15, pp. 254-57

MATINEE CONCERT, 2 FEBRUARY 1903
Dublin, Ireland, at Opera House

1. William Tell: Overture — Rossini
   Encore: The Stars and Stripes Forever, march — Sousa

2. Thoughts of Love — Pryor
   Encore: In the Deep Cellar — Fischer
   ARTHUR PRYOR, TROMBONE SOLOIST

3. Maidens Three, suite — Sousa
   I   The Coquette
   II   The Summer Girl
   III The Dancing Girl, from The Bride Elect
   Encore: Coon Band Contest — Pryor
   Encore: The Washington Post, march — Sousa

4. Indian Bell Song, from Lakme — Delibes
   Encore: The Nightingale — Mollenhauer
   ESTELLE LIEBLING, SOPRANO SOLOIST

5. Largo, from New World Symphony — Dvorak
   Encore: Reminiscences of Ireland — Godfrey

* INTERVAL *

6. In the Realm of the Dance, fantasie — Sousa
   Encore: El Capitan, march — Sousa
   Encore: The Honeysuckle and the Bee — Penn
   Encore: King Cotton, march — Sousa

7. (a)   Siziletta, novelette Von Blon
   (b)   Imperial Edward, march — Sousa
   Encore: The Invincible Eagle, march — Sousa

8. Zigeunerweisen — Sarasate
   Encore: Fantasia on St. Patrick's Day — Vieuxtemps
   MAUD POWELL, VIOLIN SOLOIST

9. Plantation Songs and Dances — Chambers

Source: Sousa Band press book no. 15, p. 252 (*Constitution*)

MATINEE CONCERT, 20 FEBRUARY 1903
Middlesbrough, England, at Royal Theatre

1. Carneval Romaine: Overture — Berlioz
   Encore: The Stars and Stripes Forever, march — Sousa

2. Love's Enchantment — Pryor
   Encore: In the Deep Cellar — Fischer
   ARTHUR PRYOR, TROMBONE SOLOIST

3. Looking Upward, suite — Sousa
   I   By the Light of the Polar Star
   II   Under the Southern Cross
   III Mars and Venus
   Encore: Coon Band Contest — Pryor
   Encore: The Washington Post, march — Sousa

4. Thou Brilliant Bird, from the Pearl of Brazil — David
   ESTELLE LIEBLING, SOPRANO SOLOIST

5. Hungarian Rhapsody No. 2 — Liszt
   Encore: Rose, Shamrock, and Thistle, fantasie — Sousa

* INTERVAL *

6. Danse Esotica — Mascagni
   Encore: The Broken Melody — Van Biene
   Encore: A Bundle of Mischief — Ziehrer

7. (a)   Country Dance — Nevin
   (b)   Imperial Edward, march — Sousa
   Encore: El Capitan, march — Sousa

8. Violin Concerto — Mendelssohn
   II   Andante
   III Allegro vivace
   Encore: Nymphalin, reverie — Sousa
   MAUD POWELL, VIOLIN SOLOIST

9. Chase of the Lion, galop de concert — Kolling

Source: Sousa Band press book no. 20, p. 11 (*Stockton Herald*)

MATINEE CONCERT, 4 FEBRUARY 1903
Belfast, Ireland, at Ulster Hall

1. William Tell: Overture — Rossini
   Encore: Hands Across the Sea, march — Sousa

2. Thoughts of Love — Pryor
   Encore: In the Deep Cellar — Fischer
   ARTHUR PRYOR, TROMBONE SOLOIST

3. Maidens Three, suite — Sousa
   I   The Coquette
   II   The Summer Girl
   III The Dancing Girl, from The Bride Elect
   Encore: Coon Band Contest — Pryor
   Encore: The Washington Post, march — Sousa

4. Indian Bell Song, from Lakme — Delibes
   Encore: The Nightingale — Mollenhauer
   ESTELLE LIEBLING, SOPRANO SOLOIST
   Flute obbligato by Marshall P. Lufsky

5. Largo, from New World Symphony — Dvorak
   Encore: Reminiscences of Ireland — Godfrey

* INTERVAL *

6. In the Realm of the Dance, fantasie — Sousa
   Encore: The Philosophic Maid, from The Charlatan — Sousa
   Encore: A Bundle of Mischief — Ziehrer

7. (a)   Siziletta, novelette — Von Blon
   (b)   Imperial Edward, march — Sousa
   Encore: Imperial Edward, march [portion repeated] — Sousa

8. Zigeunerweisen — Sarasate
   Encore: Largo — Handel
   MAUD POWELL, VIOLIN SOLOIST

9. Plantation Songs and Dances — Chambers

Source: Sousa Band press book no. 15, p. 272 (*Belfast Evening Telegraph*)

MATINEE CONCERT, 4 MARCH 1903
Wigan, England, at Court Theatre

1. Carneval Romaine: Overture — Berlioz
   Encore: El Capitan, march — Sousa
   Encore: At a Georgia Camp Meeting — Mills

2. Love's Enchantment — Pryor
   Encore: In the Deep Cellar — Fischer
   ARTHUR PRYOR, TROMBONE SOLOIST

3. Maidens Three, suite — Sousa
   I   The Coquette
   II   The Summer Girl
   III The Dancing Girl, from The Bride Elect
   Encore: Coon Band Contest — Pryor
   Encore: The Washington Post, march — Sousa

4. Thou Brilliant Bird, from the Pearl of Brazil — David
   Encore: The Nightingale — Mollenhauer
   ESTELLE LIEBLING, SOPRANO SOLOIST

5. Hungarian Rhapsody No. 2 — Liszt
   Encore: Rose, Shamrock, and Thistle, fantasie — Sousa
   Encore: The Stars and Stripes Forever, march — Sousa

* INTERVAL *

6. (a)   Siziletta, novelette — Blon
   (b)   Imperial Edward, march — Sousa

7. Zigeunerweisen — Sarasate
   Encore: Fantasia on St. Patrick's Day — Vieuxtemps
   MAUD POWELL, VIOLIN SOLOIST

8. Prelude to Act III of Lohengrin — Wagner

   God Save the King

Source: Sousa Band press book no. 20, p. 22 (*Wigan Examiner*)

EVENING CONCERT, 25 MARCH 1903
Coventry, England, at Corn Exchange

1.	Carneval Romaine: Overture	Berlioz
	Encore: The Stars and Stripes Forever, march	Sousa
2.	Love's Enchantment	Pryor
	Encore: In the Deep Cellar	Fischer
	ARTHUR PRYOR, TROMBONE SOLOIST	
3.	Looking Upward, suite	Sousa
	I By the Light of the Polar Star	
	II Under the Southern Cross	
	III Mars and Venus	
	Encore: A Coon Band Contest, cakewalk	Pryor
4.	Thou Brilliant Bird, from the Pearl of Brazil	David
	ESTELLE LIEBLING, SOPRANO SOLOIST	
5.	Hungarian Rhapsody No. 2	Liszt
	Encore: The Washington Post, march	Sousa

INTERVAL

6.	Danse Esotica	Mascagni
	Encore: Mexican Serenade	Wilson
7.	(a) Country Dance	Nevin
	(b) Imperial Edward, march	Sousa
	Encore: El Capitan, march	Sousa
8.	Violin Concerto	Mendelssohn
	II Andante	
	III Allegro vivace	
	Encore: Fantasia on St. Patrick's Day	Vieuxtemps
	MAUD POWELL, VIOLIN SOLOIST	
9.	Chase of the Lion, galop de concert	Kolling

Source: Sousa Band press book no. 20, p. 56 (*Midland Daily Telegraph*)

MATINEE CONCERT, 1 APRIL 1903
Bristol, England, at Victoria Rooms

1.	William Tell: Overture	Rossini
	Encore: The Stars and Stripes Forever, march	Sousa
2.	Thoughts of Love	Pryor
	Encore: In the Deep Cellar	Fischer
	ARTHUR PRYOR, TROMBONE SOLOIST	
3.	Maidens Three, suite	Sousa
	I The Coquette	
	II The Summer Girl	
	III The Dancing Girl, from The Bride Elect	
	Encore: Coon Band Contest	Pryor
4.	Indian Bell Song, from Lakme	Delibes
	ESTELLE LIEBLING, SOPRANO SOLOIST	
5.	Largo, from "The New World" Symphony	Dvorak
	Encore: The Washington Post, march	Sousa

* INTERVAL *

6.	In the Realm of the Dance, fantasie	Sousa
	Encore: The Patient Egg, from Chris and the Wonderful Lamp	Sousa
7.	(a) Siziletta, novelette	Von Blon
	(b) Imperial Edward, march	Sousa
	Encore: El Capitan, march	Sousa
8.	Zigeunerweisen	Sarasate
	Encore: Largo	Handel
	MAUD POWELL, VIOLIN SOLOIST	
9.	Plantation Songs and Dances	Chambers

Source: Sousa Band press book no. 20, pp. 66-67 (*Bristol Times*)

MATINEE CONCERT, 8 APRIL 1903
Taunton, England, at Assembly Rooms

1.	Carneval Romaine: Overture	Berlioz
	Encore: The Stars and Stripes Forever, march	Sousa
2.	Love's Enchantment	Pryor
	Encore: In the Deep Cellar	Fischer
	ARTHUR PRYOR, TROMBONE SOLOIST	
3.	Maidens Three, suite	Sousa
	I The Coquette	
	II The Summer Girl	
	III The Dancing Girl, from The Bride Elect	
	Encore: Coon Band Contest	Pryor
4.	Thou Brilliant Bird, from the Pearl of Brazil	David
	Encore: Maid of the Meadow	Sousa
	ESTELLE LIEBLING, SOPRANO SOLOIST	
5.	Hungarian Rhapsody No. 2	Liszt
	Encore: The Washington Post, march	Sousa

* INTERVAL *

6.	(a) Siziletta, novelette	Blon
	(b) Imperial Edward, march	Sousa
	Encore: The Patient Egg, from Chris and the Wonderful Lamp	Sousa
7.	Zigeunerweisen	Sarasate
	Encore: Largo	Handel
	MAUD POWELL, VIOLIN SOLOIST	
8.	Prelude to Act III of Lohengrin	Wagner
	God Save the King	

Source: Sousa Band press book no. 20, p. 99 (*Somerset County Herald*)

EVENING CONCERT, 16 JUNE 1903
Windsor, England, at Royal Albert Institute

1.	William Tell: Overture	Rossini
	Encore: El Capitan, march	Sousa
2.	Love's Enchantment	Pryor
	Encore: The Sunflower and the Sun	Penn
	ARTHUR PRYOR, TROMBONE SOLOIST	
3.	Looking Upward, suite	Sousa
	I By the Light of the Polar Star	
	II Under the Southern Cross	
	III Mars and Venus	
	Encore: The Passing of Ragtime	Pryor
4.	Voices of Spring	Strauss
	Encore: Maid of the Meadow	Sousa
	ESTELLE LIEBLING, SOPRANO SOLOIST	
5.	Grand Scene, from Andrea Chenier	Giordano
	Encore: The Washington Post, march	Sousa

* INTERVAL *

6.	(a) Water Sprites, caprice	Kunkel
	(b) Imperial Edward, march	Sousa
	Encore: The Stars and Stripes Forever, march	Sousa
	Encore: Whistling Rufus	Mills
	Encore: Hands Across the Sea, march	Sousa
7.	Zigeunerweisen	Sarasate
	MAUD POWELL, VIOLIN SOLOIST	
	Encore: March of the Cameron Men	Pope
8.	Plantation Songs and Dances	Chambers
	God Save the King	

Source: Sousa Band press book no. 20, p. 192 (*Windsor Express*)

MATINEE CONCERT, 17 JUNE 1903
Aldershot, England, at Royal Theatre

1. William Tell: Overture — Rossini
   Encore: El Capitan, march — Sousa
2. Love's Enchantment — Pryor
   Encore: The Sunflower and the Sun — Penn
   ARTHUR PRYOR, TROMBONE SOLOIST
3. Looking Upward, suite — Sousa
   I   By the Light of the Polar Star
   II   Under the Southern Cross
   III   Mars and Venus
   Encore: The Passing of Ragtime — Pryor
4. Voices of Spring — Strauss
   Encore: The Philosophic Maid, from The Charlatan — Sousa
   ESTELLE LIEBLING, SOPRANO SOLOIST
5. Grand Scene, from Andrea Chenier — Giordano
   Encore: Rose, Thistle and Shamrock, fantasie — Sousa
   Encore: The Washington Post, march — Sousa

* INTERVAL *

6. (a)   Water Sprites, caprice — Kunkel
   (b)   Imperial Edward, march — Sousa
   Encore: Sextette, from The Bride Elect — Sousa
   MESSRS. KENNECKE, PRYOR, LYON, HELLE, MANTIA, AND WARDWELL
   Encore: The Stars and Stripes Forever, march — Sousa
   Encore: Bamboula, Negro Dance of Trinidad — Urich
7. Zigeunerweisen — Sarasate
   Encore: Fantasia on St. Patrick's Day — Vieuxtemps
   MAUD POWELL, VIOLIN SOLOIST
8. Plantation Songs and Dances — Chambers

   God Save the King

Source: Sousa Band press book no. 20, p. 192 (*Aldershot News*)

MATINEE CONCERT, 24 JUNE 1903
Sittingbourne, England, at Bowes Park

1. Overture based on Emperor's Hymn — Haydn
2. Walther's Farewell, from The Trumpeter of Sakkingen — Nessler
   FRANZ HELLE, FLUGELHORN SOLOIST
3. Looking Upward, suite — Sousa
   I   By the Light of the Polar Star
   II   Under the Southern Cross
   III   Mars and Venus
   Encore: The Passing of Ragtime — Pryor
4. Love's Enchantment — Pryor
   Encore: The Sunflower and the Sun — Penn
   ARTHUR PRYOR, TROMBONE SOLOIST
5. Grand Scene and Ensemble, from Andrea Chenier — Giordano
   Encore: The Washington Post, march — Sousa

* INTERVAL *

6. Scenes from El Capitan — Sousa
   Encore: Rose, Shamrock, and Thistle, fantasie — Sousa
7. (a)   Sextette, from The Bride Elect — Sousa
   MESSRS. KENNECKE, PRYOR, LYON, HELLE, MANTIA, AND WARDWELL
   (b)   Imperial Edward, march — Sousa
   Encore: The Stars and Stripes Forever, march — Sousa
8. American Fantasie — Moeremans
   Encore: Old Folks at Home — Foster
   JEAN H.B. MOEREMANS, SAXOPHONE SOLOIST
9. Plantation Songs and Dances — Chambers

   God Save the King

Source: Sousa Band press book no. 20, p. 200 (*East Kent Gazette*)

EVENING CONCERT, 19 JUNE 1903
Reading, England, at Royal County Theatre

1. Overture based on Haydn's Emperor's Hymn — Westmeyer
   Encore: King Cotton, march — Sousa
2. Thoughts of Love — Pryor
   Encore: The Sunflower and the Sun — Penn
   ARTHUR PRYOR, TROMBONE SOLOIST
3. Maidens Three, suite — Sousa
   I   The Coquette
   II   The Summer Girl
   III   The Dancing Girl, from The Bride Elect
   Encore: The Passing of Ragtime — Pryor
4. Voices of Spring — Strauss
   Encore: Stolen Wings — Willeby
   ESTELLE LIEBLING, SOPRANO SOLOIST
5. Grand Scene and Ensemble, from Andrea Chenier — Giordano
   Encore: The Washington Post, march — Sousa
   Encore: Rose, Shamrock, and Thistle, fantasie — Sousa

* INTERVAL *

6. El Capitan, march — Sousa
   Encore: Way Down South, fantasie — Laurendeau
7. (a)   Water Sprites, caprice — Kunkel
   (b)   Hands Across the Sea, march — Sousa
   Encore: The Stars and Stripes Forever, march — Sousa
   Encore: The Patient Egg, from Chris and the Wonderful Lamp — Sousa
8. Fantasia based on Gounod's Faust — Wieniawski
   Encore: Fantasia on St. Patrick's Day — Vieuxtemps
   MAUD POWELL, VIOLIN SOLOIST
9. Chase of the Lion, galop de concert — Kolling

Source: Sousa Band press book no. 20, p. 191 (unidentified Berkshire newspaper)

MATINEE CONCERT, 6 JULY 1903
Bristol, England, at Victoria Rooms

1. Mysora, overture — Wettgi
   Encore: El Capitan, march — Sousa
2. American Fantasia — Moeremans
   Encore: Old Folks at Home — Foster
   JEAN H.B. MOEREMANS, SAXOPHONE SOLOIST
3. In Foreign Lands, suite — Moszkowski
   I   Spain
   II   Germany
   III   Hungary
   Encore: Way Down South, fantasie — Laurendeau
   Encore: Manhattan Beach, march — Sousa
4. Indian Bell Song, from Lakme — Delibes
   ESTELLE LIEBLING, SOPRANO SOLOIST
5. Largo, from New World Symphony — Dvorak
   Encore: The Stars and Stripes Forever, march — Sousa

* INTERVAL *

6. Scenes from Chris and the Wonderful Lamp — Sousa
   Encore: The Patient Egg, from Chris and the Wonderful Lamp — Sousa
   Encore: The Washington Post, march — Sousa
7. (a)   Rococo, serenade — Helmund
   (b)   Imperial Edward, march — Sousa
   Encore: Jack Tar, march — Sousa
8. Rondo Capriccioso — Saint-Saens
   MAUD POWELL, VIOLIN SOLOIST
9. Prelude to Act III of Lohengrin — Wagner

Source: Sousa Band press book no. 20, p. 214 (*Bristol Times*)

EVENING CONCERT, 6 JULY 1903
Bristol, England, at Victoria Rooms

1.	Overture based on Haydn's Emperor's Hymn	Westmeyer
	Encore: The Liberty Bell, march	Sousa
2.	Cujus Animam, from Stabat Mater	Rossini
	Encore: The Sunflower and the Sun	Penn
	ARTHUR PRYOR, TROMBONE SOLOIST	
3.	Looking Upward, suite	Sousa
	I By the Light of the Polar Star	
	II Under the Southern Cross	
	III Mars and Venus	
	Encore: The Passing of Ragtime Pryor	
4.	Voices of Spring	Strauss
	Encore: Stolen Wings	Willeby
	ESTELLE LIEBLING, SOPRANO SOLOIST	
5.	Grand Scene and Ensemble, from Andrea Chenier	Giordano
	Encore: The Washington Post, march	Sousa

* INTERVAL *

6.	Scenes from El Capitan	Sousa
	Encore: The Patient Egg, from Chris and the Wonderful Lamp	Sousa
7.	(a) Water Sprites, caprice	Kunkel
	(b) Jack Tar, march Sousa	
	Encore: The Stars and Stripes Forever, march	Sousa
	Encore: The High School Cadets, march	Sousa
8.	Fantasia based on Gounod's Faust	Wieniawski
	Encore: Prelude (unaccompanied)	Fiorillo
	MAUD POWELL, VIOLIN SOLOIST	
9.	Theme, Variations, and Carnival Tune, from Scenes in Naples	Massenet

Source: Sousa Band press book no. 20, p. 214 (*Western Daily Press*)

MATINEE CONCERT, 14 JULY 1903
Douglas, Isle of Man, England, at The Palace

1.	*Tannhäuser:* Overture	Wagner
	Encore: El Capitan, march	Sousa
2.	Thoughts of Love	Pryor
	Encore: The Sunflower and the Sun	Penn
	ARTHUR PRYOR, TROMBONE SOLOIST	
3.	Maidens Three, suite	Sousa
	I The Coquette	
	II The Summer Girl	
	III The Dancing Girl, from The Bride Elect	
	Encore: The Passing of Ragtime	Pryor
4.	Voices of Spring	Strauss
	ESTELLE LIEBLING, SOPRANO SOLOIST	
5.	Gralsriter, from Parsifal	Wagner
	Encore: Rose, Shamrock, and Thistle, fantasie	Sousa

* INTERVAL *

6.	Scenes from Chris and the Wonderful Lamp	Sousa
7.	(a) Rococo, serenade	Helmund
	(b) The Stars and Stripes Forever, march	Sousa
	Encore: The Washington Post, march	Sousa
8.	Fantasia based on Gounod's Faust	Wieniawski
	MAUD POWELL, VIOLIN SOLOIST	
9.	Prelude to Act III of Lohengrin	Wagner

God Save the King

Source: Sousa Band press book no. 20, p. 207 (*The Isle of Man Times*)

EVENING CONCERT, 14 JULY 1903
Douglas, Isle of Man, England, at The Palace

1.	Overture based on Haydn's Emperor's Hymn	Westmeyer
	Encore: Hands Across the Sea, march	Sousa
2.	Love's Enchantment	Pryor
	Encore: The Honeysuckle and the Bee	Penn
	ARTHUR PRYOR, TROMBONE SOLOIST	
3.	Looking Upward, suite	Sousa
	I By the Light of the Polar Star	
	II Under the Southern Cross	
	III Mars and Venus	
	Encore: Drum solo from III, Mars and Venus	
4.	Thou Brilliant Bird, from the Pearl of Brazil	David
	Encore: Maid of the Meadow	Sousa
	ESTELLE LIEBLING, SOPRANO SOLOIST	
5.	Grand Scene and Ensemble, from Andrea Chenier	Giordono
	Encore: The Washington Post, march	Sousa

* INTERVAL *

6.	Scenes from El Capitan	Sousa
7.	(a) Water Sprites, caprice	Kunkel
	(b) Jack Tar, march Sousa	
	Encore: The Stars and Stripes Forever, march	Sousa
	Encore: The High School Cadets, march	Sousa
8.	Violin Concerto	Mendelssohn
	II Andante	
	III Allegro vivace	
	MAUD POWELL, VIOLIN SOLOIST	
9.	Plantation Songs and Dances	Chambers

God Save the King

Source: Sousa Band press book no. 20, p. 207 (*The Isle of Man Times*)

MATINEE CONCERT, 15 JULY 1903
Douglas, Isle of Man, England, at The Palace

1.	William Tell: Overture	Rossini
	Encore: El Capitan, march	Sousa
2.	American Fantasie	Moeremans
	Encore: Old Folks at Home	Foster
	JEAN H.B. MOEREMANS, SAXOPHONE SOLOIST	
3.	In Foreign Lands, suite	Moszkowski
	I Spain	
	II Germany	
	III Hungary	
	Encore: The Passing of Ragtime	Pryor
4.	Mad Scene, from Hamlet	Thomas
	Encore: Stolen Wings	Willeby
	ESTELLE LIEBLING, SOPRANO SOLOIST	
5.	Toccata in E-flat	Bartlett
	Encore: The Washington Post, march	Sousa

* INTERVAL *

6.	In the Realm of the Dance, fantasie	Sousa
	Encore: Sextette, from The Bride Elect	Sousa
	Featuring six brass players	
	Encore: The Stars and Stripes Forever, march	Sousa
7.	(a) Country Dance	Nevin
	(b) Imperial Edward, march	Sousa
8.	Zigeunerweisen	Sarasate
	Encore: Fantasia on St. Patrick's Day	Vieuxtemps
	MAUD POWELL, VIOLIN SOLOIST	
9.	Chase of the Lion, galop de concert	Kolling

God Save the King

Source: Sousa Band press book no. 20, p. 207 (*The Isle of Man Times*)

EVENING CONCERT, 15 JULY 1903
Douglas, Isle of Man, England, at The Palace

1.	Carneval Romaine: Overture	Berlioz
	Encore: El Capitan, march	Sousa
2.	The Patriot	Pryor
	Encore: The Sunflower and the Sun	Penn
	ARTHUR PRYOR, TROMBONE SOLOIST	
3.	Three Quotations, suite	Sousa
	I The King of France	
	II I, Too, Was Born in Arcadia	
	III In Darkest Africa	
	Encore: The Washington Post, march	Sousa
4.	Indian Bell Song, from Lakme	Delibes
	ESTELLE LIEBLING, SOPRANO SOLOIST	
5.	Largo, from New World Symphony	Dvorak
	Encore: Rose, Shamrock, and Thistle, fantasie	Sousa

* INTERVAL *

6.	Hungarian Rhapsody No. 2	Liszt
7.	(a) Salut d'Amour	Elgar
	Encore: The Patient Egg, from Chris and the Wonderful Lamp	Sousa
	(b) Jack Tar, march	Sousa
	Encore: The Stars and Stripes Forever, march	Sousa
	Encore: The Man Behind the Gun, march	Sousa
8.	Rondo Capriccioso	Saint-Saens
	Encore: Largo	Handel
	MAUD POWELL, VIOLIN SOLOIST	
9.	Theme, Variations, and Carnival Tune, from Scenes in Naples	Massenet

God Save the King

Source: Sousa Band press book no. 20, p. 207 (*The Isle of Man Times*)

MATINEE CONCERT, 16 JULY 1903
Douglas, Isle of Man, England, at The Palace

1.	Festival Overture	Lassen
	Encore: El Capitan, march	Sousa
2.	Walther's Farewell, from The Trumpeter of Sakkingen	Nessler
	Encore: Serenade	Schubert
	FRANZ HELLE, FLUGELHORN SOLOIST	
3.	The Merchant of Venice, incidental music	Sullivan
	I Introduction and Bouree	
	II Grotesque Dance	
	III Melodrama and Finale	
4.	Maid of the Meadow, song	Sousa
	Encore: The Nightingale	Mollenhauer
	ESTELLE LIEBLING, SOPRANO SOLOIST	
5.	Sheridan's Ride, descriptive piece	Sousa
	I Waiting for the Bugle	
	II The Attack	
	III The Death of Thoburn	
	IV Coming of Sheridan	
	V Apotheosis	
	Encore: The Washington Post, march	Sousa

* INTERVAL *

6.	Danse Esotica	Mascagni
7.	(a) In a Clock Store, Idyll	Orth
	(b) Imperial Edward, march	Sousa
	Encore: The Stars and Stripes Forever, march	Sousa
	Encore: Jack Tar, march	Sousa
8.	Othello, fantasie	Ernst
	Encore: Study	Forillo
	MAUD POWELL, VIOLIN SOLOIST	
9.	Airs from The Bride Elect	Sousa

God Save the King

Source: Sousa Band press book no. 20, p. 207 (*The Isle of Man Times*)

EVENING CONCERT, 16 JULY 1903
Douglas, Isle of Man, England, at The Palace

1.	Mysora, overture	Wettgi
	Encore: El Capitan, march	Sousa
2.	Love's Enchantment	Pryor
	Encore: The Honeysuckle and the Bee	Penn
	ARTHUR PRYOR, TROMBONE SOLOIST	
3.	The Last Days of Pompeii, suite	Sousa
	I In the House of Burbo and Stratonice	
	II Nydia the Blind Girl	
	III The Destruction of Pompeii and Nydia's Death	
	Encore: The Washington Post, march	Sousa
4.	Sweet Bird, from L'Allegro il Penseroso	Handel
	Encore: Maid of the Meadow	Sousa
	ESTELLE LIEBLING, SOPRANO SOLOIST	
5.	Marche Slav	Tchaikowsky
	Encore: Rose, Shamrock, and Thistle, fantasie	Sousa

* INTERVAL *

6.	Incidental Music to Henry VIII	Sullivan
	Encore: Way Down South, fantasie Laurendeau	
	Encore: King Cotton, march	Sousa
7.	(a) Princess May Blossoms, novelette Lehmann	
	(b) Jack Tar, march	Sousa
	Encore: The Stars and Stripes Forever, march	Sousa
	Encore: The Passing of Ragtime	Pryor
8.	Zigeunerweisen	Sarasate
	Encore: Fantasia on St. Patrick's Day	Vieuxtemps
	MAUD POWELL, VIOLIN SOLOIST	
9.	Tarantella del Belphegor	Albert

God Save the King

Source: Sousa Band press book no. 20, p. 207 (*The Isle of Man Times*)

EVENING CONCERT, 15 JANUARY 1905
Southend, England, at The Kursaal

1.	The Vikings, overture	Hartman
	Encore: Hands Across the Sea, march	Sousa
2.	Sounds from the Hudson	Clarke
	Encore: The Rosary	Nevin
	HERBERT L. CLARKE, CORNET SOLOIST	
3.	At the King's Court, suite	Sousa
	I Her Ladyship the Countess	
	II Her Grace the Duchess	
	III Her Majesty the Queen	
	Encore: Dixie	Emmett
	Encore: El Capitan, march	Sousa
4.	Nightingale Song, from The Marriage of Jeanette	Massé
	Encore: Will You Love When the Lilies Are Dead?, from The Charlatan	Sousa
	ESTELLE LIEBLING, SOPRANO SOLOIST	
5.	Sunrise, from Iris	Mascagni
	Encore: The Washington Post, march	Sousa

* INTERVAL *

6.	American Character Sketches	Kroeger
	I The Gamia	
	II An Indian Lament	
	III Voodoo Night Scene	
	IV The Dancing Darkey	
	Encore: Bedilia, from The Orchid	Monckton
7.	(a) Sevilliana, Scene Espagnol	Elgar
	(b) The Diplomat, march	Sousa
	Encore: The Stars and Stripes Forever, march	Sousa
	Encore: Viens Poupoule	Gauwin
8.	Rondo Capriccioso	Saint-Saens
	MAUD POWELL, VIOLIN SOLOIST	
9.	The Merry Wives of Windsor: Overture	Nicolai

The Star Spangled Banner

God Save the King

Source: Sousa Band press book no. 22, p. 114 (*Southend Echo*)

EVENING CONCERT, 27 JANUARY 1905
Salisbury, England, at County Hall

1.	Maximillian Robespierre, tone poem	Litolff
	Encore: El Capitan, march	Sousa
	Encore: Ramona	Johnson
2.	Sounds from the Hudson	Clarke
	Encore: Ah, Cupid, from Prince Ananias	Herbert
	HERBERT L. CLARKE, CORNET SOLOIST	
3.	At the King's Court, suite	Sousa
	I Her Ladyship the Countess	
	II Her Grace the Duchess	
	III Her Majesty the Queen	
	Encore: Dixie	Emmett
	Encore: The Invincible Eagle, march	Sousa
4.	Nightingale Song, from The Marriage of Jeanette	Massé
	Encore: Will You Love When the Lilies Are Dead?, from	Sousa
	The Charlatan	
	ESTELLE LIEBLING, SOPRANO SOLOIST	
5.	Sunrise, from Iris	Mascagni
	Encore: The Washington Post, march	Sousa
	* INTERVAL *	
6.	American Character Sketches	Kroeger
	I The Gamia	
	II An Indian Lament	
	III Voodoo Night Scene	
	IV The Dancing Darkey	
	Encore: Bedilia, from The Orchid Monckton	
7.	(a) Sevilliana, Scene Espagnol	Elgar
	(b) The Diplomat, march	Sousa
	Encore: The Stars and Stripes Forever, march	Sousa
	Encore: Let's Be Lively	Myddleton
8.	Fantasia based on Gounod's Faust	Wieniawski
	Encore: The Swan, from Carnival of the Animals	Saint-Saens
	MAUD POWELL, VIOLIN SOLOIST	
9.	The Merry Wives of Windsor: Overture	Nicolai

Source: Sousa Band press book no. 20, p. 263 (*Salisbury Journal*)

EVENING CONCERT, 6 MARCH 1905
Huddersfield, England, at Town Hall

1.	The Vikings, overture	Hartman
	Encore: El Capitan, march	Sousa
2.	Sounds from the Hudson	Clarke
	Encore: Ah, Cupid, from Prince Ananias	Herbert
	HERBERT L. CLARKE, CORNET SOLOIST	
3.	At the King's Court, suite	Sousa
	I Her Ladyship the Countess	
	II Her Grace the Duchess	
	III Her Majesty the Queen	
	Encore: Dixie	Emmett
	Encore: Imperial Edward, march	Sousa
4.	Nightingale Song, from The Marriage of Jeanette	Massé
	Encore: Will You Love When the Lilies Are Dead?, from	Sousa
	The Charlatan	
	ESTELLE LIEBLING, SOPRANO SOLOIST	
5.	Sunrise, from Iris	Mascagni
	Encore: The Washington Post, march	Sousa
	* INTERVAL *	
6.	American Character Sketches	Kroeger
	I The Gamia	
	II An Indian Lament	
	III Voodoo Night Scene	
	IV The Dancing Darkey	
	Encore: Blue Bell	Morse
7.	(a) Sevilliana, Scene Espagnol	Elgar
	(b) The Diplomat, march	Sousa
	Encore: The Stars and Stripes Forever, march	Sousa
	Encore: Manhattan Beach, march	Sousa
8.	Rondo Capriccioso	Saint-Saens
	Encore: At the Brook	De Boisdeffre
	MAUD POWELL, VIOLIN SOLOIST	
9.	The Merry Wives of Windsor: Overture	Nicolai
	God Save the King	

Source: Sousa Band press book no. 22, p. 35 (*Huddersfield Daily Examiner*)

MATINEE CONCERT, 6 APRIL 1905
Leamington, England, at Winter Hall

1.	Les Preludes, symphonic poem	Liszt
	Encore: El Capitan, march	Sousa
2.	Fantasie Pastorale	Singelee
	JEAN H.B. MOEREMANS, SAXOPHONE SOLOIST	
3.	Looking Upward, suite	Sousa
	I By the Light of the Polar Star	
	II Under the Southern Cross	
	III Mars and Venus	
	Encore: Dixie	Emmett
4.	Isabella's Air, from Pré aux Clercs	Herold
	Encore: Will You Love When the Lilies Are Dead?, from	Sousa
	The Charlatan	
	ESTELLE LIEBLING, SOPRANO SOLOIST	
5.	Invitation a la Valse	Weber
	Encore: The Washington Post, march	Sousa
	* INTERVAL *	
6.	Episodes Nevin	
	I At Fountainbleau	
	II A June Night in Washington	
	Encore: Blue Bell	Morse
7.	(a) Parade of the Dwarfs	Grieg
	(b) The Diplomat, march	Sousa
	Encore: The Stars and Stripes Forever, march	Sousa
8.	Othello, fantasie	Ernst
	MAUD POWELL, VIOLIN SOLOIST	
9.	Hungarian Rhapsody No. 14	Liszt
	The Star Spangled Banner	
	God Save the King	

Source: Sousa Band press book no. 22, p. 83 (*Leamington Courier*)

EVENING CONCERT, 6 APRIL 1905
Market Harborough, England, at Assembly Room

1.	The Vikings, overture	Hartman
	Encore: El Capitan, march	Sousa
2.	Sounds from the Hudson	Clarke
	HERBERT L. CLARKE, CORNET SOLOIST	
3.	At the King's Court, suite	Sousa
	I Her Ladyship the Countess	
	II Her Grace the Duchess	
	III Her Majesty the Queen	
	Encore: Dixie	Emmett
4.	Nightingale Song, from The Marriage of Jeanette	Massé
	Encore: Will You Love When the Lilies Are Dead?, from	Sousa
	The Charlatan	
	ESTELLE LIEBLING, SOPRANO SOLOIST	
5.	Sunrise, from Iris	Mascagni
	Encore: The Washington Post, march	Sousa
	* INTERVAL *	
6.	American Character Sketches	Kroeger
	I The Gamia	
	II An Indian Lament	
	III Voodoo Night Scene	
	IV The Dancing Darkey	
	Encore: Blue Bell	Morse
7.	(a) Sevilliana, Scene Espagnol	Elgar
	(b) The Diplomat, march	Sousa
	Encore: Hands Across the Sea, march Sousa	
8.	Rondo Capriccioso	Saint-Saens
	Encore: [unnamed]	
	MAUD POWELL, VIOLIN SOLOIST	
9.	The Merry Wives of Windsor: Overture	Nicolai
	God Save the King	

Source: Sousa Band press book no. 22, p. 83 (*Midland Mail*)

MATINEE CONCERT, 14 APRIL 1905
Southhampton, England, at Philharmonic Hall

1. My Jubilee, from Symphonic Sketches — Chadwick
   Encore: El Capitan, march — Sousa

2. Kinloch o' Kinloch — Oscar
   Encore: Through the Air — Damm
   MARSHALL P. LUFSKY, PICCOLO SOLOIST

3. The Last Days of Pompeii, suite — Sousa
   I In the House of Burbo and Stratonice
   II Nydia the Blind Girl
   III The Destruction of Pompeii and Nydia's Death
   Encore: Dixie — Emmett

4. Theme and Variations — Proche
   Encore: Annie Laurie — Traditional
   ESTELLE LIEBLING, SOPRANO SOLOIST

5. Excerpts from Act III, Manon Lescaut — Puccini
   Encore: The Washington Post, march — Sousa

* INTERVAL *

6. The Musical Critic's Dream — Dix
   Encore: Blue Bell — Morse

7. (a) La Castagnette — Kitten
   (b) The Diplomat, march — Sousa
   Encore: The Stars and Stripes Forever, march — Sousa
   Encore: Manhattan Beach, march — Sousa

8. Rondo Capriccioso — Saint-Saens
   Encore: Air — Bach
   MAUD POWELL, VIOLIN SOLOIST

9. Polonaise No. 2 — Liszt

God Save the King

Source: Sousa Band press book no. 22, p. 97 (*Southhampton Independent*)

MATINEE CONCERT, 22 APRIL 1905
Brighton, England, at Brighton Dome

1. Prelude to Act III of Lohengrin — Wagner
   Encore: King Cotton, march — Sousa

2. Walther's Farewell, from The Trumpeter of Sakkingen — Nessler
   Encore: Serenade — Gounod
   FRANZ HELLE, FLUGELHORN SOLOIST

3. Maidens Three, suite — Sousa
   I The Coquette
   II The Summer Girl
   III The Dancing Girl, from The Bride Elect
   Encore: Dixie — Emmett

4. Tyrolean Air and Variations — Proche
   Encore: Indian Bell Song, from Lakme — Delibes
   ESTELLE LIEBLING, SOPRANO SOLOIST

5. Love Scene, from Feuresnoth — Strauss
   Encore: El Capitan, march — Sousa

* INTERVAL *

6. The Musical Critic's Dream — Dix
   Encore: Blue Bell — Morse
   Encore: Molly and I and the Baby — Kennedy

7. (a) Pan Pastorale, idyll — Godard
   (b) The Diplomat, march — Sousa
   Encore: The Stars and Stripes Forever, march — Sousa
   Encore: Manhattan Beach, march — Sousa

8. Andante Cantabile — Cui
   Encore: Elfin Dance — Popper
   PEARL EVELYN BRYER, CELLO SOLOIST

9. Raymond; or The Secret of the Queen: Overture — Thomas

God Save the King

Source: Sousa Band press book no. 22, p. 110 (*Brighton Daily News*)

EVENING CONCERT, 1 MAY 1905
Gravesend, England, at Public Hall

1. Les Preludes, symphonic poem — Liszt
   Encore: The High School Cadets, march — Sousa

2. Sounds from the Hudson — Clarke
   Encore: The Rosary — Nevin
   HERBERT L. CLARKE, CORNET SOLOIST

3. At the King's Court, suite — Sousa
   I Her Ladyship the Countess
   II Her Grace the Duchess
   III Her Majesty the Queen
   Encore: Dixie — Emmett
   Encore: The Washington Post, march — Sousa

4. Isabella's Air, from Pré aux Clercs — Herold
   Encore: Will You Love When the Lilies Are Dead?, from The Charlatan — Sousa
   ESTELLE LIEBLING, SOPRANO SOLOIST

5. Mars and Venus, from Looking Upward — Sousa
   Encore: The Liberty Bell, march — Sousa

* INTERVAL *

6. Themes from Rhapsody Espagnol, waltz — Waldteufel
   Encore: Bedilia, from The Orchid — Monckton

7. (a) Rondo d'Amour, idyl — Westerhout
   (b) The Diplomat, march — Sousa
   Encore: The Stars and Stripes Forever, march — Sousa
   Encore: El Capitan, march — Sousa

8. (a) The Swan, from Carnival of the Animals — Saint-Saens
   (b) Scherzo — Von Goens
   PEARL EVELYN BRYER, CELLO SOLOIST

9. Prelude to Act III of Lohengrin — Wagner

God Save the King

Source: Sousa Band press book no. 23, p. 6 (*Gravesend Northfleet Standard*)

EVENING CONCERT, 3 MAY 1905
Bromley, England, at Lyric Theatre

1. Les Preludes, symphonic pocm — Liszt
   Encore: El Capitan, march — Sousa

2. Sounds from the Hudson — Clarke
   Encore: Killarney — Balfe
   HERBERT L. CLARKE, CORNET SOLOIST

3. At the King's Court, suite — Sousa
   I Her Ladyship the Countess
   II Her Grace the Duchess
   III Her Majesty the Queen
   Encore: Dixie — Emmett

4. Isabella's Air, from Pré aux Clercs — Herold
   Encore: Will You Love When the Lilies Are Dead?, from The Charlatan — Sousa
   ESTELLE LIEBLING, SOPRANO SOLOIST

5. Mars and Venus, from Looking Upward — Sousa
   Encore: The Washington Post, march — Sousa

* INTERVAL *

6. Themes from Rhapsody Espagnol, waltz — Waldteufel
   Encore: Bedilia, from The Orchid Monckton

7. (a) Rondo d'Amour, idyl — Westerhout
   (b) The Diplomat, march — Sousa
   Encore: The Stars and Stripes Forever, march — Sousa
   Encore: Manhattan Beach, march — Sousa

8. (a) The Swan, from Carnival of the Animals — Saint-Saens
   (b) Scherzo — Von Goens
   Encore: Nymphalin, reverie — Sousa
   PEARL EVELYN BRYER, CELLO SOLOIST

9. Prelude to Act III of Lohengrin — Wagner

God Save the King

Source: Sousa Band press book no. 23, p. 9 (*Bromley Telegraph*)

EVENING CONCERT, 26 SEPTEMBER 1905
Sterling, Illinois, at Academy of Music

1. Picture in a Dream — Lumbye
   Encore: El Capitan, march — Sousa
   Encore: Ramona Johnson

2. La Veta, caprice — Clarke
   Encore: The Rosary — Nevin
   HERBERT L. CLARKE, CORNET SOLOIST

3. At the King's Court, suite — Sousa
   I   Her Ladyship the Countess
   II   Her Grace the Duchess
   III Her Majesty the Queen
   Encore: Dixie — Emmett

4. Polonaise, from Mignon — Thomas
   Encore: The Card Song, from The Bride Elect — Sousa
   ELIZABETH SCHILLER, SOPRANO SOLOIST

5. Welsh Rhapsody — German
   Encore: Sextette, from Lucia di Lammermoor — Donizetti
   Featuring six brass players

* INTERVAL *

6. Vienna Darlings, waltz — Ziehrer
   Encore: Bedilia, from The Orchid — Monckton
   Encore: The Mouse and the Clock — Whitney

7. (a) The Gypsy, air de ballet — Ganne
   (b) The Diplomat, march — Sousa
   Encore: The Stars and Stripes Forever, march — Sousa
   Encore: Manhattan Beach, march — Sousa

8. Hungarian Rhapsody — Hausa
   Encore: Madrigal — Simonetti
   JESSIE STRAUS, VIOLIN SOLOIST

9. Ride of the Valkyries, from Die Walküre — Wagner

Source: Sousa Band press book no. 24, p. 17 (*Sterling Daily Standard*)

MATINEE CONCERT, 16 JANUARY 1906
Mauch Chunk, Pennsylvania, at Opera House

1. Oberon: Overture — Weber
   Encore: El Capitan, march — Sousa

2. Bride of the Waves Clarke
   HERBERT L. CLARKE, CORNET SOLOIST
   Encore: Sextette, from Lucia di Lammermoor — Donizetti
   Clarke with five other brass players

3. At the King's Court, suite — Sousa
   I   Her Ladyship the Countess
   II   Her Grace the Duchess
   III Her Majesty the Queen
   Encore: Dixie — Emmett

4. The Card Song, from The Bride Elect — Sousa
   Encore: Love, Light of My Heart, from The Bride Elect — Sousa
   ELIZABETH SCHILLER, SOPRANO SOLOIST

5. Welsh Rhapsody — German
   Encore: Hands Across the Sea, march — Sousa

* INTERVAL *

6. Vienna Darlings, waltz — Ziehrer
   Encore: Everybody Works But Father, humoresque — Bellstedt
   Encore: The Mouse and the Clock — Whitney

7. (a) The Gypsy, air de ballet — Ganne
   (b) The Diplomat, march — Sousa
   Encore: The Stars and Stripes Forever, march — Sousa

8. Caprice Slavonic — Geloso
   Encore: Serenade — Schubert
   JEANETTE POWERS, VIOLIN SOLOIST

9. Ride of the Valkyries, from Die Walküre — Wagner

Source: Sousa Band press book no. 25, p. 26 (*Daily News*)

EVENING CONCERT, 23 JANUARY 1906
Norfolk, Virginia, at Academy of Music

1. Oberon: Overture — Weber
   Encore: El Capitan, march — Sousa
   Encore: Gleaming Star — Hager

2. Bride of the Waves — Clarke
   HERBERT L. CLARKE, CORNET SOLOIST
   Encore: Sextette, from Lucia di Lammermoor — Donizetti
   Clarke with five other brass players

3. At the King's Court, suite — Sousa
   I   Her Ladyship the Countess
   II   Her Grace the Duchess
   III Her Majesty the Queen
   Encore: Dixie — Emmett
   Encore: Hands Across the Sea, march — Sousa

4. The Card Song, from The Bride Elect — Sousa
   Encore: Love, Light of My Heart, from The Bride Elect — Sousa
   ELIZABETH SCHILLER, SOPRANO SOLOIST

5. Welsh Rhapsody — German
   Encore: The High School Cadets, march — Sousa

* INTERVAL *

6. Vienna Darlings, waltz — Ziehrer
   Encore: Everybody Works But Father, humoresque — Bellstedt
   Encore: The Mouse and the Clock — Whitney

7. (a) The Gypsy, air de ballet — Ganne
   (b) The Diplomat, march — Sousa
   Encore: The Stars and Stripes Forever, march — Sousa
   Encore: Manhattan Beach, march — Sousa

8. Violin Concerto — Mendelssohn
   II   Andante
   III Allegro vivace
   Encore: Serenade — Schubert
   Encore: Zigeunerweisen — Sarasate
   JEANETTE POWERS, VIOLIN SOLOIST

9. Ride of the Valkyries, from Die Walküre — Wagner

Source: Sousa Band press book no. 25, p. 38 (*Norfolk Landmark*)

EVENING CONCERT, 25 JANUARY 1906
Greensboro, North Carolina, at Grand Opera House

1. Coronation March — Tchaikowsky
   Encore: El Capitan, march — Sousa

2. Acreo — Zimmerman
   LEO ZIMMERMAN, TROMBONE SOLOIST
   Encore: Sextette, from Lucia di Lammermoor — Donizetti
   Zimmerman with five other brass players

3. The Last Days of Pompeii, suite — Sousa
   I   In the House of Burbo and Stratonice
   II   Nydia the Blind Girl
   III The Destruction of Pompeii and Nydia's Death
   Encore: Dixie — Emmett
   Encore: Hands Across the Sea, march — Sousa

4. Aria, from Ernani — Verdi
   Encore: Love, Light of My Heart, from The Bride Elect — Sousa
   ELIZABETH SCHILLER, SOPRANO SOLOIST

5. Excerpts from La Russea — Luigini
   Encore: King Cotton, march Sousa

* INTERVAL *

6. The Band Came Back, humoresque — Sousa
   Encore: Everybody Works But Father, humoresque — Bellstedt
   Encore: The Mouse and the Clock — Whitney

7. (a) Scaramouche, pantomime — Chaminade
   (b) Semper Fidelis, march — Sousa
   Encore: The Stars and Stripes Forever, march — Sousa

8. Violin Concerto — Mendelssohn
   II   Andante
   III Allegro vivace
   Encore: Serenade — Schubert
   Encore: [unnamed]
   JEANETTE POWERS, VIOLIN SOLOIST

9. Rákóczy March, from The Damnation of Faust — Berlioz

Source: Sousa Band press book no. 25, p. 44 (*Greensboro News*)

EVENING CONCERT, 30 JANUARY 1906
Chattanooga, Tennessee, at Chattanooga Opera House

1.	Oberon: Overture	Weber
	Encore: El Capitan, march	Sousa
	Encore: Gleaming Star	Hager
2.	Bride of the Waves	Clarke
	HERBERT L. CLARKE, CORNET SOLOIST	
	Encore: Sextette, from Lucia di Lammermoor	Donizetti
	Clarke with five other brass players	
3.	At the King's Court, suite	Sousa
	I Her Ladyship the Countess	
	II Her Grace the Duchess	
	III Her Majesty the Queen	
	Encore: Dixie	Emmett
	Encore: The Man Behind the Gun, march	Sousa
4.	The Card Song, from The Bride Elect	Sousa
	Encore: Love, Light of My Heart, from The Bride Elect	Sousa
	ELIZABETH SCHILLER, SOPRANO SOLOIST	
5.	Welsh Rhapsody	German
	Encore: King Cotton, march	Sousa

* INTERVAL *

6.	Vienna Darlings, waltz	Ziehrer
	Encore: Everybody Works But Father, humoresque	Bellstedt
	Encore: The Mouse and the Clock	Whitney
7.	(a) The Gypsy, air de ballet	Ganne
	(b) The Diplomat, march	Sousa
	Encore: The Stars and Stripes Forever, march	Sousa
	Encore: Hands Across the Sea, march	Sousa
8.	Violin Concerto	Mendelssohn
	II Andante	
	III Allegro vivace	
	Encore: Serenade	Schubert
	Encore: [unnamed]	
	JEANETTE POWERS, VIOLIN SOLOIST	
9.	Ride of the Valkyries, from Die Walküre	Wagner

Source: Sousa Band press book no. 21, p. 83 (*Chattanooga Times*)

EVENING CONCERT, 2 MARCH 1906
Hopkinsville, Kentucky, at Tabernacle

1.	Oberon: Overture	Weber
	Encore: El Capitan, march	Sousa
2.	Bride of the Waves	Clarke
	HERBERT L. CLARKE, CORNET SOLOIST	
	Encore: Sextette, from Lucia di Lammermoor	Donizetti
	Clarke with five other brass players	
3.	Looking Upward, suite	Sousa
	I By the Light of the Polar Star	
	II Under the Southern Cross	
	III Mars and Venus	
	Encore: Dixie	Emmett
4.	The Card Song, from The Bride Elect	Sousa
	Encore: Love, Light of My Heart, from The Bride Elect	Sousa
	ELIZABETH SCHILLER, SOPRANO SOLOIST	
5.	Welsh Rhapsody	German
	Encore: King Cotton, march	Sousa

* INTERVAL *

6.	Vienna Darlings, waltz	Ziehrer
	Encore: Everybody Works But Father, humoresque	Bellstedt
	Encore: I Don't Know Where I'm Goin', But I'm On My Way	Bren
	Encore: The Mouse and the Clock	Whitney
7.	(a) The Gypsy, air de ballet	Ganne
	(b) The Diplomat, march	Sousa
	Encore: The Stars and Stripes Forever, march	Sousa
	Encore: The Washington Post, march	Sousa
8.	Violin Concerto	Mendelssohn
	II Andante	
	III Allegro vivace	
	Encore: Serenade	Schubert
	JEANETTE POWERS, VIOLIN SOLOIST	
9.	Ride of the Valkyries, from Die Walküre	Wagner
	The Star Spangled Banner	

Source: Sousa Band press book no. 25, pp. 12-13 (*Hopkinsville New Era*)

MATINEE CONCERT, 7 MARCH 1906
Jacksonvile, Illinois, at Grand Opera House

1.	William Tell: Overture	Rossini
	Encore: El Capitan, march	Sousa
2.	Bride of the Waves	Clarke
	HERBERT L. CLARKE, CORNET SOLOIST	
	Encore: Sextette, from Lucia di Lammermoor	Donizetti
	Clarke with five other brass players	
3.	Looking Upward, suite	Sousa
	I By the Light of the Polar Star	
	II Under the Southern Cross	
	III Mars and Venus	
	Encore: Dixie	Emmett
4.	The Card Song, from The Bride Elect	Sousa
	Encore: Love, Light of My Heart, from The Bride Elect	Sousa
	ELIZABETH SCHILLER, SOPRANO SOLOIST	
5.	Songs of Grace and Songs of Glory, fantasie	Sousa
	Encore: Hands Across the Sea, march	Sousa

* INTERVAL *

6.	Vienna Darlings, waltz	Ziehrer
	Encore: Everybody Works But Father, humoresque	Bellstedt
	Encore: I Don't Know Where I'm Goin', But I'm On My Way	Bren
7.	(a) The Gypsy, air de ballet	Ganne
	(b) The Diplomat, march	Sousa
	Encore: The Stars and Stripes Forever, march	Sousa
	Encore: Manhattan Beach, march	Sousa
8.	Caprice Slavonic	Geloso
	Encore: Serenade	Schubert
	JEANETTE POWERS, VIOLIN SOLOIST	
9.	Ride of the Valkyries, from Die Walküre	Wagner

Source: Sousa Band press book no. 25, p. 25 (*Jacksonville Journal*)

EVENING CONCERT, 21 APRIL 1906
Manchester, New Hampshire, at Manchester Opera House

1.	Oberon: Overture	Weber
	Encore: El Capitan, march	Sousa
2.	Bride of the Waves	Clarke
	HERBERT L. CLARKE, CORNET SOLOIST	
	Encore: Sextette, from Lucia di Lammermoor	Donizetti
	Clarke with five other brass players	
3.	At the King's Court, suite	Sousa
	I Her Ladyship the Countess	
	II Her Grace the Duchess	
	III Her Majesty the Queen	
	Encore: Dixie	Emmett
4.	The Card Song, from The Bride Elect	Sousa
	Encore: Love, Light ofMy Heart, from The Bride Elect	Sousa
	ELIZABETH SCHILLER, SOPRANO SOLOIST	
5.	Welsh Rhapsody	German
	Encore: Nearer My God to Thee, hymn	Mason
	Encore: I Don't Know Where I'm Goin', But I'm On My Way	Bren

* INTERVAL *

6.	Vienna Darlings, waltz	Ziehrer
	Encore: Everybody Works But Father, humoresque	Bellstedt
7.	The Gypsy, air de ballet	Ganne
	Encore: The Diplomat, march	Sousa
	Encore: The Stars and Stripes Forever, march	Sousa
	Encore: Manhattan Beach, march	Sousa
8.	Caprice Slavonic	Geloso
	Encore: Serenade	Schubert
	JEANETTE POWERS, VIOLIN SOLOIST	
9.	Ride of the Valkyries, from Die Walküre	Wagner

Source: Sousa Band press book no. 21, p. 107 (*Manchester Union Leader*)

MATINEE CONCERT, 7 JANUARY 1908
Providence, Rhode Island, at Infantry Hall

1. Les Preludes, symphonic poem	Liszt
Encore: El Capitan, march	Sousa
Encore: Experience	Williams
2. Sounds from the Hudson	Clarke
Encore: Love Me and the World Is Mine	Ball
HERBERT L. CLARKE, CORNET SOLOIST	
3. Three Quotations, suite	Sousa
I The King of France	
II I, Too, Was Born in Arcadia	
III In Darkest Africa	
Encore: The Diplomat, march	Sousa
4. Waltz Song, from Romeo and Juliet	Gounod
Encore: Years at the Spring	Beach
LUCY ANN ALLEN, SOPRANO SOLOIST	
5. Kamenoi Ostrow, nocturne	Rubinstein

* INTERVAL *

6. My Jubilee, from Symphonic Sketches	Chadwick
Encore: Waiting at the Church, humoresque	Bellstedt
7. (a) Pan Pastoral, idyll	Godard
(b) Powhattan's Daughter, march	Sousa
Encore: The Stars and Stripes Forever, march	Sousa
Encore: Manhattan Beach, march	Sousa
8. Adagio and Moto Perpetum	Ries
Encore: Nocturne	Chopin
JEANETTE POWERS, VIOLIN SOLOIST	
9. Selections from The Free Lance	Sousa

Source: Sousa Band press book no. 21, p. 266 (*Providence Tribune*)

EVENING CONCERT, 8 FEBRUARY 1908
Urbana, Illinois, at University Auditorium

1. Overture based on Haydn's Emperor's Hymn	Westmeyer
Encore: King Cotton, march	Sousa
2. From the Shores of the Mighty Pacific	Clarke
HERBERT L. CLARKE, CORNET SOLOIST	
Encore: Sextette, from Lucia di Lammermoor	Donizetti
Clarke with five other brass players	
3. The Last Days of Pompeii, suite	Sousa
I In the House of Burbo and Stratonice	
II Nydia the Blind Girl	
III The Destruction of Pompeii and Nydia's Death	
Encore: The Free Lance, march	Sousa
4. Roberto, from Robert le Diable	Meyerbeer
Encore: Irish Love Song	Lang
LUCY ALLEN, SOPRANO SOLOIST	
5. Til Eulenspiegel's Merry Pranks, tone poem	Strauss
Encore: Illinois Loyalty	Guild
Encore: Illinois Loyalty [repeated]	Guild

* INTERVAL *

6. Peer Gynt, suite	Grieg
I Morning	
II Asa's Dance	
III Anitra's Dance	
IV In the Hall of the Mountain King	
Encore: Waiting at the Church, humoresque	Bellstedt
Encore: Selection from The Merry Widow	Lehar
7. (a) Humoseque	Dvorak
(b) Powhatan's Daughter, march	Sousa
Encore: The Stars and Stripes Forever, march	Sousa
Encore: Manhattan Beach, march	Sousa
8. Caprice Slavonic	Geloso
Encore: Serenade	Schubert
Encore: Hungarian Dance	Brahms
JEANETTE POWERS, VIOLIN SOLOIST	
9. Ride of the Valkyries, from Die Walküre	Wagner

Source: Sousa Band press book no. 29, p. 55 (unidentified Champaign, Illinois, newspaper)

EVENING CONCERT, 24 SEPTEMBER 1909
Binghamton, New York, at Armory Theater

1. In Springtime, overture	Goldmark
Encore: El Capitan, march	Sousa
2. Showers of Gold	Clarke
Encore: The Carnival of Venice	Arban
HERBERT L. CLARKE, CORNET SOLOIST	
Encore: Sextette, from Lucia di Lammermoor	Donizetti
Clarke with five other brass players	
3. People Who Live in Glass Houses, Bacchanalian suite	Sousa
I The Champagnes	
II The Rhine Wines	
IV The Whiskies	
V The Cordials	
Encore: Rondo d'Amour, idyl	Westerhout
Encore: The Diplomat, march	Sousa
4. Love, Light of My Heart, song	Sousa
Encore: Barcarolle, from Les Contes d'Hoffman	Offenbach
FRANCES AND GRACE HOYT, SOPRANO SOLOISTS	
5. Prelude to Crime and Punishment	Rachmaninoff
Encore: The Free Lance, march	Sousa

* INTERVAL *

6. Staccato Etude	Rubinstein
Encore: My Wife's Gone to the Country, humoresque	Bellstedt
Encore: Amona	Gray
7. (a) Entr' Acte	Rubinstein
(b) The Fairest of the Fair, march	Sousa
Encore: The Stars and Stripes Forever, march	Sousa
Encore: Manhattan Beach, march	Sousa
8. Fantasy Based on Gounod's Romeo and Juliet	Alard
Encore: The Shoe Dance	Ansell
Encore: To a Wild Rose	MacDowell
FLORENCE HARDEMAN, VIOLIN SOLOIST	
9. Rhapsody Espagnol	Chabrier

Source: Sousa Band press book no. 31, p. 59 (*Binghamton Republican*)

EVENING CONCERT, 15 SEPTEMBER 1910
Binghamton, New York, at Stone Opera House

1. Peer Gynt, suite	Grieg
Encore: El Capitan, march	Sousa
2. From the Shores of the Mighty Pacific	Clarke
HERBERT L. CLARKE, CORNET SOLOIST	
Encore: Sextette, from Lucia di Lammermoor	Donizetti
Clarke with five other brass players	
3. Dwellers of the Western World, suite	Sousa
I The Red Man	
II The White Man	
III The Black Man	
Encore: The Whistler's Serenade	Laurendeau
Encore: The Free Lance, march	Sousa
4. The Card Song, from The Bride Elect	Sousa
Encore: Annie Laurie	Traditional
Encore: The Goose Girl, from The Free Lance	Sousa
VIRGINIA ROOT, SOPRANO SOLOIST	
5. Til Eulenspiegel's Merry Pranks, tone poem	Strauss
Encore: The Fairest of the Fair, march	Sousa

* INTERVAL *

6. Calinda Broekhoven	
Encore: Has Anybody Here Seen Kelly?	Letters
Encore: Temptation Rag	Lodge
7. (a) Valse Triste, from Kuolema	Sibelius
(b) The Glory of the Yankee Navy, march	Sousa
Encore: The Stars and Stripes Forever, march	Sousa
Encore: Manhattan Beach, march	Sousa
8. Rhapsody Pied Montese	Sinigagia
Encore: Largo	Handel
Encore: Hungarian Dance	Brahms
NICOLINE ZEDELER, VIOLIN SOLOIST	
9. Triumphale des Boyards	Halvorsen

Source: Sousa Band press book no. 32, p. 7 (*Binghamton Republican*)

EVENING CONCERT 16 JANUARY 1911
Exeter, England, at Queen's Hall

1. Les Preludes, symphonic poem — Liszt
   Encore: El Capitan, march — Sousa
   Encore: Hobomoko — Reeves
2. Showers of Gold — Clarke
   Encore: If I Had the World to Give to You — Clarenden
   HERBERT L. CLARKE, CORNET SOLOIST
3. Dwellers of the Western World, suite — Sousa
   I   The Red Man
   II   The White Man
   III The Black Man
   Encore: The Federal, march — Sousa
4. The Card Song, from The Bride Elect — Sousa
   Encore: The Goose Girl, from The Free Lance — Sousa
   VIRGINIA ROOT, SOPRANO SOLOIST
5. Welsh Rhapsody — German
   Encore: The Washington Post, march — Sousa
   * INTERVAL *
6. The Old Cloister Clock — Kunkel
   Encore: Has Anybody Here Seen Kelly? — Letters
   Encore: Yankee Shuffle — Moreland
7. (a) Entr' Acte — Helmesberger
   (b) The Fairest of the Fair, march — Sousa
   Encore: The Stars and Stripes Forever, march — Sousa
8. Rondo Capriccioso — Saint-Saens
   Encore: [unnamed]
   NICOLINE ZEDELER, VIOLIN SOLOIST
9. Slavonic Rhapsody — Friedeman

Source: Sousa Band press book no. 36, p. 24 (*Devon Daily Gazette*)

EVENING CONCERT, 18 JANUARY 1911
Bristol, England, at Bristol Coliseum

God Save the King

1. Les Preludes, symphonic poem — Liszt
   Encore: El Capitan, march — Sousa
   Encore: Hobomoko — Reeves
2. Showers of Gold — Clarke
   Encore: If I Had the World to Give to You — Clarenden
   HERBERT L. CLARKE, CORNET SOLOIST
3. Dwellers of the Western World, suite — Sousa
   I   The Red Man
   II   The White Man
   III The Black Man
   Encore: King Cotton, march — Sousa
   Encore: The Federal, march — Sousa
4. The Card Song, from The Bride Elect — Sousa
   Encore: Annie Laurie — Traditional
   Encore: The Goose Girl, from The Free Lance — Sousa
   VIRGINIA ROOT, SOPRANO SOLOIST
5. Welsh Rhapsody — German
   Encore: The Washington Post, march — Sousa
   Encore: Rose, Shamrock, and Thistle, fantasie — Sousa
   * INTERVAL *
6. The Old Cloister Clock — Kunkel
   Encore: Has Anybody Here Seen Kelly? — Letters
7. (a) Entr' Acte — Helmesberger
   (b) The Fairest of the Fair, march — Sousa
   Encore: The Stars and Stripes Forever, march — Sousa
   Encore: Manhattan Beach, march — Sousa
8. Rondo Capriccioso — Saint-Saens
   Encore: The Swan, from Carnival of the Animals — Saint-Saens
   NICOLINE ZEDELER, VIOLIN SOLOIST
9. Slavonic Rhapsody — Friedeman

Source: Sousa Band press book no. 36, pp. 21-22 (*Bristol Times and Mirror*)

EVENING CONCERT, 23 JANUARY 1911
Northampton, England, at Corn Exchange

1. Les Preludes, symphonic poem — Liszt
   Encore: El Capitan, march — Sousa
2. Showers of Gold — Clarke
   Encore: If I Had the World to Give to You — Clarenden
   HERBERT L. CLARKE, CORNET SOLOIST
3. Dwellers of the Western World, suite — Sousa
   I   The Red Man
   II   The White Man
   III The Black Man
   Encore: Hands Across the Sea, march — Sousa
4. The Card Song, from The Bride Elect — Sousa
   Encore: Annie Laurie — Traditional
   Encore: The Goose Girl, from The Free Lance — Sousa
   VIRGINIA ROOT, SOPRANO SOLOIST
5. Welsh Rhapsody — German
   Encore: The Washington Post, march — Sousa
   * INTERVAL *
6. The Old Cloister Clock — Kunkel
   Encore: Has Anybody Here Seen Kelly? — Letters
   Encore: Yankee Shuffle — Moreland
7. (a) Entr' Acte — Helmesberger
   (b) The Fairest of the Fair, march — Sousa
   Encore: The Stars and Stripes Forever, march — Sousa
8. Rondo Capriccioso — Saint-Saens
   Encore: The Swan, from Carnival of the Animals — Saint-Saens
   NICOLINE ZEDELER, VIOLIN SOLOIST
9. Slavonic Rhapsody — Friedeman

Source: Sousa Band press book no. 36, p. 31 (*Northampton Echo* and *Northampton Chronicle*)

EVENING CONCERT, 1 MARCH 1911
Oxford, England, at Town Hall

God Save the King

1. 1812, overture solonelle — Tchaikowsky
   Encore: El Capitan, march — Sousa
   Encore: Hobomoko — Reeves
2. The Debutante — Clarke
   Encore: The Carnival of Venice — Arban
   HERBERT L. CLARKE, CORNET SOLOIST
3. Dwellers of the Western World, suite — Sousa
   I   The Red Man
   II   The White Man
   III The Black Man
   Encore: The Federal, march — Sousa
4. The Card Song, from The Bride Elect — Sousa
   Encore: Annie Laurie — Traditional
   VIRGINIA ROOT, SOPRANO SOLOIST
5. The Bells of Moscow (Prelude in C-sharp Minor) — Rachmaninoff
   Encore: The Washington Post, march — Sousa
   * INTERVAL *
6. Siegfried, grand fantasia — Wagner
   Encore: Has Anybody Here Seen Kelly? — Letters
   Encore: Yankee Shuffle — Moreland
7. (a) Entr' Acte — Helmesberger
   (b) The Fairest of the Fair, march — Sousa
   Encore: The Stars and Stripes Forever, march — Sousa
   Encore: King Cotton, march — Sousa
8. Rondo Capriccioso — Saint-Saens
   Encore: Minuet — Beethoven
   NICOLINE ZEDELER, VIOLIN SOLOIST
9. Slavonic Rhapsody — Friedeman

Source: Sousa Band press book no. 36, p. 82 (*North Berks Herald*)

MATINEE CONCERT, 3 MARCH 1911
Bristol, England, at Coliseum

God Save the King

1.	1812, overture solonelle	Tchaikowsky
	Encore: El Capitan, march	Sousa
2.	The Debutante	Clarke
	Encore: The Carnival of Venice	Arban
	HERBERT L. CLARKE, CORNET SOLOIST	
3.	Three Quotations,	Sousa
	I The King of France	
	II I, Too, Was Born in Arcadia	
	III In Darkest Africa	
	Encore: The Liberty Bell, march	Sousa
4.	Maid of the Meadow, song	Sousa
	Encore: Annie Laurie	Traditional
	VIRGINIA ROOT, SOPRANO SOLOIST	
5.	Til Eulenspiegel's Merry Pranks, tone poem	Strauss
	Encore: The Washington Post, march	Sousa

* INTERVAL *

6.	On the Beautiful Blue Danube, waltz	Strauss
	Encore: Has Anybody Here Seen Kelly?	Letters
	Encore: Yankee Shuffle	Moreland
7.	(a) Preludium	Järnefeldt
	(b) The Federal, march	Sousa
	Encore: The Stars and Stripes Forever, march	Sousa
	Encore: Manhattan Beach, march	Sousa
8.	Zigeunerweisen	Sarasate
	Encore: Minuet	Beethoven
	NICOLINE ZEDELER, VIOLIN SOLOIST	
9.	Triumphale des Boyards	Halvorsen
	Encore: Auld Lang Syne	Traditional

Source: Sousa Band press book no. 36, pp. 80-81 (*Western Daily Press*)

EVENING CONCERT, 23 MAY 1911
Maitland, Australia, at Adelphi Hall

1.	Tannhäuser: Overture	Wagner
	Encore: El Capitan, march	Sousa
2.	Showers of Gold	Clarke
	Encore: Robin Adair	Keppell
	HERBERT L. CLARKE, CORNET SOLOIST	
3.	Dwellers of the Western World, suite	Sousa
	I The Red Man	
	II The White Man	
	III The Black Man	
	Encore: King Cotton, march	Sousa
4.	Maid of the Meadow, song	Sousa
	Encore: Annie Laurie	Traditional
	VIRGINIA ROOT, SOPRANO SOLOIST	
5.	The Bells of Moscow (Prelude in C-sharp Minor)	Rachmaninoff
	Encore: The Washington Post, march	Sousa

* INTERVAL *

6.	Welsh Rhapsody	German
	Encore: Waiting at the Church, humoresque	Bellstedt
	Encore: Yankee Shuffle	Moreland
7.	(a) Entr' Acte	Helmesberger
	(b) The Federal, march	Sousa
	Encore: The Stars and Stripes Forever, march	Sousa
	Encore: Manhattan Beach, march	Sousa
8.	Zigeunerweisen	Sarasate
	Encore: Largo	Handel
	NICOLINE ZEDELER, VIOLIN SOLOIST	
9.	Ride of the Valkyries, from Die Walküre	Wagner

Source Sousa Band press book no. 34, p. 31 (*Maitland Mercury*)

EVENING CONCERT, 24 JUNE 1911
Adelaide, Australia, at Exhibition Building

1.	Tannhäuser: Overture	Wagner
	Encore: El Capitan, march	Sousa
2.	Showers of Gold	Clarke
	Encore: If I Had the World to Give to You	Clarke
	HERBERT L. CLARKE, CORNET SOLOIST	
3.	Dwellers of the Western World, suite	Sousa
	I The Red Man	
	II The White Man	
	III The Black Man	
	Encore: King Cotton, march	Sousa
4.	Maid of the Meadow, song	Sousa
	Encore: Annie Laurie	Traditional
	VIRGINIA ROOT, SOPRANO SOLOIST	
5.	The Bells of Moscow (Prelude in C-sharp Minor)	Rachmaninoff
	Encore: The Washington Post, march	Sousa

* INTERVAL *

6.	Welsh Rhapsody	German
	Encore: Waiting at the Church, humoresque	Bellstedt
	Encore: Yankee Shuffle	Moreland
7.	(a) Entr' Acte	Helmesberger
	(b) The Federal, march	Sousa
	Encore: The Stars and Stripes Forever, march	Sousa
	Encore: Manhattan Beach, march	Sousa
8.	Zigeunerweisen	Sarasate
	Encore: Minuet	Beethoven
	NICOLINE ZEDELER, VIOLIN SOLOIST	
9.	Ride of the Valkyries, from Die Walküre	Wagner

Source: Sousa Band press book no. 34, p. 52 (*Adelaide Advertiser*)

EVENING CONCERT, 28 JUNE 1911
Adelaide, Australia, at Exhibition Building

1.	Thuringa, overture	Lassen
	Encore: El Capitan, march	Sousa
2.	Sounds from the Alps	Arban
	Encore: I Need Thee Every Hour	Lowry
	HERBERT L. CLARKE AND ROSS MILLHOUSE, CORNET SOLOISTS	
3.	The Chariot Race, descriptive piece	Sousa
	Encore: The Bride Elect, march	Sousa
4.	Soldier, Take My Heart With You, song	Willeby
	Encore: Sweet Miss Industry, song	Sousa
	VIRGINIA ROOT, SOPRANO SOLOIST	
5.	Grand Chorale and Fugue, from The Well Tempered Clavier	Bach
	Encore: The Washington Post, march	Sousa

* INTERVAL *

6.	Peer Gynt, suite	Grieg
	I Morning	
	II Asa's Dance	
	III Anitra's Dance	
	IV In the Hall of the Mountain King	
	Encore: Has Anybody Here Seen Kelly?	Letters
	Encore: Turkish Patrol	Michaelis
7.	(a) Kukushka, Russian peasant dance	Lehar
	(b) The Federal, march	Sousa
	Encore: The Stars and Stripes Forever, march	Sousa
	Encore: The High School Cadets, march	Sousa
8.	Scene de la Czardas	Hubay
	Encore: Canzonetta	Chadwick
	NICOLINE ZEDELER, VIOLIN SOLOIST	
9.	Plantation Songs and Dances	Chambers

Source: Sousa Band press book no. 34, p. 54 (*Adelaide Register*)

EVENING CONCERT, 15 JULY 1911
Toowooma, Australia, at Astral Hall

1. 1812, overture solonelle — Tchaikowsky
   Encore: El Capitan, march — Sousa
2. The Debutante — Clarke
   Encore: Killarney — Balfe
   HERBERT L. CLARKE, CORNET SOLOIST
3. Three Quotations, suite — Sousa
   I   The King of France
   II   I, Too, Was Born in Arcadia
   III   In Darkest Africa
   Encore: The Federal, march — Sousa
4. The Card Song, from The Bride Elect — Sousa
   Encore: Annie Laurie — Traditional
   VIRGINIA ROOT, SOPRANO SOLOIST
5. Fantasy on Lohengrin — Wagner
   Encore: The Washington Post, march — Sousa

* INTERVAL *

6. Invitation a la Valse — Weber
   Encore: Has Anybody Here Seen Kelly? — Letters
   Encore: Yankee Shuffle — Moreland
7. (a) Preludium — Järnefeldt
   (b) The Glory of the Yankee, march — Sousa
   Encore: The Stars and Stripes Forever, march — Sousa
   Encore: Manhattan Beach, march — Sousa
8. Souvenir de Moscow — Wieniawsky
   Encore: Minuet — Beethoven
   NICOLINE ZEDELER, VIOLIN SOLOIST
9. Slavonic

   God Save the King

Source: Sousa Band press book no. 34, p. 67 (*Darling Downs Gazette*)

MATINEE CONCERT, 26 JULY 1911
Launceston, Tasmania, at Albert Hall

1. Maximilian Robspierre, tone poem — Litolff
   Encore: The Bride Elect, march — Sousa

2. Sounds from the Hudson — Clarke
   Encore: Every Little Movement — Hoschua
   HERBERT L. CLARKE, CORNET SOLOIST

3. Looking Upward, suite — Sousa
   I   By the Light of the Polar Star
   II   Under the Southern Cross
   III   Mars and Venus
   Encore: Baby's Sweetheart, song — Corri

4. Where Is Love?, from Chris and the Wonderful Lamp — Sousa
   Encore: All Through the Night, Welsh melody — Traditional
   VIRGINIA ROOT, SOPRANO SOLOIST

5. Siegfried, grand fantasia — Wagner
   With horn call by Herman Hand

* INTERVAL *

6. Hungarian Rhapsody No. 2 — Liszt
   Encore: Jolly Fellows, waltz — Vollstedt

7. (a) Song of the Nightingale — Filiposki
   With piccolo obbligato by Paul Senno
   (b) The Fairest of the Fair, march — Sousa
   Encore: The Stars and Stripes Forever, march — Sousa

8. Souvenir de Moscow — Wieniawski
   Encore: Gavotte — Gossec
   NICOLINE ZEDELER, VIOLIN SOLOIST

9. Rákóczy March, from The Damnation of Faust — Berlioz

Source: Sousa Band press book no. 34, p. 76 (*Launceston Telegraph*)

EVENING CONCERT, 26 JULY 1911
Launceston, Tasmania, at Albert Hall

1. Tannhäuser: Overture — Wagner
   Encore: El Capitan, march — Sousa
2. Showers of Gold — Clarke
   Encore: The Lost Chord — Sullivan
   HERBERT L. CLARKE, CORNET SOLOIST
3. Dwellers of the Western World, suite — Sousa
   I   The Red Man
   II   The White Man
   III   The Black Man
4. Maid of the Meadow, song — Sousa
   Encore: Annie Laurie — Traditional
   VIRGINIA ROOT, SOPRANO SOLOIST
5. The Bells of Moscow (Prelude in C-sharp Minor) — Rachmaninoff
   Encore: The Washington Post, march — Sousa

* INTERVAL *

6. Welsh Rhapsody — German
   Encore: On the Beautiful Blue Danube, waltz — Strauss
   Encore: Has Anybody Here Seen Kelly? — Letters
7. (a) Entr' Acte — Helmesberger
   (b) The Federal, march — Sousa
8. Zigeunerweisen — Sarasate
   NICOLINE ZEDELER, VIOLIN SOLOIST
9. Ride of the Valkyries, from Die Walküre — Wagner

Source: Sousa Band press book no. 34, p. 76 (*Launceston Telegraph*)

EVENING CONCERT, 27 JULY 1911
Hobart, Tasmania, at Kings Hall

1. Tannhäuser: Overture — Wagner
   Encore: El Capitan, march — Sousa
2. Showers of Gold — Clarke
   Encore: The Lost Chord — Sullivan
   HERBERT L. CLARKE, CORNET SOLOIST
3. Dwellers of the Western World, suite — Sousa
   I   The Red Man
   II   The White Man
   III   The Black Man
   Encore: The Liberty Bell, march — Sousa
4. Maid of the Meadow, song — Sousa
   Encore: Annie Laurie — Traditional
   VIRGINIA ROOT, SOPRANO SOLOIST
5. The Bells of Moscow (Prelude in C-sharp Minor) — Rachmaninoff
   Encore: The Washington Post, march — Sousa

* INTERVAL *

6. Welsh Rhapsody — German
   Encore: The Stars and Stripes Forever, march — Sousa
   Encore: Has Anybody Here Seen Kelly? — Letters
7. (a) Entr' Acte — Helmesberger
   (b) The Federal, march — Sousa
   Encore: Jolly Fellows, waltz — Vollstedt
   Encore: Manhattan Beach, march — Sousa
8. Zigeunerweisen — Sarasate
   Encore: The Swan, from Carnival of the Animals — Saint-Saens
   Encore: Gavotte — Gossec
   NICOLINE ZEDELER, VIOLIN SOLOIST
9. Ride of the Valkyries and Magic Fire Music, from Die Walküre — Wagner

Source: Sousa Band press book no. 34, p. 77 (*Hobart Daily Post*)

MATINEE CONCERT, 1 AUGUST 1911
Dunedin, New Zealand, at Garrison Hall

1. Tannhäuser: Overture — Wagner
   Encore: El Capitan, march — Sousa
2. Showers of Gold — Clarke
   Encore: Killarney — Balfe
   HERBERT L. CLARKE, CORNET SOLOIST
3. Dwellers of the Western World, suite — Sousa
   I   The Red Man
   II   The White Man
   III The Black Man
   Encore: Baby's Sweetheart, song — Corri
4. Maid of the Meadow, song — Sousa
   Encore: Annie Laurie — Traditional
   VIRGINIA ROOT, SOPRANO SOLOIST
5. The Bells of Moscow (Prelude in C-sharp Minor) — Rachmaninoff
   Encore: The Washington Post, march — Sousa

* INTERVAL *

6. Welsh Rhapsody — German
   Encore: Rose, Shamrock, and Thistle, fantasie — Sousa
   Encore: Yankee Shuffle — Moreland
7. (a) Entr' Acte — Helmesberger
   (b) The Federal, march — Sousa
   Encore: The Stars and Stripes Forever, march — Sousa
   Encore: Manhattan Beach, march — Sousa
8. Zigeunerweisen — Sarasate
   Encore: Minuet — Beethoven
   NICOLINE ZEDELER, VIOLIN SOLOIST
9. Ride of the Valkyries, from Die Walküre — Wagner

Source: Sousa Band press book no. 34, p. 80 (*Dunedin Evening Star*)

EVENING CONCERT, 1 AUGUST 1911
Dunedin, New Zealand, at Garrison Hall

1. Maximillian Robespierre, tone poem — Litolff
   Encore: The Bride Elect, march — Sousa
2. Sounds from the Hudson — Clarke
   Encore: The Lost Chord — Sullivan
   HERBERT L. CLARKE, CORNET SOLOIST
3. Looking Upward, suite — Sousa
   I   By the Light of the Polar Star
   II   Under the Southern Cross
   III Mars and Venus
   Encore: King Cotton, march — Sousa
4. Where Is Love?, from Chris and the Wonderful Lamp — Sousa
   Encore: [unnamed]
   VIRGINIA ROOT, SOPRANO SOLOIST
5. Siegfried, grand fantasia — Wagner
   With horn call by Herman Hand
6. The Band Came Back, humoresque — Sousa
   (PERFORMED DURING THE INTERVAL)
7. Hungarian Rhapsody No. 2 — Liszt
8. (a) Song of the Nightingale — Filiposki
   With piccolo obbligato by Paul Senno
   (b) The Fairest of the Fair, march — Sousa
   Encore: The Stars and Stripes Forever, march — Sousa
   Encore: The High School Cadets, march — Sousa
9. Souvenir de Moscow — Wieniawski
   Encore: [unnamed]
   NICOLINE ZEDELER, VIOLI SOLOIST
10. Rákóczy March N, from The Damnation of Faust — Berlioz

Source: Sousa Band press book no. 34, p. 80 (*Otago Times*)

EVENING CONCERT, 2 NOVEMBER 1911
Denison, Texas, at Opera House

1. 1812, overture solonelle — Tchaikowsky
   Encore: El Capitan, march — Sousa
2. From the Shores of the Mighty Pacific — Clarke
   Encore: Every Little Movement — Hoschua
   HERBERT L. CLARKE, CORNET SOLOIST
3. Dwellers of the Western World, suite — Sousa
   I   The Red Man
   II   The White Man
   III The Black Man
   Encore: King Cotton, march — Sousa
4. Maid of the Meadow, song — Sousa
   Encore: The Belle of Bayou Teche, song — Sousa
   VIRGINIA ROOT, SOPRANO SOLOIST
5. The Golden Legend, prologue — Sullivan
   Encore: Temptation Rag — Lodge

* INTERVAL *

6. The Band Came Back, humoresque — Sousa
7. (a) Preludium — Järnefeldt
   (b) The Federal, march — Sousa
8. Souvenir de Moscow — Wieniawski
   Encore: Minuet — Beethoven
   NICOLINE ZEDELER, VIOLIN SOLOIST
9. Ride of the Valkyries, from Die Walküre — Wagner

Source: Sousa Band press book no. 36, p. 114 (*Denison Herald*)

EVENING CONCERT, 20 AUGUST 1912
Delaware Water Gap, Pennsylvania, at Castle Inn Music Hall

1. 1812, overture solonelle — Tchaikowsky
   Encore: El Capitan, march — Sousa
   Encore: Shadows — Finck
2. Stars in a Velvety Sky — Clarke
   Encore: The Pink Lady — Clarke
   HERBERT L. CLARKE, CORNET SOLOIST
3. Tales of a Traveler, suite — Sousa
   I   The Kaffir on the Karoo
   II   In the Land of the Golden Fleece
   III Grand Promenade at the White House
   Encore: King Cotton, march — Sousa
   Encore: The Gliding Girl, tango — Sousa
4. Crossing the Bar, song — Willeby
   Encore: The Goose Girl, from The Free Lance — Sousa
   Encore: Annie Laurie — Traditional
   VIRGINIA ROOT, SOPRANO SOLOIST
5. The Golden Legend, prologue — Sullivan
   Encore: The Fairest of the Fair, march — Sousa

* INTERVAL *

6. Marche Militaire Francaise, from Suite Algerienne — Saint-Saens
   Encore: Everybody's Doin' It, song — Berlin
   Encore: Temptation Rag — Lodge
7. (a) Preludium — Järnefeldt
   (b) The Federal, march — Sousa
   Encore: The Stars and Stripes Forever, march — Sousa
8. Witch's Dance — Paganini
   Encore: Minuet — Beethoven
   Encore: Dixie — Emmett
   NICOLINE ZEDELER, VIOLIN SOLOIST
9. Rhapsody Pied Montese — Sinigagia

Source: Sousa Band press book no. 37, p. 3 (*Stroudsburg Daily Record*)

EVENING CONCERT, 15 OCTOBER 1912
Winona, Minnesota, at Winona Opera House

1.	Hungarian Rhapsody No. 1	Liszt
	Encore: El Capitan, march	Sousa
	Encore: Girls Who Have Loved, from The Free Lance	Sousa
2.	Southern Cross	Clarke
	Encore: Moonlit Bay	Wenrich
	Encore: Silver Threads Among the Gold, song	Danks
	HERBERT L. CLARKE, CORNET SOLOIST	
3.	Tales of a Traveler, suite	Sousa
	I The Kaffir on the Karoo	
	II In the Land of the Golden Fleece	
	III Grand Promenade at the White House	
	Encore: The Gliding Girl, tango	Sousa
4.	Voices of Spring	Strauss
	Encore: Sweet Miss Industry, song	Sousa
	VIRGINIA ROOT, SOPRANO SOLOIST	
5.	Largo, from New World Symphony	Dvorak
	Encore: The Fairest of the Fair, march	Sousa

* INTERVAL *

6.	Jewels of the Madonna, Entr' Acte	Wolf-Ferrari
	Encore: Everybody's Doin' It, song	Berlin
	Encore: With Pleasure, dance hilarious	Sousa
7.	(a) Parade of the Tin Soldiers	Jessel
	(b) The Federal, march	Sousa
	Encore: The Stars and Stripes Forever, march	Sousa
	Encore: Manhattan Beach, march	Sousa
8.	Fantasia based on Gounod's Faust	Wieniawski
	Encore: Humoresque	Dvorak
	Encore: Schön Rosmarin	Kreisler
	NICOLINE ZEDELER, VIOLIN SOLOIST	
9.	Folie Bergere, caprice	Fletcher

Source: Sousa Band press book no. 37, p. 23 (*Winona Independent*)

EVENING CONCERT, 11 NOVEMBER 1912
New Haven, Connecticut, at Woolsey Hall

1.	Hungarian Rhapsody No. 1	Liszt
	Encore: El Capitan, march	Sousa
	Encore: Girls Who Have Loved, from The Free Lance	Sousa
2.	Southern Cross	Clarke
	Encore: Moonlit Bay	Wenrich
	Encore: The Carnival of Venice	Arban
	HERBERT L. CLARKE, CORNET SOLOIST	
3.	Tales of a Traveler, suite	Sousa
	I The Kaffir on the Karoo	
	II In the Land of the Golden Fleece	
	III Grand Promenade at the White House	
	Encore: The Gliding Girl, tango	Sousa
4.	Voices of Spring	Strauss
	Encore: The Philosophic Maid, from The Charlatan	Sousa
	VIRGINIA ROOT, SOPRANO SOLOIST	
5.	Largo, from New World Symphony	Dvorak
	Encore: The Fairest of the Fair, march	Sousa
	Encore: The Team Triumphant	Schultz
	Encore: The Parabalou	Moore
	Encore: In Eli Land	Vail

* INTERVAL *

6.	Jewels of the Madonna, Entr' Acte	Wolf-Ferrari
	Encore: Everybody's Doin' It, song	Berlin
	Encore: With Pleasure, dance hilarious	Sousa
7.	(a) Parade of the Tin Soldiers	Jessel
	(b) The Federal, march	Sousa
	Encore: The Stars and Stripes Forever, march	Sousa
	Encore: Manhattan Beach, march	Sousa
8.	Fantasia based on Gounod's Faust	Wieniawski
	Encore: Humoresque	Dvorak
	Encore: Liebesfreud	Kreisler
	NICOLINE ZEDELER, VIOLIN SOLOIST	
9.	Folie Bergere, caprice	Fletcher

Source: Sousa Band press book no. 36, p. 227 (*New Haven Register*)

EVENING CONCERT, 18 NOVEMBER 1912
Fall River, Massachusetts, at Savoy Theater

1.	Hungarian Rhapsody No. 1	Liszt
	Encore: El Capitan, march	Sousa
	Encore: Girls Who Have Loved, from The Free Lance	Sousa
2.	Southern Cross	Clarke
	Encore: Moonlit Bay	Wenrich
	Encore: The Carnival of Venice	Arban
	HERBERT L. CLARKE, CORNET SOLOIST	
3.	Tales of a Traveler, suite	Sousa
	I The Kaffir on the Karoo	
	II In the Land of the Golden Fleece	
	III Grand Promenade at the White House	
	Encore: The Gliding Girl, tango	Sousa
4.	Voices of Spring	Strauss
	Encore: The Goose Girl, from The Free Lance	Sousa
	VIRGINIA ROOT, SOPRANO SOLOIST	
5.	Largo, from New World Symphony	Dvorak
	Encore: The Fairest of the Fair, march	Sousa
	Encore: King Cotton, march	Sousa

* INTERVAL *

6.	Jewels of the Madonna, Entr' Acte	Wolf-Ferrari
	Encore: Everybody's Doin' It, song	Berlin
	Encore: With Pleasure, dance hilarious	Sousa
7.	(a) Parade of the Tin Soldiers	Jessel
	(b) The Federal, march	Sousa
	Encore: The Stars and Stripes Forever, march	Sousa
	Encore: Manhattan Beach, march	Sousa
8.	Fantasia based on Gounod's Faust	Wieniawski
	Encore: Humoresque	Dvorak
	Encore: Liebesfreud Kreisler	
	NICOLINE ZEDELER, VIOLIN SOLOIST	
9.	Folie Bergere, caprice	Fletcher

Source: Sousa Band press book no. 37, p. 40 (*Fall River News*)

EVENING CONCERT, 21 NOVEMBER 1912
Portland, Maine, at Jefferson Theater

1.	Hungarian Rhapsody No. 1	Liszt
	Encore: El Capitan, march	Sousa
	Encore: Girls Who Have Loved, from The Free Lance	Sousa
2.	Southern Cross	Clarke
	Encore: Moonlit Bay	Wenrich
	Encore: The Carnival of Venice	Clarke
	HERBERT L. CLARKE, CORNET SOLOIST	
3.	Tales of a Traveler, suite	Sousa
	I The Kaffir on the Karoo	
	II In the Land of the Golden Fleece	
	III Grand Promenade at the White House	
	Encore: The Gliding Girl, tango	Sousa
4.	Voices of Spring	Strauss
	Encore: The Goose Girl, from The Free Lance	Sousa
	VIRGINIA ROOT, SOPRANO SOLOIST	
5.	Largo, from New World Symphony	Dvorak
	Encore: The Fairest of the Fair, march	Sousa
	Encore: King Cotton, march	Sousa

* INTERVAL *

6.	Jewels of the Madonna, Entr' Acte	Wolf-Ferrari
	Encore: Everybody's Doin' It, song	Berlin
	Encore: With Pleasure, dance hilarious	Sousa
7.	(a) Parade of the Tin Soldiers	Jessel
	(b) The Federal, march	Sousa
	Encore: The Stars and Stripes Forever, march	Sousa
	Encore: Manhattan Beach, march	Sousa
8.	Fantasia based on Gounod's Faust	Wieniawski
	Encore: Humoresque	Dvorak
	Encore: Liebesfreud	Kreisler
	NICOLINE ZEDELER, VIOLIN SOLOIST	
9.	Folie Bergere, caprice	Fletcher

Source: Sousa Band press book no. 36, p. 232 (*Eastern Argus*)

MATINEE CONCERT, 30 SEPTEMBER 1913
Pontiac, Michigan, at Howland Theater

1. Grand Overture de Concert — Massenet
   Encore: El Capitan, march — Sousa

2. The Debutante — Clarke
   Encore: Moonlit Bay — Wenrich
   HERBERT L. CLARKE, CORNET SOLOIST

3. The American Maid, suite — Sousa
   I   You Do Not Need a Doctor, from The American Maid
   II   The Sleeping Soldiers, from The American Maid
   III With Pleasure, dance hilarious
   Encore: The Gliding Girl, tango — Sousa

4. The Crystal Lute, from The American Maid — Sousa
   Encore: [unnamed]
   VIRGINIA ROOT, SOPRANO SOLOIST

5. Grand Festival Hymn — Bartlett

* INTERVAL *

6. A Night in Spain — Lacombe
   Encore: Snooky Ookums — Berlin
   Encore: Knock-Out Drops — Klickmann

7. (a) Kismet — Markey
   (b) From Maine to Oregon, march — Sousa
   Encore: The Stars and Stripes Forever, march — Sousa

8. Adagio and Rondo from Concerto in E — Vieuxtemps
   Encore: Madrigal — Simoette
   MARGEL GLUCK, VIOLIN SOLOIST

9. Danse Negre — Ascher

Source: Sousa Band press book no. 38, p. 34 (*Pontiac Gazette*)

EVENING CONCERT, 27 OCTOBER 1913
Fall River, Massachusetts, at Savoy Theater

1. The Chase of Prince Henry, overture — Mehul
   Encore: El Capitan, march — Sousa
   Encore: Girls Who Have Loved, from The Free Lance — Sousa

2. The Debutante — Clarke
   Encore: Moonlit Bay — Wenrich
   Encore: The Carnival of Venice — Clarke
   HERBERT L. CLARKE, CORNET SOLOIST

3. The American Maid, suite — Sousa
   I   You Do Not Need a Doctor, from The American Maid
   II   The Sleeping Soldiers, from The American Maid
   III With Pleasure, dance hilarious
   Encore: The Gliding Girl, tango — Sousa

4. Caro Nome, from Rigoletto — Verdi
   Encore: Mary of Argyle — Nelson
   VIRGINIA ROOT, SOPRANO SOLOIST

5. Kamenoi Ostrow, nocturne — Rubinstein
   Encore: The Fairest of the Fair, march — Sousa
   Encore: King Cotton, march — Sousa

* INTERVAL *

6. La Verbena, intermezzo — Lacombe
   Encore: Snookey Ookums — Berlin
   Encore: Sextette, from Lucia di Lammermoor — Donizetti
            Featuring six brass players
   Encore: Knockout Drops — Klichmann

7. (a) Kismet — Markey
   (b) From Maine to Oregon, march — Sousa
   Encore: The Stars and Stripes Forever, march — Sousa
   Encore: Manhattan Beach, march — Sousa

8. Adagio and Rondo, from Concerto in E — Vieuxtemps
   Encore: Meditation, from Thaïs — Massenet
   Encore: Liebesfreud — Kreisler
   MARGEL GLUCK, VIOLIN SOLIST

9. Danse Negre — Ascher

Source: Sousa Band press book no. 38, p. 56 (*Fall River Herald*)

10:45 a.m. CONCERT, 15 NOVEMBER 1913
Atlanta, Georgia, at Prison Chapel, Atlanta Penitentiary

1. Tone Pictures of the North and South — Bendix
   Encore: Girls Who Have Loved, from The Free Lance — Sousa

2. From the Shores of the Mighty Pacific — Clarke
   Encore: Moonlit Bay — Wenrich
   HERBERT L. CLARKE, CORNET SOLOIST

3. Songs of Grace and Songs of Glory, fantasie — Sousa

4. Will You Love When the Lilies Are Dead?, from The Charlatan — Sousa
   Encore: The Goose Girl, from The Free Lance — Sousa
   VIRGINIA ROOT, SOPRANO SOLOIST

5. (a) The Gliding Girl, tango — Sousa
   (b) With Pleasure, dance hilarious — Sousa

6. Souvenir de Moscow — Wieniawski
   Encore: Humoresque — Dvorak
   MARGEL GLUCK, VIOLIN SOLOIST

7. The Stars and Stripes Forever, march — Sousa
   Encore: Manhattan Beach, march — Sousa

(End of program)

Source: Sousa Band press book no. 40, p. 2 (*American Musician*, 17 January 1914)

MATINEE CONCERT, 4 OCTOBER 1914
Columbus, Ohio, at Southern Theater

1. Carneval Romaine: Overture — Berlioz
   Encore: El Capitan, march — Sousa
   Encore: Mama, Papa, from Chris and the Wonderful Lamp — Sousa

2. From the Shores of the Mighty Pacific — Clarke
   Encore: The Lily Bells, from Our Flirtations — Sousa
   HERBERT L. CLARKE, CORNET SOLOIST

3. The American Maid, suite — Sousa
   I   You Do Not Need a Doctor, from The American Maid
   II   The Sleeping Soldiers, from The American Maid
   III With Pleasure, dance hilarious
   Encore: The Gliding Girl, tango — Sousa
   Encore: In the Night — Gilbert
   Encore: King Cotton, march — Sousa

4. Amarella Winne
   Encore: Annie Laurie — Traditional
   VIRGINIA ROOT, SOPRANO SOLOIST

5. Polonaise No. 2 — Liszt
   Encore: The Fairest of the Fair, march — Sousa

* INTERVAL *

6. Serenade, from La Verbena — Lacomb
   Encore: Get Out and Get Under, humoresque — Bellstedt
   Encore: Ireland Forever — Myddleton

7. (a) In the Land of the Golden Fleece, from Tales of a Traveler — Sousa
   (b) The Lambs, march — Sousa
   Encore: The Stars and Stripes Forever, march — Sousa
   Encore: Manhattan Beach, march — Sousa

8. Two movements from Concerto in D Major — Wieniaswki
   Encore: Les Millious d'Arlequin — Drigo
   Encore: Liebesfreud — Kreisler
   MARGEL GLUCK, VIOLIN SOLOIST

9. Thalia, overture — Gilbert

Source: Marked program of Paul Sexauer of Sousa's Band. Courtesy Peter Sexauer, son.

EVENING CONCERT, 4 OCTOBER 1914
Columbus, Ohio, at Southern Theater

1. Pester Carnival, rhapsody — Liszt
   Encore: Hands Across the Sea, march — Sousa
   Encore: Mama, Papa, from Chris and the Wonderful Lamp — Sousa
2. Neptune's Court — Clarke
   Encore: Moonlit Bay — Wenrich
   Encore: The Carnival of Venice — Arban
   HERBERT L. CLARKE, CORNET SOLOIST
3. Impressions at the Movies — Sousa
   I   The Serenaders (The Musical Mokes)
   II   The Crafty Villain and the Timid Maid
   III Balance All and Swing Partners (The Cabaret Dancers)
   Encore: In the Night — Gilbert
4. Aria from La Boheme — Puccini
   Encore: Will You Love When the Lilies Are Dead?, from — Sousa
   The Charlatan
   Encore: The Goose Girl, from The Free Lance — Sousa
   VIRGINIA ROOT, SOPRANO SOLOIST
5. Handel in the Strand — Grainger
   Encore: The Fairest of the Fair, march — Sousa

* INTERVAL *

6. In a Haunted Forest — MacDowell
   Encore: Get Out and Get Under, humoresque — Bellstedt
   Encore: Kilties Kortship Dance — Mackenzie
7. (a)   Shepherd's Hey, danse antique — Grainger
   (b)   The Lambs, march — Sousa
   Encore: The Stars and Stripes Forever, march — Sousa
   Encore: Manhattan Beach, march — Sousa
8. Carmen Fantasia — Sarasate
   Encore: Les Millious d'Arlequin — Drigo
   Encore: Liebesfreud — Kreisler
   MARGEL GLUCK, VIOLIN SOLOIST
9. The Charlatan: Overture — Sousa

Source: Marked program of Paul Sexauer of Sousa's Band. Courtesy Peter Sexauer, son.

EVENING CONCERT, 6 APRIL 1915
Paterson, New Jersey, at Armory

1. Carneval Romaine: Overture — Berlioz
   Encore: El Capitan, march — Sousa
   Encore: Social Laws, from The Charlatan — Sousa
2. Neptune's Court — Clarke
   Encore: The Lily Bells, from Our Flirtations — Sousa
   HERBERT L. CLARKE CORNET SOLOIST
3. Impressions at the Movies — Sousa
   I   The Serenaders (The Musical Mokes)
   II   The Crafty Villain and the Timid Maid
   III Balance All and Swing Partners (The Cabaret Dancers)
   Encore: King Cotton, march — Sousa
4. La Serenata — Tosti
   Encore: Will You Love When the Lilies Are Dead?, from — Sousa
   The Charlatan
   Encore: Annie Laurie — Traditional
   VIRGINIA ROOT, SOPRANO SOLOIST
5. Selections from Tristan and Isolde — Wagner
   Encore: The Fairest of the Fair, march — Sousa

* INTERVAL *

6. Scherzo, from Symphony in D Major — Svensden
   Encore: Tipperary, fantasie — Bellstedt
7. (a)   Shepherd's Hey — Grainger
   (b)   The Pathfinder of Panama, march — Sousa
   Encore: The Stars and Stripes Forever, march — Sousa
   Encore: Manhattan Beach, march — Sousa
8. Two Movements from B Minor Concerto — Saint-Saens
   Encore: Les Millious d'Arlequin — Drigo
   MARGEL GLUCK, VIOLIN SOLOIST
9. American Dances — Shelley

Source: Sousa Band press book no. 39, p. 41 (*Paterson Guardian*)

EVENING CONCERT, 13 APRIL 1915
Hanover, Pennsylvania, at Orpheum Theater

1. Carneval Romaine: Overture — Berlioz
   Encore: El Capitan, march — Sousa
2. Neptune's Court — Clarke
   Encore: Lily Bells, from Our Flirtations — Sousa
   HERBERT L. CLARKE, CORNET SOLOIST
3. Impressions at the Movies, suite — Sousa
   I   The Musical Mokes
   II   The Crafty Villain and the Timid Maid
   III The Cabaret Dancers
   Encore: King Cotton, march — Sousa
4. La Serenata — Tosti
   Encore: Will You Love When the Lilies Are Dead?, from — Sousa
   The Charlatan
   VIRGINIA ROOT, SOPRANO SOLOIST
5. Prelude and Love Death, from Tristan and Isolde — Wagner
   Encore: The Fairest of the Fair, march — Sousa

* INTERVAL *

6. Scherzo, from Symphony in D Major — Svendsen
   Encore: Tipperary, fantasy — Bellstedt
7. (a)   Shepherd's Hey, air — Grainger
   (b)   The Pathfinder of Panama, march — Sousa
   Encore: The Stars and Stripes Forever, march — Sousa
8. Two Movements from B Minor Concerto — Saint-Saens
   MARGEL GLUCK, VIOLIN SOLOIST
   Encore: Les Million d'Arlequin — Drigo
   Harp accompaniment by Joseph Marthage
9. American Dances — Shelley

Source: *Hanover Independent*, 14 April 1915

EVENING CONCERT, 24 OCTOBER 1915
New York, New York, at Hippodrome

1. William Tell: Overture — Rossini
   Encore: King Cotton, march — Sousa
   Encore: Girls Who Have Loved, from The Free Lance — Sousa
2. Voices of Spring — Strauss
   Encore: The Goose Girl, from The Free Lance — Sousa
   VIRGINIA ROOT, SOPRANO SOLOIST
3. The American Maid, suite — Sousa
   I   You Do Not Need a Doctor, from The American Maid
   II   The Sleeping Soldiers, from The American Maid
   III With Pleasure, dance hilarious
   Encore: Hands Across the Sea, march — Sousa
4. Come, Love Divine — Leoncavallo
   Encore: Mother Machree — Olcott
   ORVILLE HARROLD, TENOR SOLOIST
5. On the Beautiful Blue Danube, waltz — Strauss
   Encore: Good-bye, Girls, I'm Through, humoresque — Bellstedt
   Encore: The Stars and Stripes Forever, march — Sousa
   Encore: Manhattan Beach, march — Sousa
6. Southern Cross — Clarke
   HERBERT L. CLARKE, CORNET SOLOIST
7. Thou Brilliant Bird, from the Pearl of Brazil — David
   BELLE STOREY, SOPRANO SOLOIST
   Flute Obbligato by Louis P. Fritze
8. The New York Hippodrome, march — Sousa

Notes: Placement of interval uncertain. The remainder of this program consisted of performances by members of the *Hip! Hip! Hooray!* show cast.

Source: Sousa Band press book no. 41, p. 124 (*Musical Courier*, 28 November 1915)

EVENING CONCERT, 29 OCTOBER 1916
Atlantic City, New Jersey, at Mixon Theater

Note: The concert below was the second half of a split program. The first half consisted of features by performers of the Hip! Hip! Hooray! *show. Sousa's Band was accompanying the show on its tour of eastern cities, and the show was playing in Philadelphia. Sunday performances were not permitted in Philadelphia in those years.*

* INTERVAL *

1. Southern Rhapsody   Hosmer
   Encore: El Capitan, march   Sousa
   Encore: Good-bye, Girls, I'm Through, humoresque   Bellstedt
   Encore: Ragging the Scale   Claypoole
2. Showers of Gold   Clarke
   Encore: A Perfect Day, song   Bond
   HERBERT L. CLARKE, CORNET SOLOIST
3. Dwellers of the Western World, suite   Sousa
   I   The Red Man
   II   The White Man
   III   The Black Man
   Encore: The Stars and Stripes Forever, march   Sousa
   Encore: Boy Scouts of America, march   Sousa
4. Scotch Fantasy   Boehm
   LOUIS P. FRITZE, FLUTE SOLOIST
5. Soldier's Chorus, from Faust   Gounod

Source: Sousa Band press book no. 44, p. 32 (*Atlantic City Press*)

EVENING CONCERT, 18 DECEMBER 1916
Pittsfield, Massachusetts, at Colonial Theater

1. Mignon: Overture   Thomas
   Encore: El Capitan, march   Sousa
   Encore: White Bird, novelette   Hager
2. The Rat Charmer of Hamelin   Thomas
   Encore: Love's Old Sweet Song   Molloy
   CLARENCE J. RUSSELL, CORNET SOLOIST
3. Dwellers of the Western World, suite   Sousa
   I   The Red Man
   II   The White Man
   III   The Black Man
   Encore: King Cotton, march   Sousa
   Encore: The Gliding Girl, tango   Sousa
4. Aria, from Samson and Delilah   Saint-Saens
   Encore: Good Bye   Tosti
   LEONORA SIMONSEN, SOPRANO
   Flute obbligato by Louis P. Fritze
5. Songs of Grace and Songs of Glory, fantasie   Sousa

* INTERVAL *

6. Southern Rhapsody   Hosmer
   Encore: Good-bye, Girls, I'm Through, humoresque   Bellstedt
   Encore: Ragging the Scale   Claypoole
7. (a)   Annie Laurie   Traditional
   Encore: Men of Harlech, patriotic air   Traditional
   JOSEPH MARTHAGE, HARP SOLOIST
   (b)   Boy Scouts of America, march   Sousa
   Encore: The Stars and Stripes Forever, march   Sousa
   Encore: Manhattan Beach, march   Sousa
8. Scotch Fantasy   Boehm
   Encore: Entr' Acte   Quensel
   LOUIS P. FRITZE, FLUTE SOLOIST
9. Rákóczy March, from The Damnation of Faust   Berlioz

Note: The soloists for this concert were not the regular touring soloists. Pittsfield was the hometown of Clarence J. Russell, the band's librarian, and as a courtesy Sousa had him substitute for Herbert L. Clarke on this concert. Leonore Simonsen was one of the stars of the *Hip! Hip! Hooray!* show, which the band was accompanying on its tour of eastern cities at this time. Joseph Marthage and Louis P. Fritze were often soloists in cities where the band played extended engagements, but they were not featured soloists on long tours.

Source: Sousa Band press book no. 44, p. 123 (*Berkshire Eagle*)

EVENING CONCERT, 20 DECEMBER 1916
Utica, New York, at Colonial Theater

1. Mignon: Overture   Thomas
   Encore: El Capitan, march   Sousa
   Encore: White Bird, novelette   Hager
2. Showers of Gold   Clarke
   HERBERT L. CLARKE, CORNET SOLOIST
   Encore: Brighten the Corner Where You Are   Gabriel
   DUET WITH FRANK SIMON
   Encore: A Perfect Day, song   Bond
   HERBERT L. CLARKE, CORNET SOLOIST
3. Dwellers of the Western World, suite   Sousa
   I   The Red Man
   II   The White Man
   III   The Black Man
   Encore: King Cotton, march   Sousa
   Encore: The Gliding Girl, tango   Sousa
4. Mad Scene, from Lucia di Lammermoor   Donizetti
   Encore: Good Bye   Tosti
   LEONORA SIMONSEN, SOPRANO
   Flute obbligato by Louis P. Fritze
5. Songs of Grace and Songs of Glory, fantasy   Sousa
   Encore: The Pathfinder of Panama, march   Sousa
   Encore [request]: Mystic Potentate March   F.A. Myers [local composer]

* INTERVAL *

6. Southern Rhapsody   Hosmer
   Encore: Good-bye, Girls, I'm Through, humoresque   Bellstedt
   Encore: Ragging the Scale   Claypoole
   Encore: Sextette, from Lucia di Lammermoor   Donizetti
   MESSRS. CLARKE, SIMON, RUSSELL, COREY, PERFETTO, AND WILLIAMS
7. (a)   Annie Laurie, song   Traditional
   Encore: Men of Harlech, patriotic air   Traditional
   JOSEPH MARTHAGE, HARP SOLOIST
   (b)   Boy Scouts of America, march   Sousa
   Encore: The Stars and Stripes Forever, march   Sousa
   Encore: Manhattan Beach, march   Sousa
8. Scotch Fantasie   Bohm
   Encore: The Waltzing Doll   Poldini
   LOUIS P. FRITZE, FLUTE SOLOIST
9. Rákóczy March, from The Damnation of Faust   Berlioz

Source: Sousa Band press book no. 44, p. 90 (*Utica Observer* and *Utica Herald Dispatch*)

EVENING CONCERT, 8 AUGUST 1917
Auburn, New York, at Auditorium

1. Mignon: Overture   Thomas
   Encore: El Capitan, march   Sousa
   Encore: White Bird, novelette   Hager
2. The Birth of Dawn   Clarke
   Encore: Sing Me to Sleep   Green
   HERBERT L. CLARKE, CORNET SOLOIST
3. Dwellers of the Western World, suite   Sousa
   I   The Red Man
   II   The White Man
   III   The Black Man
   Encore: Wisconsin Forward Forever, march   Sousa
   Encore: Throw Me a Rose, medley   Kalman
4. Amarella   Winne
   Encore: Rose of My Heart   Lohr
   Encore: The Goose Girl, from The Free Lance   Sousa
   VIRGINIA ROOT, SOPRANO SOLOIST
5. Largo, from New World Symphony   Dvorak
   Encore: The Pathfinder of Panama, march   Sousa

* INTERVAL *

6. Southern Rhapsody   Hosmer
7. (a)   Shepherd's Hey, danse antique   Grainger
   (b)   Boy Scouts of America, march   Sousa
   Encore: The Stars and Stripes Forever, march   Sousa
8. Boots, song   Sousa
   Encore: Somewhere a Voice is Calling, song   Tate
   Encore: Blue Ridge, I'm Coming Back to You, song   Sousa
   Encore: The Old Brigade, song   Barri
   PERCY HEMUS, BARITONE SOLOIST
9. Triumphale des Boyards   Halvorsen
   The Star Spangled Banner

Source: Sousa Band press book no. 46, p. 18 (*Auburn Journal*)

MATINEE CONCERT, 26 JUNE 1918
Poughkeepsie, New York, at Collingwood Opera House

1. Moorish Serenade, from Courts of Granada — Chapi
2. The Student's Sweetheart — Bellstedt
   Encore: Just a-Wearin' For You — Bond
   FRANK SIMON, CORNET SOLOIST
3. Dwellers of the Western World, suite — Sousa
   I   The Red Man
   II   The White Man
   III The Black Man
   MARJORIE MOODY, SOPRANO SOLOIST
4. Aria, from Louise — Charpentier
   Encore: [unnamed]
   ODETTE LE FONTENAY, SOPRANO SOLOIST
5. Fighting Allies, fantasie — Lake

* INTERVAL *

6. Feast of Spring — Thomas
   Encore: Over there, fantasie — Bellstedt
7. (a) Molly on the Shore — Grainger
   (b) Solid Men to the Front, march — Sousa
   Encore: The Stars and Stripes Forever, march — Sousa
8. In Flanders Fields the Poppies Grow, song — Sousa
   Encore: God Be With Our Boys Tonight — Sanderson
   RUBY HELDER, VOCAL SOLOIST
9. Southern Rhapsody — Hosmer

   The Star Spangled Banner

Source: Sousa Band press book no. 49, p. 53 (*Poughkeepsie News*)

MORNING CONCERT, 11 JULY 1918
Montreal, Canada, at Khaki Club Gardens
(unscheduled concert for returning soldiers)

1. Fighting Allies, fantasia — Lake
2. The Student's Sweetheart — Bellstedt
   FRANK SIMON, CORNET SOLOIST
3. Dwellers of the Western World, suite — Sousa
   I   The Red Man
   II   The White Man
   III The Black Man
   Encore: Lassus Trombone, rag — Fillmore
   Encore: Sextette, from Lucia di Lammermoor — Donizetti
   Featuring six brass players
4. Salut a la France — Donizetti
   Encore: The Love That Lives Forever, song — Sousa
   ODETTE LE FONTENAY, SOPRANO SOLOIST
5. (a) Over There, fantasie — Bellstedt
   (b) The Stars and Stripes Forever, march — Sousa
6. In Flanders Fields the Poppies Grow, song — Sousa
   Encore: God Be With Our Boys Tonight — Sanderson
   RUBY HELDER, VOCAL SOLOIST
7. Southern Rhapsody — Hosmer

   God Save the King

Source: Sousa Band press book no. 49, p. 58 (*Montreal Gazette*)

MATINEE CONCERT, 7 AUGUST 1918
Johnstown, Pennsylvania, at Cambria Theater

1. Southern Rhapsody — Hosmer
   Encore: El Capitan, march — Sousa
2. Valse de Concert — Green
   JOSEPH GREEN, XYLOPHONE SOLOIST
3. The American Maid, suite — Sousa
   I   You Do Not Need a Doctor, from The American Maid
   II   The Sleeping Soldiers, from The American Maid
   III With Pleasure, dance hilarious
   Encore: The U.S. Field Artillery, march — Sousa
4. Caro Nome, from Rigoletto — Verdi
   Encore: Fanny, from Chris and the Wonderful Lamp — Sousa
   Encore: Will You Love When the Lilies Are Dead?, from — Sousa
        The Charlatan
   MARJORIE MOODY, SOPRANO SOLOIST
5. Cortege de Sidar, from Caucasian Sketches — Ippolotov-Ivanov
   Encore: Boy Scouts of America, march — Sousa

* INTERVAL *

6. Andante Cantabile, from String Quartet — Tchaikowsky
   Encore: Over there, fantasie — Bellstedt
   Encore: Sally — Gilmore
7. (a) Molly on the Shore — Grainger
   (b) Anchor and Star, march — Sousa
   Encore: The Stars and Stripes Forever, march — Sousa
8. Somewhere in France — Hartmann
   Encore: God Be With Our Boys Tonight — Sanderson
   RUBY HELDER, VOCAL SOLOIST
9. The Charlatan: Overture — Sousa

Source: Sousa Band press book no. 49, p. 72 (*Johnstown Tribune*)

EVENING CONCERT, 7 AUGUST 1918
Johnstown, Pennsylvania, at Cambria Theater

1. Moorish Serenade, from Courts of Granada — Chapi
2. The Student's Sweetheart — Bellstedt
   Encore: Somewhere a Voice is Calling, song — Tate
   FRANK SIMON, CORNET SOLOIST
3. Dwellers of the Western World, suite — Sousa
   I   The Red Man
   II   The White Man
   III The Black Man
   Encore: The Gliding Girl, tango — Sousa
   Encore: The U.S. Field Artillery, march — Sousa
4. Ah, Fors e Lui, from La Traviata — Verdi
   Encore: Fanny, from Chris and the Wonderful Lamp — Sousa
   Encore: Will You Love When the Lilies Are Dead?, from — Sousa
        The Charlatan
   MARJORIE MOODY, SOPRANO SOLOIST
5. Night of the Classical Sabbath, from Mephistofele — Boito
   Encore: Solid Men to the Front, march — Sousa

* INTERVAL *

6. Mignon: Overture — Thomas
   Encore: Over there, fantasie — Bellstedt
   Encore: Lassus Trombone, rag — Fillmore
7. (a) Shepherd's Hey, danse antique — Grainger
   (b) Sabre and Spurs, march — Sousa
   Encore: The Stars and Stripes Forever, march — Sousa
   Encore: Boy Scouts of America, march — Sousa
8. In Flanders Fields the Poppies Grow, song — Sousa
   Encore: God Be With Our Boys Tonight — Sanderson
   Encore: Danny Boy — Weatherly
   RUBY HELDER, VOCAL SOLOIST
9. Southern Rhapsody — Hosmer
   The Star Spangled Banner

Source: Sousa Band press book no. 49, p. 72 (*Johnstown Tribune*)

EVENING CONCERT, 12 AUGUST 1918
Elmira, New York, at Mozart Theater

1. Moorish Serenade, from Courts of Granada — Chapi
   Encore: El Capitan, march — Sousa
   Encore: White Bird, novelette — Hager
2. The Student's Sweetheart — Bellstedt
   Encore: Somewhere a Voice is Calling, song — Tate
   FRANK SIMON, CORNET SOLOIST
3. Dwellers of the Western World, suite — Sousa
   I   The Red Man
   II   The White Man
   III The Black Man
   Encore: The U.S. Field Artillery, march — Sousa
4. Ah, Fors e Lui, from La Traviata — Verdi
   Encore: Fanny, from Chris and the Wonderful Lamp — Sousa
   Encore: Will You Love When the Lilies Are Dead?, from The Charlatan — Sousa
   MARJORIE MOODY, SOPRANO SOLOIST
5. Night of the Classical Sabbath, from Mephistofele — Boito
   Encore: Solid Men to the Front, march — Sousa

* INTERVAL *

6. Mignon: Overture — Thomas
   Encore: Over there, fantasie — Bellstedt
   Encore: Lassus Trombone, rag — Fillmore
7. (a) Shepherd's Hey, danse antique — Grainger
   (b) Sabre and Spurs, march — Sousa
   Encore: The Stars and Stripes Forever, march — Sousa
8. In Flanders Fields the Poppies Grow, song — Sousa
   Encore: God Be With Our Boys Tonight — Sanderson
   Encore: Danny Boy — Weatherly
   RUBY HELDER, VOCAL SOLOIST
9. Southern Rhapsody — Hosmer
   The Star Spangled Banner

Source: Sousa Band press book no. 49, pp. 79-81 (*Elmira Journal*, *Elmira Herald*, and *Elmira Star*)

EVENING CONCERT, 17 AUGUST 1918
Pottsville, Pennsylvania, at Hippodrome Theater

1. Moorish Serenade, from Courts of Granada — Chapi
   Encore: El Capitan, march — Sousa
2. The Student's Sweetheart — Bellstedt
   Encore: Somewhere a Voice is Calling, song — Tate
   FRANK SIMON, CORNET SOLOIST
3. Dwellers of the Western World, suite — Sousa
   I   The Red Man
   II   The White Man
   III The Black Man
   Encore: The U.S. Field Artillery, march — Sousa
4. Ah, Fors e Lui, from La Traviata — Verdi
   Encore: Fanny, from Chris and the Wonderful Lamp — Sousa
   Encore: Will You Love When the Lilies Are Dead?, from The Charlatan — Sousa
   MARJORIE MOODY, SOPRANO SOLOIST
5. Night of the Classical Sabbath, from Mephistofele — Boito
   Encore: Solid Men to the Front, march — Sousa

* INTERVAL *

6. Mignon: Overture — Thomas
   Encore: Over there, fantasie — Bellstedt
7. (a) Shepherd's Hey, danse antique — Grainger
   Encore: Lassus Trombone, rag — Fillmore
   (b) Sabre and Spurs, march — Sousa
   Encore: The Stars and Stripes Forever, march — Sousa
   Encore: We Are Coming, march-song — Sousa
8. In Flanders Fields the Poppies Grow, song — Sousa
   Encore: God Be With Our Boys Tonight — Sanderson
   Encore: Danny Boy — Weatherly
   RUBY HELDER, VOCAL SOLOIST
9. Southern Rhapsody — Hosmer
   The Star Spangled Banner

Source: Sousa Band press book no. 49, p. 80 (*Pottsville Republican*)

MATINEE CONCERT, 17 JUNE 1919
Oswego, New York, at Tioga Theater

1. Moorish Serenade, from Courts of Granada — Chapi
   Encore: El Capitan, march — Sousa
2. The Student's Sweetheart — Bellstedt
   Encore: Beneath Thy Window — Di Capua
   FRANK SIMON, CORNET SOLOIST
3. Dwellers of the Western World, suite — Sousa
   I   The Red Man
   II   The White Man
   III The Black Man
   Encore: The U.S. Field Artillery, march — Sousa
4. Ah, Fors e Lui, from La Traviata — Verdi
   Encore: The Goose Girl, from The Free Lance — Sousa
   MAY STONE, CONTRALTO SOLOIST
5. Funeral March, from Sonata No. 2 in B-flat — Chopin
   Encore: Solid Men to the Front, march — Sousa

* INTERVAL *

6. Persian Dance, from Khovanschina — Mussorgsky
   Encore: Over there, fantasie — Bellstedt
7. (a) Shepherd's Hey, danse antique — Grainger
   (b) Bullets and Bayonets, march — Sousa
   Encore: The Stars and Stripes Forever, march — Sousa
8. Thou Brilliant Bird, from the Pearl of Brazil — David
   MARY BAKER, SOPRANO SOLOIST
   Flute obbligato by Louis P. Fritze
   Encore: When the Boys Come Sailing Home, song — Sousa
9. Zampa: Overture — Herold
   The Star Spangled Banner

Source: Sousa Band press book no. 51, p. 2 (*Oswego Gazette*)

EVENING CONCERT, 17 JUNE 1919
Ithaca, New York, at Lyceum Theatre

1. Mignon: Overture — Thomas
   Encore: El Capitan, march — Sousa
   Encore: A Day at the Zoo — Hager
2. Willow Echoes — Simon
   Encore: Beneath Thy Window — Di Capua
   FRANK SIMON, CORNET SOLOIST
3. Impressions at the Movies — Sousa
   I   The Serenaders (The Musical Mokes)
   II   The Crafty Villain and the Timid Maid
   III Balance All and Swing Partners (The Cabaret Dancers)
   Encore: The U.S. Field Artillery, march — Sousa
   Encore: The Gliding Girl, tango — Sousa
4. I Am Titania, from Mignon — Thomas
   Encore: The Goose Girl, from The Free Lance — Sousa
   MAY STONE, CONTRALTO SOLOIST
5. (a) Wedding March — Sousa
   (b) The Golden Star, march — Sousa
   Encore: Bullets and Bayonets, march — Sousa

* INTERVAL *

6. Showing Off Before Company, humoresque — Sousa
   Encore: Over there, fantasie — Bellstedt
   Encore: Lassus Trombone, rag — Fillmore
7. (a) My Cairo Love, Egyptian serenade — Zamecnik
   (b) Sabre and Spurs, march — Sousa
   Encore: The Stars and Stripes Forever, march — Sousa
   Encore: Manhattan Beach, march — Sousa
8. In Flanders Fields the Poppies Grow, song — Sousa
   Encore: When the Boys Come Sailing Home, song — Sousa
   Encore: Robin, Robin Sing Me a Song — White
   RUBY HELDER, VOCAL SOLOIST
9. Southern Rhapsody — Hosmer
   The Star Spangled Banner

Source: Sousa Band press book no. 52, pp. 10 and 12 (*Ithaca News & Journal*)

EVENING CONCERT, 14 JULY 1919
Saskatoon, Canada, at Fair Grounds

1. Aida, collocation — Verdi
2. Nadine, valse caprice — Henton
   H. BENNE HENTON, SAXOPHONE SOLOIST
3. (a) Wedding March — Sousa
   (b) Willow Blossoms, legend — Sousa
   (c) The Golden Star, march — Sousa
   Encore: Canadian Patrol — Clarke
4. In Flanders Fields the Poppies Grow, song — Sousa
   Encore: When the Boys Come Sailing Home, song — Sousa
   MARY BAKER, SOPRANO SOLOIST
5. Songs of Grace and Songs of Glory, fantasie — Sousa
   Encore: The Washington Post, march — Sousa

* INTERVAL *

6. Carmen, grand fantasia — Bizet
   Encore: The U.S. Field Artillery, march — Sousa
7. Princess Alice — Bellstedt
   Encore: Beneath Thy Window — Di Capua
   FRANK SIMON, CORNET SOLOIST
8. Looking Upward, suite — Sousa
   I   By the Light of the Polar Star
   II Under the Southern Cross
   III Mars and Venus
9. Mad Scene, from Lucia di Lammermoor — Donizetti
   Encore: The Goose Girl, from The Free Lance — Sousa
   MAY STONE, CONTRALTO SOLOIST
   Flute obbligato by Louis P. Fritze
10. Chase of the Lion, galop de concert — Kolling

Source: Sousa Band press book no. 51, p. 18 (*Morning Phoenix*)

MATINEE CONCERT, 24 JULY 1919
Winnipeg, Canada, at Fair Grounds

1. La Boheme, grand fantasia — Puccini
   Encore: Liberty Loan, march — Sousa
2. Carmen Fantasie — Bizet
   Encore: [unnamed]
   FRANK SIMON, CORNET SOLOIST
3. Three Quotations, suite — Sousa
   I   The King of France
   II I, Too, Was Born in Arcadia
   III In Darkest Africa
4. Musetta's Aria, from La Boheme — Puccini
   MAY STONE, CONTRALTO SOLOIST
   Encore: The Stars and Stripes Forever, march — Sousa
   Encore: Canadian Patrol — Clarke

* INTERVAL *

5. Showing Off Before Company, humoresque — Sousa
   Encore: Smiles, humoresque — Bellstedt
6. Aria, from Louise — Charpentier
   Encore: When the Boys Come Sailing Home, song — Sousa
   MARY BAKER, SOPRANO SOLOIST
7. Folie Bergere, caprice — Fletcher

(End of concert)

Source: Sousa Band press book no. 51, p. 25 (*Free Press*)

EVENING CONCERT, 20 SEPTEMBER 1919
Lawrence, Massachusetts, at Armory

1. Mignon: Overture — Thomas
   Encore: El Capitan, march — Sousa
2. Willow Echoes — Simon
   Encore: Beneath Thy Window — Di Capua
   FRANK SIMON, CORNET SOLOIST
3. Impressions at the Movies — Sousa
   I   The Serenaders (The Musical Mokes)
   II The Crafty Villain and the Timid Maid
   III Balance All and Swing Partners (The Cabaret Dancers)
   Encore: The U.S. Field Artillery, march — Sousa
4. In Flanders Fields the Poppies Grow, song — Sousa
   MARY BAKER, SOPRANO SOLOIST
5. The Golden Star, march — Sousa
   Encore: Sabre and Spurs, march — Sousa

* INTERVAL *

6. Showing Off Before Company, humoresque — Sousa
   Encore: Smiles, humoresque — Bellstedt
7. (a) Kisses, valse lente — Zamecnik
   (b) Bullets and Bayonets, march — Sousa
   Encore: The Stars and Stripes Forever, march — Sousa
   Encore: Manhattan Beach, march — Sousa
8. Two Movements from Concerto in F-sharp Minor — Vieuxtemps
   Encore: Witch's Dance — Knezdo
   FLORENCE HARDEMAN, VIOLIN SOLOIST
9. Bohemian Suite — Ord Hume

Source: Sousa Band press book no. 51, p. 60 (*Sunday Star*)

MATINEE CONCERT, 2 AUGUST 1920
North Adams, Massachusetts, at Drury High School

1. The American Indian, rhapsody — Orem
   Encore: El Capitan, march — Sousa
   Encore: Biddy — Zamecnik
2. Souvenir of Switzerland — Liberati
   Encore: Marie, Marie — Romberg
   JOHN DOLAN, CORNET SOLOIST
3. Tales of a Traveler, suite — Sousa
   I   The Kaffir on the Karoo
   II In the Land of the Golden Fleece
   III Grand Promenade at the White House
   Encore: The Gliding Girl, tango — Sousa
   Encore: Sabre and Spurs, march — Sousa
4. Aria, from Louise — Charpentier
   Encore: The Goose Girl, from The Free Lance — Sousa
   MARJORIE MOODY, SOPRANO SOLOIST
5. (a) Theme and Variations — Pinto
   Encore: Believe Me If All Those Endearing Young Charms — Moore
   WINIFRED BAMBRICK, HARP SOLOIST
   (b) Who's Who in Navy Blue, march — Sousa

* INTERVAL *

6. A Study in Rhythms, fantasie — Sousa
   Encore: Lassus Trombone, rag — Fillmore
7. (a) Amorita, novelette — Zamecnik
   (b) Comrades of the Legion, march — Sousa
   Encore: The Stars and Stripes Forever, march — Sousa
   Encore: Manhattan Beach, march — Sousa
8. Morning, Noon, and Night in Vienna: Overture — Suppe
   Encore: [unnamed]
   GEORGE CAREY, XYLOPHONE SOLOIST
9. Marche de Szabad — Massenet

   The Star Spangled Banner

Source: Sousa Band press book no. 54, p. 2 (*North Adams Herald and Transcript*)

EVENING CONCERT, 4 AUGUST 1920
Meriden, Connecticut, at Auditorium

1. The American Indian, rhapsody — Orem
    Encore: El Capitan, march — Sousa
    Encore: Biddy — Zamecnik
2. Souvenir of Switzerland — Liberati
    Encore: Marie, Marie — Romberg
    JOHN DOLAN, CORNET SOLOIST
3. Tales of a Traveler, suite — Sousa
    I   The Kaffir on the Karoo
    II   In the Land of the Golden Fleece
    III Grand Promenade at the White House
    Encore: The Gliding Girl, tango — Sousa
    Encore: Sabre and Spurs, march — Sousa
4. Aria, from Louise — Charpentier
    Encore: The Goose Girl, from The Free Lance — Sousa
    Encore: Fanny, from Chris and the Wonderful Lamp — Sousa
    MARJORIE MOODY, SOPRANO SOLOIST
5. Andante Cantabile, from String Quartet — Tchaikowsky
    Encore: Who's Who in Navy Blue, march — Sousa

* INTERVAL *

6. Showing Off Before Company, humoresque — Sousa
    Encore: Swanee, fantasie on Gershwin's Sinbad — Sousa
    Encore: Lassus Trombone, rag — Fillmore
7. (a) Amorita, novelette — Zamecnik
    (b) Comrades of the Legion, march — Sousa
    Encore: The Stars and Stripes Forever, march — Sousa
8. Theme and Variations — Pinto
    WINIFRED BAMBRICK, HARP SOLOIST
9. Marche de Szabady — Massenet

    The Star Spangled Banner

Source: Sousa Band press book no. 54, p. 4 (*Meriden Record and Journal*)

MATINEE CONCERT, 11 AUGUST 1920
Bangor, Maine, at Auditorium

1. The Bartered Bride: Overture — Smetana
    Encore: El Capitan, march — Sousa
    Encore: Biddy — Zamecnik
2. Fantasia Brilliante — Arban
    Encore: Marie, Marie, serenade — Romberg
    JOHN DOLAN, CORNET SOLOIST
3. The Last Days of Pompeii, suite — Sousa
    I   In the House of Burbo and Stratonice
    II   Nydia the Blind Girl
    III The Destruction of Pompeii and Nydia's Death
    Encore: The U.S. Field Artillery, march — Sousa
    Encore: King Cotton, march — Sousa
4. Caro Nome, from Rigoletto — Verdi
    Encore: Fanny, from Chris and the Wonderful Lamp — Sousa
    MARJORIE MOODY, SOPRANO SOLOIST
5. (a) Theme and Variations — Pinto
    WINIFRED BAMBRICK, HARP SOLOIST
    (b) The Gliding Girl, tango — Sousa
    Encore: Sabre and Spurs, march — Sousa

* INTERVAL *

6. A Study in Rhythms, fantasie — Sousa
    Encore: Swanee, fantasie on Gershwin's Sinbad — Sousa
7. (a) The Wood Nymphs, valsette — Coates
    (b) Who's Who in Navy Blue, march — Sousa
    Encore: The Stars and Stripes Forever, march — Sousa
    Encore: Manhattan Beach, march — Sousa
8. Morning, Noon, and Night in Vienna: Overture — Suppe
    Encore: Dardanella — Bernard
    GEORGE CAREY, XYLOPHONE SOLOIST
9. Finale to Mazeppa — Liszt

    The Star Spangled Banner

Source: Sousa Band press book no. 54, p. 9 (*Bangor Daily News*)

EVENING CONCERT, 13 SEPTEMBER 1920
Trenton, New Jersey, at Armory

1. The American Indian, rhapsody — Orem
    Encore: El Capitan, march — Sousa
    Encore: Biddy — Zamecnik
2. The Carnival of Venice — Arban
    Encore: Marie, Marie, serenade — Romberg
    Encore: Once Upon a Time — Lincke
    JOHN DOLAN, CORNET SOLOIST
3. Camera Studies, suite — Sousa
    I   The Flashing Eyes of Andalusia
    II   Drifting to Loveland
    III The Children's Ball
    Encore: Sabre and Spurs, march — Sousa
    Encore: The Gliding Girl, tango — Sousa
4. Waiting — Millard
    Encore: The Crystal Lute, from The American Maid — Sousa
    MARY BAKER, SOPRANO SOLOIST
5. Andante Cantabile, from String Quartet — Tchaikowsky
    Encore: Who's Who in Navy Blue, march — Sousa

* INTERVAL *

6. A Study in Rhythms, fantasie — Sousa
    Encore: Swanee, fantasie on Gershwin's Sinbad — Sousa
    Encore: Piccolo Pic, humoresque — Slater
7. (a) The March Wind — Carey
    Encore: Annie Laurie — Traditional
    Encore: Believe Me If All Those Endearing Young Charms — Moore
    GEORGE CAREY, XYLOPHONE SOLOIST
    (b) Comrades of the Legion, march — Sousa
    Encore: The Stars and Stripes Forever, march — Sousa
8. Two Movements from Concerto in F-sharp Minor — Vieuxtemps
    Encore: Witch's Dance — Knezdo
    FLORENCE HARDEMAN, VIOLIN SOLOIST
9. Dance of the Comedians, from The Bartered Bride — Smetana
    The Star Spangled Banner

Source: Sousa Band press book no. 52, p. 78 (*Trenton Times*)

EVENING CONCERT, 20 SEPTEMBER 1920
New York, New York, at Hippodrome

1. The American Indian, rhapsody — Orem
    Encore: El Capitan, march — Sousa
2. Scintilla — Perkins
    Encore: Once Upon a Time — Lincke
    JOHN DOLAN, CORNET SOLOIST
3. Camera Studies, suite — Sousa
    I   The Flashing Eyes of Andalusia
    II   Drifting to Loveland
    III The Children's Ball
    Encore: Sabre and Spurs, march — Sousa
4. The Crystal Lute, from The American Maid — Sousa
    Encore: Carry Me Back to Old Virginny — Bland
    MARY BAKER, SOPRANO SOLOIST
5. Andante Cantabile, from String Quartet — Tchaikowsky
    Encore: Semper Fidelis, march — Sousa
    Encore: Who's Who in Navy Blue, march — Sousa

* INTERVAL *

6. A Study in Rhythms, fantasie — Sousa
    Encore: Swanee, fantasie on Gershwin's Sinbad — Sousa
    Encore: Piccolo Pic, humoresque — Slater
7. (a) The March Wind — Carey
    Encore: Annie Laurie — Traditional
    Encore: Dardanella — Bernard
    GEORGE CAREY, XYLOPHONE SOLOIST
    (b) Comrades of the Legion, march — Sousa
    Encore: The Stars and Stripes Forever, march — Sousa
    Encore: The U.S. Field Artillery, march — Sousa
8. First Movement from Concerto in F-sharp Minor — Vieuxtemps
    Encore: Souvenir — Drdla
    FLORENCE HARDEMAN, VIOLIN SOLOIST
9. Dale Dances of Yorkshire — Wood
    The Star Spangled Banner

Source: Barry Owen Furrer collection

298

MATINEE CONCERT, 28 SEPTEMBER 1920
Washington, D.C., at National Theater

1.	The American Indian, rhapsody	Orem
	Encore: El Capitan, march	Sousa
	Encore: Biddy	Zamecnik
2.	The Carnival of Venice	Arban
	Encore: Marie, Marie, serenade	Romberg
	Encore: Once Upon a Time	Lincke
	JOHN DOLAN, CORNET SOLOIST	
3.	Camera Studies, suite	Sousa
	I The Flashing Eyes of Andalusia	
	II Drifting to Loveland	
	III The Children's Ball	
	Encore: Sabre and Spurs, march	Sousa
4.	The Crystal Lute, from The American Maid	Sousa
	Encore: Carry Me Back to Old Virginny	Hosmer
	Encore: By the Waters of Minnetonka	Lieurance
	MARY BAKER, SOPRANO SOLOIST	
5.	Andante Cantabile, from String Quartet	Tchaikowsky
	Encore: Who's Who in Navy Blue, march	Sousa
	* INTERVAL *	
6.	A Study in Rhythms, fantasie	Sousa
	Encore: Swanee, fantasie on Gershwin's Sinbad	Sousa
7.	(a) The March Wind	Carey
	Encore: Annie Laurie	Traditional
	Encore: Dardanella	Bernard
	GEORGE CAREY, XYLOPHONE SOLOIST	
	(b) Comrades of the Legion, march	Sousa
	Encore: The Stars and Stripes Forever, march	Sousa
8.	Movement I, from Concerto in F-sharp Minor	Vieuxtemps
	Encore: Souvenir	Drdla
	Encore: Witch's Dance	Knezdo
	FLORENCE HARDEMAN, VIOLIN SOLOIST	
9.	Dale Dances of Yorkshire	Wood
	The Star Spangled Banner	

Source: Sousa Band press book no. 54, p. 34 (*Washington Herald*)

EVENING CONCERT, 1 OCTOBER 1920
Uniontown, Pennsylvania, at Penn Theater

1.	The American Indian, rhapsody	Orem
	Encore: El Capitan, march	Sousa
	Encore: Biddy	Zamecnik
2.	Scintilla	Perkins
	Encore: Marie, Marie	Romberg
	JOHN DOLAN, CORNET SOLOIST	
3.	Camera Studies, suite	Sousa
	I The Flashing Eyes of Andalusia	
	II Drifting to Loveland	
	III The Children's Ball	
	Encore: Sabre and Spurs, march	Sousa
4.	The Crystal Lute, from The American Maid	Sousa
	Encore: Carry Me Back to Old Virginny	Hosmer
	MARY BAKER, SOPRANO SOLOIST	
5.	Andante Cantabile, from String Quartet	Tchaikowsky
	Encore: Semper Fidelis, march	Sousa
	* INTERVAL *	
6.	A Study in Rhythms, fantasie	Sousa
	Encore: Swanee, fantasie on Gershwin's Sinbad	Sousa
7.	(a) The March Wind	Carey
	Encore: Annie Laurie	Traditional
	Encore: Dardanella	Bernard
	GEORGE CAREY, XYLOPHONE SOLOIST	
	(b) Comrades of the Legion, march	Sousa
	Encore: The Stars and Stripes Forever, march	Sousa
8.	Movement I, from Concerto in E-Minor	Vieuxtemps
	Encore: Souvenir	Drdla
	Encore: Witch's Dance	Knezdo
	FLORENCE HARDEMAN, VIOLIN SOLOIST	
9.	Dale Dances of Yorkshire	Wood
	The Star Spangled Banner	

Source: Sousa Band press book no. 54, p. 37 (*Uniontown Herald*)

EVENING CONCERT, 1 NOVEMBER 1920
Green Bay, Wisconsin, at Armory

1.	The American Indian, rhapsody	Orem
	Encore: El Capitan, march	Sousa
2.	Scintilla	Perkins
	Encore: The Fairie's Lullaby	Englander
	JOHN DOLAN, CORNET SOLOIST	
3.	Camera Studies, suite	Sousa
	I The Flashing Eyes of Andalusia	
	II Drifting to Loveland	
	III The Children's Ball	
	Encore: Sabre and Spurs, march	Sousa
4.	The Crystal Lute, from The American Maid	Sousa
	Encore: Carry Me Back to Old Virginny	Hosmer
	Encore: By the Waters of Minnetonka	Lieurance
	MARY BAKER, SOPRANO SOLOIST	
5.	Andante Cantabile, from String Quartet	Tchaikowsky
	Encore: Semper Fidelis, march	Sousa
	Encore: Who's Who in Navy Blue, march	Sousa
	* INTERVAL *	
6.	A Study in Rhythms, fantasie	Sousa
	Encore: Swanee, fantasie on Gershwin's Sinbad	Sousa
7.	(a) The March Wind	Carey
	Encore: Dardanella	Bernard
	Encore: Annie Laurie	Traditional
	GEORGE CAREY, XYLOPHONE SOLOIST	
	(b) Comrades of the Legion, march	Sousa
	Encore: The Stars and Stripes Forever, march	Sousa
8.	Movement I from Concerto in F-sharp Minor	Vieuxtemps
	Encore: Souvenir	Dvorak
	Encore: Fantasia on St. Patrick's Day	Vieuxtemps
	FLORENCE HARDEMAN, VIOLIN SOLOIST	
9.	Dale Dances of Yorkshire	Wood
	The Star Spangled Banner	

Source: Sousa Band press book no. 54, p. 57 (*Green Bay Press Gazette*)

EVENING CONCERT, 30 JULY 1921
Rome, New York, at Morris Family Theater

1.	In Springtime, overture	Goldmark
	Encore: El Capitan, march	Sousa
2.	The Carnival of Venice	Arban
	Encore: O Lassie o' Mine	Walt
	JOHN DOLAN, CORNET SOLOIST	
3.	Camera Studies, suite	Sousa
	I The Flashing Eyes of Andalusia	
	II Drifting to Loveland	
	III The Children's Ball	
	Encore: Keeping Step with the Union, march	Sousa
4.	The Wren Benedict	
	Encore: The Goose Girl, from The Free Lance	Sousa
	MARJORIE MOODY, SOPRANO SOLOIST	
5.	Angelus	Massenet
	Encore: The U.S. Field Artillery, march	Sousa
	* INTERVAL *	
6.	The Fancy of the Town, fantasie	Sousa
	Encore: Piccolo Pic, humoresque	Slater
7.	(a) The March Wind	Carey
	GEORGE CAREY, XYLOPHONE SOLOIST	
	(b) On the Campus, march	Sousa
	Encore: The Stars and Stripes Forever, march	Sousa
8.	Theme and Variations	Pinto
	Encore: Believe Me If All Those Endearing Young Charms	Moore
	WINIFRED BAMBRICK, HARP SOLOIST	
9.	Turkey in the Straw	Guion

Source: Sousa Band press book no. 56, p. 11 (*The Sentinel*)

299

EVENING CONCERT, 1 AUGUST 1921
Rochester, New York, at Convention Hall

1. In Springtime, overture — Goldmark
   Encore: El Capitan, march — Sousa
   Encore: Biddy — Zamecnik
2. The Carnival of Venice — Arban
   Encore: O Lassie o' Mine — Walt
   JOHN DOLAN, CORNET SOLOIST
3. Camera Studies, suite — Sousa
   I   The Flashing Eyes of Andalusia
   II Drifting to Loveland
   III The Children's Ball
   Encore: Keeping Step with the Union, march — Sousa
4. The Wren Benedict
   Encore: The Goose Girl, from The Free Lance — Sousa
   MARJORIE MOODY, SOPRANO SOLOIST
5. Angelus — Massenet
   Encore: The U.S. Field Artillery, march — Sousa

* INTERVAL *

6. The Fancy of the Town, fantasie — Sousa
   Encore: The Love Nest, humoresque — Garing
   Encore: Piccolo Pic, humoresque — Slater
7. (a) The March Wind — Carey
   Encore: Annie Laurie — Traditional
   Encore: [unnamed]
   GEORGE CAREY, XYLOPHONE SOLOIST
   (b) On the Campus, march — Sousa
   Encore: The Stars and Stripes Forever, march — Sousa
   Encore: Semper Fidelis, march — Sousa
8. Theme and Variations — Pinto
   WINIFRED BAMBRICK, HARP SOLOIST
9. Turkey in the Straw — Guion

Source: Sousa Band press book no. 56, p. 8 (newspaper not noted)

EVENING CONCERT, 2 AUGUST 1921
Utica, New York, at Gaiety Theatre

1. In Springtime, overture — Goldmark
   Encore: El Capitan, march — Sousa
   Encore: Biddy — Zamecnik
2. The Carnival of Venice — Arban
   Encore: O Lassie o' Mine — Walt
   JOHN DOLAN, CORNET SOLOIST
3. Camera Studies, suite — Sousa
   I   The Flashing Eyes of Andalusia
   II Drifting to Loveland
   III The Children's Ball
   Encore: Keeping Step with the Union, march — Sousa
4. The Wren Benedict
   Encore: The Goose Girl, from The Free Lance — Sousa
   MARJORIE MOODY, SOPRANO SOLOIST
5. Angelus — Massenet
   Encore: The U.S. Field Artillery, march — Sousa

* INTERVAL *

** The Golden Star, march — Sousa

6. The Fancy of the Town, fantasie — Sousa
   Encore: The Love Nest, humoresque — Garing
7. (a) The March Wind — Carey
   Encore: A Young Man's Fancy — Ager
   Encore: Twelfth Street Rag — Bowman
   GEORGE CAREY, XYLOPHONE SOLOIST
   (b) On the Campus, march — Sousa
   Encore: The Stars and Stripes Forever, march — Sousa
   Encore: Semper Fidelis, march — Sousa
8. Theme and Variations — Pinto
   Encore: Believe Me If All Those Endearing Young Charm — Moore
   WINIFRED BAMBRICK, HARP SOLOIST
9. Turkey in the Straw — Guion

**Inserted in the program as a tribute to the memory of Enrico Caruso, with Sousa addressing the audience. Placement in program is not definite.

Source: Sousa Band press book no. 56, p. 13 (*Morning Telegram*)

EVENING CONCERT, 23 SEPTEMBER 1921
New Bedford, Massachusetts, at Elm Rink

1. In Springtime, overture — Goldmark
   Encore: El Capitan, march — Sousa
   Encore: Biddy — Zamecnik
2. The Carnival of Venice — Arban
   Encore: O Lassie o' Mine — Walt
   JOHN DOLAN, CORNET SOLOIST
3. Camera Studies, suite — Sousa
   I   The Flashing Eyes of Andalusia
   II Drifting to Loveland
   III The Children's Ball
   Encore: Keeping Step with the Union, march — Sousa
4. The Wren Benedict
   Encore: Carry Me Back to Old Virginny — Hosmer
   MARY BAKER, SOPRANO SOLOIST
5. Angelus — Massenet
   Encore: Semper Fidelis, march — Sousa

* INTERVAL *

6. The Fancy of the Town, fantasie — Sousa
   Encore: Piccolo Pic, humoresque — Slater
7. (a) Rondo Capriccioso — Mendelssohn
   Encore: Humoresque — Dvorak
   Encore: Twelfth Street Rag — Bowman
   GEORGE CAREY, XYLOPHONE SOLOIST
   (b) On the Campus, march — Sousa
   Encore: The Stars and Stripes Forever, march — Sousa
8. Two Movements from Concerto in F-sharp Minor — Vieuxtemps
   Encore: Souvenir — Drdla
   FLORENCE HARDEMAN, VIOLIN SOLOIST
9. Turkey in the Straw — Guion

Note: Concert conducted by John Dolan.

Source: Sousa Band press book no. 54, p. 198 (*Morning Mercury*)

EVENING CONCERT, 21 NOVEMBER 1921
Canton, Ohio, at City Auditorium

1. In Springtime, overture — Goldmark
   Encore: El Capitan, march — Sousa
   Encore: Biddy — Zamecnik
2. The Carnival of Venice — Arban
   Encore: O Lassie o' Mine — Walt
   JOHN DOLAN, CORNET SOLOIST
3. Camera Studies, suite — Sousa
   I   The Flashing Eyes of Andalusia
   II Drifting to Loveland
   III The Children's Ball
4. The Wren Benedict
   Encore: The American Girl, from The American Maid — Sousa
   MARY BAKER, SOPRANO SOLOIST
5. Angelus — Massenet
   Encore: The U.S. Field Artillery, march — Sousa

* INTERVAL *

6. The Fancy of the Town, fantasie — Sousa
   Encore: The Love Nest, humoresque — Garing
7. (a) Rondo Capriccioso — Mendelssohn
   Encore: [unnamed] — Dvorak
   Encore: Twelfth Street Rag — Bowman
   GEORGE CAREY, XYLOPHONE SOLOIST
   (b) On the Campus, march — Sousa
   Encore: The Stars and Stripes Forever, march — Sousa
   Encore: Semper Fidelis, march — Sousa
8. Two Movements from Concerto in F-sharp Minor — Vieuxtemps
   Encore: Traumerei — Schumann
   FLORENCE HARDEMAN, VIOLIN SOLOIST
9. Turkey in the Straw — Guion

Source: Sousa Band press book no. 56, p. 31 (*Daily News*)

EVENING CONCERT, 19 DECEMBER 1921
Tacoma, Washington, at Tacoma Theater

1. In Springtime, overture — Goldmark
   Encore: El Capitan, march — Sousa
2. The Carnival of Venice — Arban
   Encore: O Lassie o' Mine — Walt
   JOHN DOLAN, CORNET SOLOIST
3. Camera Studies, suite — Sousa
   I   The Flashing Eyes of Andalusia
   II   Drifting to Loveland
   III The Children's Ball
   Encore: Keeping Step with the Union, march — Sousa
4. The Wren Benedict
   Encore: Carry Me Back to Old Virginny — Hosmer
   Encore: The American Girl, from The American Maid — Sousa
   MARY BAKER, SOPRANO SOLOIST
5. Angelus — Massenet
   Encore: The U.S. Field Artillery, march — Sousa

* INTERVAL *

6. The Fancy of the Town, fantasie — Sousa
   Encore: The Love Nest, humoresque — Garing
7. (a) Rondo Capriccioso — Mendelssohn
   Encore: Humoresque — Dvorak
   Encore: Plantation Melody — Anonymous
   GEORGE CAREY, XYLOPHONE SOLOIST
   (b) On the Campus, march — Sousa
   Encore: The Stars and Stripes Forever, march — Sousa
   Encore: Sabre and Spurs, march — Sousa
8. Two Movements from Concerto in F-sharp Minor — Vieuxtemps
   Encore: Souvenir — Drdla
   Encore: Traumerei — Schumann
   FLORENCE HARDEMAN, VIOLIN SOLOIST
9. Turkey in the Straw — Guion

Source: Sousa Band press book no. 56, p. 40 (newspaper not noted)

MATINEE CONCERT, 14 JANUARY 1922
Houston, Texas, City Auditorium

1. Hungarian Rhapsody No. 14 — Liszt
2. The Volunteer — Rogers
   Encore: O Lassie o' Mine — Walt
   JOHN DOLAN, CORNET SOLOIST
3. Three Quotations, suite — Sousa
   I   The King of France
   II   I, Too, Was Born in Arcadia
   III In Darkest Africa
   Encore: On the Campus, march — Sousa
4. Carmenia Wilson
   Encore: Carry Me Back to Old Virginny — Hosmer
   MARY BAKER, SOPRANO SOLOIST
5. Sunrise, from Iris — Mascagni
   Encore: The U.S. Field Artillery, march — Sousa

* INTERVAL *

6. Showing Off Before Company, humoresque — Sousa
7. (a) Beautiful Colorado — De Luca
   Encore: Somewhere a Voice is Calling, song — Tate
   JOSEPH DE LUCA, EUPHONIUM SOLOIST
   (b) Keeping Step with the Union, march — Sousa
   Encore: The Stars and Stripes Forever, march — Sousa
8. Polonaise in D-flat — Wieniawski
   Encore: Souvenir — Drdla
   FLORENCE HARDEMAN, VIOLIN SOLOIST
9. Dale Dances of Yorkshire — Wood

Source: Sousa Band press book no. 54, p. 143 (newspaper not noted)

EVENING CONCERT, 14 JANUARY 1922
Houston, Texas, at City Auditorium

1. In Springtime, overture — Goldmark
2. The Carnival of Venice — Arban
   Encore: O Lassie o' Mine — Walt
   JOHN DOLAN, CORNET SOLOIST
3. Camera Studies, suite — Sousa
   I   The Flashing Eyes of Andalusia
   II   Drifting to Loveland
   III The Children's Ball
   Encore: The Washington Post, march — Sousa
   Encore: El Capitan, march — Sousa
   Encore: Social Laws, from The Charlatan — Sousa
4. The Wren Benedict
   Flute obbligato by R. Meredith Willson
   Encore: Carry Me Back to Old Virginny — Hosmer
   Encore: By the Waters of Minnetonka — Lieurance
   MARY BAKER, SOPRANO SOLOIST
5. Angelus — Massenet
   Encore: The U.S. Field Artillery, march — Sousa

* INTERVAL *

6. The Fancy of the Town, fantasie — Sousa
   Encore: The Love Nest, humoresque — Garing
7. (a) Rondo Capriccioso — Mendelssohn
   Encore: Humoresque — Dvorak
   Encore: [unnamed]
   GEORGE CAREY, XYLOPHONE SOLOIST
   (b) On the Campus, march — Sousa
   Encore: The Stars and Stripes Forever, march — Sousa
   Encore: Sabre and Spurs, march — Sousa
8. Two Movements from Concerto in F-sharp Minor — Vieuxtemps
   Encore: Souvenir — Drdla
   Encore: Traumerei — Schumann
   FLORENCE HARDEMAN, VIOLIN SOLOIST
9. Turkey in the Straw — Guion

Source: Sousa Band press book no. 54, p. 143 (newspaper not noted)

EVENING CONCERT, 19 FEBRUARY 1922
Birmingham, Alabama, at Jefferson Theater

1. In Springtime, overture — Goldmark
   Encore: El Capitan, march — Sousa
   Encore: Biddy — Zamecnik
2. The Carnival of Venice — Arban
   Encore: O Lassie o' Mine — Walt
   JOHN DOLAN, CORNET SOLOIST
3. Camera Studies, suite — Sousa
   I   The Flashing Eyes of Andalusia
   II   Drifting to Loveland
   III The Children's Ball
   Encore: [unnamed]
   Encore: Bullets and Bayonets, march — Sousa
4. The Wren Benedict
   Encore: Carry Me Back to Old Virginny — Hosmer
   MARY BAKER, SOPRANO SOLOIST
5. Angelus — Massenet
   Encore: Dixie — Emmett
   Encore: The U.S. Field Artillery, march — Sousa

* INTERVAL *

6. The Fancy of the Town, fantasie — Sousa
   Encore: The Love Nest, humoresque — Garing
7. (a) Rondo Capriccioso — Mendelssohn
   Encore: Annie Laurie — Traditional
   Encore: Humoresque — Dvorak
   Encore: Somewhere in Naples — Zamecnik
   GEORGE CAREY, XYLOPHONE SOLOIST
   (b) On the Campus, march — Sousa
   Encore: The Stars and Stripes Forever, march — Sousa
   Encore: Sabre and Spurs, march — Sousa
8. Two Movements from Concerto in F-sharp Minor — Vieuxtemps
   Encore: Souvenir — Drdla
   Encore: Witch's Dance — Knezdo
   FLORENCE HARDEMAN, VIOLIN SOLOIST
9. Turkey in the Straw — Guion

Source: Sousa Band press book no. 54, p. 160 (newspaper not noted)

EVENING CONCERT, 15 MARCH 1922
Cumberland, Maryland, at Maryland Theater

1. In Springtime, overture — Goldmark
   Encore: El Capitan, march — Sousa
2. The Carnival of Venice — Arban
   Encore: O Lassie o' Mine — Walt
   JOHN DOLAN, CORNET SOLOIST
3. Camera Studies, suite — Sousa
   I   The Flashing Eyes of Andalusia
   II   Drifting to Loveland
   III The Children's Ball
   Encore: Social Laws, from The Charlatan — Sousa
   Encore: Bullets and Bayonets, march — Sousa
4. The Wren — Benedict
   Encore: O Heart That's Free — Robyn
   MARY BAKER, SOPRANO SOLOIST
5. Finale, from Symphony No. 4 — Tchaikowsky
   Encore: The U.S. Field Artillery, march — Sousa

* INTERVAL *

6. The Fancy of the Town, fantasie — Sousa
   Encore: The Love Nest, humoresque — Garing
7. (a) Rondo Capriccioso — Mendelssohn
   Encore: Somewhere in Naples — Zamecnik
   GEORGE CAREY, XYLOPHONE SOLOIST
   (b) On the Campus, march — Sousa
   Encore: The Stars and Stripes Forever, march — Sousa
8. Rondo, from Concerto No. 2 — Vieuxtemps
   Encore: Souvenir — Drdla
   Encore: Traumerei — Schumann
   FLORENCE HARDEMAN, VIOLIN SOLOIST
9. Turkey in the Straw — Guion

Source: Sousa Band press book no. 56, p. 62 (*Daily News*)

MATINEE CONCERT, 21 JULY 1922
Montpelier, Vermont, at City Hall

1. The Red Sarafan, overture — Erichs
   Encore: Keeping Step with the Union, march — Sousa
2. Centennial Polka — Bellstedt
   Encore: I Love a Little Cottage — O'Hara
   JOHN DOLAN, CORNET SOLOIST
3. Leaves from My Notebook, suite — Sousa
   I   The Genial Hostess
   II   The Campfire Girls
   III The Lively Flapper
   Encore: Bullets and Bayonets, march — Sousa
4. Caro Nome, from Rigoletto — Verdi
   Encore: The American Girl, from The American Maid — Sousa
   MARJORIE MOODY, SOPRANO SOLOIST
5. Golden Light (Agnus Dei), intermezzo — Bizet
   Encore: The U.S. Field Artillery, march — Sousa

* INTERVAL *

6. A Bouquet of Beloved Inspirations, fantasie — Sousa
   Encore: Look for the Silver Lining, humoresque — Sousa
7. (a) Nola — Arndt
   Encore: [unnamed]
   Encore: [unnamed]
   GEORGE CAREY, XYLOPHONE SOLOIST
   (b) The Gallant Seventh, march — Sousa
   Encore: The Stars and Stripes Forever, march — Sousa
8. Fantasie, Op. 35 — Alvars
   Encore: Believe Me If All Those Endearing Young Charms — Moore
   WINIFRED BAMBRICK, HARP SOLOIST
9. Turkey in the Straw — Guion

Source: Sousa Band press book no. 56, p. 124 (*Burlington Free Press*)

EVENING CONCERT, 21 JULY 1922
New Haven, Connecticut, at Woolsey Hall

1. The Red Sarafan, overture — Erichs
   Encore: El Capitan, march — Sousa
   Encore: Parade of the Wooden Soldiers — Jessel
2. Centennial Polka — Bellstedt
   Encore: I Love a Little Cottage — O'Hara
   JOHN DOLAN, CORNET SOLOIST
3. Leaves from My Notebook, suite — Sousa
   I   The Genial Hostess
   II   The Campfire Girls
   III The Lively Flapper
   Encore: Bullets and Bayonets, march — Sousa
4. Ah, Fors e Lui, from La Traviata — Verdi
   Encore: The Sweetest Story Ever Told — Stultz
   Encore: The American Girl, from The American Maid — Sousa
   MARJORIE MOODY, SOPRANO SOLOIST
5. Golden Light (Agnus Dei), intermezzo — Bizet
   Encore: The U.S. Field Artillery, march — Sousa

* INTERVAL *

6. A Bouquet of Beloved Inspirations, fantasie — Sousa
   Encore: Look for the Silver Lining, humoresque — Sousa
7. (a) Witches' Dance — MacDowell
   Encore: Nola — Arndt
   Encore: Ka-lu-a, from Good Morning, Dearie — Kern
   GEORGE CAREY, XYLOPHONE SOLOIST
   (b) The Gallant Seventh, march — Sousa
   Encore: The Stars and Stripes Forever, march — Sousa
   Encore: On the Campus, march — Sousa
8. Romance and Finale, from Concerto No. 2 — Wieniawski
   Encore: Traumerei — Schumann
   CAROLINE THOMAS, VIOLIN SOLOIST
9. Turkey in the Straw — Guion

Source: Sousa Band press book no. 56, p. 172 (newspaper not noted)

EVENING CONCERT, 21 SEPTEMBER 1922
Portland, Maine, at City Hall

1. The Red Sarafan, overture — Erichs
   Encore: El Capitan, march — Sousa
   Encore: Social Laws, from The Charlatan — Sousa
2. Centennial Polka — Bellstedt
   Encore: I Love a Little Cottage — O'Hara
   JOHN DOLAN, CORNET SOLOIST
3. Leaves from My Notebook, suite — Sousa
   I   The Genial Hostess
   II   The Campfire Girls
   III The Lively Flapper
4. Ah, Fors e Lui, from La Traviata — Verdi
   Encore: The Sweetest Story Ever Told — Stultz
   Encore: The American Girl, from The American Maid — Sousa
   MARJORIE MOODY, SOPRANO SOLOIST
5. Golden Light (Agnus Dei), intermezzo — Bizet
   Encore: The U.S. Field Artillery, march — Sousa

* INTERVAL *

6. A Bouquet of Beloved Inspirations, fantasie — Sousa
   Encore: Look for the Silver Lining, humoresque — Sousa
7. (a) Witches' Dance — MacDowell
   Encore: Nola — Arndt
   Encore: Humoresque — Dvorak
   Encore: 12th Street Rag — Bowman
   Encore: Ka-lu-a, from Good Morning, Dearie — Kern
   GEORGE CAREY, XYLOPHONE SOLOIST
   (b) The Gallant Seventh, march — Sousa
   Encore: The Stars and Stripes Forever, march — Sousa
   Encore: Parade of the Wooden Soldiers — Jessel
   Encore: Sabre and Spurs, march — Sousa
8. Romance and Finale, from Concerto No. 2 — Wieniawski
   Encore: Souvenir — Drdla
   CAROLINE THOMAS, VIOLIN SOLOIST
9. Turkey in the Straw — Guion

Source: Sousa Band press book no. 58, p. not noted (*Portland Press Herald*)

302

EVENING CONCERT, 22 SEPTEMBER 1922
Bangor, Maine, at Auditorium

1. The Red Sarafan, overture	Erichs
Encore: El Capitan, march	Sousa
Encore: Social Laws, from The Charlatan	Sousa
2. Centennial Polka	Bellstedt
Encore: I Love a Little Cottage	O'Hara
JOHN DOLAN, CORNET SOLOIST	
3. Leaves from My Notebook, suite	Sousa
I The Genial Hostess	
II The Campfire Girls	
III The Lively Flapper	
Encore: Bullets and Bayonets, march	Sousa
4. Ah, Fors e Lui, from La Traviata	Verdi
Encore: The Sweetest Story Ever Told	Stultz
MARJORIE MOODY, SOPRANO SOLOIST	
5. Golden Light (Agnus Dei), intermezzo	Bizet
Encore: The U.S. Field Artillery, march	Sousa

* INTERVAL *

6. A Bouquet of Beloved Inspirations, fantasie	Sousa
Encore: Look for the Silver Lining, humoresque	Sousa
Encore: Parade of the Wooden Soldiers	Jessel
7. (a) Witches' Dance	MacDowell
Encore: Nola	Arndt
Encore: Ka-lu-a, from Good Morning, Dearie	Kern
GEORGE CAREY, XYLOPHONE SOLOIST	
(b) The Gallant Seventh, march	Sousa
Encore: The Stars and Stripes Forever, march	Sousa
Encore: The High School Cadets, march	Sousa
8. Romance and Finale, from Concerto No. 2	Wieniawski
CAROLINE THOMAS, VIOLIN SOLOIST	
9. Turkey in the Straw	Guion

Source: Sousa Band press book no. 58, p. not noted (*Bangor Daily News*)

EVENING CONCERT, 9 OCTOBER 1922
Rochester, Minnesota, at Armory

1. The Red Sarafan, overture	Erichs
Encore: El Capitan, march	Sousa
2. Centennial Polka	Bellstedt
Encore: Berceuse, from Jocelyn	Godard
JOHN DOLAN, CORNET SOLOIST	
3. Leaves from My Notebook, suite	Sousa
I The Genial Hostess	
II The Campfire Girls	
III The Lively Flapper	
Encore: Bullets and Bayonets, march	Sousa
4. Ah, Fors e Lui, from La Traviata	Verdi
Encore: The American Girl, from The American Maid	Sousa
Encore: Our Boys Are Home Again, song	Sousa
MARJORIE MOODY, SOPRANO SOLOIST	
5. Golden Light (Agnus Dei), intemezzo	Bizet
Encore: The U.S. Field Artillery, march	Sousa

* INTERVAL *

6. A Bouquet of Beloved Inspirations, fantasie	Sousa
Encore: Look for the Silver Lining, humoresque	Sousa
7. (a) Witches' Dance	MacDowell
Encore: Nola	Arndt
Encore: Ka-lu-a, from Good Morning, Dearie	Kern
GEORGE CAREY, XYLOPHONE SOLOIST	
(b) The Gallant Seventh, march	Sousa
Encore: The Stars and Stripes Forever, march	Sousa
Encore: The High School Cadets, march	Sousa
8. Romance and Finale, from Concerto No. 2	Wieniawski
Encore: Souvenir	Drdla
CAROLINE THOMAS, VIOLIN SOLOIST	
9. Turkey in the Straw	Guion

Source: Sousa Band press book no. 58, p. not noted (newspaper not noted)

MATINEE CONCERT, 19 OCTOBER 1922
Iowa City, Iowa, at University of Iowa

1. The Red Sarafan, overture	Erichs
2. Centennial Polka	Bellstedt
Encore: [unnamed]	
JOHN DOLAN, CORNET SOLOIST	
3. Leaves from My Notebook, suite	Sousa
I The Genial Hostess	
II The Campfire Girls	
III The Lively Flapper	
Encore: Bullets and Bayonets, march	Sousa
4. Ah, Fors e Lui, from La Traviata	Verdi
Encore: The Sweetest Story Ever Told	Stultz
Encore: Comin' Thro' the Rye	Burns
MARJORIE MOODY, SOPRANO SOLOIST	
5. Golden Light (Agnus Dei), intermezzo	Bizet
Encore: The U.S. Field Artillery, march	Sousa

* INTERVAL *

6. A Bouquet of Beloved Inspirations, fantasie	Sousa
Encore: Look for the Silver Lining, humoresque	Sousa
7. (a) Witches' Dance	MacDowell
Encore: Nola	Arndt
Encore: Ka-lu-a, from Good Morning, Dearie	Kern
GEORGE CAREY, XYLOPHONE SOLOIST	
(b) The Gallant Seventh, march	Sousa
Encore: The Stars and Stripes Forever, march	Sousa
8. Romance and Finale, from Concerto No. 2	Wieniawski
Encore: Souvenir	Drdla
CAROLINE THOMAS, VIOLIN SOLOIST	
9. Turkey in the Straw	Guion

Source: Sousa Band press book no. 58, p. not noted (newapaper not noted)

EVENING CONCERT, 13 NOVEMBER 1922
Cortland, New York, at Cortland Theatre

1. The Red Sarafan, overture	Erichs
Encore: El Capitan, march	Sousa
2. Centennial Polka	Bellstedt
Encore: Berceuse, from Jocelyn	Godard
JOHN DOLAN, CORNET SOLOIST	
3. Leaves from My Notebook, suite	Sousa
I The Genial Hostess	
II The Campfire Girls	
III The Lively Flapper	
Encore: Bullets and Bayonets, march	Sousa
4. Ah, Fors e Lui, from La Traviata	Verdi
Encore: Comin' Thro' the Rye	Burns
MARJORIE MOODY, SOPRANO SOLOIST	
5. Golden Light (Agnus Dei), intermezzo	Bizet
Encore: The U.S. Field Artillery, march	Sousa

* INTERVAL *

6. A Bouquet of Beloved Inspirations, fantasie	Sousa
Encore: Look for the Silver Lining, humoresque	Sousa
7. (a) Witches' Dance	MacDowell
Encore: Nola	Arndt
GEORGE CAREY, XYLOPHONE SOLOIST	
(b) The Gallant Seventh, march	Sousa
Encore: The Stars and Stripes Forever, march	Sousa
8. Romance and Finale, from Concerto No. 2	Wieniawski
Encore: Traumerei	Schumann
CAROLINE THOMAS, VIOLIN SOLOIST	
9. Turkey in the Straw	Guion

Source: Sousa Band press book no. 58, p. not noted (*Cortland Times*)

EVENING CONCERT, 18 SEPTEMBER 1923
Portland, Maine, at City Hall

1. The American Indian, rhapsody — Orem
   Encore: El Capitan, march — Sousa
   Encore: Bambalino — Youmans
2. Cleopatra Polka — Damare
   Encore: Berceuse, from Jocelyn — Godard
   JOHN DOLAN, CORNET SOLOIST
3. At the King's Court, suite — Sousa
   I   Her Ladyship the Countess
   II   Her Grace the Duchess
   III Her Majesty the Queen
   Encore: The Glory of the Yankee Navy, march — Sousa
   Encore: Nights in the Woods — de Bozi
4. Shadow Song, from Dinorah — Meyerbeer
   Encore: A Kiss in the Dark, from Orange Blossoms — Herbert
   Encore: The American Girl, from The American Maid — Sousa
   MARJORIE MOODY, SOPRANO SOLOIST
5. The Victory Ball — Schelling
   Encore: Solid Men to the Front, march — Sousa

   * INTERVAL *

6. On with the Dance, fantasie — Sousa
   Encore: Gallagher and Shean, humoresque — Sousa
7. (a) Nocturne in E and Minute Waltz — Chopin
   Encore: Yes, We Have No Bananas, song — Silver
   Encore: Crinoline Days, from Music Box Review — Berlin
   GEORGE CAREY, XYLOPHONE SOLOIST
   (b) Nobles of the Mystic Shrine, march — Sousa
   Encore: Parade of the Wooden Soldiers — Jessel
   Encore: Semper Fidelis, march — Sousa
   Encore: The Stars and Stripes Forever, march — Sousa
8. Faust Fantasie — Sarasate
   Encore: [unnamed]
   RACHEL SENIOR, VIOLIN SOLOIST
9. Country Gardens — Grainger

Source: Sousa Band press book no. 62, p. 18 (*Portland Press Herald*)

MATINEE CONCERT, 19 SEPTEMBER 1923
Bangor, Maine, at Auditorium

1. A Bouquet of Beloved Inspirations, fantasie — Sousa
   Encore: El Capitan, march — Sousa
2. Centennial Polka — Bellstedt
   Encore: I've Made My Plans for the Summer, song — Sousa
   JOHN DOLAN, CORNET SOLOIST
3. Leaves from My Notebook, suite — Sousa
   I   The Genial Hostess
   II   The Campfire Girls
   III The Lively Flapper
   Encore: The Glory of the Yankee Navy, march — Sousa
4. Vilanelle Dell' Aqua
   Encore: Love Sends a Little Gift of Roses — Openshaw
   MARJORIE MOODY, SOPRANO SOLOIST
5. The Portrait of a Lady (Kamenoi Ostrow) — Rubinstein
   Encore: Solid Men to the Front, march — Sousa

   * INTERVAL *

6. The Merry-Merry Chorus, fantasie — Sousa
   Encore: Gallagher and Shean, humoresque — Sousa
7. (a) Valse from Suite, Op. 116 — Godard
   R. MEREDITH WILLSON, FLUTE SOLOIST
   (b) The Dauntless Battalion, march — Sousa
   Encore: The High School Cadets, march — Sousa
   Encore: El Capitan, march — Sousa
   Sousa's Band was joined by the Bangor High School
   Band for the above two encores
8. Fantasia on Weber's Oberon — Alvares
   Encore: Believe Me If All Those Endearing Young Charms — Moore
   WINIFRED BAMBRICK, HARP SOLOIST
9. When the Minstrels Came to Town — Bowron

Source: Sousa Band press book no. 61, p. not noted (*Bangor News*)

EVENING CONCERT, 24 SEPTEMBER 1923
Brockton, Massachusetts, at High School

1. The American Indian, rhapsody — Orem
   Encore: El Capitan, march — Sousa
2. Cleopatra Damare
   Encore: Berceuse, from Jocelyn — Godard
   JOHN DOLAN, CORNET SOLOIST
3. At the King's Court, suite — Sousa
   I   Her Ladyship, the Countess
   II   Her Grace, the Duchess
   III Her Majesty, the Queen
   Encore: The Gallant Seventh, march — Sousa
4. Shadow Song, from Dinorah — Meyerbeer
   Encore: A Kiss in the Dark, from Orange Blossoms — De Sylva
   MARJORIE MOODY, SOPRANO SOLOIST
5. The Victory Ball — Schelling
   Encore: Solid Men to the Front, march — Sousa

   * INTERVAL *

6. On with the Dance, medley — Arr. Sousa
   Encore: Mr. Gallagher and Mr. Shean, humoresque — Sousa
   Encore: Parade of the Wooden Soldiers — Jessel
7. Nocturne in E and Minute Waltz — Chopin
   Encore: Yes, We Have No Bananas, song — Silver
   Encore: Crinoline Days, from Music Box Review — Berlin
   Encore: Melody in F — Rubinstein
   GEORGE CAREY, XYLOPHONE SOLOIST
8. Nobles of the Mystic Shrine, march (New) — Sousa
   Encores played with Brockton, Mass. High School Orchestra:
   (a) The High School Cadets, march — Sousa
   (b) King Cotton, march — Sousa
9. Country Gardens — Grainger

Note: Rachel Senior was the violin soloist for this tour, but her performance was omitted so that the high school orchestra could perform.

Source: Sousa Band press book no. 62, p. 22 (*Rutland* [Massachusetts] *Herald*)

EVENING CONCERT, 2 OCTOBER 1923
Middletown, New York, at Stratton Theatre

1. The American Indian, rhapsody — Orem
   Encore: El Capitan, march — Sousa
   Encore: Bambalino — Youmans
2. Cleopatra Polka — Damare
   Encore: Berceuse, from Jocelyn — Godard
   JOHN DOLAN, CORNET SOLOIST
3. At the King's Court, suite — Sousa
   I   Her Ladyship the Countess
   II   Her Grace the Duchess
   III Her Majesty the Queen
   Encore: The Glory of the Yankee Navy, march — Sousa
   Encore: Nights in the Woods — de Bozi
4. Shadow Song, from Dinorah — Meyerbeer
   Encore: A Kiss in the Dark, from Orange Blossoms — Herbert
   Encore: The American Girl, from The American Maid — Sousa
   NORA FAUACHALD, SOPRANO SOLOIST
5. The Victory Ball — Schelling
   Encore: Solid Men to the Front, march — Sousa

   * INTERVAL *

6. On with the Dance, fantasie — Sousa
   Encore: Gallagher and Shean, humoresque — Sousa
7. (a) Nocturne in E and Minute Waltz — Chopin
   Encore: Yes, We Have No Bananas, song — Silver
   Encore: Crinoline Days, from Music Box Review — Berlin
   GEORGE CAREY, XYLOPHONE SOLOIST
   (b) Nobles of the Mystic Shrine, march — Sousa
   Encore: Parade of the Wooden Soldiers — Jessel
   Encore: Semper Fidelis, march — Sousa
   Encore: The Stars and Stripes Forever, march — Sousa
8. Faust Fantasie — Sarasate
   Encore: [unnamed]
   RACHEL SENIOR, VIOLIN SOLOIST
9. Country Gardens — Grainger

Source: Sousa Band press book no. 61, p. not noted (*Middletown Times*)

EVENING CONCERT, 9 OCTOBER 1923
Wilkes-Barre, Pennsylvania, at Irem Temple

1.	The American Indian, rhapsody	Orem
	Encore: King Cotton, march	Sousa
2.	Cleopatra Polka	Damare
	Encore: Berceuse, from Jocelyn	Godard
	JOHN DOLAN, CORNET SOLOIST	
3.	At the King's Court, suite	Sousa
	I Her Ladyship the Countess	
	II Her Grace the Duchess	
	III Her Majesty the Queen	
	Encore: The Gallant Seventh, march	Sousa
4.	The Lark Now Leaves Its Wat'ry Nest	Parker
	Encore: You and I	Lehmann
	NORA FAUCHALD, SOPRANO SOLOIST	
5.	The Victory Ball	Schelling
	Encore: Solid Men to the Front, march	Sousa
	* INTERVAL *	
6.	On with the Dance, fantasie	Sousa
	Encore: Gallagher and Shean, humoresque	Sousa
7.	(a) Nocturne in E and Minute Waltz	Chopin
	Encore: Yes, We Have No Bananas, song	Silver
	Encore: Humoresque	Dvorak
	GEORGE CAREY, XYLOPHONE SOLOIST	
	(b) Nobles of the Mystic Shrine, march	Sousa
	Encore: The Stars and Stripes Forever, march	Sousa
8.	Faust Fantasie	Sarasate
	Encore: Traumerei	Schumann
	RACHEL SENIOR, VIOLIN SOLOIST	
9.	Country Gardens	Grainger

Source: Sousa Band press book no. 61, p. 107 (*Wilke-Barre News*)

EVENING CONCERT, 15 NOVEMBER 1923
Akron, Ohio, at Armory

1.	The American Indian, rhapsody	Orem
	Encore: El Capitan, march	Sousa
	Encore: Bambalino	Youmans
2.	Cleopatra Polka	Damare
	Encore: Berceuse, from Jocelyn	Godard
	JOHN DOLAN, CORNET SOLOIST	
3.	At the King's Court, suite	Sousa
	I Her Ladyship the Countess	
	II Her Grace the Duchess	
	III Her Majesty the Queen	
	Encore: The Gallant Seventh, march	Sousa
4.	The Lark Now Leaves Its Wat'ry Nest	Parker
	Encore: The American Girl, from The American Maid	Sousa
	Encore: Carry Me Back to Old Virginny	Hosmer
	Encore: Dixie	Emmett
	NORA FAUCHALD, SOPRANO SOLOIST	
5.	The Victory Ball	Schelling
	Encore: Solid Men to the Front, march	Sousa
	* INTERVAL *	
6.	On with the Dance, fantasie	Sousa
	Encore: Gallagher and Shean, humoresque	Sousa
	Encore: Parade of the Wooden Soldiers	Jessel
7.	(a) Nocturne in E and Minute Waltz	Chopin
	Encore: Yes, We Have No Bananas, song	Silver
	Encore: Humoresque	Dvorak
	Encore: Crinoline Days, from Music Box Review	Berlin
	GEORGE CAREY, XYLOPHONE SOLOIST	
	(b) Nobles of the Mystic Shrine, march	Sousa
	Encore: The Stars and Stripes Forever, march	Sousa
8.	Faust Fantasie	Sarasate
	Encore: Minuet	Beethoven
	RACHEL SENIOR, VIOLIN SOLOIST	
9.	Country Gardens	Grainger

Source: Sousa Band press book no. 61, p. not noted (*Akron Journal*)

EVENING CONCERT, 5 FEBRUARY 1924
Springfield, Missouri, at Shrine Mosque

1.	The American Indian, rhapsody	Orem
	Encore: El Capitan, march	Sousa
	Encore: Bambalino	Youmans
2.	Cleopatra Polka	Damare
	Encore: Berceuse, from Jocelyn	Godard
	JOHN DOLAN, CORNET SOLOIST	
3.	At the King's Court, suite	Sousa
	I Her Ladyship the Countess	
	II Her Grace the Duchess	
	III Her Majesty the Queen	
	Encore: March of the Mitten Men	Sousa
4.	The Lark Now Leaves Its Wat'ry Nest	Parker
	Encore: The American Girl, from The American Maid	Sousa
	Encore: Carry Me Back to Old Virginny	Hosmer
	Encore: Dixie	Emmett
	NORA FAUCHALD, SOPRANO SOLOIST	
5.	The Victory Ball	Schelling
	Encore: Solid Men to the Front, march	Sousa
	* INTERVAL *	
6.	On with the Dance, fantasie	Sousa
	Encore: Gallagher and Shean, humoresque	Sousa
	Encore: No, No, Nora	Fiorita
	Encore: Parade of the Wooden Soldiers	Jessel
	Encore: Three O'clock in the Morning	Robledo
7.	(a) Nocturne and Waltz	Chopin
	Encore: Humoresque	Dvorak
	Encore: Yes, We Have No Bananas, song	Silver
	GEORGE CAREY, XYLOPHONE SOLOIST	
	(b) Nobles of the Mystic Shrine, march	Sousa
	Encore: The Stars and Stripes Forever, march	Sousa
8.	Faust Fantasie	Sarasate
	Encore: Minuet	Beethoven
	Encore: Maiden's Song	Musin
	RACHEL SENIOR, VIOLIN SOLOIST	
9.	Country Gardens	Grainger

Source: Sousa Band press book no. 61, p. 292 (newspaper not noted)

MATINEE CONCERT, 23 FEBRUARY 1924
Birmingham, Alabama, at Masonic Temple

1.	A Bouquet of Beloved Inspirations, fantasie	Sousa
	Encore: [unnamed]	
2.	Centennial Polka	Bellstedt
	Encore: I've Made My Plans for the Summer, song	Sousa
	JOHN DOLAN, CORNET SOLOIST	
3.	Leaves from My Notebook, suite	Sousa
	I The Genial Hostess	
	II The Campfire Girls	
	III The Lively Flapper	
4.	Aria, from Romeo et Juliette	Gounod
	Encore: Carry Me Back to Old Virginny	Hosmer
	Encore: Dixie	Emmett
	NORA FAUCHALD, SOPRANO SOLOIST	
5.	The Portrait of a Lady (Kamenoi Ostrow)	Rubinstein
	Encore: The U.S. Field Artillery, march	Sousa
	* INTERVAL *	

* During the interval, the combined Alabama Boys Industrial School Band and the Avondale Mills Band performed Sousa's *The Stars and Stripes Forever* and *Manhattan Beach* marches. Sousa conducted the first.

6.	The Merry, Merry Chorus, fantasie	Sousa
	Encore: Gallagher and Shean, humoresque	Sousa
	Encore: Parade of the Wooden Soldiers	Jessel
7.	(a) Valse	Godard
	Encore: [unnamed]	
	R. MEREDITH WILLSON, FLUTE SOLOIST	
	(b) The Dauntless Battalion, march	Sousa
	Encore: Semper Fidelis, march	Sousa
8.	Fantasia on Weber's Oberon	Alvares
	Encore: Believe Me If All Those Endearing Young Charms	Moore
	WINIFRED BAMBRICK, HARP SOLOIST	
9.	When the Minstrels Came to Town	Bowron

Source: Sousa Band press book no. 62, p. 84 (*Birmingham News*)

EVENING CONCERT, 4 MARCH 1924
Raleigh, North Carolina, at City Auditorium

1. The American Indian, rhapsody — Orem
   Encore: El Capitan, march — Sousa
   Encore: Bambalino — Youmans
2. Cleopatra Polka — Damare
   Encore: Berceuse, from Jocelyn — Godard
   JOHN DOLAN, CORNET SOLOIST
3. At the King's Court, suite — Sousa
   I   Her Ladyship the Countess
   II   Her Grace the Duchess
   III Her Majesty the Queen
   Encore: March of the Mitten Men — Sousa
4. The Lark Now Leaves Its Wat'ry Nest — Parker
   Encore: The Belle of Bayou Teche, song — Sousa
   Encore: Carry Me Back to Old Virginny — Hosmer
   Encore: Dixie — Emmett
   NORA FAUCHALD, SOPRANO SOLOIST
5. The Victory Ball — Schelling
   Encore: The U.S. Field Artillery, march — Sousa

* INTERVAL *

6. On with the Dance, fantasie — Sousa
   Encore: Gallagher and Shean, humoresque — Sousa
   Encore: Turkish Towel Rag — Allen
   Encore: No, No, Nora — Fiorita
   Encore: [unnamed]
7. (a) Nocturne and Waltz — Chopin
   Encore: Crinoline Days, from Music Box Review — Berlin
   Encore: Yes, We Have No Bananas, song — Silver
   Encore: [unnamed]
   GEORGE CAREY, XYLOPHONE SOLOIST
   (b) Nobles of the Mystic Shrine, march — Sousa
   Encore: The Stars and Stripes Forever, march — Sousa
8. Faust Fantasie — Sarasate
   Encore: Minuet — Beethoven
   Encore: Maiden's Song — Musin
   RACHEL SENIOR, VIOLIN SOLOIST
9. Country Gardens — Grainger

Source: Sousa Band press book no. 63, p. 39 (*Raleigh News*)

EVENING CONCERT, 24 JUNE 1924
Amsterdam, New York, at Rialto Theatre

1. My Old Stable Jacket — Bilton
   Encore: El Capitan, march — Sousa
   Encore: Peaches and Cream, fox trot — Sousa
2. La Favorita — Hartman
   Encore: If Winter Comes — Tennent
   JOHN DOLAN, CORNET SOLOIST
3. Looking Upward, suite — Sousa
   I   By the Light of the Polar Star
   II   Under the Southern Cross
   III Mars and Venus
   Encore: The Gallant Seventh, march — Sousa
4. Polonaise, from Mignon — Thomas
   Encore: The American Girl, from The American Maid — Sousa
   MARJORIE MOODY, SOPRANO SOLOIST
5. Don Juan, tone poem — R. Strauss
   Encore: The U.S. Field Artillery, march — Sousa

* INTERVAL *

6. Music of the Minute, fantasie — Sousa
   Encore: What Do You Do Sunday, Mary?, humoresque — Sousa
   Encore: Manhattan Beach, march — Sousa
7. (a) Liebesfreud — Kreisler
   Encore: [unnamed]
   Encore: Humoresque — Dvorak
   Encore: [unnamed]
   HOWARD GOULDEN, XYLOPHONE SOLOIST
   (b) Ancient and Honorable Artillery Company, march — Sousa
   Encore: The Stars and Stripes Forever, march — Sousa
   Encore: Semper Fidelis, march — Sousa
8. Fantasia on Weber's Oberon — Alvares
   Encore: Annie Laurie — Traditional
   WINIFRED BAMBRICK, HARP SOLOIST
9. Mountain Dances — Orem

Source: Sousa Band press book no. 63, p. 121 (*Amsterdam Record*)

MATINEE CONCERT, 26 JUNE 1924
Rutland, Massachusetts, at Playhouse

1. My Old Stable Jacket — Bilton
   Encore: El Capitan, march — Sousa
2. La Favorita — Hartman
   Encore: If Winter Comes — Tennent
   JOHN DOLAN, CORNET SOLOIST
3. Looking Upward, suite — Sousa
   I   By the Light of the Polar Star
   II   Under the Southern Cross
   III Mars and Venus
   Encore: The Gallant Seventh, march — Sousa
4. Polonaise, from Mignon — Thomas
   Encore: The American Girl, from The American Maid — Sousa
   MARJORIE MOODY, SOPRANO SOLOIST
5. Don Juan, tone poem — R. Strauss
   Encore: Keep Cool and Keep Coolidge — Harper

* INTERVAL *

6. Music of the Minute, fantasie — Sousa
   Encore: What Do You Do Sunday, Mary?, humoresque — Sousa
7. (a) Liebesfreud — Kreisler
   HOWARD GOULDEN, XYLOPHONE SOLOIST
   (b) Ancient and Honorable Artillery Company, march — Sousa
8. Fantasia on Weber's Oberon — Alvares
   Encore: Annie Laurie — Traditional
   WINIFRED BAMBRICK, HARP SOLOIST
9. Mountain Dances — Orem
   Encore: The Stars and Stripes Forever, march — Sousa

Source: Sousa Band press book no. 63, p. 120 (*Rutland Herald*)

EVENING CONCERT, 26 JUNE 1924
Glens Falls, New York, at Knights of Columbus Auditorium

1. My Old Stable Jacket — Bilton
   Encore: El Capitan, march — Sousa
2. La Favorita — Hartman
   Encore: If Winter Comes — Tennent
   JOHN DOLAN, CORNET SOLOIST
3. Looking Upward, suite — Sousa
   I   By the Light of the Polar Star
   II   Under the Southern Cross
   III Mars and Venus
4. Polonaise, from Mignon — Thomas
   Encore: The American Girl, from The American Maid — Sousa
   MARJORIE MOODY, SOPRANO SOLOIST
5. Don Juan, tone poem — R. Strauss
   Encore: The U.S. Field Artillery, march — Sousa
   Encore: The Liberty Bell, march — Sousa

* INTERVAL *

6. Music of the Music, fantasie — Sousa
7. (a) Liebesfreud — Kreisler
   Encore: Kitten on the Keys — Confrey
   Encore: Humoresque — Dvorak
   HOWARD GOULDEN, XYLOPHONE SOLOIST
   (b) Ancient and Honorable Artillery Company, march — Sousa
   Encore: The Stars and Stripes Forever, march — Sousa
   Encore: Manhattan Beach, march — Sousa
   Encore: The Washington Post, march — Sousa
8. Fantasia on Weber's Oberon — Alvares
   Encore: Annie Laurie — Traditional
   WINIFRED BAMBRICK, HARP SOLOIST
9. Mountain Dances — Orem

Source: Sousa Band press book no. 63, p. 120 (*Glens Falls Post*)

EVENING CONCERT, 16 SEPTEMBER 1925
Elmira, New York, at Lyceum Theatre

1. Amrain na N-Gaedeal, Op. 31, Goelic fantasy — O'Donnell
   Encore: El Capitan, march — Sousa
2. The Carnival of Venice — Arban
   Encore: [unnamed]
   DANA M. GARRETT, CORNET SOLOIST**
3. Cubaland, suite — Sousa
   I   Under the Spanish Flag
   II Under the American Flag
   III Under the Cuban Flag
   Encore: The Invincible Eagle, march — Sousa
4. I Am Titania, from Mignon — Thomas
   Encore: Danny Boy — Weatherly
   Encore: Do, Do, Do — Gershwin
   MARJORIE MOODY, SOPRANO SOLOIST
5. Love Scene, from Feuresnoth — Strauss
   Encore: The Liberty Bell, march — Sousa

* INTERVAL *

6. Jazz America, fantasie — Sousa
   Encore: Chinese Wedding Procession — Hosmer
   Encore: Follow the Swallow, humoresque — Sousa
7. (a) I Want to Be Happy, from No, No Nanette — Youmans
   Encore: On the Mississippi — Klein
   SAXOPHONE OCTET: EDWARD J. HENEY, GERALD GOODRICH, HAROLD STEPHENS,
   LEON E. WEIR, CLARENCE JOHNSON,BENJAMIN CONKLIN, AND FRED MONROE
   (b) The National Game, march — Sousa
   Encore: The Stars and Stripes Forever, march — Sousa
   Encore: Semper Fidelis, march — Sousa
8. Morning, Noon and Night in Vienna: Overture — Suppe
   Encore: Andree — Carey
   GEORGE CAREY, XYLOPHONE SOLOIST
9. Sheep and Goat Walking to Pasture — Guion
** Dana M. Garrett substituted for John Dolan
Source: Sousa Band press book no. 68, p. 27 (*Elmira Star-Gazette*)

EVENING CONCERT, 25 OCTOBER 1926
Watertown, South Dakota, at Methodist Church

1. Herod, overture — Hadley
   Encore: The Gridiron Club, march — Sousa
   Encore: Valencia — Padilla
2. Sounds from the Riviera — Boccalari
   Encore: Just a Cottage Small — Hanly
   JOHN DOLAN, CORNET SOLOIST
3. The Three S's, suite
   I   Mourning Journals — Strauss
   II The Lost Chord — Sullivan
   III Mars and Venus, from Looking Upward — Sousa
   Encore: Hands Across the Sea, march — Sousa
4. On the Beautiful Blue Danube, waltz — Strauss
   Encore: Italian Street Song, from Naughty Marietta — Herbert
   Encore: Carry Me Back to Old Virginny — Hosmer
   Encore: Comin' Thro' the Rye — Burns
   Encore: Blue Ridge, I'm Coming Back to You, song — Sousa
   MARJORIE MOODY, SOPRANO SOLOIST
5. Le Voyvode — Tchaikowsky
   Encore: The Pride of the Wolverines, march — Sousa

* INTERVAL *

6. The Mingling of the Wets and the Drys, humoresque — Sousa
   Encore: The Whistling Farmer Boy — Fillmore
7. (a) Saxerewski — Paderewski (arranged)
   Encore: Whoop 'Em Up Blues — Barnett
   Encore: Laughing Gas — Gurewich
   Encores: [several, unnamed]
   SAXOPHONE OCTET
   (b) Sesquicentennial Exposition March — Sousa
   Encore: The Stars and Stripes Forever, march — Sousa
   Encore: Semper Fidelis, march — Sousa
8. Liebesfreud — Kreisler
   Encore: Souvenir — Drdla
   Encore: Lots of Pep — Bein
   Encore: Parade of the Wooden Soldiers — Jessel
   HOWARD GOULDEN, XYLOPHONE SOLOIST
9. Juba — Dett
Source: Sousa Band press book no. 71, p. 77 (*Daily Public Opinion*)

EVENING CONCERT, 10 NOVEMBER 1926
Nashville, Tennessee, at Ryman Auditorium

1. Herod, overture — Hadley
   Encore: El Capitan, march — Sousa
   Encore: Valencia — Padilla
2. Sounds from the Riviera — Boccalari
   Encore: Just a Cottage Small — Hanly
   JOHN DOLAN, CORNET SOLOIST
3. The Three S's, suite
   I   Mourning Journals — Strauss
   II The Lost Chord — Sullivan
   III Mars and Venus, from Looking Upward — Sousa
   Encore: Power and Glory, march — Sousa
4. On the Beautiful Blue Danube, waltz — Strauss
   Encore: Dixie — Emmett
   Encore: Italian Street Song, from Naughty Marietta — Herbert
   MARJORIE MOODY, SOPRANO SOLOIST
5. Le Voyvode — Tchaikowsky
   Encore: The Pride of the Wolverines, march — Sousa

* INTERVAL *

6. The Mingling of the Wets and the Drys, humoresque — Sousa
   Encore: The Whistling Farmer Boy — Fillmore
7. (a) Saxerewski — Paderewski (arranged)
   Encores: [several, unnamed]
   SAXOPHONE OCTET
   (b) Sesquicentennial Exposition March — Sousa
   Encore: The Stars and Stripes Forever, march — Sousa
   Encore: Semper Fidelis, march — Sousa
8. Liebesfreud — Kreisler
   Encore: Souvenir — Drdla
   HOWARD GOULDEN, XYLOPHONE SOLOIST
9. Juba — Dett
Source: Sousa Band press book no. 71, p. 95 (*Nashville Tennesseean*)

EVENING CONCERT, 26 OCTOBER 1927
Pittsburg, Kansas, at Kansas State Teachers College

1. The Flying Dutchman: Overture — Wagner
   Encore: The Atlantic City Pageant, march — Sousa
   Encore: Conduit Park March — Richards
2. The Carnival of Venice — Arban
   Encore: Berceuse, from Jocelyn — Godard
   JOHN DOLAN, CORNET SOLOIST
3. The Three S's, suite
   I   Mourning Journals — Strauss
   II The Lost Chord — Sullivan
   III Mars and Venus, from Looking Upward — Sousa
4. Ah, Fors e Lui, from La Traviata — Verdi
   Encore: Danny Boy — Weatherly
   Encore: Carry Me Back to Old Virginny — Hosmer
   Encore: Italian Street Song, from Naughty Marietta — Herbert
   MARJORIE MOODY, SOPRANO SOLOIST
5. Andante Cantabile, from String Quartet — Tchaikowsky
   Encore: The Minnesota March — Sousa
   Encore: The U.S. Field Artillery, march — Sousa

* INTERVAL *

6. Feast of Spring, from Hamlet Suite — Thomas
   Encore: The Mingling of the Wets and the Drys, humoresque — Sousa
7. (a) Beautiful Colorado — De Luca
   EDWARD J. HENEY, SAXOPHONE SOLOIST
   Encore: Four unnamed numbers by the saxophone sextet
   (b) Magna Charta, march — Sousa
   Encore: The Stars and Stripes Forever, march — Sousa
   Encore: Semper Fidelis, march — Sousa
8. Ghost of the Commander — Grossman
   Encore: The World Is Waiting for the Sunrise — Lockhart
   Encore: Indian Love Call, from Rose Marie — Friml
   Encore: The Doll Dance — Brown
   HOWARD GOULDEN, XYLOPHONE SOLOIST
9. Theme, Variations and Carnival Tune, from Scenes in Naples — Massenet
Source: Sousa Band press book no. 72, p. 132 (*Pittsburgh Sun*)
Note: During the interval, Sousa conducted the massed bands from the high schools of Fort Scott, Chanute, Parsons, Joplin, and Pittsburg in two of his marches, "The High School Cadets" and "The Washington Post."

307

TYPICAL CONCERT/MOVIE TOUR CONCERT
19-25 NOVEMBER 1927
St. Louis, Missouri, at Lowe's State Theater
(4 movies/concerts per day)

1. The Washington Post, march — Sousa
   Encore: El Capitan, march — Sousa
2. The Lost Chord — Sullivan
   JOHN DOLON CORNET SOLOIST
   Accompanied by Tom Jerry, organ, and Winifred Bambrick, harp
3. Semper Fidelis, march — Sousa
   Encore: Manhattan Beach, march — Sousa
4. Italian Street Song, from Naughty Marietta — Herbert
   Encore: Dixie — Emmett
   MARJORIE MOODY, SOPRANO SOLOIST
5. The U.S. Field Artillery, march — Sousa
   Encore: The Stars and Stripes Forever, march — Sousa

(End of concert. Remainder of program was a movie, <u>Body and Soul</u>.)
Source: Sousa Band press book no. 72, p. 15 (*St. Louis Daily Globe-Democrat*)

EVENING CONCERT, 19 JULY 1928
Schenectady, New York, at Wedgeway Theater

1. Marche Militaire Francaise, from Suite Algerienne — Saint-Saens
   Encore: El Capitan, march — Sousa
2. Habanera — Sarasate
   JOHN DOLAN, CORNET SOLOIST
3. Tales of a Traveler, suite — Sousa
   I   The Kaffir on the Karoo
   II   In the Land of the Golden Fleece
   III Grand Promenade at the White House
4. Ah, Fors e Lui, from La Traviata — Verdi
   Encore: The Nightingale — Alabieff
   MARJORIE MOODY, SOPRANO SOLOIST
5. Brigg Fair, English rhapsody — Delius

* INTERVAL *

6. Among My Souvenirs, humoresque — Sousa
   Encore: The Gliding Girl, tango — Sousa
7. (a) Dance of the Mirlitrons, from Nutcracker — Tchaikowsky
   FLUTE SEXTET
   (b) The Liberty Bell, march — Sousa
   Encore: The Stars and Stripes Forever, march — Sousa
8. Rio Rita — Tierney
   Encore: Lots of Pep — Bein
   HOWARD GOULDEN, XYLOPHONE SOLOIST
9. Balance All and Swing Partners, from Impressions at the Movies — Sousa

Source: Sousa Band press book no. 75, p. 4 (*Schenectady Union-Star*)

MATINEE CONCERT, 15 AUGUST 1928
Dover, New Hampshire, at Opera House

1. Marche Militaire Francaise, from Suite Algerienne — Saint-Saens
   Encore: El Capitan, march — Sousa
2. Habanera — Sarasate
   JOHN DOLAN, CORNET SOLOIST
3. Tales of a Traveler, suite — Sousa
   I   The Kaffir on the Karoo
   II   In the Land of the Golden Fleece
   III Grand Promenade at the White House
   Encore: Semper Fidelis, march — Sousa
4. Love's Radiant Hour, song — Sousa
   Encore: Little Irish Rose, song — Zamecnik
   MARJORIE MOODY, SOPRANO SOLOIST
5. Death and Transfiguration, tone poem — Strauss
   Encore: The U.S. Field Artillery, march — Sousa

* INTERVAL *

6. Among My Souvenirs, humoresque — Sousa
7. (a) Dance of the Mirlitrons, from Nutcracker — Tchaikowsky
   MESSRS. EVANS, PETRIE, PHARES, OROSKY, ZLOTNIK, HALL, FLUTES
   (b) Golden Jubilee, march — Sousa
8. Polonaise Mignon — Tierney
   Encore: Rio Rita — Tierney
   HOWARD GOULDEN, XYLOPHONE SOLOIST
9. Balance All and Swing Partners, from Impressions at the Movies — Sousa
   Encore: The Stars and Stripes Forever, march — Sousa

Source: Sousa Band press book no. 75, p. 21 (*Foster's Daily Democrat*)

EVENING CONCERT, 15 AUGUST 1928
Portland, Maine, at City Hall

1. Marche Militaire Francaise, from Suite Algerienne — Saint-Saens
   Encore: El Capitan, march — Sousa
2. Habanera — Sarasate
   Encore: Twilight Romance — Gurewich
   JOHN DOLAN, CORNET SOLOIST
3. Tales of a Traveler, suite — Sousa
   I   The Kaffir on the Karoo
   II   In the Land of the Golden Fleece
   III Grand Promenade at the White House
   Encore: The U.S. Field Artillery, march — Sousa
4. Love's Radiant Hour, song — Sousa
   Encore: Little Irish Rose, song — Zamecnik
   Encore: Peter Pan — Stickles
   MARJORIE MOODY, SOPRANO SOLOIST
5. Death and Transfiguration, tone poem — Strauss
   Encore: Semper Fidelis, march — Sousa

* INTERVAL *

6. Among My Souvenirs, humoresque — Sousa
   Encore: The Whistling Farmer Boy — Fillmore
   Encore: Ragging the Scale — Claypoole
7. (a) Dance of the Mirlitrons, from Nutcracker — Tchaikowsky
   FLUTE SEXTET
   (b) Golden Jubilee, march — Sousa
   Encore: The Stars and Stripes Forever, march — Sousa
   Encore: The Liberty Bell, march — Sousa
8. Polonaise Mignon — Tierney
   Encore: The World Is Waiting for the Sunrise — Lockhart
   Encore: Indian Love Call, from Rose Marie — Friml
   Encore: Rio Rita — Tierney
   Encore: Lots of Pep — Bein
   HOWARD GOULDEN, XYLOPHONE SOLOIST
9. Balance All and Swing Partners, from Impressions at the Movies — Sousa

Source: Sousa Band press book no. 75, p. 21 (*Portland Press Herald*)

EVENING CONCERT, 16 AUGUST 1928
Lewiston, Maine, at Armory

1. Marche Militaire Francaise, from Suite Algerienne — Saint-Saens
    Encore: El Capitan, march — Sousa

2. Habanera — Sarasate
    Encore: Twilight Romance — Gurewich
    JOHN DOLAN, CORNET SOLOIST

3. Tales of a Traveler, suite — Sousa
    I The Kaffir on the Karoo
    II In the Land of the Golden Fleece
    III Grand Promenade at the White House
    Encore: The U.S. Field Artillery, march — Sousa

4. Love's Radiant Hour, song — Sousa
    Encore: Little Irish Rose, song — Zamecnik
    Encore: Peter Pan — Stickles
    MARJORIE MOODY, SOPRANO SOLOIST

5. Death and Transfiguration, tone poem — Strauss
    Encore: Semper Fidelis, march — Sousa

* INTERVAL *

6. Among My Souvenirs, humoresque — Sousa
    Encore: The Whistling Farmer Boy — Fillmore

7. (a) Dance of the Mirlitrons, from Nutcracker — Tchaikowsky
    FLUTE SEXTET
    (b) Golden Jubilee, march — Sousa
    Encore: The Stars and Stripes Forever, march — Sousa
    Encore: The Washington Post, march — Sousa

8. Polonaise Mignon — Tierney
    Encore: Rio Rita — Tierney
    Encore: The World Is Waiting for the Sunrise — Lockhart
    Encore: Indian Love Call, from Rose Marie — Friml
    HOWARD GOULDEN, XYLOPHONE SOLOIST

9. Balance All and Swing Partners, from Impressions at the Movies — Sousa

Source: Sousa Band press book no. 75, p. 24 (*Lewiston Daily Sun*)

EVENING CONCERT, 5 SEPTEMBER 1929
Sterling, Colorado, at Blair Hall

1. Festival Overture — Leutner
    Encore: El Capitan, march — Sousa

2. Fantasy in F Minor — Gurewich
    Encore: Pagan Love Song — Brown
    EDWARD J. HENEY, SAXOPHONE SOLOIST
    Encore: [unnamed]
    SAXOPHONE SEXET

3. I Mourning Journals — Strauss
    II The Lost Chord — Sullivan
    III Mars and Venus, from Looking Upward — Sousa
    Encore: Foshay Tower Washington Memorial, march — Sousa

4. Shadow Song, from Dinorah — Meyerbeer
    Encore: Danny Boy — Weatherly
    Encore: Italian Street Song, from Naughty Marietta — Herbert
    MARJORIE MOODY, SOPRANO SOLOIST

5. Finale, from Symphony No. 4 — Tchaikowsky
    Encore: Semper Fidelis, march — Sousa

* INTERVAL *

6. A Bouquet of Beloved Inspirations, fantasy — Sousa
    Encore: When My Dreams Come True, fantasy — Sousa

7. Ghost of the Commander — Grossman
    Encore: The World Is Waiting for the Sunrise — Lockhart
    Encore: Indian Love Call, from Rose Marie — Friml
    Encore: Lots of Pep — Bein
    HOWARD GOULDEN, XYLOPHONE SOLOIST

8. University of Illinois, march — Sousa
    Encore: The Stars and Stripes Forever, march — Sousa
    Encore: The U.S. Field Artillery, march — Sousa

9. Turkey in the Straw — Guion

Source: Sousa Band press book no. 75, p. 131 (*Sterling Advocate*)

EVENING CONCERT, 22 OCTOBER 1930
Jackson, Mississippi, at City Auditorium

1. Carneval Romaine: Overture — Berlioz
    Encore: The U.S. Field Artillery, march — Sousa

2. Tower of Jewels — Tong
    Encore: A Little Kiss Each Morning, song — Woods
    WILLIAM TONG, CORNET SOLOIST

3. The Three S's, suite
    I Mourning Journals — Strauss
    II The Lost Chord — Sullivan
    III Mars and Venus, from Looking Upward — Sousa
    Encore: Daughters of Texas, march — Sousa

4. Staccato Polka — Mulder
    Encore: Dixie — Emmett
    Encore: Kerry Dance — Molloy
    MARJORIE MOODY, SOPRANO SOLOIST

5. Knights of the Holy Grail, Grand Scene, from Parsifal — Wagner
    Encore: Semper Fidelis, march — Sousa

* INTERVAL *

6. Espana Rhapsody — Chabrier
    Encore: The Mingling of the Wets and the Drys, humoresque — Sousa

7. (a) Beautiful Colorado — De Luca
    EDWARD J. HENEY, SAXOPHONE SOLOIST
    Encore: Four unnamed numbers by the saxophone sextet
    (b) The Royal Welsh Fusiliers, march — Sousa
    Encore: The Stars and Stripes Forever, march — Sousa

8. Liebesfreud — Kreisler
    Encore: Old Folks at Home — Foster
    Encore: A Bunch of Roses, Spanish march — Chapi
    Encore: Twelfth Street Rag — Bowman
    WILLIAM PAULSON, XYLOPHONE SOLOIST

9. Turkey in the Straw — Guion

Source: Sousa Band press book no. 75, p. 165 (*Daily News*)

EVENING CONCERT, 6 NOVEMBER 1930
Greenville, South Carolina, at Textile Hall

1. Carneval Romaine: Overture — Berlioz
    Encore: The Gridiron Club, march — Sousa

2. Tower of Jewels — Tong
    Encore: A Little Kiss Each Morning, song — Woods
    WILLIAM TONG, CORNET SOLOIST

3. The Three S's, suite
    I Mourning Journals — Strauss
    II The Lost Chord — Sullivan
    III Mars and Venus, from Looking Upward — Sousa
    Encore: El Capitan, march — Sousa

4. Staccato Polka — Mulder
    Encore: [unnamed]
    Encore: Carry Me Back to Old Virginny — Hosmer
    Encore: Kerry Dance — Molloy
    MARJORIE MOODY, SOPRANO SOLOIST

5. Knights of the Holy Grail, Grand Scene, from Parsifal — Wagner
    Encore: The U.S. Field Artillery, march — Sousa

* INTERVAL *

6. Espana Rhapsody — Chabrier

7. (a) Beautiful Colorado — De Luca
    Encore: Mighty Lak' a Rose, song — Nevin
    EDWARD J. HENEY, SAXOPHONE SOLOIST
    (b) The Royal Welsh Fusiliers, march — Sousa
    Encore: The Stars and Stripes Forever, march — Sousa

8. Liebesfreud — Kreisler
    Encore: Old Folks at Home — Foster
    Encore: A Bunch of Roses, Spanish march — Chapi
    Encore: Twelfth Street Rag — Bowman
    Encore: Argonaise, from Le Cid — Massenet
    WILLIAM PAULSON, XYLOPHONE SOLOIST

9. Turkey in the Straw — Guion

Source: Sousa Band press book no. 75, p. 172 (*Greenville News*)

PART (B)
1926 WILLOW GROVE CONCERTS

The Sousa Band summer concerts at Willow Grove Park (1901-1926, except for 1911) were not the same as those played on the road. Instead of two daily concerts with intermissions, there were four shorter ones without intermissions (two each afternoon and evening, the usual times being 2:30-3:15, 4:30-5:30, 7:45-8:30, and 9:45-10:45). Every program was different, although some selections were repeated at later dates.

The only known documentation of complete Willow Grove concerts (i.e., with encores) for *any* year was compiled by percussionist John J. Heney during the 1926 engagement. In his full set of printed programs, he had written the encores in the margins.

The author was unable to reconstruct all Heney's programs. Heney marked most of them, but he used shortened titles which would identify the pieces to the musicians but not to someone unfamiliar with the band repertory. All the programs that could be reconstructed without guesswork are presented below.

In 1926, the band played 228 Willow Grove concerts in fifty-seven days, from Sunday, 18 July through Sunday, 12 September.

Heney's programs are on file at the archives of the United States Marine Band in Washington, D.C.

SUNDAY, 18 JULY
(First concert of the day)

1.	Tannhäuser, overture	Wagner
	Encore: The Pride of the Wolverines, march	Sousa
	Encore: Valencia, pasodoble	Padilla
2.	Pyramids	Liberati
	Encore: O Lassie o' Mine, song	Walt
	JOHN DOLAN, CORNET SOLOIST	
3.	Camera Studies, suite	Sousa
	I The Flashing Eyes of Andalusia	
	II Drifting to Loveland	
	III The Children's Ball	
	Encore: Song of the Vagabond, from The Vagabond King	Friml
4.	Cradle Song	Kreisler
	Encore: There's a Merry Brown Thrush, song	Sousa
	Encore: Just a Cottage Small, song	Hanley
	MARJORIE MOODY, SOPRANO SOLOIST	
5.	Benediction of the Poignards, from Les Huguenots	Meyerbeer

MONDAY, 19 JULY
(Third concert of the day)

1.	Ethiopian Rhapsody	Hosmer
	Encore: The Invincible Eagle, march	Sousa
2.	Tramp, Tramp, Tramp	Rollinson
	NOBLE B. HOWARD, EUPHONIUM SOLOIST	
3.	Dwellers of the Western World, suite	Sousa
	I The Red Man	
	II The White Man	
	III The Black Man	
4.	Sweethearts, waltz	D'Albert
5.	The U.S. Field Artillery, march	Sousa

MONDAY, 19 JULY
(Fourth concert of the day)

1.	My Old Stable Jacket, overture	Bilton
	Encore: The Pride of the Wolverines, march	Sousa
	Encore: Valencia, pasodoble	Padilla
2.	The Carnival of Venice	Clarke
	JOHN DOLAN, CORNET SOLOIST	
3.	Three Quotations, suite	Sousa
	I The King of France	
	II I, Too, Was Born in Arcadia	
	III In Darkest Africa	
	Encore: The Stars and Stripes Forever, march	Sousa
	Encore: Oh! How I've Waited for You, song	Ayer
4.	Shadow Song, from Dinorah	Meyerbeer
	Encore: Comin' Thro' the Rye, song	Burns
	MARJORIE MOODY, SOPRANO SOLOIST	
5.	The Black Horse Troop, march	Sousa

TUESDAY, 20 JULY
(Fourth concert of the day)

1.	The American Indian, rhapsody	Orem
	Encore: Keeping Step with the Union, march	Sousa
2.	My Regards	Llewellyn
	Encore: Love's Old Sweet Song	Molloy
	NOBLE P. HOWARD, EUPHONIUM SOLOIST	
3.	Grand Scene and Ensemble, from Andrea Chenier	Giordano
	Encore: The Stars and Stripes Forever, march	Sousa
4.	I Am the Rose, song	Arditi
	Encore: Just a Cottage Small, song	Hanley
	MARJORIE MOODY, SOPRANO SOLOIST	
5.	Ancient and Honorable Artillery Company, march	Sousa

WEDNESDAY, 21 JULY
(First concert of the day)

1.	Gems from Iolanthe	Sullivan
	Encore: The Fairest of the Fair, march	Sousa
2.	Hungarian Rhapsody No. 14	Liszt
	Encore: The Stars and Stripes Forever, march	Sousa
	Encore: Valencia, pasodoble	Padilla
3.	Scenes from Faust	Gounod
4.	A Cup of Coffee, song	Mayer
5.	(a) Blumengephister, idyll	Blon
	(b) The Dauntless Battalion, march	Sousa

WEDNESDAY, 21 JULY
(Third concert of the day)

1.	Selections from Orpheus in the Underworld	Offenbach
	Encore: The Washington Post, march	Sousa
2.	Centennial Polka	Bellstedt
	Encore: The Philosophic Maid, from The Charlatan	Sousa
	JOHN DOLAN, CORNET SOLOIST	
3.	Night of the Classical Sabbath, from Mephistofele	Boito
4.	Rubenesque, intermezzo	Slater
5.	(a) Love of Life, waltz	Zamzak
	(b) Power and Glory, march	Sousa

THURSDAY, 22 JULY
(First concert of the day, featuring Sousa's compositions)

1.	Tally-Ho!, overture	Sousa
	Encore: National Fencibles, march	Sousa
	Encore: Song of the Vagabond, from The Vagabond King	Friml
2.	Selections from The Bride Elect	Sousa

310

3. Jazz America, fantasie — Sousa
4. (a) The Coeds of Michigan, waltz — Sousa
   (b) The National Game, march — Sousa
5. Follow the Swallow, humoresque — Sousa

THURSDAY, 22 JULY
(Second concert of the day, featuring Sousa's compositions)

1. Selections from The Charlatan — Sousa
   Encore: On the Campus, march — Sousa
2. The Milkmaid, song — Sousa
   JOHN DOLAN, CORNET SOLOIST
3. Cubaland, suite — Sousa
   I   Under the Spanish Flag
   II   Under the American Flag
   III Under the Cuban Flag
   Encore: Sound Off, march — Sousa
4. A Serenade in Seville, song — Sousa
   Encore: The Goose Girl, from The Free Lance — Sousa
   MARJORIE MOODY, SOPRANO SOLOIST
5. Nobles of the Mystic Shrine, march — Sousa

THURSDAY, 22 JULY
(Fourth concert of the day, featuring Sousa's compositions)

1. Selections from El Capitan — Sousa
   Encore: The Gridiron Club, march — Sousa
2. I Wonder, song — Sousa
   JOHN DOLAN, CORNET SOLOIST
3. Tales of a Traveler, suite — Sousa
   I   The Kaffir on the Karoo
   II   In the Land of the Golden Fleece
   III Grand Promenade at the White House
   Encore: The Stars and Stripes Forever, march — Sousa
4. In Flanders Fields the Poppies Grow, song — Sousa
   Encore: Fanny, from Chris and the Wonderful Lamp — Sousa
   MARJORIE MOODY, SOPRANO SOLOIST
5. Hands Across the Sea, march — Sousa

FRIDAY, 23 JULY
(Second Concert of the day)

1. Selections from Aida — Verdi
   Encore: Corcoran Cadets, march — Sousa
2. Fantasia Original — Georges-Hue
   RAYMOND E. WILLIAMS, FLUTE SOLOIST
3. A Study in Rhythms, fantasie — Sousa
   Encore: The Gridiron Club, march — Sousa
4. Shadow Song, from Dinorah — Meyerbeer
   Encore: Carry Me Back to Old Virginny, song — Hosmer
   MARJORIE MOODY, SOPRANO SOLOIST
5. Sabre and Spurs, march — Sousa

SATURDAY, 24 JULY
(First concert of the day)

1. The Hunt of King Henry, overture — Mehue
   Encore: The Free Lance, march — Sousa
2. Pyramids — Liberati
   JOHN DOLAN, CORNET SOLOIST
3. Songs of Grace and Songs of Glory, fantasie — Sousa
   Encore: The Directorate, march — Sousa
4. Morning Journals, waltz — Strauss
5. The Thunderer, march — Sousa

SATURDAY, 24 JULY
(Second concert of the day)

1. Gems of Scotland — Godfrey
   Encore: The Mingling of the Wets and Drys, fantasie — Sousa
2. Parade of the Wooden Soldiers — Jessell
   HOWARD GOULDEN, XYLOPHONE SOLOIST
3. Selections from Lohengrin — Wagner
4. Aria, from Louise — Charpentier
   Encore: Italian Street Song, from Naughty Marietta — Herbert
   MARJORIE MOODY, SOPRANO SOLOIST
5. (a) The Merchant's Casino, waltz — Gung'l
   (b) The Rifle Regiment, march — Sousa

SUNDAY, 25 JULY
(Second concert of the day)

1. Pique Dame, overture — Suppe
   Encore: The Fairest of the Fair, march — Sousa
   Encore: The Mingling of the Wets and Drys, fantasie — Sousa
2. Gems from the Works of Sullivan — Sullivan
   Encore: The U.S. Field Artillery, march — Sousa
   Encore: The Gliding Girl, tango — Sousa
3. Concerto Brilliant for Flute — Chaminade
   RAYMOND E. WILLIAMS, FLUTE SOLOIST
4. There's a Merry Brown Thrush, song — Sousa
   Encore: On the Beautiful Blue Danube, waltz — Strauss
   MARJORIE MOODY, SOPRANO SOLOIST
5. When the Boys Come Sailing Home, march-song — Sousa

SUNDAY, 25 JULY
(Third concert of the day, featuring Sousa's compositions)

1. El Capitan and His Friends, suite — Sousa
   I   Excerpts from El Capitan
   II   Excerpts from The Charlatan
   III Excerpts from The Bride Elect
   Encore: The Pride of the Wolverines, march — Sousa
2. Intaglio Waltzes — Sousa
   Encore: Hands Across the Sea, march — Sousa
3. Leaves from My Notebook, suite — Sousa
   I   The Genial Hostess
   II   The Campfire Girls
   III The Lively Flapper
4. Words of Love, waltz — Sousa
5. The Dauntless Battalion, march — Sousa

SUNDAY, 25 JULY
(Fourth concert of the day, featuring Sousa's compositions)

1. Selections from The Bride Elect — Sousa
   Encore: The Mingling of the Wets and Drys, fantasie — Sousa
   Encore: The Pride of the Wolverines, march — Sousa
2. The Lily Bells, from Our Flirtations — Sousa
   Encore: The Carnival of Venice — Arban
   JOHN DOLAN, CORNET SOLOIST
3. Dwellers of the Western World, suite — Sousa
   I   The Red Man
   II   The White Man
   III The Black Man
4. The Milkmaid, song — Sousa
   Encore: On the Beautiful Blue Danube, waltz — Strauss
   MARJORIE MOODY, SOPRANO SOLOIST
5. The National Game, march — Sousa

311

MONDAY, 26 JULY
(First concert of the day)

1. Vanity Fair, overture — Fletcher
2. Les Preludes, symphonic poem — Liszt
3. Southern Cross — Clarke
   JOHN DOLAN, CORNET SOLOIST
4. The Bells of St. Mary's — Adams
   BETTY GRAY, CONTRALTO SOLOIST
5. Selections from Martha — Flotow

MONDAY, 26 JULY
(Fourth concert of the day)

1. Selections from I Pagliacci — Leoncavallo
   Encore: The Mingling of the Wets and Drys, fantasie — Sousa
   Encore: The Stars and Stripes Forever, march — Sousa
2. Through the Air — Damm
   Encore: The Whistler and His Dog, caprice — Pryor
   JOHN W. BELL, PICCOLO SOLOIST
3. The Night of Sabba, from Mephistofele — Boito
4. Caro Nome, from Rigoletto — Verdi
   Encore: There's a Merry Brown Thrush, song — Sousa
   MARJORIE MOODY, SOPRANO SOLOIST
5. (a) Fesche Geister, waltz — Strauss
   (b) The Charlatan, march — Sousa

TUESDAY, 27 JULY
(Third concert of the day)

1. Selections from The Grand Duchess — Offenbach
   Encore: Jack Tar, march — Sousa
2. Schön Rosmarin — Kreisler
   ROY SCHMIDT, CLARINET SOLOIST
   Encore: Turkey in the Straw, breakdown — Guion
3. Selections from La Cigale — Audran
4. My Heart at Thy Sweet Voice, from Samson and Delilah — Saint-Saens
   BETTY GRAY, CONTRALTO SOLIST
5. The Pathfinder of Panama, march — Sousa

WEDNESDAY, 28 JULY
(Fourth concert of the day)

1. Stradella, overture — Flotow
   Encore: Sesqui-Centennial Exposition March — Sousa
2. Our Maud — Short
   Encore: Berceuse, from Jocelyn — Godard
   JOHN DOLAN, CORNET SOLOIST
3. Maidens Three, suite — Sousa
   I   The Coquette
   II   The Summer Girl
   III The Dancing Girl, from The Bride Elect
   Encore: The Pride of the Wolverines, march — Sousa
   Encore: The Stars and Stripes Forever, march — Sousa
4. Waltz Song, from Romeo and Juliet — Gounod
   Encore: Italian Street Song, from Naughty Marietta — Herbert
   MARJORIE MOODY, SOPRANO SOLOIST
5. (a) Grosses Walzerpotpourri — Komzak
   (b) The Federal, march — Sousa

THURSDAY, 29 JULY
(First concert of the day, featuring Sousa's compositions)

1. The Glassblowers, overture — Sousa
   Encore: Marquette University March — Sousa
2. At the King's Court, suite — Sousa
   I   Her Ladyship the Countess
   II   Her Grace the Duchess
   III Her Majesty the Queen

3. Intaglio Waltzes — Sousa
4. Lovely Mary Donnelly, song — Sousa
   Encore: Neapolitan Nights, song — Zamecnik
   BETTY GRAY, CONTRALTO SOLOIST
5. (a) Willow Blossoms, concert piece — Sousa
   (b) Power and Glory, march — Sousa
   Encore: The Stars and Stripes Forever, march — Sousa

THURSDAY, 29 JULY
(Second concert of the day, featuring Sousa's compositions)

1. Selections from The Bride Elect — Sousa
   Encore: Solid Men to the Front, march — Sousa
2. The Fighting Race, song — Sousa
   Encore: Monarch Polka — Knoll
   JOHN P. SCHUELER, TROMBONE SOLOIST
3. The American Maid, suite — Sousa
   I   You Do Not Need a Doctor, from The American Maid
   II   The Sleeping Soldiers, from The American Maid
   III With Pleasure, dance hilarious
   Encore: The Volunteers, march — Sousa
4. Crossing the Bar, song — Sousa
   Encore: When You and I Were Seventeen, song — Kahn and Rosaff
   MARJORIE MOODY, SOPRANO SOLOIST
5. (a) The Gliding Girl, tango — Sousa
   (b) The Gridiron Club, march — Sousa

THURSDAY, 29 JULY
(Third concert of the day, featuring Sousa's compositions)

1. The Charlatan, overture — Sousa
   Encore: The Liberty Bell, march — Sousa
2. Selections from El Capitan — Sousa
   Encore: The U.S. Field Artillery, march — Sousa
3. Tales of a Traveler, suite — Sousa
   I   The Kaffir on the Karoo
   II   In the Land of the Golden Fleece
   III Grand Promenade at the White House
4. I Wonder, song — Sousa
   Encore: The Love That Lives Forever, song — Sousa
   BETTY GRAY, CONTRALTO SOLOIST
5. Comrades of the Legion, march — Sousa

THURSDAY, 29 JULY
(Fourth concert of the day, featuring Sousa's compositions)

1. Assembly of the Artisans, fantasie — Sousa
   Encore: The Thunderer, march — Sousa
2. The Debutante — Clarke
   WILLIAM TONG, CORNET SOLOIST
3. Three Quotations, suite — Sousa
   I   The King of France
   II   I, Too, Was Born in Arcadia
   III In Darkest Africa
4. The Milkmaid, song — Sousa
   Encore: Annie Laurie, folk song — Traditional
   MARJORIE MOODY, SOPRANO SOLOIST
5. (a) Wedding March — Sousa
   (b) Jack Tar, march — Sousa

FRIDAY, 30 JULY
(Third concert of the day)

1. Tannhäuser, overture — Wagner
   Encore: El Capitan, march — Sousa
2. (a) Serenade — Hue
   (b) The Little Shepherd, song — Debussy
   (c) Allegretto — Godard
   RAYMOND E. WILLIAMS, FLUTE SOLOIST

312

3. Selections from Cavalleria Rusticana — Masgagni

4. The Philosophic Maid, from The Charlatan — Sousa
   Encore: Neapolitan Nights, song — Zamecnik
   BETTY GRAY, CONTRALTO SOLOIST

5. (a) Themes from Rhapsody Espagnol, waltz — Waldteufel
   (b) The Washington Post, march — Sousa

SATURDAY, 31 JULY
(Third concert of the day)

1. Ballet Music from Robert le Diable — Meyerbeer
   Encore: The Birth of the Blues, song — De Sylva

2. The Skylark — Cox
   Encore: Piccolo Pic — Slater
   JOHN W. BELL, PICCOLO SOLOIST

3. Selections from Le Vivandiere — Godard

4. The Bells of St. Mary's, song — Adams
   Encore: Neapolitan Nights, song — Zamecnik
   BETTY GRAY, CONTRALTO SOLOIST

5. (a) La Gitana, waltz — Bucalossi
   (b) The Crusader, march — Sousa

SATURDAY, 31 JULY
(Third concert of the day, featuring Sousa's compositions)

1. Selections from The Free Lance — Sousa
   Encore: Oh! How I've Waited for You, song — Ayer

2. The Philosophic Maid, from The Charlatan — Sousa
   Encore: The Carnival of Venice — Arban
   WILLIAM TONG, CORNET SOLOIST

3. At the King's Court, suite — Sousa
   I   Her Ladyship the Countess
   II Her Grace the Duchess
   III Her Majesty the Queen
   Encore: The Rifle Regiment, march — Sousa

4. The Crystal Lute, from The American Maid — Sousa
   Encore: There's a Merry Brown Thrush, song — Sousa
   Encore: Comin' Thro' the Rye, song — Burns
   MARJORIE MOODY, SOPRANO SOLOIST

5. Semper Fidelis, march — Sousa

SUNDAY, 1 AUGUST
(Fourth concert of the day, featuring Sousa's compositions)

1. Selections from The Charlatan — Sousa
   Encore: The Mingling of the Wets and Drys, fantasie — Sousa

2. My Own, My Geraldine, song — Sousa
   Encore: The Carnival of Venice — Arban
   JOHN DOLAN, CORNET SOLOIST

3. Tales of a Traveler, suite — Sousa
   I   The Kaffir on the Karoo
   II In the Land of the Golden Fleece
   III Grand Promenade at the White House

4. Will You Love When the Lilies Are Dead?, from The Charlatan — Sousa
   Encore: Indian Dawn, dance — Zamecnik
   MARJORIE MOODY, SOPRANO SOLOIST

5. The National Game, march — Sousa

MONDAY, 2 AUGUST
(First concert of the day)

1. The Warrior's Festival, overture — Kling
   Encore: We Are Coming, march-song — Sousa

2. From the Land of the Sky-Blue Water — Cadman
   BETTY GRAY, CONTRALTO SOLOIST

3. Selections from Lakme — Delibes

4. Moonlight on the Alster, waltz — Fetras
   Encore: Ireland For Ever, sketch — Myddleton

Encore: The Man Behind the Gun, march — Sousa

5. The Lambs' March — Sousa

MONDAY, 2 AUGUST
(Second concert of the day)

1. Carneval Romaine, overture — Berlioz
   Encore: The Gridiron Club, march — Sousa

2. The Carnival of Venice — Clarke
   Encore: Kiss Me Again, from Mlle. Modiste — Herbert
   WILLIAM TONG, CORNET SOLOIST

3. The Bell of Mayfair — Stewart
   Encore: Look for the Silver Lining, humoresque — Sousa
   Encore: The Pride of the Wolverines, march — Sousa
   Encore: The Whistling Farmer Boy, descriptive — Fillmore

4. Italian Street Song, from Naughty Marietta — Herbert
   Encore: Ah, Sweet Mystery of Life, from Naughty Marietta — Herbert
   MARJORIE MOODY, SOPRANO SOLOIST

5. The Loyal Legion, march — Sousa
   Encore: The Man Behind the Gun, march — Sousa

MONDAY, 2 AUGUST
(Third concert of the day)

1. In May, overture — Eilenberg
   Encore: The Gridiron Club, march — Sousa

2. Allegretto — Godard
   Encore: Minute Waltz — Chopin
   RAYMOND E. WILLIAMS, FLUTE SOLOIST

3. The Scarlet Letter — Levey
   Encore: Sesqui-Centennial Exposition March — Sousa

4. The Crystal Lute, from The American Maid — Sousa
   Encore: There's a Merry Brown Thrush, song — Sousa
   MARJORIE MOODY, SOPRANO SOLOIST

5. The Fairest of the Fair, march — Sousa

TUESDAY, 3 AUGUST
(First concert of the day)

1. Kroll's Ballklange, waltz — Lumbye
   Encore: Solid Men to the Front, march — Sousa

2. Selections from The Serenade — Herbert
   Encore: Ragging the Scale — Claypoole

3. Belgravia, waltz — Godfrey

4. June Brought the Roses, song — Openshaw
   BETTY GRAY, CONTRALTO SOLOIST

5. Hail to the Spirit of Liberty, march — Sousa

TUESDAY, 3 AUGUST
(Second concert of the day)

1. Where the Citrons Bloom, waltz — Strauss
   Encore: Symphonic Poem No. 1 — DeLuca

2. Selections from Madame Butterfly — Puccini

3. Ballet Music from Romeo and Juliet — Gounod
   Encore: Sesqui-Centennial Exposition March — Sousa

4. Je Suis Titania, from Mignon — Thomas
   MARJORIE MOODY, SOPRANO SOLOIST
   Encore: Fanny, from Chris and the Wonderful Lamp — Sousa

5. Boy Scouts of America, march — Sousa

TUESDAY, 3 AUGUST
(Third concert of the day)

1. Straussiana — Seredy
   Encore: National Fencibles, march — Sousa

313

2. Flocktonian Polka   Casey
   Encore: Kilarney   Balfe
   WILLIAM TONG, CORNET SOLOIST

3. Selections from Maritana   Wallace

4. Gypsy Song, from Carmen   Bizet
   Encore: The Bells of St. Mary's, song   Adams
   BETTY GRAY, CONTRALTO SOLOIST

5. The Belle of Chicago, march   Sousa

TUESDAY, 3 AUGUST
(Fourth concert of the day)

1. Girls of Baden Waltz   Komzak
   Encore: The Mingling of the Wets and Drys, fantasie   Sousa

2. Fantasia   Georges-Hue
   RAYMOND E. WILLIAMS, FLUTE SOLOIST
   Encore: Dance of the Mirlitrons, from Nutcracker   Tchaikowsky

3. Prelude to Act III of The King's Children   Humperdinck
   Encore: The Pride of the Wolverines, march   Sousa

4. Ah, fors e lui, from La Traviata   Verdi
   Encore: There's a Merry Brown Thrush, song   Sousa
   MARJORIE MOODY, SOPRANO SOLOIST

5. Bullets and Bayonets, march   Sousa

WEDNESDAY, 4 AUGUST
(First concert of the day)

1. Hungarian Rhapsody No. 2   Liszt
   Encore: Bullets and Bayonets, march   Sousa

2. Selections from Victoria and Merry England   Sullivan
   Encore: The Lambs' March   Sousa

3. Life, Let Us Cherish, waltz   Strauss

4. By the Waters of Minnetonka, song   Lieurance
   Encore: Neapolitan Nights, song   Zamecnik
   BETTY GRAY, CONTRALTO SOLOIST

5. Sesqui-Centennial Exposition, march   Sousa
   Encore: The Whistling Farmer Boy, descriptive   Fillmore

WEDNESDAY, 4 AUGUST
(Third concert of the day)

1. Gems of Scotland   Godfrey
   Encore: The Pride of the Wolverines, march   Sousa

2. Cortege de Sardar, from Caucasian Sketches   Ippolotov-Ivanov
   Encore: The Stars and Stripes Forever, march   Sousa

3. A Highland Scene, fantasia   Moore

4. On the Beautiful Blue Danube, waltz   Strauss
   Encore: There's a Merry Brown Thrush, song   Sousa
   MARJORIE MOODY, SOPRANO SOLOIST

5. Corcoran Cadets, march   Sousa

THURSDAY, 5 AUGUST
(Third program of the day, featuring Sousa's compositions)

1. Selections from Chris and the Wonderful Lamp   Sousa
   Encore: The White Plume, march   Sousa

2. La Reine de la Mer Valses   Sousa
   Encore: Mother Goose, march   Sousa

3. Dwellers of the Western World, suite   Sousa
   I   The Red Man
   II   The White Man
   III   The Black Man

4. Lovely Mary Donnelly, song   Sousa
   Encore: The Bells of St. Mary's, song   Adams
   BETTY GRAY, CONTRALTO SOLOIST

5. The Gallant Seventh, march   Sousa

FRIDAY, 6 AUGUST
(Fourth concert of the day)

1. Selections from Aida   Verdi
   Encore: The Stars and Stripes Forever, march   Sousa

2. Gate City, march   Weldon
   Encore: Mighty Lak' a Rose, song   Nevin
   Encore: Kitten on the Keys   Confrey
   HOWARD GOULDEN, XYLOPHONE SOLOIST

3. A Study in Rhythms, fantasie   Sousa

4. Moonlight and Roses, song   Lemare
   Encore: Smilin' Through, song   Penn
   BETTY GRAY, CONTRALTO SOLOIST

5. Ben Bolt, march   Sousa

SATURDAY, 7 AUGUST
(Fourth concert of the day, devoted to Sousa's compositions)

1. The Glass Blowers, overture   Sousa
   Encore: The Gridiron Club, march   Sousa

2. The Lily Bells, from Our Flirtations   Sousa
   Encore: The Carnival of Venice   Arban
   JOHN DOLAN, CORNET SOLOIST

3. The American Maid, suite   Sousa
   I   You Do Not Need a Doctor, from The American Maid
   II   The Sleeping Soldiers, from The American Maid
   III   With Pleasure, dance hilarious
   Encore: Semper Fidelis, march   Sousa

4. Lovely Mary Donnelly, song   Sousa
   Encore: The Bells of St. Mary's, song   Adams
   BETTY GRAY, CONTRALTO SOLOIST

5. Sesqui-Centennial Exposition, march   Sousa

MONDAY, 9 AUGUST
(Fourth concert of the day)

1. Selections from The Tales of Hoffman   Offenbach
   Encore: Down South, fantasie   Laurendeau

2. Neptune's Court   Clarke
   Encore: Berceuse, from Jocelyn   Godard
   JACOB O. KNUTTUNEN, CORNET SOLOIST

3. Finlandia, tone poem   Sibelius
   Encore: Hearts and Flowers, song   Tobani

4. Vilanelle, song   Dell' Aqua
   Encore: Ah, Sweet Mystery of Life, from Naughty Marietta   Herbert
   MARJORIE MOODY, SOPRANO SOLOIST

5. National Emblem, march   Bagley

THURSDAY, 12 AUGUST
(First concert of the day, devoted to Sousa's compositions)

1. The Pride of Pittsburgh, march   Sousa
   Encore: Gypsy Love Song, from The Fortune Teller   Herbert

2. Jazz America, fantasie   Sousa

3. People Who Live in Glass Houses, Bacchanalian suite   Sousa
   I   The Champagnes
   II   The Rhine Wines
   IV   The Whiskies
   V   The Cordials

4. The Love That Lives Forever, song   Sousa
   Encore: The Lark Now Leaves Its Wat'ry Nest, song   Parker
   WINIFRED RIDGE, SOPRANO SOLOIST

5. Keeping Step with the Union, march   Sousa

THURSDAY, 12 AUGUST
(Second concert of the day, devoted to Sousa's compositions)

1. Look for the Silver Lining, humoresque   Sousa

Encore: The Pride of the Wolverines, march		Sousa
2. Selections from Desiree		Sousa
Encore: The Gridiron Club, march		Sousa
3. Looking Upward, suite		Sousa
I By the Light of the Polar Star		
II Under the Southern Cross		
III Mars and Venus		
Encore: The Whistling Farmer Boy, descriptive		Fillmore
4. A Serenade in Seville, song		Sousa
Encore: Dixie		Emmett
MARJORIE MOODY, SOPRANO SOLOIST		
5. The Liberty Bell, march		Sousa

THURSDAY, 12 AUGUST
(Fourth concert of the day, devoted to Sousa's compositions)

1. Selections from El Capitan		Sousa
Encore: The Gridiron Club, march		Sousa
2. Follow the Swallow, humoresque		Sousa
Encore: The Black Horse Troop, march		Sousa
3. Three Quotations, suite		Sousa
I The King of France		
II I, Too, Was Born in Arcadia		
III In Darkest Africa		
4. There's a Merry Brown Thrush, song		Sousa
Encore: On the Beautiful Blue Danube, waltz		Strauss
Encore: Annie Laurie, folk song		Traditional
MARJORIE MOODY, SOPRANO SOLOIST		
5. The Picador, march		Sousa

SATURDAY, 14 AUGUST
(First concert of the day)

1. Reminiscences of Mendelssohn		Arr. Godfrey
Encore: Hands Across the Sea, march		Sousa
2. Spring, ballet suite		Delibes
3. Gems of Ireland, collocation		Godfrey
4. Je Suis Titania, from Mignon		Thomas
Encore: In My Garden, song		Liddle
MARJORIE MOODY, SOPRANO SOLOIST		
5. Powhattan's Daughter, march		Sousa

SATURDAY, 14 AUGUST
(Third concert of the day)

1. Zampa, overture		Herold
2. Valse Vanite		Wiedoeft
EDWARD J. HENEY, SAXOPHONE SOLOIST		
3. Looking Upward, suite		Sousa
I By the Light of the Polar Star		
II Under the Southern Cross		
III Mars and Venus		
4. Caro Nome, from Rigoletto		Verdi
Encore: There's a Merry Brown Thrush, song		Sousa
MARJORIE MOODY, SOPRANO SOLOIST		
5. Mother Goose, march		Sousa

SUNDAY, 15 AUGUST
(Third concert of the day)

1. Franz Schubert, Overture		Suppe
Encore: Oh! How I've Waited for You, song		Ayer
2. Ethiopian Rhapsody		Hosmer
Encore: Valencia, pasodoble		Padilla
3. Jazz America, fantasie		Sousa
4. Pale Moon, song		Logan

Encore: Lo, Hear the Gentle Lark		Bishop
WINIFRED RIDGE, SOPRANO SOLOIST		
5. Power and Glory, march		Sousa

SUNDAY, 15 AUGUST
(Third concert of the day, devoted to Sousa's compositions)

1. Selections from The Bride Elect		Sousa
Encore: Sesqui-Centennial Exposition March		Sousa
2. The Lily Bells, from Our Flirtations		Sousa
Encore: Pyramids, polka		Liberati
JOHN DOLAN, CORNET SOLOIST		
3. Leaves from My Notebook, suite		Sousa
I The Genial Hostess		
II The Campfire Girls		
III The Lively Flapper		
Encore: The Thunderer, march		Sousa
4. The Milkmaid, song		Sousa
Encore: Italian Street Song, from Naughty Marietta		Herbert
MARJORIE MOODY, SOPRANO SOLOIST		
5. The Gridiron Club, march		Sousa
Encore: Blue Ridge, I'm Coming Back to You, march-song		Sousa

MONDAY, 16 AUGUST
(Second concert of the day)

1. Il Crociato, fantasia		Meyerbeer
Encore: The Federal, march		Sousa
2. Tres Jolie, waltz		Waldteufel
3. Gems from Captain Therese		Planquette
4. Scene and Cavatina, from Ernani		Verdi
Encore: When You and I Were Seventeen, song		Rosoff
MARJORIE MOODY, SOPRANO SOLOIST		
5. (a) Caster Songs		Chevalier
(b) March of the Mitten Men		Sousa

MONDAY, 16 AUGUST
(Second concert of the day)

1. 1812, overture solonelle		Tchaikowsky
Encore: The Pathfinder of Panama, march		Sousa
2. Flocktonian Polka		Casey
Encore: Kilarney		Balfe
WILLIAM TONG, CORNET SOLOIST		
3. Gems from The Dancing Doll		Bayer
4. Caro Nome, from Rigoletto		Verdi
Encore: The American Girl, from The American Maid		Sousa
WINIFRED RIDGE, SOPRANO SOLOIST		
5. El Capitan, march		Sousa

TUESDAY, 17 AUGUST
(First concert of the day)

1. Tannhäuser, overture		Wagner
Encore: The Belle of Chicago, march		Sousa
2. Selections from Dorothy		Cellier
3. (a) Serenade		Raff
(b) Naila, intermezzo		Delibes
4. Je Suis Titania, from Mignon		Thomas
Encore: Blue Ridge, I'm Coming Back to You, song		Sousa
WINIFRED RIDGE, SOPRANO SOLOIST		
5. On the Campus, march		Sousa

TUESDAY, 17 AUGUST
(Fourth concert of the day)

1. Songs of the Gael		O'Donnell

Encore: Sea Gardens, idyll — Cooke

2. Souvenir de Moscow — Fantasia
   Encore: In the Heart of the Hills, song — Lee
   JOHN DOLAN, CORNET SOLOIST

3. Selections from Well of Love — Balfe

4. Kiss Me Again, from Mlle. Modiste — Herbert
   Encore: Crossing the Bar, song — Sousa
   MARJORIE MOODY, SOPRANO SOLOIST

5. (a) Mountain Tunes — Orem
   (b) King Cotton, march — Sousa
   Encore: El Capitan, march — Sousa

WEDNESDAY, 18 AUGUST
(Fourth concert of the day)

1. Sailors Afloat, overture — Suppe
   Encore: The Rifle Regiment, march — Sousa

2. Flora — Cunard
   JOHN DOLAN, CORNET SOLOIST

3. The Foresters, fantasie — Sullivan
   Encore: National Fencibles, march — Sousa

4. Lo, Hear the Gentle Lark, song — Bishop
   Encore: The Lark Now Leaves Its Wat'ry Nest, song — Parker
   WINIFRED RIDGE, SOPRANO SOLOIST

5. (a) Irish Patrol — Puerner
   (b) Ancient and Honorable Artillery Company, march — Sousa

THURSDAY, 19 AUGUST
(First concert of the day, devoted to Sousa's compositions)

1. Tally-Ho!, overture — Sousa
   Encore: Pan Americana, characteristic — Herbert

2. Selections from The Bride Elect — Sousa
   Encore: Pizzicato Polka — Strauss

3. Jazz America, fantasie — Sousa

4. The American Girl, from The American Maid — Sousa
   Encore: The Wren, song — Benedict
   WINIFRED RIDGE, SOPRANO SOLOIST

5. Follow the Swallow, humoresque — Sousa

THURSDAY, 19 AUGUST
(Fourth concert of the day)

1. The Fancy of the Town, fantasie — Sousa
   Encore: The Pride of the Wolverines, march — Sousa

2. La Favorita — Hartman
   Encore: The Faithless Knight and the Philosophic Maid, from
   The Charlatan — Sousa
   JOHN DOLAN, CORNET SOLOIST

3. At the King's Court, suite — Sousa
   I   Her Ladyship the Countess
   II Her Grace the Duchess
   III Her Majesty the Queen
   Encore: The Fairest of the Fair, march — Sousa

4. The American Girl, from The American Maid — Sousa
   Encore: Just a Cottage Small, song — Hanley
   Encore: Comin' Thro' the Rye, song — Burns
   MARJORIE MOODY, SOPRANO SOLOIST

5. Semper Fidelis, march — Sousa

FRIDAY, 20 AUGUST
(First concert of the day)

1. Rienzi, overture — Wagner
   Encore: The Free Lance, march — Sousa

2. The Carnival of Venice — Clarke
   Encore: Drink to Me Only With Thine Eyes, song — Jonson
   WILLIAM TONG, CORNET SOLOIST

3. Gems from La Gioconda — Ponchielli

4. Just a Cottage Small, song — Hanley
   MARJORIE MOODY, SOPRANO SOLOIST

5. Marquette University March — Sousa

SATURDAY, 21 AUGUST
(First concert of the day)

1. Martha, overture — Flotow
   Encore: The Glory of the Yankee Navy, march — Sousa

2. The Old Cloister Clock, descriptive — Kunkel
   Encore: Hands Across the Sea, march — Sousa

3. Selections from La Traviata — Verdi

4. The Sweetest Story Ever Told, song — Stults
   Encore: The Crystal Lute, from The American Maid — Sousa
   MARJORIE MOODY, SOPRANO SOLOIST

5. Powhatan's Daughter, march — Sousa

SATURDAY, 21 AUGUST
(Fourth concert of the day)

1. Excerpts from Coppelia — Delibes

2. Marche Militaire Francaise, from Suite Algerienne — Saint-Saens

3. Jazz America, fantasie — Sousa

4. Just a Cottage Small, song — Hanley
   Encore: Ah, Sweet Mystery of Life, from Naughty Marietta — Herbert
   MARJORIE MOODY, SOPRANO SOLOIST

5. Solid Men to the Front, march — Sousa

SUNDAY, 22 AUGUST
(First concert of the day)

1. Comes Autumn Time, overture — Sowerby
   Encore: The Volunteers, march — Sousa

2. Cleopatra Polka — Damare
   Encore: The Lost Chord, sacred song — Sullivan
   JOHN DOLAN, CORNET SOLOIST

3. Second Suite in F — Holst

4. Lo, Hear the Gentle Lark, song — Bishop
   Encore: Blue Ridge, I'm Coming Back to You, song — Sousa
   WINIFRED RIDGE, SOPRANO SOLOIST

5. Semper Fidelis, march — Sousa

SUNDAY, 22 AUGUST
(Second concert of the day)

1. From Foreign Lands, suite — Moszkowski

2. Air Varied — Rollinson
   Encore: Beneath Thy Window, song — Di Capua
   NOBLE P. HOWARD, EUPHONIUM SOLOIST

3. El Capitan and His Friends, suite — Sousa
   I   Excerpts from El Capitan
   II Excerpts from The Charlatan
   III Excerpts from The Bride Elect
   Encore: The Mingling of the Wets and Drys, fantasie — Sousa

4. Rose of My Heart, song — Lohr
   Encore: Ah, Sweet Mystery of Life, from Naughty Marietta — Herbert
   MARJORIE MOODY, SOPRANO SOLOIST

5. Boy Scouts of America, march — Sousa

MONDAY, 23 AUGUST
(First concert of the day)

1. Poet and Peasant, overture — Suppe
   Encore: The Bohemians, march — Hadley

2. Skyrocket Polka — Barnes
   HAROLD STAMBAUGH, CORNET SOLOIST

3. Ballet Music from Carmen — Bizet

4. The Lark Now Leaves Its Wat'ry Nest, song — Parker
   Encore: Fanny, from Chris and the Wonderful Lamp — Sousa
   NORA FAUCHALD, SOPRANO SOLOIST

5. Yorktown Centennial, march — Sousa

TUESDAY, 24 AUGUST
(Third concert of the day)

1. The Flying Dutchman, fantasy — Wagner

2. Gems from Captain Therese — Planquette

3. Au Clair de Lune, waltz — Fahrbach

4. Silver Threads Among the Gold, song — Danks
   Encore: The World is Waiting for the Sunrise, song — Lockhart
   MARJORIE MOODY, SOPRANO SOLOIST

5. The Bride Elect, march — Sousa

THURSDAY, 26 AUGUST
(First concert of the day, devoted to Sousa's compositions)

1. Tally-Ho!, overture — Sousa
   Encore: The Charlatan, march — Sousa

2. Selections from The Bride Elect — Sousa

3. Jazz America, fantasie — Sousa

4. The Crystal Lute, from The American Maid — Sousa
   Encore: Smilin' Through, song — Penn
   NORA FAUCHALD, SOPRANO SOLOIST

5. Follow the Swallow, humoresque — Sousa
   Encore: The High School Cadets, march — Sousa

FRIDAY, 27 AUGUST
(First concert of the day)

1. Excerpts from Ivanhoe — Sullivan
   Encore: The Bride Elect, march — Sousa

2. Il Crociato, fantasia — Meyerbeer

3. The Forge in the Forest, idyll — Michaelis

4. The Wren, song — Benedict
   Encore: Do, Do, Do, fox trot — Gershwin
   MARJORIE MOODY, SOPRANO SOLOIST
   Flute obbligato by Raymond E. Williams

5. The Man Behind the Gun, march — Sousa

FRIDAY, 27 AUGUST
(Third concert of the day)

1. Selections from Lohengrin — Wagner
   Encore: The Rifle Regiment, march — Sousa

2. Reminiscences of Tosti — Tosti

3. The Land of Song — Fahrbach

4. Vissi d'arte, from Tosca — Puccini
   Encore: Blue Ridge, I'm Coming Back to You, song — Sousa
   MARJORIE MOODY, SOPRANO SOLOIST

5. (a) Genevieve, gavotte — Ora
   (b) The Free Lance, march — Sousa

FRIDAY, 27 AUGUST
(Fourth concert of the day)

1. Selections from Il Trovatore — Verdi
   Encore: Sea Gardens, idyll — Cooke

2. Reminiscences of Wales — Godfrey
   Encore: Sesqui-Centennial Exposition March — Sousa

3. Morning Journals, waltz — Strauss

4. Ave Maria, sacred song — Bach-Gounod

Encore: A Serenade in Seville, song — Sousa
NORA FAUCHALD, SOPRANO SOLOIST

5. Bullets and Bayonets, march — Sousa

SATURDAY, 28 AUGUST
(First concert of the day)

1. A Gaiety Girl, overture — Jones

2. Pyramids — Liberati
   Encore: I've Made My Plans for the Summer, song — Sousa
   JOHN DOLAN, CORNET SOLOIST

3. Three Quotations, suite — Sousa
   I   The King of France
   II   I, Too, Was Born in Arcadia
   III In Darkest Africa

4. Ah, fors e lui, from La Traviata — Verdi
   Encore: On the Beautiful Blue Danube, waltz — Strauss
   MARJORIE MOODY, SOPRANO SOLOIST

5. (a) Cordova, waltz — Gomez
   (b) Sabre and Spurs, march — Sousa

SATURDAY, 28 AUGUST
(Second concert of the day)

1. Meyerbeeriana — Seidel
   Encore: The Stars and Stripes Forever, march — Sousa

2. Lutzow's Wild Hunt, caprice characteristic — Weiss

3. Gems from The Pretty Parfumer — Offenbach

4. Vilanelle, song — Dell' Aqua
   Encore: At Dawning, song — Cadman
   NORA FAUCHALD, SOPRANO SOLOIST

5. (a) Immortallen, waltz — Gung'l
   (b) The National Game, march — Sousa

SATURDAY, 28 AUGUST
(Fourth concert of the day)

1. Offenbachiana — Godfrey
   Encore: Valencia, pasodoble — Padilla

2. Tales of Hoffman, fantasie — Offenbach
   Encore: The Stars and Stripes Forever, march — Sousa

3. Selections from Il Trovatore — Verdi

4. Crossing the Bar, song — Sousa
   Encore: Ah, Sweet Mystery of Life, from Naughty Marietta — Herbert
   MARJORIE MOODY, SOPRANO SOLOIST

5. The Black Horse Troop, march — Sousa

SUNDAY, 29 AUGUST
(Second concert of the day)

1. Reminiscences of Gounod — Gounod
   Encore: The Liberty Bell, march — Sousa

2. Cleopatra Polka — Damare
   Encore: Berceuse, from Jocelyn — Godard
   JOHN DOLAN, CORNET SOLOIST

3. Selections from The Pirates of Penzance — Sullivan
   Encore: The Pride of the Wolverines, march — Sousa

4. The World Is Waiting for the Sunrise, song — Lockhart
   Encore: Italian Street Song, from Naughty Marietta — Herbert
   MARJORIE MOODY, SOPRANO SOLOIST

5. The New York Hippodrome, march — Sousa

SUNDAY, 29 AUGUST
(Third concert of the day, devoted to Sousa's compositions)

1. El Capitan and His Friends, suite — Sousa
   I   Excerpts from El Capitan

    II   Excerpts from The Charlatan
    III Excerpts from The Bride Elect
    Encore: The Gridiron Club, march   Sousa

2. Intaglio Waltzes   Sousa

3. Leaves from My Notebook, suite   Sousa
    I   The Genial Hostess
    II   The Campfire Girls
    III The Lively Flapper

4. Fanny, from Chris and the Wonderful Lamp   Sousa
    Encore: Ave Maria, sacred song   Bach-Gounod
           NORA FAUCHALD, SOPRANO SOLOIST

5. The Dauntless Battalion, march   Sousa

SUNDAY, 29 AUGUST
(Fourth concert of the day, devoted to Sousa's compositions)

1. Selections from The Bride Elect   Sousa
    Encore: Sea Gardens, idyll   Cooke

2. The Lily Bells, from Our Flirtations   Sousa
           JOHN DOLAN, CORNET SOLOIST
    Encore: Triplets of the Finest, cornet trio   Henneberg
           DOLAN WITH TWO OTHER CORNETISTS

3. Tales of a Traveler, suite   Sousa
    I   The Kaffir on the Karoo
    II   In the Land of the Golden Fleece
    III Grand Promenade at the White House
    Encore: Semper Fidelis, march   Sousa
    Encore: Ireland For Ever, sketch   Myddleton

4. Crossing the Bar   Sousa
    Encore: Ah, Sweet Mystery of Life, from Naughty Marietta   Herbert
    Encore: There's a Merry Brown Thrush, song   Sousa
           MARJORIE MOODY, SOPRANO SOLOIST

5. The National Game, march   Sousa

MONDAY, 30 AUGUST
(First concert of the day)

1. Vanity Fair, overture   Fletcher
    Encore: The Gallant Seventh, march   Sousa

2. Three Characteristic Dances, suite   Saenger
    Encore: National Fencibles, march   Sousa

3. Dream of Love and You   Liszt-Taylor
    Encore: Our Flirtations, march   Sousa

4. There's a Merry Brown Thrush, song   Sousa
    Encore: Kiss Me Again, from Mlle. Modiste   Herbert
           MARJORIE MOODY, SOPRANO SOLOIST

5. Sesqui-Centennial Exposition March   Sousa
    Encore: The U.S. Field Artillery, march   Sousa

MONDAY, 30 AUGUST
(Third concert of the day)

1. The Bartered Bride, overture   Smetana
    Encore: The Pride of the Wolverines, march   Sousa

2. Excerpts from Don Carlos   Verdi

3. Selections from Le Vivandiere   Godard

4. Ol' Carolina, song   Cooke
    Encore: A Serenade in Seville, song   Sousa
           NORA FAUCHALD, SOPRANO SOLOIST

5. The Occidental, march   Sousa

TUESDAY, 31 AUGUST
(Second concert of the day)

1. Excerpts from The Chimes of Normandy   Planquette
    Encore: March of the Mitten Men   Sousa

2. Selections from A Waltz Dream   Straus

3. Selections from Patience   Sullivan
    Encore: Valencia, pasodoble   Padilla

4. June Brought the Roses, song   Openshaw
    Encore: The World is Waiting for the Sunrise, song   Lockhart
           MARJORIE MOODY, SOPRANO SOLOIST

5. Mother Goose, march   Sousa

WEDNESDAY, 1 SEPTEMBER
(Second concert of the day)

1. Comes Autumn Time, overture   Sowerby
    Encore: Valencia, pasodoble   Padilla

2. Selections from La Boheme   Puccini
    Encore: The Stars and Stripes Forever, march   Sousa

3. Jazz America, fantasie   Sousa

4. Just a Cottage Small, song   Hanley
    Encore: The Wren, song   Benedict
           MARJORIE MOODY, SOPRANO SOLOIST

5. 32nd Division, march   Steinmetz

WEDNESDAY, 1 SEPTEMBER
(Third concert of the day)

1. New Orleans Mardi Gras, overture   Wilson
    Encore: The Gridiron Club, march   Sousa

2. Nightingale Polka   Mollenhauer
    Encore: The Whistler and His Dog, caprice   Pryor
           JOHN W. BELL, PICCOLO SOLOIST

3. El Capitan and His Friends, suite   Sousa
    I   Excerpts from El Capitan
    II   Excerpts from The Charlatan
    III Excerpts from The Bride Elect

4. On the Beautiful Blue Danube, waltz   Strauss
    Encore: There's a Merry Brown Thrush, song   Sousa
           MARJORIE MOODY, SOPRANO SOLOIST

5. The Gallant Seventh, march   Sousa

THURSDAY, 2 SEPTEMBER
(Second concert of the day, devoted to Sousa's compositions)

1. Selections from The Bride Elect   Sousa
    Encore: Herod, overture   Hadley

2. The Fighting Race, song   Sousa
           JOHN P. SCHUELER, TROMBONE SOLOIST

3. The American Maid, suite   Sousa
    I   You Do Not Need a Doctor, from The American Maid
    II   The Sleeping Soldiers, from The American Maid
    III With Pleasure, dance hilarious

4. Crossing the Bar, song   Sousa
    Encore: Danny Boy, folk song   Traditional
           MARJORIE MOODY, SOPRANO SOLOIST

5. The Gridiron Club, march   Sousa

THURSDAY, 2 SEPTEMBER
(Third concert of the day, devoted to Sousa's compositions)

1. The Charlatan, overture   Sousa
    Encore: Le Voyvode, symphonic ballad   Tchaikowsky

2. Selections from El Capitan   Sousa

3. Tales of a Traveler, suite   Sousa
    I   The Kaffir on the Karoo
    II   In the Land of the Golden Fleece
    III Grand Promenade at the White House

4. I Wonder, song   Sousa
    Encore: Fanny, from Chris and the Wonderful Lamp   Sousa
           NORA FAUCHALD, SOPRANO SOLOIST

5. Comrades of the Legion, march   Sousa

THURSDAY, 2 SEPTEMBER
(Fourth concert of the day)

1. Assembly of the Artisans, fantasie — Sousa
   Encore: Valencia, pasodoble — Padilla

2. The Debutante — Clarke
   Encore: Drink to Me Only With Thine Eyes, song — Jonson
   WILLIAM TONG, CORNET SOLOIST

3. Three Quotations, suite — Sousa
   I The King of France
   II I, Too, Was Born in Arcadia
   III In Darkest Africa

4. The Milkmaid, solo — Sousa
   Encore: In Flanders Fields the Poppies Grow, song — Sousa
   MARJORIE MOODY, SOPRANO SOLOIST

5. (a) Wedding March — Sousa
   (b) Jack Tar, march — Sousa

FRIDAY 3 SEPTEMBER
(First concert of the day)

1. Roumanian Festival, overture — Keler-Bela
   Encore: The Crusader, march — Sousa

2. The New Creation — Smith
   Encore: Serenade — Schubert
   JACOB O. KNUTTUNEN, CORNET SOLOIST

3. Selections from Cox and Box — Sullivan

4. There's a Merry Brown Thrush, song — Sousa
   Encore: Smilin' Through, song — Penn
   MARJORIE MOODY, SOPRANO SOLOIST

5. (a) Wiener Bon Bons, waltz — Strauss
   (b) Sound Off, march — Sousa

FRIDAY, 3 SEPTEMBER
(Third concert of the day)

1. Hans, the Flute Player, overture — Ganne
   Encore: The Charlatan, march — Sousa

2. Selections from The Beggar's Opera — Austin

3. Selections from Sally — Kern

4. Roses of Picardy, song — Wood
   Encore: The American Girl, from The American Maid — Sousa
   NORA FAUCHALD, SOPRANO SOLOIST

5. The U.S. Field Artillery, march — Sousa

FRIDAY, 3 SEPTEMBER
(Fourth concert of the day)

1. Selections from Boccacio — Suppe
   Encore: Symphonic Poem No. 1 — DeLuca

2. Fantasia — Georges-Hue
   RAYMOND E. WILLIAMS, FLUTE SOLOIST
   Encore: Dance of the Mirlitrons, from Nutcracker — Tchaikowsky

3. (a) Sea Gardens, idyll — Cooke
   (b) Selections from Robin Hood — De Koven
   Encore: The Stars and Stripes Forever, march — Sousa
   Encore: Pan Americana, characteristic — Herbert
   Encore: March of the Mitten Men — Sousa

4. Crossing the Bar, song — Sousa
   Encore: When Bloom the Roses, song — Arditi
   MARJORIE MOODY, SOPRANO SOLOIST

5. The Pathfinder of Panama, march — Sousa

SATURDAY, 4 SEPTEMBER
(First concert of the day)

1. La Flutiste, overture — Kling
   Encore: The Charlatan, march — Sousa

2. Atlantic Zephyrs — Simons
   Encore: In the Heart of the Hills, song — Lee
   JOHN DOLAN, CORNET SOLOIST

3. The Masquerade, suite — Lacomb

4. Chanson de Florian, song — Godard
   Encore: Fanny, from Chris and the Wonderful Lamp — Sousa
   NORA FAUCHALD, SOPRANO SOLOIST

5. (a) Spirit of America, patrol — Zamecnik
   (b) Liberty Loan, march — Sousa

SATURDAY, 4 SEPTEMBER
(Third concert of the day)

1. Maximilian Robespierre, tone poem — Litolff

2. Kiss Me Again, from Mlle. Modiste — Herbert
   Encore: King Carnival, polka — Myddleton
   WILLIAM TONG, CORNET SOLOIST

3. Sylvia, ballet suite — Delibes
   Encore: Peaches and Cream, fox trot — Sousa

4. Ah, Sweet Mystery of Life, from Naughty Marietta — Herbert
   Encore: Dixie — Emmett
   MARJORIE MOODY, SOPRANO SOLOIST

5. (a) The Outpost, patrol — Mackenzie
   (b) The Federal, march — Sousa

SUNDAY, 5 SEPTEMBER
(Third concert of the day, devoted to Sousa's compositions)

1. The Merry-Merry Chorus, fantasie — Sousa
   Encore: The Pride of the Wolverines, march — Sousa

2. Selections from Chris and the Wonderful Lamp — Sousa

3. The Gliding Girl, tango — Sousa

4. In Flanders Fields the Poppies Grow, song — Sousa
   Encore: The Goose Girl, from The Free Lance — Sousa
   MARJORIE MOODY, SOPRANO SOLOIST

5. Selections from El Capitan — Sousa

MONDAY, 6 SEPTEMBER
(First concert of the day)

1. Selections from The Gondoliers — Sullivan
   Encore: The Cricket and the Bumblebee, humoresque — Chadwick
   Encore: Song of the Vagabond, from The Vagabond King — Friml

2. Our Maud — Short
   Encore: Killarney, song — Balfe
   WILLIAM TONG, CORNET SOLOIST

3. Three Quotations, suite — Sousa
   I The King of France
   II I, Too, Was Born in Arcadia
   III In Darkest Africa

4. When Myra Sings, song — Granville and A.L.
   Encore: The American Girl, from The American Maid — Sousa
   NORA FAUCHALD, SOPRANO SOLOIST

5. (a) Santiago, waltz — Corbin
   (b) The National Game, march — Sousa

MONDAY, 6 SEPTEMBER
(Second concert of the day)

1. Southern Rhapsody — Hosmer
   Encore: The Mingling of the Wets and Drys, fantasie — Sousa

2. Selections from I Pagliacci — Leoncavallo
   Encore: The Stars and Stripes Forever, march — Sousa

3. Looking Upward, suite — Sousa
   I By the Light of the Polar Star
   II Under the Southern Cross
   III Mars and Venus

4. The Cradle Song — Kreisler
   Encore: The Wren, song — Benedict
   MARJORIE MOODY, SOPRANO SOLOIST

5. March of the Mitten Men — Sousa

WEDNESDAY, 8 SEPTEMBER
(Third concert of the day)

1. Reminiscences of All Nations — Godfrey

2. Marche Slav — Tchaikowsky

3. An Evening in Spain, descriptive — Schmerling

4. Italian Street Song, from Naughty Marietta — Herbert
   Encore: Annie Laurie, folk song — Traditional
   MARJORIE MOODY, SOPRANO SOLOIST

5. (a) Visions of a Beautiful Woman, waltz — Fahrbach
   (b) The Black Horse Troop, march — Sousa

THURSDAY, 9 SEPTEMBER
(Second concert of the day, featuring Sousa's compositions)

1. Selections from The Charlatan — Sousa
   Encore: The Stars and Stripes Forever, march — Sousa

2. The Milkmaid, song — Sousa
   Encore: Fantasia di Concerto — Boccalari
   JOHN DOLAN, CORNET SOLOIST

3. Jazz America, fantasie — Sousa

4. A Serenade in Seville, song — Sousa
   Encore: Fanny, from Chris and the Wonderful Lamp — Sousa
   MARJORIE MOODY, SOPRANO SOLOIST

5. Nobles of the Mystic Shrine, march — Sousa

THURSDAY, 9 SEPTEMBER
(Third concert of the day, featuring Sousa's compositions)

1. Selections from Desiree — Sousa
   Encore: Herod, overture — Hadley

2. Selections from Chris and the Wonderful Lamp — Sousa

3. Intaglio Waltzes — Sousa

4. The Milkmaid, song — Sousa
   Encore: The American Girl, from The American Maid — Sousa
   NORA FAUCHALD, SOPRANO SOLOIST

5. The Black Horse Troop, march — Sousa

SATURDAY, 11 SEPTEMBER
(First concert of the day)

1. Moszkowskiana — Clark

2. Cortege de Sardar, from Caucasian Sketches — Ippolotov-Ivanov
   Encore: The Black Horse Troop, march — Sousa

3. Scotland's Pride, fantasie — Godfrey

4. Italian Street Song, from Naughty Marietta — Herbert
   Encore: Neapolitan Nights, song — Zamecnik
   MARJORIE MOODY, SOPRANO SOLOIST

5. (a) Blue Bells, waltz — Waldteufel
   (b) Ben Bolt, march — Sousa

SUNDAY, 11 SEPTEMBER
(First concert of the day)

1. Herod, overture — Hadley
   Encore: The Pride of the Wolverines, march — Sousa

2. Sounds from the Riviera — Boccalari
   Encore: Just a Cottage Small, song — Hanley
   JOHN DOLAN, CORNET SOLOIST

3. Le Voyvode, symphonic ballad — Tchaikowsky

4. On the Beautiful Blue Danube, waltz — Strauss
   Encore: There's a Merry Brown Thrush, song — Sousa
   MARJORIE MOODY, SOPRANO SOLOIST

5. (a) Country Gardens, Morris dance — Grainger
   (b) Sesqui-Centennial Exposition March — Sousa

SUNDAY, 11 SEPTEMBER
(Third concert of the day)

1. Yorkshire Lasses, dances — Wood
   Encore: Manhattan Beach, march — Sousa

2. Triplets of the Finest — Henneberg
   CORNET TRIO: JOHN DOLAN,
   WILLIAM TONG, AND HAROLD STAMBAUGH

3. All American, suite
   I   Pan Americana, characteristic — Herbert
   II   Song of the Flame — Gershwin
   III Her Majesty, the Queen, from At the King's Court — Sousa
   Encore: The Gliding Girl, tango — Sousa

4. Good-Bye, song — Tosti
   Encore: Carry Me Back to Old Virginny, song — Hosmer
   NORA FAUCHALD, SOPRANO SOLOIST

5. (a) Juba, from In the Bottoms — Dett
   (b) The Pride of the Wolverines, march — Sousa

SUNDAY, 11 SEPTEMBER
(Fourth concert of the day, devoted to Sousa's compositions)

1. Showing Off Before Company, humoresque — Sousa
   Encore: El Capitan, march — Sousa

2. The Mingling of the Wets and the Drys, humoresque — Sousa

3. There's a Merry Brown Thrush, song — Sousa
   Encore: Annie Laurie, folk song — Traditional

4. The Stars and Stripes Forever, march — Sousa

The Star Spangled Banner

APPENDIX V

WHAT THE BAND PLAYED

The Purpose of This Appendix

This appendix provides written documentation of the repertory of Sousa's Band and the years in which each piece was performed.

The band's contribution to America's musical heritage was enormous, and this catalog is a reflection of musical tastes during the band's forty-year period of operation (1892-1932).

A distinction should be made between the terms *repertory* and *library*. The library is the music that is at a musical organization's disposal, whereas the repertory is what was actually played. Hundreds of pieces that remained in the band's library after Sousa's death had never been played, and thousands of others had been discarded long before that time.

Sources

The primary sources used in compiling this catalog were the band's printed programs. In addition to those in my collection, others were found in the Sousa Band press books and other collections.

Other programs, for many short periods not covered by the existing press books, were found in newspaper clippings from libraries as the author was reconstructing missing legs of band tours (Appendix I). Still others were found in show business magazines such as the *New York Dramatic Mirror* and the *New York Clipper*.

Since inexact or incomplete titles often appeared on programs, it was necessary to refer to music in the sections of the band's library that still remain. When a piece of music could not be located there, the holdings of other large music libraries were consulted. In cases where an exact title could not be determined, the titles presented herein are the ones found on the printed programs.

Sousa Band programs seldom listed composers' first names, so it was necessary to consult standard reference volumes such as *The New Grove Dictionary of Music and Musicians* and *The Heritage Encyclopedia of Band Music.* These volumes are listed in the Bibliography.

Creative Titling

Sousa freely took artistic liberties in titling when creating his programs, and in the course of presenting over fifteen thousand concerts there was ample opportunity to be "creative." One might easily get the impression that he was playing games with his audiences or simply exercising his sense of humor.

It should be understandable, then, that there are likely some unidentified duplications in this appendix, although many other duplications were detected and eliminated by various computerized sortings.

One thing became overwhelmingly evident: Sousa was a clever disguise artist. When repeating a work at a later date, he would often give it a variant name, leaving the impression that it was a different work. For example, Massenet's "Scenes Neapolitaine" might show up later as "Carnival Night in Naples." He might also call a song from one of his operettas by its given name one time and later use a line or phrase from the lyrics as the title. For example, "The Card Song" (from *The Bride Elect*) might later be called "Here's a Pack." Similarly, "Oh Warrior Grim" (from *El Capitan*) might show up later as "The Tolling of the Bells."

As if Sousa's large variety of mystery titles did not cause enough confusion, other factors posed additional challenges. Printers of programs could not always interpret Sousa's handwriting. That, coupled with typographical errors and misunderstandings in verbal communication, led to a compounding of incorrect titles and composers' names.

Another cataloging difficulty arose as a result of programs not providing composers' full names. Nearly all Sousa programs listed composers' last names only, and seldom was the name of an arranger or transcriber given. Publishers of the music were almost never noted.

Reminiscences and *Selections*

Reminiscences and *Selections* were catch-all titles that were used for collections of pieces from a larger work or group of works. Because there were so many ways a piece of music was listed, there was usually no way of determining which edition was being used. For example, below is a partial list of ways titles were found on programs:

> *Reminiscences of* ____
> *Selections from* ____
> *Scenes from* ____
> *Fantasie (or Fantasy or Fantasia) from* ____
> *Grand Fantasie (or Fantasy or Fantasia)*
>   *from* ____
> *Recollections of* ____
> ____ *, Mosaic*
> ____ *, Episode Fantastic*
> *Gems from* ____
> *Gems of* ____
> *Excerpts from* ____
> *Extracts from* ____
> *Motives from* ____
> *Scenes from* ____
> *Grand Scenes from* ____
> *Airs from* ____
> *Ballet Suite from* ____
> *Some Numbers from* ____
> *Introduction of Numbers from* ____
> *Potpourri of* ____

> *Concert Suite from* ____
> *Collocation of* ____
> *Movements from* ____
> *Medley of* ____
> *Concert Suite from* ____
> *Selections from the Pen of* ____
> *Most Admired Songs of* ____
> *Scenes from the Most Admired Works of* ____
> *Themes from the Admired Works of* ____
> *Excerpts from the Works of* ____
> *Themes from the Works of* ____
> *Some Airs of* ____
> *Scenes from the Operas of* ____
> *Songs and Dances of* ____
> *Melodic Moments with* ____
> *Collection of Songs and Dances of* ____
> *Scenes from* ____ *'s Operas*
> *Extracts from the Operas of* ____
> *Fantasie on Works of* ____
> *Choice Songs of* ____
> *Scenes from Masterpieces of* ____

Favorites

It is interesting to look down this list and see which composers audiences preferred during the Sousa era – or which composers' music Sousa thought audiences should be exposed to. His favorite composer was Wagner, as confirmed by the quantity of Wagner's music that the band played.

The predominance of Sousa's own music is understandable, because his public demanded it. People paid premium prices to see him and expected to hear his music. It is also noteworthy that much of the music played by the band was composed by members of the band.

The last column is a clear indication of the music that had stood the test of time at this period in history. Asterisks (*) denote pieces that were used repeatedly on tour.

COMPOSER	TITLE	YEARS PLAYED IN
Abrams	Indian Sun Dance	02
Abt, Franz	Embarrassment, ballad	93
	Good Night (Gute Nacht), song	98
	Still is the Night, vocal solo	94
	Sweet Angel, vocal solo	93
	Woldenacht (Walkendacht), horn quartet [unaccompanied?]	98
Ackerman, H.	Divertissement on Ancient Scotch Melodies	93
	Songs and Dances of Ireland	99
Adair, Frank L.	Princeton March (Princeton Two-Step)	96
Adam	King of the Dwarfs, The: Overture	96
	Two Dances: Lisolette; Lancelot	13
Adam, Adolphe	Brewer of Preston, The: Overture	94
	Cantique de Noel	93
	Faithful Shepherd, The: Overture	93 94
	Giralda: Overture	94 96 98
	Giselle: Ballet Suite	94
	If I Were King (Si J'Etais Roi) (King for a Day): Overture	96
	Konig von Yvetot, Der (The King of Yvetot) (Le Roi d'Vyetot) (Si Jetais Roi): Overture	93 96 99
	Postillion, The, vocal solo	94
	Postillon de Lonjumeau, Le: Overture	02 24
	Poupee de Nuremberg, La (The Doll of Nuremberg): Overture	01 04 06 18 19 22
	Queen for a Day (La Reine d'Un Jour): Overture	96
	Toreador, The: Overture	94 95
Adams	Mona, vocal solo	93
Adams, A. Emmett	Bells of St. Mary's, The, vocal solo or band number	20 21 25-27
Adams, Alton A.	Governor's Own, The, march	22
	Virgin Islands, march	21
Adams, Henry C.	Victory Song [Drake University]	27
Adams, S. Jarvis	Bohemian Waltzes	03
Adams, Stephen	By the Fountain, song	94
	Holy City, The, song, vocal, violin, or cornet solo	93-96 98 99 *00 01 08 *11 13 14
	Star of Bethlehem, The, cornet solo	01
Adolph	Valse de Concert, cornet solo	*92
Ager, Milton	Happy Days Are Here Again, fox trot, saxophone ensemble	*30
	Young Man's Fancy, A, xylophone solo	*21
Ahl, George	Air and Gavotte	03
Alard, Adele	Romeo and Juliette (Fantasie on Gounod's Romeo and Juliette), violin solo	*09 10 *11 *12 16 *19 *20 *21 22
	Valse Caprice, violin solo	10
Albeniz, Isaac	Midsummer Night's Serenade, Op. 232	23 24
Albers, Fred G.	Basket of Roses, descriptive	15
Albert, Johann Joseph	Astorga: Ballet Music	96
Albert, Roch.	Tarantelle de Belphegor, La (Belphegor)	*99 *00 01 02 *03 04 05 06 08
Alexander, James Irving	Black Diamond Express March	97
Aliabiev, Alexander	Russian Nightingale (Die Nichtigall), vocal solo	02 *28 29 31
Allen, Charles Claflin	New Setting of America, A	04
Allen, Lizbeth Y.	Song of the Brownies, The	95
Allen, Thomas	Turkish Towel Rag	*24
Alvaredo	En el Mar, waltz	93
Amers, Harry G.	All on a Christmas Morning, idyll	23 24
	Wee Macgregor, The, Highland patrol	05 22 24
Amphlett, C.	Onward, march	25
Andersen	Carnival Russe, flute solo	93
	Swallows, The, flute solo	16
	Waltz Caprice, flute solo	16
Anderson	Tremolo, Le, flute solo	15
Andrews, Addison Fletcher	Oh, For a Day of Spring (Oh, Day of Spring), vocal solo	10

Andrews, M.H.	Pride of the Army, march	97
anonymous	Gavotte of the XVIII Century	96
Ansell, John	Irish Whispers	26
	Plymouth Hoe, nautical overture	15 24
	Shoe Dance, violin solo	*09
	Three Irish Dances	23 24
Anthony, Bert R.	Fan Tan, Chinese march characteristic	01
	O-B-Joyful	08
	Warm Reception, A, characteristic	99
Antressian, E.	Bijou, entr'acte (intermezzo)	94
Apiommes	Home, Sweet Home, parapharase, harp solo	93
	Last Rose of Summer, harp solo	93
Appoloni, G.	L'Ebreo, vocal solo	93
Arban, Jean Baptiste	Air Brilliante, cornet solo	98
	Air Varie (Air and Variations) (Air Varied), cornet solo	95 21 22 25 26
	Attila, cornet solo	06
	Auld Lang Syne, cornet solo	19
	Caprice Brilliante, cornet solo	22
	Carnival of Venice, cornet solo	*00 08 *09 *12 *14 *20 *21 *22 23 *24 *25 26 *27
	Fantasia Originale, cornet solo	93
	Fantasie Brillante, cornet solo	93 *20 23 24
	Polka Brilliante, cornet solo	97 21 22
	Swiss Boys, The (Sounds from the Alps) (Alpine Fantasia) (Alpine Echoes), cornet duet	06-10 *11 14 16 22 23
	Thou, Thou Variations (Du Du), euphonium solo	92
	Tyroleans, The, cornet solo/duet	06 08
Arbuckle, Matthew	Air and Variations, cornet solo	02
	Ocean View, cornet solo	29
Arditi, Luigi	Bacio, Il (The Kiss), waltz, vocal solo	22 24 27
	Bacio, Il, vocal or whistling solo [unnamed]	93 18 22 27
	Enchantress Valse, The, vocal solo	*95
	Estasi, L', waltz, vocal solo	93 97
	I Am the Rose, vocal solo	10 19-23 25 26 28
	L'Ingenue, gavotte	03 19
	Let Me Love Thee, vocal solo	95
	Love in Springtime, vocal solo	96 02
	Melba Waltz	96
	Parla Waltz, vocal solo	94 *96 97 02 05-07 10 19
	Rosebuds (Se Seran Rose) (When Bloom the Roses), vocal solo	95 96 *97 *98 *99 09 10 13 14 16-18 21-24 26-28
	Waltz Song, vocal solo	97
Armand, Charles	Poupee Automatique, La (The Mechanical Doll)	21
Armstrong, Harry	Chimes, The, reverie	13
Armstrong, William Dawson	Jota, La, Spanish dance	94
Arndt, Felix	Nola, fox trot, xylophone solo	21 *22 23-28
	Operatic Nightmare, An (Desecration No. 2), parody (potpourri)	*21
Arne, Thomas	Waltz of the Dolls	15
Arne, Thomas Augustine	Lass with the Delicate Air, The, vocal solo	10 18 26
Arne, Thomas Augustine	When Love Is Kind	09
Arnold	Grand Regent, march	94
	Passing Soldiers, patrol	02
	Tutti Frutti	98
	Un Beso, waltz	93
Arnold, Ian	Ionita, characteristic	07
	Te Escojo, The, waltz	93
Arnold, J.C.	Blennerhasset March	98
Arnold, Maurice	American Plantation Dances (Plantation Dances)	*94 *95 96 *97 01 02
	Danse de la Midway Plaisance, introducing Coochie, Coochie	96

Aronson, Rudolph	Alma, Spanish March	96
	Down the Pike, march	04
	Gallant and Gay, march	96
	Japonica, serenade	97
	Oriental Dance	94 96
	Patrol Oriental	94
	Pickaninny, serenade (Dance of the Pickaninnies)	97 *98
	Polish Mazurka	94
	Sweet Sixteen, cornet solo	93
	Syrian Patrol	94
Artemieff, N.	Russian Gypsy Songs (Uber Russische Zigeunerlieder) (Fantasia on Gypsy Airs) (Gems from Gypsy Land)	94 24
Ascher, Emil	Dance of Andalusia, A	93 94 96
	Dance of the Russian Peasants, A (National Dance of Russia)	93 94 96
	Dear Old Germany, national overture (Reminiscences of Germany)	10
	Fanfare Militaire	97 *98 99 01 02
	Rondo Militaire	04 05
Ascher, F.	L'Esperance, nocturne	94
Ascher, Joseph	Alice, Where Art Thou, romance, serenade, cornet solo, cornet duet, or band number	04 06 07 10 *11 12 13 21 22
	Danse Negre (Dance of the Darkies) (Bamboula)(Dance Founded on African Melodies), caprice	01 02 *13 14 15
Ascolese	Happy Band, The, caprice	01
Atkinson, Robert Whitman	Associated Clubs March	24
Auber, Daniel-Francois Esprit	Bronze Horse: Overture	94
	Chaperons Blancs, Les: Overture	94
	Crown Diamonds, The: Aria [unnamed], vocal solo[s]	94
	Domino Noir, Le (The Black Domino): Overture	94 96 23 26
	Fra Diavalo: Overture	*93 *94 95 96 02-04 06-09 15-24 27
	Fra Diavalo: Romance	94
	Fra Diavolo: Selections (Scenes)	94 96 01
	Gustavus III: Ballet Music	93 94 96
	Leocadie: Overture	22
	Lestocq: Overture	94 96 *98 09
	Masaniello: Ballet Music	93-96
	Masaniello: Overture	94 96 07 09 19 32
	Muette de Portici, La: Overture	96
	Part du Diable: Overture	93 94
	Premier Juor de Bonheur, Le (The First Day of Good Luck): Overture	95 96
	Reminiscences of Auber	93 96 22 24
	Sirene, La: Overture	94 23
	Slumber Song, vocal solo	95
	Zanetta: Overture	93 94 96 23 24
Aubrey, Paul	Menuet Dans le Style Ancien (Minuet in the Ancient Style)	95 96
Audran, Edmond	Cigale, La: Finale	94
	Cigale, La: Selections	92-96 *00 01 02 04 07 08 16-19 21 25-27
	Cigale, La: The Ant and the Grasshopper	94 23
	Doll, The: Selections	98
	Giselda: Ballet Suite	95
	Grand Mogel, Le: Overture	05 16 19
	In the North Sea Lives a Whale, song	96
	Indiana: Selections	93 94
	Mascot, The (La Mascotte): Overture	26
	Mascot, The (La Mascotte): Selections	93-96 01 17 18 21 23 24 25
	Mascot, The (La Mascotte): The Gobble Duet (Gobble Song), The, cornet and trombone duet	04
	Olivette: Selections	92-96 *00 01 04-07 09 15-22 24 27 28
	Poupee, Le: Selections	97-99

325

Aulin, Tor	Gavotte and Musette, violin solo	*11 12
	Humoresque, violin solo	14
Austin, Frederick	Beggar's Opera, The: Selections	26 28
Avilles	Souvenir de Granada	93
Ayer, Nat D.	If You Were the Only Girl, fox trot	26
	Yes, Uncle!, fantasia	19
Bacanggra, Francisco G. & Kozaburo Hiria	Mexicanos el Grito de Guerra, national song	98
Bach	Fantasia Brilliante, cornet solo	96
Bach, Christoph (Christian)	Fairy Tale, A (A Fairy Story), idyl	94 24
	Festival: Overture	94 95
	Honeymoon, waltz	94
	Jockey Club, galop	96
	Jubel (Jubilee) (The Day of Jubilee): Overture, Op. 66	94-98 04
	Mars and Saturn, polka rondo, cornet duet or quartet	96
	Valse Brillante, cornet solo	95 96
Bach, Emanuel	Hamlet: Overture (Scenes)	27
Bach, Johann Sebastian	Air and Sicilianna	14
	Air for the G String, violin solo	05 06 14
	Ariele, the Daughter of the Air (Ariele die Tochter der Luft): Finale	03
	Choral and Grand Fugue	20 22 23 27
	Reminiscences of Bach	22
	Sicilienne	95
	Suite in G Major: Air	01 02 *05 *11
	Third Violincello Suite: Loure	03 14
	Well-Tempered Clavier, The	09 10 *11 13 15
Bach-Caruai	Gavotte, harp solo	93
Baermann	Sonnambula, La, theme varied, clarinet solo	96
Baetens, Ch.	Albion, fantasia on Scotch, Irish and English Airs	93 94 96 06 19 22 27 28
	Rose, The Shamrock, and the Thistle, The	01
Bafunno	University of Nebraska, march	98
Bafunno, A.	Dewey's Triumphal Grand March	98
	Queen of the Raggers (The Ragger Queen), march	98
	Sir Rollo, galop	98
Bagley, Edwin Eugene	National Emblem, march	14 23-25
Bagley, Ezra Mahon	Three Star Polka (The Three Stars), cornet trio or solo	95 26
Bailey, Eben H.	Home Again, waltz	93
Baisio	Duet for Two Clarinets	93
Baker, F.G.	Japanese Dance	93
	Recessional March	93
	San Salvatore, processional march	93
Balakirev, Mily Aleksevich	Fantasie on Russian Themes	02
	Overture on Three Russian Themes (Ouverture sur Trois Themes Russes) (Fantasia on Three Russian Themes)	*98
	Rumelda: Overture	98
Balart, Jose	Ideal, waltz	12
Balfe, Michael William	Bohemian Girl, The: I Dreamt I Dwelt in Marble Halls, vocal solo	*94
	Bohemian Girl, The: Overture	93-96 04 05 17-19 21 22 27
	Bohemian Girl, The: Selections	93-96 01 03 06-10 13-18 24 27
	Bohemian Girl: The Heart Bowed Down, vocal solo	92-94 15
	Four Children of Hamon: Selections	93 95
	Killarney, ballad, vocal, cornet, or saxophone solo	98 *05 06 08-10 *11 15 16 *17 26
	Last Rose of Summer, The, vocal or trombone solo	*94 13 15 18 23
	Overture, introducing War Song of the Hussites	15
	Reminiscences of Balfe	93 94 96 07 13-15 18 22
	Satanella: Selections	96
	Talismano, Il: Introduction and two numbers (Grand Scene)	93 94 02
	Then You'll Remember Me, vocal solo	93 95
	Well of Love, The: Scenes (Grand Fantasia)	96 25 26

	When Other Lips, cornet solo	98
Balfmoor	McAlheeny's Irish Cake Walk	99
Ball	Old Daddy Peg-Leg, characteristic	08
Ball, Ernest R.	Little Bit of Heaven, A, vocal solo	*17
	Love Me and the World Is Mine, cornet solo	07 *08
	Mother Machree, vocal solo	17
Ball, Meredith	In Days of Old, suite	05
Balmer, Charles, Jr.	Branch Guards, march	93 94
Banta, Frank P.	Wheelman's Patrol	97 98
Bareuter, J.	Steeplechase, The, march	02
Barker, Leonard	Grand Irish Fantasie	98
Barker, Richard H.	Majestic Waltzes	98
	Wedding Chimes, schottische (caprice)	96
Barnard	Flirtation, cornet solo	20
Barnard, George D.	Nourhalma, waltz	02
	Old Warrior, march	98
Barnby, Joseph	Rebekah: Grand March (Bride's March)	93 95
	Sweet and Low, horn quartet [unaccompanied?]	96 *99 01 18
	Sweet and Low, paraphrase (lullaby)	94 96
Barnes	Skyrocket Polka, cornet solo	26
Barnett	Whoop 'em Up Blues, saxophone ensemble	*26
Barnhouse, Charles Lloyd	Land of Plenty, march, introducing Iowa Corn Song	29
Baron, Lizette	King Saul: Overture	96
Barr	Darling Girls, The, rube fox trot	24
	O Me! O My!	24
Barrett, A.W.	212th Artillery N.Y.N.G., march	25
Barri, Odoardo	Old Brigade, The (Boys of the Old Brigade), vocal solo/duet	*17
Bartlett, Homer Newton	Caprice Espanol	95
	Dance of the Gnomes	93
	Festival Hymn (Grand Festival Hymn)	*12
	Grand March Militaire	96
	Organ Suite: Andante and Allegro	26
	St. Anne, festival hymn	13
	Tocatta in E-flat	02 *03 04 05 24
Bartlett, James Carroll	Dream, A (Dreams) (Bartlett's Dream), vocal or cornet solo	*99 01 *15 16 23-26 *28
Bartlett, James Carroll & Celia Burt Wall	If Thou Wert Gone, vocal solo	06
Bartlett, William C.	Darling, Sweetly Sleep	94
	Philomena, idyl	94 96
Barton, Clarence	Plutocrat, The, march	07
Barwood, Arthur Vincent	Canada (Songs and Dances of Canada) (Songs of the Canadian Universities) (The Dominion) (Varsity Songs), fantasie	04 06 17 19
Baselei	Grand Concerto, cornet solo	01
Basisio	Souvenir de Cadiz	93
Basler, Horace	Claude Duval, march	03
Basquit, Heinrich	Erin, Grand fantasie (Fantasie on Irish Melodies)	95
Bassi, Luigi	Air Neapolitan, euphonium solo	93
	Fantasia for Clarinet on Themes from Rigoletto	93 26 28
	Sonnambula, La: Excerpt, clarinet solo	93
Bassler	Blooming Roses, waltz	01
Bath, Hubert	Wedding of Shon MacLean, Scotch rhapsody	14 24
Batiste, Antoine-Edouard	Communion in G: The Pilgrim's Song of Hope (offertory)	94 03 04 06 07
	Offertory in D Minor	03
	Organ Suite: Communion in E-Flat	01 03
	Pilgrim's Song of Hope	03 08 10 14 15 17 18
Batten, Ernest	Clover Blossoms (White and Red), summer idyll	13
Batten, Robert	April Morn, vocal solo	06 09 *10 *11 12-19
Battishill, Percy F.	Mediterranean Life (Along the Mediterranean) (Life in the Mediterranean), suite	06 16 17 24
Bauer	Dream of Heaven, waltz	02
	Love's Atonement, trombone solo	02
Bauer, Oscar O.	Mill in the Dale, The (The Mill in the Valley) (The Mill in the Vale) (Die Muhle im Thale), fantasie	02 06

Baxter	Southern Idyll, A	98
Bayer, Josef	Dancing Doll, The (Die Puppenfee) (The Dolls) (The Fairy Dolls): Selections (ballet suite)	05 07 08 10 16 17 21-24 26-28
Bayers, Frederick W.	Saxophones, The, medley	24
Bayly, Thomas Haynes	Long, Long Ago, vocal solo	16
Baynes, Sydney	Victory, waltz	20
Bazin, Francois Emanuel Joseph	Trompete, Le (The Trumpeter): Overture	93-96 22-26
Bazzini, Antonio	Hercules, euphonium solo	93
	King Saul: Overture	98 02 18
	Ronde des Lutins, La (The Round of the Goblins) (Dance of the Goblins): Scherzo Fantastique, violin solo	10 15 *19 *20
Beach, Amy Marcy (Mrs. H.H.A.)	Ecstacy, ballad	94
	Song of Love, A, vocal solo	95
	Year's at the Spring, The, vocal solo	06 *07 *08
Becker	Fantasie on German Songs	01
	Springtide, vocal solo	95
Beeley, Ernest L.	At Thy Window, Venetian serenade	95
Beethoven, Ludwig van	Adelaide, song	15
	Ah, Perfido	94
	Coriolan: Overture	94
	Fidelio: Aria [unnamed], vocal solo[s]	95
	Fidelio: Quartet, vocal solo	93
	King Stephan: Overture	94 98
	Leonore: Overture	95 06 23 27
	Leonore: Overture No. 3 (Fidelio)	94-96 98 99 *00 01 02 04 15 16
	Leonore: Overture No. 4	94
	Menuett, violin solo	*11 *12 *13 *24
	Morning, andante	93
	Reminiscences of Beethoven	94-96 04 06 08 24
	Sonata ("Appassionata"): Allegro	10
	Sonata ("St. Jerome's Love"): Andante Graszioso	94
	Sonata in E-flat, Op. 7: Largo	97 98 01
	Sonata in F, Op. 24 ("Spring"): Scherzo, violin solo	*03
	Sonata No. 14 in C, Op. 27 No. 2 ("Moonlight"): Movement I	96 *96 *97 16 23 24
	Sonata No. 8 in C, Op. 13 ("Pathetique"): Adagio	96
	Sonata, Op. 14: Andante	93
	Symphony No. 1 (all or separate movements)	94 95
	Symphony No. 6 ("Pastorale"): At the Brook	02
	Symphony No. 7 in A (Symphony in La Majeur): Presto	98
	Symphony No. 8: ("Unfinished"): Allegretto Scherzando	94 01 12 15
	Wellington's Victory	94
Behr, Francois	Bells, The, caprice	94
	Macarena, La: Overture	93 94 96
Behrend, A.H.	Lord Is My Shepherd, The, cornet solo	*05
Behrmann	Concerto for Clarinet	92
Bein	Lots of Pep (Plenty of Pep), xylophone solo	*26 *28 *29
Belisle	Casino, The, march	97
Bellini, Vincenzo	Norma: Aria [unnamed], vocal solo[s]	07
	Norma: At the Altar, vocal solo	94
	Norma: Excerpt, cornet solo	92
	Norma: Scene and Aria, vocal solo	06
	Old Hundred, hymn	93 95
	Puritani, I: Aria [unnamed], vocal or euphonium solo[s]	*20 22-25
	Puritani, I: Liberty Duet, trombone duet, trombone and euphonium duet, or vocal solo	01 02 *19 *20 21 27
	Puritani, I: Qui la Voce, cavatina, vocal solo	19 21 22
	Puritani, I: Theme and Variations, euphonium solo	21
	Reminiscences of Bellini	93 96
	Romeo and Juliette: Excerpt, vocal solo	93
	Sonnambula, La: Aria [unnamed], vocal solo [with humming by band]	*92 93
	Sonnambula, La: clarinet solo	06

	Sonnambula, La: Com per me Sereno, vocal solo	92
	Sonnambula, La: Recitative and Aria, vocal solo	93
	Sonnambula, La: Selections	95 96
Bellstedt, Herman	Kelly, humoresque	*10 *11
	Air Varie, cornet solo	19
	American Boy, The (The Nation's Youth) (American Youth), cornet solo	13 15-19
	American Fantasie, cornet solo	05
	Blue Bells (Good-bye, My Blue Bell), humoresque	05
	Carmen Fantasie (Airs from Carmen) (Fantasie on Themes from Carmen), cornet solo	04 05 17-19
	Centennial Polka, cornet solo	*22 *23 *24 *25 *26 28
	College Dreams, cornet solo	17
	Devil's Tongue, The, cornet solo	23-25
	Dixie Fantasia	28
	Dixie, variations, violin solo	*11 *12
	Everybody Works But Father, humoresque	05 *06 *07
	Fantasie Original (Air Originale), cornet solo	04 05
	Faust Fantasie, cornet solo	04
	Fern Leaves Waltz, cornet solo	14 16 23 24
	German Fantasie, cornet solo	04
	Get Out and Get Under, humoresque	*14
	Goodbye Girls [Good-bye, Girls, I'm Through], humoresque	15 16
	Indian War Dance	*98
	Jean Adair, cornet solo	23
	Langue de Diable, cornet solo	04 05
	Mandolinata, La, cornet solo	04 05 13-19 22
	Middletonian, cornet solo	14 16 18 19
	Midnight Choo Choo (When the Midnight Choo Choo Leaves for Alabama), descriptive	*13
	Musical Joke on Bedelia, A, humoresque	*05
	My Sweetheart, cornet solo	24
	My Wife's Gone to the Country, humoresque	*09 *11
	Napoli (Neapolitan Fantasy) (Sounds from Naples), cornet solo	16-19
	Over There, fantasie	*18 *19 *20
	Polka Caprice (Polka di Concert), cornet solo	14 17-19 22
	Polly Willis, flute solo	20
	Popular Fancy, cornet solo	17-19
	Princess Alice (The Princess), cornet solo	14-19
	Rakes of Pan (Pan's Pranks), flute solo	*20 21
	Smiles, humoresque	19
	Spanish Serenade (Spanish Fantasia), cornet solo	17 18
	Student's Sweetheart, The (Student d'Amour), cornet solo	15-17 *18 *19 *20 23-25
	Theme Varie, cornet solo	18
	Tipperary, fantasie	*14 *15 16 *17 *21
	Turkey in the Straw, humoresque	19
	Waiting at the Church, humoresque	*06 *07 *08 *11
	Waltz Caprice, cornet solo	17
	West End, march	*98
	Youth of America, cornet solo	18
	Zielerthal, cornet solo	22
	Zipcoonian Rhapsody (Zipcoonia), cornet solo	05
Bemberg, Herman	Chanson des Baisers, vocal solo	09
	Chant Venetian	*94
	Elaine: Excerpts	93
	Nymphs et Sylvain, vocal solo	93 96 *97 05 15 16
	Song-Fairy, The (La Fee Aux Chanson), vocal solo	04
Bender	Henry, march	21
Bendix , Theodore	Melodies of the Plantation (Songs and Dances of the South)	95 98 *00 16
	American Fantasie	04
	Butterfly, The (The Butterflies), characteristic (caprice)	96 *97 98 *00 06 08 18 25 26

	Chinese Episode, A (Li Hung Chang in America)	97 98
	Dawn of Love, The, serenade	04
	Good Old Times, The, fantasie	07
	Grand American Fantasia (American Songs and Dances) (Songs and Dances of America)	95 98 01
	Hungarian, The, romance	08
	Life on the Ocean Wave, A, nautical fantasia	21
	Old Chestnuts in New Burrs, fantasie	97 98 01 07 19 24
	Old Neptune, fantasie	06
	Songs of the Soldiers	95
	Songs Our Grandmothers Sang, fantasie	98
	Symposia, medley	93 94 96
	Tone Pictures of the North and South (Melodies of the North and South)	94-96 98 03 04 06 13 24
Bendix, William	American Dance, An, characteristic	94 96
Benedict, Julius	Carnival of Venice, vocal solo	20
	Eily Mavourneen, vocal solo	18
	Lily of Killarney, The: Selections	93-95 23
	Reminiscences of Benedict	93
	Wren, The, vocal solo	*21 *22 23-27 28 31
Bennet, Charles William	Refuge, medley of gospel hymns	20
Bennett, William Sterndale	Naiades, Die, Op. 15: Overture	22
Benoit, Peter	Charlotte Corday: Ent'r Acte and Valse de la Scene de Bal	94 *00 02
	Vlaamsche Volksmarsch, morceau de geme (caprice)	93
Bentley	Soldier's Song	20
Bentley, W.C.	Militaire, La, Overture	94
Bentley, William Warren	Our Starry Flag Our Glory, vocal solo	22
Beran	Dear Heart of Mine, vocal solo	*98
Berardi, Gaston	Joie d'Aimer, waltz sacred waltz	02
Bereny, Henri	Little Boy Blue: Selections	11 12
Berger & Omela	When Bright Lights Shine, fox trot	26
Berger, H.	Fantasia on Hawaiian Themes	16
Berger, Rudolphe	Amoureuse, waltz lento	05
	Reine du Danube (Queen of the Danube), waltz	05 06
Bergson, Michael	Louisa di Montfort, saxophone solo	19
Berlin, Irving	Always, vocal solo	26 27
	Crinoline Days	*23 24
	Everybody's Doing It Now, fox trot	*12
	Octette for Saxophones	24
	Snooky Ookums, song	*13
	Syncopated Walk, The, fox trot	15
Berlioz, Hector	Ball, The, symphonic fantastic	09
	Benvenuto Cellini: Overture	24
	Benvenuto Cellini: Prelude to Act II	*01
	Carneval Romaine (Roman Carnival): Overture	*98 *99 *01 *02 *03 04 07 08 *14 *15-19 21-23 25 26 *30 *31
	Damnation of Faust, The: Easter Hymn	93
	Damnation of Faust, The: Fugue and March	10 13 14
	Damnation of Faust, The: Menuet des Follets (Dance-o-the-Whisps) (Fire-fly Minuet) (Ballet des Sylphs) (Dance of the Sylphs)	95 *98 02 05
	Damnation of Faust, The: Rakoczy March	93 97 98 02 05 *06 07 09 *11 16
	Damnation of Faust, The: Reveille, Easter Hymn, and Rakocky March	93
	Damnation of Faust, The: Selections	93 94 *00 08 15 20 21 28
	Francs Juges, Des: Overture	94
	King Lear: Overture	02 24
	Reminiscences of Berlioz	05 07-09 10 *11 12-14 16 18-27
Bernard	Passions of the Heart	08
Bernard, Felix & Johnny S. Black	Dardanella, fox trot, xylophone solo or band number	*20

330

Bernicat, Fermin	Victor, the Blue Stocking: Scenes	94
Bernstein	Enthusiasm, gavotte	93
Beuger, Otto	Souvenir du Bal, intermezzo	*97
Bevan, Frederick	Dream of My Heart, The, vocal solo	*98
	Silver Path, The	94
Bevignani, Enrico	Lullaby, vocal solo	96
Beyer, Edward	Hark the Herald Angels Sing [collection of sacred themes]	93
	Recollections of the War	93
Beyer, F.	Somebody Loves Me	94
Beyer, Josef	Dolls, The: Ballet Suite (The Dancing Dolls)	06 07 09 19 20 25 26
Bial, Ernst	Bon Voyage, patrol (caprice)	96 98
	Romance, vocal solo	96
Bial, Rudolph	Baby Polka	95
Bibo, Irving	March of the Blues	27
	Sympathy Waltz, vocal solo	26
Bidgood, Thomas	Khaki Camp, A, descriptive fantasie	19 21 24 27
Bigelow, Frederick Ellsworth	Our Director March	08
Bilton, J. Manuel	My Old Stable Jacket, overture	*24 25-28
Bimbone, Giovacchino	Flower Garden, The, euphonium solo	04
Binding, Edwin	Life on the Ocean, A (Airs of the Sea), nautical selection (fantasie)	06 18 20 24
	Spanish Review, The, military fantasie	93 94
Bischoff, John W.	Bob-o-Link (Bobolink), vocal solo	92 93 01
	Love's Sorrow, vocal solo	93
	Psyche, gavotte	94
Bishop, Henry Rowley	Bloom Is On the Rye, The, sketch, vocal solo or band number	93 *09
	Collection of Glees	95
	Guy Mannering, Overture	23-26
	Home Sweet Home, paraphrase, vocal or clarinet solo	94 98
	Lo, Here the Gentle Lark, vocal solo or flute and clarinet duet	93 *95 07 08 *11 15 18 22 24 26
	My Pretty Jane, ballad	94 95
Bissell, Simeon	Endeavor, The, grand march	03
	Overture No. 1	01
Bizet, Georges	Carmen: Aria [unnamed], vocal solo[s]	93 06-08 16-19 21 27 28
	Carmen: Ballet Suite	24-26
	Carmen: Dragons d'Alcaca	*95
	Carmen: Gypsy Song, vocal solo	26
	Carmen: Habanera, vocal solo	93 95 29
	Carmen: March of the Toreadors (Toreador's Song), vocal solo	95
	Carmen: Micaela's Prayer (Micaela's Aria), vocal solo	96 97 *99 05 20 27
	Carmen: Prelude	94-97 01 07 08 19
	Carmen: Qui dei Contrabbandier, vocal solo	*97
	Carmen: Second Mosaic	93-99 *00 01-06 08-10 *11 12-16
	Carmen: Selections	95 17-28 31
	Carmen: Suite	15-24
	Carmen: This Flower	93
	Carmen: Toreadore Song, vocal solo or band number	92-94 96 97 23 26
	Carmen: Two Airs	98
	Carmen: Waltz	94 07
	Dragoons	*95
	Flower Garden, The, euphonium solo	93 94 96 05
	Golden Love, tone picture	07 08 09
	L'Arlesienne: Intermezzo and Danse Espagnole	94
	L'Arlesienne: Suite No. 1	93 94 96 03 04 06 08 *09 10 *11 12-26
	L'Arlesienne: Suite No. 2	09 10 *11 13-15 19 21 23 25 26
	L'Arlesienne: Suite No. 2: Agnus Dei (Golden Light), intermezzo	05 10 *11 15 16 *22 23 *24 25 29
	L'Arlesienne: The French Military	94
	Patrie: Overture	93 14 17 18 21 23 26 27

	Pearl Fishers, The (Les Pecheurs des Perles): Cavatina de Leila, vocal solo	24
	Pearl Fishers, The (Les Pecheurs des Perles): Selections	05 06 09 18 22 24
	Petite Suite d'Orchestra: March; The Doll, berceuse; The Spinning Top, impromptu; Little Husband and Wife, duo; The Ball, galop	05
	Tarantelle, vocal solo	05
Black	Brooklyn Times, The, march	97
Black, Alexander	Helen, waltz	*94
Black, Johnny S., SEE Bernard, Felix		
Blagrove, Richard	Village Fete, A, toy symphony	08
Blake, Eubie	Shuffle Along	22
Bland, James A.	Carry Me Back to Old Virginny, vocal solo or band number	19 *20 *21 *22 *23 *24 25 *26 *27 *30
Blattermann, Heinrich	Divertissement Antique	16
	Divertissement Fantastic (Fete Champetre) (Ballet Divertissement)	*99 08
	Fest (Uber Niederlandische Weisen) (Netherland Airs) (The United Netherlands): Overture	98
	Five Minutes in Noah's Ark, rondo	94
Bleetger, E.	German National No. 1, The, march	94
Bloch	Richard III, pageant	27
Bloch, Josef	Suite Poetique: March	04
Block, Irving Arthur	Fifes of '76, The, march	24
Blockx, Jan	Four Flemish Dances	13 15 24
Blodek, Wilhelm	At the Well, overture to a Bohemian comic opera	21 23
Bloeser, E.H.	Eleonora Polka	95
Blon, Franz von	Danseuse, La, intermezzo	01 02
	Fairy Dream (Fairy Scenes) (Traumbild), characteristic	06
	Liebestandelei, idyll	02
	Perpetum Mobile, caprice	98
	Sizilietta, serenade	*03 08 *11 17
	Whispering of the Flowers (Whispering Leaves) (Blumengefluster), idyll	*98 *99 *00 02 04 06 10 14 16 25 26
Blumenthal, Jacob	Across the Far Blue Hills, Marie, song	*98 *99 *00 02 04 06 10 14 16 21 24
	My Queen, vocal solo	95
	Sunshine and Rain, song, euphonium solo	95
Boas	Jig Medley, tuba solo	23
Boccalari, Edoardo	Air Varie, euphonium solo	14 15
	Chinese March (Marche Chinois), characteristic	06 25 26
	Dance of the Serpents, The, characteristic	28
	Fantasia di Concerto (Bolero Concerto) (Grand Fantasia) (Concerto di Concert), euphonium or cornet solo	09 *11 *28
	Hungarian, rhapsody	09
	Sounds from the Riviera, cornet solo	*26
Boccherini, Luigi	Minuet, violin solo or band number	93 94 98 01 06 08 20
Bock	Thuringian Forest Scene	06
Bock, W.E., SEE Cogley, Ed.		
Boehm	Scotch Rhapsody (In Scotland), flute solo	16 17 19
Boettger, E.	Popular Pousse Caffe: Selections	98
Bohm, Carl	Ah, Dost Thou Love, flugelhorn solo	*97 01 02
	Ballad, vocal solo (male)	93
	Cavatina	98
	Fanfare Militaire (Rondo Militaire)	*02 04 06 07 14 23 24
	Hussar's Fanfare, The (Charge of the Hussars) (Husaren Fanfare), caprice	94 95 24
	My All, vocal solo	96
	On Wings of Love (Auf Schwingen der Liebe), waltz	05 15
	Petite Bijouterie, waltz intermezzo (marceau gerni)	22 26
	Still Wie die Nacht (Still as the Night) (Calm as the Night), vocal solo	93 97 05-08 10 *11 23-25 27
	Thine, vocal solo	97 99
	Zur Parade (On Parade), march (caprice)	96
Bohn	Scotch Fantasy (Scotch Themes), flute solo	19
	Suesse Kuesse, salonstuck	93

	Zingara, La, xylophone solo	27
Boieldieu, Francois	Dame Blanche, La: Overture	93 05 07 23
	White Lady, The: Overture	18
Boieldieu, Francois Adrien	Dame Blanche, La: Aria [unnamed], vocal solo[s]	94
Boisvert, Norbert	Richelieu March	10
Boito, Arrigo	Mefistofele: In Paradise, prologue (Prologo in Cielo)	01 02
	Mefistofele: The Night of Sabba (The Night of the Classical Sabbath) (La Notte del Sabba Classico) (Easter Scene), vocal solo or band number	98 *99 *00 01 02 05 07 08 *11 *18 21 22 24-26 28
	Mefistofele: Three Motives	93 97
	Mephistofele: Selections	14 15 17-20 22-24 27
Bolbar	By the Brook, pastoral scene	02
Bond, Carrie Jacobs	A Perfect Day, vocal or cornet solo	15-17 24
	I Love You Truly, vocal or xylophone solo	21 22 *30
	Just a-Wearin' for You, vocal or cornet solo	*18 19 26 27
Bonnaud, F. Louis	Serenade Enfantine	*93 *94 *95 *96 *97 01
Bonnechope, A	Aux 3 Suisses (The Three Switzers), polka	20
Bonnisseau	Annie Laurie, march	93
	Cambria, fantasie on Welsh melodies	02
	In the Land of the Thistle	93
	Reminiscences (Gems) of Scotland, "Robert Bruce" (Grand Selection on Scotch Melodies) (Melodies that Scotchmen Love) (Songs and Dances of Scotland) (Gems of Scottish Minstrelsy, "Robert Bruce") (Gems of Scotland)	93 95 98 01 02 04-10 *11 12 13 15 16 18-26 27 31
Boos, Louis F.	Charmer, The, trombone solo	02
Bordier, Jules	Souvenir de Budapest, Hungarian dances	98
Borel, G.	Cocoyer, La (Dance Havanaise) (Cuban Dance) (Havana Dance)	98 01
Borel-Clerc, Charles	Mattchiche, La (La Sorella) (La Maxixe)	*06
Borodin, Alexander Porfirevich	From [In] the Steppes of Central Asia, tone poem	25
	Prince Igor: Ballet	16-19
	Prince Igor: Dance of Prince Igor	15
Borowski, Felix	Adoration, grand scene	23 24
	Adoration, violin solo	*21 22
Bosc, Auguste	March des Petis Pierrots	23
	Rose Mousse: Entr'acte, waltz	*01 02 06
Bosquet	Tight Little Isle, ancient and modern airs and dance tunes	95
Boucicault	Wearing of the Green, song	24
Bousquet, Georges	Golden Robin, The, piccolo solo	93
Bowman, Euday L.	12th Street Rag, xylophone solo	*21 *22 24 *30
Bowron, George	Ten Minutes with the Minstrels (Songs of the Old-Time Minstrels) (When the Minstrels Come to Town) Gems of Minstrelsy from the Days of Carncross and Dixie), medley overture	94 95 01 02 04 07 17 *23 *24
	War Time Songs and Dances	04
Bradsky	Thou Art Mine All, vocal solo	94 96
Braga, Gaetano	Angel's Serenade, The (Serenade for Violin) (Der Engel Lied), vocal or violin solo or band number	93 95 96 02 06 08 22
Braham	Fantasia on a Hungarian Folk Song	94
Braham, David	Babies on Our Block, The, song	15 16 *17
	Dad's Dinner Pail (My Dad's Dinner Pail), vocal solo	15 *17
	Squatter Sovereignty: Medley Overture (to Ed. Harrigan's comic play)	16
Braham, Edmund	Death of Nelson, The, solo	94
Braham, J.J.	Lost Love, czardas	93 94 96
Brahms, Johannes	Academic Festival (Akademische Fest), overture	94 02 14 *15 16 22-24
	Cradle Song (Wiegenlied), Op. 94	14
	Ein Deutsches Requiem, German Requiem (Brahms)	10
	Hungarian Czardas (Czardas in B-flat)	93-95
	Hungarian Dance No. 1	93 94
	Hungarian Dance No. 5	04
	Hungarian Dance No. 6	*00 01
	Hungarian Dance(s), violin solo or band number	95 96 02 *03 06 *08 *09 *10 12 13 24 28
	Lo, How a Rose E'er Blooming, song	06
	Lullaby (Lieder), Op. 49	29

	Reminiscences of Brahms	13-16 23 24
	Two Hungarian Dances	94 24
Brandeis, Frederick	Humpty Dumpty's Funeral March (Funeral March of Humpty Dumpty), humoresque	96 25
Bratton, John W.	In a Cosey Corner	02
	Paradise Alley, cornet solo	*96 *97
	Rose's Honeymoon, The, reverie	04
	Spangles, intermezzo	08
	Teddy Bear's Picnic, The	08
Bray, Charles	Dance of the Brownies	94
Bren, Joseph	I Don't Know Where I'm Goin', But I'm On My Way, song	*06 *07
Brennan, William J.	Enid Two-Step	97
Breton y Hernandez, Tomas	Dolores March, La, Spanish caprice	10 12-14 16 20
	Garin: Sardana	13
Brewer, Mark A.	Comet, The, scherzo, piccolo solo or band number	09
	Lilliputian Polka, piccolo solo	20
Briccialdi, Giulio	Carnival of Venice, piccolo solo	25
Briel, Joseph Carl	Climax, The: Song of the Soul	10
	Legend	21
Brill, Edwin S.	Game of Eyes, The, trombone solo	01
Briquet	Midnight Girl, The: Selections	15
Briquet, Jean	Adele: Selections	14 15
Bristow, George F.	Hail Columbia: Overture	98
	Seventh Regiment, grand march	97
Brockenshire, James Opie	Little Sweetheart, piccolo solo	09 10
Brockton, Lester	Beneath the Holly, selection of Christmas songs	23
Broeckoven, John van	Suite Creole (Creole Suite): Calina (Clarinda) (Creole Days); Theme and Variations	*10 *11 12 14 15 17 20 23 *24 27
Brooke	Signal, The, trombone solo	93
Brooke, Thomas Preston	Columbian Guards, march	93
	In Kansas, humoresque	06 *07
Brooks, Ellis	Bower of Beauty, The, waltz	08
	Forget Me Not, waltz	01
	In the Great Beyond, meditation	06
Broughton	Songs of the Colleges	22
Broutin, C.	Dance Israelite	94
Brown, A. Seymour	Chin Chin, I Love You, vocal solo	*15 16 *17
Brown, Nacio Herb	Doll Dance, The, descriptive	*27
	Pagan Love Song, saxophone solo	*29
Browne, John Lewis	Corsicana, La: Intermezzo	10
	Dream Time, waltz	10
	Intermezzo Gentile	09 10
	L' Egyptienne (Dance Egyptian), intermezzo	10
Bruch, Max	Arminius: Recitative and Aria, vocal solo	*97
	Kol Nidrei, ancient Hebrew hymn	07 08
	Lorely: Introduction	95
Bruckner, Anton	Symphony No. 3: Scherzo	02
Brull, Ignaz	Tales from the Champagnes, waltz	93
Bruning	Shepherd's Call	97
Bucalossi	Marche Chenois	24
Bucalossi, Ernest	Careless Cuckoos, cakewalk	22
	Darkie's Serenade (Serenade Ethiopian)	95-98 03 08 21 22
	Flying Colors, march	93 97 99 02 04-09 *11 12-15
	Love's Old Sweet Song, waltz	24 26
Bucalossi, Procida	Ciribiribin, waltz song	18 23
	Court Dance	93
	Gitana, La: Waltz	16 17 19 21-24 26 28
	Hunting Scene, A, descriptive	93-96 04-08 15 17-19 21-24
	Ideala, waltz	04 24
	Mia Cara (My Darling), waltz	93-96 24

	My Queen, waltz	03 06 07 19 21-23
	Primavera, waltz	93
	Shop Girl, The: Polka (caprice)	96
	Shop Girl, The: Waltz	96
	Sultana, waltz	94
Buck, Dudley	Annie Laurie, trombone quartet	93 94 01
	Creole Love Song, vocal solo	93 94
	Good Night, trombone quartet [unaccompanied?]	93
Budick	Tinkling Bells, The	94
Buechel, Robert	Anheuser-Busch, march	94
	Hypnotizer, The	93
	Tell Me, Adele, ballad (romance), trombone solo or band number	93-95
Buff, Anna R., SEE Stults, R.M.		
Buggerhart	My Country, 'tis of Thee, galop	95
Bunning, Herbert	Robin Hood: Dances	10 24
Burghaus	Dewdrop, intermezzo	01 02
Burleigh, Henry T.	Deep River, vocal solo	16-18
Burleigh, J.	Through the Snow, descriptive	16
Burns, Robert	Comin' Thro the Rye, vocal solo	92 *97 15 16 *22 *25 *26 27 28 *30
	John Anderson, My Jo, vocal solo	16
Burns, Robert & Johann N. Hummel	My Heart Is Fair, vocal solo	96
Busch, Carl	Chant from the Great Plains, A, symphonic episode	22
Butler, Will George	Laddie, Scottish song	18
Butterfield, Avice Louis	Garden of England, waltz	06
Butterfield, James Austin	When You and I Were Young, Maggie, vocal solo	19-21 26
Buys, Peter	Christmas Greeting, paraphrase on Silent Night	23
	Gateway to the South, The, march	22 23
	Governor, The, festive march	23
	Hot Time in the Old Town, humoresque	24
	Traveler, The, waltzes	23
Bye, George Thurmond	League of Nations, The, march	*25
Cadman, Charles Wakefield	American Indian Songs: From the Land of the Sky Blue Water, vocal solo	17 18 20-22 24-27
	Arizona, march	24
	At Dawning, vocal, cornet, or trombone solo	16 20 21 23 25 26 30
	Coq d'Or, Le	26
	Heart of Her, The, vocal solo	16
	I Hear a Thrush at Eve, vocal solo	21
	O Moon upon the Water, vocal solo	18
	Suite for Strings: Old Fiddler, xylophone solo	*28
	Youth and Old Age, caprice	03
Cadsby	Belle of Baltimore, The, march	95
Caesar, Irving	Crooning	21
Campana	Smuggler, The, vocal solo	96
Campana, Fabio	See the Pale Moon (Fair Luna), cornet and trombone duet	04 05 07 08
Campbell-Tipton, Louis	Spirit Flower, A, vocal solo	17 24
Campra, Andre	Charming Butterfly, vocal duet	*09
Canning, Irene Ackerman	Just Been Wond'ring [All Day Long], vocal solo	24
Caracciolo	Unless, vocal solo	18
Cardini	Odis et Amore: Overture	97
Carey	Heil Des im Siegerkranz [national song of the German Empire] [My Country 'Tis of Thee] (God Save the King/Queen)	93 and subsequent years
Carey	Sally in Our Alley, vocal solo	93 *94
Carey, George J.	Air Varied, xylophone solo	20
	Andree, xylophone solo	*26
	Annie Laurie, xylophone solo	21 22
	Caprice Brilliante, xylophone solo	22
	Fantasia Brilliante, xylophone solo	20
	March Wind, xylophone solo/duet	*20 *21 22 23 *24 *25 *26
	Pin Wheel, xylophone solo/duet	*25 *26
	Popular Airs, xylophone solo	21

	Reminiscenses of Suppe, xylophone solo	21
Carey, Henry	My Country 'tis of Thee, patriotic air	most, if not all, years
Carl, Karl	Collection of Tunes in March Form (Potpourri of Martial Tunes)	93
Carlin, Regina M.	Plantation Dance	95
Carlini	Fantasia Originale, euphonium solo	04 05
	Rocked in the Cradle of the Deep, trombone solo	94
Carlini, Oreste	Garden of Roses, A, euphonium solo	05
	Midnight, The (La Mezzanotte), fantasie (At Midnight) (Midnight in Santiago) (The Midnight Hour) (Come Where My Love Lies Dreaming)	97 98 *99 01 02
Carmont, Charles	Village Blacksmith, The, tone picture	98
Carolan	Echoes of Killarney: Overture	98
Carr, Frank Osmond	Black-Eyed Susan: Selections	93
	Gaiety Girl, A: Airs	94
	Marguerite of Monte Carlo, march	94
	Morocco Bound: Selections	94 95
Carrie	Strolling on the Sands	96
Carrington	Great Beyond, The, cornet solo	08-10 *11 12 13 15-17
Carrlin	Concerto for Clarinet	95
Carter	Ceaseless Echoe, The, cornet solo	01
Carter, Charles Davis	Overture	01
Carter, Stanley	She Was Bred in Old Kentucky (She Was Born in Old Kentucky), cornet solo	99
Carter, Thomas Morrill	Boston Commandery March	08
Caryll, Ivan	Baby's Sweetheart	18 20 22
	Cherry Girl, The: Selections	06
	Circus Girl, A (The Circus Girl): Selections	97-99 01 04
	Dandy Dick Whittington: Selections	95 96
	Delphine, cornet solo	27
	Duchess of Dantzig, The: Selections	05 07 09 16 19 21 22 27
	Earl and the Girl, The: Selections	05 07
	Gaiety Girl, The: Selections	94 95
	Gay Parisienne, The: Selections	96
	Girl from Kay's, The: Selections	03-05 24
	Girl from Paris, The: Selections	98 01
	Jack o' Lantern: Selections	18
	Lady Slavy, The: Selections	97
	Little Christopher Columbus: Selections	94 95
	Nelly Neil: Selections	08
	Oh! Oh! Delphine: Selections	08 24
	Pink Lady, The: My Beautiful Lady, cornet solo	*12
	Pink Lady, The: Selections	13 19 24
	Rose of Persia, The: Selections	01
	Shop Girl, The: Selections	95 96
	Spring Chicken, The: Selections	07
Caryll, Ivan & Lionel Monckton	Gaiety Echoes, The (Echoes of the Gaiety Theater): Selections	08
	Girls of [from] Gottenberg, The: Selections	08 09 24
	Messenger Boy, The: Selections	01 02 04
	Orchid, The: Selections	06 *07 08
	Runaway Girl, A: Selections	98 99 *00 01 02 04-06 21-27
	Runaway Girl, A: Soldiers in the Park	07
	Toreador, The: Selections	02
Casey, John Oscar	Flocktonian Polka, cornet solo	99 01 24-26
	Pyramid, polka, cornet solo	*21 22
	Sphinx Temple Polka, The, cornet solo	08
Catlin, Edward Noble	Berton Sec, galop	94
Catozzi, A.	Beelzebub, tuba solo	95
Cavallini, Ernesto	Air Populaire, clarinet solo	93
	Fantasia Originale (Fantasia Brilliante), euphonium solo	93 95
	Fantasie on Lucretia Borgia, clarinet solo	96
	Masked Ball, The, clarinet solo	93
	Souvenir de Naples, euphonium solo	93
Cavanass, J.M., SEE Lieurance, Thurlow		

Cavollini, Ernesto	Hercules, tuba solo	93
Cellier, Alfred	Danse Pompeuse	94 22 24 27
	Doris: Selections	*92 93 96 25 26
	Dorothy: Selections	95 96 25 26
	Little Sailors, waltz	93
	Mountebanks, The: Selections	92-94
	Queen of My Heart, ballad, vocal solo	96
	Scotch Wedding, A	94
	Sultan of Mocha, The: Selections	93
Cesar, B. Parez	Royal March [of Spain]	93
Chabrier, Emanuel	Espana, rhapsody	28 29 *30
	Gwendoline: Overture	95
	Joyeuse Marche	06
	Suite of Waltzes	23
Chadwick, George Whitefield	Ballads: Maiden and the Butterfly, The, vocal solo	14
	Cricket and the Bumble-Bee, The, humoresque	26
	Danza, The, vocal solo	96
	Fighting Men, The, march	18
	Rip Van Winkle: Overture	*98 02
	Symphonic Sketches: A Vagrom Ballad	10
	Symphonic Sketches: Canzonetta	10 *11 *15
	Symphonic Sketches: Jubilee (My Jubilee), rhapsody	*04 *05 06 *08 09 10 14 16 18 23
	Tabasco: Selections	94 95 16
	Tam O' Shanter, symphonic ballade	*26 27
Chambers	America: Overture	98
Chambers, William Paris	Darling Nelly Gray (Nelly Gray), cornet solo	*24 *26 28
	Leila, Mexican serenade	96
	Reminiscences of the Plantation (Reminiscences of Dixie) (Songs and Dances of the Plantation) (Down South), fantasie	98 99 01 04 05 08
	Songs and Dances of the North and South	98
	Southern Airs, cornet solo	20
Chamin	Sweet September, vocal solo	93
Chaminade, Cecile	Ballads, suite, vocal solos: Air de Ballet; Serenade: Callrhoe; Meditation; Valse des Cymbals	93 94 10 11 19 24
	Callirhoe: Scarf Dance (Pas des Escharges)	15 16 18 19 27 30
	Charmer, The (The Flatterer), caprice	04
	Concerto Brilliante for Flute (Concertina)	22 23 25 *26
	Fauns, The (Les Sylvains)	09
	Pierrette, air de ballet	*05
	Reminiscences of Chaminade	13 15-18 21-23 25 26 28
	Scaramouche, caprice (pantomime)	*06
	Summer (L'Ete), vocal solo	*96 *97
Chapi, Ruperto	Alhambra, The, fantasia (suite)	20 21
	Bunch of Roses, A, Spanish march	08 18 21 24 27 *30
	Collection of German Folk Songs, A	96
	Corte de Granada, La (The Courts of Granada): Fantasia (suite)	16 17 *18 *19 *20 21 22 24 30
	Corte de Granada, La (The Courts of Granada): March to the Tournament	16
	Corte de Granada, La (The Courts of Granada): Moorish Serenade	*18
	Corte de Granada, La (The Courts of Granada): Serenade	*95 96 14
Chapius, Marcel	Ke-sa-ko, Japo-niaiserie	12 15
Chaplin, Charlie	Peace Patrol, The	15 16
Chardi	Russian Fantasia, flute solo	95
Charig	Americana: Why Do Ya Roll Those Eyes	*26
Charpentier, Gustave	Impressions of Italy: Napoli (Beautiful Naples)	01 02 23
	Louise: Aria [unnamed], vocal solo[s]	08 14 16 *18 19 *20 *21 22 23 25-27
	Louise: Depuis Le Jour Me Suis Donnee, vocal solo	15 16 18-22 *24 *25 *26 28 29
	Louise: Selections	05
Chase, R.P.	Maine Capital March, The	97

Chassaigne, F.	Falka: Gipsy Chorus and Finale	94
	Falka: Selections	93-96
	Nadgy: Selections	94 96
Chattaway, J.W.	Sleeping Beauty and the Beast, grand fantasie	02
Chavallier, Albert	Coster Songs of Chavallier	96 25 26
	Coster Songs of Chevallier: Alice	94
	Coster Songs of Chevallier: The Nippers Lullaby	94
	Coster Songs of Chevallier: Who'll Buy	94
	London Costermonger's Song	95
	Chevallier's Songs of the London Costers (Songs of the London Costermonger)	92 93 95
Chiafferelli, Alberte	Lisztiana March	19
	Triumphal March	24
Chiardi	Carneval Russe (Air Russe), flute solo	94 96
	Rondo de Capricio, flute solo	94
Chick	De Auguste Durand, chaconne	02
Chopin, Frederic Francois	Grand Valse Brilliante, cornet solo	93 94
	Mazurka No. 1	95 96 *00 *04
	Mazurka, Valse, Marche Funebre, mosaic	08
	Minute Waltz, flute solo	26
	Nocturne in D-flat, Op. 27, No. 2 violin solo	*07 *08 14
	Nocturne in E Flat, violin solo	19
	Nocturne in E-flat and Minute Waltz (Nocturne and Waltz), xylophone solo	*23 *24 25 27
	Nocturne, cornet, violin, or clarinet solo	93 98 *00 06 13 15
	Polanaise in A-flat	94 95 *00
	Polonaise in B-flat	09
	Polonaise Militaire (Military Polonaise)	93 96 *06 16
	Polonaise No. 6, Op. 53	10 22
	Reminiscences of Chopin	*00 01 02 04-10 *11 12-14 15 17-26
	Sonata No. 2, Op. 32: Funeral March	93 94 *95 02 *04 *19 *20
	Three Chopin Preludes	22
	Three Mazourkas (Trois Mazurkas)	98 04 24
	Valse in D, xylophone solo	23
	Valse No. 14 in E Minor	*04
	Valse, Op. 61	94
	Valse, Op. 64	94 95 *00
	Waltz, vocal solo	16
Christern, Wilhelm	Indian Reveille (Indischer Reveille) (An Eastern Indian Reveille), idyll	*96 *97 98 99 04 08
	Scotch Wedding (A Scotch Wedding Procession)	94 12 17
Cilca, Francesco	Adrienne Lecouvreur, Intermezzo	08 09 10
Clare	Harvest Anthem	93
Clarenden	If I Had the World to Give, cornet solo	*11
Clarhouse	Nom de Plume, cornet duet	*11
Clark	Hot Time in the Old Town, A (There'll Be a Hot Time in the Old Town Tonight)	98 99 *00
Clark, Kenneth	Huskin' Bee, The, barn dance	08
Clark, Sarah Wood	Debutante, The, caprice	02
Clark, Tom	Moszkowskiana, selection of works by Moszkowski	18 21 23 25 26
Clarke	Chicago Journal, The, march	96
Clarke, Herbert Lincoln	Air Brilliante (Fantasie Brilliante) (Air Varie), cornet solo	93 01 05 07 13 14 17
	Birth of Dawn, The, cornet solo	*17
	Bride of the Waves (Queen of the Sea) (Polka Caprice) (Polka Brilliante), cornet solo	*00 *01 04 05 *06 *07 *08 09 10 *11 12-17 20 28 31
	Canadian Patrol, The	*19 25 27
	Carnival of Venice, cornet solo	*19 25 26
	Cousins, cornet and trombone duet	*06 08
	Debutante, The (Caprice Brilliante), cornet solo	*08 09 *10 *11 *12 *13 14 *15 16 17 26 27 *28

	For Love of You! (My Love for You) (I Love Thee) (I Love But You), cornet	01 04 05 09 *11 13 15
	From the Shores of the Mighty Pacific (Rondo Caprice) (Rondo Capriccioso), cornet solo	01 04 05 09 *10 *11 12 *13 *14 *15 16-18 20 22
	Neptune's Court (Court of Neptune), cornet solo	*14 *15 16-18 26 29
	Neroir, cornet solo	27
	Original Fantasie, cornet solo	15
	Passing the Cotton Fields, characteristic	17-19 21-23
	Past Glad Hours, reverie	07
	Plantation Songs and Dances (Reminiscences of Stephen Foster) (Plantation Echoes) (Songs and Dances of Our Country) (Songs and Dances of America) (Songs and Dances of the South) (A Bit of Blue and a Bit of the Gray) (Fantasie on American Melodies), medley [based on Stephen Foster melodies]	*01 *02 04-09 *11 12-21 23-25 27
	Princess May, cornet solo	06
	Reminiscences of America (Gems from America)	06 10
	Romanique (Romantique), cornet solo	13-17
	Scherzo, cornet solo	13 16 17
	Showers of Gold (Golden Showers), cornet solo	*09 10 *11 12-15 *16 17
	Side Partners, cornet duet	16 17 19
	Sounds from the Hudson (Valse Brilliante) (Valse Caprice), cornet or saxophone solo	*04 05 *07 *08 09 10 *11 12-18 20 *25 *26 27
	Southern Cross, cornet solo	*12 *13 14 15 17 21 22 24-26 *30
	Stars in a Velvety Sky, cornet solo	*12 14-17 22 25
	Tiberius Overture	93
	Twilight Dreams, cornet solo	14 16 17 19 22
	Veta Caprice, La, cornet solo	*05 *06 08-10 *11 12-17 27
Clarke, Millicent R.	Rochester Herald March	96 97
Clarke, Thomas	Danse du Ventre, polka-march	23 24
Clauder	Roma, dance characteristic	02
	Soldatenlieder	01
Clauder, Joseph	American Caprice, mazurka	98
	Lincoln Imp March, The	04
Clay	Songs of Araby (I'll Sing Thee Songs of Araby), vocal solo	96
Clay, Frederick	Princess Toto: Motives	93 96
Claypoole, Edward	Ragging the Scale, fox trot	16 26 *28
Clement	Tunes in March Form	93
Clement, Joseph	Castagnette, La	05
	Water Lily, The, cornet solo	93 24
Clendon, Hugh	Hongrois, caprice	96
Clerice, Justin/Daniel Godfrey	Pilou-Pilou, Le, dance	08 14
Clifton, William	We Won't Go Home Until Morning	93
Clitheroe, Fred W.	Fireflies of 1922: Ship o' Dreams, vocal solo	23
Clough-Leighton, Henry	Tofana: Song of the Sword	16
Clutsam	Coon, Coon, Under the Moon, fantasia	10
Coates	Songs of Our Land	24
Coates, Eric	Summer Days, Suite: Frivolette, caprice	20 21
Coates, Thomas	Plantation Echoes (Sounds from the Cotton Fields)	93 95
	Wood Nymphs, valsette (entr' acte)	*19 *20 22
Cobb, George L.	Russian Rag, xylophone solo	26
Cobb, Gerard	Barrack-Room Ballads of Rudyard Kipling	94 95
	Danny Deever	94
	On the Road to Moscow (Over the Road to Moscow), ballad	93 94
	They Are Hanging Danny Deever, ballad	94
Cobb, Walter	Yip-i-Addy-i-Ay	*09
Codivilla, Filippo	Suite di Danze	23
Cogley, Ed. & Bock, W.E.	Glory, song	04
Cohan, George Michael	Harrigan	*08 09
	Over There, song	17
	Yankee Prince, The: Selections	08

Cole, Carlota	Scotch Patrol, The	93-95
Coleridge-Taylor, Samuel	African Dance, violin solo	14
	Life and Death, vocal solo	*15
	Onaway! Awake, Beloved, vocal solo	18
	Saint Agnes' Eve, suite	25 26
Combs, Gilbert Raynolds	Calinerie	10
	Dance of the Houri	10
	Dragon Flies, polka caprice (descriptive)	10
	Manon, caprice	10
	Soubrette, The, caprice	10
Comfort, Anita	Eugenie, two-step	98
	Imogene, ballad	98
Concone	Judith, vocal solo	94
Confrey, Edward E.	Kitten on the Keys, xylophone solo	*24 26 27
Conradi, August	Berlin When It Laughs and Weeps (Berlin in Smiles and Tears) (Berlin in Joy and Sorrow) (Berlin Wie Es Weint und Lacht): Overture	95 96 02 04 06 15 23 24 27 31
	Melody Congress (Melodien Congresss) (A Congress of Overtures) (Musical Panorama), potpourri	05 09 15 23 26
	Musical Tour Through Europe, A, SEE Melody Congress, A (Conradi)	93 99
	Offenbachiana (Reminiscences of Offenbach)	93-96 01 02 19 20 22 24
	Scotch Patrol, The	95
Conrath, Louis	Air de Ballet	94
	America, intermezzo	95
Conterno, Giovanni Emanuele	Bacarolle Characteristique	94
	Clock, The, idyll	10
	Terrible, The: Overture	93
Converse, Charles	What a Friend We Have in Jesus, hymn	93
Cook, Raymond	American Progress, march	02
	Golden Memories, waltz	02
Cook, Will Marion	Exhortation, sacred song, vocal solo (A Negro sermon)	15
Cooke, James Francis	Brooklyn High School, march	94
	In My Garden, vocal solo	26
	Keltic Dance	25
	Laughing Roses, vocal solo	21 22
	Ol' Car'lina, vocal solo	20-24 26
	Old Portrait, An (A Portrait), romance	25 26
	Only to Live in Your Heart, vocal solo	19
	Ribbon Dance	25 28
	Rose of Killarney, vocal solo	23
	Sea Gardens, idyll	25 28
	Send Me a Rose from Homeland, vocal solo	19
Cooke, James Francis & Thurlow Lieurance Weed	Creole Legends No. 1: The Angelus, The, vocal solo	24
Coombs	Just One, intermezzo	10
Coote, Charles, Jr.	Before the Ball: Valse	93
	Dancing Girl, The, waltz	95
	Lights of London, The, quadrille	93 94
	Queen's Own, the, waltz	13 22 25 26
	Rob Roy March	95
	Sweethearts, waltz	23-26
Coquelet, O.	Star of Glory (Glorieuse Etoile): Overture	97-99
Corbin	Santiago, waltz	21-26
Corbin, A.F.	Mimi, intermezzo	04
Corey	Mardi Gras, march	97
Corey, W.A.	Military Maid, The, march and two-step	97-99 01
Cornelius, Peter	Barber of Baghdad, The (Der Barbier von Baghdad): Overture	10 26
Corri, W.	Baby's Sweetheart, serenade	06 07 08 *11
Cory, Edward L.	Infanta Waltzes, The	93
Costa, Michael	Reminiscences of Costa (Extracts from the Oratorios and Cantatas of Sir Michael Costa)	94
Costa, Pasquale Mario	Frangesa, A, march	01

	History of a Pierrot (Histoire d'un Pierrot): Ballet Suite	*01 02 14 18
Cottenet, R.	Chanson-Meditation, vocal solo	13 14
Coverley, Robert	Arabian March	94
	Passing Regiment, The, patrol	97 98 01 02
Cowen, Frederick Hyman	In Fairy Land: Witches Dance	01 02
	Southern Jollification	02
	Ask Nothing More of Me, Sweet, vocal solo	96
	Ballad	94
	Border Ballad, vocal solo	17
	English Dance Suite (Four English Dances in the Olden Style) (Rustic Dances)	05
	In Fairy Land: Ballet Suite	02
	Last Dream, The, waltz	23 24
	Polka Song	94
	Song and a Rose, A, vocal solo	97
	Swallows, vocal solo	*00 01 08 18
	Voice of the Father, The, cornet solo or band number	05
Cowles, Eugene	Beneath the Pines, vocal solo	97 18
	Celeste, vocal solo	06
	Forgotten, vocal solo	06 18
Cox, John S.	Bird, The (Sweet Birdie) (Birdie's Favorite) (Skylark), piccolo solo	08-10 12 20-24 26
	Scotia, piccolo solo	93
Craxton, Harold	Mavis, vocal solo	18
Cremieux, Octave	Cherries, two-step	08
	Valse d'Amour, La (Quand l'Amour Meurt), vocal solo	*13
Crisman	Emblem of the Free, The	98
	Sailing Over the Sea	98
Croft, William	O God Our Help in Ages Past, hymn	29
Crome	Fairy Voices, waltz	20 23 24
Crooke, John	'Arry and 'Arriet, caprice	93
	Lady Slavey, The: Selections	95 98
Crosby, Warner	Other Day, The, vocal solo	94
Crouch, F. Nicholls	Kathleen Mavourneen, song, vocal or cornet solo	94 95 98 10 15
Crowe	Bold Draggoons, The, waltz	93
Crowe, Alfred Gwyllym	Fairie [Fairy] Voices, waltz	93 94 22 26
	Little Sailors, waltz	93 94
Crowning	There Is a Land Mine Eye Hath Seen, vocal solo	95
Cui, Cesar	Andante Cantabile, violin or cello solo	*05
	Berceuse, violin solo	02
	Kaleidoscope: Orientale, violin solo	12
Cunard, F.W.	Flora Waltz, cornet solo	15 20 22 24 25-27
Currier	Congo, Negro dance	93
Curti	Lamentation, dramatic sketch	01 02
Curti, Carlos	Maesmawr, waltz	06
	Oscar (On Oscar), march	10
	Rosita, waltz	10
Custance, Arthur F.M.	Taps, vocal solo	20
Cyrwarner	Sweet Marie	97 99
Czibulka, Alphons	Ball Scenes (Scenes du Bal) (Ballscenen) (A Dream After the Ball) (Love's Dream After the Ball) (Ball Scenes in Vienna)	*92 93-95 *96 *97 *99 *00 01 04 07 10 22-24
	Fly, The (Der Bajazzo), minuet	*94 *95 96
	Impromptu Dramatique	93
	My Old Kentucky Home, fantasie on Stephen Foster's song	93 94 *95 96 *97 98
	Royale, gavotte	94
	To You (An Dich) (A Toi), waltz serenade	98 15
	Viennoise, waltz	94
	Woodland Whisperings, idyll	13 *15 19
D'Albert, Charles Louis Napoleon	Sweethearts, waltz	22 23 25 26
D'Albert, Eugene Francis	Improvisatore, Der: Overture	09 21 24
	Marta of the Lowlands: Fantasia	18 19 24-27
	Tiefland: Fantasie (Fantasie from Tiefland)	09 10 14 15 17
D'Alquen	In Cellar Cool, baritone solo	01

d'Ambrosio	Canzonetta, violin solo	13
	Madrigal	05
D'Azevedo, Amelie Augusta	Amerique, marche tromphale	01
d'Ernesti, Titus	Two Great Republics, The, march	93
d'Hardelot, Guy	Because, vocal solo	18
	I Know a Lovely Garden, vocal solo	13
	Mignon, vocal solo	96
	Reminiscences of d'Harlelot	24
	Say Yes!, vocal solo	96
	Selection on Guy d'Hardelot's Popular Songs	22
D'Indy, Vincent	Fervaal: Prelude to Act I	10
	Wallenstein's Camp (Le Camp de Wallenstein), descriptive	09
D'Orso, F.	Habanera, Brazilian dance	94
Dalbey, Clarence W.	Blue and Grey Patrol, The (The Blending of the Blue and Grey) (War Time Songs)	01 07
	Cuban War, The, descriptive fantasie	98 15
	My Old Kentucky Home, fantasie on Stephen Foster's song	94-96 98 *00 01 02 04 19 24
	Something Funny, humoresque	98
	Songs and Dances of America	*00
	Town Talk, novelette	04
	Twenty Minutes on Midway Plaisance, comic descriptive fantasie	95
	Way Down in Georgia, darkie dance	96
	We Won't Go Home Until Morning, fantasie	98
Dallimore, A. Holmes	Love Light, serpentine dance	96
Damare, Eugene	Air Varie, piccolo solo	17 18
	Badinage, piccolo solo	25
	Birds in the Woods, piccolo solo	*11
	Birds of Passage, piccolo solo	24
	Caprice de Concert, piccolo solo	93 18
	Carnival of Venice, piccolo solo	93
	Cleopatra, cornet solo	23 *24 *25 *26 27
	Colihu, piccolo solo	93
	Famous Ride of Tam O'Shanter, The, characteristic	95 96 20 22 *23
	Flirtation, piccolo duet	98
	Humming Bird, The, piccolo solo	93
	L'Elegante Polka, cornet solo	93
	Nightingale and the Thrush, The, piccolo duet	10
	Nightingales of the Opera	15
	Polka Caprice, piccolo solo	18
	Skylark, The, piccolo solo	23 24
	Swiss Air Varie, piccolo solo	18
	Thrush, The, piccolo solo	05 23
	Tourterelle, La, piccolo solo	21-23
	Turtle Dove, The (The Dove), piccolo solo	93 94 96-98 *00 01 02 04 05 08 10 *11 14 20 22 *24
	Valse Brilliante, cornet solo	96
	Vidette, cornet solo	94
Damm, August	Polka Caprice, piccolo solo	01 28
	Scherzo, piccolo solo	18
	Through the Air, piccolo solo	93 *00 01 02 04 *05 20 21 22 24 26
Damrosch, Walter Johannes	Danny Deever, vocal solo	17
Dancla, Charles	Romance and Bolero for Flute, flute solo	94
Daniderff, Leo	Love's Melody, waltz (berceuse tendre)	14
Daniels, Charles N.	Margery, march	98
Daniels, Mabel N.	Ballet Suite: Dance of Invitation	16
Daniels, Pollak	Philippine Welser: Divertissement, Act I	97
Danks, Hart Pease & Eben E. Rexford	Silver Threads Among the Gold, vocal or cornet solo	*11 *12 24 26
Dargomyzhsky, Alexander Sergeyevitch	Cosatschogue, fantasie on the Cossack dance (Cassol Fantasia) (Cossack Dance)	*21 22 27

Dart, Wilton	Victory March	19
Dauer, J.A.C.	Spring	30
David, Felicien	Pearl of Brazil: Thou Brilliant Bird (Thou Charming Bird) (Charmant Oiseau), vocal solo	*92 *94 95 *00 01 *02 *03 *04 05-08 15 17 18 *19 *20 21 24 25
David, N.	Arabian Nights, fox trot	19
Davidoff, Karl	Romance, cello solo	98
Davis	Mona, novelette	09
Davis, Akst	Dearest, fox trot	23
Davis-Conrad	Margie, xylophone solo	21
Dawes, Charles Gates	Melody (Melody in A Major), song	*24
de Beriot, Charles-Auguste	Concerto No. 7, violin solo	23
	Concerto, violin solo	08 09
	Fifth Concerto, cornet solo	98 22 23 25 26
	Romance, violin solo	*97
	Scene de Ballet, Op. 100, fantasie	15-17
	Seventh Air, cornet solo	27
	Sixth Air Varie (Air Varied), cornet solo	19 25
	Tremelo, La, violin solo	15
de Boisdeffre, Rene	At the Brook (Au Bord D'un Ruisseau), violin solo	*05
de Bozi, Harold	Nights in the Woods (Les Noites de Bois), descriptive fox trot	*23
De Freyne, Rollo	Where the Lazy Mississippi Flows (Lazy Mississippi), waltz	21
De Grau, Durand	Merry-Go-Round, The (Il Coricolo), galop	98
De Joncieres, Victorin	Serenade Hongroise	23
De Kontski, Anton	Awakening of the Lion, caprice	93-96 06 07 15 16 22 23
de Lajarte, Theodore-Edouard	Fete de Trianon, Une: Suite	01
De Lara, Isidore	Garden of Sleep, The, song	93
	Mine To-Day, vocal solo	96
De Loetz, Paul	On the Road to Moscow, caprice	94
	Over the Snow to Moscow, intermezzo	93
de Longpre, Paul	Souvenir of Los Angeles, waltz	01
De Luca, Joseph Orlando	American Gentlemen, The, march	22
	Beautiful Colorado, euphonium or saxophone solo	*21 22-24 26 *27 28 *29 30
	Camden Shriner's Club, march	24
	Concerto Brilliante (Concerto in B Flat), euphonium solo	*24 25
	Intermezzo, gavotte	26 27
	Symphonic March, No. 10	24
	Symphonic Poem No. 1	24 26
	The New President, march	24 26
	Valse Caprice, euphonium solo	25
	White and Red Rose March, The	28
De Smetsky, Jean	March of the Spanish Soldiery	28
De Ville, Warren	Famous Ride of Tam O'Shanter, The, characteristic	09
de Zulueta, Pedro	Claudine, waltz	24
	Phryne Waltz (intermezzo)	24
	Rendezvous Valse	13 23 24
	Starlight, intermezzo	14 24
Deakin, Earl H.	O.K. Pi (Omicron-Kappa-Pi), march and two-step	01
Deane	Royal Purple, The, march	96
Debussy, Claude Achille	Aria, vocal solo	20
	Cathedrale Engloutie, La, (The Sunken Cathedral), prelude	24
	Children's Corner, The (Le Coin des Enfants), suite	24 27
	L'en Bateau, petite suite	12
	L'Enfant Prodiue (Enfant Prodigue): Recit et Air de Lia, vocal solo	19 20
	Little Shepherd, The (Idyll), idyl, flute solo	22 26
	Marche Ecossaise sur un Theme Populaire	24
DeFuentes, Eduardo Sanchez	Tu Habanera (A Song of Havana), march	22
DeKoven, Reginald	Ask What Thou Wilt, vocal solo	94
	Down on the Bayou	07
	Highwayman, The: Selections	98 17

343

	Ma Viosine, Indian love song	95
	National Guard, march	97
	Robin Hood: Anvil Song, vocal solo	93 94 97
	Robin Hood: Finale of Act 1	*94 95 96 98
	Robin Hood: Forest Song, vocal solo	93
	Robin Hood: O, Promise Me	*94
	Robin Hood: Selections	*92 93-98 12-14 19 20 24 26 27 29
	Robin Hood: Three Songs	94
	Robin Hood: Tinker's Chorus	92 93 *94
	Roses Remind Me of You (The Rose Song), vocal solo	94
	Souvenirs of Robin Hood, vocal duet	93
	Two Loves, vocal solo	94
Del Riego, Teresa	Green Hills of Ireland	29
	Happy Song, vocal solo	08
	O Dry Those Tears, vocal, cornet, or trombone solo	09 13-15 19-23 *24 25 26
DeL'Isle, C.J. Rouget	Marseillaise, La	*00 *07
Delibes, Clement Philibert Leo	Coppelia: Ballet Suite	93 94 96 *07 08-10 *11 12 14-21 22 24-28 30 31
	Coppelia: Czardas	01 02 04-06 08 09
	Coppelia: Magyar Dance	*01
	Coppelia: Valse de la Poupee (Walzer der Puppe) (Doll Dance) (The Dolls) (Doll Waltz)	01 02
	Corsaire, Le: Pas de Fleurs, waltz	05
	Lakme: Aria [unnamed], vocal or cornet solo[s]	21 23
	Lakme: Indian Bell Song (Bell Song) (The Indian Girl), vocal or cornet solo	95 *98 *99 *02 *03 *05 10 17 21 22 24 *25 26
	Lakme: Selections	93 94 21 25 26
	Maids of Cadiz, The (Filles de Cadiz): Aria [unnamed], vocal solo[s]	96 02 30
	Maids of Cadiz, The (Filles de Cadiz): Bolero, vocal solo	93 94 *97 *24 26 27
	Masquerade, suite	31
	Naila: Intermezzo (valse lento)	93 94 15 21 26
	Regrets, vocal solo	*94
	Source, La: Ballet Suite	07 10 *11 21 22 24
	Sylvia, waltz	93
	Sylvia: Ballet Suite	96 01 02 04-07 *11 13 15-21 23 24 26 27 *29
	Sylvia: Pizzicato	*97
	Sylvia: untitled harp solo	93
	Sylvia: Valse Lente	93 94
Delibes, SEE ALSO Mincus, Ludwig		
Delius, Frederick	Brigg Fair, English rhapsody	28
	Dance Rhapsody, A	25 26
Dell' Acqua, Eva	Provencial Song (Chanson Provencal)	23 24
	Villanelle (With the Swallow), vocal or clarinet solo	*23 *24 *25 26-28
	Dolce Amour, vocal solo	*01
	Oft Have I Seen the Swift Swallow, vocal solo	25
	Provencial Song (Chanson Provencal), vocal solo	01 09 14-17 19 20 *21 22
	Villanelle, vocal solo/duet for clarinet & saxophone	93 95 *00 02 12 13 15 *19 *20 21 *22 *25
Dellinger, Rudolf	Chansonnette, Die: Reservisten (The Reserves), march	95
	Sweet Land of Providence	94
Dello Joio, C.	Belle of Mexico, The, Mexican waltz	23
Demerssemann, Jules	Air Varie, saxophone solo	94
	Carnival, The (Le Carnival) (Carnival of Venice), saxophone solo	94-96 *97 98 04
	Chant Relegieus, saxophone solo	93
	Fantasia de Concert, flute solo	18
	Fantasie on Chopin Melodie, flute solo	*15 16

	Grand Concerto, clarinet solo	94
	Souvenir de Spa, cello solo	93 *97
	Spanish Festival, A (Une Fete a Aranjuez) (Espagnole), Spanish fantasie	96 24 *26
	Tremolo, Le, flute solo	17-19
Densmore	Longing for You (For Love of You), vocal solo	21 27
Densmore, John H.	Veritas March	08
Denza, Luigi	Funiculi Funicula, cornet solo	19
	If Thou Didst Love Me, vocal solo	02
	May Morning, A, vocal solo	*98
Deppen, Jessie Louise	Eleanor, song	15 22
Deppen, Jessie Louise & Archie Bell	Japanese Sunset, A	21 25 28
Depret, M.	April Smiles (Soirire d'Avril), waltz	01
Desmarquoy, J.	Petite Marquise, La, gavotte	93
Desormes, Louis Cesar	Awake, Fairest Maid (Awake, Fair Maid), song	*96
	Ma Mie Rosette, rondo	94 24
	Scenes at a Spanish Fandango	92-95
	Serenade of [de] Mandolins	10
	Souvenir de Granada, piccolo solo	93
	Spanish Divertissement (Divertissement Espagnol)	92 93 96 24 25
Dessane, L.A.	Mercedes: Overture	21 22
Dessauer, Joseph	Bolero, vocal solo	93
	Ouvrez, vocal solo	94
	To Sevilla, vocal solo	94
DeSylva, B.G. & Ballard MacDonald	Somebody Loves Me, saxophone ensemble	*24
Dett, Robert Nathaniel	In the Bottoms: Juba Dance	*26 27
DeWitt	Reels and Jigs	27
DeWitt, Louis O.	Just One Night, medley overture (The Metropolis of Night)	95
DeWolkoff, N.	Cosatschok, Russian dance (Dance of the Cossacks)	96
Deyerberg	From a Canadian Forest (In a Canadian Forest), suite	21
Di Capua, Eduardo	Beneath Thy Window (O Sole Mio), Neapolitan song, cornet solo or band number	13 *17 *19 *20 22 23 26
Diaz, E.	Mariposa, La: Entr'Acte	01 02 08 14 15 18 22
Dillon, Carl & Calder Bramwell	O'er the Foaming Billows, song	27
Dix, Edwin Asa	Musical Critic's Dream of Annie Rooney, The, monologue (fantasie)	*94 95 *05 16
Dix, J. Arlie	Trumpeter, The, descriptive, vocal solo	17 18
Doctor, Sam	After the Ball, song	93
Dodworth, Harvey	Day in Camp, A (Episode Militaire), passing review	93 94
Dolan, John	Private Script, cornet solo	22
Don Bruno	Crème de la Crème	15
Donaldson, Walter	Thinking of You, saxophone ensemble	27
Donizetti, Gaetano	Adelia: Selections	98 02 24
	Belisario: Overture	94-96 24
	Burgomaster of Zaandam, The (The Burgomastro di Saardan): Scene	93 96
	Daughter of the Regiment: Aria [unnamed], vocal solo[s]	06
	Daughter of the Regiment: Overture	93-95
	Favorita, La: Duet, vocal duet	93
	Favorita, La: Selections	94 96
	Favorita, La: Spirito Gentil, vocal solo	15
	Favorita, La: Una Vergine Favorita, vocal solo	16
	Favorita, La: untitled saxophone or clarinet solo	19 28
	Linda di Chamounix: O Luce di Quest Anima, vocal solo	93 97 *98
	Linda di Chamounix: Selections	96
	Lucia di Lammermoor: Aria [unnamed], vocal solo[s]	*92 93 95 *97 99 01 02 16 19
	Lucia di Lammermoor: Grand Scene	93 *98
	Lucia di Lammermoor: Mad Scene, vocal solo	*92 93 03-05 07 08 15 *16 19
	Lucia di Lammermoor: Regnava nel Silenzio	94 99
	Lucia di Lammermoor: Selections	94-96 06-09 13 14 17 21 24

	Lucia di Lammermoor: Sextet [brass] (Vengeance) (What From Vengeance Yet Restrains Me?)	*93 *94 *95 96 *97 *98 *00 *01 04 *05 *06 *07 *08 *09 10 *11 12 *13 *16 17 *18 *20 22 24 26 *28
	Lucrezia Borgia: Aria [unnamed], vocal solo[s]	20 21 24 26 27
	Lucrezia Borgia: Brindisi, vocal solo	93
	Lucrezia Borgia: Cavatina, vocal solo	93
	Lucrezia Borgia: Selections	94
	Martiri, I: Overture	93
	Martyrs, The: Overture	93 94
	O Mio Fernando, vocal solo	25
	Parisina (Pariseana): Chorus	95
	Polluto, Il: Duet, clarinet & flute duet	92
	Reminiscences of Donizetti	93 95 *00 09 10 12 17 18 20 22-24
	Romance, vocal solo	96
	Salute to France (Dear France, I Adore Thee), vocal solo	*18
	Somnambula: Aria [unnamed], vocal solo[s]	93
	Ye Valleys and Mountains	*07
Doob	Lady Alice, waltz	01
Doppler, Albert Franz	Fantasie Hongraise, flute solo	93
	Hungarian Rhythm, flute duet	24
	Hungarian Scene Teka, flugelhorn solo	02
	Ilka, Hungarian overture	21 22
	L'Oiseau des Bois (Birds of the Forest), flute solo	20 21
	Mazurka de Concert (Concert Mazurka), flute solo	18
	Rondo Caprice, flute solo	18
	Two Hussars, The, Hungarian overture	21-24 27
Douglas, Shipley	Britannia (Songs of the Sea), fantasia	27
	Duncan Grey, paraphrase (humoresque)	15 16 18 19 21 24
	Tearin' o' the Green, The, paraphrase and variations (humorous paraphrase)	*06 07 08 24
	Two Gendarmes, The (The Two Guardsmen), humoresque on Offenbach	16 19 22
Downing, David L.	Railroad Galop	01
	Ride on the Limited Mail, A (On the Limited) (A Trip on the Limited Express), descriptive	93 94 96 98
Drdla, Franz	Souvenir, violin, saxophone, or xylophone solo	*19 *20 *21 *22 25 *26
Drescher, Carl Wilhelm	Ritirata Italiana, La (The Italian Tattoo), allegro marziale (march) (patrol)	12
Dresser, Paul	On the Banks of the Wabash Far Away, trombone solo	*98 *99
Dreyschoch (Dreischock), Alexander	Campanella, La (The Bells), idyll	*97 *98 01
Drigo, Riccardo	Millions d'Arlequin, Les: Reconcilliation, polka de caractere (serenade) (intermezzo)	*14 *15 16-19 21-24
	Valse Bluette, violin solo	21
Droop, E.H.	Pride of the Nation, The, march	96
Drumheller, Charles	Banjo Twang (Dance Negro)	93
	Trilby, grand valse brilliant	95
Drysdale, Learmont	Tam O'Shanter: Overture	22 23
Dubois, Theodore	Farandole, La: Ballet Music (Ballet Suite)	94 96 16 17
Dudley	Lakewood, march	94
Dukas, Paul	Sorcerer's Apprentice (Apprenti l'Sorcier), symphonic poem)	19
	Sorcerer's Apprentice (Apprenti l'Sorcier): Scherzo	*11 12-18 20-23 *24 25 26 28
Dunewaller	At the Circus, galop (rondo)	*94 98
Dunhill, Thomas Frederick	Pixies, The, fairy suite	13 14 24
Dunkler	Dance Hollandaise, cello solo	02
Dunkler, Francois, Sr.	Fantasia on Swedish Melodies	94
Dupont, Paul	Rosita, La	22
Durand	Valse di Concert (Valse Militant) (Valse Concerto), xylophone solo	18 19 21-25
Durand, Nella Wells	Tampa March	24
Dusenbery, Lillian	Signal Corps March, The	10
Duss, John S.	America Up to Date, march	97
	Fire Laddie, The, galop	98

	Jordan Rifles, cakewalk	99
	Life's Voyage, intermezzo	01
	Scarlet Letter, The, march	97
	untitled march	01
Duvall	Drummond Guards, The, march	95
Dvorak, Antonin	Bohemian Woods: In the Spinning Rooms	*12 13
	Humoresque, violin solo, xylophone solo, or band number	*07 *08 *12 15 19 20 *21 *22 *23 *24 28
	Hungarian Gypsy Song, vocal solo	96
	Husitaska, dramatic overture	95 19
	Legend	02
	Ozitska: Overture	96
	Slavonic Dance No. 1	94 *95 96 97 04
	Slavonic Dance No. 2	*00 01
	Slavonic Dance No. 5	01
	Slavonic Dances	04 06 14 15 24 31
	Symphony No. 5 ("New World"), Op. 95: Adagio and Scherzo	95
	Symphony No. 5 ("New World"), Op. 95: Largo	95 *03 *05 10 *11 *12 14 15 *17 *18 19 20 22 23 *25 *26
Dykes, J.B.	Lead Kindly Light, hymn	06 07 21
Eaton, Elsie & Katherine Lee Bates	America the Beautiful, vocal solo	29
Eckersburg, H.	Battle of Waterloo, potpourri	17
Eckert, Karl Anton Florian	Swiss Echo Song (Echo Song), vocal solo	95 16
Eckhardt	Hungarian Fantasie (Fantasie Hungarian), cornet solo	02
Edwards	I Don't Know Why I Love You, But I Do-oo-oo (I Love You, But I Can't Tell Why), trombone solo	*01
Edwards, Julian	Brian Boru: Selections	97 98 24 27
	Dolly Varden: Selections	02 04
	Gay Musician, The: Selections	08 09
	Jolly Musketeers, The: Selections	*00 01
	King Rene's Daughter: Prelude	95 96
	Love's Lottery March (Scenes)	06
	Madeline: Selections	96
	My Own United States, march	09
	Princess Chic: Selections	01
	Wedding Day, The: Selections	97 98 02 05 19
Edwards, Robert	On Dress Parade, march	93
Egghard, J.	Pearl of Madrid, The (La Perla de Madrid), descriptive bolero (idyll)	98
Ehrichs	Hungarian Prelude	98
Eilenberg, Richard	Arabian Patrol, The	06
	Bersagliere March (Marsch des Bersagliere)	28
	Blue Violets (Blaw Veilchen), mazurka caprice (album leaf)	02 05 08 24
	Charge of the Curassiers (Cuirassier-Attaque), Op. 133, galop (caprice)	93 94 96
	Christmas Bells (Weihnachtsglocken -- Les Cloches de Noel), characteristic	11 12
	Emperor's Review (Review of the German Troops), grand march (military tone picture)	93-96 *97 01 02 04-06 08-13
	Emperor's Review (Guard Mount) (Die Wachtparade Kommt) (German patrol) (United Service Passing in Review) (Emperor's Review)	93 01 04 06 12
	Evening Bells, The, nocturne	02
	Evening in Toledo, An, caprice	15
	Fanfare (and My Country 'Tis of Thee)	98
	Forest Ranger's Courtship, The, idyll	13
	Golden Blonde, The (Goldblondchen Salonstruck), descriptive (idyll)	01 05
	Husaren Fanfare, Die	94 95
	Idyllic Ballet Suite: Rose von Schiras, Die (The Rose of Shiras)	*97 * 98 *00 01 02 04 07-10 13 15 22-24
	Idyllic Ballet Suite: The Buds, polka	97
	Idyllic Ballet Suite: The Zephyr	97
	In der Waldschmeide (In the Woods), characteristic	08 09
	In May (Im Mai:), Op. 25: Overture	07 10 13 21-26
	Introduction and Polacca, cornet duet	01 02

	Japanese War March (Japanischer Siegesmarsch), Op. 175	98 06
	King Midas: Overture	95 96
	Life of a Dream (Das Leben ein Traum) (Life Is a Dream) (Life Is a Dream), Op. 106: Overture	13 16 22 25 26 30
	Manola, La, Spanish serenade	13-16 24
	Mill in the Forest, The (Die Muhle im Schwarzwald), idyll, Op. 52	93-95
	My Compliments (Mon Compliment), Op. 161, morceau de salon	96 09
	Pagenstreiche	94
	Return of the Troops, The, caprice	94
	Reveille, The, characteristic	94-96
	Sleigh Ride, galop	93
	Turkish March (Turkischer Marsch) (La Turque), Op. 165	13 23 24
	Twilight in the Mountain, idyll	24
	Two Hearts That Beat As One, cornet duet	01
	Uhlan's Call (Ulanenruf) caprice	15
Einoedshofer, Julius	Berliner Fahrten: Lieb' und Wein (Love and Wine), waltz	24
	Ein Fideler Abend (A Merry Evening) (A Jolly Evening in Berlin), fantasie	*00 01
	Fata Morgana, waltz	*00 01 02
	Life in Vienna, waltz	01
	Tugendfalle: Paradise on Earth (Ein Paradies auf Erden), waltz	06 24
Elgar, Edward	Chanson de Matin, Op. 15: Entr' Acte	24
	Choral Suite: Three Bavarian Dances	05 23 24
	Cockaigne, Op. 40: Overture	15 25
	Contrasts, The (1700-1900), gavotte	04 24
	Crown of India: Suite	13 17
	Hiawatha, idyll	02
	In the Bavarian Highlands (From the Bavarian Highlands), suite	05 09
	Land of Hope and Glory, from Pomp and Circumstance March No. 1, cornet solo or concert piece	05 14 17 18 22 *25 *26
	Lyrique, serenade (Serenade Lyrique)	21 23 24
	Pomp and Circumstance No. 1 (Land of Hope and Glory), grand march	02 03 *04 *05 *06 07 08 10 *11 12-15 17-23 *25 29
	Salut d'Amour, reverie (Morceau Mignon), reverie, (intermezzo) Op. 12	01 02 *03 04 *11 18 21 23 24 28
	Sevillana: Scenes Espagnol (Caprice Espagnol) (Dance Espagnole), idyll	*04 *05 *07 13 14 16 27
	Spanish Serenade	09
	Suite No. 2, The Wand of Youth: Little Bells	*11 12 16
	Sursam Corda: Grand Scene	04
	Sursum Corda: Adagio	02
Elli, A. Murio	Ave Maria, vocal solo	96
Elliot, Stanislaus	Medusa: Overture	94
Elliot, Zo & Stoddard King	There's a Long, Long Trail, song, vocal or euphonium solo	23-25
Elm, Robert	Darktown Wedding, A, characteristic coon march & two-step	99
Elverhoj: Overture	Elverhoj: Overture	02
Emerson, Dan	Aunt Dinah's Wedding Dance, an Ethiopian melange	95
Emerson, Walter	Carnival of Venice, The (The Carneval), cornet solo	08 23
Emmett, Daniel Decatur	Dixie, band number or vocal solo	95 *98 99 *00 04 *05 *24 *26 *27 *30 probably used as encore all years band was in southern states
Englander, Ludwig	Fairie's Lullaby, The, cornet solo	*20 *21
	Little Corporal, The: Selections	99
	Monks of Malabar: Selections	01
	Rounders, The: Selections	02
Englemann, H	Melodie d'Amour	14
Enna, August	Hexe, Die (The Witch): Spinnlied (Spinning Song)	94 95
Ennis	Comin' Thro' the Rye, trombone solo	93 *97
Erhart, Victor J.	Cold Gray Eyes, vocal solo	95
Erichs, H.	Folk Songs of Russia	27

	Sarafan: Overture (Russian Overture) (The Red Sarafan)	95 *22 23-25 27
Erkel, Franz	Hunyady-Laszlo: Overture	02
Erlanger	Daughter of the Revolution: Waltz, vocal solo	96
Ernst, Heinrich Wilhelm	Elegie	98 02
	Fantasie on Popular Viennese Melodies (Reminiscences of Suppe, Millocker, Strauss)	*03 *05 10 12 15
	Hungarian Airs, violin solo	15
Ertl, Dominik	Dreams of Love (Liebestraume)	01
Erviti, Jose	Sangre Torrera, Spanish march	24
Espinosa, Gaspar	Moraima, Spanish caprice	10
Eugene	Cupid's Gardens, intermezzo	02
Euwer, James Nelson	Steel Age - Ingot to Billet, The	06
Fahrbach, Phillip, Jr.	Au Claire de Lune, waltz	26
	Au Pays des Chanson's, waltz	93 25
	Follette, waltz	94
	In the City of Song	93
	Land of Song, The, waltz	26
	Musician's Strike, The (The Strike), humoresque	*94
	Roses Blanches, mazourka	96
	Song of the Storks, galop	93 94
	Visions of a Beautiful Woman, waltz	23-26
Fairfield, Frank	Night and Dawn, vocal solo	08
Fairlamb, J. Remington	See and the Wind, The, song	97
Fairman, George	Swanee Rose, vocal solo	15
Falkenstein	Owl's March	01
Fall, Leo	Darby and Joan (Darling and Joan), waltz	12 22-24
	Dollar Princess, The: Selections, divertissement	09 10
Fall, Richard & L. Wolfe Gilbert	O, Katherina!, fox trot	25 26
Falla, Manuel de	Jota, La	29
Fanciulli, Francesco	Grand Army Patrol	95
Faning, Eaton	Song of the Vikings, march (paraphrase)	05 17 22 24 27
Fare, Florence	Pride of Arran, The, caprice	94
Farrar, Ernest Bristow	English Pastoral Impressions, suite	22
Farrell, J.	Belle of Ireland, The, polka	94
Fassett, Raphael	G.A.R. Patrol (Patrol of the Grand Army of the Republic)	92 93
	Parade of the Guards, march	93
	Sousa's Band, march	93
Fassone, V.	Marguerite of Monte Carlo, vocal solo	93
Faure, Gabriel	Charity, vocal solo	*93
Faure, Jean Baptiste	Palms, The, vocal or trombone solo	94-96 *97 *98 26
	Rameaux, Les, vocal solo	94
Faust	Vorwarts, march	27
Faust, Carl	Lustiger Bruder, galop	94
	Tales of Long Ago, waltz	22
	With the Wind, galop	94
Fees, Sarah L.	American Boy, The, two-step	03
Felix, Hugo	Lady Dandies (The Merveilleuses) (The Marvelous One: Selections)	09 24
	Madame Sherry: Selections	06
	Pearl Girl, The: Selections	14
Fernandez, Juan	Chiquita, dance	22
Ferrari, Gustave	Mother's Prayer, A, vocal solo	18
Ferrari, P.	Gli Ultimi Giorni di Suli: Selections	96
Ferraris, Pierre	Berceuse, Op. 30, waltz	*09 *11
	Moudaine, waltz	10
Ferron	Crocodile, The, two-step	98
Ferroni, Vincenzo	Spanish Rhapsody	19
Fetras, Oscar	Carnival Secrets, waltz	97 98 01 23 24
	Court Ball Dances (Hofball Tanze), waltz	96
	Moonlight on the Alster (Mondnacht auf der Alster), waltz	99 01 02 04 06 07 12 15 24-26
	On the Elbe, waltz	22
	Rosen Auf Den Weg, waltz	96

	Spanische Weisen (Spanish Melodies) (Spanish Tales), waltz	19
	Wunderquelle, Die, Op. 121: March and Overture	24
Filipovsky, F.	Chant du Rossignol (The Nightingale) (Song of the Nightingale), concert polka, piccolo solo	96 *20 21 24-26
Fillmore, James Henry, Jr.	Billy Sunday's Successful Songs, medley	18
	Lassus Trombone, trombone rag	*18 19 *20 26
	Sally Trombone, trombone rag	19
	Whistling Farmer Boy, The [at Feeding Time], descriptive	*26 *28
Finck, Herman von der	Cheero, palace girls' dance	19
	In the Shadows, skipping rope dance	*11 *12 13 18 22
	Moonlight Dances	12
	On the Road to Zag-a-Zig, descriptive (a desert journey)	12
Finden, Amy Woodforde	Garden of Kama, The: Four Indian Love Lyrics (Some Famous Indian Love Lyrics)	13 24
	On Jhelum [Jelum] River, Kashmire love story	15
Finlay, Charles A.	Jubilee, march	98
	Swing Song	93 94
	Vivante, waltz	94
Fiorita, Ted	No, No, Nora	*24
Fischer, Carl	In the Deep Cellar, trombone and tuba ensemble	94 *03 17
Fisher & Vincent	Pucker Up and Whistle	21
Fisher, George H.	Knights of Columbus, march	97
Fitz, Albert H.	Won't You Come to My Tea Party?, waltz	95
Flegier, Ange	I've Watched the Stars at Night	95
	Stances (I Love Her), vocal or flugelhorn solo	94 95 *96 98 99 01 04
Fletcher	Folie Bergere, caprice	*12 13 16 19-21
Fletcher, Percy E.	Cairo: Selections	22-24
	Lovely Loo	*11 15-17
	Moulin Rouge, suite	18
	My Love to You, chansonette	19
	Petite Suite	17
	Rustic Revels, suite	24-26
	Three Light Pieces (Three Characteristic Pieces), suite: La Neiga (Lullaby); Fifinette; Folie Bergere	19
	Vanity Fair, comedy overture	26
	Woodland Pictures (Rustic Revels), rural suite	12 20 22 24
Fliege, H.	Chinese Patrol	93
Floersheim, Otto	Love Novel (Liebesnovelle) (Suite Miniature)	*00
Florence, Martha	Bloomer, The, march	95
Flotow, Friedrich	Albin: Overture	94
	Foerster: Scene	93 94
	Grossfurstin: Overture	94
	Martha: Good Night	93 94
	Martha: M'Appari, vocal solo	93 94 97
	Martha: Overture	98 10 *11 12-15 20-26 31
	Martha: Porti Song, vocal solo	96
	Martha: Romance, vocal solo	93
	Martha: Selections	93 94 96 98 01-08 15 22 25-28
	Martha: The Pilgrims, tenor and basso duet	93
	Mountain Sprite, The (Rubezahl): Overture	94 96
	Stradella: Finale	94 04
	Stradella: Hymn, vocal solo	94
	Stradella: Overture	93 94 *95 96-98 01-03 05-10 *11 12-15 17 20-27 30
	Stradella: Pieta Signore, vocal solo	94
	Stradella: Selections	93 94 96
Flux, Neville	Mazurka Militaire, Op. 53	10
Flynn	Off to Philadelphia	22
Foerster	At Twilight, nocturne	02

	Dream in the Forest, A, idyll	98
Foerster, Adolph Martin	Dedication March (Grand Inauguration March) (Grand Dedication March) (Founder's Day) (Festival March)	01-04 06 09 10 12-15 21 24
	Festivity, suite	16 17 21
Foerster, Rudolf	Harliquinade, caprice	93 94
Foote, Arthur	In the Mountains: Overture, Op. 14	01
	Irish Love Song (Irish Folk Song), vocal solo	*08 16
	Love Me If I Live, vocal solo	*95
	Omar Khayyam (Five Poems After Omar Khayyam), suite (tone poem)	08-10 14 16 22-24
Ford, Walter	I Love You in the Same Old Way, cornet solo	98
Forillo	Study, violin solo	*03
Fornes	Concert Mazurka, xylophone solo	04
Forrest	Onondago, two-step	07
Forster	Come For it's June, vocal solo	21
	Lorraine, march	06
Forster, Dorothy	Little Home With You, A, vocal solo	21
Forster, Joseph	Rose von Pondevedra, Die (Rose in the Bud), fantasie	21
Forsyth, Mary Isabella	American Hymn, An	99
Forsythe	Unto The, O the God of Our Fathers, hymn	*00
Foster	Famous Songs and Dances of Civil War Days	21
Foster, Fay	Prairieblumen, waltz	06 10 *11 12-15 17 18 21 22
Foster, Stephen Collins	Massa's in the Cold, Cold Ground, fanasie on Stephen Foster's song	97
	My Old Kentucky Home, violin and soprano duet	*94 *97
	Old Black Joe	25
	Old Folks at Home (Swanee River), violin, cornet, saxophone, or xylophone solo, or band selection	95 01 *03 05 08 10 13 *30
	Old Kentucky Home, fantasie	06
Fou so Ka	National Air of Japan, The	94
Fournout	In Sheltered Vale, idyll	05
France, McDermott Leila	Bon Voyage, characteristic	24
	Palm City Schottische	96
	Salero, El, march	04
	Sweetheart of the Year, song	95
Franchetti, Alberto	Asrael: Ride of the Infernals (Ridda Infernale), Act I	98 19
Francis	Chloe, song	01
Francis, Herbert	Ship o' Dreams, song, cornet solo	21
Francis, William T.	Down Ole Tampa Bay, caprice	98
Franck, Cesar	Redemption, symphonic poem	16
Franco, Jose G.	Indian, quadrille on Indian airs	95
Franke, Theo.	Russe Russian, intermezzo (Intermezzo Russe) (Russian Interlude)	*94 95 96
Franklin, Malvin Maurice	I Was Born in Michigan, fox trot	21
Franko, Nahan	Belle Creole, La, polka	94
	Marie Antoinette, gavotte	94
Fraser-Simpson, H.	Maid of the Mountains, The: Selections	20
Freman	Departed Days, nocturne	97
Frey, Hugo	Uncle Tom, fox trot	16
Friday, William H., Jr.	Home, Sweet Home, song, trombone solo	96
	Mother's Arms, song, trombone solo	96
Friedman, Carl	Attack of Cavalry (Attaque de Cavellerie) (Charge of the Cavalry),	05 08
	Slavonic Rhapsodie	09 *10 *11 12-15 17-25 27 28
Friedman, Stanleigh P. & C.W. O'Connor	Down the Field [Yale] (March on Down the Field)	08 15
Friend, Cliff	You're a Real Sweetheart, fox trot	*28
Friml, Rudolf	Chansonette, song	24
	Egyptian Dance	20
	Firefly, The: Selections	13-16 19 24 25
	High Jinks: Selections	14-16 20 24 27
	L'Amour - Toujours - L'Amour, vocal solo or band number	30
	Melodie	20
	Original, suite	19

351

	Pictures, suite	18
	Recollections of Friml	15
	Rose Marie: Indian Love Call, flute, harp & saxophone ensemble or xylophone solo	*25 *27 *28 *29
	Rose Marie: Scenes, saxophone solo	*25
	Rose Marie: Selections	26 28
	Some Time: Selections	19
	Three Musketeers, The: Selections	30
	Vagabond King, The: Song of the Vagabond, vocal solo	*26
Fritsche, Otto	Fantasie on Traviata, clarinet solo	98
Froelich, Henry	Little Dot, characteristic	*98
Fucik, Julius	Battle of Custozza, The (Die Schlacht Bei Custozza), tone picture	09
	Entry of the Gladiators, march	24
	Florentiner, The, march	09
	March of the Giants	09 24
Fuerst, William Wallace	Isle of Champagne, The: Selections	93-95
Fulton	Dream, Sweetheart, Dream, cornet solo	*09
Fumi, Vinceslav Joseph Bernard Claus	Mexican Girl's Dream, The (La Siesta de la Senorita), scherzo and habanera (idyll)	*97 98
Furchgott, Mortimer	Just As Long As the Sun Do Shine, vocal solo	98
Gabriel, Charles H.	Brighten the Corner Where You Are, hymn, cornet solo	16 *17
Gabriel-Marie	Bells of St. Malo, The, idyll	03
	Cinquantine, La, ancient dance, violin solo	98 *99 01 22
	Serenade Badine	*99 02
Gabrielsky	Quartette for Clarinets	94
Gade, Niels Wilhelm	Hamlet: Overture	04 08
	Im Hochlands (In the Highlands), Scotch overture	24
	Night Scenes of Ossian (Noachtloenge von Ossian): Overture	96
	Night Songs of Ossian: Overture	94
Gaertner, L.	Edelweiss: Overture	97 98
Gale, John J., SEE Stuckey, H.S.		
Gallo	Tarantella at Piedigrotta	*19 *20
Ganne, Gustave Louis	Arlequinade Pizzicato, mazurka	24
	Czarine, La, Russian dance	*92 93
	Gypsy, La, (The Gipsy), mazurka (idyll) (air de ballet)	04 *05 06 *07 *08 09 10 *11 12 14 15 18 20-23
	Hans the Flute Player: Selection	*21 22 23 26 27
	L'Auvergnate, mazurka (bouree)	96
	Marche Lorraine, pas redouble (march)	13 18 22-24 29
	Marche Tartare (Tartare Patrol)	05 07
	Mountebank, The, suite	21
	Mousme, La, Japanese mazurka (Mazurka Japonaise) (The Pretty Japanese)	94 *95 96-98 *00 24
	Pere de la Victoire, Le, march	28
	Saltimbanques, Les (The Mountebanks): Selections	21 22 25 28
	Tartare Patrol, SEE Marche Tartare (Ganne)	05
	Tourniquet, polka	94 *95 96-99
	Tzigane, La, Hungarian mazurka (Magyar Dance)	93 96 07
Ganz	Sing, Sweet Bird, whistling solo	93
	Vocal Polka, vocal solo	94
Garing, Athol John	Anniversary, The, march	21
	Love Nest Humoresque (Feather Your Nest)	*21 *22
	Man o' War, cornet solo	*21 22 23
	Sousa's Anniversary, march	20
	Wets, The, humoresque	22
Garner, G.	Wistful Waltz, A	23
Garnier-Marchand	Rhapsody on Themes of Chopin, No. 1 (First Rhapsody on Works of Chopin)	23
Gassner, C.	Musical Bouquet, A, fantasia	96
Gassner, G.	Mon Ami (My Friends), waltz	16 23
Gastaldon, Stanislas	Musica Proibita, romance	10
Gatti, Dominico	Air Varie, clarinet solo	96
	Caprice Rulante, euphonium solo	93

	Fantasie Brillante (Fantasie Original) (Souvenir de Naples), euphonium solo	93
	Flower Garden, The (A Garden of Roses) (A Garden of Flowers) (Il Giardino del Flori, euphonium solo	94 98 99 *00 01-03
	L'Iride, concerto for band (symphonic poem) (Grand Concerto for Band)	97 98
	Postal Tax, mazurka	93 94 96 97
	Variations on Home, Sweet Home, piccolo solo	95
Gaunt, Percy	Trip to Chinatown: Songs	93
Gautier, Leonard	Secret, Le, intermezzo	13
Gauwin, Ad.	Here! Chick! Chick! (Vien Poupoule!)	*04 21
	Viens Poupoule, polka	*05
Gay	Gems from the celebrated "Beggar's Opera"	22 23
Gay, Byron	Western Land, intermezzo	19
Gebest, Charles J.	Red Widow, The: Selections	12
Gehl	For You Alone, vocal solo	21
Geisberg, Frederick	Scarlet Letter, The, march	97
Geisler, Paul	Pied-Piper of Hamelin, The (Der Rattenfanger von Hamelin) (The Rat Charmer of Hamelin), cornet solo	17
Geloso, Cesar	Caprice Slave (Slavonic Dance), violin solo	05 *06 *07 *08 10 16 19
Genee, Richard Franz Frederick	Nanon: Selections	94-96
Gennan	Sunny South, The: Overture	95
Gennin, Jean	Fluttering Birds, Op. 31, piccolo duet or band number	21-23 *24
German, Edward	As You Like It: Rustic Dance	00 24
	Glorious Devon, cornet solo	22
	Gypsy Suite, The (The Gypsies), dance suite	*99 *00 02 04 *15 17 21 24
	Henry VIII: Incidental Music (Ballet Suite) (Dances)	92 95 09 10 *11 12-16 18-20 22-24 27
	Henry VIII: Mares Dance	93
	Henry VIII: Shepherd's Dance	93-95 96 08
	Henry VIII: Three Dances, violin solo	96 06-08
	Henry VIII: Torchlight Dance	93
	Merry England: Come to Arcadie, vocal solo or duet	*09
	Much Ado About Nothing: Bouree and Gigue	*01 *02 04-08 10 15 17 18 22 23 27
	Nell Gwyn: Three Dances	15 24
	Princess of Kensington, A: Selections	03 04 06 09
	Romany Rye	*00
	Seasons, The: Harvest Dance (Dance of the Harvesters)	02 06
	Tarantella (Tarantella and Sylvana)	02
	Tempter, The, suite	18
	Tom Jones: Selections	08 09 17 18 22 24
	Welsh Rhapsody	*05 *06 *07 08-10 *11 12-16 18 20-23
Germane	Deep Down Within the Cellar, song	94
Gershwin, George	Oh Kay: Do, Do, Do Oh (Gershwin)	*25 26
	Song of the Flame, fox trot	26
	The Man I Love, song, cornet solo	*30
	Tip Toes: Sweet and Low-Down	26
	Tip Toes: That Certain Feeling	26
Gervin	Souvenir the Liege, piccolo duet	23
Ghys, Henry	Amaryllis, air	05 06 10 *11 14 15 21-24
Giders, John Francis	Polka	92
Giesmann	Arena, The, march	94
Gilbert	Two Roses, vocal solo	19
Gilbert, Henry Franklin Belknap	Pirate Song, The, vocal solo	17
Gilbert, James L.	Bonnie Sweet Bessie, the Maid of Dundee, vocal or euphonium solo	93 94 13 22 23
Gilbert, Jean	Girl in the Taxi, The: Selections	14 22 24
	In the Night (Die Kino Konigin)	*14
	Joy-Ride Lady, The (The Gayride Lady): Selections	24

	Thalia: Overture (Lustspiel Overture)	13 *14 *15 16 18 19 21-23 27
Gilbert, Lawrence B.	Shadowland (In Shadowland), intermezzo	15-17
Gilberte, Hallet	Moonlight and Starlight, vocal solo	*19 *20
Gilchrist, William Wallace	Heart's Delight, vocal solo	*98
Gilder, John Francis	Alabama Dance, The, characteristic (Danse Africaine) (Caprice Africaine)	93-97 *98 01 04 06 16
	Aramanthus, romance	98
	Jolly Cadet, The, caprice	92 93 96
	Sunburst, novelette	04
	Tarantella Fantastique	93 94 96
	Transcendental, Op. 22, grand march	97
	Zanzibar, caprice	93 96
Gillet, Ernest	Babillage, characteristic	*00 01 02 09
	Badine, serenade	01
	Dans la Foret (In the Forest)	95 96
	Douse Caresse, intermezzo	95 *00
	Entr'Acte Gavotte	93 *96 *97 99
	Hourida, waltz caprice	*96 97
	In the Mill	94
	Lamento, Il (The Lament)	94 96
	Lettre de Manon, La (Manon's Letters), intermezzo	03 *04 05 08 10 14-17 20 24
	Loin du Bal, waltz	93 97 98
	Lost Happiness	94 96
	Passe Pied: Entr'Acte	95
	Patrol of the Children (Patrouille Enfantine)	*94
	Pendant le Bal, intermezzo	05
	Rondo de Nuit	99 *00 01 02
	Serenade Impromptu	96-98 24
	Spinning Top, The, caprice	93
	Toupie, La [The Top]	93
	Valse Lente	94 96
Gilman, C.A.	Racine Commandery, the, march	28
Gilman, S.	Fair Harvard	08
Gilmore	Sally	*18
Gilmore, Patrick S.	Columbia, patriotic air	93 96-98
	Famous 22nd Regiment, The, march	93 94
	Voice of a Departing Soul, The (Death's at the Door), dirge	92-94
Giordano, Umberto	Andrea Chenier: Aria [unnamed], vocal solo[s]	16
	Andrea Chenier: Grand Scene and Ensemble (Grand Fantasia) (Selections)	*01 *02 *03 04 05 07 09 *11 13-23 *24 25-27 31
	Fedora: Selections	01 02 24
	Springtime (Printemps), vocal solo	*01
Gioren[?]	Mass: Gloria	93
Girard	Alaskan, The: Totem Pole Dance	08
	Orchestral Suite (Le Orchestre)	01 02
	Nician Suite: Carneval Scene	*99
Glazunov, Alexander Kostantinovich	Carnival Overture (Carnival Scenes)	20 22 24
	Raymonda: Ballet Suite (Scenes)	*00 01
	Seasons, The: Ballet Suite	22
Glinka, Mikhail Ivanovich	Capriccio Brillante, overture on the theme Jota Aragonaise	*00 01 02
	Jota Aragonesa, La: Overture (Capriccio Brillante, overture on the theme Jota Aragonaise)	23
	Kamarinskaya, La (Slavonic Wedding): Fantasie	11 12 17
	Life for the Czar, A, (La Vie Pour le Tsar): Overture	19 20 23 25
	Life for the Czar, A, (La Vie Pour le Tsar): Selections	24
	Life for the Czar, A: Polonaise	14
	Ride in a Russian Droski	93
	Russian Carriage Song	93 94
	Russlan and Ludmilla (Rouslane et Ludmila): Overture	03 08 29
	Songs and Dances of Little Russia	13

354

Glogan, SEE Graff, George		
Glover	Over Hill and Dale, whistling solo	93
Glover, Charles W.	Feast of The Lanterns, The, fantasia	*98
Gluck, Christoph Willibald	Adagio and Rondo	*13
	Alceste: Allegro Gracioso	97
	Armida: Air; Gai; Siciliano	10 *18 26
	Armida: Suite	21
	Iphigenie en Aulide (Iphigenie in Tauris): Air Gai and Sicilienne	25
	Iphigenie en Aulide (Iphigenie in Tauris): Overture	*94 98
	Orfeo ed Euridice: Che Faro Senza, vocal solo	96
	Orfeo ed Eurydice: Aria [unnamed], vocal solo[s]	93 15
	Orfeo ed Eurydice: Song	94
	Reminiscences of Gluck	19
	Suite de Ballet (from Gluck's operas)	23-26
Glyn	Crusaders, The, galop	93
Godard, Benjamin	Allegretto, flute solo	*21 22 25 26
	Canzonetta, violin solo	08 09
	Concerto for Violin: Adagio et Canzonetta	02
	Concerto for Violin: Canzonetta	94 *95 02
	Concerto Romantique, violin solo (Romantique)	10
	Florian Song (Chanson de Florian), vocal solo	94 23-27
	Idyl and Allegretto, flute solo	21 23
	Idyll and Waltz, flute solo	23
	Jocelyn: Berceuse, cradle song, vocal or cornet solo	*00 02 08 19-21 *22 *23 *24 25 26 *27
	Jocelyn: Lullaby (cradle song)	01
	Marche Tzigane (Gypsy March) (The Gypsies), caprice	94-96
	Pan Pastorale, idyll	*05 *07 *08 09 10 *11 16 18 22
	Poetical (Poetic) Scenes (Scenes Poetiques) (In the Valley), suite	*19 *20 22-26 31
	Rondo, flute solo	22
	Serenade Andalouse, violin solo	02 08 09
	Tasse, Le: Danse des Bohemians	16 22
	Valse, flute solo or band number	*23 *24
	Vivandiere, The: Ballet Suite	01 06 08-10 16 17 20-22 24 26
	Vivandiere, The: untitled vocal solo	18 23-25
Godard, Charles	Dance of the Stars, waltz	98 15
Godefroid	Danse des Sylphes, La, harp solo	22
Goderman	Song of Norway, A, vocal solo	27
Godfrey	Bonnet Blue (Blue Bonnets), air and variations	93
	Dance Africaine	93
	Gems of Scotland (Reminiscences of Scotland)	23 24 *25 26 27
	Green-Eyed Monster in the Band, The, humoresque	93-96
	Guards, The, waltz, cornet solo	93 *00
	Highland Songs and Dances	02
	Melodic Moments with Wagner	01
	Moore's Irish Melodies (Moore's Melodies of Ireland)	93
	Noisy Johnnie, The, polka [galop]	93
	Offenbachiana	26
	Prussian Tattoo, The	94
	Quadrille	93
	Reminiscences of Ireland (Songs and Dances of Ireland) (Gems of Irish Minstrelsy) (Gems of Ireland)	93 *94 95 96 98 *03 04 06 08-10 *11 12 19 23 24 *25 26-28
	Scenes from Masterpieces of Italian Composers	01
	Songs and Dances of the Canadian	15
	Whirlwind Polka, cornet solo	*99 *00 01
Godfrey, Arthur Eugene	Bon Vivants, polka	96
	Boston Belle, The, barn dance (caprice) (entr'acte)	94-97 99 01 02 04 08 09 18 20-22 25-27
	Happy Darkies (The Pickaninnies), caprice	93 95 96

	Sullivanesque, fantasie	26
Godfrey, Charles, Jr.	Bonne Chance, rondo caprice	94
	Comical Contest, A (The Contest) (The Band Contest), humoresque (burlesque rondo)	92 93 96 16
	Coster Songs, selection of popular songs	26
	Friendly Rivals, (The Rivals), cornet duet	93 94
	Scotland's Pride (Pride of Scotland) [note: not same as Reminiscences of Scotland, by Frederick Godfrey]	93 94 96 02 04 06-10 12 15 17 19 21-26
	Wiener Klange (Sounds from Vienna) (Vienese Melodies), fantasie on Austrian airs	23
Godfrey, Daniel	Belgravia Waltz, The	20-26
	Hilda, waltz	*00 03 08 12 14 15 17-20 22 24
	Litany of Loretto, No. 1 and 2, ancient airs	
	Mabel Waltz, The	*00 03 04 06 12 18 22 23
Godfrey, Frederick	Airs of the Nations	92
	Jenny Jones, variations on Welsh song, piccolo solo, piccolo and flute duet, or band number	*99 02 07 19
	Miss Lucy Long, bassoon solo	94
	Reminiscences of All Nations	93 96 98 06 24-26
	Reminiscences of England (Songs and Dances of England) (Songs and Dances of Old England) (Old English Songs)	95 96 *11 13-17 19 23-26
	Reminiscences of Ireland (Songs and Dances of Ireland) (Gems of Irish Minstrelsy) (Ireland in Song and Story)	10 17
	Reminiscences of Scotland (Songs and Dances of Scotland) (Melodies that Scotchmen Love) [note: not same as Scotland's Pride, by Charles Godfrey, Jr.]	93-96 04 09 10 14 16-19 21 22 29
	Reminiscences of Wales (Wales in Song and Story) (Gems from Welsh Minstrelsy)	93-96 03 04 06-09 10 *11 12 14 17-19 21-28 31
Godfrey, Percy	Roi d'Yvetot, Le, rustic suite (Rustic Suite)	93-96 03 04 06 07 09 14 17 18 21
Goetting	Stadium, The, march	04
Goetze	Oh Happy Day, vocal solo	93 94
Goldberg, Robert	Mexican Dance No. 1 (Mexikanische Tanze No. 1)	94
Goldmark, Carl	Cricket on the Hearth, The: Prelude to Act III (Entr'Acte) (Overture)	*97 98 01 02 04 05 12 23
	In Springtime (Im Fruhling) (Spring): Overture	02 *09 10 *11 12 14-16 19 20 *21 *22 23-26
	Rustic (Country) Wedding Symphony, Op. 26: Bridal Song (Bride's Song)	15 *23 26
	Rustic (Country) Wedding Symphony, Op. 26: Selections	12 13 15-17 21 *22 24 25 27
	Rustic (Country)Wedding Symphony, Op. 26: Im Garten and Rustic Dance (No. 1)	22 28
	Sakuntala: Overture	95 98 *01 02 *03 04 05 10 *15 16-18
	Scherzo Serenade	12
Gomez	Cuore Gentil (Dear Heart), polacca, vocal solo	93 94
	Mia Piccirella, vocal solo	93
	Woodenshoe Dance	05
Gomez, Antonio Carlos	Guarany, Il: Ballata, soprano solo	96
	Guarany, Il: Overture	97 *98 *99 *00 01 02 04 15 17-20 22 24 26 28
Gomez, Juan	Cordova, waltz	26
Goodwin, Jay & Larry Shay	Tie Me to Your Apron Strings Again, fox trot	26
Gordigiani	Rosallina, vocal solo	94
Gori	Iowa Corn Song	27
Gossec, Francois-Joseph	Gavotte, violin solo	*11
Gottschalk, Louis Moreau	Banjo, The, fantasie	02 03 18 24 25

	Dying Poet, The, idyll	93-96 01 *02 04 06-10 *11 13 14 16 18 20 24
	Last Hope, The, sacred meditation	01 02 06 08 09 10
	Marche de la Nuit	93-96 01 02
	Pasquinade	*92 *93 *94 95-97 *98 99 *00 01 02 07-10 14 18-20 22-24
Gotze, Franz	Liebchen Suss, Liebchen Mein	94
Goulden, Howard	Radio Echoes, xylophone solo	*29
Gounod, Charles	Ave Maria (on J.S. Bach theme), vocal solo or band number	93-96 06 *07 09 15 24-28
	Bachantes, dance	*06
	Bells Across the Snow	19 22 29
	Chanson du Printemps	95
	Clos ta Paupiere, berceuse	93
	Close Thine Eyelids, lullaby (slumber song)	94 95
	Colombe: La, Entre' Acte	93 95 96
	Cradle Song	93
	Dance of the Nubians	93
	Dodelinette: Berceuse	93
	Dodelinette: Slumber Song	*94
	Dream on the Ocean, waltz	02
	Faust: Aria [unnamed], vocal solo[s]	95 17
	Faust: Ballet Music	*92 93-96 05 06 12 13 15 17 18 20 22 24
	Faust: Chorus of Angels and Soldiers	93
	Faust: Dio Possente, vocal solo	*93 *94 95-97
	Faust: Flower Song, vocal solo	93 97
	Faust: Grand Scene and Soldiers' Chorus (Glory and Love to the Men of Old), trombone quintet	92 93 *01 02 04-09 10 15
	Faust: Jewel Song, vocal solo	18
	Faust: Kermesse	97
	Faust: My Native Land, vocal solo	93
	Faust: Prayer, vocal solo	93
	Faust: Prelude	93
	Faust: Romanza, vocal solo	97
	Faust: Salut d'Amour, vocal solo	02
	Faust: Salve di Mora Casta e Pura, vocal solo	95 96
	Faust: Selections	92-96 *97 98 99 *00 01-10 *11 12-29
	Faust: Serenade, vocal solo	94 15
	Faust: Soldier's Chorus, band number or trombone sextet	*01 10 *11 12-14 *15 16 19 21 *26 31
	Faust: Waltz	93 29
	Funeral March of a Marionette, The	94-97 07 *08 13 14 24 25
	Gallia, motet (religious scene)	98 09 18 24
	Holy Temple, The, song (scenes)	10
	Jesus, Lover of My Soul, meditation on prelude by Bach	93
	Kermesse, King of Thule: Church Scene	93
	Meditation on Prelude of Bach	93
	Messe Solenelle: Sanctus	94
	Mireille: Aria [unnamed], vocal solo[s]	93 95 03 05
	Mireille: Mon Coeur Ne Peut Changer	*97
	Mireille: O, Legere Hirondelle, vocal solo	03
	Mireille: Overture	93 94 96
	Mireille: Waltz Song, vocal solo	96 04
	Mock Doctor, The: Selections	93 94
	Nazareth, euphonium solo	15
	O Divine Redeemer!: Prayer, vocal solo	01 19
	Pace, Pace, Mio Dio	28
	Philemon et Baucis: Entr'Acte and Danse des Bacchantes	93 *94 95 09

	Philemon et Baucis: O Riante Nature, vocal solo	05
	Philemon et Baucis: Prelude, Entr' Act and Two Scenes	94
	Philemon et Baucis: Selections	96 05 07 08 10 14 18 24
	Queen of Sheba, The (La Reine de Saba): Aria [unnamed], vocal solo[s]	*93 94 96 97 02 05-07 16-23
	Queen of Sheba, The (La Reine de Saba): Ballet Suite	10 *11 13-22 24 25
	Queen of Sheba, The (La Reine de Saba): Lend Me Your Aid, vocal solo	02
	Queen of Sheba, The (La Reine de Saba): March	93 31
	Queen of Sheba, The (La Reine de Saba): More Regal in His Low Estate,	96 06 07 16
	Queen of Sheba, The (La Reine de Saba): Plus Grand dances Sou Obscurite	06 21 25
	Queen of Sheba, The (La Reine de Saba): Plus Grand, vocal solo	06
	Queen of Sheba, The (La Reine de Saba): Selections	01 02 04 08 13 27
	Redemption: Unfold Ye Portals, choral or band number	93 24
	Reminiscences of Gounod	93 20-27
	Romeo and Juliet: Ah! Nella Calma, vocal solo	*11 12 13 15 20
	Romeo and Juliet: Aria [unnamed], vocal solo[s]	93-96 98 01-05 07-10 12 16 19-23 *24 25
	Romeo and Juliet: Ballet Music	21 22 25 26
	Romeo and Juliet: Excerpt (fantasia), violin solo	*11 18 19 22
	Romeo and Juliet: Grand Valse (Waltz Song) (Valse Aria), vocal solo	93 95 *96 *97 02 05 07 *08 *11 12 15 16 24 25 27
	Romeo and Juliet: Je Veux Vivre, vocal solo	96 20
	Romeo and Juliet: Selections (ballet suite)	96 01-03 06 08 09 16-19 22-24
	Romeo and Juliet: Valse des Fleurs	94 *07
	Ruth, vocal solo	95
	Salve Dimora, cavatina, vocal solo	*93 94
	Serenade, flugelhorn solo	02 *05
	She Alone Charmeth My Sadness, vocal solo	93
	Sing, Smile, Slumber, vocal, flugelhorn, or euphonium solo	97-99 01 02 04 05 09 24 25
	Six Sacred Pieces (Mores Et Vita): Judex	01 07 19
	Soix, Le, vocal solo	93
	There Is a Green Hill Far Away, cornet solo	93 96 01 04 06 08 10
	Valse Brilliant, vocal solo	14
Graff, George, Jr. & Jack Glogan	Wake Up, America, vocal solo	15 16
Graham	Two Little Girls in Blue, waltz	97
Grainger, Percy Aldridge	British Folk-Music Settings: Country Gardens, Morris dance	*23 24 25 *26 27 28 *29
	British Folk-Music Settings: Molly on the Shore, Irish reel	14-17 *18 21 24 27
	Colonial Song	21 24
	In a Nutshell, suite	18 19
	Irish Tune from County Derry (Tune from County Clare)	18 19
	Over the Hills and Far Away, children's march	19
	Room-Music Tid-bits: Handel in [on] the Strand, clog dance	11 *14 15-18
	Room-Music Tid-bits: Mock Morris	14 17 18 24
	Shepherd's Hey, Morris dance tune	*14 *15 16 *17 *18 *19 *20 21 24 26
Granada	Roumania, march	93
Granado	Nova Espanole, el, waltz	93
Granados, Enrique	March Militaire (A La Militaire)	20
Granichstaedten, Bruno	Rose Maid, The: Selections	11 12
Granier, Jules	Hosanna, Easter song, vocal solo	96
Grant	Leonard Wood March, SEE General Leonard Wood March (Grant)	21
Grant, Mrs. E.M.	Sevilla, song	02
A.L. & George Granville	When Myra Sings	23 *24 25 26
Graud	Bamboula, Trinidad dance	93 *95 *96
Gray	Amona	*09
Gray, Hamilton	Dawn of Redemption, The, Song	01
Graziani, M.	Parade Ecossaise (The Scotch Parade), morceau de guere	93 94
Gready, John	Hibernia: Selections	01

	Songs and Dances of Ireland	01 02
Green, George Hamilton	Fluffy Ruffles, xylophone solo	19
	Paraphrase on Dvorak's Humoresque, xylophone solo	18
	Paraphrase on Friedman's Slavonic Rhapsody, xylophone solo	18
	Paraphrase on Liszt's Hungarian Rhapsody No. 2, xylophone solo	17 18
	Paraphrase on Nicolai's Merry Wives of Windsor, xylophone solo	17 18
	Paraphrase on Rossini's William Tell Overture, xylophone solo	17-19
	Paraphrase on Suppe's Poet and Peasant Overture, xylophone solo	18 20-23 *25
	Paraphrase on Thomas' Raymond Overture	17-23 *30
	Paraphrase on Wolf-Ferrari's The Jewels of the Madonna	19
	Simco March	19
	Valse de Concert, xylophone solo	*18
Green, Joseph & Nathaniel Shilkret	Parade of the Toy Regiment, xylophone solo	*27 *30
Gregh, Louis	Arlette: Ballet Suite	94
Grey, Frank H.	Think Love of Me, vocal solo	21 22
Grieg, Edvard	Autumn Storms (Autumnal Gale), vocal solo	99
	Dream, A (Dreaming of Sweden), vocal solo	27
	Lyric Suite: The Shepherd Boy; Norwegian Rustic March; Nocturne; March of the Dwarfs	04 *05 08 09 *11 14 16 18 21
	Norwegian Dances	12-18 20-23 27
	Peer Gynt Suite [No. 1] (In the Hall of the Mountain King; Anitra's Dance; Asa's Death)	*92 93-98 06 *07 *08 *10 *11 12-14 *15 16-20 22 23 25-27
	Peer Gynt Suite No. 2: Solveg's Song	93
	Reminiscences of Grieg, Scene de Ballet (Fantasie on Works of Grieg)	02 08 13 15 16 18 19 22 27
	Sigurd Jorsalfar, suite	12 26
Griegh	Variations on He's a Jolly Good Fellow, piccolo solo	95
Griemal	Slavonic Rhapsody	26
Grisar, Albert	Bells of Bruges, The (Carillonneur de Bruge): Selections	93 94
	Duck's Bill, The: Overture	93
Gro, Josephine	Dance of the Wooden Shoes, caprice	94
	Sultan, The, patrol	95
Grobe, Charles	Tenting on the Old Camp Ground, vocal solo	16
Groedel, William	Selina Waltzes	01
Grossman, Ludwik	Ghost of the Commander (Ghost of the Warrior): Balladeeist des Wojewoden, band number or xylophone solo	94 97 16 17 23 24 *27 *28 *29 30
Grote	Venetian Gondellied, barcarolle	95 96
Grunwald, G.	Astrella: Selections	98
Guenther, K.F.W.	Country Club, March	03
Guild, Thatcher Howland	Illinois Loyalty, song	08 09
Guion, David Wendell	Sheep and Goat Walking to the Pasture, breakdown	*25 28
	Turkey in the Straw, cowboy breakdown	*21 *22 23 24 *26 *27 *29 *30
Gumbert, Ferd	Thou Art the Star, ballad	94
Gung'l, Josef	All Caught Cold (They All Caught Cold) Galop	20
	Autumn Storms (Autumnal Gale), vocal solo	*96 *97
	Dreams on the Ocean (Traume auf dem Ocean), waltz	01 02 04 07 08 16 19 21 22 24 25
	Festival March	93
	Hesperusklange, waltz	04
	Hydropaten, Die, waltz	22
	Immortellen Valse	93 95 97-99 *00 01 02 04 05 07 08 12 13 19-24 26
	In the Garden of Hesperides, fantasia	26
	Kaufmann's Casino Tanze (The Casino Waltz) (The Merchant's Casino) (The Casino Ball)	09 10 15 16 21-26
	My Beautiful Girl in Berlin, waltz	94
	On the Alps, idyl	93
	Pankeckten, Die, waltz	01
	Phantome, waltz	93 94

	Pleasures of Matrimony, The, rondo	94 95
	Soldiers' Songs (Soldaten-Lieder), waltz medley	06
	Sounds from Home	93 94 13 21 22
	Spring Jubilee in the Alps, A	94
	Zsambeki, czardas (Magyar dance)	15-17 19-21 24
Gurewich, Jascha	Emily, saxophone solo	21
	Fantasie in F Minor, saxophone solo	27 *29 *30
	Helen, saxophone solo	21
	Juliana, La, saxophone or cornet solo	20 21
	Laughing Gas, saxophone solo	21 25
	Passing Thoughts, saxophone solo	21
	Souvenir de Chamine (Chamounix), saxophone solo	21
	Souvenir Poetique, saxophone solo	21
	Twilight Romance, saxophone or cornet solo	*28
	Valse Fantasie, saxophone solo	*24 25
Gurtner, Jean	Garden of Hesperides, The (Le Jardin des Hesperides): Selections	94 20 24
Gutman, Arthur H.	Three Green Bonnets, vocal solo	95
Haakman, Georges	Primrose (Spring Idyll)	10
Haase, August	Saucilito, euphonium solo	95
	Tramp, Tramp, euphonium solo	93 94
Hacker, Phil M.	And They All Walked Away, comedy (patrol)	98
Hackh	Arlequin et Colombine, scene carnavalesque (pantomime)	04
Haddock, G. Percy	Soul's Awakening, The	94
Hadley, Henry Kimball	Aladdin: Ballet Suite	02
	Ballet Suite, Op. 16	15
	Festival March (The Bohemians)	96 24 26
	Herod: Overture	*26
	In Bohemia: Overture	*00 02 16
	Salome, symphonic poem, Op. 55	16
	Silhouettes, characteristic suite	19
	To Victory, lyric march	19
Haell	Intermezzo	94
Hager, Frederick W.	Arizona Moon, idyll	19
	Battle of the Marne (Echoes of the Marne), descriptive	19 20
	Boys and the Birds, The, characteristic	17 18 26
	Day at the Zoo, A, descriptive overture	*19 23 24
	Gleaming Star	*06
	Laughing Waters, characteristic polka	03 04
	Whistling Johnnies, The, patrol	12
	White Bird, novelette	12
Hager, Frederick W. & Justin Ring	Danse Hongroise, saxophone solo	26 27
Hager, Frederick W. & Justin Ring	Swanee Smiles	23
Haimann	Crack Regiment	*94
Haines, Chauncey	Lights Out (Out the Lights) (Taps), march	24
Haines, F.	Hibernia: Overture	98 24
Halevy	Call Me Thine Own, flute & saxophone duet	24
Halevy, Jacques Francois	Juive, La (The Jewess): Cavatina, vocal solo	93 94 97
	l'Eclaire: Overture	94
Haley, Will A.	American Beauty, The, march	97
Hall	My Clementina, piccolo solo	98
Hall, Henry A.	Plantation Chimes	*94 *95 *96
	Songs of the Navy (Songs and Dances of the Navy) (Our Navy) (Tunes for Sailors) (Life on the Ocean)	99 01 05 17 28
Hall, John T.	Wedding of the Winds, waltz	99 06 22-24
Hall, King	Cycle of Society Dances, A: Plantation Dance; Serpentine Dance; Barn Dance; Skirt Dance	17 22 24
Hall, Milt	Cotton Blossoms, idyll	97
Hall, Robert Browne	New Colonial, march	*11
Hallam	Ordway Rifles, The, march	97
Halle, R.L.	Anne Boleyn: Antique Dance	*99
	Killarney (Paraphrase on Balfe's Killarney)	15 17 21
Hallen, Johan Andreas	Swedish Rhapsody No. 2	96

360

Halton	Lark, The, vocal solo	95
Halvorsen, Johan	Triumphal Entry of the Boyards (Einzugsmarsch der Bojaren)	*10 *11 12-16 *17 18-24 29
Hamilton	Trojan League March	97
Hamm, John Valentine	Dialog for Four (The Four Gossips) (The Three Gossips), flute, clarinet, oboe	96 98 22 25
	Dream of Wagner, A	*00 01 04 08 24
	Echo from the Wagner Theatre at Bayreuth, An	93 94
	Musical Jokes (A Musical Joke) (A Musical Humoresque), potpourri	98 99 07
	Three Gossips (Drei Gespraech), fantasie flute, clarinet and oboe trio	94 *95 96-98 01 21
Hammerstein	Espagnol, march	96
	Shenandoah, march	96
Hammond, John C.	Tooty-Flooty, flute solo or band number	26
Handel, George Frederick	Arioso, violin or vocal solo	15 16
	Come and Trip It, vocal solo	96
	Harmonious Blacksmith	08 24
	Judas Maccabeus: See the Conquering Hero Comes, chorus	92 98
	Messiah: Feed His Flock (He Shall Feed His Flock)	29
	Messiah: Hallelujah Chorus	92-94 02 05-08 *11 24 26
	Peneroso: Sweet Bird, vocal solo	*03 04 05
	Reminiscences of Handel	94 96
	Rinaldo: Lascia Ch' io Pianga, paraphrase	95
	Xerxes: Largo, vocal solo, violin solo, or band number	93 94 *95 *96 97 *98 *00 01 06 07 *10 *11 12-15 17 29
Hanley, James Frederick	Just a Cottage Small [By a Waterfall], vocal or cornet solo	*26
	Little Log Cabin of Dreams, song	28
Hanser	Berceuse, cornet solo	93
Happiel	Pustenritt, xylophone solo	93
Harding	December and May, medley	94
Hariman	Irish Fantasia, An, euphonium solo	93
Harlow, Fred P.	Wanderer Polka, The, trombone solo	25
Harper	Keep Cool and Keep Coolidge	*24
Harrigan, Edward	Reilly and the 400	16
Harris	Cavalier, The, march	04
Harris, Sydney P.	Daddy's Lullaby	94
Harrison	Sambo, darkie song	96
Hartly	Valse Fantastic, trombone solo	20
Hartmann	On a German Song, euphonium solo	93
Hartmann, Emil	Souvenir des Alps (Alpensehnsucht), air varie	96
	Vikings, The (Nordische Heerfahrt), overture-tragique	03 04 *05 06 08-10 *11 13 19 20 27
Hartmann, John	Air and Variations (Air Brilliante), cornet solo	95 96 01 02
	America, fantasie, cornet solo	93
	Arbucklenian (Arbucklenian Polka), cornet solo	93 98 99 *01 04
	Banditti, caprice	93
	Belle Creole, La, caprice	93 94
	Berceuse, cornet solo	93
	Blue Bells of Scotland, cornet solo	93 95
	Caprice de Concert, cornet solo	93
	Carnival of Venice, cornet solo	04
	Collocation on Folk Songs of Germany	93
	Columbian Polka, cornet solo	02 26
	Defense of Rorke's Drift, The, battle scene, descriptive fantasia	92-94
	Du Du, euphonium solo	93 *94
	Facilita, euphonium or cornet solo	93 14 19
	Fantasia Original, cornet solo	94
	Favorite, The (Favorita, La), cornet solo	99 *00 01 *24 25 26
	German Air Varied, euphonium solo	93
	Gypsy's Warning, fantasia, euphonium or cornet solo	12
	Jaculita, euphonium solo	93
	Lizzie Polka, cornet solo	24

	Night in Berlin, A., potpourri	93 95
	Ocean View, cornet solo	01 18 20-22 *23 *24 25
	Polka Brilliant, cornet solo	14
	Robin Adair, cornet solo or cornet and trombone duet	98 05
	Russian Fantasia, cornet solo	93 94 01
	Somewhere in France, vocal solo	*18
	Weber's Last Waltz, variations, cornet solo	93
	Whirlwind Polka, cornet solo	93
Hasselmans	Valse Brillante, harp solo	20 21
Hast	Our Generals, march	26
Hastings	Red, Red, Rose, A, vocal solo	09
Hathaway, Jane	I'm a-Longin' fo' You, vocal solo	21
	It Was the Time of Lilac, vocal solo	*20
	Lilac Time, vocal solo	21 22
Hatton, John Liptrott	King Henry VIII (Koenig Heinrich VIII): Overture and Entr' Acte	*27
	Macbeth: Overture	93 *95 96 *97 99 04 09 12 15-18 20-22
Hauser, Miska	Cradle Song, violin solo	94
	Hungarian Rhapsody (Rapsodie Hongroisse) (Hungarian Dance), vocal, violin, or flute solo	*93 *95 *97 *98 04 *05 09 10 24
	Nocturne, violin solo	94
	Slumber Song, oboe solo	93 94
	Solitude, horn solo	01
Hawley, Annie Andros	Farrar "Gay Butterfly", The, waltz	08
Hawley, Charles Beach	Because I Love You Dear, vocal or trombone solo	96 10 *11 12
	Rose Fable, A, vocal solo	08
	Sweetest Flower That Blooms	15
	When Love Is Gone, vocal solo	96
Hayden, William	Shakespearian Characters: Caliban	27
Haydn, Franz Joseph	Austrian Hymn, air and variations on God Preserve the Emperor (Variations on the Austrian National Hymn)	94 96 *00 07 09 13 15
Haydn, Franz Joseph	Benedictus	94
	Creation, The: In Native Worth	94
	Gipsy Rondo (The Gypsies)	19 22 24-27
	Heavens are Telling, The	94
	Reminiscences of Haydn	93 94 96 24
	Serenade	94
	Symphony No. 94 (Surprise Symphony): Andante	*94 95 96 03 04 09 15 17 22 24
Haynes, Walter Battison	Off to Philadelphia in the Morning, euphonium solo	09
Hazel, John	Secret, Le polka, cornet solo	98 22 *23 *24
Head, Maurice L.	Sometime You'll Remember, vocal solo	19 21
Heath	Some Time You'll Remember, vocal solo	20
Heaton, Clayton	Big Six March, The	14
Hecker, Joseph	Always Jolly, galop	93
Hedges, F.R.	Romantic Fancies, idyll	11
Heed, John Clifford	At Sunrise, idyll, xylophone solo	*28
	Clipper, march	96
	Waltz Fantasia, cornet solo	21
Heinemann, Carl	Maryland, My Maryland, paraphrase	93-95
Helf, J. Fred	A Bit 'o Blarney (A Bit of Blarney)	04 05
Heller, M.	Sunset on the St. Lawrence, waltz	24
Heller, Stephen	Grand Tarantelle No. 2 in A-Flat	03 *04 05 08 13 22 24
Helmesberger, Josef	Entr'acte Valse	*09 *10 *11 28
Helmund, E.M.	Ich bin dein, vocal solo	94
Helmund, E.M.	Rococo, serenade	99 01 *03
Hemley, Alec	Little Miss Ragtime, selection on popular tunes	16 17 24 26 28
Henderson, Ray & B.G. De Sylva & Lew Brown	Birth of the Blues, The, vocal solo or band number	26
Heney, Edward J.	Good Night Ladies, saxophone solo	27
Henneberg, Paul	On Charming Themes, fantasia	23
	Sweet Old Songs, waltz	24

	Triplets of the Finest, cornet trio	26
Hennemann	Lark, The, vocal solo	95
Henning, Franz	Roses - Marechal Neil, intermezzo	01
Henri	Valse Brilliante, cornet solo	96
Henschel, George	Spring Song, vocal solo	02
Henton, H. Benne	Lanette Waltz Caprice, saxophone solo	20 25
	Laverne, saxophone solo	17 18 *19 *20 25 26
	Maritana: Scenes That Are Brightest, saxophone solo, based on melody by William Vincent Wallace	*19 *20 21 23 *24 25 26
	Nadine, saxophone solo	*19 *20
Herbert, Victor	Ah, Cupid, cornet solo	16
	Ameer, The: Selections	01
	American Fantasie (Grand American Fantasie)	98 *01 02-06 *11 26 31
	American Girl, The: Two-step (march)	96
	Babes in Toyland: March of the Toys	29
	Babes in Toyland: Selections	04
	Babes in Toyland: Slumber Song	03
	Babette: Selections	04
	Badinage, intermezzo	95 98 01 02 *03 04
	Cannibal Dance	03
	Cupid and I, vocal solo	99
	Erin, O Erin (Irish Rhapsody)	02 17 *25 26 27
	Fortune Teller, The: Gypsy Love Song (Slumber On, My Little Gypsy Sweetheart), vocal solo or xylophone solo/duet	15 *24 25 26
	Fortune Teller, The: Selections	99 01 02 04 31
	Idol's Eye: Selections	98 99 01 02 *24
	Mlle Modiste: Kiss Me Again, vocal or cornet solo	25 *26 27
	My Dream Girl, vocal solo	27
	Natoma: Selections	12 25-27 31
	Naughty Marietta: Ah! Sweet Mystery of Life, vocal solo	27 28 30
	Naughty Marietta: Italian Street Song, vocal solo	24 25 *26 *27 28 *29 *31
	Orange Blossoms: A Kiss in the Dark, vocal solo or band number	*23 24 26
	Pan Americana, characteristic	26 27 29
	Prince Ananias: Ah! Cupid, cornet solo	95 96 04 *05 15
	Prince Ananias: His Highness March	95
	Prince Ananias: Selections	96
	Princess Pat, The: Selections	31
	Punchinello	01 02
	Scherzo	96
	Serenade, The: I Love Thee, I Adore Thee	96
	Serenade, The: Selections	97-99 01 02 04 24-27
	Singing Girl: Selections	01 02 04
	Starlight, waltz	96 97
	Sweethearts: Selections	28 31
	There She Goes, polka	95
	Three Solitaires, The, cornet trio	99 01 14-17 19 21 25 29
	Wizard of the Nile, The: Selections	96-99 01 02 04 24-27
	Wizard of the Nile, The: Waltzes	96
	Yesterthoughts, song	01
Herfurth	Alpine Echoes (On the Alps) (Auf Den Allpen), fantasie (caprice), cornet duet	92-94 01 08 09 21-24
	Melodies, saxophone ensemble	27
Herley, Arthur	Once, vocal solo	94
Herman	Fiddler of St. Waast, The: Overture	23 24
Herman, Andrew	Bella Creole, La, caprice	93 94 96
	Cocoanut Dance, danse Africaine (African Cocoanut Dance)	92-95 *98
	Columbian Exposition, waltz	93
	Esmeralda Overture	23
Hermann	America: Overture	94
	Gems From The Red Hussar, Paul Jones and Poor Jonathan	93 94 24
	Magyar Fantasia	96
	Quartette for Four Cornets	93

Hernandes	Paloma Blanca, Mexican dance	93
Herold, Louis Joseph Ferdinand	Dame Blanche, La: Overture	95 96
	Duel, The: Aria [unnamed], vocal solo[s]	06-08
	Pre le Clercs, Le: Air [unnamed]	07
	Pre le Clercs, Le: Isabella's Air, vocal solo	93 *05 06 08
	Pre le Clercs, Le: Jours de Mon Enfance	94 05
	Pre le Clercs, Le: Overture	94
	Reminiscences of Herold	93 94
	White Lady, The: Overture	93 94
	Zampa: Finale	95
	Zampa: Overture	93 94 *95 96 *97 *98 *99 *00 01-10 *11 12-18 *19 *20 21-25 *26 27
Herster	What Berlin Hears, humoresque	94
Herve	Aladdin and His Wonderful Lamp: Selections	94
	Dilara, waltz	01
	Hit and Miss Galop	98
Herzeele, F. von	Belgian Patriotic Fantasie (Fantasie on Belgian Air)	95 96 20
	Grand Caprice Militaire (Grand Military Fantasie)	05 23
Heuberger, Richard	Opernball, Der (The Opera Ball): Polka-intermezzo	10
Heyser, Elwood K.	Vivandiere, La: Overture	96
Hierse, G.	Bridal Songs (Brautreigen), fantasie	96
Higgs, H.M.	Selection of Russian Folk-Songs (Songs and Dances of Russia)	15 19 24 27
Hildach, Eugen	Sparrows, The, vocal solo/duet	09
Hiller	Saul, soprano solo	*03
Hiller, F.	On the Watch	94
Hilliam, Bentley Collingwood	Freedom for All Forever	18
Hindley, Thomas W.	Patrol Comique	98
Hirsh, A.M./George L. Atwater	Yale Boola	01 08 15
Hirsuk	Melange of the Favorite Airs of Belgium	94
Hoby	Phyllis Is My Only Joy, ballad	93
Hoch, Theodor	Liebstraum, Der (Love Dreams), fantasie	95
	Pearl of the Ocean, cornet solo	98 03
	Remembrances of the Prague (Errinnerung auf Prague) (Souvenir de Prague), cornet solo	*98 99 02 03
	Souvenir de Mexico (On the Shores of the Gulf of Mexico), cornet solo	98 *02
	Valse Brillante, cornet solo	93
Hoffman	Fanfare Militaire	96
	Red Fez, The	94
	Scenes at the Fair, rustic pictures	04
Hoffman, A.W.	Banditti, salon stuck (air de ballet) (Spanish dance)	93 94
	Bianca, air de ballet	93
	Souvenir de Luyano	94
Hoffmann	Sweet Recollections	94 96
Hofmann, Heinrich Karl Johan	Kirmess, Rustic Pictures: Fantasie (Rustic Suite)	27
Hogben, Edward J.	Doozie, march	06
Holden, A., Jr.	Dame Margery, gavotte	97
Holleander, Victor	Girl from Maxim's, The (Die Herren von Maxim)	09
	Kadettenstreiche (Die Kadetten): Selections	10
Hollman	Fantasie Brillante, cornet solo	*00
Holmes	Berceuse, vocal solo	94
Holst	Secret, The, suite	25 26
Holst, Edouard	Columbian Fair, The, march	94
	Sequidilla, Spanish dance, characteristic	94-96
Holst, Gustave	Second Suite for Military Band, Op. 28: Dargason	24 26
Holstein, Franz von	Haideschacht, Der, (Die): Overture	04 05
Holzmann, Abraham	First Love Waltz	14
Homer	Dearest, vocal solo	15
Hooker, Brian & Porter Steele	Bone Dry, march	19
Hoschna, Karl	Love Dance, The: Every Little Movement, song	*11
	Madame Sherry: Selections	21

	Three Twins: Selections	08 09
Hosfeld, Samuel	Dance of the Pickaninnies	94
Hosmer, Lucius	Chinese Wedding Procession (A Chinese Wedding) (A Chinese Procession), band number or saxophone ensemble	12-14 16 22 *24 *25 *30
	Ethiopian Rhapsody	*24 25 *26 27 28 31
	L'Equestrienne Galop (Scene de Cirque)	13
	Northern Rhapsody	*20 21-23 *24 *25 26 27
	On Tiptoe, scene de ballet	95 02 14-16
	Patrouille Francaise (French Patrol), patrol	26
	Pierrot, La, caprice	13
	Songs of Uncle Sam (Songs Americans Love) (Songs and Dances of Uncle Sam) (Songs Our Soldiers Love) (American Folk Songs), fantasie	13 15-19 24 28
	Southern Rhapsody (In the South)	16 *17 *18 *19 *20 21 24-29
	War Songs of the Boys in Blue, patriotic overture	21
Housely	Mine Always, vocal solo	96
Howard	Concerto, euphonium solo	28
Howard, Joseph Edgar	Montana, state song	21
Howard, Meredith	With the Colors, march	99
Howe	Street Piano, The, humoresque (caprice)	98
Howe, Charles T.	Rustic Scenes: A Forest Idylle and Country Dance	96
Howe, Emma	Marlborough Waltz	96
Howe, Julie Ward [words]	Battle Hymn of the Republic [to tune of John Brown's Body]	99 21 24
Howgill, John Stephan	Morceau Elegant, clarinet & flute duet	13 22
Howson, Frank Alfred	Alpine Roses, mountain idyll	97 99
Hubay, Jeno	Carmen Fantasie, violin solo	02 05 08 09 16 17 *21 22
	Hejree Kati: Scenes de la Czarda (Czardas), violin solo	02 05 08 09 16-20
	Hungarian Dances, violin solo	07 09
	Violin Maker of Cremona, The (Geigenmacher von Cremona), fantasie	98 24
	Zephyr, The, violin solo	*11 12
Hubbell, Raymond	Fantana: Selections	06
	Ladder of Roses, The, two-step	16
Hubbell, Raymond & John L. Golden	Poor Butterfly, vocal solo	*17
Hue, Georges-Adolphe	Fantasia Original, flute solo	25 26
	Serenade, flute solo	25 26
Huhn, Bruno	Invictus, vocal solo	17
Hull	Fantasia on Naval Songs	15
Hummel	Mein Liebchen, Am See, flugelhorn solo	96
Hummel, J.E.	Aschanti Tanz (Ashantee War Dance)	98
Humperdinck, Engelbert	Before the Witch's House, vocal duet	09
	Hansel and Gretel: Fantasia and Angel's Pantomime	95
	Hansel and Gretel: Prelude (Vorspiel) (Overture) (Prelude)	*95 *96 *97 99 02 05 07-09 12 22 23
	Hansel and Gretel: Selections	95 96 04 23 25-27
	Hansel and Gretel: Wie Duftet's von Dorton, vocal duet	*09
	King's Children (Konigskinder): Selections	15 24-26
	Miracle, The (Das Wunder): Suite	13 24 31
	Wonder, The, pantomime	14
Huss, Henry Holden	Festival March (Grand Festival March)	98
Hussey & Gordon	There's a Kiss in This Letter for You, vocal solo	95
Hutchings, F.E.	New Cycle Path March, The	96
Ilgenfritz, B. McNair	Mozelle, La, waltz	94 96
Inman	Down on the Old Plantation, fantasie	95
Innes, Frederick Neil	Sea Shell Waltz, cornet solo	25
Ippolitov Ivanov, Mikhail	Caucasian Sketches: Cortege du Sirdar	14 31
	Caucasian Sketches: Suite	14
	Russian Lullaby, vocal solo	27
Isenman, Emil	Collection of American Songs and Dances, A	96
	Sounds from the Sunny South (Songs of the Sunny Southland)	94-97 01

Ivanovici, Josif	Carmen Sylva, waltz	05
	Waves of the Danube, waltz	93
Jackson	Nightingale and Rose, vocal solo	17
Jacobi	Deep in Your Eyes, vocal solo	21
	Tzigane, The: Ballet Suite	02
Jacobi, Georges	Zerlina, cornet solo	*94
Jacobi, Viktor	Apple Blossoms: Selections	24 27
	Apple Blossoms: You Are Free, vocal solo	21 23
	Marriage Market, The: Selections	14 16 19 24
	On Miami Shore, vocal solo or band number	20-24
	Our Army and Navy (Britain's Army and Navy), ballet suite, fantasie (grand ballet divertissement)	16 17 24
	Sybil: Selections	16 17
Jacobowsky, Eduard	Erminie: Selections	93 94 96
Jaffe, Moe	Collegiate, fox trot	*26
James, William G.	Happy Moments: Entr'acte	19
Jansen, Adolf	Ragamuffin Blues	24
	Somebody's Garden, vocal solo	25
Jarnefelt, Armas	Praeludium	*11 *12 13 14 16 21 22 24 27
Jaxone, H.L. d'Arcy	Bal des Enfants (The Enfant's Ball): Morceau (caprice) (album leaf) (intermezzo)	*92 93 94 96 *00 20
	Bicycle Ride, descriptive sketch	93 94
	Chinese Lanterns, waltz	93-95
	Clear the Course Galop	94
	My Memories Waltz, based on Francesco Paolo Tosti's music	93 24
	Serenata, La, Italian waltz	92-95
Jefferson, W.A.	National Diamond Jubilee, The (The Peace Jubilee), march	98
Jensen	Danish, suite	18
	Serenade Burlesque	21
Jensen, Adolf	In the Tavern, Op. 17	19
Jerome	Oh Willie, I Want to Go to Philly, song	26
Jessell, Leon	In the Toy Store (Im Spielwarenladen), characteristic	22
	Parade of the Tin Soldiers, The, characteristic	*12 13-15 18
	Parade of the Wooden Soldiers, xylophone solo or band number	*22 *23 *24 *25 *26 27 29
	Wedding of the Rose, The (Der Rose Hochzeitszug), intermezzo	14 24 26 27 29 30
Joachim, Joseph	Hungarian Dance, violin solo	08
John, Peyton	I Love and the World Is Mine, vocal solo	*97
Johnson	Happy Days in Dixie	*97
	Ragtime Baby, song	*99
Johnson & Bibo	Am I Wasting My Time on You, song	26
Johnson, Lee	Ma Angeline (My Baby Angeline), two -step (darkey caprice)	96 *97
	Romona March	*05
Jolson, Al	Old Fashioned Girl	22
	I'll Say She Does	19
Jomaux	Caprice Militaire	07
Jones	Girl from Paris: Selections	98
Jones, J. Sidney	Artist's Model, An: Selections	96 06
	Gaiety Girl, A, Op. 310: Selections	94-96 24 26
	Geisha, The: Selections	97 98 02 27
	Greek Slave, A: Selections	27
	King of Cambodia (King of Cadonia): Selections	09 24
	My Lady Molly: Selections	06 24
	San Toy: Rhoda's Pagoda	01
	San Toy: Selections	01 02 04 25 26
	San Toy: Soger Man	01
Jones, J. Sidney & Paul Rubens	Girl from Utah, The: Selections	15 24
Jones, Paul	Red Hussar, The: Selections	93
Jones, Stephen	What Do You Do Sunday, Mary?, fox trot	*24
Jones, William Grant	Izetta, polka	94
Jonson, Ben	Drink to Me Only With Thine Eyes, vocal or cornet solo or horn quartet	14 22 26

Jordan	World Can't Go Round Without You, The, vocal solo	21
Jordan, Julian	Song That Reached My Heart, The, vocal or cornet solo	93 11 12
Joyce	Pryne, waltz	20
Joyce, Archibald E.	Dreaming, waltz	14
	I'll (We'll) Dance Till the Sun Breaks Through, serenade, two-step	25-27
	Songe d'Automne	10
	Spanish Love Song	*95
	Vision d'Amour (Vision of Love), waltz	15 22
	Vision of Salome, Oriental waltz	10 *11
	When the Birds Began to Sing, waltz humoresque	15 18 20-25 31
Jude	Deep in the Mine (The Mighty Deep), vocal or tuba solo	94 22 23
Judson, Ben F.	Iran, Persian intermezzo	04
Juel-Frederiksen, Emil	Scandinavian Suite (Skandinavische Suite)	27
Jullien	Jordan Is a Hard Road to Travel	93
Jullien, Louis Antoine	Drum Polka, The (The Drummers), caprice	96
	Echoes of Mont Blanc, rondo	94 96
	Katy Did, polka	98 99
	Original Napolitaine, The (Neapolitaine), tarantelle des salons	08 10 *11 18
	Sleigh Ride, The	93 94 98
	Tarantelle de Belphegor	12 14
June, C.	In Cuba, Spanish waltz ballad, vocal solo	09
Jungman, Albert	Espanol, morceau	94
	Moonlight Fantasia, A	94
Justice, Herbert M.	Red Domino, The: Selections	02
Kahn, Gus & Walter Donaldson	Beside a Babbling Brook, fox trot	23
	My Buddy, fox trot	23
Kalman, Emmerich	Little Dutch Girl, A: Selections	21 22 27 28
	Queen of the Movies, The: Scenes	14 15
	Sari: Selections	14 16
	Sari: Waltz	15
	Throw Me a Rose, medley	*17
Kammermeyer, Ed [Burlington, IA]	untitled march	*98
Kantromy	Fantasie Caprice	96
Kantrowitz, N.	Mazurka Augustova	96
	Narsavia, polonaise	96
	Spring of Life, song	96
Kappey, Jacob A.	Bid Me Discourse and other themes	24 27
	Diamond Jubilee, The, patriotic fantasia (overture)	18
	Episodes in a [British] Soldier's Life, fantasia	18 27
	Excerpts from songs	24
	Fantasia on Favorite Songs of Sullivan	94
	Fantasia on National Songs of Germany	95
	Fantasia on Popular English Ballads	95 96 19
	Flying Squadron, fantasia on nautical melodies	96-98 02 19 21
	French Melodies, fantasia (Fantasie on French Melodies) (Collection of French Melodies)	96
	Hiberian Bouquet, fantasie on Irish melodies	93-95
	Last Rose of Summer, Fantasie	93-96
	Little Drummer, The, caprice	93
	Minstrel Boy, The, fantasie	24
	Potpourri of National Dances (Dance of the Nations)	96
	Reminiscences from the Grand Operas (Gems from the Operas) (Favorites Melodies from Grand Opera) (Scenes from Favorite Operas)	*00 16 17 24-27
	Rule Britannia, fantasie	95 25
	Songs and Dances of Northern Europe	92
	Terpsichoreana, potpourri (fantasia on natural dances)	96 25 26 28
	With Tommy Atkins on the Western Front, fantasie	17
	Ye Banks and Bonnie Doon (Ye Banks and Braes of Bonny Doon)	96
Kapps	Life of a Sailor, The	98
	May Day in Manila Bay	98
Kappui	Fantasie on Themes from Old Italian Operas	02
Karger, Alfred	In Cupid's Arms, waltz	*97 98

	Love's Awakening (Der Liebe Erewachen), waltz	95 96
Karren, L'eon	Enthusiastic Rhapsody (Rapsodie Enthousiaste) (Rhapsodie Enthousiasto), Italian rhapsody	97 98
Katscher, Robert	When Day Is Done, vocal solo	27
Katz	Eile-Eile, chant	21
Kaufman, Mel B. & Harry D. Kerr	Me-ow, vocal solo	19
Kebys[?]	Answer, vocal solo	93
Keler-Bela, Adabert	Consecration of the Temple (Tempelweihe Fest) (Dedication of the Temple) (The Coronation): Overture	95 98 09 17
	Csokonay, Hungarian overture	21 22
	Hungarian Comedy Overture	06 16 23 25
	Hungarian Idyll, violin solo	*97
	Hungarian Lustspiel: Overture	93
	Imperial Festival Overture	03
	Infernal, galop	93 94 96
	Kroll's Ballroom Sounds, waltz	12
	Mountaineer's Joy, The, Syrian dance	97
	On the Beautiful Rhine (On the Rhine) (Am Schoenen Rhein Gedenk' Ich Dein!), Op. 83, waltz	07 10 22 24 25
	Overture to a French Comedy	94-96
	Overture to a Hungarian Comedy	94 96 05
	Rokoczy (Rakodzky) Overture, Op. 76	26
	Romantic Drama (Romantique): Overture (Overture to a Dramatic Drama)	93 26
	Roumanian Festival: overture	23 24 27
	Storm, The	94
	Tempelweihe Fest (Consecration of the Temple): Overture	96
Kell, Nelson T.	Drill of the White Zuhrahs, march	96
Kellar	Angel of Peace, patriotic air	92
Kelley, Edgar Stillman	Phases of Love: The Lady Picking Mulberries, Chinese episode	96 22 23 26
Kellie, Lawrence	Collection of the Most Admired Songs of Lawrence Kellie (Modern Scotch Songs of Lawrence Kellie) (Recollections of Lawrence Kellie) (A Batch of Modern English Songs) (Songs of Lawrence Kellie)	93
Kellogg	Uncle Dudley, characteristic	08
Kelly, W.A.	Only a Dream of That Beautiful City	03
Kenecke, Emil	Air and Variations, cornet solo	99
Kennedy, Harry	Molly and I and the Baby	93 97 *05
	Say Au Revoir But Not Good Bye, vocal or trombone solo	94 95 *96 *97
Kenton, Maurice	Dance Irresistible, The, march and two-step	98
Kepler	Scorcher, A, caprice	95
Keppel, Keith	Robin Adair, vocal solo	*11
Kerker, Gustave	Belle of New York, The: Selections	98 99 *00 01 02 04 07 21 27
	Coquette, La, vocal solo	94
	Little Christopher: Selections	96
	Sad Regrets, vocal solo	94
	Telephone Girl: Selections	98 99 01 02
Kern, Jerome David	Ka-Lu-A, xylophone solo	*22
	Linger Awhile	24
	Oh, Boy!: Selections	18
	Sally: Selections	22-27
	Show Boat: Selections	28
	Sunny: Who, fox trot	26
Kerulf	Last Night, vocal solo	96
Kessels	Eola, Roumanian waltz	01
Kessels, Jos.	Maid of Orleans (Jungfrau von Orleans): Overture	98 16
Ketelbey, Adelbert W.	Tangled Tunes, potpourri	20
Ketten, Henry	Castagnette, La, caprice Espagnol	04 *05 07 09 *11 15 24
Ketterer, Louis F.	Hongroise, caprice (Caprice Hongroise) (Grand Pas Hongrois)	96-98 *00 01 02 08 24
Keyser, Annette	March of Freedom	24
Kiefer, William H.	Hearts and Heroes, march	24

Kienzl, Wilhelm	Evangelimann, Der (The Evangelist): Prelude and Scenes (Fantasie) (Potpourri)	97 98 *00 16 23
King, Robert A.	Beyond the Gates of Paradise, trombone solo	01 02
	Sesame, Arabian intermezzo	02
Kistler, Cyrill A.	Kunihild: Prelude to Act III (Vorspiel) (Overture)	*95 96
Klein	On the Mississippi, saxophone ensemble	*25 *26
Klein, Manuel	Auto Race: Starlight Maid, descriptive, vocal solo	08
Klemm, Gustav	Indian Lullaby	24
Klickman, Frank Henry	Knock-Out Drops	*13
Kling, Henri Adrien Louis	Ariadne: Overture (Preluade) (Military Overture)	05 16 17 19 22
	Ariadne: Selections	15
	Aus Adams Zeiten, fantasia on works of A.C. Adam (Adam's Melodies)	23
	Birds in Flight (Les Oiseaux de Passage), piccolo solo/duet	*99
	Congress of Soloists	95
	Cornetist, the Trombonist, and the Stone-Breakers, The, cornet and trombone duet (humoresque)	*92 93
	Echo des Bastions, caprice (idyll)	*98 *99 *01 04 09 10 14 15 21 22
	Echo in (im) Walde (Echo in the Forest), fantasie	98
	Fauvette et Sansonnet, concert polka for flute or piccolo	*99 02
	Flutiste, La: Overture	96-99 15 20 21 24
	Goldbeetle's Soiree, The: Gavotte of the June Bugs (The Junebug's Soiree)	*97
	Goldbeetle's Soiree, The: Humorous Fantasie	96
	Goldbeetle's Soiree, The: Race of the Race Horses	97
	Goldbeetle's Soiree, The: Waltz of the Crickets	97
	Golden Robin, The, piccolo solo	07
	King's Lieutenant, The (The Drummer of the Guard): Overture	n.d.
	Kiss Me, polka caprice	94
	Kriegerfest: Overture	99
	Life Is a Dream: Overture	19
	Merry Musicians' Tricks (Lustige Musikantenstreiche), humorous fantasia	05
	Nightingale and Blackbird, piccolo duet	98
	Road of Glory (The Road to Glory) (Le Chemin de la Gloire): Overture	97 98 02
	Robin and Wren, polka (caprice), piccolo duet	96 *97 98 99 01 02 10
	Shepherd's Life in the Alps (Life in the Alps), pastoral fantasie (descriptive idyll)	*95 96 *97 98 *00 01 02 06 08 13 14 20 22
	Stone Breakers and Lottie Collins, The, humoresque	93
	Straight Across Africa, panorama	05
	Tambour, polka, drum solo	98
	Travers des Muages: Overture	*00
	Under the Red Cross, fantasie	05
	Warrior's Festival, The (Warrior Fete): Overture	*99 02 04 05 15 16 22 24-26
Klohr, John Nicholas	Medley of Gospel Hymns (Collection of Gospel Hymns)	20 22
Klose, Hyacinthe	Air Varie, clarinet solo or band number	14 19
	Concerto for the Clarinet Choir	21-23 27 28
Kluegel, Julius	Tarantelle, cello solo	15
Kneass	Sweet Alice Ben Bolt, paraphrase (Don't You Remember Sweet Alice), vocal or cornet solo	*95 *96 *97 *07
Knezdo	Witch's Dance, violin solo	*20 *22
Knight, Joseph Philip	Rocked in the Cradle of the Deep, trombone solo	92 93 95 98 24
Knight, Launce	Crimson and Blue Waltz	08
Knoll, Anton H., Jr.	A.H. Knoll's Eccentricities	24
	Monarch Polka, cornet or trombone solo	26
	Sweet Essence of Melody	24
Koelling, Karl W.P.	Lion's Chase, The (The Chase of the Lion) (Grand Galop de Concert), galop (descriptive)	93-95 *02 *03 04-06 08 10 *11 12-15 17 19 21-24 26 27
Koenig, Hermann Louis	Post Horn (Postillion), galop	92 05 09
Koenivan	At Frensberg	19
Koennemann, Miroslav	Fremersberg, Le, grand pastorale and hunting fantasia (Hunting Fantasia)	05 15-17 21-23 *24 28 *30

369

Kohlau	Quartette for Clarinets	94
Kolling	Gypsy Life, fantasia	24
Kollo, Walter	Berlin Dances (Berlin Tanzt) (When Berlin Dances), waltz potpourri	09
Komzak	Love of Life, waltz	26
	Potpourri (Medley of Waltz Themes)	21 25 26
Komzak, Karl II	Baratavia, march	93
	Geistreich und Sinnig, fantasia	15
	Girls of Baden (Baden Girls) (Bad'ner Madl'n Waltz)	15-17 22-27
	In Military Style, caprice	95
	In the Land of the Waltz, fantasie	05
	Life of Love Is But a Day, The	94
	Love and Life in Vienna (L'Amour et la Vie a Vienne) (Vienna Life), waltz	20 22-27
	New Life, waltz	96
	Pikante Blatter: Potpourri (Fantasie)	04 15
	Vienna Life (Wiener Leben) (Life in Vienna) (Love and Life in Vienna)	94 99 *03 07
	Wasser Gigerl, caprice	93 94
	Wiener Chic - Wiener Schau, march	93
Koppitz, Charles	Golden Robin, piccolo duet	09 10
	Innesfallen, medley overture on Irish airs (Irish Recollections) (Grand Fantasie of Irish Melodies)	94 95 98
Korchke, Fred	Surf, The, march & two-step	96
Koschat, Thomas	Forsaken Am I (Verlassen Bin Ich), cornet or trombone solo	95
	Forsaken Am I (Verlassen Bin Ich), horn quartet [unaccompanied?]	95 98
Kotlar, Istvan	Monte Christo, waltz (idyll)	*00 01
Kottaun, Celian	Dance of the Lilliputians	93 94
	Princess May, court dance (intermezzo) (gavotte)	93-95
Kountz, Richard	Dawn Brought Me Love and You, The, vocal solo	29
Kraeger, Carl	Gypsies' Moonlight Dance	94
Kral, Johann Nepomuk	Pst! Herr Maier	94
	Von Pickauf, caprice	08
Kreisler, Fritz	Apple Blossoms: Selections	20 24 27 28 30
	Caprice Viennois (Cradle Song 1915), violin or vocal solo	13-16 26 27
	Liebesfreud, violin or xylophone solo	12 *13 *14 15 17 *24 *26 27 28 *30
	Liebeslied, violin solo	12
	Old Refrain, vocal solo	24
	Schon Rosmarin (The Beautiful Rosemarin), violin, clarinet, saxophone, or xylophone solo	*12 20 26 27
	Tambourin Chinois, violin solo	16 17
Kretschmer, William F.	American Festival, Op. 217, overture	15 24
	Intermezzo Americaine	98
Kreutzer, Konradin	Chapel, The (Die Kapelle), cornet quartet or horn quartet [unaccompanied?]	93 98
	Forest, The	94
	Night in Granada, A: Overture	94 96
Kroeger	Lalla Roock: Suite	14
Kroeger, Ernest Richard	American Character Sketches, suite: The Gamin; An Indian Lament; Voodoo Night Scene; The Dancing Darky; Mountain Dance	*04 05-07 14 15 27
	Pioneers, The, march	14 15
Kryl, Bohuhim	Josephine Waltz, cornet solo	26
	King Carneval, cornet solo	14 26 27
Kuchen, Frederick Wilhelm	Flight of the Swiss, The (Die Flucht Nach der Schweiz): Overture	96 01
	Crocodile on the Nile (Krokodile am Nil): Scene and Dance	*97 98 01 02
Kuehne, J.F	Dedication, vocal solo	12
	Silhouettes, Les, vocal solo	12
Kuhner, Basil	Songs and Dances of Northern Europe	93 94
Kullak, F.	Flottenschau, Die, fantasie (tone poem)	97 98
Kunkel, Charles	Alpine Storm (An Alpine Scene), idyll	92 93 *94 95 96 04-06 09 17 22
	Fo' de Wa' (Before the War), African fantasia	94 *95 96 06
	Harlequin's Pranks, caprice grotesque	*00
	Old Cloister Clock, The, descriptive	*10 *11 12 13 15 17 18 20-22 24 26

370

	Prince Pu Lun: Triumphal March	04
	Southern Jollification (The Cotton Pickers)	*01 02 04 08 25 26
	Water Sprites, caprice (polka)	*95 *96 *97 98 99 *00 01 02 *03 04 27
Kupler	All Hail! Deutscher Radfahrer (The Cyclists), galop	94
Kurscheedt, E.B.	Cyclists, march	93 94
Kussner, Albert	Moon Moths, three melodies	20
Kutschke	Burletta	02
La Dongon	Rondo, piccolo solo	19
La Jarte	Nanine, clarinet duet	01
LaBarre, Eugene	Air Original, cornet solo	19
	Gerna, cornet solo	19
	Illinois, cornet solo	19
	Raymond, cornet solo	19
Labitzky, Joseph	Remembrances of Dublin (Dublin Waltzes)	94
Lacalle, Joseph M.	Divertissement Espagnole	93
	Peace Forever March	99
Lachmund, Carl V.	Hero, The, march	04
	Japanese Overture	96
Lachner, Franz	Catharina Cornaro: Overture	96
	Four Ages of Man, The: overture	*15
Lacombe d'Estaleux, Paul Jean Jacques	Africaine (Africana): Suite	13 24
	Beneath the Balcony (Sous le Balcon), Op. 62, serenade	95
	Fair, The: At the Window	*07
	Fair, The: Suite	17
	Farandole, La: Ballet Suite	94 02 *07
	Feria, La (La Farandole) (At the Fair) (At a Spanish Fair): Spanish Suite (Ballet Suite)	08 *11 12 14 18 19 21-24 31
	Gitanilla, suite	93
	Mascarade: Ballet Suite (Scenes at a Masquerade)	*94 20 22 23 26
	Merry Musicians	19
	Night Before Xmas in Spain, The: Suite	15
	Night in Spain, A.	*13 14 15
	Pantomime (Pantomimic), suite de ballet	14 15 18 20-24 27
	Promenade Matinale, caprice	09
	Scenes at a Masquerade (The Masqueraders) (At the Masquerade) (All in Mask): Revelry of the Maskers, suite	*94 95 96 09 10 *11 13 14-18
	Soldier's Life, A: Overture	98
	Spring Morning Serenade (Aubade Printaniere) (Serenade Aubade), song	93 04 10 13-23 28
	Verbena, La, Spanish suite (intermezzo)	93 04 10 13-23
Lake, Mayhew Lester	Easter Chimes	21
	Evolution of Dixie, The, fantasie	16-18 27
	Fighting Allies, The, fantasie	*18
	In a Bird Store, descriptive	20
	Old Time, Reels and Jigs	21
	Old Timers (Old Favorites) (Songs of the Old Folks), waltz	19-24 26-28 30
	Parade of the Gendarmes, march	*28 29 *30
	Ragging "Lucia"	15
	Ragging "Lucia"	15
	Siffleur Coquet, Le Flirting Whistler, The (Le Siffleur Coquet)	16
	Songs and Dances of Hawaii (Gems from Hawaii)	17
	Victor Herbert Favorites	*28
Lalo, Edouard	Adagio, violin solo	15
	Norwegian Rhapsody (Rapsodie Norvegienne)	*97 02 10
	Roi d'Ys, Le: Overture	96 09 18 20
	Symphonie Espagnole, violin solo	13
Lamare, Edwin H. & Ben Black & Neil Moret	Moonlight and Roses, saxophone ensemble	26
Lamb	My Mary Green, cornet solo	92
Lambert	The Night Has a Thousand Eyes, vocal solo	14
Lambert, Frank	She Is Far from the Land, cornet solo or band number	22
Lamothe, Georges	Breezes of the Night, waltz	94

	Danse des Aborigines	93
	First Kiss, The, waltz	20
	Toujours et Encore, waltz	20-23
Lampe, James Bodewalt	Creole Belles, ragtime march	01
	Home Sweet Home Around the World, paraphrase	18
	Home Sweet Home the World Over, fantasie	12 13 17 18 24
	On the Way to Dublin (I'm On My Way to Dublin), humoresque	15
	Songs of Scotland (Famous Songs of Scotland), fantasie	13 14 31
	Uncle Sam, fantasia	13
Lane, Gerald	Unseen Kingdom, The, vocal solo	96
Lang, Margaret Ruthven	Irish Love Song, vocal solo	08
	Mavourneen, vocal solo	17
Lange, Gustave	Maid (Maiden) from the Highlands, The (In the Highlands), idyll (caprice)	93-96
	Pure as Snow, idyll	95
	Traum-Gluck, salon stuck	93
Langey, Carl Otto	Arabian Serenade	94
	Bella Mexicana, La, idyll (serenade)	01
	Canzonette	97
	Evening Breeze[s], idyll	07
	Felice, canzonetta	97
	Lolita, Spanish serenade	94 95 *96
	Musical Scenes from Spain, fantasie	13 27
	Musical Scenes from Switzerland, fantasie	93 96
	Our Babies, caprice	94
	Persian March (Persian Infantry on Parade)	20
	Schumann Suite (Robert Schumann)	09
	Uncle Tom: Overture	*21 22 24
Langlotz	Old Nassau [based on Auld Lang Syne]	29
Lanner, Joseph	Gems from the Works of Lanner	03 08
	Hofballtaenze, waltz	07
	Pesther, waltz	99 *00 *01 02 04 24-26
Lansing	Minstrel Echoes	93
Lansing, George L.	Pride of the South Patrol	01
Lappe, W. de Forest	On the Turf at Saratoga, march and two-step	04
Lassen, Eduard	Ach Wie Ist's Moglich Dann: Overture	01
	All Soul's Day, song	99 *00 01-03 05 18
	Fest (Festival) (Thuringia) (Thuringian Festival) (Thuringian Fete) (German Festival) (How Can I Leave Thee) (Festival): Overture	*95 *96 *97 98 99 01-05 10 *11 12 14-16 17 19-25 27
	Love Above Magic (Ueber allen Zauber Liebe): Ballet Suite	*98 02
Latann, Karl	Kladderadatsch, Der	94 96
Laurence	Salome	01
Laurendeau, Louis Philippe	Belle France, La, overture on popular French melodies	21
	Carillon, marche patriotique Canadienne-Francaise	21
	Ethiopian Carnival, Selection of Popular Melodies	95
	Laurentian Echoes, French Canadian melodies (Canadian Songs and Dances)	22
	Memories of the War 1861-1863, medley of American war songs (Melange of American War Songs) (War Songs of the Boys in Blue)	10 24
	Negro Songs and Dances	01
	Reveille, The, military sketch	01
	Spanish Review, The	93
	Way Down South (Down South), descriptive fantasie	*03
	Whistler's Serenade, The	*10
Lavallee, Calixa	Bridal Rose, The: Overture	93
	Indian Question: Scenes	94
	T.I.Q.: Selections	96
Lawler, Kate	Mansfield Post, march	94
Lax, Fred	Come Back to Erin (Bonnie Scotland), flute solo	94 95 98 23
Lazarus, H.	Air Varied, clarinet solo	93
	Fantasia on Italian Air, clarinet solo	93
	Scotch Fantasie, clarinet or flute solo	93 18
Le Grand	Air Popmeuse, cornet quartet [unaccompanied?]	93

Le Martaine	Meditations Poetiques	05
Le Thiere, Charles	Alsachiens, Les, clarinet solo	93
	Dance of the Aborigines, characteristic piece	93 94 96
	Gipsy Life, idyll (descriptive fantasie), saxophone solo or band number	92 93 96 21
	Life in an Irish Village, fantasie	98
	Little Sweetheart, piccolo solo	12
	Midnight Round of the Guards, A	94-96
	Mountain Life [Sunrise; The Muleteers; The Storm; The Mountaineers' Dance], fantasie	03 *04 05 22
	Oiseau du Bois, Le, piccolo solo	25 26
	Roman Life (Life in Rome) (Roman Days), descriptive fantasie	18 19 21-23
	Scenes at a Fandango	92
	Sylvia Scherzo, piccolo solo	25 27
	Vie Boheme, La	*11
	Village Life in the Alps (Shepherd's Life in the Alps), suite	95 19
	Village Life in the Olden Times, fantasie	94-97 02 06 08 09 17 20-22 30
Leavitt	Columbus, symphonic poem	*00 01
Lebory	Retour de Printemps, Le	93
Lecail, Clovis	Gypsy Airs, divertissement	93
	Helvetia (A Dream of Helvetia), overture dramatique	06 18
Lecalle	Hurrah Boys, march	01
Leclair, Jean Marie	Lento, violin solo	*03
	Third Sonata: Sarabande et Tambourin, violin solo	08
Lecocq, Alexandre Charles, Charles	Girofle-Girofla: Overture (Scenes)	05 16 22 27
	Grand Casimir, Le: Scenes	94
	Kasiki: Selections	93
	Little Duke, The: Selections	98
	Madame Angot (Le Fille de Mme. Angot): Selections	94 95 96
	Manola, Grand Selection	95
	Nuptial March of a Doll, The	94
	Petite Mademoiselle, La: Selections	94 96
	Scarlet Feather, The: Overture	18 19
	Scarlet Feather, The: Selections	98 99 02 07 16 17 20 21 23
Lederhaus	Troop A, march	94
Lee	One Fleeting Hour, cornet solo	24 25
Lee, Dorothy	I Love You More, vocal solo	21
	In the Heart of the Hills, vocal or cornet solo	26
	My Dreams, vocal solo	21 22
Lefebre-Wely, Louis James Alfred	Laughing, schottische	95
	Monastery Bells (Klosterglocken) (Les Cloches du Monastere), nocturne (idyll)	93-96 98 01-07 10 14 17
	Retraite Militaire, La (Military Tattoo), fanfare	93 24
Lehar, Franz	Alone at Last: Overture	16 27
	Count of Luxembourg, The: Selections	12 15
	Elfentanz (Fairy Dance), waltz	01 09 10
	Gipsy Love: Selections	13
	Gold and Silver (Gold und Silber), waltz	23-26
	Kakusha, dance	22 *23 *24 27
	Kukuska, (A La Cossack) Russian peasant dance	09 10 *11 12 21 23
	Man with Three Wives, waltz	08
	Merry Widow, The (The Jolly Widow): Selections	*07 *08 09 22-25 27
	Merry Widow, The: Waltz	*08 26
	Vienna Women, waltz	07
Lehmann, Elizabeth Nina Mary Frederika	Daisy Chain: If No One Ever Marries Me, vocal solo	10
	In a Persian Garden, suite	02 14 17
	More Daisies: Cuckoo Song, The, vocal solo	10
	Once Upon a Time: Princess May Blossom, waltz	*03 *04 05 20
	Princess Mayblossom, idyll	14
	There Are Fairies at the Bottom of Our Garden (Fairies in Our Garden), vocal solo	20

	You and I, cradle song, vocal solo	*23 24-27
Lemaire, A.	Havaz-Irani, Persian chant	98
Lenz, Max von	In the Viking's Domain (Song of the Vikings), Scandanavian fantasie	06
Lenzberg, Julius	Hungarian Rag, fox trot	21 22
Leonard	Souvenir de Haydn, violin solo	*98 *99 08 23
Leonart	Eva, march	95
Leoncavallo, Ruggerio	Arlachino, cornet solo	21
	Lesciati Amari: Come, Love Divine, vocal solo	15
	Medici, Die: Selections	94-96
	Pagliacci: Aria [unnamed], vocal solo[s]	17
	Pagliacci: Bell Chorus	95 *96 *97 98
	Pagliacci: Bird Song (Ballantell)	95 *99
	Pagliacci: Intermezzo	93 94
	Pagliacci: Prologue (Prelude), vocal or euphonium solo or band number	93-96 *97 05 15 16 18 19 22
	Pagliacci: Romance, vocal solo	18
	Pagliacci: Selections	94-99 *00 *01 02 04-10 14-25 26 28
	Pagliacci: Serenade	94 15
	Zaza: Fantasie	06
Leoni, Franco & Paul Laurence Dunbar	Birth of Morn, The, vocal solo	15
Lepinski	Concerto Militaire, violin solo	94
Leps, Wassili	America Forever, march	23
	Willow Grove, march	22
Lerman	Southern Jamboree, characteristic dance	99
Leroux, F.	Grand Pot Pourrie (based on motifs of grand masters)	93 94
	Under the Tent (Sous la Tente), fantasia (episode)	93 94 96
Leslie	Lullaby of Life	03
Lester, Eddie	Cherry Blossom, caprice	02
Letters, Will	Has Anybody Here Seen Kelly?	*10 *11
Leutner, Albert	Fest Overture (Festival Overture) (German Festival) (Grand Festival), Op. 42	96 *97 98 *00 04 06 07 *11 15 21-23 27 28 *29
Levett, David M.	Harlequinade, Op. 28, characteristic	96 *00
Levey	Scarlet Letter, The	25 26
Levey, William Charles	Matrimonee, waltz	94
	Showers of Rice	94
Levi	Soul Kiss, The: Selections	08
Levy, Jules	Grand Russian Fantasia (Russian Fantasia) (Souvenir de Moscow) (Russian Airs), cornet solo	99 21-28 31
	Whirlwind Polka, cornet solo	04 05 20-26
	Young American Polka, cornet solo	93 01
Lexhoise	Ebony Funeral, An	95
Liberati, Alessandro	Air Varie, cornet solo	05
	Felice, cornet, trombone, or saxophone solo	*92 93-99 *00 01 13
	Mia Speranza, La (My Hope), polka caprice, cornet solo	95 21 22
	Past and Future, cornet solo	94
	Polka Brilliante, cornet solo	21
	Pyramids, cornet solo	14 20-23 *24 25 26
	Souvenir de la Suisse (Souvenir de Swiss) (Swiss Melody), cornet solo	*92 96 14 *20 21-23 26
Licht, Heinrich	Auguste Victoria, march	96
Lichtenstein, Bessie F.	Triumphal America	94
Lick	Fantasia Original, saxophone solo	18
Liddle, Samuel	Abide With Me, sacred song, vocal or cornet solo	06 07
	In My Garden, vocal solo	*15 17 18
Liebling, Max	Fantasie on Sousa Airs (Fantasy on Sousa Themes), violin solo	06
	Patriotic Fantasie, violin solo	06
Liebling, Sally	Charming Women (Energetic Women) (Sparkling Women) (Fesche Frauen) (Smart Looking Girls), caprice, polka (caprice)	01 02 04 05 09 12 15 19 21 22 25 26 28
Liefield, Albert D.	Here's to Old Pittsburgh, song	08
	In the Spring, suite	05
	To the Eternal City, grand march	01

374

	Valse Espagnole	03 05
Lieurance, Thurlow Weed & J.M. Cavanass	By the Waters of Minnetonka, Indian love song, vocal solo	*20 *21 *22 26
Lilebridge	Enchantment, waltz caprice	93
Lincke, Paul	Amina, Egyptian Serenade, intermezzo	09 22 23
	Autumn Voices, reverie	09
	Frau Luna, Overture	15 27
	Frau Luna: Luna, waltz (Luna Walzer)	04 07 08 09 10
	Lysistrata: Glow Worm (Glubwurmshen), idyll	*99 *00 01 09 10 *11 13 15 22 23
	Lysistrata: Waltz	06 23
	My Jewel, waltz	03
	Nigger's Birthday (Nakris Hochzeit) (The Darkie's Birthday), The, two-step	07
	On the Bosphorus, Turkish intermezzo	10
	Once Upon a Time (Es War Einmal), song or cornet solo	01 09 10 *20
	Siamese Patrol	09
	Softly, Unawares! (Heimlich, Still und Leise!)	10
	Under My Darling's Window, waltz	22
	Unrequited Love (Verschmaehte Liebe), waltz	09-12 15 23 24
	Venus on Earth, waltz	08 09 10 *11-13 22-25
	Way to the Heart, The, gavotte (idyll)	12
Lindblad, O.	Swedish Song, vocal solo	93
Lindley	Militaire, galop	95
Lindpainter, Peter Joseph von	Camp, The: Overture	01
	Foster Children, The (Die Pflegekinder): Overture	94 95
	Jocko, the Brazillian Ape: Overture	*99
	Jubel: Overture (In Camp) (Camp Overture)	99
	Standard Watch (Die Fahnenwacht), The, Op. 114, song	24
Lindsley, H.W.	Galop Militaire	96
Line, Hans S.	Simplicity	01
Lipinski, Charles	Military Concerto, violin solo	08
Liszt, Franz	Chromatique, grand galop	04 05
	Concerto No. 1 in E-flat for Piano	16
	Hungarian Rhapsody No. 1	*97 *98 *01 02 04 10 *12 13 16 17 19 23 26 27
	Hungarian Rhapsody No. 12	01 14 28
	Hungarian Rhapsody No. 14	*94 95 *96 *00 *01 02 *05 09 10 *11 14 15 17 19 *21 *22 23 *24 26
	Hungarian Rhapsody No. 2	*92 *93 *94 *95 96 *97 *98 *00 02 *03 04-07 09 10 *11 13 *14 15 16 19 20 23-26 27 *29
	Hungarian Rhapsody No. 3	01 02
	Hungarian Rhapsody No. 6 (Pester Carneval)	92-94 96 13 *14 15 17 22-24
	Hungarian Storm (Ungarischer Sturm) (Storm March) (Martial Storm) (The Storm)	16
	Liebestraum (Dream of Love), harp solo or band number	14 15 20 *23
	Mazeppa: Finale, march	97 *20
	Mephisto, waltz (Mephisto's Waltzer)	13
	Preludes, Les, symphonic poem	94 95 96 *97 01 *02 04 *05 *06 *07 *08 *09 *10 *11 12-17 19-21 23 25 26 28
	Second Polonaise (Zweite Polonaise)	01 *02 04 *05 06 07 08 09 10 *11 12 13 *14 15-17 20-23
	Spring-Song (Fruhlingslied), vocal solo	95
	Sympathy	96
	Thou Art Like a Flower, cornet solo	96
Liszt, Franz & Taylor	Dream of Love and You	26

Litolff, Henry Charles	Knight Templars, The: Ballet Music	93 96
	Maximilian Robespierre (The Last Day of the Reign of Terror), Op. 55, overture symphonique	93 *96 *97 * 98 01 02 04 *05 06 *07 08-10 *11 *12 13-23 *24 *25 26
Lively, Katherine Allan	Within the Walls of China	25 26
Llewellyn, Edward B.	My Regards, cornet or euphonium or saxophone solo	25 26 29
	Premier Polka, The, cornet solo	18 26
	Valse Caprice, cornet solo	18
Lockhart, Eugene & Ernest Seitz	World Is Waiting for the Sunrise, The, vocal or xylophone solo	18 23-26 *27 *28 *29
Lodge, Henry	Tango Land, dance	13
	Temptation Rag	*10 *11 *12
Loehr	Out on the Deep, vocal solo	93
Loeschorn, Carl	Belle Amazone, La	94 96
Loew, Joseph	Ronde [Rondo] de la Garde (Passing of the Guard) (Rounds of the Guards) (A Return of the Guards), grand march (patrol)	98 20 22
Logan, Frederick Knight	Cheiro Waltzes	99
	Missouri Waltz, The	19
	Summer Showers, intermezzo (album leaf)	*19 *20
Logan, Frederick Knight & Jesse G.M. Glick	Pale Moon, vocal solo	21 22 26
Lohr	Heigh-Ho, vocal duet	09
Lohr, Hermann	Little Grey Home in the West, vocal or cornet solo	14 15 17 19 24-27 *30
	Reminiscences of Hermann Lohr	15 17 24
	Rose of My Heart, vocal solo	13 15 16 *17 19 24 25 26 27
	Where My Caravan Has Rested, vocal solo or band number	23-26
Loomis, Harvey Worthington	Sun Worshipers, The, Pueblo Indian Melody, vocal solo/duet	09
Loraine, William	Zamona, Arabian intermezzo	*01
Lorenz	Melody in D, trombone solo	01 02
Lorraine	Sweet Land of Provence, romance	93
Lortzing, Albert	Czar and Zimmermann (Czar and Carpenter): Holzschuh Tanz (Wooden Shoe Dance) (Dance of the Wooden Shoes)	05
	Czar and Zimmermann (Czar and Carpenter): Overture	05
	Fest: Overture	94
Losey, Frank Hoyt	Finnegan's Hornpipe, polka	21
	Zarida Polka, cornet solo	26
Lotter, Adolf	Rouge et Noir, waltz lento	07 08
Louis XIV	Amarylis, ancient air	18
Low	Morning Festival Reveille (Fest Morgen Reveille), march	98
Lowe, Charles P.	American Patrol, xylophone solo, based on Meecham's patrol	05 22 23
	Eulalic, xylophone solo	93
	Medley, A, xylophone solo [on popular themes]	93
	Melange of Popular Songs (Grand Fantasie on Popular Airs), xylophone solo	93 05
	Patriot, The, xylophone solo	07
	Sylvestrian Strains, xylophone solo	93
	Vaudeville, The, xylophone solo	93
Lowe, Helen F.	Meadowbrook Hunt, The, two-step march	95
Lowler, Charles & James Blake	Sidewalks of New York	95
Lowry, Robert	I Need Thee Every Hour, hymn, cornet solo	*11
Lowthian	Perle de Roses, xylophone solo	93
Lowthian, Caroline	Beauty's Daughters, waltz	93
	Maid of Kent, A, waltz	24
	Sweet Briar, xylophone solo	93
Lubomirsky, G.	Danse Orientale (Oriental)	18 28
Luckstone, Isadore	Delight Valses (La Diletto), vocal solo	*96 *97
	Nightingale, The, vocal solo	95
	The Latest March	94
	Waltz, vocal solo	97
Luders, Gustav Carl	Burgomaster, The: I Love You, Dear, and Only You, vocal solo	02
	Burgomaster, The: Selections	02
	Burgomaster: The Tale of a Kangaroo, trombone solo	*01 17

	Custer's Last Charge (A Cavalry Charge) (Custer's Last Chase), descriptive	*94 *96 19 21 22 24
	Grand Mogul, The: Finale	07
	King Dodo: Bumblebee Song	*02
	Prince of Pilsen, The: Selections	04 06 08 09 10 26-28
Ludwig	Laughing, polka	98
Ludwig, A.L.	San Luis, mazurka	95
Luigini, Alexandre	Ballet Russe (La Russea) (Russian Suite)	04 05 *06 08 10 13 14 17 18 22 24 27
	Egyptian Suite (Ballet Egyptian)	*99 *00 *01 04 10 13 15 16 18 21-24 27
	Egyptian Suite: Dance of the Bashibazouk	*99 *00 *01
	Egyptian Suite: The Odalisque	*99 *00 *01
	Voice of the Bells (La Voix des Cloches), reverie	01 08 10 14 19 23 24
Lumbye, Hans Christian	At the Fair, burletta	01
	Dream Pictures (Traumbilder) (Visions in a Dream) (Pictures in a Dream), fantasie (idyll)	95 96 99 01 02 04 *05 06-10 12 15-17 19 20 22 24-26
	Kermesse, burletta	01
	Kroll's Ballklange (Kroll's Ball Sounds) (Sounds from Kroll's), waltz	01 05 22-26
Lummis, Charles F. & Georgia Pierrpont Strong	Camulous, serenade, vocal solo	99
Lunt, Grace Weston	Harvard Volunteer, The, march	99
Lurvey, Hiram R.	Uncle Sam's Postman, march	08
Luscomb, Fred	Trip to the Country, A (A Day in the Country), descriptive fantasie	94
Lutz, Wilhelm Meyer	Cinder-Ellen Up too Late	93
	Reminiscences of the [London] Gaiety	93 24
	Three Jolly Cobblers, polka	13 14
Lux, Edward	Buffalo Bill's Sharpshooters	94
Luzzi	Ave Maria, vocal solo	93
Lynes	Spring Song, vocal solo	09
Macbeth, Allen	Forget Me Not (Forgetmenot), intermezzo (idyll), Op. 22	95 *96 *97 99
	Heart's-Ease, intermezzo	*12 13-15
	Love in Idleness, serenade	*97 *98 01 02 04 06 07 09 15 17 20-23
MacConnell	Such As Dare to Love, vocal solo	97
MacCunn, Hamisch	Land of the Mountain and the Flood, The: Overture (symphonic poem)	95 02 *11 12 13 15 18
Macdonald & Lawrence & O.F.Mohr	He's the Sweetest (Hottest) Little Trooper in the Army	95
Macdonald, Hamish	Ma Braw Laddie, patrol	22
MacDowell, Edward	Forest Spirits (In a Haunted Forest), Op. 42: Suite	*96 *97 98 *00 11 *14
	Forest Spirits (In a Haunted Forest), Op. 42: The Ghost	01
	Indian Suite No. 2, Op. 48: In War Time	98 *99 *00 01 02 07 27
	Moonshine, idyll	18 21
	Sonata Tragica (Stagica): Scherzo	25
	Witches' Dance, Op. 17, xylophone solo	*22 *23 *24 25 26
	Woodland Sketches: From an Indian Lodge; To a Wild Rose	04-06 10 *11 13 17 18
	Woodland Sketches: To a Wild Rose, violin solo	*09 10
Macek	Fuquet-Fuquette, cornet solo	93
MacFadyen, Alexander	Spring's Singing, vocal solo	10
MacGregor	Songs and Dances of Scotland	11
Mackenzie, Alexander Campbell	Benedictus	94
	Britannia, nautical overture, Op. 52 (Rule Brittania)	01 *11 17
	Colomba, Op. 28: Ballet Music and Rustic March	94
	Cricket on the Hearth, The, Op. 62: Overture	*96 09 21
	Dove, The: Ballet Music	96
	Kiltie's Kortship, The, intermezzo or one-step	*14
	Scotch Rhapsody No. 2 ("Burns"): Vivace	01
	Story of Sayid	94
MacKenzie, Gordon	Outpost, The, morceau militaire	20 *21 22 23 *24 26 28
	Prelude to Columbine, fairy dance	24
MacLeod, D.B.	Pythian Encampment, march	94
MacPherson, Stewart	Orchestral Ballad	21 24
Macunne, Hamish	Land of the Mountain and Flood, symphonic poem (overture)	94-96

Magine, Frank	Adoration Waltz	24
Magonier	Apollo, caprice	01
Maillart, Louis	Dragons de Villars, Les (Das Gloeckchen des Eremiten) (Hermit's Bell): Overture	97 09 17 18 21 23 24 27
Maillochand, J.B.	Fall of Jericho, The, descriptive overture	01
Malmene, Waldemar	Julia Marlowe Waltzes	98
	Triumphant March	98
Malmeni	In Memoriam, elegie militaire	04
Mama Lou	Ta-Ra-Ra Boom-Der-E, song	92
Manchielli	Triumphal, march	27
Mancinelli, Luigi	Cleopatra: Sinfonia, Intermezzo (Italian triumphal march)	93 94 19 24
	Cleopatra: Triumphal March (Cortege) (Triumphal Entrée of Cleopatra)	93 94 15
Mann	Arcadia Waltzes, saxophone solo	19
Mann, N.D.	Imam, Mohammedan serenade	12
Mansfield, Richard	Hail to the Flag, a national anthem	01 02
Mantia, Simone	Air Americaine (Old Melody with Variations) (Air and Variations) (Original Air and Variations), euphonium solo	*97 99 01 02
	Auld Lang Syne (Shall Old Acquaintance Be Forgot), euphonium solo	02 *18
	National Diamond Jubilee, The (The Peace Jubilee), march	98
Marchesi	Original Theme and Variations, euphonium solo	93
Marchetti, F.D.	Fascination, waltz tzigane	13
Marckwald, Grace	Concert Valse	96
Marckwald, Grace	Request and the Reply, A, cornet solo	*00 24
Marenco, Romualdo	Excelsior: Ballet Suite (Selection)	93 94 96 12 17-22 26 27
Margis	Kisses, The, waltz	02
	Monte Cristo, waltz	02
Margis, Alfred	Bleue, waltz (Valse Bleu)	*00 01 02 04 07
	Premier Printemps, Le, waltz	03
Marion	Only One Girl in the World for Me, song, trombone solo	95 *96 *97
Markey, J.D.	Kismet, Oriental intermezzo (oriental characteristic)	*13 14 15
Markinald, Grace	Exposition, waltz	95
Marks, Goffrey	Arab's Bride, The, vocal solo	96
Marsal, E.	Nannie, fantasie, instrumental duet	02
Marsh	Jesus, Lover of My Soul, hymn	*94
Marshall	Pick Me a Rose, vocal solo	14
Marshall, Charles	I Hear You Calling Me, vocal solo, trombone solo, or band number	14-20 26
Marshall, John	Topeka Daily Capital, The, march	97
Martin	All For You, vocal solo	21
Martini, Giovanni Battista	Plaiseur d'Amour	95
Marziales	Leaving, yet Loving, vocal solo	94
	My Love Has Come, vocal solo	93
Marzo, Eduardo	Sans Fin Waltzes	97
Masca	Intermezzo	15
Mascagni, Pietro	Cavalleria Rusticana: Ave Maria, vocal solo	94 96
	Cavalleria Rusticana: Church Scene	94 98
	Cavalleria Rusticana: Hail, the Lord Now Victorious, The, vocal solo	94
	Cavalleria Rusticana: Intermezzo	93 95 98 05
	Cavalleria Rusticana: Prelude and Sicilianna	93-95 *97 98 *99 *03 09 10 14 19 21 22
	Cavalleria Rusticana: Selections	93-95 *97 98 *99 *03 09 10 14 19 21-27
	Esotica, dance (Danze Esotica)	*03 04 13
	Eternal City, The: Grand Scene	04
	Eternal City, The: Serenata (Serenade)	05 24
	Iris: Act I, Selections	*00
	Iris: Aria [unnamed], vocal solo[s]	15 16
	Iris: Hymn to the Sun (Sunrise)	03 04 *05 06 *07 08 14 15 17 18 21 *22 23 24 26 27
	L'Amico Fritz (Friend Fritz): Selections	94 96
	Namouria: Oriental Ballet	05 06 24

	Rantzau, I: Overture (Vorspiel) (Prelude)	96
	Rantzau, I: Selections	94
	Silent Heroes	94
	William Ratcliff (Gugliemo Ratcliff) (Ratcliff's Dream): Intermezzo	95 96 *97 *01 02 22
Mascheroni, Angelo	Ave Maria, vocal solo	95 96
	For All Eternity, vocal solo	93-96
Mason, Lowell	Nearer, My God to Thee, cornet solo or band number	93 94 *01 02 06 *07 14
	Sacred Themes	13
Masse, Victor	Daughter of a Brigadier, A: Overture	93 94
	Galatea, soprano song	93
	Marriage of Jeannette, The (Noces de Jeannette): Nightingale's Song	*04 *05 06-08
	Paul and Virginia: Selections	93 94
Massenet, Jules	Cendrillon, Ballet and Fantasia (Scenes)	01
	Cid, Le: Ballet Music	95
	Cid, Le: Excerpt, vocal solo	93
	Cid, Le: Navaraise (Argonaise)	29
	Cid, Le: Pleurez Mes Yeux, vocal solo	93 96
	Elegie, vocal or xylophone solo	18-21 *22
	Erinnyes, Les: Ballet Suite	10 *11 12 16-18
	Esclarmonde: Aria [unnamed], vocal solo[s]	12-14 16 17
	Esclarmonde: Selections	93
	Favorite Songs of Massenet	94 24
	Grand Overture de Concert	*13 14 15 17 21
	Grecians, The (The Greeks) (Dance of the Classical Greeks) (Greek Dance) (Greek Dance): Ballet Suite	03 *04 *05 07 10 21
	Herodiade: Aria [unnamed], vocal solo[s]	93 15 17 18 20
	Herodiade: Il Est Doux, Il Est Bon, vocal solo	96 17
	Herodiade: Selections	09 12 24
	Last Dream of the Virgin, The (The Last Slumber of the Virgin): Prelude	93 94 05
	Manon: Aria [unnamed], vocal solo[s]	14 18
	Manon: Fabliau (Fableau), vocal solo	14 18
	Manon: Selections	96
	Navarraise, La: Selections	*97
	Parade Militaire (Air Militaire), morceau de genre	93 21-24
	Phedre: Overture	93 94 96 01 02 04 17 18 *19 *20 22 24-26
	Roi de Lahore, Le: Aria [unnamed], vocal solo[s]	93 94 24
	Roi de Lahore, Le: Selections	96
	Romance of a Harlequin, The: Columbine at the Window	92 93
	Romance of a Harlequin, The: Harlequin's Apprearance in the Pantomime	93
	Romance of a Harlequin, The: Scenes	94
	Scenes Alsaciennes, suite (Alsaciennes Suite) (The Alsaciennes): The Wine Shop; Sunday Evening	*09 10-14 16-19 22 *25 *26 28
	Scenes de Fairie (Fairy Scenes): Ballet Suite	*97
	Scenes Neapolitaine (Carnival Scene from Naples) (Carnival Scenes in Naples) (Carnival Night in Naples) (In Carnival Time) (Neapolitan Scenes)	*94 *95 *96 *97 98 99 *01 *02 *03 04 05 07 08 *11 15 16 18 24 *25 *26 *27 29 *30
	Scenes Pittoresque: Air de Ballet	94 06 07 18 28
	Scenes Pittoresque: Suite	*92 93 94 98 *00 01 02 04 08-10 13 24-26 31
	Scenes Pittoresque: The Angelus	93-95 05 08 *11 *14 *15 *21 *22 23 27
	Szabadi (Marche Heroique), Gypsy caprice	07 13 16-18 *19 *20 *21 22-24 27
	Thais: Meditation, violin solo or band number	08-10 *13 19 *21
	Werther: Selections	94
Masso	Une Nuit Cleopatra: Selections	93
Matador, Jose	Sevilla, Spanish waltz	95
Matt, Albert	Rural Dances and Scenes, suite	02
Mattei, Tito	For the Sake of the Past, romance, cornet solo	93
	Non e Ver, cornet solo	93 94

	Non Lorne, vocal solo	96
Mattie	Dear Heart, trombone solo	24
Mattioli, L.	Where Love Abides, vocal solo	94
Mayeno	Perles, Les, trombone solo	93
Mayer	Celester, reve angelique	13
	Memories of My Youth	24
Mayeur, Louis	Caprice and Polka for Clarinet (Caprice de Concert)	94 96
	Caprice Francais	15
	Fleurance, La, piccolo solo	94 21-23
Mayr, Franz	Birds of the Forest, cornet duet	94
	Meditation, reverie	97
	Waldvoglein, Die, cornet quartet	03
McAdow, W.P.	Treasure State Waltzes	27
McCanles, Josesph C.	Loyalty First, march	27
McCormick, Harry J.	Invincible Home Guards, march and two-step	12
McCoy, William J.	Bewitching Eyes (Hechiceros Ojos), Mexican dance	94
	Festival of the Flowers, waltz	96
	Hamadryads: Dance of the Young Hamadryads	19
	Hamadryads: Naiads' Idyll	09 10
	Handkerchief Dance (Jugo de Panuelos) (Hechiceros Ojos), Mexican dance	98
McGrew	McGrew Guards, The, march	95
Meacham, Frank W.	American Patrol	93 94 *95 *98 *99 *07 08 09 20 21 24
	Corncracker, The, dance	*94
Mears, O.S.	Forbidden Fruit: Overture Potpouri (Grand Fantasia)	94
Mehul, Etienne Henri	Chase of Young Henry, The (La Chasse du Jeune Henri) (The Chase of Prince Henry) (The Hunt of King Henry): Overture	94 96 *13 14 *15 16-18 21-24 26-28
	Two Blind Men of Toledo, The (Deux Avengles de Toledo) (The Two Beggars): Overture	17 27
Meinrath, Joseph	Forward March, march	20
Meisler	Babylonia, fantasia	93
Melant, Charles	In Bivouac, fantasie militaire	96
Melville, Arnold	Chrysalis, caprice (idyll)	96
Mencel	Sweet Longing, romance, oboe solo	02
Mendelssohn, Felix	Athalia, march	94
	Down in a Flowery Dell, song	96
	Elijah: Hear Ye, Israel (Hore Israel), vocal solo	06
	Elijah: Thanks Be to God, sacred song	25
	Hear My Prayer	93
	Hebrides, The (Fingal's Cave), Overture	94
	Hunter's Farewell, The, song, horn quartet [unaccompanied?]	93 96 98 15
	I Would That My Love, cornet duct or trio	01 08 09 15
	In the Forest, horn quartet	15
	Introduction and Rondo Capriccioso, violin or xylophone solo	*95 09 *24
	Midsummer Night's Dream, A: Nocturne and Scherzo	08
	Midsummer Night's Dream, A: Selections	94 97 02
	Midsummer Night's Dream: Overture	94 98
	Midsummer Night's Dream: Wedding March	93 98 03-07 09 10 *11 12 14-16 27
	Oh, For the Wings of a Dove, sacred song	93 95
	Oh, Ye Nations, chorus	03
	On Wings of Music, vocal solo	96 27
	Reminiscences of Mendelssohn	93 94 96 98 99 *00 01 02 04 06-08 10 *11 12-14 16 17 23-26
	Rondo Capriccioso, Op. 14, xylophone solo or band number	*09 10 *11 14 15 *21 *22 23 25 *26
	Ruy Blas: Overture	94 27
	Son and Stranger: Overture	93 25 26
	Songs Without Words	93 14 15 24
	Spring Song (Freuhlingslied) (Spring Is Coming)	93 94 *96 97 98 *00 20 27 28

	Spring Song, harp solo [unaccompanied?]	93
	Symphony No. 3 ("Scottish"), Op. 56: Andante and Allegro	93-95 05
	Symphony No. 3 ("Scottish"), Op. 56: Scherzo	*99 01 07
	Symphony No. 4 ("Italian"): Pilgrim's March	13 14 15 24 27
	Violin Concerto (one or two movements)	*93 94 02 *03 05 *06 07- 10 *11 12-17 19
	When Evening Twilight, song	96
Meny, P.R.	Abdulla, grand march	14
Mercadante, Saverio	Counte d'Essex, The, (The Count of Essex): Overture	93 94 96
	Elisa e Claudio: Overture	93 94 96
Mercer, Mary Speed	United, a national anthem	10
Messager, Andre	Basche, La: Selections	93 94
	Fauvette: Selections	93 96
	Little Michus, The: Selections	06 09
	Mirette: Selections	95
	Monsieur Beaucaire: Selections	28
	Two Pigeons, The, (Les Deux Pigeons) (The Two Doves), ballet suite	07 08 09 12 13 15 17 18 19 20 21 22 24
	Veronique: Selections	05 06 07 08 09 13 15 17- 24 26-28
Messinger	Romance	95
Methvan, Florence & Marian Gillespie	When You Look in the Heart of a Rose, song	19 20
Metra, Jules Louis Oliver	Serenade, La, valse Espagnole (Spanish Serenade), xylophone solo	04
	Volunteers, The, march	93 *94
	Yedda, fantasia (Japanese ballet suite)	06-10 *11 12-22 24-26 28
Metz, Theodore A.	Bird's Message, The, vocal solo	96
Metzger	Danse de Matelots	93
Meyer, George W.	Hiawatha's Melody of Love, waltz	20
Meyer, Joseph	Cup of Coffee, a Sandwich and You	26
Meyer, N. Selmar	Lulu Patrol, march	*95
Meyerbeer, Giacomo	Badinage	*98
	Corociato in Egitto, Il: Selection	96 25 26
	Dinorah (Pardon de Ploermel): Shadow Song (Shadow Dance), vocal or cornet solo	93 95 96 *97 *98 02 04 05 10 14-16 18-20 *21 22 *23 *25 *26 27 *29 31
	Dinorah: Aria [unnamed], vocal solo[s]	*93
	Dinorah: Selections	95 96
	Fackeltanz (Torch Dance) (Torchlight Dance) No. 1 in B-flat	93 04-09 12 13 15 16 19 20-22 *23 *24 *25 26
	Fackeltanz (Torch Dance) No. 3 (Third Torchlight Dance) (Marche aux Flambeaux)	93-96 99 04 05 *11
	Flambeaux, march	93
	Huguenots, Les: Aria [unnamed], vocal solo[s]	92 19-21
	Huguenots, Les: Benediction of the Poignards (Blessing of the Poignards) (Blessing of the Daggars), trombone trio or band number	93-95 97 *98 *99 *00 01 02 04-10 *11 12 15-23 25 27 28 31
	Huguenots, Les: Gypsy Dance	05
	Huguenots, Les: Love Song, vocal solo	94
	Huguenots, Les: Nobil Signor, vocal solo	93 94 96 97
	Huguenots, Les: Page Song (Lieti Signor), vocal solo	93 19 20
	Huguenots, Les: Selections	93 95 98 *00 06 09 27
	L'Africaine: Ah Paradiso (O Paradiso), grand Air	93 25
	L'Africaine: Ah Paradiso (O Paradiso), vocal solo	93
	L'Africaine: Selections	96
	L'Africaine: Unison Motive	94
	Margherite d' Anjou: Overture	93 94 96
	Meyerbeeriana, Grand Selection	25 26
	North Star, The (Star of the North): Aria [unnamed], vocal solo[s]	05
	North Star, The (Star of the North): Overture	21 22 24

	Pretty Fisher Maiden, flugelhorn solo	01
	Prophet, The, fantasie	02 04
	Prophete, Le: Ballet Suite	01 02 14 16 18-24
	Prophete, Le: Marche du Sacre (Coronation March) (Grand March) (Grand March Sacre)	01 02 07 08 *11 14 15 18 24 28
	Prophete, Le: Mio Filio, vocal solo	93
	Prophete, Le: Selections	97 01 04 05 07-10 17 21
	Reminiscences of Meyerbeer	93-96 98 04 06-10 *11 12-24 26
	Robert le Diablo (Robert the Devil): Aria [unnamed], vocal solo[s]	07
	Robert le Diablo (Robert the Devil): Ballet Suite	07 20 23 24 28 31
	Robert le Diablo (Robert the Devil): Gnaden, cavatina, vocal or cornet solo	92 94-97 01 06
	Robert le Diablo (Robert the Devil): Oh Robert, Robert (Robert, I Love Thee) (Robert, Idol of My Heart), vocal or cornet solo	95 97 01 02 *07 08-10 *11 12-15 17 19 21 22 25
	Robert le Diablo (Robert the Devil): Overture	94 96
	Robert le Diablo (Robert the Devil): Robert, Toi Que J'aime, vocal or flute	95 96 *07 *08
	Robert le Diablo (Robert the Devil): Selections	16 18 19 21 22 26 27 30
	Triomphal, grand march	05
	Vielka (The Camp in Silesia): Overture	96
Meyer-Helmund, Erik	Ball Whispers (Ball-Room Whispers) (Ballgefluester), idyll	02 24
	Burletta	01 02
	Dancing Songs, tone picture	07
	Dwarf Dance (Gnomen Tanz), burlesque polka	24
	Reminiscences of Meyer-Helmunder	01 02 04 05 10 13 15-17 20 21 23-26
	Scandinavian Fantasia	*01 02 18
	Serenade Burlesque	96 22
	Serenade Roccoco	*01 02 *11 13
	Tanzweise (Tanz Weise), characteristic dance	10
Meyrelles, Miguel C.	Bouquet of Melodies, potpourri	23
	Chinese Patrol	96
	Portuguese Revellie, fantasie	96
	Spanish National Melodies (A Medley of Spanish Airs) (Spanish Love Songs)	26-28
Michaelis, Gustav Theodor	Babillage, polka	96
	Chanteurs Hongrois, Les, polka caprice	*11
	Chinese War	94
	Clock in the Black Forest	05
	Czardas No. 1 on Hungarian National Airs	08
	Danse de Cosaques, morceau de genre	93
	Forge in the Forest, The (Schmiede Im Walde, Die), Op. 126, idyll	94 97 01 02 04-08 26
	Mill in the Forest, The	93
	Sleigh Ride, The	93
	Turkish Patrol	94 96 98 *11 14 22 24
	Winter Scene, A	93 94
Miedtke, Paul	Milwaukee First, march	15
Milanese	Air Milanese, euphonium solo	95
Mildenburg, Albert	Arabian Night, romance	19
	Gavotte Antique (Gavotte Comique)	99
Miles, Walter E.	Valse Danseuse	15
Millard, Harrison	God Save Our President, patriotic air	92
	Romona, vocal song	96 05
	Tanteum Ergo, vocal solo	94
	Waiting, vocal solo	*20 21 22
	When the Tide Comes In, flugelhorn solo	02 04
Millars, Haydn	Reve d'Amour, Le, cornet solo	27
Miller	To Thee, waltz	01
Miller, George J.	Trafalgar (Voyage in a Troopship) (Songs for Sailors) (Songs and Dances of the Sailors), nautical fantasia	93 94 08 13 24 26 27
	Trafalgar (Voyage in a Troopship), nautical fantasia	13 24 26 27
Milloecker, Carl	Apajune (The Waterman) (The Water Sprite): Selections	07 16

	Army Chaplain: Selections	94
	Beggar Student, The (Der Bettlestudent): Laura, waltz	95 06 23
	Beggar Student, The (Der Bettlestudent): Selections	96 99 07
	Beggar Student, The (Der Bettlestudent): Waltz Melodies	93 94
	Black Hussar, The: Selections	94-96
	Laura, waltz	94
Mills, Kerry	At a Georgia Camp Meeting	98 *99 *00 *03
	Sparklets	15
	Tokio, fox trot	19
	Whistling Rufus, novelty	*00 *03
Mincus, Ludwig & Delibes, C.P. Leo	Spring (Springtime), grand ballet	08 09 13-19 21 26
Minnis, F.	Little Marcia Marie, caprice	94 95
Miro, Enrique	Mercedes, waltz Espagnole	12
Missud, Jean Marie	Hurrah for the Army	01
	Manana, Chilean dance	95 96
	Paraphrase on Adeste Fidelis	01
	Rosita, Puerto Rican dance	01
Modricker	Grippertown, march	15
Moelling, Theodore	Columbia Fair, march	93
Moeremans, Jean H.B.	Air and Variations, saxophone solo	04
	American Favorites (American Fantasie), saxophone solo	02 *03 *04 05
	Carnival of Venice, The, saxophone solo	98
	Squirrel in the Forest, A	98
	Trombone King, The, march	96
	Variations on Old Folks at Home, saxophone solo	95 02 04
Mollenhauer, Emil	Dixie, paraphrase	93-95
	Nightingale, The, vocal or piccolo solo	93 01 02 *03 04 05
Moller, Max	Two Friends, The, polka	94
Molloy, James Lyman	Home, Dearie Home	94
	Kerry Dance, The	17 *30
	Love's Old Sweet Song, vocal or cornet solo or band number	92 93 *94 95 *16 17 21 22 25
Monckton, Lionel	Arcadians, The: Overture	20 24
	Bric-a-Brac, waltz	21
	Cingalee, The: Selections	05 07
	Dandy Dan: Selections	01
	Geisha, The: Selections	22
	Good Morning, Judge, fantasia	19
	Orchid, The: Bedilia	*05
	Porcupine Patrol, The, one-step	13
	Quaker Girl, The: Selections	12 13
	Soldiers in the Park March	99 01
Monckton, Lionel & Howard Talbot	Arcadians, The: Selections	09 10
Monckton, Lionel, SEE ALSO Caryll, Ivan		
Monk, William Henry	Eventide (Abide With Me), paraphrase	23
	Sun of My Soul, hymn	93
Montagu	Air Varie, saxophone solo	23
Moore	Dreaming Alone in the Twilight, vocal solo	21
	Rocky Road to Dublin, The	95 96
Moore, Douglas S.	Parabalou	*12
Moore, J. Warwick	Highland Scene, A (Highland Scenes) (In the Highlands) (At the Foot of the Highlands) (Gems of Irish Minstrelsy), descriptive fantasie (tone picture)	05 06 *07 08 15 16 22 24-27
Moore, M.M.	Moose March, The	11
Moore, Thomas	Believe Me If All Those Endearing Young Charms, vocal solo or harp solo, Irish air [unaccompanied]	17 19 *20 *21 *22 *23 *24
	Harp That Once Thro' Tara's Halls, The	95 96 *19
	Minstrel Boy [Has Gone to War], The	98
Moore, Thomas, SEE ALSO Ware, Harriet		
Moose	Salambo, intermezzo	02
Moreadante	Overture Founded on Themes of Rossini's Stabat Mater	93
Moreland, Fred L	Yankee Shuffle, The, characteristic march	*09 *11
Morelli	Dance at the Forge, The	93 94

	On the Ice, polka	93
	Sailor's Songs and Dances	93
Morelli, Albert	Alhambra, The, fantasie	93
	Reminisces of Pinsuti (Fantasia on Songs of Pinsuti) (A Collection of the Songs of Ciro Pinsuiti)	93 94 96 14 23 25 26
Morena, Camillo	Kinkerlitzchen (Sounds from the Berlin Metropole), Op. 91, potpourri of German popular songs	10
	Matador, El, Spanish waltz	10
	Souvenir de Yradier (Popular Melodies [of Mexico]) (Songs and Dances of Mexico), fantasie on Mexican melodies	03 06 09 15 24
Moret, Neil	Hiawatha, intermezzo	*03
	Yearning, saunter	27
Morgan	My Sweetheart, When a Boy, vocal solo	93
Morgen, Franz	Polish Dances	95
Mori, Emil	American Boys, march	98
Morlacchi, Francesco	Swiss Shepherd, The (Il Pastore Svizzero) (Shepherd Life), flute or piccolo solo	17 18
Morris	Remembrance of the Balkans	17
Morrison, Charles Sumner	Meditation, song	13
Morse	I've Got My Eyes on You, waltz	02
	Isis, intermezzo	02
	Meaning of U.S.A., The, two-step	02
Morse, Robert Gorham	Up the Street March	08
Morse, Theodore	Blue Bell, medley march or two-step	*05
Morse, Woolson	Wang: Selections	93-95
Moses (Moses Tobani), SEE Tobani, Theodore Moses		
Moszkowski, Moritz	Boabdil: Malaguena, vocal solo	94 16 22 24
	Boabdil: Moorish March (Moresque)	94 95 96
	From Foreign Lands (In Foreign Lands) (The Nations) (Aus Aller Herren Lander) (The Nations)[Spain; Germany; Hungary], suite	02 04 06-10 12-16 21 22 *24 25 26 28
	Guitarre, violin solo	*00 01 10 13 14 18 19 20-22
	Hungarian Dances	25
	Love's Awakening, waltz	24
	Reminiscences of Moszkowski	24-26
	Reveil d'Amour, La, waltz	95
	Scherzino, Op. 18	08 09 *11
	Serenade (Serenata), vocal or violin solo	95 04 08 10 16 24
	Spanish Dances	93-96 02 04-07 09 10 12 14-17 19-23 27
	Tone Picture	*07
	Torchlight Dance	94
Mozart, Wolfgang Amadeus	A-Major Sonata: Turkish March (March a la Turka)	93 03 15 25 27
	Astriffiamante, vocal solo	16
	Cosi Fan Tutti: Aria [unnamed], vocal solo[s]	*95
	Cosi Fan Tutti: Overture	26
	Divertissement: Minuet and French March (French March)	04 06 12 14
	Don Giovanni (Don Juan): Leperello's Aria	94
	Don Giovanni (Don Juan): Overture	94 95
	Don Giovanni (Don Juan): Selections	96
	Don Giovanni (Don Juan): Vedrai Carino, vocal solo	*15
	Idomenco: Overture	94
	Magic Flute, The: O, Isis and Osiris, vocal solo	93
	Magic Flute, The: Queen of the Night, vocal solo	05 15
	Marriage of Figaro, The (Le Nozze di Figaro): Deh Vieni Non Tardier, vocal	*15
	Marriage of Figaro, The: Aria [unnamed], vocal solo[s]	93 95
	Marriage of Figaro, The: Delightful Joy, O Come	93
	Marriage of Figaro, The: Non Pin Andrai, vocal solo	93 94
	Marriage of Figaro, The: Overture	94
	Reminiscences of Mozart	94 95 96
Mueller	Plantation Echoes	93

Mulder, Richard	Staccato Polka, vocal solo	94 01 *30 *31
Muller, Carl C.	Sonata: Andante and Fugue	96
	With Call of the Tawny Thrush, pastorale	97
Muller, Otto J.	At the Old Grist Mill, descriptive fantasie (idyll)	99 *00 01 02 06 07 15
Mundwyler	Laughing, schottische	95
Muratore, Lucien	Amore (Amora)	97
Murio-Celli	True Heart of Mine, vocal solo	94
Muscat, C.	Jolly Musicians, The	94
Musgrave, J.T.	Queenie, gavotte	94
Musin, Ovide	Caprice de Concert, violin solo	02 15
	Concert Fantasia, violin solo	14
	Maiden's Song, violin solo	*24
	Mazourka de Concerto (Mazurka in D), violin solo	97 *98 *99 13-18
Mussi, L.	Babilonia: Selections	07
	Reminiscences of the Grand Opera of Mussi	08 09 16 24
Mussorgsky, Modest	Khovantschina: Persian Dance	16 *19 *20 27
Mutchler, Erdell	New Year's Eve, humoresque	25
Myddleton, William Henry	Breezes from the South (Breezes from the Southern Seas), American tone poem (fantasia)	18 *19 *20 21 22 27 28 31
	By the Swanee River (Down by the Swanee River) (Down South), fantasie	03-06 26 28 29
	Ireland For Ever (Erin For Ever), sketch	*14 24 26
	King Carnival, burlesque polka (caprice), cornet solo	02 13 19 26
	Lalu, Ma Lubly Queen, coon serenade	04 06 17 21 24
	Let's Be Lively, episode	*05
	Phantom Brigade, The, fantasie (dream picture)	02 16 17 24
Myers, Francis A.	Mystic Potentate, march	15
Nachez, Tivadar	Danses Tzigane No. 1 (Gypsy Dances) (Hungarian Dances), violin solo	94 97 *98 *99 *01 *02 09 10 14-18 21
	Scenes Hungarian (Rhapsody Hongroise), violin solo	13 14
Napravnik, Eduard	Doubrowsky: Selections	02
Needham, Alicia Adelaide	Haymaking, vocal solo	06
Nehl, W.	Gypsy's Serenade, The	93 94
	Home, Sweet Home, paraphrase, Op. 37	93-96 *97 98 99 01 04 07 09
	In May	94
Nelson	Bonnie Sweet Bessie, vocal solo	13
Nelson, Muriel	By the Water Mill, idyll	05
Nelson, Sydney	Mary of Argyle, vocal solo	*13
Nemoir	Air de Ballet	02
Neruda, Josef N.	Berceuse Slav (Slavonic Caprice), violin solo	10
Nessler	God Bless Thee, Dear, vocal solo	96
Nessler, Victor E.	Piper of Hamelin, The	94
	Trompeter von Sakkingen, The (The Trumpeter of Sakkingen): Walter's Farewell (Walther's Farewell) (Werner's Farewell) (Young Werner's Parting	96 *97 98 *99 *00 01 02 04 *05 06 12 27
	Trompeter von Sakkingen, The: Selections	*92 93 *94 95 96
Nesvadba, Josef	How Beautiful Art Thou (How Fair Art Thou) (Wie Schone Bist Du), paraphrase	96
	Lorelei, paraphrase	93-99 *00 01 04 06-08 15 24
Neundorff, Adolph	Ratcharmer of Hamelin: The Ratcharmer's Song	16
Nevin, Ethelbert Woodbridge	Country Dance	*02 *03 04 07 12
	Day in Venice, A (A Night in Venice) (Un Giorno in Venezia), suite: Dawn; The Gondoliers; Love Song; Good Night	*02 *03 04 07 12 14-17 19 20 24 27
	En Passant, suite, Op. 30 (A June Night in Washington; Fontainebleau) (A Summer Night in Washington)	04 *05 *06 *06 07 08-10 12 14-19 21 22
	Maiden, How Sweet, vocal solo	09
	Mighty Lak' a Rose, vocal solo	03 20 26 *30
	Rosary, The, song, vocal or cornet solo	01 04 *05 06 *07 08 *10 *11 12 13 *14 15 17 18 20-24
	Water Scenes, Op. 13	96 14 15

	Water Scenes, Op. 13: Narcissus	*96 97 *98 *99 01-04 06
Nevins, George B.	Hills of God, vocal solo	96
Newcomb, A.W.	Fin de Siecle, march	93
Newman	Chinese Boxers, The, patrol	03
	Lead Kindly Night, hymn	06
Nicaloa	Li Preyo, trio	01
Nicholls, Horatio	Delilah, waltz	20 23
Nicholson	Annie Laurie, piccolo solo	93
Nicode, Jean Louis	From the South (In the South), suite	18
Nicolai, Otto	Light as a Feather, galop	93 94
	Merry Wives of Windsor: Overture	*92 93-96 03 *04 *05 07 10 12 13 15 17 18 22 23 25-27 29
	Mighty Fortress Is Our God, A (Ein Feste Burg Ist Unser Gott), Overture	98
Norrito, Giocomo	Come Back to Erin, piccolo solo	95
	Neapolitan Airs and Variations, piccolo solo	06
Norrito, Joseph	Air Italien (Italia), clarinet solo	*08 14 16
	Air Varied, clarinet solo	22
	Norma: Grand Fantasie (based on Bellini's opera), clarinet solo	98 01 *07 08 13-15 18 22
	Operatic Themes, clarinet solo	21
	Rigoletto Fantasia (based on Verdi's opera), clarinet solo	*92 93 *11 12-22
Norwood, Eille	Danse des Follettes	19 24
Nougues, Jean	Quo Vadis?, Selections	13 15 24
Novello, Ivor & Lena Guilbert Ford	Keep the Home-Fires Burning, vocal solo	18
Novin	Twas April, vocal solo	93
Nubile	My Mother's Song, euphonium solo	21 22 24 25 27
Nutting, Will L.	Crimson March, The	96
O'Brien, J. Vick	Cintra, intermezzo	03
O'Connor, C.W., SEE Friedman, Stanleigh		
O'Donnell, B. Walton	Songs of the Gael (Amrain Na N'Gaedeal), Op. 31, fantasie (Gaelic Fantasy)	*25 *26
O'Hara, Geoffrey	I Love a Little Cottage, vocal or cornet solo	*22 23-25
	Blush Rose, vocal solo	18
	I Would Weave a Song for You, vocal solo	21
	Perfect Melody, The	18 19
O'Hare, William Christopher	Cottonfield Capers, descriptive	01
	Levee Revels, Afro-American cane-hop	98 *00
	The Ruler: Selections	08
O'Neill, Florence	Marionette's Frolic	01
O'Neill, Norman	Blue Bird, The: Four Dances	15 27
Oberthur	Cascade, La, harp solo	93
Occa, J.	Kinlock o' Kinlock, piccolo solo	02-04 *05
Ochs, Siegfried	Little Bird Came Flying, A, German volkslied	93 01 02 04 09 10 *11 12 24
Ocilez	Habanera	93
Oehmier, Leo	Fatima, intermezzo	03
Oesten	Songs from the Alps	22
Offenbach, Jacques	Belle Helene, La: Fantasie	06 27
	Belle Helene, La: Overture	23 25 26
	Drum Major's Daughter, The: Selections	95
	Fatima, intermezzo	93 94 96 *00 03
	Grand Duchess, The (La Grande Duchess): Selections	94 96 06 07 09 22-28 31
	Madame Favart: Selections	94
	Madame L'Archeduchesse: Selections	93 94 96 22
	Maitre Peronilla: Overture	22 25 26 28
	Market Girls, The: Selections	98
	Monsier Choufleuri: Overture	93 94 96 27 31
	Oh, Belle Nuit	20
	Orpheus aux Enfers (Orpheus in the Underworld): Overture	08 10 16 18 21 23 24 26 31 32

386

	Orpheus aux Enfers (Orpheus in the Underworld): Selections	93-96 04 06 07 09 13 15 21-28
	Perichole, La: Selections	01 22
	Pretty Parfumer, The (La Jolie Perfumesse): Selections	95 96 26
	Princess of Trebizonde, The: Selections	97 98 02 16 21
	Reminiscences of Offenbach	23-26
	Tales of Hoffman, The (Contes d'Hoffmann, Les): Barcarolle, vocal duet	*09
	Tales of Hoffman, The (Les Contes d'Hoffman, Les): Selections	93 96 08 10 *11 12-18 20-27 30 31
	Two Gendarmes, The	18
	Vie Parisienne, La (Life in Paris): Selections	97 98 21 22
Ogarew	Caprice (Caprice Brilliante in A Minor), violin solo	*09 10 *11 12
Olcott, Chauncey	Macushla, trombone solo	20
	Mother Machree, vocal solo	15
	O'Neill, of Derry: Selections	08
Openshaw, John	Love Sends a Little Gift of Roses, vocal solo	*23 25
Openshaw, John & Ralph Stanley	June Brought the Roses, vocal solo	26
Opitz, Freidrich	On the Puesto (Auf der Pusta), czardas	94 96
Ora, Kia	Genevieve, gavotte	26
	Midsummer Ever, A, mazurka	94
Ord Hume, James	1911 (Coronation), overture	14
	Bohemian, suite	15 17 18 *19 *20 21 24-26
	Caravan, The, caprice brilliante	*19 *20
	Dawn of Peace, overture	20
	Hall of Fame, The, fantasia	16
	Malinda's Fairy Bower, intermezzo	22 24 28
	Night in Switzerland, A, cornet solo	93
	Sabbath Morning on Parade (The Sabbath) (Sabbath in Camp) (Sabbath	15-24 30
	Yule Tide, fantasia	16 17
Orem, Preston Ware	American Indian Rhapsody (Indian Love)	*19 *20 *21 22 *23 *24 *25 26 27 31
	Forest Nymph (The Wood Nymph), waltz	23 24
	Songs and Dances of the Cumberland Mountains of Kentucky (Mountain Dances) (Mountain Tunes)	*24 25 26 28
Orth, Charles J.	Advance and Retreat of the Salvation Army, patrol	92
	Birds of the American Forest, idyl	98
	Coxey's Industrial Army, patrol	94
	In a Bird Store, descriptive (idyll)	96 *97 98 *00 01 02
	In a Clock Store (In a Clock Shop), descriptive	*92 *93 *94 95-98 01 02 *03 04 06 16 21
	Spanish Beggar Girl, The, waltz	97
Orth, Lizette Emma	Eyes of Blue, vocal solo	13
Osiier, Julius	Serenade Elegante	10
Otto	Hungarian Dance	02
	Treue Deutche Herz, Das, horn quartet [unaccompanied?]	98
Owst, W.G.	What Is Love?, vocal solo	00
Pacini, G.	Dante, symphonic poem	97
Packard, E.H.	Little Queen Irene, song	95
Paderewski, Ignace Jan	Chant des Voyagers	96
	Grand Pot-Pourri (Collocation of Piano Pieces of Paderewski)	96 98 09 14 21 24 26
	Melody in G-flat	93 *94 95-97
	Menuet [Minuet] (Menuet Antique) (Minuet in B-flat), Op. 14	*93 *94 95 *97 14 17 23 28
	Saxerewski, saxophone ensemble	*26
Padilla, Jose	Valencia, pasodoble	*26
Paganini, Niccolo	Carnival of Venice, piccolo or saxophone solo	93 *95
	Carnival of Venice, The, air varie (variations for various instruments)	95 96
	Perpetual Motion (Perpetual Motion), violin or flute solo	94 21
	Witches Dance, violin or flute solo	93 *12
Paine, John Knowles	Azara: Moorish Dances	02 08
	Columbian Hymn	93

	Pieces, Piano, Op. 41: Fuga Giocosa	24 25
Paley	When It's Night Time	14
Panella, Frank	Fez, The, march	24
Panella, Louis	Pitt Panther, The	24
	University of Dayton, The, march	25
Papini, Guido	Souvenir de Sorrento (Saltarella), violin solo	*02
Paradis	Pre au Clercs, clarinet solo	92
Parenteau & Connelly	My Land, My Flag	16
Pares	Polka-Brillante, cornet solo	93
Parish-Alvars, Elias	Fantasia on Weber's Oberon (Fantasia Oberon), Op. 35, harp solo	*22 *23 *24 *25 *26 30
	Fantisie, Op. 59, harp solo	*30
Parker, Horatio	Legend of Saint Christopher, The: Iam Sol Recedit Igneus (Choral a la Capella), chorus	10 24
	Old English Songs: The Lark Now Leaves His Wat'ry Nest, vocal solo	*10 *11 12 16 *23 *24 27
	Sunlight and Shade: Overture	98
Parlow, A.	Annie, polka	22 23
	Fantasia on Tyrolean Folk Song, cornet solo	23 24
	Polka Caprice, cornet duet	93
Parry, J. Haydn	Cigarette: Scenes	94
Parsons	Fugitive Melodies: The Goldfish	02
Pary	Linger Longer Lu, waltz	94
Pattison, F.	Waltz Song	94
Payne/Bishop	Home Sweet Home, vocal solo	92 95
Pedrotti, Carlo	All in Mask (Tutti I Mascheri): Overture	93-97 18 22 24
Peek, George W.	Three Little Kittens, song	94
Peile	Belle of Cairo: Selections	98
Penfield, Smith N.	March Triomphale	96
	Morningside Souvenir, A, caprice	97
	Souvenir de Catskill	99
	Summer Reverie	94 95
Penn	Honeysuckle and the Bee, coon song	*01 *02 *03
	Ping-Pong, charasteristic	02
	Rube, A, saxophone ensemble	*26
	Sunflower and the Sun, The	02 *03
	Toreadore, fox trot	21
	Under den Linden	04
Penn, Arthur A	Coleen o' My Heart, vocal solo	24 25
	Sing Along!, vocal solo	26 27
	Smilin' Through, vocal solo	04 26 27
	Sunrise and You, vocal solo	21
Perdue	American Dances, SEE Happy Darkeys (Perdue)	
Perdue, G.	Happy Darkeys (American Barn Dance) (American Dances) (Husking Dance), barn dance (caprice)	93 *94 95 96
Perfetto, John J.	Roi d'Yvetot, Le, euphonium solo	06
Perkins, Theoron D.	Massa's in the Cold, Cold Ground, fantasie [based on Stephen Foster's song], cornet solo	94 98
	Scintilla, cornet solo	*20 21-26
Perolini	Polinto, euphonium solo	93
Peroni, Alessandro	Overture Romantique (Romantic Overture)	18
Perry	Warbler's Serenade [with whistling]	*01 02
Pesold, Arnold	McKendree Boys, march	94
Pessard, Emile	Good Day, Marie, vocal solo	95
	Pas des Marionettes (Dance of the Marionettes): Air de Ballet	22 26
Peters, V.	Jolly Coppersmith, The	93
Peterson	Scotch Wedding March	94
Pether, Henry E.	Ragtime Review, The: Selections	16
Petrella, Errico	Ione: Sinfonia (Overture)	*00
	Marco Visconti: Selections	96 97
Petrie, H.W.	Down in the Deep (Asleep in the Deep), cornet, baritone, or trombone solo	20
Petrie, H.W. & Philip Wingate	You Can't Play in Our Yard Anymore, song	94
Pflueger, Carl	1492, march	16

Phelan, Elsie Gertrude	On the Gridiron, march	08
Phelps	Dance of the Elephants	94
Phelps, Ellsworth C.	Beggar Girl's Dance, The	95
	Columbus, grand historic overture	94
	Meditation at Niagara	94 96
	Nocturne	94
	Reve d'Amour, La, gavotte	01
Phile, Philip	Hail Columbia, patriotic song	92 93 *00
Philipe	Air Americaine, saxophone or euphonium solo	*94 *95 97
	Air and Variations for Saxophone, saxophone solo	96
	Old Folks, The, saxophone solo	*95
Philips, W.A.	Star of Love, The, waltz	94
Phillips	Episodes in a Soldier's Life	98
	King of the Vikings Am I, The, trombone solo	20
Piatti, Antonio P.	Tarantelle, cello solo	15
Pierne, Gabriel	Dawn of Redemption, The	01
	March of the Little Lead [Leaden] Soldiers (Little Tin Soldiers)	*13 22 23
	Serenade, Op. 7 (Serenade Celebre)	01 08 18
Pierpont, James	Jingle Bells	07
Pinard, Al	Monarch, The, trombone solo	21 23 24 26
Pinsuti, Ciro	Bedouin's Love Song, vocal or euphonium solo	94 10
	In This Hour of Softened Splendor, chorus	24
	Merchant of Venice, The: Scenes	94 95
	Queen of the Earth, vocal solo	96
Pinto, Octavio	Grand Fantasy, harp solo	22
	Hibernian Rhapsody, harp solo	21
	Irish Rhapsody, harp solo	20 *21 22
	Kathleen Mavourneen, fantasia, harp solo	21
	One Sweetly Solemn Thought, harp solo (unaccompanied)	29
	Scotch Rhapsody, harp solo	27
	Theme and Variations, harp solo (unaccompanied)	*20 *21 *22
	Valse de Concert, harp solo	29
Pizzi, Emilio	Dolce Amor, vocal solo	*00 02
	Gabriella: Scenes	94
	Knights of Old	94
Planquette, Jean-Robert	Captain Therese: Selections	96 25 26
	Chimes of Normandy, The (Les Cloches de Corneville): Selections	94 95
	Fantasia on Themes from Paul Jones	93
	Nell Gwyne: Selections	94 95
	Rip Van Winkle: Selections	93 94 96 24
Poirier	Rhapsodie d'Airs Canadiens (Canadian Rhapsody)	22
Poldini	Marionettes: Poupee Valsante (The Waltzing Doll), waltz	04 *16
Pommer	Stripes and the Stars, The, vocal solo	98
Ponchielli, Amilcare	Air Varied, clarinet duet	93
	Gioconda, La: Aria [unnamed], vocal solo[s]	97 16
	Gioconda, La: Ballet Music	93 19
	Gioconda, La: Barcarolle	93
	Gioconda, La: Cielo e Mar, vocal solo	02
	Gioconda, La: Dance of the Hours	93 *97 98 01 02 06 09 14-18 20-24 *28 *30 31
	Gioconda, La: Finale to Act III	94 15
	Gioconda, La: Selections	93-96 06-10 *11 12-28 31
	Lituani, I: Overture	98
	Lituani, I: Recitative and Air, vocal solo	93
	Promised Bride, The (I Promessi Sposi): Overture	*97 *98 *99 01 02 *04 10 17 24
	Promised Bride, The (I Promessi Sposi): Selections	96 *97
	Promised Bride, The, clarinet solo	93
Pond, Walter J	Ring Out, Bells, waltz	12
Poniatowski, Prince	Yeoman's Wedding Song, vocal solo	94
Pontet	Big Ben, song	93 94

Pope, Douglas Alexander	March of the Cameron Men	*03
Popp	Air de Ballet	96
Popp, Wilhelm	Swiss and His Lass, The, idyl	94
	Verlecht Schelme, album leaf	94
Popper, David	Elfentanz, violin or cello solo	*00 01 03 *05 10 16
	Im Walde, cello solo	*97
Porritt, Mark	Rapid Transit, two-step	03
Porter	Old Fashioned Garden, An, vocal solo	21
Powell, John	At the Fair, suite (Sketches of American fun) (Fun at the Fair)	*26
Powell, W.C	Dream Waltz	10
Predham	March Across the Desert, The	01
Predotte	All in Mask: Overture	*09
Price, Charles B.	Belle of Chautauqua	17
	Mexican Vision	17
Prince, Charles A.	Canary and the Cuckoo, The, humoresque	11 12
Pritchard, C. E.	Noisy Johnnie, The	93 24
Proch, Heinrich	Theme (Air) and Variations, Op. 164 (Tyrolean Air and Variations) (Proch's Variations), vocal or clarinet solo	92 93 04 *05 07 08 16 22
Provent	Dance of Jephtha's Daughter	96
Pryor, Arthur Willard	Air and Variations (Air Varie) (Air Original) (Air Varied) (Theme and Variations), trombone solo	*93 *94 *95 *96 *97 *98 *99 *00 02
	American Fantasie, trombone solo	98
	Annie Laurie, fantasia, trombone or xylophone solo	*94 95 *96 *97 98 99 *00 *01 02 20 *21 *22
	Blue Bells of Scotland (Air with Variations), trombone solo	*94 95 *96 *97 98 99 *00 *01 *02
	Burlington, march	*96
	Coon Band Contest, A, cakewalk	*00 *01 *03
	Esprito d'Corpo, trombone solo	93
	Exposition Echoes, trombone solo	93
	Kansas Two-Step, A, caprice	*95 96 98 *06
	Little Nell, schottische, saxophone solo	*96 08
	Love's Enchantment (Valse de Concert), trombone solo	*02 *03 10 *11 12 15 17 18
	March King, The, march	95 *96
	Passing of Ragtime	*02 *03
	Patriot, The, trombone solo	*01 02 *03
	Petite Suzanne, La (Valse Caprice), trombone solo	*98 18
	Southern Blossoms, descriptive	*98
	Southern Hospitality, cakewalk	99
	Sweet Lorena Ray, trombone solo	*97
	Thoughts of Love (Love Thoughts) (Whispering of Love) (Valse de Concert) (Pensee d'Amour), trombone solo	*98 *99 *00 *01 *02 *03 08-10 18 21
	Trocadero, march	94
	Waltz Caprice, trombone solo	17
	Whistler and His Dog, The	26
	White Rats, march	01
	Ye Boston Tea Party, march	98 01
Puccini, Giacomo	Boheme, La: Aria [unnamed], vocal solo[s]	07 *14 18 19 21 22
	Boheme, La: Che Vita Maladetta, vocal solo	15
	Boheme, La: Love Scene	99
	Boheme, La: Musetta's Waltz, vocal solo	05-07 09 13-16 19
	Boheme, La: Quando Me'n Vo Soletta per la Via (Waltz Song), vocal solo	07
	Boheme, La: Selections	99 *00 *01 02 04-10 *11 12-24 *25 26-28 30 31
	Boheme, La: Waltz Song [unnamed], vocal solo[s]	17
	Crossing the Bar, vocal solo	13
	Madame Butterfly: Aria [unnamed], vocal solo[s]	14 15 16 18-20 *21 22
	Madame Butterfly: Night Scene	*07
	Madame Butterfly: Selections	06-10 *11 12-27 31
	Madame Butterfly: Un Bel Di Vedremo, vocal solo	*07

	Manon Lescaut: Excerpts from Act III	*05
	Manon Lescaut: Finale to Act III	98 *99 *00 01 05 07 13
	Manon Lescaut: Grand Scene	04 06 08-10
	Manon Lescaut: Prelude	98
	Manon Lescaut: Prelude	04
	Manon Lescaut: Selections	17
	Tosca, La: Aria [unnamed], vocal solo[s]	15 16 22-24
	Tosca, La: Finale to Act I (Grand Scene and Finale)	01 02 04
	Tosca, La: Selections	01 06 08 13 15 18 21
	Tosca, La: Vissi d'Arte (Prayer), vocal solo	11 12 14 16-19 21-27
	Turandot: Selections	28
Puerner, Charles J.	Darkies Patrol (The Darkies' Jubilee) (Darkey's Dream)	92
	Irish Patrol, The	93-95 16 25 26
	Japanese Cradle Song	02
	May I?, polka capriccioso	94
	On the Plantation, caprice Africaine	93 94
	Only One Girl's Trip Around the World, descripive fantasie	96 98
Pugni	Florida: Ballet Suite	93-96
Pugni, Cesare	Pharaoh's Daughter (La Fille du Pharon) (The Daughter of Pharaoh): Grand Selection (Ballet Suite)	93 94 96 14-22 24 26 27
Pupilla, L.	Presidente, Il (March Sinfonica), marcia sinfonica	17
Purdy, William T.	On, Wisconsin!, march	10
Quarrier	Victorine, waltz	04
Quensel	American Fantasia, flute solo	17
	Entr' Acte, flute solo	16
Quilter, Roger	Childrens Overture, A	21
Rabottini, Francesco Paolo	Honour and Glory (Honneur et Gloire), march	02
	South Africa, grand battle pieces (grand battle scene)	06 24
Raby	Yeux, Les, vocal solo	20
Rachmaninoff, Sergei	Bells of Moscow (Prelude in C-sharp Minor)	*09 *10 *11 12-16 18-20 23
	Crime and Punishment: Prelude	*09 *11
	Melody in E	15
	Prelude	17 27
	Prelude in G Minor, Op. 23	14 15
Raff, Joachim	Cavatina in E-flat	24
	Cavatina, violin solo or band number	94 96 97 *98 99 04 07 09 14 17 24
	Concerto Originale, euphonium solo	*92 93
	Rigaudon, No. 3	24
	Serenade in A-flat	93 94 25 26
	Symphony in No. 6 in D Minor: Funeral March (Trauer-Marsch)	97
	Symphony No. 5 in E ("Lenore"): March	*00 02 *03 04
	Symphony No. 5 in E ("Lenore"): Parting	04 07 10 21-24
	Tarantella, violin solo	*01
Raffayolo, Joseph Michele	Air Originale, euphonium solo	94
	Fantasia Original, euphonium solo	93 94
	Irish Fantasie, euphonium solo	93
	Souvenirs de Naples, euphonium solo	93
Raggi	Washington Guard, march	94
Ragone, Vincent	Declaration of Independence, historical intermezzo	12
	Souvenir de Gounod, fantasie on Meditation and Serenade	15
Rakemann, Hermann	Gridiron Club, The, march	97
Rameau	Gavotte Antique	02
Rameau, Jean Philippe	Rigodon de Dardanus	95 96 *97 17 26
Rampozzotti, Ettore	Songs and Dances of Italy (Folk Songs of Italy)	93 94 96
Ramsdell	Down in Mississippi, march	99
Randeyger	Mariners, The, trio	01
Rapoport, Ruth	Carita, vocal solo	28
Rascher, M.	Frog's, Polka	94
Ratoli	Mia Bandiera, La, vocal solo	93
Rauski, Joseph Francois	Regiment de Sambre et Meuse	18 23 24 27

Ray, Lillian	Sunshine of Your Smile, The, euphonium solo	22 25
Read, Edward M	Cloister Bells, nocturne	95
Rechzeh	Silver Bells, intermezzo	93
Reckle	Concert Trip, potpourri	93
Reckling, August	Wedding Day, A (Hochzeits-Potpourri), descriptive fantasia	96
Recordi, Giulio	Romance of Pierrot and Pierrette, The (Roman de Pierrot et Pierrette), suite	16
Reed	Singing Bird (Song Birds), intermezzo	*11 13 21 24
Reeves, David Wallis	Battery "A" Boy's Visit to His Girl, A, sentimental episode	98
	Commercial, The, patrol (Commercial Travelers)	93 94
	Deming March	99
	Evening Call, The (an Evening Call), humoresque	95-98
	Fantasie on Songs of Stephen Foster (Excerpts from the Songs of Stephen Foster)	98 99 01 02 06 07
	Fire Brigade, The, descriptive	98
	Gov. Dyer's March, two-step	98
	Keeping Step to the Music of the Union	05 *21 *22
	Nearer, My God to Thee, paraphrase	93 01 04
	Night Alarm, The, descriptive	98
	Second Regiment Connecticut National Guard, march	23 24
	United Service Passing in Review, patrol	98 02 04 24 25
	War Memories of 1862 (A Day in Camp in 1862) (1862 War Memories) (In Camp in 1862) (A Day in Camp at Mt. Gretna)	98 06 08 10 16 21
	Yankee Doodle, fantasia humoresque (Variations on Yankee Doodle)	94 95 *96 *97 02 24
Reeves, Ernest	Hobomoko, Indian romance	10 *11
Register	Fraternity, march	02
Rehm, Charles	Bell Button of West Point, galop	94
Reinboldt	Lott Ist Todt, humoresque	98
Reinecke, Carl	Governor of Tours: Farandole	95
	King Manfred (Konig Manfred), Op. 93: Prelude	01 12
	Peace Festival, Op. 105: Overture (The Dawn of Peace)	13 15 16 24
Reiner, S. Ch.	Komisch, Heiter und So Weiter (Lustig, Heiter und So Weiter) (Here, There and Everwhere) (Valse Fantasia)	02-04 06 09 12 23
Reines	Collocation (Waltz Potpourri), waltz	22
Reinhardt, Heinrich	Liebe Schatz, Der: Frauenaugen (Women's Eyes), waltz	13
	Spring Maid, The: Selections	12 13 24
Reisseger, Carl Gottlieb	Mill on the Cliff, The (The Mill on the Rock) (The Mill in the Mountain): Overture	94 96 98 09 10 22 24
	Shipwreck of the Medusa: Overture	*97 98
Reiter, J.	Juliette de Charenton, flugelhorn solo	01 02 05
Reking	Solo Performers' Congress, The	95
Relle, Moritz	Castles in Spain, ballet suite	23
	Collection of the Most Popular Folk Songs and Dances of Spain, A (Spanish Melodies) (Gems of Spanish Melody)	93
Remick, Jerome H.	Rose of the Mountain Trail, vocal solo	14
Renaud, Elyre	Elegie (Elegue), saxophone solo	93
Renelle	Marche des Moujicks	10
Resch	Flying Leaves, divertissment	94
Respighi, Ottorino	Fountains of Rome (Fontane di Roma), symphonic poem	27 28
Reuland	Parce-Parla, cornet duet	93
Reuter	Slumber Song, flugelhorn solo	97
Reveire	Around the May Pole, rustic dance (Dance of the Rustics)	93 96
Reyer, Louis-Etienne-Ernest	Sigurd: Grand Scene (Fantasie)	01 02
Reynard, Jules	Bowl of Pansies (A Bunch of Pansies), descriptive	15
	Legend of a Rose, idyll	16 19
Reznicek, Emil Nicolaus	Donna Diana: Overture	*00 01 02 07 24
	Eine Lustspiel (Lustspiel), overture	*00 02
Ricci, Joseph	San Jacinto March	24
Ricci, Luigi	Cobbler and the Fairy, The (Crispino e la Comare): Selections	22-24 27
Rice, Edward E.	Candidate, The, march	96
	Columbian Guards, The, march	94
	Excelsior March (March from 1492)	95 96
Rice, Gitz	Dear Old Pal of Mine, vocal or trombone solo	19-21 24-26

Richard	Serenade for Soprano, vocal solo	09
Richards, Joseph John	Conduit Park, march	27
Richardson	Egyptian Suite	16
Ries, Franz	Dear Blue Eyes, The, vocal solo	93
	Pleading, vocal solo	95
	Third Suite: Adagio and Moto Perpetum, violin solo	*00 *01 02 06 *07 *08 09 13 14 16 17
Rietzel, Wilhelm	Trixy Polka, piccolo solo	12
Rimsky-Korsakov, Nikolai	Capriccio Espagnol	*96 97
	Golden Cockerel, The (Le Coq d'Or): Dance of the King and Princess	22
	Golden Cockerel, The (Le Coq d'Or): Hymn to the Sun	22 25
	Golden Cockerel, The (Le Coq d'Or): Selections	22 25
	Nightingale and the Rose, vocal solo	27
	Sadko: A Song of India (Chanson Indoue), vocal solo	22 23 26 27
	Scheherazade, Op. 35: Suite	17
	Scheherezade, Op. 35: The Tale of Prince Kalender (The Story of Prince Kalender)	*97 01 *15
Ring	Call to the Feast, The, suite	20
Ring, Justin	Rocking Horse Parade, march	24
Ring, Justin & Frederick W. Hager	Danse Hongrois, saxophone solo	25
Ring, Montague	Frivolette, dance	19
	Three Arabian Dances, suite	21
Ringleben, Justus	Pen Spatterings, xylophone solo	93
	Polka Caprice, xylophone solo	93
	Straw Fiddle, The, xylophone solo	93
Ritter	Wiegenlied, flugelhorn solo	97
Ritter, Reinhold	Long, Long Ago, Op. 12, fantasie for clarinet or band number	23
Ritter, Th.	Samacueca (Souvenir de Valparaiso)	96
Riviere	Pretty Typewriter, The, caprice	07
Riviere, Jean	Melodies of Ireland	98
	Villager's Polka	94
Rix, Frank Reader	Go to Sleep My Dusky Baby, lullaby	16
Rizzi	Alpine Echoes, saxophone solo	21
Robaudi	Royal Italian March	09
Robaudi, V.	Bright Star of Hope (Alla Stella Confidente), serenade, flugelhorn or cornet solo	94 *98 99 *00 *01 02 04 05 09 15
Robbotin	Over the Top, descriptive fantasia	19
Robert, Camille	Quand Madelon (Madelon), French march	19 20
Roberts, Charles J	Old Folks at Home and in Foreign Lands (Way Down Upon the Swanee Ribber), paraphrase	20 27
	Melodies from Famous Light Operas (Master Melodies from Favorite Light	21-24
Roberts, Julia	Washington, D.C., march	22
Roberts, M.J.	Oh, Wondrous Multitude	03
Robledo, Julien & Dorothy Terris	Three O'Clock in the Morning, waltz	23 *24
Robyn, Alfred George	Answer? (Answers), ballad, vocal or cornet solo	94 96 20
	Elegie, saxophone solo	93
	Haste, Love, saxophone solo	93
	Jacintha: Manzanillo	09
	My Heart's Delight, vocal solo	21 22
	O Heart That's Free (A Heart That's Free), vocal or flute solo	*22
	There's Nothing to Say (There Is Nothing New to Say), cornet solo	04
	Yankee Consul, A: Selections	04 06
Rocereto, Mario S.	Blue Ridge Division March	25
	Longing, tone picture	01
Rodolphe, Jean Joseph	Une Corbeille de Fleurs	02 *03
Roeckel	Speed On, vocal solo	
	Storm Fiend, The	94
Roeckel, Joseph L.	Kermesse de St. Cloud, morceau de genre	93 94 96
Roederer	Love's Dreamland, waltz	93
Rogan, J. Mackenzie & Edgar F. Jacques	Indian Empire, melodies of India, fantasia	06
Rogers	Heart's Delight, vocal solo	21
	Star, The, vocal solo	16

Rogers, James Hotchkiss	At Parting, vocal solo	97
Rogers, Walter B.	Air and Variations, cornet solo	01 02
	Air Brilliante, cornet solo	02
	Auld Lang Syne, cornet solo	99 01 02
	Fantasia Originale, cornet solo	04
	Fantasie on German Airs, cornet solo	04
	Harp That Once Thro' Tara's Halls, The (The Harp of Tara), cornet solo	99 01-04
	Lulle, cornet solo	*00 01 02 04
	Minnehaha, cornet solo	*00 01 04
	Soldier's Dream, A, cornet solo	99 *01 02-04 *28 29
	Souvenir of Naples, cornet solo	99 *00 01
	Volunteer, The (The American Volunteer), cornet solo	99 01 02 *03 04 09 20 21 *22 23 24 25 27
	War Songs (War Song Variations) (Columbian Fantasy), cornet solo	04
Rolle	Songs and Dances of Spain	95
Rollinson, Thomas H.	Air Varied, euphonium solo	26
	Blue Bells of Scotland, cornet solo	93 97
	Columbia, polka, cornet or trombone solo	98 18 24 27
	Jerusalem, the Golden, paraphrase	94 96 06-08 12 22 24
	Jolly Millers, The galop	97 98
	Rocked in the Cradle of the Deep, trombone solo	*94 95 96
	Roses and Lillies, cornet solo	95
	Sea Flower Polka	02
	Silent Steed, The, galop	95
	Theme and Variations, trombone solo	93
	Tramp, Tramp, Tramp, cornet solo	26
Romberg, Sigmund	Marie, Marie, cornet solo	*20
	Your Land and My Land, march	29
Ronald, Landon	Cycle of Life, A, vocal solo	*11
Rondelle, Le Louis	Airs de Ballet: Les Coryphees	*01
	Hermione: Ballet Suite	*01 02
	Airs de Ballet: Dance des Cymbals (Dance of the Cymbal Beaters)	*01
	Belles of St. Martin, The, SEE Carillon de St. Martin (Rondelle, La)	
	Carillon de St. Martin (The Bells of St. Martin), intermezzo	14 *15 17
Rooke	Amilie: Selections	01
Root, George Frederick	Battle Cry of Freedom (Tramp, Tramp, Tramp the Boys Are Marching) (Rally Round the Flag), vocal or cornet solo	*98 24
Rosas, Juventinio	Andalusia, waltz	93
	Over the Waves (Over the Dancing Waves) (Sobre las Olas), waltz	01 02 04 06 09 14 15 22 24 31
Rosebrooke	Velma, saxophone solo	25-28
Rosenbecker	Germania Club, march	95
	In Tiefen Keller, march	95
Rosenberg	Two Little Bullfinches, piccolo duet	01
Rosenfield, Monroe H.	New York Herald, The	*94 96
	Take Him to Your Heart Again, cornet solo	94
	Virginia Skedaddle, The	94
Rosenkranz, Anton	My Austria (Mein Osterreich), fantasie, flugelhorn solo	*00 01
Rosenkranz, Fredrich	Oberon: Huons Zauberhorn, fantasie (Fantasie on Themes from Weber's Oberon)	95 96 15
Rosey, George	Anniversary, The, march	96
	Espanita, waltz	96 *00
	Handicap, The, march	96
	Honeymoon March, The	95 *96
	Scorcher, The, march	98
Roskosny	Moldaunixie, Die: Overture	98
Rosoff, Charles & Gus Kahn	When You and I Were Seventeen, vocal solo	25 26
Ross	Collection of Plantation Melodies, A	93
	Songs Our Soldiers Sang in '63, The	93 94
Rosse, Frederick	All Aboard: Selections	96
	Merchant of Venice: Incidental Music (suite)	12 17
	Mitrane: Aria [unnamed], vocal solo[s]	95

	Monsieur Beaucaire: Incidental Music (suite)	04
Rossini, Giacchino	Air Italia, euphonium solo	96 15 16
	Barber of Seville, The: Aria [unnamed], vocal solo[s]	*92 *93 04 06
	Barber of Seville, The: Barbiere (Ecco Ridente il Cielo)	16
	Barber of Seville, The: Figaro, vocal solo	93 *94
	Barber of Seville, The: Largo al Factotum, vocal solo	*92 93
	Barber of Seville, The: Overture	93 94
	Barber of Seville, The: Una Voce Poco Fa, vocal solo	93 94 05 16
	Barbiere, song	92
	Gazza Ladra, La: Overture	94 96
	Irish Fantasia for Euphonium, euphonium solo	94
	Italian in Algiers: Excerpt, clarinet solo	93
	Moses in Egypt: Prayer, chorus	93
	Reminiscences of Rossini	93
	Semiramide: Aria [unnamed] vocal solo or cornet solo/duet	93 14 21
	Semiramide: Bel Raggio Lusinghier, vocal solo	94 *95 06 *07 08
	Semiramide: Cavatina [unnamed], vocal solo[s]	95 07
	Semiramide: Ecsome Afine, vocal solo	93
	Semiramide: Overture	*92 93 *94 95-97 05 08 09 18-20 22-27
	Siege of Corinth: Overture	98
	Stabat Mater: Cujus Anima, vocal, cornet or trombone solo	93-97 *03 04 05 09 *19 20 22 26 30
	Stabat Mater: Inflammatus, vocal or cornet solo	93-96 98 99 01 02 06 *07 08-10 12-15 17 18 21 23-25 28 29 31
	Stabat Mater: Overture	94 25
	Tancredi: Aria [unnamed), vocal solo[s]	19 20 26
	Tancredi: Overture	93 94 96
	Tantum Ergo, sacred song, trombone or euphonium solo	98 04
	William Tell: Ballet Music	*92 93-96 01 04 10 14 17 18 20 21 23 24 31
	William Tell: Overture	*92 *93 *94 *95 *96 97 *98 *99 *01 *02 *03 *04 05 *06 07 *08 09 10 *11 12 13 *14 *15 16-18 20 *21 22-24 *25 26-29
	William Tell: Suite	02
	William Tell: Trio, vocal trio	93
Roth	Clown, The, caprice	94
Rothchild	Romance, flugelhorn solo	02
Rothschild	Air Sympathetique, flugelhorn solo	96
Rotoli	Daybreak, barcorolle, vocal solo	95
Routhier, Judge	Oh, Canada	19
Roy, Dudley	Ma Belle Adoree, waltz	94
Rubens, Paul A.	Balkan Princess, The: Selections	12 13 15
	Chimney Sweep, The, characteristic	18 24
	Dear Little Denmark: Selections	13 24
	Lady Madcap: Selections	06
	Little Dutch Girl, The: Selections	21
	Miss Hook of Ireland: Selections	08 24
	Sunshine Girl, The: The Argentine, tango	13
	Three Little Maids: Selections	04 07
	Tina: Selections	21
	Una, the Girl from Utah: Barcarolle	14 15
	Way We Have in the Army, A, march	22
Rubens, Paul, SEE ALSO Jones, J. Sidney		
Rubinstein, Anton	Bal Costume: Royal Tambour et Vivandiere	94 96
	Bal Costume: Selections (Ballet)	93 95 96 08 13 24
	Bal Costume: Toreador et Andalouise (Andalusia)	93 96 06

	Cavalry Canter (Cavalry Trot) (Trot de Cavalerie) (Cavalry Ride), descriptive	02 05 24
	Cossaque et Russiene, dances	95
	Feramors: Ballet Suite	*92 *93 *94 96 *97 01
	Feramors: Dance of the Bayaderes	*93 94 96 *99
	Feramors: Torchlight Dance of the Bride of Cashmere	93 *94
	Kamenoi Ostrow (Reve Angelique) (Portrait of a Lady), nocturne (portrait)	95 02 04 06 *07 *08-10 *11 12 *13 14 15 18 19 21 22 *23 *24 27
	Melody in F, paraphrase	94-96 01 06-09 15 22
	Melody in F, xylophone solo or band number	*23 27
	Since First I Met Thee, vocal solo	94
	Songs and Dances of Russia	16
	Staccato Etude, Op. 23	08 *09 10 *11 15 21
	Triomphale (Triumphal) Overture	*96 *97 98 *00 01 02 04 07 08 19
	Valse Caprice	*97 98 99 *00 20 23
Runcie, Constance F.	Prince of Asturia, The: Habanera (Gypsy Dance), Spanish dance	95
Rupprecht, Theo	Don Quixote: March Grotesque	15 16
	Don Quixote: Through Spain (Don Quixote in Spain)	13-15
Russell, James I.	Sunset, vocal solo	15
	Where the River Shannon Flows, cornet solo	15
Rybner, Cornelius	Prince Ador, ballet	21
Sabathil, Ferdinand	Dream of Lanner and Strauss, A	05
	Dream[s] on the Bosporus (Traume am Bosporus), Op. 76 waltz Orientale	23 24
	Grandfather's Wedding	94
Sabin W.D.	Phantom, The, overture	22
Sachs, Henry Everett	March Johnny	27
Saenger, Gustave	Three Characteristic Dances, suite	21 22 26
Safranek, Vincent Frank	Atlantis (The Lost Continent), suite	15 24
	Musical Panorama, A	23
	Operatic Masterpieces (Masterpieces from Grand Operas), potpourri	10 15
	Tigale, La, waltz	21 23
Saint-Saens, Camille	Ascanio: Selections (ballet music)	10 15 21
	Breton, rhapsodie (Rhapsodie Bretonne)	*95 96
	Carnival of the Animals: The Swan (Le Cygne), violin or cello solo	*95 *05 *11 12
	Cello Concerto	15
	Danse Macabre (Dance of Death), symphonic poem	97 99 01 02 *03 04 06 14 15 17 18 27
	Deluge, The: Prelude (Prelude du Deluge)	14 23 24
	Hail California, symphonic episode, with orchestra and organ	15
	Havanaise, violin solo	12
	Henry VIII (King Henry): Ballet Suite (Ballet Divertissement); Gathering of the Clans; Scotch Idylle; Gipsy Dance; Jig and Finale	*00 *01 02 10 15-20 22 24 27
	Introduction and Rondo Capriccioso, Op. 14, violin or cornet solo	93 *99 01 02 *03 *05 06 07 *10 12 14 16-18 *27
	Jota, La, a dance of Aragon (Jota Arragonese)	02 10
	Mazourka No. 1, Op. 21 (Mazurka de Concert)	98
	Night in Lisbon, A (Une Nuit a Lisbonne), barcarolle	15 17-19
	On the Banks of the Nile (Sur les Bordes du Nil), march	13
	Orient and Occident (Occident et Orient, grand march	02 08 15 18 27
	Parysatis, fantasie	14
	Phaeton, symphonic poem	15 21
	Prosperine: Selections	93
	Rondo Capriccioso, violin or cornet solo	*96 *98 *10 *11 14 15 18 23
	Samson and Delila: My Heart at Thy Sweet Voice (Mon Coeur s'Ouvre a ta Voix), vocal, cornet, or flugelhorn solo	94 96 *98 04 05 06 10 *16 18 19 21
	Samson and Delilah: Aria [unnamed], vocal or cornet solo	16 18 *19 26 27
	Samson and Delilah: Bacchanale (Air de Ballet) (Bacchanalian Ballet)	14 15 26
	Samson and Delilah: Selections	03-07 09 10 12-19 21-26

	Second Concerto, violin solo (2 movements)	94 14 *15
	Suite Algerienne	17-19 21-24 *25 26 27
	Suite Algerienne: Marche Militaire Francaise (French Military March)	94 *12 15-18 20 21 25 *28 29
	Wheel of Omphale, The (Rouet d'Omphale, Le) (Omphale's Spinning Wheel), symphonic poem	94 95
Salzer	Snow Queen, intermezzo	08
Salzer, Gustav	Spring Thoughts, novelty	13
Samson	Honor and Arms	94
Sanderson	Until, vocal solo	15
Sanderson, Wilfred	God Be With Our Boys Tonight, patriotic song, vocal solo	*18 19
Sanelli, G.	Genaro Annese: Giuramento	94 96
	Genaro Annese: The Oath	94
Santley	Only to Love Her, vocal solo	94
Sapio	Waltz, vocal solo	94
Sarakowski, G.	Arabian Dance	93
	Five Dances	94
Sarasate, Pablo de	Andalusia (Romanza Andaluza), violin solo	01-03 09 13
	Caprice Basque, violin solo	19 21
	Fantasie on Bizet's Carmen (Carmen Fantasie), violin solo	*14
	Faust Fantasie, violin solo	93 *95 10 16-18 *23 *24
	Gypsy Girl, The, (Gypsy Dance) (The Gipsies) (Gipsy Life) (Gypsy Tales) (Gypsy Airs), violin solo	*93 06 09 10 12 14-18 *19 *20 21
	Habanera, cornet solo	*28
	Jota Aragoneta [Aragonaise] (Spanish Dance No. 4), descriptive, violin solo	12 13 15
	Mignon Fantasia, violin solo	16 17 23 *24
	Reminiscences of Sarasate, violin solo	06
	Romance and Gavotte, violin solo	17 23
	Russian Airs, violin solo	15
	Spanish Dances (Dance Espagnole), violin solo	01-04 09 13 15 16 18 19
	Zapateado, violin solo	04 *11 12 15-20 *21 22
	Ziguenerweisen (Gipsy Airs, or Gipsy Tunes) (Hungarian Dance), fantasie, violin solo	93 *96 *97 *98 *99 *01 *02 *03 *04 *05 *06 *07 *09 10 *11 12 14-17
Saro, Heinrich	Grand Military Tattoo	93-96
Satta, G	Oh, How I Love Thee, romance, cornet solo	97 98
Sauret, Emile	Farfalla, violin solo	10
Savary	Lucy Long, bassoon solo	93
Savasta, G.	Bashi-Bazouk, Oriental fantasie	07
Saxone	Ma Belle Adare, waltz	93
	Santiago, Waltz	93
Saxton	Air Americaine (American Air) (Air and Variations on American Themes) (American Fantasia), saxophone or euphonium solo	96 *98 19
	I'm Lonely Since My Mother Died, euphonium solo	95 96
Sayres	Mary Green, cornet solo	*92
Schaafer, H.	Post in the Woods, The (Die Post Im Walde), fantasie, cornet solo	22
Schamortz	Los Novios, idyll	01
Scharwenka, Xavier	Gavotte	94
	Polish Dancees	93 94 96 05
Schelling, Ernest	Victory Ball, A, (At the Victory Ball), descriptive fantasie	*23 *24 28
Schermer	Gallant and Gay, medley	01
	In the Realm of the Waltz	01 02
Scheu	Sleepy Sidney	08
Schillings, Max	Ingewelde: Overture to Act I	96
Schirza, F.	I Dreamt (Sognai), song, cornet solo	93 94 96
Schleiffarth, George	Jolly Bears, The, polka caprice	93
Schlesinger, S.B.	Wedding March	94
Schlig, Martin	Down South, xylophone solo	04
Schmeling, Martin	Evening at Sea, An, romance	98

	Evening in Toledo, An (Un Nuit de Toledo), suite	97 09 10 12 13 16-20 24-27
	Evening in Spain, An	26
Schmidt	Rapid Transit, march	09
	Signal du Bal, galop, (rondo militaire), trumpet solo (The Trumpet Signal)	97 98
Schmidt, Gustav	Prince Eugene: Overture	94
Schmidt, M.E.	Orange and Black, The, march	96
Schmitt, Florent	Venetian Rhapsody (Rapsodie Viennoise), Op. 53	25 26
Schneider	Dessauer March: Overture	94
	Overture, based on America	96
Schneider, Edward Faber	Dance of the Saplings	09 10
Schoen	Veiled Prophet's Reception, march	93 94
Schoenefeld, Henry	American Rhapsody	10 *11 12 13 27
Schreiner	Military Fantasia	13
	Waltz Fantasia	14
Schreiner, Adolf	Congress Overture (Overturen Congress) (Gems from the Overtures) (A Congress of Overtures), fantasie based on famous overtures	94-96 07 20 21 23
	From Gluck to Richard Wagner, characteristic potpourri	09
	Im Zick-Zack: Potpourri (fantasie)	n.d.
	Komisch, Heiter, und So Weiter (Komischmheiter und so Weiter) (Here and There), fantasie	02 04 07
	Kurtz in Erbaulich	99
	Major and Minor (Dur und Moll), Potpourri	16
	Musical Melange, A	94
	Pandean Pastoral clarinet section soli	93
Schreiner, Otto E.	Gaudemus Igitur, paraphrase	05
Schubert, Franz	Alfonso and Estrella: Overture	94 25
	Am Meer (By the Sea), trombone solo	26
	Astres, Les, song	96
	Ave Maria, violin or vocal solo	01 14 15 16 21
	Bee, The (L'Abeille), violin solo	*03
	Chorus of the Horsemen	98
	D Minor Quartet: Death and the Maiden, variations	95
	Eloge des Larmes (Elegy of Tears), song	96
	Erlking (Erlkoenig) (The Erl King), ballad	23 24
	Fierrabras: Overture, Op. 76	95 96
	Funeral March (Trauer Marsch) (Trauermarsch)	15
	Great Jehovah, sacred air	01
	Lilac Time: Scenes	25
	Litanei (A Litany), adagio religioso	05 06
	Marche Militaire, Op. 51 (Caprice) (March Caprice)	93-96 03 04 06 13-15 23 27
	Moments Musicale (Moment Musical)	03 04 13 15 22 24 30 31
	Rosamunde: Ballet Music	*92 93 *94 95-98 01 09 14 22-24
	Rosamunde: Overture	92-95 97
	Rosamunde: Selections	93
	Schubertiana, fantasia on melodies by Franz Schubert	04
	Serenade for violin, violin solo	07
	Serenade Impromptu, band number or xylophone solo	96 24
	Serenade, song, or as cornet or flugelhorn solo	93-96 *97 *03 04 *06 *07 15
	Symphony No. 8 ("Unfinished")	93 94 23-26
	Ungedald, vocal solo	94
	Wanderer, The, vocal solo	94 99
Schulhoff, Julius	Grand Valse Brilliante (Brilliant Waltz) (Valse Brilliant)	24
Schultz	Team Triumphant, The	*12
Schumann, Georg	Amor und Psyche, Op. 3: Tanz der Nymphen und Satyrn	94 96
	Liebesfruhling, overture	12
	Love's Spring (Love in Spring) (Liebesfrueling) (Spring), overture	11 12
Schumann, Robert	Fantasiestucke, Op. 12: Warum?	Not determined

	Oriental Picture, An	96
	Reminiscences of Schumann	06 08 13 15 23
	Slumber Song	93
	Traumerei, violin solo or band number	98 01 02 *09 15 *21 *22 *23 27
	Two Grenadiers, The, vocal solo, euphonium solo, or band number	94 95 97 02 05 *06 07 08 09 15 17
	Wanderer, The, song	94
	Wiegenlied	93
Schwalm, Oskar	Forsaken Am I (Verlassen Bin I), paraphrase	05
Schwartz, Jean, Bert Kalmar, & Edgar Leslie	Hello, Hawaii, How Are You? (Hello, Aloha!, How Are You?, saxophone ensemble	*26
Scott	Within the Garden of My Heart, vocal solo	18
Scott, John Prindle	Holiday, vocal solo	24
	Wind's in the South, The, vocal solo	24
Sears, William	Haverhill Commanery March, The	25
Sebek, G.	In the Soudan (On the Soudan), Dervish chorus (idyll)	01 02 06 10 *11 15 18 22 23 27
Sebella	Air Original, cornet solo	19
Seitz, Ernest, SEE Lockhart, Eugene		
Seitz, Roland F.	Radio Pioneer, march	25
Sellenick, Adolphe Valenti	In Cairo Street, Midway Plaisance	93
	Indienne March (Caprice on Hindoo Airs) (March Hindoo) (East Indian Melodies) (Indian Air) (March Indienne)	93 94 96 01 10 24
	World's Fair	93
Sellenick, Adolphe Valenti (arranger)	Chant of the Persians (Aux Bords du Sebaou), Arab chant (Hari Irani)	93 97
Semper	Nature's Lullaby	22
Senza	May Morning, vocal solo	02
Seredy, Julius S.	Campus Memories, collection of college songs	22 30
	Old Favorites, collection of well known standard songs	22
	Straussiana, waltz	23-28
Severn, Edmund	Bacchanal, violin solo	08 09 12
	Story of Love (Storia d'Amore), violin solo	14
	Valse Caprice, violin solo	09
Sgambati, Giovanni	Gavotte in Ancient Style	96
	Gavotte in D-flat	*97
Shain	Roses from the South, waltz	20
Shannon	Favorita, A la, waltz	94
Shantz	Egyptian Patrol, An	93
Shattuck	Chiming Bells of Long Ago, cornet solo	24
Shelley, Harry Rowe	American Dances	*14 *15 16
	Love's Sorrow, vocal solo	96
	March Militaire	06
	Minstrel Boy, The, vocal solo	17
	Resurrection, saxophone solo	93 *94
Shields	Holy Friars, The, vocal solo	94
Shilkret, Nathanniel, SEE Green, Joseph		
Short	Valse Caprice, cornet solo	30 31
Short, Herbert	Battery "A" [27th Indiana Battery] March	98 99 24 30
Short, Thomas V.	Glen Island Waltz, cornet solo	98 21-26 *31
	Irish Fantasie (Irish Airs), cornet solo	08 24
	Our Maud, cornet solo	*24 *25 26
Short, William	Variations on a Well-Known Melody, fantasie	20
Sibelius, Jean	Finlandia, tone poem	09 *10 *11 12-15 20-23 *24 25 26 *28
	Krolina: Valse Triste, Op. 44	*10 *11 12 23
	Valse Triste, SEE Krolina (Sibelius)	*10
Sibella	Twilight Dreams, vocal solo	17 18
Silesu	Love, Here Is My Heart, vocal solo	21
Silesu, Lao	Little Love, a Little Kiss, A (Un Peu d'Amour), song	13 19 24
Silver, Frank & Irving Cohn	Yes, We Have No Bananas, xylophone solo	*23 *24
Silver, Lewis	April Showers, song	22

Silver, Maxwell	He Walked Right In, Turned Around, and Walked Right Out Again, humoresque	*07 *08
Silverberg, J.A.	Off to Camp, march	96
Simon, Frank & Herman Bellstedt	Willow Echoes, cornet or euphonium solo	17 18 *19 *20 21 22 28
Simonetti, Achille	Madrigale, violin solo	*02 04 *05 *13
Simons, Gardell	Atlantic Zephyrs, trombone or cornet solo	20-26 *30 31
Sinding, Christian	Suite for Violin, violin solo	02
Singelee	Fantasie Pastorale, saxophone solo	*05
Sinigaglia, Leone	Rapsodia Piedmontese, Op. 26 (Dances Piedmontese)	*10 *12 13 23
Sired, W.G.	Titania, waltz caprice	95
Sissle, Noble & EubieBlake	Shuffle Along	22
Sitt, Hans	Wiegenlied (Slumber Song), Op. 48, gavotte	*94
Skilton, Charles Sanford	Two Indian Dances: War Dance; Deer Dance	20 *21 22 27 28
Slater, Walter L.	Piccolo Pic, piccolo solo or quartet	20 22 26 28 *29
	Rubenesque, comic intermezzo	26
Slaughter, Walter	Dandy Dan, the Life Guardsman: Selections	02 07
	French Maid, The: Selections	98
	Gentleman Joe: Dance	96
	Gentleman Joe: Selections	96 26
	Lady Slavey, The: Selections	96
Sloane, Alfred Baldwin	Mary, Mary, Quite Contrary, song	16
	Strange Adventures of Jack and the Beanstalk: Jack March	16
Slowitzky, Michael	Pride of the Nation, march	23
Smareglia, Antonio	Cornelius Schutt (Cornelius Suite): Prelude (Vorspiel)	95 96 02 17 21
Smetana, Bedrich	Aus der Heimat, violin solo	13 14
	Bartered Bride, The (Die Verkaufte Braut) (Prodana Nevesta): Dance Music (Dance of the Comedians)	15 *19 *20 21-24
	Bartered Bride, The (Die Verkaufte Braut) (Prodana Nevesta): Furiant	10
	Bartered Bride, The (Die Verkaufte Braut) (Prodana Nevesta): Overture	10 15 19 *20 21-28 30
	Bartered Bride, The (Die Verkaufte Braut) (Prodana Nevesta): Polka	10
	Bartered Bride, The (Die Verkaufte Braut): Selections	23 24
	Kiss, The (Hubicka): Overture	24
	Libussa: Overture	98
	Moldau (Vltava), symphonic poem	10 15 16 24
	My Fatherland: Vysehrad, No. 1, symphonic poem	10 27
	Verkaufte Braut, Die, SEE Bartered Bride, The (Smetana)	94
Smith	Christmas Bells	01
Smith, C. Wenham	If I But Knew, vocal solo	96 19 20
	Judge, The, grand march	96
Smith, Clay	New Creation, The, cornet solo	26 28 *29
	Sorter Miss You, saxophone solo	19
Smith, Frank	39th Separate Co. Band March	98
Smith, Hubbard T.	Listen to My Tale of Woe, divertimento	*98
Smith, J. Sidney	Carillon de Noel (The Bells of Christmas) (Christmas Bells), gavotte & musette (idyll)	*99 01 02 04 05 21
	Chanson Russe, Op. 31	10 24
	Gavotte in B-flat	93
	Gavotte in F	93 94
Smith, John Stafford	Star Spangled Banner, The	all years
Smith, Lee Orean	Old Wedding Gown, The, waltz	13
Snedeker, Levengston	Polonaise No. 1	23
Sobarzo, Ed.	Naida, characteristic fantasie	07
Soderman, August	Joan of Arc (Maid of Orleans) (Jungfrau von Orleans): Overture	16 17 21
	Joan of Arc: Overture	21
	Swedish Wedding March	94 95 *96 99 06 13 18 22 23 27
Solan	Trumpet of Victory March	22
Soloman, Edward	Glee Maiden, vocal solo	97
	Venetian Dance (A Dance of Venice)	93 96
	Vicar of Bray, The: Selections	93
	Wedding Dance of the Elves	08 14 24
Solomon	Red Hussar, waltz, vocal solo	94

Son	Our Colonel, march	24
Sontag, G.	Niebelungen, march [based on themes by Wagner] (March on Themes of Richard Wagner's Operas)	01 02 04 05 09 10 13 15 16 27
Sontini, R.	Miramar, waltz	12
Sousa, John Philip	Across the Danube, march	94
	America First, march	16, succeeding years
	American Maid The (The Glass Blowers): The American Girl, vocal or cornet solo	*21 *22 *23 *24 25 26
	American Maid, The (The Glass Blowers): Overture	16 21 22-24 *25 26-28
	American Maid, The (The Glass Blowers): Suite (You Do Not Need a Doctor; The Sleeping Soldiers; With Pleasure* (*not from the operetta)	*13 *14 15 16 18-20 22 23 *25 *26 27 28 30 31
	American Maid, The (The Glass Blowers): The Crystal Lute, vocal solo	*13 *14 15-19 *20 *21 22 23 *24 25-28
	American Maid, The (The Glass Blowers): The Red Cross Nurse, vocal solo	13 15 17 24
	American Maid, The (The Glass Blowers): Waltz Song, vocal solo	16
	American Maid, The: In the Dimness of Twilight He Told His Love, vocal	24-26
	Among My Souvenirs, humoresque	*28
	Anchor and Star, march	*18, succeeding years
	Ancient and Honorable Artillery Company, march	*24, succeeding years
	Application of Jazz Tunes, An (Limehouse Blues and others)	24
	Assembly of the Artisans, The, fantasie	94 25 26
	At the King's Court: Her Grace, the Duchess (Her Royal Highness, the Princess); Her Ladyship, the Countess; Her Majesty, the Queen (Her Majesty at Westminster);	*04 *05 *06 *07 08-10 12 16 18-20 23 *24 25 *28 *30 *31
	Atlantic City Pageant, march	*27, succeeding years
	Aviators, The, march	*31 32
	Band Came Back, The (And the Band Played Annie Laurie), humoresque	93 *95 *96 97 *98 *99 *00 *01 02 *06 07 *08 09 *11 12 14-17
	Beau Ideal, The, march	*93, succeeding years
	Belle Mahone, saxophone solo	94-98 03-05
	Belle of Bayou Teche, The, vocal solo	*11, succeeding years
	Belle of Chicago, The, march	*92, succeeding years
	Ben Bolt, march	24-26
	Black Horse Troop, The, march	*25, succeeding years
	Blending of the Blue and the Gray, the, fantasie	93 94 *95 *98 24
	Bonnie Annie Laurie March	94 95
	Boots, vocal solo	16, succeeding years
	Bouquet of Beloved Inspirations, medley (fantasie)	*22 *23 *24 25-28 *29 31
	Boy Scouts of America, The, march	*16, succeeding years
	Bride Elect, The, march	*98 *99 09 22
	Bride Elect, The: Aria [unnamed], vocal solo[s]	20
	Bride Elect, The: Caprian Tarantelle (Tarantella) (The Dancing Girl)	*99 *00 01 04 06 15 18 22-24
	Bride Elect, The: Love, Light of My Heart, vocal solo/duet	05 *06 07 08 *09 19
	Bride Elect, The: Pastorella's Song, vocal solo	05
	Bride Elect, The: Second Collocation	17 19 22 23
	Bride Elect, The: Selections	98 99 *00 02 *03 04 05 07-28 30 31
	Bride Elect, The: Sextet (When Eve) (Ah, Love) (Love Kind Love), brass sextet or band number	01 02 *03 04 06 *11 13-20 22 24
	Bride Elect, The: The Card Song (Here's a Pack), vocal solo	*05 *06 *07 *10 *11 12-22
	Bride Elect, The: The Snow Baby, vocal or flugelhorn solo	*99 01-06 08 10 *11
	Bullets and Bayonets, march	*19, succeeding years
	Camera Studies: Drifting to Loveland; The Children's Ball; The Flashing (Teasing) Eyes of Andalusia	20 *21 *22 23-25 *26 28 29 31
	Capitan and His Friends, El, suite: El Capitan; The Charlatan; The Bride	*24 *25 *26 28 29 31
	Capitan, El, march	*96, succeeding years
	Capitan, El: Behold El Capitan (El Capitan's Song)	15

	Capitan, El: But a League to the South of Tampoza's Gate, chorus	96
	Capitan, El: Isabel's Song, cornet solo	19
	Capitan, El: Oh, Warrior Grim (The Bell Song) (The Tolling of the Bells), cornet solo or band number	05 06 13 16-25 27
	Capitan, El: Second Fantasie	15 17 18
	Capitan, El: Selections	*97, succeeding years
	Capitan, El: Waltzes	96-98 *00 10 24
	Capitan, El: You See in Me, vocal solo	96
	Century of Progress, A., march	31* 32
	Chantyman's March, The	*18, succeeding years
	Chariot Race, The, symphonic poem	*92, succeeding years
	Charlatan, The (The Mystical Miss): Finale to 2nd Act	21
	Charlatan, The (The Mystical Miss): Overture	01 04 05 13 *14 15-17 *18 19 21-27
	Charlatan, The (The Mystical Miss): Russian Peasant's Dance (Russian Mazurka) (Mazurka a la Russe)	*99 01 02 03 10 12 17-23 25 26
	Charlatan, The (The Mystical Miss): Selections	99 01-04 06 09 10 16-18 20-26
	Charlatan, The (The Mystical Miss): Social Laws	*15 20 21 *22 23
	Charlatan, The (The Mystical Miss): The Faithless Knight and the Philosophic Maid, vocal or cornet solo	*02 *03 *11 *12 13 17 19 21-24 *25 26 27
	Charlatan, The (The Mystical Miss): Waltzes	*99 *01 02 04 *05 08 10 *11 *12 *13 *14 *15 16 17 *18 19-24
	Charlatan, The (The Mystical Miss): Will You Love [Me] When The Lilies Are Dead?, vocal solo	18 22 24-26
	Charlatan, The, march	*98, succeeding years
	Chris and the Wonderful Lamp: Electric Ballet	01
	Chris and the Wonderful Lamp: Fanny, vocal or violin solo	13 14 17 *18 19 *20 *21 *22 23-27
	Chris and the Wonderful Lamp: Mama, Papa	*14 19-23
	Chris and the Wonderful Lamp: Overture	05 14 17 18 22 24
	Chris and the Wonderful Lamp: Selections	*00 01 02 *04 05 07-10 15-18 20-28
	Chris and the Wonderful Lamp: The Patient Egg	*03 04
	Chris and the Wonderful Lamp: Where Is Love, vocal solo	*01 02 *11 12 19
	Circumnavigator's Club, The, march	32
	Coeds of Michigan, The, waltz	*25 28
	Colonial Dames Waltzes, The	95 *98 00-02 10 15 16 19-27
	Coquette, characeristic dance (caprice)	93 95 96 *97 *00 01 12 22-24
	Corcoran Cadets, march	*93, succeeding years
	Crossing the Bar, vocal solo	*26 27
	Crusader, The, march	*93, succeeding years
	Cuba Under Three Flags (Cubaland), suite: Under the Spanish Flag; Under the American Flag; Under the Cuban Flag	*25 26 28 29
	Dauntless Battalion, The, march	*23, succeeding years
	Desiree: Overture	94 95
	Desiree: Selections	94-96 25-27
	Desiree: Waltz Song	96 17
	Dinorah: Selections	*04, succeeding years
	Directorate, The, march	*94, succeeding years
	Dwellers of the Western World: The Red Man; The White Man; The Black Man	*10, succeeding years
	Esprit du Corps, march	98
	Fairest of the Fair, The, march	*08, succeeding years
	Fancy of the Town, The (1911-1920), fantasie	*21 *22 *23 24 25 27
	Federal March, The	*11, succeeding years
	Fighting Race, The (Kelly and Burke and Shae), vocal or trombone or	17 20 22-26
	Flags of Freedom, march	19 21 22 24

	Flor de Sevilla, La, march	*29
	Follow the Swallow, humoresque	*25 26 28 29
	Foshay Tower Washington Memorial, march	*29
	Free Lance March, The (On to Victory)	*06, succeeding years
	Free Lance, The: Girls Who Have Loved	*12 *15 19-23
	Free Lance, The: Overture	21
	Free Lance, The: Selections	06 *07 *08 09 10 12 13 15-25 27 29-31
	Free Lance, The: The Carrier Pigeon, vocal solo	06 *07 08 10 *11 13 15-17 19-22
	Free Lance, The: The Goose Girl, vocal solo	08 09 *10 *11 *12 *13 *14 15 *17 *19 *20 *21 23 25-27
	Free Lance, The: Waltz Song, vocal solo	08
	From Maine to Oregon, march	*13, succeeding years
	Gallagher and Shean, humoresque	*23 *24
	Gallant Seventh, The, march	*22, succeeding years
	George Washington Bicentennial March	*30 *31
	Gladiator, The, march	09 15 19 22 23 25
	Gliding Girl, The, tango	*12, succeeding years
	Globe and Eagle, march	94 98
	Glory of the Yankee Navy, The (The Glory of the Navy) (The Pride of the Yankee Navy), march	*09, succeeding years
	Golden Jubilee, march	*28, succeeding years
	Golden Star, The, memorial march	*19 *20 21-24 27
	Good-Bye, humoresque	*92 93 *94 *95 96-98 *00 *01 26
	Great Lakes (The Boys in Navy Blue), vocal solo	18
	Gridiron Club March, The	*26, succeeding years
	Guide Right, march	93 22
	Hail to the Spirit of Liberty, march	*00, succeeding years
	Hands Across the Sea, march	*99, succeeding years
	Harmonica Wizard, march	*30 31
	High School Cadets, The, march	*92, succeeding years
	Honored Dead, The, march	93-95 98 99 01 02 04 05 14 22 23
	I Wonder (I Wonder If Over Beyond the Sea), vocal or cornet or euphonium solo	94 95 *11 12-14 16-20 22-27
	I've Made My Plans for the Summer, vocal or cornet solo	*07 08 19-21 *22 *23 *24 26
	Imperial Edward March	*02, succeeding years
	Impressions at the Movies: Balance All and Swing Partners (The Cabaret	*14, succeeding years
	In Flanders Fields, vocal solo	*18, succeeding years
	In Memoriam (Garfield's Funeral March), dirge	95
	In Parlor and Street, melange	94 95
	In Pulpit and Pew, fantasie	09 10 15 17 20 22-24 27
	In the Realm of the Dance (In the Realm of the Waltz), fantasie	*02 *03 04-07 09 *11 15 16 22-24 27
	Intaglio Waltzes	93-96 24-26
	International Congress, The (Melodies of Many Lands) (beginning sometimes programmed as Fugue on Yankee Doodle and Hail Columbia)	94 95 98 01 02 04 07 *11 24
	Invincible Eagle, The, march	*01, succeeding years
	Jack Tar, march	*03, succeeding years
	Jazz America, fantasie	*25, succeeding years
	Kansas Wildcats, march	*31 32
	Katherine: Overture	94-96 27
	Keeping Step with the Union, march	*21, succeeding years
	King Cotton, march	*95, succeeding years
	Lambs' March, The	*14, succeeding years
	Last Crusade, The, ballad, chorus	22 24 25

	Last Days of Pompeii, The, suite: In the House of Burbo and Stratonice; Nydia the Blind Girl; The Destruction of Pompeii and Nydia's Death	*93, succeeding years
	Leaves from My Notebook, suite: The Genial Hostess; The Campfire Girls: The Lively Flapper	*22 *23 *24 25 *26 27 28 29 31
	Liberty Bell, The, march	*93, succeeding years
	Liberty Loan March	*18, succeeding years
	Look for the Silver Lining, humoresque	*18, succeeding years
	Looking Upward, suite: By the Light of the Polar Star; Mars and Venus; Under the Southern Cross	*93, succeeding years
	Love that Lives Forever, The, vocal solo	*18 19-22 24-27
	Love's Radiant Hour, vocal solo	*28 *29 *31
	Lovely Mary Donnely, vocal solo	19-22 24-27
	Loyal Legion, The, march	93 94 96 98 10 12-15 22 24-26
	Magna Charta March	*27, succeeding years
	Maid of the Meadow (Today Determines All), vocal solo	*00 01 02 *03 04 05 *11 12-15 17-25
	Maidens Three, suite [suite made up of The Coquette, The Summer Girl, and The Dancing Girl (Tarantella from The Bride Elect)]	*01 *02 *03 04 *05 07-10 *11 12 15 16 18 19 21-27
	Man Behind the Gun, The, march	*99, succeeding years
	Manhattan Beach March	*94, succeeding years
	March of the Mitten Men (Power and Glory)	*24, succeeding years
	March of the Pan-Americans, medley of national airs of the Pan-American Union	15 16
	March of the Royal Trumpets	*92 93 94 98
	March of the States	*92 93 94 98
	Marquette University, march	*24, succeeding years
	Mazurka, violin solo	15
	Merrie, Merrie Chorus, The, fantasie	*23 *24 25-28
	Messiah of Nations, The, patriotic anthem	02 24-26
	Milkmaid, The, vocal solo	*14 15 21 23-25 27 28
	Mingling of the Wets and the Drys, A, humoresque	*26 *27 *30
	Minnesota March, The	*27, succeeding years
	Mother Goose, march	94 95 98 08 14-26
	Mother Hubbard, march	93 94 08 14 15 17 19
	Music of the Minute, fantasie: What'll I Do?; The Gliding Girl; Raggedy	*24 25 26 28 30 31
	My Butterfly, vocal solo	28
	My Own, My Geraldine, vocal solo	93-95 08 15 16 20 22 24-26
	Myrrha, gavotte	94 95
	National Fencibles, march	93 94 98 08 10 15 16 21-26 29
	National Game, The, march	*25, succeeding years
	Naval Reserve March (introducing Blue Ridge)	*17, succeeding years
	New Mexico (The Queen of the Plateau), march	*28, succeeding years
	New York Hippodrome, march	15, succeeding years
	Nobles of the Mystic Shrine, march	*23, succeeding years
	Non-Committal Declarations, vocal or cornet trio	21-25
	Northern Pines, The, march	*31 32
	Nymphalin (Reverie),violin or cello solo	93 94 98 08 10 13-19 21 23
	O, Ye Lilies White, vocal solo	*11 12 15 17 18
	Occidental, The, march	*11 12 15 17 18 23 24 26
	Official Air of the Pan-American	24
	Oh! How I've Waited for You!, humoresque	*26
	On Parade (The Lion Tamer), march	*21, succeeding years
	On the Campus, march	*24, succeeding years
	On the Tramp, march	22 24

	On with the Dance, fantasie	*23 *24 25 27 28 30
	Our Boys Are Home Again, vocal solo or band number	20-24
	Our Flirtations, march	93 96 15 19 25 26
	Our Flirtations: Lily Bells, cornet solo or band number	93 96 15 19 25-27
	Over the Footlights in New York, fantasie	94 *98 *99 *00 01 04 06 08 15 24
	Paroles d'Amour, waltz	25-27
	Pathfinder of Panama, The, march	*15, succeeding years
	Peaches and Cream, fox trot	*24 25 26 29
	People Who Live in Glass Houses: Convention of the Cordials, Wines,	*09, succeeding years
	Pet of the Petticoats, The	94
	Picador, The, march	93 09 10 15 17 21-25
	Plain Tunes from the Hills	94
	Powhatan's Daughter, march	*07, succeeding years
	Presidential Polonaise	93 *97 02 04 12 14, succeeding years
	Pride of Pittsburgh, The (The Belle of Pittsburgh) (Homage to Stephen Foster and Ethelbert Nevin), march	*01, succeeding years
	Pride of the Wolverines, The, march	*26, succeeding years
	Quilting Party March, The	94
	Reine de la Mer, La (The Queen of the Sea), waltz	93, succeeding years
	Resumption March	23-26
	Riders for the Flag, march	*27, succeeding years
	Rifle Regiment, The, march	93, succeeding years
	Right Forward, march	93 22 23
	Right-Left March	24
	Romance, violin solo	16
	Rose, Shamrock and Thistle (Patrol of the United Kingdom), fantasie	*01 *03 *05 *07 *09 *11
	Royal Welch Fusiliers, The, march	*30
	Sabre and Spurs, march	*18, succeeding years
	Salute of the Nations to the Columbian Exposition (Salute of the Nations) (Salute of the Nations to the St. Louis Exposition), pageant	92-95
	Semper Fidelis, march	*93, succeeding years
	Serenade, violin solo	17
	Sesqui-Centennial Exposition March	*26, succeeding years
	Sesqui-Centennial Exposition March	*92, succeeding years
	Sheridan's Ride, scenes historical, descriptive piece	*93, succeeding years
	Showing Off Before Company, humoresque	*19, succeeding years
	Smugglers, The: Love, brass quartet or quintet	14 19 20
	Solid Men to the Front!, march	*18, succeeding years
	Songs of Grace and Songs of Glory (Songs of Grace and Glory) (Five Leaves from the Hymnal) (A Collection of Sacred Themes), fantasie	*93, succeeding years
	Sound Off, march	93 16 17 23 24 26
	Sounds from the Revivals, fantasie	94
	Stag Party, The, humoresque	92 93 *94 95 96 25
	Stars and Stripes Forever, The, march	*97, succeeding years
	Study in Rhythms, A, fantasie	*20 *21 22 23 *24 25-27 *28 29 *30 *31
	Summer Girl, The, idyll, vocal solo or band number	03 06 15 17-25
	Swanee, humoresque on Gershwin's Sinbad	*20 21
	Sweet Miss Industry, vocal solo	94 *96 *97 *11 *12 24 25 26 27
	Tales of a Traveler, suite: The Kaffir on the Karoo; In the Land of the Golden Fleece: Grand Promenade at the White House	*12, succeeding years
	Tally-Ho: Overture	94 96 *97 15 21 22 25 26 27
	There's a Merry Brown Thrush (The Thrush), vocal solo	*26 27

	Three Quotations, suite: I, Too, Was Born in Arcadia; In Darkest Africa (Nigger in the Woodpile); The King of France	*96 *97 *98 *99 *00 *01 *02 *03 04-06 *08 *09 *10 12 15 16 18 19 24-26
	Three S's, The (The Internationals), suite: Morning Journals (J. Strauss); The Lost Chord (Sullivan); Mars and Venus [from Looking Upward] (Sousa)	*26, succeeding years
	Thunderer, The, march	*93, succeeding years
	Transit of Venus, march	93 94
	Triumph of Time, march	93
	Trooping of the Colors, The, fantasie	*98
	U.S. Field Artillery, The march	*18, succeeding years
	University of Illinois, march	*29 30
	University of Nebraska, march	*28, succeeding years
	Vautour (The Vulture): Overture	94-98 03 20-22 24-27
	Violets	03
	Volunteers, The, march	*18, succeeding years
	Washington Post, The, march	*92, succeeding years
	We Are Coming, vocal solo or march	*18, succeeding years
	Wedding March, The (The American Wedding March)	*19 *20 22-27
	What Is Love?, song	05 06
	When My Dreams Come True, fantasie	*29
	When the Boys Come Sailing Home, march-song, vocal solo or band number	19 25 26
	While Navy Ships Are Coaling, chanty	23 26 28
	White Plume March, The	09 15 19-22 24 26
	White Rose March, The, march	17, succeeding years
	Who's Who in Navy Blue, march	*20, succeeding years
	Willow Blossoms, legend	16, succeeding years
	Wisconsin Forward Forever (Wisconsin Forever), march	*17, succeeding years
	With Pleasure, dance hilarious	*12, succeeding years
	Words of Love, waltz	24-26 28
	Yorktown Centennial, The, march	94 09 20 21 24 25
Sousa, John Philip & Gerard Moultrie	We March, We March to Victory, march-song, vocal solo	18 22 23
Sousa, John Philip & James Francis Cooke	Serenade in Seville, A, vocal solo	*24 *25 26-28
Sousa, John Philip & William Knox	Oh, Why Should the Spirit of Mortal Be Proud, anthem, vocal solo	22-24
Sousa, John Philip (arranger)	Air of Zamboanga, An	93
	Apache Scalp Dance, An	*92 93 94
	Esia Samoa (Samoan Song)	93
	Popular Flower Song of China	93
Sowalski	Five National Dances	93
Sowerby, Leo	Comes Autumn Time (When Autumn Comes): Overture	*25 *26
	Irish Washerwoman, The	28
Spadini	Two Men of Brass, cornet duet	93
Spahn, A.	Viens Poupoule, polka	04
Spalding, Albert	Alabama, Southern melody and dance	16
	When You Know the Girl You Love Loves You, cornet solo	*96
Speaks, Oley	In May Time, vocal solo	09
	On the Road to Mandalay, vocal solo or trombone solo	15
	When the Boys Come Home, vocal solo	15 17 18 *19
Spencer	Miss Bob White: Two Numbers	01
Spencer, Herbert	My Neenyah, My Little Spanish One (My Little One), Spanish love song	25
Spencer, Willard	Princess Bonnie: Selections	*95
Spenser	Long, Long Ago, vocal solo	94
Spier, Larry & Con Conrad & B.G. De Sylva	Memory Lane, song	24
Spies	Comique: Overture	05
Spiller	Repulj Tecskem, violin solo	94
Spillman, J.E.	Flow Gently, Sweet Afton, vocal solo	13
Spindler, Fritz	Reiterlust (Trooper's Joy), characteristic	10 13
	Ride of the Hussars (Husarenritt) (Ride of the Hussars), tone picture	98 05 08 24
Spinelli, Niccola	Basso Porto, A (At the Lower Ferry): Prelude to Act III	*97 98
	Basso Porto, A (At the Lower Ferry): Prologue (Prelude)	19 24

	Basso Porto, A (At the Lower Ferry): Selections	98 02 17 25
Spohr, Louis	Rose Softly Blooming, The, romance	94
Sponacker	Lost Treasure, flugelhorn solo	02
Spontini, Gasparo	Vestal, The: Overture	94
Springer, J. Austin	March King, The, march	97
Spross, Charles Gilbert	I Know a Lovely Garden, vocal solo	18
	Robin's Song, The (Robin, Robin, Sing Me a Song), vocal solo	*19 20
	Will o' the Wisp, vocal solo	10
	Yesterday and Today, vocal solo	14 15
St. Clair, Floyd J.	Celtic, Overture	03
St. Clair, Floyd J. (arranger)	Kyah Than, song of Burma	93
Stanford, Charles Villiers	Rhapsodie Irish No. 1 (Irish Rhapsody No. 1) (Celtic Rhapsody), Op. 78	05 *06
	Shamus O'Brien: Selections	96
Stanley, Ralph, SEE Openshaw, John		
Starr, Hattie	Holy Cross, vocal solo	01
	My Sweet Girl, vocal solo	01
Stasny, Ludwig	Kutschke Polka, Op. 166, humorous fantasie (Humoresque on an Old Dance Tune) (Fantasia on an Old Dance Tune) (Burletta, fantasia on Heel and Toe Polka) (Arabasque)	*92 93 94 96 98 02 04
Statkowski, Roman	Krakowiak, Polish dance	19
Steck, Paul A.	Flirtation, caprice	93 94
	Serenade Monegasque	04 08
Steele, Porter, SEE Hooker, Brian		
Steenebrugen, Michael-Joseph	Hungarian Divertissement	93 94
	Vie Militaire, La, march	93
	Fantasie Hongroise (Divertissement Hongroise) (Grand Fantasia on Hungarian Themes)	93-96
Steffens, G.	King of Waltzes (Der Walzerkoenig), waltz	24
Steinert, Alexander L., Jr.	Rameses	23 *24
Steinhagen, P.	Halloo-Halloo, galop	93 94
Steinhauser, Frederick M.	Chevalier, Le, euphonium solo	98
Steinke, Arthur	Butterflies (Schmetterlinge), intermezzo	12
Steinmetz, Theodore A.	32nd Division March	26 30
Stephens, Harold B.	Caprice Minta, saxophone solo	*25
	Jessie, saxohone solo	25
	Varied, saxophone solo	25
Stephens, Hiram T.	Harding Memorial March	25
Stern, Leo	Springtime (Printemps), vocal solo	*01 05 06
Stewart, Humphrey John	Thespis: Entr'Act, gavotte	10
Stewart, Robert Ralsto	Lettre d'Amour, La Gipsy waltz	02
Stickles, William	Peter Pan, vocal solo	27 *28 29 *30
Stix	Habanera, waltz	96
Stix, Carl	Dream Ghosts (Trauggeister), intermezzo	96
Stobbe, W.R.	Polka Brilliante, xylophone solo	20
Stock, George Chadwick	Route Marchin', march	15 16 *19
Stoddin	Chanti di Bacchante, vocal solo	16
Strakosch, Edgar	Dear Golden Days, song	96
Strange	Damon, vocal solo	09
Straus, Oscar	Chocolate Soldier, The: My Hero, waltz	10
	Chocolate Soldier, The: Selections	10 *11 12 13 16 17 20 21-26 28
	Home from the War, descriptive	09 10 *11 17 21 22
	Lustige Eheman, vocal solo or duet	*09
	Waltz Dream, The: Selections	08-10 12 13 20-24 26
	Waltz Dream, The: Waltz	08
Strauss	New Vienna, waltz	93 24
Strauss, Eduard	Carnevals Gruss, polka-mazurka	94
	Fesche Geister (Lively Spirits), waltz	13-16 21-26
	Feuresnoth: Finale	08 09
	Feuresnoth: Love Scene	02-04 *05 06 *07 13 14 *25
	Fusionen, waltz	94

407

	Playful Spirits, SEE Fesche Geister (Strauss, E.)	20
	Wedding Songs (Hochzeitslieder) (Wedding Joys) (Wedding Sounds), waltz	95 98 99 01 02 05 09 24
Strauss, Johann, Jr.	Artist's Life, waltz	93 96 06 07 12 15 20-23 25 26 28
	Autograph, waltz	96 25 26
	Be Ye Embraced, Ye Millions!, waltz	93 02
	Beautiful Blue Danube, The (An der Schoenen Blauen Danau) (On the Beautiful Blue Danube) (On the Banks of the Beautiful Blue Danube), waltz, band number or vocal solo	93 *99 *00 01 03-07 09 10 *11 12-16 21 22 *23 *24 *25 *26 27 *28 29 *30 31
	Cagliostro, waltz	24-26
	Concurenzen, waltz	93
	Didi, waltz	12
	Eva, waltz	04
	Fledermaus, Die (The Bat): Overture	05
	Fledermaus, Die (The Bat): Selections	94 96 03-05 15 23 24
	Flying Thoughts (Gedankenflug), waltz	99 01
	Good Old Times, waltz	94
	Gypsy Baron, The (Ziguenerbaron): Excerpt, violin solo	03
	Gypsy Baron, The (Ziguenerbaron): Selections	96 06-09 12 15 21-24 27
	Gypsy Baron, The (Ziguerenbaron): Romance, flugelhorn solo	02
	Indigo: Thousand and One Nights (Tausend und Eine Nacht), waltz	05 21
	Juristen Ball, waltz	94
	Kaiser, waltz (Kaiser-Walzer) (The King's Waltz), Op. 437	26
	Life, Let Us Cherish, waltz	07 12 13 22-26
	Merry War, The: Selections	94-96 06 24-27 31
	Morning Journals (Morning Papers) (Morgenblatter), waltz	93 94 99 01 02 04 05 07-10 *11 12-16 20-25 *26 *29 31
	Night in Venice: Overture (Excerpts)	16 20
	Perpetual Motion (Perpetuum Mobile)	10 31
	Persians, The, march caprice	94 06 *11 12 24
	Prince Methusalem: Selections	94-96
	Queen's Lace Handkerchief, The: Fantasia	94
	Queen's Lace Handkerchief, The: Waltz	05
	Ritter Pasman: Czardas (Pasman Polka)	*01 02 31
	Roses from the South (Rosen aus dem Suden), waltz	01 02 04 05 12 14 22-25 29
	Tales from the Vienna Woods, waltz	32
	Thunder and Lightning, galop	93
	Umparteiische Kritiken, polka mazurka	07
	Village Swallows (Village Swallows of Austria), waltz	99 01 04 05 *07 08-10 14-17 20-26
	Voices of Spring (Fruhlingsstimmen) (Voci di Primavera) (Primavera), Op. 410, vocal solo	*99 *03 *04 05 07 08 *12 13-17
	Where the Citrons Bloom (Wo die Citronen Blue'n) (Where the Lemons Bloom), waltz	07 22 23 25-27
	Wiener Bon-Bons, waltz	94 25 26
	Wiener Type, caprice Francaise	95
	Wine, Women and Song, waltz	93 07 09 27
Strauss, Johann, Jr. & Josef Strauss	Pizzicato Polka	94 26 31
Strauss, Josef	Autumn Roses, waltz	01
Strauss, Richard	Aus Italien (Neopolitanisches Volksleben), sinfonische fantasie	15
	Death and Transfiguration (Tod und Verklarung), tone poem	*28
	Don Juan, Op. 20, symphonic poem	*24 *26
	Fueuersnot: Love Scene	02-04 *05 06 13 14 *25 *26 29 *30
	Kriegsmarsch (Battle March) (Military March), Op. 57	10
	Procession of the Knight of St. John (Feierlicher Einzug der Ritter des Johanniterorderns), investitur-march	13 14
	Rosenkavalier, Der: Suite	12 14 15

	Serenade, Op. 17, vocal solo	09
	Till Eulenspiegel's Merry Pranks, symphonic poem	*07 *08 09 *10 *11 12-15
Stravinsky, Igor	Song of the Volga Boatmen, Russian folk song, band number or harp solo	25 27
Strelezki, Anton	Happy Days, vocal solo	94 95
Strickland	Wait 'Till Your Ship Comes In, vocal solo	21
Strohm, J.E.	Darky's Temptation, The, schottische	95
Stromberg, John	Melville, polka	94
Strong	Camulos, serenade to California	*99
Stuart, Leslie	Belle of Mayfair, The: Selections	07-09 24-26
	Florodora: Selections (Flora Dance[s])	01 02 06 07 20 24
	Havana: Selections	09 10 15 24 27
	Leslie Stuart's Songs, potpourri (Fantasie on the Songs of Leslie Stuart)	02 16
	School Girl: My Little Canoe (Jolly Little Canoe)	22
	Silver Slipper, The: Selections	24
	Three Little Maids: Selections	03
	Zigana, waltz	02
Stuckey, H.S. & John J. Gale	Little Dresden Shepherdess, caprice	01 02
Stults, Robert Morrison	Birds and theBrook, The, idyll	02
Stults, Robert Morrison & Anna R. Buff	Sweetest Story Ever Told, The, ballad, vocal solo	*21 *22 23-26
Succi	Fete de Triornau: Suite	01
	Maid of Asturias: Overture	01
Suckley, Samuel	Jolly Blacksmith, The, descriptive polka (caprice)	93-95
Suddesi	Petit Pas, A, two-step	02
Suegly, E.H.	Dance at the Forge	95 96
Sullivan	Sweethearts, waltz	19 20 22
	Oh, Hush Thee, my Baby	93
Sullivan, Arthur	Brightly Gleams Our Banner, hymn	94
	Chieftain, The: Finale	96
	Chieftain, The: Selections	95
	Cox and Box: Selections	94 96 22-24 26
	Emerald Isle, The: Selections	02 06 16 17
	Favorite Songs of Arthur Sullivan	94
	Foresters: Selections	94 25 26
	Golden Legend, The: Selections	*12 13-19 21-23
	Gondoliers, The: Selections	93-96 24-27
	Grand Duke, The: Selections	96
	H.M.S. Pinafore: Selections	94-96 99 *00 01 05 07 15-19 21-24 26
	H.M.S. Pinafore: The Lass That Loves a Sailor	93
	Haddon Hall: Selections	92 93
	Henry VIII: Incidental Music	*92 93-95 96 *03 04 05 *10 *11 16 19
	Henry VIII: King Henry's Song	92
	Henry VIII: King Henry's Song and The Graceful Dance	94 02 03
	I Hear the Soft Note of an Echoing voice	93
	In Memoriam, Overture (Overture in C)	09
	Iolanthe: Finale	07 12
	Iolanthe: Lancers (March)	05 24
	Iolanthe: Selections	02 04-06 08 09 13 15-28
	Ivanhoe: Selections	93-95 26
	Light of the World, The: And God Shall Wipe Away All Tears	01 09 10
	Lord Has Risen, The	29
	Lost Chord, The, cornet solo	93-98 *99 *00 01 03 04 *05 06-08 *10 *11 12-17 20 *21 22-25 *26 *27 28 *29 *30
	Martyr of Antioch, The: Selections	01 19
	Masquerade (Mascarade): Suite	02
	Merchant of Venice, Suite: [Introduction and Bouree; Grotesque Dance; Melodrama and Finale	*02 *03 04 05 14 27

	Mikado, The: Aria [unnamed], vocal solo[s]	07
	Mikado, The: Five Airs	93
	Mikado, The: Selections	93-96 01-06 08-10 13 15-29
	Onward Christian Soldiers, hymn	05 07 08
	Overtura di Ballo	94 95 *02 04 03 13
	Patience: March	24
	Patience: Selections	94-96 02 04 06 07 09 10 19 21-26 28
	Pirates of Penzance, The: Selections	93-96 99 06 13 18 19 21-28 32
	Reminiscences of Sullivan	*92 93 94 96 05 06 08 09 *11 15 18 22 23 25-28 31
	Rose of Persia The: Selections	*00 21 24
	Ruddigore: Selections	20 26
	St. Agnes' Eve, song	94
	Trial by Jury, The: Selections	94
	Utopia Limited: Selections	94 96
	Victoria and Merrie England, ballet suite	98 02 09 17 24-26
	Yeomen of the Guard, The: Overture	94 07 15
	Yeomen of the Guard, The: Selections	25 26 28
Suppe, Franz von	Agonies of Tantalus, The (Tantalusqualen): Overture	94 *95 *96 *97 98 01 02 05 07 09 10 *11 12 14-17 22-27
	Banditensreiche: Overture	93 *97
	Beautiful Galatea, The: Overture	*92 93 94 *95 96 99 01 05-07 *11 17 23-27 30
	Boccaccio: Introduction, Duel Scene and Cooper's Chorus	93
	Boccaccio: Selections	93-96 22 26 27 *31
	Burlesque, La (Al Burletta): Overture	14 24
	Donna Juanita: Overture	01 02 04
	Donna Juanita: Selections	94 24
	Fatinitza: March	06
	Flotte Bursche (University Songs) (College Songs) (German College Songs) (Jolly Students, The): Overture	93-96 *97 98 02 04 05 07 08 14 16 22 24 25
	Forget Me Not, flugelhorn solo	94 98 04
	Frau Meisterin: Overture	93 94
	Isabella (Queen Isabella): Overture	93 94 *01 22 24
	Jolly Robbers: Overture	93-96
	Light Cavalry [Cavalerie Legere]: Overture	93-96 01 04-08 10 12-17 19-22 *23 24 26 *27 28 29 32
	Modell, Das (The Model): Overture	*97 98 99 01 04 09
	Morning, Noon and Night in Vienna: Overture	94 *95 96 *20 27
	Morning, Noon and Night, xylophone solo	*20 21-24 *25 26 28
	Opera Airs (Operatic Themes), xylophone solo	20
	Paragraph III: Overture	94-96 *99 01 02 04 05 21 24-26
	Paraphrase on Suppe's The Jolly Robbers, xylophone solo	*31
	Pensionat, Das (The Pensioner): Prelude	13
	Pensionat, Das (The Pensioner): Selections	24
	Pique Dame: Overture	93-95 96 98 03-05 07-09 15 20 22-28
	Poet and Peasant: Overture	93 *94 95-98 01 02 *04 05-10 *11 12 13 15-17 19 20-22 24 *25 26
	Pygmalion and Galatea: Overture	93
	Queen of Spades: Overture	25 26
	Sailors Afloat: Overture	94 25-27
	Schubert: Overture	93-95 25
	Shepherd's Morning Song (The Shepherd Maiden), flugelhorn solo	01

410

	Summer Night's Dream A: Overture	94 98 04 19 22 24
	Tantalusqualen: Overture	94 96
	Ten Girls and No Man (Ten Girls and No Husband) (Zehn Maedchen und Kein Man) (Ten Maidens and No Man): Overture	97-99 01 02 09 10 22
	Tricoche and Cacolet: Overture	97
	Trip to Africa, A: Rose Duet	*94
	Triumph: Overture	04 25 26
	Waltz Song, vocal solo	*94
	Wanderers' Destination (The Wanderer's Aim) (Wandrers Ziel): Overture	94 96 20-22 24
Svendsen, Johan Severin	Norwegian Carnival: Overture	18 24 25 27
	Norwegian Rhapsody (no number)	12 25 26
	Norwegian Rhapsody No. 1	96
	Norwegian Rhapsody No. 2	93 *95 *96 98 99
	Norwegian Rhapsody No. 3, Op. 21	96 26
	Parisian Carnival, A (Carneval in Paris)	*95 96 04 13 *18
	Romance, violin solo	96 02 14 18
	Symphony in D-Major, Op. 4: Scherzo	*15 23
Sweeney	Beulah Land, hymn	93
Talbar, Trabar	Daddy Won't Buy Me a Bow-Wow	93
Talbot, Howard	Chinese Honeymoon, A: Selections	02-04 06
	Girl Behind the Counter, The, Selections	27
	Pearl Girl, The: Selections	24
Tarbell, M.S.	Manhattan Two-Step	95
Tate, Arthur F.	Somewhere a Voice Is Calling, vocal, saxophone, cornet, or euphonium solo or band number	*17 *18 19 22-26 *29
	Sunshine of Your Smile, euphonium solo	24
Taubert, Wilhelm	Tempest, The (Sturm): Love Song (Liebesliedchen)	02
Taund, Eugen von & Glover	Little Genius, The: Selections	99
Tavan, E.	Sevillan Festival, A (A Festival in Seville) (Spanish Fantasia), Spanish suite	*19 21 27
Taylor	Dance African, violin solo	14
	In My Garden, vocal solo	15 26
	Valse, characteristic	02
Taylor, Franklin	America Eternal, march	23
Tchaikowsky, Peter Ilych	1812 Overture (Holy War) (Napoleon's Retreat from Moscow)	94-99 01-07 *10 *11 *12 13 19 23-26 28
Tchaikowsky, Peter Ilych	Barcarole, Reverie and Dance	10 12
	Belle Au Bois Dormant, La, air de ballet	*97
	Capriccio Italien (Caprice Italienne)	*00 *01 02-04 06 15
	Chant sans Parole (Song Without Words), romance	*11 24
	Coronation March (Imperial March) (Grand Coronation Scene)	04 *06 09 14 24 27
	Danish Coronation March	07 08
	Doll's Valse, The	14
	Dornroscher, waltz	96
	Eugene Onegin: Grand Valse	15
	Eugene Onegin: Selections	98 99 01 02 04 17
	Eugene Onegin: The Merchant's Casino, waltz	20
	Francesca da Rimini, fantasie	01
	In Autumn, idyll	20
	International, suite	09
	Itinerant Musician, The, idyll	*11
	Marche Militaire	26
	Marche Slave (Grand Russian Festival March)	95 98 01 *02 *03 04-08 10 *11 12 14 19 23-26 28
	Mazurka de Salon	96
	Nutcracker, The (Casse Noisette) Suite: Danse Russe (Trepak); Danse Chinoise; Danse des Mirlitrons	*92 *93 94 96 01 04 14 24-27 *28
	Nutcracker, The (Casse Noisette): Danse de Mirlitrons, flute sextet	26 29
	Nutcracker, The (Casse Noisette): Marche Miniature	96
	Nutcracker, The (Casse Noisette): Trepak	*99
	Nutcracker, The (Casse Noisette): Waltz of the Flowers	*30 *31
	Opritschnik, The: Overture and Ballet	22

	Pique Dame: Rustic Suite	18
	Quartet in D, Op. 11: Andante Cantabile	*12 14 15 17 *18 *20 *21 22 *27 28
	Reminiscences of Tchaikowsky	03 04 06-09 13 15 17-22 25 26
	Romance	14
	Serenade de Don Juan, vocal solo	93 96
	Sleeping Beauty: Selections	09 14
	Sleeping Beauty: Waltz	03
	Spanish Serenade	97
	Suite III (Orchestral Suite): Theme and Variations	97 02 18
	Swan Lake, The (Le Lac des Cygnes) (Lake of the Swans): Ballet Suite	13 18 27
	Sweet Memories	14
	Symphony No. 4: Allegro	*09
	Symphony No. 4: Scherzo and Finale	09 10 *11 12 17 18 *21 *22 *23 24 *25 26 *29 *31 32
	Symphony No. 6 ("Pathetique"): Allegretto	15
	Symphony No. 6 ("Pathetique"): Allegro con grazia & Finale	99 07
	Symphony No. 6 ("Pathetique"): Allegro Moderato	12
	Symphony No. 6 ("Pathetique"): Andante	*00 01 02 04
	Third Suite: Polonaise (Grand Pollacca)	18
	Three Pieces, suite (Second Series)	24
	Voyvode, Le, symphonic ballad	02 24 *26
	Yolande: Selections	05
Tchakoff, Ivan	Cossack Patrol, The	*00
	Cossack, dance	97 *98
	Dance Suite: Four Dances (Suite of Four Russian Dances) (Dance Suite No. 2) (Dansant)	98 02 04 19
	Italian Dance Suite No. 2 (Second Dance Suite) (Aus Italiens)	01 04 08
	Valse Elegant	97
Tellam, H.	Corso Blanc, polka march	93
Temple, Hope	Fond Heart, Farewell, vocal solo	95 96
	My World, vocal solo	96
	Rory Darlin	94
	Thoughts and Tears, song	93
Templeton, Fay	I Want Yer Ma Honey	*97
Tenari	Last Journal of Suli: Selections	96
Tennent	If Winter Comes, cornet solo	*24
Terry	Answer, The, vocal solo	26
Terschak	Caprice Brillante, flute solo	93
	Papillons, Les, flute solo	95
	Russian Air Varied, flute solo	93
	Souvenir de Vienne, flute solo	92
Thallon	Evening Song, An	93 94 96
Thayer, Willam Armour	Birth of Morn, The, vocal solo	16
	Dearest, vocal solo	16
	My Laddie, vocal solo	15 16 25
	Until, vocal solo	16
Thiele	Great Republic, The, patriotic march	*92 93 94
Thomas	Dost Thou Know the Land?, vocal solo	95
	My Neighbor, vocal solo	96
	Peter Gink, xylophone solo	19
	Winds in the Trees, vocal solo	96
	Syrienne, vocal solo	*94
Thomas, Ambroise	Caid, Le: Overture	94
	Hamlet: A Vos Jeux Mes Amis, Scene and Aria, vocal solo	03
	Hamlet: Ballet Music (Suite)	*93 94-96 19 27
	Hamlet: Feast of Spring, suite	*18 20 23 *27
	Hamlet: Mad Scene, vocal solo	93 *03 04-06
	Midsummer Night's Dream, A: Overture	18 27
	Mignon Fantasia, violin solo	18

	Mignon: Aria [unnamed], vocal solo[s]	95 06 25 26
	Mignon: Connais Tu Le Pays	29
	Mignon: Gavotte, vocal solo	93 94
	Mignon: Je Suis Titania (I Am Titania), recitativo and polonaise (polacca), vocal or xylophone solo	92 93 94 *05 14-16 *19 20-22 *24 *25 *26 27 28
	Mignon: Overture	94 14-16 *19 22-25 27
	Mignon: Selections	94 96 12 15
	Nadecchda: Aria [unnamed], vocal solo[s]	99
	Raymond (The Secrets of the Queen): Overture	*92 93 *94 95 96 *05 07 08 *09 12-18 23-25 27
	Summer Night, A (A Summer Night's Dream), vocal solo	96 05
Thomas, Arthur Goring	Golden Web, The: Scenes	94
	Swallows, The, vocal solo	*98 *00 01
Thomas, Jessie Beattie	Egyptian Lullaby	95
Thome, Francis	Andante Religioso, violin solo	10 14
	Badinage	*97
	Entracte Pizzicato (Entr' Acte Pizzicato) (Molto Pizzicato)	96 01
	Love Token, vocal solo	96
	Mlle. Pygmalion: L'Extase, Entr'Acte	04 08
	Simple Confession (Simple Aveu): Romanze sans Parole, violin solo	*97 00 23
	Springtime (Printemps, Le), idyll (intermezzo)	95 96
	Sunday Call, The, march	95
Thompson	Gaynell Waltz, cornet solo	24
	Yazoo, dance	94 *95
Thompson, Jack	Nightingale and the Rose, vocal solo	12
Thorne	Maid of Plymouth, vocal solo	94
Thornton, E.S.	Russian Carriage Song, characteristic piece	24 27
Thurban, T.W.	Czk, Czk, descriptive march	04 05
	Mumblin Mose, two-step (Negro air)	04 05
	Suite Americana (fantasia): The Tiger-Tail; When Melindy Sings; The Watermelon Fete	12-19 21-24
Tierney, Harry Austin	Rio Rita, xylophone solo	*28 *29
Tirindelli, Pier Adolfo	Valse Caprice (Valse di Concert), violin solo	16-18
Titl, Anton Emil	Fantasia on Bohemian Melodies	96
	King's Lieutenant, The: Overture	92 93 *94 *95 97 98 15-17 19 22 24 31
	Overture Founded on Slavonic Themes	94
	Serenade for Flute and French Horn (Celebre), Duet for Flute and Horn	93-96 99 01 13-15 17-22 24
	Tambour de Garde (Drummer of the Guard): Overture	96 98
Tobani, Theodore Moses	America, overture on national airs (patriotic overture)	96 07
	Army and Navy, The	98
	Around the Christmas Tree	31
	Auld Lang Syne, fantasie (paraphrase)	06
	College Overture (Songs of the Colleges)	10 24
	Crack Regiment, The, patrol	95
	Creme de la Creme, Op. 419, fantasia	15
	Gems from Popular Comic Operas	94-96
	Hearts and Flowers	94 10 26
	Hungarian Fantasia, Op. 207	96
	Midway Plaisance, polka caprice	94
	Nautical Fantasia, Op. 333 (Nautical Songs and Dances)	21
	Old Heidelberg, Op. 426, fantasie	08 10 24
	Opera Mirror, the, fantasie (Fantasia on Favorite Opera Themes)	13 16 17
	Poor Jonathan: Selections	93
	Providence, sacred fantasia	23
	Scenes from Light Operas	96
	Serpentine Dance	94
	U.S. Army Lancers (Lancers of the U.S. Army) (The Lancers at West Point)	01 02 21
	U.S. Army Signals, The (Signals of the U.S. Army)	01 02 19

	United States Army, The	98 01
	Warbler's Farewell, on Tyrolean melodies	24
Tobias	Weary Wraggles, dance of the hoboes	97
Toenniges, C.F.	Kansas City Journal March	98
	March Triumphal	01
Toledo, F.	On Dress Parade, march & two-step	96
Tolhurst, Frederick A.	At the King's Ball, descriptive waltz	*02
	Ballet of the Flowers, The (Fete des Fleurs), ballet suite: Marciale; The Red and the White Roses; Flirtation of the Daffodils; Estrangement of the Roses; Reconciliation of the Roses	95 96 99 02
	Bebe Minuet	97 *98
	Cupid's Serenata (Serenade Cupidon)	*98
	Whirlwind, march	97 *98
Tollman	Annie Laurie Variations, harp solo (unaccompanied) or vocal solo	*13 *16 *17 *24 *30
Tong, William	Tower of Jewels, cornet solo	*28 29 *30
Topliff	Jerusalem the Golden, paraphrase	95
Torrente	Teach Me Thy Ways (Show Me Thy Ways, O Lord), song	96
Tosca, A.	Russian Patrol	04
Tosti, F. Paolo	Ballads, vocal solo	94
	Could I, vocal solo	97
	Good-Bye (Bid Me Good-bye and Go) (Tosti's Good-bye), vocal solo	94-97 06-08 14 *16 18 20 21 23 *24 25 26
	My Dreams, vocal solo	17
	Ninon, vocal solo	14 15
	Pensee, romance, vocal solo	93
	Reminiscences of Tosti	93 05 06-10 13-18 20-28 31
	Serenade (Serenata), vocal solo	*15
	Songs of Tosti (Famous Songs of Paolo Tosti) (Love Songs)	93 94 96
	Vorrei (Romance), vocal solo	93
Tours	Mother o'Mine, vocal solo	15
Tours, Berthold	Because of Thee, vocal or cornet solo	96 04 05 07-09 16 17
	God Hath Appointed a Day, anthem	93 94 96 04-06
	Hero-Land March	22
	Hymn to the Angels, melodie religieuse	08
Tours, Frank E.	Three Dances, Suite (The Dancer)	08
Tovey, Cecile	Dulcie, dance	96
Towers, John	Miriam Grant March	20
Tracy, George	Upidee, paraphrase	95 *96
traditional	All Through the Night, vocal solo	*05 *10 *11 *12 *13 *14 *15 16 17 24 26
	Auld Lang Syne	93 96 07 *11
	Biscayan Love Song	05
	Braw, Braw Lads op' Gala Waaer, vocal solo	96
	For He's a Jolly Good Fellow, song	14
	Four Scotch Songs	95
	Gae Bring to Me a Pint of Wine, vocal solo	96
	Gospel Train am Comin', spiritual	92
	Hymn of Thanks, Netherland song	06
	Kom Kjyra, Norwegian echo song, vocal solo	16
	Loch Lomond, vocal solo	13
	Men of Harlech, band number or harp solo	93 06 13 *16
	My Lodging's in the Cold, Cold Ground	98
	My Love Is Like a Red, Red Rose, vocal or cornet solo	94 01
	Quilting Party, The (Aunt Dinah's Quilting Party), vocal solo	*21
	There'll Be No Sorrow There, cornet solo	*01
	Tua, Hawaiian song	22
	Where Are You Going, My Pretty Maid?, song	*94
	Yankee Doodle	93 *00
Traher	Old Home Town, march	24
Trinkaus, George J.	Four Winds, The: Boreas, a northern idyll	26
Trotere, Henry	Leonore, vocal solo	96

Tschetschulin	Zingaresca, violin solo	94
Tullien	Neapolitaine, tarantelle	08
Turine, Victor	Promenade du Khalif	93
Turner	Southern Idylle	01
Tuttle, H.H.	Hills of Old Ohio, The	99
Tyers, William H.	Call of the Woods, The, waltz	16
Udal	Just One Girl, song, trombone solo	*99
Uellinger, Clarence	March King, The	03
Umlauft, Paul	Evanthia: Vorspeil	94 95
undetermined	Aloha, cornet solo	12 26
	At the Brook, violin solo	*05
	Barbershop Gang, saxophone ensemble	26
	Belle Polka	95
	Celtic Rhapsody	05
	Children's Serenade	*98
	Chorus of Peddlers and Warriors	93
	Church Parade, The, medley (in collection, Six Bell Pieces)	10
	Cupid's Dart, waltz caprice	93
	Dance des Mouches	*98
	Does It Pay?, song	95
	Dream, The	92
	Epworth League, The, march	93
	Every Little Moment, cornet solo	*11
	For You Must Be a Lover of the Lord, novelty	92
	Frolics of the Coons	95
	Geluckig Vaderland, Dutch song, vocal solo	16
	Give Me Your Eye	98
	Good-By Daddy, euphonium solo	*97
	Good-by, Little Girl	05
	Great Republic, march	93
	Happy Husband(s), vocal solo	*09
	Hermit's Song, flute and clarinet duet	93
	How Swiftly the Swallows are Flying, vocal solo	25
	Hula Lou, saxophone ensemble	*24
	Hush-a-Bye, Darling, vocal solo	16
	I Love Them All, trombone solo	01
	I Saw Thee in My Dream, flugelhorn solo	*00
	In the Conservatory	93
	In Wupland: Wupland March	08
	Irish Fantasie, violin solo	*05
	It Was Not So to Be, flugelhorn solo	*99
	Jenny Jones, song	14
	Jewel, The, intermezzo	95
	Kentucky Sue	*99
	King Hotu's March	95
	Laurina Ray, trombone solo	*97
	Louisiana Cane Hop	*99
	Malbrouck Has Gone to the War, piccolo solo	95
	March of the Vehicle Owners	94
	Marseillaise, Le, and Yankee Doodle in Counterpoint	93
	Maud Mari, cornet solo	20
	Merry Husband, vocal duet	*09
	My First Love, vocal solo	05
	My Wife Won't Let Me	06
	Nancy Lee, euphonium solo	92
	Oh! My, My, My!, coon song	*05
	Oh, Maria, cornet solo	20
	Ole Swimmin' Hole, saxophone ensemble with vocal solo	*26
	On the Banks of the Sewanee, Negro fantasie	06
	Peggy Cline	92
	Plantation Jig	93
	Plantation Melody, xylophone solo	*21

	Pustak Fea, Hungarian fantasie	*97
	Roll Down That Cotton	92
	Rose Festival March	07
	Rose, xylophone solo	21
	Silverheels, march	06
	Simpfunny in Deutsche, saxophone octet	*28
	Sinbad: Boogie Man	92
	Sons of Erin	26
	Spanish Fantasie, A, cornet solo	94
	St. George, march	01
	Sunshine Above	95
	Sweetness of Your Smile, The, cornet solo	20
	They Are the Best Friends of All	*94
	Tommy Atkins	95
	True Love Is Pure	93
	Two Chinese Songs	94 96
	Watching the Moon	26
	Wha's Me for Prince Charlie, cornet solo	17
	When the Clouds Roll By, trombone solo	19
	When the Years Go Drifting By, vocal solo	26
	When You Know You're Not Forgotten, trombone solo	*07
	Whispering, xylophone solo	*21
	Whistler's Serenade	09
	Why Did I Kiss That Girl?, saxohone ensemble	25
Unger	Quartette for Flutes	02
Unrath, Carl	King Carl (Konig Karl), march	93 *94
Urich, Jean	Bamboula, Negro dance of Trinidad (Dance of the Basutuos)	93 *94 95 *03 16 24 25 26
Vail	In Eli Land	*12
Vallee, Rudy & Leon Zimmerman	I'm Just a Vagabond Lover, fox trot, saxophone ensemble	*29
Valputti	Bandilerros, Las	28
Valverde, Jaoquin	Fornarinette, La, marche Espagnole	12 27
	Gitanette, La, tango maxixa	13
	Pollo Tejada, El: Danse du Paraguay	10 24
	Three Argentine Dances: Y Como le Va; El Albaicin; Clavelitos (Carnations)	12 13
Van Alstyne, Egbert	Honey [Dat's All], waltz	25
	Hula Hula, cakewalk	01
Van Alstyne, Egbert & Schmitt & Curtis	Drifting and Dreaming (Sweet Paradise), Hawaiian love song, fox trot	26
Van Baar, Charles L.	Congo Frolic	96
	New Admiral, The, march	96
Van Biene, A.	Broken Melody, The, andante	98 *03 19
Van Buggenhoud, Edouard	America, galop	93
	Battle of Inkermann, galop	93 94 96
Van de Waten, Beardsley	King Bomba, march	97
Van der Stucken, Frank	Fallih, Fallah, vocal solo	95
	Louisiana, grand march (St. Louis World's Fair March)	04
	O Come With Me in the Spring Night (O Komm Mit Mir in die Fruhlingsnacht), vocal solo	12
Van Gael, Henri	Indienne, air characteristic (march caprice)	93
	Marlborough, piccolo solo	93
	Promenade du Khalife, morceau de guere	93
Van Goens	Scherzo, Op. 12, cello solo	*05 14
Van Hamm	Dialog Between the Flute and Clarinet, flute and clarinet duet	21
Van Maanen, J.C.	Grand Fantasia on Scotch Songs (Scotch Fantasia, A)	93 94
Van Praag, Henri J	L'Amour Defendu (Forbidden Love), waltz lento	13 23
Van Westerhout, Niccolo	Rondo d'Amour (Paroles d'Amour), idyll	97 01 *09
Vanderpool	I Did Not Know, vocal solo	24
	Magic of Your Eyes, vocal solo	20
Vandersloot, Carl	American Legion March, The	20
Vaneges	Colibois, El, waltz	01

various	All American, suite: Pan Americana (Victor Herbert); Song of the Flame (George Gershwin); Her Majesty the Queen [from At the King's Court] (Sousa)	*26
	Collection of Hymn Tunes of the American Churches	*01
	Combination Salad, jazz ensemble	*24 *26
	Press-Telegraph British War Films	17
Varney, Louis	Musketeers, The (The Musqueteers) (The Musketeers in a Convent): Selections	01 10 21-24 27
Vasseur	Marigold: Selections	93 94 96
Vclasqucz, R.	Montezuma, Mexican march	96
Vellela, Cezario A.G.	Good Night (Boa Noite), Brazilian dance	94 96
Venuto, Rocco	Kansas City Journal March	98
Venzano, Luigi	Grande Valse	*94 97
Verdi, Giuseppe	Aida: Ballet Music	*19 *20 21 22 25 *27 28
	Aida: Celeste Aida, vocal solo	*93 94 02 15
	Aida: Dance of the Slave Boys (Dance of the Slaves)	99 01 04 15
	Aida: Duet, cornet and trombone duet	02 03
	Aida: Fatal Stone, The (Oh, Fatal Stone) (The Last Finale) (Death of Aida) (Gia I Sacerdoti Adunasi), cornet and trombone solo/duet, or band number	99 *01 02 07-10 *11 12-17 19 21-23
	Aida: Final Scene	01
	Aida: Grand March	93
	Aida: Grand Scene	07 18
	Aida: Prelude to Act I	98 99
	Aida: Ritoura Vincitor, vocal solo	29
	Aida: Selections	93-96 99 00 02 04-08 10 *11 15-17 19 21-24 *25 26-29 *30 31
	Aroldo: Overture	01 02 04-06 19 24 27
	Attila: Selections	01 02 16 23 24
	Attila: Terzette and Finale	08
	Attila: Trio and Quartette	96
	Ballo in Maschera, Un (The Masked Ball): Aria [unnamed], euphonium solo	21-25 27
	Ballo in Maschera, Un (The Masked Ball): Eri Tu, vocal solo	*92 94
	Ballo in Maschera, Un (The Masked Ball): Selections	93 94
	Cavatina, cornet solo	21 27
	Don Carlos: Aria [unnamed], vocal solo[s]	96
	Don Carlos: O Don Fatale, vocal solo	96 24
	Don Carlos: Selections	95 96 01 02 04-06 08-10 13 14 16 18 19 21-27
	Due Foscari, I: Selections	02 24
	Ernani: Aria [unnamed], vocal solo[s]	*06 10 23 25 26
	Ernani: Ernani, Ernani, Involami (Scene and Cavatina), vocal or euphonium	95 96 02 21-24
	Ernani: Infelice, vocal solo	93
	Ernani: Recitative and Aria	94
	Ernani: Scene and Cavatina	93 94 02
	Ernani: Selections	93 94 96
	Falstaff: Selections	94-99 03 09 15 17 19 21 27 28
	Forza del Destino, La: Aria [unnamed], vocal solo[s]	97
	Forza del Destino, La: Overture	93
	Giovanni d'Arco: Overture	94
	Hymn to the Nations	01 02 04
	Jerusalem: Aria [unnamed], vocal solo[s]	93
	Joan of Arc: Overture	94-98 06 09 19 22 24 27
	L'Assedio di Arlem: Scene	93
	Lombardi, I: Aria [unnamed], vocal solo[s]	*93 95
	Lombardi, I: Finale	93 94
	Lombardi, I: La Mia Letezia, vocal solo	97
	Lombardi, I: Pilgrim's Chorus	94
	Lombardi, I: Selections	93

	Louisa Miller: Quando le Sere, vocal solo	02
	Macbeth: Grand Selection No. 1	94
	Mia Letizia, vocal solo	93
	Notavan: Duet, cornet and euphonium duet	93
	Oberto Conti di S. Bonifacio	93
	Othello: Selections	94 95 16 27
	Paraphrase on My Country 'tis of Thee	01
	Reminiscences of Verdi	93-96 98 99 01 02 04 05 07 08 10 *11 12-22 24
	Requiem Mass (Manzoni Mass): Excerpts	16 17
	Rigoletto: Aria [unnamed], vocal solo[s]	17 19-23
	Rigoletto: Caro Nome, vocal solo	*93 94 95 05 12 *13 *14 15-17 *18 19 *20 21 *22 *23 24 25 *26 27-31
	Rigoletto: Finale Third Act	94 24
	Rigoletto: La Donna e Mobile, vocal solo	96 15
	Rigoletto: Quartet, brass quartet	93-98 09 10 *11 14
	Rigoletto: Selections	96
	Sicilian Vespers, The (I Vespri Siciliani): Ballet Suite	96 27
	Sicilian Vespers, The (I Vespri Siciliani): Bolero, vocal solo	97 99
	Sicilian Vespers, The (I Vespri Siciliani): Overture	97 10 13-15 17 22 24
	Traviata, La: Ah, Fors e Lui, scene and aria, vocal solo	97 *99 02 13-17 *18 *19 *20 21 *22 23-25 *26 *27 28 29 31
	Traviata, La: Aria [unnamed], vocal solo[s]	*92 *02 09 10 15 17 18 20-28
	Traviata, La: Di Provenzi, vocal solo	93
	Traviata, La: Fantasie	04
	Traviata, La: Selections	93-98 01 02 04 05-10 *11 12 13 15 17-19 21-27 29
	Trovatore, Il: Anvil Chorus	93 95 05 06 23
	Trovatore, Il: Fierce Now the Flames Grow, vocal solo	93
	Trovatore, Il: Finale to Act I, vocal trio	93
	Trovatore, Il: Grand Scene, cornet and euphonium duet	93 94 21
	Trovatore, Il: Gypsy Chorus	93
	Trovatore, Il: Home to Our Mountains, contralto and tenor duet	93
	Trovatore, Il: Il Balen del Suo Sorriso, vocal solo	93 94 96 97 16
	Trovatore, Il: Prelude	93
	Trovatore, Il: Selections	93-96 98 01 04 07 09 10 13 14 16-19 21-27
	Trovatore, Il: Serenade, vocal solo	93
	Trovatore, Il: Stride la Vampa, vocal solo	96
	Trovatore, Il: Tacea la Notte, vocal solo	99
	Trovatore, Il: Tower Scene (Miserere), vocal duet or cornet and euphonium or trombone duet	93-95 98 04-06 08 09 22
	Un Ballo: Aria [unnamed], vocal solo[s]	92
Vereecken, Benjamin	Butterfly Carnival, saxophone solo	23
Verzano	Venzano Waltz	*94
Verziga	Gallant Artillerist, The: Overture	01
Vessey, Gordon H. Bowker	The Waltz We Love	18
	Valse Bebe	13
Vete, Albert	Oh, You Don't Know What You're Missin', vocal solo	26
Vickers	Guard of the Flag, song	99 07
Vieuxtemps, Henri	Ballade et Polonaise, violin solo	*96 *97 02 15 16
	Concertina in E, violin solo	*13
	Fantasia Appassionata, Op. 35, violin solo	*99
	Fantasie Caprice (Fantasie Capriccioso) (Fantasia Caprice), violin solo	*97 10
	Faust Fantasie, violin solo	*15
	Grand Concerto in E Major: Rondo, violin solo	*13 *22

	Introduction and Polonaise, violin solo	97
	Patriotic Fantasie, violin solo	07
	Polonaise Brilliante, violin solo	*19 *20
	Polonaise in A, violin solo	13
	Popular Fantasie, violin solo	07
	Reverie, violin or cello solo	93 *94 96 02
	Reveries of the Dance	93 94 96
	Russian Mazurka, violin solo	93
	St. Patrick's Day (Fantasia on St. Patrick's Day) (Reminiscences of St. Patrick's Day) (Irish Fantasie), violin solo	*03 06 *07 *08 15 16 18 *20
	Violin Concerto in F-sharp Minor: two movements	*19 *20 *21 *22 *24
Vincent, J.I.	Pixie's Dance, The (Dance of the Pixies)	*00 08 15 22 24
Violling	O Mario, violin solo	14
Viviani, Francesco	Silver Trumpets [of Rome], The, grand march	03 07 12 27
Voberon	Air and Variations, trombone solo	93
	Olympic, trombone solo	93
Vodorinska	Prelude in C Minor	20
Voelker, George, Jr.	Arkansas Traveller, The	94
	Frolics of the Sylphs, schottische	95
	Hunt in the Black Forest, A, descriptive fantasie	94-96 14-17 21 22 24-26
	Minstrelesque Minglings, olio overture	20 30
	Smiles and Tears, intermezzo	97
	Southern Patrol	*92 93 *97 98 *00
	Sultana, Oriental Dance	98
	Sword Dance, The, caprice	96
	Voyage Across the Ocean, A, descriptive fantasia	*96
	Will o th' Wisp	94
	Barn Dance	94
Vogel	Our Cruisers' Farewell	01
Voigt, Friederich Wilhelm	Imperial (Kaiser) (Emperor): Overture	96 *00
Vollstedt, Robert	Annie, polka	93
	Automatum, The, fantasie	01
	Donauperlen (La Perle du Danube) (Pearls of the Danube)	95
	In the Automat (Im Automaten Salon) (The Automaton), humorous potpourri	05
	In the Highland Freedom Dwells	95
	Japanese Patrol	04
	Japanese Patrol	94 95 *96 98 01 02 04 *11 22 23
	Jolly Girls, The, waltz	94-96
	Magic Woods, waltz	94
	Old Love Is Never Forgotten (Alte Liebe Rostet Nicht), Op. 29	95 96
	Seminary Girls, waltz	95
	Susse Kusse (Sweet Kisses), Op. 13, album blat, characteristic (salon stuck)	93 94
	Trumpeter's Dream, The	95
	Trumpeters of the Emperor, The, characteristic march	96
	Village Fair, humoresque	*97
Volpatti, F.	Los Banderilleros, Spanish march	19 22 24 27
Von Beglerbeg	Beauties of the North, waltz	05
Von Gael	Endienne, caprice	93
Voscovitz, F.	Sultana, La, gavotte	96 *97
Votteler, William G.	C.G.V., march	94 95
Wadsworth, Frank Wheeler	Belle of Frisco, gavotte (society dance)	94
Wagner, Ferdinand	Barbarossa Waltzes	96
	Iroquois, galop	96
	O Mater Dolorosa, Op.184	94
Wagner, Franz	Gimpel from Herbzut	98
Wagner, Josef Franz	Under the Double Eagle, march	06 09 11-13 16 23-26 28
	Vienna Dude's March "Gigerl"	27
	Woodlark, Cuckoo, and Frog, polka	23
	Year of the Musical Tones, The (Das Jahr in Tonen), Op. 250	96

Wagner, Richard	Album Leaf, An	93 94
	Cosatschok, caprice	93
	Fairies, The (Die Feen): Overture	98
	Flying Dutchman, The (Der Fliegende Hollander): Overture	*93 94-98 01 02 24-26 *27 28
	Flying Dutchman, The (Der Fliegende Hollander): Sailors' Chorus	93-95
	Flying Dutchman, The (Der Fliegende Hollander): Selections	93 94 96
	Flying Dutchman, The (Der Fliegende Hollander): Spinnerlied (Spinning	95
	Flying Dutchman, The (Der Fliegende Hollander): Spring Song	95
	Gotterdammerung, Die: Selections	94 98 01 04 05 12
	Gotterdammerung, Die: Siegfried's Death and Funeral March (Siegfried's Tod) (Funeral March)	*95 96-98 *99 *00 01 02 04 05 07 08 *11 12-16 23 24
	Gotterdammerung, Die: Siegfried's Rhine Journey	98 02 23
	Huldigungs-Marsch	02 04 08
	Kaiser March	94 95 02 10 *11
	Liebesmahl der Apostel (Love Feast of the Apostles)	94 95 97 99 06
	Lohengrin: Bridal Procession (Elsa's Bridal Procession) (Bridal Chorus) (Bridal Music) (Elsa's Procession to the Minister)	95 *96 *97 *98 01 02 04 05 *07 08-10 *11 12-16 22 23
	Lohengrin: Elsa's Dream (Elsa's Prayer), vocal solo	93 *96 *97 *99 *11 12 *15
	Lohengrin: Finale to Act I	15
	Lohengrin: Finale to Act II	04
	Lohengrin: Lohengrin's Farewell to the Swan, vocal solo	94
	Lohengrin: Prayer and Finale, vocal quintet	*93
	Lohengrin: Prelude (Introduction) to Act III	93 *94 *95 96 *97 *98 *99 01 *02 *03 04 *05 06-10 *11 12-17 22 23 25 26 *29 *30 31
	Lohengrin: Prelude (Vorspiel) to Act I	*94 *97 98 *00 05 07 13 15
	Lohengrin: Selections	*93 *94 95-99 02 04-10 *11 12-14 16 17 22-27
	Lohengrin: The Gathering of the Armies	93
	Meistersinger von Nurnberg, Die: Selections	94-98 *00 01 02 04 06-10 12 14 23-28 30 31
	Meistersinger von Nurnberg, Die: March of the Apprentices	95 97 98 01 04 16
	Meistersinger von Nurnberg, Die: Prelude (Vorspiel)	93 02 04 07 10 13 22
	Meistersinger von Nurnberg, Die: Prelude to Act III	24
	Meistersinger von Nurnberg, Die: Quintet	93
	Meistersinger von Nurnberg, Die: Walther's Prize Song (Walther's Preislied), vocal or violin solo	93-98 *99 *00 *04 06 07 09 10 *11 12 14 *15 16
	Parsifal: Flower Maidens, The	*04
	Parsifal: Good Friday Spell	01 02 *04
	Parsifal: Knights of the Holy Grail (March of the Knights) (Processional of the Knights of the Holy Grail) (Gralsriter) (Gralsriter March), march	*97 *98 *99 *00 *01 02 03 *04 05 06 *07 08 *11 12-15 22 24 25 27 *30 *31
	Parsifal: Prelude (Vorspiel)	93 94 *95 96-99 01 02 04 05
	Parsifal: Prelude (Vorspiel) [historical note: first performance by Sousa's Band on 15 Aug 1893 at Manhattan Beach]	93 94 *95 96-99 01 02 04 05
	Parsifal: Prelude and Glorification	95 *96
	Parsifal: Selections	*00 *04 24
	Reminiscences of Wagner	93 96 99 *00 02 04-10 *11 12-17 22-24 26
	Rheingold, Das: Entrance of the Gods into Valhalla	95 96 01 02 04 23
	Rheingold, Das: Prelude	98
	Rheingold, Das: Selections	07 12
	Rienzi: Invocation to Battle	92-94

	Rienzi: Mozaic	93 94
	Rienzi: Overture	93-95 09 10 *11 12 13 15 22-29 *30 *31
	Rienzi: Prayer, vocal solo	94
	Siegfried: Forest Echoes (Forest Murmurs) (Forest Sounds) (Waldweben)	01 09 10
	Siegfried: Forge-Song (Schmiedelieder) (Smith Scene)	*07 08 22
	Siegfried: Grand Scene	04
	Siegfried: Selections	94 95 *96 *97 98 *99 *00 01 02 04 05 *06 07-10 *11 12-15 17
	Siegfried's Idyll	02 11 12
	Tannhauser: Aria [unnamed], vocal solo[s]	07 08
	Tannhauser: Dich Theure Halle, vocal solo	94 95 06 16
	Tannhauser: Elizabeth's Prayer, vocal solo	05 *07 *08 23-26
	Tannhauser: Evening Star (Evening Song) (Bright Star of Eve) (Oh, Thou Sublime Bright Evening Star) (Wolfram's Romance), vocal or euphonium or cornet solo	*92 93-95 98 01 03 05 *07 08-10 *11 12-16 23
	Tannhauser: Fest March (Festmarsch) (Festival March) (Grand March)	94 95 97 98 01 05 09 10 15 29
	Tannhauser: Festival Chorus	93-95
	Tannhauser: Festival March and Chorus	07
	Tannhauser: Hail Bright Abode	92-94 05 *07
	Tannhauser: O, Hail, I Greet Thee, vocal solo	*94
	Tannhauser: Overture	*93 *94 *95 *96 *97 *98 *99 *00 *01 *02 03 04 *05 06-08 *09 10 *11 12-17 22 *23 *24 *25 *26 27 *29
	Tannhauser: Pilgrim's Chorus and Song of the Evening Star (Pilgrim's Chorus and Romance) (Tannhauser's Pilgrimage), band number or saxophone	93-95 *96 *98 02 04 05 08-10 *11 *15 22 24
	Tannhauser: Selections	93-99 01 02 04 05 *07 08-10 *11 12 13 15 16 22-28
	Tannhauser: Venusberg Music	*15
	Traums, cornet solo	16
	Tristan and Isolde: Dreams (Traume)	95 10
	Tristan and Isolde: Final Scene (Grand Scene)	01 04 06
	Tristan and Isolde: Isolde's Death Scene (Love Death) (Isolde's Liebestod)	94-96 01 07 20 23 *26
	Tristan and Isolde: Night Song (Night Scene) (Nachtgesang)	94-96 *97 *98 99 01 02 04 09 14 23
	Tristan and Isolde: Prelude and Liebestod (Prelude and Love Death)	96 09 10 *11 12-14 *15 16 17 23-27 *28 *30
	Tristan and Isolde: Selections	93 08 14 *15 24
	Tristan and Isolde: Tristan's Liebestod	04 08
	Walkure, Die: Introduction to Act II	02
	Walkure, Die: Love Song	93
	Walkure, Die: Magic Fire Music (Fire Charm) (Charm Music)	93 94 *95 96 *97 01 02 05 07 08 *11
	Walkure, Die: Ride of the Valkyries (Der Ritt die Walkure), band number or vocal solo	93 94 *95 96 *97 01 02 05 07 08 *11 23-25 26
	Walkure, Die: Selections	93 95 97-99 *00 01-04 07 08 *11 12-15 24 27
	Walkure, Die: Wotan's Farewell	05 07 08 *11
Wagner, Siegfried	Baerenhaeuter: Selections (Melodies from Baerenhaeuter)	02 09
Walden	Our Women (Our Ladies) (Unsere Frauen), gavotte	98
Waldorf	Cosatschok, caprice	93
	Russian National Dance (National Dance of Russia)	93
Waldron	Polka Caprice (Polka Ronda), trombone solo	13 14
	Theresa, cornet or euphonium solo	14 28
Waldteufel, Emile	Acclamations, waltz	25 26
	Amitie, waltz	96 25 26
	Bagatelle	94

421

	Barcarolle, La, waltz	28
	Blue Bells, waltz	16 18-23 25 26 28
	Comrade, polka caprice	97
	Danse Les Nuages, waltz	95
	Espana, waltz (Rhapsody Espagnol)	93 94 96 97 99 *00 01 02 04 *05 06-08 10 12 13 15-18 20-26 31
	Estudantina, waltz	93-95 15
	Etincelles, waltz	25 26
	Etoile, L' Polaire (L'Etoile Polaire), waltz	*92 93 94 98 04 09
	Grenadiers, The, valse militaire, Op. 207	25
	In the Woods, dance	94
	Jolly Fellow, waltz	93
	Kisses of Tenderness, waltz	19 22
	Love and Spring (Springtime), waltz caprice (idyll)	93-95
	Manola, waltz	94
	Nid d'Amour, waltz	96 24
	Nuit Etoilee, waltz	24
	Par Ci Par La, polka	13
	Polar Star, The, waltz	93-95 22-24
	Princess May, waltz	94
	Sentiers Fleuris (Century Flower) (Century Plant) (Country Flowers), waltz	94 07 20 22 25 26
	Skaters, waltz	94 05
	Souviens Toi (Souvenirs), waltz	23
	Sultana	94
	Tendres Basiers (Les Baisers), waltz	02
	Toujours Fidele (Always Faithful) (Ever Faithful), waltz	09 12 15 19 21-26
	Tres Jolie, waltz	25-27
	Tresor d'Amour, waltz	15 21 22 24
	Vision, waltz	93 94
Wallace	Hero and the Fairies, descriptive fantasie	01
	Southern, The, march	98
Wallace, J.A	Great Beyond, The, vocal solo	13
Wallace, William Vincent	Maritana: Grand Selection	93 20-23 26 27
	Maritana: Overture	93-95 *96 23
	Maritana: Second Mosaic	93 94
	Maritana: Selections	93 95 02 04-07 09 16 19
	Yes, Let Me Like a Soldier Fall, vocal or euphonium solo	93 08 13 17
Waller, Henry	Dance of the Sun-Feast, Americn Indian dance	04 08 15
Walt, Edward John	Lassie o' Mine (O Lassie o' Mine), vocal or cornet solo	*21 *22 26
Walthew, Richard Henry	May Day, vocal solo	01
Walton, William	Brooklyn Daily Eagle, march	94
Wanda	Zauber der Mondnacht, Der, lied	*00
Ward	The Band Played On, song	95
Ware, Harriet	Boat Song, vocal or cornet solo	09 10 *11
	Cross, The, descriptive, vocal solo	09 10 *11
	I Know a Lovely Garden, vocal solo	16
	Sunlight, vocal solo/duet	*09
Ware, Harriet & Thomas Moore	Dance the Romanika, descriptive waltz-song, vocal solo	19
Warneford, H. Launcelot	Marche Nuptiale	93
Warren	Autograph, waltz	93
Washburn	Fun on the Levee	95
	Grand Leader, The, march	95
Waterson	Fantasia Pastoral, clarinet solo	93
Watier	Corso Blane, morceau de genre	93
	Echo de Biarritz, cornet duet	93
Watson, Michael	Barn Dance	98
	Gavotte in B-flat	93
	Molto Staccato, gavotte	93 94
	Morris Dance	96 14
	Pizzicato, gavotte	93 94 96

	Royal Irish Constabulary, The, galop	93-95
	Thy Sentinel Am I, vocal solo	93
Weatherly, Fred E.	Danny Boy, vocal solo	*18 19-23 *25 26 *27 *27 *29 *31
Webb	Bells and Banjos	*94
Weber, Carl Marie von	Euryanthe: Overture	96
	Fantasia Freischuetz, saxophone solo	93
	First Concerto: Rondo, clarinet solo	26
	Freischuetz, Der: Aria [unnamed], vocal solo[s]	97
	Freischuetz, Der: Overture	96 01 04 22 23
	Freischuetz, Der: Piano, Piano, Canto Piano, vocal solo	96 97
	Freischuetz, Der: Prayer and Hunting Chorus	94 95
	Freischuetz, Der: Selections	93-95 25
	Invitation to the Dance (Invitation to the Waltz)	93 95 96 99 *00 *01 04 *05 06 *07 09 10 *11 12-17 24 27-29 *30
	Jubel (Jubilee): Overture (Prelude), based on My County 'Tis of Thee	93-96 *97 98 *98 99 01 02 05 06 *07 09 13 14 16 22-25 27
	Lutzow's Wilde Jagd (1813) (Leutzow's Wild Hunt) (Die Lustige Jager) (1813 Overture)	03 04 07 08 13 24 27 28
	Oberon: Overture	94-98 01 02 04 05 *06 07 09 10 *11 12 15-17 22-24 27 32
	Oberon: Selections	94 95 96
	Ocean, Thou Mighty Monster, vocal solo	94
	Peter Schmoll: Overture	94
	Polacca Brillante in E major (Polacca Brilliant)	07
	Preciosa, march	93
	Prelude on a Chinese Melody	96-98 14 24
	Reminiscences of Weber	93 94 98 01 04 05 08 09 13 15-17 22 23
	Romanza Appassionata (Appassionata), solo for baritone, bassoon, or trombone, or band number	07
	Second Grand Concerto for Clarinet	94 95 26
	Silvana: Jagerchor (Hunting Chorus)	04
Weckerlin, Jean-Baptiste	Menuet de Martini, vocal solo	17
Weidlinger	Serenade, vocal solo	96
Weidt, A.J.	Sounds from the Universities	05
Weil	Coquette, La, idyll	97
	Spring Song, vocal solo	96
Weisenborn	Forest Scene in the Adirondacks	02
Weiss	Lutzow's Wild Hunt, descriptive	95 96
Wekerlin, J.B. & H. Millard	Flower of the Alps (Fleur des Alpes), vocal solo	22 24
Weldon, Alfred F.	Gate City (Southern Airs), march, xylophone solo	21-26
	Grand Rapids Letter Carriers Band, The, march	01
	March Time, xylophone solo	24
	Old Favorites (American Medley), xylophone solo	21 22
	Whistling Coon, novelty	95 *96
	With Trumpet and Drum (Trumpet and Drum), march	04
Welleby	Moonlight, idyll	05
Wellesley, Arthur	Fleurette, La, dance caprice	01
Wellings	Last Night, ballad	94
Wellings, Milton	Golden Love, cornet solo	94 96
Wells	Joan of Arc: Overture	18
Wenrich, Percy	By the Camp Fire	19
	Moonlight Bay, song, cornet solo	*12 *13 *14 16
Wenzel, Leopold	Vine Land: Selections	13
Werner, F.	Love Go Hang, vocal solo	*96
Westmeyer, Wilhelm	Kaiser (Emperor): Overture (Emporer's Hymn) (Austrian Grand Overture)	93-95 96 *00 *01 *03 04 06 *07 *08 09 10 *11 12-15 24-26

Wettge, Gustave	Houris, Les, cornet duet	93
	Mysora: Episode Symphonique (Overture) (East Indian Prelude)	93 96 *03 *04 16 18 *30
	Perle de Roses, waltz	93 94
Wettman	Tiefer Keller, trombone quartet	93
Wheat, Leo	Grand Elks March, The	97
Wheeler	Cotton Blossoms, caprice	97
Wheeler, Horace O.	Humoresque	97
	Jim Chandler's March	23
Wheeler, J.W.	Laugh! Oh, Coons!, dance Africaine, schottische	93
Wheeler, Lutie Hodler	Marion, march	23 28
Whelpley, Benjamin	Phyllis Is My Only Joy, vocal solo	12
White, Clarence Cameron	Bandanna Sketches Op. 12 (Gospel Hymns), four Negro spirituals	93 23 25 26
White, Maude Valerie	Canzone di Taromina, Sicilian mountain song	14
Whiting, Richard A. & Byron Gay	Horses, fox trot	26
Whitney	Mouse and the Clock, The, novelty	*05 *06
Whitney, S.B.	Processional March	97
Widdel, J.	Fair Maid of Perth: Overture	93-95
Widmer, Henry	Pickin' on de Ole Banjo, caprice	96
Widor, Charles Marie	Korrigane, La: Ballet Suite	12
Wiedoeft, Rudy	Erica (Valse Erica), saxophone solo	20 23 24 *25 *26-28
	Favorita, La, saxophone solo	26
	Llewellyn Waltz, saxophone solo	24-26
	Saxema, saxophone solo	24
	Saxophobia, saxophone solo	24 *25 26
	Valse Vanite, saxophone solo	25 26
	Yvonne, saxophone solo	25
Wieniawski, Henryk	2nd Mazourka: Kuyiawiak, violin solo	08 09
	Airs Russes (Russian Airs), violin solo	*00 09 10 14 15
.	Ballade and Polonaise, violin solo	05
	Carmen Fantasie, violin solo	*97
	Faust Fantasie, violin solo	*03 *05 07 *12 *15 16 21
	Legende, violin solo	*97 02 08 14
	Obertass, mazourka, violin solo	94 *97 *01 02 05 08 09 *11 12 14-18
	Polonaise Brilliante in D Major, violin solo	*95 06 07 09 10 13 15-20
	Polonaise in D-flat, violin solo	21 *22
	Romance and Rondo, violin solo	14
	Romance Sans Paroles (Romance Without Words), violin solo	*97 *99 02 10
	Scherzo-Tarantelle, violin solo	*11 12
	Second Concerto for Violin in D (Concerto No. 2), 1 or 2 movements	*14 16 18 19 *22 *24
	Second Polonaise Brillante (Second Polonaise in A Major), violin solo	*01 02 09 13 *21 22
	Souvenir de Moscow, violin solo	*01 09 *10 *11 12 *13 14 17 18
	Zirgari, A La, violin solo	19
Wieprecht, W.	In the Bivouac, interlude (Intermezzo im Biwak)	95
Wilber, Harry J.	Rocky Mountain News, march	99
Wilhelm	Fantasie on Walther's Preislied, violin solo	05 09
Wilhelm, Carl	Watch on the Rhine	*00
Wilhelmi	Lover and His Mandolin (Mandolin Standchen)	93
Wilhelmj, August	Old Folks at Home (Souvenir d'Amerique), theme varie, violin solo	10
Willeby, Charles	Coming Home, vocal solo	29
	Crossing the Bar, vocal solo	*11 *12 13-15 17
	Moon Madrigal, dance	11-13 24
	Soldier, Take My Heart With You (Soldier, Will You Take My Heart?), vocal solo	*11 12 13 15-17
	Stolen Wings, vocal solo	*03
William O'Connell [Cardinal]	Hymn to the Holy Name	*24
Williams, Albert A.	Canadian Patrol	10
Williams, Ernest Samuel	Captivator, The, march	24

Williams, Hattie	Little Cherub: Experience	*07 *08
Williams, Ralph Vaughn	Folk Song Suite	24
Williams, Warwick Francis	All the Girls, Selections	05 24
	Dance of the Elves and Gnomes	93
	Marie, intermezzo	93 94
	Sorrow and Joy (Joy and Sorrow), cavatina	24
Willmers, Rudolf	Summer's Day in Norway, A (A Day in Norway), fantasie	06-08 10 13 14 17-19 21 22 24 25 27 *29
Wilson	Anieranem, march	97
	Ben Bolt	19
	Mexican Serenade	*03
Wilson, Henry Lane	Carmena, waltz, vocal solo	*09 10 *11 13 14 16 20 21 *22
Wilson, Mortimer	New Orleans Mardi Gras, Op. 64: Overture (Mardi Gras at New Orleans)	*25
Wingate, Philip, SEE Petrie, H.W.		
Winne, Jesse	Amarella, vocal solo	*14 *15 16 *17
Winner, Septimus	O Where Has My Little Dog Gone?, saxophone octet	*28
Winterbottom, Frank	America (In America), medley (Selection on American Melodies)	06 16 23
	Offenbachina	22
	Songs and Dances of Wales	08
Witkowski, Georges-Martin	Scene de Ballet	02
Witmark, F.M.	Prisoner of Zenda, waltzes	96
Witmark, I.	Lucinde's Serenade, Ethiopian sketch	08
Witte	Canzone di Toarrinia	14
Wittmann, G	Village Wedding, A (A Normandy Wedding Scene) (Noce Villageoise et Gigue)	93-95
Wolde	Dream of the Ball	98
Woldemar	Im Bunten Rock	93
Wolf-Ferari, Ermanno	Jewels of the Madonna, The: Entr' Acte (Prelude)	*12 *13 21 26
	Jewels of the Madonna, The: Selections	14 17 18 22-25 28
Wood, Arthur	Arcadians, The: Overture	22 27 29
	Fairy Dreams, intermezzo	13 14
Wood, Haydn	Cash on Delivery, fantasia	19
	Clovertown: Selections	19
	Jimmy Sale Rag, The	19
	Roses of Picardy, vocal solo	19 20 24-27
	Three Dale Dances, suite (Dale Dances of Yorkshire) (Folk Dances of Yorkshire) (Yorkshire Lasses)	*20 *21 *22 23 *24 25 *25 *26 27 28
	Virginia, Southern rhapsody (The Virginian)	*30
Woodford-Finden, Amy	Temple Bells, vocal solo	21
Woodman, Raymond Huntington	Birthday, A, vocal solo	14 24
	Open Secret, An, vocal solo	05 18
Woods	A Little Kiss Each Morning, song, cornet solo	*30
	Our National Heritage, march	23
	Silver Clouds, intermezzo	18
Woods, G.L.	Rainwater Rifles, The, march	95
Woodward	Radian Moon now Passes Away, The	93
Work, Henry Clay	Marching Through Georgia, patrol	92 93 *97
Wormser, Andre	Prodigal Son, The (L'Infant Prodigue): Selections	28
Wright, A.N.	Village Fair, The: Overture	95
Wright, Frederick Coit	General Payne's March	28
Wuerst, Richard	Dance of the Gnats, caprice	*97
Wurm, Moritz	Preacher, The, waltz (Valse of the Preachers)	18
Wynne	Sons of America, march	23
Yearsley, C. Blakesley	Ye Gods and Little Fishes, two-step caprice	14
Youmans, Vincent	No, No, Nanette: I Want to Be Happy, saxophone ensemble	*25 26
	Rainbow Girl, saxophone ensemble	26
Youmans, Vincent & Herbert Stothart	Wildflower: Bambalina, fox trot	*23
Yradier, Sebastian	Paloma, La (The Dove), Spanish serenade	93-95 *96 *97 01 03 04 06 *11 18 24 27
	Reminiscences of Yradier	04
Yuengling	Oriante, march	96

Yume	Boheme, satarelle	19
Zamara	Capricetto, flute solo	17
Zamecnik, John S.	Amorita, fox trot	*20 *21
	Biddy, fox trot	*20 *21 *22
	Dancer of Navarre, The, descriptive	18 *21 22
	Indian Dawn, dance	26
	Jealous Moon, The, fox trot	18 19
	Kisses, valse d'amour (valse lente)	*19 *20
	Little Irish Rose, vocal solo	*28
	My Cairo Love (Egyptian serenade) (Egyptia), band number or cornet solo	*19 *20 *21 26
	Neapolitan Nights, vocal solo	19 *21 26-28
	Ole South, patrol	19 21
	Only a Smile, vocal or cornet solo	22
	Somewhere in Naples, fox trot, xylophone solo	*21 *22
	Spirit of America, patrol	26
	Temple Bells, vocal solo	18 19
Zarzycki, Aleksander	Mazurka in G (Concert Mazurka), violin solo	*96 12
Zehle, W.	Japanese Tattoo (Japanischer Zapfenstreich) (In Tokyo), patrol	09
Zeller, Carl	Ach, Das Ist der Obersteiger	95
	Bist du Schoen, caprice	95
	Columbian, march	93
	Glow Worm, The, waltz	95
	Mine Boss, The: Scenes	06 08
	Obersteiger, Der: Sei Nicht Bos (Don't Be Cross), flugelhorn solo or band number	95*97 *98
	Obersteiger, Die: Martin Waltz	95
	Obersteiger, Die: Selections	95 96 04
	Tyrolean, The: Nightingale Song, vocal or flugelhorn solo	92-94 *96 *97 99
	Tyrolean, The: Selections	94-96
	Vogelhandler, Der: Selections	93
Ziehrer, Carl Michael	Bundle of Mischief, A, novelty	*02 *03
	Fantasie on Popular Viennese Melodies (Reminiscences of Suppe, Millocker, Strauss)	01 02 09 16 21 23 27
	Lovely Night (Nachtschwarmer) (Night Owls), waltz	01 *02 24
	Natursanger (Nature's Warblers), waltz	02 04 15 22
	Oh, Lovely Night!	93 01
	Sing, Laugh, and Dance (Singen, Lachen, Tanzen), waltz	03
	Street Songs of Vienna (Sounds from Vienna)	02 09 14
	This Kiss Is for the Whole World, waltz	95
	Vienna Beauties (Vienna Darlings) (Weaner Mad'ln), waltz	94 *95 *96 *97 98 99 01 04 *05 *06 07
	Vienna Songs and Dances, flugelhorn duet	04
	Wiener Burger (Vienna Citizens), waltz	02
Zikoff	March Germania	93
Zimbalist, Efrem	Suite in Alter Form (Suite in Old Style), violin solo	14
Zimmerman, Charles A	Anchors Aweigh, march	29
	In Ole Arkansas, characteristic	20 25
Zimmerman, John F.N.	Dusky Gathering, A, Negro sketch	02
	Impromptu Arabasque	22 23
	On the Delaware (Across the Delaware), march	02
	Osmanli, Oriental serenade	02 10
Zimmerman, Leopold A.	Aereo, trombone solo	*06 30
	Air Varie, trombone solo	03 04
	American Beauty Waltzes, trombone solo	03-05 07
	Leona Polka, trombone solo	03-07 *30
	My Old Kentucky Home, trombone solo	03 04
	Patriotic Medley, trombone solo	06
	Pride of the West, trombone solo	*07
	Waltz Caprice, trombone solo	04
Zitterbart	Columbus, overture	13
	Liberty, march	01
Zucca, Mana	If Flowers Could Speak, song	20 21

Zuleta	Phrynne, waltz	13 21-23 25
Miscellaneous	American Barn Dance, SEE Happy Darkeys (Perdue)	
	Batch of Modern English Songs, SEE Collection of the Most Admired Songs of Lawrence Kellie (Kellie)	
	Bit of Blue and a Bit of Gray, SEE Plantation Songs and Dances (Clarke, H.L.)	
	Burletta, SEE Kutschke Polka (Stasny)	
	Collection of Sacred Themes, A, SEE Songs of Grace and Songs of Glory (Sousa)	
	Cotton Pickers, The, SEE Southern Jollification (Kunkel)	
	Dear Heart, SEE Cuore Gentil (Gomez)	
	Episode Militaire, SEE Day in Camp, A (Dodworth)	
	Fantasie Hungarian, SEE Hungarian Fantasie (Eckhardt)	
	Fantasie on American Melodies, SEE Plantation Songs and Dances (Clarke, H.L.)	
	Fantasie Originale SEE Fantasie Brillante (Gatti)	
	Frivolette, SEE Summer Days (Coates)	
	Fugue on Yankee Doodle and Hail Columbia, SEE International Congress, The (Sousa)	
	Gems of Irish Minstrelsy, SEE ALSO Highland Scene, A (Moore, J.W.)	
	Gems of Minstrelsy from the Days of Carncross and Dixie, SEE Ten Minutes with the Minstrels (Bowron)	
	Gospel Hymns, SEE Bandanna Sketches (White, C.C.)	
	Guard Mount, SEE Emperor's Review) (Eilenberg)	
	Husking Dance, SEE Happy Darkeys (Perdue)	
	Kapelle, Die, SEE Chapel, The (Kreutzer)	
	Modern Scotch Songs of Lawrence Kellie, SEE Collection of the Most Admired Songs of Lawrence Kellie (Kellie)	
	On the Shores of the Gulf of Mexico, SEE Souvenir de Mexico (Hoch)	
	Passing of the Guard, SEE Ronde de la Garde (Loew)	
	Potpourri of Martial tunes, SEE Collection of Tunes in March Form (Carl, K.)	
	Prelude in C-sharp Minor, SEE Bells of Moscow (Rachmaninoff)	
	Prodana Nevesta, See Bartered Bride, The (Smetana)	
	Recollections of Lawrence Kellie, SEE Collection of the Most Admired Songs of Lawrence Kellie)	
	Reminiscences of Stephen Foster, SEE Plantation Songs and Dances (Clarke, H.L.)	
	Reminiscences of Victor Herbert, SEE Victor Herbert Favorites (Lake)	
	Return of the Guards, A, SEE Ronde de la Garde (Loew)	
	Rose Duet, SEE Trip to Africa, A. (Suppe)	
	Rounds of the Guards, SEE Ronde de la Garde (Loew)	
	Serenade Ethiopian, SEE Darkie's Serenade (Bucalossi, E.)	
	Slumber Song, SEE Wiegenlied (Sitt)	
	Songs and Dances of the Sailors, SEE Trafalgar (Miller)	
	Songs for Sailors, SEE Trafalgar (Miller)	
	Souvenir de Naples, SEE Fantasie Brillante (Gatti)	
	Sweet Kisses, SEE Susse Kusse (Vollstedt)	
	Tune from County Clare, SEE Irish Tune from County Derry (Grainger)	
	United Service Passing in Review, SEE Emperor's Review (Eilenberg)	
	Voyage in a Troopship, SEE Trafalgar (Miller)	

APPENDIX VI

DISCOGRAPHY

This listing of the recordings of Sousa's Band was compiled with the assistance of Melissa J. Bierley and is based on the following:

1. Extensive research by discographer Frederick P. Williams
2. *The Sousa Band: A Discography* by James R. Smart
3. *Encyclopedic Discography of Victor Recordings* by Ted Fagan and William R. Moran
4. *Berliner Gramophone Records* by Paul Charosh
5. Research by John L. Hubbard

Clarification

This discography lists all known commercial phonograph singles recordings (1,770 in number) by members of John Philip Sousa's civilian band or a mixture of those musicians and others, all of which are referred to today as "Sousa's Band."

The order in which the recordings are listed is intended to show the extent of recording activity year by year.

No additional recording sessions were required for records issued for sale outside the United States, although some have different catalog numbers. Examples of such numbers are CB (Canadian Berliner) and G&T (Gramophone & Typewriter Co., Britain). The Sousa Band did not record outside the country at any time.

Every effort was made to keep this compilation simple and straightforward, so such things as take numbers and matrix numbers are not included. Most of that information is available in volumes intended for serious collectors.

Dates

Information on recording dates is lacking for many early recordings. Manufacturers' logs, what few there might have been, have not survived.

Actual recording dates are known in some instances, particularly the Berliner discs, because the dates were often inscribed on the discs. Extensive research by discographers has made it possible to estimate most dates within a reasonable span of years. Fortunately, recording data on nearly all of the Victor Talking Machine Company discs have survived.

This list includes only those recordings that were actually put into production. Many other titles were recorded but not issued. It should be mentioned that most of the "takes" were never used.

Conductors

Conductors for many of the early recordings have not been identified. Of particular interest are the Edison cylinders. Some believe that Herbert L. Clarke, Sousa's solo cornetist and assistant conductor, directed all or most of the Edison recording sessions. He was employed by Edison during the period in question, but it must be pointed out that the Sousa Band was on tour during part of that same period, and Clarke was definitely with Sousa on those tours.

A summary of the conductors for the various companies is as follows:

Berliner Gramophone Co.	Henry Higgins, 1897-99 Arthur Pryor, 1898-1900 & others?
Columbia Phonograph Co.	Uncertain but probably Arthur Pryor & Henry Higgins
Chicago Talking Machine Co.	Unknown
Edison (United States Phonograph Co.)	Herbert L. Clarke? and others?
Victor Talking Machine Co.	Arthur Pryor, 1900-03, 1912, 1918-26 Herbert L. Clarke, 1904-06, 1915

Victor (continued)
Walter B. Rogers, 1908, 1909
Edwin G. Clarke, 1910, 1911
John Philip Sousa, 1917, 1918, 1923
Guillermo Gonzales, 1919
Joseph Pasternack, 1919-22, 1925
Nathaniel Shilkret, 1923-25
Rosario Bourdon, 1919, 1929, 1930

The Recording Companies

Among the known issuers of Sousa Band recordings, the recording and distribution activities of the Chicago Talking Machine Company are incompletely documented. Nearly all their titles also appear on known Columbia issues. However, Chicago advertised eight titles not found in Columbia catalogs, and it is known that Chicago made some recordings on their own.

Sousa's Band was involved in the recording of both cylinders and discs, as mentioned in Chapter 5, but most were discs. Cylinders were mostly two inches in diameter, but a few five-inch cylinders were made. Discs were issued in various sizes: seven-, eight-, ten-, and twelve-inch diameters before the industry standardized on ten- and twelve-inch. Before 1897 all discs were recorded on one side only.

Several other companies often mentioned as possible producers of Sousa recordings remain a mystery. Among these are the Zonophone and Vitaphone companies, both of whom might have pressed discs identical to Berliner discs with new or altered information in the label area (Berliner did not use paper labels). The Vitaphone Company was not related to a motion picture system that later used the same name.

Another questionable company was a distributor, D.E. Boswell & Company. All but one of the Boswell announced titles have been traced to other companies, and this probably indicates that their issues were copies.

Another manufacturer that could possibly have made Sousa Band recordings was the New Jersey Phonograph Company, which announced several Sousa Band titles. None of their recordings have ever turned up among record collectors, so the announcement might have been premature.

Three additional companies listed in catalogs as possible manufacturers, but which were probably just distributors, were the American Talking Machine Company, the New York Talking Machine Company, and the Kansas City Talking Machine Company.

Other possible manufacturers were the Globe Talking Machine Company, the Consolidated Talking Machine Company (from which the Victor Talking Machine Company was developed), and a company using the Climax label, which all evidently operated in the area around Philadelphia and Camden. It is suspected that if they really did produce Sousa Band disc recordings they used Berliner's stampers after Berliner went out of business.

The name of yet another possible manufacturer is occasionally mentioned, the Wonder Talking Machine Company of New York, supposedly a subsidiary of the C.G. Conn musical instrument company of Elkhart, Indiana. An advertisement claimed thirty Sousa Band titles, all bearing the same numbers used by Berliner, but none of those records are known to exist. The Wonder Label should not be confused with the Little Wonder 5½-inch records produced many years later.

Titles and Composers' Names

Music scholars have pointed out that the titles appearing on some recordings are often different from the titles on published sheet music or manuscripts. Some titles were altered or shortened, and identification in the absence of copies of the recordings makes cataloging difficult.

There are also numerous questions about composers whose names appear on labels or in catalogs. Some names are incomplete or missing, leaving a cataloger with no way to give proper attribution. The use of pseudonyms also creates problems, as does the use of composers' names not found in standard reference books.

Many of the complete names of titles and composers may be found in Appendix V or in the forthcoming book *Sousa's Band Library: Story and Catalog* (Bierley and Warfield).

Information about the types of compositions (e.g., marches, waltzes, etc.) is often missing, too, and in many instances there are no known copies of a recording to examine, thus making more exact cataloging in the future unlikely.

Record Numbers

The numbers sometimes assigned by manufacturers in the early years led to considerable confusion. Berliner in particular used more than one system of numbering, as seen in the use of the same catalog number for different titles. Victor also created cataloging problems by using the same number for re-recordings of a piece at a later date. Too, Victor used the same number for records of different sizes.

Another enigma was created when companies used a new number for a title that had been dubbed from one cylinder to another rather than re-recording it. There are not enough cylinders among the scattered holdings of collectors to make educated guesses about such things as dates of issuance.

Difficulties in Documentation

Because of the scarcity of data left by the early record manufacturers, and the absence of many of their catalogs or advertisements, a discographer's job is difficult indeed. It was made even more difficult because information about recordings was often stamped or engraved on the records, and very few of the records have survived.

Most of the old cylinders and discs were fragile, partially accounting for their scarcity. Adding to that was an unfortunate process took place in the World War II era. The growing demand for new 78-rpm records resulted in a shortage of materials, primarily shellac. Much of the material could be reclaimed by recycling old records, so manufacturers appealed to the public to donate old records for salvaging. Consequently millions of old records – including many of considerable historical value – were pulverized, melted down, and made into new records. The irony of this is that many of the very first records were made of materials other than shellac, such as hard rubber compounds, and could not be recycled. But they, too, were destroyed during the collection process and are thus lost forever.

Multiple Releases of Certain Disc Titles

From this discography the abundance of some titles might lead one to think that those pieces were more popular than they really were. Some were indeed popular at the time, but there was another reason. Only a limited number of pressings could be made from one stamper; they eventually wore out. Several hundred pressings could usually be made before a stamper had to be replaced (or, in some cases, reconditioned). After a second production run the stamper was usually beyond repair.

Since a way to make multiple stampers from a single play-through, or take (i.e., mothers), had not yet been developed, stampers were often made from several different takes. When all available stampers had outlived their usefulness, it was necessary to call for another recording session. Recording musicians' pay was much less in those days, so that wasn't a major deterrent.

The Victor Labels

Between 1900 and 1903 Victor often issued a title on both the Victor and Monarch labels. For the sake of simplicity, only "Victor" is used in this discography.

Abbreviations

Berliner	Berliner Gramophone Co., New York, Philadelphia, and Washington, D.C.
Chicago	Chicago Talking Machine Co.
Columbia	Columbia Phonograph Co., Washington, D.C.
Edison	National Phonograph Co., New York
Victor	Victor Talking Machine Co., Camden, New Jersey, and Philadelphia
cond.	conductor of recording session
cyl.	cylinder
ds	double-sided disc
ss	single-sided disc
nd	exact date of recording unknown
rec.	place and/or date of recording

1895

All issued by Columbia, recorded on 10 March in Washington. Conductor(s) unknown but possibly Arthur Pryor and Henry Higgins.

Corn Cracker Dance (Meacham)
#504 2" cyl.
La Czarina (Ganne)
#503 2" cyl.
The Directorate March (Sousa)
#518 2" cyl.
The Directorate March (Sousa)
#518 5" cyl.
Friday Night March
No number; 2" cyl.
High School Cadets (Sousa)
#501 2" cyl.
High School Cadets (Sousa)
#501 5" cyl.
The Jolly Coppersmith (Peter)
#507 2" cyl.
The Jolly Coppersmith (Peter)
#507 5" cyl.
The Liberty Bell (Sousa)
#500 2" cyl.
The Liberty Bell (Sousa)
#500 5" cyl.
Lily Bells (Sousa)
No number; cyl. size?
Manhattan Beach (Sousa)
#519 2" cyl.
Manhattan Beach (Sousa)
#519 5" cyl.
Marching Through Georgia Patrol (Sousa)
No number; cyl. size?
Plantation Chimes (Hall)
#513 2" cyl.
Semper Fidelis (Sousa)
#530 2" cyl.
Semper Fidelis (Sousa)
#530 5" cyl.
The Washington Post (Sousa)
#520 2" cyl.
The Washington Post (Sousa)
#520 5" cyl.
William Tell: Overture; Finale (Rossini)
No number; cyl. size?
Yazoo Dance (W.L. Thompson)
#502 2" cyl.

1895-1900

All issued by Chicago. Place(s) of recording unknown. Conductor(s) unknown.

America
#300 2" cyl; nd.
The Beau Ideal (Sousa)
#301 2" cyl; nd.
The Beau Ideal (Sousa)
#301 5" cyl; nd.
The Belle of New York: Selections (Kerker)
#315 2" cyl; nd.
The Belle of New York: Selections (Kerker)
#327 2" cyl; nd.
The Belle of New York: Selections (Kerker)
#701 2" cyl; nd.
The Belle of New York: Selections (Kerker)
#1026 2" cyl; nd.
The Bride Elect (Sousa)
#317 2" cyl; nd.
El Capitan: March (Sousa)
#306 2" cyl; nd.
Circus Gallop (Donnawell)
#1054 2" cyl; nd.

Constellation March (Clark)
#302 2" cyl; nd.
Corn Cracker Dance (Meacham)
#710 2" cyl; nd.
Corn Cracker Dance (Meacham)
#1051 2" cyl; nd.
Cuban Patriots March (Murden)
#303 2" cyl; nd.
Cuban Patriots March (Murden)
#1038 2" cyl; nd.
La Czarina (Ganne)
#711 2" cyl; nd.
La Czarina (Ganne)
#1052 2" cyl; nd.
The Directorate March (Sousa)
#316 2" cyl; nd.
The Directorate March (Sousa)
#316 5" cyl; nd.
The Directorate March (Sousa)
#704 2" cyl; nd.
The Directorate March (Sousa)
#1029 2" cyl; nd.
Hands Across the Sea (Sousa)
#304 5" cyl; nd.
High School Cadets (Sousa)
#329 2" cyl; nd.
High School Cadets (Sousa)
#703 2" cyl; nd.
High School Cadets (Sousa)
#1028 2" cyl; nd.
Honeymoon March (Rosey)
#307 2" cyl; nd.
Honeymoon March (Rosey)
#1037 2" cyl; nd.
Image of the Rose (Reichardt)
#1058 2" cyl; nd.
In the Sweet Bye and Bye (Webster)
#318 2" cyl; nd.
In the Sweet Bye and Bye (Webster)
#318 5" cyl; nd.
The Jolly Coppersmith (Peter)
#1063 2" cyl; nd.
Kansas Two-step (Pryor)
#1034 2" cyl; nd.
King Cotton (Sousa)
#308 2" cyl; nd.
King Cotton (Sousa)
#1036 2" cyl; nd.
The Liberty Bell (Sousa)
#309 2" cyl; nd.
The Liberty Bell (Sousa)
#328 2" cyl; nd.
The Liberty Bell (Sousa)
#702 2" cyl; nd.
The Liberty Bell (Sousa)
#1027 2" cyl; nd.
Little Duke: Selections (Lecocq)
#1001 2" cyl; nd.
Little Marcia Marie Polka (Pryor)
Trombone solo by Arthur Pryor. #1059 2" cyl; nd.
Little Nell (Pryor)
Trombone solo by Arthur Pryor. #1057 2" cyl; nd.
Manhattan Beach (Sousa)
#706 2" cyl; nd.
Manhattan Beach (Sousa)
#1031 2" cyl; nd.
The March King (Pryor)
#1035 2" cyl; nd.
Marching Through Georgia Patrol (Sousa)
#708 2" cyl; nd.
Marching Through Georgia Patrol (Sousa)
#1033 2" cyl; nd.
Nearer My God to Thee (Mason)
#320 2" cyl; nd.

Off to Camp March (Frederick)
  #311 2" cyl; nd.
Only One Girl in the World for Me (D. Marion)
  Trombone solo by Arthur Pryor. #1056 2" cyl; nd.
The Picador March (Sousa)
  #312 2" cyl; nd.
The Picador March (Sousa)
  #705 2" cyl; nd.
The Picador March (Sousa)
  #1030 2" cyl; nd.
Semper Fidelis (Sousa)
  #313 2" cyl; nd.
Semper Fidelis (Sousa)
  #707 2" cyl; nd.
Semper Fidelis (Sousa)
  #1032 2" cyl; nd.
The Sidewalks of New York (Lawlor)
  #1061 2" cyl; nd.
The Stars and Stripes Forever (Sousa)
  #321 2" cyl; nd.
The Stars and Stripes Forever (Sousa)
  #321 5" cyl; nd.
The Sunshine of Paradise Alley (Bratton)
  #1060 2" cyl; nd.
Sweet Marie (Moore)
  #633[?] 2" cyl; nd.
The Washington Post (Sousa)
  #314 2" cyl; nd.
The Washington Post (Sousa)
  #326 2" cyl; nd.
The Washington Post (Sousa)
  #700 2" cyl; nd.
The Washington Post (Sousa)
  #1025 2" cyl; nd.
Water Sprites (Kunkel)
  #1062 2" cyl; nd.
William Tell: Overture; Finale (Rossini)
  #712 2" cyl; nd.
William Tell: Overture; Finale (Rossini)
  #1000 2" cyl; nd.
Yazoo Dance (W.L. Thompson)
  #709 2" cyl; nd.
Yazoo Dance (W.L. Thompson)
  #1050 2" cyl; nd.

1896

All Columbia. Recorded in Washington. Conductor(s) unknown but possibly Arthur Pryor and Henry Higgins.
El Capitan: March (Sousa)
  #514 2" cyl; [ca. 1896].
El Capitan: March (Sousa)
  #514 5" cyl; nd.
Circus Gallop (Donnawell)
  #509 2" cyl; [ca. 1896].
Circus Gallop (Donnawell)
  #509 5" cyl; [ca. 1896].
The Columbia Phonograph Company March (Burton)
  #515 2" cyl; [ca. 1896].
Dancing in the Dark
  #529 2" cyl; nd.
Dancing in the Dark
  #529 5" cyl; nd.
The Darky's Temptation (Srohm)
  #510 2" cyl; [ca. 1896].
Honeymoon March (Rosey)
  #526 2" cyl; nd.
Honeymoon March (Rosey)
  #526 5" cyl; nd.
Kansas Two-step (Pryor)
  #511 2" cyl; [ca. 1896].
King Cotton (Sousa)
  #506 2" cyl; nd.

King Cotton (Sousa)
  #506 5" cyl; nd.
Little Marcia Marie Polka (Pryor)
  Trombone solo by Arthur Pryor. #517 2" cyl; [ca. 1896].
Little Nell (Pryor)
  Trombone solo by Arthur Pryor. No number; nd.
The March King (Pryor)
  No number; cyl. size? nd.
Midway Plaisance Medley
  #508 2" cyl; [ca. 1896].
Off to Camp March (Frederick)
  #521 2" cyl; nd.
Off to Camp March (Frederick)
  #521 5" cyl; nd.
Only One Girl in the World for Me (D. Marion)
  No number; cyl. size? nd.
Say Au Revoir, But Not Goodbye (Kennedy)
  Trombone solo by Arthur Pryor. #516 2" cyl; [ca. 1896].
Say Au Revoir, But Not Goodbye (Kennedy)
  Trombone solo by Arthur Pryor. #516 5" cyl; nd.
The Sidewalks of New York (Lawlor)
  #512 2" cyl; [ca. 1896].
The Sunshine of Paradise Alley (Bratton)
  #505 2" cyl; nd.

1897

America
  Columbia #525 2" cyl; rec. ca. 1897, Washington.
Answer (Robyn)
  Cornet solo by Henry Higgins. Berliner #67 7" ss; cond. Higgins; rec. 18 Aug., New York.
At a Georgia Camp Meeting (Mills)
  Berliner #64 7" ss; rec. ca. 1897, NY.
The Beau Ideal (Sousa)
  Columbia #523 2" cyl; rec. ca. 1897, Washington.
The Butterfly (Bendix)
  Berliner #60V 7" ss; cond. Higgins; rec. 10 or 18 Aug., New York.
The Butterfly (Bendix)
  Berliner #60X 7" ss; rec. ca. 1897, New York.
El Capitan: March (Sousa)
  Berliner #42V 7" ss; cond. Higgins; rec. Aug., New York.
El Capitan: March (Sousa)
  Berliner #42X 7" ss; cond. Higgins; rec. 18 Aug., New York.
El Capitan: March (Sousa)
  Berliner #42ZZ 7" ss; cond. Higgins; rec. Oct., New York.
Carmen: Selections (Bizet)
  Berliner #27 7" ss; cond. Higgins; rec. Aug., New York
The Crack Regiment (Tobani)
  Berliner #79 7" ss; cond. Higgins; rec. 10 or 18 Aug., New York.
The Crack Regiment (Tobani)
  Berliner #79X 7" ss; rec. ca. 1897, New York.
The Crack Regiment (Tobani)
  Berliner 79Z 7" ss; rec. ca. 1897, New York.
La Czarina (Ganne)
  Berliner #66Z 7" ss; cond. Higgins; rec. 18 Aug., New York.
La Czarina (Ganne)
  Berliner #66X 7" ss; cond. Higgins; rec. Oct., New York.
La Czarina (Ganne)
  Berliner #66 7" ss; cond. Higgins; rec. ca. 1897, New York.
The Directorate March (Sousa)
  Berliner #23 7" ss; cond. Higgins; rec. 18 Aug., New York.
The Directorate March (Sousa)
  Berliner #23Y 7" ss; rec. 18 Aug., New York.
The Directorate March (Sousa)
  Berliner #23V 7" ss; rec. ca. 1897, New York.
The Enquirer Club March (Brand)
  Columbia #531 2" cyl; rec. 1897, Washington.
The Enquirer Club March (Brand)
  Columbia #531 5" cyl; rec. ca. 1897, Washington.
Flirtation (Steck)
  Berliner #76 7" ss; cond. Higgins; rec. 1 Sept., New York.
The Gladiator March (Sousa)
  Berliner #13Z 7" ss; cond. Higgins; rec. 1 Sept., New York.

The Gladiator March (Sousa)
Berliner #13W 7" ss; cond. Higgins; rec. 2 Sept., New York.

Glass in Hand Polka (Fahrbach)
Berliner #80Z 7" ss; cond. Higgins; rec. 1 Sept., New York.

Handicap March (Rosey)
Berliner #41w 7" ss; cond. Higgins; rec. 10 or 18 Aug., New York.

Handicap March (Rosey)
Columbia #522 2" cyl; rec. ca. 1897, Washington.

Handicap March (Rosey)
Columbia #522 5" cyl; rec. ca. 1897, Washington.

Happy Days in Dixie (Mills)
Berliner #56Z 7" ss; cond. Higgins; rec. 18 Aug., New York.

The Jolly Fellows Waltz (Vollstedt)
Berliner #51U 7" ss; cond. Higgins; rec. ca. 1897, New York.

The Jolly Fellows Waltz (Vollstedt)
Berliner #51X 7" ss; cond. Higgins; rec. 10 or 18 Aug., New York.

The Jolly Fellows Waltz (Vollstedt)
Berliner #51V 7" ss; cond. Higgins; rec. ca. 1897, New York.

Levee Revels (O'Hare)
Berliner #38Z 7" ss; cond. Higgins; rec. 10 or 18 Aug., New York.

Levee Revels (O'Hare)
Berliner #38Y 7" ss; cond. Higgins; rec. ca. 1897, New York.

Lily Bells (Sousa)
Berliner #70 7" ss; cond. Higgins; rec. 1 Sept., New York

Lily Bells (Sousa)
Berliner #70W 7" ss; cond. Higgins; rec. 1 Sept., New York.

Lily Bells (Sousa)
Berliner #70ZZ 7" ss; rec. ca. 1897, New York.

Little Coquette Polka
Berliner #71 7" ss; cond. Higgins; rec. 1 Sept., New York.

Little Flatterer (Eilenberg)
Berliner #82 7" ss; cond. Higgins; rec. 10 or 18 Aug., New York.

Little Flatterer (Eilenberg)
Berliner #82W 5" cyl; rec. ca. 1897, New York.

Little Marcia Marie Polka
Trombone solo by Arthur Pryor. Berliner #69Z 7" ss; cond. Higgins; rec. 1 Sept., New York.

Loin du Bal (Gillet)
Berliner #15X 7" ss; cond. Higgins; rec. Oct., New York.

The March King (Pryor)
Berliner #83 7" ss; rec. ca. 1897, New York.

The March King (Pryor)
Berliner #83Y 7" ss; cond. Higgins; rec. 1 Sept., New York.

Midsummer Night's Dream (Mendelssohn)
Berliner #20Y 7" ss; cond. Higgins; rec. Aug., New York.

My Angeline (L. Johnson)
Berliner #39X 7" ss; cond. Higgins; rec. 23 Nov., New York.

Oriental Echoes (Rosey)
Berliner #40 7" ss; cond. Higgins; rec. Aug., New York.

The Picador March (Sousa)
Columbia #524 2" cyl; rec. ca. 1897, Washington.

Plantation Chimes (Hall)
Berliner #72V 7" ss; cond. Higgins; rec. Sept., New York.

Plantation Chimes (Hall)
Berliner #72W 7" ss; rec. ca. 1897, New York.

Plantation Chimes (Hall)
Berliner #72Z 7" ss; rec. ca. 1897, New York.

The Soposis March
Berliner #78 7" ss; rec. ca. 1897, New York.

Southern Blossoms (Orange Blossoms) (Pryor)
Berliner #65 7" ss; cond. Higgins; rec. 18 Aug., New York.

Starlight Waltz (Herbert)
Berliner #73Z 7" ss; cond. Higgins; rec. 1 Sept., New York.

The Stars and Stripes Forever (Sousa)
Berliner #61T 7" ss; rec. ca. 1897, New York.

The Stars and Stripes Forever (Sousa)
Berliner #61V 7" ss; cond. Higgins; rec. 18 Aug., New York.

The Stars and Stripes Forever (Sousa)
Berliner #61U 7" ss; rec. ca. 1897, New York.

The Stars and Stripes Forever (Sousa)
Berliner #61W 7" ss; rec. ca. 1897, New York.

The Stars and Stripes Forever (Sousa)
Columbia #532 2" cyl; rec. ca. 1897, Washington.

The Stars and Stripes Forever (Sousa)
Columbia #532 5" cyl; rec. ca. 1897, Washington.

The Thunderer (Sousa)
Berliner #30V 7" ss; rec. ca. 1897, New York.

The Thunderer (Sousa)
Berliner #30W 7" ss; rec. ca. 1897, New York.

The Thunderer (Sousa)
Berliner #30Y 7" ss; cond. Higgins; rec. 10 Aug., New York.

The Thunderer (Sousa)
Berliner #30X 7" ss; cond. Higgins; rec. Oct., New York.

Uncle Rastus (Clappe)
Columbia #527 2" cyl; rec. ca. 1897, Washington.

The Washington Post (Sousa)
Berliner 140Z 7" ss; cond. Higgins; rec. 18 Aug., New York.

The Washington Post (Sousa)
Berliner 140Y 7" ss; cond. Higgins; rec. Oct., 1897, New York.

Water Sprites (Kunkel)
Columbia no number; cyl. size? rec. ca. 1897, Washington.

Way Down in Georgia (Dalbey)
Columbia #528 2" cyl; rec. ca. 1897, Washington.

William Tell: Overture; Finale (Rossini)
Berliner #7W 7" ss; cond. Higgins; rec. 10 or 18 Aug., New York.

Yazoo Dance
Berliner #77 7" ss; rec. Oct., New York.

1898

At a Georgia Camp Meeting (Mills)
Berliner #136Z 7" ss; cond. Higgins; rec. April, New York

At a Georgia Camp Meeting (Mills)
Berliner #136X 7" ss; rec. ca. 1898, New York

The Blue Danube Waltz (J. Strauss, II)
Berliner #109 7" ss; cond. Higgins; rec. 9 April, New York.

The Bride Elect: March (Sousa)
Berliner #92 7" ss; cond. Higgins; rec. 3 Feb., New York.

The Bride Elect: March (Sousa)
Berliner #92Y 7" ss; cond. Higgins; rec. 8 April, New York.

The Bride Elect: March (Sousa)
Berliner #92Z 7" ss; cond. Higgins; rec. 8 April, New York.

The Bride Elect: March (Sousa)
Columbia #533 2" cyl; rec. ca. 1898, Washington.

The Bride Elect: March (Sousa)
Columbia #533 5" cyl; rec. ca. 1898, Washington.

Canadian Medley March (Baugh)
Berliner #142 7" ss; cond. Higgins; rec. 1 or 2 Sept., New York.

El Capitan: March (Sousa)
Berliner #42YY 7" ss; cond. Higgins; rec. 7April, New York.

Cavalleria Rusticana: Intermezzo (Mascagni)
Berliner #123 7" ss; cond. Higgins; rec. April, New York.

Cavalleria Rusticana: Intermezzo (Mascagni)
Berliner #123Y 7" ss; cond. Pryor. rec. 1 Sept., New York.

Cavalleria Rusticana: Intermezzo (Mascagni)
Berliner #123Z 7" ss; rec. 2 Sept. 1898, New York.

The Charlatan: March (Sousa)
Berliner #36 7" ss; cond. Higgins; rec. Sept., New York

The Charlatan: March (Sousa)
Berliner #36Z 7" ss; cond. Higgins; rec. ca. 1898, New York.

Colonial Dames Waltzes (Sousa)
Berliner #112 7" ss; cond. Higgins; rec. 8 April, New York.

Coon Band Contest (Pryor)
Columbia #538 2" cyl; nd., Washington.

Coon Band Contest (Pryor)
Columbia #538 5" cyl; nd., Washington.

Cotton Blossoms (Hall)
Berliner #104 7" ss; cond. Higgins; rec. 7 April, New York.

Dancing in the Dark
Berliner #114 7" ss; cond. Higgins; rec. 9 April, New York.

The Directorate March (Sousa)
Berliner #23ZZ 7" ss; cond. Higgins; rec. 8 April, New York.

Dixie (Emmett)
Berliner #102 7" ss; cond. Higgins; rec. 7 April, New York.

Enquirer Club March (Brand)
Berliner #110 7" ss; cond. Higgins; rec. 8 April, New York.

First Heart Throbs (Eilenberg)
Berliner #127 7" ss; cond. Higgins; rec. April, New York.

Flee as a Bird (Dana)
Berliner #133 7" ss; cond. Higgins; rec. April, New York.

Flee as a Bird (Dana)
Berliner #133Z 7" ss; cond. Higgins; rec. 28 May, New York.
The Fortune Teller: Gypsy Love Song and Hungarian Movement (Herbert)
Berliner #8007 7" ss; rec. Dec., 1898; rec. place?
Funiculi-Funicula – A Merry Heart (Denza)
Berliner #119 7" ss; cond. Higgins? rec. April, New York.
The Gladiator March (Sousa)
Berliner #13W 7" ss; cond. Pryor; rec. 2 Sept., New York.
God Save the Queen
Berliner #148Y 7" ss; cond. Higgins; rec. 3 Dec., New York.
A Hot Time in the Old Town (Metz)
Berliner #139 7" ss; cond. Higgins; rec. 2 Sep, New York.
A Hot Time in the Old Town (Metz)
Berliner #139Y 7" ss; cond. Higgins; rec. ca. 1898, New York.
King Cotton (Sousa)
Berliner #143 7" ss; cond. Higgins; rec. 1 or 2 Sept., New York.
King Cotton (Sousa)
Berliner #143ZZ 7" ss; cond. Higgins; rec. 1 or 2 Sept., New York.
Loin du Bal (Gillet)
Berliner #15W 7" ss; cond. Higgins; rec. 3 Feb, New York.
Lorelei (Nesvadba)
Berliner #130 7" ss; cond. Higgins; rec. 28 May, New York.
Lorelei (Nesvadba)
Berliner #130Y 7" ss; cond. Higgins; rec. 1 or 2 Sept., New York.
The Man Behind the Gun (Sousa)
Columbia #537 2" cyl; nd., Washington.
The Man Behind the Gun (Sousa)
Columbia #537 5" cyl; nd., Washington.
Manhattan Beach (Sousa)
Berliner #149W 7" ss; cond. Higgins; rec. 1 Sept., New York.
Manhattan Beach (Sousa)
Berliner #149V 7" ss; cond. Higgins? rec. ca. 1898, New York.
La Marseillaise (Rouget de l'Isle)
Berliner #117X 7" ss; cond. Higgins; rec. 1 Sept., New York.
La Marseillaise (Rouget de l'Isle)
Berliner #117Y 7" ss; cond. Higgins; rec. 2 Sept., New York.
The Matinee Girl March (Pryor)
Berliner #108 7" ss; cond. Higgins; rec. 9 April, New York.
The Meeting of the Blue and the Gray (T.F. Morse)
Berliner #128 7" ss; cond. Higgins; rec. 29 May, New York.
The Meeting of the Blue and the Gray (T.F. Morse)
Berliner #128X 7" ss; cond. Higgins; rec. 1 or 2 Sept., New York.
Mexican National Hymn
Berliner #101 7" ss; cond. Higgins; rec. April, New York.
A Midsummer Night's Dream: Wedding March (Mendelssohn)
Berliner #20Z 7" ss; cond. Higgins; rec. 28 May, New York.
A Midsummer Night's Dream: Wedding March (Mendelssohn)
Berliner #20Y 7" ss; cond. Higgins; rec. 29[?] May, New York.
Mother Hubbard March (Sousa)
Berliner #107 7" ss; cond. Higgins; rec. 9 Apr, New York.
My Old Kentucky Home Fantasy (Foster/Dalbey)
Berliner #129 7" ss; cond. Higgins; rec. 26 May, New York.
My Old Kentucky Home Fantasy (Foster/Dalbey)
Berliner #129Z 7" ss; cond. Higgins; rec. Sept., New York.
Red Cross March (Philips)
Columbia #536 2" cyl; nd., Washington.
Red Cross March (Philips)
Columbia #536 5" cyl; nd., Washington.
Robin Hood: Selections (De Koven)
Berliner #131 7" ss; cond. Higgins; rec. Sept., New York.
Robin Hood: Selections (De Koven)
Berliner #131X 7" ss; cond. Higgins; rec. ca. 1898, New York.
Robin Hood: Selections (De Koven)
Berliner #131Z 7" ss; cond. Higgins; rec. ca. 1898, New York.
Robin Hood: Waltz (De Koven)
Berliner #132 7" ss; cond. Higgins; rec. 28 May, New York.
Robin Hood: Waltz (De Koven)
Berliner #132Z 7" ss; cond. Higgins; rec. 1 or 2 Sept., New York.
The Serenade: Waltz (Herbert)
Berliner #113Y 7" ss; cond. Higgins; rec. April, New York.
The Serenade: Waltz (Herbert)
Berliner #113 7" ss; cond. Higgins; rec. 28 May, New York.

Songs of Scotland
Berliner #141Z 7" ss; cond. Higgins; rec. 1 Sept., New York.
Songs of Scotland
Berliner #141 7" ss; cond. Pryor; rec. ca. 2 Sept., New York.
The Star Spangled Banner (arr. Sousa)
Berliner #103 7" ss; cond. Higgins; rec. 8 April, New York.
The Star Spangled Banner (arr. Sousa)
Berliner #0227 7" ss; cond. Higgins; rec. 7 April, New York.
The Stars and Stripes Forever (Sousa)
Berliner #103Y 7" ss; cond. Higgins; rec. 7 April, New York.
The Thunderer (Sousa)
Berliner #30V 7" ss; cond. Higgins; rec. ca. 1898, New York.
The Thunderer (Sousa)
Berliner #30W 7" ss; cond. Higgins; rec. ca. 1898, New York.
The Thunderer (Sousa)
Berliner #30X 7" ss; conc. Pryor; rec. 28 May, New York.
Il Trovatore: Home to Our Mountains (Verdi)
Cornet and trombone duet by Herbert L. Clarke and Arthur Pryor. Columbia #534 2" cyl; nd., Washington.
Way Down in Georgia (Dalbey)
Berliner #111 7" ss; cond. Higgins; rec. 9 April, New York
The Washington Post (Sousa)
Berliner #140X 7" ss; cond. Higgins; rec. 1 Sept., New York.
The Washington Post (Sousa)
Berliner #140W 7" ss; rec. ca. 1898, New York.
Ye Boston Tea Party (Pryor)
Berliner #93 7" ss; cond. Higgins; rec. April, New York.
Ye Boston Tea Party (Pryor)
Berliner #93W 7" ss; cond. Higgins; rec. ca. 1898, New York.

Ca. 1898

Issued by the United States Phonograph Company of Newark, New Jersey. Most, if not all, believed to be copies of Columbia Phonograph Machine Company cylinders. Size(s), numbers, exact dates, and conductor(s) unknown.

America
The Beau Ideal (Sousa)
The Belle of New York: March (Kerker)
El Capitan: March (Sousa)
Constellation March (Clark)
Cuban Patriots March (Murden)
The Directorate March (Sousa)
Handicap March (Rosey)
High School Cadets (Sousa)
Honeymoon March (Rosey)
King Cotton (Sousa)
The Liberty Bell (Sousa)
Manhattan Beach (Sousa)
The New York Girl March (Katzenstein)
Off to Camp March (Frederick)
The Picador March (Sousa)
Semper Fidelis (Sousa)
The Stars and Stripes Forever (Sousa)
The Washington Post (Sousa)

1899

An African Beauty (Pryor)
Berliner #080 7" ss; cond. Pryor; rec. 22 April, Philadelphia.
American Marine's March (Tocaben)
Berliner #0188 7" ss; cond. Pryor; rec. 6 June, New York.
American Republic March (Thiele)
Berliner #0208 7" ss; cond. Pryor; rec. 10 June, New York.
An Arkansaw Huskin' Bee (Pryor)
Berliner #0191 7" ss; cond. Pryor; rec. 7 June, New York.
At a Georgia Camp Meeting (Mills)
Berliner #0247 7" ss; cond. Pryor; rec. June, New York.
Because (Bowers)
Berliner #0183 7" ss; cond. Pryor; rec. 6 June, New York.
The Blue Danube Waltz (J. Strauss, II)
Berliner #0246 7" ss; cond. Pryor; rec. 6 June, New York.
The Bride Elect: March (Sousa)
Berliner #0229 7" ss; cond. Pryor; rec. June, New York.

The Bride Elect: Tarantella (Sousa)
Berliner #077 7" ss; cond. Pryor; rec. 22 April, Philadelphia.
Canadian Medley March (Baugh)
Berliner #0196 7" ss; cond. Pryor; rec. June, New York.
El Capitan: March (Sousa)
Berliner #0230 7" ss; cond. Pryor; rec. 8 June, New York.
Cavalleria Rusticana: Intermezzo (Mascagni)
Berliner #0175 7" ss; cond. Pryor; rec. June, New York.
The Charlatan: March (Sousa)
Berliner #076 7" ss; cond. Higgins; rec. 22 April, Philadelphia.
The Charlatan: Mazurka (Sousa)
Berliner #078 7" ss; cond. Pryor; rec. 22 April, Philadelphia.
The Christian: Waltzes (Furst)
Berliner #0187 7" ss; cond. Pryor; rec. 6 June, New York.
Cotton Blossoms (Hall)
Berliner #0197 7" ss; cond. Pryor; rec. June, New York.
Cyrano de Bergerac: Waltzes (Herbert)
Berliner #8014 7" ss; cond. Higgins; rec. 22 April, Philadelphia.
La Czarina (Ganne)
Berliner #0225 7" ss; cond. Pryor; rec. 8 June, New York.
Dance of the Sprites (Cowan)
Berliner #0224 7" ss; cond. Pryor; rec. June, New York.
Danza Mexicana (Chambers)
Berliner #0219 7" ss; cond. Pryor; rec. 10 June, New York.
The Directorate March (Sousa)
Berliner #0216 7" ss; cond. Pryor; rec. June, New York.
Dixie (Emmett)
Berliner #0213 7" ss; cond. Pryor; rec. 7 June, New York.
Dixie (Emmett)
Berliner #0213 7" ss; cond. Pryor; rec. 9 June, New York.
Enquirer Club March (Brand)
Berliner #0178 7" ss; cond. Pryor; rec. 5 June, New York.
First Heart Throbs (Eilenberg)
Berliner #0199 7" ss; cond. Pryor; rec. 7 June, New York.
The Fortune Teller: Gypsy Love Song (Herbert)
Euphonium solo by Simone Mantia. Berliner #0217 7" ss; cond. Pryor; rec. June, New York.
The Fortune Teller: Gypsy Love Song and Hungarian Movement (Herbert)
Berliner #8007Z 7" ss; cond. Higgins; rec. ca. 1898, Philadelphia.
The Fortune Teller: March (Herbert)
Berliner #8001Z 7" ss; cond. Higgins; rec. 22 April, Philadelphia.
The Fortune Teller: March (Herbert)
Berliner #0184 7" ss; cond. Pryor; rec. 7 June, New York.
The Fortune Teller: Selections (Herbert)
Berliner #0186 7" ss; cond. Pryor; rec. June, New York.
The Fortune Teller: Waltz (Herbert)
Berliner #8008Z 7" ss; cond. Higgins; rec. 22 April, Philadelphia.
The Fortune Teller: Waltz and March (Herbert)
Berliner #0185 7" ss; cond. Pryor; rec. June, New York.
The Gladiator March (Sousa)
Berliner #0236 7" ss; cond. Pryor; rec. 8 June, New York.
God Save the Queen (arr. Sousa)
Berliner #0211 7" ss; cond. Pryor; rec. June, New York.
Handicap March (Rosey)
Berliner #0240 7" ss; cond. Pryor; rec. 8 June, New York.
Hands Across the Sea (Sousa)
Berliner #075 7" ss; cond. Pryor; rec. 22 April, Philadelphia.
Hands Across the Sea (Sousa)
Columbia #535 2" cyl; rec. nd., Washington.
Hands Across the Sea (Sousa)
Columbia #535 5" cyl; rec. nd., Washington.
The Hercules March (Mantia)
Berliner #0204 7" ss; cond. Pryor; rec. 9 June, New York.
A Hot Time in the Old Town (Metz)
Berliner #0201 7" ss; cond. Pryor; rec. 8 June, New York.
Pousse Café: How I Love My Lou (Smith-De Lange – Stromberg)
Berliner #8005 7" ss; cond. Higgins; rec. 22 April, Philadelphia.
Just One Girl (Udall)
Berliner #8000 7" ss; cond. Higgins; rec. 22 April, Philadelphia.
Just One Girl (Udall)
Berliner #0179 7" ss; cond. Pryor; rec. 7 June, New York.
King Cotton (Sousa)
Berliner #0231 7" ss; cond. Pryor; rec. June, New York.

Levee Revels (O'Hare)
Berliner #0214 7" ss; cond. Pryor; rec. June, New York.
Little Flatterer (Eilenberg)
Berliner #0223 7" ss; cond. Pryor; rec. 8 June, New York.
Little Nell (Pryor)
Berliner #079 7" ss; cond. Higgins; rec. 22 April, Philadelphia.
Loin du Bal (Gillet)
Berliner #0177 7" ss; cond. Pryor; rec. 5 June, New York.
Lorelei (Nesvadba)
Berliner #0176 7" ss; cond. Pryor; rec. 5 June, New York.
Love Thoughts (Pryor)
Trombone solo by Arthur Pryor. Berliner #0190 7" ss; rec. 6 June, New York.
Mammy's Little Pumpkin Colored Coon (Perrin)
Cornet solo by Emil Kenecke. Berliner #8013 7" ss; cond. Higgins; rec. 22 April, Philadelphia.
Mammy's Little Pumpkin Colored Coon (Perrin)
Cornet solo by Emil Kenecke. Berliner #0203 7" ss; cond. Pryor. rec. 8 June, New York.
The March King (Pryor)
Berliner #0237 7" ss; cond. Pryor; rec. June, New York.
The Matinee Girl March (Pryor)
Berliner #0192 7" ss; cond. Pryor; rec. June, New York.
Medley of Irish Airs
Berliner #8009 7" ss; cond. Higgins; rec. 22 April, Philadelphia.
Medley of Irish Air
Berliner #8009Z 7" ss; rec. ca. 1899, place?
Meeting of the Blue and the Gray (T.F. Morse)
Berliner #0239 7" ss; cond. Pryor; rec. 9 June, New York.
A Midsummer Night's Dream: Wedding March (Mendelssohn)
Berliner #0238 7" ss; cond. Pryor; rec. 8 June, New York.
The Mikado March (George Wiegand) [incorrectly attributed to Sousa]
Berliner #0206 7" ss; cond. Pryor; rec. 10 June, New York
Mother Hubbard March (Sousa)
Berliner #0198 7" ss; cond. Pryor; rec. 5 June, New York.
Narcissus (Nevin)
Berliner #0220 7" ss; cond. Pryor; rec. 10 June, New York.
Nearer My God to Thee (Mason)
Berliner #8004 7" ss; rec. 22 April, Philadelphia.
Nearer My God to Thee (Mason)
Berliner #8004Z 7" ss; cond. Higgins; rec. 22 April, Philadelphia.
Nearer My God to Thee (Mason)
Berliner #0210 7" ss; cond. Pryor; rec. 10 June, New York.
Nibelungen March (Sonntag-Wagner)
Berliner #0215 7" ss; cond. Pryor; rec. 10 June, New York.
The Old 100 (Bourgeois)
Berliner #0207 7" ss; cond. Pryor; rec. 6 June, New York.
I Pagliacci: Serenade (Leoncavallo)
Euphonium solo by Simone Mantia. Berliner #0205 7" ss; cond. Pryor; rec. 9 June, New York.
Parson Ringtail's Wedding Dance (Isenman)
Berliner #0218 7" ss; cond. Pryor; rec. June, 1899, New York.
The Phroso Waltzes (Furst)
Berliner #0244 7" ss; cond. Pryor; rec. 6 June, New York.
The Picador March (Sousa)
Berliner #8012 7" ss; cond. Higgins; rec. 22 April, Philadelphia.
Robin Hood: Selections (De Koven)
Berliner #0189 7" ss; cond. Pryor; rec. 6 June, New York.
Robin Hood: Waltz (De Koven)
Berliner #0209 7" ss; cond. Pryor; rec. June, New York.
Rubber Neck Jim (Bratton)
Berliner #0182 7" ss; cond. Pryor; rec. 5 June, New York.
A Runaway Girl: Soldiers in the Park (Monckton)
Berliner #0195 7" ss; cond. Pryor; rec. 7 June, New York.
Scorcher March (Rosey)
Berliner #8015 7" ss; cond. Higgins; rec. 22 April, Philadelphia
Scorcher March (Rosey)
Berliner #0241 7" ss; cond. Pryor; rec. June, New York.
Serenade [Opus 15, No. 1] (Moszkowski)
Berliner #0200 7" ss; cond. Pryor; rec. 8 June, New York.
The Serenade: Waltz (Herbert)
Berliner #0243 7" ss; cond. Pryor; rec. 8 June, New York.

Songs of Scotland
Berliner #0226 7" ss; cond. Pryor; rec. 9 June, New York.

Southern Hospitality (Pryor)
Berliner #081 7" ss; cond. Pryor; rec. 22 April, Philadelphia.

A Southern Idyll (Baxter)
Berliner #8006 7" ss; cond. Pryor; rec. 22 April, Philadelphia.

The Star Spangled Banner (arr. Sousa)
Berliner #0227 7" ss; cond. Pryor; rec. 9 June, New York.

The Stars and Stripes Forever (Sousa)
Berliner #0228 7" ss; cond. Pryor; rec. 9 June, New York.

The Stars and Stripes Forever (Sousa)
Berliner #61 7" ss; cond. Pryor; rec. 17 April.

A Sylvan Dream
Berliner #8010 7" ss; cond. Higgins; rec. 22 April, Philadelphia.

When You Ain't Got No Money, Well You Needn't Come Around (Brewster-Sloan)
Berliner #082 7" ss; cond. Pryor; rec. 22 April, Philadelphia.

Whirlwind Polka (Levy)
Cornet solo by Herbert L. Clarke. Berliner #0202 7" ss; cond. Pryor; rec. 8 June 1899, New York.

Whistling Rufus (Mills)
Berliner #0181 7" ss; cond. Pryor; rec. 6 June, New York.

William Tell: Overture; Finale (Rossini)
Berliner #0222 7" ss; cond. Pryor; rec. June, New York.

Ye Boston Tea Party (Pryor)
Berliner #0193 7" ss; cond. Pryor; rec. June, New York.

Ca. 1899

The following recordings were issued by the D.E. Boswell Company of Chicago. Most, if not all, are believed to be copies of Columbia Phonograph Company cylinders. Size(s), numbers, and conductor(s) unknown.

The American National March (Heinzinger)
The Beau Ideal (Sousa)
High School Cadets (Sousa)
Lily Bells (Sousa)
Manhattan Beach (Sousa)
The Picador March (Sousa)
Semper Fidelis (Sousa)
The Washington Post (Sousa)

1900

"A Frangesa" March (Costa)
Berliner #01204 7" ss; cond. Pryor; rec. April, Philadelphia.

"A Frangesa" March (Costa)
Victor #352 7" ss; cond. Pryor; rec. 1 Oct., Philadelphia.

Ah! 'Twas a Dream (Lassen)
Cornet solo by Walter B. Rogers. Berliner #01188 7" ss; cond. Pryor; rec. April, Philadelphia.

Ah! 'Twas a Dream (Lassen)
Cornet solo by Walter B. Rogers. Victor #349 7" ss; cond. Pryor; rec. 5 Oct., Philadelphia.

The Ameer: March (Herbert)
Berliner #01206 7" ss; cond. Pryor; rec. April, Philadelphia.

The Ameer: Selections (Herbert)
Berliner #01207 7" ss; cond. Pryor; rec. April, Philadelphia.

American Patrol (Meacham)
Victor #382 7" ss; cond. Pryor; rec. 6 Oct, Philadelphia.

An Arkansaw Huskin' Bee (Pryor)
Victor #314 7" ss; cond. Pryor; rec. 1 Oct., Philadelphia.

Asleep in the Deep (Petrie)
Trombone solo by Arthur Pryor. Berliner #01184 7" ss; rec. April, Philadelphia.

At a Georgia Camp Meeting (Mills)
Victor #315 7" ss; cond. Pryor; rec.1 Oct., Philadelphia.

Auld Lang Syne (arr. Rogers)
Cornet solo by Walter B. Rogers. Victor #375 7" ss; cond. Rogers; rec. 5 Oct., Philadelphia.

Baby Polka (Bial)
Victor #370 7" ss; cond. Pryor; rec. 3 Oct., Philadelphia.

Balscenen Waltz (Czibulka)
Berliner #01174 7" ss; cond. Pryor; rec. April, Philadelphia.

Balscenen Waltz: Love's Dream After the Ball (Czibulka)
Victor #342 7" ss; cond. Pryor; rec. 3 Oct., Philadelphia.

The Belle of New York: Finale (Kerker)
Victor #378 7" ss; cond. Pryor; rec. 5 Oct., Philadelphia.

Blue Bells of Scotland
Trombone solo by Arthur Pryor. Berliner #01179 7" ss; rec. 14 April, Philadelphia.

Blue Bells of Scotland
Trombone solo by Arthur Pryor. Victor #311 7" ss; rec. 6 Oct., Philadelphia.

The Blue Danube Waltz (J. Strauss, II)
Victor #343 7" ss; cond. Pryor; rec. 4 Oct., Philadelphia.

The Bride Elect: March (Sousa)
Victor #303 7" ss; cond. Pryor; rec. 2 Oct., Philadelphia.

The Bride Elect: Tarantella (Sousa)
Victor #335 7" ss; cond. Pryor; rec. 5 Oct., Philadelphia.

Bride of the Waves (Clarke)
Cornet solo by Herbert L. Clarke. Berliner #01185 7" ss; cond. Pryor; rec. April, Philadelphia.

Bride of the Waves (Clarke)
Cornet solo by Herbert L. Clarke. Victor #346 7" ss; cond. Pryor; rec. 5 Oct., Philadelphia.

Butterfly Dance (Bendix)
Victor #374 7" ss; cond. Pryor; rec. 5 Oct., Philadelphia.

El Capitan: March (Sousa)
Victor #304 7" ss; cond. Pryor; rec. 4 Oct., Philadelphia.

Cavalleria Rusticana: Intermezzo
Victor #353 7" ss; cond. Pryor; rec. 3 Oct., Philadelphia.

Cavalleria Rusticana: Siciliana (Mascagni)
Victor #372 7" ss; cond. Pryor; rec. 4 Oct., Philadelphia.

The Charlatan: March (Sousa)
Victor #302 7" ss; cond. Pryor; rec. 4 Oct., Philadelphia.

Chopin's Mazurka (Chopin)
Victor #364 7" ss; cond. Pryor; rec. 2 Oct., Philadelphia.

Chopin's Polonaise (Chopin)
Victor #318 7" ss; cond. Pryor; rec. 2 Oct., Philadelphia.

Chopin's Waltz (Chopin)
Victor #317 7" ss; cond. Pryor; rec. 2 Oct., Philadelphia.

Chris and the Wonderful Lamp: Fanny Waltz (Sousa)
Trombone solo by Arthur Pryor. Berliner #01182 7" ss; rec. April, Philadelphia.

Chris and the Wonderful Lamp: Fanny Waltz (Sousa)
Trombone solo by Arthur Pryor. Victor #309 7" ss; rec. 6 Oct., Philadelphia.

Circus Galop (Donnawell)
Berliner #01172 7" ss; cond. Pryor; rec. April, Philadelphia.

Circus Galop (Donnawell)
Victor #319 7" ss; cond. Pryor; rec. 2 Oct., Philadelphia.

The Conquerer March (Corey)
Victor #373 7" ss; cond. Pryor; rec. 4 Oct., Philadelphia.

Coon Band Contest (Pryor)
Berliner #01170 7" ss; cond. Pryor; rec. 12 April, Philadelphia.

Coon Band Contest (Pryor)
Victor #312 7" ss; cond. Pryor; rec. 2 Oct., Philadelphia.

The Crack Regiment Patrol (Tobani)
Berliner #01178 7" ss; cond. Pryor; rec. April, Philadelphia.

The Crack Regiment Patrol (Tobani)
Victor #338 7" ss; cond. Pryor; rec. 3 Oct., Philadelphia.

Cyrano de Bergerac: March (Herbert)
Berliner #01205 7" ss; cond. Pryor; rec. April, Philadelphia.

La Czarina Mazurka Russe (Ganne)
Victor #326 7" ss; cond. Pryor; rec. 1 Oct., Philadelphia.

Danse des Paysans Russes (Ascher)
Berliner #01193 7" ss; cond. Pryor; rec. April, Philadelphia.

Dear Golden Days Waltz (Strakosch)
Victor #530 7" ss; rec. 20 Nov., Philadelphia.

The Directorate March (Sousa)
Victor #308 7" ss; cond. Pryor; rec. 4 Oct., Philadelphia.

Dixie Cheers (Emmett)
Victor #320 7" ss; cond. Pryor; rec. 2 Oct., Philadelphia.

A Dream of Wagner (Hamm)
Berliner #01176 7" ss; cond. Pryor; rec. April, Philadelphia.

A Dream of Wagner (Hamm)
Victor #313 7" ss; cond. Pryor; rec. 1 Oct., Philadelphia.

Echo de Bastions (Kling)
Berliner #01195 7" ss; cond. Pryor; rec. April, Philadelphia.

Eugen Onegin (Chaikovskii) [Tchaikovsky]
Berliner #01190 7" ss; cond. Pryor; rec. April, Philadelphia.

Eugen Onegin: Waltz (Chaikovskii) [Tchaikovsky]
Victor #341 7" ss; cond. Pryor; rec. 4 Oct., Philadelphia.

Felice Waltz (Liberati)
Berliner #01181 7" ss; cond. Pryor; rec. April, Philadelphia.

Flirtation Waltz (Steck)
Victor # 366 7" ss; cond. Pryor; rec. 2 Oct., Philadelphia.

Flirtation Waltz (Steck)
Victor # 366 7" ss; cond. Pryor; rec. 5 Oct., Philadelphia.

The Fortune Teller: Gypsy Love Song (Herbert)
Euphonium solo by Simone Mantia. Victor #350 7" ss; cond. Pryor; rec. 5 Oct., Philadelphia.

Frau Luna: Luna Walzer (Lincke)
Victor #377 7" ss; cond. Pryor; rec. 6 Oct., Philadelphia.

Fresche Frauen (Brilliant Women) (Liebling)
Victor #376 7" ss; cond. Pryor; rec. 6 Oct., Philadelphia.

German Sounds (arr. Rogers)
Cornet solo by Walter B. Rogers. Victor #531 7" ss; rec. 20 Nov., Philadelphia.

God Save the Queen (arr. Sousa)
Victor #322 7" ss; cond. Pryor. Rec. 6 Oct., Philadelphia.

Golden Wedding March (Rogers)
Berliner #01202 7" ss; cond. Pryor; rec. April, Philadelphia.

Hail to the Spirit of Liberty (Sousa)
Victor #365 7" ss; cond. Pryor; rec. 6 Oct., Philadelphia.

Hands Across the Sea (Sousa)
Victor #300 7" ss; cond. Pryor; rec. 1 Oct., Philadelphia.

A Hot Time in the Old Town (Metz)
Victor #316 7" ss; cond. Pryor; rec. 2 Oct., Philadelphia.

Les Huguenots: Benediction of the Poignards (Meyerbeer)
Berliner #01196 7" ss; cond. Pryor; rec. April, Philadelphia.

Les Huguenots: Benediction of the Poignards (Meyerbeer)
Victor #327 7" ss; Pryor; rec. 4 Oct., Philadelphia.

Hula Hula Cake Walk (Van Alstyne)
Berliner #01201 7" ss; cond. Pryor; rec. April, Philadelphia.

Indian War Dance (Bellstedt)
Berliner #01175 7" ss; cond. Pryor; rec. April, Philadelphia.

Indian War Dance (Bellstedt)
Victor #324 7" ss; cond. Pryor; rec. 2 Oct., Philadelphia.

Just Sweet Sixteen (Thornton)
Cornet solo by Walter B. Rogers. Victor #526 7" ss; rec. 19 Nov., Philadelphia.

King Cotton (Sousa)
Victor #301 7" ss; cond. Pryor; rec. 4 Oct., Philadelphia.

Levee Revels (O' Hare)
Victor #328 7" ss; cond. Pryor; rec. 3 Oct., Philadelphia.

Lily Bells (Sousa)
Berliner #01198 7" ss; cond. Pryor; rec. April, Philadelphia.

Lily Bells (Sousa)
Victor #339 7" ss; cond. Pryor; rec. 2 Oct., Philadelphia.

Listen to My Tale of Woe (H.F. Smith)
Berliner #01200 7" ss; cond. Pryor; rec. April, Philadelphia.

Listen to My Tale of Woe (H.F. Smith)
Victor #323 7" ss; cond. Pryor; rec. 3 Oct., Philadelphia.

Little Nell (Pryor)
Trombone solo by Arthur Pryor. Victor #330 7" ss; rec. 1 Oct., Philadelphia.

Loin du Bal (Gillet)
Victor #329 7" ss; cond. Pryor; rec. 5 Oct., Philadelphia.

Lolita (Langey)
Victor #381 7" ss; cond. Pryor; rec. 6 Oct., Philadelphia.

Lorelei Paraphrase (Nesvadba)
Victor #356 7" ss; cond. Pryor; rec. 1 Oct., Philadelphia.

Love Thoughts (Pryor)
Trombone solo by Arthur Pryor. Berliner #01180 7" ss; cond. Pryor; rec. April, Philadelphia.

Love Thoughts (Pryor)
Trombone solo by Arthur Pryor. Victor #310 7" ss; rec. 5 Oct., Philadelphia.

Lucia di Lammermoor: Sextet (Donizetti)
Brass sextet by Herbert L. Clarke, Henry Higgins, Simone Mantia, Arthur Pryor, Marcus Lyon, and Edward A. Williams. Berliner #01177 7" ss; rec. April, Philadelphia.

Lucia di Lammermoor: Sextet (Donizetti)
Brass sextet by Herbert L. Clarke, Henry Higgins, Simone Mantia, Arthur Pryor, Marcus Lyon, and Edward A. Williams. Victor #334 7" ss; rec. 4 Oct., Philadelphia.

Man Behind the Gun (Sousa)
Berliner #01169 7" ss; cond. Pryor; rec. 19 April, Philadelphia.

The Man Behind the Gun (Sousa)
Victor #307 7" ss; cond. Pryor; rec. 1 Oct., Philadelphia.

The March King (Pryor)
Victor #340 7" ss; cond. Pryor; rec. 4 Oct., Philadelphia.

The Mosquito Parade (Whitney)
Berliner #01199 7" ss; cond. Pryor; rec. April, Philadelphia.

The Mosquito Parade (Whitney)
Victor #337 7" ss; cond. Pryor; rec. 4 Oct., Philadelphia.

Mother Hubbard March (Sousa)
Victor #305 7" ss; cond. Pryor; rec. 1 Oct., Philadelphia.

My Love for You (Little/Pritzkow)
Cornet solo by Herbert L. Clarke. Berliner #01186 7" ss; cond. Pryor; rec. April, Philadelphia.

My Love For You (Little/Pritzkow)
Cornet solo by Herbert L. Clarke. Victor #345 7" ss; cond. Pryor; rec. 5 Oct., Philadelphia.

Narcissus (Nevin)
Victor #354 7" ss; cond. Pryor; rec. 6 Oct., Philadelphia.

Nearer My God to Thee (Mason)
Victor #355 7" ss; cond. Pryor; rec. 2 Oct., Philadelphia.

Not Long Ago
Cornet solo by Walter B. Rogers. Victor #528 7" ss; rec. 20 Nov., Philadelphia.

Old Black Joe with Variations (Foster/Rogers)
Cornet solo by Walter B. Rogers. Victor #527 7" ss; rec. 19 Nov., Philadelphia.

I Pagliacci: Serenade (Leoncavallo)
Euphonium solo by Simone Mantia. Victor #351 7" ss; cond. Pryor; rec. 5 Oct., Philadelphia.

Peace Forever March (Lacalle)
Berliner #01203 7" ss; cond. Pryor; rec. April, Philadelphia.

Peace Forever March (Lacalle)
Victor # 357 7" ss; cond. Pryor; rec. 1 Oct., Philadelphia.

Pixies' Dance (Vincent)
Berliner #01194 7" ss; cond. Pryor; rec. April, Philadelphia.

Pixies' Dance (Vincent)
Victor #331 7" ss; cond. Pryor; rec. 2 Oct., Philadelphia.

Pixies' Dance (Vincent)
Victor #331 7" ss; cond. Pryor; rec. 4 Oct., Philadelphia.

Polka Des Clowns (Allier)
Victor #379 7" ss; cond. Pryor; rec. 6 Oct., Philadelphia.

Polonaise (Chopin)
Berliner #01192 7" ss; cond. Pryor; rec. April, Philadelphia.

Primrose March (Carlton)
Victor #367 7" ss; cond. Pryor; rec. 3 Oct., Philadelphia.

Rose Mousse (Bosc)
Victor #383 7" ss; cond. Pryor; rec. 6 Oct., Philadelphia.

A Runaway Girl: Selections (Monckton)
Berliner #01197 7" ss; cond. Pryor; rec. April, Philadelphia.

A Runaway Girl: Selections (Monckton)
Victor #332 7" ss; cond. Pryor; rec. 4 Oct., Philadelphia.

Salome (Loraine)
Berliner #01173 7" ss; cond. Pryor; rec. April, Philadelphia.

Salome (Loraine)
Victor # 325 7" ss; cond. Pryor; rec. 1 Oct., Philadelphia.

Semiramide: Overture (Rossini)
Victor # 359 7" ss; cond. Pryor; rec. 4 Oct., Philadelphia.

Serenade (Moszkowski)
Victor #333 7" ss; cond. Pryor; rec. 1 Oct., Philadelphia.

The Serenade: Waltz (Herbert)
Victor # 368 7" ss; cond. Pryor; rec. 3 Oct., Philadelphia.

A Soldiers Dream (Rogers)
Cornet solo by Walter B. Rogers. Victor #524 7" ss; cond. Pryor; rec. 19 Nov., Philadelphia.

A Southern Dance (Rogers)
Cornet solo by Walter B. Rogers. Victor #525 7" ss; cond. Pryor; rec. 19 Nov., Philadelphia.

A Souvenir of Naples (arr. Puntillo)
Cornet solo by Walter B. Rogers. Berliner #01187 7" ss; cond. Pryor; rec. April, Philadelphia.

A Souvenir of Naples (arr. Puntillo)
Cornet solo by Walter B. Rogers. Victor #348 7" ss; cond. Pryor; rec. 5 Oct., Philadelphia

The Star Spangled Banner (arr. Sousa)
Victor #336 7" ss; cond. Pryor; rec. 6 Oct., Philadelphia.

The Stars and Stripes Forever (Sousa)
Berliner #0228 7" ss; cond. Pryor; rec. 11 April, Philadelphia.

The Stars and Stripes Forever (Sousa)
Victor #306 7" ss; cond. Pryor; rec. 2 Oct., Philadelphia.

The Three Solitaires (Herbert)
Cornet trio by Herbert L. Clarke, Walter B. Rogers, and Henry Higgins. Berliner #01189 7" ss; cond. Pryor; rec. April, Philadelphia.

The Trumpeter of Sackingen: Werner's Farewell (Nessler)
Trombone solo by Arthur Pryor. Berliner #01183 7" ss; rec. April, Philadelphia.

Waltz (Chopin)
Berliner #01191. 7" ss; cond. Pryor; rec. ca. 1900, Philadelphia.

Whistling Rufus (Mills)
Victor #361 7" ss; cond. Pryor; rec. 1 Oct., Philadelphia.

The White Rat March (Pryor)
Victor #371 7" ss; cond. Pryor; rec. 4 Oct., Philadelphia.

Whirl-i-gig: The Sun Do Move (Stromberg)
Berliner #01171 7" ss; cond. Pryor; rec. 9 April, Philadelphia.

Whirlwind Polka (Levy)
Cornet solo by Herbert L. Clarke. Victor 347 7" ss; cond. Pryor; rec. 5 Oct., Philadelphia.

Who Say Dat Chickin in Dis Crowd? (W. Marion)
Berliner #01208 7" ss; cond. Pryor; rec. April, Philadelphia.

Who Say Dat Chickin in Dis Crowd? (W. Marion)
Victor #362 7" ss; cond. Pryor; rec. 3 Oct., Philadelphia.

William Tell: Overture; Finale (Rossini)
Victor #321 7" ss; cond. Pryor; rec. 5 Oct., Philadelphia.

Yankee Doodle with Variations (Round/Rogers)
Cornet solo by Walter B. Rogers. Victor #532 7" ss; rec. 20 Oct., Philadelphia.

Ye Boston Tea Party (Pryor)
Victor #344 7" ss; cond. Pryor; rec. 3 Oct., Philadelphia.

Zampa: Overture (Herold)
Victor #363 7" ss; cond. Pryor; rec. 4 Oct., Philadelphia.

1901

"A Frangesa" March (Costa)
Victor #352 7" ss; cond. Pryor; rec. 2 April, Philadelphia.

"A Frangesa" March (Costa)
Victor #352 10" ss; cond. Pryor; rec. 30 Dec., Philadelphia.

Aida: The Fatal Stone (Verdi)
Victor #3243 10" ss; cond. Pryor; rec. 4 April, Philadelphia.

American Fantasie (Bendix)
Victor #1170 7" ss; cond. Pryor; rec. 31 Dec., Philadelphia.

American Fantasie (Bendix)
Victor #1170 10" ss; cond. Pryor; rec. 31 Dec., Philadelphia.

American Fantasie (Bendix)
Victor #3259 10" ss; cond. Pryor; rec. 5 April, Philadelphia.

American Patrol (Meacham)
Victor #382 7" ss; cond. Pryor; rec. 5 April, Philadelphia.

An Arkansaw Huskin' Bee (Pryor)
Victor #314 7" ss; cond. Pryor; rec. 5 April, Philadelphia.

At a Georgia Camp Meeting (Mills)
Victor #315 7" ss; cond. Pryor; rec. 2 April, Philadelphia.

At the Old Grist Mill (Muller)
Victor #3440 10" ss; cond. Pryor; rec. 7 June, Philadelphia.

Auld Lang Syne (arr. Rogers)
Cornet solo by Walter B. Rogers. Victor #375 7" ss; cond. Pryor; rec. 2 April, Philadelphia.

Auld Lang Syne
Cornet solo by Walter B. Rogers. Victor #375 10" ss; cond. Pryor; rec. 21 June, Philadelphia.

Auld Lang Syne (arr. Rogers)
Cornet solo by Walter B. Rogers. Victor #375 7" ss; cond. Pryor; rec. 5 Oct., Philadelphia.

Balscenen Waltz (Czibulka)
Victor #342 7" ss; cond. Pryor; rec. 5 April, Philadelphia.

The Belle of New York: Finale (Kerker)
Victor #378 7" ss; cond. Pryor; rec. 4 April, Philadelphia.

The Belle of New York: Finale (Kerker)
Victor #3236 10" ss; cond. Pryor; rec. 4 April, Philadelphia.

The Belle of New York: Finale (Kerker)
Victor #378 7" ss; cond. Pryor; rec. 5 June, Philadelphia.

The Blue and the Gray Partol (Dalbey)
Victor #3260 10" ss; cond. Pryor; rec. 5 April, Philadelphia.

The Blue and the Gray Partol (Dalbey)
Victor #1171 7" ss; cond. Pryor; rec. 31 Dec., Philadelphia.

The Blue and the Gray Partol (Dalbey)
Victor #1171 10" ss; cond. Pryor; rec. 31 Dec., Philadelphia.

Blue Bells of Scotland
Trombone solo by Arthur Pryor. Victor # 3251 10" ss; rec. 5 April, Philadelphia.

Blue Bells of Scotland
Trombone solo by Arthur Pryor. Victor #311 7" ss; rec. 5 June, Philadelphia.

Blue Bells of Scotland
Trombone solo by Arthur Pryor. Victor #311 10" ss; rec. 5 April, Philadelphia.

The Blue Danube Waltz (J. Strauss, II)
Victor #343 7" ss; cond. Pryor; rec. 5 April, Philadelphia.

The Bride Elect: March (Sousa)
Victor #303 7" ss; cond. Pryor; rec. 5 June, Philadelphia.

The Bride Elect: Sextet (Sousa)
Brass sextet, soloists unknown. Victor #3235 10" ss; cond. Pryor; rec. 3 April, Philadelphia.

The Bride Elect: Tarantella (Sousa)
Victor #335 7" ss; cond. Pryor; rec. 5 June, Philadelphia.

Bride of the Waves (Clarke)
Cornet solo by Herbert L. Clarke. Victor #346 7" ss; cond. Pryor; rec. 5 June, Philadelphia.

The Burgomaster: The Tale of a Kangaroo (Luders)
Victor #728 7" ss; cond. Pryor; rec., 2 April, Philadelphia.

El Capitan: March (Sousa)
Victor #304 7" ss; cond. Pryor; rec. 5 June, Philadelphia.

Carmen: Selections (Bizet)
Victor #3445 10" ss; cond. Pryor; rec. 7 June, Philadelphia.

Cavalleria Rusticana: Intermezzo (Mascagni)
Victor #353 7" ss; cond. Pryor; rec. 2 April, Philadelphia.

Chopin's Polonaise (Chopin)
Victor #318 7" ss; cond. Pryor; rec. 5 April, Philadelphia.

Coon Band Contest (Pryor)
Victor #312 7" ss; cond. Pryor; rec. 2 April, Philadelphia.

Coon Band Contest (Pryor)
Victor #312 7" ss; cond. Pryor; rec. 31 Dec., Philadelphia.

Coon Band Contest (Pryor)
Victor #312 10" ss; cond. Pryor; rec. 31 Dec., Philadelphia.

The Crack Regiment Patrol (Tobani)
Victor #338 7" ss; cond. Pryor; rec. 5 April, Philadelphia.

La Czarina (Ganne)
Victor #326 7" ss; cond. Pryor; rec. 1 April, Philadelphia.

Danse Des Cymbals (La Rondelle)
Victor #3248 10" ss; cond. Pryor; rec. 4 April, Philadelphia.

The Directorate March (Sousa)
Victor #308 7" ss; cond. Pryor; rec. 5 June, Philadelphia.

A Dream of Wagner (Hamm)
Victor #313 7" ss; cond. Pryor; rec. 5 April, Philadelphia.

Evening Zephyrs (Eilenberg)
Victor #3442 10" ss; cond. Pryor; rec. 7 June, Philadelphia.

Fantasie on American Airs
Flute solo by Darius Lyons. Victor #3421 10" ss; cond. Pryor; rec. 1 June, Philadelphia.

Faust Selections (Gounod)
Victor #3247 10" ss; cond. Pryor; rec. 4 April, Philadelphia.

Flirtation Waltz (Steck)
Victor #366 7" ss; cond. Pryor; rec. 1 April, Philadelphia.
Forever (Pryor)
Trombone solo by Arthur Pryor. Victor #3253 10" ss; rec. 5 April, Philadelphia.
Gate City March (Weldon)
Victor #3237 10" ss; cond. Pryor; rec. 4 April, Philadelphia.
German Sounds
Victor #531 7" ss; cond. Pryor; rec. 31 May, Philadelphia.
God Save the Queen (arr. Sousa)
Victor #322 7" ss; cond. Pryor; rec. 2 April, Philadelphia.
La Gazelle (Bendix)
Victor #3245 10" ss; cond. Pryor; rec. 4 April, Philadelphia.
The Gladiator (Sousa)
Victor #3228 10" ss; cond. Pryor; rec. 3 April, Philadelphia.
Hail to the Flag! (Mansfield)
Victor #1187 7" ss; cond. Pryor; rec. 4 Jan., Philadelphia.
Hail to the Spirit of Liberty (Sousa)
Victor #365 7" ss; cond. Pryor; rec. 2 April 1901, Philadelphia.
Hail to the Spirit of Liberty (Sousa)
Victor #3224 10" ss; cond. Pryor; rec. 3 April, Philadelphia.
Hail to the Spirit of Liberty (Sousa)
Columbia #31483 2" cyl; rec. ca. 1901, Washington.
Hail to the Spirit of Liberty (Sousa)
Columbia #31483 5" cyl; rec. ca. 1901, Washington.
Hands Across the Sea (Sousa)
Victor #300 7" ss; cond. Pryor; rec. 1 April, Philadelphia.
Hands Across the Sea (Sousa)
Victor #3226 10" ss; cond. Pryor; rec. 3 April, Philadelphia.
Hearts and Flowers (Tobani)
Cornet solo by Herbert L. Clarke. Victor #1172 7" ss; cond. Pryor; rec. 31 Dec., Philadelphia.
Hearts and Flowers (Tobani)
Cornet solo by Herbert L. Clarke. Victor #1172 10" ss; cond. Pryor; rec. 31 Dec., Philadelphia.
The Honeysuckle and the Bee (Penn)
Victor #1169 7" ss; cond. Pryor; rec. 30 Dec., Philadelphia.
The Honored Dead (Sousa)
Victor #3244 10" ss; cond. Pryor; rec. 4 April, Philadelphia.
Les Huguenots: Benediction of the Poignards (Meyerbeer)
Victor #327 7" ss; cond. Pryor; rec. 2 April, Philadelphia.
Les Huguenots: Benediction of the Poignards (Meyerbeer)
Victor #327 10" ss; cond. Pryor; rec. 3 April, Philadelphia.
Les Huguenots: Benediction of the Poignards (Meyerbeer)
Victor #3231 10" ss; cond. Pryor; rec. 3 April, Philadelphia.
Les Huguenots: Benediction of the Poignards (Meyerbeer)
Victor #327 7" ss; cond. Pryor; rec. 5 April, Philadelphia.
Hula, Hula Cakewalk (Van Alstyne)
Victor #3263 10" ss; cond. Pryor; rec. 5 April, Philadelphia.
I Can't Tell Why I Love You, But I Do (Edwards)
Trombone solo by Arthur Pryor. Victor #727 7" ss; rec. 2 April, Philadelphia.
Indian War Dance (Bellstedt)
Victor #324 7" ss; cond. Pryor; rec. 2 April, Philadelphia.
The Invincible Eagle (Sousa)
Victor #844 7" ss; cond. Pryor; rec. 5 June, Philadelphia.
The Invincible Eagle (Sousa)
Victor #844 10" ss; cond. Pryor; rec. 5 June, Philadelphia.
The Invincible Eagle (Sousa)
Victor #3435 10" ss; cond. Pryor; rec. 7 June, Philadelphia.
The Jolly Fellows Waltz (Vollstedt)
Victor #3246 10" ss; cond. Pryor; rec. 4 April, Philadelphia.
The Jolly Fellows Waltz (Vollstedt)
Victor #1174 7" ss; cond. Pryor; rec. 31 Dec., Philadelphia.
The Jolly Fellows Waltz (Vollstedt)
Victor #1174 10" ss; cond. Pryor; rec. 31 Dec., Philadelphia.
King Cotton (Sousa)
Victor #301 7" ss; cond. Pryor; rec. 1 April, Philadelphia.
Levee Revels (O' Hare)
Victor #328 7" ss; cond. Pryor; rec. 5 April, Philadelphia.
The Lily Bells (Sousa)
Victor #339 7" ss; cond. Pryor; rec. 5 April, Philadelphia.
Lohengrin: Selections (R. Wagner)
Victor #3234 10" ss; cond. Pryor; rec. 3 April, Philadelphia.

Lohengrin (R. Wagner) and Tannhauser (R. Wagner)
Victor #3258 10" ss; cond. Pryor; rec. 5 April, Philadelphia.
Loin du Bal (Gillet)
Victor #329 7" ss; cond. Pryor; rec. 1 April, Philadelphia.
Lorelei Paraphrase (Nesvadba)
Victor #319 7" ss; cond. Pryor; rec. 1 April, Philadelphia.
Love Thoughts (Pryor)
Victor #310 7" ss; rec. 5 June, Philadelphia.
Lucia di Lammermoor: Sextet (Donizetti)
Brass sextet by Herbert L. Clarke, Henry Higgins, Simone Mantia, Arthur Pryor, Marcus Lyon, and Edward A. Williams. Victor #334 7" ss; cond. Pryor; rec. 2 April, Philadelphia.
Lucia di Lammermoor: Sextet (Donizetti)
Brass sextet by Herbert L. Clarke, Henry Higgins, Simone Mantia, Arthur Pryor, Marcus Lyon, and Edward A. Williams. Victor #334 10" ss; rec. 2 April, Philadelphia.
Lucia di Lammermoor: Sextet (Donizetti)
Brass sextet by Herbert L. Clarke, Henry Higgins, Simone Mantia, Arthur Pryor, Marcus Lyon, and Edward A. Williams. Victor #3230 10" ss; rec. 5 April, Philadelphia.
The Man Behind the Gun (Sousa)
Victor #307 7" ss; cond. Pryor; rec. 1 April, Philadelphia.
The Man Behind the Gun (Sousa)
Victor #3227 10" ss; cond. Pryor; rec. 3 April, Philadelphia.
The March King (Pryor)
Victor #340 7" ss; cond. Pryor; rec. 2 April, Philadelphia.
La Mariposa (Diaz)
Victor #3439 10" ss; cond. Pryor; rec. 7 June, Philadelphia.
Minnehaha Waltz (Roger)
Cornet solo by Walter B. Rogers. Victor #3241 10" ss; cond. Pryor; rec. 4 April, Philadelphia.
Miss Bob White: Selections (Spencer)
Victor #3448 10" ss; cond. Pryor; rec. 7 June, Philadelphia.
The Mosquito Parade (Whitney)
Victor #337 7" ss; cond. Pryor; rec. 1 April, Philadelphia.
Mother Hubbard March (Sousa)
Victor #305 7" ss; cond. Pryor; rec. 5 June, Philadelphia.
My Black Pearl
Victor #3436 10" ss; cond. Pryor; rec. 7 June, Philadelphia.
My Japanese Cherry Blossom (Stromberg)
Victor #1176 7" ss; cond. Pryor; rec. 31 Dec., Philadelphia.
My Japanese Cherry Blossom (Stromberg)
Victor #1176 10" ss; cond. Pryor; rec. 31 Dec., Philadelphia.
My Old Kentucky Home Fantasy (Foster-Dalbey)
Victor #3264 10" ss; cond. Pryor; rec. 5 April, Philadelphia.
Nearer My God to Thee (Mason)
Victor 355 7" ss; cond. Pryor; rec. 1 April, Philadelphia.
Nearer My God to Thee (Mason)
Victor 355 7" ss; cond. Pryor; rec. 2 Oct., Philadelphia.
I Pagliacci: Serenata (Leoncavallo)
Victor #3229 10" ss; cond. Pryor; rec. 4 April, Philadelphia.
La Paloma (Yradier)
Victor #3437 10" ss; cond. Pryor; rec. 7 June, Philadelphia.
Pasquinade (Gottschalk)
Victor #3438 10" ss; cond. Pryor; rec. 7 June, Philadelphia.
The Patriot (Pryor)
Trombone solo by Arthur Pryor. Victor #3252 10" ss; rec., 5 April, Philadelphia.
Peace Forever March (Lacalle)
Victor #357 7" ss; cond. Pryor; rec. 5 June, Philadelphia.
Pesther Waltzes (Lanner)
Victor #3249 10" ss; cond. Pryor; rec. 4 April, Philadelphia.
The Picador March (Sousa)
Victor #3229 10" ss; cond. Pryor; rec. 3 April, Philadelphia.
Polka des Clownes (Allier)
Victor #379 7" ss; cond. Pryor; rec. 5 June, Philadelphia.
Portuguese Hymn
Victor #729 7" ss; cond. Pryor; rec. 5 April, Philadelphia.
Reminiscences of Wagner (arr. Fred Godfrey)
Victor #3257 10" ss; cond. Pryor; rec. 5 April, Philadelphia.
Ritter Pasman: Czardas (J. Strauss, II)
Victor #3250 10" ss; cond. Pryor; rec. 4 April, Philadelphia.
Robin Hood: Selections (De Koven)
Victor #358 7" ss; cond. Pryor; rec. 1 April, Philadelphia.

439

Romanza (Tertschak)
Flute solo by Darius Lyons. Victor #3422 10" ss; cond. Pryor; rec.
1 June, Philadelphia.

Rose Mousse (Bosc)
Victor #3256 10" ss; cond. Pryor; rec. 5 April, Philadelphia.

Rose Mousse (Bosc)
Victor #383 7" ss; cond. Pryor; rec. 5 June, Philadelphia.

The Rose of Shiras: Rose Buds Polka (Eilenberg)
Victor #3441 10" ss; cond. Pryor; rec. 7 June, Philadelphia.

The Rose of Shiras: Rose Waltzes (Eilenberg)
Victor #3443 10" ss; cond. Pryor; rec. 7 June, Philadelphia.

A Runaway Girl: Selections (Monckton)
Victor #332 7" ss; cond. Pryor; rec. 4 Oct., Philadelphia.

A Runaway Girl: Selections (Monckton)
Victor #3232 10" ss; cond. Pryor; rec. 3 April, Philadelphia.

Salome Intermezzo (Loraine)
Victor #325 7" ss; cond. Pryor; rec. 5 April, Philadelphia.

San Toy: Selections (Jones)
Victor #3233 10" ss; cond. Pryor; rec. 3 April, Philadelphia.

The Scandinavian Songs of Meyer-Helmund (arr. Wright)
Victor #3254 10" ss; cond. Pryor; rec. 5 April, Philadelphia.

Scenes Pittoresques: Fete Boheme (Massenet)
Victor #3444 10" ss; cond. Pryor; rec. 7 June, Philadelphia.

Semiramide: Overture (Rossini)
Victor #359 7" ss; cond. Pryor; rec. 5 June, Philadelphia.

Semper Fidelis (Sousa)
Victor #1175 7" ss; cond. Pryor; rec. 31 Dec., Philadelphia.

Semper Fidelis (Sousa)
Victor #1175 10" ss; cond. Pryor; rec. 31 Dec., Philadelphia.

The Serenade: Waltz (Herbert)
Victor #368 7" ss; cond. Pryor; rec. 1 April, Philadelphia.

Serenade [Opus 15, No. 1] (Moszkowski)
Victor #333 7" ss; cond. Pryor; rec. 1 April, Philadelphia.

Serenade Rococo (Meyer-Helmund)
Victor #3255 10" ss; cond. Pryor; rec. 5 April, Philadelphia.

A Soldiers Dream (Rogers)
Cornet solo by Walter B. Rogers. Victor #3242 10" ss; cond. Pryor;
rec. 4 April, Philadelphia.

A Soldiers Dream (Rogers)
Cornet solo by Walter B. Rogers. Victor #524 7" ss; cond. Pryor;
rec. 31 May, Philadelphia.

Songs and Dances of the Navy (Hall)
Victor #3446 10" ss; cond. Pryor; rec. 7 June, Philadelphia.

A Southern Dance (Rogers)
Cornet solo by Walter B. Rogers. Victor #3242 10" ss; cond. Pryor;
rec. 4 April, Philadelphia.

Souvenir of Naples (Rogers)
Cornet solo by Walter B. Rogers. Victor #348 7" ss; cond. Pryor;
rec. 2 April, Philadelphia.

The Star Spangled Banner (arr. Sousa)
Victor #336 7" ss; cond. Pryor; rec. 2 April, Philadelphia.

The Stars and Stripes Forever (Sousa)
Victor #306 7" ss; cond. Pryor; rec. 3 April, Philadelphia.

The Stars and Stripes Forever (Sousa)
Victor #3225 10" ss; cond. Pryor; rec. 3 April, Philadelphia.

The Stars and Stripes Forever (Sousa)
Victor #306 7" ss; cond. Pryor; rec. 30 Dec., Philadelphia.

The Stars and Stripes Forever (Sousa)
Victor #306 10" ss; cond. Pryor; rec. 30 Dec., Philadelphia.

Il Trovatore: Miserere (Verdi)
Cornet and Trombone duet by Walter B. Rogers and Arthur Pryor.
Victor #3238 10" ss; rec., 4 April, Philadelphia.

The Warbler's Serenade (Perry)
Victor #3447 10" ss; cond. Pryor; rec. 7 June, Philadelphia.

The Warbler's Serenade (Perry)
Victor #1168 7" ss; cond. Pryor; rec. 30 Dec., Philadelphia.

The Warbler's Serenade (Perry)
Victor #1168 10" ss; cond. Pryor; rec. 30 Dec., Philadelphia/

'Way Down South
Victor #1173 7" ss; cond. Pryor; rec. 31 Dec., Philadelphia.

'Way Down South
Victor #1173 10" ss; cond. Pryor; rec. 31 Dec., Philadelphia.

When You Were Sweet Sixteen (Thornton)
Cornet solo by Walter B. Rogers. Victor #3262 10" ss; cond. Pryor;
rec. 5 April, Philadelphia.

Whirlwind Polka (Levy)
Cornet solo by Herbert L. Clarke. Victor #347 7" ss; cond. Pryor;
rec. 5 June, Philadelphia.

Whistling Rufus (Mills)
Victor #361 7" ss; cond. Pryor; rec. 5 April, Philadelphia.

The White Rat March (Pryor)
Victor #371 7" ss; cond. Pryor; rec. 5 June, Philadelphia.

Yankee Doodle with Variations (Round/Rogers)
Cornet solo by Walter B. Rogers. Victor #532 7" ss; cond. Pryor;
rec. 31 May, Philadelphia.

Ye Boston Tea Party (Pryor)
Victor #344 7" ss; cond. Pryor; rec. 1 April, Philadelphia.

Zamona (Loraine)
Victor #3261 10" ss; cond. Pryor; rec. 5 April, Philadelphia.

Zampa: Overture (Herold)
Victor #363 7" ss; cond. Pryor; rec. 5 June, Philadelphia.

1902

"A Frangesa" March (Costa)
Victor #352 7" ss; cond. Pryor; rec. 16 Dec., Philadelphia.

"A Frangesa" March (Costa)
Victor #352 10" ss; cond. Pryor; rec. 16 Dec., Philadelphia.

American Patrol (Meacham)
Victor #382 7" ss; cond. Pryor; rec. 18 Dec., Philadelphia.

American Patrol (Meacham)
Victor #382 10" ss; cond. Pryor; rec. 18 Dec., Philadelphia.

An Arkansaw Huskin' Bee (Pryor)
Victor #314 7" ss; cond. Pryor; rec. 21 June, Philadelphia.

An Arkansaw Huskin' Bee (Pryor)
Victor #314 10" ss; cond. Pryor; rec. 21 June, Philadelphia.

Army Bugle Calls
Victor #1303 10" ss; rec. by Sousa's Cornets on 7 March,
Philadelphia.

Army Bugle Calls
Victor #1303a 7" ss; rec. by Sousa's Cornets on 7 March,
Philadelphia.

Army Bugle Calls
Victor #1303b 7" ss; rec. by Sousa's Cornets on 7 March,
Philadelphia.

At a Georgia Camp Meeting (Mills)
Victor #315 10" ss; cond. Pryor; rec. 1 Jan., Philadelphia.

At a Georgia Camp Meeting (Mills)
Victor #315 7" ss; cond. Pryor; rec. 14 Aug., Philadelphia.

At a Georgia Camp Meeting (Mills)
Victor #315 10" ss; cond. Pryor; rec. 14 Aug., Philadelphia.

The Belle of New York: Finale (Kerker)
Victor #378 7" ss; cond. Pryor; rec. 3 Jan., Philadelphia.

The Belle of New York: Finale (Kerkcr)
Victor #378 10" ss; cond. Pryor; rec. 3 Jan., Philadelphia.

Ben Hur Chariot Race (Sousa)
Victor #1196 7" ss; cond. Pryor; rec. 7 Jan., Philadelphia.

Ben Hur Chariot Race (Sousa)
Victor #1196 10" ss; cond. Pryor; rec. 7 Jan., Philadelphia.

Berlin in Joy and Sorrow Overture (Conradi)
Victor #1431 7" ss; cond. Pryor; rec. 18 June, Philadelphia.

Berlin in Joy and Sorrow Overture (Conradi)
Victor #1431 10" ss; cond. Pryor; rec. 18 June, Philadelphia.

The Blue and the Gray Patrol (Dalbey)
Victor #1171 10" ss; cond. Pryor; rec. 5 April, Philadelphia.

The Blue and the Gray Patrol (Dalbey)
Victor #1171 7" ss; cond. Pryor; rec. 24 June, Philadelphia.

Blue and Gray Patrol (Dalbey)
Victor #1171 7" ss; cond. Pryor; rec. 24 June, Philadelphia.

Blue Bells of Scotland
Victor #311 10" ss; cond. Pryor; rec. 2 Jan., Philadelphia.

The Blue Danube Waltz (J. Strauss, II)
Victor #343 7" ss; cond, Pryor; rec. 4 Jan., Philadelphia.

The Blue Danube Waltz (J. Strauss, II)
Victor #343 10" ss; cond, Pryor; rec. 4 Jan., Philadelphia.

The Blue Danube Waltz (J. Strauss, II)
Victor #343 10" ss; cond. Pryor; rec. 18 June, Philadelphia.

The Bride Elect: Sextet (Sousa)
Victor #3235 10" ss; cond. Pryor; rec. 4 Jan., Philadelphia.

The Bride Elect: Sextet (Sousa)
Victor #3235 10" ss; cond. Pryor; rec. 20 June, Philadelphia.
Bunch of Mischief Polka
Victor #1200 7" ss; cond. Pryor; rec. 7 Jan., Philadelphia.
Bunch of Mischief Polka
Victor #1200 10" ss; cond. Pryor; rec. 7 Jan., Philadelphia.
El Capitan: March (Sousa)
Victor #304 10" ss; cond. Pryor; rec. 3 Jan., Philadelphia.
Carmen: Selections (Bizet)
Victor #1449 7" ss; cond. Pryor; rec. 24 June, Philadelphia.
Carmen: Selections (Bizet)
Victor #1449 10" ss; cond. Pryor; rec. 24 June, Philadelphia.
Carmen: Toreador Song (Bizet)
Vocal solo by Emilio de Gogorzo. Victor #1453 10" ss; cond. Pryor;
rec. 25 June, Philadelphia.
Chopin's Polonaise (Chopin)
Victor #318 7" ss; cond. Pryor; rec. 16 Dec., Philadelphia.
Chopin's Polonaise (Chopin)
Victor #318 10" ss; cond. Pryor; rec. 16 Dec., Philadelphia.
Chopin's Waltz (Chopin)
Victor #317 7" ss; cond. Pryor; rec. 16 Dec., Philadelphia.
Circus Galop (Donnawell)
Victor #319 7" ss; cond. Pryor; rec. 25 June, Philadelphia.
Circus Galop (Donnawell)
Victor #319 10" ss; cond. Pryor; rec. 25 June, Philadelphia.
Coon Smiles (Clarke)
Victor #1555 7" ss; cond. Pryor; rec. 14 Aug., Philadelphia.
Coon Smiles (Clarke)
Victor #1555 10" ss; cond. Pryor; rec. 14 Aug., Philadelphia.
The Crack Regiment Patrol (Tobani)
Victor #338 7" ss; cond. Pryor; rec. 17 June, Philadelphia.
The Crack Regiment Patrol (Tobani)
Victor #338 10" ss; cond. Pryor; rec. 17 June, Philadelphia.
Creole Bells (Lampe)
Victor #1182 7" ss; cond. Pryor; rec. 2 Jan., Philadelphia.
Creole Bells (Lampe)
Victor #1182 10" ss; cond. Pryor; rec. 24 June, Philadelphia.
Creole Bells (Lampe)
Victor #1182 7" ss; cond. Pryor; rec. 24 June, Philadelphia.
Custer's Last Charge (Luders)
Victor #1192 7" ss; cond. Pryor; rec. 6 Jan., Philadelphia.
Custer's Last Charge (Luders)
Victor #1192 10" ss; cond. Pryor; rec. 6 Jan., Philadelphia.
Dixie Cheers (Emmett)
Victor #320 7" ss; cond. Pryor; rec. 3 June, Philadelphia.
Fackeltanz (Meyebeer)
Tuba solo by Herman Conrad. Victor #1446 7" ss; cond. Pryor;
rec. 24 June, Philadelphia.
Fackeltanz (Meyebeer)
Tuba solo by Herman Conrad. Victor #1446 10" ss; cond. Pryor;
rec. 24 June, Philadelphia.
Faust (Gounod) and Il Trovatore (Verdi): Selections
Victor #1553 7" ss; cond. Pryor; rec. 12 Aug., Philadelphia.
Faust (Gounod) and Il Trovatore (Verdi): Selections
Victor #1553 10" ss; cond. Pryor; rec. 12 Aug., Philadelphia.
Faust Selections (Gounod)
Victor #1838 7" ss; cond. Pryor; rec. 19 Dec., Philadelphia.
Faust Selections (Gounod)
Victor #1838 10" ss; cond. Pryor; rec. 19 Dec., Philadelphia.
First Heart Throbs (Eilenberg)
Victor #1836 7" ss; cond. Pryor; rec. 18 Dec., Philadelphia.
First Heart Throbs (Eilenberg)
Victor #1836 10" ss; cond. Pryor; rec. 18 Dec., Philadelphia.
Gate City March (Weldon)
Victor #1444 7" ss; cond. Pryor; rec. 23 June, Philadelphia.
Gate City March (Weldon)
Victor #1444 10" ss; cond. Pryor; rec. 23 June, Philadelphia.
German Sounds (arr. Rogers)
Cornet solo by Walter B. Rogers. Victor #531 10" ss; cond. Pryor;
rec. 8 Aug., Philadelphia.
The Gladiator March (Sousa)
Victor #1177 7" ss; cond. Pryor; rec. 1 Jan., Philadelphia.
The Gladiator March (Sousa)
Victor #1177 10" ss; cond. Pryor; rec. 16 Dec., Philadelphia.

Hail to the Bride (Rosey)
Columbia #31781 2" cyl; nd., Washington.
Hail to the Flag (Mansfield)
Victor #1187 7" ss; cond. Pryor; rec. 4 Jan., Philadelphia.
Hail to the Flag (Mansfield)
Victor #1187 10" ss; cond. Pryor; rec. 4 Jan., Philadelphia.
Hail to the Spirit of Liberty (Sousa)
Victor #365 10" ss; cond. Pryor; rec. 8 Jan., Philadelphia.
Hands Across the Sea (Sousa)
Victor #300 10" ss; cond. Pryor; rec. 3 Jan., Philadelphia.
Hands Across the Sea (Sousa)
Victor #300 10" ss; cond. Pryor; rec. 15 Dec., Philadelphia.
Hearts and Flowers (Tobani)
Cornet solo by Herbert L. Clarke. Victor #1172 7" ss; cond. Pryor;
rec. 19 June, Philadelphia.
Hearts and Flowers (Tobani)
Cornet solo by Herbert L. Clarke. Victor #1172 10" ss; cond. Pryor;
rec. 23 June, Philadelphia.
The Honeysuckle and the Bee (Penn)
Victor #1169 10" ss; cond. Pryor; rec. 1 Jan., Philadelphia.
A Hot Time in the Old Town (Metz)
Victor #316 7" ss; cond. Pryor; rec. 18 June, Philadelphia.
A Hot Time in the Old Town (Metz)
Victor #316 10" ss; cond. Pryor; rec. 18 June, Philadelphia.
Humpty Dumpty March (Penn)
Victor #1427 7" ss; cond. Pryor; rec. 16 June, Philadelphia.
Humpty Dumpty March (Penn)
Victor #1427 10" ss; cond. Pryor; rec. 16 June, Philadelphia.
I Can't Tell Why I Love You, But I Do (Edwards)
Victor #727 10" ss; cond. Pryor; rec. 6 Jan., Philadelphia.
I Can't Tell Why I Love You, But I Do (Edwards)
Victor #727 10" ss; cond. Pryor; rec. 19 Dec., Philadelphia.
Imperial Edward Coronation March (Sousa)
Victor #1418 7" ss; cond. Pryor; rec. 9 June, Philadelphia.
Imperial Edward Coronation March (Sousa)
Victor #1418 7" ss; cond. Pryor; rec. 17 June, Philadelphia.
Imperial Edward Coronation March (Sousa)
Victor #1418 10" ss; cond. Pryor; rec. 17 June, Philadelphia.
Imperial Edward Coronation March (Sousa)
Columbia #31762 2" cyl; nd., Washington.
In the Good Old Summer Time (Evans)
Walter B. Rogers, cornet; Arthur Pryor, trombone; S.H. Dudley & Harry
Macdonough, vocal. Victor #1833 7" ss; rec. 17 Dec., Philadelphia.
In the Good Old Summer Time (Evans)
Walter B. Rogers, cornet; Arthur Pryor, trombone; S.H. Dudley & Harry
Macdonough, vocal. Victor #1833 10" ss; rec. 17 Dec., Philadelphia.
In the Realm of the Waltz (Sousa)
Victor #1438 7" ss; cond. Pryor; rec. 20 June, Philadelphia.
In the Realm of the Waltz (Sousa)
Victor #1438 10" ss; cond. Pryor; rec. 20 June, Philadelphia.
In the Realm of the Waltz (Sousa)
Victor #1438 7" ss; cond. Pryor; rec. 14 Aug., Philadelphia.
Indian War Dance (Bellstedt)
Victor #324 7" ss; cond. Pryor; rec. 18 June, Philadelphia.
Indian War Dance (Bellstedt)
Victor #324 10" ss; cond. Pryor; rec. 18 June, Philadelphia.
The Invincible Eagle (Sousa)
Victor #844 7" ss; cond. Pryor; rec. 1 Jan., Philadelphia.
The Invincible Eagle (Sousa)
Victor #844 10" ss; cond. Pryor; rec. 1 Jan., Philadelphia.
The Invincible Eagle (Sousa)
Columbia #31633 2" cyl; nd., Washington.
The Jolly Coppersmith (Peter)
Victor #1450 7" ss; cond. Pryor; rec. 24 June, Philadelphia.
The Jolly Coppersmith (Peter)
Victor #1450 10" ss; cond. Pryor; rec. 24 June, Philadelphia.
The Jolly Fellows Waltz (Vollstedt)
Victor #1174 10" ss; cond. Pryor; rec. 19 Dec., Philadelphia.
King Broadway (Wardwell)
Victor #1222 7" ss; cond. Pryor; rec. 30 Jan., Philadelphia.
King Broadway (Wardwell)
Victor #1222 10" ss; cond. Pryor; rec. 30 Jan., Philadelphia.
King Broadway (Wardwell)
Victor #1222 10" ss; cond. Pryor; rec. 16 June, Philadelphia.

King Cotton (Sousa)
Victor #301 10" ss; cond. Pryor; rec. 3 Jan., Philadelphia.
The Lark (Damare)
Victor #1439 7" ss; cond. Pryor; rec. 20 June, Philadelphia.
The Lark (Damare)
Victor #1439 10" ss; cond. Pryor; rec. 20 June, Philadelphia.
Levee Revels (O' Hare)
Victor #328 7" ss; cond. Pryor; rec. 5 April, Philadelphia.
Levee Revels (O' Hare)
Victor #328 10" ss; cond. Pryor; rec. 17 Dec., Philadelphia.
The Liberty Bell (Sousa)
Victor #1193 7" ss; cond. Pryor; rec. 6 Jan., Philadelphia.
The Liberty Bell (Sousa)
Victor #1193 10" ss; cond. Pryor; rec. 6 Jan., Philadelphia.
The Liberty Bell (Sousa)
Victor #1193 7" ss; cond. Pryor; rec. 20 June, Philadelphia.
The Liberty Bell (Sousa)
Victor #1193 10" ss; cond. Pryor; rec. 20 June, Philadelphia.
Lily Bells (Sousa)
Victor #339 7" ss; cond. Pryor; rec. 21 June, Philadelphia.
Lily Bells (Sousa)
Victor #339 10" ss; cond. Pryor; rec. 21 June, Philadelphia.
Lily Bells (Sousa)
Victor #339 10" ss; cond. Pryor; rec. 18 Dec., Philadelphia.
A Little Boy in Blue (Brown)
Cornet solo by Walter B. Rogers. Victor #1435 7" ss; cond. Pryor; rec. 24 June, Philadelphia.
A Little Boy in Blue (Brown)
Cornet solo by Walter B. Rogers. Victor #1435 10" ss; cond. Pryor; rec. 24 June, Philadelphia.
A Little Boy in Blue (Brown)
Cornet solo by Walter B. Rogers. Victor #1435 10" ss; cond. Pryor; rec. 19 Dec., Philadelphia.
The Little Duchess: Pretty Molly Shannon (Wolff)
Victor #1425 7" ss; cond. Pryor; rec. 9 June, Philadelphia.
The Little Duchess: Pretty Molly Shannon (Wolff)
Victor #1425 10" ss; cond. Pryor; rec. 9 June, Philadelphia.
Little Nell (Pryor)
Trombone solo by Arthur Pryor. Victor #330 7" ss; rec. 8 Jan., Philadelphia.
Little Nell (Pryor)
Trombone solo by Arthur Pryor. Victor #330 10" ss; rec. 8 Jan., Philadelphia.
Lorelei (Nesvadba)
Victor #1835 7" ss; cond. Pryor; rec. 18 Dec., Philadelphia.
Lorelei (Nesvadba)
Victor #1835 10" ss; cond. Pryor; rec. 18 Dec., Philadelphia.
Love Thoughts (Pryor)
Trombone solo by Arthur Pryor. Victor #310 10" ss; rec. 8 May, Philadelphia.
Love Thoughts (Pryor)
Trombone solo by Arthur Pryor. Victor #310 7" ss; rec. 3 June, Philadelphia.
Love's Enchantment (Pryor)
Trombone solo by Arthur Pryor. Victor #1428 7" ss; rec. 19 June, Philadelphia.
Love's Enchantment (Pryor)
Trombone solo by Arthur Pryor. Victor #1428 10" ss; rec. 21 June, Philadelphia.
Lucia di Lammermoor: Sextet (Donizetti)
Brass sextet by Herbert L. Clarke, Henry Higgins, Simone Mantia, Arthur Pryor, Marcus Lyon, and Edward A. Williams. Victor #3230 7" ss; rec. 20 June, Philadelphia.
Maidens Three: I. The Coquette (Sousa)
Victor #1179a 7" ss; cond. Pryor; rec. 1 Jan., Philadelphia.
Maidens Three: I. The Coquette (Sousa)
Victor #1179a 10" ss; cond. Pryor; rec. 1 Jan., Philadelphia.
Maidens Three: II. The Summer Girl (Sousa)
Victor #1179b 7" ss; cond. Pryor; rec. 1 Jan., Philadelphia.
Maidens Three: II. The Summer Girl (Sousa)
Victor #1179b 10" ss; cond. Pryor; rec. 1 Jan., Philadelphia.
Maidens Three: III. The Dancing Girl (Sousa)
Victor #1179c 7" ss; cond. Pryor; rec. 2 Jan., Philadelphia.
Maidens Three: III. The Dancing Girl (Sousa)
Victor #1179c 10" ss; cond. Pryor; rec. 2 Jan., Philadelphia.

The Man Behind the Gun (Sousa)
Victor #307 7" ss; cond. Pryor; rec. 21 June, Philadelphia.
The Man Behind the Gun (Sousa)
Victor #307 10" ss; cond. Pryor; rec. 21 June, Philadelphia.
Minnehaha Waltz (Rogers)
Cornet solo by Walter B. Rogers. Victor #1202 10" ss; cond. Pryor; rec. 8 Jan., Philadelphia.
Miss Bob White: Selections (Spencer)
Victor #1205 7" ss; cond. Pryor; rec. 8 Jan., Philadelphia.
Miss Bob White: Selections (Spencer)
Victor #1205 10" ss; cond. Pryor; rec. 8 Jan., Philadelphia.
Miss Bob White: Selections (Spencer)
Victor #1205 10" ss; cond. Pryor; rec. 14 Aug., Philadelphia.
Morning, Noon and Night in Vienna: Overture (Suppe)
Victor #1430 7" ss; cond. Pryor; rec. 19 June, Philadelphia.
Morning, Noon and Night in Vienna: Overture (Suppe)
Victor #1430 10" ss; cond. Pryor; rec. 19 June, Philadelphia.
Morning, Noon and Night in Vienna: Overture (Suppe)
Victor #1420 10" ss; cond. Pryor; rec. 23 June, Philadelphia.
Much Ado About Nothing: Bourree (German)
Victor #1188 7" ss; cond. Pryor; rec. 4 Jan., Philadelphia.
Much Ado About Nothing: Bourree (German)
Victor #1188 10" ss; cond. Pryor; rec. 4 Jan., Philadelphia.
Much Ado About Nothing: Gigue (German)
Victor #1189 7" ss; cond. Pryor; rec. 4 Jan., Philadelphia.
Much Ado About Nothing: Gigue (German)
Victor #1189 10" ss; cond. Pryor; rec. 4 Jan., Philadelphia.
My Old Kentucky Home Fantasy (Foster-Dalbey)
Victor #3264 10" ss; cond. Pryor; rec. 16 June, Philadelphia.
Narcissus (Nevin)
Victor #354 7" ss; cond. Pryor; rec. 4 Jan., Philadelphia.
Narcissus (Nevin)
Victor #354 10" ss; cond. Pryor; rec. 4 Jan., Philadelphia.
Nymphalin Reverie (Sousa)
Violin solo by Dorothy Hoyle. Victor #1201 7" ss; cond. Pryor; rec. 7 Jan., Philadelphia.
Nymphalin Reverie (Sousa)
Violin solo by Dorothy Hoyle. Victor #1201 10" ss; cond. Pryor; rec. 7 Jan., Philadelphia.
On a Sunday Afternoon (arr. Von Tilzer)
Victor #1433 7" ss; cond. Pryor; rec. 18 June, Philadelphia.
On a Sunday Afternoon (arr. Von Tilzer)
Victor #1433 10" ss; cond. Pryor; rec. 18 June, Philadelphia.
On Tip Toe (Loomis)
Victor #1225 7" ss; cond. Pryor; rec. 30 Jan., Philadelphia.
On Tip Toe (Loomis)
Victor #1225 10" ss; cond. Pryor; rec. 30 Jan., Philadelphia.
On Tip Toe (Loomis)
Victor #1225 7" ss; cond. Pryor; rec. 19 June, Philadelphia.
Orpheus in the Underworld: Overture (Offenbach)
Victor #1434 10" ss; cond. Pryor; rec. 19 June, Philadelphia.
I Pagliacci: Prologue (Leoncavallo)
Vocal solo by Emilio de Gogorza. Victor #1452 10" ss; cond. Pryor; rec. 25 June, Philadelphia.
I Pagliacci: Serenade (Leoncavallo)
Trombone solo by Arthur Pryor. Victor #3239 10" ss; rec., 3 Jan., Philadelphia.
La Paloma (Yradier)
Victor #1190 7" ss; cond. Pryor; rec. 6 Jan., Philadelphia.
La Paloma (Yradier)
Victor #1190 10" ss; cond. Pryor; rec. 6 Jan., Philadelphia.
La Paloma (Yradier)
Victor #1190 10" ss; cond. Pryor; rec. 16 June, Philadelphia
Parsifal: Knights of the Holy Grail (R. Wagner)
Victor #3623 10" ss; cond. Pryor; rec. 25 June, Philadelphia.
The Passing of Ragtime (Pryor)
Victor #1417 7" ss; cond. Pryor; rec. 3 June, Philadelphia.
The Passing of Ragtime (Pryor)
Victor #1417 7" ss; cond. Pryor; rec. 9 June, Philadelphia.
The Passing of Ragtime (Pryor)
Victor #1417 10" ss; cond. Pryor; rec. 9 June, Philadelphia.
The Passing of Ragtime (Pryor)
Victor #1417 10" ss; cond. Pryor; rec. 17 June, Philadelphia.
The Passing of Ragtime (Pryor)
Victor #1417 7" ss; cond. Pryor; rec. 17 Dec., Philadelphia.

The Patriot (Pryor)
Trombone solo by Arthur Pryor. Victor #3252 10" ss; rec. 17 June, Philadelphia.

The Picador March (Sousa)
Victor #1181 7" ss; cond. Pryor; rec. 2 Jan., Philadelphia.

The Picador March (Sousa)
Victor #1181 10" ss; cond. Pryor; rec. 2 Jan., Philadelphia.

Plantation Songs (Clarke)
Victor #1197 7" ss; cond. Pryor; rec. 7 Jan., Philadelphia.

Plantation Songs (Clarke)
Victor #1197 10" ss; cond. Pryor; rec. 7 Jan., Philadelphia.

Poet and Peasant Overture (Suppe)
Victor #1552 7" ss; cond. Pryor; rec. 12 Aug., Philadelphia.

Poet and Peasant Overture (Suppe)
Victor #1552 10" ss; cond. Pryor; rec. 12 Aug., Philadelphia.

The Presidential Polonaise (Sousa)
Victor #1195 7" ss; cond. Pryor; rec. 7 Jan., Philadelphia.

The Presidential Polonaise (Sousa)
Victor #1195 10" ss; cond. Pryor; rec. 7 Jan., Philadelphia.

Rajah March (Louka)
Victor #1443 7" ss; cond. Pryor; rec. 23 June, Philadelphia.

Rajah March (Louka)
Victor #1443 10" ss; cond. Pryor; rec. 23 June, Philadelphia.

The Ranting Rube (Rosadye)
Victor #1554 10" ss; cond. Pryor; rec. 12 Aug., Philadelphia.

The Ranting Rube (Rosadye)
Victor #1554 10" ss; cond. Pryor; rec. 12 Aug., Philadelphia.

The Reuben and the Maid (Levi)
Victor #1185 7" ss; cond. Pryor; rec. 3 Jan., Philadelphia.

The Reuben and the Maid (Levi)
Victor #1185 10" ss; cond. Pryor; rec. 3 Jan., Philadelphia.

Ritter Pasman: Czardas (J. Strauss, II)
Victor #1186 7" ss; cond. Pryor; rec. 3 Jan., Philadelphia.

Ritter Pasman: Czardas (J. Strauss, II)
Victor #1186 10" ss; cond. Pryor; rec. 3 Jan., Philadelphia.

The Rose of Shiras: Rose Buds Polka (Eilenberg)
Victor #1832 10" ss; cond. Pryor; rec. 15 Dec., Philadelphia.

The Rose of Shiras: Rose Buds Polka (Eilenberg)
Victor #1832 7" ss; cond. Pryor; rec. 15 Dec., Philadelphia.

The Rose of Shiras: Rose Waltzes (Eilenberg)
Victor #1831 7" ss; cond. Pryor; rec. 15 Dec., Philadelphia.

The Rose of Shiras: Rose Waltzes (Eilenberg)
Victor #1831 10" ss; cond. Pryor; rec. 15 Dec., Philadelphia.

The Rose, The Thistle and the Shamrock Patrol (Sousa)
Victor #1194 7" ss; cond. Pryor; rec. 7 Jan., Philadelphia.

The Rose, the Thistle and the Shamrock Patrol (Sousa)
Victor #1194 10" ss; cond. Pryor; rec. 7 Jan., Philadelphia.

A Runaway Girl: Selections (Caryll)
Victor #332 10" ss; cond. Pryor; rec. 16 Dec., Philadelphia.

Salome Intermezzo (Loraine)
Victor #325 7" ss; cond. Pryor; rec. 2 Jan., Philadelphia.

Salome Intermezzo (Loraine)
Victor #325 10" ss; cond. Pryor; rec. 2 Jan., Philadelphia.

Salut d'Amour (Elgar)
Victor #1199 7" ss; cond. Pryor; rec. 7 Jan., Philadelphia.

Salut d'Amour (Elgar)
Victor #1199 10" ss; cond. Pryor; rec. 7 Jan., Philadelphia.

San Toy: Selections (Jones)
Victor #1184 7" ss; cond. Pryor; rec. 2 Jan., Philadelphia.

San Toy: Selections (Jones)
Victor #1184 10" ss; cond. Pryor; rec. 2 Jan., Philadelphia.

Semiramide: Overture (Rossini)
Victor #359 7" ss; cond. Pryor; rec. 6 Jan., Philadelphia.

Semiramide: Overture (Rossini)
Victor #359 10" ss; cond. Pryor; rec. 6 Jan., Philadelphia.

Semiramide: Overture (Rossini)
Victor #359 10" ss; cond. Pryor; rec. 23 June, Philadelphia.

Semper Fidelis (Sousa)
Victor #1175 7" ss; cond. Pryor; rec. 23 June, Philadelphia.

Semper Fidelis (Sousa)
Victor #1175 10" ss; cond. Pryor; rec. 23 June, Philadelphia.

The Serenade: Waltz (Herbert)
Victor #368 7" ss; cond. Pryor; rec. 21 June, Philadelphia.

The Serenade: Waltz (Herbert)
Victor #368 10" ss; cond. Pryor; rec. 21 June, Philadelphia.

Sheridan's Ride (Sousa)
Victor #1203 7" ss; cond. Pryor; rec. 8 Jan., Philadelphia.

Sheridan's Ride (Sousa)
Victor #1203 10" ss; cond. Pryor; rec. 8 Jan., Philadelphia.

A Soldiers Dream (Rogers)
Cornet solo by Walter B. Rogers. Victor #524 10" ss; cond. Pryor; rec. 24 June, Philadelphia.

A Soldiers Dream (Rogers)
Cornet solo by Walter B. Rogers. Victor #524 7" ss; cond. Pryor; rec. 24 June, Philadelphia.

A Soldiers Dream (Rogers)
Cornet solo by Walter B. Rogers. Victor #524 10" ss; cond. Pryor; rec. 24 June, Philadelphia.

Songs and Dances of the Navy (Hall)
Victor #1556 7" ss; cond. Pryor; rec. 14 Aug., Philadelphia.

Songs and Dances of the Navy (Hall)
Victor #1556 10" ss; cond. Pryor; rec. 14 Aug., Philadelphia.

Songs of Grace and Songs of Glory (Sousa)
Victor #1198 10" ss; cond. Pryor; rec. 7 Jan., Philadelphia.

Songs of Grace and Songs of Glory (Sousa)
Victor #1198 7" ss; cond. Pryor; rec. 25 June, Philadelphia.

Songs of Grace and Songs of Glory (Sousa)
Victor #1198 10" ss; cond. Pryor; rec. 25 June, Philadelphia.

A Southern Dance (Rogers)
Cornet solo by Walter B. Rogers. Victor #525 10" ss; cond. Pryor; rec. 4 April, Philadelphia.

A Southern Dance (Rogers)
Cornet solo by Walter B. Rogers. Victor #525 7" ss; cond. Pryor; rec. 23 June, Philadelphia.

A Southern Dance (Rogers)
Cornet solo by Walter B. Rogers. Victor #525 10" ss; cond. Pryor; rec. 23 June, Philadelphia.

A Souvenir of Naples (Puntillo)
Cornet solo by Walter B. Rogers. Victor #348 7" ss; cond. Pryor; rec. 25 June, Philadelphia.

A Souvenir of Naples (Puntillo)
Cornet solo by Walter B. Rogers. Victor #348 10" ss; cond. Pryor; rec. 25 June, Philadelphia.

The Star Spangled Banner (arr. Sousa)
Victor #336 7" ss; cond. Pryor; rec. 18 June, Philadelphia.

The Star Spangled Banner (arr. Sousa)
Victor #336 10" ss; cond. Pryor; rec. 18 June, Philadelphia.

The Stars and Stripes Forever (Sousa)
Victor #306 10" ss; cond. Pryor; rec. 16 June, Philadelphia.

Stay in Your Own Backyard (Udall)
Trombone solo by Arthur Pryor. Victor #1551 7" ss; rec., 12 Aug., Philadelphia.

Stay in Your Own Backyard (Udall)
Trombone solo by Arthur Pryor. Victor #1551 10" ss; rec., 12 Aug., Philadelphia.

Sylvia (Le Thiere)
Flute solo by Darius Lyons. Victor #1441 7" ss; cond. Pryor; rec. 20 June, Philadelphia.

Sylvia (Le Thiere)
Flute solo by Darius Lyons. Victor #1441 10" ss; cond. Pryor; rec. 20 June, Philadelphia.

Tambour Der Garde: Overture (Titl)
Victor #1837 7" ss; cond. Pryor; rec. 18 Dec., Philadelphia.

Tambour Der Garde: Overture (Titl)
Victor #1837 10" ss; cond. Pryor; rec. 18 Dec., Philadelphia.

There is a Green Hill Far Away (Gounod)
Victor #1448 7" ss; cond. Pryor; rec. 24 June, Philadelphia.

There is a Green Hill Far Away (Gounod)
Victor #1448 10" ss; cond. Pryor; rec. 24 June, Philadelphia.

Three Quotations: 1. King of France (Sousa)
Victor #1180a 7" ss; cond. Pryor; rec. 2 Jan., Philadelphia.

Three Quotations: 1. King of France (Sousa)
Victor #1180a 10" ss; cond. Pryor; rec. 2 Jan., Philadelphia.

Three Quotations: 2. I Too Was Born in Arcadia (Sousa)
Victor #1180b 7" ss; cond. Pryor; rec. 6 Jan., Philadelphia.

Three Quotations: 2. I Too Was Born in Arcadia (Sousa)
Victor #1180b 10" ss; cond. Pryor; rec. 6 Jan., Philadelphia.

Three Quotation: 3. In Darkest Africa (Sousa)
Victor #1180c 7" ss; cond. Pryor; rec. 8 Jan., Philadelphia.

Three Quotation: 3. In Darkest Africa (Sousa)
Victor #1180c 10" ss; cond. Pryor; rec. 8 Jan., Philadelphia.
The Thunderer (Sousa)
Victor #1437 7" ss; cond. Pryor; rec. 20 June, Philadelphia.
The Thunderer (Sousa)
Victor #1437 10" ss; cond. Pryor; rec. 20 June, Philadelphia.
The Toreador: The Espada March (Caryll)
Victor #1178 7" ss; cond. Pryor; rec. 1 Jan., Philadelphia.
The Toreador: The Espada March (Caryll)
Victor #1178 10" ss; cond. Pryor; rec. 1 Jan., Philadelphia.
A Trip Through Dixie (Casey)
Victor #1840 7" ss; cond. Pryor; rec. 18 Dec., Philadelphia.
A Trip Through Dixie (Casey)
Victor #1840 10" ss; cond. Pryor; rec. 18 Dec., Philadelphia.
Trombone Sneeze (Sorrensen) [incorrectly attributed to Pryor]
Victor #1223 7" ss; cond. Pryor; rec. 30 Jan., Philadelphia
Trombone Sneeze (Sorrensen) [incorrectly attributed to Pryor]
Victor #1223 10" ss; cond. Pryor; rec. 30 Jan., Philadelphia
Trombone Sneeze (Sorrensen) [incorrectly attributed to Pryor]
Victor #1123 7" ss; cond. Pryor; rec. 16 June, Philadelphia.
Trombone Sneeze (Sorrensen) [incorrectly attributed to Pryor]
Victor #1123 10" ss; cond. Pryor; rec. 16 June, Philadelphia.
Il Trovatore: Anvil Chorus (Verdi)
Victor #1226 7" ss; cond. Pryor; rec. 30 Jan., Philadelphia.
Il Trovatore: Anvil Chorus (Verdi)
Victor #1226 10" ss; cond. Pryor; rec. 30 Jan., Philadelphia.
Il Trovatore: Miserere (Verdi)
Cornet & trombone duet by Walter B. Rogers & Arthur Pryor. Victor #3238 10" ss; rec., 23 June, Philadelphia.
The United States Passing in Review (Reeni)
Victor #1432 7" ss; cond. Pryor; rec. 18 June, Philadelphia.
The United States Passing in Review (Reeni)
Victor #1432 10" ss; cond. Pryor; rec. 18 June, Philadelphia.
Valse Bleue (Margis)
Victor #1445 7" ss; cond. Pryor; rec. 23 June, Philadelphia.
Valse Bleue (Margis)
Victor #1445 10" ss; cond. Pryor; rec. 23 June, Philadelphia.
The Volunteer Polka (Rogers)
Cornet solo by Walter P. Rogers. Victor #1429 7" ss; cond. Pryor; rec. 17 June, Philadelphia.
The Volunteer Polka (Rogers)
Cornet solo by Walter P. Rogers. Victor #1429 10" ss; cond. Pryor; rec. 17 June, Philadelphia.
The Volunteer Polka (Rogers)
Cornet solo by Walter P. Rogers. Victor #1429 7" ss; cond. Pryor; rec. 18 Dec., Philadelphia.
Waltz and Mazurka (Chopin/Sousa)
Victor #317 10" ss; cond. Pryor; rec. 16 Dec., Philadelphia.
The Warbler's Serenade (Perry)
Whistling solo by Edward Wardwell. Victor #1168 7" ss; cond. Pryor; rec. 9 June, Philadelphia.
The Warbler's Serenade (Perry)
Whistling solo by Edward Wardwell. Victor #1168 10" ss; cond. Pryor; rec. 9 June, Philadelphia.
The Warbler's Serenade (Perry)
Whistling solo by Edward Wardwell. Victor #1168 10" ss; cond. Pryor; rec. 17 Dec., Philadelphia.
The Washington Post (Sousa)
Victor #1183 7" ss; cond. Pryor; rec. 2 Jan., Philadelphia.
The Washington Post (Sousa)
Victor #1183 7" ss; cond. Pryor; rec. 12 Aug., Philadelphia.
The Washington Post (Sousa)
Victor #1183 10" ss; cond. Pryor; rec. 12 Aug., Philadelphia.
Water Sprites (Kunkel)
Victor #1204 7" ss; cond. Pryor; rec. 8 Jan., Philadelphia.
Water Sprites (Kunkel)
Victor #1204 10" ss; cond. Pryor; rec. 8 Jan., Philadelphia.
'Way Down South
Victor #1173 10" ss; cond. Pryor; rec. 19 Dec., Philadelphia.
Will You Love When the Lilies Are Dead? (Sousa)
Soprano solo by Maud Reese Davies. Victor #1224 7" ss; cond. Pryor; rec. 30 Jan., Philadelphia.
Will You Love When the Lilies Are Dead? (Sousa)
Soprano solo by Maud Reese Davies. Victor #1224 10" ss; cond. Pryor; rec. 30 Jan., Philadelphia.

William Tell: Ballet Music (Rossini)
Victor #1442 7" ss; cond. Pryor; rec. 21 June, Philadelphia.
William Tell: Ballet Music (Rossini)
Victor #1442 10" ss; cond. Pryor; rec. 21 June, Philadelphia.
William Tell: Overture; Finale (Rossini)
Victor #321 10" ss; cond. Pryor; rec. 4 Jan., Philadelphia.
William Tell: Overture; Finale (Rossini)
Victor #321 7" ss; cond. Pryor; rec. 19 June, Philadelphia.
William Tell: Overture; Finale (Rossini)
Victor #321 10" ss; cond. Pryor; rec. 19 June, Philadelphia.
Xerxes: Largo (Handel)
Victor #1440 7" ss; cond. Pryor; rec. 20 June, Philadelphia.
Xerxes: Largo (Handel)
Victor #1440 10" ss; cond. Pryor; rec. 20 June, Philadelphia.
The Yale Boola March (Hirsh)
Victor #1839 7" ss; cond. Pryor; rec. 19 Dec., Philadelphia.
The Yale Boola March (Hirsh)
Victor #1839 10" ss; cond. Pryor; rec. 19 Dec., Philadelphia.
Yankee Doodle with Variations (arr. Rogers)
Cornet solo by Walter B. Rogers. Victor #532 7" ss; cond. Pryor; rec. 8 Aug., Philadelphia.
Yankee Doodle with Variations (arr. Rogers)
Cornet solo by Walter B. Rogers. Victor #532 10" ss; cond. Pryor; rec. 8 Aug., Philadelphia.
Ye Boston Tea Party (Pryor)
Victor #344 7" ss; cond. Pryor; rec. 21 June, Philadelphia.
Ye Boston Tea Party (Pryor)
Victor #344 10" ss; cond. Pryor; rec. 21 June, Philadelphia.
Zampa: Overture (Herold)
Victor #363 7" ss; cond. Pryor; rec. 3 Jan., Philadelphia.
Zampa: Overture (Herold)
Victor #363 10" ss; cond. Pryor; rec. 3 Jan., Philadelphia.

1903
Aida: Selection (The Fatal Stone) (Verdi)
Victor #4008 10" ss; cond. Pryor; rec. 28 Aug., Philadelphia.
American Patrol (Meacham)
Victor #382 7" ss; cond. Pryor; rec. 12 Aug., Philadelphia.
American Patrol (Meacham)
Victor #382 10" ss; cond. Pryor; rec. 12 Aug., Philadelphia.
American Patrol (Meacham)
Victor #382 7" ss; cond. Pryor; rec. 14 Aug., Philadelphia.
Andrea Chenier: Selections (Giordano)
Victor #2650 7" ss; cond. Pryor; rec. 12 Aug., Philadelphia.
Andrea Chenier: Selections (Giordano)
Victor #2650 10" ss; cond. Pryor; rec. 12 Aug., Philadelphia.
Andrea Chenier: Selections (Giordano)
Victor #31080 12" ss; cond. Pryor; rec. 12 Aug., Philadelphia.
Army Bugle Calls
Victor #1303a 7" ss; rec. by Sousa's Cornets on 5 Sept., Philadelphia.
Army Bugle Calls
Victor #1303b 7" ss; rec. by Sousa's Cornets on 5 Sept., Philadelphia.
Army Bugle Calls
Victor #1303 10" ss; rec. by Sousa's Cornets on 5 Sept., Philadelphia.
Army Bugle Calls
Victor #31113 12" ss; rec. by Sousa's Cornets on 5 Sept., Philadelphia.
At the Old Grist Mill (Muller)
Victor #2482 7" ss; cond. Pryor; rec. 20 Aug., Philadelphia.
At the Old Grist Mill (Muller)
Victor #2482 10" ss; cond. Pryor; rec. 20 Aug., Philadelphia.
The Blue and the Gray Patrol (Dalbey)
Victor #1171 7" ss; cond. Pryor; rec. 11 Aug., Philadelphia.
The Blue and the Gray Patrol (Dalbey)
Victor #1171 10" ss; cond. Pryor; rec. 11 Aug., Philadelphia.
Blue Bells of Scotland
Trombone solo by Arthur Pryor. Victor #2477 7" ss; rec. 28 Aug., Philadelphia.
Blue Bells of Scotland
Trombone solo by Arthur Pryor. Victor #2477 10" ss; rec. 28 Aug., Philadelphia.

444

Blue Bells of Scotland
Trombone solo by Arthur Pryor. Victor #31109 12" ss; rec. 28 Aug., Philadelphia.

The Blue Danube Waltz (J. Strauss, II)
Victor #343 7" ss; cond. Pryor; rec., 14 Aug., Philadelphia.

The Blue Danube Waltz (J. Strauss, II)
Victor #343 10" ss; cond. Pryor; rec., 14 Aug., Philadelphia.

The Blue Danube Waltz (J. Strauss, II)
Victor #31450 12" ss; cond. Pryor; rec. 4 Sept., Philadelphia.

The Bride Elect: Selections (Sousa)
Victor #2494 10" ss; cond. Pryor; rec. 24 Aug., Philadelphia.

Bunch of Mischief Polka
Victor #1200 7" ss; cond. Pryor; rec. 13 Aug., Philadelphia.

Bunch of Mischief Polka
Victor #1200 10" ss; cond. Pryor; rec. 13 Aug., Philadelphia.

Cavalleria Rusticana: Selections (Mascagni)
Victor #2461 7" ss; cond. Pryor; rec. 24 Aug., Philadelphia.

Concert Polka (Losey)
Cornet duet by Walter B. Rogers & Henry Higgins. Victor #31115 12" ss; cond. Pryor; rec. 28 Aug., Philadelphia.

Coon Smiles (Clarke)
Victor #1555 7" ss; cond. Pryor; rec. 11 Aug., Philadelphia.

Coon Smiles (Clarke)
Victor #1555 10" ss; cond. Pryor; rec. 11 Aug., Philadelphia.

Country Dance (Nevin)
Victor #2614 7" ss; cond. Pryor; rec. 14 Aug., Philadelphia.

Country Dance (Nevin)
Victor #2614 10" ss; cond. Pryor; rec. 14 Aug., Philadelphia.

Country Dance (Nevin)
Victor #2614 10" ss; cond. Pryor; rec. 24 Aug., Philadelphia.

Country Dance (Nevin)
Victor #31101 12" ss; cond. Pryor; rec. 26 Aug., Philadelphia.

Custer's Last Charge (Luders)
Victor #1192 7" ss; cond. Pryor; rec. 25 Aug., Philadelphia.

Custer's Last Charge (Luders)
Victor #1192 10" ss; cond. Pryor; rec. 25 Aug., Philadelphia.

La Danseuse (Blon)
Victor #2613 7" ss; cond. Pryor; rec. 21 Aug., Philadelphia.

La Danseuse (Blon)
Victor #2613 10" ss; cond. Pryor; rec. 21 Aug., Philadelphia.

La Danseuse (Blon)
Victor #31085 12" ss; cond. Pryor; rec. 28 Aug., Philadelphia.

A Dream of the Ballet (Uhl)
Victor #2484 7" ss; cond. Pryor; rec. 28 Aug., Philadelphia.

A Dream of the Ballet (Uhl)
Victor #2484 10" ss; cond. Pryor; rec. 28 Aug., Philadelphia.

Dream of the Ballet (Uhl)
Victor #31087 12" ss; cond. Pryor; rec. 28 Aug., Philadelphia.

A Dream of the Ballet (Uhl)
Victor #31087 10" ss; cond. Pryor; rec. 4 Sept., Philadelphia.

A Dream of the Ballet (Uhl)
Victor #31087 12" ss; cond. Pryor; rec. 4 Sept., Philadelphia.

Faust Selections (Gounod)
Victor #1838 7" ss; cond. Pryor; rec. 17 Aug., Philadelphia.

Faust Selections (Gounod)
Victor #1838 10" ss; cond. Pryor; rec. 17 Aug., Philadelphia.

Faust Selections (Gounod)
Victor #31104 12" ss; cond. Pryor; rec. 17 Aug., Philadelphia.

Faust: Selections (Gounod)
Victor #1838 7" ss; cond. Pryor; rec. 24 Aug., Philadelphia.

Faust Selections (Gounod)
Victor #1838 10" ss; cond. Pryor; rec. 24 Aug., Philadelphia.

Faust Selections (Gounod)
Victor #31104 12" ss; cond. Pryor; rec. 24 Aug., Philadelphia.

Funeral March of a Marionette (Gounod)
Victor #2524 7" ss; cond. Pryor; rec. 17 Aug., Philadelphia.

Funeral March of a Marionette (Gounod)
Victor #2524 10" ss; cond. Pryor; rec. 17 Aug., Philadelphia.

Funeral March of a Marionette (Gounod)
Victor #31081 12" ss; cond. Pryor; rec. 18 Aug., Philadelphia.

Funeral March of a Marionette (Gounod)
Victor #2524 7" ss; cond. Pryor; rec. 25 Aug., Philadelphia.

Funeral March of a Marionette (Gounod)
Victor #2524 10" ss; cond. Pryor; rec. 25 Aug., Philadelphia.

Gladiator March (Sousa)
Victor #1177 7" ss; cond. Pryor; rec. 11 Aug., Philadelphia.

Gladiator March (Sousa)
Victor #1177 10" ss; cond. Pryor; rec. 11 Aug., Philadelphia.

Graceful Dance (German)
Victor 2440 7" ss; cond. Pryor; rec. 25 Aug., Philadelphia.

Graceful Dance (German)
Victor #2440 10" ss; cond. Pryor; rec. 25 Aug., Philadelphia.

Il Guarany: Overture (Gomez)
Victor #31116 12" ss; cond. Pryor; rec. 24 Aug., Philadelphia.

The Harp That Once Thro' Tara's Halls (Rogers)
Cornet solo by Walter Rogers. Victor #2663 7" ss; rec. 14 Aug., Philadelphia.

The Harp That Once Thro' Tara's Halls (Rogers)
Cornet solo by Walter Rogers. Victor #31110 12" ss; cond. Pryor; rec. 14 Aug., Philadelphia.

Hearts and Flowers (Tobani)
Cornet solo by Herbert L. Clarke. Victor #1172 7" ss; cond. Pryor; rec. 11 Aug., Philadelphia.

Hearts and Flowers (Tobani)
Cornet solo by Herbert L. Clarke. Victor #1172 10" ss; cond. Pryor; rec. 11 Aug., Philadelphia.

Hiawatha (Moret)
Victor #2443 7" ss; cond. Pryor; rec. 14 Aug., Philadelphia.

Hiawatha (Moret)
Victor #2443 10" ss; cond. Pryor; rec. 14 Aug., Philadelphia.

High School Cadets (Sousa)
Victor #2442 7" ss; cond. Pryor; rec. 11 Aug., Philadelphia.

High School Cadets (Sousa)
Victor #2442 10" ss; cond. Pryor; rec. 11 Aug., Philadelphia.

"His Master's Voice" Concert Polka (Losey)
Victor #31115 12" ss; cond. Pryor; rec. 28 Aug., Philadelphia.

A Hot Time in the Old Town (Metz)
Victor #316 7" ss; cond. Pryor; rec. 13 Aug., Philadelphia.

A Hot Time in the Old Town (Metz)
Victor #316 10" ss; cond. Pryor; rec. 13 Aug., Philadelphia.

A Hot Time in the Old Town (Metz)
Victor #316 10" ss; cond. Pryor; rec. 13 Aug., Philadelphia.

A Hot Time in the Old Town (Metz)
Victor #316 10" ss; cond. Pryor; rec. 15 Aug., Philadelphia.

A Hot Time in the Old Town (Metz)
Victor #316 10" ss; cond. Pryor; rec. 19 Aug., Philadelphia.

Hungarian Rhapsody, No. 2 (Liszt)
Victor #31083 12" ss; cond. Pryor; rec. 12 Aug., Philadelphia.

Hungarian Rhapsody, No. 2 (Liszt)
Victor #2617 10" ss; cond. Pryor; rec. 17 Aug., Philadelphia.

Hungarian Rhapsody, No. 2 (Liszt)
Victor #31083 12" ss; cond. Pryor; rec. 17 Aug., Philadelphia.

Hungarian Rhapsody, No. 2 (Liszt)
Victor #2617 10" ss; cond. Pryor; rec. 25 Aug., Philadelphia.

I Need Thee Every Hour (Lowry)
Cornet solo by Walter B. Rogers. Victor #2469 7" ss; cond. Pryor; rec. 24 Aug., Philadelphia.

I Need Thee Every Hour (Lowry)
Cornet solo by Walter B. Rogers. Victor #2469 10" ss; cond. Pryor; rec. 24 Aug., Philadelphia.

Imperial Edward Coronation March (Sousa)
Victor #1418 7" ss; cond. Pryor; rec. 18 Aug., Philadelphia.

Imperial Edward Coronation March (Sousa)
Victor #1418 10" ss; cond. Pryor; rec. 18 Aug., Philadelphia.

Imperial Kaiser Overture (Westmeyer)
Victor #2526 10" ss; cond. Pryor; rec. 12 Aug., Philadelphia.

Imperial Kaiser Overture (Westmeyer)
Victor #2526 10" ss; cond. Pryor; rec. 14 Aug., Philadelphia.

Imperial Kaiser Overture (Westmeyer)
Victor #31082 12" ss; cond. Pryor; rec. 17 Aug., Philadelphia.

Imperial Kaiser Overture (Westmeyer)
Victor #2526 10" ss; cond. Pryor; rec. 19 Aug., Philadelphia.

In the Realm of the Waltz (Sousa)
Victor #1438 7" ss; cond. Pryor; rec. 14 Aug., Philadelphia.

In the Realm of the Waltz (Sousa)
Victor #1438 10" ss; cond. Pryor; rec. 14 Aug., Philadelphia.

In the Soudan: Dervish Chorus (Sebek)
Victor #2463 7" ss; cond. Pryor; rec. 20 Aug., Philadelphia.

In the Soudan: Dervish Chorus (Sebek)
Victor #2463 10" ss; cond. Pryor; rec. 20 Aug., Philadelphia.
The Invincible Eagle (Sousa)
Victor #844 7" ss; cond. Pryor; rec. 18 Aug., Philadelphia.
The Invincible Eagle (Sousa)
Victor #844 10" ss; cond. Pryor; rec. 18 Aug., Philadelphia.
Invitation to the Dance (Weber)
Victor #31105 12" ss; cond. Pryor; rec. 18 Aug., Philadelphia.
Jack Tar (Sousa)
Victor #2419 7" ss; cond. Pryor; rec. 12 Aug., Philadelphia.
Jack Tar (Sousa)
Victor #2419 10" ss; cond. Pryor; rec. 12 Aug., Philadelphia.
Jack Tar (Sousa)
Victor #31051 12" ss; cond. Pryor; rec. 12 Aug., Philadelphia.
Jack Tar (Sousa)
Victor #2419 7" ss; cond. Pryor; rec. 4 Sept., Philadelphia.
Jack Tar (Sousa)
Victor #2419 10" ss; cond. Pryor; rec. 4 Sept., Philadelphia.
Jack Tar (Sousa)
Victor #31051 12" ss; cond. Pryor; rec. 4 Sept., Philadelphia.
Jack Tar (Sousa)
Columbia #32297 2" cyl; rec. nd., Washington.
The Jolly Fellows Waltz (Vollstedt)
Victor #1174 7" ss; cond. Pryor; rec. 13 Aug., Philadelphia.
The Jolly Fellows Waltz (Vollstedt)
Victor #1174 10" ss; cond. Pryor; rec. 13 Aug., Philadelphia.
The Jolly Fellows Waltz (Volstadt)
Victor #1174 7" ss; cond. Pryor; rec. 17 Aug., Philadelphia.
The Jolly Fellows Waltz (Vollstedt)
Victor #1174 10" ss; cond. Pryor; rec. 17 Aug., Philadelphia.
The Liberty Bell (Sousa)
Victor #1193 7" ss; cond. Pryor; rec. 13 Aug., Philadelphia.
The Liberty Bell (Sousa)
Victor #1193 10" ss; cond. Pryor; rec. 13 Aug., Philadelphia.
The Liberty Bell (Sousa)
Victor #1193 10" ss; cond. Pryor; rec. 17 Aug., Philadelphia.
The Liberty Bell (Sousa)
Victor #1173 7" ss; cond. Pryor; rec. 18 Aug., Philadelphia.
Light Cavalry: Overture (Suppe)
Victor #2471 7" ss; cond. Pryor; rec. 20 Aug., Philadelphia.
Light Cavalry: Overture (Suppe)
Victor #2471 10" ss; cond. Pryor; rec. 20 Aug, Philadelphia.
Light Cavalry: Overture (Suppe)
Victor #31095 12" ss; cond. Pryor; rec. 24 Aug., Philadelphia.
Lily Bells (Sousa)
Victor #339 7" ss; cond. Pryor; rec. 13 Aug., Philadelphia.
Lily Bells (Sousa)
Victor #339 10" ss; cond. Pryor; rec. 13 Aug, Philadelphia.
Lohengrin: Selections (R. Wagner)
Victor #2479 7" ss; cond. Pryor; rec. 19 Aug., Philadelphia.
Lohengrin: Selections (R. Wagner)
Victor #2479 10" ss; cond. Pryor; rec. 19 Aug., Philadelphia.
Looking Upward: I. By the Light of the Polar Star (Sousa)
Victor #2486 7" ss; cond. Pryor; rec. 19 Aug., Philadelphia.
Looking Upward: I. By the Light of the Polar Star (Sousa)
Victor #2486a 10" ss; cond. Pryor; rec. 19 Aug., Philadelphia.
Looking Upward: I. By the Light of the Polar Star (Sousa)
Victor #2486 10" ss; cond. Pryor; rec. 21 Aug., Philadelphia.
Looking Upward: I. By the Light of the Polar Star (Sousa)
Victor #31088 12" ss; cond. Pryor; rec. 21 Aug., Philadelphia.
Looking Upward: II. Under the Southern Cross (Sousa)
Victor #2487 7" ss; cond. Pryor; rec. 19 Aug, Philadelphia.
Looking Upward: II. Under the Southern Cross (Sousa)
Victor #2487 10" ss; cond. Pryor; rec. 19 Aug, Philadelphia.
Looking Upward: III. Mars and Venus (Sousa)
Victor #2488 7" ss; cond. Pryor; rec. 19 Aug., Philadelphia.
Looking Upward: III. Mars and Venus (Sousa)
Victor #2488 10" ss; cond. Pryor; rec. 19 Aug., Philadelphia.
Looking Upward: III. Mars and Venus (Sousa)
Victor #2488 10" ss; cond. Pryor; rec. 21 Aug., Philadelphia.
Love Thoughts (Pryor)
Trombone solo by Arthur Pryor. Victor #310 7" ss; rec. 27 Aug., Philadelphia.
Love Thoughts (Pryor)
Trombone solo by Arthur Pryor. Victor #310 10" ss; rec. 27 Aug., Philadelphia.
Love Thoughts (Pryor)
Trombone solo by Arthur Pryor. Victor #31108 12" ss; rec. 27 Aug., Philadelphia.
Love's Enchantment (Pryor)
Trombone solo by Arthur Pryor. Victor #1428 7" ss; rec. 19 Aug., Philadelphia.
Love's Enchantment (Pryor)
Trombone solo by Arthur Pryor. Victor #1428 10" ss; rec. 19 Aug., Philadelphia.
Love's Enchantment (Pryor)
Trombone solo by Arthur Pryor. Victor #31107 12" ss; rec. 27 Aug., Philadelphia.
Lulle Waltz (Rogers)
Cornet solo by Walter B. Rogers. Victor #2439 7" ss; cond. Pryor; rec. 26 Aug., Philadelphia.
Lulle Waltz (Rogers)
Cornet solo by Walter B. Rogers. Victor #2439 10" ss; cond. Pryor; rec. 26 Aug., Philadelphia.
Lulle Waltz (Rogers)
Cornet solo by Walter B. Rogers. Victor #31112 12" ss; cond. Pryor; rec. 26 Aug., Philadelphia.
Maidens Three: Coquette (Sousa)
Victor #1179a 7" ss; cond. Pryor; rec. 13 Aug., Philadelphia.
Maidens Three: Coquette (Sousa)
Victor #1179a 10" ss; cond. Pryor; rec. 13 Aug., Philadelphia.
Maidens Three: Summer Girl (Sousa)
Victor #1179b 7" ss; cond. Pryor; rec. 13 Aug., Philadelphia.
Maidens Three: Summer Girl (Sousa)
Victor #1179b 10" ss; cond. Pryor; rec. 13 Aug., Philadelphia.
Maidens Three: Dancing Girl (Sousa)
Victor #1179c 7" ss; cond. Pryor; rec. 13 Aug., Philadelphia.
Maidens Three: Dancing Girl (Sousa)
Victor #1179c 10" ss; cond. Pryor; rec. 13 Aug., Philadelphia.
La Mandolinata (Paladilhe)
Victor #2485 7" ss; cond. Pryor; rec. 17 Aug., Philadelphia.
La Mandolinata (Paladilhe)
Victor #2485 10" ss; cond. Pryor; rec. 17 Aug., Philadelphia.
La Mandolinata (Paladilhe)
Victor #31098 12" ss; cond. Pryor; rec. 26 Aug., Philadelphia.
Mexican Serenade (Wilson)
Victor #2444 7" ss; cond. Pryor; rec. 15 Aug., Philadelphia.
Mexican Serenade (Wilson)
Victor #2444 10" ss; cond. Pryor; rec. 15 Aug., Philadelphia.
Minnehaha Waltz (Rogers)
Cornet solo by Walter B. Rogers. Victor #1202 7" ss; cond. Pryor; rec. 26 Aug., Philadelphia.
Minnehaha Waltz (Rogers)
Cornet solo by Walter B. Rogers. Victor #1202 10" ss; cond. Pryor; rec. 26 Aug., Philadelphia.
Minnehaha Waltz (Rogers)
Cornet solo by Walter B. Rogers. Victor #31111 12" ss; cond. Pryor; rec. 26 Aug., Philadelphia.
Minuet (Paderewski)
Victor #2460 10" ss; cond. Pryor; rec. 28 Aug., Philadelphia.
Minuet (Paderewski)
Victor #31120 12" ss; cond. Pryor; rec. 28 Aug., Philadelphia.
Morning, Noon and Night in Vienna: Overture (Suppe)
Victor #1430 7" ss; cond. Pryor; rec. 15 Aug., Philadelphia.
Morning, Noon and Night in Vienna: Overture (Suppe)
Victor #1430 10" ss; cond. Pryor; rec. 15 Aug., Philadelphia.
My Old Kentucky Home Fantasy (Foster/Dalbey)
Victor #2481 7" ss; cond. Pryor; rec. 20 Aug., Philadelphia.
My Old Kentucky Home Fantasy (Foster/Dalbey)
Victor #2481 10" ss; cond. Pryor; rec. 20 Aug., Philadelphia.
Nancy Brown: Congo Love Song (J.R. Johnson)
Trombone solo by Arthur Pryor. Victor #2436 7" ss; cond. Pryor; rec. 28 Aug., Philadelphia.
Nancy Brown: Congo Love Song (J.R. Johnson)
Trombone solo by Arthur Pryor. Victor #2436 10" ss; cond. Pryor; rec. 28 Aug., Philadelphia.

Narcissus (Nevin)
Victor #354 7" ss; cond. Pryor; rec. 18 Aug., Philadelphia.
Narcissus (Nevin)
Victor #354 10" ss; cond. Pryor; rec. 18 Aug., Philadelphia.
Nearer My God to Thee (Mason)
Victor #355 7" ss; cond. Pryor; rec. 21 Aug., Philadelphia.
Nearer My God to Thee (Mason)
Victor #355 10" ss; cond. Pryor; rec. 21 Aug., Philadelphia.
La Paloma (Yradier)
Victor #1190 7" ss; cond. Pryor; rec. 20 Aug., Philadelphia
La Paloma (Yradier)
Victor #1190 10" ss; cond. Pryor; rec. 20 Aug., Philadelphia
Parsifal: Gralsritter Marsch (R. Wagner)
Victor #2527 10" ss; cond. Pryor; rec. 28 Aug., Philadelphia.
Parsifal: Gralsritter Marsch (R. Wagner)
Victor #31103 12" ss; cond. Pryor; rec. 28 Aug., Philadelphia.
The Passing of Rag Time (Pryor)
Victor #1417 7" ss; cond. Pryor; rec. 18 Aug., Philadelphia.
The Passing of Rag Time (Pryor)
Victor #1417 10" ss; cond. Pryor; rec. 18 Aug., Philadelphia.
The Patriot (Pryor)
Trombone solo by Arthur Pryor. Victor #2498 7" ss; rec. 26 Aug., Philadelphia.
The Patriot (Pryor)
Trombone solo by Arthur Pryor. Victor #2498 10" ss; rec., 26 Aug., Philadelphia.
Picador March (Sousa)
Victor #1181 7" ss; cond. Pryor; rec. 11 Aug., Philadelphia.
Picador March (Sousa)
Victor #1181 10" ss; cond. Pryor; rec. 11 Aug., Philadelphia.
The Prince of Pilsen: The Message of the Violet (Luders)
Victor #2437 7" ss; rec., 18 Aug., Philadelphia.
The Prince of Pilsen: The Message of the Violet (Luders)
Victor #2437 10" ss; rec., 18 Aug., Philadelphia.
The Prince of Pilsen: A Tale of the Seashell (Luders)
Cornet solo by Walter B. Rogers. Victor #2470 7" ss; cond. Pryor; rec. 18 Aug., Philadelphia.
The Prince of Pilsen: A Tale of the Seashell (Luders)
Cornet solo by Walter B. Rogers. Victor #2470 10" ss; cond. Pryor; rec. 18 Aug., Philadelphia.
Rienzi: Overture (R. Wagner)
Victor #2612 7" ss; cond. Pryor; rec. 26 Aug., Philadelphia.
Rienzi: Overture (R. Wagner)
Victor #2612 10" ss; cond. Pryor; rec. 26 Aug., Philadelphia.
Rienzi: Overture (R. Wagner)
Victor #31099 12" ss; cond. Pryor; rec. 26 Aug., Philadelphia.
Robespierre Overture (Litolff)
Victor #31093 12" ss; cond. Pryor; rec. 21 Aug., Philadelphia.
The Rose, The Thistle and the Shamrock Patrol (Sousa)
Victor #1194 7" ss; cond. Pryor; rec. 19 Aug., Philadelphia.
The Rose, The Thistle and the Shamrock Patrol (Sousa)
Victor #1194 10" ss; cond. Pryor; rec. 19 Aug., Philadelphia.
Salut d'Amour (Elgar)
Victor #1199 10" ss; cond. Pryor; rec. 25 Aug., Philadelphia.
Scenes Pittoresques: Angelus (Massenet)
Victor #31091 12" ss; cond. Pryor; rec. 26 Aug., Philadelphia.
Scenes Pittoresques: Fete Boheme (Massenet)
Victor #31091 12" ss; cond. Pryor; rec. 21 Aug., Philadelphia.
Scenes Pittoresques: March (Massenet)
Victor #31089 12" ss; cond. Pryor; rec. 21 Aug., Philadelphia.
Semper Fidelis (Sousa)
Victor #1175 7" ss; cond. Pryor; rec. 11 Aug., Philadelphia.
Semper Fidelis (Sousa)
Victor #1175 10" ss; cond. Pryor; rec. 11 Aug., Philadelphia.
Semper Fidelis (Sousa)
Victor #1175 7" ss; cond. Pryor; rec. 14 Aug., Philadelphia.
Semper Fidelis (Sousa)
Victor #1175 10" ss; cond. Pryor; rec. 14 Aug., Philadelphia.
Serenade (Titl)
Victor #31084 12" ss; cond. Pryor; rec. 4 Sept., Philadelphia.
The Skaters (Waldteufel)
Victor #31097 12" ss; cond. Pryor; rec. 28 Aug., Philadelphia.
Songs of Grace and Songs of Glory (Sousa)
Victor #31086 12" ss; cond. Pryor; rec. 28 Aug., Philadelphia.

Songs of Grace and Songs of Glory (Sousa)
Victor #31086 12" ss; cond. Pryor; rec. 4 Sept., Philadelphia.
Stabat Mater: Cujus Animam (Rossini)
Victor #2472 7" ss; rec., 28 Aug., Philadelphia.
Stabat Mater: Cujus Animam (Rossini)
Victor #2472 10" ss; rec., 28 Aug., Philadelphia.
Stabat Mater: Cujus Animam (Rossini)
Victor #31106 12" ss; rec., 28 Aug., Philadelphia.
The Stars and Stripes Forever (Sousa)
Victor #306 7" ss; cond. Pryor; rec. 14 Aug., Philadelphia.
The Stars and Stripes Forever (Sousa)
Victor #306 10" ss; cond. Pryor; rec. 14 Aug., Philadelphia.
The Stars and Stripes Forever (Sousa)
Victor #31102 12" ss; cond. Pryor; rec. 27 Aug., Philadelphia.
The Stars and Stripes Forever (Sousa)
Victor #306 10" ss; cond. Pryor; rec. 3 Sept., Philadelphia.
The Sunflower and the Sun (Penn)
Victor #2438 7" ss; rec., 26 Aug., Philadelphia.
The Sunflower and the Sun (Penn)
Victor #2438 10" ss; rec., 26 Aug., Philadelphia.
Sylvia: Selections (Delibes)
Victor #2651 7" ss; cond. Pryor; rec. 15 Aug., Philadelphia.
Sylvia: Selections (Delibes)
Victor #2651 10" ss; cond. Pryor; rec. 15 Aug., Philadelphia.
Sylvia: Selections (Delibes)
Victor #31094 12" ss; cond. Pryor; rec. 15 Aug., Philadelphia.
Tambour Der Garde: Overture (Titl)
Victor #1837 7" ss; cond. Pryor; rec. 17 Aug., Philadelphia.
Tambour Der Garde: Overture (Titl)
Victor #1837 10" ss; cond. Pryor; rec. 17 Aug., Philadelphia.
Tambour Der Garde: Overture (Titl)
Victor #31092 12" ss; cond. Pryor; rec. 18 Aug., Philadelphia.
Three Quotations: The King of France (Sousa)
Victor #1180a 7" ss; cond. Pryor; rec. 17 Aug., Philadelphia.
Three Quotations: The King of France (Sousa)
Victor #1180a 10" ss; cond. Pryor; rec. 17 Aug., Philadelphia.
Three Quotations: I Too Was Born in Arcadia (Sousa)
Victor #1180b 10" ss; cond. Pryor; rec. 17 Aug., Philadelphia.
The Thunderer (Sousa)
Victor #1437 7" ss; cond. Pryor; rec. 11 Aug., Philadelphia.
The Thunderer (Sousa)
Victor #1437 10" ss; cond. Pryor; rec. 11 Aug., Philadelphia.
The Thunderer (Sousa)
Victor #1437 7" ss; cond. Pryor; rec. 18 Aug., Philadelphia.
The Thunderer (Sousa)
Victor #1437 10" ss; cond. Pryor; rec. 18 Aug., Philadelphia.
Under the Double Eagle (J.F. Wagner)
Victor #31100 12" ss; cond. Pryor; rec. 27 Aug., Philadelphia.
The United Service Passing in Review (Reeves)
Victor #31096 12" ss; cond. Pryor; rec. 19 Aug., Philadelphia.
The Washington Post (Sousa)
Victor #1183 7" ss; cond. Pryor; rec. 18 Aug., Philadelphia.
The Washington Post (Sousa)
Victor #1183 10" ss; cond. Pryor; rec. 18 Aug., Philadelphia.
The Washington Post (Sousa)
Victor #1183 7" ss; cond. Pryor; rec. 19 Aug., Philadelphia.
The Washington Post (Sousa)
Victor #1183 10" ss; cond. Pryor; rec. 19 Aug., Philadelphia.
Water Sprites (Kunkel)
Victor #1204 7" ss; cond. Pryor; rec. 12 Aug., Philadelphia.
Water Sprites (Kunkel)
Victor #1204 10" ss; cond. Pryor; rec. 12 Aug., Philadelphia.
William Tell: Ballet Music (Rossini)
Victor #1442 10" ss; cond. Pryor; rec. 15 Aug., Philadelphia.
William Tell: Overture; Alpine Duet (Rossini)
Victor #2525 10" ss; cond. Pryor; rec. 15 Aug., Philadelphia.
William Tell: Overture; Finale (Rossini)
Victor #321 7" ss; cond. Pryor; rec. 15 Aug., Philadelphia.
William Tell: Overture; Finale (Rossini)
Victor #321 10" ss; cond. Pryor; rec. 15 Aug., Philadelphia.
Xerxes: Largo (Handel)
Victor #1440 7" ss; cond. Pryor; rec. 11 Aug., Philadelphia.
Xerxes: Largo (Handel)
Victor #1440 10" ss; cond. Pryor; rec. 11 Aug., Philadelphia.

1904

American Patrol (Meacham)
Victor #382 7" ss; cond. H.L. Clarke; rec. 7 Dec., Philadelphia.

American Patrol (Meacham)
Victor #382 10" ss; cond. H.L. Clarke; rec. 7 Dec., Philadelphia.

American Patrol (Meacham)
Victor #382 7" ss; cond. H.L. Clarke; rec. 12 Dec., Philadelphia.

American Patrol (Meacham)
Victor #382 10" ss; cond. H.L. Clarke; rec. 12 Dec., Philadelphia.

An Arkansaw Huskin' Bee (Pryor)
Victor #314 7" ss; cond. H.L. Clarke; rec. 8 Dec., Philadelphia.

An Arkansaw Huskin' Bee (Pryor)
Victor #314 10" ss; cond. H.L. Clarke; rec. 8 Dec., Philadelphia.

Andrea Chenier: Selections (Giordano)
Victor #31080 12" ss; cond. H.L. Clarke; rec. 20 Dec., Philadelphia.

At a Georgia Camp Meeting (Mills)
Victor #315 7" ss; cond. H.L. Clarke; rec. 7 Dec., Philadelphia.

At a Georgia Camp Meeting (Mills)
Victor #315 10" ss; cond. H.L. Clarke; rec. 7 Dec., Philadelphia.

At a Georgia Camp Meeting (Mills)
Victor #315 7" ss; cond. H.L. Clarke; rec. 12 Dec., Philadelphia.

At a Georgia Camp Meeting (Mills)
Victor #315 10" ss; cond. H.L. Clarke; rec. 12 Dec., Philadelphia.

The Blue and the Gray Patrol (Dalbey)
Victor #1171 10" ss; cond. H.L. Clarke; rec. 7 Dec., Philadelphia.

The Blue and the Gray Patrol (Dalbey)
Victor #1171 10" ss; cond. H.L. Clarke; rec. 12 Dec., Philadelphia.

The Blue Danube Waltz (J. Strauss, II)
Victor #343 7" ss; cond. H.L. Clarke; rec. 13 Dec., Philadelphia.

The Blue Danube Waltz (J. Strauss, II)
Victor #343 10" ss; cond. H.L. Clarke; rec. 13 Dec., Philadelphia.

Bride of the Waves (Clarke)
Cornet solo by Herbert L. Clarke. Victor #4263 10" ss; rec. 22 Dec., Philadelphia.

Bride of the Waves (Clarke)
Cornet solo by Herbert L. Clarke. Victor #16194 10" ds; cond. H.L. Clarke; rec. 21 Dec., Philadelphia.

Bride of the Waves (Clarke)
Cornet solo by Herbert L. Clarke. Victor #31077 10" ss; cond. H.L. Clarke; rec. 21 Dec., Philadelphia.

Bride of the Waves (Clarke)
Cornet solo by Herbert L. Clarke. Victor #62559 10" ds; rec. 21 Dec., Philadelphia.

El Capitan: March (Sousa)
Victor #304 10" ss; cond. H.L. Clarke; rec. 6 Dec., Philadelphia.

Carmen: Selections (Bizet)
Victor #35000 12" ds; cond. H.L. Clarke; rec. 16 Dec., Philadelphia.

Country Dance (Nevin)
Victor #2614 10" ss; cond. H.L. Clarke; rec. 13 Dec., Philadelphia.

Country Dance (Nevin)
Victor #31101 12" ss; cond. H.L. Clarke; rec. 13 Dec., Philadelphia.

Creole Bells (Lampe)
Victor #1182 7" ss; cond. H.L. Clarke; rec. 14 Dec., Philadelphia.

Creole Bells (Lampe)
Victor #1182 10" ss; cond. H.L. Clarke; rec. 14 Dec., Philadelphia.

Custer's Last Charge (Luders)
Victor #1192 10" ss; cond. H.L. Clarke; rec. 22 Dec., Philadelphia.

La Danseuse (Blon)
Victor #31085 12" ss; cond. H.L. Clarke; rec. 16 Dec., Philadelphia.

The Diplomat March (Sousa)
Victor #4180 10" ss; cond. H.L. Clarke; rec. 6 Dec., Philadelphia.

The Diplomat March (Sousa)
Victor #31334 12" ss; cond. H.L. Clarke; rec. 6 Dec., Philadelphia.

The Diplomat March (Sousa)
Victor #62473 10" ds; cond. H.L. Clarke; rec. 6 Dec., Philadelphia.

The Diplomat March (Sousa)
Victor 4180 10" ss; cond. H.L. Clarke; rec. 7 Dec., Philadelphia.

Faust Selections (Gounod)
Victor #31104 12" ss; cond. H.L. Clarke; rec. 20 Dec., Philadelphia.

Faust Selections (Gounod)
Victor 68159 12" ds; cond. H.L. Clarke; rec. 20 Dec., Philadelphia.

Favorite Songs of Canada
Victor #4453 10" ss; cond. H.L. Clarke; rec. 19 Dec., Philadelphia.

Der Freischutz: Overture (Weber)
Victor #35000 12" ds; cond. H.L. Clarke; rec. 21 Dec., Philadelphia.

Funeral March of a Marionette (Gounod)
Victor #31081 12" ss; cond. H.L. Clarke; rec. 16 Dec., Philadelphia.

The Harp That Once Thro' Tara's Halls (Rogers)
Cornet solo by Walter B. Rogers. Victor #2663 10" ss; cond. H.L. Clarke; rec. 14 Aug., Philadelphia.

The Harp That Once Thro' Tara's Halls
Trombone solo. Victor #31110 12" ss; recorded ca. 1904.

Hail to the Spirit of Liberty (Sousa)
Victor #365 10" ss; cond. H.L. Clarke; rec. 6 Dec., Philadelphia.

Hail to the Spirit of Liberty (Sousa)
Victor #365 10" ss; cond. Pryor; rec. 10 Dec., Philadelphia.

Hands Across the Sea (Sousa)
Victor #300 10" ss; cond. H.L. Clarke; rec. 6 Dec., Philadelphia.

Hearts and Flowers (Tobani)
Cornet solo by Herbert L. Clarke. Victor #1172 10" ss; rec. 8 Dec., Philadelphia.

Hearts and Flowers (Tobani)
Cornet solo by Herbert L. Clarke. Victor #62472 10" ss; rec. 8 Dec., Philadelphia.

Hiawatha (Moret)
Victor #2443 10" ss; cond. H.L. Clarke; rec. 19 Dec., Philadelphia.

Hiawatha (Moret)
Victor #31368 12" ss; cond. H.L. Clarke; rec. 19 Dec., Philadelphia.

High School Cadets (Sousa)
Victor #2442 10" ss; cond. H.L. Clarke; rec. 12 Dec., Philadelphia.

A Hot Time in the Old Town (Metz)
Victor #316 10" ss; cond. H.L. Clarke; rec. 7 Dec., Philadelphia.

A Hot Time in the Old Town (Metz)
Victor #316 10" ss; cond. H.L. Clarke; rec. 12 Dec., Philadelphia.

A Hot Time in the Old Town (Metz)
Victor #316 10" ss; cond. H.L. Clarke; rec. 12 Dec., Philadelphia.

Hungarian Rhapsody, No. 2 (Liszt)
Victor #2617 10" ss; cond. H.L. Clarke; rec. 16 Dec., Philadelphia.

Hungarian Rhapsody, No. 2 (Liszt)
Victor #31083 12" ss; cond. H.L. Clarke; rec. 16 Dec., Philadelphia.

Imperial Edward Coronation March (Sousa)
Victor #1418 10" ss; cond. H.L. Clarke; rec. 7 Dec., Philadelphia.

In the Realm of the Waltz (Sousa)
Victor #1438 10" ss; cond. H.L. Clarke; rec. 15 Dec., Philadelphia.

Invitation to the Dance (Weber)
Victor #31105 12" ss; cond. H.L. Clarke; rec. 13 Dec., Philadelphia.

Kaiser Overture (Westmeyer)
Victor #31082 12" ss; cond. H.L. Clarke; rec. 16 Dec., Philadelphia.

Kinloch O' Kinloch (Occa)
Victor #4266 10" ss; cond. H.L. Clarke; rec. 22 Dec., Philadelphia.

Kinloch O' Kinloch (Occa)
Victor #16090 10" ds; cond. H.L. Clarke; rec. 22 Dec., Philadelphia.

Kinloch O' Kinloch (Occa)
Victor #62584 10" ss; cond. H.L. Clarke; rec. 22 Dec., Philadelphia.

The Liberty Bell (Sousa)
Victor #1193 10" ss; cond. H.L. Clarke; rec. 7 Dec., Philadelphia.

Light Cavalry: Overture (Suppe)
Victor #31095 12" ss; cond. H.L. Clarke; rec. 13 Dec., Philadelphia.

Lucia di Lammermoor: Sextette (Donizetti)
Brass sextet. Victor #3230 10" ss; rec. 13 Dec., Philadelphia.

The Man Behind the Gun (Sousa)
Victor #307 10" ss; cond. H.L. Clarke; rec. 6 Dec., Philadelphia.

La Marsillaise (Rouget de l'isle)
Victor #4198 10" ss; cond. H.L. Clarke; rec. 14 Dec., Philadelphia.

Masaniello: Overture (Auber)
Victor #31361 12" ss; cond. H.L. Clarke; rec. 23 Dec., Philadelphia.

Minuet (Paderewski)
Victor #2460 10" ss; cond. H.L. Clarke; rec. 15 Dec., Philadelphia.

Minuet (Paderewski)
Victor #31120 12" ss; cond. H.L. Clarke; rec. 15 Dec., Philadelphia.

Minuet (Paderewski)
Victor #35152 12" ss; cond. H.L. Clarke; rec. 15 Dec., Philadelphia.

A Musical Joke on Bedelia (Schwartz/Bellstedt)
Victor #4181 10" ss; cond. H.L. Clarke; rec. 8 Dec., Philadelphia.

A Musical Joke on Bedelia (Schwartz/Bellstedt)
Victor #31335 12" ss; cond. H.L. Clarke; rec. 8 Dec., Philadelphia.

A Musical Joke on Bedelia (Schwartz/Bellstedt)
    Victor #4181 10" ss; cond. H.L. Clarke; rec. 14 Dec., Philadelphia.
National Air of Bohemia: War Song of the Hussites
    Victor #4223 10" ss; cond. H.L. Clarke; rec. 14 Dec., Philadelphia.
National Air of Bohemia: War Song of the Hussites
    Victor #62445 10" ss; cond. H.L. Clarke; rec. 14 Dec., Philadelphia.
La Paloma (Yradier)
    Victor #1190 7" ss; cond. H.L. Clarke; rec. 13 Dec., Philadelphia
La Paloma (Yradier)
    Victor #1190 10" ss; cond. H.L. Clarke; rec. 13 Dec., Philadelphia
Parsifal: Gralsritter March (Wagner)
    Victor #31103 12" ss; cond. H.L. Clarke; rec. 14 Dec., Philadelphia.
Patriotic Airs of Italy
    Victor #4199 10" ss; cond. H.L. Clarke; rec. 14 Dec., Philadelphia.
Patriotic Airs of Italy
    Victor #16136 10" ds; cond. H.L. Clarke; rec. 14 Dec., Philadelphia.
Patriotic Airs of Italy
    Victor #62455 10" ds; cond. H.L. Clarke; rec. 14 Dec., Philadelphia.
Patriotic Song of Poland (Sowinski)
    Victor #4222 10" ss; cond. H.L. Clarke; rec. 14 Dec., Philadelphia.
Patriotic Song of Poland (Sowinski)
    Victor #62500 10" ds; cond. H.L. Clarke; rec. 14 Dec., Philadelphia.
Patriotic Song of Wales: Men of Harlech
    Victor #4221 10" ss; cond. H.L. Clarke; rec. 14 Dec., Philadelphia.
Poet and Peasant Overture (Suppe)
    Victor #1552 10" ss; cond. H.L. Clarke; rec.15 Dec., Philadelphia.
Poet and Peasant Overture (Suppe)
    Victor #31354 12" ss; cond. H.L. Clarke; rec. 15 Dec., Philadelphia.
Pomp and Circumstance [Opus 39, No. 1] (Elgar)
    Victor #31351 12" ss; cond. H.L. Clarke; rec. 21 Dec., Philadelphia.
Ramona (Johnson)
    Victor #4218 10" ss; cond. H.L. Clarke; rec. 9 Dec., Philadelphia.
The Ranting Rube (Rosadye)
    Victor #1554 10" ss; cond. H.L .Clarke; rec. 22 Dec., Philadelphia.
Rienzi: Overture (R. Wagner)
    Victor #2612 10" ss; cond. H.L. Clarke; rec. 15 Dec., Philadelphia.
Rienzi: Overture (R. Wagner)
    Victor #31099 12" ss; cond. H.L. Clarke; rec. 15 Dec., Philadelphia.
Robespierre Overture (Litolff)
    Victor #31093 12" ss; cond. H.L. Clarke; rec. 13 Dec., Philadelphia.
The Rose, The Thistle and the Shamrock Patrol (Sousa)
    Victor #1194 10" ss; rec. 19 Aug., Philadelphia.
Semper Fidelis (Sousa)
    Victor #1175 10" ss; cond. H.L. Clarke; rec. 6 Dec., Philadelphia.
Semper Fidelis (Sousa)
    Victor #1175 7" ss; cond. H.L. Clarke; rec. 12 Dec., Philadelphia.
Semper Fidelis (Sousa)
    Victor #1175 10" ss; cond. H.L. Clarke; rec. 12 Dec., Philadelphia.
The Sho-Gun: Selections (Luders)
    Victor #4235 10" ss; cond. H.L. Clarke; rec. 23 Dec., Philadelphia.
The Skaters (Waldteufel)
    Victor #31097 12" ss; cond. H.L. Clarke; rec. 23 Dec., Philadelphia.
The Stars and Stripes Forever (Sousa)
    Victor #31102 12" ss; rec. 27 April, Philadelphia.
The Stars and Stripes Forever (Sousa)
    Victor #306 10" ss; cond. H.L. Clarke; rec. 6 Dec., Philadelphia.
The Stars and Stripes Forever (Sousa)
    Victor #31102 12" ss; cond. H.L. Clarke; rec. 6 Dec., Philadelphia.
Tambour Der Garde: Overture (Titl)
    Victor #31092 12" ss; cond. H.L. Clarke; rec. 15 Dec., Philadelphia.
Tancredi: Overture (Rossini)
    Victor #31369 12" ss; cond. H.L. Clarke; rec. 23 Dec., Philadelphia.
Il Trovatore: Miserere (Verdi)
    Cornet & trombone duet by Herbert L. Clarke & Leo Zimmerman.
    Victor #4006 10" ss; rec., 20 Dec., Philadelphia.
Under the Double Eagle (J.F. Wagner)
    Victor #31100 12" ss; cond. H.L. Clarke; rec. 19 Dec., Philadelphia.
The United Service Passing in Review (Reeni)
    Victor #1432 10" ss; cond. H.L. Clarke; rec. 21 Dec., Philadelphia.
The United Service Passing in Review (Reeni)
    Victor #31096 12" ss; cond. H.L. Clarke; rec. 21 Dec., Philadelphia.
Valse Bleue (Margis)
    Victor #1445 10" ss; cond. H.L .Clarke; rec. 8 Dec., Philadelphia.
Waltz and Mazurka (Chopin)
    Victor #317 10" ss; cond. H.L. Clarke; rec. 13 Dec., Philadelphia.

The Washington Post (Sousa)
    Victor #1183 7" ss; cond. H.L. Clarke; rec. 6 Dec., Philadelphia.
The Washington Post (Sousa)
    Victor #1183 10" ss; cond. H.L. Clarke; rec. 6 Dec., Philadelphia.
The Washington Post (Sousa)
    Victor #1183 10" ss; cond. H.L. Clarke; rec. 14 Dec., Philadelphia.
The Watch on the Rhine (Wilhelm)
    Victor #4196 10" ss; cond. H.L. Clarke; rec. 14 Dec., Philadelphia.
The Watch on the Rhine (Wilhelm)
    Victor #16138 10" ds; cond. H.L. Clarke; rec. 14 Dec., Philadelphia.
'Way Down South (Myddleton)
    Victor #1173 7" ss; cond. H.L. Clarke; rec. 7 Dec., Philadelphia.
Whistling Rufus (Mills)
    Victor #361 7" ss; cond. H.L. Clarke; rec. 12 Dec., Philadelphia.
Zampa: Overture (Herold)
    Victor #31350 12" ss; cond. H.L. Clarke; rec. 9 Dec., Philadelphia.
Zampa: Overture (Herold)
    Victor #363 10" ss; cond. H.L. Clarke; rec. 20 Dec., Philadelphia.
Zampa: Overture (Herold)
    Victor #31350 12" ss; cond. H.L. Clarke; rec. 20 Dec., Philadelphia.

1905

America
    Victor #4452 10" ss; cond. H.L. Clarke; rec. 12 June, Philadelphia.
America
    Victor #16137 10" ds; cond. H.L. Clarke; rec. 12 June, Philadelphia.
Amoureuse Waltz (Berger)
    Victor #4454 10" ss; cond. H.L. Clarke; rec. 12 June, Philadelphia.
Amoureuse Waltz (Berger)
    Victor #31572 12" ss; cond. H.L. Clarke; rec. 14 June, Philadelphia.
An Arkansaw Huskin' Bee (Pryor)
    Victor #314 8" ss; cond. H.L. Clarke; rec. 11 April, Philadelphia.
Blue Bell (T.F. Morse)
    Victor #4376 10" ss; cond. H.L. Clarke; rec. 12 June, Philadelphia.
The Blue Danube Waltz (J. Strauss, II)
    Victor #31450 12" ss; cond. H.L. Clarke; rec. 8 Sept., Philadelphia.
Breeze of the Night (Lamothe)
    Victor #31454 12" ss; cond. H.L. Clarke; rec. 8 Sept., Philadelphia.
Cavalleria Rusticana: Intermezzo (Mascagni)
    Victor #2461 10" ss; cond. H.L. Clarke; rec. 26 Oct., Philadelphia.
Creole Bells (Lampe)
    Victor #1182 10" ss; cond. H.L. Clarke; rec. 26 Oct., Philadelphia.
The Damnation of Faust: Minuet and Presto (Berlioz)
    Victor #4414 10" ss; cond. H.L. Clarke; rec. 15 June, Philadelphia.
The Damnation of Faust: Rakoczy March (Berlioz)
    Victor #31424 12" ss; cond. H.L. Clarke; rec. 15 June, Philadelphia.
The Darky and the Mule (Thurban)
    Victor #4540 10" ss; cond. H.L. Clarke; rec. 24 Oct., Philadelphia.
The Dying Poet (Gottschalk)
    Victor #31469 12" ss; cond. H.L. Clarke; rec. 27 Oct., Philadelphia.
The Dying Poet (Gottschalk)
    Victor #68075 12" ds; cond. H.L. Clarke; rec. 27 Oct., Philadelphia.
Faust Selections (Gounod)
    Victor #31104 12" ss; cond. H.L. Clarke; rec. 7 Sept., Philadelphia.
Favorite Songs of Canada
    Victor #4453 10" ss; cond. H.L. Clarke; rec. 12 June, Philadelphia.
Die Fledermaus: Selections (J. Strauss, II)
    Victor #31439 12" ss; cond. H.L. Clarke; rec. 14 June, Philadelphia.
Friendly Rivals (Godfrey)
    Cornet duet by Herbert L. Clarke & Herman Bellstedt. Victor #4423
    10" ss; rec. 16 June, Philadelphia.
Hapsburg March (Kral)
    Victor #4415 10" ss; cond. H.L. Clarke; rec. 12 June, Philadelphia.
Hapsburg March (Kral)
    Victor #62445 10" ds; cond. H.L. Clarke; rec. 12 June, Philadelphia.
Les Huguenots: Benediction of the Poignards (Meyerbeer)
    Victor #31574 12" ss; cond. H.L. Clarke; rec. 25 Oct., Philadelphia.
Hungarian Rhapsody, No. 2 (Liszt)
    Victor #31400 [Part I] 12" ss; cond. H.L. Clarke; rec. 14 June, Philadelphia.
Hungarian Rhapsody, No. 2 (Liszt)
    Victor #31401 [Part II] 12" ss; cond. H.L. Clarke; rec. 14 June, Philadelphia.

In the Good Old Summer Time (Evans)
Walter B. Rogers, cornet; unidentified, trombone; S.H. Dudley & Harry Macdonough, vocal. Victor #1833 7" ss; cond. H.L. Clarke; rec. 27 Oct., Philadelphia.
In the Good Old Summer Time (Evans)
Walter B. Rogers, cornet; unidentified, trombone; S.H. Dudley & Harry Macdonough, vocal. Victor #1833 10" ss; cond. H.L. Clarke; rec. 27 Oct., Philadelphia.
The Invincible Eagle (Sousa)
Victor #844 10" ss; cond. H.L. Clarke; rec. 23 Oct., Philadelphia.
Invitation to the Dance (Weber)
Victor #31105 12" ss; cond. H.L. Clarke; rec. 8 Sept., Philadelphia.
Jack Tar (Sousa)
Victor #2419 7" ss; cond. H.L. Clarke; rec. 9 Sept., Philadelphia.
Jack Tar (Sousa)
Victor #2419 10" ss; cond. H.L. Clarke; rec. 9 Sept., Philadelphia.
Jack Tar (Sousa)
Victor #2419 10" ss; cond. H.L. Clarke; rec. 26 Oct., Philadelphia.
Jack Tar (Sousa)
Victor #31051 12" ss; cond. H.L. Clarke; rec. 26 Oct., Philadelphia.
The Liberty Bell (Sousa)
Victor #1193 10" ss; cond. H.L. Clarke; rec. 26 Oct., Philadelphia.
Lohengrin: Selections (Wagner)
Victor #31425 12" ss; cond. H.L. Clarke; rec. 16 June, Philadelphia.
Lucia di Lammermoor: Sextet (Donizetti)
Brass sextet by Herbert L. Clarke, Henry Higgins, Arthur Pryor, Marcus Lyon, and two unidentified. Victor #3230 10" ss; rec. 8 Sept., Philadelphia.
The Man Behind the Gun (Sousa)
Victor #307 10" ss; cond. H.L. Clarke; rec. 25 Oct., Philadelphia.
Manhattan Beach (Sousa)
Victor #4565 10" ss; cond. H.L. Clarke; rec. 25 Oct., Philadelphia.
A Medley of Remick Hits (arr. Lampe)
Victor #31399 12" ss; cond. H.L. Clarke; rec. 13 June, Philadelphia.
A Medley of Remick Hits (Lampe)
Victor #4377 10" ss; cond. H.L. Clarke; rec. 15 June, Philadelphia.
A Medley of Remick Hits (Lampe)
Victor #31399 12" ss; cond. H.L. Clarke; rec. 15 June, Philadelphia.
Die Meistersinger: March (R. Wagner)
Victor #31427 12" ss; cond. H.L. Clarke; rec. 15 June, Philadelphia.
Die Meistersinger: March (R. Wagner)
Victor #35044 12" ss; cond. H.L. Clarke; rec. 15 June, Philadelphia.
Die Meistersinger: Prize Song (R. Wagner)
Victor #31440 12" ss; cond. H.L .Clarke; rec. 13 June, Philadelphia.
Die Meistersinger: Prize Song (R. Wagner)
Victor #35044 12" ss; cond. H.L .Clarke; rec. 13 June, Philadelphia.
Messiah: Hallelujah Chorus (Handel)
Victor #31770 12" ss; cond. H.L. Clarke; rec. 9 Sept., Philadelphia.
Moonlight Serenade (Moret)
Victor #4528 7" ss; cond. H.L. Clarke; rec. 23 Oct., Philadelphia.
Moonlight Serenade (Moret)
Victor #4528 10" ss; cond. H.L. Clarke; rec. 23 Oct., Philadelphia.
Narcissus (Nevin)
Victor #354 10" ss; cond. H.L. Clarke; rec. 13 June, Philadelphia.
Nightingale Polka (Mollenhauer)
Piccolo solo by Marshall P. Lufsky. Victor #4416 10" ss; cond. H.L. Clarke; rec. 15 June, Philadelphia.
Orpheus in the Underworld: Overture (Offenbach)
Victor #31447 12" ss; cond. H.L. Clarke; rec. 6 Sept., Philadelphia.
Orpheus in the Underworld: Overture (Offenbach)
Victor #31447 12" ss; cond. H.L. Clarke; rec. 8 Sept., Philadelphia.
The Pearl Fishers: Selections (Bizet)
Victor #31466 12" ss; cond. H.L. Clarke; rec. 27 Oct., Philadelphia.
The Pearl Fishers: Selections (Bizet)
Victor #35033 12" ss; cond. H.L. Clarke; rec. 27 Oct., Philadelphia.
The Pearl Fishers: Selections (Bizet)
Victor #68186 12" ss; cond. H.L. Clarke; rec. 27 Oct., Philadelphia.
Peter Piper (Henry)
Victor #4530 7" ss; cond. H.L. Clarke; rec. 24 Oct., Philadelphia.
The Queen of Sheba: March (Gounod)
Victor #31453 12" ss; cond. H.L. Clarke; rec. 9 Sept., Philadelphia.
The Queen of Sheba: March (Gounod)
Victor #68189 12" ss; cond. H.L. Clarke; rec. 9 Sept., Philadelphia.
Reminiscences of Tosti (arr. Fred Godfrey)
Victor #31448 12" ss; cond. H.L. Clarke; rec. 7 Sept., Philadelphia.

Reminiscences of Tosti (arr. Fred Godfrey)
Victor #31448 12" ss; cond. H.L. Clarke; rec. 9 Sept., Philadelphia.
Ruy Blas Overture (Mendelssohn)
Victor #31452 12" ss; cond. H.L. Clarke; rec. 8 Sept., Philadelphia.
Scenes Pittoresques: Angelus (Massenet)
Victor #31090 12" ss; cond. H.L. Clark; rec. 27 Oct., Philadelphia.
Silence and Fun (Mullen)
Victor #4538 10" ss; cond. H.L. Clarke; rec. 25 Oct., Philadelphia.
The Skaters (Waldteufel)
Victor #31097 12" ss; cond. H.L. Clarke; rec. 27 Oct., Philadelphia.
The Stars and Stripes Forever (Sousa)
Victor #306 10" ss; cond. H.L. Clarke; rec. 6 Sept., Philadelphia.
Tannhauser: Festival March (R. Wagner)
Victor #4512 10" ss; cond. H.L. Clarke; rec. Philadelphia.
Tannhauser: Festival March (R. Wagner)
Victor #31423 12" ss; cond. H.L. Clarke; rec. Philadelphia.
Tannhauser: Festival March (R. Wagner)
Victor #62655 12" ss; cond. H.L. Clarke; rec. Philadelphia.
The Three Solitaires (Herbert)
Cornet trio by Herbert L. Clarke, Walter B. Rogers, & Herman Bellstedt. Victor #4456 10" ss; rec., 16 June, Philadelphia.
The Three Solitaires (Herbert)
Cornet trio by Herbert L. Clarke, Walter B. Rogers, & Herman Bellstedt. Victor #16317 10" ds; rec., 16 June, Philadelphia.
The Three Solitaires (Herbert)
Cornet trio by Herbert L. Clarke, Walter B. Rogers, & Herman Bellstedt. Victor #62537 10" ds; rec., 16 June, Philadelphia.
The Troubadour (Powell)
Victor 4529 10" ss; cond. H.L. Clarke; rec. 23 Oct., Philadelphia.
The Turtle Dove (Damare)
Piccolo solo by Marshall P. Lufsky. Victor #4455 10" ss; cond. H.L. Clarke; rec. 15 June, Philadelphia.
Valse Bleue (Margis)
Victor #1445 10" ss; cond. H.L. Clarke; rec. 26 Oct., Philadelphia.
Valse Bleue (Margis)
Victor #16922 10" ds; cond. H.L. Clarke; rec. 26 Oct., Philadelphia.
Vienna Bon Bons (J. Strauss, II)
Victor #31449 12" ss; cond. H.L. Clarke; rec. 8 Sept., Philadelphia.
The Warbler's Serenade (Perry)
Whistling solo by Edward Wardwell. Victor #1168 10" ss; cond. H.L. Clarke; rec. 8 Sept., Philadelphia.
The Wee Macgregor (Amers)
Victor #4417 10" ss; cond. H.L. Clarke; rec. 16 June, Philadelphia.
Xerxes: Largo (Handel)
Victor #1440 10" ss; cond. H.L. Clarke; rec. 7 Sept., Philadelphia.
Xerxes: Largo (Handel)
Victor #1440 10" ss; cond. H.L. Clarke; rec. 26 Oct., Philadelphia.
Zampa: Overture (Herold)
Victor #31350 12" ss; cond. H.L. Clarke; rec. 7 Sept., Philadelphia.
Zampa: Overture (Herold)
Victor #363 10" ss; cond. H.L. Clarke; rec. 26 Oct., Philadelphia.

1906

El Alfidor (Corretjer)
Victor #3130 10" ss; cond. H.L.Clarke; rec. 4 Sept., Camden.
El Alfidor (Corretjer)
Victor #62609 10" ss; cond. H.L.Clarke; rec. 4 Sept., Camden.
America
Victor #4452 8" ss; cond. H.L. Clarke; rec. 11 April, Camden.
American Patrol (Meacham)
Victor #382 8" ss; cond. H.L. Clarke; rec. 10 April, Camden.
American Patrol (Meacham)
Victor #382 10" ss; cond. H.L. Clarke; rec. 10 April, Camden.
An Arkansaw Huskin' Bee (Pryor)
Victor #314 8" ss; cond. H.L. Clarke; rec. 11 April, Camden.
At a Georgia Camp Meeting (Mills)
Victor #315 8" ss; cond. H.L. Clarke; rec. 11 April, Camden.
Bamboula (Urich)
Victor #31622 12" ss; cond. H.L. Clarke; rec. 12 April, Camden.
Blue Danube Waltz (J. Strauss II)
Victor #343 10" ss; cond. H.L. Clarke; rec. 11 April, Camden.
Breeze of the Night (Lamothe)
Victor #5036 8" ss; cond. H.L. Clarke; rec. 13 April, Camden.

El Capitan: March (Sousa)
Victor #304 8" ss; cond. H.L. Clarke. rec. 9 April, Camden.
Cherry March (Albert)
Victor #4867 8" ss; cond. H.L. Clarke; rec. 7 Sept., Camden.
Cherry March (Albert)
Victor #4867 10" ss; cond. H.L. Clarke; rec. 7 Sept., Camden.
Cousins (Clarke)
Cornet and trombone duet by Herbert L. Clarke and Leo Zimmerman.
Victor #62564 10" ds; cond. H.L. Clarke; rec. 12 April, Camden.
Cousins (Clarke)
Cornet and trombone duet by Herbert L. Clarke and Leo Zimmerman.
Victor #4716 10" ss; cond. H.L. Clarke; rec. 13 April, Camden.
The Darky and the Mule (Thurban)
Victor #4540 8" ss; cond. H.L. Clarke; rec. 12 April, Camden.
The Dream of the Rarebit Fiend (Thurban)
Victor #4919 10" ss; cond. H.L. Clarke; rec. 7 Sept., Camden.
Everybody Works But Father (Hazen)
Victor #31536 12" ss; cond. H.L. Clarke; rec. 10 April, Camden.
The Flying Arrow Two-Step (Holzman)
Victor #4718 10" ss; cond. H.L. Clarke; rec. 10 April, Camden.
The Flying Arrow Two-Step (Holzman)
Victor #16091 10" ds; cond. H.L. Clarke; rec. 10 April, Camden.
The Free Lance (Sousa)
Victor #4699 10" ss; cond. H.L. Clarke; rec. 9 April, Camden.
The Free Lance (Sousa)
Victor #16383 10" ds; cond. H.L. Clarke; rec. 9 April, Camden.
The Free Lance (Sousa)
Victor #31528 12" ss; cond. H.L. Clarke; rec. 9 April, Camden,
The Free Lance (Sousa)
Victor #35163 12" ds; cond. H.L. Clarke; rec. 9 April, Camden.
The Free Lance (Sousa)
Victor #4699 8" ss; cond. H.L. Clarke; rec. 11 April, Camden.
The Gypsy Baron: My Treasure Waltz (J. Strauss, II)
Victor #31591 12" ss; cond. H.L. Clarke; rec. 13 April, Camden.
The Gypsy Baron: My Treasure Waltz (J. Strauss, II)
Victor #68104 12" ds; cond. H.L. Clarke; rec. 13 April, Camden.
Hail to the Spirit of Liberty (Sousa)
Victor #365 8" ss; cond. H.L. Clarke; rec. 12 April, Camden.
Hands Across the Sea (Sousa)
Victor #300 8" ss; cond. H.L. Clarke; rec. 4 Sept., Camden.
Hands Across the Sea (Sousa)
Victor #300 10" ss; cond. H.L. Clarke; rec. 10 April, Camden.
High School Cadets (Sousa)
Victor #2442 8" ss; cond. H.L. Clarke; rec. 4 Sept., Camden.
I Would That My Love (Mendelssohn)
Cornet duet by Herbert L. Clarke and Ross Millhouse. Victor #4717
10" ss; rec. 12 April, Camden.
I Would That My Love (Mendelssohn)
Cornet duet by Herbert L. Clarke and Ross Millhouse. Victor #62592
10" ds; rec. 12 April, Camden.
The Invincible Eagle (Sousa)
Victor #844 8" ss; cond. H.L. Clarke; rec. 12 April, Camden.
Iola (Johnson)
Victor #4862 8" ss; cond. H.L. Clarke; rec. 5 Sept., Camden.
Iola (Johnson)
Victor #4862 10" ss; cond. H.L. Clarke; rec. 5 Sept., Camden.
Lazo de Amor (Nipatra)
Victor #3195 10" ss; cond. H.L. Clarke; rec. 5 Sept., Camden.
Lazo de Amor (Nipatra)
Victor #62151 10" ds; cond. H.L. Clarke; rec. 5 Sept., Camden.
The Liberty Bell (Sousa)
Victor #1193 8" ss; cond. H.L. Clarke; rec. 9 April, Camden.
Lojos Del Bien Amado (Metallo)
Victor #3202 10" ss; cond. H.L. Clarke; rec. 5 Sept., Camden.
Lojos Del Bien Amado (Metallo)
Victor #62153 10" ds; cond. H.L. Clarke; rec. 5 Sept., Camden.
El Manevo (Lopez)
Victor #3197 10" ss; cond. H.L. Clarke; rec. 4 Sept., Camden.
El Manevo (Lopez)
Victor #65152 10" ds; cond. H.L. Clarke; rec. 4 Sept., Camden.
Mi Corazon Te Pertanece (Mantallo)
Victor #3199 10" ss; cond. H.L. Clarke; rec. 5 Sept., Camden.
Mi Corazon Te Pertanece (Mantallo)
Victor #62156 10" ds; cond. H.L. Clarke; rec. 5 Sept., Camden.

Moonlight Serenade (Moret)
Victor #4528 8" ss; cond. H.L. Clarke; rec. 11 April, Camden.
El Negro (Lopez)
Victor #3192 10" ss; cond. H.L. Clarke; rec. 5 Sept., Camden.
El Negro (Lopez)
Victor #62609 10" ds; cond. H.L. Clarke; rec. 5 Sept., Camden.
One of the Boys March (Bloom)
Victor #4704 8" ss; cond. H.L. Clarke; rec. 10 April, Camden.
One of the Boys March (Bloom)
Victor #4704 10" ss; cond. H.L. Clarke; rec. 10 April, Camden.
La Paloma (Yradier)
Victor #1190 8" ss; cond. H.L. Clarke; rec. 10 April, Camden.
Peter Piper (Henry)
Victor #4530 8" ss; cond. H.L. Clarke; rec. 12 April, Camden.
The Preacher and the Bear (Arzonia)
Victor #4981 10" ss; cond. H.L. Clarke; rec. 6 Sept., Camden.
Recuerdos de la Pampa (Bevilacqua)
Victor #3203 10" ss; cond. H.L. Clarke; rec. 7 Sept., Camden.
Recuerdos de la Pampa (Bevilacqua)
Victor #62175 10" ds; cond. H.L. Clarke; rec. 7 Sept., Camden.
Semper Fidelis (Sousa)
Victor #1175 8" ss; cond. H.L. Clarke; rec. 10 April, Camden.
Semper Fidelis (Sousa)
Victor #1175 10" ss; cond. H.L. Clarke; rec. 10 April, Camden.
A Shady Lane (Eugene)
Victor #5035 10" ss; cond. H.L. Clarke; rec. 5 Sept., Camden.
Siegfried Fantasy (R. Wagner)
Victor #31621 12" ss; cond. H.L. Clarke; rec. 13 April, Camden.
Siegfried Fantasy (R. Wagner)
Victor #68193 12" ds; cond. H.L. Clarke; rec. 13 April, Camden.
La Sorella (Gallini)
Victor #4744 10" ss; cond. H.L. Clarke; rec. 9 April, Camden.
The Stars and Stripes Forever (Sousa)
Victor #306 8" ss; cond. H.L. Clarke; rec. 9 April, Camden.
The Swiss Boy (de Ville)
Cornet duet by Herbert L. Clarke and Ross Millhouse. Victor #4753
10" ss; rec., 12 April, Camden.
The Thunderer (Sousa)
Victor #1437 8" ss; cond. H.L. Clarke; rec. 5 Sept., Camden.
The Washington Post (Sousa)
Victor #1183 8" ss; cond. H.L. Clarke; rec. 9 April, Camden.
The Whistlers (Reiterer)
Victor #4705 8" ss; cond. H.L. Clarke; rec. 12 April, Camden.
The Whistlers (Reiterer)
Victor #4705 10" ss; cond. H.L. Clarke; rec. 12 April, Camden.
Whistling Rufus (Mills)
Victor #361 8" ss; cond. H.L. Clarke; rec. 11 April, Camden.

1907
Army Bugle Calls
Victor #1303 10" ss; recorded by Sousa's cornets on 27 June,
Camden.
Army Bugle Calls
Victor #16056 10" ds; rec. by Sousa's Cornets on 27 June,
Camden.
Army Bugle Calls
Victor #31113 12" ss; rec. by Sousa's Cornets on 27 June,
Camden.
Army Bugle Calls
Victor #35056 12" ds; rec. by Sousa's Cornets on 27 June,
Camden.
Army Bugle Calls
Victor #62543 12" ds; rec. by Sousa's Cornets on 27 June,

1908
At a Georgia Camp Meeting (Mills)
Victor #16402 10" ds; cond. Rogers; rec. 23 Oct., Camden.
The Blue Danube Waltz (J. Strauss, II)
Victor #31450 12" ss; cond. Rogers; rec. 20 Oct., Camden.
The Blue Danube Waltz (J. Strauss, II)
Victor #31450 12" ss; cond. Rogers; rec. 22 Oct., Camden.
The Blue Danube Waltz (J. Strauss, II)
Victor #68075 12" ds; cond. Rogers; rec. 22 Oct., Camden.

Bride of the Waves (Clarke)
Cornet solo by Herbert L. Clarke. Victor #16194 10" ds; cond. Rogers; rec. 21 Oct., Camden.
Bride of the Waves (Clarke)
Cornet solo by Herbert L. Clarke. Victor #62559 10" ds; cond. Rogers; rec. 21 Oct., Camden.
A Bunch of Mischief Polka (Chapi)
Victor #5665 10" ss; cond. Rogers; rec. 22 Oct., Camden.
A Bunch of Mischief Polka (Chapi)
Victor #16420 10" ds; cond. Rogers; rec. 22 Oct., Camden.
A Bunch of Mischief Polka (Chapi)
Victor #62610 10" ds; cond. Rogers; rec. 22 Oct., Camden.
El Capitan: March (Sousa)
Victor #17302 10" ds; cond. Rogers; rec. 23 Oct., Camden.
El Capitan: March (Sousa)
Victor #35052 12" ds; cond. Rogers; rec. 23 Oct., Camden.
El Capitan: March (Sousa)
Victor #62493 10" ds; cond. Rogers; rec. 23 Oct., Camden.
Caprice Brilliante (Clarke)
Cornet solo by Herbert L. Clarke. Victor #31721 12" ss; cond. Rogers; rec. 21 Oct., Camden.
Caprice Brilliante (Clarke)
Cornet solo by Herbert L. Clarke. Victor #35090 12" ss; cond. Rogers; rec. 21 Oct., Camden.
Caprice Brilliante (Clarke)
Cornet solo by Herbert L. Clarke. Victor #68250 12" ds; cond. Rogers; rec. 21 Oct., Camden.
Fairest of the Fair (Sousa)
Victor #5621 10" ss; cond. Roger; rec. 21 Oct., Camden.
Fairest of the Fair (Sousa)
Victor #16777 10" ds; cond. Rogers; rec. 21 Oct., Camden.
Fairest of the Fair (Sousa)
Victor #62741 10" ds; cond. Rogers; rec. 21 Oct., Camden.
Hands Across the Sea (Sousa)
Victor #16190 10" ds; cond. Rogers; rec. 22 Oct., Camden.
High School Cadets (Sousa)
Victor #2442 10" ss; cond. Rogers; rec. 23 Oct., Camden.
High School Cadets (Sousa)
Victor #16200 10" ds; cond. Rogers; rec. 23 Oct., Camden.
The Invincible Eagle (Sousa)
Victor #844 10" ss; cond. Rogers; rec. 21 Oct., Camden.
The Invincible Eagle (Sousa)
Victor #16273 10" ds; cond. Rogers; rec. 21 Oct., Camden.
Iola (Johnson)
Victor #4862 10" ss; cond. Rogers; rec. 22 Oct., Camden.
Iola (Johnson)
Victor #16776 10" ds; cond. Rogers; rec. 22 Oct., Camden.
Iola (Johnson)
Victor #62484 10" ds; cond. Rogers; rec. 22 Oct., Camden.
Jack Tar (Sousa)
Victor #2419 10" ss; cond. Rogers; rec. 21 Oct., Camden.
Jack Tar (Sousa)
Victor #16151 10" ds; cond. Rogers; rec. 21 Oct., Camden.
The Liberty Bell (Sousa)
Victor #1193 10" ss; cond. Rogers; rec. 22 Oct., Camden.
The Liberty Bell (Sousa)
Victor #62446 10" ds; cond. Rogers; rec. 22 Oct., Camden.
Light Cavalry: Overture (Suppe)
Victor #35045 12" ds; cond. Rogers; rec. 20 Oct., Camden.
Light Cavalry: Overture (Suppe)
Victor #68088 12" ds; cond. Rogers; rec. 20 Oct., Camden.
The Man Behind the Gun (Sousa)
Victor #16395 10" ds; cond. Rogers; rec. 21 Oct., Camden.
Manhattan Beach (Sousa)
Victor #4565 10" ss; cond. Rogers; rec. 22 Oct., Camden.
Manhattan Beach (Sousa)
Victor #16383 10" ds; cond. Rogers; rec. 22 Oct., Camden.
Manhattan Beach (Sousa)
Victor #62492 10" ds; cond. Rogers; rec. 22 Oct., Camden.
Die Meistersinger: March (R. Wagner)
Victor #35044 12" ds; cond. H.L. Clarke; rec. 23 Oct., Philadelphia.
Die Meistersinger: March (R. Wagner)
Victor #68180 12" ds; cond. H.L. Clarke; rec. 23 Oct., Philadelphia.

Die Meistersinger: Prize Song (R. Wagner)
Victor #35044 12" ds; cond. Rogers; rec. 23 Oct., Philadelphia.
Die Meistersinger: Prize Song (R. Wagner)
Victor #68180 12" ds; cond. Rogers; rec. 23 Oct., Philadelphia.
La Paloma (Yradier)
Victor #1190 10" ss; cond. Rogers; rec. 20 Oct., Camden.
La Paloma (Yradier)
Victor #16529 10" ds; cond. Rogers; rec. 20 Oct., Camden.
La Paloma (Yradier)
Victor #31727 12" ss; cond. Rogers; rec. 20 Oct., Camden.
La Paloma (Yradier)
Victor #62499 10" ds; cond. Rogers; rec. 20 Oct., Camden.
The Rose of Shiras: Rose Waltzes (Eilenberg)
Victor #31726 12" ss; cond. Rogers; rec. 23 Oct., Camden.
The Rose of Shiras: Rose Waltzes (Eilenberg)
Victor #35152 12" ds; cond. Rogers; rec. 23 Oct., Camden.
The Rose of Shiras: Rose Waltzes (Eilenberg)
Victor #68100 12" ds; cond. Rogers; rec. 23 Oct., Camden.
The Rose of Shiras: Rose Waltzes (Eilenberg)
Victor #68103 12" ds; cond. Rogers; rec. 23 Oct., Camden.
Semper Fidelis (Sousa)
Victor #16190 10" ds; cond. Rogers; rec. 21 Oct., Camden.
Sleepy Sidney (Scheu)
Victor #16278 10" ds; cond. Rogers; rec. 21 Oct., Camden.
The Stars and Stripes Forever (Sousa)
Victor #35286 12" ds; cond. Rogers; rec. 22 Oct., Camden.
The Stars and Stripes Forever (Sousa)
Victor #35709 12" ds; cond. Rogers; rec. 22 Oct., Camden.
The Stars and Stripes Forever (Sousa)
Victor #75361 12" ds; cond. Rogers; rec. 22 Oct., Camden.
The Stars and Stripes Forever (Sousa)
Victor #306 10" ss; cond. Rogers; rec. 23 Oct., Camden.
The Stars and Stripes Forever (Sousa)
Victor #16777 10" ds; cond. Rogers; rec. 23 Oct., Camden.
The Stars and Stripes Forever (Sousa)
Victor #31102 12" ss; cond. Rogers; rec. 22 Oct., Camden.
The Thunderer (Sousa)
Victor #16151 10" ds; cond. Rogers; rec. 21 Oct., Camden.
Under the Double Eagle (J.F. Wagner)
Victor #5639 10" ss; cond. Rogers; rec. 20 Oct., Camden.
Under the Double Eagle (J.F. Wagner)
Victor #16960 10" ds; cond. Rogers; rec. 20 Oct., Camden.
Under the Double Eagle (J.F. Wagner)
Victor #31100 12" ss; cond. Rogers; rec. 20 Oct., Camden.
Under the Double Eagle (J.F. Wagner)
Victor #35286 12" ds; cond. Rogers; rec. 20 Oct., Camden.
Under the Double Eagle (J.F. Wagner)
Victor #62444 10" ds; cond. Rogers; rec. 20 Oct., Camden.
Under the Double Eagle (J.F. Wagner)
Victor #72488 10" ds; cond. Rogers; rec. 20 Oct., Camden.
Venus on Earth (Licke)
Victor #31722 12" ss; cond. Rogers; rec. 22 Oct., Camden.
Venus on Earth (Licke)
Victor #31564 12" ds; cond. Rogers; rec. 22 Oct., Camden.
Venus on Earth (Licke)
Victor #68103 12" ds; cond. Rogers; rec. 22 Oct., Camden.

1909

American Patrol (Meacham)
Victor #16523 10" ds; cond. Rogers; rec. 28 Dec., Camden.
Amina (Lincke)
Victor #31771 12" ss; cond. Rogers; rec. 31 Dec., Camden.
Amina (Lincke)
Victor #68202 12" ss; cond. Rogers; rec. 31 Dec., Camden.
Amoureuse Waltz (Berger)
Victor #4454 10" ss; cond. Rogers; rec. 31 Dec., Camden.
Amoureuse Waltz (Berger)
Victor #17228 10" ds; cond. Rogers; rec. 31 Dec., Camden.
Amoureuse Waltz (Berger)
Victor #62446 10" ds; cond. Rogers; rec. 31 Dec., Camden.
Autumn Voices (Lincke)
Victor #16468 10" ds; cond. Rogers; rec. 28 Dec., Camden.
Bachelor's Button (Powell)
Edison #10379 2" cyl; cond. H.L. Clarke; rec. 7 Aug., New York.

El Capitan: March (Sousa) and Manhattan Beach (Sousa)
Edison #319 2" cyl. (4 min.); cond; H.L. Clarke; rec. 7 Aug., New York.

El Capitan: March (Sousa) and Manhattan Beach (Sousa)
Edison #1711 2" cyl. (4 min.); cond. H.L. Clarke; rec. 7 Aug., New York.

The Damnation of Faust: Rakoczy March (Berlioz)
Victor #68052 12" ds; cond. Rogers; rec. 30 Dec., Camden.

Dixieland (Haines)
Edison #10335 2" cyl; cond. H.L. Clarke; rec. 7 Aug., New York.

Florentiner March (Fucik)
Victor #5764 10" ss; cond. Rogers; rec. 28 Dec., Camden.

Florentiner March (Fucik)
Victor #62483 10" ds; cond. Rogers; rec. 28 Dec., Camden.

The Gladiator (Sousa) and The Thunderer (Sousa)
Edison #404 2" cyl. (4 min.); cond. H.L. Clarke; rec. 7 Aug., New York.

Glory of the Yankee Navy (Sousa)
Victor #5818 10" ss; cond. Rogers; rec. 30 Dec., Camden.

Glory of the Yankee Navy (Sousa)
Victor #17229 10" ds; cond. Rogers; rec. 30 Dec., Camden.

La Gipsy (Ganne)
Edison #413 2" cyl. (4 min.); cond. H.L. Clarke; rec. 7 Aug., New York.

La Gispy (Ganne)
Edison #5390 2" cyl. (4 min.); cond. H.L. Clarke; rec. 7 Aug., New York.

High School Cadets (Sousa) and The Washington Post (Sousa)
Edison #325 2" cyl. (4 min.); cond. H.L. Clarke; rec. 7 Aug., New York.

High School Cadets (Sousa) and The Washington Post (Sousa)
Edison #5301 2" cyl. (4 min.); cond. H.L. Clarke; rec. 7 Aug., New York.

Les Huguenots: Benediction of the Poignards (Meyerbeer)
Edison #350 2" cyl. (4 min); rec. 7 Aug., New York.

Les Huguenots: Benediction of the Poignards (Meyerbeer)
Victor #31574 12" ss; cond. Rogers; rec. 30 Dec., Camden.

Les Huguenots: Benediction of the Poignards (Meyerbeer)
Victor #35118 12" ds; cond. Rogers; rec. 30 Dec., Camden.

Les Huguenots: Benediction of the Poignards (Meyerbeer)
Victor #68055 12" ds; cond. Rogers; rec. 30 Dec., Camden.

Kukushka (Lehar)
Edison #474 2" cyl. (4 min.); rec. H.L. Clarke; rec. ca. Dec., New York.

La Lettre de Manon (Gillet)
Edison #10317 2" cyl; cond. H.L. Clarke; rec. 7 Aug., New York.

Lohengrin: Selections (Wagner)
Victor #35114 12" ds; cond. Rogers; rec. 30 Dec., Camden.

Lohengrin: Selections (Wagner)
Victor #68175 12" ds; cond. Rogers; rec. 30 Dec., Camden.

Maidens Three: The Dancing Girl (Sousa)
Edison #10300 2" cyl; rec. 7 Aug., New York.

Maidens Three: The Summer Girl (Sousa)
Edison #10277 2" cyl; rec. 7 Aug., New York.

La Marseillaise (Rouget de l'Isle)
Victor #16514 10" ds; cond. Rogers; rec. 30 Dec., Camden.

La Marseillaise (Rouget de l'Isle)
Victor #17668 10" ds; cond. Rogers; rec. 30 Dec., Camden.

La Marseillaise (Rouget de l'Isle)
Victor #63500 10" ds; cond. Rogers; rec. 30 Dec., Camden.

March Tartare (Ganne)
Edison #540 2" cyl; (4 min) cond. H.L. Clarke; rec. ca. Dec., New York.

Messiah: Hallelujah Chorus (Handel)
With Victor Chorus. Victor #31770 12" ss; cond. Rogers; rec. 29 Dec., Camden.

Mondaine (Bosc)
Edison #10387 2" cyl; cond. H.L. Clarke; rec. ca. Dec., New York.

Morgenblaetter Waltz (J. Strauss, II)
Edison #452 2" cyl. (4 min.); cond. H.L. Clarke; rec. 7 Aug., New York.

Narcissus (Nevin)
Edison #10350 2" cyl; rec. 7 Aug., New York.

Narcissus (Nevin)
Victor #16525 10" ds; cond. Rogers; rec. 27 Dec., Philadelphia.

Narcissus (Nevin)
Victor #62496 10" ds; cond. Rogers; rec. 27 Dec., Philadelphia.

Once Upon a Time (Lincke)
Cornet solo by Herbert L. Clarke. Victor #16447 10" ds; cond. Rogers; rec. 29 Dec., Camden.

Once Upon a Time (Lincke)
Cornet solo by Herbert L. Clarke. Victor #62588 10" ds; cond. Rogers; rec. 29 Dec., Camden.

Poet and Peasant Overture (Suppe)
Victor #31354 12" ss; cond. Rogers; rec. 30 Dec., Camden.

Poet and Peasant Overture (Suppe)
Victor #35287 12" ds; cond. Rogers; rec. 31 Dec., Camden.

Poet and Peasant Overture (Suppe)
Victor #68188 12" ds; cond. Rogers; rec. 31 Dec., Camden.

Powhatan's Daughter (Sousa)
Edison #10237 2" cyl; rec. 7 Aug., New York.

Rose of Shiras: Rose Waltzes (Eilenberg)
Edison #365 2" cyl. (4 min.); cond. H.L. Clarke; rec. 7 Aug., New York.

Saludo Militar Marcha (Sciutti)
Victor #62437 10" ds; cond. Rogers; rec. 30 Dec., Camden.

San Lorenzo (Silva)
Victor #62437 10" ds; cond. Rogers; rec. 30 Dec., Camden.

San Lorenzo (Silva)
Victor #72376 10" ds; cond. Rogers; rec. 30 Dec., Camden.

Siamese Patrol (Lincke)
Victor #5766 10" ss; cond. Rogers; rec. 28 Dec., Camden.

Siamese Patrol (Lincke)
Victor #62483 10" ds; cond. Rogers; rec. 28 Dec., Camden.

The Skaters (Waldteufel)
Victor #35119 12" ds; cond. Rogers; rec. 30 Dec., Camden.

Slavonic Rhapsody (Friedmann)
Edison #463 2" cyl. (4 min.); cond. H.L. Clarke; rec. ca. Dec., New York.

Slavonic Rhapsody (Friedmann)
Edison #5363 2" cyl. (4 min.); rec. ca. Dec., New York.

Slavonic Rhapsody (Friedmann)
Victor #35099 12" ds; cond. Rogers; rec. 28 Dec., Camden.

Slavonic Rhapsody (Friedmann)
Victor #68097 12" ds; cond. Rogers; rec. 28 Dec., Camden.

Softly, Unawares (Lincke)
Edison #580 2" cyl. (4 min.); rec. ca. Dec., New York.

Softly, Unawares (Lincke)
Edison #5272 2" cyl. (4 min.); rec. ca. Dec., New York.

La Sorella (Gallini)
Victor #16523 10" ds; cond. Rogers; rec. 27 Dec., Camden.

La Sorella (Gallini)
Victor #62488 10" ds; cond. Rogers; rec. 27 Dec., Camden.

Sounds from the Hudson (Clarke)
Cornet solo by Herbert L. Clarke. Victor #16679 10" ds; cond. Rogers; rec. 3 Feb., Camden.

Sounds from the Hudson (Clarke)
Cornet solo by Herbert L. Clarke. Victor #62590 10" ds; cond. Rogers; rec. 3 Feb., Camden.

The Stars and Stripes Forever (Sousa)
Edison #285 2" cyl. (4 min.); rec. 7 Aug., New York.

The Stars and Stripes Forever (Sousa)
Edison #2104 2" cyl. (4 min.); rec. 7 Aug., New York.

Tannhauser: Festival March (R. Wagner)
Victor #16514 10" ds; cond. Rogers; rec. 30 Dec., Camden.

Tannhauser: Festival March (R. Wagner)
Victor #62653 10" ds; cond. Rogers; rec. 30 Dec., Camden.

Unrequited Love (Lincke)
Victor #35101 12" ds; cond. Rogers; rec. 29 Dec., Camden.

Unrequited Love (Lincke)
Victor #68230 12" ds; cond. Rogers; rec. 29 Dec., Camden.

Xerxes: Largo (Handel)
Victor #16525 10" ds; cond. Rogers; rec. 30 Dec., Camden.

Yankee Shuffle (Moreland)
Edison #10272 2" cyl. (4 min.); rec. 7 Aug., New York.

1910

Corcoran Cadets (Sousa)
Edison #10466 2" cyl; cond. H.L. Clarke; rec. ca. Aug., New York.

Dwellers in the Western World: I. Red Man (Sousa)
Edison #779 2" cyl. (4 min.); cond. H.L. Clarke; rec. ca. Aug., New York.

Dwellers in the Western World: I. Red Man (Sousa)
Edison #5222 2" cyl. (4 min.); rec. ca. Aug., New York.

Dwellers in the Western World: I. Red Man (Sousa)
Victor #35185 12" ds; cond. E.G. Clarke; rec. 20 Dec., New York.

Dwellers in the Western World: II. White Man (Sousa)
Edison #807 2" cyl. (4 min.); rec. ca. Aug., New York.

Dwellers in the Western World: II. White Man (Sousa)
Edison #5242 2" cyl. (4 min.); rec. ca. Aug., New York.

Dwellers in the Western World: III. Black Man (Sousa)
Edison #839 2" cyl. (4 min.); rec. ca. Aug., New York.

Dwellers in the Western World: III. Black Man (Sousa)
Edison #5256 2" cyl. (4 min.); rec. ca. Aug., New York.

Elfentanz Valse (Lehar)
Edison #656 2" cyl. (4 min.); cond. H.L. Clarke; rec. ca. Aug., New York.

Elfentanz Valse (Lehar)
Edison #5332 2" cyl. (4 min.); cond. H.L. Clarke; rec. ca. Aug., New York.

The Federal March (Sousa)
Victor #5824 10" ss; cond. E.G. Clarke; rec. 20 Dec., New York.

The Federal March (Sousa)
Victor #63270 10" ss; cond. E.G. Clarke; rec. 20 Dec., New York.

Florentiner March (Fucik)
Edison #10546 2" cyl; cond. H.L. Clarke; rec. ca. Aug., New York.

Glory of Yankee Navy (Sousa)
Edison #740 2" cyl. (4 min.); cond. H.L. Clarke; rec. ca. Aug., New York.

Glory of Yankee Navy (Sousa)
Edison #5211 2" cyl. (4 min.); cond. H.L. Clarke; rec. ca. Aug., New York.

Glory of the Yankee Navy (Sousa)
Victor #17229 10" ds; cond. E.G. Clarke; rec. 20 Dec., New York.

Has Anybody Here Seen Kelly? (Letters)
Edison #935 2" cyl. (4 min.); cond. H.L. Clarke; rec. ca. Aug., New York.

Hobomoko (Reeves)
Edison #10476 2" cyl; cond. H.L. Clarke; rec. ca. Aug., New York.

The Jolly Fellows Waltz (Vollstedt)
Edison #636 2" cyl. (4 min); cond. H.L. Clarke; rec. ca. Aug., New York.

The Jolly Fellows Waltz (Vollstedt)
Edison #1878 2" cyl. (4 min.); cond. H.L. Clarke; rec. ca. Aug., New York.

Lion Chase (Kolling)
Edison #10511 2" cyl; cond. H.L. Clarke; rec. ca. Aug., New York.

Tannhauser: Festival March (R. Wagner)
Victor #31423 12" ss; cond. E.G. Clarke; rec. 20 Dec., Camden.

Three Quotations: I. King of France (Sousa)
Edison #679 2" cyl (4 min.); rec. ca. Aug., New York.

Three Quotations: I. King of France (Sousa)
Edison #5441 2" cyl. (4 min.); rec. ca. Aug., New York.

Three Quotations: II. I Too Was Born in Arcadia (Sousa)
Edison #739 2" cyl. (4 min.); rec. ca. Aug., New York.

Three Quotations: II. I Too Was Born in Arcadia (Sousa)
Edison #5474 2" cyl. (4 min.); rec. ca. Aug., New York.

Three Quotations: III. In Darkest Africa (Sousa)
Edison #889 2" cyl. (4 min.); cond. H.L. Clarke; rec. ca. Aug., New York.

Three Quotations: III. In Darkest Africa (Sousa)
Edison #5507 2" cyl. (4 min.); cond. H.L. Clarke; rec. ca. Aug., New York.

The United Service Passing in Review
Edison #2644 2" cyl. (4 min.); cond. H.L. Clarke; rec. ca. Aug., New York.

1911

Aloha Oe (Queen Liliuokalani)
Herbert L. Clarke, cornet soloist. Victor #17035 10" ds; cond. E.G. Clarke; rec. 14 Dec., Camden.

America
Victor #16137 10" ds; cond. E.G. Clarke; rec. 12 Dec., Camden.

Amoureuse Waltz (Berger)
Victor #31572 12" ss; cond. E.G. Clarke; rec. 12 Dec., Camden.

Amoureuse Waltz (Berger)
Victor #68108 12" ds; cond. E.G. Clarke; rec. 12 Dec., Camden.

Carmen: Selections (Bizet)
Victor #35000 12" ds; cond. E.G. Clarke; rec. 13 Dec., Camden.

Carmen: Selections (Bizet)
Victor #68146 12" ds; cond. E.G. Clarke; rec. 13 Dec., Camden.

Celebre Jamacueca (Niemeyer)
Victor #63581 10" ds; cond. E.G. Clarke; rec. 14 Dec., Camden.

Count of Luxembourg: Waltz (Lehar)
Victor #63582 12" ds; cond. E.G. Clarke; rec. 14 Dec., Camden.

Creole Belles (Lampe)
Victor #17252 10" ds; cond. E.G. Clarke; rec. 13 Dec., Camden.

Custer's Last Charge (Luders)
Victor #1192 10" ss; cond. E.G. Clarke; rec. 12 Dec., Camden.

Danza Elida (Cavalli)
Victor #63581 10" ds; cond. E.G. Clarke; rec. 14 Dec., Camden.

The Dollar Princess: Waltz (Fall)
Victor #63582 10" ds; cond. E.G. Clarke; rec. 14 Dec., Camden.

The Dollar Princess: Waltz (Fall)
Victor #98685 10" ds; cond. E.G. Clarke; rec. 14 Dec., Camden.

Faust Selections (Gounod)
Victor #31104 12" ss; cond. E.G. Clarke; rec. 12 Dec., Camden.

Die Fledermaus: Selections (J. Strauss, II)
Victor #31439 12" ss; cond. E.G. Clarke; rec. 13 Dec., Camden.

Die Fledermaus: Selections (J. Strauss, II)
Victor #68159 12" ss; cond. E.G. Clarke; rec. 13 Dec., Camden.

Die Fledermaus: Selections (J. Strauss, II)
Victor #68158 12" ds; cond. E.G. Clarke; rec. 13 Dec., Camden.

Funeral March of a Marionette (Gounod)
Victor #31081 12" ss; cond. E.G. Clarke; rec. 14 Dec., Camden.

Funeral March of a Marionette (Gounod)
Victor #68101 12" ds; cond. E.G. Clarke; rec. 14 Dec., Camden.

Invitation to the Dance (Weber)
Victor #31105 12" ss; cond. E.G. Clarke; rec. 13 Dec., Camden.

Invitation to the Dance (Weber)
Victor #68100 12" ds; cond. E.G. Clarke; rec. 13 Dec., Camden.

Minuet (Paderewski)
Victor #2460 10" ss; cond. E.G. Clarke; rec. 13 Dec., Camden.

Minuet (Paderewski)
Victor #35152 12" ds; cond. E.G. Clarke; rec. 13 Dec., Camden.

Tancredi: Overture (Rossini)
Victor #31369 12" ss; cond. E.G. Clarke; rec. 13 Dec., Camden.

Tancredi: Overture (Rossini)
Victor #35287 12" ds; cond. E.G. Clarke; rec. 13 Dec., Camden.

Tancredi: Overture (Rossini)
Victor #68195 12" ds; cond. E.G. Clarke; rec. 13 Dec., Camden.

Valse Bleue (Margis)
Victor #16922 10" ds; cond. E.G. Clarke; rec. 13 Dec., Camden.

Valse Bleue (Margis)
Victor #62493 10" ds; cond. E.G. Clarke; rec. 13 Dec., Camden.

The Watch on the Rhine (Wilhelm)
Victor #17669 10" ds; cond. E.G. Clarke; rec. 12 Dec., Camden.

The Watch on the Rhine (Wilhelm)
Victor #62457 10" ds; cond. E.G. Clarke; rec. 12 Dec., Camden.

Woodland Sketches: From and Indian Lodge (MacDowell)
Victor 17035 10" ds; cond. E.G. Clarke; rec. 13 Dec., Camden.

Zampa: Overture (Herold)
Victor #31350 12" ss; cond. E.G. Clarke; rec. 12 Dec., Camden.

Zampa: Overture (Herold)
Victor #68195 12" ds; cond. E.G. Clarke; rec. 12 Dec., Camden.

1912

The Ben Hur Chariot Race March (Paull)
Victor #17110 10" ds; cond. Pryor; rec. 16 May, Camden.

The Ben Hur Chariot Race March (Paull)
Victor #63866 10" ds; cond. Pryor; rec. 16 May, Camden.

The Blue Danube Waltz (J. Strauss, II)
Victor #31450 12" ss; cond. Pryor; rec. 17 May, Camden.

The Blue Danube Waltz (J. Strauss, II)
Victor #35289 12" ds; cond. Pryor; rec. 17 May, Camden.

The Blue Danube Waltz (J. Strauss, II)
Victor #68075 12" ds; cond. Pryor; rec. 17 May, Camden.

Canadian Medley March, No. 1
Victor #17304 10" ds; cond. Pryor; rec. 12 Dec., Camden.
Chant Du Rossignol (Fillipovsky)
Piccolo solo by Clement Barone. Victor #17134 10" ds; cond. Pryor; rec. 16 May, Camden.
Chant Du Rossignol (Fillipovsky)
Piccolo solo by Clement Barone. Victor #63961 10" ds; cond. Pryor; rec. 16 May, Camden.
Chimes of Normandy: Selections (Planquette)
Victor #31180 12" ss; cond. Pryor; rec. 13 May, Camden.
Chimes of Normandy: Selections (Planquette)
Victor #35134 12" ds; cond. Pryor; rec. 13 May, Camden.
Chimes of Normandy: Selections (Planquette)
Victor #68114 12" ds; cond. Pryor; rec. 13 May, Camden.
Creole Bells (Lampe)
Victor #17252 10" ds; cond. Pryor; rec. 13 Dec., Camden.
Don Carlos: Grand March (Verdi)
Victor #17133 10" ds; cond. Pryor; rec. 14 May, Camden.
Don Carlos: Grand March (Verdi)
Victor #63960 10" ds; cond. Pryor; rec. 14 May, Camden.
Duke Street (Hattan)
Victor #17258 10" ds; cond. Pryor; rec. 13 Dec., Camden.
The Dying Poet (Gottschalk)
Victor #35467 12" ds; cond. Pryor; rec. 14 May, Camden.
The Dying Poet (Gottschalk)
Victor #68075 12" ds; cond. Pryor; rec. 14 May, Camden.
Der Freischutz: Overture (Weber)
Victor #35000 12" ds; cond. Pryor; rec. 14 May, Camden.
Der Freischutz: Overture (Weber)
Victor #68146 12" ds; cond. Pryor; rec. 14 May, Camden.
The Four Dance
Victor #17329 10" ds; cond. Pryor; rec. 11 Dec., Camden.
The Free Lance: March (Sousa)
Victor #16383 10: ds; cond. Pryor; rec. 12 Dec., Camden
Golden Trumpets (Rollinson)
Victor #35228 12" ds; cond. Pryor; rec. 14 May, Camden.
Golden Trumpets (Rollinson)
Victor #68349 12" ds; cond. Pryor; rec. 14 May, Camden.
Gustaf's Skal
Victor #17330 10" ds; cond. Pryor; rec. 11 Dec., Camden.
Hansel and Gretel: Selections (Humperdinck)
Victor #17103 10" ds; cond. Pryor; rec. 14 May, Camden.
Hiawatha (Moret)
Victor #17252 10" ds; cond. Pryor; rec. 13 Dec., Camden.
Hiawatha (Moret)
Victor #62443 10" ds; cond. Pryor; rec. 13 Dec., Camden.
A Hot Time in the Old Town (Metz)
Victor #316 10" ss; cond. Pryor; rec. 17 May, Camden.
In the Spring (Duyckinck)
Victor #17103 10" ds; cond. Pryor; rec. 14 May, Camden.
Indian War Dance (Bellstedt)
Victor #324 10" ds; cond. Pryor; rec. 18 June, Camden.
The Joker (Lake)
Victor #17125 10" ds; cond. Pryor; rec. 15 May, Camden.
Kull-Dansen
Victor #17330 10" ds; cond. Pryor; rec. 11 Dec., Camden.
Light Cavalry: Overture (Suppe)
Victor #35045 12" ds; cond. Pryor; rec. 11 Dec., Camden.
Light Cavalry: Overture (Suppe)
Victor #68088 12" ds; cond. Pryor; rec. 11 Dec., Camden.
London Bridge and the Mulberry Bush
Victor #17104 10" ds; cond. Pryor; rec. 14 May, Camden.
My Maryland March (Mygrant)
Victor #17142 10" ds; cond. Pryor; rec. 13 May, Camden.
Nigarepolska
Victor #17327 10" ds; cond. Pryor; rec. 11 Dec., Camden.
On the Mississippi - Medley
Victor #17249 10" ds; cond. Pryor; rec. 10 Dec., Camden.
Over the Waves (Rosas)
Victor #35068 12" ds; cond. Pryor; rec. 15 May, Camden.
Over the Waves (Rosas)
Victor #68105 12" ds; cond. Pryor; rec. 15 May, Camden.
The Prince of Pilsen: Selections (Luders)
Victor #16527 10" ds; cond. Pryor; rec. 16 May., Camden.
The Prince of Pilsen: Selections (Luders)

Victor #16919 10" ds; cond. Pryor; rec. 16 May., Camden.
Reminiscences of Verdi (arr. Fred Godfrey)
Victor #35230 12" ds; cond. Pryor; rec. 13 May, Camden.
Reminiscences of Verdi (arr. Fred Godfrey)
Victor #68348 12" ds; cond. Pryor; rec. 13 May, Camden.
Ribbon Dance
Victor #17329 10" ds; cond. Pryor; rec. 11 Dec., Camden.
Round and Round the Village
Victor #17104 10" ds; cond. Pryor; rec. 14 May, Camden.
Royal Arcanum: Opening Ode - Rock of Ages (Hastings)
Victor #17123-A 10" ds; cond. Pryor; rec. 17 May, Camden.
Royal Arcanum: Closing Mode
Victor #17123-B 10" ds; cond. Pryor; rec. 17 May, Camden.
Sardina March (Gabetti)
Victor #17162 10" ds; cond. Pryor; rec. 13 May, Camden.
Sardinia March (Gabetti)
Victor #63953 10" ds; cond. Pryor; rec. 13 May, Camden.
Semper Fidelis March (Sousa)
Victor #16190 10" ds; cond. Pryor; rec. 13 May, Camden.
Seventh Regiment March (Neyer)
Victor #17162 10" ds; cond. Pryor; rec. 17 May, Camden.
Seventh Regiment March (Neyer)
Victor #63953 10" ds; cond. Pryor; rec. 17 May, Camden.
The Skaters (Mullen)
Victor #35119 12" ds; cond. Pryor; rec. 17 May, Camden.
The Skaters (Mullen)
Victor #68101 12" ds; cond. Pryor; rec. 17 May, Camden.
The Stars and Stripes Forever (Sousa)
Victor #16777 10" ds; cond. Pryor; rec. 13 Dec., Camden.
Tannhauser: Festival March (R. Wagner)
Victor #31423 12" ds; cond. Pryor; rec. 11 Dec., Camden.
Tannhauser: Festival March (R. Wagner)
Victor #68068 12" ds; cond. Pryor; rec. 11 Dec., Camden.
The Washington Post (Sousa)
Victor #17302 10" ds; cond. Pryor; rec. 13 Dec., Camden.
The Washington Post (Sousa)
Victor #62467 10" ds; cond. Pryor; rec. 13 Dec., Camden.
Xerxes: Largo (Handel)
Victor #16525 10" ds; cond. Pryor; rec. 13 Dec., Camden.
You're My Baby – Medley
Victor #17249 10" ds; cond. Pryor; rec. 10 Dec., Camden.

1915

Chinese Blues - Medley
Victor #35514 12" ds; cond. H.L. Clarke; rec. 19 Nov., Camden.
The Gliding Girl (Sousa)
Victor #17976 10" ds; cond. H.L. Clarke; rec. 9 Nov., New York.
The Lambs March (Sousa)
Victor #17976 10" ds; cond. H.L. Clarke; rec. 9 Nov., New York.
The New York Hippodrome (Sousa)
Victor #17901 10" ds; cond. H.L. Clarke; rec. 9 Nov., New York.
The New York Hippodrome (Sousa)
Victor #17901 10" ds; cond. H.L. Clarke; rec. 19 Nov., New York.
The Pathfinder of Panama (Sousa)
Victor #17901 10" ds; cond. H.L. Clarke; rec. 9 Nov., New York.
The Pathfinder of Panama (Sousa)
Victor #17901 10" ds; cond. H.L. Clarke; rec. 19 Nov., New York.

1917

Liberty Loan (Sousa)
Victor #18430 10" ds; cond. John Philip Sousa; rec. 21 Dec., Camden.
The U.S. Field Artillery (Sousa)
Victor #18430 10" ds; cond. John Philip Sousa; rec. 21 Dec., Camden.

1918

Sabre and Spurs (Sousa)
Victor #18504 10" ds; cond. John Philip Sousa; rec. 6 Sept., Camden.
Solid Men to the Front (Sousa)
Victor #18504 10" ds; cond. John Philip Sousa; rec. 6 Sept., Camden.
Wedding March (Sousa)
Victor #35683 12" ds; cond. Pryor; rec. 13 Dec., Camden.

1919

Bullets and Bayonets (Sousa)
Victor #18752 10" ds; cond. Pasternack; rec. 2 Oct., Camden.
The Darky and the Mule (Thurban)
Victor #16139 10" ds; cond. Bourdon; rec. 10 March, Camden.
Golden Star March (Sousa)
Victor #35709 12" ds; cond. Pasternack; rec. 2 Oct., Camden.
Ituzaingo
Victor #72405 10" ds; cond. Bourdon; rec. 6 March, Camden.
National Hymn of Argentina (Conradi)
Victor #72405 10" ds; cond. Bourdon; rec. 6 March, Camden.
National Hymn of Argentina (Conradi)
Victor #72405 10" ds; cond. Guillermo Gonzales; rec. 8 Aug., Camden.
La Pericon Por Maria (Podesta)
Victor #72376 10" ds; cond. Bourdon; rec. 5 April, Camden.
San Lorenzo (Silva)
Victor #72376 10" ds; cond. Bourdon; rec. 6 March, Camden.
San Lorenzo (Silva)
Victor #72376 10" ds; cond. Bourdon; rec. 5 April, Camden.

1920

Comrades of the Legion (Sousa)
Victor #18683 10" ds; cond. Pasternack; rec. 10 June, Camden.
Fairest of the Fair (Sousa)
Victor #16777 10" ds; cond. Pasternack; rec. 9 Nov., Camden.
Who's Who in the Navy (Sousa)
Victor #18683 10" ds; cond. Pasternack; rec. 10 June, Camden.

1921

The Free Lance (Sousa)
Victor #16383 10" ds; cond. Pasternack; rec. 24 May, Camden.
On the Campus (Sousa)
Victor #18752 10" ds; cond. Pasternack; rec. 5 April, Camden.

1922

The Gallant Seventh (Sousa)
Victor #18929 10" ds; cond. Pasternack; rec. 20 July, Camden.
Keeping Step With the Union (Sousa)
Victor #18929 10" ds; cond. Pasternack; rec. 20 July, Camden.

1923

The Dauntless Battalion (Sousa)
Victor #19056 10" ds; cond. John Philip Sousa; rec. 29 March, New York.
The Free Lance: March (Sousa)
Victor #16383 10" ds; cond. Shilkret; rec. 20 July, New York.
The Free Lance: March (Sousa)
Victor #62492 10" ds; cond. Shilkret; rec. 20 July, New York.
Hands Across the Sea (Sousa)
Victor #16190 10" ds; cond. Shilkret; rec. 10 April, New York.
Hands Across the Sea (Sousa)
Victor #73823 10" ds; cond. Shilkret; rec. 10 April, New York.
Hands Across the Sea (Sousa)
Victor #73912 10" ds; cond. Shilkret; rec. 10 April, New York.
High School Cadets (Sousa)
Victor #19064 10" ds; cond. Shilkret; rec. 16 Jan., New York.
The Invincible Eagle (Sousa)
Victor #16273 10" ds; cond. Shilkret; rec. 20 July, New York.
Jack Tar (Sousa)
Victor #16151 10" ds; cond. Shilkret; rec. 16 Jan., New York.
Manhattan Beach (Sousa)
Victor #16383 10" ds; cond. Shilkret; rec. 20 July, New York.
Nobles of the Mystic Shrine (Sousa)
Victor #19056 10" ds; cond. John Philip Sousa; rec. 29 March, New York.
La Paloma (Yradier)
Victor #16529 10" ds; cond. Pryor; rec. 2 Nov., Camden.
Semper Fidelis (Sousa)
Victor #16190 10" ds; cond. Shilkret; rec. 14 Nov., New York.
The Thunderer (Sousa)
Victor #16151 10" ds; cond. Shilkret; rec. 23 April, Camden.
The Thunderer (Sousa)
Victor #16151 10" ds; cond. Shilkret; rec. 2 Nov., Camden.

Under the Double Eagle (J.F. Wagner)
Victor #19064 10" ds; cond. Shilkret; rec. 10 April, New York.
Under the Double Eagle (J.F. Wagner)
Victor #73912 10" ds; cond. Shilkret; rec. 10 April, New York.
Under the Double Eagle (J.F. Wagner)
Victor #73823 10" ds; cond. Shilkret; rec. 10 April, New York.
The Washington Post (Sousa)
Victor #17302 10" ds; cond. Shilkret; rec. 2 Nov., Camden.
The Washington Post (Sousa)
Victor #62467 10" ds; cond. Shilkret; rec. 2 Nov., Camden.

1924

The Ancient and Honorable Artillery Company (Sousa)
Victor #19400 10" ds; cond. Shilkret; rec. 19 June, New York.
El Capitan: March (Sousa)
Victor #17302 10" ds; cond. Shilkret; rec. 19 June, New York.
El Capitan: March (Sousa)
Victor #62493 10" ds; cond. Shilkret; rec. 19 June, New York.
The Chantyman's March (Sousa)
Victor #19400 10" ds; cond. Shilkret; rec. 14 May, New York.
Fairest of the Fair (Sousa)
Victor #16777 10" ds; cond. Shilkret; rec. 14 May, New York.

1925

The Black Horse Troop (Sousa)
Victor #19741 10" ds; cond. Pasternack; rec. 24 July, Camden.
High School Cadets (Sousa)
Victor #19871 10" ds; cond. Shilkret; rec. 22 Oct., Camden.
The National Game (Sousa)
Victor #19741 10" ds; cond. Pasternack; rec. 24 July, Camden.
Under the Double Eagle (J.F. Wagner)
Victor #19871 10" ds; cond. Shilkret; rec. 22 Oct., Camden.

1926

El Capitan: March (Sousa)
Victor #20191 10" ds; cond. Pryor; rec. 15 June, Camden.
Fairest of the Fair (Sousa)
Victor #20132 10" ds; cond. Pryor; rec. 28 May, Camden.
The Gridiron Club (Sousa)
Victor #20276 10" ds; cond. Pryor; rec. 13 May, Camden.
The Pride of the Wolverines (Sousa)
Victor #20276 10" ds; cond. Pryor; rec. 5 Oct., Camden.
Sabre and Spurs (Sousa)
Victor #20305 10" ds; cond. Pryor; rec. 6 Oct., Camden.
The Sesquicentennial Exposition March (Sousa)
Victor #20054 10" ds; cond. Pryor; rec. 13 May., Camden.
Solid Men to the Front (Sousa)
Victor #20305 10" ds; cond. Pryor; rec. 5 Oct., Camden.
The Stars and Stripes Forever (Sousa)
Victor #20132 10" ds; cond. Pryor; rec. 28 May, Camden.
The Washington Post (Sousa)
Victor #20191 10" ds; cond. Pryor; rec. 28 May, Camden.

1929

Golden Jubilee March (Sousa)
Victor #22020 10" ds; cond. Bourdon; rec. 28 May, Camden.
The Riders of the Flag (Sousa)
Victor #22020 10" ds; cond. Bourdon; rec. 28 May, Camden.

1930

Hands Across the Sea (Sousa)
Victor #22940 10" ds; cond. Bourdon; rec. 1 July, Camden.
The Royal Welch Fusiliers (Sousa)
Victor #22940 10" ds; cond. Bourdon; rec. 1 July, Camden.

Bibliography

BOOKS

ASCAP Biographical Dictionary. Fourth ed. New York: R. R. Bowker, 1980.

Baker's Biographical Dictionary of Musicians, Fifth Edition with 1965 Supplement. New York: G. Schirmer, 1958.

Barnouw, Erik. *A Tower in Babel: The History of Broadcasting in the United States to 1933.* New York: Oxford University Press, 1966.

Berger, Kenneth. *Band Encyclopedia.* Evansville: Band Associates, 1960.

———. *Bandmen.* Biloxi: Clark D. Shaughnessy Press, 1955.

———. *The March King and His Band: The Story of John Philip Sousa.* New York: Exposition Press, 1957.

Bierley, Paul E. *John Philip Sousa, American Phenomenon.* Rev. ed. Miami: Warner Brothers Publications, 2001.

———. *Sousa Band Fraternal Society News Index.* Westerville, Ohio: Integrity Press, 1998.

———. *The Works of John Philip Sousa.* Westerville, Ohio: Integrity Press, 1984.

———. and Suzuki, Kozo. *All about Sousa Marches.* Tokyo: Ongaku No Toma Shaw, 2001.

Blain, Virginia, Patricia Clements, and Isobel Grundy, eds. *The Feminist Companion to Literature in English: Women Writers from the Middle Ages to the Present.* New Haven: Yale University Press, 1990.

Bordman, Gerald. *The Oxford Companion to American Theatre.* New York: Oxford University Press, 1984.

Bridges, Glenn D. *Pioneers in Brass.* Detroit: Sherwood Publications, 1965.

Burford, Cary Clive. *We're Loyal to You, Illinois.* Urbana: Self-published, 1952.

Charles, Henry. *The Grand Opera Singers of Today.* Boston: Page, 1912.

Charosh, Paul. *Berliner Gramophone Records, American Issues, 1892–1900.* Westport: Greenwood Press, 1995.

Clarke, Herbert L. *How I Became a Cornetist.* Kenosha: Leblanc Educational Publications, n.d.

Cook, Rob, comp. *Leedy Drum Topics Complete from 1923 to 1941.* Anaheim Hills: Cedarcreek Publishing, 1993.

Cross, Milton. *Complete Stories of the Great Operas.* Garden City: Doubleday, 1947.

Dearborn, L. E., ed. *Appleton's Cyclopaedia of American Biography: A Supplement, 1918–1931.* New York: Press Association Compilers, 1961.

Delaplaine, Edward S. *John Philip Sousa and the National Anthem.* Frederick: Great Southern Press, 1983.

Dunlop, Orrin E., Jr. *The Story of Radio.* New York: Dial Press, 1935.

Ewen, David. *All the Years of American Popular Music.* Inglewood Cliffs: Prentice-Hall, 1977.

———. *Encyclopedia of Concert Music.* New York: Hill and Wang, 1959.

———. *The New Encyclopedia of the Opera.* New York: Hill and Wang, 1971.

———. *Panorama of American Popular Music.* Englewood Cliffs: Prentice-Hall, 1957.

Fagan, Ted, and William R. Moran. *The Encyclopedic Discography of Victor Recordings.* Westport: Greenwood Press, 1983.

———. *The Encyclopedic Discography of Victor Recordings, Matrix Series: 1 through 4999.* Westport: Greenwood Press, 1986.

Freedland, Michael. *Music Man: The Story of Frank Simon.* Ilford, Essex, Eng.: Vallentine Mitchell, 1994.

Garraty, John A., and Mark C. Carnes, eds. *American National Biography.* New York: Oxford University Press, 1999.

Graham, Alberta Powell. *Great Bands of America.* New York: Thomas Nelson and Sons, 1951.

Green, Stanley. *Encyclopedia of the Musical Theatre.* New York: Dodd, Mead, 1976.

Hamilton, David, ed. *The Metropolitan Opera Encyclopedia.* New York: Simon and Schuster, 1987.

Hazen, Margaret Hindle, and Robert M. Hazen. *The Music Men.* Washington: Smithsonian Institution Press, 1987.

Heslip, Malcolm. *Nostalgic Happenings in the Three Bands of John Philip Sousa.* Westerville: Integrity Press, 1982.

Hitchcock, Wiley, and Stanley Sadie, eds. *The New Grove Dictionary of American Music.* London: Macmillan, 1986.

———, eds. *The New Grove Dictionary of Opera.* New York: Macmillan, 1986.

Hopper, DeWolf. *Reminiscences of DeWolf Hopper: Once a Clown Always a Clown.* Garden City: Garden City Publishing, 1927.

Ireland, Norma Olin. *Index to Women of the World from Ancient to Modern Times.* Westwood: F. W. Faxon, 1970.

Kinnell, Susan K. *People in History.* Santa Barbara: ABC-Clio, 1988.

Lake, Mayhew Lester. *Great Guys.* Grosse Pointe Woods: Bovaco Press, 1983.

Leonard, John William, ed. *Woman's Who's Who of America.* New York: American Commonwealth, 1914.

Levy, Felice, comp. *Obituaries on File.* New York: Facts on File, 1979.

Lingg, Ann M. *John Philip Sousa.* New York: Henry Holt, 1954.

Luper, Loren J. *Arthur Pryor.* Santa Barbara: Kimberly Press, 1987.

McCoy, Guy. *Portraits of the World's Best-Known Musicians.* Philadelphia: Theodore Presser, 1946.

———. *Portraits of the World's Best Women Musicians.* Philadelphia: Theodore Presser, 1946.

Midgley, Ned. *The Advertising Business Side of Radio.* Englewood Cliffs: Prentice-Hall, 1948.

Mitziga, Walter, comp. *The Sound of Sousa: John Philip Sousa Compositions Recorded.* Chicago: South Shore Printers, 1986.

The National Cyclopaedia of American Biography. New York: James T. White, 1926.

Newsom, John, ed. *Perspectives on John Philip Sousa.* Washington: Library of Congress, 1983.

Notable Names in the American Theatre. Clifton: James T. White, 1976.

Pratt, Waldo Selden, ed. *The New Encyclopedia of Music and Musicians.* New York: Macmillan, 1924.

Ragan, David. *Who's Who in Hollywood, 1900–1976.* New Rochelle: Arlington House, 1976.

Rehrig, William H. *The Heritage Encyclopedia of Band Music,* edited by Paul E. Bierley. Westerville: Integrity Press, 1991.

———. *Supplement* (vol. 3) to *The Heritage Encyclopedia of Band Music,* edited by Paul E. Bierley. Westerville: Integrity Press, 1996.

Rigdon, Walter, ed. *The Biographical Encyclopedia and Who's Who of the American Theatre.* New York: James H. Heineman, 1966.

Rust, Brian. *The American Record Label Book.* New York: DaCapo Press, 1978.

Sadie, Stanley, ed. *The New Grove Dictionary of Music and Musicians.* New York: Macmillan, 1980.

Saied, James G. *A Rag Merchant's Son.* Tulsa: Self-published, 1997.

Schwartz, Harry W. *Bands of America.* Garden City: Doubleday, 1957.

Seltsam, William, ed. *Metropolitan Opera Annals: A Chronicle of Artists and Performances.* New York: H. W. Wilson, in association with the Metropolitan Opera Guild, 1947.

Seymour-Smith, Martin, and Andrew C. Kimmens, eds. *Women Authors, 1900–1950.* New York: H. W. Wilson, 1996.

Shaffer, Karen A., and Neva Garner Greenwood. *Maud Powell: Pioneer American Violinist.* Ames: Iowa State University Press, 1988.

Slide, Anthony. *Encyclopedia of Vaudeville.* Westport: Greenwood Press, 1994.

Smart, James R., comp. *The Sousa Band: A Discography.* Washington: Library of Congress, 1970.

Sousa, John Philip. *Marching Along.* Rev. ed. Westerville: Integrity Press, 1994.

Summers, Harrison B. *A Thirty-Year History of Programs Carried on National Radio Networks in the United States, 1926–1956.* Columbus: Ohio State University, 1958.

Truitt, Evelyn Mack. *Who Was Who on Screen.* New York: R. R. Bowker, 1983.

Uglow, Jennifer S., ed. *The Continuum Dictionary of Woman's Biography.* New York, Continuum Publishing, 1989.

Waters, Edward N. *Victor Herbert: A Life of Music.* New York: Macmillan, 1955.

Who Is Who in South Dakota. Pittsburgh: University of Pittsburgh Press, 1951.

Who Was Who in America. Wilmette: Marquis Who's Who, 1976.

Who's Who of American Women. Wilmette: Marquis Who's Who, various years.

Who's Who in Entertainment. Wilmette: Marquis Who's Who, 1992.

Willson, Meredith. *And There I Stood with My Piccolo.* Garden City: Doubleday, 1948.

Zilboorg, Caroline, ed. *Women's Firsts.* Detroit: Gale Research, 1997.

Zimmerman, Oscar G., and George Murphy. *Once More . . . from the Beginning.* Self-published, 1993.

DISSERTATIONS AND THESES

Bly, Leon J. "The March in American Society." Ph.D. diss., University of Miami, 1977.

Church, Charles Fremont. "The Life and Influence of John Philip Sousa." Ph.D. diss., Ohio State University, 1942.

Frizane, Daniel E. "Arthur Pryor (1870–1942) American Trombonist, Bandmaster, Composer." Ph.D. diss., University of Kansas, 1984.

Hester, Michael E. "A Study of the Saxophone Soloists Performing with the John Philip Sousa Band: 1893–1930." Ph.D. diss., University of Arizona, 1995.

Madeja, James T. "The Life and Work of Herbert L. Clarke (1867–1945)." Ph.D. diss., University of Illinois, 1988.

Ullery, Victoria L. "Frank Simon: History and Influence." Honors paper, Wright State University, 1984.

Warfield, Patrick. "Salesman of Americanism, Globetrotter, and Musician: The Nineteenth-Century John Philip Sousa, 1854–1893." Ph.D. diss., Indiana University, 2003.

DIARIES AND DAYBOOKS

[Holt, Frank.] "The Drummer." Diary of 1928 tour, edited by George L. Stone, in *Jacobs' Band Monthly,* May, June, July, Aug. 1929.

Knecht, Albert A. Daybook. Scattered entries from 1900–1914. Unpublished.

———. World Tour Diary, 1911. Unpublished. Copy in the Paul E. Bierley Papers, the Sousa Archives and Center for American Music, University of Illinois at Urbana-Champaign.

Morris, Louis. Daybook. Scattered entries, 1914, 1915, 1919.

Russell, Clarence. J. Daybook, Sept. 27, 1911–Sept. 9, 1917. Published as "Around the World with Sousa." *Musical America,* Feb. 4–Nov. 8, 1911. Copy also in the Paul E. Bierley Papers, the Sousa Archives and Center for American Music, University of Illinois at Urbana-Champaign.

———. World Tour Diary, Dec. 24, 1910–Sept. 27, 1911. Unpublished.

PERIODICALS AND NEWSPAPERS

The Etude, various issues, 1898–1933; *The Instrumentalist,* various issues, 1960–2003; *Jacobs' Band Monthly,* various issues, 1915–41; *J. W. Pepper Musical Times and Band Journal,* various issues, 1893–98; *Metronome,* various issues, 1892–1930; *Musical Courier,* various issues, 1915; *Musical Messenger,* various issues, 1912–24; *Musical Truth,* various issues, 1892–1935; *New York Clipper,* various issues, 1892–1900; *New York Commercial Tribune,* radio logs in various issues, 1929–32; *New York Dramatic Mirror,* various issues, 1892–1910; *Sousa Band Fraternal Society News,* all issues, 1949–90; *Variety,* obituaries in various issues, 1919–61.

ARTICLES

Bierley, Paul E. "Sousa's Mystery March." *The Instrumentalist* (Feb. 1966): 55.

———. "That Curious Sousa Voice Tape." *Journal of Band Research* (Fall 1986): 45.

———. "Why Are Sousa's Marches Still So Popular?" *Grand Band Companion,* Nov. 6, 1999, 3.

Clarke, Herbert L. "A World's Tour with Sousa." *Musical Messenger,* July 1918–May 1919.

Cohen, Donna L. "The Attractions of Willow Grove Park." *Old York Road Historical Society Bulletin* 56 (1996).

Hunsberger, Donald. "Defining the Wind Band Sound." *Wind Works* (Spring 2001).

Johnston, Herbert N. "Along the Old York Road with John Philip Sousa." *Old York Road Historical Society Bulletin* 56 (1996).

Peterson, A. O. "The Human Side of Sousa." *Musical Messenger,* May 1916, 3–4.

Radio Digest. Nov. 1931.

Rehrig, William H. "Around the World with Sousa." *Grand Band Companion* [Virginia Grand Military Band], Nov. 6, 1999, 5.

———. "John Philip Sousa, Some Notes on His Leisure Activities." *Grand Band Companion,* Dec. 2, 2000.

———. "A Lost March, a Derailment, and Bronchitis." *Grand Band Companion,* Feb. 14, 1999.

Smiley, Anita R. "Memories of Willow Grove Park." *Old York Road Historical Society Bulletin* 56 (1996).

"Sousa's Band." *Musical Messenger,* Dec. 1920, 1.

Walsh, James. "Favorite Pioneer Recording Artists: Estella Louise Mann." *Hobbies* (April 1952): 24–27.

Williams, Frederick P. "The Willow Grove Park Concerts, 1896–1925." *Old York Road Historical Society Bulletin* 56 (1996).

Zanine, Louis J. "Willow Grove in 1895–1896: Trolley Car and Park Transform a Community." *Old York Road Historical Society Bulletin* 56 (1996).

COLLECTIONS

Allentown (Pa.) Band Archives. Photographs, programs, historical documents, music.

Barry Owen Furrer Collection. Bound Brook, N.J. Autographs, photographs, programs, manuscripts, music, paintings, memorabilia.

Clyde Hall Collection. U.S. Marine Band, Washington, D.C. Music, clippings, photographs, correspondence.

David Blakely Collection. New York Public Library. Financial papers, correspondence, programs, memorabilia.

George Ford Collection. U.S. Marine Band, Washington, D.C. Photographs, clippings, route sheets, correspondence.

George Foreman Collection. Danville, Ky. Sherley Thompson Collection as well as photographs, sheet music, and band memorabilia.

Harold B. Stephens Collection. U.S. Marine Band, Washington, D.C. Career scrapbooks.

Herbert L. Clarke Music and Personal Papers. The Sousa Archives and Center for American Music, University of Illinois at Urbana-Champaign. Music, photographs, recordings, programs, clippings.

John J. Heney Collection. U.S. Marine Band, Washington, D.C. Programs, clippings, route sheets, correspondence, photographs.

Joseph De Luca Career Scrapbook. University of Arizona Music Department. Clippings, photographs, programs.

Kenneth Berger Collection. University of Minnesota School of Music, Minneapolis. Correspondence between Kenneth Berger and former Sousa Band musicians.

Library of Congress Music Division Collections. Manuscripts, music, correspondence, Sousa Band music library (partial), photographs, *Sousa Band Fraternal Society News,* memorabilia.

Owen Kincaid Collection. Youngstown State University. Photographs, programs, clippings, route sheets, correspondence.

Paul E. Bierley Papers. Sousa Archives and Center for American Music, University of Illinois at Urbana-Champaign. Photographs, programs, music, rosters, files of band personnel, files of Sousa music, correspondence, notes on interviews, route sheets, *Sousa Band Fraternal Society News,* timelines, log of Sousa activities, databases, memorabilia.

Rudolph Becker Collection. U.S. Marine Band, Washington, D.C. Photographs, music, clippings, programs, correspondence, other memorabilia.

Sousa Archives and Center for American Music, University of Illinois at Urbana-Champaign. Herbert L. Clarke Music and Personal Papers, Paul E. Bierley Papers, and Virginia Root Collection as well as Sousa Band music library (majority), manuscripts, photographs, correspondence, and memorabilia.

U.S. Marine Band/Sousa Collection, Washington, D.C. Sousa Band press books, Sousa Band music library (partial), photographs, financial records, correspondence, uniforms, *Sousa Band Fraternal Society News,* memorabilia.

Virginia Root Collection. Sousa Archives and Center for American Music, University of Illinois at Urbana-Champaign. Vocal music, programs, clippings, photographs, memorabilia.

RECORDINGS

The Complete Marches of John Philip Sousa. Detroit Concert Band. Leonard B. Smith, conductor. Walking Frog Records WFR 300 (five compact discs; the same recordings as *Sousa American Bicentennial Collection*).

The Heritage of John Philip Sousa. U.S. Marine Band. Jack T. Kline, conductor. Privately produced by Robert Hoe (eighteen LPs).

John Philip Sousa at the Symphony. Razumovsky Symphony Orchestra. Keith Brion, conductor. Naxos 8.559013 (compact discs).

John Philip Sousa Music for Wind Band. Vols. 1– . Royal Artillery Band. Keith Brion, conductor. Naxos 8.559058– (compact discs).

Marching along with John Philip Sousa. New Sousa Band, Rochester Philharmonic Orchestra. Keith Brion, conductor. Bainbridge BCD 6250 (compact disc).

On Wings of Lightning. Razumovsky Symphony Orchestra. Keith Brion, conductor. Naxos 8.559029 (compact disc).

The Original All-American Sousa! New Sousa Band. Keith Brion, conductor. Delos DE 3102 (compact disc).

Semper Fidelis. U.S. Marine Band. John R. Bourgeois, conductor. U.S. Marine Band issue (compact disc).

Sousa. Air Combat Command Heritage of the American Band, Langley Air Force Base. Lowell E. Graham, conductor. U.S. Air Force issue (compact disc).

Sousa American Bicentennial Collection. Detroit Concert Band. Leonard B. Smith, conductor. H&L Records (ten LPs; also boxed set by Book-of-the-Month Club Records).

Sousa Marches Original Complete Works. Ground Self-Defense Force First Band. Masahiro Yoshinaga, conductor. Crown CRCI-35025–35034 (ten compact discs; 135 marches recorded chronologically.)

Sousa Marches as Played by the Sousa Band. Various conductors, including Sousa. Crystal Records CD461–3 (three compact discs).

Stars and Stripes and Sousa! Washington Winds. Keith Brion, conductor. Walking Frog Records WFR 137 (compact disc).

MISCELLANEOUS

Kraushaar, Otto J. No title. Unpublished autobiography, ca. 1975.

Lest We Forget. All-time membership history of American Bandmasters Association, issued periodically.

Levy, Lester S. Autograph book. Autographs of twenty-six Sousa Band musicians. Dated Nov. 1895. Dallas, Tex.

Morris, Louis. "History of My Life as a Musician." Unpublished autobiography, ca. 1960.

Osmund Varela Collection. Approximately five thousand negatives by Varela and his father (Sousa's brother-in-law), dating from 1893 (includes several Sousa Band and U.S. Marine Band musicians).

Schwann Opus. Woodland, Calif.: Schwann Publications, 1998.

Sousa Band Press Books. Eighty-five scrapbooks of clippings and programs. U.S. Marine Band/Sousa Collection, Washington, D.C.

Sousa Oral History Project. David Whitwell, director; transcribed by Frank Byrne. Northridge: California State University (Northridge) Bands, 1984.

Wadsworth, Frank W., and Lillian June Wadsworth. Unpublished collection of memorabilia of a Sousa Band flutist and his daughter, compiled by Thomas and Virginia VanDerMeid, early 1960s. Copy in the Paul E. Bierley Papers, Sousa Archives and Center for American Music, University of Illinois at Urbana-Champaign.

Wall, Edmund A. World tour poem, 1911. *Sousa Band Fraternal Society News,* Dec. 1951 issue.

Wiedner, Eugene. "The Last Days of John Philip Sousa." Unpublished paper, 1932. Copy in the Paul E. Bierley Papers, Sousa Archives and Center for American Music, University of Illinois at Urbana-Champaign.

Index

PAUL EDMUND BIERLEY has passed through three careers: engineer, musician, and music historian/author. He spent his early life in Portsmouth, Ohio, until World War II, when he served as a radio operator/gunner on B-25 bombers in the U.S. Army Air Forces. After earning an aeronautical engineering degree, he worked in the aerospace industry for thirty-five years as an airplane/missile designer, data manager, and technical writer.

As a musician, he played tuba with the Columbus Symphony Orchestra, the Detroit Concert Band, the Virginia Grand Military Band, the Brass Band of Columbus, and the Village Brass quintet. He also toured with the World Symphony Orchestra and the New Sousa Band and led an industrial band.

His intensive research on John Philip Sousa began in 1963, and this is his eighth book on the subject. He received an honorary doctorate from his alma mater, the Ohio State University, in 2001 for his contributions to American musical history. He has also received numerous awards and honorary memberships from musical organizations.

Music in American Life

Only a Miner: Studies in Recorded Coal-Mining Songs   *Archie Green*

Great Day Coming: Folk Music and the American Left
    R. Serge Denisoff

John Philip Sousa: A Descriptive Catalog of His Works
    Paul E. Bierley

The Hell-Bound Train: A Cowboy Songbook   *Glenn Ohrlin*

Oh, Didn't He Ramble: The Life Story of Lee Collins, as Told to Mary
    Collins   *Edited by Frank J. Gillis and John W. Miner*

American Labor Songs of the Nineteenth Century   *Philip S. Foner*

Stars of Country Music: Uncle Dave Macon to Johnny Rodriguez
    Edited by Bill C. Malone and Judith McCulloh

Git Along, Little Dogies: Songs and Songmakers of the American West
    John I. White

A Texas-Mexican *Cancionero:* Folksongs of the Lower Border
    Américo Paredes

San Antonio Rose: The Life and Music of Bob Wills   *Charles R.
    Townsend*

Early Downhome Blues: A Musical and Cultural Analysis
    Jeff Todd Titon

An Ives Celebration: Papers and Panels of the Charles Ives Centennial
    Festival-Conference   *Edited by H. Wiley Hitchcock and Vivian Perlis*

Sinful Tunes and Spirituals: Black Folk Music to the Civil War
    Dena J. Epstein

Joe Scott, the Woodsman-Songmaker   *Edward D. Ives*

Jimmie Rodgers: The Life and Times of America's Blue Yodeler   *Nolan
    Porterfield*

Early American Music Engraving and Printing: A History of Music Pub-
    lishing in America from 1787 to 1825, with Commentary on Earlier
    and Later Practices   *Richard J. Wolfe*

Sing a Sad Song: The Life of Hank Williams   *Roger M. Williams*

Long Steel Rail: The Railroad in American Folksong   *Norm Cohen*

Resources of American Music History: A Directory of Source Materials
    from Colonial Times to World War II   *D. W. Krummel, Jean Geil, Doris
    J. Dyen, and Deane L. Root*

Tenement Songs: The Popular Music of the Jewish Immigrants
    Mark Slobin

Ozark Folksongs   *Vance Randolph; edited and abridged by Norm Co-
    hen*

Oscar Sonneck and American Music   *Edited by
    William Lichtenwanger*

Bluegrass Breakdown: The Making of the Old Southern Sound   *Robert
    Cantwell*

Bluegrass: A History   *Neil V. Rosenberg*

Music at the White House: A History of the American Spirit
    Elise K. Kirk

Red River Blues: The Blues Tradition in the Southeast   *Bruce Bastin*

Good Friends and Bad Enemies: Robert Winslow Gordon and the Study
    of American Folksong   *Debora Kodish*

Fiddlin' Georgia Crazy: Fiddlin' John Carson, His Real World, and the
    World of His Songs   *Gene Wiggins*

America's Music: From the Pilgrims to the Present (rev. 3d ed.)
    Gilbert Chase

Secular Music in Colonial Annapolis: The Tuesday Club, 1745–56
    John Barry Talley

Bibliographical Handbook of American Music   *D. W. Krummel*

Goin' to Kansas City   *Nathan W. Pearson, Jr.*

"Susanna," "Jeanie," and "The Old Folks at Home": The Songs of Ste-
    phen C. Foster from His Time to Ours (2d ed.)
    William W. Austin

Songprints: The Musical Experience of Five Shoshone Women
    Judith Vander

"Happy in the Service of the Lord": Afro-American Gospel Quartets in
    Memphis   *Kip Lornell*

Paul Hindemith in the United States   *Luther Noss*

"My Song Is My Weapon": People's Songs, American Communism, and
    the Politics of Culture, 1930–50   *Robbie Lieberman*

Chosen Voices: The Story of the American Cantorate   *Mark Slobin*

Theodore Thomas: America's Conductor and Builder of Orchestras,
    1835–1905   *Ezra Schabas*

"The Whorehouse Bells Were Ringing" and Other Songs Cowboys
    Sing   *Guy Logsdon*

Crazeology: The Autobiography of a Chicago Jazzman   *Bud Freeman,
    as Told to Robert Wolf*

Discoursing Sweet Music: Brass Bands and Community Life in Turn-of-
    the-Century Pennsylvania   *Kenneth Kreitner*

Mormonism and Music: A History   *Michael Hicks*

Voices of the Jazz Age: Profiles of Eight Vintage Jazzmen
    Chip Deffaa

Pickin' on Peachtree: A History of Country Music in Atlanta, Georgia
    Wayne W. Daniel

Bitter Music: Collected Journals, Essays, Introductions, and Librettos
    Harry Partch; edited by Thomas McGeary

Ethnic Music on Records: A Discography of Ethnic Recordings Produced
    in the United States, 1893 to 1942   *Richard K. Spottswood*

Downhome Blues Lyrics: An Anthology from the Post–World War II Era
    Jeff Todd Titon

Ellington: The Early Years   *Mark Tucker*

Chicago Soul   *Robert Pruter*

That Half-Barbaric Twang: The Banjo in American Popular Culture
    Karen Linn

Hot Man: The Life of Art Hodes   *Art Hodes and Chadwick Hansen*

The Erotic Muse: American Bawdy Songs (2d ed.)   *Ed Cray*

Barrio Rhythm: Mexican American Music in Los Angeles   *Steven Loza*

The Creation of Jazz: Music, Race, and Culture in Urban America
    Burton W. Peretti

Charles Martin Loeffler: A Life Apart in Music   *Ellen Knight*

Club Date Musicians: Playing the New York Party Circuit
    Bruce A. MacLeod

Opera on the Road: Traveling Opera Troupes in the United States,
    1825–60   *Katherine K. Preston*

The Stonemans: An Appalachian Family and the Music That Shaped
    Their Lives   *Ivan M. Tribe*

Transforming Tradition: Folk Music Revivals Examined   *Edited by
    Neil V. Rosenberg*

The Crooked Stovepipe: Athapaskan Fiddle Music and Square Dancing
    in Northeast Alaska and Northwest Canada   *Craig Mishler*

Traveling the High Way Home: Ralph Stanley and the World of Tradi-
    tional Bluegrass Music   *John Wright*

Carl Ruggles: Composer, Painter, and Storyteller   *Marilyn Ziffrin*

Never without a Song: The Years and Songs of Jennie Devlin, 1865–1952   *Katharine D. Newman*

The Hank Snow Story   *Hank Snow, with Jack Ownbey and Bob Burris*

Milton Brown and the Founding of Western Swing   *Cary Ginell, with special assistance from Roy Lee Brown*

Santiago de Murcia's "Códice Saldívar No. 4": A Treasury of Secular Guitar Music from Baroque Mexico   *Craig H. Russell*

The Sound of the Dove: Singing in Appalachian Primitive Baptist Churches   *Beverly Bush Patterson*

Heartland Excursions: Ethnomusicological Reflections on Schools of Music   *Bruno Nettl*

Doowop: The Chicago Scene   *Robert Pruter*

Blue Rhythms: Six Lives in Rhythm and Blues   *Chip Deffaa*

Shoshone Ghost Dance Religion: Poetry Songs and Great Basin Context   *Judith Vander*

Go Cat Go! Rockabilly Music and Its Makers   *Craig Morrison*

'Twas Only an Irishman's Dream: The Image of Ireland and the Irish in American Popular Song Lyrics, 1800–1920   *William H. A. Williams*

Democracy at the Opera: Music, Theater, and Culture in New York City, 1815–60   *Karen Ahlquist*

Fred Waring and the Pennsylvanians   *Virginia Waring*

Woody, Cisco, and Me: Seamen Three in the Merchant Marine   *Jim Longhi*

Behind the Burnt Cork Mask: Early Blackface Minstrelsy and Antebellum American Popular Culture   *William J. Mahar*

Going to Cincinnati: A History of the Blues in the Queen City   *Steven C. Tracy*

Pistol Packin' Mama: Aunt Molly Jackson and the Politics of Folksong   *Shelly Romalis*

Sixties Rock: Garage, Psychedelic, and Other Satisfactions   *Michael Hicks*

The Late Great Johnny Ace and the Transition from R&B to Rock 'n' Roll   *James M. Salem*

Tito Puente and the Making of Latin Music   *Steven Loza*

Juilliard: A History   *Andrea Olmstead*

Understanding Charles Seeger, Pioneer in American Musicology   *Edited by Bell Yung and Helen Rees*

Mountains of Music: West Virginia Traditional Music from *Goldenseal*   *Edited by John Lilly*

Alice Tully: An Intimate Portrait   *Albert Fuller*

A Blues Life   *Henry Townsend, as told to Bill Greensmith*

Long Steel Rail: The Railroad in American Folksong (2d ed.)   *Norm Cohen*

The Golden Age of Gospel   *Text by Horace Clarence Boyer; photography by Lloyd Yearwood*

Aaron Copland: The Life and Work of an Uncommon Man   *Howard Pollack*

Louis Moreau Gottschalk   *S. Frederick Starr*

Race, Rock, and Elvis   *Michael T. Bertrand*

Theremin: Ether Music and Espionage   *Albert Glinsky*

Poetry and Violence: The Ballad Tradition of Mexico's Costa Chica   *John H. McDowell*

The Bill Monroe Reader   *Edited by Tom Ewing*

Music in Lubavitcher Life   *Ellen Koskoff*

Zarzuela: Spanish Operetta, American Stage   *Janet L. Sturman*

Bluegrass Odyssey: A Documentary in Pictures and Words, 1966–86   *Carl Fleischhauer and Neil V. Rosenberg*

That Old-Time Rock & Roll: A Chronicle of an Era, 1954–63   *Richard Aquila*

Labor's Troubadour   *Joe Glazer*

American Opera   *Elise K. Kirk*

Don't Get above Your Raisin': Country Music and the Southern Working Class   *Bill C. Malone*

John Alden Carpenter: A Chicago Composer   *Howard Pollack*

Heartbeat of the People: Music and Dance of the Northern Pow-wow   *Tara Browner*

My Lord, What a Morning: An Autobiography   *Marian Anderson*

Marian Anderson: A Singer's Journey   *Allan Keiler*

Charles Ives Remembered: An Oral History   *Vivian Perlis*

Henry Cowell, Bohemian   *Michael Hicks*

Rap Music and Street Consciousness   *Cheryl L. Keyes*

Louis Prima   *Garry Boulard*

Marian McPartland's Jazz World: All in Good Time   *Marian McPartland*

Robert Johnson: Lost and Found   *Barry Lee Pearson and Bill McCulloch*

Bound for America: Three British Composers   *Nicholas Temperley*

Lost Sounds: Blacks and the Birth of the Recording Industry, 1890–1919   *Tim Brooks*

Burn, Baby! BURN! The Autobiography of Magnificent Montague   *Magnificent Montague with Bob Baker*

Way Up North in Dixie: A Black Family's Claim to the Confederate Anthem   *Howard L. Sacks and Judith Rose Sacks*

The Bluegrass Reader   *Edited by Thomas Goldsmith*

Colin McPhee: Composer in Two Worlds   *Carol J. Oja*

Robert Johnson, Mythmaking, and Contemporary American Culture   *Patricia R. Schroeder*

Composing a World: Lou Harrison, Musical Wayfarer   *Leta E. Miller and Fredric Lieberman*

Fritz Reiner, Maestro and Martinet   *Kenneth Morgan*

That Toddlin' Town: Chicago's White Dance Bands and Orchestras, 1900–1950   *Charles A. Sengstock Jr.*

Dewey and Elvis: The Life and Times of a Rock 'n' Roll Deejay   *Louis Cantor*

Come Hither to Go Yonder: Playing Bluegrass with Bill Monroe   *Bob Black*

Chicago Blues: Portraits and Stories   *David Whiteis*

The Incredible Band of John Philip Sousa   *Paul E. Bierley*

The University of Illinois Press
is a founding member of the
Association of American University Presses.

_____

Composed in 9/13.5 Meta Book
with Meta display
by Celia Shapland
for the University of Illinois Press
Designed by Paula Newcomb
Manufactured by Sheridan Books, Inc.

University of Illinois Press
1325 South Oak Street
Champaign, IL 61820-6903
www.press.uillinois.edu